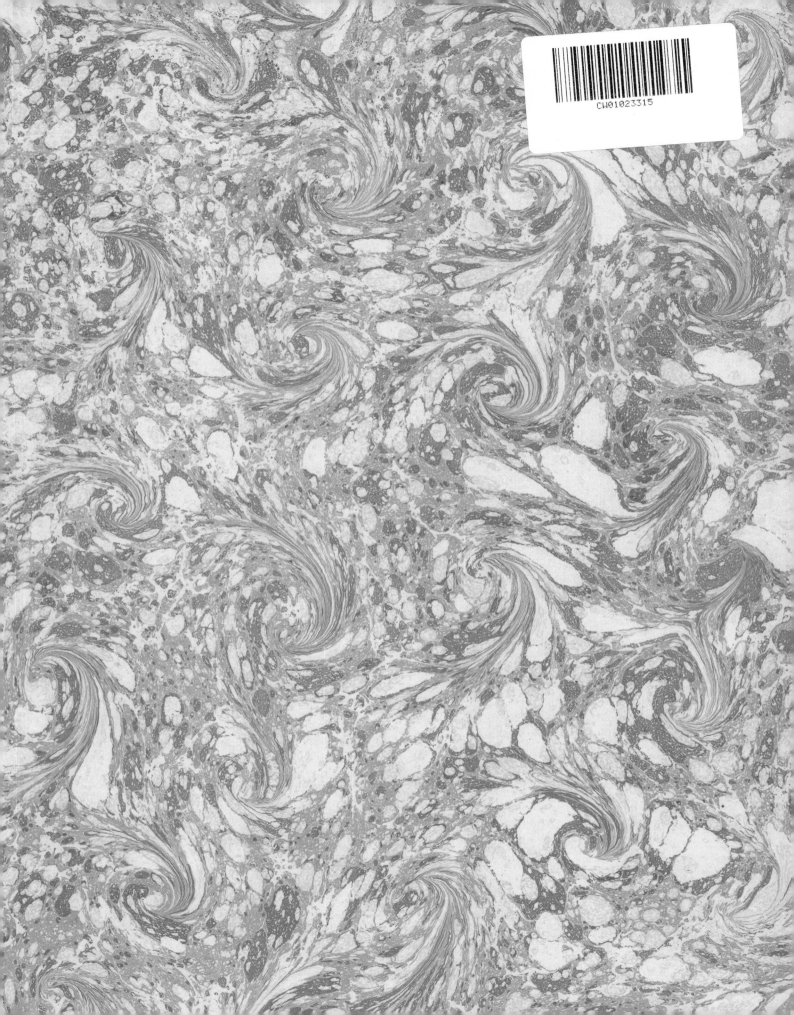

Aircraft Histories of the Ling-Temco-Vought A-7 Corsair II

AIRCRAFT HISTORIES OF THE LING-TEMCO-VOUGHT
A-7 CORSAIR II

Michael L. Roberts

Schiffer Military History
Atglen, PA

DEDICATION

This publication is dedicated to all hands that designed, built, supported, flew, or maintained the A-7 Corsair II aircraft.

Book Design by Michael L. Roberts & Stephanie Daugherty.
Copyright © 2009 by Michael L. Roberts.
Library of Congress Control Number: 2009923148

Printed in China.
ISBN: 978-0-7643-3238-8
We are interested in hearing from authors with book ideas on related topics.

Published by Schiffer Publishing Ltd.
4880 Lower Valley Road
Atglen, PA 19310
Phone: (610) 593-1777
FAX: (610) 593-2002
E-mail: Info@schifferbooks.com.
Visit our web site at: www.schifferbooks.com
Please write for a free catalog.
This book may be purchased from the publisher.
Please include $5.00 postage.
Try your bookstore first.

In Europe, Schiffer books are distributed by:
Bushwood Books
6 Marksbury Avenue
Kew Gardens
Surrey TW9 4JF, England
Phone: 44 (0) 20 8392-8585
FAX: 44 (0) 20 8392-9876
E-mail: Info@bushwoodbooks.co.uk.
Visit our website at: www.bushwoodbooks.co.uk

THE VOUGHT A-7 CORSAIR II

CONTENTS

* 156734 - 156740 (BLK I)   *Procured as A-7E, with TF-30 Engine, redesignated A-7C by the U.S. Navy after in service*
** 156741 - 156761 (BLK II)   *Procured as A-7E, with TF-30 Engine, redesignated A-7C by the U.S. Navy after in service*
*** 156762 - 156800 (BLK III)   *Procured as A-7E, with TF-30 Engine, redesignated A-7C by the U.S. Navy after in service*

+ 159662 - 159667 (BLK XVIII)   *was the first block for the Greek A-7H*

ACKNOWLEDGMENTS

Dick Atkins *Vought Aircraft Industries, Retirees Club; Dallas, TX.*
David Dollarhide *CAPT. USNR, Ret., Seventh C.O. VA-203; NAS Cecil Field, FL..*
Mike Dugan *Aircraft Records 309 AMARG; Davis Monthan AFB; Tucson, AZ.*
Rudi Brito Elvas *A-7P List*
Rul A. Ferreira *Luso Fanatics*
William C. Fields *Former member VA-204; NAS New Orleans, LA.*
Dale J. Gordon *Naval Historical Center, WA., D.C. (Archivist)*
Roy A. Grosnick, *Naval Historical Center, WA., D.C. (Archivist)*
Craig Hall *TA-7C Corsair II owner; Chino, CA.*
Dick Hassler *Former AMS1; VA-304, VA-305*
Robert W. Hodson *Capt. USN, Ret., former pilot VA-30; NAS Point Mugu, CA*
Don Howell *Owner of Haveco Aircraft Surplus, Tucson, AZ.*
P. Susie Kent *Vought Aircraft Industries, Law Department; Dallas, TX.*
John Maysick *ADCS, USN, Ret. Former member VA-303, VA-305*
Burt Noble *Vought Aircraft Industries, Retirees Club; Dallas, TX.*
Fred Noyes *AECS, USN, Ret. Former member VA-304; NAS Alameda, CA.*
Naval Historical Center *Microfilm and data*
Jimmy Price *NAWCWD China Lake, CA. Weapons Loading Standardization Team.*
Jay Roberts *Technical Advisor*
Judy Roberts *Dictation of data*
Paul Ryplewski *Aircraft Records 309 AMARG; Davis Monthan AFB; Tucson, AZ.*
Jill Schaefer *Thomson Aviation; El Mirage, CA.*
Bob Southerland *Air Forces Research*
Tailhook Association *Photos, Micro film, and Carrier Cruises*
Mark Thomson *Owner of Thomson Aviation; El Mirage, CA.*
Scott Thompson *NAWC China Lake, CA., Survivability Range*
Rob Van Lijf *Aircraft Historian, Netherlands*
Teresa Vanden-Heuvel *Public Affairs Officer 309 AMARG; Davis Monthan AFB; Tucson, AZ.*
Joao M. Vidal *A-7P list*
Dan Winsett *Aircraft Records 309 AMARG; Davis Monthan AFB; Tucson, AZ.*
Vought Corporation *Articles and data*

Photographic credits:

www.http;//Aircraft Slide.Ccom
DOD Photo Archives; Washington, DC.
DOD Still Media Records Center; Washington, DC.
Goodrich / Stencil Corporation
Hughes Aircraft Company; Conoga Park, CA.
Naval Photographic Center
Public Relations, AMARG, Davis Monrthan AFB, AZ.
The Tailhook Association; San Diego, CA.
Vought Corporation; Dallas, TX.
www.http;//phileppecolin.net
Chadwick J. Addie; La Porte, IN.
Robert N. Abbott Jr. collection
Fabio AcuOa
Tom Brower
Al Adcock collection
Robert Atkinson
Gary Baker collection; Roswell, NM.
Michael Ballcock
Rod Bankston
Rex Barker
J. D. Bass Jr., Vintage Photos and Postcards; Newport, KY.
Sergio Battaro
David F. Brown collection; Thomasville, PA.
Gary Campbell collection
John M. Campbell collection
Guiseppe Candiani
William Carmody
Tom Chee
Aldo Ciarini
Major Eric L. Clinton
Terry Cove
Thomas Cuddy II
Bill Curry
Derek Daniel
Reagean Dansereau
Kelvin Darling collection; Wales, UK
James F. Davis
David Dollarhide collection; Orange Park, FL.
Robert Dorr
Rolf Flinzher
Stephon Fox
Michael J. Freer collectin, Touchdown Aviation; Evesham, UK
Stuert J. Freer, Fighter Control
Jack Friell
Steve Galeener collection; Bellflower, CA
Theodore van Geffan
Richardo Gouveia
Bob Greby
Michael Grote
Michael Grove
Eddy Gual collection; Miami, FL.
Craig Hall collection; Chino, CA.
Joseph Handelman
Jean-Marie Hanon
Ian Harding collection; UK
Nelson Hare
R.W. Harrison, candid Aero collection; Indian Orchard, MA.
Gerald Helmer
Jose' Almansur Herculano collection
Marty Isham
Andre Jans
Duane Kasulika
Rodger Kelly collection
Nancy Kerr collection; Ringwood, NJ.
Ben Knoeles
Jacob Dahlgaard Kristensen
Bois LaBouy

Robert Lawson
John Leen Houts
Roy Lock
Chris Lofting collection; Burnham, England
Terry Love
Ralf Manteueel
Gerald Markgraf
Jim Marrow
Charles Mayer
John Maysick collection; Castle Rock, WA.
Christopher McCall, Mach 1 collectables; Goodyear, AZ.
Thomas P. McManus
Frank McSurley
Jake Melampy
David Menard
Peter Mencus collection
Stephen Miller collection; Frederickaburg, VA.
Robert Mills
Jack Morris
Jim Morrow
Harold P. Myers
Mark Nankivi collection; St. Louis, MO.
Wolodymir Ncldwkin
David Ostroski
Lionel Paul
Lindsay Peacock
Steve Pelts
Ralph Peterson
Stephano Piceilli
Ian Powell
JO1 J.D. Randall, USN
Doug Remington
Ed Richardson
Michael L. Roberts collection; Long Beach, CA.
Mick Roth
Rotramel
William F. Ruck Jr. collection
Jorge Manual Antao Ruivo
Giargio Salerno
Henk Scharringa collection; de Bilt, Netherlands
Art Schorni
Hans Joschim Schroder
John Shea collection; Santa Clara, CA.
W.D. Siuru JR. collection; Colorado Springs, CO.
Rick Sleight collection; UK
Slowiak
Bill Spidle
Peter Steelhouwer collection
Alberto Storti
Jim Sullivan
Richard Sullivan
Eric Tammer
Jean M. Tellier collection; Nashua, NH.
Steve Tobey
Toshiyoki Toda
Bruce Trombecky
Vance Vasquez
Jan van Waarde collection; Rotterdam, The Netherlands
Nickolas J. Waters
Kevin Whitehead
Bryan Williams collection; Mission Viejo, CA.
Steve Williams
Peter Zastro
Steven Zink
Eugene Zorn

FOREWORD

I was just another skinny kid at Mississippi State University when the Navy recruiters showed up on the campus my senior year. Just seeing them in their "summer white" uniforms and hearing stories of adventures at sea, I was hooked.

It was 1964 when I reported to preflight training in Pensacola. A few months later, after primary training in the T-34B, I was fortunate to find myself assigned to fly jets. The T-2A Buckeye was followed by the F-9 Panther, then the F-11 Tiger, and I received my Wings of Gold in '66. Excitedly, I fired up my old '60 Corvette for the trip to NAS Cecil in Jacksonville, FL, to fly the A-4 Skyhawk with the VA-46 Clansmen.

In the summer of '67, our combat cruise to Vietnam aboard *USS Forrestal* ended abruptly after a tragic accident with fire and bombs exploding on the flight deck. In my cockpit surrounded by the chaos on the flight deck, I was fortunate to call myself a survivor. We lost one hundred and thirty-four shipmates, and all but five of our A-4Es were severely damaged or lost.

Back at NAS Cecil, we were assigned older model A-4Bs, as we waited a few months to train in the Navy's new replacement aircraft, the A-7 Corsair II. One of the Skyhawks tried to end my career in '68, as the engine seized just south of Cecil Field. A safe ejection let me dodge another "bullet" and continue on to fly the new Corsair.

Our squadron made the transition and was assigned the second generation Corsair, the A-7B. All of the previous A-7As had gone to combat in Vietnam, but our next cruise was aboard *USS Saratoga*, and we would be the first A-7 equipped Air Wing deployed to the Mediterranean.

"You are therefore directed to travel to CONUS for release from active duty," read my sudden orders three months into the cruise. The Navy decided to let thousands of us USNR types go, and after eighteen months of flying the new bird, I was released from active duty in '69. I later spent twelve years with the reserves, flying mostly the A-7A and A-7B with VA-203, and eventually retired with 3,000 flight hours, 1,500 of which were in the Corsair.

The A-7 was a very different airplane from the A-4. It had a much slower roll rate and was not as maneuverable as the "Scooter." However, it was a little faster, could carry tons of fuel, and had a much larger ordinance load.

As a "transonic" jet the A-7A/B's advertised maximum mach number was 1.12 (645 knots), and a few times when diving from 40,000' I actually saw the mach meter on 1.1. At sea level and full throttle it would usually ease up to an indicated speed of 575 kts. A four "G" pull to the vertical and you could roll over on your back, level at 20,000 feet; respectable performance for a non-afterburning attack plane.

With an internal fuel capacity of 10,500 pounds and the fuel efficient TF-30 fan engine, the Corsair II had an incredible range for a fighter type airplane. We seldom carried drop tanks for extra fuel. Two Sidwinder missile stations were mounted on the fuselage and there were six wing pylons, giving it tremendous flexibility in the amount and types of ordinance it could carry.

Though the later A-7E was equipped with the real "magic," we loved the new gizmos in the cockpit of the "Bravo," especially the nice autopilot. The CP-741 bombing computer was unique for us Skyhawk drivers, and though it was an interim system, it improved our bombing scores by fifty percent over the A-4. A Doppler unit fed ground speed to the ASN-67 "Roller Map" for low level missions. The AN/APQ-116 radar was a tremendous improvement, and though designed primarily for terrain mapping and terrain following (TF), it could be also used for weather avoidance. However, the Roller Map and TF systems were poorly designed and mostly not used in fleet squadrons.

While the Marines continued to fly the A-4, the Navy entrusted the A-7 as the workhorse of light attack. From drawing board to delivery of the first airplane in just under two years, the A-7 was rushed into production and continued to serve for twenty-six years. Then, with the disestablishment of Attack Squadrons 46 and 72 in 1991, the A-7 was suddenly gone, replaced by the F/A-18 Hornet. The Skyhawk remained with the Marines and Training Command for many years, but the Corsair just disappeared from the U.S. Navy inventory. A number of them still sit baking in the sun of an Arizona "boneyard," and other remnants of the fleet can be found at museums or on display at small airports, parks, and school yards around the country.

Little has been written about the A-7 to date, but "Rob" Roberts' years of research to document the past actually brings the machine back to life for many. *Aircraft Histories of the Ling-Temco A-7 Corsair II* touches the souls of those who maintained and flew the airplane, as the book meticulously documents the travels and disposition of individual aircraft. His collection of photographs is unmatched, and offers a unique visual connection to the past. Whether you are a researcher, hobbyist, or have an emotional connection with the Corsair II, you'll treasure your copy of this book. I'm proud to have assisted with my small contribution.

Dave Dollarhide
CAPT USNR (ret)

PREFACE

Each naval aircraft is assigned a bureau number by the Director, Air Warfare (N88). The history of that particular aircraft is tracked by this number. The history card is transferred to microfilm, and usually includes the date of acceptance, duty stations, and sometimes the date stricken from the Navy inventory.

The data for this reference was gathered from numerous sources, ie articles, magazines, books, websites, Aircraft Historians both Foreign and domestic, photographs, the manufacturer, former U.S. Navy personnel, Government manuals, and microfilm. The two major sources of information came from the Vought Corporation and the U.S. Navy (Declassified) Flight record card microfilm. The Flight Record Cards were invaluable, as they gave the acceptance dates and a continuous flow of duty stations and dates of transfer, as well as the date of loss if that were the case. Unfortunately, the U.S. Navy discontinued the Flight Record Cards due to budgetary restraints in September 1987. Since the Navy A-7 Corsair II's first acceptance was in October 1965 and the last Navy A-7 transferred to AMARG (the Boneyard) in 1991, there is a four year gap of U.S. Navy operational or strike data. The only other source of information is from the computers and aircraft records of the storage facility at AMARG, Davis Monthan AFB, Tucson, AZ. The AMARG facility has the terminal data on the aircraft which contains the last squadron that had custody prior to the transfer to AMARG, the aircraft Bureau Number, Modex (nose) number, Tail code (which IDs the air wing), the storage code number assigned by AMARG, items of equipment removed from the aircraft, date of transfer to another squadron, facility, DRMO, or scrap, and the name of salvage company or museum. Unfortunately, the AMARG facility does not archive their aircraft documents, and many of the earlier A-7 documents have been destroyed.

Explanatory Notes:
Example #1, E-069 156803 Navy acceptance from NPRO Rep. LTV, Dallas, TX., 26 OCT 65 *

The first two sets of numbers are in bold print for separation and ease of finding the next aircraft history. Aircraft histories are also separated by a space. The first set of numbers **E-069** is the (CSN) Contract Sequence Number. The **E** indicates this is an A-7E. The number **069** indicates it is the 69th A-7E to be produced. The second set of numbers **156803** is the aircraft bureau number. The next entry is the Navy acceptance date.

Example #2, ** Transferred to VA-147/CVW-9, NG/400, USS Constellation (CV-64), 17 JUL 72;

Transferred to Attack Squadron **VA-147**. The **CVW-9** is the carrier air wing the squadron belongs to. The Tail code is **NG**. The modex (nose number) is 400. If the modex number is known, it will be given. If the number is not known the correct prefix number will be followed with a double XX, as **in 4XX**. The **USS Constellation** is where it went. The **(CV-64)** is the type of carrier. The **CV** indicates Aircraft Carrier. The hull number is **64**. The date, **17 JUL 72**, is the day it was transferred.

Example #3, AMARG storage code 210816 = Area 21, Row 08, Spot 16.

For easier reading a double asterisk ** is utilized to separate transfers between commands, or other data. The semicolon (;) is used for separation when the aircraft is traveling between destinations in the same command. Strikes are separated by the accent sign ~. Acronyms, abbreviations, and initialisms may be found in the glossary.

To find the total history on bureau number **156803** from acceptance on 26 OCT 65 to a strike on 31 MAY 82, nineteen different reels of microfilm had to be reviewed. Some aircraft have shorter histories, others longer. The production run on the A-7 Corsair II was 1,545 aircraft.

The data presented in this publication is as accurate and complete as possible. All known existing government data has been reviewed. Hopefully all the mistakes have been corrected, but in reality there are probably some mistakes still hiding somewhere.

Note:
1. The Contract Sequence Number was used in this publication vice the Vought Number, which is different.
2. According to the LTV A-7 Aircraft Correlation List the Contract Sequence Numbers E-157 and E-317 were not used.
3. Contract Sequence Number E-409 was used on two aircraft, Vought number 399, A-7E 159261 and Vought number 410, A-7E 159272.
4. Aircraft photographs cover all operating commands except NAEF and NAEL of which I was unable to locate.
5. Patches cover the aircraft, airwings, and all operating commands except NAEF and NAEL of which I was unable to locate.

GLOSSARY

A-7 Corsair II Single seat Attack Aircraft unless prefixed with TA, which would indicate two seats, as in TA-7C, TA-7H, and TA-7P. The A-7K and EA-7L were also two seat.

AFB Air Force Base

AMARC Aerospace Maintenance and Regeneration Center; Davis Monthan AFB, Tucson, AZ, (Post Oct. 85)

AMARG Aerospace Maintenance and Regeneration Group; Davis Monthan AFB, Tucson, AZ (As of 02 MAY 07). Title changed due to the F-117 being stored at AMARG Tonopa, NV., and other special aircraft at different locations.

AP Airport

AZ. Arizona

BE. Belgium

Bureau Number Serial Number of the aircraft

CA. California

CBC Construction Battalion Center

C/O Care of

COSA Unknown

CRAA Unknown

CSAR Combat Search and Rescue

CSN Contract Sequence Number

CV Aircraft Carrier

CVA Attack Aircraft Carrier

CVAN Nuclear Attack Aircraft Carrier

CVN Aircraft Carrier Nuclear

CVW Carrier Air Wing

DCASO Defense Contract Administration Services Office

DIC Died in Captivity

DRMO Defense Reutilization and Marketing Office (Surplus sales)

FAC Forward Air Control

FAP Forca Aerea Portuguesa, Portuguese Air Force, (Portugal)

FAWPRA Fleet Air wing Pacific Repair Activity

FEWSG Fleet Electronic Warfare Support Group

FL. Florida

FLIR Forward Looking Infra Red

FMS Foreign Military Sales

FRS Fleet Replacement Squadron

FY Fiscal Year

GA. Georgia

GE. Germany, Federal Republic of

GR. Greece

HAF Elliniki Palaniki Aeroporia, Helenic Air Force, (Greece)

HI. Hawaii

IAP International Airport

IT. Italy

JRB Joint Reserve Base

JP. Japan

KIA Killed in Action

LA. Louisiana

LE. Lebanon

LTV Ling Temco Vought Corp.

MA. Massachusetts

MAP Municipal Airport and/or Military Assistance Program

MASDC Military Aircraft Storage and Disposal Center; Davis Monthan AFB, Tucson, AZ. (Pre Oct. 85)

MCAS Marine Corps Air Station

MD. Maryland

MIA Missing in Action

MLG Main Landing Gear

Modex Nose number

NAD Naval Air Depot

NADC Naval Air Development Center

NAEC Naval Air Engineering Center

NAEL Naval Air Engineering Laboratory

NAF Naval Air Facility

NALF Unknown

NARF Naval Air Rework Facility

NARF Naval Aerospace Recovery Facility (El Centro, CA.) 1964 – 1973

NARF Naval Air Rework Facility

NAS Naval Air Station

NASC Naval Air Systems Command

NASC Naval Air Service Center

NATF Naval Air Test Facility

NASM National Air and Space Museum
NATC Naval Air Test Center
NATSI Unknown
NATTC Naval Air Technical Training Center
NAWS Naval Air Warfare Station
NJ. New Jersey
NLG Nose Landing Gear
NM. New Mexico
NPRO Naval Plant Representative Office
NPTR National Parachute Test Range (El Centro, CA.,) 1973-1979
NSWC National Strike Warfare Center
NTPS Naval Test Pilot School
NV. Nevada
NVN North Vietnam
NWC Naval Weapons Center
NWEF Naval Weapons Evaluation Facility

OK. Oklahoma

PA. Pennsylvania
PI. Philippine Islands
PO. Portugal
POW Prisoner of War
PR. Puerto Rico

RAG Replacement Air Group
RAP Regional Airport
RI. Rhode Island
R & T Research and Test
RDT & E Research, Development, Test and Evaluation
RTND Royal Thai Navy Division, (Thailand)

S 1SO strike Major damage (Accident) or (crash)(Capital damage)
S 2SO strike Depreciation (Not economical or Practical to restore to serviceability)
S 3SO strike Administrative
S 4SO strike Service completed (Has reached the end of its service life)
SAM Surface to Air Missile
SARDIP Stricken Aircraft and Disposal Program
SC. South Carolina
S/N Serial number
SOC Struck Off Charge
SP. Spain
SVN South Vietnam

TH. Thailand
TN. Tennessee
TX. Texas

USS United States Ship

VA. Virginia
VFN Vought Fabrication Number

WA. Washington
WFU Withdrawn from use
W/O Written Off

INTRODUCTION

THE VOUGHT A-7 CORSAIR II

In May 1963, the Navy began a design competition for a light-attack, carrier-based aircraft to supplement and later replace the Douglas A-4 Skyhawk. The new aircraft was to carry a larger ordnance payload and fly a greater combat radius than the Skyhawk. Douglas, Grumman, North American, and Vought responded to the Navy's invitation to bid. Vought was selected as the winner in FEB 64. In March, the designation A-7A was approved for the new aircraft. The Ling Temco Vought A-7 production line started on 19 MAR 64 and continued until SEP 84; 1,545 were manufactured. Its first flight, powered by a Pratt & Whitney TF3O-P-6 turbofan engine, was on 27 SEP 65. Navy Preliminary Evaluations were underway in JAN 66. Test programs were accomplished with wartime urgency, and the first fleet delivery to VA-174 was on 14 OCT 66.

The name Corsair has its origins in a series of famous biplanes built for the Navy by the Vought Corporation between World Wars I and II. Later the name was applied to the Vought F4U series of fighters flown by Navy and Marine pilots during World War II. The modern-day descendant of these historic aircraft is the Vought A-7 Corsair II.

The proposal by Vought engineers was based on their F-8 Crusader but with many significant differences. By using a proven design and engine, development of the A-7 was greatly accelerated over what it would have been if both the airframe and power plant were entirely new concepts.

The high wing of the A-7 has less sweepback, but is closely related in geometry and physical size to that of the F-8. Outboard ailerons were introduced on the A-7 wing, and the structure was strengthened to allow the wings and fuselage to carry a total ordnance load of 15,000 lbs on eight stations (two fuselage each with 500 lb capacity, two inboard on the wings with 2,500 lb capacity each, and four on the outer wings with 3,500 lb capacity each), with more than 200 combinations of different stores.

Leading edge flaps and single-slotted trailing-edge flaps are fitted to the wing, as are upper surface spoilers located ahead of the flaps. Not used on the A-7 is the variable-incidence wing of the F-8. Other features of the F-8 are characterized by a low horizontal tail. Because of the larger mass flow of the turbofan engine, the chin inlet is larger than the turbojet-powered fighter, and short landing-gear retracts into the fuselage. Since the A-7 is a subsonic aircraft, no area rule is incorporated in the fuselage. The shorter length of the fuselage together with the slight "upsweep" of the underside of the afterbody allow the A-7 to be rotated to a significantly higher pitch angle on takeoff and landing, without tail scrape, than was possible for the F-8. With the higher ground pitch attitude, together with the capability of the high-lift system, the Variable-incidence wing was not needed. The nine foot speed brake is located on the bottom of the fuselage about midway between the nose and the tail. The A-7A incorporated the 11,350 lb thrust Pratt & Whitney TF30-P-6 turbo-fan engine, which had been developed for the F-111. The A-7A, A-7B, and A-7C were eventually upgraded to the TF-30-P-8 and TF-30-P-408 Turbo-fan engines. The A-7E had a greatly improved Allison TF-41-A-2 Turbo-fan Engine. The engine for the A-7 did not have an after-burner.

The A-7 is a modern, sophisticated, integrated, highly versatile airborne weapon system capable of performing a variety of search, surveillance, and attack missions. It is capable of carrying four external wing-mounted 300 gallon fuel tanks, coupled with a variety of ordnance on remaining stations. The A-7 can also conduct in-flight refueling operations, and is capable of transferring over 12,000 pounds of fuel. The A-7 has a fully integrated digital navigation/weapon delivery system, and the integration technique is common to all current U.S. Navy and U.S. Air Force attack aircraft of the time. The avionics system, based on state-of-the-art electronics, digital computing techniques, and an automation philosophy, provide unparalleled mission effectiveness and flexibility. With its Forward-Looking Infrared (FLIR) capability, the A-7's night attack accuracy is equivalent to its day attack accuracy. A wide assortment of external stores can be accommodated on the A-7. Eight store-mounting positions are provided. There are three pylons under each wing, and a single mounting station is located on each side of the fuselage. A total of 15,000 pounds of stores can be carried. A total of 6,560 pounds can be carried on a typical mission with a radius of 556 miles. The A-7A/B/C had two MK-12 20 MM gun systems, one on each side of the fuselage. The A-7E had an M61A-1, six-barrel 20 MM Vulcan cannon located on the left side of the fuselage near the bottom of the aircraft.

The A-7A began Vietnam combat operations in DEC 67, and proved to be one of the most effective Navy close support and strike aircraft in that conflict. The A-7E Corsair IIs were part of the two-carrier battle group that conducted a joint strike on selected Libyan terrorist-related targets in 1986. Together with carrier-based F/A-18s, A-7s used anti-radiation missiles to neutralize Libyan air defenses. During Desert Storm, the A-7 demonstrated over 95% operational readiness and did not miss a single combat sortie.

The A-7 is one of those aircraft with a demonstrated capability of performing well in a wide variety of missions. Other aircraft are faster or have a greater range-payload capability, or have a faster rate of climb; sometimes, certain of these characteristics are deemed so important that it dominates the entire design. What results is a "point design" aircraft that can perform one mission extremely well but is relatively much less effective in any other mission. The design parameters of the A-7 were chosen so that the aircraft has great mission versatility. It was successfully employed in just about every conceivable attack role during the Vietnam conflict.

Retirements of the last two U.S. Navy A-7 operational squadrons were VA-46 and VA-72 in May 91. In addition to service in the U.S. Navy, Corsair IIs were flown by the U.S. Naval Air Reserve, U.S. Marines, U.S. Air Force, Air National Guard, Greek Air Force, Portuguese Air Force, and Thailand's Naval Division. Thailand and Portugal have long since retired their A-7's, but the Greek Air Force is scheduled to fly the A-7 until 2015 and possibly longer.

A-7 Models:

A-7A U.S. Navy, U.S. Naval Air Reserve

A-7B U.S. Navy, U.S. Naval Air Reserve

A-7C U.S. Navy, TF-30 powered A-7Es, production numbers E-001 thru E-067 were re-designated A-7C by the Navy after they were placed in service.

TA-7C U.S. Navy, Helenic Air Force (Greece), Thailand Naval Division (Thailand), converted from A-7B, A-7C, A-7E

A-7D U.S. Air Force, U.S. Air National Guard

A-7E U.S. Navy, U.S. Naval Air Reserve, Helenic Air Force (Greece)

TA-7E U.S. Navy

A-7F U.S. Air Force, 2 Demonstrators built; afterburner (supersonic), with drag chute, no contract.

A-7G Proposal for Switzerland, no contract

A-7H Helenic Air Force (Greece), production

TA-7H Helenic Air Force (Greece), production

A-7K U.S. Air Force, U.S. Air National Guard, Two seat, production

EA-7L U.S. Navy, Two seat, converted from TA-7C, configured to FEWSG standards

A-7P Portuguese Air Force (Portugal), converted from A-7A

TA-7P Portuguese Air Force (Portugal), converted from A-7A

V-531 Proposed U.S.AF two place / Twin engine, (with F-404, {F-18}, non-afterburning engines), to be converted from the A-7D, no contract

Vought Corporation

SECTION 1

A-7A

152580/152582 LTV YA-7A-1-CV Corsair II; (Block I) FY 64, Contract NOw 64-0363f (Lot I), (3) A-7A; A-001 Thru A-003

A-001 152580 Navy acceptance from NPRO Rep., LTV, Dallas, TX., Date unknown, unable to verify data on microfilm ** First YA-7A Prototype ** First flight, 27 SEP 65 ** Transferred to NAF China Lake, CA., Modex 1, for flight tests ~ S 1SO strike, 23 MAR 66 ** Crashed at NAF China Lake, Ca., while testing the efficiency of the Ram Air Turbine (RAT) and dead stick landing requirements.

A-002 152581 Navy acceptance from NPRO Rep., LTV, Dallas, TX., 13 OCT 65 ** Second YA-7A Prototype ** Used for Special Weapons Test ** Changed to NA-7A ** Remained at NPRO Rep., LTV, Dallas, TX., for R & T, 14 OCT 65 ** Transferred to NATC, Service Test, NAS Patuxent River, MD., 23 SEP 68 ** Transferred to NPRO REP., LTV, Dallas, TX., for R & T, 10 JUN 69 ** Transferred to NATC, Service Test, NAS Patuxent River, MD., Modex 581,, 08 AUG 69 ** Transferred to NATC, NAS Patuxent River, MD., for RDT & E, 01 SEP 72 ** Transferred to MASDC, Davis Monthan AFB; Tucson, AZ., assigned Park Code; 6A0041, 06 OCT 76 ** Interservice transfer to the USAF, changed to park code AE003, 18 JAN 77 ** Transferred to LTV; Dallas, TX, to be the prototype structural demo for the YA-7F.

A-003 152582 Navy acceptance from NPRO Rep., LTV, Dallas, TX., 12 NOV 65 ** Third YA-7A Prototype ** Remained at NPRO Rep., LTV , Dallas, TX., for R & T, 18 AUG 66 ~ S 1SO Strike, 16 FEB 68 ** Crashed near Cleburn, TX., due to a stall.

152647/152650 LTV A-7A-2-CV Corsair II; (Block II) FY 65, Contract NOw 64-0363f (Lot II) (4) A-7A; A-000/A-007

A-004 152647 Navy acceptance from NPRO Rep., LTV, Dallas, TX., 31 MAR 66 ** Transferred to NATC, Weapons System Test, NAS Patuxent River, MD., 15 SEP 66, Transferred to NATC, NAS Patuxent River, MD., for RDT & E, 01 JUN 73, NATC and a Lightning (W) on tail / No Modex ** Transferred to VA-125/FRS, NJ/525, NAS LeMoore, CA., 27 FEB 76 ** Transferred to MASDC, Davis Monthan AFB; Tucson, AZ., assigned park code 6A0044, 17 JAN 77 ~ S 3SO strike, 07 MAY 80 ** No data on strike ** On conditional loan from the National Museum of Naval Aviation; Pensacola, FL., to the School Board of Alachua, Fl.

A-005 152648 Navy acceptance from NPRO Rep., LTV, Dallas, TX., 06 JAN 66 ** Transferred to NATC, Service Test, NAS Patuxent River, MD., 28 OCT 66, with NATC Patuxent River tail marking ** Transferred to Edwards AFB, CA to conduct Intra service testing ** Transferred to MASDC, Davis Monthan AFB; Tucson, AZ., 28 APR 70 ** Transferred to NARF, NAS Alameda, CA., 12 AUG 72 ** Transferred to VA-125/FRS, NJ/5XX, NAS LeMoore, CA., 18 OCT 73 ~ S 3S0 strike, 17 NOV 76 ** No data on strike.

A-006 152649 Navy acceptance from NPRO Rep., LTV, Dallas, TX., 31 JAN 66 ** Remained at NPRO Rep., LTV, Dallas, TX., for RDT & E, 02 FEB 66 ** Transferred to NATC, Service Test, NAS Patuxent River, MD., 11 APR 69 ** Transferred to NATC, Weapon Systems Test, NAS Patuxent River, MD., 11 APR 69 ** Transferred to MASDC, Davis Monthan AFB; Tucson, AZ., 16 DEC 70 ** Transferred to NARF, NAS Alameda, CA., 13 AUG 72 ** Transferred to VA-125/FRS, NJ/5XX, NAS LeMoore, CA., 02 NOV 73; To VA-125, USS Ranger (CV-61), 23 MAY 74; To VA-125 NAS LeMoore, CA., 01 JUL 74 ~ S 3SO strike, 17 NOV 76 ** No data on strike.

A-007 152650 Navy acceptance from NPRO Rep., LTV, Dallas, TX., 28 FEB 66 ** Transferred to NATC, Weapons Test, NAS Patuxent River, MD., 07 OCT 66 ** Transferred to NATC, Service Test, NAS Patuxent River, MD., 07 OCT 66 ** Transferred to NATSI, NAS Lakehurst, NJ., 10 JAN 69, Used to conduct carrier suitability trials ** Transferred to NATC, Service Test, NAS Patuxent River, MD., 10 MAR 69 ** Transferred to NATC, Service Test, NAS Patuxent River, MD., 03 JUN 69 ** Transferred to NARF, NAS Jacksonville, FL., 06 NOV 70 ~ S 3SO strike 03 NOV 75 ** No data on strike ** On conditional loan from the National Museum of Naval Aviation; Pensacola, FL., to Don Garletts Racing Museum; Ocala, FL., APR 95.

152651/152660 LTV A-7A-3a-CV Corsair II Block IIIa) FY 65, Contract NOw 64-0363f (Lot 111) (35) A-7A; A-008/A-042

A-008 152651 Navy acceptance from NPRO Rep., LTV, Dallas, TX., 21 MAR 66 ** Transferred to NWEF, Kirtland AFB; Albuquerque, NM., 13 SEP 66 ** Transferred to NPRO Rep., LTV, Dallas, TX., for R & T, 09 FEB 67 ** Transferred to NATC, Service Test, NAS Patuxent River, MD., 17 JAN 68 **

Transferred to NAS Point Mugu, CA., for RDT & E, 18 SEP 68 ** Transferred to NMC, NAS Point Mugu, CA, NMC tail code, 65 Modex, JUL 72 ** Transferred to PMTC, NAS Point Mugu, CA., PMTC/65, 01 JUN 76 ** Transferred to MASDC, Davis Monthan AFB, assigned Park Code 6A080, 08 OCT 77 ~ S 3SO strike, 14 MAR 83 ** No data on strike ** Transferred to the Portuguese AF (FAP) to be used as spare parts, for the A-7P program.

A-009 152652 Navy acceptance from NPRO Rep., LTV, Dallas, TX., 20 APR 66 ** Transferred to NATC, Weapon Systems Test, NAS Patuxent River, MD., 13 SEP 66 ~ S 1SO Strike, 02 AUG 67 ** Crashed at Tinker AFB; Oklahoma City, OK., due to engine failure.

A-010 152653 Navy acceptance from NPRO Rep., LTV, Dallas, TX., 09 MAY 66 ** Transferred to NATC, Weapon Systems Test, NAS Patuxent River, MD., 15 SEP 66 ** Transferred to NATC, Service Test, NAS Patuxent River, MD., 04 MAR 68 ** Transferred to NATC, Weapons Systems Test, NAS Patuxent River, MD., 06 MAY 68 ** Transferred to VA-174/FRS, AD/ 2XX, NAS Oceana., VA., 27 FEB 69 ** Transferred to VA-122/FRS, NJ/2XX, NAS LeMoore, CA., 21 MAY 69 ** Transferred to VA-153/CVW-19 , NM/3XX, USS Oriskany (CVA-34), 23 OCT 69 ** Transferred to VA-174/FRS, AD/2XX, NAS Cecil Field, FL., 22 DEC 69 ** Transferred to NATC, NAS Patuxent River, MD., for RDT & E, 20 NOV 73, NATC Decal on tail, Modex 653; To NATC at NAS Jacksonville, FL., for RDT & E 14 APR 76; To NATC, NAS Patuxent River, MD., 15 APR 76 ~ S 1SO strike, 15 NOV 78 ** Crashed near NAS Patuxent River, MD., due to engine failure.

A-011 152654 Navy acceptance from NPRO Rep., LTV, Dallas, TX., 19 MAY 66; Remained at NAVPRO Rep., LTV, Dallas, TX., for RDT& E, 08 JUN 66 ** Transferred to NATC, Service Test, NAS Patuxent River, MD., 12 JUL 68 ** Transferred to NWEF, Kirtland AFB; Albuquerque, NM., 30 SEP 68 ** Transferred to NATC, Service Test, NAS Patuxent River, MD., 26 NOV 68 ** Transferred to NWEF, Kirtland AFB; Albuquerque, NM., 04 MAR 69 ~ S 1SO strike, 26 JUL 76 ** Crashed near NWEF Kirtland AFB, NM., due to fuel starvation.

A-012 152655 Navy acceptance from NPRO Rep., LTV, Dallas, TX., 10 JUN 66 ** Transferred to VA-122/FRS, NJ/2XX, NAS LeMoore, CA., 22 DEC 66 ** Transferred to VA-174/FRS, AD/2XX, NAS Oceana, VA., 04 JAN 67 ** Transferred to VC-2 Det., Quonset Point, RI., 21 AUG 67 ** Transferred to NATC, Weapon Systems Test, NAS Patuxent River, MD., 22 AUG 67 ** Transferred to NARF, NAS Jacksonville, FL., 18 SEP 67 ** Transferred to VA-174/FRS, AD/2XX, NAS Cecil Field, FL., 21 JUN 68 ** Transferred to MASDC, Davis Monthan AFB; Tucson, AZ., assigned park code 6A unknown; 20 OCT 70 ** Transferred to NARF, NAS Alameda, CA., 09 AUG 72 ** Transferred to VA-125/FRS, NJ/5XX, NAS LeMoore, CA., 19 JUN 73 ** Transferred to Naval Test Pilot School, NAS Patuxent River, MD., TPS Tail Code, 05 Modex, 11 SEP 73 ** Transferred to MASDC, Davis Monthan AFB; Tucson, AZ., Assigned Park Code 6A0040, 25 JUL 75 ~ S 3SO strike 08 OCT 77 ** No data on strike ** Transferred to the Portuguese AF (FAP) to be used as spare parts, for the A-7P program, 05 OCT 83.

A-013 152656 Navy acceptance from NPRO Rep., LTV, Dallas, TX., 16 JUN 66 ** Transferred VA-174/FRS, AD/2XX, NAS Oceana, VA., 02 FEB 67 ** Transferred to NAF China Lake CA., for RDT&E, 25 SEP 67; China Lake on tail ** Transferred to PMTC, NAS Point Mugu, CA., 01 SEP 75 ** Transferred to NAS Point Mugu, CA., 01 JUN 76 ** Transferred to PMTC, NAS Point Mugu, CA., PMTC/63, 01 JUL 77 ** Transferred to MASDC, Davis Monthan AFB; Tucson, CA., assigned park code 6A0079, 08 OCT 77 ~ S 3SO strike, 14 MAR 83 ** No data on strike ** Transferred to the Portuguese AF (FAP) to be used as spare parts, for the A-7P program.

A-014 152657 Navy acceptance from NPRO Rep., LTV, Dallas, TX., 29 JUN 66 ** Transferred to VA-174/FRS, AD/2XX, NAS Cecil Field, FL., 14 FEB 67 ** Transferred to VA-122/FRS, NJ/2XX, NAS LeMoore, CA.,25 SEP 67 ** VA-174/FRS, AD/2XX, NAS Cecil Field, FL., 18 JAN 70 ** Transferred to MASDC, Davis Monthan AFB; Tucson, AZ., assigned park code 6Aunknown; 30 JAN 71 ** Transferred to NARF, NAS Alameda, CA., 11 AUG 72 ** Transferred to VA-125/FRS, NJ/5XX, NAS LeMoore, CA., 13 JUN 73 ** Transferred to NTPS, NAS Patuxent River, MD., TPS/XXX, 03 OCT 73 ** Transferred to NATC, NAS Patuxent River, MD., for RDT & E, 14 JUN 76; to NATC, NAS Jacksonville, FL., for RDT & E, 16 JUN 76 ** Transferred to NTPS, NAS Patuxent River, MD., 16 JUN 76; to NTPS, NAS Jacksonville, FL., 29 JUL 76 ** Transferred to NWEF, Thunderbird/657, Kirtland AFB; Albuquerque, NM., 24 AUG 76 ** Transferred to MASDC, Davis Monthan AFB; Tucson, AZ., assigned park code 6A0045, 25 MAR 77 ~ S 3SO strike, 14 MAR 83 ** No data on strike ** Transferred to the Portuguese AF (FAP) to be used as spare parts, for the A-7P program.

A-015 152658 Navy acceptance from NPRO Rep., LTV, Dallas, TX., 12 JUL 66 ** Transferred to NATC, Weapon Systems Test, NAS Patuxent River, MD., 02 NOV 66 ** Transferred to NATC, Service Test, NAS Patuxent River, MD., 15 AUG 67 ** Transferred to NPRO Rep., LTV, Dallas, TX., for RDT & E, 26 MAY 68** Re-designated to NA-7A ** Transferred to NATC, Service Test, NAS Patuxent River, MD., 11 SEP 69 ** Transferred to NATF, NAS Lakehurst, NJ., for catapult trials, This was the first A-7 Corsair II to land on a carrier ** Transferred to NATC, NAS Patuxent River, MD, for RDT & E, 01 SEP 72 ~ S 3SO strike, 01 NOV 78 ** No data on strike ** On conditional loan from the National Museum of Naval Aviation, Pensacola, Fl., to the Naval Air Test and Evaluation, Test Wing Atlantic, Naval Air Museum; Patuxent, MD., since 79. Marked as an A-7C (incorrect), but carried correct Bureau Number.

A-016 152659 Navy acceptance from NPRO Rep., LTV, Dallas, TX., 28 SEP 66 ** Transferred to NASC, LTV, Dallas, TX., for RDT & E, 28 APR 66 ** Transferred to VA-174/FRS, AD/201, NAS Oceana,VA., 3 OCT 66 ** Transferred to MASDC, Davis Monthan AFB; Tucson, AZ., Assigned park code 6A042, 30 JUL 70 ** Transferred to NARF, NAS Alameda, CA., 11 AUG 72 ** Transferred to VA-125/FRS, NJ/5XX, NAS LeMoore, CA., 15 JUN 73 ** Transferred to PMTC, NAS Point Mugu, CA., PMTC/64, for RDT & E, 25 APR 75 ** Transferred to MASDC, Davis Monthan AFB; Tucson, AZ., assigned park code 6A0042, 05 NOV 75 ~ S 3SO strike, 01 NOV 78 ** No data on strike.

A-017 152660 Navy acceptance from NPRO Rep., LTV, Dallas, TX., 28 SEP 66 ** Transferred to NASC, LTV, Dallas, TX., 28 SEP 66 ** Transferred to VA-174/FRS, AD/202, NAS Oceana, VA., 14 OCT 66 ** Transferred to VA-122/FRS, NJ/2XX, NAS LeMoore, CA., 23 MAY 69 ** Transferred to VA-125/FRS, NJ/5XX, NAS LeMoore, CA., 26 NOV 69 ** Transferred to VA-174/FRS, AD/2XX, NAS Oceana, VA., 22 JAN 70 ** Transferred to MASDC, Davis Monthan AFB; Tucson, AZ., assigned park code unknown, 03 AUG 70 ** Transferred to NARF, NAS Alameda, CA., 11 AUG 72 ** Transferred to VA-125/FRS, NJ/5XX, NAS LeMoore, CA., 09 JUL 73 ** Transferred to NATF, NAS Lakehurst, NJ., XX/XXX, 12 SEP 73; to NATF, NAS Jacksonville, FL., 25 MAR 76; Return to NATF, NAS Lakehurst, NJ., 13 MAY 76 ** Transferred to NAEC, NAS Lakehurst, NJ., XX/XXX, 20 JUL 77 ** Transferred to NWEF, Kirtland AFB; Albuquerque, NM., Thunderbird/XXX, 22 JAN 79 ** Transferred to NARF, NAS Jacksonville, FL., 30 SEP 80 ** Transferred to MASDC, Davis Monthan AFB; Tucson, AZ., assigned park code 6A0121, 29 DEC 81** 3294.9 flight hours ** TF30P6E engine S/N 652078 ** Interservice transfer to USAF, park code assigned, AE005 ** Aircraft released from storage and shipped overland to 355 TFS at Davis Monthan AFB; Tucson, AZ., Engine to be removed and returned to AMARC, 09 MAR 83 ~ S 3SO strike, 31 MAR 83 ** No data on strike ** Transferred to England AFB; Alexandria, LA. ** On display at England AFB; Alexandria, LA., Marked as USAF A-7D 69-6234.

152661/152685 LTV A-7A-3b-CV Corsair II; (Block IIIb)

A-042 152661 Navy acceptance from NPRO Rep., LTV, Dallas, TX., 24 JAN 67 ** Transferred to NASC, Dallas, TX., 24 JAN 67 ** Remained at NPRO Rep. for RDT & E, 25 JAN 67 ** Transferred to NATC, Service Test, NAS Patuxent River, MD., 12 FEB 70 ** Transferred to NATF, NAS Lakehurst, NJ., 14 APR 72 ** Transferred to NTPS, NAS Patuxent River, Md., TPS Tail Code/07 Modex, 25 OCT 73 ~ S 3SO strike, 01 AUG 75 ** No data on strike ** On display at NATF, NAS Lakehurst, NJ., US Naval Sea Cadets on tail, Modex 07, USS Eisenhower on tail cone, 78.

A-018 152662 Navy acceptance from NPRO Rep., LTV, Dallas, TX., 28 SEP 66 ** Transferred to NAS Point Mugu, CA., 18 OCT 66 ** Transferred to VX-5, XE/XXX, NAF China Lake, CA., 08 MAR 67 ** Transferred to VA-122/FRS, NJ/2XX, NAS LeMoore, CA., 28 AUG 68 ~ S 1SO strike, 18 MAR 69 ** Crashed near NAS LeMoore, CA., due to stall/spin.

A-019 152663 Navy acceptance from NPRO Rep., LTV, Dallas, TX., 21 OCT 66 ** Transferred to NASC, LTV, Dallas, TX., 21 OCT 66 ** Transferred to VA-174/FRS, AD/2XX, NAS Cecil Field, FL., 11 NOV 66 ** Transferred to VA-86/CVW-6, AE/4XX, NAS Cecil Field, FL., 20 APR 67 ** to VA-86, USS America (CV-66), 20 APR 67 ** Transferred to VA-174/FRS, AD/2XX, NAS Cecil Field, FL., 11 JAN 68 ~ S 1SO, 23 JUN 70 ** Crashed near NAS Cecil Field, due loss of control.

A-020 152664 Navy acceptance from NPRO Rep., LTV, Dallas, TX., 21 OCT 66 ** Transferred to NASC, LTV, Dallas, TX., 21 OCT 66 ** Transferred to VA-122/FRS, NJ/201, NAS LeMoore, CA., 11 NOV 66 ** Transferred to VA-97/CVW-14, NK/5XX, USS Constellation (CVA-64), 09 NOV 67 ** Transferred to VA-122/FRS, NJ/2XX, NAS LeMoore, CA., 26 JUN 67 ~ S 1SO Strike, 07 MAY 69 ** Crashed into the ground.

A-021 152665 Navy acceptance from NPRO Rep., LTV, Dallas, TX., 21 OCT 66 ** Transferred to NASC, LTV, Dallas, TX., 21 OCT 66 ** Transferred to VA-122FRS, NJ/2XX, NAS LeMoore, CA., 10 NOV 66 ** Transferred to VA-82/CVW-6, AE/ 3XX, NAS Cecil Field, FL., 19 DEC 68 ** Transferred to MASDC, Davis Monthan AFB; Tucson, AZ., 23 JUL 70 ** Transferred to NARF, NAS Alameda, CA, 11 AUG 72 ** Transferred to VA-125/FRS, NJ/5XX, NAS LeMoore, CA., 05 FEB 73 ** Transferred to VA-56/CVW-5, NF/410, NAS LeMoore, CA., 10 MAY 73; To VA-56, USS Midway (CVA-41), 15 JUN 73; To VA-56, NAF Atsugi, JP., 20 JAN 75; To VA-56, USS Midway (CVA-41), 10 MAR 75; To VA-56, NAF Atsugi, JP., 05 SEP 75; To VA-56, USS Midway (CVA-41), 06 SEP 75; To VA-56, NAF Atsugi, JP., 12 SEP 75; To VA-56, USS Midway (CVA-41), 01 OCT 75; To VA-56, NAF Atsugi, JP., 06 NOV 75; To VA-56, USS Midway (CVA-41), 08 NOV 75; To VA-56, NAF Atsugi, JP., 09 NOV 75; To VA-56, USS Midway (CVA-41), 12 MAR 76; To VA-56, NAF Atsugi, JP., 08 SEP 76; To VA-56, USS Midway (CVA-41), 23 SEP 76; TO VA-56, NAF Atsugi, JP., 27 OCT 76; To VA-56, USS Midway (CVA-41), 30 OCT 76 ~ S 1SO Strike, 13 JAN 77 ** Aircraft rolled off the Flight Deck.

A-022 152666 Navy acceptance from NPRO Rep., LTV, Dallas, TX., 23 SEP 66 ** Transferred to VA-122/FRS, NJ/2XX, NAS LeMoore, CA., 01 FEB 67 ** Transferred to NPRO Rep., LTV, Dallas, TX., for R & T, 09 SEP 67 ** Transferred to VA-122/FRS, NJ/2XX, NAS LeMoore, CA., 04 MAR 68 ~ S 1SO strike, 17 MAY 68 ** Crashed at Visalia, CA. due to a mid air collision with A-7A 153172.

A-023 152667 Navy acceptance from NPRO Rep., LTV, Dallas, TX., 22 NOV 66 ** Transferred to NASC, LTV, Dallas, TX., 22 NOV 66 ** Transferred to VA-122/FRS, NJ/2XX, NAS LeMoore, CA., 06 DEC 66 ** Transferred to VA-174/FRS, AD/ 2XX, NAS Cecil Field, FL., 21 JUN 72 ** Transferred to MASDC, Davis Monthan AFB; Tucson, AZ., assigned park code 6A055; 01

SEP 70 ** Transferred to NARF Alameda, CA., 18 JUN 72 ** Transferred to VA-125/FRS, NJ/5XX, NAS LeMoore, CA., 02 JAN 73 ** Transferred to VA-93/CVW-5, NF/310, NAS LeMoore, CA., 26 APR 73; To VA-93, USS Midway (CV-41), 19 JUN 73; To VA-93, NAF Atsugi, JP., 15 NOV 74; To VA-93, USS Midway (CV-41), 20 NOV 74; To VA-93, NAF Atsugi, JP., 10 DEC 74; ToVA-93, USS Midway (CV-41), 27 DEC 74; To VA-93, NAF Atsugi, JP., 23 JUL 75; To VA-93, USS Midway (CV-41), 24 JUL 75; To VA-93, NAF Atsugi, JP., 28 JUL 75; To VA-93, USS Midway (CV-41), 24 DEC 75; To VA-93, NAF Atsugi, JP., 01 DEC 76; To VA-93, USS Midway (CV-41), 09 DEC 76; To VA-93, NAF Atsugi, JP., 13 DEC 76; To VA-93, USS Midway (CV-41), 07 MAR 77; To VA-93, NAS North Island, CA., 24 MAY 77 ** Transferred to MASDC, Davis Monthan AFB; Tucson, AZ., assigned park code 6A0055, 26 MAY 77 ~ S 3SO strike, 27 SEP 80 ** No data on strike ** Transferred to the Portuguese AF (FAP) to be used as spare parts, for the A-7P program.

A-024 152668 Navy acceptance from NPRO Rep., LTV, Dallas, TX., 23 NOV 66 ** Transferred to NASC, LTV, Dallas, TX., 23 NOV 66 ** Transferred to VA-174/FRS, AD/2XX, NAS Cecil Field, CA., 17 DEC 68 ** Transferred to VA-86/CVW-6, AE/4XX, NAS Cecil Field, FL., 20 APR 67; To VA-86, USS America (CV-66), 20 APR 67 ** Transferred to VA-174/FRS, AD/2XX, NAS Cecil Field, FL., 21 DEC 67 ** Transferred to MASDC, Davis Monthan AFB; Tucson, AZ., 03 SEP 70 ** Transferred to NARF, NAS Alameda, CA., 05 JUL 72 ** Transferred to VA-303/CVWR-30, ND/300, NAS Alameda, CA., 16 DEC 72 ** Transferred to VA-203/CVWR-20, AF/302, NAS Jacksonville, FL., 09 APR 74 ** Transferred to VA-305/ CVWR-30, ND/5XX, NAS Point Mugu, CA., 17 NOV 76 ** Transferred to VA-203/CVWR-20, AF/3XX, NAS Jacksonville, FL., 04 DEC 76 ~ S 3SO strike, 15 SEP 77 ** No data on strike ** Sectioned Airframe on conditional loan from the National Museum of Naval Aviation; Pensacola, FL., to the Chicago Museum of Science and Industry, Chicago, IL.

A-025 152669 Navy acceptance from NPRO Rep., LTV, Dallas, TX., 22 NOV 66 ** Transferred to NASC, LTV, Dallas, TX., 22 NOV 66 ** Transferred to VA-174/FRS, AD/2XX, NAS Cecil Field, FL., 08 DEC 66 ** Transferred to VA-86/CVW-6, AE/4XX, NAS Cecil Field, FL., 20 APR 67; To VA-86, USS America (CVA-66), 20 APR 67 ** Transferred to VA-174/FRS, AD/2XX, NAS Cecil Field, FL., 26 DEC 67 ** Transferred to VA-86/CVW-6, AE/4XX, NAS Cecil Field, FL., 01 FEB 69 ** Transferred to MASDC, Davis Monthan AFB; Tucson, AZ., assigned park code 6A Unknown; 25 AUG 70 ** Transferred to NARF, NAS Alameda, CA., 11 JUL 72 ** Transferred to VA-93/ CVW-5, NF/306, NAS LeMoore, CA., 25 MAY 73; To VA-93, USS Midway (CVA-41), 21 JUN 73; To VA-93, NAF Atsugi, JP., 22 DEC 75; To VA-93, USS Midway (CVA-41), 01 NOV 76; To VA-93, NAS North Island, CA., 24 MAY 77 ** Transferred to MASDC, Davis Monthan AFB; Tucson, AZ., assigned park code 6A0053, 26 MAY 77 ~ S 3SO strike, 14 MAR 83 ** No data on strike ** Transferred to the Portuguese AF (FAP) to be used as spare parts, for the A-7P program.

A-026 152670 Navy acceptance from NPRO Rep., LTV, Dallas, TX., 22 NOV 66 ** Transferred to NASC, LTV, Dallas, TX., 22 NOV 66 ** Transferred to VA-122/FRS, NJ/2XX, NAS LeMoore, CA., 07 DEC 66 ~ S 1SO strike, 08 DEC 66 ** Crashed near MCAS Yuma, AZ., due to a spin.

A-027 152671 Navy acceptance from NPRO Rep., LTV, Dallas, TX., 30 NOV 66 ** Transferred to NASC, LTV, Dallas, TX., 30 NOV 66 ** Transferred to VA-122/FRS, NJ/2XX, NAS LeMoore, CA., 18 DEC 66 ~ S 1SO strike, 24 SEP 68 ** Crashed at MCAS Yuma, AZ., Due to port wing folded on take off.

A-028 152672 Navy acceptance from NPRO Rep., LTV, Dallas, TX., 28 NOV 66 ** Transferred to NASC, LTV, Dallas, TX., 28 NOV 66 ** Transferred to VA-174/FRS, AD/2XX, NAS Cecil Field, FL., 14 DEC 66 ~ S 1SO strike, 26 JAN 67 ** Crashed near NAS Cecil Field, FL., Due to a failed engine bearing.

A-029 152673 Navy acceptance from NPRO Rep., LTV, Dallas, TX., 20 DEC 66 ** Transferred to NASC, LTV, Dallas, TX., 20 DEC 66 ** Transferred to VX-5, XE/XXX, NAF China Lake, CA., 10 JAN 67 ** Transferred to VA-122/FRS, NJ/2XX, NAS LeMoore, CA., 26 MAR 68 ** Transferred to VA-82/CVW-15, NL/3XX, NAS Cecil Field, FL., 23 DEC 68 ** Transferred to VA-174/FRS, AD/2XX, NAS Cecil Field, FL., 30 JUL 69, Transferred to NARF, NAS Alameda, CA., 02 JUL 72 ** Transferred to VA-125/FRS, NJ/5XX, NAS LeMoore, CA., 26 DEC 72 ** Transferred to VA-93/CVW-5, NF/300, NAS LeMoore, CA., 17 APR 73; To VA-93, USS Midway (CVA-41), 18 JUN 73; To VA-93, NAF Atsugi, JP., 20 JAN 76; To VA-93, USS Midway (CVA-41), 18 MAY 76; To VA-93, NAF Atsugi, JP., 16 NOV 76; To VA-93, USS Midway (CVA-41), 02 DEC 76; To VA-93, NAS North Island, CA., 24 MAY 77 ** Transferred to MASDC, Davis Monthan AFB, Tucson, AZ., assigned park code 6A059; 27 MAY 77 ~ S 3SO strike, 14 MAR 83 ** No data on strike ** Located in North Hollywood, Ca., Airframe less engine, instruments, panels & other parts, for sale on E-bay, 02 AUG 04.

A-030 152674 Navy acceptance from NPRO Rep., LTV, Dallas, TX., 14 DEC 66 ** Transferred to NASC, LTV, Dallas, TX., 14 DEC 66 ** Transferred to VX-5, XE/XXX, NAF China Lake, CA., 20 DEC 66 ** S 1SO strike, 01 AUG 67 ** Crashed, Due to a Mid Air Collision with a civilian Cessna 210B N9771X over Owens Peak, CA. while flying passive SHRIKE runs; LCDR Tom Ewell and three civilians were killed.

A-031 152675 Navy acceptance from NPRO Rep., LTV, Dallas, TX., 22 DEC 66 ** Transferred to NASC, LTV, Dallas, TX., 22 DEC 66 ** Transferred to VA-27/CVW-14, NK/6XX, USS Constellation (CVA-64), 19 DEC 67 ** Transferred to VA-122/FRS, NJ/2XX, NAS LeMoore, CA., 30 APR 68 ** Transferred to VA-82/CVW-15, NL/3XX, USS Coral Sea (CVA-43), 14 JAN 69; To VA-82, NAS Cecil Field, FL., 24 MAY 70 ** Transferred to MASDC, Davis Monthan AFB; Tucson, AZ., assigned park code 6Aunknown; 17 AUG 70 ** Transferred to NARF, NAS Alameda, CA., 16 JUL 72 ** Transferred to VA-56/ CVW-5, NF/400, NAS LeMoore, CA., 02 MAY 73; To VA-56, USS Midway (CVA-41), 15 JUN 73; To VA-56, NAF Atsugi, JP., 21 AUG 74; To VA-56, USS Midway (CVA-41), 25 OCT 74; To VA-56, NAF Atsugi, JP., 17 MAR 75; To VA-56, USS Midway (CVA-41), 01 APR 75; To VA-56, NAF Atsugi, JP., 21 JUL 75; To VA-56, USS Midway (CV-41), 26 JUL 75; To VA-56, NAF Atsugi, JP., 06 JAN 76; To VA-56, USS MIDWAY (CV-41), 14 JAN 76; To VA-56, NAF Atsugi, JP., 06 MAY 76; To VA-56, USS Midway (CV-41), 26 NOV 76; To VA-56, NAF Atsugi, JP.,03 MAR 77; To VA-56, USS Midway (CV-41), 22 MAR 77; To VA-56, North Island, CA., 27 MAY 77 ** Transferred to MASDC, Davis Monthan AFB; Tucson, AZ., assigned park code 6A0065, 31 MAY 77 ~ S 3SO strike, 13 APR 83 ** No data on strike ** Transferred to the Portuguese AF (FAP) to be used as spare parts, for the A-7P program.

A-032 152676 Navy acceptance from NPRO Rep., LTV, Dallas, TX., 22 DEC 66 ** Transferred to NASC, LTV, Dallas, TX., 22 DEC 66 ** Transferred to VA-122/FRS, NJ/2XX, NAS LeMoore, CA., 17 JAN 67 ** Transferred to VA-86/CVW-15, NL/ 4XX, USS Coral Sea (CVA-43), 29 DEC 69 ** Transferred to VA-25/CVW-15, NL/3XX, NAS LeMoore, CA., 09 APR 70 ** Transferred to VA-86/CVW-15, NL/4XX, NAS Cecil Field, FL., 16 MAY 70 ** Transferred to MASDC, Davis Monthan AFB; Tucson, AZ., assigned park code 6A unknown; 25 AUG 70 ** Transferred to NARF, NAS Alameda, CA., 02 JUL 72 ** Transferred to VA-304/CVWR-30, ND/406, NAS ALAMEDA, CA., 06 DEC 72; To VA-304, NAS Jacksonville, FL., 16 MAR 75; To VA-304 NAS Alameda, CA., 15 MAY 75; To VA-304, NAS Jacksonville, FL., 21 MAY 75; To VA-304, NAS Alameda, CA., 22 JUL 75 ** Transferred to MASDC, Davis Monthan AFB; Tucson, CA., assigned park code 6A0087, 18 NOV 77 ~ S 3SO strike, 15 APR 83 ** No data on strike ** Transferred to the Portuguese AF (FAP) to be used as spare parts, for the A-7P program.

A-033 152677 Navy acceptance from NPRO Rep., LTV, Dallas, TX., 20 DEC 66 ** Transferred to NASC, LTV, Dallas, TX., 20 DEC 66 ** Transferred to VA-174/FRS, AD/2XX, NAS Oceana, VA., 10 JAN 67 ** Transferred to VA-86/CVW-6, AE/4XX, NAS Cecil Field, FL., 20 APR 67; To VA-86,USS America (CVA-66), 20 APR 67 ** Transferred to VA-37/CVW-11, NH/3XX, NAS Cecil Field, FL., 13 DEC 67; To VA-37, USS Kitty Hawk (CVA-63), 13 DEC 67 ** Transferred to VA-174/FRS, AD/2XX, NAS Cecil Field, FL., 24 SEP 68 ** Transferred to VA-86/CVW-6, AE/4XX, NAS Cecil Field, FL., 14 FEB 69 ** Transferred to VA-86/CVW-15, NL/4XX, USS Coral Sea (CVA-43), 30 MAY 69; To VA-86, NAS Cecil Field, FL., 16 MAY 70 ** Transferred to MASDC, Davis Monthan AFB; Tucson, AZ., assigned park code 6A068; 10 SEP 70 ** Transferred to NARF, NAS Alameda, CA., 04 JUL 72 ** Transferred to VA-125/FRS, NJ/5XX, NAS LeMoore, CA., 03 JAN 73 ** Transferred to VA-56/CVW-5, NF/407, NAS LeMoore, CA., 18 APR 73; To VA-56, USS Midway (CVA-41), 15 JUN 73; To VA-56, NAF Atsugi, JP., 07 JUL 76; To VA-56, USS Midway (CV-41), 31 DEC 76; To VA-56, NAS North Island, CA., 26 MAY 77 ** Transferred to MASDC, Davis Monthan AFB; Tucson, AZ., assigned park code 6A0068; 01 JUN 77 ** Transferred to NWEF, Kirtland AFB, Albuquerque, NM., 23 SEP 80 ** Transferred to MASDC, Davis Monthan AFB; Tucson, AZ., assigned park code 6A122, 29 DEC 81 ** 2736.9 flight hours ** Engine TF30P6E, S/N P652086 ~ S 3SO strike, 17 APR 83 ** No data on strike ** Aircraft released from storage and prepared for overland shipment to Holloman AFB; Alamogordo, NM., as a range target, 11 APR 05.

A-034 152678 Navy acceptance from NPRO Rep., LTV, Dallas, TX., 22 DEC 66 ** Transferred to NASC, LTV, Dallas, TX., 22 DEC 66 ** Transferred to VA-122/FRS, NJ/2XX, NAS LeMoore, CA., 14 JAN 67 ** Transferred to VA-82/CVW-15, NL/3XX, NAS Cecil Field, FL., 23 DEC 68; To VA-82, USS Coral Sea (CVA-43), 13 MAY 69; To VA-82, NAS Cecil Field, FL., 22 APR 70 ** Transferred to MASDC, Davis Monthan AFB; Tucson, AZ., 21 AUG 70 ** Transferred to NARF, NAS Alameda, CA., 15 JUL 72 ** Transferred to VA-93/CVW-5, NF/307, NAS LeMoore, CA., 06 MAY 73; To VA-93, USS Midway (CVA-41), 29 JUN 73; VA-93, NAF Atsugi, JP., 02 JUL 74; To VA-93, USS Midway (CV-41), 04 JUN 74; To VA-93, NAF Atsugi, JP., 15 JUL 74; To VA-93, USS Midway (CV-41), 15 JUL 74; To VA-93, NAF Atsugi, JP.,15 OCT 74; To VA-93, USS Midway (CV-41), 12 NOV 74; To VA-93, NAF Atsugi, JP., 12 DEC 75; To VA-93, USS Midway (CV-41), 09 APR 77; To VA-93, NAS North Island, CA., 26 MAY 77 ** Transferred to MASDC, Davis Monthan AFB; Tucson, AZ., assigned park code 6A0062, 31 MAY 77~ S 3SO strike, 26 SEP 80 ** No data on strike ** Transferred to the Portuguese AF (FAP) to be used as spare parts, for the A-7P program.

A-035 152679 Navy acceptance from NPRO Rep., LTV, Dallas, TX., 23 JAN 67 ** Transferred to NASC, LTV, Dallas, TX., 23 JAN 67 ** Transferred to VA-86/CVW-6, AE/4XX, NAS Cecil Field, FL., 30 JAN 67; ToVA-86, USS America (CVA-66), 17 FEB 67 ** Transferred to VA-174/FRS, AD/2XX, 27 DEC 67 ** Transferred to VA-86/CVW-15, NL/4XX, NAS Cecil Field, FL., 27 FEB 69; VA-86, USS Coral Sea (CVA-43), 02 MAY 69 ~ S 1SO strike, 15 NOV 69 ** Lost due to engine failure over SE Asia, pilot survived.

A-036 152680 Navy acceptance from NPRO Rep., LTV, Dallas, TX., 23 JAN 67 ** Transferred to NASC, LTV, Dallas, TX., 23 JAN 67 ** Transferred to VA-86/CVW-6, AE/4XX, NAS Cecil Field, FL., 30 JAN 67; To VA-86, USS America (CVA-66), 30 JAN 67 ** Transferred to VA-37/CVW-17, NH/3XX, NAS Cecil Field, FL., 13 DEC 67; To VA-37, USS Kitty Hawk (CVA-63), 01 MAY 68 ** Transferred to VA-174/FRS, AD/2XX, NAS Cecil Field, FL., 24 SEP 68 ** Transferred to VA-82/ CVW-15, NL/3XX, USS Coral Sea (CVA-43), 19 SEP 69 ~ S 1SO strike, 01 MAY 70 ** Lost due to engine failure over SE Asia, pilot survived.

A-037 152681 Navy acceptance from NPRO Rep., LTV, Dallas, TX., 24 JAN 67 ** Transferred to NASC, LTV, Dallas, TX., 24 JAN 67 ** Transferred to VA-122/FRS, NJ/2XX, NAS LeMoore, CA., 25 JAN 67 ** Transferred to NATC, Service Test, NAS Patuxent

River, MD., 24 SEP 67 ** Transferred to VA-122/FRS, NJ/2XX, NAS LeMoore, CA., 28 FEB 69 ** Transferred to VA-125/FRS, NJ/5XX, NAS LeMoore, CA., 01 DEC 69 ** Transferred to VA-305/CVWR-30, ND/502, NAS Point Mugu, CA., 11 JUL 72; To VA-305, NAS Alameda, CA., 28 OCT 72; To VA-305, NAS Whidbey Island, WA., 29 OCT 72; To VA-305, NAs Point Mugu, CA., 29 OCT 72 ** Transferred to VA-203/CVWR-20, AF/306, NAS Jacksonville, FL., 07 APR 74 ** Transferred to NATTC; Millington, TN., date unknown, ., sitting outside the Airframes shop, to be used as an instructional airframe ~ S 3SO strike, 01 MAY 70 ** No data on strike ** On conditional loan from the National Museum of Naval Aviation; Pensacola, FL., to the Prairie Aviation Museum, Bloomington, IL., APR 01.

A-038 152682 Navy acceptance from NPRO Rep., LTV, Dallas, TX., 23 JAN 67 ** Transferred to NASC, LTV, Dallas, TX., 23 JAN 67 ** Transferred to VA-86/CVW-6, AE/4XX, NAS Cecil Field, FL., 02 FEB 67; To VA-86, USS America (CVA-66), 02 FEB 67 ** Transferred to VA-37/CVW-11, NH/3XX, NAS Cecil Field, FL., 21 DEC 67; To VA-37, USS Kitty Hawk (CVA-63), 14 MAY 68 ** Transferred to VA-174/FRS, AD/2XX, NAS Cecil Field, FL., 23 SEP 68 ** Transferred to VA-82/CVW-15, NL/3XX, NAS Cecil Field, FL., 29 APR 69; To VA-82, USS Coral Sea (CVA-43), 24 JUN 69; To VA-82, NAS Cecil Field, FL., 19 MAY 70 ** Transferred to MASDC, Davis Monthan AFB; Tucson, AZ., assigned park code 6A057; 05 AUG 70 ** Transferred to NARF, NAS Alameda, CA., 05 JUL 72 ** Transferred to VA-125/FRS, NJ/5XX, NAS LeMoore, CA., 23 JAN 73 ** Transferred to VA-56/CVW-5, NF/405, NAS LeMoore, CA., 02 MAY 73; To VA-56, USS Midway (CVA-41), 15 JUN 73; To VA-56, NAF Atsugi, JP, 21 DEC 73 ** Transferred to VA-93/CVW-5, NF/3XX, NAF Atsugi, JP., 21 JUN 74; To VA-93, USS Midway (CVA-41), 09 OCT 74 ** Transferred to VA-56/CVW-5, NF/405, USS Midway (CV-41), 26 JUN 75; To VA-56, NAF Atsugi, JP., 27 FEB 76; To VA-56, USS Midway (CV-41), 03 JUL 76; To VA-56, NAF Atsugi, JP., 20 AUG 76; To VA-56, USS Midway (CV-41), 28 AUG 76; To VA-56, NAF Atsugi, JP., 21 DEC 76; To VA-56, USS Midway (CV-41), 09 APR 77; To VA-56, NAS Atsugi, JP., 18 APR 77; To VA-56, USS Midway (CV-41), 20 APR 77; To VA-56, NAS North Island, CA., 23 MAY 77 ** Transferred to MASDC, Davis Monthan AFB; Tucson, AZ., assigned park code unknown, 27 MAY 77~ S 3SO strike, 25 SEP 80 ** No data on strike ** Transferred to the Portuguese AF (FAP) to be used as spare parts, for the A-7P program.

A-039 152683 Navy acceptance from NPRO Rep., LTV, Dallas, TX., 23 JAN 67 ** Transferred to NASC, LTV, Dallas, TX., 23 JAN 67 ** Transferred to VA-122/FRS, NJ/201, NAS LeMoore, CA., 03 FEB 67 ~ S 1SO, 03 AUG 68 ** Crashed Near NAS Fallon, NV., due to hydraulic failure and loss of control.

A-040 152684 Navy acceptance from NPRO Rep., LTV, Dallas, TX., 23 JAN 67 ** Transferred to NASC, LTV, Dallas, TX., 23 JAN 67 ** Transferred to VA-86/CVW-6, AE/4XX, NAS Cecil Field, FL., 10 FEB 67; To VA-86, USS America (CVA-66), 17 FEB 67 ** Transferred to VA-174/FRS, AD/2XX, NAS Cecil Field, FL., 28 DEC 67 ~ S 1SO strike ** Crashed near NAS Cecil Field, FL., due to an engine failure.

A-041 152685 Navy acceptance from NPRO Rep., LTV, Dallas, TX., 25 JAN 67 ** Transferred to NASC, LTV, Dallas, TX., 25 JAN 67 ** Transferred to VA-86/CVW-6, AE/4XX, NAS Cecil Field, FL.,10 FEB 67; To VA-86, USS America (CVA-66), 10 FEB 66 ** Transferred to VA-174/FRS, AD/2XX, NAS Cecil Field, FL., 27 DEC 67 ** Transferred to VA-82/CVW-15, NL/3XX, USS Coral Sea (CVA-43), 30 JUN 69; To VA-82, NAS Cecil Field, FL., 03 MAR 70 ** Transferred to MASDC, Davis Monthan AFB; Tucson, AZ., 24 AUG 70 ** Transferred to NARF, NAS Alameda, CA., 11 JUL 72 ** Transferred to VA-56/CVW-5, NF/413, USS Midway (CVA-41), 24 JUL 73; To VA-56 NAS Atsugi, Japan, 23 DEC 74; To VA-56, USS Midway (CVA-41), 18 JAN 75 ~ S 1SO strike, 24 MAY 75 ** Pilot ejected, reason unknown, and was rescued. The aircraft continued to fly and was shot down by another A-7.

153134/153181 LTV A-7A-4a-CV Corsair II; (Block IVa) FY 66, Contract NOw 64-0363f (Lot IV) (157) A-7A; A-043/A-199

A-090 153134 Navy acceptance from NPRO Rep., LTV, Dallas, TX., 31 MAY 67 ** Transferred to NASC, LTV, Dallas, TX., 31 MAY 67, Transferred to VA-122/FRS, NJ/2XX, NAS LeMoore, CA., 15 JUN 67 ** Transferred to VX-5, XE/XXX, NAF China Lake, CA., 04 OCT 67 ** Transferred to VA-122/FRS, NJ/2XX, NAS LeMoore, CA., 26 JAN 68; To VA-122, COSA, NAs LeMoore, CA., 12 SEP 69 ** Transferred to VA-27/CVW-14, NK/4XX, 15 DEC 69 ** Transferred to VA-125/FRS, NJ/5XX, NAS LeMoore, CA., 09 JUN 70 ** Transferred to VA-304/CVWR-30, ND/4XX, NAS Alameda, CA., 25 SEP 72 ** Transferred to VA-305/CVWR-30, ND/506, NAS Point Mugu, CA., 09 AUG 72; To VA-305, NAS Jacksonville, FL., 04 FEB 76; To VA-305, NAS Point Mugu, CA., 31 MAR 76; To VA-305, NAS Dallas, TX., 04 APR 78; To VA-305, NAS Point Mugu, CA., 26 APR 78 ** Transferred to MASDC assigned park code 6A0104, 08 MAY 78 ~ S 3SO strike, 13 MAY 83 ** No data on strike ** Sent to LTV, Dallas, TX., to be converted to A-7P ** Transferred to the Portuguese AF, (FAP) as S/N 5521 ** Transferred to Esquadra 304 "Magnificoes" , BA-5; Monte Real, PO., 1984 ** S/N changed to 15521 ** Applied special paint scheme "64,000 horas" ** W/O and on display at Monte Real, PO., 2000.

A-043 153135 Navy acceptance from NPRO Rep., LTV, Dallas, TX., 30 JAN 67 ** Transferred to NASC, LTV, Dallas, TX., 30 JAN 67 ** Transferred to VX-5 , XE/XXX, NAF China Lake, CA., 09 FEB 67 ** Transferred to VA-122/FRS, NJ/2XX, NAS LeMoore, CA., 09 DEC 68 ** Transferred to VA-97/CVW-14, NK/5XX, NAS LeMoore, CA. ** Transferred to VA-97/CVW-14, NK/5XX, USS Constellation (CVA-64), 01 MAY 69 ** Transferred to VA-25/CVW-2, NE/4XX, NAS LeMoore, CA., 03 JUN 70 ** Transferred to VA-153/CVW-19, NM/3XX, USS Oriskany (CVA-34), 17 JAN 72 ** Transferred to VA-125/ FRS, NJ5XX, NAS LeMoore, CA., 21 APR 72 ** Transferred to VA-305/CVWR-30, ND/501, NAS Point Mugu, CA., 27 JUN 72 ** Transferred to MASDC, Davis Monthan AFB; Tucson, AZ., 08 DEC 77, assigned park code 6A0097; 08 DEC 77 ~ S 3SO strike, 07 MAY 80 ** No data on strike ** Transferred to NS Great Lakes Naval Recruit Depot, near Haineville, IL. to be used as an instructional airframe ** Transferred to NATTC, Millington, TN., sitting outside the airframes shop, to be used as an instructional airframe, 07 OCT 89 ** On conditional loan from the National Museum of Naval Aviation, Pensacola, Fl. to the Valliant Air Command Museum; Titusville, FL., MAR 97.

A-044 153136 Navy acceptance from NPRO Rep., LTV, Dallas, TX., 30 JAN 67 ** Transferred to NASC, LTV, Dallas, TX., 30 JAN 67 ** Transferred to VA-122/FRS, NJ/2XX, NAS LeMoore, CA., 09 FEB 67 ** Transferred to VA-86/CVW-15, NL/400, NAS Cecil Field, FL., 03 FEB 69; To VA-86, USS Coral Sea (CVA-43), 02 MAY 69 ~ S 1SO strike, 04 MAR 70 ** Lost due to a bad catapult shot.

A-045 153137 Navy acceptance from NPRO Rep., LTV, Dallas, TX., 16 FEB 67 ** Transferred to NASC, LTV, Dallas, TX., 16 FEB 67 ** Transferred to VA-122/FRS, NJ/2XX, NAS LeMoore, CA., 17 FEB 67 ** Transferred to VA-97/CVW-14, NK/ 5XX, USS Constellation (CVA-64), 31 OCT 67 ** Transferred to VA-122/FRS, NJ/2XX, NAS LeMoore, CA., 01 MAR 68 ~ S 1SO, 08 MAR 68 ** Crashed due to a spin.

A-046 153138 Navy acceptance from NPRO Rep., LTV, Dallas, TX., 23 FEB 67 ** Transferred to NASC, LTV, Dallas, TX., 23 FEB 67 ** Transferred to VA-86/CVW-6, AE/4XX, NAS Cecil Field, FL., 24 FEB 67; To VA-86, USS America (CVA-66), 24 FEB 67 ** Transferred to VA-174/FRS, AD/2XX, NAS Cecil Field, FL., 12 JAN 68 ** Transferred to VA-86/CVW-15, NL/4XX, NAS Cecil Field, FL., 24 APR 69; To VA-86, USS Coral Sea (CVA-43), 23 JUN 69; To VA-86, NAS Cecil Field, 17 APR 70 ** Transferred to MASDC, Davis Monthan AFB; Tucson, AZ., assigned park code 6A078; 10 SEP 70 ** Transferred to NARF, NAS Alameda. CA., 07 AUG 72 ** Transferred to VA-305/CVWR-30, ND/504, NAS Point Mugu, CA., 14 MAR 73; To VA-305 NAS Jacksonville, FL., 14 APR 75;

To VA-305, NAS Point Mugu, CA., 14 APR 75; To VA-305, NAS alameda, CA., 05 MAR 76; To VA-305, 05 MAR 76 ** Transferred to MASDC, Davis Monthan AFB; Tucson, AZ., assigned park code 6A0078, 26 SEP 77 ~ S 3SO strike, 13 MAY 83 ** No data on strike ** Transferred to the Portuguese AF (FAP) to be used as spare parts, for the A-7P program.

A-047 153139 Navy acceptance from NPRO Rep., LTV, Dallas, TX., 23 FEB 67 ** Transferred to NASC, LTV, Dallas, TX., 20 FEB 67 ** Transferred to VA-86/CVW-6, AE/4XX, NAS Cecil Field, FL., 08 MAR 67; To VA-86, USS America (CVA-66), 08 MAR 67 ** Transferred to VA-174/FRS, AD/2XX, NAS Cecil Field, FL., 14 JAN 69 ~ S 1SO, 30 JUL 69 ** Crashed near MCAS Yuma, AZ., due to loss of control.

A-048 153140 Navy acceptance from NPRO Rep., LTV, Dallas, TX., 20 FEB 67 ** Transferred to NASC, LTV, Dallas, TX., 20 FEB 67 ** Transferred to VA-86/CVW-6, AE/4XX, NAS Cecil Field, FL., 01 MAR 67; To VA-86, USS America (CVA-66), 01 MAR 67 ** Transferred to VA-174/FRS, AD/2XX, NAS Cecil Field, FL., 16 JAN 68 ** Transferred to VA-86/CVW-15, NL/4XX, NAS Cecil Field, FL., 10 MAR 69; To VA-86, USS Coral Sea (CVA-43), 23 JUN 69; To VA-86, NAS Cecil Field, FL., 03 MAY 70 ** Transferred to MASDC, Davis Monthan AFB; Tucson, AZ., assigned park code unknown, 14 SEP 70 ** Transferred to NARF, NAS Alameda, CA., 26 AUG 72 ** Transferred to VA-93/CVW-5, NF/3XX, NAS LeMoore, CA., 05 APR 73; To VA-93, USS Midway (CVA-41), 14 JUN 73; To VA-93, NAF Atsugi, JP., 03 JUL 75; To VA-93, USS Midway (CVA-41), 17 DEC 75; To VA-93, NAF Atsugi, JP., 30 AUG 76 ** Transferred to VA-56/CVW-5, NF/412, USS Midway (CV-41), 15 FEB 77; To VA-56, NAF Atsugi, JP., 08 MAR 77; To VA-56, USS Midway (CV-41), 17 MAR 77; To VA-56, NAS North Island, CA., 25 MAY 77 ** Transferred to MASDC, Davis Monthan AFB; Tucson, AZ., assigned park code 6A0058, 27 MAY 77 ~ S 3SO strike, 26 SEP 80 ** No data on strike ** Transferred to the Portuguese AF (FAP) to be used as spare parts, for the A-7P program.

A-049 153141 Navy acceptance from NPRO Rep., LTV, Dallas, TX., 20 FEB 67 ** Transferred to NASC, LTV, Dallas, TX., 20 FEB 67 ** Transferred to VA-122/FRS, NJ/2XX, NAS LeMoore, CA., 11 MAR 67 ** Transferred to VA-97/CVW-14, NK/5XX, USS Constellation (CVA-64), 25 OCT 67 ** Transferred to VA-122/FRS, NJ/2XX, NAS LeMoore, CA., 26 FEB 68 ** Transferred to VA-27/CVW-14, NK/4XX, USS Constellation (CVA-64), 25 OCT 69; To VA-27, NAS LeMoore, CA., 12 JUN 69; To VA-27, USS Enterprise (CVAN-65), 10 JUN 70 ** Transferred to VA-125/FRS, NJ/5XX, NAS LeMoore, CA., 12 NOV 70 ~ S 1SO strike, 12 FEB 72 ** Crashed near NAS Miramar, CA., due to engine failure.

A-050 153142 Navy acceptance from NPRO Rep., LTV, Dallas, TX., 20 FEB 67 ** Transferred to NASC, LTV, Dallas, TX., ** Transferred to VA-86/CVW-6, AE/4XX, NAS Cecil Field, FL., 08 MAR 67 ** Transferred to VA-174/FRS, AD/2XX, 19 JAN 68 ** Transferred to VA-86/CVW-15, NL/4XX, USS Coral Sea (CVA-43), 09 MAY 69; To VA-86, NAS Cecil Field, FL., 11 MAY 70 ** Transferred to MASDC, Davis Monthan AFB; Tucson, AZ., 25 AUG 70 ** Transferred to NARF, NAS Alameda, CA., 15 JUL 72 ** Transferred to VA-304/CVWR-30, ND/411, NAS Alameda, CA.; (Cyclops) on MLG door, 15 MAR 73 ** Transferred to VA-203/CVWR-20, AF/303, NAS Jacksonville, FL., 24 APR 74 ~ S 3SO strike, 15 SEP 77 ** No data on strike ** On display at the Forest Barber AP; Alliance, OH.

A-051 153143 Navy acceptance from NPRO Rep., LTV, Dallas, TX., 23 FEB 67 ** Transferred to NASC, LTV, Dallas, TX., 23 FEB 67 ** Transferred to VA-122/FRS, NJ/2XX, NAS Cecil Field, FL., 04 MAR 67 ** Transferred to VA-97/CVW-14, NK/5XX, USS Constellation (CVA-64), 27 OCT 67 ** Transferred to VA-122/FRS, NJ/2XX, NAS Cecil Field, FL., 04 MAR 68; To VA-122, COSA, NAS LeMoore, CA., 29 JUL 69 ** Transferred to VA-27/CVW-14, NK/411, NAS LeMoore, CA., 05 AUG 69 ~ S 1SO strike, 01 MAR 70 ** No data on strike.

A-052 153144 Navy acceptance from NPRO Rep., LTV, Dallas, TX., 24 FEB 67 ** Transferred to NASC, LTV, Dallas, TX., 24 FEB 67 ** Transferred to VA-122/FRS, NJ/2XX, NAS LeMoore, CA., 08 MAR 67 ** Transferred to VA-97/CVW-14, NK/507, USS Constellation (CVA-64), 02 NOV 67 ** Transferred to VA-122/FRS, NJ/2XX, NAS LeMoore, CA., 07 MAR 68 ** Transferred to VA-86/CVW-14, NL/4XX, NAS LeMoore, CA., 21 JAN 69; To VA-86, USS Coral Sea (CVA-43), 25 APR 69; To VA-86, NAS Cecil Field, FL., 03 JUN 70 ** Transferred to MASDC, Davis Monthan AFB; Tucson, AZ., assigned park code 6A064; 25 JUL 70 ** Transferred to NARF, NAS Alameda, CA., 15 JUN 72 ** Transferred to VA-174/FRS, AD/2XX, NAS Cecil Field, FL., 09 DEC 72 ** Transferred to VA-56/CVW-5, NF/4XX, NAS LeMoore, CA., 26 MAR 73; To VA-56, USS Midway (CVA-41), 19 JUN 73; To VA-93/CVW-5, NF/3XX NAF Atsugi, JP., 20 JAN 75; To VA-93, USS Midway (CVA-41), 26 FEB 75; To VA-93, NAF Atsugi, JP., 29 MAY 75 ** Transferred to VA-56/CVW-5, NF/411, NAF Atsugi, JP., 29 MAY 75; To VA-56, USS Midway (CVA-41), 21 DEP 75; VA-56, NAF Atsugi, JP., 19 DEC 75; To VA-56, USS Midway (CV-41), 27 DEC 75; To VA-56, NAF Atsugi, JP., 07 SEP 76; To VA-56, USS Midway (CV-41), 01 OCT 76; To VA-56, NAF Atsugi, JP., 20 OCT 76; To VA-56, USS Midway (CV-41), 27 OCT 76; To VA-56, NAF Atsugi, JP., 25 JAN 77; To VA-56, USS Midway (CV-41), 27 JAN 77 ** Transferred to MASDC, Davis Monthan AFB; Tucson, AZ., 6A0064, 31 MAY 77 ~ S 3SO strike, 26 SEP 80 ** No data on strike ** Transferred to the Portuguese AF (FAP) to be used as spare parts, for the A-7P program.

A-053 153145 Navy acceptance from NPRO Rep. LTV Dallas, TX., 24 FEB 67 ** Transferred to NASC, LTV, Dallas, TX., 24 FEB 67 ** Transferred to VA-97/CVW-14, NK/5XX, USS Constellation (CVA-64), 31 OCT 67 ** Transferred to VA-122/ FRS, NJ/2XX, NAS LeMoore, CA., 10 MAR 67 ** Transferred to VA-97/CVW-14, NK/3XX, USS Constellation (CVA-64), 12 MAY 69 ** Transferred to VA-125/FRS, NJ/5XX, NAS LeMoore, CA., 26 JUN 70 ** Transferred to VA-303/CVWR-30, ND/313, NAS Alameda, CA., 21 JUN 71 ** Transferred to VA305/CVWR-30, ND/505, NAS Point Mugu, CA., 25 JUL 72; City seal of Thousand Oaks, CA., painted on port fuselage; in different time frames, this aircraft had LCDR Bob Hodson & LCDR Rob Lind assigned & painted on the port side of cockpit ; To VA-305, NAS Alameda, CA., 19 MAR 75; To VA-305, NAS Point Mugu, CA., 24 JUL 75** Transferred to MASDC, Davis Monthan AFB; Tucson, AZ., assigned park code 6A0077; 15 SEP 77 ** Transferred to NATTC, Millington, TN., to be used as an instructional airframe 07 JUN 81 ~ S 3SO strike, 08 JUN 81 ** No data on strike ** Outside Airframes NATTC Millington, TN., 07 Oct 89 ** Noted in poor condition outside Flying Tigers Warbird Museum, Kissimmee, FL., awaiting restoration, SEP 03.

A-054 153146 Navy acceptance from NPRO Rep., LTV, Dallas, TX., 28 FEB 67 ** Transferred to NASC, LTV, Dallas, TX., 28 FEB 67 ** Transferred to VA-86/CVW-6, AE/4XX, NAS Cecil Field, FL., 21 MAR 67 ** Transferred to VA-174/FRS, AD/2XX, NAS Oceana, VA., 20 APR 67 ** Transferred to VA-82/CVW-17, AA/3XX, NAS Cecil Field, FL., 15 JAN 69 ** Transferred to VA-82/CVW-15, NL/3XX, USS Coral Sea (CVA-43), 14 JUN 69 ~ S 1SO strike, 22 MAR 70 ** Lost over SE Asia due to engine failure, pilot was rescued.

A-055 153147 Navy acceptance from NPRO Rep., LTV, Dallas, TX., 28 FEB 67 ** Transferred to NASC, LTV, Dallas, TX., 28 FEB 67 ** Transferred to VA-97/CVW15, NK/5XX, USS Constellation (CVA-64), 04 NOV 67 ** Transferred to VA-122/ FRS, NJ/2XX, NAS LeMoore, CA., 23 MAR 67 ** Transferred to VA-105/CVW-11, NH/407, USS Kitty Hawk (CVA-63), 22 JUN 69; To VA-105/CVW-3, AC/407, USS Saratoga (CV-60),22 JUN 69; To VA-105, NAS Cecil Field, FL., 25 MAY 72 ~ S 1SO strike, 06 AUG 72. No data on the crash.

A-056 153148 Navy acceptance from NPRO Rep., LTV, Dallas, TX., 28 FEB 67 ** Transferred to NASC, LTV, Dallas, TX., 28 FEB 67 ** Transferred to VA-174/FRS, AD/2XX, NAS Oceana, VA., 20 APR 67 ** Transferred to VA-37/CVW-11, NH/3XX, USS Kitty Hawk (CVA-64), 10 SEP 68; To VA-37/CVW-3, AC/3XX, USS Saratoga

CVA-60), 21 JUN 69; To VA-37, NAS Cecil Field, FL., 25 MAY 72 ** Transferred to NARF, NAS Jacksonville, FL., 10 APR 73 ~ S 3SO strike, 23 JUN 80 ** No data on strike.

A-057 153149 Navy acceptance from NPRO Rep., LTV, Dallas, TX., 20 MAR 67 ** Transferred to NASC, LTV, Dallas, TX., 20 MAR 67 ** Transferred to VA-122/FRS, NJ/2XX, NAS LeMoore, CA., 06 APR 67 ** Transferred to VA-97/CVW-14, NK/5XX, USS Constellation (CVA-64), 28 OCT 67 ** Transferred to VA-122/FRS, NJ/2XX, NAS LeMoore, CA., 01 APR 68 ** Transferred to VA-174/FRS, AD/2XX, NAS Cecil Field, FL., 15 JAN 70 ~ S 1SO strike, 15 JUN 70 ** Crashed at Patrick AFB; Cocoa Beach, FL., due to pilot error.

A-058 153150 Navy acceptance from NPRO Rep., LTV, Dallas, TX., 14 MAR 67 ** Transferred to NASC, LTV, Dallas, TX., 14 MAR 67 ** This was one of two A-7's used to conduct carrier qualifications for aircraft type ** Transferred to VA-147/ CVW-2, NE/3XX, NAS LeMoore, CA., 27 JUN 67 ** Transferred to VA-122/FRS, NJ/2XX, NAS LeMoore, CA., 27 APR 68 ** Transferred to VA-37/CVW-11, NH/3XX, USS Kitty Hawk (CVA-63), 23 DEC 68; To VA-37/CVW-3, AC/3XX, USS Saratoga (CV-60), 21 JUN 69; To VA-37, NAS Cecil Field, FL., 25 MAY 72 ** Transferred to NARF, NAS Jacksonville, FL., 12 JUL 73 ** Transferred to VA-203/CVWR-20, AF/311, NAS Jacksonville, FL., 05 NOV 74 ** Transferred to NATTC; Millington, TN., date unknown, sitting outside the Airframes shop, to be used as an instructional airframe ~ S 3SO strike, 15 SEP 77 ** No data on strike ** On conditional loan from the National Museum of Naval Aviation; Pensacola, FL., to the Black River Technical College; Pocahontas, AR., date unknown.

A-059 153151 Navy acceptance from NPRO Rep., LTV, Dallas, TX., 06 APR 67 ** Transferred to NASC, LTV, Dallas, TX., 16 MAR 67 ** Transferred to VA-122/FRS, NJ/2XX, NAS LeMoore, CA., 06 APR 67 ** Transferred to VA-97/CVW-25, NK/5XX, USS Constellation (CVA-64), OCT 67 ** Transferred to VA-122/FRS, NJ/2XX, NAS LeMoore, CA., 01 APR 68 ** Transferred to NARF, NAS Alameda, CA., 14 NOV 69 ** Transferred to VA-125/FRS, NJ/5XX, NAS LeMoore, Ca., 08 JUL 70 ** Transferred to VA-153/CVW-19, NM/304, CA./USS Oriskany (CVA-34), 06 MAR72 ** Transferred to VA-125/FRS, NJ/5XX, NAS LeMoore, CA., 11 JUN 73 ** Transferred to VA-56/CVW-5, NF/413, USS Midway (CV-41), 03 NOV 75; To VA-56, NAS Atsugi, JP., 25 NOV 75; To VA-56, USS Midway (CV-41), 10 DEC 75; To VA-56, NAF Atsugi, JP., 27 JAN 76; To VA-56, USS Midway (CV-41), 10 FEB 76; To VA-56, NAF Atsugi, JP., 16 NOV 76; To VA-56, USS Midway (CV-41), 21 NOV 76; To VA-56, NAF Atsugi, JP., 22 JAN 77; To VA-56, USS Midway (CV-41), 29 JAN 77; To VA-56 NAS North Island, CA., 25 MAY 77 ** Transferred to MASDC, Davis Monthan AFB; Tucson, AZ., assigned park code 6A0066; 01 JUN 77 ~ S 3SO strike, 13 MAY 83 ** Transferred to LTV, Dallas, TX. to be converted to A-7P ** Transferred to the Portuguese AF (FAP) as S/N 5530 ** Transferred to Esquadra 304 "Magnificoes", BA-5; Monte Real, PO., 1985 ~ Strike, 1987 ** W/O, Destroyed in accident near Mira d Aire, Portugal.

A-060 153152 Navy acceptance from NPRO Rep., LTV, Dallas, TX., 16 MAR 67 ** Transferred to NASC, LTV, Dallas, TX., 16 MAR 67 ** Transferred to VA-147/CVW-2, NE/3XX, NAS LeMoore, CA., 29 JUN 67 ** Transferred to VA-122/FRS, NJ/2XX, NAS LeMoore, CA., 11 OCT 67 ** Transferred to VA-27/CVW-14, NK/4XX, USS Constellation (CVA-64), 26 MAY 69; To VA-27, NAS LeMoore, CA., 18 JUN 69 ** Transferred to VA-125/FRS, NJ/5XX, NAS LeMoore, CA., 08 JUN 70 ** Transferred to VA-153/CVW-19, NM/307, USS Oriskany (CVA-34), 17 FEB 72 ** Transferred to VA-125/ FRS, NJ/5XX, NAS LeMoore, CA., 19 MAY 73 ** Transferred to VA-93/CVW-5, NF/301, USS Midway (CV-41), 15 MAR 74, Tiger teeth painted on intake ** To VA-93, Atsugi, 02 MAR 76; To VA-93, USS Midway (CV-41), 01 JUL 76; To VA-93, NAS North Island, CA., 27 MAY 77 ** Transferred to MASDC, Davis Monthan AFB; Tucson, AZ., assigned park code 6A0070, 01 JUN 77 ~ S 3SO strike, 20 JUN 80 ** No data on strike ** Transferred to LTV, Dallas, TX. to be converted to A-7P ** Transferred to the Portuguese AF (FAP) S/N 5510 ** Transferred to Esquadra 302 "Falcões", BA-5; Monte Real, PO., 1982 ~ Strike 1989 ** Destroyed in an accident near Vila Vicosa, PO.

A-061 153153 Navy acceptance from NPRO Rep., LTV, Dallas, TX., 28 MAR 67 ** Transferred to NASC, LTV, Dallas, TX., 28 MAR 67 ** Transferred to VA-122/FRS, NJ/2XX, NAS LeMoore, CA., 19 APR 67 ** Transferred to VA-147/CVW-2, NE/3XX, NAS LeMoore, CA., 28 JUN 67 ** Transferred to VA-122/FRS, NJ/2XX, NAS LeMoore, CA., 01 NOV 67 ** Transferred to VA-97/CVW-14, NK/307, USS Constellation (CVA-64), 27 MAY 69 ~ S 1SO strike, 07 APR 70 ** Lost over NVN due to Engine failure, pilot ejected safely.

A-062 153154 Navy acceptance from NPRO Rep., LTV, Dallas, TX., 20 MAR 67 ** Transferred to NASC, LTV, Dallas, TX., 20 MAR 70 ** Transferred to VA-122/FRS, NJ/2XX, NAS LeMoore, CA., 04 APR 67 ~ S 1SO strike, 14 JUN 68 ** No data on strike.

A-063 153155 Navy acceptance from NPRO Rep., LTV, Dallas, TX., 29 MAR 67 ** Transferred to NASC, LTV, Dallas, TX., 29 MAR 67 ** Transferred to VA-122/FRS, NJ/2XX, NAS LeMoore, CA., 14 APR 67 ** Transferred to VA-147/CVW-2, NE/3XX, NAS LeMoore, CA., 28 JUN 67 ** Transferred to VA-122/FRS, NJ/2XX, 07 OCT 67 ** Transferred to VA-97/CVW-14, NK/3XX, NAS LeMoore, CA., 23 JUN 69; To VA-97, USS Constellation (CVA-64), 23 JUN 69; To VA-97/CVW-14, NK/3XX, USS Enterprise (CVAN-65), 03 MAY 70 ** Transferred to VA-125/FRS, NJ/5XX, NAS LeMoore, CA., 03 JUL 70 ** Transferred to VA-303/CVWR-30, ND/311, NAS Alameda, CA., 07 JUN 71 ** Transferred to VA-305/CVWR-30, ND/503, NAS Point Mugu, CA., 25 JUL 72, Green contrail on tail; To VA-305, NAS Alameda, CA., 10 MAY 73; To VA-305, NAS Point Mugu, CA., 10 MAY 73; To VA-305, NAS Jacksonville, FL., 29 JUN 76; To VA-305, NAS Point Mugu, CA., 25 AUG 76; To VA-305, NAS Alameda, CA., 04 OCT 76; To VA-305, NAS Point Mugu, CA., 08 OCT 76; To VA-305, NAS Alameda, CA., 17 SEP 77; To VA-305, NAS Point Mugu, CA., 17 SEP 77 ** Transferred to MASDC, Davis Monthan AFB; Tucson, AZ., assigned park code 6A0103; 15 MAY 78 ~ S 3SO strike, 15 MAY 83 ** No data on strike ** Transferred to LTV, Dallas, TX., to be converted to A-7P ** Transferred to the Portuguese AF (FAP) S/N 5522 ** Transferred to Esquadra 304 "Magnificoes" , BA-5; Monte Real, PO., 1984 ** S/N changed to 15522 ** W/O and transferred to DGMFA Alverca, PO., for storage, 1994.

A-064 153156 Navy acceptance from NPRO Rep., LTV, Dallas, TX., 27 MAR 67 ** Transferred to NASC, LTV, Dallas, TX., 27 MAR 67 ** Transferred to VA-122/FRS, NJ/2XX, NAS LeMoore, CA., 21 APR 67 ** Transferred to VA-147/CVW-2, NE/3XX, NAS LeMoore, CA., 29 JUN 67 ** Transferred to VA-122/FRS, NJ/2XX, NAS LeMoore, CA., 21 JUN 68 ** Transferred to VA-27/CVW-14, NK/4XX, USS Constellation (CVA-64), 15 MAY 69 ** Transferred to VA-125/FRS, NJ/5XX, NAS LeMoore, CA., 30 JUN 69 ~ S 1SO strike, 15 NOV 69 ** No data on strike.

A-065 153157 Navy acceptance from NPRO Rep., LTV, Dallas, TX., 27 MAR 67 ** Transferred to NASC, LTV, Dallas, TX., 27 MAR 67 ** Transferred to VA-174/FRS, AD/2XX, NAS CECIL FIELD, FL., 20 APR 67 ** Transferred to VA-82/CVW-15, NL/3XX, USS Coral Sea (CVA-43), 30 JUL 69; To VA-82, NAS Cecil Field, FL., 11 APR 70 ** Transferred to MASDC, Davis Monthan AFB; Tucson, AZ., assigned park code 6A063; 24 JUL 70 ** Transferred to NARF, NAS Alameda, CA., 31 JUL 72 ** Transferred to VA-125/FRS, NJ/5XX, NAS LeMoore, CA., 15 FEB 73 ** Transferred to VA-56/CVW-5, NF/403, NAS LeMoore, CA., 21 MAY 73; To VA-56, USS Midway (CVA-41), 15 JUN 73; To VA-56, NAF Atsugi, JP., 12 JUL 74; To VA-56, USS Midway (CVA-41), 02 AUG 74; To VA-56, NAF Atsugi, JP., 05 MAR 76; To VA-56, USS Midway (CV-41), 13 JUL 76; To VA-56, NAF Atsugi, JP., 18 FEB 77; To VA-56, USS Midway (CV-41), 20 FEB 77; To VA-56, NAF Atsugi, JP., 07 MAR 77; To VA-56, USS Midway (CV-41), 17 MAR 77; To VA-56, NAS North Island, CA., 23 MAY 77 ** Transferred to MASDC, Davis Monthan AFB; Tucson, AZ., assigned park code 6A0063, 31 MAY 77 ~ S 3SO strike, 02 JUL 80 ** No data on strike.

A-066 153158 Navy acceptance from NPRO Rep., LTV, Dallas, TX., 27 MAR 67 ** Transferred to NASC, LTV, Dallas, TX., 27 MAR 67 ** Transferred to VA-122/FRS, NJ/2XX, NAS LeMoore, CA., 19 APR 67 ** Transferred to VA-147/CVW-2, NE/3XX, NAS LeMoore, CA., 29 JUN 67 ** Transferred to VA-122/FRS, NJ/2XX, NAS LeMoore,m CA., 26 OCT 67 ** Transferred to VA-27/CVW-14, NK/4XX, NAS LeMoore, CA., 13 JUN 69; To VA-27, NAS Atsugi, JP., 01 MAY 70; To NAS Atsugi, JP., A & T, 01 MAY 70; To VA-27 ** Transferred to NARF, NAS Alameda, CA., 19 JAN 71 ** Transferred to VA-303/ CVWR-30, ND/3XX, NAS Alameda, CA., 06 JUL 71** Transferred to VA-304/CVWR-30, ND/4XX, NAS Alameda, CA., 07 AUG 71 ** Transferred to VA-305/CVWR-30, ND/507, NAS Point Mugu, CA., 09 AUG 72, First allocation A-7 with Green Diamonds on the rudder, LT Ken Matlock painted on nose, 13 NOV 73; To VA-305, NAS Miramar, CA., 14 FEB 73; To VA-305, NAS LeMoore, CA., 15 FEB 73; To VA-305, NAS Point Mugu, CA., 15 FEB 73; To VA-305, USS Ranger (CV-61), Nov 76 ~ S 1SO strike, 16 NOV 76 ** Lost at sea after a night ramp strike on the USS Ranger (CV-61) that sheared the Port MLG, Pilot CDR Michael Louis Plattis, (Squadron XO), ejected, landed in the ocean. Neither the pilot nor the aircraft were found. The Air Wing was on a congressionally mandated TACAIR Test, NOV 76.

A-067 153159 Navy acceptance from NPRO Rep., LTV, Dallas, TX., 28 MAR 67 ** Transferred to NASC, LTV, Dallas, TX., 28 MAR 67 ** Transferred to VA-86/CVW-6, AE/4XX, NAS Cecil Field, FL., 04 MAY 67 ** Transferred to VA-174/FRS, AD/2XX, NAS Cecil Field, FL., 28 DEC 67 ** Transferred to VA-105/CVW-3, AC/4XX, NAS Cecil Field, FL., 14 OCT 68; To VA-105, USS Saratoga CV-60, 14 MAY 69; To VA-105, NAS Cecil Field, FL., 25 MAY 72 ** Transferred to NARF, NAS Jacksonville, FL., 02 JUL 73 ** Transferred to VA-203/CVWR-20, AF/313, NAS Jacksonville, FL., 26 MAR 75 ** Transferred to VA-305/CVWR-30, ND/513, NAS Point Mugu, CA., 26 AUG 77 ** Transferred to MASDC, Davis Monthan AFB; Tucson, AZ., assigned park code 6A0108; 30 MAY 78 ~ S 3SO strike, 15 MAY 83 ** Sent to LTV, Dallas, TX., to be converted to A-7P ** Transferred to the Portuguese AF (FAP) S/N 5523 ** Transferred to Esquadra 304 "Magnificoes" , BA-5; Monte Real, PO., 1984 ~ Strike, 1992 ** W/O, destroyed in accident near Montijo, and located at the dump in Montijo, Portugal.

A-068 153160 Navy acceptance from NPRO Rep., LTV, Dallas, TX., 29 MAR 67 ** Transferred to NASC, LTV, Dallas, TX., 29 MAR 67 ** Transferred to VA-174/FRS, AD/2XX, NAS Cecil Field, FL., 01 MAY 67 ** Transferred to VA-82/CVW-15, NL/3XX, NAS Cecil Field, FL., 22 JAN 69; To VA-82, USS Coral Sea (CVA-43), 23 JUN 69; To VA-82, NAS Cecil Field, FL., 19 APR 70 ** Transferred to MASDC, Davis Monthon AFB; Tucson, AZ., 31 AUG 70 ** Transferred to NARF, NAS Alameda, CA., 10 AUG 72 ** Transferred to VA-93/CVW-5, NF/304, NAS LeMoore, CA., 05 APR 73; To VA-93, USS Midway (CVA-41), 26 MAR 74 ~ S 1SO strike, 11 JUL 74 ** No data on strike.

A-069 153161 Navy acceptance from NPRO Rep., LTV, Dallas, TX., 29 MAR 67 ** Transferred to NASC, LTV, Dallas, TX., 29 MAR 67 ** Transferred to VA-174/FRS, AD/2XX, NAS Cecil Field, FL., 26 APR 67 ** Transferred to VA-37/CVW-11, NH/300, USS Kitty Hawk (CVA-63), 09 SEP 68; To VA-37/CVW-3, AC/300, USS Saratoga (CV-60), 30 DEC 71; To VA-37, NAS Cecil Field, FL., 19 JUN 72 ~ S 1SO strike, 10 NOV 72 ** No data on strike.

A-070 153162 Navy acceptance from NPRO Rep. LTV Dallas, TX., 29 MAR 67 ** Transferred to NASC, LTV, Dallas, TX., 29 MAR 67 ** Transferred to VA-174/FRS, AD/2XX, NAS Cecil Field, FL., 18 MAY 67 ** Transferred to VA-82/CVW-15, NL/3XX, NAS Cecil Field, FL., 15 JAN 69; To VA-82, USS Coral Sea (CVA-43), 06 JUN 69; To VA-82, NAS Cecil Field, FL., 28 MAY 70 ** Transferred to MASDC, Davis Monthan AFB; Tucson, AZ., assigned park code unknown, 14 AUG 70 ~ S 1SO strike, 31 JAN 72 ** No data on strike ** Transferred to NARF, NAS Alameda, CA., 15 JUL 72 ** Transferred to VA-93/CVW-5, NF/3XX, USS Midway(CVA-41), 14

AUG 73; To VA-93, NAF Atsugi, JP., 25 AUG 75; To VA-93, USS Midway (CV-41), 09 SEP 75; To VA-93, NAF Atsugi, JP., 19 SEP 75; To VA-93, USS Midway (CV-41), 27 NOV 75; To VA-93, NAS Alameda, CA., 13 JAN 76 ** Transferred to VA-125/FRS, NJ/527, NAS Lemoore, CA., 18 FEB 76 **Transferred to MASDC, assigned park code 6A0048, 11 MAY 77 ~ S 3SO strike, 15 M AY 83 ** No data on strike ** Transferred to LTV, Dallas, TX. to be converted to A-7P ** Transferred to the Portuguese AF (FAP), S/N 5524 ** Transferred to Esquadra 304 "Magnificoes" , BA-5; Monte Real, PO., 1984 ** S/N changed to 15524 ** W/O and transferred to BA-5; Monte Real, PO., for display, 1999.

A-071 153163 Navy acceptance from NPRO Rep., LTV, Dallas, TX., 19 APR 67 ** Transferred to NASC, LTV, Dallas, TX., 19 APR 67 ** Transferred to VA-174/FRS, AD/2XX, NAS Oceana, VA., 06 MAY 67 ** Transferred to VA-37/CVW-11, NH/3XX, USS Kitty Hawk (CVA-63), 06 SEP 68; To VA-37/CVW-3, AC/3XX, USS Saratoga (CVA-60), 08 APR 69; To VA-37, NAS Cecil Field, FL., 15 JUN 72 ** Transferred to NARF, NAS Jacksonville, FL., 12 JUL 73 ** Transferred to VA-305/CVWR-30, ND/5XX, NAS Point Mugu, CA., 19 MAR 74 ** Transferred to VA-203/CVWR-20, AF/300, NAS Jacksonville, FL., 20 APR 74 ** Transferred to NATTC; Millington, TN., date unknown, ., sitting outside the Airframes shop, to be used as an instructional airframe ~ S 3SO, 15 SEP 77 ** No data on strike.

A-072 153164 Navy acceptance from NPRO Rep., LTV, Dallas, TX., 21 APR 67 ** Transferred to NASC, LTV, Dallas, TX., 21 APR 67 ** Transferred to VA-174/FRS, AD/2XX, NAS Cecil Field, FL., 06 MAY 67 ** Transferred to VA-37/CVW-11, NH/3XX, USS Kitty Hawk (CVA-63), 28 AUG 67 ~ S 1SO strike, 28 APR 69 ** Lost over SE Asia due to engine failure, pilot survived.

A-073 153165 Navy acceptance from NPRO Rep., LTV, Dallas, TX., 19 APR 67 ** Transferred to NASC, LTV, Dallas, TX., 21 APR 67 ** Transferred to VA-122/FRS, NJ/2XX, NAS LeMoore, CA., 07 JUN 67 ** Transferred to VA-147/CVW-2, NE/3XX, NAS LeMoore, CA., 29 JUN 67 ** Transferred to VA-122/FRS, NJ/2XX, NAS LeMoore, CA., 06 OCT 67 ~ S 1SO strike, 21 JAN 69 ** Crashed near MCAS Yuma, AZ., Due to a spin.

A-074 153166 Navy acceptance from NPRO Rep., LTV, Dallas, TX., 19 APR 67 ** Transferred to NASC, LTV, Dallas, TX., 19 APR 67 ** Transferred to VA-122/FRS, NJ/2XX, NAS LeMoore, CA., 07 JUN 67 ** Transferred to VA-147/CVW-9, NG/3XX, NAS LeMoore, CA., 31 JUL 67 ** Transferred to VA-122/FRS, NJ/2XX, NAS LeMoore, CA., 14 OCT 67 ** Transferred to VA-97/CVW-14, NK/3XX, USS Constellation (CVA-64), 28 MAY 69 ** Transferred to VA-125/FRS, NJ/5XX, NAS LeMoore, CA., 01 JUN 70 ** Transferred to NARF, NAS Jacksonville, FL., 08 MAR 74 ~ S 3SO strike, 15 JUN 78 ** No data on strike.

A-075 153167 Navy acceptance from NPRO Rep., LTV, Dallas, TX., 21 APR 67 ** Transferred to NASC, LTV, Dallas, TX., 21 APR 67 ** Transferred to VA-174/FRS, AD/204, NAS Cecil Field, FL., 10 MAY 67 ** Transferred to NARF, NAS Jacksonville, FL., 02 FEB 68 ~ S 1SO strike, 27 AUG 73 ** No data on strike.

A-076 153168 Navy acceptance from NPRO Rep., LTV, Dallas, TX., 20 APR 67 ** Transferred to NASC, LTV, Dallas, TX., 20 APR 67 ** Transferred to VA-122/FRS, NJ/2XX, NAS LeMoore, CA., 30 MAY 67 ** Transferred to VA-147/CVW-2, NE/3XX, NAS LeMoore, CA., 05 JUL 67 ~ S 1SO strike, 28 SEP 67 ** Crashed on USS Ranger (CVA-61), due to a ramp strike.

A-077 153169 Navy acceptance from NPRO Rep., LTV, Dallas, TX., 26 APR 67 ** Transferred to NASC, LTV, Dallas, TX., 26 APR 67 ** Transferred to VA-122/FRS, NJ/2XX, NAS LeMoore, CA., 14 JUN 67 ** Transferred to VA-105/CVW-11, NH/4XX, USS Kitty Hawk (CVA-63), 20 DEC 68; To VA-105/CVW-3, AC/3XX, USS Saratoga (CVA-60), 06 APR 69 ** Transferred to VA-174/FRS, AD/2XX, NAS Cecil Field, FL., 25 MAR 70 ** Transferred to MASDC, Davis

Monthan AFB; Tucson, AZ., 19 OCT 70 ** Transferred to NARF, NAS Alameda, CA., 18 JUN 72 ** Transferred to VA-174/FRS, AD/2XX, NAS Cecil Field, FL., 20 SEP 72 ** Transferred to VA-37/CVW-3, AC/3XX, NAS Cecil Field, FL., 26 OCT 72 ** Transferred to VA-174/FRS, AD/2XX, NAS Cecil Field, FL., 08 MAR 73 ~ S 1SO strike, 06 APR 73 ** Crashed near MCAS Yuma, AZ., due to engine failure.

A-078 153170 Navy acceptance from NPRO Rep., LTV, Dallas, TX., 26 APR 67 ** Transferred to NASC, LTV, Dallas, TX., 26 APR 67 ** Transferred to VA-147/CVW-2, NE/3XX, NAS LeMoore, CA., 07 JUL 67 ** Transferred to VA-122/FRS, NJ/232, NAS LeMoore, CA., 06 OCT 67; To VA-122, USS Coral Sea (CVA-43), 18 JUL 69 ** Transferred to VA-153/CVW-19, NM/3XX, USS Oriskany CVA-34), 25 NOV 69 ** Transferred to VA-125/FRS, NJ/5XX, NAS LeMoore, CA., CRAA, 17 APR 72 ** Transferred to VA-125/FRS, NJ/5XX, NAS LeMoore, CA., 16 APR 73 ** Transferred to VA-93/CVW-5, NF/3XX, USS Midway (CV-41), 11 JAN 76; To VA-93, NAF Atsugi, JP., 18 SEP 76; To VA-93; USS Midway (CV-41), 27 SEP 76; To VA-93, NAF Atsugi, JP., 29 SEP 76; To VA-93, USS Midway (CV-41), 05 OCT 76; To VA-93, NAF Atsugi, JP., 26 OCT 76; To VA-93, USS Midway (CV-41), 29 OCT 76 ** VA-125/FRS, NJ/523, NAS LeMoore, CA., 10 DEC 76 ** Transferred to MASDC, Davis Monthan AFB; Tucson, AZ., assigned park code 6A0047; 10 MAY 77 ~ S 3SO strike, 02 JUL 80 ** Transferred to LTV, Dallas, TX. to be converted to A-7P ** Transferred to the Portuguese AF (FAP), S/N 5512 ** Transferred to Esquadra 302 "Falcões" , BA-5; Monte Real, PO., 1982 ** S/N changed to 15512 ** W/O and transferred to DGMFA Alverca, PO., for storage, 1988.

A-079 153171 Navy acceptance from NPRO Rep., LTV, Dallas, TX., 21 APR 67 ** Transferred to NASC, LTV, Dallas, TX., 21 APR 67 ** Transferred to VA-122/FRS, NJ/2XX, NAS LeMoore, CA., 01 JUN 67 ** Transferred to NAS Cubi Point, PI., 05 OCT 68 ** Transferred to VA-82/CVW-6, AE/3XX, NAS Cecil Field, FL., 08 OCT 68 ** Transferred to VA-27/CVW-14, NK/6XX, USS Constellation (CVA-64), 04 NOV 68 ** Transferred to VA-122/FRS, NJ/2XX, NAS LeMoore, CA., 26 MAY 69 ** Transferred to VA-153/CVW-19, NM/3XX, USS Oriskany (CVA-34), 26 NOV 69 ** Transferred to VA-86/CVW-15, NL/4XX, USS Coral Sea (CVA-43), 13 FEB 70 ** Transferred to VA-97/CVW-14, NK/3XX, USS Constellation (CVA-64), 10 APR 70 ** Transferred to VA-86/ CVW-15, NL/4XX, USS Coral Sea (CVA-43), 22 APR 70; To VA-86, NAS Cecil Field, FL., 28 APR 70 ** Transferred to VA-174/FRS, AD/2XX, 28 AUG 70 ** Transferred to MASDC, Davis Monthan AFB; Tucson, AZ., 26 OCT 70 ** Transferred to NARF, NAS Alameda, CA., 10 JUN 71 ** Transferred to VA-304/CVWR-30, ND/400, NAS Alameda, CA., 08 SEP 71, Pegasus painted on MLG doors; To VA-304, NAS Jacksonville, FL., 23 APR 74; To VA-304, NAS Alameda, CA., 23 APR 74; To VA-304, NAS Jacksonville, FL.,28 AUG 74; To VA-304, NAS Alameda, CA., 28 AUG 74 ** Transferred to MASDC, Davis Monthan AFB; Tucson, AZ., assigned park code 6A081; 14 NOV 77 ~ S 3SO strike, 15 MAY 83 ** Transferred to LTV, Dallas, TX., to be converted to A-7P ** Transferred to the Portuguese AF (FAP), S/N 5525 ** Transferred to Esquadra 304 "Magnificoes", BA-5; Monte Real, PO., 1984 ** S/N changed to 15525 ~ Strike, 1992 ** W/O, Crashed in Germany.

A-080 153172 Navy acceptance from NPRO Rep., LTV, Dallas, TX., 27 APR 67 ** Transferred to NASC, LTV, Dallas, TX., 27 APR 67 ** Transferred to VA-122/FRS, NJ/2XX, NAS LeMoore, CA., 01 JUN 67 ~ S 1SO strike, 17 MAY 68 ** Crashed near Visalia, CA., due to a mid air collision with A-7A 152666.

A-081 153173 Navy acceptance from NPRO Rep., LTV, Dallas, TX., 15 MAY 67 ** Transferred to NASC, LTV, Dallas, TX., 15 MAY 67 ** Transferred to VA-122/FRS, NJ/2XX, NAS LeMoore, CA., 01 JUN 67 ** Transferred to VA-97/CVW-14, NK/ 5XX, USS Constellation (CVA-64), 12 APR 68 ** Transferred to VA-122/FRS, NJ/2XX, NAS LeMoore, CA., 09 MAY 69 **

Transferred to VA-153/CVW-19, NM/302, USS Oriskany (CVA-34), 13 NOV 69 ** Transferred to VA-125/FRS, NJ/5XX, NAS LeMoore, CA., 04 APR73; To VA-125, USS Ranger (CV-61), 01 JUN 74; To VA-125, NAS LeMoore, CA., 01 JUL 74; To VA-125, NAS Jacksonville, FL.,25 JUN 75; VA-125, NAS LeMoore, CA., 20 JUN 75; To VA-125, NAS Jacksonville, FL., 23 JUN 75 ** Transferred to VA-93/CVW-5, NF/315, USS Midway (CV-41), 11 JAN 76; To VA-93, NAF Atsugi, JP., 07 MAY 76; To VA-93, USS Midway (CV-41), 11 MAY 76; To VA-93, NAF Atsugi, JP., 01 SEP 76; To VA-93, USS Midway(CV-41), 09 SEP 76; To VA-93, NAS North Island, CA., 27 MAY 77 ** Transferred to MASDC, Davis Monthan AFB; Tucson, AZ., assigned park code 6A0073; 04 JUN 77 ~ S 3SO strike, 15 MAY 83, ** Transferred to LTV, Dallas, TX. to be converted to A-7P ** Transferred to the Portuguese AF (FAP), S/N 5533 ** Transferred to Esquadra 304 "Magnificoes" , BA-5; Monte Real, PO. ** S/N changed to 15533 ~ Strike, 1995 ** W/O, Destroyed in accident near Baleizao, Portugal.

A-082 153174 Navy acceptance from NPRO Rep., LTV, Dallas, TX., 26 APR 67 ** Transferred to NASC, LTV, Dallas, TX., 26 APR 67 ** Transferred to VA-122/FRS, NJ/2XX, NAS LeMoore, CA., 26 MAY 67 ** Transferred to VA-147/CVW-2, NE/3XX, NAS LeMoore, CA., 29 JUN 67 ** Transferred to VA-122/FRS, NJ/2XX, 07 OCT 67 ~ S 1SO strike, 11 FEB 68 ** Crashed on USS Constellation (CVA-64), when pilot ejected by mistake.

A-083 153175 Navy acceptance from NPRO Rep., LTV, Dallas, TX., 11 MAY 67 ** Transferred to NASC, LTV, Dallas, TX., 11 MAY 67 ** Transferred to VA-122/FRS, NJ/2XX, NAS LeMoore, CA., 18 MAY 67 ** VA-147/CVW-2, NE/300, NAS LeMooere, CA., 28 JUN 67 ** Transferred to VA-122/FRS, NJ/2XX, NAS LeMoore, CA., 01 NOV 67 ** Transferred to NAS Cubi Point, PI., 02 OCT 68 ** Transferred to VA-27/CVW-14, NK/6XX, USS Constellation (CVA-64), 08 OCT 68 ~ S 1SO strike, 31 OCT 68 ** Lost due to engine failure on a combat mission. Pilot ejected safely.

A-084 153176 Navy acceptance from NPRO Rep., LTV, Dallas, TX., 18 MAY 67 ** Transferred to NASC, LTV, Dallas, TX., 18 MAY 67 ** Transferred to VA-122/FRS, NJ/2XX, NAS LeMoore, CA., 09 JUN 67 ** Transferred to VA-27/CVW-14, NK/ 6XX, USS Constellation (CVA-64), 19 DEC 67 ** Transferred to VA-122/FRS, NJ/2XX, NAS LeMoore, CA., 08 MAR 68 ** Transferred to VA-27/CVW-14, NK/6XX, USS Constellation (CVA-64), 10 MAY 68 ** Transferred to VA-82/CVW-6, AE/ 3XX, USS America (CVA-66), 12 JUN 68; To VA-82, NAS Cecil Field, FL., 12 JUN 68 ** Transferred to VA-27/CVW-14, NK/6XX, USS Constellation (CVA-64), 07 NOV 68 ** Transferred to VA-122/FRS, NJ/2XX, NAS LeMoore, CA., 08 MAY 69 ** Transferred to VA-153/CVW-19, NM/3XX, USS Oriskany (CVA-34), 06 OCT 69 ~ S 1SO strike, 29 JUN 70 ** CDR D.D. Aldern, KIA when shot down over Laos by AAA.

A-085 153177 Navy acceptance from NPRO Rep., LTV, Dallas, TX., 25 MAY 67 ** Transferred to NASC, LTV, Dallas, TX., 25 MAY 67 ** Transferred to VAW-121, Det. 9, XX/XXX, USS Essex (CVS-9), 07 JUN 67, for carrier suitability trials ** Transferred to VA-82/CVW-6, AE/3XX, USS America (CVA-66), 08 JUN 67 ** Transferred to VA-174/FRS, AD/2XX, NAS Cecil Field, FL., 08 JAN 68 ** Transferred to VA-105/CVW-11, NH/4XX, NAS Cecil Field, FL., 13 MAR 68; To VA-105, USS Kitty Hawk (CVA-63), 27 JUN 68; To VA-105/CVW-3, AC/4XX, USS Saratoga (CV-60), 18 APR 69 ** Transferred to VA-174/FRS, AD/2XX, NAS Cecil Field, FL., 02 JUN 71 ** Transferred to VA-37/CVW-3, AC/3XX, 12 SEP 72 **Transferred to NARF, NAS Jacksonville, FL., 17 JUL 73 ** Transferred to VA-303/CVWR-30, ND/3XX, NAS Alameda, CA., 18 DEC 73 ** Transferred to VA-203/CVWR-20, AF/301, NAS Jacksonville, FL., 10 DEC 75 ** Transferred to VA-305/ CVWR-30, ND/515, NAS Point Mugu, Ca., 26 AUG 77; To VA-305, USS Enterprise (CVN-65), 05 OCT 77; To VA-305, NAS Point Mugu, CA., 05 OCT 77 ** Transferred to MASDC, Davis Monthan AFB; Tucson, AZ., assigned park code 6A0114; 17 SEP 78 ~ S 3SO strike, 15 JUN 83 ** Transferred to LTV, Dallas, TX. to be converted to A-7P ** Transferred to the Portuguese AF (FAP), S/N 5526 ** Transferred to Esquadra 304 "Magnificoes" , BA-5; Monte Real, PO., 1984 ** S/N changed to 15526 ** W/O and transferred DGMFA Alverca, PO., for storage, 1994.

A-086 153178 Navy acceptance from NPRO Rep., LTV, Dallas, TX., 18 MAY 67 ** Transferred to NASC, LTV, Dallas, TX., 18 MAY 67 ** Transferred to VA-122/FRS, NJ/2XX, NAS LeMoore, CA., 14 JUN 67 ** Transferred to VA-97/CVW-14, NK/5XX, USS Constellation (CVA-64), 11 APR 68 ** Transferred to VA-82/CVW-6, AE/3XX, NAS Cecil Field, FL., 12 JUN 68 ** Transferred to VA-27/CVW-14, NK/6XX, USS Constellation (CVA-64), 07 NOV 68 ** Transferred to VA-122/FRS, NJ/2XX, NAS LeMoore, CA., 31 MAY 69 ** Transferred to VA-153/CVW-19, NM/3XX, USS Oriskany (CVA-34), 25 NOV 69 ** Transferred to VA-125/FRS, NJ/5XX, NAS LeMoore, CA., 19 MAR 71 ** Transferred to VA-153/CVW-19, NM/3XX, USS Oriskany (CVA-34), 21 APR 72; To VA-153, NAS LeMoore, CA., 26 JUN 72 ** Transferred to VA-125/FRS, NJ/5XX, NAS LeMoore, CA., 01 MAY 73 ** Transferred to VA-93/CVW-5, NF/3XX, USS Midway (CVA-41) 18 FEB 75; To VA-93, NAF Atsugi, JP., 16 SEP 75; To VA-93, USS Midway (CV-41), 30 SEP 75 ~ S 1SO strike, 06 OCT 75 ** Crashed due to engine failure during a simulated strafing run, pilot ejected safely.

A-087 153179 Navy acceptance from NPRO Rep. LTV Dallas, TX., 25 MAY 67 ** Transferred to NASC, LTV, Dallas, TX., 25 MAY 67 ** Transferred to NPRO REP., LTV, Dallas, TX., for RDT & E, 21 JUN 67 ** Transferred to VA-82/CVW-6, AE/3XX, USS America (CVA-66), 21 JUN 67 ** Transferred to VA-174/FRS, AD/2XX, NAS Cecil Field, FL., 12 JAN 68 ** Transferred to VA-105/CVW-11, NH/4XX, NAS Cecil Field, FL.,04 MAR 68; To VA-105, USS Kitty Hawk (CVA-63), 17 JUN 68; To VA-105/CVW-3, AC/4XX, USS Saratoga, (CV-60), 30 JUN 69 ** Transferred to VA-174/FRS, NAS Cecil Field, FL., 15 JUN 70 ** Transferred to VA-105/ CVW-3, AC/4XX, USS Saratoga (CV-60), 17 JUN 70; To VA-105, NAS Cecil Field, FL., 26 MAY 72 ** Transferred to VA-303/CVWR-30, ND/3XX, NAS Alameda, CA., 19 JUN 73; To VA-303, NAS Jacksonville, FL., 02 MAY 75; To VA-303, NAS Alameda, CA., 14 AUG 75 ** Transferred to VA-305/CVWR-30, ND/514, NAS Alameda, CA., 24 JAN 78 ** To VA-305, NAS Point Mugu, CA., 24 JAN 78 ** Transferred to MASDC, Davis Monthan AFB; Tucson, AZ., assigned park code 6A0111; 06 JUL 78 ~ S 3SO strike, 15 JUN 83 ** Transferred to LTV, Dallas, TX. to be converted to A-7P ** Transferred to the Portuguese AF (FAP), S/N 5527 ** Transferred to Esquadra 304 "Magnificoes" , BA-5; Monte Real, PO., ** S/N changed to 15527 ** W/O and transferred to DGMFA Alverca, PO., for storage, 1995.

A-088 153180 Navy acceptance from NPRO Rep., LTV, Dallas, TX., 19 MAY 67 ** Transferred to NASC, LTV, Dallas, TX., 19 MAY 67 ** Transferred to VAW-121, Det. 9, XX/XXX, USS Essex (CVS-9), 07 JUN 67, for carrier suitability trials ** Transferred to VA-82/CVW-6, AE/3XX, USS America (CVA-66), 08 JUN 67 ** Transferred to VA-174/FRS, AD/2XX, NAS Cecil Field, FL., 14 NOV 67 ** Transferred to VA-105/CVW-11, NH/ 413, NAS Cecil Field, FL., 07 MAR 68; To VA-105, USS Kitty Hawk (CVA-63), 27 JUN 68 ~ S 1SO strike, 02 MAY 69 ** LCDR W.J. O' Conner was rescued after being shot down by AAA near Route 920, Shea Valley, SVN. Pilot ejected and was rescued.

A-089 153181 Navy acceptance from NPRO Rep., LTV, Dallas, TX., 29 MAY 67 ** Transferred to NASC, LTV, Dallas, TX., 29 MAY 67 ** Transferred to VAW-121, Det. 9, XX/XXX, USS Essex (CVS-9), 08 JUN 67; for carrier suitability trials ** Transferred to VA-82/CVW-6, AE/3XX, USS America (CVA-66), 08 JUN 67 ** Transferred to VA-174/ FRS, AD/2XX, NAS Cecil field, FL., 20 NOV 67 ** Transferred to VA-105/CVW-11, NH/4XX, NAS Cecil Field, FL., 28 MAR; To VA-105, USS Kitty Hawk (CVA- 63), 28 JUN 68 ~ S 1SO strike, 15 FEB 69 ** LTJG W.C. Niedecken KIA when shot down by SAM over Laos.

153182/153233 LTV A-7A-4b-CV Corsair II; (Block IVb)

A-142 153182 Navy acceptance from NPRO Rep., LTV, Dallas, TX., 25 SEP 67; ** Transferred to NPRO Rep., for R &T, 20 APR 67 ** Transferred to NASC, LTV, Dallas, TX., 25 SEP 67 ** Transferred to VA-37/CVW-11, NH/310, NAS Cecil Field, FL., 28 SEP 67; To VA-37, USS Kitty Hawk (CVA-63), 17 APR 68; To VA-37/CVW-3, AC/3XX, USS Saratoga (CVA-63), 29 JUN 69 ~ S 1SO strike, 21 MAR 71 ** Crashed at NAS Cecil Field, FL., Due to both wings folded on takeoff.

A-091 153183 Navy acceptance from NPRO Rep., LTV, Dallas, TX., 18 APR 67 ** Transferred to NASC, LTV, Dallas, TX., 18 APR 67 ** Transferred to NPRO Rep., LTV, Dallas, TX., for R & T, 19 APR 67 ** Transferred to VA-27/CVW-14, NK/ 4XX, USS Constellation (CVA-64), 17 JUN 69; To VA-27, NAS LeMoore, CA., 30 JUN 69; To VA-27/CVW-14, NK/4XX, USS Enterprise (CVAN-65), 28 MAY 70 ** Transferred to VA-125/FRS,NJ/5XX, NAS LeMoore, CA., 15 JUL 70 ** Transferred to VA-153/CVW-19, NM/305, USS Oriskany (CVA-34),22 FEB 72; To VA-153, NAS LeMoore, CA., 11 JUN 72 ** Transferred to VA-125/FRS, NJ/5XX, NAS LeMoore, CA., 27 APR 73 ~ S 1SO strike, 29 JAN 74 ** Crashed near Blythe, CA., due to engine failure.

A-092 153184 Navy acceptance from NPRO Rep., LTV, Dallas, TX., 31 MAY 67 ** Transferred to NASC, LTV, Dallas, TX., 31 MAY 67 ** Transferred to VA-82/CVW-6, AE/3XX, USS America (CVA-66), 22 JUN 67 ** Transferred to VA-174/FRS, AD/2XX, NAS Cecil Field, FL., 04 JAN 68 ** Transferred to VA-105/CVW-11, NH/4XX, NAS Cecil Field, FL., 07 MAR 68; To VA-105/CVW-3, AC/3XX, USS Saratoga (CV-60), 06 APR 69; To VA-105, NAS Cecil Field, FL., 18 JUN 72 ** Transferred to VA-305/CVWR-30, ND/507 and ND/512, NAS Point Mugu, CA., 30 APR 73; To VA-305, NAS Jacksonville, FL., 03 AUG 74; To VA-305, NAS Point Mugu, CA., 27 AUG 74 ** Transferred to MASDC, Davis Monthan AFB; Tucson, AZ., assigned park code 6A0095; 07 DEC 77 ~ S 3SO strike, 15 APR 80 ** Sent to LTV Dallas, TX. to be converted to A-7P ** Transferred to the Portuguese AF (FAP), S/N 5504 ** Transferred to Esquadra 302 "Falcões" , BA-5; Monte Real, PO., 1981 ** S/N changed to 15504 ** W/O and located at AM1 Figo Maduro, PO., 1997.

A-093 153185 Navy acceptance from NPRO Rep., LTV, Dallas, TX., 24 MAY 67 ** Transferred to NASC, LTV, Dallas, TX., 24 MAY 67 ** Transferred to NPRO Rep., LTV, Dallas, TX., for R & T, 27 MAY 67 **Transferred to VA-37/CVW-14, NK/6XX, NAS Cecil Field, FL., 16 SEP 67; To VA-37, USS Kitty Hawk (CVA-64),05 JUN 68 ~ S 1SO strike, 02 AUG 69 ** LCDR George E. Talkin KIA when he crashed in SE Asia.

A-094 153186 Navy acceptance from NPRO Rep., LTV, Dallas, TX., 31 MAY 67 ** Transferred to NASC, LTV, Dallas, TX., 31 MAY 67 ** Transferred to VA-82/CVW-6, AE/3XX, USS America (CVA-66), 15 JUN 67 ** Transferred to VA-174/FRS, AD/2XX, NAS Cecil Field, FL., 29 DEC 67 ** Transferred to VA-105/CVW-11, NH/410, NAS Cecil Field, FL., 07 MAR 68; To VA-105, USS Kitty Hawk (CVA-63), 27 JUN 68; To VA-105/CVW-3, AC/4XX, USS Saratoga (CV-60), 02 MAY 69; To VA-105, NAS Cecil Field, FL., 18 JUN 72 ** Transferred to NARF, NAS Jacksonville, FL., 10 JAN 73 ** Transferred to VA-105/CVW-3, AC/4XX, NAS Cecil Field, FL., 24 JAN 73 ** Transferred to NARF, NAS Jacksonville, FL., 20 MAR 73 ~ S 3SO strike, 23 JUN 80.

A-095 153187 Navy acceptance from NPRO Rep., LTV, Dallas, TX., 31 MAY 67 ** Transferred to NASC, LTV, Dallas, TX., 31 MAY 67 ** Transferred to VA-122/FRS, NJ/2XX, NAS LeMoore, CA., 27 JUN 67 ** To VA-97/CVW-14, NK/5XX,, USS Constellation (CVA-64), 25 APR 68; To VA-97, NAS LeMoore, CA., 22 MAY 68 ** Transferred to VA-122/FRS, NJ/2XX, NAS LeMoore, CA., 27 MAY 69 ** Transferred to NARF, NAS Alameda, CA., 22 JUL 69 ** Transferred to VA-125/FRS, NJ/5XX, NAS LeMoore, CA., 05 DEC 70 ** Transferred to VA-303/CVWR-30, ND/304, NAS Alameda, CA., 22 APR 71 ** Transferred to VA-125/FRS, NJ/5XX, NAS

LeMoore, CA., 27 OCT 72 ** Transferred to VA-303/CVWR-30, ND/304, NAS Alameda, CA., 06 FEB 74 ** Transferred to MASDC, Davis Monthan AFB; Tucson, AZ., assigned park code 6A0100, 27 DEC 77 ~ S 3SO strike, 15 JUN 83 ** Transferred to LTV, Dallas, TX., to be converted to A-7P ** Transferred to the Portuguese AF (FAP), S/N 5528 ** Transferred to Esquadra 304 "Magnificoes" , BA-5; Monte Real, PO., 1985 ** S/N changed to 15528 ** W/O and transferred BA-11; Beja, PO., for storage, 1989.

A-096 153188 Navy acceptance from NPRO Rep., LTV, Dallas, TX.,16 JUN 67 ** Transferred to NASC, LTV, Dallas, TX., 16 JUN 67 ** Transferred to VA-82/CVW-6, AE/3XX, NAS Cecil Field, FL., 30 JUN 67 ** Transferred to VA-174/FRS, AD/2XX, NAS Cecil Field, FL., 22 DEC 67 ** Transferred to VA-105/CVW-11, NH/4XX, NAS Cecil Field, FL., 12 MAR 68; To VA-105, USS Kitty Hawk (CVA-63), 24 MAY 68 ** Transferred to FAWPRA, NAF Atsugi, JP., 15 MAY 69 ** Transferred to NARF, NAS Alameda, CA., 16 JUL 70 ** Transferred to MASDC, Davis Monthan AFB; Tucson, AZ., assigned park code 6A071; 25 NOV 70 ** Transferred to NARF, NAS Alameda, CA., 04 JUL 72 ** Transferred to VA-125/FRS, NJ/5XX, NAS LeMoore, CA., 03 NOV 72 ** Transferred to VA-56/CVW-5, NF/402, NAS LeMoore, CA., 02 APR 73; To VA-56, USS Midway (CVA-41), 15 JUN 73; To VA-56, NAF Atsugi, Japan, 20 NOV 74; To VA-56, USS Midway (CVA-41), 12 DEC 74; To VA-56, NAF Atsugi, JP., 02 JUN 75; To VA-56, USS Midway (CV-41), 18 DEC 75; To VA-56, NAF Atsugi, JP., 02 MAR 76; To VA-56, USS Midway (CV-41), 31 MAR 76; To VA-56, NAF Atsugi, JP., 16 JUL 76; To VA-56, USS Midway (CV-41), 17 JUL 76; To VA-56, NAF Atsugi, JP., 11 OCT 76; To VA-56, USS Midway (CV-41), 14 OCT 76; To VA-56, NAF Atsugi, JP., 15 OCT 76; To VA-56, USS Midway (CV-41), 20 OCT 76; To VA-56, NAF Atsugi, JP., 25 OCT 76; To VA-56, USS Midway (CV-41), 30 OCT 76; To VA-56, NAF Atsugi, JP., 25 JAN 77; To VA-56, USS Midway (CV-41), 29 JAN 77; To VA-56, NAS North Island, CA., 26 MAY 77 ** Transferred to MASDC, Davis Monthan AFB; Tucson, AZ., assigned park code 6A0071, 01 JUN 77 ~ S 3SO strike, 11 JUL 80 ** Sent to LTV, Dallas, TX. to be converted to A-7P ** Transferred to the Portuguese AF (FAP), S/N 5513 ** Transferred to Esquadra 302 "Falcões" , BA-5; Monte Real, PO., 1982 ** S/N changed to 15513 ** Transferred to BA-11; Beja, PO., 1989 ** W/O and stored at BA-11 Beja, PO., 1990.

A-097 153189 Navy acceptance from NPRO Rep., LTV, Dallas, TX., 16 JUN 67 ** Transferred to NPRO Rep., LTV, Dallas, TX., for R & T, 16 JUN 67 ** Transferred to NARF, NAS Jacksonville, FL., 21 MAR 69 ** Transferred to VA-125/FRS, NJ/5XX, 10 MAR 70 ** Transferred to VA-153/CVW-19, NM/3XX, USS Oriskany (CVA-34), 16 JUL 70 ~ S 1SO strike, 01 NOV 71 ** LT Thomas P. Frank was killed when the Launch bar failed on catapult shot.

A-098 153190 Navy acceptance from NPRO Rep., LTV, Dallas, TX., 20 JUN 67 ** Transferred to VA-82/ CVW-6, AE/3XX, USS America (CVA-66), 02 JUL 67 ** Transferred to VA-122/ FRS, NJ/2XX, NAS LeMoore, CA., 07 AUG 67 ** Transferred to VA-82/CVW-6, AE/3XX, USS America (CVA-66), 24 OCT 67 ** Transferred to VA-174/FRS, AD/2XX, NAS Cecil Field, FL., 21 NOV 67 ** Transferred to VA-105/CVW-11, NH/4XX, NAS LeMoore, CA., 30 APR 68; To VA-105/CVW-3, AC/4XX, USS Saratoga (CV-60), 30 MAY 68 ** Transferred to VA-174/FRS, AD/2XX, NAS Cecil Field, FL., 28 MAY 71 ** Transferred to VA-105/CVW-3, AC/4XX, USS Saratoga (CV-60), 09 NOV 71; To VA-105, NAS Cecil Field, FL., 25 MAY 72 ** Transferred to VA-174/FRS, AD/2XX, NAS Cecil Field, FL., 07 MAR 73; To VA-174, NAS Jacksonville, FL., 27 JAN 75; To VA-174, NAS Cecil Field, FL., 16 APR 75 ** Transferred to VA-303/CVWR-30, ND/3XX, NAS Alameda, CA., 30 JUN 75 ** Transferred to MASDC, Davis Monthan AFB; Tucson, AZ., assigned park code 6A0091; 24 NOV 77 ~ S 3SO strike, 31 MAY 80 ** Sent to LTV Dallas, TX. to be converted to A-7P ** Transferred to the Portuguese AF (FAP), S/N 5505 ** Transferred to Esquadra 302 "Falcões", BA-5; Monte Real, PO., 1981 ~ Strike, 1985 ** Destroyed in accident in Belguim.

A-099 153191 Navy acceptance from NPRO Rep., LTV, Dallas, TX., 16 JUN 67 ** Transferred to VA-122/FRS, NJ/2XX, NAS LeMoore, CA., 30 JUN 67 ** Transferred to VA-27/CVW-14, NK/6XX, USS Constellation (CVA-64), 20 DEC 67 ** Transferred to VA-122/FRS, NJ/2XX, NAS LeMoore, CA., 27 MAR 72 ** Transferred to VA-125/FRS, NJ/XXX, NAS LeMoore, CA., 27 MAR 72 ** Transferred to VA-93/CVW-5, NF/311, NAS LeMoore, CA., 10 APR 73; To VA-93, USS Midway (CVA-41), NF/3XX, 14 JUN 73; To VA-93, NAF Atsugi, JP., 24 NOV 75; To VA-93, USS Midway (CVA-41), 01 MAR 76; TO VA-93, NAF Atsugi, JP., 23 AUG 76; To VA-93, USS Midway (CV-41), 26 AUG 76 ~ S 1SO strike, 30 MAR 77 ** Due to a cold catapult shot.

A-100 153192 Navy acceptance from NPRO Rep., LTV, Dallas, TX., 20 JUN 67 ** Transferred to VA-82/CVW-6, AE/3XX, NAS Cecil Field, FL., 06 JUL 67 ** Transferred to VA-174/FRS, AD/2XX, NAS Cecil Field, FL., 10 JAN 68 ** Transferred to VA-105/CVW-11, NH/4XX, NAS Cecil Field, FL., 04 MAR 68; To VA-105, USS Kitty Hawk (CVA-63), 27 JUN 68 ~ S 1SO strike, 03 OCT 68 ** Crashed near McCoy, (Pinecastle), AFB; Orlando, FL., due to engine gearbox failure.

A-101 153193 Navy acceptance from NPRO Rep., LTV, Dallas, TX., 21 JUN 67 ** Transferred to VA-82/CVW-6, AE/3XX, USS America (CVA-66), 21 JUL 67 ** Transferred to VA-174/FRS, AD/2XX, NAS Cecil Field, FL., 21 NOV 67 ** Transferred to VA-105/CVW-11, NH/4XX, NAS Cecil Field, FL., 07 MAR 68 ** To VA-105, USS Kitty Hawk (CVA-63), 27 JUN 68; To VA-105/ CVW-3, AE/4XX, USS Saratoga (CV-60), 06 MAY 69 ** Transferred to VA-174/FRS, AD/2XX, NAS Cecil Field, FL., 16 JUN 70 ** Transferred to VA-105/CVW-3, AE/4XX, USS Saratoga (CV-60), 02 AUG 70; To VA-105, NAS Cecil Field, FL., 22 JUN 72 ~ S 1SO strike, 31 JUL 72 ** Crashed due to engine failure, pilot survived.

A-102 153194 Navy acceptance from NPRO Rep., LTV, Dallas, TX., 27 JUN 67 ** Transferred to VA-82/CVW-6, AE/3XX, USS America (CVA-66), 25 JUL 67 ** Transferred to VA-174/FRS, AD/2XX, NAS Cecil Field, FL., 12 DEC 67 ** Transferred to VA-105/CVW-11, NH/4XX, NAS Cecil Field, FL., 12 MAR 68 ** To VA-105, USS Kitty Hawk (CVA-63), 28 JUN 68; To VA-105/CVW-3, AE/4XX, USS Saratoga (CV-60), 06 JUN 69; To VA-105, NAS Cecil Field, FL., 25 MAY 72 ** Transferred to VA-303/CVWR-30, ND/312, NAS Alameda, CA., 17 JUN 73; To VA-303, NAS Jacksonville, FL., 18 DEC 74; To VA-303, NAS Alameda, CA., 11 MAR 75 ** Transferred to MASDC, Davis Monthan AFB; Tucson, AZ., assigned park code 6A0085; 17 NOV 77 ~ S 3SO strike, 10 JUN 80 ** Sent to LTV, Dallas, TX., to be converted to A-7P ** Transferred to the Portuguese AF (FAP), S/N 5507 ** Transferred to Esquadra 302 "Falcões" , BA-5; Monte Real, PO., 1982 ** S/N changed to 15507 ** W/O and transferred to DGMFA; Alverca, PO., for storage, 1997.

A-103 153195 Navy acceptance from NPRO Rep., LTV, Dallas, TX., 23 JUN 67 ** Transferred to VA-122/FRS, NJ/2XX, NAS LEMOORE, CA., 19 DEC 67 ** Transferred to VA-27/CVW-14, NK/6XX, USS Constellation (CVA-64), 19 DEC 67 ** Transferred to VA-122/FRS, NJ/2XX, NAS LeMoore, CA., 29 FEB 68 ** Transferred to NARF, NAS Alameda, CA., 22 JUL 69 ** Transferred to VA-27/CVW-14, NK/4XX, USS Enterprise (CVAN-65), 15 JUL 50 ** Transferred to VA-125/FRS, NJ/5XX, NAS LeMoore, CA., 20 JUL 70 ** Transferred to VA-303/CVWR-30, ND/305, NAS Alameda, CA., 22 APR 71 ** Transferred to VA-305/CVWR-30, ND/5XX, NAS Point Mugu, CA., 11 MAR 75 ** To VA-303, NAS Jacksonville, FL., 27 JAN 76; To VA-303, NAS Alameda, CA., 22 MAR 76 ** ** Transferred to MASDC, Davis Monthan AFB; Tucson, AZ., assigned park code 6A0107; 17 NOV 77 ~ S 3SO strike, 10 JUN 80 ** Transferred to LTV, Dallas, TX. to be converted to A-7P ** Transferred to the Portuguese AF (FAP), S/N 5529 ** Transferred to Esquadra 304 "Magnificoes" , BA-5; Monte Real, PO., 1985 ** S/N changed to 15529 ** W/O and located at DGMFA; Alverca, PO., 1994

A-104 153196 Navy acceptance from NPRO Rep., LTV, Dallas, TX., 28 JUN 67 ** Transferred to VA-105/CVW-11, NH/4XX, NAS Cecil Field, FL., 10 JUN 68 ** Transferred to VA-82/CVW-6, AE/3XX, USS America, (CVA-66), 24 JUL 67 ** VA-174/FRS, AD/2XX, NAS Cecil Field, FL., 14 NOV 67 ** Transferred to VA-105/CVW-11, NH/4XX, NAS Cecil Field, FL., 11 MAR 68; To VA-105, USS Kitty Hawk (CVA-63), 10 JUN 68; To VA-105/CVW-3, AC/4XX, USS Saratoga (CV-60), 24 JUN 69; To VA-105, NAS Cecil Field, FL., 25 MAY 72 ** Transferred to NARF, NAS Jacksonville, FL., 28 JAN 74 ** Transferred to VA-203/CVWR-20, AF/3XX, NAS Jacksonville, FL., 19 DEC 74 ** Transferred to VA-30/CVWR-30, ND/502, & ND/503, NAS Point Mugu, CA., 06 AUG 77 ** Transferred to MASDC, Davis Monthan AFB; Tucson, AZ., assigned park code 6A0102; 08 MAY 78 ~ S 3SO strike, 15 JUN 83 ** Transferred to LTV, Dallas, TX. to be converted to TA-7P ** Transferred to the Portuguese AF (FAP), S/N 5546 ** Transferred to BA-5; Monte Real, PO., 1985 ** S/N changed to 15546 ** W/O and transferred to BA-5; Monte Real, PO., for storage, 1999.

A-105 153197 Navy acceptance from NPRO Rep., LTV, Dallas, TX., 28 JUN 67 ** Transferred to VA-82/CVW-6, AE/3XX, USS America (CVA-66), 22 JUL 67 ** Transferred to VA-174/FRS, AD/2XX, NAS Cecil Field, FL., 03 JAN 68 ** Transferred to VA-105/CVW-11, NH/4XX, NAS Cecil Field, FL., 04 MAR 68; To VA-105, USS Kitty Hawk (CVA-63), 28 JUN 68; To VA-105/CVW-3, AC/4XX, USS Saratoga (CV-63), 28 JUN 69 ~ S 1SO strike, 16 JUN 72 ** LT John J. Cabral killed when he flew into the water.

A-106 153198 Navy acceptance from NPRO Rep., LTV, Dallas, TX., 30 JUN 67 ** Transferred to VA-82/CVW-6, AE/3XX, USS America (CVA-66), 22 JUL 67 ** Transferred to VA-174/FRS, AD/2XX, NAS Cecil Field, FL., 07 NOV 67 ** Transferred to VA-105/CVW-11, NH/4XX, NAS Cecil Field, FL., 07 MAR 68; To VA-105, USS Kitty Hawk (CVA-63), 24 JUN 68; To VA-105/CVW-3, AC/4XX, USS Saratoga (CV-60), 09 APR 69 ~ S 1SO strike, 10 JUL 72 ** Crashed after catapult shot, due to loss of control.

A-107 153199 Navy acceptance from NPRO Rep., LTV, Dallas, TX., 29 JUN 67 ** Transferred to VA-147/CVW-2, NE/3XX, NAS LeMoore, CA., 20 JUL 67 ** Transferred to VA-122/FRS, NJ/2XX, NAS LEMOORE, CA., 17 OCT 67 ** Transferred to NAS Cubi Point, PI., 13 JUL 68 ** Transferred to VA-86/CVW-6, AE/4XX, NAS Cecil Field, FL., 19 JUL 68 ** Transferred to VA-97/CVW-14, NK/5XX, USS Constellation (CVA-64), 05 NOV 68 ** Transferred to VA-122/FRS, NJ/2XX, NAS LeMoore, CA., 10 MAR 69 ** Transferred to VA-153/CVW-19, NM/3XX, USS Oriskany (CVA-34), 03 OCT 69 ** Transferred to VA-125/FRS, NJ/5XX, NAS LeMoore, CA., 06 MAY 71 ** Transferred to VA-153/CVW-19, NM/306, USS Oriskany (CVA-34), 20 JAN 72; To VA-153, NAS LeMoore, CA., 19 JUN 72 ** Transferred to VA-125/FRS, NJ/5XX, NAS LeMoore, CA., 17 MAY 73 ** Transferred to VA-56/CVW-5, NF/415, USS Midway (CV-41), 16 OCT 75; To VA-56, NAF Atsugi, JP., 27 APR 76; To VA-56, USS Midway (CV-41), 18 MAY 76; To VA-56, NAF Atsugi, JP., 22 DEC 76; To VA-56, USS Midway (CV-41), 29 DEC 76; To VA-56, NAF Atsugi, JP., 07 JAN 77; To VA-56, USS Midway (CV-41), 11 JAN 77; To VA-56, NAF Atsugi, JP., 18 FEB 77; To VA-56, USS Midway (CV-41), 24 FEB 77; To VA-56, NAF Atsugi, JP., 07 MAR 77; To VA-56, USS Midway (CV-41), 17 MAR 77; To VA-56, NAS North Island, CA., 26 MAY 77 ** Transferred to MASDC, Davis Monthan AFB; Tucson, AZ., assigned park code 6A0069, 01 JUN 77 ~ S 3SO strike, 20 AUG 80 ** No data on strike ** Transferred to the Portuguese AF (FAP) to be used as spare parts, for the A-7P program.

A-108 153200 Navy acceptance from NPRO Rep., LTV, Dallas, TX., 30 JUN 67 ** Transferred to VA-37/CVW-11, NH/3XX, NAS Cecil Field, FL., 02 AUG 67; To VA-37, USS Kitty Hawk (CVA-63,), 18 JUN 68; To VA-37/CVW-3, AC/3XX, USS Saratoga (CVA-60), 06 MAR 69 ** Transferred to VA-174/FRS, AD/2XX, NAS Cecil Field, FL., 23 JUN 70 ** Transferred to MASDC, Davis Monthan AFB; Tucson, AZ., 08 FEB 71 ** Transferred to NARF, NAS Alameda, CA., 25 JUN 71 ** VA-303/CVWR-30, ND/300 & ND/314, NAS

Alameda, CA., 22 SEP 71 ** Transferred to MASDC, Davis Monthan AFB; Tucson, AZ., assigned park code 6A0088, 18 NOV 77 ~ S 3SO strike, 06 MAY 80 ** No data on strike ** Sent to LTV Dallas, TX. to be converted to A-7P ** Transferred to the Portuguese AF (FAP), S/N 5502 ** Transferred to Esquadra 302 "Falcões" , BA-5; Monte Real, PO., 1981 ** W/O and transferred to BA-11; Beja, PO., for storage, 1990.

A-109 153201 Navy acceptance from NPRO Rep., LTV, Dallas, TX., 30 JUN 67 ** Transferred to VA-122/FRS, NJ/2XX, NAS LeMoore, CA., 03 AUG 67 ** Transferred to VA-27/CVW-14, NK/6XX, USS Constellation (CVA-64), 17 APR 68 ** Transferred to VA-147/CVW-2, NE/3XX, NAS LeMoore, CA., 15 OCT 68 ** Transferred to VA-122/FRS, NJ/2XX, NAS LeMoore, CA., 18 MAR 69 ** Transferred to VA-153/CVW-19, NM/3XX, USS Oriskany (CVA-34), 19 NOV 69 ** Transferred to VA-125/FRS, NJ/ 5XX, NAS LeMoore, CA., 02 FEB 71 ** Transferred to VA-304/CVWR-30, ND/404, NAS Alameda, CA., 11 JAN 72 ** Transferred to VA-125/FRS, NJ/5XX, 27 OCT 72 ** Transferred to VA-304/CVWR-30, ND/404, NAS Alameda, CA., 14 NOV 72; To VA-304, NAS Jacksonville, FL., 10 DEC 75; To VA-304, NAS Alameda, CA., 08 FEB 76 ** Transferred to MASDC, Davis Monthan AFB; Tucson, AZ., assigned park code 6A0116, 23 SEP 78 ~ S 3SO strike, 15 JUN 83 ** No data on strike ** Transferred to LTV, Dallas, TX., to be converted to TA-7P ** Transferred to the Portuguese AF (FAP), S/N 5545 ** Transferred BA-5; Monte Real, PO., 1985 ** S/N changed to 15545 ** W/O and transferred DGMFA, Alverca, PO., for storage, 1995.

A-110 153202 Navy acceptance from NPRO Rep., LTV, Dallas, TX., 13 JUL 67 ** Transferred to VA-147/CVW-9, NG/3XX, NAS Cecil Field, FL., 22 APR 69 ~ S 1SO strike, 26 SEP 67 ** Crashed near USS Ranger (CV-61), due to engine failure.

A-111 153203 Navy acceptance from NPRO Rep., LTV, Dallas, TX., 13 JUL 67 ** Transferred to VX-5, XE/XXX, NAF China Lake, CA., 17 MAY 68 ~ S 1SO strike, 08 JAN 69 ** Crashed near MCAS Yuma, AZ., Due to Mid air collision with A-7A 154347.

A-112 153204 Navy acceptance from NPRO Rep., LTV, Dallas, TX., 24 JUL 67 ** Transferred to VA-37/CVW-11, NH/3XX, NAS Cecil Field, FL., 14 AUG 67; To VA-37, USS Kitty Hawk (CVA-63), 21 JUN 68; To VA-37/CVW-3, AC/3XX, USS Saratoga (CVA-60), 06 APR 69 ** Transferred to VA-174/FRS, AD/2XX, NAS Cecil Field, FL., 21 MAY 70 ** Transferred to VA-37/CVW-3, AC/3XX, USS Saratoga (CVA-60), 29 MAY 70 ** Transferred to VA-174/ FRS, AD/2XX, NAS Cecil Field, FL., 13 JUN 70 ** Transferred to NATF, NAS Lakehurst, NJ., 19 DEC 70 ** Transferred to MASDC, Davis Monthan AFB; Tucson, AZ., 07 JUL 71 ** Transferred to NARF, NAS Alameda, CA., 04 JUL 72 ** Transferred to VA-174/ FRS, AD/2XX, NAS Cecil Field, FL., 25 NOV 72 ** Transferred to VA-56/CVW-5, NF/4XX, NAS LeMoore, CA., 27 FEB 73; To VA-56, USS Midway (CVA-41), 18 APR 73 ~ S 1SO strike, 22 DEC 73 ** Crashed due to mid air collision with EA-6B.

A-113 153205 Navy acceptance from NPRO Rep., LTV, Dallas, TX., 31 JUL 67 ** Transferred to VA-122/FRS, NJ/2XX, NAS LeMoore, CA., 18 AUG 67 ** Transferred to VA-97/CVW-14, NK/5XX, USS Constellation (CVA-64), 09 MAY 68 ** Transferred to VA-82/CVW-6, AE/3XX, NAS Cecil Field, FL., 14 JUN 68 ** Transferred to VA-27/CVW-14, NK/6XX, USS Constellation (CVA-64), 07 NOV 68 ** Transferred to VA-122/FRS, NJ/2XX, NAS LeMoore, CA., 11 MAR 69 ** Transferred to VA-153/CVW-19 NM/3XX, USS Oriskany (CVA-34), 21 NOV 69 ~ S 1SO strike, 09 JUN 71 ** No data on strike.

A-114 153206 Navy acceptance from NPRO Rep., LTV, Dallas, TX., 24 JUL 67 ** Transferred to VA-37/CVW-11, NH/3XX, NAS Cecil Field, FL., 17 AUG 67; To VA-37, USS Kitty Hawk (CVA-63), 06 JUN 68; To VA-37/CVW-3, AC/313, USS Saratoga (CV-60), 22 APR 69 ~ S 1SO strike, 14 JUN 72 ** LCDR F.J. Davis KIA when he was shot down by a SAM over North Vietnam.

A-115 153207 Navy acceptance from NPRO Rep., LTV, Dallas, TX., 31 JUL 67 ** Transferred to VA-37/CVW-11, NH/306, NAS Cecil Field, FL., 16 AUG 67; To VA-37, USS Kitty Hawk (CVA-63), 13 JUN 68; To VA-37/CVW-3, AC/313, USS Saratoga (CV-60), 18 JUN 69; To VA-37, NAS Cecil Field, FL.., 15 JUN 72 ~ S 1SO strike, 17 AUG 72 ** No data on strike.

A-116 153208 Navy acceptance from NPRO Rep., LTV, Dallas, TX., 19 MAY 67 ** Transferred to NPRO Rep., LTV, Dallas, TX., for R & T, 20 MAY 67 ** Transferred to NATC, Weapons System Test, NAS Patuxent River, MD., 20 DEC 67 ** Transferred to NPRO Rep., LTV, Dallas, TX., for R & T, 04 FEB 68 ** Transferred to NATC, Weapons Systems Test, NAS Patuxent River, MD., 17 JUN 68 ** Transferred to VA-122/FRS, NJ/2XX, NAS LeMoore, CA., 18 JUN 68 ** Transferred to NAS Cubi Pt., PI., XX/XXX, 13 JUL 68 ** Transferred to VA-82/CVW-6, AE/3XX, NAS Cecil Field, FL., 18 JUL 68; To VA-82/CVW-15, NL/3XX, USS Coral Sea (CVA-43), 10 JAN 69 ** Transferred to VA-174/FRS, AD/2XX, NAS Cecil Field, FL., 15 JUL 69 ** Transferred to NWEF, Kirtland AFB; Albuquerque, NM., 06 NOV 70 ** Transferred to MASDC, Davis Monthan AFB; Tucson, AZ., assigned park code 6A071, 23 DEC 70 ** Transferred to NARF, NAS Alameda, CA., 01 JUL 72 ** Transferred to VA-125/FRS, NJ/5XX, NAS LeMoore, CA., 27 OCT 72 ** Transferred to VA-93/CVW-5, NF/302, NAS LeMoore, CA., 02 APR 73; To VA-93, USS Midway (CVA-41), 15 JUN 73; To VA-93, NAF Atsugi, JP., 21 AUG 74; To VA-93, USS Midway (CVA-41), 27 AUG 74; To VA-93, NAF Atsugi, JP., 24 NOV 75; To VA-93, USS Midway (CV-41), 31 DEC 75; To VA-93, NAF Atsugi, JP., 01 NOV 76; To VA-93, USS Midway (CV-41), 02 NOV 76; To VA-93, NAF Atsugi, JP., 04 NOV 76; To VA-93, USS Midway (CV-41), 08 NOV 76; To VA-93, NAS North Island, CA., 24 MAY 77 ** Transferred to MASDC, Davis Monthan AFB; Tucson, AZ., assigned park code 6A0054, 26 MAY 77 ~ S 3SO strike, 15 JUN 83 ** No data on strike ** Transferred to LTV, Dallas, TX. to be converted to A-7P ** Transferred to the Portuguese AF (FAP), S/N 5536 ** Transferred to Esquadra 304 "Magnificoes", BA-5; Monte Real, PO., 1985 ** S/N changed to 15536 ** W/O and transferred DGMFA Alverca, PO., for storage, 1995.

A-117 153209 Navy acceptance from NPRO Rep., LTV, Dallas, TX., 24 JUL 67 ** Transferred to VA-37/CVW-11, NH/3XX, NAS Cecil Field, FL., 23 AUG 67; To VA-37, USS Kitty Hawk (CVA-63), 06 MAY 68 ** To VA-37/CVW-3, AC/3XX, USS Saratoga (CV-60), 18 JUN 69 ~ S 1SO strike, 03 MAY 71 ** Crashed due to engine failure.

A-118 153210 Navy acceptance from NPRO Rep., LTV, Dallas, TX., 24 JUL 67 ** Transferred to VA-37/CVW-11, NH/3XX, NAS Cecil Field, FL., 10 JUN 68 ~ S 1SO strike, 10 JUN 68 ** Crashed near NAS Cecil Field due to a stall/spin.

A-119 153211 Navy acceptance from NPRO Rep., LTV, Dallas, TX., 31 JUL 67 ** Transferred to VA-122/FRS, NJ/2XX, NAS LeMoore, CA., 25 AUG 67 ~ S 1SO strike, 07 JUN 68 ** Crashed on USS Hancock (CVA-19), due to a ramp strike.

A-120 153212 Navy acceptance from NPRO Rep., LTV, Dallas, TX., 28 JUL 67 ** Transferred to VA-37/CVW-11, NH/3XX, NAS Cecil Field, FL., 11 AUG 67; To VA-37, USS Kitty Hawk (CVA-63), 28 JUN 68; To VA-37/CVW-3, AC/311, Cecil Field, FL., USS Saratoga (CV-60), LT Lei painted on side of cockpit, 30 JUN 69; To VA-37, NAS Cecil Field, FL., 25 MAY 72 ** Transferred to VA-303/CVWR-30, ND/320, NAS Alameda, CA., 30 APR 73 ** Transferred to MASDC, Davis Monthan AFB; Tucson, AZ., assigned park code 6A0090; 23 NOV 77 ~ S 3SO strike, 15 JUL 83 ** No data on strike ** Transferred to LTV, Dallas, TX., to be converted to A-7P ** Transferred to the Portuguese AF (FAP), S/N 5531** Transferred to Esquadra 304 "Magnificoes", BA-5; Monte Real, PO. ** S/N changed to 15531 ** W/O and Transferred BA5, Monte Real, PO., 1999.

A-121 153213 Navy acceptance from NPRO Rep., LTV, Dallas, TX., 31 JUL 67 ** Transferred to VA-37/CVW-11, NH/3XX, NAS Cecil Field, FL., 17 AUG 67; To VA-37/CVW-3, AC/3XX, USS Saratoga (CV-60), 29 MAY 68; To VA-37, NAS Cecil Field, FL., 30 MAY 72 ~ S 1SO strike, 13 SEP 72 ** No data on strike.

A-122 153214 Navy acceptance from NPRO Rep., LTV, Dallas, TX., 28 JUL 67 ** Transferred to VA(F)-122/FRS, NJ/2XX, NAS LeMoore, CA., Corsair College on side in large letters, 18 AUG 67 ** VA-97/CVW-14, NK/5XX, USS Constellation (CVA-64), 22 MAY 68 ~ S 1SO strike, 18 SEP 68 ** LCDR B.D. Woods became a POW after being shot down over North Vietnam by AAA .

A-123 153215 Navy acceptance from NPRO Rep., LTV, Dallas, TX., 31 JUL 67 ** Transferred to VA-122/FRS, NJ/2XX, NAS LeMoore, CA., 21 JUN 68 ** Transferred to NAS Cubi Point., PI., 05 OCT 68 ** Transferred to VA-86/CVW-6, AE/4XX, NAS Cecil Field, FL., 08 OCT 68; To VA-86/CVW-15, NL/4XX, USS Coral Sea (CVA-43), 16 JUN 69; To VA-86, NAS Cecil Field, FL., 22 APR 70 ** Transferred to MASDC, Davis Monthan AFB; Tucson, AZ., assigned park code unknown, 25 AUG 71 ** Transferred to NARF, NAS Alameda, CA., 14 JUN 72 ** Transferred to VA-125/FRS, NJ/5XX, NAS LeMoore, CA., 26 OCT 72 ** Transferred to VA-93/CVW-5, NF/305, NAS LeMoore, CA.,09 MAY 73; To VA-93, USS Midway (CVA-4), 14 OCT 73; To VA-93, NAF Atsugi, JP., 11 JUL 74; To VA-93, USS Midway (CVA-41), 06 AUG 74; To VA-93, NAF Atsugi, JP., 20 DEC 74 **Transferred to USS Midway (CVA-41), 27 DEC 74; To VA-93, NAF Atsugi, JP., 24 FEB 75; To VA-93, USS Midway (CVA-41), 27 FEB 75; To VA-93, NAF Atsugi, JP., 02 JUN 75; To VA-93, USS Midway (CV-41), 14 SEP 75; To VA-93, NAF Atsugi, JP., 06 JAN 77; To VA-93, USS Midway (CV-41), 11 JAN 77; To VA-93, NAF Atsugi, JP., 11 MAR 77; To VA-93, USS Midway (CV-41), 06 APR 77; To VA-93, NAS North Island, CA., 24 MAY 77 88 ** Transferred to MASDC, Davis Monthan AFB; Tucson, AZ. assigned park code 6A0052, 26 MAY 77 ~ S 3SO strike, 11 JUL 80 ** No data on strike ** Transferred to LTV, Dallas, TX., to be converted to A-7P ** Transferred to the Portuguese AF (FAP), S/N 5514 ** Transferred to Esquadra 302 "Falcões" , BA-5; Monte Real, PO., 1982 ** S/N changed to 15514 ** W/O and transferred to DGMFA Alverca, PO., for storage, 1998.

A-124 153216 Navy acceptance from NPRO Rep., LTV, Dallas, TX., 31 JUL 67 ** Transferred to VA-37/CVW-11, NH/3XX, NAS Cecil Field, FL., 18 AUG 67; To VA-37, USS Kitty Hawk (CVA-63), 27 JUN 68; To VA-37/CVW-3, AC/3XX, USS Saratoga (CV-60), 18 JUN 69; To VA-37, NAS Cecil Field, FL., 30 JUN 72 ** Transferred to VA-174/FRS, AD/2XX, NAS Cecil Field, FL.,24 APR 72 ** Transferred to VA-304/CVWR-30, ND/403, NAS Alameda, CA., 21 MAR 74; To VA-304, NAS Jacksonville, FL., 10 JAN 75; To VA-304, NAS Alameda, CA., 19 MAR 75 ** Transferred to MASDC, Davis Monthan AFB; Tucson, AZ., assigned park code 6A0084, 26 SEP 77 ~ S 3SO strike, 15 JUL 83 ** No data on strike ** Transferred to LTV, Dallas, TX. to be converted to A-7P ** Transferred to the Portuguese AF (FAP), S/N 5532 ** Transferred to Esquadra 304 "Magnificoes" , BA-5; Monte Real, PO., 1985 ** S/N changed to 15532 ** W/O and transferred to DGMFA Alverca, PO., for storage, 1995.

A-125 153217 Navy acceptance from NPRO Rep., LTV, Dallas, TX., 18 AUG 67 ** Transferred to VA-122/FRS, NJ/2XX, NAS LeMoore, CA., 23 AUG 67 ** Transferred to VA-97/CVW-14, NK/5XX, USS Constellation (CVA-64), 22 NOV 67 ** Transferred to VA-122/FRS, NJ/2XX, NAS LeMoore, CA., 24 FEB 68 ** Transferred to VA-97/CVW-14, NK/5XX, USS Constellation (CVA-64), 07 AUG 68 ** Transferred to VA-105/CVW-11, NH/4XX, USS Kitty Hawk (CVA-63), 22 JUN 69; To VA-105/CVW-3, AC/4XX, USS Saratoga (CV-60), 22 JUN 69 ** Transferred to VA-174/FRS, AD/2XX, NAS Cecil Field, FL., 18 FEB 72 ** Transferred to VA-105/CVW-3, AC/3XX, NAS Cecil Field, FL.,24 JUN 72 ** Transferred to VA-305/CVWR-30, ND/502 & ND/513, NAS Point Mugu, CA., 01 MAY 73; To VA-305, NAS Alameda, CA., 28 JUN 74; To VA-305, NAS Point Mugu, CA., 22 AUG 74; To VA-305, NAS Jacksonville, FL., 05 MAY 75; To VA-305, NAS Point Mugu, CA., 20 OCT 75 ** Transferred to MASDC, Davis Monthan AFB; Tucson, AZ., assigned park code 6A0106, 17 MAY 78 ~ S 3SO strike, 15 JUL 83 ** No data on strike ** Transferred to the Portuguese AF (FAP), to be used for spare parts for the A-7P program.

A-126 153218 Navy acceptance from NPRO Rep., LTV, Dallas, TX., 28 AUG 67 ** Transferred to VA-122/ FRS, NJ/2XX, NAS LeMoore, CA., 31 MAR 67 ** Transferred to VA-82/CVW-8, AJ/3XX, NAS Cecil Field, FL., 08 AUG 68 ** Transferred to VA-97/CVW-14, NK/5XX, USS Constellation (CVA-64), 03 NOV 68 ** Transferred to VA-122/ FRS, NJ/2XX, NAS LeMoore, CA., 17 MAY 69 ** Transferred to VA-105/CVW-11, NH/4XX, USS Kitty Hawk (CVA-63), 22 JUN 69; To VA-105/ CVW-3, AC/3XX, USS Saratoga (CV-60), 22 JUN 69 ** Transferred to VA-122/FRS, NJ/2XX, NAS LeMoore, CA., 14 SEP 69 ** Transferred to VA-153/ CVW-19, NM/313, USS Oriskany (CVA-34), 23 OCT 69; TO VA-153, NAS LeMoore, CA., 28 JUN 72 ** Transferred to NARF, NAS Alameda, CA., 05 APR 73 ~ S 3SO strike, 16 NOV 76, No data on strike.

A-127 153219 Navy acceptance from NPRO Rep., LTV, Dallas, TX., 24 AUG 67 ** Transferred to NATC, Weapons Systems Test, NAS Patuxent River, MD., 11 SEP 67 ** Transferred to VA-147/CVW-2, NE/315, NAS Lemoore, CA., 27 SEP 67; ** Transferred to VA-122/ FRS, NJ/2XX, NAS LeMoore, CA., 13 JUN 69 ** Transferred to VA-153/CVW-19, NM/312, USS Oriskany (CVA-34), 15 SEP 69; To VA-153, NAS LeMoore, CA., 26 JUN 72 ** Transferred to VA-125/ FRS, NJ/5XX, NAS LeMoore, CA., 10 APR 73; To VA-125, NAS Jacksonville, FL., 15 JAN 75; To VA-125, NAS LeMoore, CA., 25 FEB 75 ** Transferred to VA-56/CVW-5, NF/414, USS Midway (CVA-41), 19 APR 75; To VA-56, NAF Atsugi, JP., 11 MAR 76; To VA-56, USS Midway (CV-41), 06 APR 76; To VA-56, NAF Atsugi, JP., 01 JUL 76; To VA-56, USS Midway (CV-41), 18 JUL 76; To VA-56, NAS North Island, CA., 25 MAY 77 ** Transferred to MASDC, Davis Monthan AFB; Tucson, AZ., assigned park code 6A0060, 27 MAY 77 ~ S 3SO strike, 18 JUN 80 ** No data on strike ** Transferred to LTV, Dallas, TX. to be converted to A-7P ** Transferred to the Portuguese AF (FAP), S/N 5508 ** Transferred to Esquadra 302 "Falcões", BA-5; Monte Real, PO., 1981 ** S/N changed to 15508 ** Retired in 1999 ** W/O and located at Museu do Ar - Alverca, Portugal for display.

A-128 153220 Navy acceptance from NPRO Rep., LTV, Dallas, TX., 24 AUG 67 ** Transferred to VA-147/CVW-2, NE/3XX, NAS LeMoore, CA., 14 SEP 67 ** Transferred to VA-122/FRS, NJ/2XX, NAS LeMoore, CA., 09 JUN 69 ** Transferred to VA-153/CVW-19, NM/311, USS Oriskany (CVA-34), 10 SEP 69; To VA-153, NAS LeMoore, CA., 26 JUN 72 ** Transferred to VA-125/FRS, NJ/5XX, NAS LeMoore, CA., 10 APR 73 ** Transferred to VA-56/CVW-5, NF/4XX, USS Midway (CVA-41), 11 JUL 73; To VA-56, NAS Cubi Point, PI., 28 MAR75; To VA-56, USS Midway (CV-41), 16 JUN 75 ** Transferred to VA-56, NAS Alameda, CA., 17 JUL 75 ** Transferred to VA-125/FRS, NJ/520, NAS LeMoore, CA., 01 FEB 76 ** Transferred to MASDC, Davis Monthan, AFB; Tucson, AZ., assigned park code 6A0046; 15 APR 77 ~ S 3SO strike, 07 MAY 80 ** No data on strike ** On display at American Legion Post 1170; Round Lake, IL.

A-129 153221 Navy acceptance from NPRO Rep., LTV, Dallas, TX., 30 AUG 67 ** Transferred to VA-147/CVW-2, NE/3XX, NAS LeMoore, CA., 22 SEP 67 ** Transferred to VA-122/FRS, NJ/2XX, NAS LeMoore, CA., 12 JUN 69 ** Transferred to VA-125/FRS, NJ/5XX, NAS LeMoore, CA.,17 JAN 70; To VA-125, USS Coral Sea CVA-43, 10 AUG 70; To VA-125, NAS LeMoore, CA., 01 JAN 71 ** Transferred to NAS Point Mugu, CA., for RDT&E, 25 FEB 71 ** Transferred to VA-125/FRS, NJ/522, NAS LeMoore, CA.,15 AUG 73 ** Transferred to MASDC, Davis Monthan AFB; Tucson, AZ., assigned park code 6A0043; 08 JAN 77 ~ S 3SO strike, 19 JUL 80 ** No data on strike ** Transferred to LTV, Dallas, TX. to be converted to A-7P ** Transferred to the Portuguese AF (FAP), S/N 5515 ** Transferred to Esquadra 302 "Falcões", BA-5; Monte Real, PO., 1982 ** S/N changed to 15515 ** W/O and transferred to DGMFA Alverca, PO., for storage, 1990.

A-130 153222 Navy acceptance from NPRO Rep., LTV, Dallas, TX., 28 AUG 67 ** Transferred to VA-147/CVW-2, NE/305, NAS LeMoore, CA., 26 SEP 67 ~ S 1SO strike, 12 APR 69 ** No data on strike.

A-131 153223 Navy acceptance from NPRO Rep., LTV, Dallas, TX., 31 AUG 67 ** Transferred to VA-147/CVW-2, NE/302, NAS LeMoore, CA., 17 SEP 67 ** Transferred to VA-122/FRS, NJ/2XX, NAS LeMoore,

CA., 06 JUN 69 ** Transferred to VA-153/CVW-19, NM/3XX, USS Oriskany (CVA-34), 10 DEC 69 ~ S 1SO strike, 08 SEP 71 ** Crashed due to engine failure on launch. Pilot ejected and was rescued.

A-132 153224 Navy acceptance from NPRO Rep., LTV, Dallas, TX., 30 AUG 67 ** Transferred to VA-147/CVW-2, NE/3XX, NAS LeMoore, CA., 22 JUL 68 ** Transferred to VA-122/FRS, NJ/2XX, NAS LeMoore, CA., 09 OCT 69 ** Transferred to VA-125/FRS, NJ/5XX, NAS LeMoore, CA., 07 JAN 70; To VA-125, USS Coral Sea (CVA-43), 10 AUG 70; To VA-125, NAS LeMoore, CA., 01 JAN 71 ** Transferred to VA-304/CVWR-30, ND/405, NAS Alameda, CA., 18 AUG 71; To VA-304, NAS Jacksonville, FL., 03 MAY 76, NAS Alameda, CA., 27 JUN 76 ** Transferred to MASDC as 6A0105, 09 MAY 78 ** S 3SO strike, 15 JUL 83 ** No data on strike ** Transferred to LTV, Dallas, TX., to be converted to TA-7P ** Transferred to the Portuguese AF (FAP), S/N 5547 ** Transferred to BA-5; Monte Real, PO., 1985 ** S/N changed to 15547 ** W/O and located at BA5; Monte Real, Portugal, 1995.

A-133 153225 Navy acceptance from NPRO Rep., LTV, Dallas, TX., 28 AUG 67 ** Transferred to VA-147/CVW-2, NE/307, NAS LeMoore, CA., 02 OCT 67 ** Transferred to VA-86/CVW-6, AE/4XX, NAS Cecil Field, FL., 09 JUL 68 ~ S 1SO strike, 02 SEP 68 ** No data on strike.

A-134 153226 Navy acceptance from NPRO Rep., LTV, Dallas, TX., 29 AUG 67 ** Transferred toVA-147/CVW-2, NE/3XX, NAS LeMoore, CA., 28 SEP 67 ** Transferred to VA-122/FRS, NJ/2XX, NAS LeMoore, CA., 17 JUN 69 ** Transferred to VA-153/CVW-19, NM/305, USS Oriskany (CVA-34), 11 DEC 69 ** Transferred to VA-125/FRS, NJ/5XX, NAS LeMoore, CA., 18 APR 72 ** Transferred to VA-93/CVW-5, NF/312, NAS LeMoore, CA., 12 APR 73; To VA-93, USS Midway (CVA-41), 14 JUN 73; To VA-93, NAF Atsugi, JP., 21 AUG 74; To VA-93, USS Midway (CVA-41), 30 AUG 74; To VA-93, NAF Atsugi, JP., 02 APR 75; To VA-93, USS Midway (CVA-41), 09 APR 75; To VA-93, NAF Atsugi, JP., 10 APR 75; To VA-93, USS Midway (CV-41), 01 AUG 75; To VA-93, NAF Atsugi, JP., 07 JAN 76; To VA-93, USS Midway (CV-41), 14 JAN 76; To VA-93, NAF Atsugi, JP., 04 MAR 76; To VA-93, USS Midway (CV-41), 12 MAR 76; To VA-93, NAF Atsugi, JP., 04 AUG 76; To VA-93, USS Midway (CV-41), 13 AUG 76; To VA-93, NAF Atsugi, JP., 06 SEP 76; To VA-93, USS Midway (CV-41), 05 OCT 76; To VA-93, NAF Atsugi, JP., 22 MAR 77; To VA-93, USS Midway (CV-41), 08 APR 77; To VA-93, NAS North Island, CA., 27 MAY 77 ** Transferred to MASDC, Davis Monthan AFB; Tucson, AZ., assigned park code 6A0061, 27 MAY 77 ~ S 3SO strike, 15 AUG 83 ** No data on strike ** Transferred to LTV, Dallas, TX., to be converted to A-7P ** Transferred to the Portuguese AF (FAP), S/N 5539 ** Transferred to Esquadra 304 "Magnificoes", BA-5; Monte Real, PO., 1985 ** S/N changed to 15539 ** W/O and transferred to BA-11; Beja, PO., for storage, 1990.

A-135 153227 Navy acceptance from NPRO Rep., LTV, Dallas, TX., 31 AUG 67 ** Transferred to VA-147/CVW-2, NE/3XX, NAS LeMoore, CA., 03 OCT 67 ** Transferred to VA-122/FRS, NJ/2XX, NAS LeMoore, CA., 12 OCT 69 ** Transferred to VA-125/FRS, NJ/5XX, NAS LeMoore, CA., 07 JAN 70 ** Transferred to VA-86/ CVW-15, NL/4XX, USS Coral Sea (CVA-43), 26 MAR 70; To VA-86, NAS Cecil Field, FL., 17 APR 70 ** Transferred to VA-174/ FRS, AD/2XX, NAS Cecil Field, FL., 28 AUG 70 ** Transferred to NARF, NAS Jacksonville, FL., 07 APR 71 ** Transferred to NATC, Service Test, XX/XXX, NAS Patuxent River, MD., for RTD & E, 10 DEC 71; To NATC, Service Test, NAS Jacksonville, FL., for RDT & E, 13 JUN 75 ** To NATC, Service Test, NAS Patuxent River, MD., for RTD & E, 01 JUL 75; To NATC, Service Test, NAS Jacksonville, FL., for RDT & E, 27 AUG 75; To NATC, Service Test, Modex 227, NAS Patuxent River, MD., for RTD & E, 28 AUG 75 ** Transferred to MASDC, Davis Monthan AFB; Tucson, AZ., assigned park code 6A0112, 01 SEP 78 ~ S 3SO strike, 22 JUL 80 ** No data on strike ** Sent to LTV, Dallas, TX., to be converted to A-7P ** Transferred to the Portuguese AF (FAP), S/N 5516 ** Transferred to Esquadra 302 "Falcões", BA-5; Monte Real, PO., 1982 ~ Stike, 1988 ** W/O, destroyed in accident near Peniche, PO.

A-136 153228 Navy acceptance from NPRO Rep., LTV, Dallas, TX., 31 AUG 67 ** Transferred to VA-147/CVW-2, NE/312, NAS LeMoore, CA., 02 OCT 67 ** Transferred to NATC, Weapons Systems Test, NAS Patuxent River, Md., XX/XXX, 06 JUL 68; Transferred to VA-147/CVW-2, NE/3XX, NAS LeMoore, CA., 30 JUL 68; To VA-147/CVW-9, NG/4XX, USS America (CVA-66), 10 JUN 69 ** Transferred to VA-122/FRS, NJ/2XX, NAS LeMoore, CA., 17 OCT 69 ** Transferred to VA-153/ CVW-19, NM/314, USS Oriskany (CVA-34), 31 JAN 70; To VA-153, NAS LeMoore, CA., 10 JUN 72 ** Transferred to VA-125/FRS, NJ/5XX, NAS LeMoore, CA., 04 APR 73 ** VA-93/CVW-5, NF/312 & NF/313, USS Midway (CVA-41), 05 JUL 73; To VA-93, NAF Atsugi, Japan, 28 JUN 74; To VA-93, USS Midway CVA-41), 02 JUL 74; To VA-93, NAF Atsugi, JP., 24 FEB 75; To VA-93, USS Midway (CV-41), 13 JUN 75; To VA-93, NAF Atsugi, JP., 17 SEP 75; To VA-93, USS Midway (CV-41), 14 OCT 76; To VA-93, NAF Atsugi, JP., 18 OCT 76; To VA-93, USS Midway (CV-41), 01 NOV 76; To VA-93, NAS North Island, CA., 24 MAY 77 ** Transferred to MASDC, Davis Monthan AFB, Tucson, AZ., assigned park code 6A0056, 27 MAY 77 ~ S 3SO strike, 25 JUL 80 ** No data on strike ** Sent to LTV, Dallas, TX., to be converted to A-7P ** Transferred to the Portuguese AF (FAP), S/N 5517 ** Transferred to Esquadra 302 "Falcões", BA-5; Monte Real, PO., 1982 ** S/N changed to 15517 ** W/O and transferred to DGMFA; Alverca, PO., for storage, 1994.

A-137 153229 Navy acceptance from NPRO Rep., LTV, Dallas, TX., 31 AUG 67 ** Transferred to VA-147/CVW-2, NE/3XX, NAS LeMoore, CA. 07 OCT 67 ** Transferred to VA-86/CVW-6, AE/4XX, NAS Cecil Field, FL., 09 JUL 68; To VA-86/CVW-15, NL/4XX, USS Coral Sea (CVA-43), 29 JUN 69; To VA-86, NAS Cecil Field, FL., 03 MAY 70 ** Transferred to NARF, NAS Alameda, CA., 10 MAR 71 ** Transferred to VA-303/CVWR-30, ND/3XX, NAS Alameda, CA., 01 JUL 71 ** Transferred to VA-304/CVWR-30, ND/414, NAS Alameda, CA., 14 AUG 71; To VA-304, NAS Jacksonville, FL., 11 JUN 74; To VA-304, NAS Alameda, CA., 11 JUN 74; To VA-304, NAS Jacksonville, FL., 11 SEP 74; To VA-304, NAS Alameda, CA., 15 OCT 74 ** Transferred to MASDC, Davis Monthan AFB; Tucson, AZ., assigned park code 6A0076; 28 AUG 77 ~ S 3SO strike, 15 AUG 83 ** No data on strike ** Sent to LTV, Dallas, TX. to be converted to A-7P ** Transferred to the Portuguese AF (FAP), S/N 5534 ** Transferred to Esquadra 304 "Magnificoes", BA-5; Monte Real, PO., 1985 ** S/N changed to 15534 ** W/O and transferred to DGMFA Alverca, PO., for storage, 1995.

A-138 153230 Navy acceptance from NPRO Rep., LTV, Dallas, TX., 23 OCT 67 ** Transferred to VA-82/CVW-6, AE/3XX, NAS Cecil Field, FL., 02 APR 68; To VA-82, USS America, (CVA-66), 21 DEC 67 ** Transferred to VA-174/FRS, AD/2XX, NAS Cecil Field, FL., 15 MAY 69 ** Transferred to VA-105/CVW-3, AC/4XX, USS Saratoga (CV-60), 15 APR 71 ~ S 1SO strike, 18 JUN 72 ** Shot down by AAA, Pilot MIA.

A-139 153231 Navy acceptance from NPRO Rep., LTV, Dallas, TX., 29 NOV 67 ** Transferred to VA-86/CVW-6, AE/4XX, USS America (CVA-66), 21 DEC 67; To VA-86, NAS Cecil Field, FL., 25 MAR 68; To VA-86/ CVW-15, NL/4XX, CA./USS Coral Sea (CVA-43), 29 JUN 69 ~ S 1SO strike, 07 JAN 70 ** LCDR M.G. Hoff KIA when shot down by AAA over Laos.

t**A-140 153232** Navy acceptance from NPRO Rep., LTV, Dallas, TX.,15 NOV 67 ** Transferred to VA- 27/CVW-14, NK/6XX, USS Constellation (CVA-64), 22 JAN 68; To VA-27/CVW-14, NK/4XX, NAS LeMoore, CA., 10 JUN 69; To VA-27, USS Enterprise (CVAN-65), 20 MAY 70 ** Transferred to VA-125/FRS, NJ/5XX, NAS LeMoore, CA., 29 SEP 70 ~ S 1SO strike, 12 NOV 70 ** No data on strike.

A-141 153233 Navy acceptance from NPRO Rep., LTV, Dallas, TX., 21 NOV 67 ** Transferred to VA-97/ CVW-14, NK/5XX, USS Constellation (CVA-64), 07 FEB 68 ~ S 1SO strike, 16 JUL 68 ** LT M.P. Hamilton was rescued after being shot down by AAA over Laos.

153234/153273 LTV A-7A-4c-CV Corsair II

A-143 153234 Navy acceptance from NPRO Rep., LTV, Dallas, TX., 14 DEC 67 ** Transferred to VA-97/ CVW-14, NK/505, USS Constellation (CVA-64), 21 FEB 68 ~ S 1SO strike, 16 JUL 68 ** Crashed due to fuel starvation in holding pattern, pilot ejected and was rescued.

A-144 153235 Navy acceptance from NPRO Rep., LTV, Dallas, TX., 19 DEC 67 ** Transferred to VA-97/CVW-14, NK/5XX, USS Constellation (CVA-64), 24 FEB 68 ** Transferred to VA-125/FRS, NJ/5XX, NAS LeMoore, CA., 22 OCT 70 ** Transferred to VA-153/CVW-19, NM/310, USS Oriskany (CVA-34), 14 JUL 71; To VA-153, NAS LeMoore, CA., 26 JUN 72 ** Transferred to VA-125/FRS, NJ/5XX, NAS LeMoore, CA., 25 APR 73 ** Transferred to VA-56/CVW-5, NF/4XX, USS Midway (CVA-41), 08 MAR 74 ** To VA-56/CVW-5, NAF Atsugi, JP., 16 OCT 75; To VA-56, USS Midway (CV-41), 01 MAR 76; To VA-56, NAF Atsugi, JP., 26 OCT 76; To VA-56, USS Midway (CV-41), 30 OCT 76 ** Transferred to NARF, NAS Alameda, Ca., 11 DEC 76 ~ S 3SO strike, 01 JUN 78 ** No data on strike.

A-145 153236 Navy acceptance from NPRO Rep., LTV, Dallas, TX., 19 DEC 67 ** Transferred to VA-97/CVW-14, NK/5XX, USS Constellation (CVA-64), 06 MAR 68 ** Transferred to VA-125/FRS, NJ/5XX, NAS LeMoore, CA., 23 JUN 70 ** Transferred to VA-303/CVWR-30, ND/301, NAS Alameda, CA., 05 APR 71 ** Transferred to MASDC, Davis Monthan AFB; Tucson, AZ., assigned park code 6A0099, 12 DEC 77 ~ S 3SO strike, 27 NOV 79, No data on strike.

A-146 153237 Navy acceptance from NPRO Rep., LTV, Dallas, TX., 07 DEC 67 ** Transferred to VA-27/CVW-14, NK/6XX, USS Constellation (CVA064), 25 FEB 68; To VA-27, NAS LeMoore, CA., 23 JUN 69; To VA-27/CVW-14, NK/4XX, USS Enterprise (CVAN-65), 16 MAY 70 ** Transferred to VA-125/FRS, NJ/5XX, NAS LeMoore, CA., 15 OCT 70 ** Transferred to VA-125/FRS, NJ/5XX, CRAA, NAS LeMoore, CA., 04 AUG 71 ** Transferred to VA-153/CVW-19, NM/300, USS Oriskany (CVA-34), 02 JUL 71; To VA-153, NAS LeMoore, CA., 14 JUN 72 ** Transferred to VA-125/FRS, NJ/5XX, NAS LeMoore, CA., 04 OCT 73 ** Transferred to VA-93/ CVW-5, NF/3XX, USS Midway (CV-41), 20 AUG 74; To VA-93, NAF Atsugi, JP., 30 MAR 76; To VA-93, USS Midway (CV-41), 05 OCT 76; To VA-93, NAS North Island, CA., 24 MAY 76 ** Transferred to MASDC, Davis Monthan AFB; Tucson, AZ., assigned park code 6A0067; 31 MAY 77 ~ S 3SO strike, 27 NOV 79 ** No data on strike ** Sent to LTV Dallas, TX. to be converted to A-7P ** Transferred to the Portuguese AF (FAP), S/N 5518 ** Transferred to Esquadra 302 "Falcões", BA-5; Monte Real, PO., 1982 ~ Strike, 1983 ** W/O, Destroyed in accident near Leiria, PO.

A-147 153238 Navy acceptance from NPRO Rep., LTV, Dallas, TX., 29 DEC 67 ** Transferred to VA-97/CVW-14, NK/5XX, USS Constellation (CVA-64), 29 FEB 68; To VA-97, NAS LeMoore, CA., 25 JUN 69 ** Transferred to VA-125/FRS, NJ/5XX, NAS LeMoore, CA., 24 JUN 70 ** Transferred to VA-153/CVW-19, NM/301, USS Oriskany (CVA-34), date unknown ** Transferred to VA-303/CVWR-30, ND/310 & ND/376, NAS Alameda, CA., 27 MAY 71, Painted in Bicentennial paint scheme ** Transferred to MASDC, Davis Monthan AFB; Tucson, AZ., assigned park code 6A0086; 18 NOV 77 ~ S 3SO strike, 27 NOV 79, No data on strike.

A-148 153239 Navy acceptance from NPRO Rep., LTV, Dallas, TX., 10 OCT 67 ** Transferred to VA-147/CVW-2, NE/313, NAS LeMoore, CA., USS Ranger (CVA-61), LCDR Jim Hickerson painted on Port side under cockpit, First combat loss in Vietnam ~ S 1SOstrike, 22 DEC 67, LCDR Jim Hickerson became a POW after being shot down by a SAM over North Vietnam.

A-149 153240 Navy acceptance from NPRO Rep., LTV, Dallas, TX., 27 SEP 67 ** Transferred to VA-147/CVW-2, NE/3XX, NAS LeMoore, CA., 12 OCT 67 ** Transferred to VA-37/CVW-11, NH/3XX, USS Kitty Hawk (CVA-63), 25 JUN 69; To VA-37/CVW-3, AC/3XX, USS Saratoga (CV-60), 25 JUN 69; To VA-37, NAS Cecil Field, FL. 25 MAY 72 ** Transferred to VA-304/CVWR-30, ND/412, NAS Alameda, CA., 27 APR 73; To VA-304, NAS Jacksonville, FL., 25 OCT 74; To VA-304, NAS Alameda, CA., 07 JAN 75 ** Transferred to MASDC, Davis Monthan AFB; Tucson, AZ., assigned park code 6A0082, 15 NOV 77 ~ S 3SO strike, 15 AUG 83 ** No data on strike ** Transferred to LTV Dallas, TX., to be converted to A-7P ** Transferred to the Portuguese AF (FAP), S/N 5535 ** Transferred to Esquadra 304 "Magnificoes" , BA-5; Monte Real, PO., 1985 ~ Strike, 1986 ** W/O, Destroyed in accident near Pocarica, Portugal.

A-150 153241 Navy acceptance from NPRO Rep., LTV, Dallas, TX., 28 SEP 67 ** Transferred to VA-147/ CVW-2, NE/3XX, NAS LeMoore, CA., 11 JUN 68 ** Transferred to VA-147/CVW-2, NE/3XX, NAS LeMoore, CA., 26 JUL 68; To VA-147, USS America (CVA-66), 30 JUN 69 ** Transferred to VA-125/FRS, NJ/XXX, NAS LeMoore, CA., 07 DEC 69 ** Transferred to VA-153/ CVW-19, NM/3XX, USS Oriskany (CVA-34), 04 FEB 70 ** Transferred to VA-125/FRS, NJ/5XX, NAS LeMoore, CA., 18 APR 72 ** Transferred to VA-56/CVW-5, NF/401, NAS LeMoore, CA., 12 APR 73; To VA-56, USS Midway (CVA-41), 29 JUN 73; To VA-56, NAF Atsugi, JP., 15 JUL 74; To VA-56, USS Midway (CVA-41), 31 JUL 74; To VA-56, NAF Atsugi, JP., 24 SEP 74 ; To VA-56, USS Midway (CVA-41), 29 SEP 74; To VA-56, NAF Atsugi, JP., 22 MAR 75; To VA-56, USS Midway (CVA-41), 26 MAR 75; To VA-56, NAF Atsugi, JP., 22 JUL 75; To VA-56, USS Midway (CV-41), 21 NOV 75; To VA-56, NAF Atsugi, JP., 10 MAY 76; To VA-56, USS Midway (CV-41), 15 MAY 76; To VA-56, NAF Atsugi, JP., 17 NOV 76; To VA-56, USS Midway (CV-41), 05 JUN 77; To VA-56, NAF Atsugi, JP., 21 JUN 77; To VA-56, USS Midway (CV-41), 22 JUN 77; To VA-56, NAS Alameda, CA., 13 JUL 77 ** Transferred to MASDC, Davis Monthan AFB; Tucson, AZ., assigned park code 6A0075, 08 AUG 77 ~ S 3SO strike, 15 AUG 83 ** No data on strike ** Aircraft deleted from inventory and released to DRMO for disposition, date unknown ** Sold to unknown buyer ** Located in Scottsdale, AZ., for sale, Complete aircraft, (not de-milled), has all the wing stations. Drop tanks and simulated missiles are available, engine missing the starter and tailpipe. On web site at Controller.com for $275,000.00 with a spare airframe, Bureau Number unknown, 25 FEB 06 ** For sale on E-Bay, Auction number 180147277286, $25,000.00, Seller in WA. State; both A/C located in AZ.,, TF-30 Engine, missing CSD and tailpipe, 15 AUG 07.

A-151 153242 Navy acceptance from NPRO Rep. LTV Dallas, TX., 29 SEP 67 ** Transferred to VA-147/CVW-2, NE/317, NAS LeMoore, CA., 22 APR 68; To VA-147/CVW-9, NG/4XX USS America (CVA-66), 30 JUN 69 ** Transferred to VA-125/FRS, NJ/5XX, NAS LeMoore, CA., 14 OCT 69 ** Transferred to VA-153/CVW-19, NM/3XX, USS Oriskany (CVA-34), 17 FEB 70 ** Transferred to VA-125/FRS, NJ/5XX, NAS LeMoore, CA., 01 FEB 71 ** Transferred to VA-153/ CVW-19, NM/3XX, USS Oriskany (CVA-34), 01 FEB 71 ** Transferred to VA-125/FRS, NJ/5XX, NAS LeMoore, CA., 01 FEB 71 ** Transferred to VA-304/CVWR-30, ND/410, NAS Alameda, CA., 24 AUG 71 ** Transferred to VA-174/FRS, AD/2XX, NAS Cecil Field, FL., 22 AUG 72 ** Transferred to VA-37/CVW-3, AC/3XX, NAS Cecil Field, FL., 04 DEC 72 ** Transferred to NARF, NAS Jacksonville, FL., 17 JUL 73 ** Transferred to VA-203/CVWR- 20, AF/310, NAS Jacksonville, FL., 18 OCT 74 ** Crashed at NAS Jacksonville, FL., structural damage ~ S 3SO strike 15 SEP 77 ** Transferred to NATTC; Millington, TN., date unknown, ., sitting outside the Airframes shop, to be used as an instructional airframe ** On conditional loan from the National Museum of Naval Aviation, Pensacola, Fl. to The U.S. Space and Rocket Center; Aviation Challenge Museum; Huntsville, AL. 1996.

A-152 153243 Navy acceptance from NPRO Rep. LTV Dallas, TX., 29 SEP 67 ** Transferred to VA-147/CVW-2, NE/3XX, NAS LeMoore, 18 OCT 67 ~ S 1SO strike, 17 JUN 69 ** Crashed near LeMoore due to engine failure.

A-153 153244 Navy acceptance from NPRO Rep., LTV, Dallas, TX., 28 SEP 67 ** Transferred to VA-147/CVW-2, NE/3XX, NAS LeMoore, CA., 17 OCT 67 ** Transferred to VA-122/FRS, NJ/2XX, NAS LeMoore, CA., 11 JUN 68 ** Transferred to NAS Cubi Point, PI, XX/XXX, 02 OCT 68 ** Transferred to VA-97/ CVW-14, NK/5XX, USS Constellation (CVA-64), 19 OCT 68 ** Transferred to VA-122/FRS, NJ/2XX, NAS LeMoore, CA., 07 MAR 69 ** Transferred to VA-82/CVW-15, NL/3XX, USS Coral Sea (CVA-43), 25 MAR 70 ** Transferred to VA-97/CVW-14, NK/3XX, USS Constellation (CVA-64), 10 APR 70 ** Transferred to VA-82/ CVW-15, NL/3XX, USS Coral Sea (CVA-43), 22 APR 70; To VA-82, NAS Cecil Field, FL., 15 MAY 70 ** Transferred to VA-174/FRS, AD/2XX, NAS Cecil Field, FL., 30 JUL 70 ** Transferred to NARF, NAS Jacksonville, FL., 06 APR 71 ** Transferred to VA-37/CVW-3, AC/3XX, USS Saratoga (CVA-60), 22 NOV 71 ** Transferred to VA-174/FRS, AD/2XX, NAS Cecil Field, FL., 17 FEB 72 ** Transferred to VA-105/CVW-3, AC/4XX, NAS Cecil Field, FL., 02 AUG 72 ** Transferred to VA-174/FRS, AD/2XX, NAS Cecil Field, FL., 06 MAR 73; To VA-174, NAS Jacksonville, FL., 19 NOV 74; To VA-174, NAS Cecil Field, FL., 01 FEB 75 ** Transferred to VA-125/ FRS, NJ/5XX, NAS LeMoore, CA., 24 FEB 75 ** Transferred to VA-93/CVW-5, NF/3XX, USS Midway (CV-41), 11 JAN 76 ** To VA-93, NAF Atsugi, JP., 17 AUG 76; To VA-93, Midway (CV-41), 20 AUG 76; To VA-93, NAF Atsugi, JP., 21 FEB 77; To VA-93, USS Midway (CV-41), 13 MAR 77; To VA-93, NAS North Island, CA., 26 MAY 77 ** Transferred to MASDC, Davis Monthan AFB; Tucson, AZ., assigned park code 6A0072, 01 JUN 77 ~ S 3SO strike, 20 JUN 80 ** No data on strike ** Transferred to LTV, Dallas, TX., to be converted to A-7P ** Transferred to the Portuguese AF (FAP), S/N 5509 ** Transferred to Esquadra 302 "Falcões" , BA-5; Monte Real, PO., 1981 ** S/N changed to 15509 ** W/O and located at BA-5; Monte Real, PO., 1999.

A-154 153245 Navy acceptance from NPRO Rep., LTV, Dallas, TX., 28 SEP 67 ** Transferred to VA-147/ CVW-2, NE/3XX, NAS LeMoore, CA., 03 OCT 67; To VA-147/CVW-9, NG/3XX, USS America (CVA-66), 19 JUN 69 ** Transferred to VA-125/FRS, NJ/5XX, NAS LeMoore, CA., 16 OCT 69 ** Transferred to VA-153/ CVW-19, NM/3XX, USS Oriskany (CVA-34), 06 FEB 70 ** Transferred to VA-125/FRS, NJ/5XX, NAS LeMoore, CA., 12 JUN 72 ** Transferred to VA-56/ CVW-5, NF/406, USS Midway (CVA-41), 15 JUN 73; To VA-56, NAF Atsugi, JP., 02 APR 75, Painted in bi-centennial Scheme, 04 JUL 76; To VA-56, USS Midway (CV-41), 12 JUL 75; To VA-56, NAF Atsugi, JP., 08 OCT 76; To VA-56, USS Midway (CV-41), 31 OCT 76; To VA-56, NAF Atsugi, JP., 08 MAR 77; To VA-56, 19 MAR 77 ** Transferred to MASDC, Davis Monthan AFB; Tucson, AZ., assigned park code 6A0049, 18 APR 77 ~ S 3SO strike, 15 SEP 83 ** No data on strike ** Transferred to LTV, Dallas, TX., to be converted to A-7P ** Transferred to the Portuguese AF (FAP), S/N 5544 ** Transferred to Esquadra 304 "Magnificoes , BA-5; Monte Real, PO., 1986 ** S/N changed to 15544 ** W/O and transferred BA-5; Monte Real, PO., for storage, 1996.

A-155 153246 Navy acceptance from NPRO Rep., LTV, Dallas, TX., 28 SEP 67 ** Transferred to VA-82/CVW-6, AE/3XX, USS America (CVA-66), 16 NOV 67; To VA-82, NAS Cecil Field, FL., 25 MAR 68; To VA-82/CVW-15, NL/3XX, USS Coral Sea (CVA-43), 31 MAY 69 ~ S 1SO strike, 22 AUG 69 ** Crashed due to ramp strike.

A-156 153247 Navy acceptance from NPRO Rep., LTV, Dallas, TX., 30 SEP 67 ** Transferred to VA-86/CVW-6, AE/4XX, USS America (CVA-66), 25 NOV 67; To VA-86, NAS Cecil Field, FL., 27 MAR 68; To VA-86/CVW-15, NL/4XX, USS Coral Sea (CVA-43) 04 JUN 69; To VA-86, NAS Cecil Field, FL., 08 MAY 70 ** Transferred to VA-174/FRS, AD/2XX, NAS Cecil Field, FL., 18 SEP 70 ~ S 1SO strike, 04 JUN 71 ** Crashed near White House, FL., due to engine failure.

A-157 153248 Navy acceptance from NPRO Rep., LTV, Dallas, TX., 30 OCT 67 ** Transferred to VA-22/CVW-15, NL/3XX, NAS Cecil Field, CA., 22 MAR 68 ** Transferred to VA-86/CVW-6, AE/4XX,

USS America (CVA-66), 04 DEC 67; To VA-86, NAS Cecil Field, FL., 22 MAR 68 ** Transferred to VA-174/FRS, AD/2XX, NAS Cecil Field, FL., 19 FEB 69 ** Transferred to MASDC, Davis Monthan AFB; Tucson, AZ., assigned park code 6A074; 01 APR 71 ** Transferred to NARF, NAS Alameda, CA., 01 JUL 72 ** Transferred to VA-125/FRS, NJ/5XX, NAS LeMoore, CA., 02 NOV 72 ** Transferred to VA-56/CVW-5, NF/404, NAS LeMoore, CA., 11 APR 73; To VA-56, USS Midway (CVA-41), 15 JUN 73; To VA-56, NAF Atsugi, JP., 20 FEB 75; To VA-56, USS Midway (CVA-41), 07 MAR 75; To VA-56, NAF Atsugi, JP., 16 OCT 75; To VA-56, USS Midway (CV-41), 23 DEC 75; To VA-56, NAF Atsugi, JP., 02 APR 76; To VA-56, USS Midway (CV-41), 17 APR 76; To VA-56, NAF Atsugi, JP., 22 JAN 77; To VA-56, USS Midway (CV-41), 27 JAN 77; To VA-56, NAS North Island, CA., 25 MAY 77 ** Transferred to MASDC, Davis Monthan AFB; Tucson, AZ., assigned park code 6A0074, 02 JUN 77 ~ S 3SO strike, 15 AUG 80 ** No data on strike ** Sent to LTV, Dallas, TX., to be converted to A-7P ** Transferred to the Portuguese AF (FAP), S/N 5519 ** Transferred to Esquadra 302 "Falcões", BA-5; Monte Real, PO., 1982 ** S/N changed to 15519 ** W/O and transferred to BA-5; Monte Real, PO., for storage, 1998.

A-158 153249 Navy acceptance from NPRO Rep., LTV, Dallas, TX., 07 DEC 67 ** Transferred to VA-27/CVW-14, NK/614, USS Constellation (CVA-64), LTJG Rich Banks pained on side of cockpit, 25 FEB 68; To VA-27, NAS LeMoore, CA., 24 JUN 69 ** Transferred to VA125/FRS, NJ/5XX, NAS LeMoore, CA., 02 JUN 70 ** Transferred to VA-304/CVWR-30, ND/410, NAS Alameda, CA., 15 SEP 71; To VA-304, NAS Jacksonville, FL., 17 AUG 76; To VA-304, NAS Alameda, CA., 04 OCT 76 ** Transferred to MASDC, Davis Monthan AFB; Tucson, AZ., assigned park code 6A0113, 18 SEP 78 ~ S 3SO strike, 15 SEP 83 ** Transferred to LTV, Dallas, TX. to be converted to TA-7P ** Transferred to the Portuguese AF (FAP), S/N 5548 ** Transferred to BA-5; Monte Real, PO.,1985 ~ Strike, 13 MAY 94 ** W/O, crashed near Rosas, Spain, both crew killed.

A-159 153250 Navy acceptance from NPRO Rep., LTV, Dallas, TX., 14 DEC 67 ** Transferred to VA-97/CVW-14, NK/5XX, USS Constellation (CVA-64), 17 FEB 68; To VA-97/CVW-14, NK/3XX, USS Enterprise (CVAN-65), 09 JUN 70 ** Transferred to VA-125/FRS, NJ/5XX, NAS LeMoore, CA., 14 OCT 70 ** Transferred to VA-303/CVWR-30, ND/302 & ND/303; NAS Alameda, CA., 05 APR 71; To VA-303, Jacksonville, FL., 23 MAY 76; To VA-303, NAS Alameda, CA., 25 MAY 76; To VA-303, NAS Jacksonville, FL., 01 JUL 76; To VA-303, NAS Alameda, CA., 18 JUL 76 ** Transferred to VMO-6, MCAS Futenma, 27 JUL 77 ** Transferred to NWEF Kirtland AFB, NM., XX/XXX, 28 JUL 77 ** Transferred to MASDC, Davis Monthan, AFB; Tucson, AZ., assigned park code 6A0118; 17 MAR 79 ~ S 3SO strike, 31 MAY 80 ** No data on strike ** Sent to LTV, Dallas, TX., to be converted to A-7P ** Transferred to the Portuguese AF (FAP), S/N 5506 ** Transferred to Esquadra 302 "Falcões", BA-5; Monte Real, PO., 1981 ** S/N changed to 15506 ** W/O and transferred to CFMTFA Ota, Portugal, for storage, 1996.

A-160 153251 Navy acceptance from NPRO Rep., LTV, Dallas, TX., 14 DEC 67 ** Transferred to VA-97/CVW-14, NK/5XX, USS Constellation (CVA-64), 28 FEB 68 ~ S 1SO strike, 09 MAR 68 ** Crashed near NAS LeMoore, Ca., due to a Mid air Collision with A-7A 154348.

A-161 153252 Navy acceptance from NPRO Rep., LTV, Dallas, TX., 28 SEP 67 ** Transferred to VA-86/CVW-6, AE/403, USS America (CVA-66), 20 NOV 67 ** Transferred to NARF, NAS Jacksonville, FL., 05 MAR 68 ** Transferred to VA-97/ CVW-14, NK/5XX, USS Constellation (CVA-64), 07 MAR 69 ~ S 1SO strike, 02 OCT 69 ** LT P.E. Mallowney was rescued after being shot down by AAA, over SE Asia.

A-162 153253 Navy acceptance from NPRO Rep., LTV, Dallas, TX., 28 SEP 67 ** Transferred to VA-82/CVW-6, AE/3XX, USS America (CVA-66), 11 NOV 67 ~ S 1SO strike, 24 JUL 68 ** No data on strike.

A-163 153254 Navy acceptance from NPRO Rep., LTV, Dallas, TX., 28 SEP 67 ** Transferred to VA-82/CVW-6, AE/3XX, USS America (CVA-66), 16 NOV 67; To VA-82, NAS Cecil Field, FL., 29 MAR 68; To VA-82/CVW-15, NL/3XX, USS Coral Sea (CVA-43), 27 JUN 69; To VA-82, NAS Cecil Field, FL., 09 JUN 70 ** Transferred to MASDC, Davis Monthan AFB; Tucson, AZ., 23 JUL 70 ** Transferred to NARF, NAS Alameda, CA., 11 JUN 71 ** Transferred to VA-304/CVWR-30, ND/407, NAS Alameda, CA., 09 SEP 71, Apocalypse painted on MLG Doors ** Transferred to MASDC, Davis Monthan, AFB; Tucson, AZ., assigned park code 6A092, 29 NOV 77 ~ S 3SO strike, 15 SEP 83 ** No data on strike ** Transferred to LTV, Dallas, TX. to be converted to A-7P ** Transferred to the Portuguese AF (FAP), S/N 5537 ** Transferred to Esquadra 304 "Magnificoes" , BA-5; Monte Real, PO., 1985 ** S/N changed to 15537 ** On display at Alcochete, PO., firing range, as gate guard, 1995.

A-164 153255 Navy acceptance from NPRO Rep., LTV, Dallas, TX., 29 SEP 67 ** Transferred to VA-82/CVW-6, AE/304, USS America (CVA-66), 12 NOV 67 ~ S 1SO strike, 31 MAY 68 ** LT K.W. Fields ejected and was rescued after being shot down by AAA near Ban Kate, Laos ** First Navy A-7 loss of Vietnam War.

A-165 153256 Navy acceptance from NPRO Rep., LTV, Dallas, TX., 29 SEP 67 ** Transferred to VA-82/CVW-6, AE/3XX, USS America (CVA-66), 02 NOV 67; To VA-82, NAS Cecil Field, FL., 24 MAR 68; To VA-82/CVW-15, NL/3XX, USS Coral Sea (CVA-43), 21 JUN 69; To VA-82, NAS Cecil Field, FL., 09 JUN 70 ** Transferred to NARF, NAS Jacksonville, FL., 06 AUG 70 ** Transferred to VA-174/FRS, AD/2XX, 29 JAN 73 ** Transferred to VA-93/CVW-5, NF/3XX, NAS LeMoore, CA., 26 MAR 73; To VA-93, USS Midway (CVA-43), 14 JUN 73 ~ S 1SO strike, 12 NOV 73 ** No data on crash.

A-166 153257 Navy acceptance from NPRO Rep., LTV, Dallas, TX., 30 SEP 67 ** Transferred to VA-82/CVW-6, AE/3XX, USS America (CVA-66), 23 DEC 67 ~ S 1SO strike, 22 JUN 68 ** Pilot survived after engine failure over SE Asia.

A-167 153258 Navy acceptance from NPRO Rep., LTV, Dallas, TX., 23 OCT 67 ** Transferred to VA-82/CVW-6, AE/307, USS America (CVA-66), 08 DEC 67 ~ S 1S0 strike, 31 MAY 68 ** Pilot rescued after fuel starvation near USS America (CVA-66), while attempting in flight refueling, pilot ejected and was rescued.

A-168 153259 Navy acceptance from NPRO Rep., LTV, Dallas, TX., 30 OCT 67 ** Transferred to VA-82/CVW-6, AE/3XX, USS America (CVA-66), 17 NOV 67 ~ S 1S0 strike, 27 APR 68 ** No data on strike.

A-169 153260 Navy acceptance from NPRO Rep., LTV, Dallas, TX., 30 OCT 67 ** Transferred to VA-86/CVW-6, AE/4XX, USS America (CVA-66), 19 DEC 67; Transferred to VA-86, NAS Cecil Field, FL., 28 MAR 68 ** Transferred to VA-174/FRS, AD/2XX, NAS Cecil Field, FL., 27 FEB 69 ** Transferred to VA-105/CVW-3, AC/4XX, USS Saratoga (CV-60), 09 NOV 71 ** Transferred to VA-174/FRS, AD/2XX, NAS Cecil Field, FL., 09 APR 72 ** Transferred to VA-105/CVW-3, AC/4XX, NAS Cecil Field, FL., 22 SEP 72 ** Transferred to VA-305/CVWR-30, ND/514, NAS Point Mugu, CA.,10 JUN 73; To VA-305, NAS Alameda, CA., 26 JUL 74; To VA-305, NAS Point Mugu, CA., 04 AUG 74; To VA-305, NAS Alameda, CA., 13 JUN 75; To VA-305, NAS Point Mugu, CA., 20 JUN 75 ** Transferred to MASDC, Davis Monthan AFB; Tucson, AZ., assigned park code 6A0096, 07 DEC 77~ S 3SO strike, 15 SEP 83 ** No data on strike ** Transferred to LTV, Dallas, TX. to be converted to A-7P ** Transferred to the Portuguese AF (FAP), S/N 5538 ** Transferred to Esquadra 304 "Magnificoes", BA-5; Monte Real, PO., 1985 ** S/N changed to 15538 ** W/O and transferred to BA-11; Beja, Portugal, for storage, 1990.

A-170 153261 Navy acceptance from NPRO Rep., LTV, Dallas, TX., 23 OCT 67 ** Transferred to VA-82/CVW-6, AE/3XX, USS America (CVA-66), 29 DEC 67; To VA-82, NAS Cecil Field, FL., 01 APR 68 **

Transferred to VA-174/FRS, AD/2XX, NAS Cecil Field, FL., 27 MAY 69 ** Transferred to VA-37/CVW-3, AC/3XX, USS Saratoga (CV-60), 22 DEC 69 ** Transferred to VA-174/FRS, AD/2XX, NAS Cecil Field, FL., 26 FEB 70 ** Transferred to VA-105/CVW-3, AC/4XX, USS Saratoga (CV-60), 31 AUG 70 ** Transferred to VA-174/FRS, AD/2XX, NAS Cecil Field, Fl., 12 JUL 71 ** Transferred to VA-37/CVW-3, AC/3XX, USS Saratoga (CV-60), 05 NOV 71 ** Transferred to VA-174/FRS, AD/2XX, NAS Cecil Field, FL., 14 FEB 72 ** Transferred to VA-105/CVW-3, AC/4XX, NAS Cecil Field, FL., 14 JUL 72 ** Transferred to VA-304/CVWR-30, ND/411, NAS Alameda, CA., 07 JUN 73 ** Transferred to MASDC, Davis Monthan AFB; Tucson, AZ., assigned park code 6A0093, 30 NOV 77 ~ S 3SO strike, 30 APR 80 ** No data on strike ** Transferred to LTV Dallas, TX., to be converted to A-7P ** Transferred to the Portuguese AF (FAP), S/N 5520 ** Transferred to Esquadra 302 "Falcões", BA-5; Monte Real, PO., 1982 ~ Strike, 1989 ** W/O, destroyed in accident near Monte Real, Portugal.

A-171 153262 Navy acceptance from NPRO Rep., LTV, Dallas, TX., 20 OCT 67 ** Transferred to VA-27/CVW-14, NK/6XX, USS Constellation (CVA-64), 20 JAN 68; To VA-27, NAS LeMoore, Ca., 22 MAR 68 ** Transferred to VA-125/ FRS, NJ/5XX, NAS LeMoore, CA., 09 JUN 70 ** Transferred to VA-303/CVWR-30, ND/306, NAS Alameda, CA., 06 MAY 71 ~ S 1SO strike, 06 APR 75 ** Pilot ejected safely on approach at NAS LeMoore, CA., Due to Engine failure.

A-172 153263 Navy acceptance from NPRO Rep., LTV, Dallas, TX., 27 NOV 67 ** Transferred to VA-86/CVW-6, AE/4XX, USS America (CVA-66), 13 JAN 68; To VA-86, NAS Cecil Field, FL., 22 MAR 68; To VA-86/CVW-15, NL/4XX, USS Coral Sea (CVA-43), 16 JUN 69; To VA-86, NAS Cecil Field, FL., 13 MAY 70 ** Transferred to VA-174/FRS, AD/2XX, NAS Cecil Field, FL., 04 AUG 70 ** Transferred to VA-86/CVW-15, NL/4XX, NAS Cecil Field, FL., 04 AUG 70 ** Transferred to VA-174/FRS, AD/2XX, NAS Cecil Field, FL., 04 AUG 70 ** Transferred to VA-105/CVW-3, AC/4XX, NAS Cecil Field, FL., 25 AUG 72 ** Transferred to VA-174/FRS, AD/2XX, NAS Cecil Field, FL., 05 MAR 73 ** Transferred to NARF, NAS Jacksonville, FL., 21 AUG 73 ~ S 3SO strike, 23 JUN 80 No data on strike.

A-173 153264 Navy acceptance from NPRO Rep., LTV, Dallas, TX., 20 NOV 67 ** Transferred to VA-27/CVW-14, NK/6XX, USS Constellation (CVA-64), 17 JAN 68; To VA-27, NAS LeMoore, CA., 30 JUN 69 ** Transferred to VA-125/FRS, NJ/5XX, NAS LeMoore, CA., 26 JUN 70 ** Transferred to VA-303/CVWR-30, ND/300, NAS Alameda, CA., 30 JUN 71 ** Transferred to VA-174/FRS, AD/2XX, NAS Cecil Field, FL., 21 AUG 72 ** Transferred to VA-37/CVW-3, AC/3XX, NAS Cecil Field, FL., 15 OCT 72 ** Transferred to NARF, NAS Jacksonville, FL., 17 JUL 73 ** Transferred to VA-203/CVWR-20, AF/307, NAS Jacksonville, FL., 02 AUG 74 ~ S 1SO strike, 22 JUL 76 ** Lost near NAS Jacksonville, FL., Due to Engine failure, (Ground).

A-174 153265 Navy acceptance from NPRO Rep., LTV, Dallas, TX., 30 OCT 67 ** Transferred to VA-86/CVW-6, AE/404, USS America (CVA-66), 12 DEC 67 ~ S 1SO strike, 11 JUN 68 ** LCDR R.W. Ford crashed in NVN, survived and became a POW, DIC.

A-175 153266 Navy acceptance from NPRO Rep., LTV, Dallas, TX., 27 OCT 67 ** Transferred to VA-97/CVW-14, NK/5XX, USS Constellation (CVA-64), 09 FEB 68; To VA-97/CVW-14, NK/3XX, USS Enterprise (CVAN-65), 01 JUN 70 ** Transferred to VA-125/ FRS, NJ/5XX, NAS LeMoore, CA., 16 JUL 70 ** Transferred to VA-303/CVWR-30, ND/312, NAS Alameda, CA., 11 JUN 71 ** Transferred to VA-305/CVWR-30, ND/511, NAS Point Mugu, CA., 29 AUG 72; To VA-305, NAS Jacksonville, FL., 20 AUG 76; To VA-305, NAS Point Mugu, CA., 06 OCT 76 ** Transferred to MASDC, Davis Monthan AFB;Tucson, AZ., assigned park code 6A0115, 18 SEP 78 ~ S 3SO strike, 07 MAY 80 ** No data on strike ** Transferred to NATTC Memphis, TN. as an instructional airframe, sitting outside the airframe shop. ** Transferred to NS Great Lakes Naval Recruit Depot, near Haineville, IL. to be used as an instructional airframe.

A-176 153267 Navy acceptance from NPRO Rep., LTV, Dallas, TX., 27 OCT 67 ** Transferred to VA-86/CVW-6, AE/4XX, USS America (CVA-66), 12 DEC 67; To VA-86, NAS Cecil Field, FL., 02 APR 68 ** Transferred to VA-174/FRS, AD/2XX, NAS Cecil Field, FL., 27 FEB 69 ** Transferred to MASDC, Davis Monthan AFB; Tucson, AZ., 02 NOV 70 ** Transferred to NARF, NAS Alameda, CA., 04 JUN 71 ** Transferred to VA-304/CVWR-30, ND/4XX, NAS Alameda, CA., 24 AUG 71 ~ S 1SO strike, 21 OCT 72 ** Crashed at NAS Alameda, Due to a Flame Out.

A-177 153268 Navy acceptance from NPRO Rep., LTV, Dallas, TX., 20 OCT 67 ** Transferred to VA-86/CVW-6, AE/4XX, USS America (CVA-66), 05 DEC 67; To VA-86, NAS Cecil Field, FL., 27 MAR 68 ** Transferred to VA-174/FRS, AD/2XX, NAS Cecil Field, FL., 27 FEB 69 ** Transferred to VA-37/CVW-3, AC/3XX, USS Saratoga (CV-60), 05 APR 71; To VA-37, NAS Cecil Field, FL., 30 JUN 72 ** Transferred to VA-305/CVWR-30, ND/500, NAS Point Mugu, CA., 12 JUN 73, had bi-centennial paint scheme 04 JUL 76, CDR Campbell on port side of cockpit ; To VA-305, NAS Jacksonville, FL., 16 MAR 76; To VA-305, NAS Point Mugu, CA., 05 MAY 76 ** Transferred to MASDC, Davis Monthan AFB; Tucson, AZ., assigned park code 6A0110, 21 JUN 78 ~ S 3SO strike, 15 OCT 83 ** No data on strike ** Transferred to LTV, Dallas, TX. to be converted to TA-7P ** Transferred to the Portuguese AF (FAP), S/N 5549 ** Transferred BA-5; Monte Real, PO., 1985 ** S/N changed to 15549 ** W/O and located at BA-5; Monte Real, Portugal, 1999.

A-178 153269 Navy acceptance from NPRO Rep., LTV, Dallas, TX., 23 OCT 67 ** Transferred to VA-86/CVW-6, AE/411, USS America (CVA-66), 19 DEC 67 ~ S 1SO strike, 21 JUN 68 ** Pilot was rescued when the aircraft was lost in the Tonkin Gulf due to Flight Control Hydraulic Failure on a test flight.

A-179 153270 Navy acceptance from NPRO Rep., LTV, Dallas, TX., 27 OCT 67 ** Transferred to VA-86/CVW-6, AE/4XX, USS America (CVA-66), 17 DEC 67; To VA-86, NAS Cecil Field, FL., 01 APR 68 ** Transferred to VA-174/FRS, AD/2XX, NAS Cecil Field, FL., 19 JUN 69 ** Transferred to NATC, Weapon System Test, XX/XXX, NAS Patuxent River, MD., 23 OCT 70 ** Transferred to NATC, Sevice Test, for RDT & E, XX/XXX, NAS Patuxent River, MD., 01 SEP 72 ** Transferred to NARF, NAS Jacksonville, FL., 03 OCT 72 ~ S 3SO strike, 15 JUN 78 ** No data on strike.

A-180 153271 Navy acceptance from NPRO Rep., LTV, Dallas, TX., 30 OCT 67 ** Transferred to VA-86/CVW-6, AE/412, USS America (CVA-66), 28 DEC 67 ~ S 1SO strike, 25 JUN 68 ** Pilot survived when the aircraft was lost over NVN, due to a generator failure.

A-181 153272 Navy acceptance from NPRO Rep., LTV, Dallas, TX., 30 OCT 67 ** Transferred to VA-82/CVW-6, AE/3XX, 29 DEC 67 ** Transferred to VX-5, XE/XXX, NAF China Lake, CA., 11 APR 68 ** Transferred to NPRO Rep., LTV, Dallas, TX, XX/XXX, for RDT & E, 06 AUG 68 ** Transferred to NARF, NAS Jacksonville, FL, 04 NOV 66 ** Transferred to VA-174/FRS, AD/2XX, NAS Cecil Field, FL., 21 OCT 69 ** Transferred to VA-37/CVW-3, AC/3XX, USS Saratoga (CV-60), 22 DEC 69 ** Transferred to VA-174/FRS, AD/2XX, NAS Cecil Field, FL., 03 APR 70 ** Transferred to NATC, Service Test, XX/XXX, for RDT & E, NAS Patuxent River, MD., 14 JUL 71 ** Transferred to VA-125/FRS, NJ/5XX, NAS LeMoore, CA., 23 MAY 74; To VA-125, USS Ranger (CVA-61), 23 MAY 74; To VA-125/FRS, NJ/526, NAS LeMoore, CA., 01 AUG 74 ** Transferred to MASDC, Davis Monthan AFB; Tucson, AZ., assigned park code 6A0051, 23 MAY 77 ~ S 3SO strike, 31 MAY 80 ** No data on strike ** Transferred to LTV Dallas, TX. to be converted to A-7P ** Transferred to the Portuguese AF (FAP), S/N 5503 ** Transferred to Esquadra 302 "Falcões" , BA-5; Monte Real, PO., 1981 ** S/N changed to 15503 ** W/O and transferred to Sintra Museo Do Ar, BA-1; Sintrus Pole air Museum, Portugal, for display, 1996.

A-182 153273 Navy acceptance from NPRO Rep., LTV, Dallas, TX., 08 DEC 67 ** Transferred to VA-27/CVW-14, NK/612, USS Constellation (CVA-64), 12 FEB 68 ~ S 1SO strike, 06 OCT 68 ** Pilot safely ejected over water and was rescued after being shot down by a SAM near Vinh, NVN.

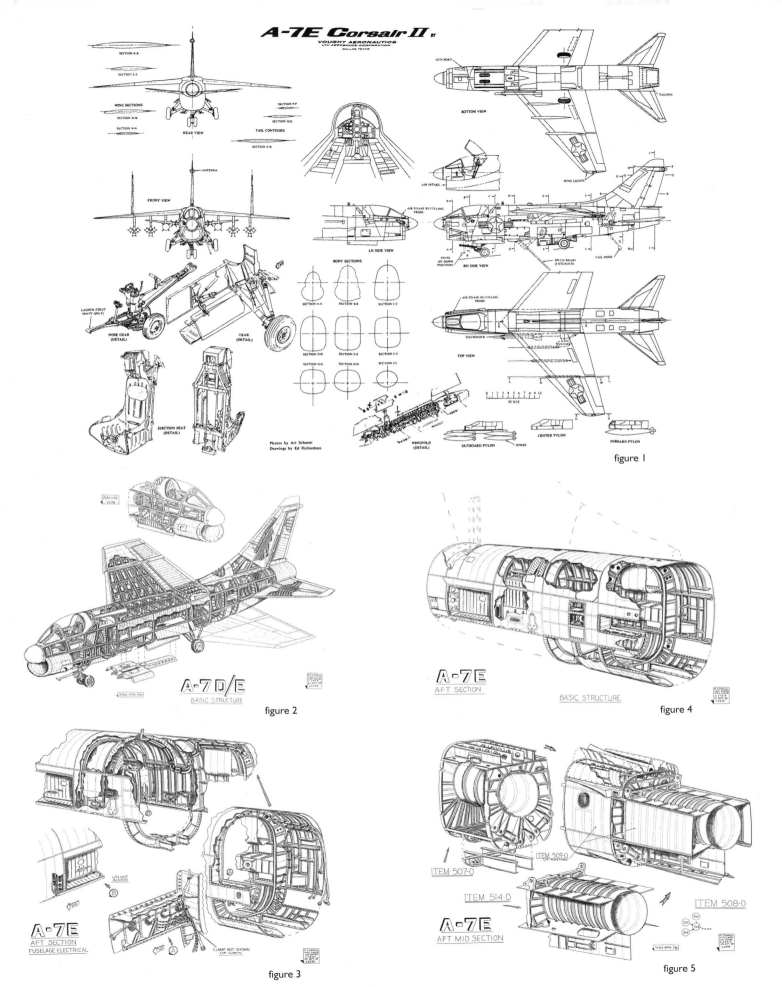

A-7E Corsair II by
VOUGHT AERONAUTICS
LTV AEROSPACE CORPORATION
DALLAS, TEXAS

SECTION K-K
SECTION L-L
WING SECTIONS
SECTION M-M
SECTION N-N
REAR VIEW
SECTION P-P
SECTION Q-Q
TAIL CONTOURS
SECTION R-R

ANTENNA

FRONT VIEW

LAUNCH STRUT
(NAVY ONLY)
NOSE GEAR
(DETAIL)
GEAR
(DETAIL)

EJECTION SEAT
(DETAIL)

Photos by Art Schoeni
Drawings by Ed Richardson

BODY SECTIONS
SECTION A-A   SECTION B-B   SECTION C-C
SECTION D-D   SECTION E-E   SECTION F-F
SECTION G-G   SECTION H-H   SECTION J-J

WINGFOLD
(DETAIL)

SCALE

OUTBOARD PYLON   BOMBS   CENTER PYLON   INBOARD PYLON

GUN PORT
BOTTOM VIEW
TAILPIPE
WING LIGHTS

AIR INTAKE

AIR-TO-AIR REFUELING
PROBE
LH SIDE VIEW
STEPS
(IN DOWN
POSITION)
RH SIDE VIEW
SPEED BRAKE
(EXTENDED)
TAIL HOOK

AIR-TO-AIR REFUELING
PROBE
SIDEWINDER
TOP VIEW

figure 1

R/H SIDE VIEW

A-7 D/E
BASIC STRUCTURE

SCALE APPX 1/24

figure 2

A-7E
AFT SECTION
BASIC STRUCTURE

figure 4

L/H UHT ACCESS

CLAMP NOT SHOWN FOR CLARITY

A-7E
AFT SECTION
FUSELAGE ELECTRICAL

figure 3

ITEM 507-0
ITEM 509-0
ITEM 514-0
ITEM 508-0

A-7E
AFT MID SECTION

SCALE APPX 1/8

figure 5

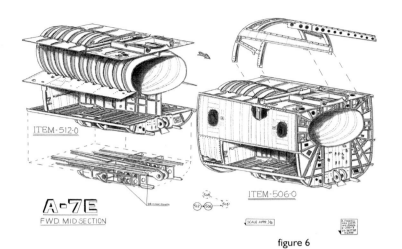

A-7E
FWD. MID SECTION

ITEM-512·0

ITEM-506·0

SCALE APPR ⅛

figure 6

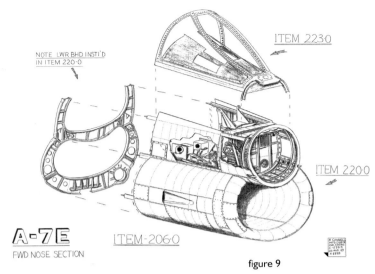

NOTE LWR. BHD. INSTL'D
IN ITEM 220·0

ITEM 223·0

ITEM 220·0

A-7E
FWD NOSE SECTION

ITEM-206·0

figure 9

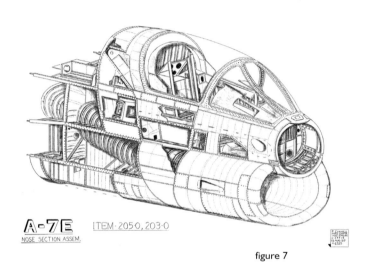

A-7E
NOSE SECTION ASSEM.

ITEM-205·0, 203·0

figure 7

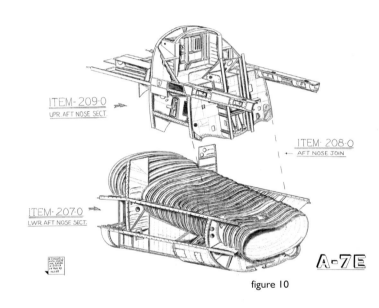

ITEM-209·0
UPR. AFT NOSE SECT.

ITEM-208·0
AFT NOSE JOIN

ITEM-207·0
LWR. AFT NOSE SECT.

A-7E

figure 10

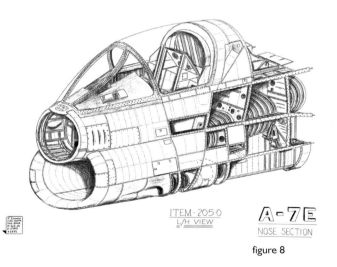

ITEM-205·0
L/H VIEW

A-7E
NOSE SECTION

figure 8

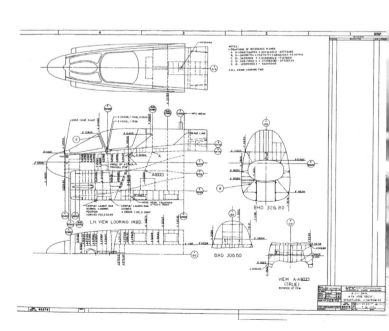

figure 11

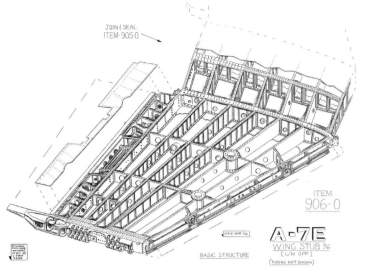

JOIN & SEAL
ITEM-905-0

ITEM
906-0

A-7E
WING STUB ¾
(L/H OPP.)
(TUBING NOT SHOWN)

BASIC STRUCTURE

figure 12

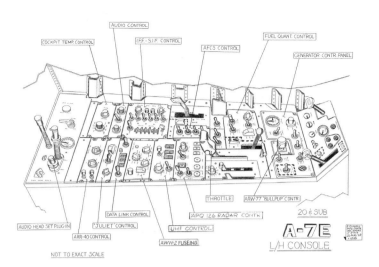

COCKPIT TEMP. CONTROL
AUDIO CONTROL
I.F.F.- S.I.F. CONTROL
AFCS CONTROL
FUEL QUANT. CONTROL
GENERATOR CONTR. PANEL

AUDIO HEAD SET PLUG-IN
ARR-40 CONTROL
"JULIET" CONTROL
DATA LINK CONTROL
AWW-2 FUSEING
UHF CONTROL
APQ 126 RADAR CONTR.
THROTTLE
ARW-77 "BULLPUP" CONTR.

A-7E
L/H CONSOLE
20 & SUB

NOT TO EXACT SCALE

figure 15

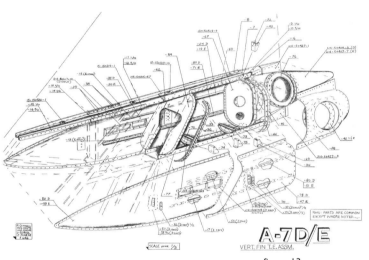

A-7D/E
VERT. FIN T.E. ASSM.

SCALE APPR. 1/3

figure 13

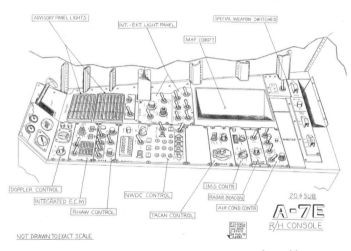

ADVISORY PANEL LIGHTS
INT.- EXT. LIGHT PANEL
SPECIAL WEAPON SWITCHES
MAP COMPT.

DOPPLER CONTROL
INTEGRATED E.C.M.
RHAW CONTROL
NWDC CONTROL
TACAN CONTROL
IMS CONTR
RADAR BEACON
AIR COND. CONTR.

A-7E
R/H CONSOLE
20 & SUB

NOT DRAWN TO EXACT SCALE

figure 16

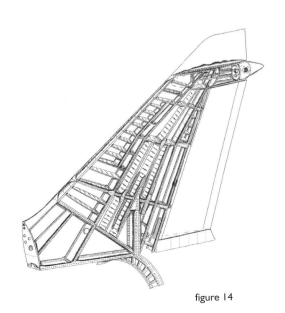

figure 14

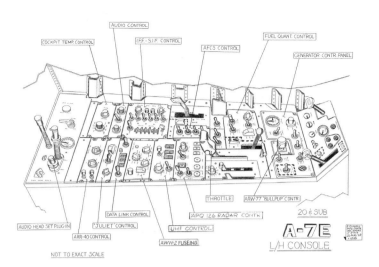

A-7E
INSTRUMENT PANEL
20 & SUB.

figure 17

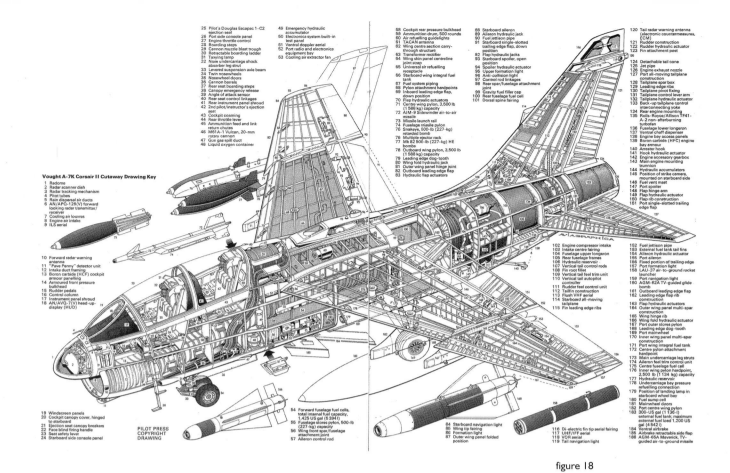

Vought A-7K Corsair II Cutaway Drawing Key

1 Radome
2 Radar scanner dish
3 Radar tracking mechanism
4 Pitot tubes
5 Rain dispersal air ducts
6 AN/APQ-126(V) forward looking radar transmitter/receiver
7 Cooling air louvres
8 Engine air intake
9 ILS aerial

10 Forward radar warning antenna
11 "Pave Penny" detector unit
12 Intake duct framing
13 Boron carbide (HCF) cockpit armour panelling
14 Armoured front pressure bulkhead
15 Rudder pedals
16 Control column
17 Instrument panel shroud
18 AN/AVQ-7(V) head-up-display (HUD)

19 Windscreen panels
20 Cockpit canopy cover, hinged to starboard
21 Ejection seat canopy breakers
22 Face blind firing handle
23 Seat safety lever
24 Starboard side console panel

25 Pilot's Douglas Escapac 1-C2 ejection seat
26 Port side console panel
27 Engine throttle control
28 Boarding steps
29 Cannon muzzle blast trough
30 Retractable boarding ladder
31 Taxying lamp
32 Nose undercarriage shock absorber leg strut
33 Levered suspension axle beam
34 Twin nosewheels
35 Nosewheel doors
36 Cannon barrels
37 Rear seat boarding steps
38 Canopy emergency release
39 Angle of attack sensor
40 Rear seat control linkages
41 Rear instrument panel shroud
42 2nd pilot/instructor's ejection seat
43 Cockpit coaming
44 Rear throttle lever
45 Ammunition feed and link return chutes
46 M61A-1 Vulcan, 20-mm rotary cannon
47 Gun gas spill duct
48 Liquid oxygen container

49 Emergency hydraulic accumulator
50 Electronics system built-in test panel
51 TACAN aerial
52 Port radio and electronics equipment bay
53 Cooling air extractor fan

54 Forward fuselage fuel cells, total internal fuel capacity, 1,425 US gal (5 394 l)
55 Fuselage stores pylon, 500-lb (227-kg) capacity
56 Wing front spar/fuselage attachment joint
57 Aileron control rod

58 Cockpit rear pressure bulkhead
59 Ammunition drum, 500 rounds
60 Air refuelling guidelights
61 TACAN antenna
62 Wing centre section carry-through structure
63 Transformer rectifier
64 Wing skin panel centreline joint strap
65 Universal air refuelling receptacle
66 Starboard wing integral fuel tank
67 Fuel system piping
68 Pylon attachment hardpoints
69 Inboard leading edge flap, down position
70 Flap hydraulic actuators
71 Centre wing pylon, 3,500 lb (1 588 kg) capacity
72 AIM-9 Sidewinder air-to-air missile
73 Missile launch rail
74 Fuselage missile pylon
75 Snakeye, 500-lb (227-kg) retarded bomb
76 Multiple ejector rack
77 Mk 82 500-lb (227-kg) HE bombs
78 Outboard wing pylon, 3,500 lb (1 588 kg) capacity
79 Leading edge dog-tooth
80 Wing fold hydraulic jack
81 Outer wing panel hinge joint
82 Outboard leading edge flap
83 Hydraulic flap actuators

84 Starboard navigation light
85 Wing tip fairing
86 Formation light
87 Outer wing panel folded position

88 Starboard aileron
89 Aileron hydraulic jack
90 Fuel jettison pipe
91 Starboard single-slotted trailing edge flap, down position
92 Flap hydraulic jacks
93 Starboard spoiler, open position
94 Spoiler hydraulic actuator
95 Upper formation light
96 Anti-collision light
97 Control rod linkages
98 Rear spar/fuselage attachment joint
99 Gravity fuel filler cap
100 Rear fuselage fuel cell
101 Dorsal spine fairing

102 Engine compressor intake
103 Intake centre fairing
104 Fuselage upper longeron
105 Rear fuselage frames
106 Hydraulic reservoir
107 Vertical tail control rods
108 Fin root fillet
109 Vertical tail feel trim unit
110 Vertical tail autopilot controller
111 Rudder feel control unit
112 Tailfin construction
113 Starboard all-moving tailplane
114 Fin leading edge ribs
115 Rudder feel control unit

116 Di-electric fin tip aerial fairing
117 UHF/IFF aerial
118 VOR aerial
119 Tail navigation light

120 Tail radar warning antenna (electronic countermeasures, ECM)
121 Rudder construction
122 Rudder hydraulic actuator
123 Fin attachment post

124 Detachable tail cone
125 Jet pipe
126 Engine exhaust nozzle
127 Port all-moving tailplane construction
128 Tailplane spar box
129 Leading edge ribs
130 Tailplane pivot fixing
131 Tailplane control lever arm
132 Tailplane hydraulic actuator
133 Back-up tailplane control interconnecting yoke
134 Rear engine mounting
135 Rolls-Royce/Allison TF41-A-2 non-afterburning turbofan
136 Fuselage lower longeron
137 Ventral chaff dispenser
138 Engine bay access panels
139 Boron carbide (HFC) engine bay armour
140 Arrester hook
141 Hook hydraulic actuator
142 Engine accessory gearbox
143 Main engine mounting trunnion
144 Hydraulic accumulators
145 Position of strike camera, mounted on starboard side
146 Fuel vent mast
147 Port spoiler
148 Flap hinge arm
149 Flap hydraulic actuator
150 Rail construction
151 Port single-slotted trailing edge flap

152 Fuel jettison pipe
153 External fuel tank tail fins
154 Aileron hydraulic actuator
155 Port aileron
156 Fixed portion of trailing edge
157 Port formation light
158 LAU-37 air-ground rocket launcher
159 Port navigation light
160 AGM-82A TV-guided glide bomb
161 Outboard leading edge flap
162 Leading edge flap rib construction
163 Flap hydraulic actuators
164 Outer wing panel multi-spar construction
165 Wing hinge rib
166 Wing fold hydraulic actuator
167 Port outer stores pylon
168 Leading edge dog-tooth
169 Port mainwheel
170 Inner wing panel multi-spar construction
171 Port wing integral fuel tank
172 Centre pylon attachment hardpoint
173 Main undercarriage leg struts
174 Aileron feel trim control unit
175 Centre fuselage fuel cell
176 Inner wing pylon hardpoint, 2,500 lb (1 134 kg) capacity
177 Hydraulic reservoir
178 Undercarriage bay pressure refuelling connection
179 Position of landing lamp in starboard wheel bay
180 Fuel sump cell
181 Mainwheel doors
182 Port centre wing pylon
183 300-US gal (1 136-l) external fuel tank; maximum capacity of fuel 1,200 US gal (4 550-l)
184 Ventral airbrake
185 Airbrake retractable side flap
186 AGM-65A Maverick, TV-guided air-to-ground missile

PILOT PRESS
COPYRIGHT
DRAWING

figure 18

Development

YA-7A

A-7A/A-7P

A-7B

TA-7C

A-7D

A-7E

YA-7F

A-7K

figure 19

LTV A-7A production line

LTV TA-7C production line

LTV A-7A production line

LTV A-7B production line

LTV A-7E production line

LTV VA-305 A-7A No/502 restored by Vought Retiree Club

LTV A-7E production line

LTV A-7E 159979 production line

LTV A-7A 152581 test flight line

LTV A-7A, F-8140488, RF-8G waiting to be reworked for restoration

LTV A-7P production line

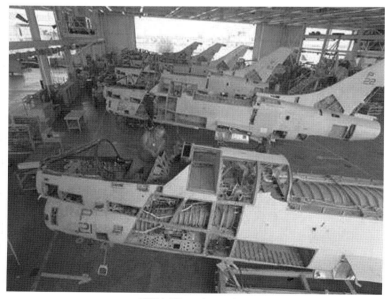

LTV A-7P production line

LTV ready for test flight line

LTV TA-7C 154477 test flight

LTV A-7A 03 flight test

LTV A-7 test flight

LTV A-7A 03 flight test

LTV A-7A 152580 test line

LTV A-7 flight test line

LTV A-7C 152580 test flight

LTV A-7E 160880 test flight

LTV A-7C 152580 test flight

LTV A-7A, F-8 test flight

LTV flight line

LTV WR-93/VMF 312/N33693, A-7, TA-7C

LTV TA-7C 154544 test flight

LTV A-7 armament display

LTV TA-7C 156801 test flight

LTV TA-7C 154544 flight test. This aircraft is now privately owned in Chino, CA.

LTV A-7 award

LTV TA-7C on test line

40

LTV TA-7C 154477 test flight

LTV TA-7C 156801 test flight

LTV TA-7C test line

LTV 156801 test line

LTV TA-7C 158801 test line

41

LTV TA-7C 154477 test flight

LTV TA-7C snort rocket test sled

LTV TA-7C 7 rocket test sled

LTV TA-7B/E SRT-2 rocket test sled

LTV TA-7D 3 rocket test sled

NADC NA-7E 156802

NADC A-7C 156770

NADC A-7E 156874

NADC A-7E 156874

NADC A-7B 154373

NAEC A-7B 154373

NATC A-7A 152653

NATC A-7A 152653

NATC NA-7A 152581

NATC NA-7A 152581

NATC A-7 SD/401 and SD/406

NATC NA-7A 152581

NATC A-7A 152658

NATC A-7E 159256 SD/401

NATC A-7E 156752

NATC A-7C 156776

NATC A-7 SD/403

NATC A-7 156874 7T/405

NATC A-7 404

NATC 156874 SD/405

NATC A-7C 156752

NATC A-7E 159256 SD/401

NATC A-7A 152656

NATC A-7 USS America CV-66

46

NATC A-7A 152658

NATC A-7A 152658

NATC A-7A 152581

NATC TA-7C 154477 7T/440

NATC A-7A 152581

NAWC TA-7Cs

NATC A-7C 156797

NAWC line: nose numbers 86, 84, 85, and 82, TA-7C 156787 foreground

NATC A-7A 152658

NAWC TA-7C 85

NATC A-7A 152660

NAWC TA-7C 94

NMC A-7

NMC TA-7C 156738

NMC A-7A 152651

NMC A-7A 152662

NSAWC A-7

NTPS (top to bottom): TA-7C 154544, TA-4J, T-2C 157032, and T-38A 158200.

NSAWC A-7 foreground

NTPS TA-7C 154544

48

NTPS TA-7C 154544

NTPS TA-7C 154544

NTPS A-7A 152655

NWC A-7

NATC TA-7C 154544 in lead. Left is TA-4J, right is T-2C 157032, and trailing is T-38A 158200

NWC A-7C 156739

NTPS TA-7C Clockwise from top left: TA-4J, TA76 154544 in lead, T-2C 157082, and T38A 158200

NWC A-7

NWC A-7A 152655

NWC A-7C 156785

NWC A-7C 156782

NWC A-7Es 160566 and 156883

NWC A-7E 160566 foreground, and 156883

NWC A-7E 160566

NWC A-7E

NWC TA-7C 156768

NWEF A-7C 156776

NWEF A-7C 156776

NWEF TA-7C 156750

NWEF TA-7C 156750

NWEF TA-7C 156750

NWEF TA-7C 156750

NWEF TA-7C 156750

NWEF A-7 with blivet

NWEF A-7C 156772

NWEF A-7

51

PMTC A-7C 156787 84

PMTC TA-7C 156787 84

PMTC TA-7C 154544

PMTC TA-7C 154464

PMTC A-7A 152651 65

PMTC TA-7C 85

PMTC A-7 83

RTC A-7A 153135

VA-12 A-7E AG/403

VA-12 A-7E 157578 AG/404, 157472 AG/400

VA-12 A-7E AG/410

VA-12 A-7 AG/4XX

VA-12 A-7E AG/4XX

VA-12 A-7E 156844 AG/406

VA-12 A-7E 157574 AG/403

VA-12 A-7E 157452 AG/400

VA-12 A-7 AG/412

VA-12 A-7E 157478 AG/404

VA-12 A-7E 157484 AG/414, 157459 AG/407

VA-15 A-7B 154402 AE/307

VA-15 A-7 AE/314

VA-15 A-7 AE/305

VA-15 A-7B 154492 AE/300 USS Roosevelt

VA-15 A-7Es 160859 AE/301, 304, 300

VA-15 A-7 AE/310

VA-15 A-7E 160863 AE/301, 160869 AE/304

VA-15 A-7 AE/3XX

VA-15 A-7B 154402 AE/3XX USS Roosevelt

VA-22 A-7E 160537 NH/301

VA-82 A-7E 160537 NH/301

VA-22 A-7E 156821 NL/303

VA-22 A-7E 156013 NH/302

VA-22 A-7E 156013 NH/302

VA-22 A-7 NL/301

VA-22 A-7E 159982 NL/302

VA-22 A-7 NL/314 USS Kitty Hawk

VA-22 A-7E 159975 NL/301 Bicentenial, USS Coral Sea

VA-22 A-7 NL/300 USS Kitty Hawk

VA-25 A-7E 155224 NE/416. This is the BuNo but this BuNo was issued to a T-2B.

VA-25 A-7E 157451 NE/400 USS Ranger

VA-25 A-7E 156807 NE/403

VA-25 A-7E 157483 NE/400 USS Ranger

VA-25 A-7E 156804 NE/406 USS Ranger

VA-25 A-7E 157483 NE/400 USS Ranger

VA-113 A-7 NE/300

VA-25 A-7E 156846 NE/501

VA-25 A-7 line: NE/403, 407, 401, 405, and 406

VA-25 A-7B 154441 AH/502

VA-25 A-7s: NE/405, 413, 407, 4XX, and 4XX

VA-27 A-7E 158658 NK/402 USS Enterprise

VA-27 A-7E 158832 NK/400 USS Enterprise

VA-27 A-7E 158658 NK/402 USS Enterprise

VA-27 A-7E 158658 NK/402 USS Enterprise

VA-27 A-7E 158832 NK/400 USS Enterprise

VA-27 A-7E 158658 NK/402 USS Enterprise

VA-27 A-7E 156851 NK/407, 157460 NK/401, USS Enterprise

VA-27 A-7E 156808 NK/403 USS Enterprise

VA-27 A-7s: NK/604, 614, 617, and 602, USS Constellation

VA-27 A-7 NK/411 USS Enterprise

VA-27 A-7E 157441 NK/404 USS Enterprise

VA-27 A-7A 153249 NK/614 and 610, USS Constellation

VA-27 A-7E 157460 NK/407 USS Enterprise

VA-27 A-7E 159651 NK/401 USS Enterprise

VA-27 A-7E 157454 NK/405 USS Enterprise

VA-27 A-7E 158658 NK/402 USS Enterprise

VA-27 A-7Es NK/415 and 400, USS Enterprise

VA-27 A-7Es Clockwise from top left: 158832, 158657

VA-27 A-7 NK/410

VA-27 A-7E 159651 NK/401 USS Enterprise

VA-27 A-7s NK/4XX

VA-27 A-7 NK/406

VA-27 A-7E 158657 NK/401, 157460 NK/407 USS Enterprise

VA-27 A-7E 159645 NK/402

VA-27 A-7 402

VA-37 A-7E 158826 AC/300 USS Saratoga

VA-37 A-7A 154243 with MK-82s, NH/307 USS Kitty Hawk

VA-37 A-7E with MK-76, 157470 AC/301 USS Saratoga

VA-37 A-7E 157579 AC/305 USS Saratoga

VA-37 A-7A 153212 NH/311 USS Kitty Hawk

VA-37 A-7s USS Saratoga

VA-37 A-7E 160550 AC/306 USS Forrestal

VA-37 A-7s AE/3XX

63

VA-37 A-7E 302

VA-37 A-7 AE/307 USS Forrestal

VA-37 A-7A 153161 NH/300 USS Kitty Hawk

VA-37 A-7A 153207 AC/306

VA-37 A-7 AC/300

VA-37 A-7E 158826 AC/300

VA-37 A-7A 153150 AC/302 USS Saratoga

VA-37 A-7As NH/304, 310 USS Kitty Hawk

VA-37 A-7E 157559 AC/300 USS Saratoga

VA-37 A-7E 160879 AC/300

VA-37 A-7E158830 AC/300 USS Saratoga

VA-37 A-7E 159264 AC/314 USS Saratoga

VA-37 A-7E 157455 AE/315, loaned to VA-174 as 025

VA-37 A-7A 153161 AC/300

VA-37 A-7s AC/312 and 306

VA-37 A-7s AC/312 and 301 near Mt. Fuji

VA-46 A-7B 154488 AB/304 USS John F Kennedy

VA-46 A-7E 160547 AB/306 USS John F Kennedy

VA-46 A-7B 154488 with MK-82s and drop tanks, AB/304 USS John F Kennedy

VA-46 A-7E 160547 AB/306 USS John F Kennedy

VA-46 A-7E 169544 with shrike, droptanks, and sidewinders, AB/305 USS JFK

VA-46 A-7E 159997 AB/307 USS John F Kennedy

VA-46 A-7E 160549 AB/305 USS John F Kennedy with MK-82s

VA-46 A-7 AB/310 USS John F Kennedy with MK-82s

VA-46 A-7E 158549 AB/305 USS John F Kennedy

VA-46 A-7B 154502 AB/311 USS John F Kennedy

VA-46 A-7B 154502 with drop tanks, AB/311 USS John F Kennedy

VA-46 A-7E with MK-76, 159988 AB/312 USS John F Kennedy

VA-46 A-7E 157455 AB/311

VA-46 A-7E 157455 AB/311

VA-46 A-7s AB/3XX

VA-46 A-7E 157455 AB/311

VA-46 A-7s AB/3XX, 1988 Med cruise. Pilots are (clockwise from top left: Lt Andy "Ziggy" Zigler, CDR Ed "Fast" Fahy (XO), and LCDR John Leenhouts. (photo by John Leenhouts)

VA-46 A-7Es 158549 and 159997, AB/305, 307

VA-46 A-7B 154488 (at left), AB/301, 303, and 304 (l to r)

VA-46 A-7B AB/301, 303, and 304

VA-46 A-7E AB/3XX, 1988 Med Cruise (photo by pilot LCDR John Leenhouts)

VA-46 A-7E AB/311, 300 with missiles, MK-82s, and drop tanks, USS JFK

VA-46 A-7E 160558 (foreground) and 160553, AB/301, 303 USS Kennedy

VA-46 A-7Es 158549 with FLIR pods, AB/305, 312

VA-46 A-7s AB/304, 300, and 305

VA-46 A-7 AB/3XX, 1988 Med Cruise. (photo by LCDR John Leenhouts)

VA-46 A-7E 160551 AB/304

VA-46 A-7s AB/3XX

VA-46 A-7E 159988 AB/312

VA-46 A-7B 154486 AC/300 USS Saratoga

VA-46 A-7s AB/3XX

VA-46 A-7B 154502 with rocket pod, AB/ 311 USS John F. Kennedy

VA-46 A-7B 154475 AB/313 USS John F Kennedy

VA-46 A-7B 154438 AB/307 taking the barrier (no nose gear) due to PC2 hydraulic failure, USS Saratoga 1968 Med Cruise. Pilot is LTJG Marty Hayes. (photo by wingman LT David Dollarhide)

VA-46 A-7B 154552 AB/310 USS John F Kennedy

VA-46 A-7E 160556 AB/301 USS America

VA-46 A-7E 159285 AG/306 USS Dwight D Eisenhower

VA-46 in Air Wing flyover, A-7, A-6, F-14, and EA-6

VA-46 A-7E 160713 AC/307 USS John F Kennedy

VA-46 A-7E 160713 AC/307 USS John F Kennedy

VA-46 A-7E 160713 AC/307, Desert Storm USS John F Kennedy

VA-46 A-7 pass over USS Dwight D Eisenhower

VA-46 A-7B AB/305

VA-46 A-7B 154481 AG/305 USS John F Kennedy escorting Russian bomer

VA-46 A-7E 160560 AG/312, 305 USS Dwight D Eisenhower

VA-46 A-7B 154487 AB USS John F Kennedy

VA-46 A-7E 154482 AG/307 USS John F Kennedy

VA-46 A-7B 154496 AC/314

VA-46 A-7B 154482 AB/301 USS John F Kennedy

VA-46 A-7 AC/306, 302 in flight refueling

VA-56 A-7B 154547 NF/400 USS Midway

VA-56 A-7Bs NE/401, 414, 415, and 407 with MK-82s

VA-56 A-7E 159651 NF 401

VA-56 A-7Bs 154517, 154542 NE/401, 414, 415, and 407 with MK-82s, USS Ranger

VA-56 A-7A 152665 NF/410 USS Midway

VA-56 A-7B 154547 AH/400 USS Midway

VA-56 A-7B 154535 AH/404 USS Midway

VA-56 A-7B 154531 NE/407 USS Ranger

VA-56 A-7B 154539 NF/412 USS Midway

VA-56 A-7B 154547 NF/400

VA-56 A-7B line AH/405, 401, 412, 403, 404, 402, and 416 USS Midway

VA-56 A-7B 154531 NE/407 USS Ranger

VA-56 A-7B 154531 NE/407 USS Ranger

VA-56 A-7B NE/401 USS Ranger

VA-56 A-7B NF/404 USS Midway

VA-56 A-7 NF/401, 413, 404, and 400

VA-66 A-7E 159273, 157443 with drop tanks, AB/301 USS Independence

VA-66 A-7E 160564 AG/301 USS Dwight D Eisenhower

VA-66 A-7E AG/306, 301 USS Independence

VA-66 A-7E 159268 AG/306 USS Dwight D Eisenhower

VA-66 A-73E 158669, 157538 AG/303, 305, -, 314 USS Dwight D Eisenhower

VA-66 A-7E 159268 AG/306 USS Dwight D Eisenhower

VA-66 A-7E 159268 AG/306 USS Dwight D Eisenhower

VA-66 A-7E 159268 AG/306 USS Dwight D Eisenhower

VA-66 A-7E 159268 AG/306 USS Dwight D Eisenhower

VA-66 A-7E 159268 AG/306 USS Dwight D Eisenhower

VA-66 A-7E AG/300 USS Dwight D Eisenhower

VA-66 A-7E 157449 AG/302 USS Dwight D Eisenhower

VA-66 A-7E 159268 AG/306 USS Dwight D Eisenhower

VA-66 A-7E 157572 AG/310 USS Dwight D Eisenhower

VA-66 A-7E AG/307, 311, 300, and 313. 300 has FLIR. USS Dwight D Eisenhower

VA-66 A-7s AG/303, 306, 310, and 314 USS Dwight D Eisenhower

VA-66 A-7E AG/300 USS Dwight D Eisenhower

VA-72 A-7E AC/410

VA-15 A-7 AG/3XX (USS Indy) and VA-66 A-7E AG/301 (USS Ike)

VA-72 A-7E AB/402 on deck with ordnance

VA-67 A-7B 154492 AE/300 USS Roosevelt

VA-72 A-7E AC/412

VA-72 A-7 firing rockets

VA-72 A-7s AC/403, 405

VA-72 A-7s pass over USS Dwight D Eisenhower

VA-72 A-7 AC/400

VA-72 A-7s in formation

VA-72 A-7 AB/402

VA-72 A-7 AB/402

VA-72 A-7 AC/403

VA-72 A-7 AC/412

VA-72 A-7s IFR from USAF KC-135: AC/401, 411, and 412

VA-72 A-7 AC/403

VA-72 A-7s AC/403, 407, 411 and 414 USS John F Kennedy

VA-72 A-7Es AC/401, 406, 400, and 410

VA-72 A-7Es AC/404, 400

VA-72 A-7Es AC/404, 407, and 414

VA-72 A-7Es 1589992, 160550 AB/402, 407 USS America

VA-72 A-7Es 159992, 160550 AB/402, 407 IFR from an A-6

VA-72 A-7E 160548 AB/406 and F-14 USS John F Kennedy

VA-72 A-7Es 159992, 160550 AB/402, 407 USS America

VA-72 A-7Es AC/400, 405

VA-72 A-7Es AB/4XX

VA-72 A-7Es 159995, 159992 AB/410, 402 USS America

VA-72 A-7Es AB/4XX

VA-72 A-7s AB/401, 400, 405, and 407 USS America

VA-72 A-7Es AC/403, 400, 405, 411, and 404

VA-72 A-7Es AB/4XX

VA-72 A-7Es AB/4XX

VA-72 A-7 AC/4XX

VA-72 A-7s

VA-72 A-7E with Sidewinder missiles

VA-72 A-7s AC/406, 412, and 400

VA-72 A-7Es AC/412, 4XX

VA-72 A-7E 157585 AG/407

VA-72 A-7Es AC/404

VA-72 A-7B 154375 AB/407

VA-72 A-7 AG/411 on elevator

VA-72 A-7Es AC/411, 4XX

VA-72 A-7B 154375 AB/407

VA-72 A-7E AC/400

154344/154360 LTV A-7A-4c-CV Corsair II; (Block IVc)

A-183 154344 Navy acceptance from NPRO Rep., LTV, Dallas, TX., 09 NOV 67 ** Transferred to VA-27/CVW-14, NK/610, USS Constellation (CVA-64), 17 JAN 68 ~ S 1SO strike, 25 SEP 68 ** Aircraft hit by AAA, lost fuel, caught fire, made emergency landing at DaNang, SVN., arresting cable broke, aircraft left the runway, the pilot safely ejected and was rescued.

A-184 154345 Navy acceptance from NPRO Rep., LTV, Dallas, TX., 09 NOV 67 ** Transferred to VA-82/CVW-6, AE/3XX, USS America (CVA-66), 14 JAN 68; To VA-82, NAS Cecil Field, FL., 25 MAR 68; To VA-82/CVW-15, NL/3XX, USS Coral Sea (CVA-43), 09 MAY 69 ; To VA-82, NAS Cecil Field, FL., 25 JUN 70 ** Transferred to VA-174/FRS, AD/2XX, NAS Cecil Field, FL., 03 AUG 70 ** Transferred to VA-37/CVW-3, AC/3XX, USS Saratoga (CV-60), 20 MAY 71 ** Transferred to VA-37/ CVW-3, AC/3XX, USS Saratoga (CV-60), 20 JUN 71; To VA-37, NAS Cecil Field, FL., 14 JUN 72 ** Transferred to NARF, NAS Jacksonville, FL., 17 JUL 73 ** Transferred to VA-203/CVWR-20, AF/305, NAS Jacksonville, FL., 26 JUN 74 ~ S 3SO strike, 15 SEP 77 ** No data on strike ** On conditional loan from the National Museum of Naval Aviation, Pensacola, Fl. to Hickory, MAP, NC. JAN 03.

A-185 154346 Navy acceptance from NPRO Rep., LTV, Dallas, TX., 09 NOV 67 ** Transferred to VA-27/CVW-14, NK/6XX, USS Constellation (CVA-64), 20 JAN 68; To VA-27, NAS LeMoore, CA., 15 MAY 69 ** Transferred to VA-125/ FRS, NJ/5XX, NAS LeMoore, CA., 16 JUN 70 ** Transferred to VA-303/CVWR-30, ND/307, ND/314, & ND/325, NAS Alameda, CA., 13 MAY 71 ** Transferred to MASDC, Davis Monthan AFB; Tucson, AZ., assigned park code 6A0098; 12 DEC 77 ~ S 3SO strike, 15 OCT 83 ** No data on strike ** Transferred to LTV, Dallas, TX., to be converted to A-7P ** Transferred to the Portuguese AF (FAP), S/N 5540 ~ Strike 1985 ** W/O, Crashed during test flight from Vought; Dallas, TX.

A-186 154347 Navy acceptance from NPRO Rep., LTV, Dallas, TX., 14 NOV 67 ** Transferred to VX-5, XE/XXX, NAF China Lake, CA., 12 JAN 68 ~ S 1SO strike, 08 JAN 69 ** Crashed near MCAS Yuma, AZ., Due to mid air collision with A-7A 153203.

A-187 154348 Navy acceptance from NPRO Rep., LTV, Dallas, TX., 14 NOV 67 ** Transferred to VA-97/CVW-14, NK/5XX, USS Constellation (CVA-64), 23 FEB 68 ~ S 1SO strike, 09 MAR 68 ** Crashed near NAS LeMoore, Ca., Due to a Mid air Collision with A-7A 153251.

A-188 154349 Navy acceptance from NPRO Rep., LTV, Dallas, TX., 15 NOV 67 ** Transferred to VX-5, XE/XXX, NAF China Lake, CA., 12 JAN 68 ** Transferred to VA-153/CVW-19, NM/3XX, USS Oriskany (CVA-34), 15 NOV 69 ** Transferred to VA-125/FRS, NJ/5XX, NAS LeMoore, CA., 12 DEC 69 ** Transferred to VA-22/CVW-15, NL/3XX, NAS LeMoore, CA., 25 MAR 70 ** Transferred to VA-125/FRS, NJ/5XX, NAS LeMoore, CA., 01 JUN 70 ** Transferred to NAS Point Mugu, CA., for RDT & E, 08 OCT 70 ** Transferred to MASDC, Davis Monthan AFB; Tucson, AZ., assigned park code 6A0101; 28 DEC 70 ** Transferred to NARF, NAS Alameda, CA., 02 JUL 72 ** Transferred to VA-174/FRS, AD/2XX, NAS Cecil Field, FL., 12 OCT 72 ** Transferred to VA-303/CVWR-30, ND/314, NAS Alameda, CA., 07 OCT 73; To VA-303 NAS Jacksonville, FL., 07 MAR 75; To VA-303, NAS Alameda, CA., 01 MAY 75 ** Transferred to MASDC, Davis Monthan AFB; Tucson, AZ., assigned park code 6A0101, 27 JAN 78 ~ S 3SO strike, 15 OCT 83 ** No data on strike ** Transferred to LTV, Dallas, TX., to be converted to A-7P ** Transferred to the Portuguese AF (FAP), S/N 5541 ** Transferred to Esquadra 304 "Magnificoes" , BA-5; Monte Real, PO., 1985 ~ Strike, 1987 ** W/O, Destroyed in accident near Boticus, PO.

A-189 154350 Navy acceptance from NPRO Rep., LTV, Dallas, TX., 15 NOV 67 ** Transferred to VA-27/CVW-14 NK/6XX, USS Constellation (CVA-64), 25 JAN 68 ** To VA-27/CVW-14 NK/4XX, NAS LeMoore, CA., 26 JUN 69; To VA-27, USS Enterprise (CVAN-65), 26 MAY 70 ** Transferred to VA-125/FRS, NJ/5XX, NAS LeMoore, CA., 04 AUG 70 ** Transferred to VA-304/ CVWR-30, ND/4XX, NAS Alameda, CA., 31 AUG 71 ~ S 1SO strike, 28 SEP 74 ** Crashed at NAS LeMoore, CA., SEP 74, due to a Hydraulic failure.

A-190 154351 Navy acceptance from NPRO Rep., LTV, Dallas, TX., 20 NOV 67 ** Transferred to VA-27/CVW-6, NK/ 6XX, USS Constellation (CVA-64), 20 JAN 68; To VA-27/CVW-14, NK/4XX, NAS LeMoore, CA., 07 JUN 69; To VA-27, USS Enterprise (CVAN-65), 13 MAY 70 ** Transferred to NARF, NAS Alameda, CA., 07 JUL 70 ** Transferred to VA-304/ CVWR-30, ND/4XX, NAS Alameda, CA., 18 AUG 71 ** Transferred to VA-305/CVWR-30, ND/510, NAS Point Mugu, CA., 26 AUG 72, City of Santa Paula. city seal painted on port fuselage, First assigned A-7 with green diamonds on rudder; To VA-305, NAS Alameda, CA., 15 NOV 74; To VA-305, NAS Point Mugu, CA., 15 NOV 74; To VA-305, NAS North Island, CA., 22 SEP 76; To VA-305, NAS Point Mugu, CA., 06 OCT 76 ** Transferred to MASDC, Davis Monthan AFB; Tucson, AZ., assigned park code 6A0094; 07 DEC 77 ~ S 3SO strike, 15 OCT 83 ** No data on strike ** Transferred to LTV Dallas, TX. to be converted to A-7P ** Transferred to the Portuguese AF (FAP), S/N 5542 ** Transferred to Esquadra 304 "Magnificoes" , BA-5; Monte Real, PO., 1985 ** S/N changed to 15542 ~ Strike, 1994 ** W/O, destroyed in accident near Monte Real, Portugal.

A-191 154352 Navy acceptance from NPRO Rep., LTV, Dallas, TX., 21 NOV 67 ** Transferred to VA-27/CVW-14, NK/6XX, USS Constellation (CVA-64), 30 JAN 68; To VA-27/CVW-14, NK/4XX, NAS LeMoore, CA., 11 JUN 69; To VA-27, USS Enterprise (CVAN-65), 13 MAY 70 ** Transferred to VA-125/ FRS, NJ/5XX, NAS LeMoore, CA., 24 JUL 70 ** Transferred to VA-304/CVWR-30, ND/401, NAS Alameda, CA., 08 SEP 71 ** Transferred to MASDC, Davis Monthan AFB; Tucson, AZ., assigned park code 6A0083; 16 NOV 77 ~ S 3SO strike, 30 APR 80 ** No data on strike ** Transferred to LTV, Dallas, TX. to be converted to A-7P ** Transferred to the Portuguese AF (FAP), S/N 5501 ** Transferred to Esquadra 302 "Falcões" , BA-5; Monte Real, PO., 1981 ~ Strike, 1985 ** W/O, destroyed in accident in Belgium.

A-192 154353 Navy acceptance from NPRO Rep., LTV, Dallas, TX., 21 NOV 67 ** Transferred to VA-27/CVW-14, NK/6XX, USS Constellation (CVA-64), 07 FEB 68; To VA-27/CVW-14, NK/4XX, NAS LeMoore, CA., 12 JUN 69 ** Transferred to VA-122/FRS, NJ/2XX, NAS LeMoore, CA., 05 AUG 69 ** Transferred to VA-125/FRS, NJ/5XX, NAS LeMoore, CA., 21 APR 70 ** Transferred to VA-153/CVW-19, NM/314, USS Oriskany (CVA-34), 16 JUL 70; To VA-153, NAS LeMoore, CA., 28 JUN 72 ** Transferred to VA-125/FRS, NJ/5XX, NAS LeMoore, CA., 17 MAY 73; To VA-125, USS Ranger (CV-61), 21 MAR 74; To VA-125, NAS LeMoore, CA., 01 AUG 74 ** Transferred to VA-97/CVW-14, NK/3XX, NAS LeMoore, CA., 16 SEP 74 ** Transferred to VA-56/CVW-5, NF/4XX, USS Enterprise (CVAN-65), 20 OCT 74; To VA-56, USS Midway (CVA-41), 29 OCT 74; To VA-56, NAF Atsugi, JP., 20 NOV 74; To VA-56, USS Midway (CVA-41), 29 NOV 74; To VA-56, NAF Atsugi, JP., 21 OCT 75 ~ S 1SO strike, 22 OCT 75 ** Pilot was rescued when the aircraft ran off the runway.

A-193 154354 Navy acceptance from NPRO Rep., LTV, Dallas, TX., 08 DEC 67 ** Transferred to VA-97/CVW-14, NK/5XX, USS Constellation (CVA-64), 07 FEB 68 ** Transferred to NARF, NAS Alameda, CA., 05 JUN 69 ** Transferred to VA-125/ FRS, NJ/5XX, NAS LeMoore, CA., 22 SEP 70 ** Transferred to VA-303/CVWR-30, ND/303, NAS Alameda, CA., 14 APR 71; To VA-303, NAS Jacksonville, FL., 23 AUG 76; To VA-303, NAS

Alameda, CA., 31 AUG 76 ** Transferred to VA-305/CVWR-30, ND/507, NAS Point Mugu, CA., 04 DEC 76 ** Transferred to MASDC, Davis Monthan AFB; Tucson, AZ., assigned park code 6A0109; 06 JUN 78 ~ S 3SO strike, 31 OCT 83 ** No data on strike ** Transferred to LTV, Dallas, TX. to be converted to TA-7P ** Transferred to the Portuguese AF (FAP), S/N 5550 ** Transferred BA-5; Monte Real, PO., 1985 ** S/N changed to 15550 ** W/O and transferred to DGMFA Alverca, PO., for storage, 1997.

A-194 154355 Navy acceptance from NPRO Rep., LTV, Dallas, TX., 08 DEC 67 ** Transferred to VA-82/CVW-6, AE/3XX, USS America (CVA-66), 10 FEB 68; To VA-82, NAS Cecil Field, FL., 29 MAR 68; To VA-82/CVW-15, NL/3XX, USS Coral Sea (CVA-43), 05 SEP 69; To VA-82, NAS Cecil Field, FL., 01 JUN 70 ** Transferred to VA-174/FRS, AD/2XX, NAS Cecil Field, FL., 27 JUL 70 ** Transferred to VA-37/CVW-3, AC/3XX, USS Saratoga (CV-60), 24 NOV 71; To VA-174/FRS, AD/ 2XX, NAS Cecil Field, FL., 23 FEB 72; To VA-37, NAS Cecil Field, FL., 19 JUN 72 ** Transferred to NARF, NAS Jacksonville, FL., 12 JUL 73 ** Transferred to VA-303/CVWR-30, ND/3XX, NAS Alameda, CA., 12 FEB 74 ** Transferred to VA-203/CVWR-20, AF/3XX, NAS Jacksonville, FL., 11 MAY 74 ** Transferred to VA-305/CVWR-30, ND/505 & ND/525, NAS Point Mugu, CA., 14 AUG 77 ** Transferred to MASDC, Davis Monthan AFB; Tucson, AZ., assigned park code 6A0117; 14 OCT 78 ~ S 3SO strike, 31 OCT 83 ** No data on strike ** Transferred to LTV, Dallas, TX. to be converted to A-7P ** Transferred to the Portuguese AF (FAP), S/N 5543 ** Transferred to Esquadra 304 "Magnificoes" , BA-5; Monte Real, PO., 1985 ** S/N changed to 15543 ~ Strike, 1986 ** W/O, Destroyed in accident near Pocarica, PO.

A-195 154356 Navy acceptance from NPRO Rep., LTV, Dallas, TX., 08 DEC 67 ** Transferred to VA-86/CVW-6, AE/4XX, USS America (CVA-66), 09 FEB 68; To VA-86, NAS Cecil Field, FL., 27 MAR 68; To VA-86/CVW-15, NL/403, USS Coral Sea (CVA-43), LCDR J.M. McDermott painted on side cockpit, 16 MAY 69; To VA-82, NAS Cecil Field, FL., 01 JUN 70 ** Transferred to VA-174/FRS, AD/2XX, NAS Cecil Field, FL., 28 AUG 70 ** Transferred to VA-105/CVW-3, AC/4XX, USS Saratoga (CV-60), 19 APR 71 ** Transferred to VA-304/CVWR-30, ND/402, NAS Alameda, CA., 08 JUN 73 ** Transferred to MASDC, Davis Monthan AFB; Tucson, AZ., assigned park code 6A0089; 23 NOV 77 ~ S 3SO strike, 31 OCT 80 ** No data on strike ** Transferred to the Portuguese AF (FAP) to be used as spare parts, for the A-7P program.

A-196 154357 Navy acceptance from NPRO Rep., LTV, Dallas, TX., 08 DEC 67 ** Transferred to VA-97/CVW-14, NK/3XX, USS Constellation (CVA-64), 28 FEB 68; To VA-97, USS Enterprise (CVAN-65), 15 JUN 70 ** Transferred to VA-125/FRS, NJ/5XX, NAS LeMoore, CA., 24 AUG 70 ~ S 1SO strike, 02 OCT 70 ** Crashed near NAS LeMoore, CA., due to Engine failure.

A-197 154358 Navy acceptance from NPRO Rep., LTV, Dallas, TX., 07 DEC 67 ** Transferred to VA-97/CVW-14, NK/5XX, USS Constellation (CVA-64), 29 FEB 68 ~ S 1SO Strike, 03 APR 70 ** LT H.P. Hoffman was rescued after being shot down by AAA over Laos.

A-198 154359 Navy acceptance from NPRO Rep., LTV, Dallas, TX., 07 DEC 67 ** Transferred to VA-27/CVW-14, NK/613, USS Constellation (CVA-64), 21 FEB 68 ~ S 1SO strike, 25 AUG 68 ** LT J.R. Lee ejected over water and was rescued after being hit by AAA near Vinh, NVN.

A-199 154360 Navy acceptance from NPRO Rep., LTV, Dallas, TX., 12 DEC 67 ** Last production A-7A ** Transferred to VA-97/CVW-14, NK/5XX, USS Constellation (CVA-64), 05 MAR 68; To VA-97/CVW-14, NK/3XX, USS Enterprise (CVAN-65), 08 JUN 70 ** Transferred to VA-125/FRS, NJ/521, NAS LeMoore, CA., 19 AUG 70; To VA-125, USS Ranger (CVA-61), 14 MAY 74; To VA-125, NAS LeMoore, CA., 14 MAY 74; To VA-125, NAS Alameda, CA., 02 JUL 76; To VA-125, NAS LeMoore, CA., 11 JUL 76 ** Transferred to MASDC, Davis Monthan AFB; Tucson, AZ., assigned park code 6A0050; 11 MAY 77 ~ S 3SO strike, 19 AUG 80 ** No data on strike ** Transferred to LTV, Dallas, TX. to be converted to A-7P ** Transferred to the Portuguese AF (FAP), S/N 5511 ** Transferred to Esquadra 302 "Falcões" , BA-5; Monte Real, PO., 1981 ** S/N changed to 15511 ** W/O and transferred to BA-5; Monte Real, PO., 1998.

154913/154929 Cancelled contract for LTV A-7A Corsair II (Block IVc)

A---- 154913 Cancelled	A---- 154914 Cancelled
A---- 154915 Cancelled	A---- 154916 Cancelled
A---- 154917 Cancelled	A---- 154918 Cancelled
A---- 154919 Cancelled	A---- 154920 Cancelled
A---- 154921 Cancelled	A---- 154922 Cancelled
A---- 154923 Cancelled	A---- 154924 Cancelled
A---- 154925 Cancelled	A---- 154926 Cancelled
A---- 154927 Cancelled	A---- 154928 Cancelled
A---- 154929 Cancelled	

SECTION 2

A-7B

154361/154417 LTV A-7B-1-CV Corsair II; (Block I)
FY 67, Contract N00019-67-C-0082, (196) A-7B; B-001/B-196
FY 75, Contract N00019-75-C-0342, (3) TA-7C
*   from (3) A-7B; B-001 thru B-003; CSN 1-3*
FY 76-7T, Contract N00019-76-C-0229 (21) TA-7C
*   from (14) A-7B B-004 Thru B-017; CSN 4-24*
FY 76-7T, Contract N00019-76-C-0229, (7) TA-7C
*   from 018/B-024; CSN 25-31*

Note: As a newly formed squadron, VA-67 merged with the disestablishing VA-15, A-4 squadron, adopting their designation but keeping there A-7B's, 69.

B-057 154361 Navy acceptance from NPRO Rep., LTV, Dallas, TX., 24 APR 68 ** First production A-7B ** Transferred to VA-174/FRS, AD/200, NAS Cecil Field, FL., 18 JUL 68 ** Transferred to NPRO Rep., LTV, Dallas, TX., to be converted to TA-7C, 15 JUL 75 ** Re-designated to TA-7C, 24 JUL 75 ** Transferred to VA-122/FRS, NJ/2XX, NAS LeMooore, CA., 28 DEC 78 ** Transferred to VX-5, XE/XXX, NAS Cecil field, FL., 12 NOV 79; To VX-5, NWC China Lake, CA., 10 SEP 80 ** Transferred to NARF, NAS Jacksonville, FL., 17 SEP 81 ** Transferred to VX-5, XE/XXX, NAS Jacksonville, FL,, 29 AUG 84 ** Transferred to NARF, NAS Jacksonville, FL., 26 OCT 85 ** End of flight record card ** Transferred to NPRO Rep., LTV, Dallas, TX., 02 AUG 87 ** Transferred to NATC, NAS Patuxent River, MD., date unknown ** Transferred to AMARC, Davis Monthan AFB; Tucson, AZ., assigned park code 6A0368, 27 JUN 90 ** 4,202.8 flight hours ** TF41A402D engine S/N 141401 ** Storage location 111510 ** Located at AMARG, Davis Monthan AFB; Tucson, AZ., 15 JUN 07.

B-001 154362 Navy acceptance from NPRO Rep. LTV, Dallas, TX., 29 JAN 68 ** Converted from A-7A to A-7B, 01 FEB 68 ** Transferred to NATC, Weapons Systems Test, NAS Patuxent River, MD., 26 APR 68 ** Transferred to VA-122/ FRS, NJ/2XX, NAS LeMoore, CA., 08 JAN 69; To VA-122,COSA, NAS LeMoore, CA., 18 JUL 69 ** Transferred to VA-125/ FRS, NJ/5XX, NAS LeMoore, CA., 01 DEC 69 ** Transferred to VA-56/CVW-2, NE/4XX, NAS LeMoore, CA., 30 JAN 70; To VA-56/ CVW-5, NF/4XX, USS Midway (CVA-41), 18 JUN 70; To VA-56, NAS LeMoore, CA., 06 APR 72 ** Transferred To VA-153/CVW-19, NM/3XX, NAS LeMoore, CA., 12 APR 73; To VA-153, NAS Jacksonville, FL., 26 JUN 74; To VA-153, NAS LeMoore, CA., 15 AUG 74; To VA-153, NAS Glynco, GA., 07 OCT 74; To VA-153, NAS LeMoore, CA., 23 OCT 74; To VA-153, NAS Fallon, NV., 23 OCT 74; To VA-153, NAS LeMoore, CA., 11 APR 75; To VA-153, USS Oriskany (CV-34), 30 JUN 75; To VA-153, NAF Atsugi, JP., 17 DEC 75; To VA-153, USS Oriskany (CV-34), 20 DEC 75; To VA-153, NAS LeMoore, CA., 20 DEC 75; To VA-153 USS Franklin D. Roosevelt (CV-42), 21 APR 77; To VA-153, NAS LeMoore, CA., 21 APR 77 ** Transferred to VA-304/CVWR-30, ND/4XX, NAS Alameda, CA., 31 JUL 77; To VA-304, NAS Jacksonville, FL., 03 AUG 77; To VA-304, NAS Alameda, CA., 03 DEC 77; To VA-304, NAS Dallas, TX., 19 MAY 78; To VA-304, NAS Alameda, CA., 31 MAY 78 ~ S 3SO strike, 23 APR 86. No data on strike.

B-002 154363 Navy acceptance from NPRO Rep. LTV, Dallas, TX., 29 JAN 68 ** Converted from A-7A to A-7B, 01 FEB 68 ** Transferred to NATC, Service Test, NAS Patuxent River, MD., 26 APR 68 ** Transferred to NAS Point Mugu, CA., for R & T, 07 JUL 68 ** Transferred to VX-5, XE/XXX, NAF China Lake, CA., 07 SEP 68 ** Transferred to VA-155/ CVW-19, NM/502, USS Oriskany (CVA-34),18 NOV 69 ~ S 1SO strike, 20 SEP 72 ** Operational loss due to engine failure over Gulf of Tonkin, Pilot ejected and was rescued.

B-003 154364 Navy acceptance from NPRO Rep. LTV, Dallas, TX., 29 JAN 68 ** Converted from A-7A to A-7B, 01 FEB 68 ** Transferred to VA-122/FRS, NJ/2XX, NAS LeMoore, CA., 28 MAY 68 ** Transferred to VA-125/FRS, NJ/5XX, NAS LeMoore, CA., 24 DEC 69 ~ S 1SO strike, 26 FEB 70 ** No Data on strike.

B-004 154365 Navy acceptance from NPRO Rep. LTV, Dallas, TX., 29 JAN 68 ** Converted from A-7A to A-7B, 01 FEB 68 ** Transferred to VX-5, XE/XXX, NAF China Lake, CA., 15 MAY 68 ** Transferred to VA-125/FRS, NJ/5XX, NAS LeMoore, CA., 19 APR 70 ~ S 1SO strike, 15 JUN 71 ** No data on strike.

B-005 154366 Navy acceptance from NPRO Rep. LTV, Dallas, TX., 29 JAN 68 ** Converted from A-7A to A-7B, 01 FEB 68 ** Transferred to VX-5, XE/11, NAF China Lake, CA., 30 APR 68 ** Transferred to VA-125/FRS, NJ/5XX, NAS LeMoore, CA., 23 DEC 74 ** Transferred to VA-203/CVWR-20, AF/313, NAS Jacksonville, FL., 03 AUG 77 ** Transferred to MASDC, Davis Monthan AFB; Tucson, AZ., assigned park code 6A0130; 18 JUL 83 ** End of flight record card ** 4925.4 flight hours ** Engine removed upon arrival ** Aircraft deleted from inventory and sent to DRMO for disposition, 21 MAR 98 ** Sold as surplus to Fritz Enterprises; Taylor, MI., delivered to HVF West's yard; Tucson, AZ., 13 AUG 99.

B-006 154367 Navy acceptance from NPRO Rep. LTV, Dallas, TX., 29 JAN 68 ** Converted from A-7A to A-7B, 01 FEB 68 ** Transferred to VA-122/FRS, NJ/2XX, NAS LeMoore, CA., 30 APR 69 ~ S 1SO strike, 19 JUN 69 ** No data on strike.

B-007 154368 Navy acceptance from NPRO Rep. LTV, Dallas, TX., 29 JAN 68 ** Converted from A-7A to A-7B, 01 FEB 68 ** Transferred to VA -122/FRS, NJ/2XX, NAS LeMoore, CA., 20 JUN 68 ** Transferred to VA-174/FRS, AD/2XX, NAS Cecil Field, FL., 28 OCT 69 ** Transferred to VA-72/CVW-1, AB/4XX, NAS Cecil Field, FL., 28 JAN 70; To VA-72, USS John F. Kennedy (CVA-67), 22 JUN 71; To VA-72, NAS Cecil Field, FL., 06 SEP 72; To VA-72, USS John F. Kennedy (CVA-67), 13 FEB 75; To VA-72, NAS Cecil Field, FL., 08 APR 75; To VA-72, USS John F. Kennedy (CVA-67), 30 MAR 76; To VA-72, NAS Cecil Field, FL., 12 APR 76; To VA-72, USS John F. Kennedy (CVA-67), 27 APR 76; NAS Cecil Field, FL., 27 APR 76 To VA-72, USS John F. Kennedy (CVA-67), 27 APR 76; To VA-72, NAS Cecil Field, FL., 17 JUL 77 ** Transferred to VA-203/CVWR-20, AF/310, NAS Jacksonville, FL., 26 AUG 77 ** Transferred to MASDC, Davis Monthan AFB; Tucson, AZ., assigned park code 6A0129; 12 JUL 83 ** End of flight record card ** 5046.8 flight hours ** Engine removed on arrival ** Aircraft deleted from inventory and released to DRMO for disposition, 13 AUG 99 ** Sold to Fritz Enterprises; Taylor, MI., and shipped to HVF West's salvage yard Tucson, AZ., per DRMO letter dated 02 SEP 99.

B-008 154369 Navy acceptance from NPRO Rep. LTV, Dallas, TX., 29 JAN 68 ** Converted from A-7A to A-7B, 01 FEB 68 ** Transferred to VA-122/FRS, NJ/2XX, NAS LeMoore, CA., 02 JUN 68 ** Transferred to VA-174/FRS, AD/2XX, NAS Cecil Field, FL., 07 DEC 69 ~ S 1SO strike, 23 APR 73 ** No data on strike.

B-009 154370 Navy acceptance from NPRO Rep. LTV, Dallas, TX., 29 JAN 68 ** Converted from A-7A to A-7B, 01 FEB 68 ** Transferred to VA-87/CVW-16, AH/3XX, NAS Cecil Field, FL., 08 JUN 68; To VA-87, USS Ticonderoga (CVA-14), 27 JUN 68 ** Transferred to VA-174/FRS, AD/2XX, NAS Cecil Field, FL., 23 SEP 68 ** Transferred to VA-15/CVW-6, AE/3XX, USS Intrepid (CVS-11), 08 APR 69; To VA-15, USS Franklin D. Roosevelt (CVA-42), 26 JUN 69; To VA-15, NAS Cecil Field, FL., 05 APR 73; To VA-15, NAS Jacksonville, FL., 22 AUG 74; Transferred to VA-15/CVW-6, AE/3XX, MCAS Yuma, AZ., 13 SEP 74; To VA-15, NAS Cecil Field, FL., 23 SEP 74; To VA-15, USS John F. Kennedy (CVA-67), 23 SEP 74; To VA-15, USS Franklin D. Roosevelt (CVA-42), 22 JUN 75; To VA-15, NAS Cecil Field, FL., 22 JUN 75 ** Transferred to VA-205/CVWR-20, AF/5XX, NAS Atlanta, GA., 22 NOV 75; To VA-205, NAS Jacksonville, FL., 21 NOV 77 ** Transferred to VA-304/CVWR-30, ND/4XX, NAS Alameda, CA., 04 FEB 78; To VA-304, NAS Jacksonville, FL., 07 JUL 83; To VA-304, NAS Alameda, CA., 08 JUL 83; To VA-304, NAS Jacksonville, FL., 30 SEP 83; To VA-304, NAS Alameda, CA., 23 NOV 83 ** Transferred to VA-205/CVWR-20, AF/5XX, NAS Atlanta, GA., 24 NOV 83 ** Transferred to VA-204/CVWR-20, AF/4XX, NAS New Orleans, LA., 01 JUN 84 ** Transferred to VA-305/ CVWR-30, ND/5XX, NAS Point Mugu, CA., 04 JUN 86 ** Transferred to and stored at NAD, NAS North Island, CA., 19 DEC 86 ~ S 3SO strike 30 JAN 87 ** No data on strike ** End of flight record card ** On conditional loan from National Naval Museum; Pensacola, FL., to the USS Midway (CV-41) museum San Diego, CA. for display.

B-010 154371 Navy acceptance from NPRO Rep. LTV, Dallas, TX., 29 JAN 68 ** Converted from A-7A to A-7B, 01 FEB 68 ** Transferred to VA-122/FRS, NJ/2XX, NAS LeMoore, CA., 08 JUN 68 ** Transferred to VA-174/FRS, AD/2XX, NAS Cecil Field, FL., 21 NOV 69 ** Transferred to VA-72/CVW-1, AB/4XX, NAS Cecil Field, FL.,13 FEB 70; To VA-72, USS John F. Kennedy (CVA-67), 09 JUN 71; To VA-72, NAS Cecil Field, FL., 10 SEP 72; To VA-72, NAS Jacksonville, FL., 13 DEC 74; To VA-72, USS John F. Kennedy (CV -67), 25 FEB 75; To VA-72, NAS Cecil Field, FL., 25 FEB 75; To VA-72, USS John F. Kennedy (CV-67), 25 FEB 75; To VA-72, NAS Cecil Field, FL., 25 FEB 75; To VA-72, USS John F. Kennedy (CV-67), 05 NOV 75; To VA-72, NAS Cecil Field, FL., 05 NOV 75;

To VA-72, USS John F. Kennedy (CV-67), 19 DEC 76; To VA-72, NAS Cecil Field, FL., 17 JUL 77 ** Transferred to VA-203/CVWR-20, AF/311, NAS Jacksonville, FL., 26 AUG 77 ** Transferred to MASDC, Davis Monthan AFB; Tucson, AZ., assigned park code 6A0131, 25 JUL 83 ** End of flight record card ** 4678.9 flight hours ** Engine removed upon arrival ** Aircraft deleted from inventory and sent to DRMO for disposition, 17 AUG 99 ** Sold to Fritz Enterprises; Taylor, MI. and shipped to HVF West's salvage yard Tucson, AZ., per DRMO letter dated 02 SEP 99.

B-011 154372 Navy acceptance from NPRO Rep. LTV, Dallas, TX., 29 JAN 68 ** Converted from A-7A to A-7B, 01 FEB 68 ** Transferred to VA-122/FRS, NJ/2XX, NAS LeMoore, CA., 05 JUN 68 ** Transferred to VA-174/FRS, AD/2XX, NAS Cecil Field, FL., 31 OCT 69 ** Transferred to VA-72/CVW-1, AB/4XX, NAS Cecil Field, FL., 27 FEB 70; To VA-72, John F. Kennedy (CVA-67), 17 JUN 71; To VA-72, NAS Cecil Field, FL., 17 OCT 72; To VA-72, John F. Kennedy (CV-67), 19 SEP 74; To VA-72, NAS Jacksonville, FL., 26 APR 75; To VA-72, John F. Kennedy (CV-67), 26 APR 75; To VA-72, NAS Jacksonville, FL., 01 MAY 75; To VA-72, John F. Kennedy (CV-67), 13 JUN 75; To VA-72, NAS Cecil Field, FL., 30 JUN 75; To VA-72, John F. Kennedy (CV-67), 30 JUN 75; To VA-72, NAS Cecil Field, FL., 30 JUN 75; To USS John F. Kennedy (CV-67), 30 JUN 75; To VA-72, NAS Cecil Field, FL., 17 JUL 77 ** Transferred to VA-205/CVWR-20, AF/503, NAS Atlanta, GA., 24 AUG 77; To VA-205, NAS Jacksonville, FL., 21 APR 78; To VA-205, NAS Atlanta, GA., 30 AUG 78; To VA-205, NAS Jacksonville, FL., 26 FEB 81; To VA-205, NAS Atlanta, GA., 26 JUN 81; To VA-205, NAS Jacksonville, FL., 19 JAN 83; To VA-205, NAS Atlanta, GA., 06 MAY 83 ** Transferred to MASDC, Davis Monthan AFB; Tucson, AZ., assigned park code 6A0151; 12 JUN 84 ** End of flight record card ** 5019.2 flight hours ** Engine removed on arrival ** Aircraft released from storage and prepared for overland shipment to Holloman AFB; Alamogordo, NM., to be used as a range target, 11 APR 05.

B-012 154373 Navy acceptance from NPRO Rep. LTV, Dallas, TX., 29 JAN 68 ** Converted from A-7A to A-7B, 01 FEB 68 ** Transferred to VA -122/FRS, NJ/2XX, NAS LeMoore, CA., 11 JUN 68 ** Transferred to VA-146/CVW-9, NG/3XX, NAS Alameda, CA., 13 JUN 68; To VA-146, USS Enterprise (CVAN-65), 13 JUN 68 ** Transferred to VA-122/FRS, NJ/2XX, NAS LeMoore, CA., 18 OCT 68 ** Transferred to VA-174/FRS, AD/2XX, NAS Cecil Field, FL., 11 JAN 70 ** Transferred to NATC, Service Test, NAS Patuxent River, MD., 12 JUL 72, ** Transferred to NATC, NAS Patuxent River, MD., for RDT & E, 01 SEP 72, Tail has 4373 & NATC Decal, no Modex ;To NATC, NAS Jacksonville, FL., for RDT & E, 25 MAY 76; To NATC, NAS Patuxent River, MD., 03 AUG 76 ** Transferred to NAF Warminster, PA., for RDT & E, 13 JUN 78 ** Transferred to NAEC, NAS LAKEHURST, NJ. 15 NOV 78, NAEC under a bat on tail /373, Jet intake warning has teeth; To NAEC, NAS Jacksonville, FL., 12 MAR 81; To NAEC, modex 373, NAS Lakehurst, NJ., 27 MAY 81 ** Transferred to AMARC, Davis Monthan AFB; Tucson, AZ., assigned park code 6A0206; 26 SEP 86 ** End of flight record card ** Deleted and sent to DRMO for disposition, 13 AUG 02.

B-013 154374 Navy acceptance from NPRO Rep. LTV, Dallas, TX., 29 JAN 68 ** Converted from A-7A to A-7B, 01 FEB 68 ** Transferred to VA-122/FRS, NJ/2XX, NAS LeMoore, CA., 28 MAY 68 ** Transferred to VA-113/CVW-3, AC/4XX, USS Saratoga (CVA-60), 06 MAY 69 ** Transferred to VA-174/FRS, AD/2XX, NAS Cecil Field, FL., 05 JUN 69 ** Transferred to VA-15/CVW-6, AE/3XX, USS Franklin D. Roosevelt (CVA-42), 02 DEC 69; To VA-15, NAS Cecil Field, FL., 28 JAN 72 ~ S 1SO strike, 19 AUG 74 ** No data on strike.

B-014 154375 Navy acceptance from NPRO Rep. LTV, Dallas, TX., 29 JAN 68 ** Converted from A-7A to A-7B, 01 FEB 68 ** Transferred to VA-122/FRS, NJ/2XX, NAS LeMoore, CA., 15 JUN 68; VA-122, COSA, NAS LeMoore, CA. 18 JUL 69 ** Transferred to VA-174/FRS, AD/2XX, NAS Cecil Field, FL., 24 NOV 69 ** Transferred to VA-72/CVW-1, AB/4XX, NAS Cecil Field, FL., 05

FEB 70; To VA-72,USS John F. Kennedy (CVA-67), 17 JUN 71; To VA-72, NAS Cecil Field, FL., 07 NOV 72; To VA-72, USS John F. Kennedy (CVA-67), 11 APR 74; To VA-72, NAS Jacksonville, FL., 09 MAY 75; To VA-72, NAS Cecil Field, FL., 09 MAY 75; To VA-72, NAS Jacksonville, FL., 12 MAY 75; To VA-72, USS John F. Kennedy (CV-67), 23 JUN 75; To VA-72, NAS Cecil Field, FL., 05 APR 76; To VA-72, USS John F. Kennedy (CV-67), 12 APR 76; To VA-72, NAS Cecil Field, FL., 12 APR 76; To VA-72, USS John F. Kennedy (CV-67), 12 APR 76; To VA-72, NAS Cecil Field, FL., 17 JUL 77 ** Transferred to VA-204/CVWR-20, AF/4XX, NAS Memphis, TN., 16 SEP 77 ** Transferred to VA-203/CVWR-20, AF/302, NAS Jacksonville, FL., 29 NOV 77; VA-203, NAS Dallas, TX., 17 MAY 78; VA-203, NAS Jacksonville, FL., 25 MAY 78 ** Transferred to VA-204/CVWR-20, AF/413, NAS Jacksonville, FL., 02 JUN 83; To VA-204, NAS New Orleans, LA., 24 AUG 83 ** Transferred to MASDC, Davis Monthan AFB; Tucson, AZ., assigned park code 6A0153, 12 JUL 84 ** End of flight record card ** 6098.5 flight hours ** Engine removed on arrival ** Aircraft deleted from inventory and sent to DRMO for disposition, 21 MAR 98 ** Sold as surplus to Fritz Enterprises; Taylor, MI., delivered to HVF West's yard; Tucson, AZ., 13 AUG 99.

B-015 154376 Navy acceptance from NPRO Rep. LTV, Dallas, TX., 29 JAN 68 ** Converted from A-7A to A-7B, 01 FEB 68 ** Transferred to VA-122/FRS, NJ/2XX, NAS LeMoore, CA., 18 JUN 68 ** Transferred to VA-146/CVW-9, NG/3XX, NAS Alameda, CA., 19 JUN 68; To VA-146, USS Enterprise (CVAN-65), 19 JUN 68 ** Transferred to VA-122/FRS, NJ/2XX, NAS LeMoore, CA., 11 SEP 68 ~ S 1SO strike, 07 MAR 69 ** No data on strike.

B-016 154377 Navy acceptance from NPRO Rep. LTV, Dallas, TX., 29 FEB 68 ** Transferred to VA-122/FRS, NJ/2XX, NAS LeMoore, CA., 29 MAY 68 ** Transferred to VA-146/CVW-9, NG/3XX, NAS Alameda, CA., 04 JUN 68; To VA-146, USS Enterprise (CVAN-65), 30 JUN 68 ** Transferred to VA-122/FRS, NJ/2XX, NAS LeMoore, CA., 30 SEP 68 ** Transferred to VA-146/CVW-9, NG/3XX, USS Enterprise (CVAN-65), 30 JUN 68 ** Transferred to VA-122/FRS, NJ/2XX, NAS LeMoore, CA., 30 SEP 68 ** To VA-122, COSA, NAS LeMoore, CA., 18 JUL 69 ** Transferred to VA-125/FRS, NJ/511, NAS LeMoore, CA., 24 DEC 69; To VA-125, COSA, NAS LeMoore, CA., 15 JUN 71; To VA-125, CRAA, NAS LeMoore, CA., 28 JUN 71; To VA-125, NAS LeMoore, CA., 01 JAN 72 ** Transferred to NPRO Rep. LTV, Dallas, TX. to be converted to TA-7C, 25 NOV 75 ** Re-designated TA-7C, 04 DEC 75 ** Transferred to VA-122/FRS, NJ/2XX, NAS LeMoore, CA., 14 OCT 78; To VA-122, NAS Jacksonville, FL., 03 MAR 81; To VA-122, NAS LeMoore, CA., 04 MAR 81; To VA-122, NAS Jacksonville, FL., 02 APR 81; To VA-122, NAS LeMoore, CA., 17 NOV 81; To VA-122, NAS Jacksonville, FL., 01 FEB 85 ** Transferred to NARF, NAS Jacksonville, FL., 29 MAR 85 ** Transferred to VA-122/FRS, NJ/2XX, NAS LeMoore, CA., 18 APR 85; To VA-122, NAS Dallas, TX., 19 FEB 86; To VA-122, NAS LeMoore, CA., 24 FEB 86 thru 28 MAY 87 ** End of flight record card ** Transferred to VAQ-34, GD/06, NAS Point Mugu, CA., date unknown ** Transferred to AMARC, Davis Monthan AFB; Tucson, AZ., assigned park code 6A0330, 29 MAR 90 ** 6850.1 flight hours ** TF41A402D engine S/N 142618 ** Storage location 111512 ** Located at AMARG, Davis Monthan AFB; Tucson, AZ., 15 NOV 07.

B-017 154378 Navy acceptance from NPRO Rep. LTV, Dallas, TX., 29 FEB 68 ** Transferred to VA-122/FRS, NJ/2XX, NAS LeMoore, CA., 21 JUN 68 ~ S 1SO strike, 06 MAY 69 ** No data on strike.

B-018 154379 Navy acceptance from NPRO Rep. LTV, Dallas, TX., 29 FEB 68 ** Transferred to VA-122/FRS, NJ/2XX, NAS LeMoore, CA., 06 JUN 68 ** Transferred to VA-146/CVW-9, NG/3XX, NAS Alameda, CA., 10 JUN 68; To VA-146, USS Enterprise (CVAN-65), 10 JUN 68 ** Transferred to VA-122/FRS, NJ/2XX, NAS LeMoore, CA., 02 OCT 68 ** Transferred to VA-146/CVW-9, NG/3XX, USS Enterprise (CVAN-65), 27 FEB 69 ** Transferred to VA-25/CVW-16, AH/500, USS Ticonderoga (CVA-14), 18 JUN 69 ** Transferred to VA-155/CVW-19, NM/5XX, USS Oriskany (CVA-34), 20 MAR 70

** Transferred to VA-125/FRS, NJ/5XX, NAS LeMoore, CA., 20 MAR 70 ** Transferred to VA-93/CVW-5, NF/300, USS Midway (CVA-41), 01 OCT 70; To VA-93, NAS LeMoore, CA., 23 MAT 72 ** Transferred to NARF, NAS Alameda, CA., 06 JUL 72 ** Transferred to VA-215/CVW-19, NM/4XX, NAS LeMoore, CA., 11 JUL 73; To VA-215, USS Oriskany (CVA-34), 05 JUN 74; To VA-215, NAS LeMoore, CA., 05 JUN 74; To VA-215, NAS Fallon, NV., 09 NOV 74; To VA-215, NAS LeMoore, CA., 12 FEB 75; To VA-215, NAS Fallon, NV., 27 FEB 75; To VA-215, NAS LeMoore, CA., 11 APR 75; To VA-215, USS Oriskany (CV-34), 04 JUN 75; To VA-215, NAF Atsugi, JP., 24 DEC 75; To VA-215, USS Oriskany (CV-34), 06 FEB 76; To VA-215, NAS LeMoore, CA., 06 FEB 76 ** Transferred to VA-125/FRS, NJ/5XX, NAS LeMoore, CA., 15 JUN 76 ** Transferred to NPRO Rep. LTV, Dallas, TX. to be converted to TA-7C, 29 JUL 76 ** Re-designated TA-7C, 07 AUG 76 ** Transferred to VA-122/FRS, NJ/2XX, NAS LeMoore, CA., 23 MAY 78 ** To VA-122, NAS Alameda, CA., 13 JUN 80; To VA-122, NAS LeMoore, CA., 09 JUL 80; To VA-122, NAS Jacksonville, FL., 30 JUL 80; To VA-122, NAS LeMoore, CA., 12 SEP 80; To VA-122, NAS Jacksonville, FL., 20 JUN 85; To VA-122, NAS LeMoore, CA., 07 OCT 85 ** Transferred to NATC, SD/421, NAS Patuxent River, MD., for RDT & E, 04 SEP 86 thru 04 SEP 87, end of flight record card ** Transferred to AMARC, Davis Monthan AFB; Tucson, AZ., assigned park code 6A0394, 27 MAR 91 ** Prepare for overland and above deck shipment to Stellar Freight; Galveston, TX., for the government of Greece, no later than, 30 AUG 95 ** Transferred to the Helenic Air Force (Greece).

B-019 154380 Navy acceptance from NPRO Rep. LTV, Dallas, TX., 29 FEB 68 ** Transferred to VA-122/FRS, NJ/2XX, NAS LeMoore, CA., 28 MAY 68 ** Transferred to VA-146/CVW-9, NG/3XX, NAS Alameda, CA., 29 MAY 68; To VA-146, USS Enterprise (CVAN-65), 09 JUL 68 ** Transferred to VA-122/FRS, NJ/2XX, NAS LeMoore, CA., 07 OCT 68 ** Transferred to VA-146/CVW-9, NG/3XX, USS Enterprise, (CVAN-65), 09 MAR 69 ** Transferred to VA-25/CVW-16, AH/5XX, USS Ticonderoga (CVA-14), 18 JUN 69; To VA-25, NAS LeMoore, CA., 18 JUN 69 ** Transferred to VA153/CVW-19, NM/3XX, USS Oriskany (CVA-34), 23 OCT 69 ** Transferred to VA-125/FRS, NJ/5XX, NAS LeMoore, CA., 28 NOV 69 ** Transferred to VA-155/CVW-19, NM/5XX, USS Oriskany (CVA-34), 13 JUL 70; To VA-155, NAS LeMoore, 11 JUN 71 ** Transferred to VA-125/FRS, NJ/5XX, NAS LeMoore, CA., 21 JAN 72 ** Transferred to VA-93/CVW-5, NF/3XX, NAS LeMoore, CA., 07 NOV 72 ** VA-153/CVW- 19, NM/3XX, NAS LeMoore, CA., 08 MAY1973 ~ S 1SO, 04 DEC 73 ** No data on strike.

B-020 154381 Navy acceptance from NPRO Rep. LTV, Dallas, TX., 29 FEB 68 ** Transferred to VA-122/FRS, NJ/2XX, NAS LeMoore, CA., 13 JUN 68 ** Transferred to VA-146/CVW-9, NG/3XX, NAS Alameda, CA., 14 JUN 68; To VA-146, USS Enterprise (CVAN-65), 14 JUN 68 ** Transferred to VA-122/FRS, NJ/2XX, NAS LeMoore, CA., 28 AUG 68 ** Transferred to VA-125/FRS, NJ/5XX, NAS LeMoore, CA., 04 FEB 70 ** Transferred to VA-93/CVW-5, NF/3XX, USS Midway (CVA-41), 29 JUL 70; To VA-93, NAS LeMoore, CA., 10 APR 72; To VA-93, USS Midway (CVA-41), 22 JUN 73 ** Transferred to VA-215/CVW-19, NM/400, NAS LeMoore, CA., 23 JUN 73; To VA-215, USS Oriskany (CVA-34), 05 JUN 74; To VA-215, NAS LeMoore, CA., 05 JUN 74; To VA-215, NAS Fallon, NV., 14 NOV 74; To VA-215, NAS LeMoore, CA., 04 FEB 75; To VA-215, NAS Jacksonville, FL., 04 FEB 75; To VA-215, NAS LeMoore, CA., 23 MAR 75; To VA-215, NAS Jacksonville, FL., 23 MAR 73; To VA-215, NAS LeMoore, CA., 11 APR 75; To VA-215, USS Oriskany (CV-34), 15 JUL 75; To VA-215, NAS LeMoore, CA., 31 MAR 76; To VA-215, USS Franklin D. Roosevelt (CV-42), 22 APR 77; To VA-215, NAS Alameda, CA., 12 MAY 77; To VA-215, NAS LeMoore, CA., 06 JUN 77; To VA-215, NAS Alameda, CA., 01 JUL 77; To VA-215, NAS LeMoore, CA., 21 JUL 77 ** Transferred to VA-304/CVWR-30, ND/4XX, NAS Alameda, CA., 22 JUL 77 ** Transferred to NARF, NAS Jacksonville, FL., 17 JUN 78 ** Transferred to VA205/CVWR-20, AF/504, NAS Atlanta, GA., 29 AUG 78; To VA-205, NAS Jacksonville, FL., 27 MAR 81; To VA-205, NAS Atlanta, GA., 06 JUL 81; To VA-205, NAS Jacksonville, FL., 25 MAR 83; To VA-205,

NAS Atlanta, GA., 17 OCT 83 ** Transferred to MASDC, Davis Monthan AFB; Tucson, AZ., assigned park code 6A0147, 31 MAY 84 ** End of flight record card ** 3896.5 flight hours ** Engine removed on arrival ** Aircraft deleted from inventory and released to DRMO for disposition, 21 MAR 99 ** Sold as surplus to Fritz Enterprises; Taylor, MI., delivered to HVF West's yard; Tucson, AZ., 16 AUG 99.

B-021 154382 Navy acceptance from NPRO Rep. LTV, Dallas, TX., 19 JUN 68 ** Transferred to VA-146/CVW-9, NG/3XX, NAS Alameda, CA., 21 JUN 68; To VA-146, USS Enterprise (CVAN-65), 28 JUN 68 ** Transferred to VA-122/FRS, NJ/2XX, NAS LeMoore, CA., 23 AUG 68 ** Transferred to VA-125/FRS, NJ/5XX, NAS LeMoore, CA., 14 JAN 70 ** Transferred to VA-93/CVW-5, NF/3XX, USS Midway (CV-41), 14 OCT 70; To VA-93, NAS LeMoore, CA., 12 APR 72 ** Transferred to VA-153/CVW-19, NM/3XX, NAS LeMoore, CA., 07 MAY 73; To VA-153, USS Oriskany (CVA-34), 04 JUN 74; To VA-153, NAS LeMoore, CA., 04 JUN 74; To VA-153, NAS Jacksonville, FL., 13 JAN 75; To VA-153, NAS Fallon, NV., 24 MAR 75; To VA-153, NAS LeMoore, CA., 11 APR 75; To VA-153, USS Oriskany (CV-34), 30 JUN 75; To VA-153, NAF Atsugi, JP., 27 NOV 75; To VA-153, USS Oriskany (CV-34), 05 DEC 75; To VA-153, NAS LeMoore, CA., 05 DEC75; To VA-153, USS Franklin D. Roosevelt (CV-42), 20 APR 77; To VA-153, NAS LeMoore, CA., 20 APR 77 ** Transferred to VA-303/CVWR-30, ND/3XX, NAS Alameda, CA., 07 JUL 77 ** Transferred to VA-204/CVWR-20, AF/4XX, NAS Memphis, TN., 05 NOV 77; To VA-204, NAS Dallas, TX., 24 NOV 77; To VA-204, NAS Jacksonville, FL., 11 APR 78; To VA-204, NAS New Orleans, LA., 18 APR 78 ** Transferred to VA-305/CVWR-30, ND/514, NAS Point Mugu, CA., 29 AUG 78; To VA-305 NAS Jacksonville, FL., 11 AUG 83; Transferred to VA-205/CVWR-20, AF/5XX, NAS Atlanta, GA., 07 JAN 84 ** Transferred to VA-305/CVWR-30, ND/514, NAS Point Mugu, CA., 01 JUN 84 ** Transferred to VA-204/CVWR-20, AF/4XX, NAS New Orleans, LA., 19 JUN 84 ** Transferred to VA-305/CVWR-30, ND/514, NAS Point Mugu, CA., 25 APR 86 ** Transferred to NATTC,;Millington, TN., sitting outside the Airframes shop, to be used as an instructional airframe, 16 JAN 87 ~ S 3SO strike, 17 JAN 87 ** No data on strike.

B-022 154383 Navy acceptance from NPRO Rep. LTV, Dallas, TX., 29 FEB 68 ** Transferred to VA-122/FRS, NJ/2XX, NAS LeMoore, CA., 27 JUN 68 ** Transferred to VA-146/CVW-9, NG/3XX, USS Enterprise (CVAN-65), 02 JUL 68 ** Transferred to VA-122/FRS, NJ/2XX, 04 OCT 68 ** Transferred to VA-215/CVW-9, NG/4XX, USS Enterprise (CVAN-65), 27 FEB 69 ~ S 1SO strike, 08 JUN 69 ** No data on strike.

B-023 154384 Navy acceptance from NPRO Rep. LTV, Dallas, TX., 29 FEB 68 ** Transferred to VA-87/CVW-16, AH/3XX, USS Ticonderoga (CVA-14), 12 JUL 68 ** Transferred to VA-174/FRS, AD/2XX, NAS Cecil Field, FL., 01 NOV 68 ** Transferred to VA-15/CVW-6, AE/3XX, USS Intrepid (CVS-11), 26 MAR 69; To VA-15, NAS South Weymouth, MA., 12 JUN 69; To VA-15, USS Intrepid (CVS-11), 19 JUN 69; To VA-15/CVW-6, AE/3XX, USS Franklin D. Roosevelt (CVA-42), 19 JUN 69; To VA-15, NAS Cecil Field, FL., 10 FEB 72 ~ S 1SO strike, 10 JUL 72 ** No data on strike.

B-024 154385 Navy acceptance from NPRO Rep. LTV, Dallas, TX., 29 FEB 68 ** Transferred to VA-122/FRS, NJ/2XX, NAS LeMoore, CA., 20 JUN 68 ~ S 1SO strike, 13 NOV 69 ** No data on strike.

B-025 154386 Navy acceptance from NPRO Rep. LTV, Dallas, TX., 29 FEB 68 ** Transferred to VA-87/CVW-16, AH/3XX, USS Ticonderoga (CVA-14), 09 JUL 68 ** Transferred to VA-174/FRS, AD/2XX, NAS Cecil Field, FL., 27 JAN 70 ** Transferred to VA-72/CVW-1, AB/4XX, NAS Cecil Field, FL., 27 JAN 70; To VA-72, USS John F. Kennedy (CVA-67), 08 JAN 71 ~ S 1SO strike, 20 MAY 72 ** No data on strike.

B-026 154387 Navy acceptance from NPRO Rep. LTV, Dallas, TX., 29 FEB 68 ** Transferred to VA-122/FRS, NJ/2XX, NAS LeMoore, CA., 20 JUN 68~ S 1SO strike, 06 MAY 69 ** No data on strike.

B-027 154388 Navy acceptance from NPRO Rep. LTV, Dallas, TX., 29 FEB 68 ** Transferred to VA-122/FRS, NJ/2XX, NAS LeMoore, CA., 03 JUL 68 ** Transferred to VA-146/CVW-9, NG/3XX, USS Enterprise (CVAN-65), 09 JUL 68 ** Transferred to VA-122/FRS, NJ/2XX, NAS LeMoore, CA., 11 SEP 68 ** Transferred to VA-87/CVW-6, AE/4XX, NAS Cecil Field, FL., 24 NOV 69; To VA-87, USS Franklin D. Roosevelt (CVA-42), 02 JUN 70 ** Transferred to VA-174/FRS, AD/2XX, NAS Cecil Field, FL., 06 APR 71 ** Transferred to VA-46/CVW-1, AB/3XX, USS John F. Kennedy (CVA-67), 29 JUN 72 ** Transferred to VA-174/FRS, AD/2XX, NAS Cecil Field, FL., 06 OCT 72 ** Transferred to VA-125/FRS, NJ/5XX, NAS LeMoore, CA., 25 NOV 72 ** Transferred to VA-174/FRS, AD/2XX, NAS Cecil Field, FL., 21 JUL 73; To VA-174, NAS Jacksonville, FL., 24 JUN 74; To VA-174, NAS Cecil Field, FL., 20 AUG 74 ** Transferred to VA-15/CVW-6, AE/304, USS Franklin D. Roosevelt (CVA-42), 24 DEC 74; To VA-15, NAS Cecil Field, FL., 22 JUN 75 ** Transferred to VA-46/CVW-1, AB/3XX, USS John F. Kennedy (CV-67), 08 JUL 75; To VA-46, NAS Cecil Field, FL., 08 JUL 75; To VA-46, NAS Cecil Field, FL., 08 JUL 75; To VA-46, USS John F. Kennedy (CV-65), 03 DEC 76; To VA-46, NAS Cecil Field, FL., 03 DEC 76; To VA-46, USS John F. Kennedy (CV-67), 11 AUG 77 ** Transferred to VA-203/CVWR-20, AF/XXX, NAS Jacksonville, FL., 16 AUG 77, ** Transferred to VA-303/CVWR-30, ND/3XX, NAS Alameda, CA., 03 FEB 78 ** Transferred to VA-204/CVWR-20, AF/404, NAS Memphis, TN., 27 APR 78; To VA-204, NAS New Orleans, LA., 27 APR 78; To VA-204, NAS Jacksonville, FL., 29 APR 82; To VA-204, NAS New Orleans, LA., 10 SEP 82 ** Transferred to MASDC, Davis Monthan AFB; Tucson, AZ., assigned park code 6A0157, 24 JUL 84 ** End of flight record card. 6219.7 flight hours ** Engine removed on arrival ** Aircraft released from storage and prepared for overland shipment to Holloman AFB; Alamogordo, NM., to be used as a range target, 11 APR 05.

B-028 154389 Navy acceptance from NPRO Rep. LTV, Dallas, TX., 29 FEB 68 ** Transferred to VA-87/ CVW16, AH/3XX, USS Ticonderoga (CVA-14), 18 JUL 68 ** Transferred to VA-174/FRS, AD/2XX, NAS Cecil Field, FL., 02 OCT 68 ** Transferred to NARF, NAS Jacksonville, FL., 14 NOV 69 ** Transferred to VA-174/ FRS, AD/2XX, NAS Cecil Field, FL., 15 MAR 71 ** Transferred to VA-46/CVW-1, AB/4XX, USS John F. Kennedy (CVA-67), 01 JUL 72; To VA-46, NAS Cecil Field, FL., 04 DEC 72; To VA-46, USS John F. Kennedy (CV-67), 06 DEC 74; To VA-46, NAS Cecil Field, FL., 06 DEC 74; To VA-46, USS John F. Kennedy (CV-67), 13 DEC 74; To VA-46, NAS Cecil Field, FL., 13 DEC 74; To VA-46, USS John F. Kennedy (CV-67), 13 DEC 74; TO VA-46, NAS Cecil Field, FL., 26 FEB 76; To VA-46, USS John F. Kennedy (CV-67), 05 MAY 76; To VA-46, NAS Cecil Field, FL., 10 DEC 76; To VA-46, USS John F. Kennedy (CV-67), 18 JAN 77; TO VA-46, NAS Cecil Field, FL., 01 JUN 77 ** Transferred to VA-204/CVWR-20, AF/4XX, NAS Memphis, TN., 30 AUG 77; To VA-204, NAS Jacksonville, FL., 28 SEP 77 ** Transferred to VA-303/CVWR-30, ND/300, NAS Alameda, CA., 05 NOV 77; To VA-303, NAS Jacksonville, FL., 30 NOV 77; To VA-303, NAS Alameda, CA., 04 JAN 78; To VA-303, NAS Jacksonville, FL., 05 JUN 80; To VA-303, NAS Alameda, CA., 03 AUG 80; To VA-303, NAS Jacksonville, FL., 30 SEP 82; To VA-303, NAS Alameda, CA., 02 MAR 83 ** Transferred to VA-204/CVWR-20, AF/4XX, NAS New Orleans, LA., 17 SEP 83 ** Transferred to VA-305/CVWR-30, ND/5XX, NAS Point Mugu, CA., 05 JUN 86 ** Transferred to NWEF, Kirtland AFB; Albuquerque, NM., 22 OCT 86 ~ S 3SO strike, 23 OCT 86 ** No data on strike.

B-029 154390 Navy acceptance from NPRO Rep. LTV, Dallas, TX., 29 FEB 68 ** Transferred to VA-122/FRS, NJ/2XX, NAS LeMoore, CA., 30 JUL 68 ** Transferred to VA-125/FRS, NJ/5XX, NAS LeMoore, CA.,06 JAN 70 ** Transferred to VA-215/CVW-19, NM/4XX, USS Oriskany (CVA-34), 06 JAN 71 ** Transferred to VA-56/CVW-5, NF/4XX, USS Midway (CVA-41), 09 APR 72; To VA-56, NAS LeMoore, CA., 22 JUN 72 ** Transferred to VA-155/CVW-19, NM/5XX, NAS LeMoore, CA. 24 APR 73; To VA-155, USS Oriskany (CVA-34), 04 JUN 74; To VA-155, NAS LeMoore, CA., 04 JUN 74; To VA-155, NAS Jacksonville, FL., 29 OCT 74; To

VA-155, NAS Fallon, NV., 07 JAN 75; To VA-155, NAS LeMoore, CA., 11 APR 75; To VA-155, USS Oriskany (CV-34), 15 JUL 75; To VA-155, NAS LeMoore, CA., 12 SEP 75; To VA-155/CVW-19, NM/5XX, Franklin D. Roosevelt (CV-42), 15 OCT 76; To VA-155, NAS LeMoore, CA., 06 JUL 77 ** Transferred to VA-304/CVWR-30, ND/4XX, NAS Alameda, CA., 07 JUL 77 ** Transferred to NARF, NAS Jacksonville, FL., 24 MAR 78 ** Transferred to VA-305/CVWR-30, ND/513, NAS Point Mugu, CA., 29 AUG 78; To VA-305, NAS Jacksonville, FL., 05 FEB 81; To VA-305, NAS Point Mugu, CA., 26 MAR 81; To VA-305, NAS Jacksonville, FL., 30 AUG 82; To VA-305, NAS Point Mugu, CA., 04 JAN 83; ** Transferred to AMARC, Davis Monthan AFB; Tucson, AZ., assigned park code 6A0169, 12 JUN 86 ~ S 3SO strike, 29 SEP 86 ** No data on strike ** 5663.1 flight hours ** TF30P408 Engine S/N 664311 ** Engine records released, 13 MAR 00 ** Aircraft deleted from inventory and sent to DRMO for disposition, 13 AUG 02.

B-030 154391 Navy acceptance from NPRO Rep. LTV, Dallas, TX., 19 MAR 68 ** Transferred to VA-122/FRS, NJ/2XX, NAS LeMoore, CA., 13 JUN 68; To VA-122, COSA, NAS LeMoore, CA., 18 JUL 69 ** Transferred to VA-93/CVW-2, NE/3XX, NAS LeMoore, CA., 11 DEC 69 ~ S 1SO strike, 05 FEB 70 ** No data on strike.

B-031 154392 Navy acceptance from NPRO Rep. LTV, Dallas, TX., 19 MAR 68 ** Transferred to VA-122/FRS, NJ/2XX, NAS LeMoore, CA., 19 JUN 68 ** Transferred to VA-146/CVW-9, NG/3XX, NAS Alameda, CA., 24 JUN 68; To VA-146, USS Enterprise (CVAN-65), 24 JUN 68 ** Transferred to VA-122/FRS, NJ/2XX, NAS LeMoore, CA., 11 SEP 68 ~ S 1SO strike, 09 JUN 69 ** No data on strike.

B-032 154393 Navy acceptance from NPRO Rep. LTV, Dallas, TX., 19 MAR 68 ** Transferred to VA-122/FRS, NJ/2XX, NAS LeMoore, CA., 24 JUN 68 ** Transferred to VA-146/CVW-9, NG/3XX, USS Enterprise (CVAN-65), 30 JUL 68 ** Transferred to VA-122/FRS, NJ/2XX, NAS LeMoore, CA., 11 SEP 68 ** Transferred to VA-125/FRS, NJ/5XX, NAS LeMoore, CA., 19 JAN 70 ** Transferred to VA-93/CVW-5, NF/3XX, USS Midway (CVA-41), 28 JUL 70; To VA-93, NAS LeMoore, CA., 10 JUN 72 ~ S 1SO strike, 08 SEP 72 ** No data on strike.

B-033 154394 Navy acceptance from NPRO Rep. LTV, Dallas, TX., 19 MAR 68 ** Transferred to VA-122/FRS, NJ/2XX, NAS LeMoore, CA., 19 JUN 68 ** Transferred to VA-125/FRS, NJ/5XX, NAS LeMoore, CA., 28 JAN 70 ~ S 1SO strike, 08 MAR 70 ** No data on strike.

B-034 154395 Navy acceptance from NPRO Rep. LTV, Dallas, TX., 19 MAR 70 ** Transferred to VA-87/CVW-16, AH/3XX, NAS Cecil Field, FL., 11 JUN 68; To VA-87, USS Ticonderoga (CVA-14), 27 JUN 68 ** Transferred to VA-174/ FRS, AD/2XX, NAS Cecil Field, FL., 09 OCT 68 ** Transferred to VA-72/CVW-1, AB/4XX, NAS Cecil Field, FL., 28 JAN 70; To VA-72, USS John F. Kennedy (CVA-67), 23 JUN 71; To VA-72, NAS Cecil Field, FL., 07 DEC 72; To VA-72, USS John F. Kennedy (CV-67), 13 AUG 74 ** To VA-72, NAS Jacksonville, FL., 14 MAR 75; To VA-72, NAS Cecil Field, FL., 03 MAY 75; To VA-72, USS John F. Kennedy (CV-67), 30 JUN 75; To VA-72, NAS Cecil Field, FL., 30 JUN 75; To VA-72, USS John F. Kennedy (CV-67), 30 JUN 75; To VA-72, NAS Cecil Field, FL., 30 JUN 75; To VA-72, USS John F. Kennedy (CV-67), 30 JUN 75; To VA-72, NAS Cecil Field, FL., 17 JUL 77 ** Transferred to VA-203/CVWR-20, AF/307, NAS Jacksonville, FL., 25 AUG 77 ~ S 1SO strike, 26 NOV 82 ** No data on strike.

B-035 154396 Navy acceptance from NPRO Rep. LTV, Dallas, TX., 19 MAR 68 ** Transferred to VA-122/FRS, NJ/2XX, NAS LeMoore, CA., 15 JUN 68 ** Transferred to VA-125/FRS, NJ/5XX, NAS LeMoore, CA., 19 JAN 70 ** Transferred to VA-93/CVW-5, NF/3XX, USS Midway (CVA-41), 21 JUL 70; To VA-93, USS Midway (CVA-41), 28 JUN 72; To VA-93, USS Midway (CVA-41), 02 MAR 72 ** Transferred to NARF, NAS Jacksonville, FL., 25 JUL 73 ** Transferred to VA-203/CVWR-20, AF/312, NAS Jacksonville,

FL. 02 SEP 77 ** Transferred to MASDC, Davis Monthan AFB; Tucson, AZ., assigned park code 6A0125, 28 JUN 83 thru 29 JUN 83 ** End of flight record card ** 3953.2 flight hours ** Engine removed on arrival ** Aircraft deleted from inventory and released to DRMO for disposition, 21 MAR 99 ** Sold as surplus to Fritz Enterprises; Taylor, MI., delivered to HVF West's yard; Tucson, AZ., 13 AUG 99.

B-036 154397 Navy acceptance from NPRO Rep. LTV, Dallas, TX., 19 MAR 68 ** Transferred to VA-122/FRS, NJ/2XX, NAS LeMoore, CA., 20 JUN 68 ** Transferred to VA-125/FRS, NJ/5XX, NAS LeMoore, CA., 30 DEC 69 ** Transferred to VA-93/CVW-5, NF/3XX, USS Midway (CVA-41), 29 JUL 70; To VA-93, NAS LeMoore, CA., 28 JUN 72 ** Transferred to VA-153/CVW-19, NM/310, NAS LeMoore, CA., 03 JUL 73; To VA-153, USS Oriskany (CVA-34), 04 JUN 74; To VA-153, NAS LeMoore, CA., 04 JUN 74; To VA-153, NAS Fallon, NV., 13 MAR 75; To VA-153, NAS Jacksonville, FL., To VA-153, NAS LeMoore, CA., 06 MAY 75; To VA-153, USS Franklin D. Roosevelt (CV-42), 20 APR 77; To VA-153, NAS LeMoore, CA., 14 JUL 77 ** Transferred to VA-303/CVWR-30, ND/3XX, NAS Alameda, CA., 14 MAR 75 ** Transferred to VA-204/ CVWR-20, AF/407, NAS Memphis, TN., 05 NOV 77; To VA-204, NAS Dallas, TX., 24 NOV 77; To VA-204, NAS Memphis, TN., 11 MAY 78; To VA-204, NAS New Orleans, LA., 11 MAY 78 ** Transferred to NPRO Rep. LTV, Dallas, TX., for RDT & E, 30 APR 80 ** Transferred to VA-204/CVWR-20, AF/407, NAS New Orleans, LA., 09 FEB 81; To VA-204, NAS Jacksonville, FL., 23 MAR 81; To VA-204, NAS New Orleans, LA., 24 APR 81 ** Transferred to MASDC, Davis Monthan AFB; Tucson, AZ., assigned park code 6A0138, 23 SEP 83 ** End of flight record card ** 5363.7 flight hours ** Engine removed on arrival ** Aircraft released from storage and prepared for overland shipment to Holloman AFB; Alamogordo, NM., to be used as a range target, 11 APR 05.

B-037 154398 Navy acceptance from NPRO Rep. LTV, Dallas, TX., 19 MAR 68 ** Transferred to VA-122/FRS, NJ/2XX, NAS LeMoore, CA., 25 JUN 68 ** Transferred to VA-146/CVW-9, NG/3XX, USS Enterprise (CVAN-65), 01 JUL 68 ** Transferred to VA-122/FRS, NJ/2XX, NAS LeMoore, CA., 02 OCT 68 ** Transferred to VA-215/CVW- 9, NG/4XX, USS Enterprise (CVAN-65), 27 FEB 69; To VA-215/CVW-6, AE/4XX, USS Franklin D. Roosevelt (CVA-42), 30 MAR 69 ** Transferred to VA-122/FRS, NJ/2XX, NAS LeMoore, CA., 21 AUG 69 ** Transferred to VA-125/FRS, NJ/5XX, NAS LeMoore, CA., 13 JAN 70 ** Transferred to VA-93/CVW-5, NF/3XX, USS Midway (CVA-41), 07 OCT 70 ** Transferred to NARF, NAS Alameda, CA., 05 APR 73 ~ S-3SO strike 16 NOV 76 ** No data on strike.

B-038 154399 Navy acceptance from NPRO Rep. LTV, Dallas, TX., 19 MAR 68 ** Transferred to VA-122/FRS, NJ/2XX, NAS LeMoore, 18 JUN 68 ** Transferred to VA-155/CVW-19, NM/5XX, USS Oriskany (CVA-34), 28 OCT 69 ** Transferred to VA-56/ CVW-2, NE/4XX, NAS LeMoore, CA., 30 JAN 70; To VA-56/CVW-5, NF/4XX, USS Midway (CVA-41), 22 JUN 70; To VA-56, NAS LeMoore, CA., 19 MAY 72 ~ S 1SO strike, 11 NOV 72 ** No data on strike.

B-039 154400 Navy acceptance from NPRO Rep. LTV, Dallas, TX., 19 MAR 68 ** Transferred to VA-122/FRS, NJ/2XX, NAS LeMoore, CA., 25 JUN 68 ** Transferred to VA-125/FRS, NJ/5XX, NAS LeMoore, CA., 13 JAN 70 ** Transferred to VA-56/CVW-5, NF/4XX, NAS LeMoore, CA., 11 NOV 72 ** Transferred to VA-153/CVW-19, NM/3XX, NAS LeMoore, CA., 24 APR 73; To VA-153, USS Oriskany (CVA-34), 04 JUN 74; To VA-153, NAS Jacksonville, FL., 26 AUG 74; To VA-153, NAS LeMoore, CA., 27 OCT 74; To VA-153, NAS Fallon, NV., 27 OCT 74; To VA-153, NAS Fallon, NV., 26 FEB 75; To VA-153, NAS LeMoore, CA., 11 APR 75; To VA-153, USS Oriskany (CV-34), 30 JUN 75; To VA-153, NAS LeMoore, CA., 16 SEP 75; To VA-153/CVW-19, NM/3XX, USS Franklin D. Roosevelt (CV-42), 10 MAR 77 ~ S 1SO strike, 10 MAR 77 ** No data on strike.

B-040 154401 Navy acceptance from NPRO Rep. LTV, Dallas, TX., 26 MAR 68 ** Transferred to VA-87/CVW-16, AH/3XX, USS Ticonderoga (CVA-14), 19 JUL 68 ** Transferred to VA-174/FRS, AD/2XX, NAS Cecil Field, FL., 04 SEP 68 ** Transferred to VA-15/CVW6, AE/3XX, USS Intrepid, (CVS-11), 17 APR 69; To VA-15, USS Franklin D. Roosevelt (CVA-42), 23 JUN 69 ~ S 1SO strike, 01 MAR 70 ** No data on strike.

B-041 154402 Navy acceptance from NPRO Rep. LTV, Dallas, TX., 26 MAR 68 ** Transferred to VA-174/FRS, AD/2XX, NAS Cecil Field, FL., 24 JUL 68 ** Transferred to VA-15/CVW-6, AE/307, USS Intrepid (CVS-11), 14 MAR 69; To VA-15 CVW-6, AE/307, USS Franklin D. Roosevelt (CVA-42), 23 JUN 69; To VA-15, NAS Cecil Field, FL., 23 OCT 71; To VA-15, MCAS Yuma, AZ., 10 JUN 74; To VA-15, NAS Cecil Field, FL.,10 JUN 74; To VA-15, MCAS Yuma, AZ., 10 JUN 74; To VA-15, NAS Cecil Field, FL., 03 OCT 74; To VA-15, USS Franklin D. Roosevelt (CVA-42), 13 NOV 74; To VA-15, NAS Cecil Field, FL., 22 JUN 75 ** Transferred to VA-174/FRS, AD/2XX, NAS Cecil Field, FL., 01 DEC 75 ** Transferred to NPRO Rep. LTV, Dallas, TX., to be converted to TA-7C, 21 JUN 76 ** Re-designated TA-7C, 30 JUN 76 ** Transferred to VA-122/FRS, NJ/2XX, NAS LeMoore, CA., 26 MAY 79; To VA-122, NAS Jacksonville, FL., 06 FEB 82; To VA-122, NAS LeMoore, CA., 21 MAR 82; To VA-122, NAS Alameda, CA., 26 JUL 82; To VA-122, NAS LeMoore, CA., 17 SEP 82; To VA-122, NAS Dallas, TX., 19 NOV 85; To VA-122, NAS Jacksonville, FL., 21 OCT 86; To VA-122, NAS LeMoore, CA., 21 OCT 86; To VA-122, NAS Jacksonville, FL., 19 DEC 86 ** Transferred to NARF, NAS Jacksonville, FL., 08 APR 87 ** Transferred to NATC, Strike Test, SD/421, NAS Patuxent River, MD., for RDT & E, 10 APR 87 ** End of flight record card ** Transferred to AMARC, Davis Monthan AFB; Tucson, AZ., assigned park code 6A0370, 19 JUL 90 ** 5715.3 flight hours ** TF41A402D engine S/N 141581 ** Storage location 211961 ** Transferred to FMS, 06 APR 04 ** Located at AMARG, Davis Monthan AFB; Tucson, AZ., 15 JUN 07.

B-042 154403 Navy acceptance from NPRO Rep. LTV, Dallas, TX., 26 MAR 68 ** Transferred to VA-87/CVW-16, AH/3XX, USS Ticonderoga (CVA-14), 17 JUL 68 ** Transferred to VA-174/FRS, AD/2XX, NAS Cecil Field, FL., 04 OCT 68 ** Transferred to VA-15/CVW-6, AE/3XX, USS Intrepid (CVS-11), 14 MAR 69; To VA-15, USS Franklin D. Roosevelt (CVA-42), 25 JUN 69 ~ S 1SO strike, 12 NOV 69 ** No data on strike.

B-043 154404 Navy acceptance from NPRO Rep. LTV, Dallas, TX., 26 MAR 68 ** Transferred to VA-122/FRS, NJ/2XX, NAS LeMoore, CA., 26 JUN 68 ** Transferred to VA-174/FRS, AD/2XX, NAS Cecil Field, FL., 01 DEC 69, Transferred to VA-72/CVW-1, AB/4XX, NAS Cecil Field, FL., 28 JAN 71; To VA-72/CVW-1, AB/ 4XX, USS John F. Kennedy (CVA-67), 08 NOV 72; To VA-72, NAS Cecil Field, FL., 08 NOV 72 ** Transferred to VA-87/CVW-6, AE/4XX, NAS Cecil Field, FL., 18 NOV 73; To VA-87, NAS Cecil Field, FL., 18 NOV 73; To VA-87, NAS Jacksonville, FL., 07 AUG 74; To VA-87, MCAS Yuma, AZ., 12 SEP 74; To VA-87, NAS Cecil Field, FL., 04 OCT 74; To VA-87, USS Franklin D. Roosevelt (CVA-42), 24 OCT 74; To VA-87, NAS Cecil Field, FL., 24 OCT 74; To VA-87, USS Franklin D. Roosevelt (CVA-42), 24 OCT 74; To VA-87, NAS Cecil Field, FL., 24 JUL 75 ** Transferred to VA-174/FRS, AD/2XX, NAS Cecil Field, FL., 02 OCT 75 ** Transferred to NPRO Rep. LTV, Dallas, TX., to be converted to TA-7C, 28 JAN 76 ** Re-designated to TA-7C, 06 FEB 76 ** Transferred to NPRO Rep. LTV, Dallas, TX. for RDT & E, 00 APR 79 ** Transferred to the Portuguese AF, for lease, 1982 ** Transferred back to U.S. Navy, 1985 ** Transferred to PMTC, NAS Point Mugu, CA., 18 APR 85; To PMTC, NAS Dallas, TX., 17 SEP 85 ** Transferred to HC-7, NAS Imperial Beach, CA., 30 SEP 85 ** Transferred to NATC, Service Test, NAS Patuxent River, MD., 01 OCT 85 ** Transferred to NAEL, NAS Lakehurst, NJ., 19 AUG 86 ** End of flight record card **Transferred to AMARC, Davis Monthan AFB; Tucson, AZ., assigned park code 6A0369, 29 JUN 90 ** 4891.0 flight hours ** TF41A402D engine S/N 141989 ** Prepare for overland and above deck shipment to Stellar Freight; Galveston, TX., for the government of Greece, no later than 15 AUG 95 ** Transferred to the Helenic Air Force (Greece).

B-044 154405 Navy acceptance from NPRO Rep. LTV, Dallas, TX., 26 MAR 68 ** Transferred to VA-122/FRS, NJ/2XX, NAS LeMoore, CA., 26 JUN 68 ** Transferred to NARF, NAS Alameda, CA., 13 APR 69 ** Transferred to VA-125/FRS, NJ/5XX, NAS LeMoore, CA., 02 MAR 70 ** Transferred to VA-93/CVW-2, NE/3XX, NAS LeMoore, CA., 22 MAR 70; To VA-93/CVW-5, NF/3XX, USS Midway (CVA-41), 22 MAR 70 ~ S 1SO strike, 23 MAY 72 ** CDR C.E. Barnett KIA when shot down by SAM over North Vietnam.

B-045 154406 Navy acceptance from NPRO Rep. LTV, Dallas, TX., 24 APR 68 ** Transferred to VA-174/FRS, AD/2XX, NAS Cecil Field, FL., 30 JUL 68 ** Transferred to VA-15/CVW-6, AE/3XX, NAS Cecil Field, FL., 12 JUN 69 ** Transferred to VA-15, USS Intrepid (CVS-11), 09 APR 69; To VA-15, USS Franklin D. Roosevelt (CVA-42), 12 JUN 69; To VA-15, NAS Cecil Field, FL., 19 FEB 72; To VA-15, MCAS Yuma, AZ., 31 JUL 74; To VA-15, NAS Cecil Field, FL., 25 SEP 74; To VA-15, USS Franklin D. Roosevelt (CVA-42), 25 SEP 74; To VA-15, NAS Cecil Field, FL., 24 JUL 75; ** Transferred to VA-125/FRS, NJ/5XX, NAS LeMoore., CA., 20 NOV 75 ** Transferred to VA-304/CVWR-30, ND/406, NAS Alameda, CA., 11 AUG 77; To VA-304, NAS Jacksonville, FL., 26 APR 78; To VA-304, NAS Alameda, CA., 30 AUG 78 ** To VA-304, NAS Jacksonville, FL., 30 NOV 80; To VA-304, NAS Alameda, CA., 13 MAR 81; To VA-304, NAS Jacksonville, FL., 21 SEP 83 ** Transferred to VA-204/CVWR-20, AF/4XX, NAS New Orleans, LA., 13 JAN 84; Transferred to VA-304/CVWR-30, ND/4XX NAS Alameda, CA., 27 JAN 84; To VA-304, NAS Jacksonville, FL., 08 FEB 84 ** Transferred to VA-204/CVWR-20, AF/406, NAS New Orleans, LA., 20 JUN 84 ** Transferred to AMARC, Davis Monthan AFB; Tucson, AZ., assigned park code 6A0181, 11 JUL 86 ~ S 3SO strike, 29 SEP 86 ** End of flight record card ** 6222.9 flight hours ** TF30P408 engine S/N 664309 ** Aircraft deleted from inventory and released to DRMO for disposition, 13 AUG 02.

B-046 154407 Navy acceptance from NPRO Rep. LTV, Dallas, TX., 24 APR 68 ** Transferred to VA-122/FRS, NJ/2XX, NAS LeMoore, CA., 03 JUL 68 ** Transferred to VA-146/CVW-9, NG/3XX, USS Enterprise (CVAN-65), 09 JUL 68 ** Transferred to VA-122/FRS, NJ/2XX, NAS LeMoore, CA., 10 OCT 68; To VA-122, COSA, 18 JUL 69 ** Transferred to VA-155/CVW-19, NM/5XX, USS Oriskany (CVA-34), 29 OCT 69 ** Transferred to VA-113/CVW-2, NE/3XX, NAS LeMoore, CA., 17 FEB 70 ** Transferred to VA-125/FRS, NJ/5XX, NAS LeMoore, CA., 29 JUN 70 ** Transferred to VA-46/CVW-1, AB/3XX, NAS Cecil Field, FL., 06 MAY 71; To VA-46, USS John F. Kennedy (CVA-67), 24 JUN 71 ** Transferred to VA-174/FRS, AD/2XX, NAS Cecil Field, FL., 06 OCT 72 ** Transferred to VA-125/FRS, NJ/5XX, 25 NOV 72 ** Transferred to VA-174/FRS, AD/2XX, NAS Cecil Field, FL., 21 JUL 73 ** Transferred to VA-15/CVW-6, AE/3XX, MCAS Yuma, AZ., 17 JUL 74; To VA-15, NAS Cecil Field, FL., 23 SEP 74; To VA-15, USS Franklin D. Roosevelt (CVA-42), 23 OCT 74 ** Transferred to VA-174/FRS, AD/2XX, NAS Cecil Field, FL., 19 AUG 75 ** Transferred to NPRO Rep. LTV, Dallas, TX. to be converted to TA-7C, 22 APR 76 ** Re-designated TA-7C, 30 APR 76 ** Transferred to VA-122/FRS, NJ/2XX, NAS LeMoore, CA., 01 SEP 78; VA-122, NAS Alameda, CA., 25 NOV 80; To VA-122, NAS LeMoore, CA., 19 JAN 81; To VA-122, NAS Jacksonville, FL., 26 FEB 81; To VA-122, NAS LeMoore, CA., 19 APR 81; To VA-122, NAS Jacksonville, FL., 10 MAY 85; To VA-122, NAS LeMoore, CA., 11 NOV 85 ** Transferred to NATC, NAS Patuxent River, MD. for RDT & E, 05 DEC 86 thru 13 MAY 87 ** End of flight record card.

B-047 154408 Navy acceptance from NPRO Rep. LTV, Dallas, TX., 24 APR 68 ** Transferred to VA-174/FRS, AD/2XX, NAS Cecil Field, FL., 23 JUL 68 ** Transferred to VA-15/CVW-6, AE/3XX, USS Intrepid (CVS-11), FL., 09 JUN 69; To VA-15, USS Franklin D. Roosevelt (CVA-42), 27 APR 69 ~ S 1SO strike, 04 SEP 69 ** No data on strike.

B-048 154409 Navy acceptance from NPRO Rep. LTV, Dallas, TX., 24 APR 68 ** Transferred to VA-122/FRS, NJ/2XX, NAS LeMoore, CA., 28 JUN 68 ** Transferred to VA-155/CVW-19, NM/5XX, USS Oriskany (CVA-34), 25 SEP 69 ** Transferred to VA-125/FRS, NJ/5XX, NAS LeMoore, CA., 22 MAR 70 ** Transferred to VA-155/CVW-19, NM/5XX, NAS LeMoore, CA., 04 DEC 72; To VA-155, USS Oriskany (CVA-34), 04 JUN 74 ** To VA-155, NAS LeMoore, CA., 04 JUN 74; To VA-155, NAS Fallon, NV., 16 OCT 74; To VA-155, NAS LeMoore, CA., 06 FEB 75; To VA-155, NAS Jacksonville, FL., 10 FEB 75; To VA-155, NAS Fallon, NV., 22 MAR 75; To VA-155, NAS LeMoore, CA., 11 APR 75; To VA-155, USS Oriskany (CV-34), 15 JUL 75; To VA-155, NAS LeMoore, CA., 12 SEP 75; To VA-155, NAS Alameda, CA., 06 MAY 76; To VA-155, NAS LeMoore, CA., 08 MAY 76; To VA-155, NAS Alameda, CA., 28 MAY 76; To VA-155, NAS LeMoore, CA., 25 JUN 76, Painted in bi-centennial scheme, 04 JUL 76; To VA-155, USS Franklin D. Roosevelt (CV-42), 15 OCT 76; To VA-155, NAS LeMoore, CA., 07 JUL 77 ** Transferred to VA-303/CVWR-30, ND/3XX, NAS Alameda, CA., 07 JUL 77 ** Transferred to VA-204/CVWR-20, AF/4XX, NAS Memphis, TN, 05 NOV 77; To VA-204, NAS Dallas, TX., 22 NOV 77** Transferred to NARF, NAS Jacksonville, FL., 28 APR 78 ** Transferred to VA-204/CVWR-20, AF/410, NAS New Orleans, LA., 30 AUG 78; To VA-204, NAS Jacksonville, FL., 26 OCT 82; To VA-204, NAS New Orleans, LA., 24 MAR 83 ** Transferred to MASDC, Davis Monthan AFB; Tucson, CA., assigned park code 6A0148, 31 MAY 84 ** End of flight record card ** 5273.6 flight hours ** Engine removed on arrival ** ** Aircraft released from storage and prepared for overland shipment to Holloman AFB; Alamogordo, NM., 11 APR 05.

B-049 154410 Navy acceptance from NPRO Rep. LTV, Dallas, TX., 24 APR 68 ** Transferred to VA-87/CVW-16, AH/3XX, USS Ticonderoga (CVA-14), 17 JUL 68 ** Transferred to VA-174/FRS, AD/2XX, NAS Cecil Field, FL., 20 JUL 68 ** Transferred to VA-15/CVW-6, AE/3XX, USS Intrepid (CVS-11), 11 MAR 69 ** To VA-15, USS Franklin D. Roosevelt (CVA-42), 10 JUN 69; To VA-15, NAS Cecil Field, FL., 07 JAN 72; To VA-15, MCAS Yuma, AZ., 25 JUN 74; To VA-15, NAS Cecil Field, FL., 15 OCT 74; To VA-15, USS Franklin D. Roosevelt (CVA-42), 16 OCT 74 ** Transferred to VA-174/ FRS, AD/2XX, NAS Cecil Field, FL., 28 JAN 75 ** Transferred to NPRO Rep. LTV, Dallas, TX. to be converted to TA-7C, 07 OCT 76 ** Re-designated TA-7C,07 OCT 76 ** Transferred to VA-122/ FRS, NJ/203, NAS LeMoore, CA., 06 JUN 78; To VA-122, NAS Jacksonville, FL., 12 AUG 80; To VA-122, NAS LeMoore, CA., 01 OCT 80 ~ S 1SO strike, 17 JAN 84 ** Engine failure near NAS Fallon, NV., both pilots ejected safely.

B-050 154411 Navy acceptance from NPRO Rep. LTV, Dallas, TX., 24 APR 68 ** Transferred to VA-122/FRS, NJ/2XX, NAS LeMoore, CA., 02 JUL 68 ** Transferred to VA-146/CVW-9, NG/3XX, USS Enterprise (CVAN-65), 08 JUL 68 ** Transferred to VA-122/FRS, NJ/2XX, NAS LeMoore, CA., 11 OCT 68 ** Transferred to VA-125/FRS, NJ/5XX, NAS LeMoore, CA., 18 JUN 70 ** Transferred to VA-215/CVW-19, NM/404, USS Oriskany (CVA-34), 28 DEC 70; To VA-215, NAS LeMoore, CA., 11 JUN 72; To VA-215, USS Oriskany (CVA-34), 05 JUN 74; To VA-215, NAS LeMoore, CA., 05 JUN 74; To VA-215, NAS Fallon, NV., 09 NOV 74; To VA-215, NAS Jacksonville, FL., 09 DEC 74; To VA-215, NAS LeMoore, CA., 12 FEB 75; To VA-215, NAS Fallon, NV., 24 MAR 75; To VA-215, NAS LeMoore, CA., 16 APR 75; To VA-215, USS Oriskany (CV-34), 15 JUL 75; To VA-215, NAF Atsugi, JP., 03 NOV 75; To VA-215, USS Oriskany (CV-34), 06 NOV 75; To VA-215, NAS LeMoore, CA., 06 NOV 75; To VA-215, USS Franklin D. Roosevelt (CV-42), 22 APR 77; To VA-215, NAS LeMoore, CA., 25 MAY 77 ** Transferred to VA-303/CVWR-30, ND/3XX, NAS Alameda, CA., 02 JUL 77 ** Transferred to VA-204/CVWR-20, AF/4XX, NAS Memphis, TN., 05 NOV 77; To VA-204, NAS Dallas, TX., 30 NOV 77; To VA-204, NAS Jacksonville, FL., 08 MAY 78; To VA-204, NAS New Orleans, LA., 09 MAY 78 ** Transferred to VA-305/ CVWR-30, ND/ 5XX, NAS Point Mugu, CA., 24 MAR 79; To VA-305, NAS Alameda, CA., 06 JUN 80; To VA-305, NAS Point Mugu, CA., 21 JUL 80; To VA-305, NAS Alameda, CA., 25 JUL 80; To VA-305, NAS Point Mugu,

CA., 05 AUG 80; To VA-305 NAS Jacksonville, FL., 21 APR 81; To VA-305, NAS Point Mugu, CA., 03 JUN 81; To VA-305 NAS Jacksonville, FL., 08 JUN 83; To VA-305, NAS Point Mugu, CA., 05 DEC 83; To VA-305 NAS Jacksonville, FL., 09 JAN 84 ; To VA-305, NAS Point Mugu, CA., 13 JAN 84 ** Transferred to NWEF, Kirtland AFB, Albuquerque, NM., 28 OCT 86 ~ S 3SO strike, 29 OCT 86 ** End of flight record card.

B-051 154412 Navy acceptance from NPRO Rep. LTV, Dallas, TX., 28 APR 68 ** Transferred to VA-87/CVW-16, AH/3XX, USS Ticonderoga (CVA-14), 12 JUL 68 ** Transferred to VA-174/FRS, AD/2XX, NAS Cecil Field, FL., 28 SEP 68 ** Transferred to VA-15/CVW-6, AE/3XX, USS Franklin D. Roosevelt (CVA-42), 18 OCT 69 ** Transferred to VA-174/FRS, AD/2XX, NAS Cecil Field, FL., 07 JUL 72 ** Transferred to VA-87/CVW-6, AE/4XX, Franklin D. Roosevelt (CVA-42), 24 FEB 72; To VA-87, NAS Cecil Field, FL., 31 MAR 72; To VA-87, NAS Jacksonville, FL., 13 AUG 74; To VA-87, NAS Cecil Field, FL., 30 NOV 73; To VA-87, NAS Jacksonville, FL., 13 AUG 74; To VA-87, NAS Cecil Field, FL., 24 OCT 74; To VA-87, NAS Jacksonville, FL., 18 NOV 74; To VA-87, USS Franklin D. Roosevelt (CVA-42), 22 JUN 75; To VA-87, NAS Cecil Field, FL., 24 JUL 75; To VA 87, USS Saratoga (CV-60), 01 OCT 75 ** Transferred to VA-174/FRS, AD/2XX, NAS Cecil Field, FL., 20 NOV 75 ** Transferred to NPRO Rep. LTV, Dallas, TX., to be converted to TA-7C, 25 AUG 76 ** Re-designated to TA-7C, 03 SEP 76 ** Transferred to NATC, NAS Patuxent, River, MD., for RDT & E, 02 MAY 78, ** Re-designated to JTA-7C, 03 MAY 78 ** Re-designated to TA-7C, 01 JUL 78 ** Transferred to VA-122/FRS, NJ/206, NAS LeMoore, CA., 14 AUG 78; To VA-122, NAS Jacksonville, FL., 19 SEP 80; To VA-122, NAS LeMoore, CA., 29 OCT 80; To VA-122, NAS Jacksonville, FL., 31 MAY 85; To VA-122, NAS LeMoore, CA., 31 MAY 85; To VA-122, NAS Jacksonville, FL., 04 JUN 85; To VA-122, NAS LeMoore, CA., 02 SEP 85; To VA-122, NAS Dallas, TX., 09 SEP 85 ** VA-174/FRS, AD/2XX NAS Cecil Field, FL., 28 JUL 86 thru 17 MAR 87 ** End of flight record card.

B-052 154413 Navy acceptance from NPRO Rep. LTV, Dallas, TX., 28 APR 68 ** Transferred to VA-122/FRS, NJ/2XX, NAS LeMoore, CA., 02 JUL 68 ** Transferred to VA-215/CVW-9, NG/4XX, USS Enterprise (CVAN-65), 22 JUL 68 ** Transferred to VA-122/FRS, NJ/2XX, NAS LeMoore, CA., 11 SEP 68 ** Transferred to VA-125/FRS, NJ/5XX, NAS LeMoore, CA., 25 MAR 70 ** Transferred to VA-174/FRS, AD/2XX, NAS Cecil Field, FL., 13 APR 71 ** Transferred to VA-15/CVW-6, AE/311, NAS Cecil Field, FL., 19 JUL 72; To VA-15, MCAS Yuma, AZ., 03 JUL 74; To VA-15, NAS Cecil Field, FL., 18 SEP 74; VA-15, USS Franklin D. Roosevelt (CVA-42), 10 DEC 74; To VA-15, NAS Cecil Field, FL., 24 JUL 75 ** Transferred to VA-205/CVWR-20, AF/501, NAS Atlanta, GA., 25 SEP 75; To VA-205, NAS Jacksonville, FL., 04 MAY 82; To VA-205, NAS Atlanta, GA., 15 MAY 82 ** Transferred to MASDC, Davis Monthan AFB; Tucson, AZ., assigned park code 6A0149; 06 JUN 84 ** End of flight record card ** 5311.8 flight hours ** Engine removed on arrival ** Aircraft released from storage and prepared for overland shipment to Holloman AFB; Alamogordo, NM., to be used as a range target, 11 APR 05.

B-053 154414 Navy acceptance from NPRO Rep. LTV, Dallas, TX., 28 APR 68 ** Transferred to VA-174/FRS, NAS Cecil Field, FL., 09 JUL 68 ** Transferred to VA-15/CVW-6, AE/3XX, USS Intrepid (CVS-11), 07 APR 69; To VA-15, USS Franklin D. Roosevelt (CVA-42), 03 JUN 69 ~ S 1SO strike, 04 SEP 69 ** No data on strike.

B-054 154415 Navy acceptance from NPRO Rep. LTV, Dallas, TX., 28 APR 68 ** Transferred to VA-87/CVW-16, AH/3XX, USS Ticonderoga (CVA-14), 17 JUL 68 ** Transferred to VA-174/FRS, AD/2XX, NAS Cecil Field, FL., 20 JUL 68 ** Transferred to VA-15/CVW-6, AE/3XX, NAS Cecil Field, FL./USS Intrepid (CVS-11), 14 APR 69 ** To VA-15, USS Franklin D. Roosevelt (CVA-42), 03 JUN 69; To VA-15, NAS Cecil Field, FL.,28 SEP 71; To VA-15, NAS Jacksonville, FL., 12 AUG 74; To VA-15, NAS Cecil Field, FL., 27 SEP 74; To VA-15, USS Franklin D. Roosevelt (CVA-42), 08 OCT 74; To VA-15, NAS Cecil Field, FL., 24 JUL 75 ** Transferred to VA-205/

CVWR-20, AF/5XX, NAS Atlanta, GA., 19 SEP 75 ** Transferred to NARF, NAS Jacksonville, FL., 11 FEB 78 ** Transferred to VA-204/CVWR-20, AF/403, NAS Memphis, TN., 25 APR 78; To VA-204, NAS New Orleans, LA., 25 APR 78; To VA-204, NAS Jacksonville, FL., 03 OCT 82; To VA-204, NAS New Orleans, LA., 03 OCT 82; To VA-204 NAS Jacksonville, FL., 07 OCT 82; To VA-204, NAS New Orleans, LA., 28 JUL 83 ** Transferred to MASDC, Davis Monthan AFB; Tucson, AZ., assigned park code 6A0154; 12 JUL 84 ** End of flight record card ** 5471.1 flight hours ** Engine removed on arrival ** Aircraft deleted from inventory and released to DRMO for disposition, 21 MAR 99 ** Sold as surplus to Fritz Enterprises; Taylor, MI., delivered to HVF West's yard; Tucson, AZ., 14 AUG 99.

B-055 154416 Navy acceptance from NPRO Rep. LTV, Dallas, TX., 28 APR 68 ** Transferred to VA-174/FRS, AD/2XX, NAS Cecil Field, FL., 12 JUL 68 ** Transferred to VA-15/CVW-6, AE/3XX, USS Intrepid (CVS-11), 24 MAR 69; To VA-15, USS Franklin D. Roosevelt (CVA-42), 23 JUN 69; To VA-15, NAS Cecil Field, FL., 10 JAN 72; To VA-15, NAS Jacksonville, FL., 13 AUG 74; To VA-15; NAS Cecil Field, FL., 20 AUG 74; To VA-15, USS Franklin D. Roosevelt (CVA-42), 03 OCT 74; To VA-15, NAS Cecil Field, FL., 24 JUL 75 ** Transferred to VA-205/CVWR-20, AF/5XX, NAS Atlanta, GA., 08 APR 76; To VA-205, NAS Jacksonville, FL., 23 NOV 77; To VA-205, NAS Dallas, TX., 03 MAY 78 ** Transferred to VA-305/CVWR-30, ND/510 and ND/514, NAS Point Mugu, CA., 12 MAY 78; To VA-305, NAS Jacksonville, FL., 12 JUN 80; To VA-305, NAS Point Mugu, CA., 03 SEP 80 ** Transferred to AMARC, Davis Monthan AFB; Tucson, AZ., assigned park code 6A0186; 24 JUL 86 ~ S 3SO strike, 29 SEP 86 ** End of flight record card ** 6375.1 flight hours ** TF30P408 engine S/N 664193 ** Aircraft deleted from inventory and released to DRMO for disposition, 13 AUG 02.

B-056 154417 Navy acceptance from NPRO Rep. LTV, Dallas, TX., 28 APR 68 ** Transferred to VA-174/FRS, AD/2XX, NAS Cecil Field, FL., 25 JUL 68 ~ S 1SO strike, 25 NOV 68 ** No data on strike.

154418/154474 LTV A-7B-2-CV Corsair II; (Block II)

B-114 154418 Navy acceptance from NPRO Rep. LTV, Dallas, TX., 28 APR 68 ** Transferred to VA-122/FRS, NJ/2XX, NAS LeMoore, CA., 14 NOV 68 ~ S 1SO strike, 03 JUN 69 ** No data on strike ** Cockpit on display at the Fantasy of Flight Museum, Polk City, FL., SEP 03.

B-058 154419 Navy acceptance from NPRO Rep. LTV, Dallas, TX., 28 APR 68 ** Transferred to NATC, Service Test, NAS Patuxent River, MD., 02 AUG 68 ** Transferred to VA-122/FRS, NJ/2XX, NAS LeMoore, CA., 23 AUG 68; To VA-122, COSA, NAS Lemoore, CA., 18 JUL 69 ** Transferred to VA-125/FRS, NJ/5XX, NAS LeMoore, CA., 16 MAR 70; To VA-125, COSA, NAS LeMoore, CA., 15 JUN 71; To VA-125, CRAA, NAS LeMoore, CA., 15 JUN 71; To VA-125, NAS LeMoore, CA., 01 JAN 72 ~ S 1SO strike, 30 JAN 72 ** No data on strike.

B-059 154420 Navy acceptance from NPRO Rep. LTV, Dallas, TX., 28 APR 68 ** Transferred to VA-122/FRS, NJ/2XX, NAS LeMoore, CA., 12 AUG 68 ** Transferred to VA-215/CVW-9, NG/4XX, USS Enterprise (CVAN-65), 19 AUG 68 ** Transferred to VA-122/FRS, NJ/2XX, NAS LeMoore, CA., 15 FEB 69 ** Transferred to VA-93/CVW-2, NE/3XX, NAS LeMoore, CA., 22 JUL 69 ** Transferred to VA-155/CVW-19, NM/3XX, USS Oriskany (CVA-34), 10 DEC 69 ** Transferred to VA-113/CVW-2, NE/3XX, NAS LeMoore, CA., 17 FEB 70 ** Transferred to VA-125/FRS, NJ/5XX, NAS LeMoore, CA., 08 APR 70 ** Transferred to NARF, NAS Pensacola, FL., 13 JUL 70 ** Transferred to NARF, NAS Jacksonville, FL., 14 SEP 70 ** Transferred to VA-204/CVWR-20, AF/4XX, NAS New Orleans, LA., 19 NOV 79 ~ S 1SO strike, 12 OCT 83 ** No data on strike ** On display at NAS Fallon, NV., Airpark.

B-060 154421 Navy acceptance from NPRO Rep. LTV, Dallas, TX., 28 APR 68 ** Transferred to VA-87/CVW-16, AH/311 & 314, USS Ticonderoga (CVA-14), 24 JUL 68 ** To VA-87, NAS Cecil Field, FL., 27 MAR 69; To VA-87, USS Franklin D. Roosevelt (CVA-42), 19 JUN 70; To VA-87, NAS Cecil Field, FL., 25 FEB 72 ~ S 1SO strike, 22 OCT 73 ** No data on strike.

B-061 154422 Navy acceptance from NPRO Rep. LTV, Dallas, TX., 28 MAY 68 ** Transferred to VA-215/CVW-9, NG/4XX, USS Enterprise, (CVAN-65), 28 AUG 68; To VA-215/CVW-6, AE/4XX, USS Franklin D. Roosevelt (CVA-42), 01 JUN 69; To VA-215/CVW-19, NM/4XX, USS Oriskany (CVA-34), 17 MAY 70 ~ S 1SO strike, 22 OCT 73 ** No data on strike.

B-062 154423 Navy acceptance from NPRO Rep. LTV, Dallas, TX., 28 MAY 68 ** Transferred to VA-87/CVW-16, AH/3XX, USS Ticonderoga (CVA-14), 30 JUL 68 ** To VA-87, NAS Cecil Field, FL., 02 JUN 69 ~ S 1SO strike, 20 JUL 69 ** No data on strike.

B-063 154424 Navy acceptance from NPRO Rep. LTV, Dallas, TX., 28 MAY 68 ** Transferred to VA-87/CVW-16, AH/3XX, USS Ticonderoga (CVA-14), 27 JUL 68; To VA-87, NAS Cecil Field, FL., 03 JUN 69 ** Transferred to VA-72/CVW-1, AB/4XX, NAS Cecil field, FL., 20 FEB 70 ** Transferred to VA-174/FRS, AD/261, NAS Cecil Field, FL., 19 AUG 70 ** Transferred to NPRO Rep. LTV, Dallas, TX., to be converted to TA-7C, 08 JAN 76 ** Re-designated to TA-7C, 17 JAN 76 ** Transferred to VA-174/FRS, AD/3XX, NAS Cecil Field, FL., 26 FEB 79; To VA-174, NAS Jacksonville, FL., 12 AUG 81; To VA-174, NAS Cecil Field, FL., 06 OCT 81; To VA-174, NAS Jacksonville, FL., 09 JUL 85; To VA-174, NAS Cecil Field, FL., 09 JUL 85; To VA-174, NAS Jacksonville, FL., 10 JUL 85; To VA-174, NAS Cecil Field, FL., 04 DEC 85 thru 20 OCT 86 ** End of flight record card ** Transferred to AMARC, Davis Monthan AFB; Tucson, AZ., assigned park code 6A0400, 30 AUG 91 ** 3668.1 flight hours ** TF41A402D engine S/N AE141893 ** Prepare for overland and above deck shipment to Stellar Freight; Galveston, TX., for the government of Greece, no later than, 15 SEP 95 ** Transferred to the Helenic Air Force (Greece).

B-064 154425 Navy acceptance from NPRO Rep. LTV, Dallas, TX., 28 MAY 68 ** Transferred to NARF, NAS Jacksonville, FL., 20 AUG 68 ** Transferred to VA-87/CVW-16, AH/3XX, USS Ticonderoga (CVA-14), 03 SEP 68; To VA-87, NAS Cecil Field, FL., 01 MAY 69; To VA-87/CVW-6, AE/4XX, USS Franklin D. Roosevelt (CVA-42), 01 JUN 70; To VA-87, NAS Cecil Field, FL., 20 FEB 72; To VA-87, MCAS Yuma, AZ., 30 NOV 73; To VA-87, NAS Cecil Field, FL., 08 OCT 74; To VA-87, NAS Jacksonville, FL., 09 OCT 74; To VA-87, USS Franklin D. Roosevelt (CVA-42), 17 DEC 74; To VA-87, NAS Cecil Field, FL., 22 JUN 75 ** Transferred to VA-174/FRS, AD/2XX, NAS Cecil Field, FL., 13 AUG 75 ** Transferred to NPRO Rep. LTV, Dallas, TX. to be converted to TA-7C, 08 JAN 76 ** Re-designated to TA-7C, 09 AUG 76 ** Transferred to NAF China Lake, CA., 19 APR 78 ** Transferred to VA-122/FRS, NJ/203, NAS LeMoore, CA., 16 OCT 78; To VA-122, NAS Jacksonville, FL., 16 MAY 80 ** Transferred to NPRO Rep. LTV, Dallas, TX., 26 MAY 85 ** Transferred to VA-122/FRS, NJ/203, NAS LeMoore, CA., 13 JUL 80 ** To VA-122, NAS Jacksonville, FL., 02 OCT 85; To VA-122, NAS LeMoore, CA., 22 MAY 85 thru 12 MAR 87 ** End of flight record card ** Transferred to AMARC, Davis Monthan AFB; Tucson, AZ., assigned park code 6A0320, 21 MAR 90, with FLIR ** 5809.8 flight hours ** TF41A402D engine S.N 141407 ** Storage location 111507 ** Located at AMARG, Davis Monthan AFB; Tucson, AZ., 15 JUN 07.

B-065 154426 Navy acceptance from NPRO Rep. LTV, Dallas, TX., 28 MAY 68 ** Transferred to VA-122/FRS, NJ/2XX, NAS LeMoore, CA., 29 AUG 68 ** Transferred to VA-146/CVW-9, NG/3XX, USS Enterprise (CVAN-65), 03 SEP 68 ~ S 1SO strike, 14 JAN 69, No data on strike.

B-066 154427 Navy acceptance from NPRO Rep. LTV, Dallas, TX., 28 MAY 68 ** Transferred to VA-87/CVW-16, AH/3XX, USS Ticonderoga (CVA-14), 13 AUG 68; To VA-87, NAS Cecil Field, FL., 24 FEB 69; To VA-87, NAS Jacksonville, FL., 22 AUG 74; To VA-87/CVW-6, AE/4XX, USS Franklin D. Roosevelt (CVA-42), 22 JUN 75; To VA-87, NAS Cecil Field, FL., 24 JUL 75 ** Transferred to VA-205/CVWR-20, AF/5XX, NAS Atlanta, GA., 30 SEP 75; To VA-205, NAS Jacksonville, FL., 12 MAY 78 ~ S 1SO strike, 03 JUN 78 ** No data on strike.

B-067 154428 Navy acceptance from NPRO Rep. LTV, Dallas, TX., 28 MAY 68 ** Transferred to VA-174/FRS, AD/2XX, NAS Cecil Field, FL., 09 SEP 68 ~ S 1SO strike, 14 JAN 69, No data on strike.

B-068 154429 Navy acceptance from NPRO Rep. LTV, Dallas, TX., 28 MAY 68 ** Transferred to VA-122/FRS, NJ/2XX, NAS LeMoore, CA., 09 SEP 68 ** Transferred to VA-146/CVW-9, NG/3XX, USS Enterprise (CVAN-65), 11 SEP 68 ~ S 1SO strike, 14 JAN 69 ** No data on strike.

B-069 154430 Navy acceptance from NPRO Rep. LTV, Dallas, TX., 28 MAY 68 ** Transferred to VA-122/FRS, NJ/2XX, NAS LeMoore, CA., 10 SEP 68 ** Transferred to VA-146/CVW-9, NG/3XX, USS Enterprise (CVAN-65), 01 OCT 68; To VA-146/CVW-9, NG/3XX, USS America (CVA-66), 23 JUN 69 ** Transferred to VA-215/CVW-6, AE/4XX, USS Franklin D. Roosevelt (CVA-42), 28 JUN 69; To VA-215/CVW-19, NM/411, USS Oriskany (CVA-34), 28 APR 70 ~ S 1SO strike, 22 SEP 71 ** Due to engine failure during weapons strike, pilot ejected safely.

B-070 154431 Navy acceptance from NPRO Rep. LTV, Dallas, TX., 28 MAY 68 ** Transferred to VA-122/FRS, NJ/2XX, NAS LeMoore, CA., 28 SEP 68 ** Transferred to VA-146/CVW-9, NG/3XX, USS Enterprise (CVAN-65), 01 OCT 68; To VA-146, USS America (CVA-66), 06 JUN 69 ** Transferred to VA-174/FRS, AD/ 2XX, NAS Cecil Field, FL., 10 OCT 69 ** Transferred to VA-87/CVW-16, AH/3XX, NAS Cecil Field, FL., 25 NOV 69; To VA-87/CVW-6, AE/4XX, USS Franklin D. Roosevelt (CVA-42), 26 JUN 70; To VA-87, NAS Cecil Field, FL., 17 FEB 72; To VA-87, MCAS Yuma, AZ., 10 SEP 74; To VA-87, NAS Cecil Field, FL., 16 SEP 74; To VA-87, USS Franklin D. Roosevelt (CVA-42), 24 OCT 74; To VA-87, NAS Cecil Field, FL., 24 OCT 74; To VA-87, USS Franklin D. Roosevelt (CVA-42), 24 OCT 74; To VA-87, NAS Cecil Field, FL., 24 JUL 75 ** Transferred to VA-125/FRS, NJ/5XX, NAS LeMoore, CA., 23 SEP 75 ** Transferred to VA-303/CVWR-30, ND/304, NAS Alameda, CA., 08 SEP 77 ** Transferred to NARF, NAS Jacksonville, FL., 09 APR 78 ** Transferred to VA-303/CVWR-30, ND/304, NAS Alameda, CA., 04 FEB 79 ** Transferred to VA-305/CVWR-30, ND/510, NAS Point Mugu, CA., 14 NOV 79; To VA-305, NAS Jacksonville, FL., 19 MAR 81; To VA-305, NAS Point Mugu, CA., 21 MAY 81; To VA-305, NAS Jacksonville, FL., 26 JUN 84 ** Transferred to VA-204/CVWR-20, AF/4XX, NAS New Orleans, LA., 20 JUL 84 ** Transferred to VA-305/CVWR-30, ND/5XX, NAS Point Mugu, CA., 08 MAY 86 ** Transferred to NATTC; Millington, TN., ., sitting outside the Airframes shop, to be used as an instructional airframe, 26 JAN 87 ~ S 3SO strike, 27 JAN 87 ** End of flight record card ** On conditional loan from the National Museum of Naval Aviation, Pensacola, Fl. to the Texas Air Museum, Caprock Chapter; Slaton, TX. JAN 03.

B-071 154432 Navy acceptance from NPRO Rep. LTV, Dallas, TX., 28 MAY 68 ** Transferred to NARF, NAS Jacksonville, FL., 12 SEP 68 ** Transferred to VA-87/CVW-16, AH/3XX, USS Ticonderoga (CVA-14), 25 SEP 68; To VA-87, NAS Cecil Field, FL., 24 OCT 74; To VA-87, USS Franklin D. Roosevelt (CVA-42), 26 JAN 70 ~ S 1SO strike, 23 JUN 72 ** No data on strike.

B-072 154433 Navy acceptance from NPRO Rep. LTV, Dallas, TX., 28 MAY 68 ** Transferred to VA-122/FRS, NJ/2XX, NAS LeMoore, CA., 05 SEP 68 ** Transferred to VA-146/CVW-9, NG/3XX, USS Enterprise (CVAN-65), 06 JUN 68; To VA-146, USS America (CVA-66), 29 JUN 69 ** Transferred to VA-122/FRS, NJ/2XX, NAS LeMoore, CA., 18 AUG 69 ** Transferred to VA-125/FRS, NJ/5XX, NAS LeMoore, CA., 20 NOV 69 ** Transferred to VA-215/CVW-19, NM/4XX, USS Oriskany (CVA-34), 17 SEP 70 ** Transferred to VA-125/FRS, NJ/5XX, NAS LeMoore, CA., 08 JAN 71 ** Transferred to VA-215/CVW-19, NM/401, USS Oriskany (CVA-34), 07 APR 71; To VA-215, NAS LeMoore, CA., 24 JUN 72; To VA-215, NAS Jacksonville, FL., 28 JUN 74; To VA 215, NAS LeMoore, CA., 29 JUN 74; To VA-215, NAS Fallon, NV., 10 OCT 74; To VA-215, NAS LeMoore, CA., 09 NOV 74; To VA-215, NAS Fallon, NV., 09 NOV 74; To VA-215, NAS LeMoore, CA., 09 NOV 74; To VA-215, Fallon, NV., 09 NOV 74; To VA-215, NAS LeMoore, CA., 11 APR 75; To VA-215, USS Oriskany (CV-34), 15 JUL 75; To VA-215, NAS Alameda, CA., 11 MAR 76; To VA-215, NAS LeMoore, CA., 18 MAR 76; To VA-215, NAS Alameda, CA., 21 MAY 76; To VA-215, NAS LeMoore, CA., 22 MAY 76; To VA-215, USS Franklin D. Roosevelt (CV-42), 30 AUG 76; To VA-215, NAS LeMoore, CA., 25 MAY 77 ** Transferred to VA-303/CVWR-30, ND/305, NAS Alameda, CA., 05 AUG 77 ** Transferred to VA-205/CVWR-20, AF/5XX, NAS Atlanta, GA., 09 SEP 83 ** Transferred to VA-204/CVWR-20, AF/4XX, NAS Atlanta, GA., 08 JUN 84; To VA-204, NAS New Orleans, LA., 19 SEP 84; VA-204, NAS Jacksonville, FL., 02 MAY 85; To VA-204, NAS New Orleans, LA., 02 JUL 85 ** Transferred to VA-304/CVWR-30, ND/411, NAS Alameda, CA., 22 NOV 85 ** Transferred to AMARC, Davis Monthan AFB; Tucson, AZ., assigned park code 6A0200, 12 Sep 86 ** S 3SO strike, 29 SEP 86 ** End of flight record card ** 6464.8 flight hours ** TF30P408 Engine S/N 664435 ** Aircraft deleted from inventory and released to DRMO for disposition, 13 AUG 02 ** On conditional loan from the National Museum of Naval Aviation, Pensacola, Fl. to NAES, NAS Lakehurst, NJ., for display.

B-073 154434 Navy acceptance from NPRO Rep. LTV, Dallas, TX., 28 MAY 68 ** Transferred to NARF, NAS Jacksonville, FL., 16 SEP 68 ** Transferred to VA-87/CVW-16, AH/3XX, USS Ticonderoga (CVA-14), 04 OCT 68; To VA-87, NAS Cecil Field, FL., 14 JUN 69; To VA-87, USS Franklin D. Roosevelt (CVA-42), 08 JUN 70 ~ S 1SO strike, 19 FEB 72 ** No data on strike.

B-074 154435 Navy acceptance from NPRO Rep. LTV, Dallas, TX., 28 MAY 68 ** Transferred to VA-122/FRS, NJ/2XX, NAS LeMoore, CA., 01 OCT 68 ** Tr5ansferred to VA-25/CVW-16, AH/5XX, USS Ticonderoga (CVA-14), 11 OCT 68; To VA-25, NAS LeMoore, CA., 09 APR 69 ** Transferred to VA-155/CVW-19, NM/5XX, USS Oriskany (CVA-34), 01 OCT 69 ** Transferred to NARF, NAS Alameda, CA., 08 MAY 70 ** Transferred to VA-174/FRS, AD/2XX, NAS Cecil Field, FL., 07 APR 72 ** Transferred to VA-87/CVW-6, AE/4XX, NAS LeMoore, CA., 10 JUL 72 ~ S 1SO strike, 25 JUL 72 ** No data on strike.

B-075 154436 Navy acceptance from NPRO Rep. LTV, Dallas, TX., 28 MAY 68 ** Transferred to VA-122/FRS, NJ/2XX, NAS LeMoore, CA., 29 OCT 68 ** Transferred to VA-25/CVW-16, USS Ticonderoga (CVA-14), 30 OCT 68; To VA-25, NAS LeMoore, CA., 29 MAY 69 ** Transferred to VA-125/FRS, NJ/5XX, NAS LeMoore, CA., 25 SEP 69 ** VA-155/CVW-19, NM/500, USS Oriskany (CVA-34), 01 OCT 69; To VA-155, NAS LeMoore, CA., 04 JUN 72 ~ S 1SO strike, 24 SEP 72 ** Combat Loss.

B-076 154437 Navy acceptance from NPRO Rep. LTV, Dallas, TX., 28 MAY 68 ** Transferred to VA-174/FRS, AD/2XX, NAS Cecil Field, FL., 10 OCT 68 ** Transferred to VA-46/CVW-1, AB/3XX, USS John F. Kennedy (CVA-67), 21 JUN 71; To VA-46, NAS Cecil Field, FL., 04 DEC 72 ** Transferred to VA-87/CVW-6, AE/4XX, NAS Cecil Field, FL., 18 NOV 73; To VA-87, MCAS Yuma, AZ., 21 MAY 74; To VA-87, NAS Cecil Field, FL., 24 OCT 74; To VA-87, USS Franklin D. Roosevelt (CVA-42), 26 OCT 74; To VA-87, NAS Cecil Field, FL., 26 OCT 74; To VA-87, USS Franklin D. Roosevelt (CVA-42), 26 OCT 74; To VA-87, NAS Cecil Field, FL., 01 AUG 75; To VA-87, USS Saratoga (CV-60), 15 SEP 75; To VA-87, NAS Cecil Field, FL., 15 SEP 75; To VA-87, USS America (CV-66), 15 SEP 75 ** Transferred to NPRO Rep. LTV, Dallas, TX. to be converted to TA-7C, 24 SEP 75 ** Re-designated to TA-7C, 03

OCT 75 ** Transferred to VA-174/FRS, AD/3XX, NAS Cecil Field, FL., 14 DEC 78; To VA-174, NAS Jacksonville, FL., 11 MAR 81; To VA-174, NAS Cecil Field, FL., 10 APR 81; To VA-174, Jacksonville, FL., 13 APR 81; To VA-174, NAS Cecil Field, FL., 22 JUN 81 ~ S 1SO strike, 24 AUG 82 ** No data on strike.

B-077 154438 Navy acceptance from NPRO Rep. LTV, Dallas, TX., 27 JUN 68 ** Transferred to VA-174/FRS, AD/2XX, NAS Cecil Field, FL., 05 NOV 68 ** Transferred to VA-46/CVW-3, AC/307, NAS Cecil Field, FL., 21 NOV 68, This aircraft had a barricade engagement on board the USS Saratoga (CVA-60) in 69, aircraft was repaired; To VA-46/CVW-1, AB/301, USS John F. Kennedy (CVA-67), 19 APR 71; To VA-46, NAS Cecil Field, FL., 08 DEC 72; To VA-46, USS John F. Kennedy (CVA-67), 06 NOV 74; To VA-46, NAS Cecil Field, FL., 06 NOV 74; To VA-46, USS John F. Kennedy (CVA-67), 06 NOV 74; To VA-46, NAS Cecil Field, FL., 06 NOV 74; To VA-46, USS John F. Kennedy (CVA-67), 06 NOV 74; To VA-46, NAS Cecil Field, FL., 01 JUL 75; To VA-46, USS John F. Kennedy (CVA-67), 01 JUL 75; To VA-46, NAS Cecil Field, FL., 01 JUL 75; To VA-46, USS John F. Kennedy (CVA-67), 19 DEC 76; To VA-46, NAS Cecil Field, FL., 01 MAY 77; To VA-204/CVWR-20, AF/4XX, NAS Memphis, TN., 24 AUG 77; To VA-204, NAS Jacksonville, FL., 07 SEP 77 ** Transferred to VA-303/CVWR-30, ND/301, NAS Alameda, CA., 05 NOV 77, Blue tail with outstretched Golden Hawk; To VA-303, NAS Dallas, TX., 01 JUN 78; To VA-303, NAS Alameda, CA., 01 MAY 80; To VA-303, NAS Jacksonville, FL., 04 AUG 81; To VA-303, NAS Alameda, CA., 25 AUG 8 ** Transferred to VA-204/CVWR-20, AF/405, NAS New Orleans, LA., 10 SEP 83 ** Transferred to AMARC, Davis Monthan AFB; Tucson, AZ., assigned park code 6A0174, 19 JUN 86 ~ S 3SO strike, 29 SEP 86 ** End of flight record card ** 6966.3 flight hours ** TF30P408 engine S/N 664360 ** Aircraft deleted from inventory and released to DRMO for disposition, 13 AUG 02.

B-078 154439 Navy acceptance from NPRO Rep. LTV, Dallas, TX., 27 JUN 68 ** Transferred to VA-174/FRS, AD/2XX, NAS Cecil Field, FL., 25 NOV 68 ** Transferred to NARF, NAS Jacksonville, FL., 20 JUN 72 ** Transferred to VA-305/ CVWR-30 ND/507, NAS Point Mugu, CA., 18 APR 78, Green contrail on tail; To VA-305, NAS Dallas, TX., 04 MAY 78; To VA-305, NAS Point Mugu, CA., 17 MAY 78; To VA-305, NAS Jacksonville, FL., 28 SEP 81; To VA-305, NAS Point Mugu, CA., 20 NOV 81 ** Transferred to AMARC, Davis Monthan AFB; Tucson, AZ., assigned park code 6A0165, 29 MAY 86 ** End of flight record card ** 4303.7 flight hours ** TF30P408 engine S/N P664404 ** Aircraft deleted from inventory and released to DRMO for disposition, 13 AUG 02.

B-079 154440 Navy acceptance from NPRO Rep. LTV, Dallas, TX., 27 JUN 68 ** Transferred to NARF, NAS Jacksonville, FL., 23 SEP 68 ** Transferred to VA-87/CVW-16, AH/3XX, USS Ticonderoga (CVA-14), 11 OCT 68; To VA-87, NAS Cecil Field, FL., 08 MAY 69; To VA-87/CVW-6, AE/4XX, USS Franklin D. Roosevelt (CVA-42), 08 JUN 70; To VA-87, NAS Cecil Field, FL., 06 JAN 72; To VA-87, NAS Jacksonville, FL., 15 AUG 74; To VA-87, NAS Cecil Field, FL., 19 AUG 74; To VA-87, USS Franklin D. Roosevelt (CVA-42), 24 OCT 74; To VA-87, NAS Cecil Field, FL., 24 OCT 74; To VA-87, USS Franklin D. Roosevelt (CVA-42), 24 OCT 74; To VA-87, NAS Cecil Field, FL., 22 JUN 75 ** Transferred to VA-205/CVWR-20, AF/5XX, NAS Atlanta, GA., 20 SEP 75; To VA-205, NAS Jacksonville, FL., 29 NOV 77; To VA-205, NAS Dallas, TX., 25 APR 78 ** Transferred to VA-305/CVWR-30, ND/506, NAS Point Mugu, CA., 03 MAY 78 ** Transferred to VA-204/ CVWR-20, AF/415, NAS New Orleans, LA., 01 MAY 80; To VA-204, NAS Jacksonville, FL., 15 AUG 80; To VA-204, NAS New Orleans, LA., 22 SEP 80; To VA-204, NAS Jacksonville, FL., 05MAY 82; To VA-204, NAS New Orleans, LA., 05 MAY 82; To VA-204, NAS Jacksonville, FL., 11 MAY 82; To VA-204, NAS New Orleans, LA., 25 AUG 82; To VA-204, NAS Jacksonville, FL., 08 SEP 82; To VA-204, NAS New Orleans, LA., 18 SEP 82 ** Transferred to MASDC, Davis Monthan AFB; Tucson, AZ., assigned park code 6A0155, 20 Jul 84 ** End of flight record card ** 4958.0 flight hours ** Engine removed on arrival **Transferred to the Navy Test Site; Mercury, NV., 11 MAR 02.

B-080 154441 Navy acceptance from NPRO Rep. LTV, Dallas, TX., 27 JUN 68 ** Transferred to VA-122/FRS, NJ/2XX, NAS LeMoore, CA., 27 SEP 68 ** Transferred to VA-25/CVW-16, AH/5XX, USS Ticonderoga (CVA-14), 14 OCT 68 ~ S 1SO strike, 13 MAY 69 ** Pilot ejected and was rescued after a tanker accident off the coast of NVN.

B-081 154442 Navy acceptance from NPRO Rep. LTV, Dallas, TX., 27 JUN 68 ** Transferred to VA-122/FRS, NJ/2XX, NAS LeMoore, CA., 01 OCT 68 ** Transferred to VA-25/CVW-16, AH/5XX, USS Ticonderoga (CVA-14), 22 OCT 68; To VA-25, NAS LeMoore, CA., 24 MAY 69 ** Transferred to VA-125/FRS, NJ/5XX, NAS LeMoore, CA., 03 OCT 69 ** Transferred to VA-93/CVW-5, NF/3XX, NAS LeMoore, CA., 07 NOV 72 ** Transferred to VA-153/CVW-19, NM/3XX, NAS LeMoore, CA., 25 APR 73 ** Transferred to VA-125/FRS, NJ/5XX, NAS LeMoore, CA., 10 OCT 73 ** Transferred to VA-153/CVW-19, NM/310, NAS LeMoore, CA., 11 MAR 74; To VA-153, USS Oriskany (CVA-34), 04 JUN 74; To VA-153, NAS LeMoore, CA., 04 JUN 74; To VA-153, USS Oriskany (CVA-34), 04 JUN 74; To VA-153, NAS LeMoore, CA., 28 AUG 74; To VA-153, NAS Fallon, NV., 17 DEC 74; To VA-153, NAS LeMoore, CA., 11 APR 75; To VA-153, USS Oriskany (CVA-34), 30 JUN 75 ~ S 1SO strike, 20 JAN 76 ** Aircraft broke up and went over the side on a ramp strike, pilot ejected.

B-082 154443 Navy acceptance from NPRO Rep. LTV, Dallas, TX., 27 JUN 68 ** Transferred to VA-122/FRS, NJ/2XX, NAS LeMoore, CA., 01 OCT 68 ** Transferred to VA-25/CVW-16, AH/5XX, USS Ticonderoga (CVA-14), 11 OCT 68 ** Transferred to VA-125/FRS, NJ/ 5XX, NAS LeMoore, CA., 03 OCT 69, ** Transferred to VA-215/CVW-19, NM/4XX, USS Oriskany (CVA-34), 22 SEP 70 ** Transferred to VA-125/FRS, NJ/5XX, 04 JAN 71** Transferred to VA-93/CVW-5, NF/3XX, NAS LeMoore, CA., 17 NOV 72 ** Transferred to VA-125/ FRS, NJ/5XX, 21 MAY 73; To VA-125, USS Ranger (CV-61), 17 APR 74 ** Transferred to VA-203/CVWR-20, AF/3XX, NAS Jacksonville, FL., 09 APR 78; To VA-125, NAS LeMoore, CA., 17 APR 74 ** Transferred to VA-203/CVWR-20, AF/3XX, NAS Jacksonville, FL., 11 AUG 77 ** Transferred to VA-204/CVWR-20, AF/406, NAS Memphis, TN., 23 MAY 78; To VA-204, NAS New Orleans, LA., 25 MAY 78; To VA-204, NAS Jacksonville, FL., 10 SEP 81; VA-204, NAS New Orleans, LA., 24 NOV 8 ** Transferred to NATTC, NAS Lakehurst, NJ., 01 AUG 84 ~ S 3SO strike, 02 AUG 84 ** On conditional loan from the National Museum of Naval Aviation; Pensacola, Fl. to NAWC Lakehurst, NJ.

B-083 154444 Navy acceptance from NPRO Rep. LTV, Dallas, TX., 27 JUN 68 ** Transferred to VA-122/FRS, NJ/2XX, NAS LeMoore, CA., 19 SEP 68 ** Transferred to VA-146/CVW-9, NG/3XX, USS Enterprise (CVAN-65), 24 SEP 68 ~ S 1SO strike, 14 JAN 69 ** No data on strike.

B-084 154445 Navy acceptance from NPRO Rep. LTV, Dallas, TX., 27 JUN 68 ** Transferred to VA-122/FRS, NJ/2XX, NAS LeMoore, CA., 25 SEP 68 ** Transferred to VA-25/CVW-16, AH/5XX, USS Ticonderoga (CVA-14), 14 OCT 68 ** Transferred to VA-25/CVW-16, AH/5XX, NAS LeMoore, CA., 26 JUN 69 ** Transferred to VA-125/FRS, NJ/5XX, NAS LeMoore, CA., 28 NOV 69 ** Transferred to VA-215/CVW-19, NM/4XX, USS Oriskany (CVA-34), 21 SEP 70 ** Transferred to VA-125/FRS, NJ/5XX, NAS LeMoore, CA., 18 JAN 71 ** Transferred to VA-56/CVW-5, NF/4XX, NAS LeMoore, CA., 03 AUG 72 ** Transferred to VA-155/CVW-19, NM/5XX, NAS LeMoore, CA./USS Oriskany (CV-34), 17 SEP 75 ** VA-155/ CVW-19, NM/5XX, NAS LeMoore, CA., 16 MAY 73; To VA-155, NAS Jacksonville, FL., 17 JUN 74; To VA-155, NAS LeMoore, CA., 31 JUL 74; To VA-155, NAS Fallon, NV., 09 NOV 74; To VA-155, NAS LeMoore, CA., 30 JAN 75; To VA-155, NAS Fallon, NV., 04 MAR 75; To VA-155, NAS LeMoore, CA., 11 APR 75; To VA-155, USS Oriskany (CVA-34), 01 JUL 75; To VA-155, NAS LeMoore, CA., 12 SEP 75; To VA-155, NAS Alameda, CA., 26 MAY 76; To VA-155, NAS LeMoore, CA., 04 JUN 76; To VA-155, NAS Alameda, CA., 14 JUN 76; To VA-

155, NAS LeMoore, CA., 25 JUN 76; To VA-155, USS Franklin D. Roosevelt (CV-42), 15 OCT 76; To VA-155, NAS LeMoore, CA., 10 JUL 77 ** Transferred to VA-304/CVWR-30, ND/400 & ND/404, NAS Alameda, CA., 16 JUL 77; To VA-304, NAS Jacksonville, FL., 06 AUG 81; To VA-304, NAS Alameda, CA., 06 AUG 81 ~ 1SO strike, 27 MAR 86 ** No data on strike.

B-085 154446 Navy acceptance from NPRO Rep. LTV, Dallas, TX., 27 JUN 68 ** Transferred to VA-122/FRS, NJ/2XX, NAS LeMoore, CA., 01 AUG 68 ** Transferred to VA-215/CVW-9, NG/4XX, USS Enterprise (CVAN-65), 02 AUG 68 ~ S 1SO strike, 14 JAN 69 ** No data on strike.

B-086 154447 Navy acceptance from NPRO Rep. LTV, Dallas, TX., 27 JUN 68 ** Transferred to VA-122/FRS, NJ/2XX, NAS LeMoore, CA., 13 AUG 68 ** Transferred to VA-215/CVW-9, NG/4XX, USS Enterprise (CVAN-65), 14 AUG 68; To VA-215/CVW-6, AE/4XX, USS Franklin D. Roosevelt (CVA-42), 20 JUN 69; To VA-215/CVW-19, NM/4XX, USS Oriskany (CVA-34), 22 JUN 70 ~ S 1SO strike, 18 NOV 70 ** No data on strike.

B-087 154448 Navy acceptance from NPRO Rep. LTV, Dallas, TX., 27 JUN 68 ** Transferred to VA-122/FRS, NJ/2XX, NAS LeMoore, CA., 14 AUG 68 ** Transferred to VA-215/CVW-9, NG/4XX, USS Enterprise (CVAN-65), 29 AUG 68; To VA-215/CVW-6, AE/4XX, NAS Franklin D. Roosevelt (CVA-42), 12 APR 69; To VA-215/CVW-19, NM/4XX, USS Oriskany (CVA-34), 09 SEP 70; To VA-215, NAS LeMoore, CA., 22 JUN 72 ** Transferred to VA-125/FRS, NJ/5XX, NAS LeMoore, CA., 19 JUL 73 ** Transferred to VA-153/CVW-19, NG/ 4XX, NAS LeMoore, CA., 23 JUL 74; To VA-153/CVW-19, NM/3XX,USS Oriskany (CV-34), 30 JUN 75; To VA-153, NAF Atsugi, JP., 19 DEC 75; To VA-153, USS Oriskany (CV-34), 29 JAN 76; To VA-153, NAS LeMoore, CA., 03 FEB 76; To VA-153, USS Franklin D. Roosevelt (CV-42), 20 APR 77; To VA-153, NAS LeMoore, CA., 20 APR 77 ** Transferred to VA-303/CVWR-30, ND/3XX, NAS Alameda, CA., 30 JUN 77; To VA-303, NAS Jacksonville, FL., 06 JUL 77; To VA-303, NAS Alameda, CA., 07 SEP 77 ** Transferred to VA-204/CVWR-20, AF/401and AF/406, NAS New Orleans, LA.., 26 MAR 78; To VA-204, NAS Jacksonville, FL., 08 MAY 81; To VA-204, NAS New Orleans, LA., 19 OCT 81 ** Transferred to MASDC, Davis Monthan AFB; Tucson, AZ., assigned park code 6A0143, 07 OCT 83 ** End of flight record card ** 5522.7 flight hours ** Engine removed on arrival ** Aircraft released from storage and prepared for overland shipment to Holloman AFB; Alamogordo, NM., to be used as a range target, 11 APR 05.

B-088 154449 Navy acceptance from NPRO Rep. LTV, Dallas, TX., 27 JUN 68 ** Transferred to VA-122/FRS, NJ/2XX, NAS LeMoore, CA., 21 AUG 68 ** Transferred to VA-215/CVW-9, NG/4XX, USS Enterprise (CVAN-65), 31 APR 69 ** To VA-215/CVW-6, AE/4XX, NAS Franklin D. Roosevelt (CVA-42), 31 MAY 69; To VA-215/CVW-19, NM/413, USS Oriskany (CVA-34), 26 MAY 70; To VA-215, NAS LeMoore, CA., 07 JUN 72 ** Transferred to VA-155/CVW-19, NM/5XX, NAS LeMoore, CA., 19 NOV 75; To VA-155/USS Oriskany (CV-42), 04 JUN 74; To VA-155, NAS LeMoore, CA., 04 JUN 74; To VA-155, NAS Fallon, NV., 09 NOV 74; To VA-155, NAS Jacksonville, FL., 26 JAN 75; To VA-155, NAS Fallon, NV., 09 NOV 74; To VA-155, NAS LeMoore, CA., 11 APR 75; To VA-155, USS Oriskany (CV-34), 15 JUL 75; To VA-155, NAS LeMoore, CA., 15 JUL 75; To VA-155, USS Franklin D. Roosevelt (CV-42), 15 OCT 76; To VA-155, NAS LeMoore, CA., 18 MAY 77 ** Transferred to VA-303/CVWR-30, ND/3XX, NAS Alameda, CA., 13 JUL 77 ** Transferred to NARF, NAS Jacksonville, FL., 27 APR 78 ** Transferred to VA-305/CVWR-30, ND/505, NAS Point Mugu, CA.,17 NOV 78; To VA-305, NAS Jacksonville, FL., 16 MAR 83; To VA-305, NAS Point Mugu, CA., 12 NOV 83 thru 26 JAN 87 ** End of flight record card ** Being restored next to Blackbird Air Park; Palmdale, CA., OCT 02.

B-089 154450 Navy acceptance from NPRO Rep. LTV, Dallas, TX., 27 JUN 68 ** Transferred to VA-87/CVW-16, AH/3XX, USS Ticonderoga (CVA-14), 28 JUL 68; To VA-87, NAS Cecil Field, 26 JUN 69 ** Transferred to VA-174/FRS, AD/2XX, NAS Cecil Field, FL., 01 SEP 70 ** Transferred to VA-72/CVW-1, AB/4XX, USS John F. Kennedy (CVA-67), 16 JUL 72 ** Transferred to VA-174/FRS, AD/2XX, NAS Cecil Field, FL., 26 OCT 72 ** Transferred to VA-15/CVW-6, AE/306, NAS Cecil Field, FL., 29 MAY 74; To VA-15, MCAS Yuma, AZ., 29 MAY 74; To VA-15, NAS Cecil Field, FL., 07 OCT 74; To VA-15, USS Franklin D. Roosevelt (CVA-42), 16 OCT 74; To VA-15, NAS Cecil Field, FL., 24 JUL 75 ** Transferred to VA-174/FRS, AD/2XX, NAS Cecil Field, FL., 27 AUG 75 ** Transferred to NPRO Rep. LTV, Dallas, TX., to be converted to TA-7C, 27 MAR 76 ** Re-designated to TA-7C, 05 APR 76 ** Transferred to VA-174/FRS, AD/3XX, NAS Cecil Field, FL., 06 AUG 78; To VA-174, NAS Jacksonville, FL., 14 DEC 80; To VA-174, NAS Cecil Field, FL., 23 JAN 81; To VA-174, NAS Jacksonville, FL., 16 NOV 82; To VA-174, NAS Cecil Field, FL., 25 FEB 83; To VA-174, NAS Jacksonville, FL., 16 MAR 83; To VA-174, NAS Cecil Field, FL., 12 OCT 83 ~ S 1SO strike, 29 NOV 84 ** Crashed into the ocean on a bomb run near the Pinecastle Range, McCoy AFB; Orlando, FL., both pilots ejected safely.

B-090 154451 Navy acceptance from NPRO Rep. LTV, Dallas, TX., 27 JUN 68 ** Transferred to VA-122/FRS, NJ/2XX, NAS LeMoore, CA., 02 AUG 68 ** Transferred to VA-215/CVW-9, NG/4XX, USS Enterprise (CVAN-65), 03 AUG 68; To VA-215/CVW-6, AE/4XX, USS Franklin D. Roosevelt (CVA-42), 28 MAY 69; To VA-215/CVW-19, NM/4XX, USS Oriskany (CVA-34), 26 APR 70 ** Transferred to VA-155/CVW-19, NM/507, USS Oriskany (CVA-34), 27 JAN 71; To VA-155, NAS LeMoore, CA., 28 JUN 72 ** Transferred to VA-125/FRS, NJ/5XX, NAS LeMoore, CA., 31 MAY 73 ** Transferred to VA-174/FRS, AD/2XX, NAS Cecil Field, FL., 18 DEC 73 ** Transferred to VA-72/CVW-1, AB/4XX, NAS Cecil Field, FL., 01 AUG 74; To VA-72, USS John F. Kennedy (CV-67), 09 DEC 74; To VA-72, NAS Cecil Field, FL., 09 DEC 74; To VA-72, USS John F. Kennedy, (CV-67), 01 JUL 75; To VA-72, NAS Cecil Field, FL., 23 MAR 76; To VA-72, NAS Jacksonville, FL., 14 JUN 76; To VA-72, USS John F. Kennedy (CV-67), 26 JUN 76; To VA-72, NAS Cecil Field, FL., 26 JUN 76; To VA-72, USS John F. Kennedy (CV-67), 26 JUN 76; To VA-72, NAS Cecil Field, FL., 26 JUN 76; To VA-72, USS John F. Kennedy (CV-67), 21 DEC 76; To VA-72, NAS Cecil Field, FL., 17 JUL 77 ** Transferred to VA-203/CVWR-20, AF/303, NAS Jacksonville, FL., 18 AUG 77, NAS ** Transferred to MASDC, Davis Monthan AFB; Tucson, AZ., assigned park code 6A0127, 07 JUL 83 Thru 08 JUL 83 ** End of flight record card ** 4824.0 flight hours ** Engine removed on arrival ** Aircraft deleted from inventory and released to DRMO for Disposition, 21 MAR 99.

B-091 154452 Navy acceptance from NPRO Rep. LTV, Dallas, TX., 27 JUN 68 ** Transferred to VA-87/CVW-16, AH/3XX, USS Ticonderoga (CVA-14), 28 JUL 68; To VA-87, NAS Cecil Field, FL., 30 JUN 69; To VA-87, USS Franklin D. Roosevelt (CVA-42), 12 MAY 70; To VA-87, NAS Cecil Field, FL., 28 DEC 71; To VA-87, MCAS Yuma, AZ., 09 SEP 74; To VA-87, NAS Cecil Field, FL., 02 OCT 74; To VA-87, NAS Jacksonville, FL., 21 OCT 74; To VA-87, NAS Cecil Field, FL., 24 OCT 74; To VA-87, USS Franklin D. Roosevelt (CVA-42), 23 DEC 74 ** Transferred to VA-174/FRS, AD/220, NAS Cecil Field, FL. 24 DEC 74 ** Transferred to VA-203/CVWR-20, AF/306, NAS Jacksonville, FL., 19 AUG 7 ** Transferred to VA-205/CVWR-20, AF/5XX, NAS Atlanta, GA., 02 JUN 83 ** Transferred to MASDC, Davis Monthan AFB; Tucson, AZ., assigned park code 6A0136, 13 SEP 83 ** End of flight record card ** 4865.2 flight hours ** Engine removed on arrival ** Aircraft released from storage and prepared for overland shipment to Holloman AFB; Alamogordo, NM., to be used as a range target, 11 APR 05.

B-092 154453 Navy acceptance from NPRO Rep. LTV, Dallas, TX., 27 JUN 68 ** Transferred to VA-122/FRS, NJ/2XX, NAS LeMoore, CA., 01 AUG 68 ** Transferred to VA-146/CVW-9, NG/3XX, USS Enterprise (CVAN-65), 07 AUG 68; To VA-146, USS America (CVA-66), 08 JUN 69 ** Transferred to VA-174/FRS, AD/2XX, NAS Cecil Field, FL., 22

DEC 69 ** Transferred to VA-72/CVW-1, AB/4XX, NAS Cecil Field, FL., 21 JAN 70; To VA-72, USS John F. Kennedy (CVA-67), 08 JUN 71; To VA-72 NAS Cecil Field, FL., 08 NOV 72; To VA-72, USS John F. Kennedy (CVA-67), 07 MAY 74; To VA-72, NAS Jacksonville, FL., 11 MAR 75; To VA-72, NAS Cecil Field, FL., 27 APR 75; To VA-72, USS John F. Kennedy (CVA-67), 30 JUN 75; To VA-72 NAS Cecil Field, FL., 30 JUN 75; To VA-72, USS John F. Kennedy (CV-67), 30 JUN 75; To VA-72 NAS Cecil Field, FL., 30 JUN 75; To VA-72, USS John F. Kennedy (CVA-67), 30 JUN 75; To VA-72 NAS Cecil Field, FL., 17 JUL 77 ** Transferred to VA-204/CVWR-20, AF/4XX, NAS Memphis, TN., 16 SEP 77 ** Transferred to VA-305/CVWR-30, ND/504, NAS Point Mugu, CA., 16 APR 78; To VA-305, NAS Dallas, TX., 29 MAY 78; To VA-305, NAS Point Mugu, CA., 29 AUG 78; To VA-305, NAS Alameda, CA., 01 MAY 81; To VA-305, NAS Point Mugu, CA., 01 MAY 81; To VA-305, NAS Jacksonville, FL., 23 JUL 81; To VA-305, NAS Point Mugu, CA., 23 JUL 81; To VA-305, NAS Jacksonville, FL., 30 SEP 81; To VA-305, NAS Point Mugu, CA., 13 NOV 82 ** Transferred to AMARC, Davis Monthan AFB; Tucson, AZ., assigned park code 6A0163, 15 MAY 86 ** End of flight record card ** At AMARC, Davis Monthan AFB; Tucson, AZ., 31 DEC 97 ** 6952.7 flight hours ** TF30P408 engine S/N 664401 ** Aircraft deleted from inventory and released to DRMO for disposition, 13 AUG 02.

B-093 154454 Navy acceptance from NPRO Rep. LTV, Dallas, TX., 26 JUL 68 ** Transferred to VA-122/FRS, NJ/2XX, NAS LeMoore, CA., 28 AUG 68 ** Transferred to VA-215/CVW-9, NG/4XX, USS Enterprise (CVAN-65), 29 AUG 68; To VA-215/CVW-6, AE/4XX, USS Franklin D. Roosevelt (CVA-42), 29 JUN 69; To VA-215/CVW-19, NM/410, CA., USS Oriskany (CVA-34), 20 APR 70; To VA-215, NAS LeMoore, CA.,, 04 JUN 72 ** Transferred to VA-125/FRS, NJ/5XX, NAS LeMoore, CA., 20 AUG 73; To VA-125, NAS Alameda, CA., 23 AUG 76; To VA-125, NAS LeMoore, CA., 03 SEP 76; To VA-125, NAS Alameda, CA., 20 MAY 77; To VA-125, NAS LeMoore, CA., 20 JUL 77 ** Transferred to VA-204/CVWR-20, AF/4XX, NAS Memphis, TN., 29 JUL 77; To VA-204, NAS Dallas, TX., 30 SEP 77; To VA-204, NAS Jacksonville, FL., 07 NOV 77 ** Transferred to VA-304/CVWR-30, ND/411, NAS Alameda, CA., 14 MAR 78; To VA-304, NAS Jacksonville, FL., 18 OCT 82; To VA-304, NAS Alameda, CA., 22 OCT 82 **Transferred to AMARC, Davis Monthan AFB; Tucson, AZ., assigned park code 6A0203; 19 SEP 86 ** End of flight record card ** 6403.9 flight hours ** TF30P408 engine S/N 664384 ** Aircraft deleted from inventory and released to DRMO for disposition, 13 AUG 02.

B-094 154455 Navy acceptance from NPRO Rep. LTV, Dallas, TX., 26 JUL 68 ** Transferred to VA-122/ FRS, NJ/2XX, NAS LeMoore, CA., 29 JUL 68 ** Transferred to VA-215/CVW-9, NG/4XX, USS Enterprise (CVAN-65), 30 JUL 68; To VA-215/CVW-6, AE/4XX, USS Franklin D. Roosevelt (CVA-42), 30 MAY 69; To VA-215,NAS LeMoore, CA., 28 MAY 70 ** Transferred to VA-125/FRS, NJ/5XX, NAS LeMoore, CA., 16 JUN 70; To VA-125, COSA, NAS LeMoore, CA., 15 JUN 71; To VA-125, CRAA, NAS LeMoore, CA., 29 JUN 71; To VA-125, NAS LeMoore, CA., 22 SEP 71 ** Transferred to VA-174/ FRS, AD/221, NAS Cecil Field, FL., 01 NOV 73; To VA-174, NAS Jacksonville, FL., 30 JUN 74; To VA-174, NAS Cecil Field, FL., 20 AUG 74 ** Transferred to NPRO Rep. LTV, Dallas, TX. to be converted to TA-7C, 04 SEP 76 ** Re-designated to TA-7C, 04 SEP 76 ** Transferred to VA-122/FRS, NJ/204, NAS LeMoore, CA., 15 OCT 78; To NAS Jacksonville, FL., 02 JAN 85; To VA-122, NAS LeMoore, CA., 18 JUN 85; To VA-122, NAS Dallas, TX., 21 APR 86; To VA-122, NAS LeMoore, CA. 22 APR 86 thru 28 FEB 87 ** End of flight record card ** Transferred to AMARC, Davis Monthan AFB; Tucson, AZ., assigned park code 6A0321; 21 MAR 90, with FLIR ** 5,697.4 flight hours ** TF41A402D engine S/N 141443 ** Storage location 111210 ** Transferred to FMS, 06 APR 04 ** Located at AMARG, Davis Monthan AFB; Tucson, AZ., 15 JUN 07.

B-095 154456 Navy acceptance from NPRO Rep. LTV, Dallas, TX., 26 JUL 68 ** Transferred to VA-122/FRS, NJ/2XX, NAS LeMoore, CA., 03 AUG 68 ** Transferred to VA-215/CVW-9, NG/4XX, USS Enterprise (CVAN-65), 05 AUG 68; To VA-215/CVW-6, AE/4XX, USS Franklin D. Roosevelt (CVA-42), 04 JUN 69; To VA-215/CVW-

19, NM/405, USS Oriskany (CVA-34), 03 JUN 70 ** To VA-215, NAS LeMoore, CA., 04 JUN 72 ** Transferred to VA-125/FRS, NJ/5XX, NAS LeMoore, CA., 19 JUL 73 ** Transferred to VA-155/CVW-19, NM/ 5XX, NAS LeMoore, CA., 03 JUL 74; To VA-155, NAS Fallon, NV., 09 NOV 74; To VA-155, NAS LeMoore, CA., 11 FEB 75; To VA-155, NAS Fallon, NV., 13 FEB 75; To VA-155, NAS LeMoore, CA., 13 FEB 75; To VA-155, NAS Fallon, NV., 31 MAR 75; To VA-155, NAS LeMoore, CA., 11 APR 75; To VA-155, USS Oriskany (CV-34), 15 JUL 75; To VA-155, NAS LeMoore, CA., 31 MAR 76; To VA-155, USS Franklin D. Roosevelt (CV-42), 10 AUG 76 ** Transferred to VA-125/FRS, NJ/5XX, NAS LeMoore, CA., 20 MAY 77 ** Transferred to VA-304/ CVWR-30, ND/405, NAS Dallas, TX., 30 MAY 78; To VA-304, NAS Alameda, CA., 24 JUN 78 ** Transferred to NATTC Millington , TN., ., sitting outside the Airframes shop, to be used as an instructional airframe, , 28 AUG 86 ~ S 3SO strike, 29 AUG 86 ** End of flight record card ** Transferred to AMARC, Davis Montham AFB; Tucson, AZ., date unknown ** Sold to private party for $20,000.00 at auction, plus $3500.00 shipping, from DRMO Davis Monthan AFB; Tucson, AZ., 11 NOV 96 ** For sale on E-Bay for $17,500.00, auction number 120215142574, ending 31 JAN 08; Wings are with the aircraft but have been cut off at the fuselage; missing tail, horizontal stabilizers, engine and canopy, located in Rosamond, CA. ** For sale on E-Bay Stores, (Buy it Now), 12 FEB 08, for $19,000.00, auction number 120218533038, end date unknown.

B-096 154457 Navy acceptance from NPRO Rep. LTV, Dallas, TX., 26 JUL 68 ** Transferred to VA-122, NJ/2XX, NAS LeMoore, CA., 22 AUG 68 ** Transferred to VA-215/CVW-9, NG/4XX, USS Enterprise (CVAN-65), 23 AUG 68 ~ S 1SO strike, 14 JAN 69 ** No data on strike.

B-097 154458 Navy acceptance from NPRO Rep. LTV, Dallas, TX., 26 JUL 68 ** Transferred to VA-122/FRS, NJ/2XX, NAS LeMoore, CA., 16 AUG 68 ** Transferred to VA-146/CVW-9, NG/3XX, USS Enterprise (CVAN-65), 21 AUG 68; To VA-146, USS America (CVA-66), 06 JUN 69 ** Transferred to VA-122/FRS, NJ/2XX, NAS LeMoore, CA., 14 AUG 69 ** Transferred to VA-125/FRS, NJ/5XX, NAS LeMoore, CA., 22 APR 70 ** Transferred to VA-215/CVW-19, NM/406, USS Oriskany (CVA-34), 28 DEC 70; To VA-215, NAS LeMoore, CA., 11 JUN 72 ** Transferred to VA-125/FRS, NJ/5XX, NAS LeMoore, CA., 10 OCT 73; To VA-125, USS Ranger (CV-61), 19 APR 74; To VA-125, NAS LeMoore, CA., 19 APR 74 ** Transferred to NPRO Rep. LTV, Dallas, TX. to be converted to TA-7C, 24 AUG 76 ** Re-designated to TA-7C, 02 SEP 76 ** Transferred to VX-5, XE/07, NAF China Lake, CA., 25 APR 78; To VX-5, NAS Alameda, CA., 10 JAN 83; To VX-5, NWC China Lake, CA., 10 FEB 83 ** Transferred to VA-122/FRS, NJ/207, NAS LeMoore, CA., 06 OCT 83; To VA-122, NAS Jacksonville, FL., 27 MAR 85; To VA-122, NARF, NAS Jacksonville, FL., 16 JUL 85; To VA-122, NAS LeMoore, CA., 22 JUL 85; To VA-122, NAS Dallas, TX., 05 AUG 85; To VA-122, NAS LeMoore, 17 JUN 86 thru 13 SEP 87 ** End of flight record card ** Note: Crashed in New Mexico and was eventually put back into service, date unknown. Transferred to AMARC, Davis Monthan AFB; Tucson, AZ., assigned park code 6A0322; 21 MAR 90, with FLIR ** 5964.9 flight hours ** TF41A402D engine S/N AE141617 ** Storage location 111209 ** Stored at EL Dorado Aircraft Supplies, date unknown ** Located at AMARG, Davis Monthan AFB; Tucson, AZ., 15 JUN 07.

B-098 154459 Navy acceptance from NPRO Rep. LTV, Dallas, TX., 26 JUL 68 ** Transferred to VA-122/FRS, NJ/2XX, NAS LeMoore, CA., 29 AUG 68 ** Transferred to VA-146/CVW-9, NG/3XX, USS Enterprise (CVAN-65), 03 SEP 68 ~ S 1SO strike, 07 DEC 68 ** No data on strike.

B-099 154460 Navy acceptance from NPRO Rep. LTV, Dallas, TX., 26 JUL 68 ** Transferred to VA-122/FRS, NJ/2XX, NAS LeMoore, CA., 15 AUG 68 ** Transferred to VA-215/CVW-9, NG/410, USS Enterprise (CVAN-65), Painted white bottom with light gray top, LTJG J.B, Mason pained on side of nose, 19 AUG 68; To VA-215, USS Franklin D. Roosevelt (CVA-42), 13 JUN 69

** Transferred to VA-125/FRS, NJ/5XX, NAS LeMoore, CA., 19 DEC 69 ** Transferred to NPRO Rep. LTV, Dallas, TX., for RDT & E, 09 FEB 71 ** Transferred to NATC, Weapons Systems Test, NAS Patuxent River, MD., 03 SEP 71 ** Transferred to VA-174/FRS, AD/2XX, NAS Cecil Field, FL., 13 DEC 71 ** Transferred to VA-72/CVW-1, AB/4XX, USS John F. Kennedy (CVA-67), 17 JUN 72 ** Transferred to VA-174/FRS, AD/2XX, NAS Cecil Field, FL., 06 OCT 72 ** Transferred to VA-155/CVW-19, NM/5XX, USS Franklin D. Roosevelt (CV-42), 31 JAN 77; To VA-155, NAS LeMoore, CA., 27 JUN 77 ** Transferred to VA-304/CVWR-30, ND/403 & ND/405, NAS Alameda, CA., 07 SEP 77; To VA-304, NAS Dallas, TX., 25 MAY 78; To VA-304, NAS Alameda, CA., 01 JUN 78; To VA-304, NAS Jacksonville, FL., 16 SEP 79; To VA-304, NAS Alameda, CA., 13 MAR 81 ** Transferred to AMARC, Davis Monthan AFB; Tucson, AZ., assigned park code 6A0161; 19 FEB 86 ** End of flight record card ** 5382.8 flight hours ** TF30P408 engine S/N P664366 ** Aircraft deleted from inventory and released to DRMO for disposition, 13 AUG 02.

B-100 154461 Navy acceptance from NPRO Rep. LTV, Dallas, TX., 26 JUL 68 ** Transferred to VA-122/FRS, NJ/2XX, NAS LeMoore, CA., 21 AUG 68 ** Transferred to VA-215/CVW-9, NG/4XX, USS Enterprise (CVAN-65), 22 AUG 68
~ S 1SO strike, 14 JAN 69 ** No data on strike.

B-101 154462 Navy acceptance from NPRO Rep. LTV, Dallas, TX., 26 JUL 68 ** Transferred to NARF, NAS Jacksonville, FL., 13 SEP 68 ** Transferred to VA-87/CVW-16, AH/3XX, USS Ticonderoga (CVA-14), 27 SEP 68 ** Transferred to VA-174/FRS, AD/2XX, NAS Cecil Field, FL., 26 JAN 69 ** Transferred to VA-15/CVW-6, AE/3XX, USS Intrepid (CVS-11), 11 MAR 69 ** Transferred to VA-46/CVW-3, AC/3XX, NAS Cecil Field, FL., 24 APR 69; To VA-46/CVW1, AB/300, USS John F. Kennedy (CVA-67), 28 JUN 71; To VA-46, NAS Cecil Field, FL., 07 NOV 72; To VA-46, USS John F. Kennedy (CV-67), 31 JUL 74; To VA-46, NAS Cecil Field, FL., 31 JUL 74; To VA-46, NAS Jacksonville, FL., 27 FEB 75; To VA-46, USS John F. Kennedy (CV-67), 27 FEB 75; To VA-46, NAS Jacksonville, FL., 03 MAR 75; To VA-46, USS John F. Kennedy (CV-67), 08 APR 75; To VA-46, NAS Cecil Field, FL., 06 APR 76; To VA-46, USS John F. Kennedy (CV-67), 13 APR 76; To VA-46, NAS Cecil Field, FL., 13 APR 76; To VA-46, USS John F. Kennedy (CV-67), 22 DEC 76; To VA-46, NAS Cecil Field, FL., 11 MAR 77; To VA-46, USS Dwight D. Eisenhower, (CVN-69), 11 MAR 77; To VA-46, NAS Cecil Field, FL., 11 MAR 77 ** Transferred to VA-304/CVWR-30, ND/407, NAS Alameda, CA., 05 NOV 77 ** Transferred to AMARC, Davis Monthan AFB; Tucson, AZ., assigned park code 6A0172, 13 JUN 86 ** End of flight record card ** 6742.4 flight hours ** TF30P408 engine S/N 664361 ** Transferred to the Nevada Test Site; Mercury, NV., 11 MAR 02.

B-102 154463 Navy acceptance from NPRO Rep. LTV, Dallas, TX., 26 JUL 68 ** Transferred to VA-122/FRS, NJ/2XX, NAS LeMoore, CA., 21 AUG 68 ** Transferred to VA-215/CVW-9, NG/4XX, USS Enterprise (CVAN-65), 27 AUG 68; To VA-215/CVW-6, AE/412, USS Franklin D. Roosevelt (CVA-42), 11 FEB 69; To VA-215/CVW-19, NM/412, USS Oriskany (CVA-34), 22 JUN 70; To VA-215, NAS LeMoore, CA., 21 JUN 72 ** Transferred to VA-122/FRS, NJ/2XX, NAS LeMoore, CA., 24 JUL 73 ** Transferred to VA-174/FRS, AD/2XX, NAS Cecil Field, FL., 01 NOV 73 ** Transferred to VA-203/CVWR-20, AF/314, NAS Jacksonville, FL., 03 AUG 77 ** Transferred to VA-204/CVWR-20, AF/4XX, NAS New Orleans, LA., 02 JUN 83 ** Transferred to MASDC, Davis Monthan AFB; Tucson, AZ., assigned park code 6A0156, 20 JUL 84 ** End of flight record card ** 4805.1 flight hours ** Engine removed on arrival ** Aircraft released from storage and prepared for overland shipment to Holloman AFB; Alamogordo, NM., to be used as a range target, 11 APR 05.

B-103 154464 Navy acceptance from NPRO Rep. LTV, Dallas, TX., 26 JUL 68 ** Transferred to VA-122/FRS, NJ/2XX, NAS LeMoore, CA., 28 AUG 68 ** Transferred to VA-146/CVW-9, NG/3XX, USS Enterprise (CVAN-65), 30 AUG 68; To VA-146, USS America (CVA-66), 26 JUN 69 ** Transferred to VA-174/FRS, AD/271, NAS Cecil

Field, FL., 09 OCT 69 ** Transferred to NPRO Rep. LTV, Dallas, TX. to be converted to TA-7C, 06 JUL 75 ** Re-designated to TA-7C, 06 JUL 75; To NPRO for RDT & E, 03 MAR 77 ** Transferred to NATC, NAS Patuxent River, MD., for RDT & E, 17 APR 78 ** Re-designated to JTA-7C, 24 APR 78 ** Re-designated TA-7C, 14 JUL 78 ** Transferred to the Naval Test Pilot School, NAS Patuxent River, MD., No tail code, Modex 02, 09 JUN 80 ** Transferred to NATC, NAS Patuxent River, MD., for RDT & E, 09 JUN 80 ** Transferred to the Naval Test Pilot School, NAS Patuxent River, MD., 01 AUG 80; To NTPS, NAS Jacksonville, FL., 28 JUN 84; To NTPS, NAS Patuxent River, MD., 24 NOV 84 ** Transferred to Pacific Missile Test Center, PMTC/81, NAS Point Mugu, CA., 27 MAR 85; To PMTC, NAS Dallas, TX., 19 DEC 85; To PMTC, PMTC/81, NAS Point Mugu, CA., 20 DEC 85 thru 12 DEC 86 ** End of flight record card ** Transferred to AMARC, Davis Monthan AFB; Tucson, AZ., assigned park code 6A0381; 25 SEP 90 ** 5636.2 flight hours TF41A402D engine S/N 141607 ** Storage location 111408 ** Transferred to FMS, 06 APR 04 ** Located at AMARG, Davis Monthan AFB; Tucson, AZ., 15 JUN 07.

B-104 154465 Navy acceptance from NPRO Rep. LTV, Dallas, TX., 26 JUL 68 ** Transferred to VA-122/FRS, NJ/2XX, NAS LeMoore, CA., 28 AUG 68 ** Transferred to VA-146/CVW-9, NG/3XX, USS Enterprise (CVAN-65), 30 AUG 68 ** Transferred to VA-122/FRS, NJ/2XX, NAS LeMoore, CA., 16 FEB 69 ** Transferred to VA-93/CVW-2, NE/3XX, NAS LeMoore, CA. 26 SEP 69; To VA-93/CVW-5, NF/3XX, USS Midway (CVA-41), 01 JUN 70; To VA-93, NAS LeMoore, CA., 10 APR 72 ** Transferred to VA-153/CVW-19, NM/306, NAS LeMoore, CA., 29 MAY 73; To VA-153, USS Oriskany (CVA-34), 04 JUN 74; To VA-153, NAS LeMoore, Ca., 04 JUN 74; To VA-153, NAS Fallon, NV., 04 NOV 74; To VA-153, NAS LeMoore, CA., 12 NOV 74; To VA-153, NAS Jacksonville, FL., 21 JAN 75; To VA-153, NAS Fallon, NV., 22 JAN 75; To VA-153, NAS LeMoore, CA., 03 APR 75; To VA-153, NAS Jacksonville, FL., 03 APR 75; To VA-153, NAS LeMoore, CA., 11 APR 75; To VA-153, USS Oriskany (CV-34), 30 JUN 75; To VA-153, NAS LeMoore, CA., 16 SEP 75, Painted in bicentennial scheme 04 JUL 76; To VA-153, USS Franklin D, Roosevelt (CV-42), 20 APR 77; To VA-153, NAS LeMoore, CA., 20 APR 77 ** Transferred to VA-304/CVWR-30, ND/4XX, NAS Alameda, CA., 08 JUL 77 ** Transferred to VA-204/CVWR-20, AF/413, NAS Memphis, TN., 05 NOV 77 ** Transferred to VA-304/CVWR-30, ND/4XX, NAS Alameda, CA., 24 NOV 77 ** Transferred to NARF, NAS Jacksonville, FL., 16 JUN 78 ** Transferred to VA-204/ CVWR-20, AF/4XX, NAS New Orleans, LA., 30 AUG 78 ~ S 1SO strike, 24 AUG 79 ** No data on strike.

B-105 154466 Navy acceptance from NPRO Rep. LTV, Dallas, TX., 26 JUL 68 ** Transferred to NARF, NAS Jacksonville, FL., 17 SEP 68 ** Transferred to VA-87/CVW-16, AH/3XX, USS Ticonderoga (CVA-14), 08 OCT 68; To VA-87, NAS Cecil Field, FL., 24 MAY 69; To VA-87, USS Franklin D. Roosevelt (CVA-42), 13 SEP 70 ** Transferred to VA-174/FRS, AD/2XX, NAS Cecil Field, FL., 14 JAN 71 ** Transferred to VA-87/CVW-6, AE/4XX, NAS Cecil Field, FL., 11 SEP 72; To VA-87, NAS Jacksonville, FL., 27 JUN 74; To VA-87, NAS Cecil Field, FL., 16 AUG 74; To VA-87, USS Franklin D. Roosevelt (CVA-42), 24 OCT 74; To VA-87, NAS Cecil Field, FL., 24 OCT 74 ** To VA-87, USS Franklin D. Roosevelt (CVA-42), 24 OCT 74; To VA-87, NAS Cecil Field, FL., 24 JUL 75; To VA-87, USS Saratoga (CV-60), 24 JUL 75 ** Transferred to VA-205/CVWR-20, AF/506, NAS Atlanta, GA., 21 NOV 75; To VA-205, NAS Jacksonville, FL., 03 APR 78; To VA-205, NAS Atlanta, GA., 08 APR 78; To VA-205, NAS Jacksonville, FL., 03 JUL 80; To VA-205, NAS Atlanta, GA., 08 AUG 80 ** Transferred to MASDC, Davis Monthan AFB; Tucson, AZ., assigned park code 6A0145, 03 NOV 83 thru 06 AUG 83 ** End of flight record card ** 3981.4 flight hours ** Engine removed on arrival ** Aircraft released from storage and prepared for overland shipment to Holloman AFB; Alamogordo, NM., to be used as a range target, 11 APR 05.

B-106 154467 Navy acceptance from NPRO Rep. LTV, Dallas, TX., 26 JUL 68 ** Transferred to VA-122/FRS, NJ/2XX, NAS LeMoore, CA., 23 AUG 68 ** Transferred to VA-146/CVW-9, NG/3XX, USS Enterprise (CVAN-65), 27 AUG 69; To VA 146, USS America (CVA-66), 23 JUN 69 ** Transferred to VA-174/FRS, AD/260, NAS Cecil

Field, FL., 04 OCT 69 ** Transferred to NPRO Rep. LTV, Dallas, TX., to be converted to TA-7C, 20 FEB 76 ** Re-designated to TA-7C, 01 MAR 76 ** Transferred to VA-122/FRS, NJ/2XX, NAS LeMoore, CA., 05 OCT 78; To VA-122, NAS Jacksonville, FL., 20 NOV 81; To VA-122, NAS LeMoore, CA., 19 JAN 82 ** Transferred to VA-174/FRS, AD/2XX, NAS Cecil Field, FL., 16 APR 84; To VA-174, NAS Jacksonville, FL., 06 AUG 84; To VA-174, NAS Cecil Field, FL., 08 NOV 84 ** Transferred to VA-122/FRS, NJ/2XX, NAS LeMoore, CA., 21 JAN 86 ~ S 3SO strike, 15 OCT 86 ** No data on strike.

B-107 154468 Navy acceptance from NPRO Rep. LTV, Dallas, TX., 26 JUL 68 ** Transferred to VA-122/FRS, NJ/2XX, NAS LeMoore, CA., 10 SEP 68 ** Transferred to VA-215/CVW-9, NG/4XX, USS Enterprise (CVAN-65), 11 SEP 68; To VA-215CVW-6, AE/4XX, USS Franklin D. Roosevelt (CVA-42), 15 JUN 69; To VA-215CVW-19, NM/400, USS Oriskany (CVA-34), 03 APR 70; To VA-215, NAS LeMoore, CA., 26 JUN 72 ** Transferred to VA-125/FRS, NJ/5XX, NAS LeMoore, CA., 18 JUN 73 ** Transferred to VA-155/CVW-19, NM/5XX, NAS LeMoore, CA., 25 JUN 75; To VA-155, USS Oriskany (CV-34), 15 JUL 75; To VA-155, NAS LeMoore, CA., 18 JAN 76 ** Transferred to VA-125/FRS, NJ/5XX, NAS LeMoore, CA., 24 JUN 76 ** To VA-215/CVW-19, NM/4XX, USS Franklin D. Roosevelt (CV-42), 02 FEB 77; To VA-215, NAS LeMoore, CA., 01 JUN 77 ** Transferred to VA-304/CVWR-30, ND/4XX, NAS Alameda, CA., 16 JUL 77; To VA-304, NAS Jacksonville, FL., 19 JUL 77; To VA-304, NAS Alameda, CA., 05 OCT 77 ** Transferred to VA-204/CVWR-20, AF/405, NAS Memphis, TN., 11 MAY 77; To VA-204, NAS New Orleans, LA., 11 MAY 77; To VA-204, NAS Jacksonville, FL., 26 JUN 81; To VA-204, NAS New Orleans, LA., 28 JUN 81; To VA-204, NAS Jacksonville, FL., 25 AUG 81; To VA-204, NAS New Orleans, LA., 20 DEC 81 ** Transferred to MASDC, Davis Monthan AFB; Tucson, AZ., assigned park code 6A0134, 08 SEP 83 ** End of flight record card ** 4799.6 flight hours ** Engine removed on arrival ** Aircraft deleted from inventory and released to DRMO for disposition, 21 MAR 99 ** Sold as surplus to Fritz Enterprises; Taylor, MI., delivered to HVF West's yard; Tucson, AZ., 16 AUG 99.

B-108 154469 Navy acceptance from NPRO Rep. LTV, Dallas, TX., 21 AUG 68 ** Transferred to NARF, NAS Jacksonville, FL., 12 SEP 68 ** Transferred to VA-87/CVW-16, AH/301, USS Ticonderoga (CVA-14), 21 SEP 68; To VA-87, NAS Cecil Field, FL., 17 APR 69; To VA-87/CVW-6, AE/4XX, USS Franklin D. Roosevelt (CVA-42), 10 APR 70; To VA-87, NAS Cecil Field, FL., 04 APR 72; To VA-87, MCAS Yuma, AZ., 05 JUN 74; To VA-87, NAS Cecil Field, FL., 05 JUN 74; To VA-87, MCAS Yuma, AZ., 05 JUN 74; To VA-87, NAS Cecil Field, FL., 24 SEP 74; To VA-87, USS Franklin D. Roosevelt (CVA-42), 24 OCT 74; To VA-87, NAS Cecil Field, FL., 24 OCT 74 ** To VA-87, USS Franklin D. Roosevelt (CVA-42), 24 OCT 74; To VA-87, NAS Cecil Field, FL., 24 JUL 75; To VA-87, USS Saratoga (CV-60), 24 JUL 75 ** Transferred to VA-205/CVWR-20, AF/500, NAS Atlanta, GA., CDR. Mel Seibel painted on side of nose, 25 NOV 75; To VA-205, NAS Jacksonville, FL., 21 SEP 77; To VA-205, NAS Atlanta, GA., 04 DEC 77; To VA-205, NAS Jacksonville, FL., 31 AUG 81; To VA-205, NAS Atlanta, GA., 08 NOV 81 ** Transferred to MASDC, Davis Monthan AFB; Tucson, AZ., assigned park code 6A0144, 20 OCT 83 ** End of flight record card ** 5121.8 flight hours ** Engine removed on arrival ** Deleted from inventory and released to DRMO for disposition, 21 MAR 99 ** Sold as surplus to Fritz Enterprises; Taylor, MI., delivered to HVF West's yard; Tucson, AZ., 13 AUG 99.

B-109 154470 Navy acceptance from NPRO Rep. LTV, Dallas, TX., 21 AUG 68 ** Transferred to VA-122/FRS, NJ/2XX, NAS LeMoore, CA., 06 SEP 68 ** Transferred to VA-146/CVW-9, NG/3XX, USS Enterprise (CVAN-69), 09 SEP 68; VA-146, USS America (CVA-66), 19 MAY 69 ** Transferred to VA-174/FRS, AD/2XX, NAS Cecil Field, FL., 14 OCT 69 ~ S 1SO strike, 01 APR 70 ** No data on strike.

B-110 154471 Navy acceptance from NPRO Rep. LTV, Dallas, TX., 21 AUG 68 ** Transferred to NARF, NAS Jacksonville, FL., 14 SEP 68 ** Transferred to VA-87/CVW-16, AH/3XX, USS Ticonderoga (CVA-14),01 OCT 68; To VA-87, NAS Cecil Field, FL., 11 MAY 69; To VA-87, USS Franklin D. Roosevelt (CVA-42), 23 APR 70; To VA-87, NAS Cecil Field, FL., 23 JAN 72; To VA-87, NAS Jacksonville,

FL., 08 AUG 74; To VA-87, NAS Cecil Field, FL., 24 OCT 74; To VA-87, USS Franklin D. Roosevelt (CVA-42), 24 OCT 74; To NAS Cecil Field, FL., 24 OCT 74; To VA-87, USS Franklin D. Roosevelt (CVA-42), 24 OCT 74; To VA-87, NAS Cecil Field, FL., 24 JUL 75 ** Transferred to VA-174/FRS, AD/2XX, NAS Cecil Field, FL., 02 SEP 75 ** Transferred to NPRO Rep. LTV, Dallas, TX. to be converted to TA-7C, 23 JUL 76 ** Re-designated to TA-7C, 01 AUG 76 ** Transferred to VA-174/FRS, AD/3XX, NAS Cecil Field, FL., 09 JAN 79; To VA-174, NAS Jacksonville, FL., 16 JUL 81; To VA-174, NAS Cecil Field, Fl., 06 OCT 81; To VA-174, NAS Jacksonville, FL., 23 MAY 85; To VA-174, NAS Cecil Field, Fl., 23 MAY 85; To VA-174, NAS Jacksonville, FL., 28 AUG 85; To VA-174, NAS Cecil Field, FL., 13 JAN 85; TO VA-174, NAS Dallas, TX., 07 JAN 87; To VA-174, NAS Cecil Field, Fl., 06 FEB 87 ** Transferred to NPRO Rep. LTV, Dallas, TX., 06 FEB 87 ** Transferred to Naval Test Pilot School, NAS Patuxent River, MD., 28 SEP 87 thru 29 SEP 87 ** End of flight record card ** Transferred to NATC, Strike Test, SD/425, NAS Patuxent River, MD., date unknown ** Transferred to AMARC, Davis Monthan AFB; Tucson, AZ., assigned park code 6A0377, 22 AUG 90 ** 4,867.8 flight hours ** TF41A402D engine S/N 141920 ** Storage location 111410 ** Transferred to FMS, 06 APR 04 ** Located at AMARG, Davis Monthan AFB; Tucson, AZ., 15 JUN 07.

B-111 154472 Navy acceptance from NPRO Rep. LTV, Dallas, TX., 21 AUG 68 ** Transferred to VA-122/FRS, NJ/2XX, NAS LeMoore, CA., 20 SEP 68 ** Transferred to VA-146/CVW-9, NG/3XX, USS Enterprise (CVAN-65), 24 SEP 68 ** Transferred to VA-122/FRS, NJ/2XX, NAS LeMoore, CA., 19 AUG 69 ** Transferred to VA-174/FRS, AD/2XX, NAS Cecil Field, FL, 29 DEC 69 ** Transferred to VA-87/CVW-6, AE/4XX, USS Franklin D. Roosevelt (CVA-42), 06 DEC 71; To VA-87, NAS Cecil Field, FL., 07 JAN 72 ** Transferred to NARF, NAS Jacksonville, FL., 19 JUL 74 ** Transferred to VA-205/CVWR-20, AF/513, NAS Atlanta, GA., 13 NOV 76 ** Transferred to MASDC, Davis Monthan AFB; Tucson, AZ., assigned park code 6A0142, 07 OCT 83 ** End of flight record card ** 4551.6 flight hours ** Engine removed on arrival ** Aircraft deleted from inventory and released to DRMO for disposition, 13 AUG 02.

B-112 154473 Navy acceptance from NPRO Rep. LTV, Dallas, TX., 21 AUG 68 ** Transferred to VA-122/FRS, NJ/2XX, NAS LeMoore, CA., 26 SEP 68 ** Transferred to VA-25/CVW-16, AH/5XX, USS Ticonderoga (CVA-14), 14 OCT 68 ~ S 1SO strike, 09 MAR 69 ** Pilot survived and was rescued after having an engine failure over SE Asia.

B-113 154474 Navy acceptance from NPRO Rep. LTV, Dallas, TX., 21 AUG 68 ** Transferred to VA-122/FRS, NJ/2XX, NAS LeMoore, CA., 04 SEP 68 ** Transferred to VA-146/CVW-9, NG/3XX, USS Enterprise (CVAN-65), 06 SEP 68; To VA-146, USS America (CVA-66), 11 JUN 69 ** Transferred to VA-155/CVW-19, NM/501, USS Oriskany (CVA-34), 01 JAN 70; To VA-155, NAS LeMoore, CA., 08 JUN 72; To VA-155, USS Oriskany (CVA-34), 04 JUN 74; To VA-155, NAS LeMoore, CA., 01 JUL 74; To VA-155, NAS Jacksonville, FL., 25 OCT 74; To VA-155, NAS LeMoore, CA., 01 NOV 74; To VA-155, NAS Fallon, NV., 09 NOV 74; VA-155, NAS LeMoore, CA., 11 DEC 74; To VA-155, NAS Fallon, NV., 31 MAR 75; To VA-155, NAS LeMoore, CA., 11 APR 75; To VA-155, USS Oriskany (CV-34), 11 JUL 75; To VA-155, NAS LeMoore, CA., 12 SEP 75; To VA-155, USS Franklin D. Roosevelt (CV-42), 15 OCT 76; To VA-155, NAS LeMoore, CA.,19 JUL 77 ** Transferred to VA-304/CVWR-30, ND/4XX, NAS Alameda, CA., 21 JUL 77; To VA-304, NAS Dallas, TX., 11 OCT 77 ** Transferred to VA-204/CVWR-20, AF/4XX, NAS Memphis, TN., 05 NOV 77; To VA-204, NAS Dallas, TX., 19 NOV 77 ** Transferred to NARF, NAS Jacksonville, FL., 16 FEB 78 ** Transferred to VA-305/CVWR-30, ND/503, NAS Point Mugu, CA., 03 MAY 78; To VA-305, NAS Jacksonville, FL., 25 JUL 80; To VA-305, NAS Point Mugu, CA., 22 MAY 81; To VA-305, NAS Jacksonville, FL., 19 JAN 83; To VA-305, NAS Point Mugu, CA., 08 JUL 83 ** Transferred to NATTC Millington, TN., sitting outside the Airframes shop, to be used as an instructional airframe, 02 DEC 87 ~ S 3SO strike, 03 DEC 87 ** End of flight record card ** On conditional loan from the National Museum of Naval Aviation; Pensacola, Fl. to the Stennis Space Center, Ms.

VA-72 A-7E AC/400

VA-72 A-7E AC/400

VA-72 A-7 AB/400

VA-72 A-7E AC/400

VA-72 A-7Es AC/4XX with KC-135 tanker Pathfinder escort.

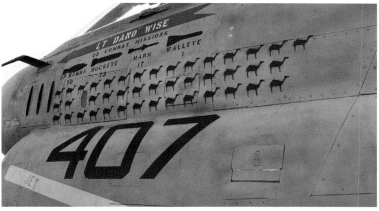

VA-72 A-7E AC/407

VA-72 A-7E AC/411

VA-72 A-7E AC/410

VA-72 A-7E AC/400

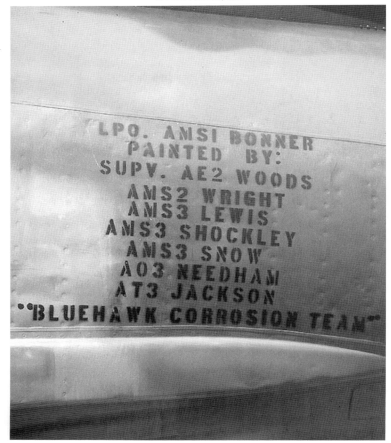

VA-72 A-7E AC/4XX Corrosion Team

VA-72 A-7E AC/4XX

VA-72 A-7E AC/401

VA-72 A-7Es AC/404, 405, 401, 400, 402, and 403

VA-72 A-7Es 159286 AC/400, 405

VA-72 A-7E AC/403

VA-72 AC/414, 412, and 401 USS John F Kennedy

VA-72 A-7Es AC/404, 402, 405, 407, and 411

VA-72 A-7E AC/400

VA-72 A-7E AC/403 in the barrier

VA-81 A-7E 157446 AA/411 USS Forrestal

VA-81 A-7E AA/401 USS Forrestal

VA-81 A-7E 158827 AA/400 USS Forrestal

VA-81 A-7E 160718 AA/404 USS Forrestal

VA-81 A-7E 160718 AA/404 USS Forrestal

VA-81 A-7 AA/400

VA-81 A-7E 160718 AA/404 USS Forrestal

VA-81 A-7 AA/400 USS Forrestal

VA-81 A-7E 160718 AA/404 USS Forrestal

VA-81 A-7E 157460 AA/404

VA-81 A-7Es 157625 AA/410, 158008 AA/406 USS Forrestal

VA-83 A-7Es (back two) AA/301, 310 and VA-81 A-7E 160718 AA/404

VA-81 A-7E AA/414

VA-81 A-7Es AA/401, 157571 AA/403 USS Forrestal

VA-81 A-7Es 157446, 157470, and 157452 AA/400, 404, 411, and 402 over NAS Cecil Field, FL.

VA-81 A-7E AA/414 dropping a MK-82

VA-81 A-7E 157450 AA/412 USS Forrestal

VA-81 A-7 AA/403 with huffer hose attached

VA-81 A-7E 159303 AA/301 USS Saratoga

VA-81 A-7Es AA/414, 412, and 401 USS Forrestal

VA-82 A-7C 156794 AJ/302 USS America over St John River

VA-82 A-7E 157569 AJ/312 USS Nimitz

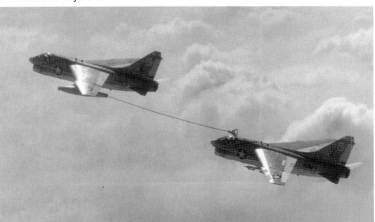

VA-82 A-7s IFR from a D-704 buddy store

VA-82 A-7 AJ/304

VA-82 A-7E 157585 AJ/307

VA-82 A-7E 158827 AJ/300 with tow bar attached

VA-82 A-7E 157571 AJ/311 shared with VA-86, USS Nimitz

VA-82 A-7 AJ/310 taking the wire

VA-82 A-7E 157460 AJ/303 USS Nimitz

VA-82 A-7C 156768 AJ/311 USS America

VA-82 A-7C 156794 AJ/302 USS America

VA-82 A-7 AJ/305

VA-82 A-7 AJ/313 taking the wire. On the side are VA-82 A-7 AJ/307 and A-5 AJ/602, USS America.

VA-82 A-7C 156768 NL/311

VA-83 A-7E 157439, 157473, 157457, and 157458 AA/304, 300, 305, and 307 USS Forrestal over NAS Cecil Field, FL.

VA-83 A-7E 159298 AA/300

VA-83 A-7E 158008 AA/304 USS Forrestal

VA-83 A-7E 157550 AA/302 USS Forrestal

VA-83 A-7E 160717 AA/310 USS Saratoga

VA-83 A-7E 159294 AA/301 USS Forrestal

VA-83 A-7E 158008 AA/304 USS Forrestal

VA-83 A-7 AA/3XX

VA-86 A-7 USS Coral Sea

VA-86 A-7C 156738 AJ/413 on catapult

VA-86 A-7s AJ/411, 405, 401, and 402 USS Nimitz

VA-86 A-7 AJ/408 tow bar attached

VA-86 A-7 AJ/406 USS Amercia on catapult

VA-86 A-7A 154356 NL-403 USS Coral Sea

VA-86 A-7A 152680 AG/221

23

VA-86 A-7A 153136 NL/400 USS Coral Sea

VA-86 A-7Es 157510 AJ/407, 412, 406, 413, 403, 402, and 411

VA-86 A-7E 157510 AJ/412 USS Nimitz next to USAF C-141

VA-86 A-7E 157482 AJ/405 USS Nimitz

VA-86 A-7A 154356 NL/403 USS Coral Sea

VA-86 A-7E AJ/406 USS Nimitz

VA-86 A-7E 157510 AJ/412 on the cat

VA-86 A-7A 152680 AE/403 USS Coral Sea

VA-87 A-7E 159977 AE/413 next to A-6

VA-87 A-7E 159977 AE/413 USS America

VA-87 A-7E 154469 AE/400 USS Roosevelt

VA-87 A-7Es AE/405, 401

VA-87 A-7E 159977 AE/413 USS America

VA-87 A-7s on board USS Ticonderoga (CVS-14). Other aircraft are A-4, F-8, E-1, and S-2.

VA-87 A-7Es AE/400, 404

VA-87 A-7 AE/405

VA-87 A-7B 154471 AE/401 USS Roosevelt

VA-87 154471 AE/402 USS Independence

VA-87 A-7B 154471 AE/402 USS Independence

VA-93 A-7B 154379 NF/300 USS Midway

VA-93 A-7E 160537 NF/314 USS Midway

VA-93 A-7 NF/3XX with drop tanks and D-704 buddy store, USS Midway

VA-93 A-7Es NF/3XX USS Midway

VA-93 A-7Bs 154379 and 154396, NF/301, 300, 306, and 311

VA-93 A-7E NF/313 with tow bar attached

VA-93 A-7B 154379 NF/300 USS Midway

VA-93 A-7B 154397 AH/310

VA-93 A-7B 154396 NF/311 USS Midway

VA-93 A-7B 154479 NF/300 USS Midway

VA-93 A-7B 154379 NF/300 USS Midway

VA-93 A-7B 154479 NF/300 USS Midway

VA-93 A-7A 153226 NF/312 USS Midway

VA-93 A-7B 154490 NF/314 USS Midway

VA-94 A-7E 159976 NL/400 with MK-76 USS Kitty Hawk

VA-94 A-7E 158011 NL/400 USS Coral Sea

VA-94 A-7E 158011 NL/400 USS Coral Sea

VA-94 A-7 NL/404

VA-94 A-7 NL/403 USS Coral Sea on the cat with JBD up

VA-94 A-7E NH/400

VA-94 A-7E 159989 NH/401 USS Enterprise

VA-94 A-7E 158017 NL/406 USS Kitty Hawk

VA-94 A-7E 159989 NL/403 USS Coral Sea

VA-94 A-7E 159976 NL/400 USS Coral Sea

VA-94 A-7E 159976 NL/400 USS Kitty Hawk

VA-94 A-7E 160728 NL/415 USS Kitty Hawk

VA-97

VA-97 A-7A 153144 NK/507 with MK-82s

VA-97 A-7E 158656 NK/301 USS Enterprise

VA-97 A-7A 153250 NK/504 USS Constellation with drop tanks

VA-97 A-7E NL/313 with drop tanks

VA-97 A-7A NK/304 at NAS Fallon, NV.

VA-97 A-7E 157486 NL/301 USS Carl Vinson

VA-97 A-7E 156872

VA-97 A-7E 156872 NK/300 USS Enterprise

VA-97 A-7E NK/300 USS Enterprise

VA-97 A-7A 153252 NK/500 USS Constellation

VA-97 A-7E NK/312 USS Enterprise on the cat

VA-97 A-7A 153235 NK/506 USS Constellation

VA-97 A-7A 153234 NK/505 USS Constellation

VA-97 A-7 line front to back: NK/301, 305, 311, 310, 315, 316, and 303

VA-97 A-7As 152664, 153144 NK/509, 507

VA-97 A-7A 153144 NK/507

VA-97 A-7A 153144 NK/507 with MK-82s

VA-97 A-7As NK/503, 505, 513, and 514

VA-105 A-7A AC/404

VA-105 A-7A

VA-105 A-7A AC/407 USS Saratoga

VA-105 A-7A 153186 NH/410

VA-105 A-7Es AC/404, 403, 402, and 401 over Mt Fuji

VA-105 A-7E 158831 AC/400 USS Saratoga

VA-105 A-7E 159970 NL/400 USS Carl Vinson

VA-105 A-7E 158831 AC/400 USS Saratoga

VA-105 A-7E 156882 AC/415 USS Saratoga

VA-105 A-7A 153190 NH/406 USS Kitty Hawk

VA-105 A-7Es AC/4XX

VA-105 A-7E 157477 AC/414 USS Saratoga being towed

VA-105 A-7Es AC/4XX (159309 in foreground)

VA-113 154477 AC-416 USS Saratoga

VA-113 A-7E 158664 NE/300 USS Ranger

VA-113 A-7E 159304 NE-301

VA-113 A-7E 158664 NE/300 USS Ranger

VA-113 A-7E 159288 NE/307 USS Ranger

VA-113 A-7E 158664 NE/300 USS Ranger with tail cone and engine pan removed

VA-113 A-7Bs 154529, 154527, AC/401, 402, 404, 405, 406, 407, 411, and 412 flight line

VA-113 A-7E 159304 NE/314 well starter in foreground

VA-113 A-7E 159281 NE/302 USS Ranger

VA-113 A-7E NE/302 USS Ranger with drop tanks

VA-113 A-7E 159998 NE/305 USS Ranger

VA-113 A-7E 159281 NE/302 USS Ranger

VA-113 A-7E NE/316

VA-122 A-7C 156761 still with VA-113 paint

VA-122 TA-7C 154487 NJ/211

VA-122 A-7E NJ/233 USS Lexington painted on side

VA-122 A-7E NJ/233 USS Lexington painted on side

VA-122 A-7E 156830 NJ/237 USS Lexington painted on side

VA-122 A-7 NJ/247 dropping a snakeye

VA-122 A-7 NJ/247 dropping snakeyes

VA-122 A-7 NJ/247 with snakeyes

VA-122 A-7 NJ/250 firing rockets

VA-122 A-7, and TA-7C NJ 237, 203

VA-122 A-7 and TA-7C NJ/237, 203

Top-to-bottom: fins 24, 26, 34, 40

VA-122 A-7 and TA-7C NJ/206, 201 with MK-76

VA-122 A-7E 156841 NJ/201 USS Lexington painted on side

VA-122 TA-7C NJ/203

VA-122 A-7A 153170 NJ/232, 1966

VA-122 TA-7C 154407 NJ/211

VA-122 TA-7C 156741 NJ/220

VA-122 A-7E NJ/201

156774

VA-122 TA-7C NJ/210 with FLIR

VA-122 TA-7C NJ/210 with FLIR, VFA-125 F/A-18 NL/562

VA-125 A-7 NJ/550 in maintenance check

VA-125 A-7 NJ/540 with VFA-125 F/A-18 NJ/500

VA-125 A-7s NJ/530, 504, 525, and 526 over NAS LeMoore, CA.

VA-125 A-7A 153155 NJ/573

VA-125 A-7A 153162 NJ/527

VA-125 A-7B 154442 NJ/502

VA-125 A-7B NJ/506

VA-125 154436

154443

VA-125 A-7B 154443 NJ/406 with towbar and tug

VA-125 A-7s (top to bottom) 525, 504, 530, and 557

VA-146 A-7E 160728 NG/305 USS Constellation

VA-146 A-7E 160728 NG/305 USS Constellation

VA-146 A-7E 160726 NG/303 USS Constellation

VA-146 A-7 AG/314 with FLIR pod catching the wire

VA-146 A-7E 160866 NE/300 USS Kitty Hawk

VA-146 A-7E NG/302 USS Constellation with MK-82s

VA-146 A-7E 160730 NG/307 USS Constellation with FLIR pod

VA-146 A-7E 160723 NG/301 USS Constellation with FLIR pod

VA-146 A-7E 160729 NG/306 USS Constellation

VA-146 A-7E 160726 NG/303 USS Constellation with FLIR pod

VA-146 A-7E 160726 NG/303 USS Constellation with FLIR pod

VA-146 A-7E 160729 NG/306, 3XX USS Constellation with MK-82s

127

VA-146 A-7Es 160732, NG/306, 311 with FLIR pods

VA-146 A-7Es 160726, 160731 NG/303, 310 USS Constellation with FLIR pods

VA-146 A-7Es 160732, NG/306, 311 with FLIR pods

VA-146 A-7Es NG/300, 304, and 302

VA-146 A-7Es 160732, NG 307, 311 USS Constellation with FLIR pods

VA-146 A-7Es 160728, NG/312, 305 USS Constellation with FLIR pods

VA-146 A-7Es NG/307, 313, and 310 USS Constellation ready to land flyby

VA-146 A-7Es 160731, 160730 NG/310, 307 with FLIR pods and MK-82s

VA-146 A-7Es 160731, 160732, 160729 NG/310, 300, 311, and 306 USS Constellation with FLIR pods

VA-146 A-7E 160732 NG/311 USS Constellation with FLIR pods and sidewinder

VA-146 A-7Es NG/304, 313 USS Constellation

VA-146 A-7E NG/301 USS Kitty Hawk with drop tanks and power plugged in

VA-146 A-7E 160872 NG/301 USS Constellation with FLIR pods

VA-146 A-7E 150831 NG/311 USS Constellation catching the wire

VA-146 A-7E 160731 NG/310 USS Constellation taking the wire

VA-146 A-7E NE/312 USS Kitty Hawk escorting Russian Bear

VA-146 A-7E 160723 NG/313 USS Constellation

VA-147 A-7B 154436 NG-400 USS America

VA-147 A-7A 153175 NE/300 USS Ranger

VA-147 A-7B 154436 NG/400 USS America

VA-147 A-7E 158009 NG/405 USS Constellation

VA-147 A-7As NE/300, 310, 306, and 304 USS Ranger ready for launch

VA-147 A-7E 157491 NG/407 USS Constellation

VA-147 A-7Es 157491 NG/404, 407 USS Constellation

VA-147 A-7E 158837 NG/401 USS Constellation

VA-147 A-7E 158837 NG/401 USS Constellation

VA-147 A-7Es -, -, 157491 NG/400, 404, and 407 USS Constellation in the break to land

VA-147 A-7E 156819 NG/411 USS Constellation

VA-147 A-7E 159639 NG/413 USS Constellation

VA-147 A-7E 156815 NG/401 USS Constellation, bicentennial paint

VA-147 A-7E 156819 NE/310 USS America with drop tanks

VA-147 A-7 NE/312 on cat JBD-up

VA-147 A-7 NE-311 over USS Ranger with rocket pods and sidewinders

VA-147 A-7 NE/312 with snakeyes in foreground and liquid oxygen and avionics bays open

VA-147 A-7As 153175, 153168 NE/300, 310 USS America

VA-147 A-7 NG/405 inflight refueling from VAG-308 KL-30 ND/633, USS Constellation

AV-147 A-7A 153175 NE/300 USS America and F4U 138193 N693M

VA-147 A-7E NG/401 with VQ-1 A-3 PRO3, South China Sea 20 Sep 74

VA-147 A-7A NE/314 landing on the USS Ranger in the Tonkin Gulf, 13 Dec 67

VA-147 A-7 NG/412

VA-153 A-7A 153237 NM/300 USS Oriskany

VA-153 A-7A 153173 NM/302 USS Oriskany with drop tanks

VA-153 A-7A 153237 NM/300 USS Oriskany

VA-153 A-7A 153237 NM/302 USS Oriskany with drop tanks

VA-153 A-7A 153176 nm/306 USS Oriskany

VA-153 A-7B 154535 NM/300

VA-153 A-7A 153220 NM/311 USS Oriskany

VA-153 A-7B 154535 NM/300 USS Roosevelt bicentennial paint

VA-153 A-7B 154465 NM/306 USS Oriskany

VA-153 A-7B 154465 NM/306 USS Roosevelt bicentennial paint

VA-153 A-7B 154403 NM/307 USS Roosevelt bicentennial paint

VA-153 A-7B 154535 NM/300 USS Roosevelt

VA-153 A-7 NM/314

VA-153 A-7s NM/313, 305 on the pier

VA-155 A-7B 154456 NM/501 USS Oriskany

VA-155 A-7B 154520 NM/500 USS Oriskany

VA-155 A-7B 154456 NM/501 USS Oriskany

VA-155 A-7B 154528 NM/516 USS Oriskany

VA-155 A-7B 154456 NM/501 USS Oriskany

VA-155 A-7B 154465 NM/512 USS Oriskany

VA-155 A-7B 154548 NM/500 USS Roosevelt

VA-155 A-7B 154548 NM/500 USS Roosevelt bicentennial paint

VA-155 A-7Bs 154526, 154520 NM/504, 520 USS Oriskany

VA-174 A-7C 156762 AD/240. VA-174 was the east coast training squadron.

VA-174 A-7E 157489 AD/401 with MK-82s

VA-174 A-7E 158842 AD/401

VA-174 A-7E 157472 AD/413 USS Lexington (on tail cone)

VA-174 A-7E 157469 AD/400 USS Lexington (on tailcone)

VA-174 A-7E 156812 AD/425 USS Lexington (on tail cone)

VA-174 A-7Es (clockwise from top) 156806, 160561, 157489 AD/405, 431, and 401 inflight refueling from a KC-135

VA-174 A-7E 156812 AD/425 USS Lexington (on tail cone)

VA-174 A-7E 157489 AD/401 with MK-82s

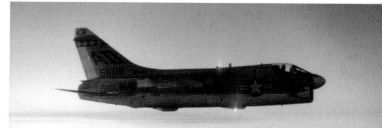

VA-174 A-7E 156808 AD/431 USS Lexington (on tail cone)

VA-174 A-7E 156815 AD/435

VA-174 A-7Es 157581, AD/442, 437

VA-174 A-7Es 157489, 157549 AD/401, 402

VA-174 A-7Es 157489, 158672 AD/401, 405 inflight refueling

VA-174 A-7E and TA-7C 156786, 156820 AD/353, 410

VA-174 A-7Es 157472, 158531, 154476 AD/413, 426, and 411 with MK-82s

VA-174 A-7Es 157549, 157489 AD 402, 401 with USAF KC-135 00317

VA-174 A-7Es 157453, 157556, 156819 AD/404, 447, and 442

VA-174 A-7Es 156819, 1575814 AD/442, 437

VA-174 TA-7Cs *Clockwise from top left:* 156744, 156757, 156767 AD/357, 350, and 372 with MK-82s

VA-174 A-7Es 156834, 156819, 156868, 156812 AD/422, 442, 441, and 425 USS Lexington

VA-174 A-7Es 156834, 156819, 156868, 156812 AD/427, 442, 441, and 425

VA-174 A-7Es 157581, 156815, 156819, 157556 AD/437, 435, 442, and 447

VA-174 A-7Es Clockwise from left: 156746, *156743*, 156751, 157489 AD/373, 420, 3? and 401

VA-174 A-7Es 156834, 156819, 156868, 156812 AD/422, 442, 441, and 425

VA-174 A-7Es bottom-to-top: 156834, 156819, 156868, 156812 AD/422, 442, 441, and 42?

VA-174 A-7Es *Clockwise from top left: 156868, 156812, 156819, 156834 AD/441, 425, 442, and 422*

VA-174 A-7Es 156834, 156819, 156868, 156812 AD/422, 442, 441, and 425

VA-174 TA-7C 154489 AD/360

-174 3 TA-7Cs and 1 A-7E Clockwise from top left: 156767, 154450, 157489, 156746
D/372, 354, 401, and 372

VA-174 A-7E 156820 AD/410

VA-174 A-7Es 156868, 156834, 157549, -, 156806 AD/441, 422, 402, 454, and 405

VA-174 A-7E 160736 AD/450

VA-174 A-7Bs 154424, 154467, 154537, 154455 AD/251, 260, 231, and 221

VA-174 A-7Es 158672, 156878, 159307, 157453 AD/454, 415, 421, 402, and 414

VA-174 A-7Bs 154455, 154424, 154537, 154467 AD/221, 251, 231, and 260

VA-174 A-7C 156800 AD/355

VA-174 A-7A 152659 AD/201

VA-174 A-7C 156781 AD/ 233

VA-174 A-7E AD/446

VA-174 A-7A 153167 AD/204

VA-192 A-7E NH/305 USS Enterprise

VA-192 A-7E 157530 NH/300 USS Kitty Hawk with MK-82s

VA-192 A-7 NL/04 with mines

VA-192 A-7E 157530 NH/300 USS Kitty Hawk with MK-82s

VA-192 A-7E NH/304 being positioned on flight deck

VA-192 A-7Es NG/304, 310, and 303 USS Ranger with FLIR pods

VA-192 A-7 ordnancemen loading weapons

VA-192 A-7 ordnanceman loading MK-82s

VA-192 A-7 NH/311 being positioned on flight deck of USS Kitty Hawk

VA-192 A-7E 157524 NH/303 USS Enterprise

VA-192 A-7Es NH/301, 304, 307, 302, 315, and 311 USS Kitty Hawk

VA-192 A-7E 157508 NH/301 USS Kitty Hawk

VA-192 A-7E 157524 NH/303 on elevator of USS Enterprise

VA-192 A-7E 1578002 NL/XXX with laser guided MK-83

VA-192 A-7E 158002 with laser guided MK-83

VA-192 A-7E NG/312 USS Ranger

VA-192 A-7 NH/311 on final

VA-192 A-7E 157537 NH/310 USS Kitty Hawk catching the wire

VA-192 A-7E 159647 NG/300

VA-192 A-7E NH/508

VA-195 A-7E 158828 NH/400

VA-195 A-7E 158833 NH/400 over USS Ranger

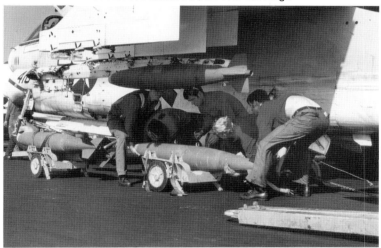

VA-195 A-7E ordnance loading MK-82

VA-195 A-7Es 155817, 155813 NG/412, 413 USS Ranger

VA-195 A-7Es NG/412, 403, 402 over USS Ranger

VA-195 A-7 NH/401 with MK-82s on the cat during ordnance final check

VA-195 A-7E 158828 NH/400

VA-195 A-7E 156888 NH/408 tail hook down during check flight, RAT and IFR probe out

VA-195 A-7Es 157526, 156873 NH/406, 407 USS Kitty Hawk

VA-195 A-7 NH/405 catching the wire

VA-195 A-7E 156865 NH/406 USS Kitty Hawk

VA-195 A-7E 158828 NH/400 USS Kitty Hawk

VA-195 A-7E

VA-195 A-7E 158828 NH/400 USS Kitty Hawk

VA-195 A-7 NH/401 from USS Kitty Hawk on USS Coral Sea with flight deck graffi

B-162 154475 Navy acceptance from NPRO Rep. LTV, Dallas, TX., 25 NOV 68 ** Transferred to VA-174/FRS, AD/2XX, NAS Cecil Field, FL., 02 DEC 68 ** Transferred to VA-46/CVW-3, AC/3XX, NAS Cecil Field, FL., 07 APR 70; To VA-46/ CVW-1, AB/3XX, USS John F. Kennedy (CVA-67), 29 JUN 71 ** Transferred to NATC, NAS Patuxent River, MD., for RDT & E, 05 DEC 72 ** Transferred to VA-46/CVW-1, AB/3XX, USS John F. Kennedy (CVA-67), 21 JAN 73; To VA-46, NAS Cecil Field, FL., 01 JAN 73; To VA-46, USS John F. Kennedy (CVA-67), 03 DEC 74; To VA-46, NAS Cecil Field, FL., 03 DEC 74; To VA-46, USS John F. Kennedy (CVA-67), 03 DEC 74; To VA-46, NAS Cecil Field, FL., 10 DEC 74; To VA-46, USS John F. Kennedy (CVA-67), 10 DEC 74; To VA-46, NAS Cecil Field, FL., 10 DEC 74; To VA-46, USS John F. Kennedy (CVA-67), 10 DEC 74; To VA-46, NAS Cecil Field, FL., 24 MAR 76; To VA-46, USS John F. Kennedy (CV-67), 15 APR 76; To VA-46, NAS Cecil Field, FL., 15 APR 76; To VA-46, USS John F. Kennedy (CV-67),18 JAN 77; To VA-46, NAS Cecil Field, FL., 18 JAN 77 ** Transferred to VA-203/CVWR-20, AF/3XX, NAS Jacksonville, FL., 01 SEP 77 ** Transferred to VA-205/CVWR-20, AF/514, NAS Atlanta, GA., 02 JUN 83 ** Transferred to MASDC, Davis Monthan AFB; Tucson, AZ., assigned park code 6A0152, 12 JUN 84 ** End of flight record card ** 6331.4 flight hours ** engine removed on arrival ** Transferred to DMI Aviation for Yanks Air Museum; Chino, CA., thru GSA, 24 APR 02.

B-115 154476 Navy acceptance from NPRO Rep. LTV, Dallas, TX., 21 AUG 68 ** Transferred to VA-122/FRS, NJ/2XX, 05 OCT 68 ** Transferred to VA-25/CVW-16, AH/5XX, USS Ticonderoga (CVA-14), 28 OCT 68; To VA-25, NAS LeMoore, Ca., 20 JUN 69 ** Transferred to VA-155/CVW-19, NM/5XX, USS Oriskany (CVA-34), 01 DEC 69 ** Transferred to VA-125/ FRS, NJ/513, NAS LeMoore, CA., 18 DEC 69 ** Transferred to VA-93/CVW-5, NF/3XX, NAS LeMoore, CA., 10 JAN 73 ** Transferred to VA-155/CVW-19, NM/5XX, NAS LeMoore, CA., 12 FEB 73 ** Transferred to VA-125/FRS, NJ/5XX, NAS LeMoore, CA., 15 OCT 73; To VA-125, USS Ranger (CV-61), 17 APR 74; To VA-125, NAS LeMoore, CA., 17 APR 74 ** Transferred to VA-204/CVWR-20, AF/4XX, NAS Memphis, TN., 29 JUL 77; To VA-204, NAS Jacksonville, FL., 15 NOV 77 ** Transferred to VA-303/CVWR-30, ND/307, NAS Alameda, CA., 25 FEB 78; To VA-303, NAS Jacksonville, FL., 11 JUL 80; To VA-303, NAS Alameda, CA., 04 SEP 80; To VA-303, NAS Jacksonville, FL., 12 AUG 83; To VA-303, NAS Alameda, CA., 26 AUG 83 ** Transferred to VA-305/CVWR-30, ND/5XX, NAS Point Mugu, CA., 26 SEP 83; To VA-305, NAS Jacksonville, FL., 28 OCT 83; To VA-305, NAS South Weymouth, MA., 16 NOV 83; To VA-305, NAS Jacksonville, FL., 18 NOV 83; To VA-305, NAS Point Mugu, CA., 19 NOV 83 ** Transferred to NAF EL Centro, CA., 10 APR 87 thru 13 APR 87 ** End of flight record card ** On display at NAF El Centro, CA., OCT 95.

B-116 154477 Navy acceptance from NPRO Rep. LTV, Dallas, TX., 21 AUG 68 ** Transferred to NATC, Service Test, NAS Patuxent River, MD., 10 OCT 68 ** Transferred to VA-122/FRS, NJ/2XX, NAS LeMoore, CA., 08 NOV 68 ** Transferred to VA-113/CVW-3, AC/4XX, USS Saratoga (CVA-60), 20 JAN 69; To VA-113, NAS LeMoore, CA., 10 JUN 69 ** Transferred to VA-155/CVW-19, NM/512, USS Oriskany (CVA-34), 10 APR 70; To VA-155, NAS LeMoore, CA., 04 JUN 72 ** Transferred to VA-125/FRS, NJ/5XX, NAS LeMoore, CA., 15 OCT 73 ** Transferred to VA-174/FRS, AD/2XX, NAS Cecil Field, FL., 02 NOV 73 ** Transferred to NPRO Rep. LTV, Dallas, TX. to be converted to TA-7C, 28 FEB 75 ** First A-7B to be converted to a TA-7C ** Re-designated to TA-7C, 09 MAR 75 ** Transferred to NPRO Rep. LTV, Dallas, TX., for RTD & E, 01 FEB 77 ** Transferred to NATC, NAS Patuxent River, MD., for RTD & E, 10 MAY 78, Tail had 4477 and NATC decal/477 & later NAWC/420, Tail and wing tips painted orange, Re-designated JTA-7C, 27 JUN 78 ** Re-designated TA-7C, 09 MAR 75, needle nose added at NATC & removed at NAWC, 16 JUL 81; To NATC, NAS Jacksonville, FL., for RTD & E, 29 NOV 82; To NATC, NAS Patuxent River, MD., for RTD & E, 30 NOV 82 ; To NATC, NAS

Jacksonville, FL., for RTD & E, 08 DEC 82; To NATC, NAS Patuxent River, MD., for RTD & E, 21 APR 83 ; To NATC, NAS Jacksonville, FL., for RTD & E, 25 MAY 83; To NATC, NAS Patuxent River, MD., for RTD & E, 17 JUN 83; To NATC, NAS Dallas, TX., for RTD & E, 23 AUG 84; To NATC, NAS Patuxent River, MD., for RTD & E, 20 AUG 85 thru 16 SEP 87 ** End of flight record card ** Transferred to Thunderbird Avionics, Inc. with FAA S/N N164TB, 17 OCT 96 ** Transferred to AMARC, Davis Monthan AFB; Tucson, AZ., assigned park code 6A0420, 22 OCT 96 ** 5009.9 flight hours ** TF41A402D engine S/N 141910 ** Aircraft contained limited quantities of radiation material, contains 20 micro curies of Cesium 137 and 3.27 milli cures of depleted Uranium , 24 MAR 00 ** Prepare (AS-IS), for overland and above deck shipment to M / V Efdim Hops, Woodhouse Terminal; Galveston, TX., at no cost to the government, for the government of Greece, 16 MAR 00 ** Transferred to the Helenic Air Force (Greece).

B-117 154478 Navy acceptance from NPRO Rep. LTV, Dallas, TX., 21 AUG 68 ** Transferred to VA-122/FRS, NJ/2XX, 04 OCT 68 ** Transferred to VA-25/CVW-16, AH/5XX, USS Ticonderoga (CVA-14), 25 OCT 68; To VA-25, NAS LeMoore, CA., 02 JUN 69 ** Transferred to VA-125/FRS, NJ/5XX, NAS LeMoore, CA., 20 NOV 69 ** Transferred to VA-25/CVW-2, NE/4XX, NAS LeMoore, CA., 20 NOV 69 ** Transferred to VA-125/FRS, NJ/5XX, NAS LeMoore, CA., 20 NOV 69 ** Transferred to VA-174/FRS, AD/2XX, NAS Cecil Field, FL., 15 APR 71 ** Transferred to VA-205/CVWR-20, AF/510, NAS Atlanta, GA., 05 SEP 75; To VA-205, NAS Jacksonville, FL., 13 JAN 76; To VA-205, NAS Atlanta, GA., 19 MAR 76; To VA-205, NAS Dallas, TX., 08 MAY 78; To VA-205, NAS Atlanta, GA., 21 MAY 78 ** Transferred to MASDC, Davis Monthan AFB; Tucson, AZ., assigned park code 6A0139; 23 Sep 83 ** End of flight record card ** 5511.0 flight hours ** Engine removed on arrival ** Aircraft deleted from inventory and released to DRMO for disposition, 13 AUG 02.

B-118 154479 Navy acceptance from NPRO Rep. LTV, Dallas, TX., 21 AUG 68 ** Transferred to VA-122/FRS, NJ/2XX, 28 SEP 68 ** Transferred to VA-25/CVW-16, AH/5XX, USS Ticonderoga (CVA-14), 14 OCT 68; To VA-25, NAS LeMoore, CA., 26 JUN 69 ** Transferred to VA-125/FRS, NJ/5XX, NAS LeMoore, CA., 28 NOV 69 ** Transferred to VA-93/CVW-5, NF/ 3XX, USS Midway (CVA-41), 09 JUN 72; To VA-93, NAS LeMoore, CA., 27 JUN 72; To VA 93, USS Midway (CVA-41), 11 JUN 73 ** Transferred to VA-215/CVW-19, NM/4XX, NAS LeMoore, CA., 06 SEP 73; To VA-215, USS Oriskany (CVA-34), 05 JUN 74; To VA-215, NAS LeMoore, CA., 21 AUG 74; To VA-215, NAS Fallon, NV., 09 NOV 74; To VA-215, NAS LeMoore, CA., 10 FEB 75; To VA-215, NAS Fallon, NV., 12 FEB 75; To VA-215, NAS LeMoore, CA., 17 APR 75; To VA-215, NAS Jacksonville, FL., 18 APR 75; To VA-215, NAS LeMoore, CA., 20 APR 75; To VA-215, NAS Jacksonville, FL., 02 JUN 75; To VA-215, NAS LeMoore, CA., 13 JUN 75; To VA-215, USS Oriskany (CV-34), 15 JUL 75; To VA-215, NAF Atsugi, JP., 04 FEB 76; To VA-215, USS Oriskany (CV-34), 13 FEB 76; To VA-215, NAS Alameda, CA., 11 MAR 76; To VA-215, NAS LeMoore, CA., 29 MAR 76; To VA-215, USS Franklin D. Roosevelt (CV-42), 20 JUL 76, Painted in Bicentennial colors 04 JUL 76; To VA-215, NAS LeMoore, CA., 19 MAY 77 ** Transferred to VA-304/CVWR-30, ND/412, NAS Alameda, CA., 10 SEP 77; To VA-304, NAS Jacksonville, FL., 30 SEP 83 ** Transferred to VA-205/CVWR-20, AF/5XX, NAS Atlanta, GA., 07 JAN 84; To VA-205, NAS Jacksonville, FL., 27 JAN 84; To VA-205, NAS Atlanta, GA., 08 FEB 84 ** Transferred to VA-304/ CVWR-30, ND/412, NAS Alameda, CA., 01 JUN 84 ** Transferred to VA-204/CVWR-20, AF/4XX, NAS New Orleans, LA., 07 JUN 84 ** Transferred to AMARC, Davis Monthan AFB; Tucson, AZ., assigned park code 6A0182; 11 JUL 86 ** End of flight record card ** 6038.2 flight hours ** TF30P408 engine S/N 664284 ** On conditional loan from the National Naval Aviation, Museum; Pensacola, FL., to the Texas Aviation Historical Society; Dumas, TX., 18 JUL 02, Transfer accountability to GSA ** On conditional loan from the National Naval Aviation Museum; Pensacola, FL., to the English Field Air and Space Museum, Tradewind AP; Amarillo, TX., early 03.

B-119 154480 Navy acceptance from NPRO Rep. LTV, Dallas, TX., 21 AUG 68 ** Transferred to VA-122/FRS, NJ/2XX, NAS LeMoore, CA., 01 OCT 68 ** Transferred to VA-25/CVW-16, AH/504, USS Ticonderoga (CVA-14), 14 OCT 68; To VA-25, NAS LeMoore, CA., 15 JUN 69 ** Transferred to VA-153/CVW-19, NM/3XX, USS Oriskany (CVA-34), 23 OCT 69 ** Transferred to VA-125/FRS, NJ/5XX, NAS LeMoore, CA., 26 JAN 70 ~ S 1SO strike, 27 AUG 70 ** No data on strike.

B-120 154481 Navy acceptance from NPRO Rep. LTV, Dallas, TX., 21 AUG 68 ** Transferred to VA-174/FRS, AD/2XX, NAS Cecil Field, FL., 03 OCT 68 ** Transferred to VA-46/CVW-3, AC/3XX, NAS Cecil Field, FL., 18 NOV 68; To VA-46/ CVW-1, AB/3XX, USS John F. Kennedy (CVA-67), 22 JUN 71; To VA-46, NAS Cecil Field, FL., 26 DEC 72; To VA-46, NAS Jacksonville, FL., 19 DEC 74; To VA-46, NAS Cecil Field, FL., 19 DEC 74; To VA-46, NAS Jacksonville, FL., 20 DEC 74; To VA-46, NAS Cecil Field, FL., 13 DEC 75; To VA-46, USS John F. Kennedy (CVA-67), 21 FEB 75; To VA-46, NAS Cecil Field, FL., 30 JUN 75; To VA-46, USS John F. Kennedy (CV-67), 23 AUG 76; To VA-46, NAS Cecil Field, FL., 23 AUG 76; To VA-46, USS John F. Kennedy (CV-67), 23 AUG 76; To VA-46, NAS Cecil Field, FL., 23 AUG 76; To VA-46, USS Dwight D. Eisenhower (CVN-69), 23 AUG 76; To VA-46, NAS Cecil Field, FL., 23 AUG 76; To VA-46, USS John F. Kennedy (CV-67), 23 AUG 76; To VA-46, NAS Cecil Field, FL., 23 AUG 76 ** Transferred to VA-205/CVWR-20, AF/507, NAS Atlanta, GA., 24 APR 78 ** Transferred to VA-204/CVWR-20, AF/4XX, NAS Memphis, TN., 03 OCT 77 ** Transferred to VA-205/CVWR-20, AF/507, NAS Atlanta, GA., 18 NOV 77; To VA-205, NAS Jacksonville, FL., 29 AUG 80; To VA-205, NAS Atlanta, GA., 17 DEC 80 ** To VA-205, NAS Jacksonville, FL., 27 MAY 82; To VA-205, NAS Atlanta, GA., 25 FEB 83 ** Transferred to MASDC, Davis Monthan AFB; Tucson, AZ., assigned park code 6A0150, 06 JUN 84 ** End of flight record card ** 6261.8 flight hours ** Engine removed on arrival ** Aircraft deleted from inventory and released to DRMO for disposition, 13 AUG 02.

B-121 154482 Navy acceptance from NPRO Rep. LTV, Dallas, TX., 21 AUG 68 ** Transferred to VA-46/CVW-3, AC/302, NAS Cecil Field, FL. 16 NOV 68; To VA-46/CVW-1, AB/3XX, USS John F. Kennedy (CVA-67), 11 MAY 71 ** To VA-46, NAS Cecil Field, FL., 12 DEC 72; To VA-46, USS John F. Kennedy (CVA-67), 11 DEC 74; To VA-46, NAS Cecil Field, FL., 11 DEC 74; To VA-46, USS John F. Kennedy (CVA-67), 11 DEC 74; To VA-46, NAS Cecil Field, FL., 28 APR 76; To VA-46, USS John F. Kennedy (CV-67), 11 MAY 76; To VA-46, NAS Cecil Field, FL., 11 MAY 76; To VA-46, USS John F. Kennedy (CV-67), 21 DEC 76; To VA-46, NAS Cecil Field, FL., 01 MAY 77 ** Transferred to VA-203/CVWR-20, AF/3XX, NAS Jacksonville, FL., 16 JUN 77 ** Transferred to VA-204/CVWR-20, AF/400, NAS Memphis, TN., 17 MAR 78; To VA-204, NAS New Orleans, LA., 24 MAY 78; To VA-204 NAS Jacksonville, FL., 25 AUG 79; To VA-204, NAS New Orleans, LA., 06 MAR 81 ~ S 1SO strike, 06 MAR 81 ** No data on strike.

B-122 154483 Navy acceptance from NPRO Rep. LTV, Dallas, TX., 21 AUG 68 ** Transferred to VA-174/FRS, AD/2XX, NAS Cecil Field, FL., 19 NOV 69 ~ S 1SO strike, 10 APR 69 ** No data on strike.

B-123 154484 Navy acceptance from NPRO Rep. LTV, Dallas, TX., 26 SEP 68 ** Transferred to VA-174/FRS, AD/2XX, NAS Cecil Field, FL., 21 NOV 68 ** Transferred to NPRO Rep. LTV, Dallas, TX., for RDT & E, 11 FEB 72 ** Transferred to NATC, Service Test, Patuxent River, MD., 23 MAY 72 ** Transferred to VA-174/ FRS, AD/2XX, NAS Cecil Field, FL., 25 JUL 72 ** Transferred to VA-87/CVW-6, AE/4XX, NAS Cecil Field, FL., 11 JUN 74; To VA-87, MCAS Yuma, AZ., 11 JUN 74; To VA-87, NAS Cecil Field, FL., 26 SEP 74; To VA-87, USS Franklin D. Roosevelt (CVA-42), 24 OCT 74; To VA-87, NAS Cecil Field, FL., 24 OCT 74; To VA-87, USS Franklin D. Roosevelt (CVA-42), 24 OCT 74; To VA-87, NAS Cecil Field, FL., 24 JUL 75 ** Transferred to VA-205/CVWR-20, AF/511, NAS Atlanta, GA., 19 SEP 75; To VA-205, NAS Jacksonville, FL., 17 JAN 77; To VA-205, NAS Atlanta, GA., 20 JAN 77; To VA-205,

NAS Jacksonville, FL., 01 FEB 79; To VA-205, NAS Atlanta, GA., 12 MAR 79; To VA-205, NAS Jacksonville, FL., 05 DEC 80; To VA-205, NAS Atlanta, GA., 31 MAR 81; ** Transferred to MASDC, Davis Monthan AFB; Tucson, AZ., assigned park code 6A0140, 27 SEP 83 ** End of flight record card ** 6453.3 flight hours ** Engine removed on arrival ** Aircraft deleted from inventory and released to DRMO for disposition, 13 AUG 02.

B-124 154485 Navy acceptance from NPRO Rep. LTV, Dallas, TX., 26 SEP 68 ** Transferred to VA-56/CVW-2, NE/4XX, NAS LeMoore, CA., 12 FEB 69 ** To VA-146/CVW-9, NG/3XX, USS America (CVA-66), 01 APR 69 ** Transferred to VA-93/CVW-2, NE/3XX, NAS LeMoore, CA., 17 JUL 69; To VA-93/CVW-5, NF/3XX, USS Midway (CVA-41), 12 MAY 70 ** Transferred to VA-155/CVW-19, NM/503, USS Oriskany (CVA-34), 07 APR 72; To VA-155, NAS LeMoore, CA., 04 JUN 72 ** Transferred to VA-125/FRS, NJ/5XX, 11 OCT 73; To VA-125, USS Ranger (CVA-61), 01 JUN 74 ** Transferred to VA-153/CVW-19, NM/3XX, NAS LeMoore, CA., 09 MAY 75; To VA-153, USS Oriskany (CVA-34), 30 JUN 75; To VA-153, NAS LeMoore, CA., 16 SEP 75; To VA-153, USS Franklin D. Roosevelt (CV-42), 20 APR 77; To VA-153, NAS LeMoore, CA., 20 APR 77 ** Transferred to VA-303/CVWR-30, ND/3XX, NAS Alameda, CA., 24 JUL 77 ** Transferred to NARF, NAS Jacksonville, FL., 27 JAN 78 ** Transferred to VA-303/CVWR-30, ND/310, NAS Alameda, CA., 05 MAY 78; To VA-303, NAS Jacksonville, FL., 11 SEP 80; To VA-303, NAS Alameda, CA., 13 NOV 80; To VA-303, NAS Jacksonville, FL., 06 OCT 82 ** Transferred to VA-304/CVWR-30, ND/4XX, NAS Alameda, CA., 19 AUG 83 ** Transferred to NATTC Millington, TN., sitting outside the Airframes shop, to be used as an instructional airframe, 16 OCT 86 ~ S 3SO strike, 16 OCT 86 ** End of flight record card, 17 OCT 86 ** On conditional loan from the National Museum of Naval Aviation; Pensacola, FL. to the American Military Heritage Foundation St John, AP, Reserve, LA.; JUL 95.

B-125 154486 Navy acceptance from NPRO Rep. LTV, Dallas, TX., 26 SEP 68 ** Transferred to NARF, NAS Jacksonville, FL., 11 OCT 68 ** Transferred to VA-174/FRS, AD/2XX, NAS Cecil Field, FL., 24 OCT 68 ** Transferred to VA-46/CVW-3, AC/306, NAS Cecil Field, FL., 08 NOV 68 ~ S 1SO strike, 11 APR 69 ** No data on strike.

B-126 154487 Navy acceptance from NPRO Rep. LTV, Dallas, TX., 26 SEP 68 ** Transferred to NARF, NAS Jacksonville, FL., 15 OCT 68 ** Transferred to VA-174/FRS, AD/2XX, NAS Cecil Field, FL., 26 OCT 68 ** Transferred to VA-86/CVW-6, AE/4XX, NAS Cecil Field, FL., 20 NOV 68 ** Transferred to VA-46/CVW-1, AB/306, NAS Cecil Field, FL., 26 AUG 69; To VA-46, USS John F. Kennedy (CVA-67), 22 JUN 71; To VA-46, NAS Cecil Field, FL., 04 DEC 72; To VA-46, USS John F. Kennedy (CV-67), 29 JUN 74; To VA-46, NAS Cecil Field, FL., 29 JUN 74; To VA-46, NAS Jacksonville, FL., 07 MAR 75; To VA-46, USS John F. Kennedy (CV-67), 22 APR 75; To VA-46, NAS Jacksonville, FL., 07 MAR 75; To VA-46, USS John F. Kennedy (CV-67), 22 APR 75 ~ S 1SO strike, 06 JUL 75 ** No data on strike.

B-127 154488 Navy acceptance from NPRO Rep. LTV, Dallas, TX., 26 SEP 68 ** Transferred to NARF, NAS Jacksonville, FL., 31 OCT 68 ** Transferred to VA-46/CVW-3, AC/304, NAS Cecil Field, FL., 18 NOV 68; To VA-46/CVW-1, AB/3XX, USS John F. Kennedy (CVA-67), 07 JUN 71; To VA-46, NAS Cecil Field, FL., 13 DEC 72; To VA-46, USS John F. Kennedy (CV-67), 14 NOV 74; To VA-46, NAS Cecil Field, FL., 14 NOV 74; To VA-46, USS John F. Kennedy (CV-67), 14 NOV 74; To VA-46, NAS Cecil Field, FL., 20 APR 76; To VA-46, USS John F. Kennedy (CV-67), 30 AUG 76; To VA-46, NAS Cecil Field, FL., 05 OCT 76; To VA-46, USS John F. Kennedy (CV-67), 10 FEB 77; To VA-46, NAS Cecil Field, FL., 10 FEB 77; To VA-46, USS Dwight D. Eisenhower (CVN-69), 11 AUG 77; To VA-46, NAS Cecil Field, FL., 11 AUG 77 ** Transferred to VA-204/CVWR-20, AF/4XX, NAS Memphis, TN., 07 SEP 77 ** Transferred to VA-303/CVWR-30, ND/302, NAS Alameda, CA., 05 NOV 77; To VA-303, NAS Jacksonville, FL., 01 JUN 82; To VA-303,

NAS Alameda, CA., 24 JUL 82 ** Transferred to VA-204/CVWR-20, AF/400, NAS New Orleans, LA., ** Transferred to AMARC, Davis Monthan AFB; Tucson, AZ., assigned park code 6A0175, 19 JUN 86 ~ S 3SO strike, 29 SEP 86 ** No data on strike ** End of flight record card ** 7115.0 flight hours ** TF30P408 engine S/N P664336 ** Aircraft deleted from inventory and released to DRMO for disposition, 13 AUG 02.

B-128 154489 Navy acceptance from NPRO Rep. LTV, Dallas, TX., 26 SEP 68 ** Transferred to VA-122/FRS, NJ/2XX, NAS LeMoore, CA., 03 DEC 68 ** Transferred To VA-25/CVW-16, AH/5XX, NAS LeMoore, CA., 25 JUN 69 ** Transferred to VA-155/CVW-19, NM/506, USS Oriskany (CVA-34), 24 DEC 69; To VA-155, NAS LeMoore, CA., 28 JUN 72; To VA-155, USS Oriskany (CVA-34), 04 JUN 74; To VA-155, NAS LeMoore, CA., 29 JUL 74; To VA-155, NAS Fallon, NV., 09 OCT 74; To VA-155, NAS LeMoore, CA., 28 JAN 75; To VA-155, NAS Fallon, NV., 06 MAR 75; To VA-155, NAS LeMoore, CA., 11 APR 75; To VA-155, USS Oriskany (CV-34), 15 JUL 75; To VA-155, NAS LeMoore, CA., 22 MAR 76 ** Transferred to NPRO Rep. LTV, Dallas, TX. to be converted to TA-7C, 12 JUN 76 ** Re-designated TA-7C, 21 JUN 76 ** Transferred to VA-174/FRS, AD/3XX, NAS Cecil Field, FL., 17 OCT 78; To VA-174, NAS Jacksonville, FL., 05 FEB 81; To VA-174, NAS Cecil Field, FL., 09 JUN 81; To VA-174, NAS Jacksonville, FL., 08 APR 85; To VA-174, NAS Cecil Field, FL., 24 JUN 85; To VA-174, NAS Dallas, TX., 29 APR 86; To VA-174, NAS Cecil Field, FL., 07 MAY 86 ** Transferred to the Naval Test Pilot School, NAS Patuxent River, Md., 21 SEP 87 thru 22 SEP 87 ** End of flight record card ** Transferred to NATC, NAS Patuxent River, MD., Date unknown ** Transferred to AMARC, Davis Monthan AFB; Tucson, AZ., assigned park code 6A0392, 11 FEB 91 ** 4730.9 flight hours ** TF41A402D engine S/N 142602 ** Prepared for overland and above deck shipment to Stellar Freight; Galveston, TX., for the government of Greece, no later than, 15 SEP 95 ** Transferred to the Helenic Air Force (Greece).

B-129 154490 Navy acceptance from NPRO Rep. LTV, Dallas, TX., 26 SEP 68 ** Transferred to NARF, NAS Jacksonville, FL., 14 JAN 69 ** Transferred to VA-125/FRS, NJ/5XX, NAS LeMoore, CA., 02 MAY 70 ** Transferred to VA-93/CVW-5, NF/3XX, USS Midway (CVA-41), 08 OCT 70; To VA-93, NAS LeMoore, CA., 09 JUN 72 ** Transferred to VA-153/CVW-19, NM/303, NAS LeMoore, CA., 07 MAY 73; To VA-153, USS Oriskany (CVA-34), 04 JUN 74; To VA-153, NAS Fallon, NV., 02 NOV 74; To VA-153, NAS LeMoore, CA., 11 APR 75; To VA-153, NAS Jacksonville, FL., 14 APR 75; To VA-153, NAS LeMoore, CA., 02 JUN 75; To VA-153, USS Oriskany (CV-34), 16 JUL 75; To VA-153, NAF Atsugi, JP., 26 NOV 75; To VA-153, NAS LeMoore, CA., 27 NOV 75; To VA-153, USS Franklin D. Roosevelt (CV-42), 20 APR 77; To VA-153, NAS LeMoore, CA., 25 JUN 77 ** Transferred to VA-304/CVWR-30, ND/4XX, NAS Alameda, CA., 29 JUN 77 ** Transferred to NARF Jacksonville, FL. 25 MAY 78 ** VA-204/CVWR-20, AF/412, NAS New Orleans, LA., 30 AUG 78 ** Transferred to MASDC, Davis Monthan AFB; Tucson, AZ., assigned park code 6A0124, 24 JUN 83 ** End of flight record card ** 4196.8 flight hours ** Engine removed on arrival ** Aircraft deleted from inventory and released to DRMO for disposition, 08 NOV 04.

B-130 154491 Navy acceptance from NPRO Rep. LTV, Dallas, TX., 26 SEP 68 ** Transferred to NARF, NAS Jacksonville, FL., 06 NOV 68 ** Transferred to VA-46/CVW-3, AC/3XX, NAS Cecil Field, FL., 02 DEC 68 ** Transferred to VA-72/CVW-1, AB/4XX, NAS Cecil Field, FL., 13 FEB 70; To VA-72, USS John F. Kennedy (CVA-67), 25 MAY 71; To VA-72, NAS Cecil Field, FL., 26 OCT 72; To VA-72, USS John F. Kennedy (CVA-67), 26 NOV 74; To VA-72, NAS Cecil Field, FL., 26 NOV 74; To VA-72, USS John F. Kennedy (CV-67), 30 JUN 75; To VA-72, NAS Cecil Field, FL., 20 APR 76; To VA-72, USS John F. Kennedy (CV-67), 27 APR 76; To VA-72, NAS Cecil Field, FL., 12 DEC 76; To VA-72, USS John F. Kennedy (CV-67), 13 DEC 76; To VA-72, NAS Cecil Field, FL., 13 DEC 76; To VA-72, USS John F. Kennedy (CV-67), 11 AUG 77; To VA-72, NAS Jacksonville, FL., 20 SEP 77; To VA-72, Dwight D. Eisenhower (CVN-69), 20 SEP 77; To VA-72, NAS Cecil Field, FL., 20 SEP 77 ** Transferred to VA-304/CVWR-30, ND/4XX, NAS Alameda, CA., 05 NOV 77 ** Transferred to VA-204/CVWR-20, AF/4XX, NAS New Orleans, LA., 17 SEP 78 ** Transferred to NARF, NAS Jacksonville, FL., 31 MAR 82 ** End of flight record card ** Transferred to MASDC, Davis Monthan AFB; Tucson, AZ., assigned park code 6A0158, 25 JUL 84 ** 6315.7 flight hours ** Engine removed on arrival ** Storage location 210810 ** Located at AMARG, Davis Monthan AFB; Tucson, AZ., 04 NOV 04.

B-131 154492 Navy acceptance from NPRO Rep. LTV, Dallas, TX., 26 SEP 68 ** Transferred to VA-174/FRS, AD/2XX, NAS Cecil Field, FL., 09 FEB 69 ** Transferred to VA-67/CVW-6, AE/300 then VA-67 merged into VA-15/CVW-6, AE/300, USS Intrepid (CVS-11), 17 APR 69; To VA-15, USS Franklin D. Roosevelt (CVA-42), 28 JUN 69, CDR T.S. Rogers painted on nose; To VA-15, NAS Cecil Field, FL., 14 JAN 72; To VA-15, MCAS Yuma, AZ., 30 JUN 74; To VA-15, NAS Cecil Field, FL., 30 JUN 74; To VA-15, MCAS Yuma, AZ., 30 JUN 74; To VA-15, NAS Cecil Field, FL., 20 SEP 74; To VA-15, USS Franklin D. Roosevelt (CVA-42), 27 SEP 74 ~ S 1SO strike, 25 MAY 75 ** No data on strike.

B-132 154493 Navy acceptance from NPRO Rep. LTV, Dallas, TX., 26 SEP 68 ** Transferred to VA-174/FRS, AD/2XX, NAS Cecil Field, FL., 04 DEC 68 ** Transferred to VA-72/CVW-1, AB/4XX, NAS Cecil Field, FL., 27 FEB 70; To VA-72, USS John F. Kennedy (CVA-67), 28 JUN 71; To VA-72, NAS Cecil Field, FL., 02 NOV 72; To VA-72, USS John F. Kennedy (CV-67), 06 DEC 74; To VA-72, NAS Cecil Field, FL., 06 DEC 74; To VA-72, USS John F. Kennedy (CV-67), 06 DEC 74; To VA-72, NAS Cecil Field, FL., 01 JUL 75; To VA-72, USS John F. Kennedy (CV-67), 24 JUL 75; To VA-72, NAS Cecil Field, FL., 24 JUL 75; To VA-72, USS John F. Kennedy (CV-67), 21 DEC 76; To VA-72, NAS Cecil Field, FL., 01 JUN 77 ** Transferred to VA-203/CVWR-30, AF/3XX, NAS Jacksonville, FL., 02 AUG 77 ** Transferred to MASDC, Davis Monthan AFB; Tucson, AZ., assigned park code 6A0133; 02 AUG 83 ** End of flight record card ** 5698.5 flight hours ** Engine removed on arrival ** Aircraft deleted from inventory and released to DRMO for disposition, 08 NOV 04.

B-133 154494 Navy acceptance from NPRO Rep. LTV, Dallas, TX., 26 SEP 68 ** Transferred to VA-174/FRS, AD/2XX., NAS Cecil Field, FL., 11 DEC 68 ** Transferred to VA-15/CVW-6, AE/3XX, NAS Cecil Field, FL., 13 MAR 70; To VA-15, USS Franklin D. Roosevelt (CVA-42), 25 MAR 71; To VA-15, NAS Cecil Field, FL., 12 JAN 72; To VA-15, NAS Jacksonville, FL., 31 JUL 74; To VA-15, NAS Cecil Field, FL., 05 AUG 74; To VA-15, USS Franklin D. Roosevelt (CVA-42), 01 OCT 74; To VA-15, NAS Cecil Field, FL., 24 JUL 75 ** Transferred to VA-205/CVWR-20, AF/512, NAS Atlanta, GA., 19 SEP 75; To VA-205, NAS Jacksonville, FL., 14 AUG 77; To VA-205, NAS Atlanta, GA., 11 OCT 77; To VA-205, NAS Jacksonville, FL., 10 SEP 79; To VA-205, NAS Atlanta, GA., 17 DEC 80; To VA-205, NAS Jacksonville, FL., 16 JUN 81; To VA-205, NAS Atlanta, GA., 05 AUG 81; To VA-205, NAS Jacksonville, FL., 01 SEP 81; To VA-205, NAS Atlanta, GA., 01 OCT 81;** Transferred to MASDC, Davis Monthan AFB; Tucson, AZ., assigned park code 6A0146, 14 NOV 83 ** End of flight record card ** 4655.0 flight hours ** Engine removed on arrival ** Transferred to Barry Goldwater Range; Yuma, AZ., to be used as a target, 27 OCT 03.

B-134 154495 Navy acceptance from NPRO Rep. LTV, Dallas, TX., 26 SEP 68 ** Transferred to VA-174/FRS, AD/2XX, NAS Cecil Field, FL., 25 OCT 68 ** Transferred to VA-46/CVW-3, AC/3XX, NAS Cecil Field, FL., 25 NOV 68 ~ S 1SO strike, 25 JAN 71 ** No data on strike.

B-135 154496 Navy acceptance from NPRO Rep. LTV, Dallas, TX., 26 SEP 68 ** Transferred to VA-174/FRS, AD/2XX, NAS Cecil Field, FL., 04 NOV 68 ** Transferred to VA-46/CVW-3, AC/3XX, NAS Cecil Field, FL., 27 NOV 68 ~ S 1SO strike, 23 MAR 70 ** No data on strike.

B-136 154497 Navy acceptance from NPRO Rep. LTV, Dallas, TX., 26 SEP 68 ** Transferred to VA-122/FRS, NJ/2XX, NAS LeMoore, CA., 30 OCT 68 ** Transferred to VA-56/CVW-2, NE/4XX, NAS LeMoore, CA., 10 FEB 69 ** Transferred to VA-215/CVW-9, NG/4XX, USS Enterprise (CVAN-65), 26 FEB 69; To VA-215/CVW-6, AE/4XX, USS Franklin D. Roosevelt (CVA-42), 09 JUN 69; To VA-215/CVW-19, NM/403, USS Oriskany (CVA-34), 05 JUN 70; To VA-215, NAS LeMoore, CA., 30 JUN 72 ** Transferred to VA-125/FRS, NJ/5XX, NAS LeMoore, CA., 15 OCT 73 ** Transferred to VA-174/FRS, AD/2XX, NAS Cecil Field, FL., 15 DEC 73 ** Transferred to VA-205/CVWR-20, AF/5XX, NAS Atlanta, GA., 19 SEP 75; To VA-205, NAS Jacksonville, FL., 02 AUG 76; To VA-205, NAS Atlanta, GA., 28 SEP 76 ** Transferred to VA-204/CVWR-20, AF/4XX, NAS Memphis, TN., 13 APR 78; To VA-204, NAS Dallas, TX., 26 MAY 78; To VA-204, NAS New Orleans, LA., 26 MAY 78 ~ S 1SO strike, 11 FEB 79 ** No data on strike.

B-137 154498 Navy acceptance from NPRO Rep. LTV, Dallas, TX., 14 OCT 68 ** Transferred to VA-122/FRS, NJ/2XX, NAS LeMoore, CA., 15 OCT 68 ** Transferred to VA-25/CVW-16, AH/5XX, USS Ticonderoga (CVA-14), 17 OCT 68; To VA-25, NAS Miramer, CA., 17 DEC 68 ** Transferred to NARF, NAS Alameda, CA., 18 JAN 69 ** Transferred to VA-87/ CVW-6, AE/4XX, NAS Cecil Field, FL., 17 JUN 70; To VA-87, USS Franklin D. Roosevelt (CVA-42), 25 JUN 70; To VA-87, NAS Cecil Field, FL., 11 JAN 72 ** Transferred to VA-72/CVW-1, AB/4XX, USS John F. Kennedy (CVA-67), 09 SEP 72; To VA-72, NAS Cecil Field, FL., 28 NOV 72; To VA-72, USS John F. Kennedy (CV-67), 26 AUG 74; To VA-72, NAS Cecil Field, FL., 05 MAY 75; To VA-72, NAS Jacksonville, FL., 05 MAY 75; To VA-72, USS John F. Kennedy (CV-67), 17 JUN 75; To VA-72, NAS Cecil Field, FL., 26 JUN 75; To VA-72, USS John F. Kennedy (CV-67), 26 JUN 75; To VA-72, NAS Cecil Field, FL., 26 JUN 75; To VA-72, USS John F. Kennedy (CV-67), 19 DEC 76; To VA-72, NAS Cecil Field, FL., 17 JUL 77 ** Transferred to VA-205/CVWR-20, AF/505, NAS Atlanta, GA., 22 SEP 77; To VA-205, NAS Jacksonville, FL., 14 SEP 81; To VA-205, NAS Atlanta, GA., 24 NOV 81 ** Transferred to MASDC, Davis Monthan AFB; Tucson, AZ., assigned park code 6A0137, 13 SEP 83 ** End of flight record card ** 5347.2 flight hours ** Engine removed on arrival ** Transferred to Barry Goldwater Range; Yuma, AZ., to be used as a target, 27 OCT 03.

B-138 154499 Navy acceptance from NPRO Rep. LTV, Dallas, TX., 29 OCT 68 ** Transferred to VA-122/FRS, NJ/2XX, NAS LeMoore, CA., 01 NOV 68 ** Transferred to VA-113/CVW-3, AC/4XX, USS Saratoga (CVA-60), 19 DEC 68 ~ S 1SO strike, 16 APR 69 ** No data on strike.

B-139 154500 Navy acceptance from NPRO Rep. LTV, Dallas, TX., 11 OCT 68 ** Transferred to VA-122/FRS, NJ/2XX, NAS LeMoore, CA., 19 OCT 68 ** Transferred to VA-25/CVW-16, AH/5XX, USS Ticonderoga (CVA-14), 21 OCT 68; Transferred to NAS Miramar, CA., 17 DEC 68 ** Transferred to NARF, NAS Alameda, CA., 18 JAN 69, Transferred to VA-125/FRS, NJ/5XX, NAS LeMoore, CA., 02 APR 70 ** Transferred to VA-155/ CVW-19, NM/500, USS Oriskany (CVA-34), 14 JUL 70 ** Transferred to VA-125/FRS, NJ/5XX, NAS LeMoore, CA., 07 JAN 72 ** Transferred to VA-153/ CVW-19, NM/3XX, NAS LeMoore, CA., 07 MAY 73; To VA-153, USS Oriskany (CV-34), 04 JUN 74; To VA-153, NAS LeMoore, CA., 04 JUN 74; To VA-153, NAS Fallon, NV., 26 FEB 75; To VA-153, NAS LeMoore, CA., 11 MAY 75; To VA-153, USS Oriskany (CV-34), 16 JUL 75; To VA-153, NAF Atsugi, JP., 08 DEC 75; To VA-153, USS Oriskany (CV-34), 10 JAN 76; To VA-153, NAS LeMoore, CA., 25 MAR 76 ** Transferred to NPRO Rep. LTV, Dallas, TX. to be converted to TA-7C, 22 JUN 76 ** Re-designated to TA-7C, 01 JUL 76 ** Transferred to VA-174/FRS, AD/3XX, NAS Cecil Field, FL., 01 DEC 78; To VA-174, NAS Jacksonville, FL., 28 MAY 81; To VA-174, NAS Cecil Field, FL., 24 AUG 81; To VA-174, NAS Jacksonville, FL., 28 JAN 85; To VA-174, NAS Cecil Field, FL., 18 APR 85 ** Transferred to the Naval Test Pilot School, NAS Patuxent River, MD., 09 SEP 87 thru 14 SEP 87 ** End of flight record card ** On display at the American Wings Air Museum, Anoka County-Blaine, AP, MN., painted as a Blue Angel with Naval Air Reserve Center Minneapolis decal on the tail, 30 SEP 04.

B-140 154501 Navy acceptance from NPRO Rep. LTV, Dallas, TX., 31 OCT 68 ** Transferred to VA-46/CVW-3, AC/3XX, NAS Cecil Field, FL., 08 NOV 68 ** Transferred to VA-174/FRS, AD/2XX, NAS Cecil Field, FL., 20 FEB 70 ** Transferred to NPRO Rep. LTV, Dallas, TX., for RDT & E, 10 JAN 72 ** Transferred to VA-174/FRS, AD/2XX, NAS Cecil Field, FL., 16 JUL 73 ** Transferred to NATC, NAS Patuxent River, MD., for RTD & E, 29 APR 73 ** Transferred to VA-174/FRS, AD/2XX, NAS Cecil Field, FL., 16 JUL 73 ** Transferred to NATC, NAS Patuxent River, MD., for RTD & E, 23 OCT 73 ~ S 1SO strike, 03 AUG 74 ** No data on strike.

B-141 154502 Navy acceptance from NPRO Rep. LTV, Dallas, TX., 30 OCT 68 ** Transferred to VA-174/FRS, AD/2XX, NAS Cecil Field, FL., 01 NOV 68 ** Transferred to VA-46/CVW-1, AB/3XX, NAS Cecil Field, FL., 25 NOV 68; To VA-46, USS John F. Kennedy (CVA-67), 17 JUN 71 ** Transferred to VA-174/FRS, AD/2XX, NAS Cecil Field, FL., 06 OCT 72 ** Transferred to VA-46/CVW-1, AB/3XX, USS John F. Kennedy (CVA-67), 31 OCT 72; To VA-46, NAS Cecil Field, FL., 08 DEC 72; To VA-46, NAS Jacksonville, FL., 18 FEB 75; To VA-46, USS John F. Kennedy (CV-67), 27 MAR 75; To VA-46, NAS Cecil Field, FL., 18 FEB 76; To VA-46, USS John F. Kennedy (CV-67), 29 MAR 76; To VA-46, NAS Cecil Field, FL., 13 DEC 76; To VA-46, USS John F. Kennedy (CV-67), 18 JAN 76; To VA-46, NAS Cecil Field, FL., 18 JAN 77 ** Transferred to VA-204/ CVWR-20, AF/4XX, NAS Memphis, TN., 22 SEP 77 ** Transferred to VA-203/CVWR-20, AF/3XX, NAS Jacksonville, FL., 20 NOV 77; To VA-203, NAS Dallas, TX., 27 APR 78; To VA-203, NAS Jacksonville, FL., 05 MAY 78 ** Transferred to VA-305/CVWR-30, ND/502, NAS Point Mugu, CA., 13 MAY 78; To VA-305, NAS Jacksonville, FL., 23 SEP 80; To VA-305, NAS Point Mugu, CA., 31 OCT 80; To VA-305, NAS Dallas, TX., 17 APR 81; To VA-305, NAS Point Mugu, CA., 01 AUG 81; To VA-305, NAS Jacksonville, FL., 30 AUG 85; To VA-305, NAS Point Mugu, CA., 30 NOV 83; To VA-305, NAS Jacksonville, FL., 08 FEB 84; To VA-305, NAS Point Mugu, CA., 28 JUN 84** Transferred to NATTC Millington, TN., 29 DEC 86, sitting outside the Airframes shop, to be used as an instructional airframe ** End of flight record card ** Sitting outside Airframes, NATTC Millington, TN., 07 OCT 89 ** On conditional loan from the National Museum of Naval Aviation; Pensacola, FL. to LTV Dallas, TX., Jul 99. The Vought Retiree Club, restored this aircraft in VA-305/CVWR-30, ND/502 colors and was displayed at LTV; Dallas, TX., JUL 03 ** Vought loaned this aircraft to Frontiers of Flight at Love Field; Dallas, TX., JUL 04.

B-142 154503 Navy acceptance from NPRO Rep. LTV, Dallas, TX., 30 OCT 68 ** Transferred to VA-174/FRS, AD/2XX, NAS Cecil Field, FL., 01 NOV 68 ** Transferred to VA-46/CVW-3, AC/312, NAS Cecil Field, FL., 26 NOV 68 ~ S 1SO strike, 17 APR 71 ** No data on strike.

B-143 154504 Navy acceptance from NPRO Rep. LTV, Dallas, TX., 30 OCT 68 ** Transferred to VA-174/FRS, AD/2XX, NAS Cecil Field, FL., 01 NOV 68 ** Transferred to VA-46/CVW-3, AC/315, NAS Cecil Field, FL., 28 NOV 68 ~ S 1SO strike, 16 MAR 70 ** No data on strike.

B-144 154505 Navy acceptance from NPRO Rep. LTV, Dallas, TX., 30 OCT 68 ** Transferred to VA-122/FRS, NJ/2XX, NAS LeMoore, CA., 16 NOV 68 ** Transferred to VA-146/ CVW-9, NG/3XX, USS Enterprise (CVAN-65), 20 DEC 68 ** Transferred to VA-174/FRS, AD/2XX, NAS Cecil Field, FL., 29 JUL 69 ** Transferred to VA-46/CVW-1, AB/303, NAS Cecil Field, FL., 02 APR 70; To VA-46, USS John F. Kennedy (CVA-67), 25 JUN 71; To VA-46, NAS Cecil Field, FL., 06 OCT 72; To VA-46, USS John F. Kennedy (CV-67), 31 OCT 74; To VA-46, NAS Cecil Field, FL., 31 OCT 74; To VA-46, USS John F. Kennedy (CV-67), 31 OCT 74; To VA-46, NAS Cecil Field, FL., 31 OCT 74; To VA-46, USS John F. Kennedy (CV-67), 31 OCT 74; To VA-46, NAS Cecil Field, FL., 26 FEB 76; To VA-46, USS John F. Kennedy (CV-67), 13 AUG 76; To VA-46, NAS Cecil Field, FL., 19 AUG 76; To VA-46, USS John F. Kennedy (CV-67), 19 AUG 76; To VA-46, NAS Cecil Field, FL., 13 DEC

76; To VA-46, USS John F. Kennedy (CV-67), 18 JAN 76; To VA-46, NAS Cecil Field, FL., 18 JAN 77; To VA-46, USS John F. Kennedy (CV-67), 10 MAR 77; To VA-46, NAS Cecil Field, FL., 11 MAR 77 ** Transferred to VA-204/CVWR-20, AF/ 4XX, NAS Memphis, TN., 07 SEP 77 ** Transferred to VA-304/CVWR-30, ND/402, NAS Alameda, CA., 05 NOV 77; To VA-304, NAS Jacksonville, FL., 07 JUN 82; To VA-304, NAS Alameda, CA., 22 SEP 82 ** Transferred to AMARC, Davis Monthan AFB; Tucson, AZ., assigned park code 6A0201, 12 SEP 86 ** End of flight record card ** 7116.4 flight hours ** Engine removed on arrival ** Aircraft deleted from inventory and released to DRMO for disposition, 13 AUG 02.

B-145 154506 Navy acceptance from NPRO Rep. LTV, Dallas, TX., 30 OCT 68 ** Transferred to VA-122/FRS, NJ/2XX, NAS LeMoore, CA., 07 NOV 68 ** Transferred to VA-113/CVW-3, AC/4XX, USS Saratoga (CVA-60), 19 DEC 68; To VA-113, NAS LeMoore, CA., 09 JUN 69 ** Transferred to VA-125/FRS, NJ/5XX, NAS LeMoore, CA., 25 MAY 70 ** Transferred to VA-93/CVW-5, NF/314, USS Midway (CVA-41), 10 JUN 72; To VA-93, NAS LeMoore, CA., 28 JUN 72 ~ S 1SO strike, 10 NOV 72 ** No data on strike.

B-146 154507 Navy acceptance from NPRO Rep. LTV, Dallas, TX., 30 OCT 68 ** Transferred to VA-174/FRS, AD/2XX, NAS Cecil Field, FL., 19 DEC 68 ** Transferred to VA-72/CVW-1, AB/4XX, USS John F. Kennedy (CVA-67), 16 AUG 72 ** Transferred to VA-174/FRS, AD/2XX, NAS Cecil Field, FL., 06 OCT 72 ** Transferred to VA-87/CVW-6, AE/407, NAS Cecil Field, FL., 03 JUL 74; To VA-87, MCAS Yuma, AZ., 03 JUL 74; To VA-87, NAS Cecil Field, FL., 30 SEP 74; To VA-87, USS Franklin D. Roosevelt (CVA-42), 24 OCT 74; To VA-87, NAS Cecil Field, FL., 24 OCT 74; To VA-87, USS Franklin D. Roosevelt (CVA-42), 24 OCT 74; To VA-87, NAS Cecil Field, FL., 24 JUL 75 ** Transferred to VA-174/FRS, AD/2XX, NAS Cecil Field, FL., 19 AUG 75 ** Transferred to NPRO Rep. LTV, Dallas, TX., to be converted to TA-7C, 20 MAY 76 ** Re-designated to TA-7C, 29 MAY 76 ** Transferred to VA-174/FRS, AD/3XX, NAS Cecil Field, Fl., 23 JUL 78; To VA-174, NAS Jacksonville, FL., 18 JUL 80; To VA-174, NAS Cecil Field, FL., 23 JUL 80; To VA-174, NAS Jacksonville, FL., 05 SEP 84; To VA-174, NAS Cecil Field, FL., 08 NOV 84 Thru 19 MAR 87 ** End of flight record card ** Transferred to VA-304/CVWR-30, ND/4XX, date unknown ** Transferred to AMARC, Davis Monthan AFB; Tucson, AZ., assigned park code 6A0417, 08 NOV 94 ** 6143.5 flight hours ** TF41A402D S/N 141941 ** Prepare for overland shipment to FMS, NAS Jacksonville, FL., for the government of Greece no later than, 31 JAN 96.

B-147 154508 Navy acceptance from NPRO Rep. LTV, Dallas, TX., 30 OCT 68 ** Transferred to VA-122/FRS, NJ/2XX, NAS LeMoore, CA., 27 JAN 69 ** Transferred to VA-56/CVW-2, NE/4XX, NAS LeMoore, CA., 25 JAN 69; To VA-56/CVW-5, NF/3XX, USS Midway (CVA-41), 13 APR 70; To VA-56, NAS LeMoore, CA., 10 APR 72 ~ S 1SO strike, 06 AUG 72 ** No data on strike.

B-148 154509 Navy acceptance from NPRO Rep. LTV, Dallas, TX., 30 OCT 68 ** Transferred to VA-122/FRS, NJ/2XX, NAS LeMoore, CA., 26 JAN 69 ** Transferred to VA-56/CVW-5, NF/4XX, NAS LeMoore, CA., 27 JAN 69; To VA-56, USS Midway (CVA-41), 15 JUN 70; To VA-56, NAS LeMoore, CA., 27 JUN 72 ** Transferred to VA-155/CVW-19, NM/5XX, NAS LeMoore, CA., 23 MAY 73; To VA-155, USS Oriskany (CVA-34), 04 JUN 74; To VA-155, NAS LeMoore, CA., 12 AUG 74; To VA-155, NAS Jacksonville, FL., 14 NOV 74; To VA-155, NAS Fallon, NV., 16 NOV 74; To VA-155, NAS LeMoore, CA., 16 NOV 74; TO VA-155, NAS Fallon, NV., 31 MAR 75; To VA-155, NAS LeMoore, CA., 11 APR 75 ** Transferred to VA-125/FRS, NJ/5XX, NAS LeMoore, CA., 07 MAY 75; To VA-125, NAS Alameda, CA., 18 SEP 75; To VA-125, NAS LeMoore, CA., 24 DEC 75; To VA-125, NAS Alameda, CA., 19 APR 76; To VA-125, NAS LeMoore, CA.,

09 JUN 76 ** Transferred to VA-205/CVWR-20, AF/5XX, NAS Atlanta, GA., 14 AUG 77; To VA-205, NAS Dallas, TX., 12 APR 78; To VA-205, NAS Atlanta, GA., 05 MAY 78 ** Transferred to NARF, NAS Jacksonville, FL., 30 JUN 78 ** Transferred to VA-205/CVWR-20, AF/502, NAS Atlanta, GA., 11 SEP 78; To VA-205, NAS Jacksonville, FL., 03 NOV 80; To VA-205, NAS Atlanta, GA., 03 FEB 81 ** Transferred to MASDC, Davis Monthan AFB; Tucson, AZ., assigned park code 6A0132, 28 JUL 83 ** End of flight record card ** 5633.6 flight hours ** Engine removed on arrival ** Aircraft deleted from inventory and released to DRMO for disposition, 13 AUG 02.

B-149 154510 Navy acceptance from NPRO Rep. LTV, Dallas, TX., 30 OCT 68 ** Transferred to VA-122/FRS, NJ/2XX, NAS LeMoore, CA., 03 DEC 68 ** Transferred to VA-25/CVW-16, AH/5XX, USS Ticonderoga (CVA-14), 18 DEC 68 ~ S 1SO strike, 07 JAN 69 ** No data on strike.

B-150 154511 Navy acceptance from NPRO Rep. LTV, Dallas, TX., 31 OCT 68 ** Transferred to VA-122/FRS, NJ/2XX, NAS LeMoore, CA., 25 NOV 68 ** Transferred to VA-113/CVW-3, AC/4XX, USS Saratoga,(CVA-60), 03 JAN 69; To VA-113, NAS Cecil Field, FL. , 26 JUN 69 ~ S 1SO strike, 10 NOV 69 ** No data on strike.

B-151 154512 Navy acceptance from NPRO Rep. LTV, Dallas, TX., 31 OCT 68 ** Transferred to VA-174/FRS, AD/2XX, NAS Cecil Field, FL., 25 NOV 68 ** Transferred to VA-15/CVW-6, AE/310, USS Franklin D. Roosevelt (CVA-42), 04 APR70; To VA-15, NAS Cecil Field, FL., 15 OCT 71; To VA-15, NAS Jacksonville, FL., 20 AUG 74; To VA-15, NAS Cecil Field, FL., 27 SEP 74; To VA-15, USS Franklin D. Roosevelt (CVA-42), 09 OCT 74; To VA-15, NAS Cecil Field, FL., 24 JUL 75 ** Transferred to VA-205/ CVWR-20, AF/514, NAS Atlanta, GA., 02 OCT 75; To VA-205, NAS Jacksonville, FL., 20 JUN 80; To VA-205, NAS Atlanta, GA., 09 SEP 80 ** Transferred to MASDC, Davis Monthan AFB; Tucson, AZ., assigned park code 6A0123; 24 JUN 83 ** End of flight record card ** 5455.7 flight hours ** Engine removed on arrival ** Located at AMARC, Davis Monthan AFB; Tucson, AZ., 31 DEC 97.

B-152 154513 Navy acceptance from NPRO Rep. LTV, Dallas, TX., 25 NOV 68 ** Transferred to VA-174/FRS, AD/2XX, NAS Cecil Field, FL., 26 NOV 68 ** Transferred to VA-15/CVW-6, AE/306, USS Franklin D. Roosevelt (CVA-42), 22 DEC 69; VA-15, NAS Cecil Field, FL., 14 NOV 71 ~ S 1SO strike, 08 MAY 74 ** No data on strike.

B-153 154514 Navy acceptance from NPRO Rep. LTV, Dallas, TX., 25 NOV 68 ** Transferred to VA-122/FRS, NJ/2XX, NAS LeMoore, CA., 07 DEC 68 ** Transferred to VA-113/CVW-3, AC/4XX, USS Saratoga(CVA-60), 12 DEC 68 ~ S 1SO strike, 03 JAN 69 ** No data on strike.

B-154 154515 Navy acceptance from NPRO Rep. LTV, Dallas, TX., 27 NOV 68 ** Transferred to VA-174/FRS, AD/2XX, NAS Cecil Field, FL., 23 DEC 68 ~ S 1SO strike, 25 JAN 69 ** No data on strike.

B-155 154516 Navy acceptance from NPRO Rep. LTV Dallas, TX., 25 NOV 68 ** Transferred to VA-122/FRS, NJ/2XX, NAS LeMoore, CA., 26 NOV 68 ** Transferred to VA-113/CVW-3, AC/4XX, USS Saratoga (CVA-60), 10 DEC 68; To VA-113, NAS LeMoore, CA., 26 JUN 69 ** Transferred to VA-155/CVW-19, NM/5XX, USS Oriskany (CVA-34), 26 FEB 70 ** Transferred to VA-93/CVW-5, NF/3XX, USS Oriskany (CVA-34), 07 APR 72; To VA-93, NAS LeMoore, CA., 22 MAY 72; To VA-93, USS Midway (CVA-41), 29 JUN 73 ** Transferred to VA-215/CVW-19, NM/405, NAS LeMoore, CA., 12 JUL 73; Transferred to VA-215, USS Oriskany (CVA-34), 05 JUN 74; To VA-215, NAS LeMoore, CA., 05 JUN 74; To VA-215, NAS Fallon, NV., 09 NOV 74; To VA-215, NAS Jacksonville, FL., 20 MAR 75; To VA-215,

NAS Fallon, NV., 20 MAR 75; To VA-215, NAS Jacksonville, FL., 26 MAR 75; To VA-215, NAS LeMoore, CA., 26 MAR 75; To VA-215, NAS Jacksonville, FL., 11 JUN 75; To VA-215, NAS LeMoore, CA., 01 JUL 75; To VA-215, USS Oriskany (CVA-34), 15 JUL 75; To VA-215, NAS LeMoore, CA., 15 SEP 75; To VA-215, USS Franklin D. Roosevelt (CV-42), 19 AUG 76 ** Transferred to VA-125/FRS, NJ/5XX, NAS LeMoore, CA., 18 MAY 77 ** Transferred to VA-303/CVWR-30, ND/3XX, NAS Alameda, CA., 11 AUG 77; To VA-303, NAS Jacksonville, FL., 06 APR 78; To VA-303, NAS Alameda, CA., 31 MAY 78 ** Transferred to VA-204/CVWR-20, AF/412, NAS New Orleans, LA., 23 SEP 83 ** Transferred to AMARC, Davis Monthan AFB; Tucson, AZ., assigned park code 6A0160, 01 FEB 86 ** End of flight record card ** 5022.4 flight hours ** TF30P408 engine S/N 664282 ** Aircraft deleted from inventory and released to DRMO for disposition, 13 AUG 02.

B-156 154517 Navy acceptance from NPRO Rep. LTV, Dallas, TX., 27 NOV 68 ** Transferred to VA-122/FRS, NJ/2XX, NAS LeMoore, CA., 21 JAN 69 ** Transferred to VA-56/CVW-2, NE/401, NAS LeMoore, CA., 22 JAN 69 ~ S 1SO strike, 26 DEC 69 ** No data on strike.

B-157 154518 Navy acceptance from NPRO Rep. LTV, Dallas, TX., 25 NOV 68 ** Transferred to VA-122/FRS, NJ/2XX, NAS LeMoore, CA., 03 DEC 68 ** Transferred to VF-114, XX/XXX, USS Kitty Hawk (CVA-63), 10 DEC 68; Transferred to VA-113/CVW-3, AC/4XX, USS Saratoga (CVA-60), 11 DEC 68; To VA-113, NAS LeMoore, CA., 21 JUN 69 ** Transferred to VA-155/CVW-19, NM/505, USS Oriskany (CV-34), 06 MAY 70; To VA-155, NAS LeMoore, CA., ~ S 1SO strike, 12 MAY 74 ** No data on strike.

B-158 154519 Navy acceptance from NPRO Rep. LTV, Dallas, TX., 27 NOV 68 ** Transferred to VA-122/FRS, NJ/2XX, NAS LeMoore, CA., 09 DEC 68 ** Transferred to VA-113/CVW-3, AC/4XX, USS Saratoga (CVA-60), 12 DEC 68; To VA-113, NAS LeMoore, Ca., 13 JUN 69 ** Transferred to VA-155/CVW-19, NM/5XX, USS Oriskany (CVA-34), 17 MAR 70 ** Transferred to VA-56/CVW-5, NF/3XX, USS Midway (CVA-41), 27 MAR 71; To VA-56, NAS LeMoore, CA., 28 JUN 72 ** Transferred to NARF, NAS Alameda, CA., 05 APR 73 ~ S 1SO strike, 16 NOV 76 ** No data on strike.

B-159 154520 Navy acceptance from NPRO Rep. LTV, Dallas, TX., 27 NOV 68 ** Transferred to VA-174/FRS, AD/2XX, NAS Cecil Field, FL., 05 DEC 68 ** Transferred to VA-113/CVW-3, AC/4XX, NAS LeMoore, CA., 03 JUL 69 ** Transferred to VA-155/CVW-19, NM/5XX, USS Oriskany (CVA-34), 11 FEB 70; To VA-155, NAS LeMoore, CA., 04 JUN 72 ** Transferred to NARF, NAS Alameda, CA., 05 APR 73 ** Transferred to VA-303/CVWR-30, ND/312, NAS Alameda, CA., 05 APR 73 ** Transferred to VA-205/CVWR-20, AF/5XX, NAS Atlanta, GA., 29 SEP 83 ** Transferred to VA-204/CVWR-20, AF/4XX, NAS New Orleans, LA., 05 JUN 84 ** Transferred to AMARC, Davis Monthan AFB; Tucson, AZ., assigned park code 6A0173, 13 JUN 86 ** End of flight record card ** 4461.8 flight hours ** TF30P408 engine S/N P664265 ** Aircraft deleted from inventory and released to DRMO for disposition, 13 AUG 02.

B-160 154521 Navy acceptance from NPRO Rep. LTV, Dallas, TX., 27 NOV 68 ** Transferred to VA-174/FRS, AD/2XX, NAS Cecil Field, FL., 22 DEC 68 ** Transferred to VA-113/CVW-3, AC/4XX, NAS LeMoore, CA., 25 JUN 69 ** Transferred to VA-155/CVW-19, NM/510, USS Oriskany (CVA-34), 28 JAN 70; To VA-155, NAS LeMoore, CA., 04 JUN 72 ~ S 1SO strike, 17 JUL 72 ** Combat loss.

B-161 154522 Navy acceptance from NPRO Rep. LTV, Dallas, TX., 27 NOV 68 ** Transferred to VA-174/FRS, AD/2XX, NAS Cecil Field, FL., 18 DEC 68 ** ~ S 1SO strike, 06 MAY 69 ** No data on strike.

154523/154556 LTV A-7B-4-CV Corsair II; (Block IV)

B-163 154523 Navy acceptance from NPRO Rep. LTV, Dallas, TX., 26 NOV 68 ** Transferred to VA-113/CVW-3, AC/4XX, USS Saratoga (CVA-60), 05 NOV 69; To VA-113, NAS LeMoore, CA., 10 JUN 69 ** Transferred to VA-155/CVW-19, NM/514 & NM/502, USS Oriskany (CVA-34), 28 JAN 70; To VA-155, NAS LeMoore, CA., 04 JUN 72; To VA-155, NAS Jacksonville, FL., 07 AUG 74; To VA-155, NAS LeMoore, CA., 17 AUG 74; To VA-155, NAS Fallon, NV., 17 SEP 74; To VA-155, NAS LeMoore, CA., 26 SEP 74; To VA-155, NAS Fallon, NV., 31 MAR 75; To VA-155, NAS LeMoore, CA., 11 APR 75; To VA-155, USS Oriskany (CV-34), 09 JUL 75; To VA-155, NAS LeMoore, CA., 01 APR 76; To VA-155, USS Franklin D. Roosevelt (CV-42), 25 JUN 76; To VA-155, NAS LeMoore, CA., 27 MAY 77 ** Transferred to VA-303/CVWR-30, ND/316, NAS Alameda, CA., 22 JUL 77; To VA-303, NAS Jacksonville, FL., 28 JUL 77; To VA-303, NAS Alameda, CA., 02 AUG 77; To VA-303, NAS Jacksonville, FL., 07 OCT 77; To VA-303, NAS Alameda, CA.,03 JAN 78; To VA-303, NAS Jacksonville, FL., 13 MAY 83 ** Transferred to VA-304/CVWR-30, ND/4XX, NAS Alameda, CA., 30 AUG 83 ** Transferred to VA-305/CVWR-30, ND/5XX, NAS Point Mugu, CA., 29 JUL 86 ** Transferred to NATTC Millington, TN., 08 JAN 87, as an instructional aid ~ S 3SO strike, 09 JAN 87 ** End of flight record card ** On conditional loan from the National Museum of Naval Aviation; Pensacola, FL. to the Arkansas Air Museum at Drake Field; Fayetteville, AR.

B-164 154524 Navy acceptance from NPRO Rep. LTV, Dallas, TX., 26 NOV 68 ** Transferred to VA-113/CVW-3, AC/4XX, USS Saratoga (CVA-60), 10 JAN 69 ~ S 1SO strike, 24 JUN 69 ** No data on strike.

B-165 154525 Navy acceptance from NPRO Rep. LTV, Dallas, TX., 26 NOV 68 ** Transferred to VA-25/CVW-16, AH/5XX, USS Ticonderoga (CVA-14), 14 JAN 69; To VA-25, NAS LeMoore, CA., 28 APR 69 ** Transferred to VA-125/FRS, NJ/5XX, NAS LeMoore, CA., 13 NOV 69 ** VA-155/CVW-19, NM/5XX, USS Oriskany (CVA-34), 29 JAN 70 ~ S 1SO strike, 25 JUN 70 ** Crashed due to engine failure.

B-166 154526 Navy acceptance from NPRO Rep. LTV, Dallas, TX., 19 DEC 68 ** Transferred to VA-113/CVW-3, AC/4XX, USS Saratoga (CVA-60), 12 JAN 69; To VA-113, NAS LeMoore, CA., 13 JUN 69 ** Transferred to VA-155/CVW-19, NM/504, NAS LeMoore, CA., 04 JUN 72; To VA-155, USS Oriskany (CVA-34), 04 JUN 74; To VA-155, NAS Jacksonville, FL., 01 AUG 74; To VA-155, NAS LeMoore, CA., 25 SEP 74; To VA-155, NAS Fallon, NV., 09 NOV 74; To VA-155, NAS LeMoore, CA., 03 DEC 74; To VA-155, NAS Fallon, NV., 31 MAR 75; To VA-155, NAS LeMoore, CA., 11 APR 75; To VA-155, USS Oriskany (CV-34), 15 JUL 75; To VA-155, NAF Atsugi, JP., 03 NOV 75; To VA-155, USS Oriskany (CV-34), 05 NOV 75; To VA-155, NAS LeMoore, CA., 23 FEB 76; To VA-155, USS Franklin D. Roosevelt (CV-42), 15 OCT 76 ~ S 1SO strike, 05 DEC 76 ** No data on strike.

B-167 154527 Navy acceptance from NPRO Rep. LTV, Dallas, TX., 18 DEC 68 ** Transferred to VA-113/CVW-3, AC/4XX, USS Saratoga (CVA-60), 10 JAN 69; To VA-113, NAS LeMoore, CA., 16 JUN 69 ** Transferred to VA-155/CVW-19, NM/ 5XX, USS Oriskany (CVA-34), 05 FEB 70 ** Transferred to VA-125/FRS, NJ/5XX, NAS LeMoore, CA., 16 APR 71 ** Transferred to VA-215/CVW-19, NM/411, USS Oriskany (CVA-34), 15 FEB 72; To VA-215, NAS LeMoore, CA., 04 JUN 72; To VA-215; USS Oriskany (CVA-34), 05 JUN 74; To VA-215, NAS LeMoore, CA., 19 AUG 74; To VA-215, NAS Fallon, NV., 09 NOV 74; To VA-215, NAS LeMoore, CA., 27 JAN 75; To VA-215, NAS Fallon, NV., 28 JAN 75; To VA-215, NAS LeMoore, CA., 28 JAN 75; To VA-215, USS Oriskany (CV-34), 15 JUL 75; To VA-215, NAS LeMoore, CA., 23 MAR 76; To VA-215, USS Franklin D. Roosevelt (CV-42), 13 JAN 77; To VA-215, NAS LeMoore, CA., 12 MAY 77 ** Transferred to VA-304/CVWR-30, ND/414, NAS Alameda, CA., 01 JUL 77; To VA-304, NAS Dallas, TX., 16 MAY 78; To VA-304, NAS Alameda, CA., 29

MAY 78; To VA-304, NAS Jacksonville, FL., 17 SEP 81; To VA-304, NAS Alameda, CA., 03 DEC 81 ** Transferred to NATTC; Millington, TN., ., sitting outside the Airframes shop, to be used as an instructional airframe, 28 AUG 86 ~ S 3SO strike, 29 AUG 86 ** End of flight record card ** Transferred to the Fire Training Compound NATTC; Millington, TN., date unknown.

B-168 154528 Navy acceptance from NPRO Rep. LTV, Dallas, TX., 18 DEC 68 ** Transferred to VA-113/CVW-3, AC/4XX, USS Saratoga (CVA-60), 14 JAN 69; To VA-113, NAS LeMoore, CA., 10 JUN 69 ** Transferred to VA-155/CVW-19, NM/ 511, USS Oriskany (CVA-34), 28 JAN 70 ** Transferred to VA-125/FRS, NJ/5XX, NAS LeMoore, CA., 16 APR 71 ** Transferred to VA-155/CVW-19, NM/5XX, USS Oriskany (CVA-34), 07 JAN 72 ~ S 1SO strike, 14 APR 72 ** No data on strike.

B-169 154529 Navy acceptance from NPRO Rep. LTV, Dallas, TX., 18 DEC 68 ** Transferred to VA-113/CVW-3, AC/4XX, USS Saratoga (CVA-60), 03 JAN 69; To VA-113, NAS LeMoore, CA., 10 JUN 69 ** Transferred to VA-155/CVW-19, NM/ 5XX, USS Oriskany (CVA-34), 29 JAN 70 ** Transferred to VA-125/FRS, NJ/5XX, NAS LeMoore, CA., 16 APR 71 ** Transferred to VA-155/CVW-19, NM/5XX, USS Oriskany (CVA-34), 31 JAN 72; To VA-155, NAS LeMoore, CA., 26 JUN 72; To VA-155, NAS Fallon, NV., 09 NOV 74; To VA-155, NAS LeMoore, CA., 26 FEB 75; To VA-155, NAS Fallon, NV., 28 FEB 75; To VA-155, NAS LeMoore, CA., 17 MAR 75; To VA-155, USS Oriskany (CV-34), 15 JUL 75; To VA-155, NAF Atsugi, JP., 11 NOV 75; To VA-155, USS Oriskany (CV-34), 30 NOV 75; To VA-155, NAF Atsugi, JP., 07 JAN 76; To VA-155, USS Oriskany (CV-34), 14 JAN 76; To VA-155, NAS LeMoore, CA., 18 JAN 76; To VA-155, NAS Alameda, CA., 28 MAY 76; To VA-155, NAS LeMoore, CA., 15 JUN 76; To VA-155, USS Franklin D. Roosevelt (CV-42), 15 OCT 76; To VA-155, NAS LeMoore, CA., 06 JUL 77 ** Transferred to VA-303/CVWR-30, ND/314, NAS Alameda, CA., 06 JUL 77 ** Transferred to NARF, NAS Jacksonville, FL. 02 MAR 78 ** Transferred to VA-303/CVWR-30, ND/314, NAS Alameda, CA., 24 MAY 78 ** Transferred to VA-205/CVWR-20, AF/5XX, NAS Atlanta, GA., 30 AUG 83 ** Transferred to VA-204/CVWR-20, AF/404, NAS New Orleans, LA., 01 JUN 84 ** Transferred to AMARC, Davis Monthan AFB; Tucson, AZ., assigned park code 6A0167, 02 JUN 86 ~ S 3SO strike, 29 SEP 86 ** No data on strike ** End of flight record card ** 6057.1 flight hours ** TF30P408 engine S/N 664423 ** Aircraft deleted from inventory and released to DRMO for disposition, 13 AUG 02.

B-170 154530 Navy acceptance from NPRO Rep. LTV, Dallas, TX., 18 DEC 68 ** Transferred to VA-113/CVW-3,AC/4XX, USS Saratoga (CVA-60), 15 JAN 69; To VA-113/CVW-3, AC/4XX, NAS LeMoore, CA., 10 JUN 69 ** Transferred to VA-155/ CVW-19, NM/5XX, USS Oriskany (CVA-34), 27 JAN 70 ~ S 1SO strike, 09 APR 70 ** No data on strike.

B-171 154531 Navy acceptance from NPRO Rep. LTV, Dallas, TX., 18 DEC 68 ** Transferred to VA-56/CVW-2, NE/407, NAS LeMoore, CA., 10 FEB 69; ** To VA-56/CVW-5, NF/404, USS Midway (CVA-41), 20 APR 70; To VA-56, NAS LeMoore, CA., 29 JUN 72 ~ S 1SO strike, 23 JUL 72 ** No data on strike.

B-172 154532 Navy acceptance from NPRO Rep. LTV, Dallas, TX., 18 DEC 68 ** Transferred to VA-122/FRS, NJ/2XX, NAS LeMoore, CA., 07 FEB 69 ** Transferred to VA-56/CVW-2, NE/4XX, NAS LeMoore, CA., 10 FEB 69 ** Transferred to VA-155/CVW-19, NM/5XX, USS Oriskany (CVA-34), 09 OCT 69 ** Transferred to VA-56/CVW-5, NF/400, USS Midway (CVA-41), 09 APR 72; To VA-56, NAS LeMoore, CA., 23 JUN 72 ~ S 1SO strike, 23 JUL 72 ** No data on strike.

B-173 154533 Navy acceptance from NPRO Rep. LTV, Dallas, TX., 18 DEC 68 ** Transferred to VA-56/CVW-2, NE/4XX, NAS LeMoore, CA., 12 FEB 69 ** Transferred to VA-146/CVW-9, NG/3XX, USS Enterprise (CVAN-65), 27 FEB 69; To VA-146, USS America (CVA-66), 19 MAY 69 ** Transferred to VA-56/CVW-2, NE/4XX, NAS

LeMoore, CA., 15 JUL 69; To VA-56/CVW-5, NF/4XX, USS Midway (CVA-41), 19 MAR 70; To VA-56, NAS LeMoore, CA., 05 JUN 72 ** Transferred to VA-153/CVW-19, NM/310, NAS LeMoore, CA., 04 MAY 73 ~ S 1SO strike, 19 MAR 74 ** No data on strike.

B-174 154534 Navy acceptance from NPRO Rep. LTV, Dallas, TX., 18 DEC 68 ** Transferred to VA-174/FRS, AD/2XX, NAS Cecil Field, FL., 24 JAN 69 ** Transferred to VA-72/CVW-1, AB/4XX, NAS Cecil Field, FL., 16 FEB 70; To VA-72, USS John F. Kennedy (CVA-67), 28 JUN 71 ~ S 1SO strike, 27 JUN 72 ** No data on strike.

B-175 154535 Navy acceptance from NPRO Rep. LTV, Dallas, TX., 18 DEC 68 ** Transferred to VA-122/FRS, NJ/2XX, NAS LeMoore, CA., 30 JAN 69 ** Transferred to VA-56/CVW-2, NE/404, NAS LeMoore, CA., 31 JAN 69; To VA-56, USS Midway (CVA-41), 17 APR 70; To VA-56, NAS LeMoore, CA., 29 APR 72 ** Transferred to VA-153/CVW-19, NM/300, NAS LeMoore, CA., 27 JUN 73; To VA-153, USS Oriskany (CVA-34), 04 JUN 74; To VA-153, NAS Jacksonville, FL., 06 AUG 74; To VA-153, NAS LeMoore, CA., 25 OCT 74; To VA-153, NAS Fallon, NV., 27 NOV 74; To VA-153, NAS LeMoore, CA., 11 APR 75; To VA-153, USS Oriskany (CV-34), 30 JUN 75; To VA-153, NAS Alameda, CA., 27 JUL 75; To VA-153, USS Oriskany (CV-34), 28 JUL 75; To VA-153, NAS LeMoore, CA.,16 SEP 75; To VA-153, USS Franklin D. Roosevelt (CV-42), 20 APR 77; To VA-153, NAS LeMoore, CA., 21 APR 77 ** Transferred to VA-304/CVWR-30, ND/4XX, NAS Alameda, CA., 6 JUL 77; To VA-304, NAS Dallas, TX., 05 DEC 77; To VA-304, NAS Jacksonville, FL., 12 MAY 78; To VA-304, NAS Alameda, CA., 01 JUN 78 ** Transferred to VA-305/CVWR-30, ND/501, NAS Point Mugu, CA., 20 JAN 79; To VA-305, NAS Jacksonville, FL., 19 NOV 80; To VA-305, NAS Point Mugu, CA., 02 FEB 81 ** To VA-305, NAS Jacksonville, FL., 30 SEP 82; To VA-305, NAS Point Mugu, CA., 16 NOV 82 ** Transferred to AMARC, Davis Monthan AFB; Tucson, AZ., assigned park code 6A0184, 17 JUL 86 ~ S 3SO strike, 29 SEP 86 ** No data on strike ** 6534.0 flight hours ** TF30P408 engine S/N 664422 ** Aircraft deleted from inventory and released to DRMO for disposition, 13 AUG 02.

B-176 154536 Navy acceptance from NPRO Rep. LTV, Dallas, TX., 18 DEC 68 ** Transferred to VA-125/FRS, NJ/5XX, NAS LeMoore, CA., 30 JAN 69 ** Transferred to VA-56/CVW-2, NE/4XX, NAS LeMoore, CA., 31 JAN 69; To VA-56/CVW-5, NF/4XX, USS Midway (CVA-41), 27 JUN 70; To VA-56, NAS LeMoore, CA., 28 MAY 72 ** Transferred to NARF, NAS Alameda, CA., 06 JUL 72 ** Transferred to VA-215/CVW-19, NM/4XX, NAS LeMoore, CA., 09 JUL 73; To VA-215, USS Oriskany (CVA-34), 05 JUN 74; To VA-215, NAS LeMoore, CA., 05 JUN 74; To VA-215, NAS Fallon, NV., 09 NOV 74; To VA-215, NAS LeMoore, CA., 03 FEB 75; To VA-215, NAS Fallon, NV., 27 FEB 75; To VA-215, NAS LeMoore, CA., 27 FEB 75; To VA-215, USS Oriskany (CV-34),27 FEB 75; To VA-215, NAF Atsugi, JP., 12 NOV 75; To VA-215, USS Oriskany (CV-34), 30 DEC 75; To VA-215; NAS LeMoore, CA., 30 DEC 75 ** Transferred to VA-125/FRS, NJ/5XX, NAS LeMoore, CA., 16 JUN 76 ** Transferred to NPRO Rep. LTV, Dallas, TX., to be converted to TA-7C, 01 OCT 76 ** Re-designated to TA-7C, 08 OCT 76 ** Transferred to VA-122/FRS, NJ/207, NAS LeMoore, CA., 31 JAN 79 ~ S 1SO strike, 02 OCT 79 ** No data on strike.

B-177 154537 Navy acceptance from NPRO Rep. LTV, Dallas, TX., 30 JAN 69 ** Transferred to VA-56/CVW-2, NE/4XX, NAS LeMoore, CA., 20 FEB 69; To VA-56/CVW-5, NF/4XX, USS Midway (CVA-41), 13 APR 70 ** Transferred to NARF, NAS Alameda, CA., 12 MAY 71 ** Transferred to VA-125/FRS, NJ/5XX, NAS LeMoore, CA., 31 MAY 73 ** Transferred to VA-174/FRS, AD/231, NAS Cecil Field, FL., 01 NOV 73 ** Transferred to NPRO Rep. LTV Dallas, TX., to be converted to TA-7C, 15 JUL 75 ** Re-designated to TA-7C, 24 JUL 75 ** Transferred to VA-174/FRS, AD/3XX, NAS Cecil Field, FL., 31 OCT 78; To VA-174, NAS Jacksonville, FL., 22 DEC 80; To VA-174, NAS Cecil Field, FL., 26 JAN 81; To VA-174, NAS Jacksonville, FL., 22 JAN 81; To VA-174, NAS Cecil Field, FL., 28 MAR 81 ** Transferred to NARF, NAS Jacksonville, FL., 18 OCT 82 ~ S 1SO strike, 28 JUN 84 ** No data on strike.

B-178 154538 Navy acceptance from NPRO Rep. LTV, Dallas, TX., 18 DEC 68 ** Transferred to VA-56/CVW-2, NE/404, NAS LeMoore, CA., 15 FEB 69 ** Transferred to VA-215/CVW-9, NG/4XX, USS Enterprise (CVAN-65), 27 FEB 69; To VA-215/CVW-6, AE/401, USS Franklin D. Roosevelt (CVA-42), 12 APR 69; To VA-215/CVW19, NM/414, USS Oriskany (CVA-34), 20 MAR 70; To VA-215, NAS LeMoore, CA., 04 JUN 72; To VA-215, USS Oriskany (CVA-34), 05 JUN 74; To VA-215, NAS LeMoore, CA., 05 JUN 74; To VA-215, NAS Fallon, NV., 09 NOV 74; To VA-215, NAS LeMoore, CA., 15 JAN 75; To VA-215, NAS Fallon, NV., 15 JAN 75; To VA-215, NAS LeMoore, CA., 11 APR 75; To VA-215, NAS Jacksonville, FL., 24 JUN 75; To VA-215, NAS LeMoore, CA., 24 JUN 75; To VA-215, NAS Jacksonville, FL., 25 JUN 75; To VA-215, USS Oriskany (CV-34), 30 AUG 75; To VA-215, NAS LeMoore, CA., 15 SEP 75; To VA-215, USS Franklin D. Roosevelt (CV-42), 30 AUG 76 ** Transferred to NARF, NAS Jacksonville, FL., 01 OCT 76 ** Transferred to VA-204/CVWR-20, AF/4XX, NAS New Orleans, LA., 04 APR 79; To VA-204, NAS Jacksonville, FL., 27 SEP 79 ** Transferred to VA-305/CVWR-30, ND/510, NAS Point Mugu, CA., 11 DEC 80 ** Transferred to AMARC, Davis Monthan AFB; Tucson, AZ., assigned park code 6A0159, 15 NOV 86 ** End of flight record card ** 4978.5 flight hours ** TF30P408 engine S/N 671450 ** Sent to DMI Aviation for Yanks Air Museum; Chino, CA., thru GSA. ** Located in compound behind restoration hangar at Yanks Air Museum; Chino, CA. SEP 06.

B-179 154539 Navy acceptance from NPRO Rep. LTV, Dallas, TX., 30 JAN 69 ** Transferred to VA-56/CVW-2, NE/4XX, NAS LeMoore, CA., 27 FEB 69; To VA-56/CVW-5, NF/4XX, USS Midway (CVA-41), 17 JUN 70 ~ S 1SO strike, 19 OCT 71 ** No data on strike .

B-180 154540 Navy acceptance from NPRO Rep. LTV, Dallas, TX., 30 JAN 69 ** Transferred to VA-122/FRS, NJ/2XX, NAS LeMoore, CA., 04 APR 69 ** Transferred to VA-93/CVW-5, NF/3XX, NAS LeMoore, CA., 18 JUN 69; To VA-93, USS Midway (CVA-41), 22 JUN 70 ** Transferred to VA-155/CVW-19, NM/5XX, USS Oriskany (CVA-34), 27 JAN 71 ** Transferred to VA-125/FRS, NJ/511, NAS LeMoore, CA., 26 APR 71; To VA-125, CRAA, NAS LeMoore, CA., 28 JUL 71; VA-125, NAS LeMoore, CA., 01 JAN 72 ** Transferred to VA-56/CVW-5, NF/403, NAS LeMoore, CA., 15 SEP 72 ~ S 1SO strike, 06 NOV 72 ** No data on strike.

B-181 154541 Navy acceptance from NPRO Rep. LTV, Dallas, TX., 30 JAN 69 ** Transferred to VA-56/CVW-2, NE/4XX, NAS LeMoore, CA., 27 FEB 69; To VA-56/CVW-5, NF/411,USS Midway (CVA-34), 23 JUN 70 ~ S 1SO strike, 19 MAY 72 ** LT Aubrey A. Nichols ejected with facial burns and became a POW after being shot down by AAA over North Vietnam.

B-182 154542 Navy acceptance from NPRO Rep. LTV, Dallas, TX., 30 JAN 69 ** Transferred to VA-56/CVW-2, NE/414, NAS LeMoore, 07 MAR 69 ~ S 1SO strike, 18 DEC 69 ** No data on strike.

B-183 154543 Navy acceptance from NPRO Rep. LTV, Dallas, TX., 30 JAN 69 ** VA-56/CVW-2, NE/4XX, NAS LeMoore, CA., 04 MAR 69 ** Transferred to VA-125/FRS, NJ/5XX, NAS LeMoore, CA., 16 APR 71 ** Transferred to VA-56/CVW-5, NF/4XX, NAS LeMoore, CA., 10 JUL 72 ~ S 1SO strike, 06 JAN 73 ** No data on strike.

B-184 154544 Navy acceptance from NPRO Rep. LTV, Dallas, TX., 30 JAN 69 ** Transferred to VA-56/CVW-2, NE/4XX, NAS LeMoore, CA., 07 MAR 69; To VA-56/CVW-5, NF/4XX, USS Midway (CVA-41), 10 JUN 70 ** Transferred to VA-215/ CVW-19. NM/402, USS Oriskany (CVA-34), 08 APR 72; To VA-215, NAS LeMoore, CA., 23 JUN 72 ** Transferred to VA-125/FRS, NJ/5XX, NAS LeMoore, CA. 15 OCT 73 ** Transferred to NPRO Rep. LTV, Dallas, TX., to be converted to TA-7C, 21 NOV 75 ** Re-designated to TA-7C, 30 NOV 75 ** This was the last A-7B to be converted to TA-7C ** Transferred to NPRO Rep. LTV, Dallas, TX., for RDT & E, 30 MAR 77, had TA-7C on the tail in large letters ** Transferred to NATC, NAS Patuxent River, MD. for RDT & E, 18 APR 78 ** Transferred to the Naval Test Pilot School, TPS/ XX, NAS Patuxent River, MD., 30 AUG 78 ** Transferred to NATC, NAS Patuxent River, MD. for RDT & E, 23 JUL 82 ** Transferred to Naval Test Pilot School, NAS Patuxent River, MD., 24 JUL 82; To NTPS, NAS Jacksonville, FL., 13 OCT 82; To NTPS, NAS Patuxent River, MD., 02 NOV 82 ** Transferred to the Pacific Missile Test Center, NAS Point Mugu, CA., PMTC logo on tail, 82 Modex, 23 DEC 85 thru 09 DEC 86 ** End of flight record card ** Transferred to DRMO/ CBC Port Hueneme, Ca., for disposition ** Sold to private party and hangared at Chino, AP, CA., 27 NOV 95 ** At same location, 15 APR 08.

B-185 154545 Navy acceptance from NPRO Rep. LTV, Dallas, TX., 27 FEB 69 ** Transferred to VA-122/FRS, NJ/5XX, NAS LeMoore, CA., 27 MAR 69 ** Transferred to VA-93/CVW-5, NF/3XX, USS Midway (CVA-41), 01 JUN 70; To VA-93, NAS LeMoore, CA., ** Transferred to VA-215/CVW-19, NM/4XX, NAS LeMoore, CA., 20 APR 73; To VA-215, USS Oriskany (CVA-34), 05 JUN 74; To VA-215, NAS LeMoore, CA., 05 JUN 74; To VA-215, NAS Jacksonville, FL., 24 SEP 74; To VA-215, NAS Fallon, NV., 05 DEC 74; To VA-215, NAS LeMoore, CA., 15 JAN 75; To VA-215, USS Oriskany (CV-34), 15 JUL 75; To VA-215, NAS LeMoore, CA., 23 MAR 76; To VA-215, NAS Alameda, Ca., 21 APR 76; To VA-215, NAS LeMoore, CA., 13 MAY 76; To VA-215 USS Franklin D. Roosevelt (CV-42), 22 APR 77; To VA-215, NAS LeMoore, CA., 25 MAY 77; To VA-215, NAS Alameda, CA., 03 JUN 77; To VA-215, NAS LeMoore, CA., 08 JUL 77 ** Transferred to VA-304/ CVWR-30, ND/415, NAS Alameda, CA., 06 AUG 77; To VA-304, NAS Jacksonville, FL., 17 SEP 82; To VA-304, NAS Alameda, CA., 18 SEP 82; To VA-304, NAS Jacksonville, FL., 11 JAN 82; To VA-304, NAS Alameda, CA., 09 NOV 83 ** Transferred to AMARC, Davis Monthan AFB; Tucson, AZ., assigned park code 6A0204, 19 SEP 86 ** S 3SO strike, 29 SEP 86 ** No data on strike ** End of flight record card ** 6361.9 flight hours ** TF30P408 engine S/N 664290 ** Aircraft deleted from inventory and released to DRMO for disposition, 13 AUG 02.

B-186 154546 Navy acceptance from NPRO Rep. LTV, Dallas, TX., 27 FEB 69 ** Transferred to VA-122/FRS, NJ/2XX, NAS LeMoore, CA., 07 APR 69 ** Transferred to VA-93/CVW-2, NE/3XX, NAS LeMoore, CA., 25 APR 69 ~ S 1SO strike, 21 OCT 69 ** No data on strike.

B-187 154547 Navy acceptance from NPRO Rep. LTV, Dallas, TX., 30 JAN 69 ** Transferred to VA-56/CVW-2, NE/4XX, NAS LeMoore, CA., 27 MAR 69; To VA-56/CVW-5, NF/4XX, USS Midway (CVA-41), 24 JUN 70 ** Transferred to VA-125/ FRS, NJ/5XX, NAS LeMoore, CA., 09 APR 72 ** Transferred to VA-56/ CVW-5, NF/4XX, USS Midway (CVA-41), 09 JUN 72; To VA-56, NAS LeMoore, CA., 05 JUN 72 ** Transferred to VA-153/CVW-19, NM/3XX, NAS LeMoore, CA., 25 APR 73; To VA-153, USS Oriskany (CVA-34), 04 JUN 74; To VA-153, NAS LeMoore, CA., 04 JUN 74; To VA-153, NAS Jacksonville, FL., 20 NOV 74;To VA-153, NAS LeMoore, CA., 27 NOV 74; To VA-153, NAS Jacksonville, FL., 02 DEC 74; To VA-153, NAS LeMoore, CA., 02 DEC 74; To VA-153, NAS Fallon, NV., 02 DEC 74; To VA-153, NAS LeMoore, CA., 02 DEC 74 ** Transferred to VA-125/FRS, NJ/5XX, NAS LeMoore, CA., 13 MAR 75; To VA-125, NAS Alameda, CA., 03 FEB 76; To VA-125, NAS LeMoore, CA., 06 MAY 76 ** Transferred to VA-215/ CVW-19, NM/4XX, USS Franklin D. Roosevelt (CV-42), 13 SEP 76; To VA-215, NAS LeMoore, CA., 25 MAY 77 ** Transferred to VA-303/CVWR-30, ND/3XX, NAS Alameda, CA., 19 JUL 77; To VA-303, NAS Dallas, TX., 10 JAN 78; To VA-303, NAS Jacksonville, FL., 26 MAY 78 ** Transferred to NARF, NAS Jacksonville, FL., 26 MAY 78 ** Transferred to VA-305/CVWR-30, ND/5XX, NAS Point Mugu, CA., 29 AUG 78; To VA-305, NAS Jacksonville, FL., 16 MAR 81 Transferred to VA-204/CVWR-20, AF/4XX, NAS New Orleans, LA., 10 JUN 81 ** Transferred to MASDC, Davis Monthan AFB; Tucson, AZ., assigned park code 6A0135, 13 SEP 83 ** End of flight record card ** 4888.9 flight hours ** Engine removed on arrival ** Aircraft deleted from in inventory and sent to DRMO for disposition, 13 AUG 02.

B-188 154548 Navy acceptance from NPRO Rep. LTV, Dallas, TX., 27 FEB 69 ** Transferred to VA-122/FRS, NJ/2XX, NAS LeMoore, CA., 15 APR 69 ** Transferred to VA-93/CVW-2, NE/3XX, NAS LeMoore, CA., 20 JUN 69; To VA-93/CVW-5, NF/3XX, USS Midway (CVA-41), 21 MAY 70 ** Transferred to VA-56/CVW-5, NF/4XX, USS Midway (CVA-41), 06 OCT 70 ** Transferred to VA-155/CVW-19, NM/5XX, USS Oriskany (CVA-34), 04 FEB 71 ** Transferred to VA-125/FRS, NJ/5XX, NAS LeMoore, CA., 11 MAY 71 ** Transferred to VA-155/CVW-19, NM/5XX, USS Oriskany (CVA-34), 11 MAY 71 ** Transferred to VA-125/FRS, NJ/5XX, NAS LeMoore, CA., 11 MAY 71 ** Transferred to VA-56/CVW-5, NF/4XX, NAS LeMoore, CA., 03 AUG 72 ** Transferred to VA-155/CVW-19, NM/5XX, NAS LeMoore, CA., 12 FEB 73; To VA-155, USS Oriskany (CVA-34),04 JUN 74; To VA-155, NAS LeMoore, CA.,22 AUG 74; To VA-155, NAS Jacksonville, FL., 28 AUG 74; To VA-155, NAS LeMoore, CA., 31 AUG 74; To VA-155, NAS Fallon, NV., 09 NOV 74; To VA-155, NAS LeMoore, CA., 18 FEB 75; To VA-155, NAS Fallon, NV., 19 FEB 75; To VA-155, NAS LeMoore, CA., 11 APR 75; To VA-155, USS Oriskany (CV-34) 01 JUL 75; To VA-155, NAS LeMoore, CA., 15 AUG 75;To VA-155, USS Franklin D. Roosevelt (CV-42), 23 AUG 76; To VA-155, NAS LeMoore, Ca., 21 JUL 77 ** Transferred to VA-303/CVWR-30, ND/3XX, NAS Alameda, CA., 22 JUL 77; To VA-303, NAS Jacksonville, FL., 28 JUL 77; To VA-303, NAS Alameda, CA., 28 NOV 77; To VA-303, NAS Jacksonville, FL., 06 SEP 83 ** Transferred to VA-304/CVWR-30, ND/4XX, NAS Alameda, CA., 26 SEP 83 ** Transferred to VA-305/CVWR-30, ND/5XX, NAS Point Mugu, CA., 14 OCT 83 ** Transferred to VA-304/CVWR-30, ND/4XX, NAS Alameda, CA., 31 OCT 83 ** Transferred to NATTC Millington, TN., as an instructional airframe 16 OCT 86 ** S 3SO strike, 16 OCT 86 ** End of flight record card. ** On conditional loan from the National Museum of Naval Aviation; Pensacola, Fl., to the USS Lexington (CVT-16), Museum on the Bay; Corpus Christi, TX., NOV 95.

B-189 154549 Navy acceptance from NPRO Rep. LTV, Dallas, TX., 27 FEB 69 ** Transferred to VA-122/FRS, NJ/2XX, NAS LeMoore, CA., 03 APR 69 ** Transferred to VA-93/CVW-2, NE/3XX, NAS LeMoore, CA., 04 JUN 69; To VA-93/CVW-5, NF/3XX, USS Midway (CVA041), 15 JUN 70 ** Transferred to VA-56/CVW-5, NF/4XX, USS Midway (CVA-41), 06 OCT 70 ** Transferred to VA-155/CVW-19, NM/5XX, USS Oriskany (CVA-34), 04 FEB 71 ** Transferred to VA-125/FRS, NJ/503, NAS LeMoore, CA.,11 MAY 71 ** Transferred to VA-56/CVW-5, NF/4XX, NAS LeMoore, CA., 15 SEP 72 ** Transferred to VA-153/CVW-19, NM/302, NAS LeMoore, CA., 12 APR 73; To VA-153, USS Oriskany (CV-34), 04 JUN 74; To VA-153,NAS LeMoore, CA., 04 JUN 74; To VA-153, NAS Jacksonville, FL., 27 SEP 74; To VA-153, NAS Fallon, NV., 27 SEP 74; To VA-153, NAS Jacksonville, FL., 08 NOV 74; To VA-153, NAS LeMoore, CA., 23 NOV 74; To VA-153, NAS Fallon, NV., 23 NOV 74; To VA-153, NAS LeMoore, CA., 11 APR 75; To VA-153, USS Oriskany (CV-34), 30 JUN 75; To VA-153, NAS LeMoore, CA., painted in Bicentennial paint scheme, 04 JUL 76; To VA-153, USS Franklin D. Roosevelt (CV-42), 20 APR 77; To VA-153, NAS LeMoore, CA., 20 APR 77 ** Transferred to VA-304/CVWR-30, ND/410, NAS Alameda, CA., 05 AUG 77; To VA-304, NAS Jacksonville, FL., 06 JUL 80; To VA-304, NAS Alameda, CA., 08 MAY 81; To VA-304, NAS Jacksonville, FL., 13 MAY 83; To VA-304, NAS Alameda, CA., 26 AUG 83 ~ S 1SO strike, 02 NOV 84.

B-190 154550 Navy acceptance from NPRO Rep. LTV, Dallas, TX., 27 FEB 69 ** Transferred to VA-122/FRS, NJ/2XX, NAS LeMoore, CA., 10 MAY 69 ** Transferred to VA-93/CVW-2, NE/3XX, NAS Lemoore, CA.; 12 JUN 69; To VA-93/ CVW-5, NF/3XX, USS Midway (CVA-41), 21 MAY 70 ** Transferred to VA-87/CVW-6, AE/4XX, USS Franklin D. Roosevelt (CVA-42); 30 JUL 70 ** Transferred to VA-174/FRS, AD/2XX, NAS Cecil Field, FL.; 12 JAN 71 ** Transferred to VA-87/ CVW-6, AE/4XX, NAS Cecil Field FL., 11 SEP 72 ** Transferred to VA-46/CVW-1, AB/3XX, NAS Cecil Field, FL., 15 NOV 73; To VA-46, NAS Jacksonville, FL., 12 SEP 74; To VA-46, NAS Cecil Field, FL.,

12 SEP 74; To VA-46, USS John F. Kennedy (CV-67), 04 DEC 74; To VA-46, NAS Cecil Field, FL., 04 DEC 74; To VA-46, USS John F. Kennedy (CV-67), 04 DEC 74; To VA-46, NAS Cecil Field, FL., 06 APR 76; To VA-46, USS John F. Kennedy (CV-67), 29 APR 76; To VA-46, NAS Cecil Field, FL., 29 APR 76; To VA-46, USS John F. Kennedy (CV-67), 18 JAN 77; To VA-46, NAS Cecil Field, FL., 18 JAN 77 ** Transferred to VA-203/CVWR-20 AF/3XX, NAS Jacksonville; 16 AUG 77 ** Transferred to VA-303/CVWR-30 ND/306, NAS Alameda, CA., 10 APR 78; To VA-303, NAS Dallas, TX., 18 MAY 78; To VA-303, NAS Alameda, CA., 25 MAY 78; To VA-303, NAS Jacksonville, FL., 25 AUG 80; To VA-303, NAS Alameda, CA., 03 MAY 81; To VA-303, NAS Jacksonville, FL., 02 FEB 83 ** Transferred to VA-305/ CVWR-30, ND/5XX, NAS Point Mugu, CA., 26 SEP 83; To VA-305, NAS Jacksonville, FL., 14 OCT 83; To VA-305, NAS Point Mugu, CA., 01 SEP 84 ** Transferred to NATTC Millington, TN., as an instructional aid, 26 JAN 87 ~ S 3SO strike, 26 JAN 87 ** End of flight record card, 27 JAN 87 ** On conditional loan from the National Museum of Naval Aviation; Pensacola, Fl. to the Air Victory Museum, South Jersey Regional Airport; Medford, NJ., 26 Dec 87.

B-191 154551 Navy acceptance from NPRO Rep. LTV, Dallas, TX., 27 FEB 69 ** Transferred to VA-93/CVW-2, NE/3XX, NAS LeMoore, CA., 29 JUN 69; To VA-93/CVW-5, NF/3XX, USS Midway (CVA-41), 01 JUN 70 ** Transferred to VA-15/ CVW-6, AE/3XX, USS Franklin D. Roosevelt (CVA-42), 01 AUG 70 ** Transferred to VA-174/FRS, AD/2XX, NAS Cecil Field, FL., 12 JAN 71 ** Transferred to VA-72/CVW-1, AB/4XX, USS John F. Kennedy (CVA-67), 27 JUN 72; To VA-72, NAS Cecil Field, FL., 30 OCT 72; To VA-72, USS John F. Kennedy (CV-67), 20 NOV 74; To VA-72, NAS Cecil Field, FL., 20 NOV 74; To VA-72, USS John F. Kennedy (CV-67), 20 NOV 74; To VA-72, NAS Cecil Field, FL., 13 JUN 76; To VA-72, USS John F. Kennedy (CV-67), 30 JUL 76; To VA-72, NAS Cecil Field, FL., 06 AUG 76; To VA-72, USS John F. Kennedy (CV-67), 09 AUG 76; To VA-72, NAS Jacksonville, FL., 15 OCT 76; To VA-72, NAS Cecil Field, FL., 17 DEC 76; To VA-72, USS John F. Kennedy (CV-67), 18 DEC 76; To VA-72, NAS Cecil Field, FL., 17 JUL 77 ** Transferred to VA-203/CVWR-20, AF/305, NAS Jacksonville, FL., 19 SEP 77 ** Transferred to MASDC, Davis Monthan AFB; Tucson, AZ., assigned park code 6A0128, 12 JUL 83 ** End of flight record card ** 5820.0 flight hours ** Engine removed on arrival ** Aircraft deleted from inventory and released to DRMO for disposition., 21 MAR 99 ** Sold as surplus to Fritz Enterprises; Taylor, MI., delivered to HVF West's yard; Tucson, AZ., 17 AUG 99.

B-192 154552 Navy acceptance from NPRO Rep. LTV, Dallas, TX., 28 FEB 69 ** Transferred to VA-122/FRS, NJ/2XX, NAS LeMoore, CA., 15 MAY 69 ** Transferred to VA-93/CVW-2, NE/3XX, NAS LeMoore, CA., 16 MAY 69; To VA-93/ CVW-5, NF/3XX, USS Midway (CVA-41), 01 JUN 70 ** Transferred to VA-174/FRS, AD/2XX, NAS Cecil Field, FL., 29 JUL 70 ** Transferred to VA-15/CVW-6, AE/3XX, USS Franklin D. Roosevelt (CVA-42), 29 JUL 70 ** Transferred to VA-174/FRS, AD/2XX, NAS Cecil Field, FL., 13 JAN 71 ** Transferred to VA-46/CVW-1, AB/3XX, NAS Cecil Field, FL., 01 APR 71; To VA-46, USS John F. Kennedy (CVA-67), 27 APR 71 ** To VA-46, NAS Cecil Field, FL., 13 APR 73; To VA-46, USS John F. Kennedy (CV-67), 20 NOV 74; To VA-46, NAS Cecil Field, FL., 20 NOV 74; To VA-46, USS John F. Kennedy (CV-67), 20 NOV 74; To VA-46, NAS Cecil Field, FL., 20 NOV 74; To VA-46, USS John F. Kennedy (CV-67), 20 NOV 74; To VA-46, NAS Cecil Field, FL., 02 MAR 76; To VA-46, USS John F. Kennedy (CV-67), 07 JUN 76; To VA-46, NAS Cecil Field, FL., 07 JUN 76; To VA-46, USS John F. Kennedy (CV-67), 07 JUN 76; To VA-46, NAS Cecil Field, FL., 01 MAY 77; To VA-46, USS Dwight D. Eisenhower (CVN-69), 11 AUG 77; To VA-46, NAS Cecil Field, FL., 11 AUG 77 ** Transferred to VMFA-251, Beaufort, SC., 24 AUG 77 ** Transferred to VA-303/CVWR-30, ND/303, NAS Alameda. CA., 05 NOV 77; To VA-303, NAS Jacksonville, FL., 30 JUL 81 ** Transferred to VA-205/

CVWR-20, AF/5XX, NAS Atlanta, GA., 17 SEP 85 ** Transferred to VA-204/CVWR-20, AF/401, NAS New Orleans, LA., 01 JUN 84 ** Transferred to AMARC, Davis Monthan AFB; Tucson, AZ., assigned park codes 6A0171, 13 JUN 86 ** End of flight record card ** 6343.8 flight hours ** TF30P408 engine S/N 664270 ** Aircraft generator and CSD removed from engine ** Interservice transfer to the Air Force assigned park code AE0004 ** Classified equipment removed and aircraft demilled, 04 APR 95 ** Aircraft deleted from inventory and released to DRMO for disposition, 26 SEP 95.

B-193 154553 Navy acceptance from NPRO Rep. LTV, Dallas, TX., 26 MAR 69 ** Transferred to VA-122/FRS, NJ/2XX, NAS LeMoore, CA., 27 MAR 69 ** Transferred to VA-93/CVW-2, NE/3XX, NAS LeMoore, CA., 29 APR 69; To VA-93/ CVW-5, NF/3XX, USS Midway (CVA-41), 01 JUN 70; To VA-93, NAS LeMoore, CA., 06 APR 72 ** Transferred to VA-215/ CVW-19, NM/4XX, NAS LeMoore, CA., 04 MAY 73; To VA-215, USS Oriskany (CVA-34), 05 JUN 74 ** To VA-215, NAS LeMoore, CA., 07 AUG 74; To VA-215, NAS Fallon, NV., 02 JAN 75; To VA-215, NAS Jacksonville, FL., 03 JAN 75; To VA-215, NAS LeMoore, CA., 18 FEB 75; To VA-215, NAS Fallon, NV., 18 FEB 75; To VA-215, NAS LeMoore, CA., 18 FEB 75; To VA-215, USS Oriskany (CV-34), 15 JUL 75, To VA-215, NAS LeMoore, CA., 15 SEP 75; To VA-215, USS Franklin D. Roosevelt (CV-42), 03 DEC 76; To VA-215, NAS Norfolk, VA., 14 FEB 77; To VA-215, USS Franklin D. Roosevelt (CV-42), 15 FEB 77; To VA-215, NAS Norfolk, VA., 06 APR 77 ** Transferred to NARF, NAS Jacksonville, FL., 27 APR 77 ** Transferred to VA-204/CVWR-20, AF/414, NAS New Orleans, LA., 03 AUG 79 ** To VA-204, NAS Jacksonville, FL., 11 MAY 81; To VA-204, NAS New Orleans, LA., 03 AUG 81 ** Transferred to MASDC, Davis Monthan AFB; Tucson, AZ., assigned park code 6A0141, 27 SEP 83 ** End of flight record card ** 4976.8 flight hours ** Engine removed on arrival ** Aircraft deleted from inventory and released to DRMO for disposition, 13 AUG 02.

B-194 154554 Navy acceptance from NPRO Rep. LTV, Dallas, TX., 26 MAR 69 ** Transferred to VA-122/FRS, NJ/2XX, NAS LeMoore, CA., 22 APR 69 ** Transferred to VA-93/CVW-2, NE/3XX, NAS LeMoore, CA., 23 APR 69; To VA-93/CVW-5, NF/3XX, USS Midway (CVA-41), 19 JUN 70 ** Transferred to VA-56/CVW-5, NF/4XX, USS Midway (CVA-41), 04 NOV 70 ** Transferred to VA-155/CVW-19, NM/5XX, USS Oriskany (CVA-34), 08 FEB 71 ** Transferred to VA-125/ FRS, NJ/5XX, NAS LeMoore, CA., 27 MAY 71 ** Transferred to NPRO Rep. LTV, Dallas, TX, for RDT & E, 12 AUG 71 ** Transferred to VA-56/CVW-5, NF/4XX, USS Midway (CVA-41), 29 NOV 71; To VA-56, NAS LeMoore, CA., 27 JUN 72 ** Transferred to VA-215/CVW-19, NM/406, NAS LeMoore, CA., 20 JUN 73; To VA-215, NAS Jacksonville, FL., 10 SEP 74; To VA-215, NAS LeMoore, CA., 02 NOV 74; To VA-215, NAS Fallon, NV., 09 NOV 74; To VA-215, NAS LeMoore, CA., 23 JAN 75; To VA-215, USS Oriskany (CV-34), 15 JUL 75; To VA-215, NAS LeMoore, CA., 24 MAR 76; To VA-215, USS Franklin D. Roosevelt (CV-42), 22 APR 77; To VA-215, NAS LeMoore, CA., 25 MAY 77 ** Transferred to VA-303/CVWR-30, ND/3XX, NAS Alameda, CA., 23 JUL 77 ** Transferred to VA-204/CVWR-20, AF/4XX, NAS Memphis, TN., 05 NOV 77; To VA-204, NAS Dallas, TX., 12 NOV 77 ** Transferred to NARF, NAS Jacksonville, FL., 27 FEB 78 ** Transferred to VA-305/CVWR-30, ND/5XX, NAS Point Mugu, CA., 29 AUG 78; To VA-305, NAS Jacksonville, FL., 25 NOV 80; To VA-305, NAS Point Mugu, CA., 09 FEB 81 ** Transferred to NAS North Island, CA., 14 JAN 87 ~ S 3SO strike, 14 JAN 87 ** End of Flight Record Card, 15 JAN 87 ** On conditional loan from the National Museum of Naval Aviation; Pensacola, Fl., to the San Diego Aerospace Museum; San Diego, CA.

B-195 154555 Navy acceptance from NPRO Rep. LTV, Dallas, TX., 26 MAR 69 ** Transferred to VA-122/FRS, NJ/2XX, NAS LeMoore, CA., 30 APR 69 ** Transferred to VA-93/CVW-2, NE/3XX, NAS LeMoore, CA.,01 MAY 69 ~ S 1SO strike, 09 MAY 70 ** Crashed due to tailhook failure.

B-196 154556 Last production A-7B ** Navy acceptance from NPRO Rep. LTV, Dallas, TX., 30 APR 69 ** Transferred to VA-122/FRS, NJ/2XX, NAS LeMoore, CA., 08 MAY 69 ** Transferred to VA-93/CVW-2, NE/3XX, NAS LeMoore, CA., 13 MAY 69; To VA-93/CVW-5, NF/3XX, USS Midway (CVA-41), 18 JUN 70 ** Transferred to VA-174/FRS, AD/2XX, NAS Cecil Field, FL., 29 JUL 70 ** Transferred to VA-15/CVW-6, AE/3XX, USS Franklin D. Roosevelt (CVA-42), 29 JUL 70 ** Transferred to VA-174/FRS, AD/2XX, NAS Cecil Field, FL., 29 JUL 70 ** Transferred to VA-15/CVW-6, AE/3XX, USS Franklin D. Roosevelt (CVA-42), 26 AUG 70 ** Transferred to VA-174/FRS, AD/2XX, NAS Cecil Field, FL., 12 JAN 71** Transferred to VA-72/CVW-1, AB/4XX, NAS Cecil Field, FL., 30 MAR 71; To VA-72, USS John F. Kennedy (CVA-67), 30 MAR 71 ** To VA-72, NAS Cecil Field, FL., 10 NOV 72; To VA-72, USS John F. Kennedy (CV-67), 02 NOV 74; To VA-72, NAS Cecil Field, FL., 02 NOV 74; To VA-72, USS John F. Kennedy (CV-67), 30 JUN 75; To VA-72, NAS Cecil Field, FL., 23 MAR 76; To VA-72, USS John F. Kennedy (CV-67), 30 MAR 76; To VA-72, NAS Cecil Field, FL., 30 MAR 76; To VA-72, USS John F. Kennedy (CV-67), 30 MAR 76; To VA-72, NAS Cecil Field, FL., 30 MAR 76; To VA-72, USS John F. Kennedy (CV-67), 11 AUG 77 ** Transferred to VA-203/CVWR-20, AF/301, NAS Jacksonville, FL., 23 SEP 77 ** Transferred to MASDC, Davis Monthan AFB; Tucson, AZ., assigned park code 6A0126, 05 JUL 83 ** End of flight record card ** 5853.7 flight hours ** Engine removed on arrival ** Aircraft deleted and released to DRMO for disposition, 13 AUG 02.

154557/154573 Cancelled contract for LTV (17) A-7B Corsair II

B---- 154557 Cancelled	B---- 154558 Cancelled
B---- 154559 Cancelled	B---- 154560 Cancelled
B---- 154561 Cancelled	B---- 154562 Cancelled
B---- 154563 Cancelled	B---- 154564 Cancelled
B---- 154565 Cancelled	B---- 154566 Cancelled
B---- 154567 Cancelled	B---- 154568 Cancelled
B---- 154569 Cancelled	B---- 154570 Cancelled
B---- 154571 Cancelled	B---- 154572 Cancelled
B---- 154573 Cancelled	

154913/154929 Cancelled contract for LTV (17) A-7B Corsair II

B---- 154913 Cancelled	B---- 154914 Cancelled
B---- 154915 Cancelled	B---- 154916 Cancelled
B---- 154917 Cancelled	B---- 154918 Cancelled
B---- 154919 Cancelled	B---- 154920 Cancelled
B---- 154921 Cancelled	B---- 154922 Cancelled
B---- 154923 Cancelled	B---- 154924 Cancelled
B---- 154925 Cancelled	B---- 154926 Cancelled
B---- 154927 Cancelled	B---- 154928 Cancelled
B---- 154929 Cancelled	

156178 / 156417 Cancelled contract for LTV (239) A-7B Corsair II

B---- 156178 Cancelled	B---- 156179 Cancelled
B---- 156180 Cancelled	B---- 156181 Cancelled
B---- 156182 Cancelled	B---- 156183 Cancelled
B---- 156184 Cancelled	B---- 156185 Cancelled
B---- 156186 Cancelled	B---- 156187 Cancelled
B---- 156188 Cancelled	B---- 156189 Cancelled
B---- 156190 Cancelled	B---- 156191 Cancelled
B---- 156192 Cancelled	B---- 156193 Cancelled
B---- 156194 Cancelled	B---- 156195 Cancelled
B---- 156196 Cancelled	B---- 156197 Cancelled
B---- 156198 Cancelled	B---- 156199 Cancelled
B---- 156200 Cancelled	B---- 156201 Cancelled
B---- 156202 Cancelled	B---- 156203 Cancelled
B---- 156204 Cancelled	B---- 156205 Cancelled
B---- 156206 Cancelled	B---- 156207 Cancelled
B---- 156208 Cancelled	B---- 156209 Cancelled
B---- 156210 Cancelled	B---- 156211 Cancelled
B---- 156212 Cancelled	B---- 156213 Cancelled

B---- 156214 Cancelled
B---- 156216 Cancelled
B---- 156218 Cancelled
B---- 156220 Cancelled
B---- 156222 Cancelled
B---- 156224 Cancelled
B---- 156226 Cancelled
B---- 156228 Cancelled
B---- 156230 Cancelled
B---- 156232 Cancelled
B---- 156234 Cancelled
B---- 156236 Cancelled
B---- 156238 Cancelled
B---- 156240 Cancelled
B---- 156242 Cancelled
B---- 156244 Cancelled
B---- 156246 Cancelled
B---- 156248 Cancelled
B---- 156250 Cancelled
B---- 156252 Cancelled
B---- 156254 Cancelled
B---- 156256 Cancelled
B---- 156258 Cancelled
B---- 156260 Cancelled
B---- 156262 Cancelled
B---- 156264 Cancelled
B---- 156266 Cancelled
B---- 156268 Cancelled
B---- 156270 Cancelled
B---- 156272 Cancelled
B---- 156274 Cancelled
B---- 156276 Cancelled
B---- 156278 Cancelled
B---- 156280 Cancelled
B---- 156282 Cancelled
B---- 156284 Cancelled
B---- 156286 Cancelled
B---- 156288 Cancelled
B---- 156290 Cancelled
B---- 156292 Cancelled
B---- 156294 Cancelled
B---- 156296 Cancelled
B---- 156298 Cancelled
B---- 156300 Cancelled
B---- 153302 Cancelled
B---- 156304 Cancelled
B---- 156306 Cancelled
B---- 156308 Cancelled
B---- 156310 Cancelled
B---- 156312 Cancelled
B---- 156314 Cancelled

B---- 156215 Cancelled
B---- 156217 Cancelled
B---- 156219 Cancelled
B---- 156221 Cancelled
B---- 156223 Cancelled
B---- 156225 Cancelled
B---- 156227 Cancelled
B---- 156229 Cancelled
B---- 156231 Cancelled
B---- 156233 Cancelled
B---- 156235 Cancelled
B---- 156237 Cancelled
B---- 156239 Cancelled
B---- 156241 Cancelled
B---- 156243 Cancelled
B---- 156245 Cancelled
B---- 156247 Cancelled
B---- 156249 Cancelled
B---- 156251 Cancelled
B---- 156253 Cancelled
B---- 156255 Cancelled
B---- 156257 Cancelled
B---- 156259 Cancelled
B---- 156261 Cancelled
B---- 156263 Cancelled
B---- 156265 Cancelled
B---- 156267 Cancelled
B---- 156269 Cancelled
B---- 156271 Cancelled
B---- 156273 Cancelled
B---- 156275 Cancelled
B---- 156277 Cancelled
B---- 156279 Cancelled
B---- 156281 Cancelled
B---- 156283 Cancelled
B---- 156285 Cancelled
B---- 156287 Cancelled
B---- 156289 Cancelled
B---- 156291 Cancelled
B---- 156293 Cancelled
B---- 156295 Cancelled
B---- 156297 Cancelled
B---- 156299 Cancelled
B---- 156301 Cancelled
B---- 156303 Cancelled
B---- 156305 Cancelled
B---- 156307 Cancelled
B---- 156309 Cancelled
B---- 156311 Cancelled
B---- 156313 Cancelled
B---- 156315 Cancelled

B---- 156316 Cancelled
B---- 156318 Cancelled
B---- 156320 Cancelled
B---- 156322 Cancelled
B---- 156324 Cancelled
B---- 156326 Cancelled
B---- 156328 Cancelled
B---- 156330 Cancelled
B---- 156332 Cancelled
B---- 156334 Cancelled
B---- 156336 Cancelled
B---- 156338 Cancelled
B---- 156340 Cancelled
B---- 156342 Cancelled
B---- 156344 Cancelled
B---- 156346 Cancelled
B---- 156348 Cancelled
B---- 156350 Cancelled
B---- 156352 Cancelled
B---- 156354 Cancelled
B---- 156356 Cancelled
B---- 156358 Cancelled
B---- 156360 Cancelled
B---- 156362 Cancelled
B---- 156364 Cancelled
B---- 156366 Cancelled
B---- 156368 Cancelled
B---- 156370 Cancelled
B---- 156372 Cancelled
B---- 156374 Cancelled
B---- 156376 Cancelled
B---- 156378 Cancelled
B---- 156380 Cancelled
B---- 156382 Cancelled
B---- 156384 Cancelled
B---- 156386 Cancelled
B---- 156388 Cancelled
B---- 156390 Cancelled
B---- 156392 Cancelled
B---- 156394 Cancelled
B---- 156396 Cancelled
B---- 156398 Cancelled
B---- 156400 Cancelled
B---- 156402 Cancelled
B---- 156404 Cancelled
B---- 156406 Cancelled
B---- 156408 Cancelled
B---- 156410 Cancelled
B---- 156412 Cancelled
B---- 156414 Cancelled
B---- 156416 Cancelled

B---- 156317 Cancelled
B---- 156319 Cancelled
B---- 156321 Cancelled
B---- 156323 Cancelled
B---- 156325 Cancelled
B---- 156327 Cancelled
B---- 156329 Cancelled
B---- 156331 Cancelled
B---- 156333 Cancelled
B---- 156335 Cancelled
B---- 156337 Cancelled
B---- 156339 Cancelled
B---- 156341 Cancelled
B---- 156343 Cancelled
B---- 156345 Cancelled
B---- 156347 Cancelled
B---- 156349 Cancelled
B---- 156351 Cancelled
B---- 156353 Cancelled
B---- 156355 Cancelled
B---- 156357 Cancelled
B---- 156359 Cancelled
B---- 156361 Cancelled
B---- 156363 Cancelled
B---- 156365 Cancelled
B---- 156367 Cancelled
B---- 156369 Cancelled
B---- 156371 Cancelled
B---- 156373 Cancelled
B---- 156375 Cancelled
B---- 156377 Cancelled
B---- 156379 Cancelled
B---- 156381 Cancelled
B---- 156383 Cancelled
B---- 156385 Cancelled
B---- 156387 Cancelled
B---- 156389 Cancelled
B---- 156391 Cancelled
B---- 156393 Cancelled
B---- 156395 Cancelled
B---- 156397 Cancelled
B---- 156399 Cancelled
B---- 156401 Cancelled
B---- 156403 Cancelled
B---- 156405 Cancelled
B---- 156407 Cancelled
B---- 156409 Cancelled
B---- 156411 Cancelled
B---- 156413 Cancelled
B---- 156415 Cancelled
B---- 156417 Cancelled

SECTION 3

A-7C

156734/156740 LTV A-7C-1-CV Corsair II;
Multi-YR 67, Contract N00019-68-C-0075,
    (7) A-7E; E-001/E-007 & E-028; (Block I)
FY 76-7T Contract N00019-76-C-0229 (21) TA-7C
    from (14) A-7B & (7) A-7C; C-001/C-007; CSN 25-31

Note: TF-30 powered A-7E's, production numbers E-001 thru E-067 were-designated A-7C by the Navy after they were placed in service.

E-001 156734 Navy acceptance from NPRO Rep. LTV, Dallas, TX., 27 NOV 68 ** First re-designated A-7C ** First of three A-7C's to be Re-designated NA-7C ** Transferred to NPRO Rep. LTV, Dallas, TX., for R & T, 28 NOV 68 ** Transferred to NAF China Lake, CA., for RTD & E, 26 MAY 71; To NAF China Lake, at NAS Jacksonville, FL., 15 AUG 74; To NAF China Lake, CA., 18 OCT 74; To NAF China Lake, at NAS Jacksonville, FL., 31 OCT 74, Re-designated to NA-7C; To NAF China Lake, CA., 05 NOV 74; NAF China Lake, at NAS Jacksonville, FL., 02 MAY 79; To NWC China Lake, CA., 10 AUG 79 thru 31 AUG 84 ** End of flight record card.

E-002 156735 Navy acceptance from NPRO Rep. LTV, Dallas, TX., 27 NOV 68 ** Transferred to NPRO Rep. LTV, Dallas, TX., for RDT & E, 28 NOV 68 ** Re-designated NA-7C ~ S 1SO strike, 17 JUL 69 ** No data on strike.

E-003 156736 Navy acceptance from NPRO Rep. LTV, Dallas, TX., 23 DEC 68 ** Transferred to NPRO Rep. LTV, Dallas, TX., for RDT & E, 24 DEC 68 ** Re-designated NA-7C ** Transferred to NATC, Weapons Systems Test, NAS Patuxent River, MD.; 28 JUN 69 ** Transferred to NATC, Service Test, NAS Patuxent River, MD., 22 SEP 70 ** Transferred to NATC, NAS Patuxent River, MD., for RTD & E, 02 JUL 75 ~ S 1SO strike, 02 JUL 75 ** No data on strike.

E-028 156737 Navy acceptance from NPRO Rep. LTV, Dallas, TX., 28 FEB 69 ** Transferred to NPRO Rep. LTV, Dallas, TX., for RDT & E, 26 JUN 69 ** Transferred to NARF, NAS Jacksonville, FL., 03 JAN 71 ** Transferred to VA-174/FRS, AD/3XX, NAS Cecil Field, FL., 06 APR 73 ** Transferred to NPRO Rep. LTV, Dallas, TX., to be converted to TA-7C, 06 JAN 76 ** Re-designated to TA-7C, 15 JAN 76 ** Transferred to VA-174/FRS, AD/3XX, NAS Cecil Field, FL., 20 APR 79; To VA-174, NAS Jacksonville, FL.,04 SEP 81; To VA-174, NAS Cecil Field, FL., 02 NOV 81 ~ S 1SO strike, 10 NOV 83 ** No data on strike.

E-004 156738 Navy acceptance from NPRO Rep. LTV, Dallas, TX., 27 MAR 69 ** Transferred to NPRO Rep. LTV, Dallas, TX., for RDT & E, 29 MAR 69 ** Transferred to NARF, NAS Jacksonville, FL., 09 FEB 71 ** Transferred to VA-174/FRS, AD/3XX, NAS Cecil Field, FL., 21 AUG 72 ** Transferred to VA-86/CVW-8, AJ/413, USS America (CVA-66), 28 AUG 73; To VA-86, NAS Cecil Field, FL., 28 AUG 73 ** Transferred to VA-174/FRS, AD/3XX, NAS Cecil Field, FL., 14 NOV 74 ** Transferred to NARF, NAS Jacksonville, FL., 06 SEP 75 ** Transferred to VA-122/FRS, NJ/2XX, NAS LeMoore, CA., 29 OCT 75 ** Transferred to NPRO Rep. LTV, Dallas, TX., to be converted to TA-7C, 23 MAR 76 ** Re-designated to TA-7C, 01 APR 76 ** Transferred to NAF China, CA., 23 MAR 78; To NWC China Lake at NAS Alameda, CA., 29 DEC 82; To NWC China Lake, CA., 09 MAR 83; To NWC China Lake at NAS Jacksonville, FL., 26 AUG 83; To NWC China Lake, CA., 01 FEB 84; To NWC China Lake at NAS Dallas, TX., 08 AUG 85; To NWC China Lake, CA., thru 05 AUG 87 ** End of flight record card ** Transferred to AMARC, Davis Monthan AFB; Tucson, AZ., assigned park code 6A0421, 22 OCT 96 ** 3786.2 flight hours ** TF41A402D engine S/N 141541 ** Aircraft contains limited quantities of radiation material, contains 20 micro curies of Cesium 137 and 3.27 milli cures of depleted Uranium , 24 MAR 00 ** Transferred to Thunderbird Aviation on FAA S/N, N165TB; Deer Valley, AZ. ** The FAA states that registration N165TB apparently reserved for this aircraft, has been un-reserved (declared not taken up), and that the aircraft remains at AMARC, Davis Monthan AFB; Tucson, AZ., 12 JUN 03 Prepare (AS-IS), for overland and above deck shipment to M/V Efdim Hops, Woodhouse Terminal; Galveston, TX., at no cost to the government, for the government of Greece, 16 MAR 04 ** Transferred to the Helenic Air Force (Greece).

E-005 156739 Navy acceptance from NPRO Rep. LTV, Dallas, TX., 15 SEP 69 ** Transferred to NAS Point Mugu, CA., for RDT & E, 27 AUG 69, Second A-7C to be re-designated NA-7C ** Transferred to NATC, Weapons Systems test, NAS Patuxent River, MD., 07 OCT 69 ** Transferred to NAS Point Mugu, CA., Point Mugu/XXX, for RDT & E, 03 JAN 70 ** Transferred to NWEF Kirtland AFB, NM., XX/XXX, 24 JUL 70 ** Transferred to NAS Point Mugu, CA., for RDT & E, 12 OCT 72 ** Transferred to NAF China Lake, CA., for RDT & E, 15 AUG 73; Transferred to NAF China Lake, CA., China Lake/739, 01 JUL 75, to conduct Special Weapons Tests, later re-designated NA-7C; To NAF China Lake at NAS Jacksonville, FL., 26 FEB 76; To NAF China Lake, CA., 15 MAR 76; To NAF China Lake at NAS Jacksonville, FL.,

31 MAY 78; To NWC China Lake, CA., 27 MAR 80; To NWC China Lake at NAS Jacksonville, FL., 16 JUL 80; To NWC China Lake, CA., 18 SEP 80 thru 20 OCT 84 ** End of flight record card ** Transferred to NWC China Lake, CA., to be used as a target on the Survivability range ** On conditional loan from the National Museum of Naval Aviation; Pensacola, Fl. to the USAF museum at Wright Patterson AFB, OH.

E-006 156740 Navy acceptance from NPRO Rep. LTV, Dallas, TX., 17 SEP 69 ** Transferred to VA-122/FRS, NJ/2XX, NAS LeMoore, CA., 16 SEP 69 ** Transferred to VA-174/FRS, AD/3XX, NAS Cecil Field, FL., 08 NOV 72 ** Transferred to NPRO Rep. LTV, Dallas, TX. to be converted to TA-7C, 06 JAN 75 ** Re-designated to TA-7C, 15 JAN 75 ** Transferred to NPRO Rep. LTV, Dallas, TX., for RDT & E, 03 OCT 78 ** Transferred to VA-146/CVW-9, NG/3XX, NAS Cubi Point, PI., 21 JUN 79; To VA-146, NAS LeMoore, CA., 31 JUL 79 ** Transferred to VA-122/FRS, NJ/2XX, NAS LeMoore, CA., 07 SEP 79 ** Transferred to VA-174/FRS, AD/3XX, NAS Cecil Field, FL., 27 FEB 80 ** Transferred to VA-122/FRS, NJ/2XX, NAS LeMoore, 15 MAY 80; To VA-122, NAS Alameda, CA., 30 AUG 82; To VA-122, NAS LeMoore, CA., 22 SEP 82 ~ S 1SO strike, 21 SEP 83 ** Both pilots ejected safely when aircraft lost altitude and crashed.

156741/156761 LTV A-7C-2-CV Corsair II; Multi-YR 68,
  Contract N00019-68-C-0075 (150) A-7E,
    from E-008/E-157; (Block II)
FY 77 Contract N00019-77-C-0030 (15) TA-7C
  from A-7C C-008/C-022; CSN 32-46;
FY 78 Contract N00019-78-C-0005 (14) TA-7C
  From C-023/C-036; CSN 47-60

E-007 156741 Navy acceptance from NPRO Rep. LTV, Dallas, TX., 10 JUN 69 ** Transferred to VA-122/FRS, NJ/2XX, NAS LeMoore, CA., 18 SEP 69 ** Transferred to VA-174/FRS, AD/3XX, NAS Cecil Field, FL., 05 OCT 72 ** Transferred to VA-86/CVW-8, AJ/4XX, NAS Cecil Field, FL., 07 DEC 72; To VA-86, USS America (CVA-66), 30 MAY 73; To VA-86, NAS Cecil Field, FL., 01 JAN 75 ** Transferred to NARF, NAS Jacksonville, FL., 19 MAY 75 ** Transferred to VA-174/FRS, AD/3XX, NAS Cecil Field, FL., 18 SEP 75 ** Transferred to NPRO Rep. LTV Dallas, TX. to be converted to TA-7C, 30 JUN 77 ** Re-designated to TA-7C, 30 JUN 77 ** Transferred to VA-122/FRS, NJ/220, NAS LeMoore, CA., 31 JAN 79; To VA-122, NAS Jacksonville, FL., 18 FEB 82; To VA-122, NAS LeMoore, CA., 11 JAN 83 ** Transferred to VAQ-34, GD/201, FEWSG, NAS Point Mugu, CA. 26 JAN 83; Converted to EA-7L, 01 MAY 84; Changed Modex to GD/08; To VAQ-134, NAS Jacksonville, FL., 02 DEC 84; To VAQ-34, NAS Point Mugu, CA., 02 DEC 84; To VAQ-134, NAS Jacksonville, FL., 04 DEC 84; To VAQ-34, NAS Point Mugu, CA., 26 FEB 85; To VAQ-34, NAS Dallas, TX., 04 SEP 85; To VAQ-34, NAS Point Mugu, CA., 24 MAY 86 thru 13 JAN 87 ** End of flight record card ** Transferred to AMARC, Davis Monthan AFB; Tucson, AZ., assigned park code 6A0404, 25 SEP 91 ** 5634.6 flight hours ** TF41A402D engine S/N AE141385 ** Storage location 111508 ** At AMARG, Davis Monthan AFB; Tucson, AZ., 15 JUN 07.

E-008 156742 Navy acceptance from NPRO Rep. LTV, Dallas, TX., 10 JUN 69 ** Transferred to NATC, Weapons Systems Test, NAS Patuxent River, MD., 25 JUN 69 ~ S 1SO strike, 23 SEP 70 ** No data on strike.

E-009 156743 Navy acceptance from NPRO Rep. LTV, Dallas, TX., 27 MAR 69 ** Transferred to VA-174/FRS, AD/3XX, NAS Cecil Field, FL., 29 AUG 70 ** Transferred to NPRO Rep. LTV, Dallas, TX., 29 AUG 70 ** Transferred to VA-174/FRS, AD/3XX, NAS Cecil Field, FL., 29 AUG 70 ** Transferred to VA-86/CVW-8, AJ/4XX, USS America (CVA-66), 27 APR 72; To VA-86, NAS Cecil Field, FL., 27 APR 72; To VA-86, USS America (CVA-66), 13 JUN 73 ** Transferred to NATF, NAS Lakehurst, NJ, XX/XXX, 07 APR 75 ** Transferred to NPRO Rep. LTV, Dallas, TX. to be converted to TA-7C, 31 OCT 76 ** Re-designated to TA-7C, 26 NOV 76 ** Transferred to VA-174/FRS, AD/3XX, NAS Cecil Field, FL., 23 JUN 78; To VA-174, NAS Jacksonville, FL., 01 JUL 80; To VA-174, NAS Cecil Field, FL., 03 JUL 80; To VA-174, NAS Jacksonville, FL., 07 AUG 80; To VA-174, NAS Cecil Field, FL., 27 AUG 80; To VA-174, NAS Jacksonville, Fl.,

20 JUL 82; To VA-174, NAS Cecil Field, FL., 20 JUL 82; To VA-174, NAS Jacksonville, FL., 21 JUL 82 ** Transferred to VAQ-34, GD/202, FEWSG, NAS Point Mugu, CA. 12 MAY 83; Converted to EA-7L, 01 MAY 84; To VAQ-34, NAS Dallas, TX., 24 MAY 85; To VAQ-34, NAS Point Mugu, CA., 25 MAY 85; To VAQ-34, NAS Dallas, TX., 24 MAY 85; VAQ-34, NAS Point Mugu, CA., 25 MAY 85; To VAQ-34, NAS Jacksonville, FL., 06 APR 86; To VAQ-34, NAS Point Mugu, CA., 09 APR 86 thru 01 AUG 87 ** End of flight record card ~ S 1SO strike, 19 JUL 90 ** Crashed into the hills above Santa Barbara, Ca. near Gibralter dam in Los Padres National Forest.

E-010 156744 Navy acceptance from NPRO Rep. LTV, Dallas, TX., 27 MAR 69 ** Transferred to NATC, Weapons Systems Test, NAS Patuxent River, MD., 11 JUL 69 ** Transferred to NAS Point Mugu, CA., for RDT & E, 18 FEB 70 ** Transferred to NAF China Lake, CA., for RDT & E, 02 MAR 70 ** Transferred to NARF, NAS Alameda, CA., 15 MAR 71 ** Transferred to VA-174/FRS, AD/3XX, NAS Cecil Field, FL., 30 MAR 72 ** Transferred to VA-86/CVW-8, AJ/412, USS America (CVA-66), 04 MAY 72; To VA-86, NAS Cecil Field, FL., 04 MAY 72; To VA-86, USS America (CVA-66), 14 JUN 73; To VA-86, NAS Cecil Field, FL., 01 JAN 75 ** Transferred to NARF, NAS Jacksonville, FL., 20 MAY 75 ** Transferred to VA-125/FRS, NJ/5XX, NAS LeMoore, CA., 30 AUG 75 ** Transferred to VA-122/FRS, NJ/2XX, NAS LeMoore, CA., 29 OCT 75 ** Transferred to NPRO Rep. LTV, Dallas, TX. to be converted to TA-7C, 01 APR 77 ** Re-designated to TA-7C, 07 APR 77 ** Transferred to VA-174/FRS, AD/357, NAS Cecil Field, FL., 08 OCT 78; To VA-174, NAS Jacksonville, FL., 17 FEB 81; To VA-174, NAS Cecil Field, FL., 24 MAR 81; To VA-174, NAS Jacksonville, FL., 25 MAR 81; To VA-174, NAS Cecil Field, FL., 10 JUN 81; To VA-174, NAS Jacksonville, FL., 26 FEB 85; To VA-174, NAS Cecil Field, FL., 28 MAY 85 thru 09 JUL 87 ** End of flight record card.

E-011 156745 Navy acceptance from NPRO Rep. LTV, Dallas, TX., 02 AUG 69 ** Transferred to VX-5, XE/XXX, NAF China Lake, CA., 03 AUG 69 ** Transferred to VA-82/CVW-8, AJ/3XX, USS America (CVA-66), 11 APR 72; To VA-82, NAS Cecil Field, FL., 24 APR 72; To VA-82, USS America (CVA-66), 04 APR 73; To VA-82, NAS Cecil Field, FL., 15 NOV 74 ** Transferred to VA-174/FRS, AD/3XX, NAS Cecil Field, FL., 12 MAR 75 ** Transferred to NARF, NAS Jacksonville, FL., 05 JUN 75 ** Transferred to VA-174/FRS, AD/3XX, NAS Cecil Field, FL., 23 AUG 75 ** Transferred to NPRO Rep. LTV Dallas, TX. to be converted to TA-7C, 24 JUN 77 ** Re-designated to TA-7C, 28 JUN 77 ** Transferred to VA-122/FRS, NJ/2XX, NAS LeMoore, CA., 19 MAY 79 ** Transferred to VAQ-34/FEWSG, GD/200, NAS Point Mugu, CA., 03 JUN 83; Converted to EA-7L, changed Modex to GD/00, 01 MAY 84; To VAQ-34, NAS Jacksonville, FL., 23 JUL 84; To VAQ-34, NAS Point Mugu, CA., 23 JUL 84; To VAQ-34, NAS Jacksonville, FL., 25 JUL 84; To VAQ-34, NARF, NAS Jacksonville, FL., 27 JUL 84; To VAQ-34, NAS Point Mugu, CA., 15 NOV 84; To VAQ-34, NAS Dallas, TX, 31 AUG 85; To VAQ-34, NAS Point Mugu, CA., 31 AUG 85 ** To VAQ-34, NAS Dallas, TX, 25 FEB 86; To VAQ-34, NAS Whidbey Island, WA., 02 APR 86; To VAQ-34, NAS Point Mugu, CA., 04 APR 86 thru 29 JUN 87 ** End of flight record card ** Transferred to AMARC, Davis Monthan AFB; Tucson, AZ., assigned park code 6A0405, 25 SEP 91 ** 5608.5 flight hours ** TF41A402D engine S/N AE141235 ** Storage location 111509 ** Transferred to MDC FMS, 06 APR 04 ** At AMARG, Davis Monthan AFB; Tucson, AZ., 15 JUN 07.

E-012 156746 Navy acceptance from NPRO Rep. LTV, Dallas, TX., 14 JUL 69 ** Transferred to VA-122/FRS, NJ/2XX, NAS LeMoore, CA., 15 JUL 69 ** Transferred to VA-82/CVW-8, AJ/3XX, USS America (CVA-66), 09 MAY 72; To VA-82, NAS Cecil Field, FL., 15 MAY 72; To VA-82, USS America (CVA-66), 30 APR 73; To VA-82, NAS Cecil Field, FL., 01 JAN 75; To VA-82, NAS Jacksonville, FL., 02 APR 75; To VA-82, NAS Cecil Field, FL., 03 APR 75; To VA-82, NAS Jacksonville, FL., 08 MAY 72; To VA-82, NAS Cecil Field, FL., 14 MAY 75 ** Transferred to VA-174/FRS, AD/373, NAS Cecil Field, FL., 29 MAY 75 ** Transferred to NPRO Rep. LTV Dallas, TX., to be converted to TA-7C, 17 NOV 77 ** Re-designated to TA-7C, 17 NOV 77 ** Transferred to VA-174/FRS, AD/3XX, NAS Cecil Field, FL., 31 OCT 79 ** Transferred to VA-

122/FRS, NJ/2XX, NAS LeMoore, CA., 28 MAY 80 ** Transferred to VA-174/FRS, AD/3XX, NAS Cecil Field, FL., 29 JUL 80; To VA-174, NAS Jacksonville, FL., 21 DEC 81; To VA-174, NAS Cecil Field, FL., 05 FEB 82; To VA-174, NAS Jacksonville, FL., 09 NOV 83; To VA-174, NAS Cecil Field, FL. 17 FEB 84; To VA-174, NAS Jacksonville, FL., 09 MAR 84 ** Transferred to VA-122/FRS, NJ/2XX, NAS LeMoore, CA., 31 MAR 84; To VA-122, NAS Dallas, TX., 09 APR 86 ** Transferred to VX-5, XE/XXX, NWC China Lake, CA., 31 MAR 87 ** End of flight record card ** Transferred to AMARC, Davis Monthan AFB; Tucson, AZ., assigned park code 6A0357, 22 MAY 90 ** 7412.6 flight hours ** TF41A402D engine S/N 141945 ** Transferred to the Royal Thai Navy, S/N 1415, JUL 95.

E-013 156747 Navy acceptance from NPRO Rep. LTV, Dallas, TX., 16 JUL 69 ** Transferred to VA-122/FRS, NJ/2XX, NAS LeMoore, CA., 17 JUL 69 ** Transferred to VA-25/CVW-2, NE/4XX, NAS LeMoore, CA., 06 APR 72 ** Transferred to VA-122/FRS, NJ/2XX, NAS LeMoore, CA., 01 MAY 72 ** Transferred to VA-82/CVW-8, AJ/3XX, NAS Cecil Field, FL., 30 OCT 72 ** Transferred to VA-86/CVW-8, AJ/4XX; 06 NOV 72; To VA-86, USS America (CVA-66), 04 APR 73; To VA-86, NAS Cecil Field, FL., 01 JAN 75 ** Transferred to NARF, NAS Jacksonville, FL., 19 MAY 75 ** Transferred to VA-174/FRS, AD/454, NAS Cecil Field, FL., 31 AUG 75 ** Transferred to NPRO Rep. LTV, Dallas, TX. to be converted to TA-7C, 07 NOV 77 ** Re-designated to TA-7C, 17 NOV 77 ** Transferred to VA-122/FRS, NJ/2XX, NAS LeMoore, CA., 19 SEP 79; To VA-122, NAS Jacksonville, FL., 10 MAY 85; To VA-122, NAS LeMoore, CA., 06 NOV 85 ** Transferred to VA-174/FRS, AD/3XX, NAS Cecil Field, FL., 03 SEP 86 Thru 20 OCT 86 ** End of flight record card ** Transferred to VAQ-34/FEWSG, GD/208, NAS Point Mugu, CA. ** Transferred to the Helinic Air Force (Greece).

E-014 156748 Navy acceptance from NPRO Rep. LTV, Dallas, TX., 15 JUL 69 ** Transferred to VA-122/FRS, NJ/2XX, NAS LeMoore, CA., 16 JUL 69 ** Transferred to VA-82/CVW-8, AJ/3XX, NAS Cecil Field, FL., 30 OCT 63; To VA-82, USS America (CVA-66), 13 JUN 73; To VA-82, NAS Cecil Field, FL., 01 JAN 75 ** Transferred to VA-174/FRS, AD/3XX, NAS Cecil Field, FL., 18 MAR 75 ** Transferred to NPRO Rep. LTV, Dallas, TX. to be converted to TA-7C, 19 SEP 75 ** Re-designated to TA-7C, 24 SEP 75 ** Transferred to VX-5, XE/XXX, NAF China Lake, CA., 08 MAY 78 ~ S 1SO strike, 21 NOV 79 ** Crashed while simulating close air support at Ft. Irwin, CA., Both pilots killed.

E-015 156749 Navy acceptance from NPRO Rep. LTV, Dallas, TX., 03 AUG 69 ** Transferred to VA-122/FRS, NJ/205, NAS LeMoore, CA., 05 AUG 69 ~ S 1SO strike, 19 JUN 72 ** No data on strike.

E-016 156750 Navy acceptance from NPRO Rep. LTV, Dallas, TX., 16 JUL 69 ** Transferred to VA-122/FRS, NJ/2XX, NAS LeMoore, CA., 23 JUL 69 ** Transferred to VA-25/CVW-2, NE/4XX, NAS LeMoore, CA, 09 APR 72 ** Transferred to NPRO Rep. LTV, Dallas, TX. to be converted to TA-7C, 08 JUL 77 ** Re-designated to TA-7C, 26 JUL 77 ** Transferred to NWEF, Kirtland AFB, NM., 09 APR 79, Thunderbird with NAVWPNFACILTY on tail, 02 Modex; To NWEF, at NAS Jacksonville, FL., 09 MAR 83; To NWEF, Kirtland AFB, NM., 20 MAY 83; To NWEF, at NAS Dallas, TX., 15 JUL 85 thru 18 JUN 87 ** End of flight record card.

E-017 156751 Navy acceptance from NPRO Rep. LTV, Dallas, TX., 12 AUG 69 ** Transferred to VA-122/FRS, NJ/2XX, NAS LeMoore, CA., 13 AUG 69 ** Transferred to VA-25/CVW-2, NE/4XX, NAS LeMoore, CA., 07 APR 72 ** Transferred to VA-122/FRS, NJ/2XX, NAS LeMoore, CA., 01 MAY 72 ** Transferred to VA-174/FRS, AD/3XX, NAS Cecil Field, FL., 21 NOV 72 ** Transferred To NARF, NAS Jacksonville, FL., 04 DEC 75 ** Transferred to VA-122/FRS, NJ/2XX, NAS LeMoore, CA., 18 SEP 75 ** Transferred to NPRO Rep. LTV, Dallas, TX. to be converted to TA-7C, 16 JUL 77 ** Re-designated to TA-7C, 26 JUL 77 ** Transferred to VA-174/FRS, AD/371, NAS Cecil Field, FL., 27 MAY 79; To VA-174, NAS Jacksonville, FL., 27 OCT 81; To VA-174, NAS Cecil Field, FL., 22 DEC 81; To VA-174, NAS Jacksonville, FL., 06 OCT 83; To VA-174, NAS Cecil Field, FL., 15 DEC 83 ** To VA-174, NAS Dallas, TX.,

29 JAN 85 ** Transferred to NATC, Patuxent River, MD., for RDT & E, 29 JAN 85 ** Transferred to VA-174/FRS, AD/3XX, NAS Cecil Field, FL., 13 MAR 85 thru 20 OCT 86 ** End of flight record card ** Located at the Kenosha Military Museum.

E-018 156752 Navy acceptance from NPRO Rep. LTV, Dallas, TX., 30 APR 69 ** Transferred to NPRO Rep. LTV, Dallas, TX., for R & T, 30 APR 69 ** Transferred to NATC, Weapon Systems Test; NAS Patuxent River, MD., 29 SEP 69 ** Transferred to NATC, Service Test; NAS Patuxent River, MD., 30 JUL 70, ** Transferred to NATC, NAS Patuxent River, MD., for RDT & E, Paint was white with orange nose and tail, NATC/752; 13 NOV 75; To NATC, at NAS Jacksonville, FL., 13 NOV 75; To NATC, NAS Patuxent River, MD., 13 NOV 75; NATC, at NAS Jacksonville, FL., 13 NOV 75; To NATC, NAS Patuxent River, MD., 24 NOV 75; To NATC, NAS Jacksonville, FL., 18 OCT 79; NATC, NAS Patuxent River, MD., 14 DEC 79; To NATC, at NAS Jacksonville, FL., 05 APR 83; To NATC, NAS Patuxent River, MD., 31 AUG 83 ** Transferred to NWEF Kirtland AFB, NM., 04 SEP 84, light gray on dark gray, thunderbird on tail; To NWEF, at NAS Jacksonville, FL., 20 AUG 85; To NWEF, Kirtland AFB, NM., 21 AUG 85 ** End of flight record card ** Nose Section of Aircraft, Modex 752, Sitting in front of the El Real Nursery in Santa Clara, CA. 24 JUL 05, For sale on E-Bay for $8500.00, 24 JUL 05.

E-019 156753 Navy acceptance from NPRO Rep. LTV, Dallas, TX., 02 AUG 69 ** Transferred to VA-122/FRS, NJ/2XX, NAS LeMoore, CA., 04 AUG 69 ** Transferred to VA-113/CVW-2, NE/3XX, NAS LeMoore, CA., 10 APR 72 ** Transferred to VA-122/FRS, NJ/2XX, NAS LeMoore, CA., 01 JUN 72 ** Transferred to NATC, NAS Patuxent River, MD., for RDT & E, 19 JAN 76 ** Transferred to NATF, NAS Lakehurst, NJ., 19 JAN 76 ** Transferred to NAEC, NAS Lakehurst, NJ., 01 MAY 77 ** Transferred to NPRO Rep. LTV, Dallas, TX. to be converted to TA-7C, 22 FEB 78 ** Re-designated to TA-7C, 28 FEB 78 ** Transferred to VA-122/FRS, NJ/225 NAS LeMoore, CA. 01 APR 80; To VA-122, NAS Dallas, TX., 19 NOV 85 ** Transferred to VX-5, XE/07, NWC China Lake, CA., 22 SEP 86 thru 21 SEP 87 ** End of flight record card ** Transferred to the Helenic Air Force (Greece).

E-020 156754 Navy acceptance from NPRO Rep. LTV, Dallas, TX., 30 APR 69 ** Transferred to NPRO Rep. LTV, Dallas, TX., for RDT & E, 30 APR 69 ** Transferred to NATC, Service Test, NAS Patuxent River, MD., XX/XXX, for RDT & E, 11 DEC 69 ** Transferred to NPRO Rep. LTV, Dallas, TX., for RDT & E, 03 APR 72 ** Transferred to NATC, Service Test, NAS Patuxent River, MD., 29 APR 72 ** Transferred to NATC, NAS Patuxent River, MD., for RDT & E, 21 SEP 72; To NATC, at NAS Jacksonville, FL., 03 SEP 76; Transferred to NATC, NAS Patuxent River, MD., 26 OCT 76; To NATC, at NAS Jacksonville, FL., 10 NOV 76; Re-designated NA-7E, 07 JUN 78; To NATC, NAS Jacksonville, FL., 16 NOV 79; To NATC, NAS Patuxent River, MD.,MD., 25 MAR 80; To NATC, FS, NAS Patuxent River, MD., 04 MAR 86; Transferred to NATC, NAS Patuxent River, MD., 20 OCT 86 ~ S 3SO strike, 21 OCT 86 ** No data on strike.

E-021 156755 Navy acceptance from NPRO Rep. LTV, Dallas, TX., 29 MAY 69 ** Transferred to VA-122/FRS, NJ/2XX, NAS LeMoore, CA., 12 SEP 69 ** Transferred to VA-174/FRS, AD/4XX, NAS Cecil Field, FL., 02 NOV 72 ** Transferred to VA-82/CVW-17, AA/3XX, NAS Cecil Field, FL., 05 FEB 73; To VA-82, USS America, (CVA-66), 04 JUN 73; VA-82, NAS Cecil Field, FL., 02 DEC 74 ~ S 1SO strike, 02 DEC 74 ** No data on strike.

E-022 156756 Navy acceptance from NPRO Rep. LTV, Dallas, TX., 29 MAY 69 ** Transferred to VA-147/CVW-9, NG/4XX, USS America (CVA-66), 30 SEP 69 ** Transferred to VA-122/FRS, NJ/2XX, NAS LeMoore, CA., 08 JAN 70 ** Transferred to VA-25/CVW-2, NE/4XX, NAS LeMoore, CA., 09 APR 72 ** Transferred to VA-122/FRS, NJ/2XX, NAS LeMoore, CA., 01 MAY 72 ** Transferred to VA-174/FRS, AD/3XX, NAS Cecil Field, FL., 16 AUG 73 ~ S 1SO strike, 30 JUN 75 ** No data on strike.

E-023 156757 Navy acceptance from NPRO Rep. LTV, Dallas, TX., 04 SEP 69 ** Transferred to VA-122/FRS, NJ/2XX, NAS LeMoore, CA., 05 SEP 69 ** Transferred to NAF China Lake, CA., for RDT & E, 26 FEB 71 ** Transferred to NARF, NAS Jacksonville, FL., 20 APR 72 ** Transferred to VA-174/FRS, AD/350, NAS Cecil Field, FL., 06 JUL 72 ** Transferred to VA/82/CVW-8, AJ/3XX, NAS Cecil Field, FL., 03 AUG 72; To VA-82, USS America (CVA-66), 31 MAY 73; To VA-82, NAS Cecil Field, FL., 01 JUL 73 ** Transferred to VA-174/FRS, AD/3XX, NAS Cecil Field, FL., 27 NOV 74 ** Transferred to NARF, NAS Jacksonville, FL., 29 AUG 75 ** Transferred to VA-122/FRS, NJ/2XX, NAS LeMoore, CA., 29 OCT 75 ** Transferred to NPRO Rep. LTV, Dallas, TX. to be converted to TA-7C, 25 FEB 76 ** Re-designated to TA-7C, 03 MAY 76 ** Transferred to VA-174/FRS, AD/3XX, NAS Cecil Field, FL., 09 JUN 78; To VA-174, NAS Jacksonville, FL., 22 OCT 80; To VA-174, NAS Cecil Field, FL., 19 NOV 80 ** To VA-174, NAS Jacksonville, FL., 20 NOV 80; To VA-174, NAS Cecil Field, FL., 02 FEB 81; To VA-174, NAS Jacksonville, FL., 14 NOV 82; To VA-174, NAS Cecil Field, FL., 14 NOV 82; To VA-174, NAS Jacksonville, FL., 18 NOV 82 ** Transferred to VAQ-34/FEWSG, GD/204, Later Red Star on tail/04 Modex, NAS Point Mugu, CA., 19 AUG 83; To VAQ-34, NARF, NAS Jacksonville, FL., 29 JUN 83; Converted to EA-7L, 01 MAY 84; To VAQ-34, NAS Dallas, TX., 20 AUG 85; To VAQ-34, NAS Point Mugu, CA., 01 OCT 86; To VAQ-34, NAS Whidbey Island, CA., 16 DEC 86; To VAQ-34, NAS Point Mugu, CA., 08 JAN 87 thru 20 APR 87 ** End of flight record card ** Transferred to AMARC, Davis Monthan AFB; Tucson, AZ., assigned park code 6A0399, 22 AUG 91 ** 6453.2 flight hours ** TF41A402D engine S/N AE141916 ** Storage location 111305 Transferred to MDC FMS, 06 APR 07 ** At AMARG, Davis Monthan AFB; Tucson, AZ., 15 JUN 07.

E-024 156758 Navy acceptance from NPRO Rep. LTV, Dallas, TX., 29 AUG 69 ** Transferred to VA-122/FRS, NJ/2XX, NAS LeMoore, CA., 30 AUG 69 ~ S 1SO strike, 13 AUG 70 ** No data on strike.

E-025 156759 Navy acceptance from NPRO Rep. LTV, Dallas, TX., 27 AUG 69 ** Transferred to VA-122/FRS, NJ/2XX, NAS LeMoore, CA., 28 AUG 69 ** Transferred to VA-25/CVW-2, NE/4XX, NAS LeMoore, CA.,06 APR 72 ** Transferred to VA-122/FRS, NJ/2XX, NAS LeMoore, CA., 02 JUN 72 ** NAF China Lake, CA., 23 FEB 73 ~ S 1SO strike, 25 JUL 74 ** No data on strike.

E-026 156760 Navy acceptance from NPRO Rep. LTV, Dallas, TX., 20 SEP 69 ** Transferred to VA-146/CVW-9, NG/3XX, USS America (CVA-66), 21 SEP 69 ** Transferred to VA-122/FRS, NJ/2XX, NAS LeMoore, CA., 22 DEC 69 ** Transferred to VA-86/CVW-8, AJ/4XX, USS America (CVA-66), 08 MAY 72; To VA-86, NAS Cecil Field, FL., 15 MAY 72 ~ S 1SO strike, 26 JUL 73 ** No data on strike.

E-027 156761 Navy acceptance from NPRO Rep. LTV, Dallas, TX., 29 MAY 69 ** Transferred to VA-147/CVW-9, NG/3XX, USS America (CVA-66), 17 SEP 69 ** Transferred to VA-122/FRS, NJ/2XX, NAS LeMoore, CA., 12 JAN 70 ** Transferred to VA-113/CVW-3, AC/4XX, NAS LeMoore, CA., 07 APR 72 ** Transferred to VA-122/FRS, NJ/2XX, NAS LeMoore, CA., 04 MAY 72 ** Transferred to VA-174/FRS, AD/3XX, NAS Cecil Field, FL., 28 JUL 73 ** Transferred to NPRO Rep. LTV, Dallas, TX. to be converted to TA-7C, 14 MAY 76 ** Re-designated to TA-7C, 23 MAY 76 ** Transferred to NATC, NAS Patuxent River, MD., for RDT & E, 28 APR 78 ** Transferred to VA-122/FRS, NJ/2XX, NAS LeMoore, CA., 01 AUG 78; To VA-122, NAS Jacksonville, FL., 12 JUN 80; To VA-122, NAS LeMoore, CA., 25 SEP 80 ** To VA-122, NAS Jacksonville, FL., 31 MAR 83; To VA-122, NAS LeMoore, CA., 20 JUN 83 ** Transferred to VAQ-34/FEWSG, GD/205, NAS Point Mugu, CA., 30 JUL 83; Converted to EA-7L, 18 MAY 84; Modex 84; To VAQ-34, NAS Dallas, TX., 18 MAY 86; To VAQ-34, NAS Point Mugu, CA., 01 OCT 86; To VAQ-34, NAS Dallas, TX., 07 OCT 87; To VAQ-34, NAS Point Mugu, CA., 16 JAN 87; To VAQ-34, NAS Dallas, TX., 30 JAN 87; To VAQ-34, NAS Point Mugu, CA., 10 FEB 87 thru 23 SEP 87 ** End of flight record card ** Transferred to NADEP, NAS Jacksonville, FL., 15 MAY 90 ** Transferred to AMARC, Davis Monthan AFB; Tucson, AZ., assigned park code 6A0418, 17 NOV 94 ** 7188.8 flight hours TF41A402D engine S/N 141540 ** Storage location 211843 ** Transferred to MDC FMS, 06 APR 04 ** At AMARG, Davis Monthan AFB; Tucson, AZ., 15 JUN 07.

156762/156800 LTV A-7C-3-CV Corsair II; (Block III)

E-067 156762 Navy acceptance from NPRO Rep. LTV, Dallas, TX., 31 AUG 69 ** Transferred to VA-174/FRS, AD/3XX, NAS Cecil Field, FL., 05 MAR 70 ** Transferred to VA-86/CVW-8, AJ/404, USS America (CVA-66), 28 APR 72; To VA-86, NAS Cecil Field, FL., 28 APR 72 ~ S 1SO strike, 29 OCT 72 ** LCDR James E. Sullivan Ejected safely when hit by AAA near Vinh, NVN. Killed in captivity, seen laying face down in boat.

E-029 156763 Navy acceptance from NPRO Rep. LTV, Dallas, TX., 11 SEP 69 ** Transferred to VA-122/FRS, NJ/2XX, NAS LeMoore, CA., 12 SEP 69 ** Transferred to VX-5, XE/XXX, NAF China Lake, CA., 27 APR 71 ** Transferred to NARF, NAS Alameda, CA, 02 MAR 73 ~ S 1SO strike, 06 NOV 75 ** No data on strike ** On display at NAS LeMoore, with Bureau Number 160122, MAR 95.

E-030 156764 Navy acceptance from NPRO Rep. LTV, Dallas, TX., 08 OCT 69 ** Transferred to VA-147/CVW-9, NG/4XX, USS America (CVA-66), 09 OCT 69 ** Transferred to VA-122/FRS, NJ/2XX, NAS LeMoore, CA., 31 DEC 69 ** Transferred to VA-174/ FRS, AD/3XX, NAS Cecil Field, FL., 29 JUN 72 ** Transferred to VA-86/CVW-8, AJ/4XX, NAS Cecil Field, FL., 03 AUG 72 ~ S 1SO strike, 09 NOV 72 ** Due to brake failure on landing, aircraft over side, Pilot ejected and rescued.

E-031 156765 Navy acceptance from NPRO Rep. LTV, Dallas, TX., 03 SEP 69 ** Transferred to VA-122/FRS, NJ/2XX, NAS LeMoore, CA., 05 SEP 69 ** Transferred to VA-25/CVW-14, NK/4XX, NAS LeMoore, CA., 07 APR 72 ** Transferred to VA-122/FRS, NJ/2XX, NAS LeMoore, CA., 23 MAY 72; To VA-122, NAS Jacksonville, FL., 28 OCT 74; To VA-122, NAS LeMoore, CA., 30 DEC 74 ** Transferred to VA-125/FRS, NJ/5XX, NAS LeMoore, CA., 05 MAR 76 ** Transferred to VA-122/FRS, NJ/2XX, NAS LeMoore, CA., 09 SEP 77 ** Transferred to NPRO Rep. LTV, Dallas, TX., to be converted to TA-7C, 12 DEC 77 ** Re-designated to TA-7C, 16 DEC 77 ** Transferred to VA-122/FRS, NJ/2XX, NAS LeMoore, CA., 27 NOV 79; To VA-122, NAS Jacksonville, FL., 25 JUL 85; To VA-122, NAS LeMoore, CA., 25 JUL 85; To VA-122, NAS Jacksonville, FL., 30 JUL 85; To VA-122, NAS LeMoore, CA., 12 NOV 85 ** Transferred to NSWC, NSWC/XXX, NAS Fallon, NV., 24 SEP 86 thru 23 JUL 87 ** End of flight record card ** On display at the Pacific Coast Division of the United States Aviation Museum, Inyokern, CA. ** Museum has closed, aircraft no longer there, AUG 04 ** Located at the VX-31 Preservation Yard, NAWC China Lake, CA., NOV 04.

E-032 156766 Navy acceptance from NPRO Rep. LTV, Dallas, TX., 17 SEP 69 ** Transferred to VX-5/XE/01, NAF China Lake, CA., 24 SEP 69 ** Transferred to NPRO Rep. LTV, Dallas, TX. to be converted to TA-7C, 30 JAN 76 ** Re-designated to TA-7C, 08 FEB 76 ** Transferred to VA-122/FRS, NJ/2XX, NAS LeMoore, CA., 23 JUN 78; To VA-122, NAS Jacksonville, FL., 29 AUG 80; To VA-122, NAS LeMoore, CA., 05 MAY 81 ~ S 1SO strike, 13 OCT 81 ** Both pilots ejected safely, due to an engine flame out.

E-033 156767 Navy acceptance from NPRO Rep. LTV, Dallas, TX., 14 OCT 69 ** Transferred to VA-146/CVW-9, NG/3XX, USS America (CVA-66), 15 OCT 69 ** Transferred to VA-122/ FRS, NJ/2XX, NAS LeMoore, CA., 14 JAN 70 ** Transferred to VA-174/FRS, AD/372, NAS Cecil Field, FL., 31 MAR 70 ** Transferred to VA-82/CVW-8, AJ/3XX, USS America (CVA-66), 16 APR 72; To VA-82, NAS Cecil Field, FL., 05 MAY 72; To VA-82, USS America (CVA-66), 16 MAY 73; To VA-82, NAS Cecil Field, FL., 01 SEP 74 ** Transferred to NARF, NAS Jacksonville, FL., 31 JUL 75 ** Transferred to VA-125/FRS, NJ/5XX, NAS LeMoore, CA., 06 DEC 75 ** Transferred to NPRO Rep. LTV, Dallas, TX., to be converted to TA-7C, 21 JUL 77 ** Re-designated to TA-7C, 26 JUL 77 ** Transferred to VA-174/FRS,

AD/3XX, NAS Cecil Field, FL., 21 JUN 79; To VA-174, NAS Jacksonville, FL., 04 DEC 81; To VA-174, Bloomfield, 08 FEB 82; To VA-174, NAS Jacksonville, FL., 11 FEB 82; To VA-174, NAS Cecil Field, FL., 12 FEB 82; To VA-174, NAS Dallas, TX., 16 APR 82; To VA-174, NAS Cecil Field, FL., 27 JUL 82; To VA-174, NAS Jacksonville, FL., 10 JUL 84; To VA-174, NAS Cecil Field, FL., 17 JAN 85 thru 17 SEP 87 ** End of flight record card ** Transferred to VA-122/FRS, NJ/217, NAS LeMoore, CA., date unknown ** Transferred to AMARC, Davis Monthan AFB; Tucson, AZ., assigned park code 6A0323, 21 MAR 90 ** 5194.9 flight hours ** TF41A402D engine S/N 142623 ** FLIR pods removed and placed in storage account for A-7E 156810 ** Prepare for overland and above deck shipment to Stellar Freight; Galveston, TX., for the government of Greece, no later than, 15 SEP 95 ** Transferred to the Helenic Air Force (Greece).

E-034 156768 Navy acceptance from NPRO Rep. LTV, Dallas, TX., 12 SEP 69 ** Transferred to VA-122/FRS, NJ/2XX, NAS LeMoore, CA., 13 SEP 69 ** Transferred to VA-174/FRS, AD/3XX, NAS Cecil Field, FL., 16 APR 70 ** Transferred to NPRO Rep. LTV, Dallas, TX., for RDT & E, 13 APR 71 ** Transferred to VA-174/FRS, AD/3XX, NAS Cecil Field, FL.,, 11 JUN 71 ** Transferred to VA-82/CVW-8, AJ/311, USS America (CVA-66), 05 APR 72; To VA-82, NAS Cecil Field, FL., 05 APR 72; To VA-82, USS America (CVA-66), 14 JUN 73; To VA-82, NAS Cecil Field, FL., 14 JUN 73 ** Transferred to VA-174/FRS, AD/3XX, NAS Cecil Field, FL., 13 FEB 75 ** Transferred to NARF, NAS Jacksonville, FL., 26 AUG 75 ** Transferred to VA-174/FRS, AD/3XX, NAS Cecil Field, FL., 11 OCT 75 ** Transferred to NPRO Rep. LTV, Dallas, TX. to be converted to TA-7C, 15 NOV 77 ** Re-designated to TA-7C, 21 NOV 77 ** Transferred to NWC China Lake, CA., NWC/768, Black tail with two pirates in white circles and NWC China Lake on tail, no Modex but 768 on tail cap, 20 DEC 79; To NWC, NAS Jacksonville, FL., 22 OCT 84; To NWC, NWC China Lake, CA., 22 OCT 84; To NWC, at NAS Jacksonville, FL., 24 OCT 84; To NWC, at NAS Dallas, TX., 18 JAN 85; To NWC, NWC China Lake, CA., 04 DEC 85 thru 31 AUG 87 ** End of flight record card ** Transferred to the Helenic Air Force (Greece).

E-035 156769 Navy acceptance from NPRO Rep. LTV, Dallas, TX., 11 SEP 69 ** Transferred to VA-122/FRS, NJ/2XX, NAS LeMoore, CA., 12 SEP 69 ~ S 1SO strike, 07 DEC 70 ** No data on crash.

E-036 156770 Navy acceptance from NPRO Rep. LTV, Dallas, TX., 05 SEP 69 ** Transferred to VA-122/FRS, NJ/2XX, NAS LeMoore, CA., 06 SEP 69 ** Transferred to VX-5, XE/06, NAF China Lake, CA., 16 APR 71; To VX-5, at NAS Jacksonville, FL., 11 DEC 74 ** Transferred to NAF Warminster, PA., XX/XXX, for RDT & E, 27 FEB 75 ** Transferred to NPRO Rep. LTV, Dallas, TX. to be converted to TA-7C, 23 MAY 78 ** Re-designated to TA-7C, 25 MAY 78 ** Transferred to NTPS, NAS Patuxent River, MD., 09 JUN 80 ** Transferred to VA-174/FRS, AD/3XX, NAS Cecil Field, FL., 03 APR 81 ~ S 1SO strike, 13 JAN 83 ** No data on strike.

E-037 156771 Navy acceptance from NPRO Rep. LTV, Dallas, TX., 30 SEP 69 ** Transferred to VA-147/CVW-9, NG/4XX, USS America (CVA-66), 01 OCT 69 ** Transferred to VA-122/FRS, NJ/2XX, NAS LeMoore, CA., 12 JAN 70 ** Transferred to VA-174/FRS, AD/3XX, NAS Cecil Field, FL., 29 MAR 70 ** Transferred to VA-86/CVW-8, AJ/4XX, USS America (CVA-66), 14 APR 72; To VA-86, NAS Cecil Field, FL., 16 APR 72 ~ S 1SO strike, 17 JUL 72 ** Lead aircraft in a three plane formation flying A-7C 156792 and an F-4. When the bombs were dropped, one exploded prematurely badly damaging all three aircraft. All four pilots ejected and were rescued.

E-038 156772 Navy acceptance from NPRO Rep. LTV, Dallas, TX., 18 OCT 69 ** Transferred to VA-122/FRS, NJ/2XX, NAS LeMoore, CA., 20 OCT 69 ** Transferred to VA-174/FRS, AD/3XX, NAS Cecil Field, FL., 04 OCT 72 ** Transferred to VA-86/CVW-8, AJ/4XX, NAS Cecil Field, FL., 07 DEC 72 ** Transferred to VA-86, USS America (CVA-

66), 14 MAY 73; To VA-86, NAS Cecil Field, FL., 01 JAN 75 ** Transferred to NATF, NAS Lakehurst, NJ., 03 MAY 75; To NATF, at NAS Jacksonville, FL., 03 SEP 75 ** Transferred to NWEF Kirtland AFB, Albuquerque, NM., Thunderbird on tail/4 , 04 NOV 75; To NWEF, at NAS Alameda, CA., 05 OCT 76; To NWEF, Kirtland AFB; Albuquerque, NM., 12 OCT 76; To NWEF, at NAS Jacksonville, FL., 02 APR 80; To NWEF, Kirtland AFB; Albuquerque, NM. ** Transferred to NWC China Lake, CA., NWC/XX, 02 JUL 86 ** End of flight record card.

E-039 156773 Navy acceptance from NPRO Rep. LTV, Dallas, TX., 10 OCT 69 ** Transferred to NATC, Weapons Systems Test, NAS Patuxent River, MD., 13 OCT 69 ** Transferred to VA-174/FRS, AD/3XX, NAS Cecil Field, FL., 18 DEC 69 ** Transferred to VA-86/CVW-8, AJ/4XX, USS America (CVA-66), 15 APR 72; To VA-86, NAS Cecil Field, FL., 15 APR 72; To VA-86, USS America (CVA-66), 04 APR 73; To VA-86, NAS Cecil Field, FL., 01 SEP 74 ** Transferred to NARF, NAS Jacksonville, FL., 19 MAY 75 ** Transferred to VA-174/FRS, AD/3XX, NAS Cecil Field, FL., 01 AUG 75 ** Transferred to NPRO Rep. LTV, Dallas, TX., to be converted to TA-7C, 24 MAY 77 ** Re-designated to TA-7C, 01 JUN 77 ** Transferred to VA-122/FRS, NJ/2XX, NAS LeMoore, CA., 06 DEC 78; To VA-122, NAS Jacksonville, FL., 16 FEB 82; To VA-122, NAS LeMoore, CA., 03 JUL 82; To VA-122, NAS Dallas, TX., 27 NOV 85; To VA-122, NAS LeMoore, CA., 25 OCT 86; To VA-122, NAS Jacksonville, FL., 28 APR 87; To VA-122, NAS LeMoore, CA., 28 APR 87 thru 28 SEP 87 ** End of flight record card ** Transferred to NSWC, Strike/32 NAS Fallon, NV., date unknown ** Transferred to AMARC, Davis Monthan AFB; Tucson, AZ., assigned park code 6A0331, 02 APR 90 ** 5738.0 flight hours ** TF41A402D engine S/N 141888 ** Prepared for overland shipment to Jacksonville, FL., 06 JUN 94.

E-040 156774 Navy acceptance from NPRO Rep. LTV, Dallas, TX., 30 SEP 69 ** Transferred to VA-146/CVW-9, NG/3XX, USS America (CVA-66), 01 OCT 69 ** Transferred to VA-174/FRS, AD/3XX, NAS Cecil Field, FL., 04 JUN 70 ** Transferred to VA-82/CVW-8, AJ/3XX, USS America (CVA-66), 11 APR 72; To VA-82, NAS Cecil Field, FL., 11 APR 72; To VA-82, USS America (CVA-66), 03 MAY 73; To VA-82, NAS Cecil Field, FL.,01 SEP 74 ** Transferred to NTPS, NAS Patuxent River, MD., 29 APR 75; To NTPS, NAS Jacksonville, FL., 29 APR 75; To NTPS, NAS Patuxent River, MD., 24 JUL 75 ** Transferred to NPRO Rep. LTV, Dallas, TX. to be converted to TA-7C, 18 AUG 78 ** Re-designated to TA-7C, 23 AUG 78 ** Transferred to VA-174/FRS, AD/3XX, NAS Cecil Field, FL., 02 AUG 80; To VA-174, NAS Jacksonville, FL., 10 AUG 82; To VA-174, NAS Cecil Field, FL., 17 JAN 83; To VA-174, NAS Jacksonville, FL., 16 APR 85; To VA-174, NAS Cecil Field, FL., 19 APR 85 thru 20 OCT 86 ** End of flight record card ** Transferred to the Helenic Air Force (Greece).

E-041 156775 Navy acceptance from NPRO Rep. LTV, Dallas, TX., 07 OCT 69 ** Transferred to VA-147/CVW-9, NG/4XX, USS America (CVA-66), 09 OCT 69 ** Transferred to VA-122/FRS, NJ/2XX, NAS LeMoore, CA., 18 JUN 70 ** Transferred to VA-174/FRS, AD/3XX, NAS Cecil Field, FL., 29 JUN 72 ** Transferred to VA-86/CVW-8, AJ/401, NAS Cecil Field, FL., 03 AUG 72 ~ S 1SO strike, 28 OCT 72 ** No data on strike.

E-042 156776 Navy acceptance from NPRO Rep. LTV, Dallas, TX., 17 OCT 69 ** Transferred to VA-146/CVW-9, NG/3XX, USS America (CVA-66), 18 OCT 69 ** Transferred to VA-122/FRS, NJ/2XX, NAS LeMoore, CA., 02 OCT 70 ** Transferred to VA-174/FRS, AD/3XX, NAS Cecil Field, FL., 03 APR 70 ** Transferred to NATC, Weapons Systems Test, NAS Patuxent River, MD., No tail markings, No Modex ** 20 APR 71 ** Transferred to VA-174/FRS, AD/3XX, NAS Cecil Field, FL., 20 APR 71 ** Transferred to NATC, Weapons Systems Test, NAS Patuxent River, MD., 20 APR71 ** Transferred to NWEF, Kirtland AFB; Albuquerque, NM., Thunderbird emblem/XXX, 30 JUN 72 ** Transferred to NATC, NAS Patuxent River, MD., for RDT

VA-195 A-7E 158833 NG/400 over USS Ranger

VA-195 A-7E NH/400 USS Kitty Hawk

VA-195 on board USS Ranger

VA-203 A-7B 154493 AF/300

VA-203 A-7A 153177 AF/301, pilot CDR Dollarhide, C.O.

VA-203 A-7 AF/300

VA-203 A-7B 154452 AF/306

VA-203 A-7E 156829 AF/311

VA-203 A-7E 157553 AF/300, Mt Rainier in the background

VA-203 A-7Bs 154493, 154475, - AF/300, 304, and 313

VA-203 A-7Bs AF/3XX with missiles

VA-203 A-7s AF/3XX fly over Pyramid Lake, NV.

VA-203 A-7A 153163 AF/300

VA-203 A-7A 154345 AF/305, pilot CDR Dave Dollarhide, C.O.

VA-203 A-7s AF/301, 312, and 3XX

VA-203 A-7 AF/301 and 2 A-7Ds PRANG

VA-203 A-7A AF/313 with 9' speed brake extended

VA-203 A-7 AF/302 firing rockets

VA-203 A-7 90° bank bonzo AF/313 with MK-76s

VA-203 A-7B 154493 AF/300

VA-203 A-7B AF/301 with MK-82s

VA-203 A-7A 153277 AF/301

VA-203 A-7B 154556 AF/301

VA-203 A-7A AF/300

VA-203 A-7B 154551 AF/313

VA-203 A-7B AF/314

VA-203 A-7B AF/300

VA-203 A-7B 154556 AF/301

VA-203 A-7 AF/3XX sand blower

VA-204 A-7B 154468 AF/405

VA-204 A-7B 154491 AF/411

VA-204 A-7E 157514 AF/414

VA-204 line of A-7Bs, 154482 AF/400

VA-204 A-7B 154552 AF/401

VA-204 A-7Bs AF/4XX

VA-204 A-7E AF/406

VA-204 A-7B 154520 AF/410

VA-204 A-7E AF/413 firing rockets

VA-204 A-7B 154454 AF/401 display

VA-205

VA-205 A-7B 154472 AF/513 with missile

VA-205 A-7B 154472 AF/513 with missile

VA-205 A-7Bs 154478, 154372, 154381 AF/510, 503, and 504

VA-205 A-7Bs over Stone Mountain Park, GA.

VA-205 A-7B af/513 ready to taxi

VA-205 A-7B 154453 AF/500

VA-205 A-7B 154454 AF/511 with MK-82s

VA-205 A-7B 154454 AF/511 with MK-76s

VA-205 A-7B 154454 AF/511 with MK-82s

VA-205 A-7 in museum

VA-205 A-7B 154370 AF/500 with engine pan and tail cone removed

VA-205 A-7B AF/506 dropping 2 MK-82s on the range

VA-205 A-7E AF-503 with drop tanks

166

VA-215 A-7B 154381 NM/300 with drop tanks

VA-215 A-7B 154463 AE/412

VA-215 A-7s NM/400, 403, and 404

VA-215 A-7B 154475 AE/401 USS Roosevelt over target

VA-215 A-7B AE/400 with drop tanks

VA-215 A-7B 154437 NM/403 USS Oriskany

VA-215 A-7 on flight deck with F-8 landing

VA-215 154433 NM/412 sandblower

VA-215 A-7B NM/410

VA-215 A-7B 154553 NM/410 taking the wire

VA-215 A-7 NM/4XX over Niagara Falls, NY

VA-215 A-7 NM/407, 404, and 401

VA-215 A-7 NM/405 taking the wire

VA-215 A-7B 154475 NM/401 on cat USS Oriskany

VA-215 A-7B 154475 NM/401 USS Roosevelt bicentennial paint scheme

VA-215 A-7B 154475 NM/401 USS Roosevelt bicentennial paint scheme

VA-215 A-7Bs AE/400, 4XX with D-704 buddy store

VA-303 A-7A 153264 ND/300

VA-303 A-7 ND/3XX

VA-303 A-7 ND/316 with MK-82s

VA-303 A-7B 154389 ND/300

VA-303 A-7As 153250 ND/302, 301, 305, and 311 over the Golden Gate

VA-303 A-7 ND/3XX AO and MK-82s

VA-303 A-7B 154438 ND/301

VA-303 A-7A ND/376 with bicentennial paint

VA-303 A-7 ND/300 on USS Ranger

VA-303 A-7 ND/303 with old yellow starter pod on port side

VA-303 A-7 ND/302 with AO's and rocket pod

VA-303 A-7A ND/376 USS Ranger bicentennial

VA-303 A-7 ND/3XX ready to take off along estuary at Alameda

VA-303 A-7B 154520 ND/312

VA-304 A-7A 153171 ND/400 over San Francisco

VA-304 wash rack wall built with sheets of 3/4" steel by AMSI Mike Kolter

VA-304 A-7B 154505 on ramp, San Francisco in background

VA-304 A-7B 154549 ND/417

VA-304 A-7A 153224 ND/405 on the wash ramp

VA-304 A-7A 154352 ND/401

VA-304 A-7A 153254 ND/407 with 9' speed brake down

VA-304 A-7A 153254 ND/407

VA-304 A-7As 153261, 154356, 153171, 153229, 152676 ND/411, 402, 400, 414, and 406 over NAS Alameda

VA-304 A-7A 153254 ND/407

VA-304 A-7A 153171 ND/400

VA-304 A-7As 153243, 152675 ND/410, 406

VA-304 A-7 ND/405

VA-304 A-7As 154352, 153240, 153201, 153249 ND/401, 412, 404, and 410

VA-304 A-7As 154356, 154352 ND/402, 401

VA-304 A-7As 153201, 152676 ND/404, 401, and 406

VA-304 A-7B 154370 ND/401

VA-304 A-7A 153201 ND/404 USS Lexington

VA-304 A-7A 153254 ND/407

VA-304 A-7A 153171 ND/400

VA-304 A-7A 153261 ND/411

VA-304 A-7A 153229 ND/414

VA-304 A-7E ND/4XX refueling with VF-301 F-14s (2) and VFA-303 F/A-18s

VA-304 A-7A 153224 ND/405

VA-304 A-7B 154362 ND/400

VA-304 A-7A 154356 ND/402 USS Ranger

VA-304 A-7E ND/401

VA-304 A-7Bs 154549 ND/410, 4XX

VA-304 A-7 ND/400

VA-304 A-7A 152676 ND/414

VA-304 A-7A 153134 ND/506

174

VA-305 A-7A 153135 ND/501

VA-305 A-7A 153134 ND/506

VA-305 A-7A 153155 ND/503 refueling from VAQ-309 A-3 ND/632

VA-305 A-7As 153155, 152681 ND/503, 502

VA-305 A-7 ND/505 taxiing

VA-305 A-7A ND/5XX going to the cat

VA-305 A-7B ND/501

VA-305 A-7A 153158 ND/507

VA-305 A-7 waiting for F-14s on carrier

VA-305 A-7s in formation with (2) ANG A-7Ds

VA-305 A-7Bs in route to fleet exercise

VA-305 A-7 ND/506 on carrier

VA-305 A-7Bs returning home from deployment

VA-305 A-7 ND/502 parking

VA-305 A-7Bs returning home from deployment

VA-305 A-7Bs flyby at NAS Whidbey Is, WA

VA-305 A-7Bs in route to fleet exercise

VA-305 A-7Bs 511 and 501 in front of new hangar

VA-305 A-7 ND/502

VA-305 A-7B ND/5XX 5000 flight hours

VA-305 A-7Bs 500, 5XX, 505, 506, 507, 510, 514, and 5XX with crew at NAS Fallon, NV

VA-305 A-7B 154554 ND/500 sporting the "E" award

VA-305 A-7B 154390 ND/513

VA-305 A-7B 154390 ND/513

VA-305 A-7A ND/504 at San Clementi Is, CA

VA-305 A-7A ND/500 lands on USS Ranger. Foreground is VAW-88 E-1 ND/712.

VA-305 A-7A ND/500 at airshow with plane captain Barker at intake.

VA-305 A-7 ND/5XX refueling from USAF tanker

VA-305 A-7s ND/501, 504, and 512

VA-305 A-7A 153158 ND/507 at air show

VA-305 A-7B 154538 ND/512 with bombs

VA-305 A-7A 153138 ND/504 USS Ranger

VA-305 A-7A 153145 ND/505 USS Ranger

VA-305 A-7B ND/501

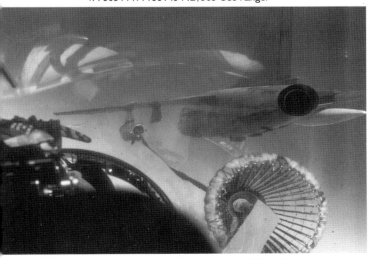

VA-305 A-7A refueling another aircraft with a D-704 buddy store.

VA-305 A-7A 153250 ND/514 refueling from VAQ-308 A-3 138929 ND/632

VA-305 A-7A 153268 ND/500 refueling from S-3 157956

VA-305 A-7A 154351 ND/510 with MK-76s

VA-305 A-7Bs ND/507, 510, 505, 506, 5XX, and 514

VA-305 A-7Bs 154453, 154390, 154411 ND/504, 513, and 511

VA-305 A-7Bs ND/514, 5XX, 506, 505, 510, and 507

VA-305 A-7 ND/5XX performing FCLPs

VA-305 A-7A ND/5XX being fueled by Plane CAPT Nickerson

VA-305 A-7B 154439 ND/507 at the boneyard

VA-305 A-7B 154538 ND/512 at Champs Museum, Chino, CA.

VA-305 A-7B 154538 ND/512 at Champs Museum, Chino, CA.

VA-305's first A-7A with LCDR Winslow exiting the a/c. Markings are for VA-125 NJ/550.

VA-305 A-7A 153134 ND/506

VA-305 A-7 waiting to taxi

VA-305 A-7A 153135 ND/501

VA-305 A-7A 153134 with a HARM missile

VA-305 A-7A ND/501, unknown ladies in intake at airshow.

VA-305 A-7A flight line with engine screen at NAS Fallon, NV.

VA-305 A-7As on flight line at NAS Fallon, NV

VA-305 line (153155 foreground) at NAS Point Mugu, CA

VA-305 A-7A ND/506 (author bottom row third from left)

VA-305 A-7s ND/512, 506, 510, and 507

VA-305 A-7 ND/5XX AOs loading MK-82s on carrier

VA-305 A-7B 154449 ND/505

VA-305 A-7A 152631 ND/502 on the cat of USS Ranger a

VA-305 A-7 ND/502 catching the wire on USS Ranger, '76

VA-305 A-7 with crew

VA-305 A-7A ND/503 with VXE-6 C-130 JD in the background (author is bottom row, 7th from the left)

VA-305 A-7A 153145 ND/505 with a Walleye

VA-305 A-7A ND/505 on the cat of USS Ranger

VA-305 A-7A ND/503 with MK-102s

VA-305 A-7A 153268 ND/515

VA-305 A-7A 153268 ND/515

VA-305 A-7A 152681 ND/502 cat shot

VA-305 A-7As ND/5XX

VA-305 A-7A ND/5XX FCLPs

VA-305 A-7A 153155 ND/503 over Camarillo, CA, with city seal painted on side

VA-305 A-7A 153158, 154360 ND/507, 510

VA-305 A-7A firing rockets

VA-305 A-7A 153268 ND/515

VA-305 A-7A 153268 ND/500

VA-305 A-7Bs ND/5XX, 514, and 506

VA-305 A-7A 153155 ND/503

VA-305 A-7A 154351 ND/510 with MK-76s

VA-305 A-7As ND/5XX with plane captains and pilots at NAS Point Mugu, CA.

VA-305 A-7A 153155 ND/503 with ordnance

VA-305 A-7Bs ND/5XX enroute to Whidbey Is, WA.

VA-305 A-7As ND/510, 500, and 514 over USS Ranger with VF-4B on approach below.

VA-305 A-7A 153268 ND/500

VA-305 A-7 line at NAS Fallon, NV

VA-305 A-7As ND/513, 505, and 504 with OV-10

VA-305 A-7B 154538 ND/512 in restoration yard at Champs Museum, Chino, CA.

VA-305 A-7B 154474 ND/503 with ordnance

VA-305 A-7As 153135, 153268 ND/501, 500

VA-305 A-7A 153681 ND/502 USS Ranger

VA-305 A-7s ND 515, 512, 511, 506, and 505

VA-305 A-7A ND/5XX on carrier

VA-305 A-7Bs ND/521, 500

VA-305 A-7A 153138 ND/504

VA-305 A-7A 153268 ND/500 in storage at AMARC

VA-305 A-7B ND/503

VA-305 A-7A 153268 ND/500

VA-305 A-7A 153268 ND/500

VA-305 A-7A 153268 ND/500

VA-305 A-7s (153155 foreground) at NAS Point Mugu, CA.

VA-305 A-7A 153134 ND/506

VA-305 A-7A 153217 ND/502

VA-305 A-7A 153268 ND/500

188

VAQ-33 TA-7C GD/120

VAQ-33 TA-7C 156786 GD/115

VAQ-33 TA-7C 156737 GD/114

VAQ-33 TA-7C 156754 GD/119

VAQ-34 TA-7C 156743 ★02

VAQ-34 TA-7C 156743 GD/202

VAQ-34 TA-7Cs ★06, ★XX

VAQ-34 TA-7C 156757 ★04

VAQ-34 TA-7C ★00

VAQ-34 TA-7Cs ★00 (left) ★04 (foreground)

VAQ-34 TA-7C 156741 GD/204

VAQ-34 TA-7C 156757 ★04

VAQ-34 TA-7C 156757 ★04

VAQ-34 TA-7C 156757 ★04

VAQ-34 TA-7C 156741 GD/201

VAQ-34 TA-7C 156741 GD/201

VAQ-34 TA-7C 156757 GD/204

VAQ-34 TA-7C 156743 ★02

VAQ-34 TA-7C 156761 GD/205

VAQ-34 TA-7C 156741 GD/204

VAQ-34 TA-7Cs GD/XXX, 213

VAQ-34 TA-7C 156743 GD/202 at NAS Point Mugu, CA

VX-5 A-7 160722 XE/05 with ordnance

VAQ-34 TA-7C 156761 GD/205

VX-5 A-7 160722 XE/05 with ordnance

VX-5 A-7E 156805 XE/03

VX-5 A-7 160722 XE/05 with ordnance

VX-5 A-7E 156770 XE/06

VX-5 A-7E 160722 XE/05 with drop tanks and ordnance

VX-5 A-7C 156748 XE/08

VX-5 A-7E 160722 XE/05 with drop tanks and ordnance

VX-5 A-7E XE/XX

VX-5 TA-7C 154458 XE/07

VX-5 A-7A 153135 XE/17

VX-5 TA-7C 154458 XE/07

VX-5 A-7 XE/05

VX-5 A-7 152673 XE/15 NAWS China Lake, CA

VX-5 TA-7C XE/08

& E, 05 DEC 72; To NATC, at NAS Jacksonville, FL., 20 APR 76; To NATC, NAS Patuxent River, MD., 23 APR 76; To NATC, at NAS Jacksonville, FL., 02 JUL 78; To NATC, NAS Patuxent River, MD., 05 JUL 78; To NATC, NAS Jacksonville, FL., 15 APR 80; To NATC, NAS Patuxent River, MD., 15 APR 80; To NATC, at NAS Jacksonville, FL., 16 APR 80; To NATC, NARF, NAS Jacksonville, FL., 18 JUN 80; To NATC, NAS Patuxent River, MD., 25 JUN 80 ** Transferred to NWEF, Thunderbird on tail, Modex 20, Kirtland AFB; Albuquerque, NM., 21 NOV 81 ** Transferred to AMARC, Davis Monthan AFB; Tucson, AZ., assigned park code 6A0162, 06 MAY 86 ** 3702.1 flight hours ** TF30P408 engine S/N P664228 ** Storage location 211614 ** Located at AMARG, Davis Monthan AFB; Tucson, AZ., 15 JUN 07.

E-043 156777 Navy acceptance from NPRO Rep. LTV, Dallas, TX., 05 OCT 69 ** Transferred to VA-146/CVW-9, NG/3XX, USS America (CVA-66), 06 OCT 69 ** Transferred to VA-122/FRS, NJ/2XX, NAS LeMoore, CA., 13 JAN 70 ** Transferred to VX-5, XE/07, NAF China Lake, CA., 09 AUG 74; To VX-5, NAS Alameda, CA., 10 SEP 76; To VX-5, NAF China Lake, CA., 20 OCT 76 ** Transferred to NPRO Rep. LTV, Dallas, TX. to be converted to TA-7C, 21 NOV 77 ** Re-designated to TA-7C, 23 NOV 77 ** Transferred to PMTC, XX/XXX, NAS Point Mugu, CA. 18 DEC 79 ~ S 1SO strike, 29 SEP 81 ** Crashed near California City, Ca., both pilots ejected safely.

E-044 156778 Navy acceptance from NAVPRO Rep. LTV, Dallas, TX., 27 SEP 69 ** Transferred to VA-147/CVW-9, NG/4XX, USS America (CVA-66), 28 SEP 69 ** Transferred to VA-122/FRS, NJ/2XX, NAS LeMoore, CA., 12 JAN 70 ~ S 1SO strike, 15 JUN 70 ** No data on strike.

E-045 156779 Navy acceptance from NPRO Rep. LTV, Dallas, TX., 27 SEP 69 ** Transferred to VA-146/CVW-9, USS America (CVA-66), 29 SEP 69 ** VA-122/FRS, NJ/2XX, NAS LeMoore, CA., 30 DEC 69 ** Transferred to VA-113/ CVW-2, NE/3XX, NAS LeMoore, CA., 09 APR 72 ** Transferred to VA-122/FRS, NJ/2XX, NAS LeMoore, CA., 12 JUN 72 ** Transferred to VX-5, XE/05, NAF China Lake, CA., 23 FEB 73; To VX-5, NAS Jacksonville, FL., 03 DEC 74; To VX-5, NAF China Lake, CA., 30 JAN 75; To VX-5, NAS Jacksonville, FL., 07 FEB 75; To VX-5, NAF China Lake, CA., 07 FEB 75; To VX-5, NAS Alameda, CA., 23 OCT 75; To VX-5, NAF China Lake, CA., 11 NOV 75; To VX-5, NAS Alameda, CA., 01 NOV 76; To VX-5, NAF China Lake, CA., 18 NOV 76 ** Transferred to NPRO Rep. LTV, Dallas, TX. to be converted to TA-7C, 21 MAR 78 ** Re-designated to TA-7C, 24 MAR 78 ** Transferred to VA-174/FRS, AD/3XX, NAS Cecil Field, FL., 19 APR 80; To VA-174, NAS Jacksonville, FL., 27 APR 82; To VA-174, NAS Cecil Field, FL., 11 JUN 82; To VA-174, NAS Jacksonville, FL., 30 APR 85; To VA-174, NAS Cecil Field, FL., 28 MAY 85; To VA-174, NAS Dallas, TX., 28 APR 86; To VA-174, NAS Cecil Field, FL., 05 MAY 86 thru 20 OCT 86 ** End of flight record card ** Transferred to VX-5, XE/06, NWC China Lake, CA., date unknown ** Transferred to AMARC, Davis Monthan AFB; Tucson, AZ., assigned park code 6A0327, 28 MAY 90 ** 4174.6 flight hours ** TF41A402D engine S/N 141311 ** Transferred to the Royal Thai Navy, S/N 1416, JUL 95.

E-046 156780 Navy acceptance from NPRO Rep. LTV, Dallas, TX., 23 OCT 69 ** Transferred to VA-122/FRS, NJ/2XX, NAS LeMoore, CA., 24 OCT 69 ** Transferred to VA-113/CVW-2, NE/3XX, NAS LeMoore, CA., 07 APR 72 ** Transferred to VA-215/CVW-19, NM/4XX, USS Oriskany (CVA-34), 30 MAY 72 ** Transferred to VA-122/FRS, NJ/ 201, NAS LeMoore, CA., 30 MAY 72 ** Transferred to VA-113/CVW-2, NE/3XX, NAS LeMoore, CA., 30 MAY 72 ** Transferred to VA-122/ FRS, NJ/2XX, NAS LeMoore, CA., 30 MAY 72 ** Transferred to VA-215/CVW-19, NM/4XX, USS Oriskany (CVA-34), 30 MAY 72; Transferred to VA-122/FRS, NJ/2XX, NAS LeMoore, CA., 03 JUN 72 ** S 1SO strike, 07 JUN 72 ** No data on strike.

E-047 156781 Navy acceptance from NPRO Rep. LTV, Dallas, TX., 07 NOV 69 ** Transferred to VA-174/FRS, AD/3XX, NAS Cecil Field, FL., 01 FEB 70 ** Transferred to VA-82/CVW-8, AJ/3XX, USS America (CVA-66), 07 APR 72 ** Transferred to NARF, NAS Jacksonville, FL., 10 JAN 73 ~ S 1SO strike, 15 JUN 78 ** No data on strike.

E-048 156782 Navy acceptance from NPRO Rep. LTV, Dallas, TX., 28 OCT 69 ** Transferred to VA-122/FRS, NJ/201, NAS LeMoore, CA., 30 OCT 69 ** Transferred to VX-5, XE/XXX, NWC China Lake, CA., 23 FEB 73 ** Transferred to NAF Warminster. PA., for RDT & E, 25 MAY 74; To NAF Warminster, at NAS Jacksonville, FL., 20 FEB 75; To NAF Warminster, PA., 16 APR 75 ** Transferred to NAF China Lake, CA., for RDT & E, 01 MAY 75 ** Transferred to NPRO Rep. LTV, Dallas, TX., to be converted to TA-7C, 27 APR 78 ** Re-designated TA-7C, 01 MAY 78 ** Transferred to VA-122/ FRS, NJ/2XX, NAS LeMoore, CA., 29 MAR 80; To VA-122, NAS Jacksonville, FL., 27 MAR 85; To VA-122, NAS LeMoore, CA., 19 AUG 85 thru 01 OCT 85 ** End of flight record card ** On display at the Naval Air Museum; Olathe, KS.

E-049 156783 Navy acceptance from NPRO Rep. LTV, Dallas, TX., 07 NOV 69 ** Transferred to VA-174/FRS, AD/3XX, NAS Cecil Field, FL., 03 FEB 70 ** Transferred to VA-82/CVW-8 AJ/303, USS America (CVA-66), 07 APR 72; To VA-82, NAS Cecil Field, FL., 07 APR 72 ~ S 1SO strike, 20 DEC 72 ** No data on strike.

E-050 156784 Navy acceptance from NPRO Rep. LTV, Dallas, TX., 08 NOV 69 ** Transferred to VA-174/FRS, AD/3XX, NAS Cecil Field, FL., 13 FEB 70 ** Transferred to VA-86/CVW-8, AJ/4XX, USS America (CVA-66), 07 APR 72; To VA-86, NAS Cecil Field, FL., 07 APR 72; To VA-86; USS America (CVA-66), 04 JUN 73; To VA-86, NAS Cecil Field, FL., 01 SEP 74 ** Transferred to NARF, NAS Jacksonville, FL., 20 MAY 75 ** Transferred to VA-174/FRS, AD/3XX, NAS Cecil Field, FL., 31 JUL 75 ** Transferred to NPRO Rep. LTV, Dallas, TX. to be converted to TA-7C, 25 MAY 77 ** Re-designated to TA-7C, 01 JUN 77 ** Transferred to VA-174/FRS, AD/3XX, NAS Cecil Field, FL., 22 DEC 78; To VA-174, NAS Jacksonville, FL., 13 MAY 81; To VA-174, NAS Cecil Field, FL., 21 JUL 81; To VA-174, NAS Jacksonville, FL., 29 MAY 85; To VA-174, NAS Cecil Field, FL., 29 MAY 85; To VA-174, NAS Jacksonville, FL., 30 MAY 85; To VA-174, NAS Cecil Field, FL., 27 AUG 85 thru 20 OCT 86 ** End of flight record card ** Transferred to VAQ-33/FEWSG, GD307, NAS Key West, FL., date unknown ** Transferred to AMARC, Davis Monthan AFB; Tucson, AZ., assigned park code 6A0376; 08 AUG 90 ** 5582.9 flight hours ** TF41A402D engine S/N 141427 ** Prepare (AS-IS), for overland and above deck shipment to M / V Thelisis, Stellar Lines S.A., C/O Southern Cresent Shipping Co., NC. State port, Warehouse #3, Wilmington, NC., 28402, 03 APR 01 ** for the government of Greece, Transferred to the Helinic Air Force (Greece) ** Transferred to 116 Pteriga Makhis ~ Strike, 09 OCT 03 ** Crashed near Araxos AB, Greece due to loss of control on a training flight** Both pilots ejected safely.

E-051 156785 Navy acceptance from NPRO Rep. LTV, Dallas, TX., 22 OCT 69 ** Transferred to VA-122/FRS, NJ/2XX, NAS LeMoore, CA., 23 OCT 69; To VA-122, NAS Jacksonville, FL., 03 DEC 74; To VA-122, NAS LeMoore, CA., 28 JAN 75 ** Transferred to NAF China Lake, CA., XX/XXX, 15 APR 76; To NWC, at NAS Jacksonville, FL., 27 SEP 85; To NWC, China Lake, CA., 28 JAN 86 thru 14 JUN 87 ** End of flight record card ** Transferred to NAWC China Lake, Ca., as a target on the Survivability range, Nov 04.

E-052 156786 Navy acceptance from NPRO Rep. LTV, Dallas, TX., 29 OCT 69 ** Transferred to VA-174/FRS, AD/3XX, NAS Cecil Field, FL., 10 FEB 70 ** Transferred to VA-82/CVW-8, AJ/3XX, USS America (CVA-66), 03 APR 72; To VA-72, NAS Cecil Field, FL., 03 APR 72; To VA-82, USS America (CVA-66), 04 APR 73; To VA-82, NAS Cecil Field, FL., 01 OCT 75 ** Transferred to

MASDC, Davis Monthan AFB; Tucson, AZ., assigned park code 6A0037, 16 APR 75 ** Transferred to NARF, NAS Jacksonville, FL., 21 OCT 76 ** Transferred to NPRO Rep. LTV, Dallas, TX., to be converted to TA-7C, 03 DEC 76 ** Re-designated to TA-7C, 06 DEC 76 ** Transferred to VA-174/FRS, AD/353, NAS Cecil Field, FL., 02 AUG 78; To VA-174, NAS Jacksonville, FL., 12 NOV 80; To VA-174, NAS Cecil field, FL., 15 DEC 80; To VA-174, NAS Jacksonville, FL., 16 DEC 80; To VA-174, NAS Cecil field, FL., 14 JAN 81; To VA-174, NAS Jacksonville, FL., 27 SEP 82; To VA-174, NAS Cecil Field, FL., 27 SEP 82; To VA-174, NAS Jacksonville, FL., 29 SEP 82 ** Transferred to VAQ-34/ FEWSG, GD/203, NAS Point Mugu, CA., 12 JUL 83; Converted to EA-7L, 01 MAY 84; To VAQ-34, NAS Dallas, TX., 09 APR 86; To VAQ-34, NAS Point Mugu, CA., 10 APR 86; To VAQ-34, NAS Dallas, TX., 30 JAN 87; To VAQ-34, NAS Point Mugu, CA., 20 FEB 87 thru 23 SEP 87 ** End of flight record card ** Transferred to AMARC, Davis Monthan AFB; Tucson, AZ., assigned park code unknown, date unknown.

E-053 156787 Navy acceptance from NPRO Rep. LTV, Dallas, TX., 15 OCT 69 ** Transferred to VA-122/FRS, NJ/2XX, NAS LeMoore, CA., 16 OCT 69; To VA-122, NAS Jacksonville, FL., 02 DEC 74; To VA-122, NAS LeMoore, CA., 18 APR 75 ** Transferred to NPRO Rep. LTV, Dallas, TX. to be converted to TA-7C, 08 FEB 78 ** Re-designated TA-7C, 13 FEB 78 ** Transferred to PMTC, PMTC/84, NAS Point Mugu, CA., 09 FEB 80; To PMTC, at NAS Dallas, TX., 09 APR 85; To PMTC, NAS Point Mugu, CA., 20 DEC 85 thru 09 DEC 86 ** End of flight record card ** Transferred to AMARC, Davis Monthan AFB; Tucson, AZ., assigned park code 6A0416; 28 OCT 94 ** 5343.2 flight hours ** TF41A402D engine S/N 142562 ** Prepare (AS-IS), for overland and above deck shipment to M/V Thelisis, Stellar Lines S.A., C/O Southern Cresent Shipping Co., NC. State port, Warehouse #3, Wilmington, NC., 03 APR 01, for the government of Greece ** Transferred to the Helinic Air Force (Greece).

E-054 156788 Navy acceptance from NPRO Rep. LTV, Dallas, TX., 17 NOV 69 ** Transferred to VA-25/CVW-2, NE/4XX, NAS LeMoore, CA., 11 DEC 69 ** Transferred to VA-174/FRS, AD/3XX, NAS Cecil Field, FL., 10 MAR 70 ** Transferred to VA-86/CVW-8, AJ/4XX, NAS Cecil Field, FL., 24 APR 72; To VA-86, USS America (CVA-66), 15 MAY 73; To VA-86, NAS Cecil Field, FL., 01 SEP 74 ** Transferred to NARF, NAS Jacksonville, FL., 19 MAY 75 ** Transferred to VA-174/FRS, AD/3XX, NAS Cecil Field, FL., 26 SEP 75 ** Transferred to NPRO Rep. LTV, Dallas, TX. to be converted to TA-7C, 18 NOV 77 ** Re-designated to TA-7C, 23 NOV 77 ** Transferred to VA-122/FRS, NJ/ 2XX, NAS LeMoore, CA., 01 NOV 79; To VA-122, NAS Jacksonville, FL., 31 MAY 85; To VA-122, NAS LeMoore, CA., 24 JUN 85 thru 23 JAN 87 ** End of flight record card ** Transferred to AMARC, Davis Monthan AFB; Tucson, AZ., assigned park code 6A0361 ** Transferred to the Royal Thai Navy, S/N 1417, JUL 95.

E-055 156789 Navy acceptance from NPRO Rep. LTV, Dallas, TX., 31 AUG 69 ** Transferred to VA-174/FRS, AD/3XX, NAS Cecil Field, FL., 07 MAR 70 ** Transferred to VA-86/CVW-8, AJ/400, USS America (CVA-66), 11 APR 72; To VA-86, NAS Cecil Field, FL., 11 APR 72; To VA-86, USS America (CVA-66), 30 APR 73; To VA-86, NAS Cecil Field, FL., 01 JUL 73 ** Transferred to VA-174/FRS, AD/3XX, NAS Cecil Field, FL., 12 NOV 74 ** Transferred to NARF, NAS Jacksonville, FL., 23 SEP 75 ** Transferred to VA-125/FRS, NJ/5XX, NAS LeMoore, CA., 24 NOV 75 ** Transferred to NPRO Rep. LTV, Dallas, TX. to be converted to TA-7C, 21 JUL 77 ** Re-designated TA-7C, 26 JUL 77 ** Transferred to VA-174/FRS, AD/3XX, NAS Cecil Field, FL., 29 APR 79; To VA-174, NAS Jacksonville, FL., 21 AUG 81; To VA-174, NAS Cecil Field, FL., 27 NOV 81; To VA-174, NAS Jacksonville, FL., 10 DEC 84; To VA-174, NAS Cecil Field, FL., 13 MAR 85 thru 22 JUL 87 ** End of flight record card ** On display at NAS Jacksonville, FL.

E-056 156790 Navy acceptance from NPRO Rep. LTV, Dallas, TX., 31 AUG 69 Transferred to VA-174/FRS, AD/3XX, NAS Cecil Field, FL., 21 MAR 70 ** Transferred to VA-86/CVW-8, AJ/4XX, USS America (CVA-66), 08 APR 72; To VA-86, NAS Cecil Field, FL., 08 APR 72; To VA-86, USS America (CV-66), 20 JUN 73; To VA-86, NAS Cecil Field, FL., 01 SEP 74 ** Transferred to NARF, NAS Jacksonville, FL., 20 MAY 75; Transferred to VA-125/FRS, NJ/5XX, NAS LeMoore, CA., 03 SEP 75 ** Transferred to VA-122/FRS, NJ/2XX, NAS LeMoore, CA., 07 OCT 75 ** Transferred to VA-125/FRS, NJ/5XX, NAS LeMoore, CA., 04 AUG 76 ** Transferred to NPRO Rep. LTV, Dallas, TX., to be converted to TA-7C, 28 APR 77 ** Re-designated TA-7C, 24 MAY 77 ** Transferred to VA-122/FRS, NJ/2XX, NAS LeMoore, CA., 24 OCT 78; To VA-122, NAS Alameda, CA., 22 JUL 81; To VA-122, NAS Whidbey Island, WA., 24 JUL 81; To VA-122, NAS LeMoore, CA., 27 AUG 81; To VA-122, NAS Jacksonville, FL., 18 NOV 81; To VA-122, NAS LeMoore, CA., 25 FEB 82; To VA-122, NAS Dallas, TX., 15 MAR 82; To VA-122, NAS LeMoore, CA., 11 AUG 82; To VA-122, NAS Jacksonville, FL., 06 MAR 84 ** Transferred to VA-174/FRS, AD/3XX, NAS Cecil Field, FL., 21 JUL 84; To VA-174, NAS Jacksonville, FL., 04 NOV 85; To VA-174, NAS Cecil Field, FL., 13 FEB 86; To VA-174, NAS Dallas, TX., 23 DEC 86; To VA-174, NAS Cecil Field, FL., 06 FEB 87 ** Transferred to NSWC, NAS Fallon, NV., 25 MAY 87 thru 30 SEP 87 ** End of flight record card ** Transferred to AMARC, Davis Monthan AFB; Tucson, AZ., assigned park code 6A0410; 03 FEB 92 ** 6697.7 flight hours ** TF41A402D engine S/N 141994 ** Prepare (AS-IS), for overland and above deck shipment to M/V Efdim Hops, Woodhouse Terminal; Galveston, TX., at no cost to the government, for the government of Greece, 16 MAR 00 ** Transferred to the Helenic Air Force (Greece).
.

E-057 156791 Navy acceptance from NPRO Rep. LTV, Dallas, TX., 26 SEP 69 ** Transferred to VA-174/FRS, AD/3XX, NAS Cecil Field, FL., 03 FEB 70 ** Transferred to VA-86/CVW-8, AJ/4XX, USS America (CVA-66), 08 APR 72; To VA-86, NAS Cecil Field, FL., 08 APR 72; To VA-86, USS America (CVA-66), 13 JUN 73; To VA-86, NAS Cecil Field, FL., 01 NOV 74 ** Transferred to NTPS, NAS Patuxent River, MD., 28 APR 75; To NTPS, at NAS Jacksonville, FL., 11 JUN 75; To NTPS, NAS Patuxent River, MD., 23 JUN 75 ** Transferred to NPRO Rep. LTV Dallas, TX., to be converted to TA-7C, 31 AUG 78 ** Re-designated TA-7C, 05 SEP 78 ** Transferred to VA-122/FRS, NJ/2XX, NAS LeMoore, CA., 29 AUG 80; To VA-122, NAS Whidbey Island, WA., 05 FEB 86 ** Transferred to VA-174/FRS, AD/3XX, NAS Cecil Field, FL., 07 JAN 87 thru 08 JAN 87 ** End of flight record card ** Transferred to VAQ-34/FEWSG, GD/206, NAS Point Mugu, CA. ** Converted to EA-7L ** Modex 86 ** End of flight record card ** Transferred to NADEP, NAS Alameda, CA., 21 NOV 91 ** Transferred to NAS Point Mugu, CA., date unknown **Transferred to AMARC, Davis Monthan AFB; Tucson, AZ., assigned park code 6A0419, 17 NOV 94 ** 5606.8 flight hours ** TF41F engine S/N 141939 ** On FMS list, 31DEC 97 ** Storage location 211962 ** Transferred to MDC FMS, 06 APR 04 ** Located at AMARG, Davis Monthan AFB; Tucson, AZ., 15 JUN 07.

E-058 156792 Navy acceptance from NPRO Rep. LTV, Dallas, TX., 31 AUG 69 ** Transferred to VA-174/FRS, AD/2XX, NAS Cecil Field, FL., 07 MAY 70 ** Transferred to VA-86/CVW-8, AJ/405, USS America (CVA-66), 27 APR 72; To VA-86, NAS Cecil Field, FL., 27 APR 72 ~ S ISO strike, 17 JUL 72 ** CDR W.D. Yonke, (Squadron C.O.), Aircraft was in a three plane formation with A-7C 156771 and an F-4. When the bombs were dropped, one exploded prematurely badly damaging all three aircraft. All four Pilots ejected and were rescued.

E-059 156793 Navy acceptance from NPRO Rep. LTV, Dallas, TX., 30 OCT 69 ** Transferred to VA-122/FRS, NJ/2XX, NAS LeMoore, CA., 30 OCT 69 ** Transferred to NPRO Rep. LTV, Dallas, TX., 30 OCT 69 ** Transferred to VA-122/FRS, NJ/2XX,

NAS LeMoore, CA., 31 OCT 69 ** Transferred to VA-125/FRS, NJ/5XX, NAS LeMoore, CA., 01 JUN 76 ** Transferred to VA-122/FRS, NJ/2XX, NAS LeMoore, CA., 09 SEP 77 ** Transferred to VX-5, XE/06, NAF China Lake, CA., 13 DEC 77 ** Transferred to NPRO Rep. LTV, Dallas, TX. to be converted to TA-7C, 20 JUN 78 ** Re-designated to TA-7C, 22 JUN 78 ** Transferred to VA-122/FRS, NJ/2XX, NAS LeMoore, CA., 27 JUN 80 ~ S 1SO strike, 17 AUG 83 ** Pilot ejected safely when canopy separated from aircraft on descent.

E-060 156794 Navy acceptance from NPRO Rep. LTV, Dallas, TX., 11 JAN 70 ** Transferred to VA-174/FRS, AD/3XX, NAS Cecil Field, FL., 05 NOV 70 ** Transferred to VA-82/CVW-8, AJ/302, USS America (CVA-66), 05 APR 72; To VA-82, NAS Cecil Field, FL., 05 JUN 72; To VA-82, USS America (CVA-66), 09 MAY 73; To VA-82, NAS Cecil Field, FL., 03 MAR 75 ** Transferred to MASDC, Davis Monthan AFB; Tucson, AZ.,16 APR 75 ** Transferred to NARF, NAS Jacksonville, FL., 27 DEC 76 ** Transferred to NPRO Rep. LTV, Dallas, TX. to be converted to TA-7C, 17 FEB 77 ** Re-designated to TA-7C, 22 FEB 77 ** Transferred to VA-174/FRS, AD/3XX, NAS Cecil Field, FL., 02 OCT 78; To VA-174, NAS Jacksonville, FL., 15 JAN 81; To VA-174, NAS Cecil Field, FL., 12 FEB 81; To VA-174, NAS Jacksonville, FL., 13 FEB 81; To VA-174, NAS Cecil Field, FL., 13 MAR 81; To VA-174, NAS Jacksonville, FL., 12 AUG 83; To VA-174, NAS Cecil Field, FL., 18 NOV 83; To VA-174, NAS Jacksonville, FL., 22 DEC 83; To VA-174, NAS Cecil Field, FL., 02 OCT 84; To VA-174, NAS Jacksonville, FL., 18 DEC 85; To VA-174, NAS Cecil Field, FL., 18 DEC 85; To VA-174, NAS Jacksonville, FL., 06 MAR 86; To VA-174, NAS Cecil Field, FL., 17 MAR 86; To VA-174, NAS Dallas, TX.,07 JAN 87; To VA-174, NAS Cecil Field, FL., 03 APR 87 ** End of flight record card ** Transferred to AMARC, Davis Monthan AFB; Tucson, AZ., assigned park code 6A0036 ** Transferred to the Royal Thai Navy, S/N 1418, JUL 95.

E-061 156795 Navy acceptance from NPRO Rep. LTV, Dallas, TX., 21 DEC 69 ** Transferred to VA-25/CVW-2, NE/4XX, NAS LeMoore, CA., 22 DEC 69 ** Transferred to VA-174/FRS, AD/3XX, NAS Cecil Field, FL., 10 MAR 70 ** Transferred to VA-82/CVW-8, AJ/3XX, USS America (CVA-66), 16 APR 72; To VA-82, NAS Cecil Field, FL., 05 MAY 72; To VA-82, USS America (CVA-66), 01 MAY 73 ** Transferred to MASDC, Davis Monthan AFB; Tucson, AZ., assigned park code 6A0039, 18 JUN 75 ** Transferred to NARF, NAS Jacksonville, FL., 05 AUG 76 ** Transferred to NPRO Rep. LTV, Dallas, TX. to be converted to TA-7C, 10 SEP 76 ** Re-designated to TA-7C, 11 SEP 76 ** Transferred to VA-122/FRS, NJ/204, NAS LeMoore, CA., 19 JUN 78; To VA-122, NAS Jacksonville, FL., 25 AUG 80; To VA-122, NAS LeMoore, CA., 25 MAY 81; To VA-122, NAS Jacksonville, FL., 24 APR 85; To VA-122, NAS LeMoore, CA., 22 JUL 85; To VA-122, NAS Dallas, TX., 27 MAY 86; To VA-122, NAS LeMoore, CA., 29 MAY 86 thru 01 OCT 86 ** End of flight record card ** Transferred to AMARC, Davis Monthan AFB; Tucson, AZ., assigned park code 6A0336; 03 APR 90 ** 5168.8 flight hours ** TF41A402D engine S/N 141233 ** Prepare (AS-IS), for overland and above deck shipment to M /V Thelisis, Stellar Lines S.A., C/O Southern Cresent Shipping Co., NC. State port, Warehouse #3, Wilmington, NC., 28402, 03 APR 01 ** for the government of, Greece.

E-062 156796 Navy acceptance from NPRO Rep. LTV, Dallas, TX., 19 JAN 70 ** Transferred to VA-174/FRS, AD/3XX, NAS Cecil Field, FL., 21 JAN 70 ~ S 1SO strike, 24 JUN 70 ** No data on strike.

E-063 156797 Navy acceptance from NPRO Rep. LTV, Dallas, TX., 31 AUG 69 ** Transferred to VA-174/FRS, AD/3XX, NAS Cecil Field, FL., 22 AUG 70 ** Transferred to NATC, Weapons Systems Test, NAS Patuxent River, MD., 04 OCT 70 ** Transferred to NATC, NAS Patuxent River, MD., for RDT & E, 01 SEP 72 ** Transferred to NAF China Lake, CA., for RDT & E, 11 MAR 74; To China lake at NAS Jacksonville, FL., 11 MAR 75 ** Transferred to NATC, NAS Patuxent River, MD., for RDT & E, 27 MAR 75; To NATC, NAS Jacksonville, FL.; 12 JUN 79; To NATC, NAS Patuxent River, MD., 13 AUG 79 ** Transferred to PMTC, NAS Point Mugu, CA., 29 APR 82 thru 09 DEC 86 ** End of flight record card ** Transferred to AMARC, Davis Monthan AFB; Tucson, AZ. ** At AMARC, Davis Monthan AFB; Tucson, AZ., 31 DEC 97 ** On conditional loan from the National Museum of Naval Aviation; Pensacola, FL., to the Weapons Test Squadron Museum NAWC China Lake, Ca.; Nov 04.

E-064 156798 Navy acceptance from NPRO Rep. LTV, Dallas, TX., 31 AUG 69 ** Transferred to VA-174/FRS, AD/3XX, NAS Cecil Field, FL., 22 MAY 70 ** Transferred to VA-82/CVW-8, AJ/3XX, USS America (CVA-66), 27 APR 72; To VA-82, NAS Cecil Field, FL., 27 APR 72 ~ S 1SO strike, 10 SEP 72 ** No data on strike.

E-065 156799 Navy acceptance from NPRO Rep. LTV, Dallas, TX., 24 SEP 69 ** Transferred to VA-174/FRS, AD/3XX, NAS Cecil Field, FL., 30 JUN 70 ** Transferred to NARF, NAS Jacksonville, FL., 06 JAN 71 ~ S 1SO strike, 15 JUN 78 ** No data on strike.

E-066 156800 Navy acceptance from NPRO Rep. LTV, Dallas, TX., 24 SEP 69 ** Last A-7C ** Transferred to VA-174/FRS, AD/3XX, NAS Cecil Field, FL., 12 APR 70 ** Transferred to VA-82/CVW-8, AJ/3XX, USS America (CVA-66), 22 APR 72; To VA-82, NAS Cecil Field, FL., 22 APR 72; To VA-82, USS America (CVA-66), 22 MAY 73; To VA-82, NAS Cecil Field, FL., 29 AUG 73 ** Transferred to MASDC, Davis Monthan AFB; Tucson, AZ., assigned park code 6A0038; 28 MAY 75 ** Transferred to NARF, NAS Jacksonville, FL., 08 SEP 76 ** Transferred to NPRO Rep. LTV, Dallas, TX., to be converted to TA-7C, 28 OCT 76 ** Re-designated to TA-7C, 30 OCT 76 ** Transferred to VA-174/FRS, AD/355, NAS Cecil Field, FL., 18 AUG 78; To VA-174, NAS Jacksonville, FL., 09 JUN 81; To VA-174, NAS Cecil Field, FL., 01 SEP 81; To VA-174, NAS Jacksonville, FL., 18 SEP 85; To VA-174, NAS Cecil Field, FL., 18 SEP 85; To VA-174, NAS Jacksonville, FL., 19 SEP 85; To VA-174, NAS Cecil Field, FL., 28 JAN 86 thru 05 DEC 86 ** End of flight record card ** Transferred to NATC, Strike Test, NAS Patuxent River, MD., Date unknown ** Transferred to AMARC, Davis Monthan AFB; Tucson, AZ., assigned park code 6A0415, 28 JAN 93 ** 4382.2 flight hours ** TF41A402D engine S/N 142596 ** ** Prepare for overland and above deck shipment to Stellar Freight; Galveston, TX., for the government of Greece, no later than, 30 AUG 95 ** Transferred to the Helinic Air Force (Greece) ** Transferred to 336 Mira ~ Strike, 09 DEC 99 ** Crashed near Araxas, Greece after an engine failure ** Both pilots ejected safely.

Section 4

A-7E

Note: TF-30 powered A-7E's, production numbers E-001 thru E-067 were re-designated A-7C by the Navy after they were placed in service.

156801/156840 LTV A-7E-4-CV Corsair II (Block IV)

E-108 156801 Navy acceptance from NPRO Rep. LTV, Dallas, TX., 30 JUL 69 ** First Production A-7E ** Transferred to VA-174/FRS, AD/4XX, NAS Cecil Field, FL., 05 MAY 70 ** Transferred to NPRO Rep, LTV, Dallas, TX., for RTD & E, 01 JUL 74 ** Redesignated YA-7E ** End of flight record card, 18 NOV 86 ** Converted to YA-7H, A-7 Corsair II 2 painted on tail in large letters ** Loaned to Martin- Marietta to test the Pathfinder Navigation System ** Privately owned.

E-068 156802 Navy acceptance from NPRO Rep. LTV, Dallas, TX., 30 JUL 69 ** Transferred to NPRO Rep. LTV, Dallas, TX., for RDT & E, 18 NOV 69 ** Redesignated NA-7E and held for RDT & E, 01 JUL 75 ** Transferred to NADC Warminster, PA., for RDT & E, NADC on tail, no modex, 14 SEP 81; To NAF Warminster, NAS Jacksonville, FL., 22 SEP 81; To NADC, NAF Warminster, PA., NADC in a darter with 156802 under it, on the tail, 20 JAN 82; To NADC, NAS Jacksonville, FL., 09 FEB 82; To NADC, NAF Johnsville, PA., 09 FEB 82 thru 01 APR 87 ** End of flight record card.

E-069 156803 Navy acceptance from NPRO Rep. LTV, Dallas, TX., 26 OCT 69 ** Transferred to VA-147/CVW-9, NG/400, USS America (CVA-66), 28 OCT 69; To VA-147, NAS Fallon, NV., 15 MAY 70 ** Transferred to VA-122/FRS, NJ/2XX, NAS LeMoore, CA., 25 MAY 71 ** Transferred to VA-147/CVW-9, NG/400, USS Constellation (CV-64), 17 JUL 72; To VA-147, NAS Jacksonville, FL., 03 MAR 75; To VA-147, NAS LeMoore, CA., 21 APR 75; To VA-147, NAS Fallon, NV., 23 JUN 75; To VA-147, MCAS Yuma, AZ., 09 OCT 75; To VA-147, NAS LeMoore, CA., 28 OCT 75; To VA-147, USS Constellation (CV-64), 11 AUG 76; To VA-147, NAS LeMoore, CA., 27 OCT 76; To VA-147, USS Constellation (CV-64), 23 JUL 77; To VA-147, NAF Atsugi, JP., 06 OCT 77; To VA-147, USS Constellation (CV-64), 08 OCT 77; To VA-147, NAF Atsugi, JP.,18 OCT 77; To VA-147, USS Constellation (CV-64), 20 OCT 77; To VA-147, NAS LeMoore, CA., 19 NOV 77; To NAS Jacksonville, FL., 31 JAN 78; To VA-147, NAS LeMoore, CA., 01 FEB 78; To VA-147, USS Constellation (CV-64), 25 SEP 78; To VA-147, NAS Cubi Point, PI., 06 NOV 78; To VA-147, USS Constellation (CV-64), 31 DEC 78; To VA-147, NAF Atsugi, JP., 19 MAR 79; To VA-147, USS Constellation (CV-64), 21 MAR 79; To VA-147, NAS LeMoore, CA., 19 JUN 79; To VA-147, NAS Jacksonville, FL., 07 DEC 79; To VA-147, USS Constellation (CV-64), 10 DEC 79; To VA-147, NAS LeMoore, CA., 23 JAN 80; To VA-147, USS Constellation (CV-64), 26 FEB 80; To VA-147, NAS Cubi Point, PI., 18 APR 80; To VA-147, USS Constellation (CV-64), 18 SEP 80; To VA-147, NAS LeMoore, CA., 18 SEP 80; To VA-147, NAS El Centro, CA., 02 APR 81; To VA-147, USS Constellation (CV-64), 30 APR 81; To VA-147, NAS LeMoore, CA., 13 MAY 81; To VA-147, USS Constellation (CV-64), 07 JUL 81; To VA-147, NAS LeMoore, CA., 06 AUG 81; To VA-147, NAS Alameda, CA., 22 SEP 81; To VA-147, NAS LeMoore, CA., 11 OCT 81; To VA-147, USS Constellation (CV-64), 19 OCT 81; To VA-147, NAS Cubi Point, PI., 19 OCT 81; To VA-147, NAF Atsugi, JP., 01 FEB 82; To VA-147, USS Constellation (CV-64), 05 FEB 82; To VA-147, NAS LeMoore, CA., 31 MAY 82 ~ S 1SO strike, 31 MAY 82 ** Emergency landing due to fire warning, ran off runway, pilot ejected safely.

E-070 156804 Navy acceptance from NPRO Rep. LTV, Dallas, TX., 08 OCT 69 ** Transferred to VA-146/CVW-9, NG/ 3XX, USS America (CVA-66), 09 OCT 69; To VA-146, NAS Fallon, NV., 28 JUN 70; To VA-146, NAS LeMoore, CA., 29 JUN 71 ** Transferred to VA-94/CVW-15, NL/4XX, USS Coral Sea (CVA-34), 15 JUN 72 ** Transferred to VA-146/ CVW-9, NG/3XX, USS Constellation (CVA-64), 01 NOV 72; To VA-146, NAS LeMoore, CA., 14 FEB 75; To VA-146, NAS Fallon, NV., 08 MAY 75; To VA-146, NAS LeMoore, CA., 08 JUN 75; To VA-146, USS Constellation (CV-64), 14 SEP 76; To VA-146, NAS LeMoore, CA., 15 DEC 76; To VA-146, USS Constellation (CV-64), 15 DEC 76; To VA-146, NAS LeMoore, CA., 05 FEB 77; To VA-146, NAS Cubi Point, PI., 14 MAY 77; To VA-146, USS Constellation (CV-64), 25 OCT 77; To VA-146, NAS LeMoore, CA., 19 NOV 77; To VA-146, NAS Jacksonville, FL., 07 DEC 77; To VA-146, NAS LeMoore, CA., 07 DEC 77; To VA-146, NAS Jacksonville, FL., 12 DEC 77 ** Transferred to VA-174/FRS, AD/4XX, NAS Cecil Field, FL., 12 APR 78 ** Transferred to VA-86/CVW-8, AJ/4XX, NAS Cecil Field, FL., 02 OCT 78; To VA-86, NAS Roosevelt Roads, PR., 02 OCT 78; To VA-86, NAS Cecil Field, FL., 02 OCT 78; To VA-86, USS Nimitz (CVN-68), 02 OCT 78; To VA-86, NAS Cecil Field, FL., 02 OCT 78 ** Transferred to VA-12/ CVW-7, AG/4XX, USS Dwight D. Eisenhower (CVN-67), 23 JUL 79; To VA-12, NAS Cecil Field, FL., 23 OCT 79; To VA-12, USS Dwight D. Eisenhower (CVN-67), 05 NOV 79 ** Transferred to VA-146/CVW-9, NG/3XX, USS Constellation (CV-64), 12 SEP 80

** Transferred to VA-147/CVW-9, NG/4XX, NAS Cubi Point, PI., 28 AUG 80; To VA-147, USS Constellation (CV-64), 12 SEP 80; To VA-147, NAS LeMoore, CA., 17 SEP 80 ** Transferred to VA-174/FRS, AD/4XX, NAS Cecil Field, FL., 02 NOV 80; To VA-174, NAS Jacksonville, FL., 21 MAY 81 ** Transferred to VA-25/CVW-2, NE/406, NAS LeMoore, CA., 13 AUG 81; To VA-25 NAS Fallon, NV., 10 SEP 81; To VA-25, USS Ranger (CV-61), 30 OCT 81; To VA-25, NAS LeMoore, CA., 23 NOV 81; To VA-25, USS Ranger (CV-61), 15 JAN 82; To VA-25, NAS LeMoore, 15 JAN 82; To VA-25, USS Ranger (CV-61), 15 JAN 82; To VA-25, NAS Cubi Point, PI., 15 JAN 82; To VA-25, NAF Atsugi, JP., 25 JUN 82; To VA-25, NAS Cubi Point, PI., 01 JUL 82; To VA-25, NAF Atsugi, JP., 06 JUL 82; To VA-25, NAS Cubi Point, PI., 12 JUL 82; To VA-25, USS Ranger (CV-61), 12 JUL 82 ** Transferred to VA-56/CVW-5, NF/4XX, NAF Atsugi, JP., 26 AUG 82; To VA-56, NAS Cubi Point, PI., 20 JUN 84; To VA-56, NAF Atsugi, JP., 25 JUN 84 ** Transferred to VA-22/CVW-11, NH/3XX, USS Enterprise (CVN-65), 02 NOV 84; To VA-22, NAS LeMoore CA., 02 NOV 84; To VA-22, NAS Fallon, NV., 05 FEB 85; To VA-22, NAS LeMoore, CA., 05 FEB 85; To VA-22, USS Enterprise (CVN-65), 19 DEC 85** Transferred to VA-203/CVWR-20, AF/3XX, NAS Jacksonville, FL., 02 JAN 86 Thru 05 JUN 87 ** End of flight record card ** On display at National   Museum of Naval Aviation, Pensacola, FL., OCT 94

E-071 156805 Navy acceptance from NPRO Rep. LTV, Dallas, TX., 13 NOV 69 ** Transferred to VX-5, XE/03, NAF China Lake, CA., 19 NOV 69; To VX- 5, NAS Jacksonville, FL., CA., 05 DEC 76; To VX-5, NAF China Lake, CA. ** Transferred to VA-122/FRS, NJ/2XX, NAS LeMoore, CA., 17 MAR 77; To VA-122, NAS Jacksonville, FL., 10 MAR 79; To VA-122, NAS LeMoore, CA., 16 APR 79 ** Transferred to VA-97/CVW-14, NK/3XX, NAS LeMoore, CA., 16 SEP 82; To VA-97, NAS Alameda, CA., 08 FEB 83; To VA-97, USS Coral Sea (CV-43), 09 JUN 83 ** Transferred to VA-147/CVW-9, NE/3XX, NAS LeMoore, CA., 08 JUL 83; To VA-147, USS Kitty Hawk (CV-63), 02 SEP 83; To VA-147, NAF Atsugi, JP., 01 APR 84; To VA-147, USS Kitty Hawk (CV-63), 22 MAY 84; To VA-147, NAF Atsugi, JP., 28 MAY 84; To VA-147, USS Kitty Hawk (CV-63), 30 MAY 84; To VA-147, NAF Atsugi, JP., 22 JUN 84; To VA-147, USS Kitty Hawk (CV-63), 04 JUL 84; To VA-147, NAS LeMoore, CA., 02 OCT 84; To VA-147, USS Kitty Hawk (CV-63), 10 JUL 85; To VA-147, NAS LeMoore, CA., 08 DEC 86 ** Transferred to VA-205/CVWR-20, AF/507, NAS Atlanta, GA., 29 JAN 86; To VA-205, NAS Jacksonville, FL., 19 MAY 86; To VA-205, NAS Atlanta, GA., 23 MAY 86 thru 27 SEP 87 ** End of flight record card ** Transferred to AMARC, Davis Monthan AFB; Tucson, AZ., assigened park code 6A0264, 29 APR 88 ** 5218.2 flight hours ** TF41A402D engine S/N 141559 ** Prepared for overland and above deck shipment for the government of Greece ** Transferred to the Helenic Air force (Greece).

E-072 156806 Navy acceptance from NPRO Rep. LTV, Dallas, TX., 26 NOV 69 ** Transferred to VA-146/CVW-9, NG/ 3XX, USS America (CVA-66), 29 NOV 69; To VA-146, NAS Fallon, NV., 26 JUN 70 ** Transferred to VA-122/FRS, NJ/2XX, NAS LeMoore, CA., 24 MAY 71 ** Transferred to NATC, Service Test, NAS Patuxent River, MD., 13 APR 72 ** Transferred to NATC, NAS Patuxent River, MD., for RDT & E, 01 SEP 72 ** Transferred to VA-174/FRS, AD/405, NAS Cecil Field, FL., 01 OCT 73; To VA-174, NAS Jacksonville, FL., 07 JUL 78; To VA-174, NAS Cecil Field, FL., 07 SEP 74 ** Transferred to VA-66/CVW-7, AG/3XX, USS Dwight D. Eisenhower (CVN-69), 13 JAN 81; To VA-66, NAS Cecil Field, FL., 28 MAY 81; To VA-66, USS Dwight D. Eisenhower (CVN-69), 28 MAY 81; To VA-66, NAS Jacksonville, FL., 21 JUL 81; To VA-66, USS Dwight D. Eisenhower (CVN-69), 21 JUL 81; To VA-66, NAS Cecil Field, FL., 06 AUG 81; To VA-66, USS Dwight D. Eisenhower (CVN-69), 06 AUG 81; To VA-66, NAS Cecil Field, FL., 06 AUG 81** Transferred to VA-81/CVW-17, AA/4XX, NAS Jacksonville, FL., 06 APR 83; To VA-81, NAS Cecil Field, FL., 06 APR 83; To VA-81, NAS Fallon, NV., 01 AUG 83; To VA-81, NAS Cecil Field, FL., 01 AUG 83; To VA-81, USS Saratoga (CV-60).,19 OCT 83; To VA-81, NAS Cecil Field, FL., 14 NOV 83; To VA-81, USS Saratoga (CV-60)., 13 FEB 84; To VA-81, NAS Cecil Field, FL., 09 AUG 84 ** Transferred to VA-174/FRS, AD/4XX, NAS Cecil Field, FL., 17 AUG 84; To VA-174, NAS Jacksonville, FL., 09

OCT 85; To VA-174, NAS Cecil Field, FL., 02 NOV 85; To VA-174, NAS Jacksonville, FL., 11 DEC 85 ** Transferred to VA-86/CVW-8, AJ/4XX, NAS Jacksonville, FL., 20 JUN 86; To VA-86, NAS cecil Field, FL., 20 JUN 86 ** Transferred to VA-205/CVWR-20, AF/5XX, NAS Jacksonville, FL., 02 JUL 86 ** Transferred to VA-304/CVWR-30, ND/4XX, NAS Alameda, CA., 05 AUG 86 ** Transferred To VA-205/CVWR-20, AF/5XX, NAS Atlanta, GA., 26 NOV 86 thru 21 MAY 87 ** End of flight record card ** Transferred to AMARC, Davis Monthan AFB; Tucson, AZ., assigned park code 6A0252, 07 MAR 88 ** Aircraft demilled, 13 JAN 05 ** Aircraft deleted from inventory and released to DRMO for disposition, 13 JAN 05.

E-073 156807 Navy acceptance from NPRO Rep. LTV, Dallas, TX., 06 NOV 69 ** Transferred to VA-147/CVW-9, NG/ 4XX, USS America (CVA-66), 07 NOV 69; To VA-147, NAS Fallon, NV, 15 JUN 70 ** Transferred to VA-122/FRS, NJ/2XX, NAS LeMoore, CA., 02 APR 71 ** Transferred to VA-97/CVW-14, NK/3XX, NAS LeMoore, CA., 18 FEB 72 ** Transferred to VA-25/CVW-2, NE/4XX, NAS LeMoore, CA., 05 DEC 72; To VA-25, USS Ranger (CV-61), 21 JUN 73; To VA-25, NAS Jacksonville, FL., 24 OCT 74; To VA-25, NAS LeMoore, CA., 08 JAN 75; To VA-25, NAS Fallon, NV., 02 JUL 75; To VA-25, USS Ranger (CV-61), 04 SEP 75; To VA-25, NAS LeMoore, CA., 23 SEP 75; To VA-25, USS Ranger (CV-61), 23 SEP 75; To VA-25, NAF Atsugi, JP., 14 JUN 76; To VA-25, USS Ranger (CV-61), 19 JUN 76; To VA-25, NAS LeMoore, CA., 28 SEP 76; To VA-25, NAS Fallon, NV., 31 JUL 77; To VA-25, NAS LeMoore, CA., 12 AUG 77; To VA-25, NAS Jacksonville, FL., 15 DEC 77; To VA-25, MCAS Yuma, AZ., 15 DEC 77; To VA-25, NAS Jacksonville, FL., 31 JAN 78; To VA-25, NAS LeMoore, CA., 12 MAR 78; To VA-25, USS Ranger (CV-61), 13 NOV 78; To VA-25, NAS LeMoore, CA., 15 DEC 78; To VA-25, USS Ranger (CV-61), 15 DEC 78; To VA-25, NAS Cubi Point, PI., 20 FEB 79; To VA-25, NAS LeMoore, CA., 24 OCT 79; To VA-25, NAS Jacksonville, FL., 25 OCT 79; To VA-25, NAS LeMoore, CA., 30 OCT 79; To VA-25, NAS Fallon, NV., 30 OCT 79; To VA-25, NAS LeMoore, CA., 04 JAN 80; To VA-25, USS Ranger (CV-61), 04 JAN 80; To VA-25, NAS LeMoore, CA., 09 JUL 80; To VA-25, USS Ranger (CV-61), 18 JUL 80; To VA-25, NAS LeMoore, CA., 06 AUG 80; To VA-25, USS Ranger (CV-61), 10 SEP 80 ** Transferred to VA-87/CVW-6, AE/4XX, USS Independence (CV-62), 25 FEB 81; To VA-87, NAS Cecil Field, FL., 25 FEB 81; To VA-87, USS Independence (CV-62), 25 FEB 81; To VA-87, NAS Cecil Field, FL., 02 FEB 82; To VA-87, USS Independence (CV-62), 04 FEB 82; To VA-87, NAS Cecil Field, FL., 04 FEB 82; To VA-87, USS Independence (CV-62), 04 FEB 82; To VA-87, NAS Cecil Field, FL., 11 MAR 82; To VA-87, USS Independence (CV-62), 13 MAY 83; To VA-87, NAS Cecil Field, FL., 09 JUL 83; To VA-87, USS Independence (CV-62), 12 AUG 83; To VA-87, NAS Cecil Field, FL., 12 AUG 83; To VA-87, USS Independence (CV-62), 12 AUG 83; To VA-87, NAS Cecil Field, FL., 25 APR 85; To VA-87, USS Independence (CV-62), 17 JUL 84 ** Transferred to VA-174/FRS, AD/4XX, NAS Cecil Field, FL., 06 AUG 84; To VA-174, NAS Jacksonville, FL., 30 JUL 85; To VA-174, NAS Cecil Field, FL., 31 JUL 85; To VA-174, NAS Jacksonville, FL., 19 AUG 85 ** Transferred to VA-87/CVW-6, AE/4XX, NAS Cecil Field, FL., 20 AUG 85 ** Transferred to VA-86/CVW-8, AJ/4XX, NAS Cecil Field, FL., 07 JAN 86; To VA-86, USS Nimitz (CVN-68), 07 JAN 86 ** Transferred to VA-83/CVW-17, AA/314, NAS Cecil Field, FL., 17 MAY 86; To VA-83, USS Saratoga (CV-60), 17 MAY 86; To VA-83, NAS Cecil Field, FL., 15 OCT 86; To VA-83, USS Saratoga (CV-60), 15 OCT 86 ** Transferred to CLAW-1, NAS Cecil Field, FL., date unknown ** Transferred to AMARC, Davis Monthan AFB; Tucson, AZ., assigned park code 6A0218; 10 FEB 87 ** End of flight record card ** 5443.7 flight hours ** TF41A2B engine S/N 142367 ** Project changed per FSO letter, 06 APR 04 Engine records released to DRMO for disposition, 21 DEC 04 ** Aircraft deleted from inventory and released to DRMO for disposition, 19 AUG 05 ** Transferred to NAS Fallon, NV. as a range target.

E-074 156808 Navy acceptance from NPRO Rep. LTV, Dallas, TX., 17 NOV 69 ** Transferred to VA-147/CVW-9, NG/ 4XX, USS America (CVA-66), 18 NOV 69; To VA-147, NAS Fallon, NV., 12 MAY 70 ** Transferred to VA-122/FRS, NJ/ 2XX, NAS LeMoore, CA., 14 JUN 71 ** Transferred to VA-27/CVW-14, NK/4XX, NAS LeMoore,

CA., 10 APR 72; To VA-27, USS Enterprise (CVN-65), 01 MAR 75; To VA-27, NAS LeMoore, Ca., 20 MAY 75; To VA-27, NAS Fallon, NV., 04 SEP 75; To VA-27, NAS Jacksonville, FL., 17 DEC 75; To VA-27, NAS LeMoore, CA., 19 DEC 75; To VA-27, USS Enterprise (CVN-65), 12 MAR 76; To VA-27, NAS LeMoore, CA., 10 MAY 76; To VA-27, USS Enterprise (CVN-65), 30 JUN 76; To VA-27, NAS LeMoore, CA., 30 JUN 76; To VA-27, USS Enterprise (CVN-65), 28 JUL 76; To VA-27, NAS LeMoore, CA., 28 MAR 77; To VA-27, USS Enterprise (CVN-65), 06 JAN 78; To VA-27, NAS LeMoore, CA., 03 MAR 78; To VA-27, USS Enterprise (CVN-65), 15 SEP 78; To VA-27, NAS Cubi Point, PI., 29 SEP 78; To VA-27, NAS LeMoore, CA., 08 OCT 78; To VA-27, NAS Jacksonville, FL., 02 NOV 78; To VA-27, NAS LeMoore, CA., 18 DEC 78 ** Transferred to VA-25/CVW-2, NE/4XX, NAS LeMoore, CA., 04 JAN 79; To VA-25, USS Ranger (CV-61), 04 JAN 79; To VA-25, NAF Atsugi, JP., 31 MAR 79 ** Transferred to VA-113/CVW-2, NE/3XX, Cubi Point, PI., 04 APR 79; To VA-113, NAF Atsugi, JP., 06 APR 79; To VA-113, NAF Cubi Point, PI., 07 APR 79 ** Transferred to VA-25/CVW-2, NE/4XX, USS Ranger (CV-61), 19 APR 79; To VA-25, NAS Cubi Point, PI., 19 APR 79; To VA-25, NAS Fallon, NV., 21 SEP 79; To VA-25, NAS LeMoore, CA., 22 JAN 80; To VA-25, NAS Jacksonville, FL., 16 MAY 80; To VA-25, NAS LeMoore, CA., 16 MAY 80 ** Transferred to VA-174/FRS, AD/4XX, NAS Cecil Field, FL., 10 JUN 80 ** Transferred to VA-66/CVW-7, AG/3XX, NAS Cecil Field, FL., 01 JUN 81; To VA-66, USS Dwight D. Eisenhower (CVN-69), 01 JUN 81; To VA-66, NAS Cecil Field, FL., 01 JUN 81; To VA-66, USS Dwight D. Eisenhower (CVN-69), 01 JUN 81; To VA-66, NAS Jacksonville, FL., 15 JUL 82 ** Transferred to VA-12/CVW-7, AG/4XX, NAS Cecil Field, FL., 03 SEP 82; To VA-12, USS Eisenhower (CVN-68), 13 APR 83; To VA-12, NAS Cecil Field, FL., 13 APR 83; To VA-12, USS Eisenhower (CVN-68), 17 FEB 84; To VA-12, NAS Cecil Field, FL., 01 JUN 84; To VA-12, USS Eisenhower (CVN-68), 25 JUL 84; To VA-12, NAS Cecil Field, FL., 31 JUL 84; To VA-12, USS Eisenhower (CVN-68), 26 JUN 85; To VA-12, NAS Jacksonville, FL., 02 DEC 85; To VA-12, NAS Cecil Field, FL., 03 DEC 85; To VA-12, NAS Pensacola, FL., 22 AUG 86; To VA-12, NAS Cecil Field, FL., 23 AUG 86; Transferred to VA-205/CVWR-20, AF/514, NAS Atlanta, GA., 25 AUG 86; To VA-205, NAS Pensacola, FL., 09 SEP 86; To VA-205, NAS Atlanta, GA., 30 NOV 86; To VA-205, NAS Pensacola, FL., 06 MAY 87; To VA-205, NAS Atlanta, GA., 08 MAY 87 thru 12 JUN 87 ** End of flight record card ** Transferred to AMARC, Davis Monthan AFB; Tucson, AZ., assigned park code 6A0279; 08 JUL 88 ** 6739.7 flight hours ** TF41A402D engine S/N 141918 ** Engine records released to DRMO for disposition, 27 JUL 05 ** Aircraft deleted from inventory and released to DRMO for disposition, 01 AUG 05.

E-075 156809 Navy acceptance from NPRO Rep. LTV, Dallas, TX., 03 DEC 69 ** Transferred to VA-147/CVW-9, NG/4XX, USS America (CVA-66), 07 DEC 69; To VA-147, NAS Fallon, NV., 13 JUN 70 ** Transferred to VA-122/FRS, NJ/2XX, NAS LeMoore, CA., 27 APR 71; To VA-122, CRAA, 26 JUL 72 ** Transferred to VA-22/CVW-15, AE/3XX, USS Coral Sea (CVA-43), 16 OCT 72 ~ S 1SO strike, 18 MAY 73 ** No data on strike.

E-076 156810 Navy acceptance from NPRO Rep. LTV, Dallas, TX., 06 NOV 69 ** Transferred to VA-146/CVW-9, NG/ 3XX, USS America (CVA-66), 07 NOV 69; To VA-146, NAS Fallon, NV., 26 JUN 70 ** Transferred to VA-122/FRS, NJ/2XX, NAS LeMoore, CA., 11 APR 71 ** Transferred to VA-97/CVW-14, NK/3XX, NAS LeMoore, CA., 07 MAR 72; To VA-146, USS Enterprise (CVAN-65), 13 NOV 74; To VA-97, NAS LeMoore, CA., 20 MAY 75; To VA-97, NAS Jacksonville, FL., 04 JUN 75; To VA-97, NAS LeMoore, CA.,12 AUG 75; To VA-97, NAS Fallon, NV., 04 SEP 75; To VA-97, NAS LeMoore, CA., 04 SEP 75; To VA-97, USS Enterprise (CVN-65), 20 FEB 76; To VA-97, NAS Alameda, CA., 15 MAR 76; To VA-97, NAS LeMoore, CA., 09 APR 76 ** Transferred to VA-195/CVW-11, NH/4XX, NAS LeMoore, CA., 07 JUN 76; To VA-195, USS Kitty Hawk (CV-63), 26 JUL 77; To VA-195, NAS LeMoore, CA., 26 JUL 77; To VA-195, USS Kitty Hawk (CV-63), 29 SEP 77; To VA-195, USS Kitty Hawk (CV-63), 29 SEP 77; To VA-195, NAS LeMoore, CA., 09 MAR 78; To VA-195, NAS Jacksonville, FL., 21 JUL 78; To VA-195, NAS LeMoore, CA., 30 JUL 78; To VA-195, NAS Jacksonville, FL., 22 AUG 78; To VA-195, NAS LeMoore,

CA., 28 AUG 78; To VA-195, USS America (CV-66), 05 JUL 79; To VA-195, NAS LeMoore, CA., 05 JUL 79; To VA-195, NAS Jacksonville, FL., 06 OCT 79; To VA-195, NAS LeMoore, CA.,06 NOV 79; To VA-195, NAS Jacksonville, FL., 08 NOV 79; To VA-195, NAS LeMoore, CA., 02 FEB 80; To VA-195, NAS Fallon, NV., 19 OCT 80; To VA-195, NAS LeMoore, CA., 07 NOV 80; To VA-195, USS America (CV-66), 23 JAN 81; To VA-195, NAS LeMoore, CA., 09 APR 71; To VA-195, NAS Jacksonville, FL., 08 FEB 82; To VA-195, NAS LeMoore, CA., 22 MAR 82 ** Transferred to VA-113/CVW-2, NE/3XX, USS Ranger (CV-61), 30 MAR 82; To VA-113, NAS Cubi Point, PI., 30 MAR 82 ** Transferred to VA-56/CVW-5, NF/4XX , NAF Atsugi, JP., 28 MAY 82 ** Transferred to FS, FAWPRA, JP., 20 DEC 74 ** Transferred to VA-192/CVW-9, NG/3XX, NAS Cubi Point, PI., 14 NOV 85; To VA-192, NAS LeMoore, CA., 30 DEC 85; To VA-192, NAS Jacksonville, FL., 27 JAN 86 ** Transferred to VA-203/CVWR-20, AF/3XX, NAS Jacksonville, FL., 27 JAN 86 thru 01 DEC 86 ** End of flight record card ** Transferred to VA-122/FRS, NJ/2XX, NAS LeMoore, CA., date unknown ** Transferred to AMARC, Davis Monthan AFB; Tucson, AZ., assigned park code 6A0245; 28 JAN 88 ** 6592.1 flight hours ** TF41A402D engine S/N 142608 released to DRMO ** FLIR pods from TA-7C 156767 placed in storage account for this aircraft, 15 SEP 95 ** Engine records released to DRMO for disposition, 29 JUN 05 ** Aircraft deleted from inventory and released to DRMO for disposition, 01 AUG 05

E-077 156811 Navy acceptance from NPRO Rep. LTV, Dallas, TX., 19 NOV 69 ** Transferred to VA-146/CVW-9, NG/ 3XX, USS America (CV-66), 21 NOV 69; To VA-146, NAS Fallon, NV., 26 JUN 70; To VA-146, NAS LeMoore, CA., 27 JUN 71 ** Transferred to VA-122/FRS, NJ/2XX, NAS LeMoore, CA., 02 AUG 71 ** Transferred to VA-27/CVW-14, NK/4XX, NAS LeMoore, CA., 21 APR 72 ** Transferred to VA-147/CVW-9, NG/4XX, USS Constellation (CV-64), 29 MAY 73 ** Transferred to VA-22/CVW-15, NL/314, NAS LeMoore, CA., 19 SEP 73; To VA-22, USS Coral Sea (CVA-43), 29 NOV 74; To VA-22, NAS LeMoore, CA., 29 JUL 75; To VA-22, NAS Fallon, NV., 07 AUG 75; VA-22, NAS Jacksonville, FL., 19 SEP 75; To VA-22, NAS LeMoore, CA., 23 SEP 75; To VA-22, NAS Jacksonville, FL., 10 NOV 75; To VA-22, NAS LeMoore, CA., 11 DEC 75; To VA-22, NAS Fallon, NV., 30 APR 76; To VA-22, NAS Lemoore, CA., 30 APR 76; To VA-22, Painted in Bicentennial scheme, 04 JUL 76; To VA-22, USS Coral Sea (CV-43), 25 FEB 77; To VA-22, NAF Atsugi, JP., 17 MAR 77; To VA-22, USS Coral Sea (CV-43), 28 MAR 77; To VA-22, NAS LeMoore, CA., 26 OCT 77; To VA-22, NAS Jacksonville, FL., 22 MAR 78; To VA-22, NAS LeMoore, CA., 23 APR 78; To VA-22, NAS Kingsville, TX., 23 AUG 78; To VA-22, NAS LeMoore, CA., 23 AUG 78; To VA-22, USS Kitty Hawk (CV-63), 26 APR 79; To VA-22, NAF Atsugi, JP., 07 NOV 79; To VA-22, USS Kitty Hawk (CV-63), 22 NOV 79; To VA-22, NAS LeMoore, CA., 22 NOV 79; To VA-22, NAS Jacksonville, FL., 10 JUL 80; To VA-22, NAS LeMoore, CA., 10 JUL 80; To VA-22, NAS Jacksonville, FL., 14 JUL 80; To VA-22, USS Kitty Hawk (CV-63), 02 OCT 80; To VA-22, NAS LeMoore, CA., 13 JAN 81; To VA-22, USS Kitty Hawk (CV-63), 22 JAN 81 ** Transferred to VA-94/CVW-15, NL/4XX, USS Kitty Hawk (CV-63), 02 APR 81; To VA-94, NAS Cubi Point, PI., 13 MAY 81; To VA-94, NAF Atsugi, JP., 29 SEP 81; To VA-94, USS Kitty Hawk (CV-63), 24 OCT 81; To VA-94, NAS LeMoore, CA., 24 OCT 81; To VA-97/CVW-14, NK/3XX, NAS LeMoore, CA., 24 JUN 82; To VA-97, NAS Jacksonville, FL., 04 NOV 82; To VA-97, NAS LeMoore, CA., 21 DEC 82; To VA-97, USS Coral Sea (CV-43), 03 MAR 83; To VA-97, NAS LeMoore, CA., 05 MAY 83 ** Transferred to VA-174/FRS, AD/4XX, NAS Cecil Field, FL., 09 SEP 83; To VA-174, NAS Jacksonville, FL., 15 AUG 85 ** Transferred to VA-15/CVW-6, AE/3XX, NAS Cecil Field, FL., 15 AUG 85 ** Transferred to NARF, NAS Jacksonville, FL., 15 AUG 85 ** Transferred to VA-37/CVW-6, AE/311, NAS Cecil Field, FL., 13 SEP 85; To VA-37, USS Forrestal (CV-59), 03 JAN 86; To VA-37, NAS Cecil Field, FL., 28 MAR 86; To VA-37, USS Forrestal (CV-59), 03 MAY 86; To VA-37, NAS Cecil Field, FL., 01 APR 87 ** Transferred to AMARC, Davis Monthan AFB; Tucson, AZ., assigned park code 6A0223; 01 APR 87 ** 5627.3 flight hours ** TF41A2B engine S/N 141234 ** Project changed IAW FSO letter, 06 APR 04 ** At AMARC; Davis Monthan AFB; Tucson, AZ., 11 JAN 06.

E-078 156812 Navy acceptance from NPRO Rep. LTV, Dallas, TX., 26 NOV 69 ** Transferred to VA-146/CVW-9, NG/ 3XX, USS America (CVA-66), 21 DEC 69; To VA-146, NAS Fallon, NV., 06 JUN 70 ** Transferred to VA-97/CVW-14, NK/3XX, USS Enterprise (CVAN-65), 06 APR 71; To VA-97, NAS LeMoore, CA., 16 MAY 71; To VA-97, USS Enterprise (CVAN-65), 01 FEB 75; To VA-97, NAS LeMoore, CA., 20 MAY 75; To VA-97, NAS Jacksonville, FL., 24 JUL 75; To VA-97, NAS LeMoore, CA., 17 OCT 75; To VA-97, NAS Fallon, NV., 30 NOV 75; To VA-97, NAS LeMoore, CA., 20 FEB 76; To VA-97, USS Enterprise (CVN-65), 20 FEB 76; To VA-97, NAS LeMoore, CA., 25 MAR 76; To VA-97, USS Enterprise (CVN-65), 28 JUL 76; To VA-97, NAS LeMoore, CA., 30 JUN 76; To VA-97, USS Enterprise (CVN-65), 28 JUL 76; To VA-97, NAS LeMoore, CA., 06 JUN 77; To VA-97, USS Enterprise (CVN-65), 10 MAR 78; To VA-97, NAF Atsugi, JP., 28 JUN 78; To VA-97, USS Enterprise (CVN-65), 05 JUL 78; To VA-97, NAS LeMoore, CA., 30 OCT 78; To NAS Jacksonville, FL., 12 NOV 78 ** Transferred to VA-174/ FRS, AD/425, NAS Cecil Field, FL., 13 FEB 79; To VA-174, Jacksonville, FL., 18 AUG 81; To VA-174, NAS Cecil Field, FL., 23 OCT 81; To VA-174, NAS Jacksonville, FL., 23 JAN 84; To VA-174, NAS Cecil Field, FL., 06 APR 84 ** Releasor to AMARC from Tinker AFB; Oklahoma City, OK., Date unknown ** Transferred to AMARC, Davis Monthan AFB; Tucson, AZ., assigned park code 6A0213; 12 JAN 87 ** End of flight record card 5638.8 flight hours ** TF41A2C engine S/N 141473 ** Ejection seat S/N 0275 removed from aircraft, 09 MAR 89 ** Aircraft deleted from inventory and released to DRMO for disposition, 20 DEC 95 ** Sold as surplus to Fritz Enterprises; Taylor, MI., delivered to HVF West's yard; Tucson, AZ., 10 SEP 96.

E-079 156813 Navy acceptance from NPRO Rep. LTV, Dallas, TX., 25 NOV 69 ** Transferred to VA-146/CVW-9, NG/ 3XX, USS America (CVA-66), 26 NOV 69; To VA-146, NAS Fallon, NV., 24 JUN 70 ** Transferred to VA-122/FRS, NJ/2XX, NAS LeMoore, CA., 08 JUN 71 ** Transferred to VA-97/CVW-14, NK/3XX NAS LeMoore, CA., 30 MAR 72; To VA-97,NAS Jacksonville, FL., 23 DEC 75; To VA-97, NAS LeMoore, CA., 22 JAN 76; To VA-97, USS Enterprise (CVN-65), 20 FEB 76 To VA-97, NAS LeMoore, CA., 29 APR 76; To VA-97, USS Enterprise (CVN-65), 28 JUL 76; To VA-97, NAF Atsugi, JP., 08 JAN 77; To VA-97, USS Enterprise (CVN-65), 10 JAN 77; To VA-97, NAS LeMoore, CA., 19 JUN 77; To VA-97, USS Enterprise (CVN-65), 01 FEB 78; To VA-97, NAF Atsugi, JP., 28 JUN 78; To VA-97, USS Enterprise (CVN-65), 05 JUL 78; To VA-97, NAS LeMoore, CA., 30 OCT 78 ** Transferred to NARF, NAS Alameda, CA., 29 MAR 79 ** Transferred to NARF, NAS Jacksonville, FL., 04 JUN 79 ** Transferred to VA-195/CVW-9, NG/413, NAS LeMoore, CA., 01 NOV 82; To VA-195, USS Ranger (CV-61), 06 JUL 83; To VA-195, NAS LeMoore, CA., 01 MAR 84; To VA-195, NAS Jacksonville, FL., 13 APR 85 ** Transferred to VA-97/ CVW-14, NK/3XX, NAS LeMoore, CA., 17 JUN 85 ** Transferred to VA-174/FRS, AD/4XX, NAS Cecil Field, FL., 21 AUG 85 ** Transferred to VA-97/CVW-14, NK/3XX, NAS LeMoore, CA., 21 AUG 85 ** Transferred to VA-174/FRS, AD/4XX, NAS Cecil Field, FL., 22 AUG 85 ** Transferred to AMARC, Davis Monthan AFB; Tucson, AZ., assigned park code 6A0178, 27 JUN 86 ** End of flight record card ** 4078.6 flight hours ** TF41A2B engine S/N 141945 ** Ejection seat S/N 0151 removed from aircraft, 09 MAR 89 ** Aircraft deleted from inventory and released to DRMO for disposition, 09 SEP 05.

E-080 156814 Navy acceptance from NPRO Rep. LTV, Dallas, TX., 11 DEC 69 ** Transferred to VA-147/CVW-9, NG/ 4XX, USS America (CVA-66), 13 DEC 69; To VA-147, NAS Fallon, NV., 28 JUN 70; To VA-147, NAS LeMoore, Ca., 10 JUN 71 ** Transferred to VA-122/ FRS, NJ/2XX, NAS LeMoore, CA., 04 AUG 71 ** Transferred to VA-146/CVW-9, NG/3XX, USS Constellation (CVA-64), 24 JUL 72 ** Transferred to VA-122/FRS, NJ/2XX, NAS LeMoore, CA., 09 SEP 74 ** Transferred to VA-146/CVW-9, NG/3XX, NAS LeMoore, CA., 25 FEB 75; To VA-146, NAS Fallon, NV., 13 MAY 75; To VA-146, NAS LeMoore, CA., 27 MAY 75; To VA-146, NAS Jacksonville, FL., 07 JUN 76; To VA-146, USS Constellation (CV-64), 24 SEP 76; To VA-146, NAS LeMoore, CA., 15 DEC 76; To VA-146, USS Constellation (CV-64), 15 DEC 76; To VA-146, NAS Cubi Point, PI., 14 MAY 77; To VA-146, USS Constellation (CV-64), 25 OCT 77; To VA-146, NAS LeMoore, CA., 19 NOV 77; To VA146, NAS Fallon, NV., 10 MAY 78; To VA-146, NAS LeMoore, CA., 28 JUN 78 ** Transferred to VA-25/ CVW-2, NE/4XX, NAS LeMoore, CA., 24 JUL 78; To VA-25, USS Ranger (CV-61), 13 NOV 78; To VA-25, NAS Jacksonville, FL., 21 NOV 78; To VA-25, NAS LeMoore, CA., 25 DEC 78; To VA-25, NAF Atsugi, JP., 21 MAR 79; To VA-25, USS Ranger (CV-61), 28 MAR 79; To VA-25, NAS Cubi Point, PI., 28 MAR 79; To VA-25, NAS LeMoore, CA., 14 NOV 79; To VA-25, NAS Fallon, NV., 03 DEC 79; To VA-25, NAS LeMoore, CA., 26 JAN 80 ** Transferred to VA-195/ CVW-11, NH/4XX, NAS LeMoore, CA., 05 MAR 80; To VA-195, NAS Fallon, NV., 16 AUG 80; To VA-195, NAS LeMoore, CA., 16 AUG 80; To VA-195, USS America (CV-66), 16 AUG 80; To VA-195, NAS LeMoore, CA., 21 JAN 81 ** Transferred to VA-97/CVW-14, NK/3XX, NAS LeMoore, CA., 13 MAR 81; To VA-97, USS Coral Sea (CV-43), 04 APR 81; To VA-97, NAS LeMoore, CA., 11 JUN 81; To VA-97, USS Coral Sea (CV-43), 20 AUG 81; To VA-97, NAS LeMoore, CA., 27 JUN 82; To VA-97, USS Enterprise (CVN-65), 27 JUN 82; To VA-97, NAF Atsugi, JP., 20 OCT 82; To VA-97, USS Enterprise (CVN-65), 26 OCT 86 ** Transferred to VA-56/CVW-5, NF/4XX, NAF Atsugi, JP., 10 FEB 83 ** Transferred to VA-122/ CVW-11, NH/3XX, USS Enterprise (CVN-65), 17 NOV 84; To VA-22, NAS Fallon, NV., 20 MAR 85; To VA-22, NAS LeMoore, CA., 20 MAR 85 ** Transferred to VA-174/FRS, AD/4XX, NAS Cecil Field, FL., 06 OCT 85 ** Transferred to AMARC, Davis Monthan AFB; Tucson, AZ., assigned park code 6A0168, 05 JUN 86 ** End of flight record card ** 4916.1 flight hours ** TF41A2C engine S/N 142608 ** ** Ejection seat S/N 0445 removed from aircraft, 09 MAR 89 ** Aircraft deleted from inventory and released to DRMO for disposition, 31 OCT 95 ** Sold as surplus to Fritz Enterprises; Taylor, MI., delivered to HVF West's yard; Tucson, AZ., 10 SEP 96..

E-081 156815 Navy acceptance from NPRO Rep. LTV, Dallas, TX., 29 NOV 69 ** Transferred to VA-146/CVW-9, NG/ 3XX, USS America (CVA-66), 30 NOV 69; To VA-146, NAS Fallon, NV., 12 JUN 70 ** Transferred to VA-122/FRS, NJ/2XX, NAS LeMoore, CA., 11 MAY 71; To VA-122, CRAA, NAS LeMoore, CA., 26 JUL 72 ** Transferred to VA-94/CVW-15, NL/ 4XX, USS Coral Sea (CVA-43), 31 JAN 73 ** Transferred to VA-147/CVW-9, NG/4XX, USS Constellation (CVA-64), 29 MAR 73 ** Transferred to VA-122/FRS, NJ/2XX, NAS LeMoore, CA., 17 JUN 74 ** Transferred to VA-147/ CVW-9, NG/401, NAS LeMoore, CA., 24 MAR 75; To VA-147, NAS Fallon, NV., 22 MAY 75; To VA-147, NAS LeMoore, CA., 05 JUN 75; To VA-147, NAS Jacksonville, FL., 07 JUN 75; To VA-147, NAS LeMoore, CA., 14 AUG 75; To VA-147, MCAS Yuma, AZ., 28 OCT 75; To VA-147, NAS LeMoore, CA., 29 DEC 75; To VA-147, Painted in Bicentennial scheme with City of LeMoore on nose; CDR P.B. Austin on port nose, 04 JUL 76 ** To VA-147, USS Constellation (CV-64), 28 SEP 76; To VA-147, NAS LeMoore, CA., 22 OCT 76; To VA-147, USS Constellation (CV-64), 23 JUL 77; To VA-147, NAS LeMoore, CA., 19 NOV 77; To VA-147, NAS Jacksonville, FL., 29 NOV 77; To VA-147, NAS LeMoore, CA., 19 JAN 78; To VA-147, USS Constellation (CV-64), 28 AUG 78; Transferred to VA-195/ CVW-11, NH/4XX, NAS LeMoore, CA., 11 SEP 78 ** Transferred to VA-97/CVW-14, NK/3XX, NAS LeMoore, CA., 08 DEC 78; To VA-97, USS Coral Sea (CV-43), 23 AUG 79 ** Transferred to VA-174/FRS, AD/435, NAS Cecil Field, FL., 10 JUN 82; To VA-174, NAS Jacksonville, FL., 10 JUN 82; To VA-174, NAS Cecil Field, FL., 13 AUG 82; To VA-174, NAS Jacksonville, FL., 28 MAR 85; To VA-174, NAS Cecil Field, FL., 29 MAR 85 ** Transferred to AMARC, Davis Monthan AFB; Tucson, AZ., assigned park code 6A0179, 10 JUL 86 ** End of flight record card ** 5440.3 flight hours ** TF41A2C engine S/N 141232 ** Aircraft deleted from inventory and released to DRMO for disposition, 09 SEP 05.

E-082 156816 Navy acceptance from NPRO Rep. LTV, Dallas, TX., 20 NOV 69 ** Transferred to VA-147/CVW-9, NG/ 4XX, USS America (CVA-66), 22 NOV 69; To VA-147, NAS Fallon, NV., 07 JUN 70 ** Transferred to VA-122/FRS, NJ/2XX, NAS LeMoore, CA., 07 MAY 71 ** Transferred to VA-27/CVW-14, NK/4XX, NAS LeMoore, CA., 19 APR 72; To VA-27, USS Enterprise (CVN-65), 05 NOV 74; To VA-

27, NAS LeMoore, CA.,20 MAY 75; To VA-27, NAS Fallon, NV., 24 OCT 75; To VA-27, NAS Jacksonville, FL., 25 NOV 75; To VA-27, NAS LeMoore, CA., 09 FEB 76; To VA-27, USS Enterprise (CVN-65), 09 FEB 76; To VA-27, NAS LeMoore, CA., 09 FEB 76; To VA-27, USS Enterprise (CVN-65), 29 APR 76; To VA-27, NAS LeMoore, CA., 17 MAY 76; To VA-27, USS Enterprise (CVN-65), 30 JUN 76; To VA-27, NAS LeMoore, CA., 30 JUN 76; To VA-27, USS Enterprise (CVN-65), 28 JUL 76; To VA-27, NAS LeMoore, CA., 28 MAR 77; To VA-27, USS Enterprise (CVN-65), 12 NOV 78; To VA-27, NAS LeMoore, CA., 03 MAR 78; VA-27, NAF Atsugi, JP., 30 JUN 78; To VA-27, USS Enterprise (CVN-65), 10 JUL 78; VA-27, NAS Cubi Point, PI., 10 JUL 78; To VA-27, NAS LeMoore, CA., 10 OCT 78; To VA-27, NAS Jacksonville, FL., 18 NOV78; To VA-27, NAS LeMoore, CA., 05 JAN 79 Transferred to VA-25/ CVW-2, NE/4XX, 16 JAN 79; To VA-25, USS Ranger (CV-61), 22 JUN 79; To VA-25, NAF Atsugi, JP., 22 MAY 79; To VA-25, USS Ranger (CV-61), 23 MAY 79; To VA-25, NAS Cubi Point, PI., 23 MAY 79; To VA-25, NAS Fallon, NV., 21 SEP 79; To VA-25, NAS LeMoore, CA., 26 JAN 80; To VA-25, NAS Jacksonville, FL., 30 APR 80; To VA-25, USS Ranger (CV-61), 29 MAY 80; To VA-25, NAS LeMoore, CA., 29 JUN 80; To VA-25, USS Ranger (CV-61), 14 JUL 80; To VA-25, NAS LeMoore, CA., 18 JUL 80; To VA-25, USS Ranger (CV-61), 10 SEP 80 ** Transferred to VA-56/ CVW-5, NF/4XX, USS Midway (CV-41), 28 MAR 81; To VA-56, NAF Atsugi, JP., 19 MAY 81; To VA-56, USS Midway (CV-61), 02 SEP 81; To VA-56, NAF Atsugi, JP., 30 OCT 81 ** Transferred to VA-25/CVW-2, NE/4XX, NAS Cubi Point, PI., 21 AUG 82; To VA-25, USS Ranger (CV-61), 21 AUG 82; To VA-25, NAS LeMoore, CA., 21 AUG 82; Transferred to VA-195/CVW-9, NG/4XX, NAS LeMoore, CA., 10 DEC 82; To VA-195, NAS Jacksonville, FL., 24 JAN 83; To VA-195, NAS LeMoore, CA., 23 MAR 83; To VA-195, USS Ranger (CV-61), 05 JUL 83; To VA-195, NAS LeMoore, CA., 25 JUL 83; To VA-195, NAS Jacksonville, FL., 08 OCT 85 ** Tansferred to NSWC, NAS Fallon, NV., 16 OCT 85 thru 23 JAN 87 ** End of flight record card.

E-083 156817 Navy acceptance from NPRO Rep. LTV, Dallas, TX., 13 DEC 69 ** Transferred to VA-146/CVW-9,NG/3XX, USS America (CVA-66), 15 DEC 69; To VA-146, NAS Fallon, NV., 24 JUN 70; To VA-146 NAS LeMooree, CA., 11 JUN 71; To VA-146, USS Constellation (CVA-64), 30 JUN 72; To VA-146, NAS LeMoore, CA., 22 DEC 74; To VA-146, NAS Jacksonville, FL., 13 MAY 75; To VA-146, NAS Fallon, NV., 13 MAY 75; To VA-146, NAS Jacksonville, FL., 14 MAY 75; To VA-146, NAS LeMoore, CA., 07 JUL 75; To VA-146, USS Constellation (CV-64), 27 AUG 76; To VA-146, NAS LeMoore, CA., 15 DEC 76; To VA-146, USS Constellation (CV-64), 15 DEC 76; To VA-146, NAS LeMoore, CA., 05 FEB 77; To VA-146, NAS Cubi Point, PI., 14 MAY 77; To VA-146, USS Constellation (CVA-64), 25 OCT 77; To VA-146, NAS LeMoore, CA., 19 NOV 77; To VA-146, NAS Jacksonville, FL., 17 MAR 78; To VA-146, NAS LeMoore, CA., 01 MAY 76; To VA-146, NAS Fallon, NV., 10 MAY 78; To VA-146, NAS LeMoore, CA., 12 JUN 78; To VA-146, USS Constellation, (CV-64), 16 JUL 78; To VA-146, NAS LeMoore, CA., 24 AUG 78; To VA-146, USS Constellation, (CV-64), 21 SEP 78; To VA-146, NAS Cubi Point, PI., 21 DEC 78; To VA-146, NAF Atsugi, JP., 08 OCT 79; To VA-146, NAS Cubi Point, PI., 16 JAN 79 ** Transferred To VA-122/FRS, NJ/2XX, NAS LeMoore, CA., 18 JUN 79; To VA-122, NAS Alameda, CA., 16 JUL 79; To VA-122, NAS LeMoore, CA., 17 JUL 79; To VA-122, NAS Jacksonville, FL., 25 APR 80; To VA-122, NAS LeMoore, CA., 10 JUL 80 ** To VA-192/CVW-11, NH/3XX, NAS LeMoore, CA., 14 JUL 80; To VA-192, NAS Fallon, NV., 20 OCT 80; To VA-192, NAS LeMoore, CA.,07 NOV 80; To VA-192, USS America (CV-66), 29 JAN 81; To VA-192, NAS LeMoore, CA., 08 APR 81; Transferred to VA-195/CVW-11, NH/4XX, NAS LeMoore, CA., 26 JUL 82; To VA-195, NAS Jacksonville, FL., 24 AUG 82; To VA-195, NAS LeMoore, CA., 30 SEP 82; To VA-195/ CVW-9, NG/4XX, USS Ranger (CV-61), 06 JUL 83; To VA-195, NAS LeMoore, CA., 21 NOV 83 ** Transferred to VA-122/FRS, NJ/247, NAS LeMoore, CA., 01 MAR 84; To VA-122, NAS Jacksonville, FL., 24 DEC 85; To VA-122, NAS LeMoore, CA., 03 JAN 86 ** Transferred to AMARC, Davis Monthan AFB; Tucson, AZ., assigned park code 6A0187; 31 JUL 86 ** End of flight record card ** 5364.5 flight hours ** TF-41A2B engine S/N 142584 ** Project changed per FSO letter, 06 APR 04 ** Aircraft deleted from inventory and released to DRMO for disposition, 05 OCT 05.

E-084 156818 Navy acceptance from NPRO Rep. LTV, Dallas, TX., 30 NOV 69 ** Transferred to VA-147/CVW-9, NG/407, USS America (CVA-66), 04 DEC 69; To VA-147, NAS Fallon, NV., 31 MAY 70; To VA-147, NAS LeMoore, CA., 23 JUN 71; To VA-147, USS Constellation (CVA-64), 30 JUN 72; To VA-147, NAS LeMoore, CA., 06 FEB 75; To VA-147, NAS Fallon, NV., 26 MAY 75; To VA-147, NAS LeMoore, CA., 05 JUN 75; To VA-147 MCAS Yuma, AZ., 28 OCT 75; To VA-147, NAS LeMoore, CA., 29 NOV 75; To VA-147, NAS Jacksonville, FL., 16 SEP 76 ** Transferred to VA-37/CVW-3, AC/3XX, NAS Cecil Field, FL., 12 NOV 76; To VA-37, USS Saratoga (CVA-60), 22 NOV 76; To VA-37, NAS Cecil Field, FL., 22 NOV 76; To VA-37, USS Saratoga (CV-60), 22 NOV 76; To VA-37, NAS Cecil Field, FL., 16 JUL 77; To VA-37, NAS Jacksonville, FL., 02 NOV 78; To VA-37, NAS Cecil Field, FL., 27 DEC 78; To VA-37, MCAS Yuma, AZ., 27 DEC 78; To VA-37, NAS Cecil Field, FL., 27 DEC 78; To VA-37, USS Saratoga (CV-60), 28 NOV 79; To VA-37, NAS Cecil Field, FL., 28 NOV 79, USS Saratoga (CV-60), 28 NOV 79; To VA-37, NAS Cecil Field, FL., 16 MAR 80; To VA-37, NAS Jacksonville, FL., 06 MAR 81; To VA-37, NAS Cecil Field, FL., 05 MAY 81; To VA-37, NAS Fallon, NV., 05 MAY 81; To VA-37, NAS Cecil Field, FL., 05 MAY 81; To VA-37, USS John F. Kennedy (CV-67), 05 MAY 81; To VA-37, NAS Cecil Field, Fl., 05 MAY 81; To VA-37, USS John F. Kennedy (CV-67), 05 MAY 81; To VA-37, NAS Cecil Field, FL., 05 MAY 81; To VA-37/CVW-15, NL/3XX, USS Carl Vinson (CVN-70), 13 SEP 82; To VA-37, NAS Jacksonville, FL., 21 NOV 83; To VA-37, NAS Roosevelt Roads, PR., 31 JAN 84; To VA-37, NAS Cecil Field, FL., 31 JAN 84; To VA-37, NWC China Lake, CA., 22 MAR 84; To VA-37, NAS Cecil Field, FL., 01 APR 84; To VA-37, MCAS Twenty Nine Palms, CA., 20 APR 84; To VA-37, NAS Cecil Field, FL., 20 SEP 84; To VA-37, MCAS Iwacuni, JP., 25 OCT 84; To VA-37, Korea, 06 MAR 85; To VA-37, MCAS Iwacuni, JP., 12 MAR 85; To VA-37, NAS Cecil Field, FL., 26 JUN 85 **Transferred to VA-174/FRS, AD/4XX, NAS Cecil Field, FL., 04 DEC 85 ** Transferred to AMARC, Davis Monthan AFB; Tucson, AZ., assigned park code 6A0164, 23 MAY 86 ** End of flight record card ** 5580.9 flight hours ** TF41A2B engine S/N 142545 ** ** Ejection seat S/N 0194 removed from aircraft, 09 MAR 89 ** Aircraft deleted from inventory and released to DRMO for disposition, 31 OCT 95 ** Sold as surplus to Fritz Enterprises; Taylor, MI., delivered to HVF West's yard; Tucson, AZ., 10 SEP 96.

E-085 156819 Navy acceptance from NPRO Rep. LTV, Dallas, TX., 23 DEC 69 ** Transferred to VA-147/CVW-9, NG/4XX, USS America (CVA-66),03 JAN 70; To VA-147, NAS Fallon, NV., 07 APR 70; To VA-147, NAS LeMoore, CA., 11 JUN 71; To VA-147, USS Constellation (CVA-64), 28 JUN 73; To VA-147/CVW-9, NG/4XX, NAS LeMoore, CA., 14 APR 75; To VA-147, NAS Fallon, NV., 14 MAY 75; To VA-147, NAS Jacksonville, FL., 07 MAY 75; To VA-147, NAS LeMoore, CA., 30 JUN 75; To VA-147, MCAS Yuma, AZ., 28 OCT 75; To VA-147, NAS LeMoore, CA., 28 OCT 75; To VA-147, USS Constellation (CV-64), 29 SEP 76; To VA-147, NAS LeMoore, CA., 22 OCT 76; To VA-147, USS Constellation (CV-64), 23 JUL 77; To VA-147, NAS LeMoore, CA., 19 NOV 77; To VA-147, NAS Jacksonville, FL., 16 MAR 78; To VA-147, NAS LeMoore, CA., 27 APR 78; To VA-147, USS Constellation (CV-64), 18 SEP 78; To VA-147, NAS Cubi Point, PI., 06 NOV 78; To VA-147, NAF Atsugi, JP., 07 DEC 78; To VA-147, USS Constellation (CV-64), 13 DEC 78; To VA-147, NAS Alameda, CA., 09 AUG 79; To VA-147, USS Constellation (CV-64), 13 SEP 79; To VA-147, NAS LeMoore, CA., 02 DEC 79; To VA-147, USS Constellation (CV-64), 13 DEC 79; To VA-147, NAS LeMoore, CA., 03 DEC 80; To VA-147, NAS Jacksonville, FL., 28 MAR 80 ** Transferred to VA-174/FRS, AD/442, NAS Cecil Field, FL. 28 APR 80 ** Transferred to VA-66/CVW-7, AG/3XX, NAS Cecil Field, FL., 28 APR 80; To VA-66, USS Dwight D. Eisenhower (CVN-69), 14 APR 81; To VA-66, NAS Cecil Field, FL., 14 APR 81; To VA-66, USS Dwight D. Eisenhower (CVN-69), 14 APR 81; To VA-66, NAS Cecil Foield, FL., 14 APR 81; To VA-66, USS Dwight D. Eisenhower (CVN-69), 16 DEC 81; To VA-66, NAS Jacksonville, FL., 29 JUL 82 ** Transferred to VA-12/CVW-7, AG/4XX, NAS Cecil Field, FL., 29 SEP 82; To VA-12, USS Dwight D. Eisenhower (CVN-69), 04 NOV 82; To VA-12, NAS Cecil Field, FL., 24 JUL 83 ** Transferred to VA-37/CVW-6, AE/314,

NAS Cecil Field, FL., 24 APR 84; To VA-37, MCAS Twenty Nine Palms, CA., 31 JUL 84; To VA-37, NAS Cecil Field, FL., 07 SEP 84; To VA-37, MCAS Iwacuni, JP., 07 SEP 84; To VA-37, Korea, 07 MAR 85; To VA-37, MCAS Iwacuni, JP., 25 MAR 85; To VA-37, NAS Cecil Field, FL., 25 MAR 85; To VA-37, USS Forrestal (CV-59), 23 DEC 85; To VA-37, NAS Cecil Field, FL., 23 DEC 85; To VA-37, USS Forrestal (CV-59), 23 DEC 85; To VA-37, NAS Cecil Field, FL., 05 MAR 87 ** Transferred to AMARC, Davis Monthan AFB; Tucson, AZ., assigned park code 6A0221; 06 MAR 87 ** End of flight record card ** 6477.8 flight hours ** TF41A2B engine S/N 141583 ** Aircraft deleted from inventory and released to DRMO for disposition, 01AUG 05.

E-086 156820 Navy acceptance from NPRO Rep. LTV, Dallas, TX., 30 NOV 69 ** Transferred to VA-147/CVW-9, NG/4XX, USS America (CVA-66), 01 DEC 69 ** Transferred to VA-122/FRS, NJ/2XX, NAS LeMoore, CA., 28 MAY 70; To VA-122, CRAA, NAS LeMoore, Ca., 14 OCT 71 ** Transferred to VA-22/CVW-15, NL/3XX, USS Coral Sea (CVA-43), 22 OCT 71 ** Transferred to NARF, NAS Alameda, CA., 17 JUL 72 ** Transferred to NARF, NAS Jacksonville, FL., 16 OCT 73 ** Transferred to VA-174/FRS, AD/410, NAS Cecil Field, FL., 16 OCT 73; To VA-174, NAS Jacksonville, FL., 11 JUL 78; To VA-174, NAS Cecil Field, FL., 13 OCT 78 ** Transferred to VA-86/CVW-8, AJ/4XX, USS Nimitz (CVN-68), 29 AUG 80; To VA-86, NAS Cecil Field, FL., 11 NOV 80; To VA-86, NAS Jacksonville, FL., 30 MAR 81; To VA-86, NAS Cecil Field, FL., 30 APR 81; To VA-86, USS Nimitz (CVN-68), 30 APR 81; To VA-86, NAS Cecil Field, FL., 30 APR 81; To VA-86, USS Nimitz (CVN-68), 30 APR 81; To VA-86, NAS Cecil Field, FL., 30 APR 81 ** Transferred to VA-174/FRS, AD/4XX, NAS Cecil Field, FL., 05 APR 82; To VA-174, NAS Cecil Field, FL., 15 NOV 82; To VA-174, NAS Cecil Field, FL., 15 NOV 82; To VA-174, NAS Jacksonville, FL., 17 NOV 82 ** Transferred to VA-81/CVW-17, AA/4XX, NAS Cecil Field, FL., 18 FEB 83; To VA-81, NAS Fallon, NV., 12 AUG 83; To VA-81, NAS Cecil Field, FL., 16 AUG 83; To VA-81, USS Saratoga (CV-60), 07 NOV 83; To VA-81, NAS Cecil Field, FL., 25 JAN 84; To VA-81, USS Saratoga (CV-60), 30 MAR 84; To VA-81, NAS Cecil Field, FL., 05 AUG 84 ~ S ISO strike, 07 FEB 85 ** No data on strike.

E-087 156821 Navy acceptance from NPRO Rep. LTV, Dallas, TX., 18 DEC 69 ** Transferred to VA-147/CVW-9, NG/4XX, USS America (CVA-66), 19 DEC 69; To VA-147, NAS Fallon, NV., 23 MAY 70; To VA-147, NAS LeMoore, CA., 28 MAY 71 ** Transferred to VA-122/ FRS, NJ/2XX, NAS LeMoore, CA., 17 SEP 71 ** Transferred to VA-22/CVW-15, NL/3XX, USS Coral Sea (CVA-43), 02 OCT 72; To VA-22, NAS LeMoore, CA., 06 JUN 73; To VA-22, USS Coral Sea (CVA-43), 29 NOV 74; To VA-22, NAS LeMoore, CA., 30 JUL 75; To VA-22, NAS Fallon, NV., 07 AUG 75; To VA-22, NAS LeMoore, CA., 16 OCT 75; To VA-22, NAS Jacksonville, FL., 17 OCT 75; To VA-22, NAS LeMoore, CA., 22 OCT 75; To VA-22, NAS Jacksonville, FL., 14 JAN 76; To VA-22, NAS LeMoore, CA., 23 JAN 76; To VA-22, To VA-22, USS Coral Sea (CV-43), 10 JUL 77; To VA-22, NAS LeMoore, CA., 17 OCT 77; To VA-22, NAS NAS Jacksonville, FL., 08 MAR 78; To VA-22, NAS LeMoore, Ca., 05 MAY 78; To VA-22, NAS Kingsville, TX., 23 AUG 78; To VA-22, NAS LeMoore, CA., 23 AUG 78; To VA-22, USS kitty Hawk (CV-63), 26 APR 79; To VA-22, NAF Atsugi, JP., 23 OCT 79; To VA-22, USS Kitty Hawk (CV-63), 04 NOV 79; To VA-22, NAS LeMoore, CA., 04 NOV 79; To VA-22, NAS Jacksonville, FL., 06 APR 80; To VA-22, NAS LeMoore, CA., 06 APR 80; To VA-22, NAS Jacksonville, FL., 08 APR 80; To VA-22, NAS LeMoore, CA., 21 JUN 80; To VA-22, USS Kitty Hawk (CV-63), 11 SEP 80; To VA-22, NAS LeMoore, CA., 13 JAN 81; To VA-22, USS Kitty Hawk (CV-63), 22 JAN 81** Transferred to VA-94/CVW-15, NL/4XX, NAS Cubi Point, PI., 13 MAY 81; To VA-94, NAF Atsugi, JP., 21 JUL 81; To VA-94, NAS Cubi Point, PI., 25 JUL 81; To VA-94, USS Kitty Hawk (CV-63), 25 JUL 81; To VA-94, NAS LeMoore, CA., 04 OCT 81; To VA-94, NAS Jacksonville, FL., 30 JUN 82 ** Transferred to VA-122/ FRS, NJ/2XX, NAS LeMoore, CA., 02 SEP 82 ** Transferred to VA-174/FRS, AD/4XX, NAS Cecil Field, FL., 09 JAN 84; To VA-174, NAS Jacksonville, FL., 14 DEC 84; To VA-174, NAS Jacksonville, FL., 18 DEC 84; To VA-174, NAS Jacksonville, FL., 09 APR 85 ** Transferred to AMARC, Davis Monthan AFB; Tucson,

AZ., assigned park code 6A0209, 19 DEC 86 ** End of flight record card ** Project changed per FSO letter, 06 APR 04 ** 5171.3 flight hours ** TF41A2B engine S/N 142502 ** Aircraft deleted from inventory and released to DRMO for disposition, 09 JUN 05. Transferred to NAS Fallon, NV., as a range target, 04 NOV 05..

E-088 156822 Navy acceptance from NPRO Rep. LTV, Dallas, TX., 13 MAR 70 ** Transferred to VA-192/CVW-11, NH/3XX, NAS LeMoore, CA., 17 MAR 70; To VA-192, USS Kitty Hawk (CVA-63), 25 JUN 70 ** Transferred to FS, NAS LeMoore, CA., 30 SEP 70 ** Transferred to VA-122/FRS, NJ/2XX, NAS LeMoore, CA., 16 FEB 70; To VA-122, USS Coral Sea (CVA-43), 24 JUN 71 ** Transferred to VA-146/CVW-9, NG/ 3XX, USS Constellation (CVA-64), 20 DEC 72; To VA-146, NAS LeMoore, CA., 22 DEC 74; To VA-146, NAS Fallon, NV., 08 MAY 75; To VA-146, NAS LeMoore, CA., 27 MAY 75; To VA-146, NAS Jacksonville, FL., 20 JUL 76; To VA-146, NAS Pensacola, FL., 20 SEP 76; To VA-146, NAS Jacksonville, FL., 05 OCT 76 ** Transferred to VA-105/CVW-3, AC/4XX, NAS cecil Field, FL., 05 OCT 76; To VA-105, USS Saratoga (CV-60), 26 DEC 77; To VA-105, NAS Cecil Field, FL., 04 FEB 77; To VA-105, USS Saratoga, (CV-60), 04 FEB 77; To VA-105, NAS Cecil Field, FL., 18 JUL 77; To VA-105, USS Saratoga (CV-60), 29 JUN 78; To VA-105, NAS Cecil Field, FL., 08 JUL 78; To VA-105, USS Saratoga (CV-60), 08 JUL 78 ** Transferred to VA-86/CVW-8, AJ/4XX, NAS Cecil Field, FL., 07 SEP 78; To VA-86, NAS Roosevelt Roads, PR., 07 SEP 78; To VA-86, NAS Cecil Field, FL., 07 SEP 78; To VA-86, NAS Jacksonville, FL., 10 JAN 79; To VA-86, NAS Cecil Field, FL., 15 JAN 79; To VA-86, USS Nimitz (CVN-68), 15 JAN 79; To VA-86, NAS Cecil Field, FL., 15 JAN 79 ** Transferred to VA-83/CVW-17, AA/3XX, NAS Cecil Field, FL., 07 JAN 80; To VA-83, USS Forrestal (CV-59), 04 FEB 80; To VA-83, NAS Cecil Field, FL., 20 MAR 80 ** Transferred To VA-82/CVW-8, AJ/3XX, USS Nimitz (CVN-68), 22 JUL 80; To VA-82, NAS Jacksonville, FL., 10 FEB 81; To VA-82, NAS Cecil Field, FL., 20 APR 81; To VA-82, USS Nimitz (CVN-68), 24 APR 81; To VA-82, NAS Cecil Field, FL., 29 APR 81; To VA-82, USS Carl Vinson (CVN-70), 29 APR 81; To VA-82, NAS Cecil Field, FL., 23 JUN 82; To VA-82, USS Nimitz (CVN-68), 01 JUL 82; To VA-82, NAS Cecil Field, FL., 01 JUL 82; To VA-82, USS Nimitz (CVN-68), 01 JUL 82; To VA-82, NAS Cecil Field, FL., 05 MAR 83; To VA-82, NAS Jacksonville, FL., 01 FEB 84 ** Transferred to VA-12/CVW-7, AG/4XX, NAS Cecil Field, FL., 02 FEB 84; To VA-12, USS Dwight D. Eisenhower (CVN-69), 09 APR 84; To VA-12, NAS Cecil Field, FL., 09 APR 84; To VA-12, USS Dwight D. Eisenhower (CVN-69), 20 AUG 84; To VA-12, NAS Cecil Field, FL., 22 AUG 84; To VA-12, USS Dwight D. Eisenhower (CVN-69), 19 JUN 85; To VA-12, NAS Cecil Field, FL., 04 JUL 85; To VA-12, NAS Jacksonville, FL., 13 MAY 86 ** Transferred to VA-304/CVWR-30, ND/4XX, NAS Alameda, CA., 29 SEP 86 thru 10 JUL 87 ** End of flight record card ** Transferred to VA-205/CVWR-30, AF/5XX, NAS Atlanta, GA., date unknown ** Transferred to AMARC, Davis Monthan AFB; Tucson, AZ., assigned park code 6A0324, 22 MAR 90 ** 7210.5 flight hours ** TF41A402D engine S/N 141337 ** Storage location 211845 ** At AMARG, Davis Monthan AFB; Tucson, AZ.,15 JUN 07.

E-089 156823 Navy acceptance from NPRO Rep. LTV, Dallas, TX., 11 DEC 69 ** Transferred to VA-146/CVW-9, NG/ 3XX, USS America (CV-66), 12 DEC 69; To VA-146, NAS Fallon, NV., 27 JUN 70 ** Transferred to VA-122/FRS, NJ/2XX, NAS LeMoore, CA., 16 JUN 71 ** Transferred to VA-147/CVW-9, NG/4XX, USS Constellation (CVA-64), 11 AUG 72; To VA-147, NAS LeMoore, CA., 22 APR 75; To VA-147, NAS Jacksonville, FL., 23 APR 75; To VA-147, NAS Fallon, NV., 29 APR 75; To VA-147, NAS Jacksonville, FL., 11 JUN 75; To VA-147, NAS LeMoore, CA., 27 JUN 75; To VA-147, MCAS Yuma, AZ., 17 SEP 75; To VA-147, NAS LeMoore, CA., 20 NOV 75; To VA-147, USS Constellation (CV-64), 27 AUG 76; To VA-147, NAS LeMoore, CA., 12 OCT 76; To VA-147, NAS Alameda, CA., 23 NOV 76; To VA-147, NAS LeMoore, CA., 17 DEC 76; To VA-147, NAS Alameda, CA., 24 DEC 76; To VA-147, NAS LeMoore, CA., 21 JAN 77; To VA-147, NAF Atsugi, JP., 09 MAY 77; To VA-147, NAS LeMoore, CA., 18 MAY 77; To VA-147, USS Constellation (CV-64), 23 JUL 77; To VA-147, NAS LeMoore, CA., 19 NOV 77; To VA-147,

NAS Jacksonville, FL., 05 APR 78; To VA-147, NAS LeMoore, CA., 23 MAY 78; To VA-147, USS Constellation (CV-64), 25 SEP 78; To VA-147, NAS Cubi Point, PI., 06 NOV 78; To VA-147, USS Constellation (CV-64), 31 DEC 78 ** Transferred to VA-113/CVW-2, NE/3XX, NAS LeMoore, CA., 13 JAN 80; To VA-113, USS Ranger (CV-61), 21 APR 80 ** Transferred to VA-192/CVW-11, NH/3XX, NAS LeMoore, CA., 23 MAY 80; To VA-192, NAS Jacksonville, FL., 08 JUN 80; To VA-192, NAS LeMoore, CA., 11 AUG 80; To VA-192, NAS Fallon, NV., 20 OCT 80; To VA-192, NAS LeMoore, CA., 07 NOV 80; To VA-192, USS America (CV-66), 29 JAN 81; To VA-192, NAS LeMoore, CA., 29 JAN 81 ** Transferred to VA-195/CVW-9, NG/4XX, NAS LeMoore, CA., 02 NOV 82; To VA-195, NAS Jacksonville, FL., 17 JAN 83; To VA-195, NAS LeMoore, CA., 10 MAR 83; To USS Ranger (CV-61), 01 JUN 83; To VA-195, NAS LeMoore, CA., 03 DEC 83 ** Transferred to VA-122/FRS, NJ/246, NAS LeMoore, CA., 01 MAR 84; To VA-122, NAS Jacksonville, FL., 28 FEB 85; To VA-122, NAS LeMoore, CA., 09 MAR 85 ** Transferred To AMARC, Davis Monthan AFB, Tucson, AZ., Assigned park code 6A0208, 26 SEP 86 ** End of flight record card ** 4936.5 flight hours ** TF41A2B engine S/N 141615 ** Aircraft deleted from inventory and released to DRMO for disposition, 26 MAY 05 **. Transferred to NAS Fallon, NV., as a range target, 04 NOV 05

E-090 156824 Navy acceptance from NPRO Rep. LTV, Dallas, TX., 23 DEC 69 ** Transferred to VA-146/CVW9, NG/3XX, USS America (CVA-66), 02 JAN 70; To VA-146, NAS Fallon, NV., 21 JUN 70; To VA-146, NAS LeMoore, CA., 26 JUN 71; To VA-146 USS Constellation (CVA-64), 30 JUN 72; To VA-146, NAS LeMoore, CA., 07 FEB 75; To VA-146, NAS Fallon, NV., 14 MAY 75; To VA-146, NAS LeMoore, CA., 01 JUL 75; To VA-146, USS Constellation (CV-64), 22 SEP 76; To VA-146, NAS Jacksonville, FL., 22 NOV 76; To VA-146, NAS LeMoore, CA., 24 NOV 76; To VA-146, NAS Jacksonville, FL., 07 JAN 77; To VA-146, NAS LeMoore, CA., 01 FEB 77; To VA-146, NAS Cubi Point, PI., 14 MAY 77; To VA-146, USS Constellation (CV-64), 31 AUG 77; To VA-146, NAS LeMoore, CA., 19 NOV 77; To VA-146, NAS Fallon, NV., 10 MAY 78; To VA-146, USS Constellation (CV-64), 16 JUL 78; To VA-146, NAS LeMoore, CA., 29 AUG 78; To VA-146, USS Constellation (CV-64), 21 SEP 78; To VA-146, NAS Cubi Point, PI., 21 DEC 78 ** Transferred to VA-147/CVW-9, NG/4XX, USS Constellation (CV-64), 23 AUG 79; To VA-147, NAS LeMoore, CA., 12 OCT 79; To VA-147, USS Constellation (CV-64), 02 DEC 79; To VA-147, NAS LeMoore, CA., 02 DEC 79; To VA-147, USS Constellation (CV-64), 26 FEB 80; To VA-147, NAS Cubi Point, PI., 18 APR 80; To VA-147, USS Constellation (CV-64), 20 SEP 80; To VA-147, NAS LeMoore, CA., 20 SEP 80; To VA-147, NAS Alameda, CA., 02 FEB 81; To VA-147, NAS LeMoore, CA., 13 MAR 81; To VA-147, NAF El Centro, CA., 02 APR 81; To VA-147, USS Constellation (CV-64), 29 APR 81; To VA-147, NAS Jacksonville, FL., 30 APR 81; To VA-147, USS Constellation (CV-64), 30 APR 81; To VA-147, NAS Jacksonville, FL., 26 JUN 81; To VA-147, USS Constellation (CV-64), 02 JUL 81; To VA-147, NAS LeMoore, CA., 06 AUG 81; To VA-147, USS Constellation (CV-64), 19 OCT 81; To VA-147, NAS Cubi Point, PI., 19 OCT 81; To VA-147, USS Constellation (CV-64), 19 OCT 81; To VA-147, NAS LeMoore, CA., 19 OCT 81 ** Transferred to VA-27/CVW-14, NK/4XX, NAS LeMoore, CA., 25 OCT 82; To VA-27, USS Coral Sea (CV-43), 17 FEB 83; To VA-27, NAS LeMoore, CA., 10 MAR 83 ** Transferred to VA-82/CVW-8, AJ/3XX, NAS Cecil Field, FL., 09 SEP 83 ** Transferred to VA-37/CVW-15, NL/3XX, USS Carl Vinson (CVN-70), 28 OCT 83; To VA-37, NAS Roosevelt Roads, PR., 21 NOV 83; To VA-37, NAS Cecil Field, FL., 29 FEB 84; To VA-37, NWC China Lake, CA., 29 FEB 84; To VA-37, NAS Cecil Field, FL., 29 FEB 84; To VA-37, MCAS Twenty Nine Palms, CA., 16 JUL 84; To VA-37, NAS Cecil Field, FL., 12 SEP 84; To VA-37, MCAS Iwacuni, JP., 27 DEC 84; To VA-37, Korea, 07 JAN 85; To VA-37, MCAS Iwacuni, JP., 07 JAN 85; To VA-37, NAS Cecil Field, FL., 07 JAN 85; To VA-37/CVW-6, AE/3XX, NAS Jacksonville, FL., 30 JAN 86 To VA-37, USS Forrestal (CV-59), 30 JAN 86; To VA-37, NAS Cecil Field, FL., 03 MAR 86 ** Transferred to VA-204/CVWR-20, AF/4XX, NAS Jacksonville, FL., 03 MAR 86; To VA-204, NAS New Orleans, LA., 01 AUG 86 thru 10 SEP 87 ** End of flight record card.

E-091 156825 Navy acceptance from NPRO Rep. LTV, Dallas, TX., 05 DEC 69 ** Transferredto VA-146/CVW-9, NG/3XX, USS America (CVA-66), 08 DEC 69; To VA-146, NAS Fallon, NV., 27 JUN 70 ** Transferred to VA-122/FRS, NJ/2XX, NAS LeMoore, CA. 03 MAY 71; To VA-122, CRAA, NAS LeMoore, CA., 21 DEC 72 ** Transferred to VA-113/CVW-2, NE/3XX, NAS LeMoore, CA., 21 JAN 73; To VA-113, USS Ranger (CV-61), 21 JUN 73 ~ S 1SO strike, 12 MAY 74 ** No data on strike.

E-092 156826 Navy acceptance from NPRO Rep. LTV Dallas, TX., 16 DEC 69 ** Transferred to VA-147/CVW-9, NG/4XX, USS America (CVA-66), 17 DEC 69; To VA-146, NAS Fallon, NV., 28 JUN 70 ~ S 1SO strike, 29 JUN 71 ** No data on strike.

E-093 156827 Navy acceptance from NPRO Rep. LTV, Dallas, TX., 26 NOV 69 ** Transferred to VA-147/CVW-9, NG/405, USS America (CV-66), 29 NOV 69; To VA-147, NAS Fallon, NV., 26 MAY 70 ** Transferred to NARF, NAS Jacksonville, FL., 02 FEB 71 ** Transferred to VA-122/FRS, NJ/2XX, NAS LeMoore, CA., 18 FEB 83; To VA-122, NAS Jacksonville, FL., 24 FEB 78; To VA-122, NAS LeMoore, CA., 03 JUN 78 ** Transferred to VA-27/CVW-14, NK/4XX, USS Coral Sea (CV-43), 01 APR 81; To VA-27, NAS LeMoore, CA., 11 JUN 81; To VA-27, USS Coral Sea (CV-43), 20 JUL 81 ** Transferred to VA-122/FRS, NJ/2XX, NAS LeMoore, CA., 14 AUG 81; To VA-122, NAS Alameda, CA., 26 APR 83; To VA-122, NAS LeMoore, CA.,01 AUG 83; To VA-122, NAS Jacksonville, FL., 01 AUG 83 ** Transferred to VA-203/CVWR-20, AF/3XX, NAS Jacksonville, FL., 13 AUG 83 ** Transferred to VA-205/CVWR-20, AF/5XX, NAS Atlanta. GA., 20 SEP., 84 thru 31 AUG 87** End of flight record card ** Transferred to AMARC, Davis Monthan AFB; Tucson, AZ., assigned park code 6A0281, 11 JUN 88 ** 5651.0 flight hours ** TF41A402D engine S/N 141242 ** Prepare for overland and above deck shipment, for the government of Greece ** Transferred to the Helenic Air force (Greece).

E-094 156828 Navy acceptance from NPRO Rep. LTV, Dallas, TX., 19 DEC 69 ** Transferred to VA-147/CVW-9, NG/ 4XX, USS America (CVA-66), 24 DEC 69; To VA-147, NAS Fallon, NV., 29 JUN 70; To VA-147, NAS LeMoore, CA., 16 JUN 71; To VA-147, USS Constellation (CVA-64), 30 JUN 72 ** Transferred to VA-122/FRS, NJ/2XX, NAS LeMoore, CA., 06 FEB11, 73 ** Transferred to VA-192/CVW-11, NH/3XX, USS Kitty Hawk (CV-63), 15 MAY 75; To VA-192, NAS Cubi Point, PI., 16 SEP 75; To VA-192, USS Kitty Hawk (CV-63), 19 NOV 75; To VA-192, NAS LeMoore, CA., 18 FEB 76; To VA-192, MCAS Yuma, AZ., 30 NOV 76; To VA-192, NAS LeMoore, CA., 01 FEB 77; To VA-192, NAS Jacksonville, FL., 05 FEB 77; To VA-192, NAS LeMoore, CA., 01 APR 77; To VA-192, USS Kitty Hawk (CV-63), 20 JUL 77; To VA-192, NAS LeMoore, CA., 31 AUG 77; To VA-192, USS Kitty Hawk (CV-63), 19 SEP 77; To VA-192, NAS LeMoore, CA., 30 SEP 77; To VA-192, USS Kitty Hawk (CV-63), 30 SEP 77 ** Transferred to VA-94/CVW-15, NL/4XX, NAS LeMoore, CA., 26 OCT 77; To VA-94, NAS Cubi Point, PI., 29 MAY 79; To VA-94, USS Kitty Hawk (CV-63), 06 JUN 79; To VA-94, NAS LeMoore, CA., 21 SEP 79; To VA-94, NAS Jacksonville, FL., 30 APR 80; To VA-94, NAS LeMoore, CA., 10 MAY 80; VA-192, USS Kitty Hawk (CV-63), 27 JUL 80; To VA-94, NAS LeMoore, CA., 27 JUL 80 ** Transferred to VA-192/CVW-11, NH/3XX, USS Kitty Hawk (CV-63), 05 AUG 80; To VA-94, NAS LeMoore, CA., 05 AUG 80 ** Transferred to VA-122/FRS, NJ/2XX, NAS LeMoore, CA., 20 MAR 81 ** Transferred to VFA-125/FRS, NJ/5XX, NAS LeMoore, CA., 06 APR 81; To VFA-125, NAS Jacksonville, FL., 21 APR 82 ** Transferred to VA-97/CVW-14, NK/3XX, NAS LeMoore, CA., 23 APR 82; To VA-97, USS Coral Sea (CV-43), 28 FEB 83; To VA-97, NAS LeMoore, CA., 28 FEB 83 ** Transferred to VA-82/CVW-8, AJ/3XX, NAS Cecil Field, FL., 09 SEP 83 ** Transferred to VA-37/CVW-6, AE/3XX, NAS Jacksonville, FL., 30 JUL 84; To VA-37, MCAS Twenty Nine Palms, CA., 30 JUL 84; To VA-37, NAS Jacksonville, FL., 26 SEP 84; To VA-37, NAS Cecil Field, FL., 03 OCT 84; To VA-37, MCAS Iwacuni, JP., 26 OCT 84; To VA-37, Korea, 28 OCT 84; To VA-37, MCAS Iwacuni, JP., 30 APR 85; To VA-37, NAS Cecil Field, FL., 30 MAY 85 ** Transferred to VA-174/FRS, AD/4XX, NAS Cecil Field, FL., 09 DEC 85 ** Transferred to AMARC, Davis Monthan AFB; Tucson, AZ., assigned park code 6A0180, 10 JUL 86 ** End of flight record card ** 5792.8 flight hours ** TF41A2E engine S/N 142507 ** Project changed per FSO letter, 06 APR 04 ** Engine released to DRMO for disposition, 26 MAY 05 ** Aircraft deleted from inventory and released to DRMO for disposition, 31 OCT 95.

E-095 156829 Navy acceptance from NPRO Rep. LTV, Dallas, TX., 22 DEC 69 ** Transferred to VA-146/CVW-9, NG/ 3XX, USS America (CVA-66), 29 DEC 69; To VA-146, NAS Fallon, NV., 10 JUN 70; To VA-146, NAS LeMoore, CA., 05 JUN 71 ** Transferred to VA-122/FRS, NJ/2XX, NAS LeMoore, CA., 16 SEP 71; To VA-122, CRAA, NAS LeMoore, CA., 26 JUL 72; To VA-122, NAS LeMoore, CA., 07 NOV 73; To VA-122, NAS Jacksonville, FL., 11 JAN 78; To VA-122, NAS LeMoore, CA., 11 JAN 78; To VA-122, NAS Jacksonville, FL., 18 JAN 78; To VA-122, NAS LeMoore, CA., 27 MAY 78; To VA-122, NAS Alameda, CA., 03 APR 80; To VA-122, NAS LeMoore, CA., 11 APR 80; To VA-122, NAS Jacksonville, FL., 18 SEP 80; To VA-122, NAS LeMoore, CA., 30 OCT 80 ** Transferred to VA-97/CVW-14, NK/3XX, NAS LeMoore, CA, 02 FEB 81; To VA-97, USS Coral Sea (CV-43), 04 APR 81; To VA-97, NAS LeMoore, CA., 11 JUN 81; To VA-97, USS Coral Sea (CV-43), 20 AUG 81; To VA-97, NAS LeMoore, CA., 22 MAR 82 ** Transferred to VA-25/CVW-2, NE/4XX, NAS LeMoore, CA., 20 JAN 83; TO VA-25, NAS Jacksonville, FL., 08 JUN 83 ** Transferred to VA-203/CVWR-20, AF/3XX, NAS Jacksonville, FL., 08 JUN 83 ** Transferred to VA-205/CVWR-20, AF/5XX, NAS Atlanta, GA., 08 JUL 84 thru 24 SEP 87 ** End of flight record card ** Transferred to AMARC, Davis Monthan AFB; Tucson, AZ., assigned park code 6A0280, 08 JUL 88 ** 5668.2 flight hours ** TF41A402D engine S/N 141422 ** Engine records released to DRMO for disposition, 29 JUN 05 ** Aircraft deleted from inventory and released to DRMO for disposition, 01 AUG 05.

E-096 156830 Navy acceptance from NPRO Rep. LTV, Dallas, TX., 13 JAN 70 ** Transferred to VX-5, XE/XXX, NAF China Lake, CA., 19 JAN 70 ** Transferred to VA-122/FRS, NJ/237, NAS LeMoore, CA., 26 JAN 73; To VA-122, NAS Jacksonville, FL., 31 JAN 79; To VA-122, NAS LeMoore, CA., 27 FEB 79; To VA-122, NAS Jacksonville, FL., 07 MAR 79; To VA-122, NAS LeMoore, CA., 09 MAR 79; TO VA-122, NAS Jacksonville, FL., 20 FEB 81; To VA-122, NAS LeMoore, CA., 23 APR 81 ** Transferred to VA-27/CVW-14, NK/4XX, NAS LeMoore, CA., 28 APR 81; To VA-27, USS Coral Sea (CV-43), 28 APR 81; To VA-27, NAS LeMoore, CA., 11 JUN 81; To VA-27, USS Coral Sea (CV-43), 29 JUL 81; To VA-27, NAS LeMoore, CA., 22 MAR 82 ** Transferred to VA-147/CVW-9, NE/3XX, NAS LeMoore, CA., 03 NOV 82; To VA-147, NAS Jacksonville, FL., 30 JUL 83; To VA-147, NAS LeMoore, CA., 03 NOV 83; To VA-147, USS Kitty Hawk (CV-63), 03 NOV 83; To VA-147, NAS LeMoore, CA., 02 OCT 84; To VA-147, USS Kitty Hawk (CV-63), 14 MAY 85; To VA-147, NAF Atsugi, JP., 27 AUG 85; To VA-147, USS Kitty Hawk (CV-63), 11 SEP 85; To VA-147, NAF Atsugi, JP., 14 SEP 85; To VA-147, USS Kitty Hawk (CV-63), 18 SEP 85; To VA-147, NAS LeMoore, CA., 07 JAN 86; To VA-147, NAS Jacksonville, FL., 07 JAN 86 ** Transferred to VA-122/FRS, NJ/2XX, NAS LeMoore, CA., 05 APR 86 ** Transferred to AMARC, Davis Monthan AFB; Tucson, AZ., assigned park code 6A0237; 02 SEP 87 ** 5632.7 flight hours ** TF41A2B engine S/N 142508 ** Aircraft demilled, 13 JAN 05 ** Engine released to DRMO for disposition, 09 SEP 05 ** Aircraft deleted from inventory and released to DRMO for disposition, 09 SEP 05.

E-097 156831 Navy acceptance from NPRO Rep. LTV, Dallas, TX., 17 DEC 69 ** Transferred to VA-146/CVW-9, NG/ 3XX, USS America (CVA-66), 19 DEC 69; To VA-146, NAS Fallon, NV., 26 JUN 70; To VA-146, NAS LeMoore, CA., 04 JUN 71; To VA-146, USS Constellation (CVA-64), 30 JUN 72; To VA-146, NAS LeMoore, CA., 27 FEB 75; To VA-146, NAS Fallon, NV., 27 MAY 75; To VA-146, NAS LeMoore, CA., 13 JUN 75; To VA-146, NAS Jacksonville, FL., 14 JUN 75; To VA-146, NAS LeMoore, CA., 06 AUG 75; To VA-146, USS Constellation (CV-64), 09 JUN 76; To VA-146, NAS LeMoore, CA., 13 DEC 76; To VA-146, USS Constellation (CV-64), 15 DEC 76; To VA-146, NAS LeMoore, CA., 16 FEB 77; To VA-146, NAS Cubi Point, PI., 14 MAY 77; To VA-146, NAF Atsugi, JP., 23 JUL 77; To VA-146, NAS Cubi Point, PI., 31 AUG 77; To VA-146, USS Constellation (CV-64), 25 OCT 77; To VA-146, NAS LeMoore, CA., 19 NOV 77; To VA-146, NAS Jacksonville, FL., 24 FEB 78; To VA-146, NAS LeMoore, CA., 24 APR 78; To VA-146, NAS Fallon, NV., 24 APR 78; To VA-146, NAS LeMoore, CA., 20 JUN 78; To VA-146, USS Constellation (CV-64), 16 JUL 78; To VA-146, NAS LeMoore, CA., 24 AUG 78; To VA-146, USS Constellation (CV-64), 21 SEP 78; To VA-146, NAS Cubi Point, PI., 21 DEC 78; To VA-146, NAF Atsugi, JP., 21 FEB 79; To VA-146, NAS Cubi Point, PI., 26 FEB 79 ** Transferred to VA-122/FRS, NJ/2XX, NAS LeMoore, CA., 18 JUN 79; To VA-122, NAS Jacksonville, FL., 25 JAN 80; To VA-122, NAS LeMoore, CA., 07 APR 80 ** Transferred to VA-97/ CVW-14, NK/3XX, NAS LeMoore, CA., 12 JAN 81; To VA-97, USS Coral Sea (CV-43), 04 APR 81; To VA-97, NAS LeMoore, CA., 11 JUN 81; To VA-97, USS Coral Sea (CV-43), 20 AUG 81; To VA-97, NAS LeMoore, CA., 22 MAR 82; To VA-97, NAS Jacksonville, FL., 28 MAY 82; To VA-97, NAS LeMoore, Ca., 09 AUG 82; To VA-97, USS Coral Sea (CV-43), 04 MAR 83; To VA-97, NAS LeMoore, CA., 14 MAR 83 ** Transferred to VA-82/CVW-8, AJ/3XX, NAS Cecil Field, FL., 09 SEP 83 ** Transferred to VA-37/CVW-15, NL/3XX, USS Carl Vinson (CVN-70), 28 OCT 83; To VA-37, NAS Roosevelt Roads, PR., 02 FEB 84; To VA-37, NAS Cecil Field, FL., 03 MAR 84; To VA-37, MCAS Twenty Nine Palms, CA., 20 JUL 84; To VA-37, NAS Cecil field, Fl., 31 AUG 84; Toi VA-37, MCAS Iwacuni, JP., 26 SEP 84; To VA-37, Korea, 24 JAN 85; To VA-37, MCAS Iwacuni, JP., 24 JAN 85; To VA-37, NAS Cecil Field, FL., 28 JUN 85; To VA-37/CVW-6, AE/3XX, NAS Jacksonville, FL., 18 JUL 85; To VA-37, NAS Cecil Field, FL., 25 OCT 85; To VA-37, USS Forrestal (CV-59), 05 MAR 86; To VA-37, NAS Cecil Field, FL., 05 MAR 86 ** Transferred to VA-12/CVW-7, AG/417, NAS Cecil Field, FL., Date unknown ** Transferred to AMARC, Davis Monthan AFB; Tucson, AZ., assigned park code 6A0192, 21 AUG 86 ** End of flight record card ** 6004.9 flight hours ** TF41A2B engine S/N 141348 ** Engine released to DRMO for disposition, Date unknown ** Aircraft deleted from inventory and released to DRMO for disposition, 01 AUG 05 ** Transferred to NAS Fallon, NV., to be used as a range target, 04 NOV 05.

E-098 156832 Navy acceptance from NPRO Rep. LTV, Dallas, TX., 22 DEC 69 ** Transferred to VA-146/CVW-9, NG/3XX, USS America (CVA-66), 23 DEC 69; To VA-146, NAS Fallon, NV., 07 JUN 70; To VA-146, NAS LeMoore, CA., 07 JUN 71; To VA-146, USS Constellation (CVA-64), 30 JUN 72; To VA-146, NAS LeMoore, CA., 22 DEC 74; To VA-146, NAS Fallon, NV., 07 MAY 75; To VA-146, NAS Jacksonville, FL., 16 JUN 75 ** Transferred to VA-174/ FRS, AD/4XX, NAS Cecil Field, FL.,27 AUG 75; To VA-174, NAS Jacksonville, FL., 08 AUG 78; To VA-174, NAS Cecil Field, FL., 07 SEP 78 **Transferred to VA-105/CVW-3, AC/4XX, USS Saratoga (CV-60), 10 SEP 79; To VA-105, NAS Cecil Field, FL., 10 SEP 79; To VA-105, USS Saratoga (CV-60), 24 FEB 80; To VA-105, NAS Jacksonville, FL., 05 SEP 80; To VA-105, USS Saratoga (CV-60), 03 NOV 80; To VA-105, NAS Cecil Field, FL., 11 FEB 81; To VA-105, NAS Fallon, NV., 16 MAR 81; To VA-105, NAS Cecil Field, FL., 16 MAR 81; To VA-105, USS John F. Kennedy (CV-67), 16 MAR 81 ** Transferred to VA-87/CVW-6, AE/411, NAS Cecil Field, FL./ USS Independence (CV-62), 16 MAR 81 ** Transferred to VA-87/ CVW-6, AE/4XX, NAS Cecil Field, FL., 19 AUG 81; To VA-87, USS Independence (CV-62), 01 OCT 81; To VA-87, NAS Cecil Field, FL., 01 OCT 81; To VA-87, USS Independence (CV-62), 01 OCT 81; To VA-87, NAS Cecil Field, FL., 13 MAY 82; To VA-87, USS Independence (CV-62), 24 MAY 82; To VA-87, NAS Cecil Field, FL., 24 MAY 82; To VA-87, USS Independence (CV-62), 31 MAY 83; To VA-87, NAS Jacksonville, FL., 01 JUN 83; To VA-87, USS Independence (CV-62), 02 JUN 83; To VA-87, NAS Cecil Field, FL., 02 JUN 83; To VA-87, USS Independence (CV-62), 18 AUG 83; To VA-87, NAS Cecil Field, FL., 02 SEP 83; To VA-87, USS Independence (CV-62), 02 SEP 83; To VA-87, NAS Cecil Field, FL., 04 MAY 84; To VA-87, USS Independence (CV-62), 4 MAY 84; To VA-87, NAS Cecil Field, FL., 04 SEP 84; To VA-87, USS Independence (CV-62), 13 SEP 84; To VA-87, NAS Cecil Field,

FL., 13 SEP 84; To VFA-87, NAS Jacksonville, FL., 19 JUN 86 ** Transferred to VA-174/FRS, AD/402, NAS Cecil Field, FL., 19 JUN 86 ** Transferred to AMARC, Davis Monthan AFB; Tucson, AZ., assigned park code 6A0220; 25 FEB 87 ** 4846.6 flight hours ** TF41A2C engine S/N 141890 ** End of flight record card ** Project changed per FSO letter, 06 APR 04 ** At AMARC; Davis Monthan AFB; Tucson, AZ., 11 JAN 06.

E-099 156833 Navy acceptance from NPRO Rep. LTV, Dallas, TX., 19 DEC 69 ** Transferred to VA-147/CVW-9, NG/400, City of Hanford and NG/402, City of Alongapo painted on side, USS America (CVA-66), 03 JAN 70; To VA-147, NAS Fallon, NV., 25 MAY 70; To VA-147, NAS LeMoore, CA., 17 MAY 71; To VA-147, USS Constellation (CVA-64), 30 JUN 72; To VA-147, NAS Cubi Point, PI., 19 NOV 74; To VA-147, USS Constellation (CVA-64), 09 DEC 74; To VA-147, NAS Jacksonville, FL., 08 DEC 75 ** Transferred to NARF, NAS Jacksonville, FL., 28 APR 75 ** Transferred to VA-174/FRS, AD/4XX, NAS Cecil Field, FL., 27 FEB 75 ** Transferred to VA-83/CVW-17, AA/3XX, NAS Cecil Field, FL., 02 MAR 76; To VA-83, USS Forrestal (CV-59), 02 MAR 76; To VA-83, NAS Cecil Field, FL., 02 MAR 76; To VA-83, USS Franklin D. Roosevelt (CV-42), 02 MAR 76; To VA-83, NAS Cecil Field, FL., 02 MAR 76; To VA-83, USS Forrestal (CV-59), 20 JUL 77; To VA-83, NAS Cecil Field, FL., 20 JUL 77; To VA-83, USS Forrestal (CV-59), 20 JUL 77; To VA-83, USS Cecil Field, FL., 28 FEB 78; To VA-83, USS Forrestal (CV-59), 03 MAR 78; To VA-83, NAS Jacksonville, FL., 14 SEP 78; To VA-83, NAS Cecil Field, FL., 24 OCT 78; To VA-83, USS Forrestal (CV-59), 24 OCT 78; To VA-83, NAS Cecil Field, FL. 24 OCT 78; To VA-83, USS Forrestal (CV-59), 24 OCT 78; To VA-83, NAS Cecil Field, FL., 24 OCT 78; To VA-83, USS Forrestal (CV-59), 24 OCT 78; To VA-83, NAS Cecil Field, FL., 24 OCT 78; To VA-83, USS Forrestal (CV-59), 24 OCT 78 ** Transferred to NATC, NAS Patuxent River, MD., for RDT & E, 01 SEP 80 ** Transferred to VX-5, XE/XXX, NWC China Lake, CA., 04 DEC 80 ** Transferred to NWC China Lake, CA., NWC/ XXX, 06 DEC 80 ** Transferred to NATC, NAS Patuxent River, MD., for RDT & E, 01 MAY 82 ** Transferred to VA-205/CVWR-20, AF/505, NAS Atlanta, GA., 05 JUN 84 thru 19 AUG 87 ** End of flight record card ** Transferred to AMARC, Davis Monthan AFB; Tucson, AZ., assigned park code 6A0259, 22 APR 88 ** Aircraft released from storage and prepared for overland and above deck shipment to Greece, 15 SEP 94 ** Transferred to the Helinic Air Force (Greece).

E-100 156834 Navy acceptance from NPRO Rep. LTV, Dallas, TX., 29 DEC 69 ** Transferred to VA-122/FRS, NJ/2XX, NAS LeMoore, CA., 04 JAN 70; To VA-122, COSA, NAS LeMoore, CA. 06 APR 70; To VA-122, NAS LeMoore, CA., 30 MAR 71 ** Transferred to VA-147/CVW-9, NG/4XX, USS Constellation (CVA-64), 19 JUL 72; To VA-147, NAS LeMoore, CA., 01 FEB 75; To VA-147, NAS Jacksonville, FL., 24 APR 75; To VA-147, NAS Fallon, NV., 06 MAY 75; To VA-147, NAS LeMoore, CA., 05 JUN 75; To VA-147, MCAS Yuma, AZ., 10 OCT 75; To VA-147, NAS LeMoore, CA., 06 NOV 75; To VA-147, USS Constellation (CV-64), 15 JUN 76; To VA-147, NAS LeMoore, CA., 15 JUN 76; To VA-147, USS Constellation (CV-64), 23 JUL 77; To VA-147, NAF Atsugi, JP., 13 OCT 77; To VA-147, USS Constellation (CV-64), 19 OCT 77; To VA-147, NAF Atsugi, JP., 26 OCT 77; To VA-147, NAS LeMoore, CA., 19 NOV 77; To VA-147, NAS Jacksonville, FL., 24 FEB 78; To VA-147, NAS LeMoore, CA., 06 APR 78 ** Transferred to VA-22/CVW-15, NL/3XX, NAS LeMoore, 16 AUG 78; To VA-22, NAS Kingsville, TX., 23 AUG 78; To VA-22, NAS LeMoore, CA., 23 AUG 78 ** Transferred to VA-27/CVW-14, NK/4XX, NPTR El Centro, CA., 09 APR 79; To VA-27, NAS Jacksonville, FL., 20 SEP 79; To VA-27, USS Coral Sea (CV-43), 27 SEP 79 ** Transferred to VA-174/FRS, AD/4XX, NAS Cecil Field, FL., 20 NOV 79; To VA-174, NAS Jacksonville, FL., 22 FEB 82; To VA-174, NAS Cecil Field, FL., 31 MAR 82 ** Transferred to VA-12/CVW-7, AG/4XX, USS Dwight D. Eisenhower (CVN-69), 13 APR 83; To VA-12, NAS Cecil Field, FL., 23 OCT 83; To VA-12, NAS Jacksonville, FL., 03 FEB 84; To VA-12, USS Dwight D. Eisenhower (CVN-69), 03 MAY 84; To VA-12, NAS Cecil Field, FL., 03 MAY 84; To VA-12, USS Dwight D. Eisenhower (CVN-69),

03 MAY 84; To VA-12, NAS Cecil Field, FL., 03 MAY 84; To VA-12, USS Dwight D. Eisenhower (CVN-69), 03 MAY 84; To VA-12, NAS Cecil Field, FL., 03 MAY 84; To VA-12, NAS Jacksonville, FL., 20 MAY 86; To VA-12, NAS Cecil Field, FL., 27 MAY 86; To VA-12, NAS Jacksonville, FL., 12 SEP 86 ** Transferred to VA304/CVWR-30, ND/4XX, NAS Alameda, CA., 17 SEP 86 thru 24 MAY 87 ** End of flight record card ** Transferred to AMARC, Davis Monthan AFB; Tucson, AZ., assigned park code 6A0263; 29 APR 88 ** 6650.8 flight hours ** TF41A402B engine S/N 141573 ** Engine records released to DRMO for disposition, 26 JUL 05 ** Aircraft deleted from inventory and released to DRMO for disposition, 01 AUG 05.

E-101 156835 Navy acceptance from NPRO Rep. LTV, Dallas, TX., 21 JAN 70 ** Transferred to VA-25/CVW-2, NE/4XX, NAS LeMoore, CA., 31 JAN 70 ** Transferred to VA-97/CVW-14, NK/3XX, USS Enterprise (CVAN-65), 04 AUG 70; To VA-97, NAS LeMoore, CA., 08 APR 71; To VA-97, USS Enterprise (CVAN-65), 01 MAY 75; To VA-97, NAS LeMoore, CA., 20 MAY 75; To VA-97, NAS Jacksonville, FL., 22 NOV 75; To VA-97, NAS LeMoore, CA., 24 NOV 75; To VA-97, NAS Jacksonville, FL., 24 JAN 76; To VA-97, NAS LeMoore, CA., 28 JAN 76; To VA-97, USS Enterprise (CVN-65), 20 SEP 76; To VA-97, NAS LeMoore, CA., 27 APR 76; To VA-97, USS Enterprise (CVN-65), 28 JUL 76; To VA-97, NAF Atsugi, JP., 09 MAR 77; To VA-97, USS Enterprise (CVN-65), 10 MAR 77; To VA-97, NAS LeMoore, CA., 19 JUN 77; To VA-97, USS Enterprise (CVN-65), 12 AUG 77; To VA-97, NAS LeMoore, CA., 29 AUG 77; To VA-97, USS Enterprise (CVN-65), 10 MAR 78; To VA-97, NAF, Atsugi, JP., 05 JUN 78; To VA-97, USS Enterprise (CVN-65), 22 JUN 78; To VA-97, NAF Atsugi, JP, 08 SEP 78; To VA-97, USS Enterprise (CVN-65), 15 SEP 78; To VA-97, NAS LeMoore, CA., 30 OCT 78; To VA-97, NAS Jacksonville, FL., 27 DEC 78; To VA-97, NAS LeMoore, CA., 15 JAN 79 ** Transferred to VA-113/CVW-2, NE/ 3XX, NAS LeMoore, CA., 18 JAN 79; To VA-113, USS Ranger (CV-61), 22 MAR 79; To VA-113, NAF Atsugi, JP., 05 MAY 79; To VA-113, NAS Cubi Point, PI., 13 JUN 79; To VA-113, NAS Fallon, NV., 22 SEP 79; To VA-113, NAS LeMoore, CA., 22 SEP 79; To VA-113, USS Ranger (CV-61), 21 APR 80 ** Transferred to VA-195/CVW-11, NH/4XX, NAS LeMoore, CA., 13 MAY 80; To VA-195, NAS Jacksonville, FL., 14 MAY 80; To VA-195, NAS LeMoore, CA., 15 JUL 80; To VA-195, NAS Fallon, NV., 19 OCT 80; To VA-195, NAS LeMoore, CA., 07 NOV 80; To VA-195, USS America (CV-66), 25 JAN 81; To VA-195, NAS LeMoore, CA., 09 APR 81; To VA-195, NAS Jacksonville, FL., 12 JUL 82; To VA-195, NAS LeMoore, CA., 25 AUG 82; To VA-195, USS Ranger (CV-61), 21 JUL 83; To VA-195, NAF Atsugi, JP., 28 SEP 83; To VA-195, USS Ranger (CV-61), 04 OCT 83; To VA-195, NAF Atsugi, JP., 22 DEC 83; To VA-195, USS Ranger (CV-61), 01 JAN 84; To VA-195, NAS LeMoore, CA., 01 JAN 84; To VA-195, NAS Jacksonville, FL., 28 FEB 85 ** Transferred to NARF, NAS Jacksonville, FL., 28 FEB 85 ** Transferred to VA-122/FRS, NJ/2XX, NAS LeMoore, CA., 07 MAR 85 ** Transferred to VA-204/CVWR-20, AF/4XX, NAS NEW Orleans, LA., 04 APR 86 ** Transferred to VA-304/CVWR-30, ND/401, NAS Alameda, CA., 27 AUG 86 thru 30 AUG 87 ** End of flight record card ** Transferred to AMARC, Davis Monthan AFB; Tucson, AZ., assigned park code 6A0270; 26 MAY 88 ** 6637.1 flight hours ** TF41A402D engine S/N 141343 ** Project changed per FSO letter, 06 APR 04, PLO ** At AMARC, Davis Monthan AFB; Tucson, AZ., 11 JAN O6.

E-102 156836 Navy acceptance from NPRO Rep. LTV, Dallas, TX., 19 JAN 70 ** Transferred to VA-25/CVW-2, NE/4XX, NAS LeMoore, CA., 20 JAN 70 ** Transferred to VA-97/CVW-14, NK/3XX, USS Enterprise (CVAN-65), 02 JUL 70; To VA-97, NAS LeMoore, CA., 07 APR 71; To VA-97 USS Enterprise (CVAN-65), 01 MAR 75; To VA-97, NAS LeMoore, CA., 20 MAY 75; To VA-97, NAS Jacksonville, FL., 03 NOV 75; To VA-97, NAS Fallon, NV., 14 DEC 75; To VA-97, NAS LeMoore, CA., 20 FEB 76; To VA-97, USS Enterprise (CVN-65), 20 FEB 76; To VA-97, NAS LeMoore, CA., 13 APR 76; To VA-97, USS Enterprise (CVN-65), 28 JUL 76; To VA-97, NAS LeMoore, CA., 17 JUN 77; To VA-97, USS Enterprise (CVN-65), 01 FEB 78; To VA-97, NAF Atsugi, JP., 26

JUN 78; To VA-97, USS Enterprise (CVN-65), 05 JUL 78; To VA-97, NAF Atsugi, JP., 30 AUG 78; To VA-97, USS Enterprise (CVN-65), 02 SEP 78; To VA-97, NAS LeMoore, CA., 30 OCT 78; To VA-97, NAS Jacksonville, FL., 21 DEC 78; To VA-97, NAS LeMoore, CA., 05 APR 79 ** Transferred to VA-94/CVW-15, NL/4XX, NAS LeMoore, CA., 09 APR 79; To VA-94, NAS Cubi Point, PI., 29 MAY 79; To VA-94, USS Kitty Hawk (CV-63), 06 JUN 79; To VA-94, NAS LeMoore, CA., 23 NOV 79; To VA-94, USS Kitty Hawk (CV-63), 28 JUL 80; To VA-94, NAS LeMoore, CA., 28 JUL 80; To VA-94, USS Kitty Hawk (CV-63), 11 SEP 80; To VA-94, NAS LeMoore, CA., 06 NOV 80 Transferred to VA-122/FRS, NJ/2XX, NAS LeMoore, CA., 12 DEC 81; To VA-122, NAS Jacksonville, FL., 02 AUG 81 ** Transferred to VA-25/CVW-2, NE/4XX, USS Ranger (CVA-61), 14 OCT 81; To VA-25, NAS LeMoore, CA., 29 OCT 81; To VA-25, USS Ranger (CV-61), 14 JAN 82; To VA-25, NAS LeMoore, CA., 14 JAN 82; To VA-25, USS Ranger (CV-61), 14 JAN 82; To VA-25, NAS LeMoore, CA., 14 JAN 82; USS Ranger (CV-61), 09 MAR 82; To VA-25, NAS Cubi Point, PI., 28 MAY 82; To VA-25, NAF Atsugi, JP., 20 JUL 82; To VA-25, NAS Cubi Point, PI., 23 JUL 82; To VA-25, NAF Atsugi, JP., 30 JUL 82 ** Transferred to VA-56/CVW-5, NF/4XX, NAF Atsugi, JP., 30 JUL 82 ** Transferred to VA-94/CVW-11, NH/ 4XX, USS Enterprise (CVN-65), 10 FEB 83; To VA-94, NAS Cubi Point, PI., 10 FEB 83; To VA-94, NAS LeMoore, CA., 16 APR 83 ** Transferred to VA-37/CVW-15, NL/3XX, USS Carl Vinson (CVN-70), 12 MAY 83 ** Transferred to VA-122/ FRS, NJ/2XX, NAS LeMoore, CA., 28 OCT 83; To VA-122, NAS Jacksonville, FL., 30 MAR 84 ** Transferred to VX-5, XE/XXX, NWC China Lake, CA., 27 JUN 84 ** Transferred to VA-122/FRS, NJ/2XX, NAS LeMoore, CA., 04 OCT 84 ** Transferred to VA-204/CVWR-20, AF/406, NAS New Orleans, LA., 19 MAR 86; VA-204, NAS Jacksonville, FL., 31 JUL 86; To VA-204, NAS New Orleans, LA., 08 AUG 86 thru 06 MAR 87 ** End of flight record card ** Transferred to AMARC, Davis Monthan AFB; Tucson, AZ., assigned park code 6A0337; 12 APR 90 ** 6849.1 flight hours ** TF41A402B engine S/N AE141625 ** Aircraft demilled, 13 JAN 05 ** Aircraft deleted from inventory and released to DRMO for disposition, 25 NOV 03 ** Engine records released to DRMO for disposition, 09 SEP 05.

E-103 156837 Navy acceptance from NPRO Rep. LTV, Dallas, TX., 07 JAN 70 ** Transferred to VA-122/ FRS, NJ/2XX, NAS LeMoore, CA., 09 JAN 70 ** Transferred to VA-147/CVW-9, NG/4XX, USS America (CVA-66), 18 MAR 70; To VA-147, NAS Fallon, NV., 11 JUN 70; To VA-147, NAS LeMoore, CA., 30 JUN 71; To VA-147, USS Constellation (CVA-64), 30 JUN 72 ~ S 1SO strike, 23 JAN 73 ** CDR T.R. Wilkinson was killed when he crashed on a routine training flight ** Final Navy A-7 loss of the Vietnam War.

E-104 156838 Navy acceptance from NPRO Rep. LTV, Dallas, TX., 23 FEB 70 ** Transferred to VA-195/CVW-11, NH/4XX, NAS LeMoore, CA., 26 FEB 70; To VA-195, USS Kitty Hawk (CVA-63), 01 MAY 70 ** Transferred to FS, NAS LeMoore, CA., 30 SEP 70 ** Transferred to VA-94/CVW-15, NL/4XX, 15 MAR 71; To VA-94, USS Coral Sea (CVA-43), 30 JUN 71 ** Transferred to VA-122/FRS, NJ/2XX, NAS LeMoore, CA., 25 JUL 72 ** Transferred to VA-147/CVW-9, NG/4XX, NAS LeMoore, CA., 26 MAY 76; To VA-147, USS Constellation (CV-64), 13 SEP 76; To VA-147, NAS LeMoore, CA., 22 OCT 76; To VA-147, USS Constellation (CV-64), 23 JUL 77; To VA-147, NAS LeMoore, CA., 19 NOV 77; To VA-147, NAS Jacksonville, FL., 17 JUL 78; To VA-147, USS Constellation (CV-64), 20 SEP 78; To VA-147, NAS Cubi Point, PI., 06 NOV 78; To VA-147, USS Constellation (CV-64), 31 DEC 78; To VA-147, To VA-147, NAF Atsugi, JP., 22 FEB 79; To VA-147, USS Constellation (CV-64), 24 FEB 79; To VA-147, NAS Jacksonville, FL., 15 JUN 79; To VA-147, USS Constellation (CV-64), 20 JUN 79; To VA-147, NAS Jacksonville, FL., 21 JUN 79; To VA-147, USS Constellation (CV-64), 07 SEP 79; To VA-147, NAS LeMoore, CA., 02 DEC 79; To VA-147, USS Constellation (CV-64), 13 DEC 79; To VA-147, NAS LeMoore, CA., 23 JAN 80; To VA-147, USS Constellation (CV-64), 26 FEB 80, To VA-147, NAS Cubi Point, PI., 18 APR 80; To VA-147, USS Constellation (CV-64), 18 SEP 80; To VA-147, NAS LeMoore, CA., 18 SEP 80; To VA-147, NAF El Centro, CA., 13 DEC 80 ** Transferred to VFA-125/FRS, NJ/5XX, 14 MAR 81; To VFA-125, NAS Jacksonville, FL., 18 OCT 81** Transferred to VA-195/CVW-11, NH/4XX, NAS LeMoore, CA., 10 DEC 81 ** Transferred to VA-94/CVW-9, NG/4XX, NAS LeMoore, CA., 10 DEC 81 ** Transferred to VA-94/CVW-11, NH/4XX, NAS LeMoore, CA., 16 MAR 82; To VA-94, USS Enterprise (CVN-65), 24 JUN 82; To VA-94, NAF Atsugi, JP., 05 APR 83; To VA-94, NAS LeMoore, CA., 15 APR 83 ** Transferred to VA-27/CVW-15, NL/4XX, NAS LeMoore, CA., 18 NOV 83; To VA-27, NAS Jacksonville, FL., 20 MAR 84; To VA-27, USS Carl Vinson (CVN-70), 24 MAR 84; To VA-27, NAS LeMoore, CA., 24 MAR 84; To VA-27, USS Carl Vinson (CVN-70), 24 MAR 84; To VA-27, NAS LeMoore, CA., 24 MAR 84; To VA-27, USS Carl Vinson (CVN-70), 24 MAR 84; To VA-27, NAS LeMoore, CA., 24 MAR 84 ** Transferred to NSWC, NAS Fallon, NV., 25 JUL 85 ~ S 1SO strike, 20 AUG 85 ** No data on strike.

E-105 156839 Navy acceptance from NPRO Rep. LTV, Dallas, TX., 23 JAN 70 ** Transferred to VA-25/CVW-2, NE/4XX, NAS LeMoore, CA., 23 JAN 70 ** Transferred to VA-97/CVW-14, NK/3XX, USS Enterprise (CVAN-65), 19 AUG 70 ~ S 1SO strike, 03 MAR 71 ** No data on strike.

E-106 156840 Navy acceptance from NPRO Rep. LTV, Dallas, TX., 23 DEC 69 ** Transferred to VA-122/FRS, NJ/2XX, 01 FEB 70 ** Transferred to VA-146/CVW-9, NG/3XX, USS Constellation (CV-64), 26 JUL 72; To VA-146, NAS Jacksonville, FL., 10 JAN 75; To VA-146, NAS LeMoore, CA., 04 MAR 75; To VA-146, NAS Fallon, NV., 27 MAY 75; To VA-146, NAS LeMoore, CA., 23 JUN 75; To VA-146, USS Constellation (CV-64), 06 AUG 76; To VA-146, NAS LeMoore, CA., 28 OCT 76; To VA-146, USS Constellation (CV-64), 28 OCT 76; To VA-146, NAS LeMoore, CA., 22 JAN 77; To VA-146, NAS Cubi Point, PI., 14 MAY 77; To VA-146, NAF Atsugi, JP., 19 JUL 77; To VA-146, Cubi Point, PI., 31 AUG 77; To VA-146, USS Constellation (CV-64), 31 AUG 77; To VA-146, NAS LeMoore, CA., 19 NOV 77; To VA-146, NAS Fallon, NV., 10 MAY 76; To VA-146, NAS LeMoore, CA., 20 JUN 78; To VA-146, USS Constellation (CV-64), 16 JUL 78; To VA-146, NAS LeMoore, CA., 24 AUG 78, To VA-146, USS Constellation (CV-64), 21 SEP 78; To VA-146, NAS Cubi Point, PI., 21 DEC 78; To VA-146, NAS Jacksonville, FL., 21 JUN 79; To NAS Cubi Point, PI., 29 AUG 79; To VA-146, USS Constellation (CV-64), 29 AUG 79 ** Transferred to VA-147/CVW-9, NG/4XX, USS Constellation (CV-64), 15 OCT 79; To VA-147, NAS LeMoore, CA., 02 DEC 79; To VA-147, USS Constellation (CV-64), 13 DEC 79; To VA-147, NAS LeMoore, CA., 23 JAN 80; To VA-147, USS Constellation (CV-64), 26 FEB 80; To VA-147, NAS Cubi Point, PI., 18 APR 80; To VA-147, USS Constellation (CV-64), 18 SEP 80; To VA-147, NAS LeMoore, CA., 18 SEP 80; To VA-147, NAS El Centro, CA., 19 NOV 80; To VA-147, USS Constellation (CV-64), 24 MAY 81; To VA-147, NAS LeMoore, CA., 12 JUN 81; To VA-147, USS Constellation (CV-64), 07 JUL 81; To VA-147, NAS LeMoore, CA., 06 AUG 81; To VA-147, NAS Jacksonville, FL., 28 AUG 81; To VA-147, USS Constellation (CV-64), 10 OCT 81; To VA-147, NAS Cubi Point, PI., 19 OCT 81; To VA-147, USS Constellation (CV-64), 19 OCT 81; To VA-147, NAS LeMoore, CA., 19 OCT 81; To VA-147, NAS Jacksonville, FL., 23 OCT 83 ** Transferred to VA-27/CVW-15, NL/4XX, NAS LeMoore, CA., 04 FEB 84; To VA-27, USS Carl Vinson (CVN-70), 04 FEB 84; To VA-27, NAS LeMoore, CA., 04 FEB 84; To VA-27, USS Carl Vinson (CVN-70), 04 FEB 84; To VA-27, NAS LeMoore, CA., 04 FEB 84; To VA-27, USS Carl Vinson (CVN-70), 04 FEB 84; To VA-27, NAS LeMoore, CA., 07 MAY 85 ** Transferred to VA-174/FRS, AD/4XX, NAS Cecil Field, FL., 30 AUG 85; To VA-174, NAS Jacksonville, FL., 27 FEB 86; To VA-174, NAS Cecil Field, FL., 07 MAR 86; To VA-174, NAS Jacksonville, FL., 11 APR 86 ** Transferred to VA-204/CVWR-20, AF/410, NAS Jacksonville, FL., 14 APR 86; To VA-204, NAS New Orleans, LA., 08 AUG 86 thru 01 MAY 87 ** End of flight record card **** Transferred to AMARC, Davis Monthan AFB; Tucson, AZ., assigned park code 6A0276; 21 JUN 88 ** 7549.3 flight hours ** TF41A402D engine S/N 141379 ** Aircraft deleted from inventory and released to DRMO for disposition, 17 OCT 05 ** Engine released to DRMO for disposition, 17 NOV 05.

E-157 156841 Navy acceptance from NPRO Rep. LTV, Dallas, TX., 26 FEB 70 ** Transferred to VA-122/FRS, NJ/2XX, NAS LeMoore, CA., 28 FEB 70 ** Transferred to VA-147/CVW-9, NG/4XX, USS Constellation (CV-64), 15 NOV 72 ** Transferred to VA-122/FRS, NJ/201, NAS LeMoore, CA., 14 DEC·72; To VA-122, CRAA, NAS LeMoore, CA., 21 DEC 72, To VA-122, NAS LeMoore, CA., 03 DEC 73; To VA-122, NAS Jacksonville, FL., 06 APR 76; To VA-122, NAS LeMoore, CA., 13 APR 76 ** Transferred to VA-147/CVW-9, NG/4XX, NAS LeMoore, CA., 19 OCT 81; To VA-147/CVW-9, NE/3XX, NAS Jacksonville, FL., 23 OCT 83 ** Transferred to VA-27/CVW-15, NL/4XX, NAS LeMoore, CA., 04 FEB 84; To VA-27, USS Carl Vinson (CVN-70), 04 FEB 84; To VA-27, NAS LeMoore, CA., 04 FEB 84; To VA-27, USS Carl Vinson (CVN-70), 04 FEB 84; NAS LeMoore, CA., 04 FEB 84 ** Transferred to VA-122/FRS, NJ/201, NAS LeMoore, CA., 13 APR 76, Painted in bicentenial scheme, 04 JUL 76; To VA-122, NAS Jacksonville, FL., 21 FEB 78; To VA-122, NAS LeMoore, CA., 04 APR 78; To VA-122, NAS Jacksonville, FL., 03 JUN 80 ** Transferred to VA-195/CVW-11, NH/4XX, NAS LeMoore, CA., 13 AUG 80; To VA-195, NAS Fallon, NV., 19 OCT 80; To VA-195, NAS LeMoore, CA., 07 NOV 80; To VA-195, USS America (CV-66), 25 JAN 81; To VA-195, NAS LeMoore, CA., 09 APR 81; To VA-195, NAS Jacksonville, FL., 16 SEP 82; To VA-195, NAS LeMoore, CA., 24 OCT 82; To VA-195/CVW-9, NG/4XX, USS Ranger (CV-61), 10 MAY 83 ** Transferred to VA-27/CVW-15, NL/4XX, NAS LeMoore, CA., 26 SEP 83 ** Transferred to VA-147/CVW-9, NE/3XX, NAS LeMoore, CA., 30 DEC 83; To VA-147, USS Kitty Hawk (CV-63), 30 DEC 83 ** Transferred to VA-27/CVW-15, NL/4XX, NAS LeMoore, CA., 09 JAN 84 ** Transferred to VA-122/FRS, NJ/236, NAS LeMoore, CA., 14 FEB 84 ~ S 1SO strike, 04 APR 84 ** Pilot killed when aircraft ran off the flight deck due to brake failure on USS Lexington (AVT-16).

E-107 156842 Navy acceptance from NPRO Rep. LTV, Dallas, TX., 26 FEB 70 ** Transferred to VA-25/CVW-16, AH/5XX, NAS LeMoore, CA., 10 FEB 70 ** Transferred to VA-97/CVW-14, NK/311, USS Enterprise (CVAN-65), 28 JUL 70; To VA-97, NAS LeMoore, CA., 22 MAR 71 ** Transferred to VA-122/FRS, NJ/2XX, NAS LeMoore, CA., 26 JUN 72 ** Transferred to VA-192/CVW-11, NH/3XX, NAS LeMoore, CA., 18 OCT 72; To VA-192, USS Kitty Hawk (CV-63), 29 JUN 73; To VA-192, NAS LeMoore, CA., 17 AUG 74; To VA-192, NAS Jacksonville, FL., 16 JAN 75; To VA-192, NAS LeMoore, CA., 05 MAR 75 ** Transferred to VA-122/FRS, NJ/2XX, NAS LeMoore, CA., 23 JUN 75 ** Transferred to VA-97/CVW-14, NK/3XX, NAS LeMoore, CA., 16 JUL 75; To VA-97, NAS Fallon, NV., 30 NOV 75; To VA-97, NAS LeMoore, CA., 20 FEB 76; To VA-97, USS Enterprise (CVN-65), 20 FEB 76; To VA-97, NAS LeMoore, CA., 27 APR 76; To VA-97, USS Enterprise (CVN-65), 28 JUL 76; To VA-97, NAS LeMoore, CA., 06 JUN 77; To VA-97, NAS Jacksonville, FL., 16 NOV 77; To VA-97, NAS LeMoore, CA., 03 JAN 78; To VA-97, USS Enterprise (CVN-65), 10 MAR 78; To VA-97, NAF Atsugi, JP., 30 JUN 78; To VA-97, USS Enterprise (CVN-65), 05 JUL 78; To VA-97, NAS LeMoore, CA., 30 OCT 78; To VA-97, NAS Jacksonville, FL., 14 MAY 79 ** Transferred to VA-37/CVW-3, AC/3XX, NAS Cecil Field, FL., 03 JUL 79; To VA-37, MCAS Yuma, AZ., 03 JUL 79; To VA-37, NAS Cecil Field, FL., 03 JUL 79; To VA-37, USS Saratoga (CV-60), 03 JUL 79; To VA-37, NAS Cecil Field, FL., 03 JUL 79; To VA-37, USS Saratoga (CV-60), 03 JUL 79; To VA-37, NAS Cecil Field, FL., 03 JUL 79; To VA-37, NAS Fallon, NV., 25 OCT 80; To VA-37, NAS Cecil Field, FL., 25 OCT 80 ** Transferred to VA-46/CVW-1, AB/3XX, NAS Cecil Field, FL., 7 JUL 81; To VA-46, NAS Jacksonville, FL., 23 DEC 81; To VA-46, NAS Cecil Field, FL., 12 FEB 82 ~ S 1SO strike, 18 APR 82 ** Pilot lost power on approach to NAS Cecil Field, FL., Ejected safely, Aircraft crashed in residential area, casualties unknown.

E-109 156843 Navy acceptance from NPRO Rep. LTV Dallas, TX., 19 JAN 70 ** Transferred to VA-25/CVW-2, NE/4XX, NAS LeMoore, CA., 20 JAN 70 ** Transferred to VA-97/CVW-14, NK/3XX, USS Enterprise (CVAN-65), 04 AUG 70; To VA-97, NAS LeMoore, CA., 26 JUN 71 ~ S-1SO strike, 30 SEP 71 ** No data on strike.

E-110 156844 Navy acceptance from NPRO Rep. LTV, Dallas, TX., 19 DEC 69 ** Transferred to VA-174/FRS, AD/4XX, NAS Cecil field, FL., 04 JUN 70 ** Transferred to VA-122/FRS, NAS LeMoore, CA., 06 MAY 71; To VA-122, CRAA, NAS LeMoore, CA., 14 NOV 71; To VA-122, NAS LeMoore, CA., 17 NOV 71; To VA-122, CRAA, NAS LeMoore, CA., 22 NOV 71 ** Transferred to VA-147/CVW-9, NG/4XX, NAS LKeMoore, CA., 04 JUN 72 ** Transferred to VA-22/CVW-15, NL/3XX, USS Coral Sea (CVA-43), 16 JUN 72; To VA-22, NAS LeMoore, CA., 02 JUN 73; To VA-22, USS Coral Sea (CVA-43), 12 NOV 74 ** Transferred to VA-122/FRS, NJ/2XX, NAS LeMoore, CA., 26 NOV 74 ** Transferred to NARF, NAS Jacksonville, FL., 07 DEC 74 ** Transferred to VA-25/CVW-2, NE/4XX, NAS LeMoore, CA., 28 APR 75; To VA-25, NAS Fallon, NV., 13 JUL 75; To VA-25, USS Ranger (CV-61), 14 AUG 75; To VA-25, NAS LeMoore, CA., 23 SEP 75; To VA-25, NAS Fallon, NV., 30 APR 76 ** Transferred to VA-22/CVW-15, NL/3XX, NAS LeMoore, Ca., 03 MAY 76; To VA-22, USS Coral Sea (CV-43), 20 SEP 77; To VA-22, NAS LeMoore, CA., 19 OCT 77; To VA-22, NAS Jacksonville, FL., 28 FEB 78; To VA-22, NAS LeMoore, CA., 06 APR 78; To VA-22, NAS Kingsville, TX., 23 AUG 78; To VA-22, NAS LeMoore, CA., 23 AUG 78 ** Transferred to VA-27/CVW-14, NK/4XX, NAS El Centro, CA., 06 APR 79; To VA-27, USS Coral Sea (CV-43), 09 MAY 79 ** Transferred to VA-12/CVW-7, AG/4XX, NAS Cecil Field, FL., 24 NOV 79; To VA-12, USS Dwight D. Eisenhower (CVN-69), 24 NOV 79; To VA-12, NAS Cecil Field, FL., 31 JAN 80; To VA-12, USS Dwight D. Eisenhower (CVN-69), 31 JAN 80 ~ S 1SO strike, 05 SEP 81 ** No data on strike.

E-111 156845 Navy acceptance from NPRO Rep. LTV, Dallas, TX., 26 JAN 70 ** Transferred to VA-25/CVW-2, NE/4XX, NAS LeMoore, CA., 01 FEB 70 ** Transferred to VA-97/CVW-14, NK/3XX, USS Enterprise (CVAN-65), 31 JUL 70; To VA-97, NAS LeMoore, CA., 26 JUN 71; To VA-97, USS Enterprise (CVAN-65), 01 FEB 75 ** To VA-97, NAS LeMoore, CA., 20 MAY 75; To VA-97, NAS Jacksonville, FL., 18 SEP 75; To VA-97, NAS LeMoore, CA., 18 DEC 75; To VA-97, USS Enterprise (CVN-65), 20 FEB 76; To VA-97, NAS LeMoore, CA., 30 APR 76; To VA-97, USS Enterprise (CVN-65), 28 JUL 76; To VA-97, NAS LeMoore, CA., 19 JUN 77; To VA-97, USS Enterprise (CVN-65), 19 AUG 77; To VA-97, NAS LeMoore, CA., 01 SEP 77; To VA-97, USS Enterprise (CVN-65), 10 MAR 78; To VA-97, NAF Atsugi, JP., 28 JUN 78; To VA-97, USS Enterprise (CVN-65), 05 JUL 78; To VA-97, NAS LeMoore, CA., 30 OCT 78; To VA-97, NAS Jacksonville, FL., 21 JAN 79; VA-97, NAS LeMoore, CA., 05 JUL 79; To VA-97, USS Coral Sea (CV-43), 11 OCT 79 ** Transferred to VA-195/CVN-11, NH/4XX, NAS LeMoore, CA., 09 NOV 79; To VA-195, NAS Alameda, CA., 28 APR 80; To VA-195, NAS LeMoore, CA., 29 APR 80; To VA-195, NAS Fallon, NV., 19 OCT 80; To VA-195, NAS LeMoore, CA., 07 NOV 80; To VA-195, USS America (CV-66), 07 NOV 80 ** Transferred to VA-147/CVW-9, NG/4XX, NAS LeMoore, CA., 08 JAN 81; To VA-147, NAF El Centro, CA., 02 APR 81; To VA-147, USS Constellation (CV-64), 30 APR 81; To VA-147, NAS LeMoore, CA., 08 JUN 81; To VA-147, NAS Jacksonville, FL., 09 JUN 81; To VA-147, NAS LeMoore, CA., 01 AUG 81; To VA-147, USS Constellation (CV-64), 19 OCT 81; To VA-147, NAS Cubi Point, PI., 19 OCT 81; To VA-147. USS Constellation (CV-64), 08 JAN 82; To VA-147, NAS LeMoore, CA., 08 JAN 82; To VA-147, NAS Alameda, CA., 14 MAR 83; To VA-147, NAS LeMoore, CA., 15 MAR 83; To VA-147, NAS Jacksonville, FL., 29 JUL 83; To VA-147, NAS LeMoore, CA., 19 NOV 83; To VA-147, USS Kitty Hawk (CV-63), 19 NOV 83; To VA-147, NAS LeMoore, CA., 25 SEP 84; To VA-147, USS Kitty Hawk (CV-63), 09 MAY 85; To VA-147, NAS LeMoore, CA., 10 JUL 86; To VA-147, NAS Jacksonville, FL., 14 JUL 86 ** Transferred to VA-205/CVWR-20, AF/5XX, NAS Jacksonville, FL., 14 JUL 86 ** To VA-204/CVWR-20, AF/4XX, NAS Jacksonville, FL., 02 DEC 86; To VA-204, NAS New Orleans, LA., 04 DEC 86 ** Transferred to VA-205/CVWR-20, AF/5XX, NAS Atlanta, GA., 10 DEC 86 ** To VA-204/CVWR-20, AF/405, NAS New Orleans, LA., 11 DEC 86 thru 01 APR 87 ** End of flight record card ** Transferred to AMARC, Davis Monthan AFB, Tucson, AZ., assigned park code 6A0278; 7 JUN 88 ** 6271.3 flight hours ** TF41A402D engine S/N 141232 ** Engine records released to DRMO for disposition, 05 OCT 05 ** Aircraft deleted from inventory and released to DRMO for disposition, 05 AUG 05.

E-112 156846 Navy acceptance from NPRO Rep. LTV, Dallas, TX. 14 JAN 70 ** Transferred to VA-25/CVW-2, NE/4XX, NAS LeMoore, CA., 17 JAN 70 ** Transferred to VA-97/CVW-14, NK/3XX, CA., USS Enterprise (CVAN-65), 09 JUL 70; To VA-97, NAS LeMoore, CA., 26 JUN 71 ** Transferred to VA-22/CVW-15, NL/3XX, USS Coral Sea (CVA-43), 16 SEP 72; To VA-22, NAS LeMoore, CA., 27 MAY 73 ~ S 1SO strike, 02 SEP 73 ** No data on strike.

E-113 156847 Navy acceptance from NPRO Rep. LTV, Dallas, TX., 24 FEB 70 ** Transferred to VA-192/CVW-11, NH/3XX, NAS LeMoore, CA., 26 FEB 70; To VA-192, USS Kitty Hawk (CVA-63), 22 JUN 70 ** Transferred to FS, NAS LeMoore, CA., 30 SEP 70 ** Transferred to VA-22/CVW-15, NL/3XX, NAS LeMoore, CA., 02 MAR 71; To VA-22, USS Coral Sea (CVA-43), 02 JUN 71 ** Transferred to VA-122/FRS, NJ/2XX, NAS LeMoore, CA., 05 NOV 71 ** Transferred to VA-94/CVW-15, NL/407, USS Coral Sea (CVA-43), 22 NOV 72; To VA-94, NAS LeMoore, CA., 27 JUN 73; To VA-94, USS Coral Sea (CVA-43), 03 DEC 74; To VA-94, NAS Fallon, NV., 01 SEP 75; To VA-94, NAS LeMoore, CA., 21 OCT 75; To VA-94, NAS Jacksonville, FL., 19 JAN 76 ** Transferred to VA-174/FRS, AD/4XX, NAS Cecil Field, FL., 24 MAR 76 ** Transferred to VA-83/CVW-17, AA/3XX, NAS Cecil Field, FL., 30 JUN 77; To VA-83, USS Forrestal (CV-59), 20 JUL 77; To VA-83, NAS Cecil Field, FL., 20 JUL 77; To VA-83, USS Forrestal (CV-59), 20 JUL 77; To VA-83, NAS Jacksonville, FL., 08 FEB 78; To VA-83, USS Forrestal (CV-59), 13 MAR 78; To VA-83, NAS Cecil Field, FL., 13 MAR 78; To VA-83, USS Forrestal (CV-59), 14 MAR 79; To VA-83, NAS Cecil Field, FL., 14 MAR 79; To VA-83, USS Forrestal (CV-59), 14 MAR 79; To VA-83, NAS Cecil Field, FL., 20 MAR 80; To VA-83, USS Forrestal (CV-59), 02 JUN 80 ** Transferred to VA-86/CVW-8, AJ/4XX, USS Nimitz (CVN-68), 06 OCT 80; To VA-86, NAS Cecil Field, FL., 01 DEC 80; To VA-86, USS Nimitz (CVN-68), 01 DEC 80; To VA-86, NAS Cecil Field, FL., 01 DEC 80; To VA-86, USS Nimitz (CVN-68), 01 DEC 80; To VA-86, NAS Cecil Field, FL., 01 DEC 80 ** Transferred to VA-82/CVW-8, AJ/3XX, USS Carl Vinson (CVN-70), 22 MAR 82; To VA-82, NAS Cecil Field, FL., 22 MAR 82; To VA-82, USS Nimitz (CVN-68), 22 MAR 82; To VA-82, NAS Cecil Field, FL., 22 MAR 82; To VA-82, USS Nimitz (CVN-68), 22 MAR 82; To VA-82, NAS Cecil Field, FL., 22 MAR 82; To VA-82, NAS Jacksonville, FL., 03 JUN 83; To VA-82, NAS Cecil Field, FL., 04 JUN 83; To VA-82, NAS Jacksonville, FL., 01 AUG 83; To VA-82, NAS Cecil Field, FL., 02 AUG 83 ** Transferred to VA-174/FRS, AD/4XX, NAS Cecil Field, FL., 28 JUN 84; To VA-174, NAS Jacksonville, FL., 08 MAR 85 ** Transferred to VA-81/CVW-17, AA/400, NAS Cecil Field, FL., 08 MAR 85; To VA-81, USS Saratoha (CV-60), 09 APR 85; To VA-81, NAS Cecil Field, FL., 09 APR 85; To VA-81, USS Saratoga (CV-60), 09 APR 85; To VA-81, NAS Cecil Field, FL., 09 APR 85; To VA-81, USS Saratoga (CV-60),26 SEP 86; To VA-81, NAS Cecil Field, FL., 21 OCT 86 ** Transferred to AMARC, Davis Monthan AFB; Tucson, AZ., assigned park code 6A0214; 14 JAN 87 ** 5838.1 flight hours ** TF41A2B engine S/N 141945 ** Storage location 210534 ** End of flight record card ** ** Ejection Seat S/N 0269 removed, FEB 89 ** Under GSA control ** At AMARG , Davis Monthan AFB; Tucson, AZ., 15 JUN 07.

E-114 156848 Navy acceptance from NPRO Rep. LTV, Dallas, TX., 31 JAN 70 ** Transferred to VA-122/FRS, NJ/2XX, NAS LeMoore, CA., 04 FEB 70 ** Transferred to VA-94/CVW-15, NL/405, USS Coral Sea (CVA-43), 05 SEP 72; To VA-94, NAS LeMoore, CA., 25 JUN 73; To VA-94 ,USS Coral Sea (CVA-43), 24 MAY 75; To VA-94, NAS LeMoore, CA., 26 JUL 75; To VA-94, NAS Fallon, NV., 01 SEP 75; To VA-94, NAS LeMoore, CA., 01 NOV 75; To VA-94, NAS Jacksonville, FL., 30 NOV 75; To VA-94, NAS LeMoore, CA., 08 MAR 76; To VA-94, NAS Fallon, NV., 30 APR 76; To VA-94, NAS LeMoore, CA., 30 APR 76; To VA-94, USS Coral Sea (CV-43), 09 DEC 76; To VA-94, NAS LeMoore, CA., 08 JAN 77; To VA-94, USS Coral Sea (CV-43), 31 AUG 77; To VA-94, NAS LeMoore, CA., 26 OCT 77; To VA-94, NAS Fallon, NV., 09 MAY 78; To VA-94, NAS Alameda, CA., 11 MAY 78; To VA-94, NAS LeMoore, CA., 15 MAY 78; To VA-94, NAS Alameda, CA., 28 AUG 78; To VA-94, NAS LeMoore, CA., 29 AUG 78; To VA-94, NAS Jacksonville, FL., 16 SEP 78; To VA-94, NAS LeMoore, CA., 02 NOV 78; To VA-94, NAS

Cubi Point, PI., 29 MAY 79; To VA-94, USS Kitty Hawk (CV-63), 15 NOV 79; To VA-94, NAS LeMoore, CA., 15 NOV 79; To VA-94, USS Kitty Hawk (CV-63), 27 JUN 80; To VA-94, NAS LeMoore, CA., 27 JUN 80; To VA-94, USS Kitty Hawk (CV-63), 27 JUN 80; To VA-94, NAS LeMoore, CA., 12 NOV 80; To VA-94, NAS Jacksonville, FL., 13 DEC 80; To VA-94, NAS LeMoore, CA., 19 FEB 81; To VA-94, USS Kitty Hawk (CV-63), 19 FEB 81; To VA-94, NAS Cubi Point, PI., 13 MAY 81; To VA-94, USS Kitty Hawk (CV-63), 24 OCT 81; To VA-94, NAS LeMoore, CA., 24 OCT 81; To VA-94/CVW-11, NH/4XX, USS Enterprise (CVN-65), 09 JUN 82 ** Transferred to VA-56/CVW-5, NF/4XX, NAF Atsugi, JP., 10 FEB 83 ** Transferred to VA-22/CVW-11, NH/302, USS Enterprise (CVN-65), 11 NOV 84 ~ S 1SO strike, 23 NOV 84 ** Crashed into the sea on approach to USS Enterprise (CVN-65), Pilot ejected safely.

E-115 156849 Navy acceptance from NPRO Rep. LTV, Dallas, TX., 31 JAN 70 ** Transferred to VA-122/FRS, NJ/2XX, NAS LeMoore, CA., 01 FEB 70; To VA-122, COSA, NAS LeMoore, CA., 23 JUN 70 ** Transferred to VA-147/CVW-9 NG/4XX, NAS Fallon, NV., 13 JUL 70; Transferred to VA-146/CVW-9, NG/3XX, NAS Fallon, NV., 10 OCT 70; To VA-146, NAS LeMoore, CA., 26 MAY 71 ~ S 1SO strike, 22 JAN72 ** No data on crash.

E-116 156850 Navy acceptance from NPRO Rep. LTV, Dallas, TX., 31 JAN 70 ** Transferred to VA-122/FRS, NJ/2XX, NAS LeMoore, CA., 04 FEB 70 ~ S 1SO strike, 10 FEB 72 ** No data on strike.

E-117 156851 Navy acceptance from NPRO Rep. LTV, Dallas, TX., 04 MAR 70 ** Transferred to VA-192/CVW-11, NH/3XX, NAS LeMoore, CA., 06 MAR 70; To VA-192, USS Kitty Hawk (CVA-63), 22 MAY 70 ** Transferred to FS, NAS LeMoore, CA., 30 SEP 70 ** Transferred to VA-22/CVW-11, NH/3XX, NAS LeMoore, CA., 01 MAR 71; To VA-22, USS Coral Sea (CVA-43), 21 JUN 71 ** Transferred to NARF, NAS Alameda, CA., 17 JUL 72 ** Transferred to NARF, NAS Jacksonville, FL., 23 JAN 73 ** Transferred to VA-174/FRS, AD/4XX, NAS Cecil Field, FL., 03 AUG 73; To VA-174, NAS Jacksonville, FL., 01 JUL 75; To VA-174, NAS Cecil Field, FL., 12 APR 76; To VA-174, NAS Jacksonville, FL., 15 MAR 78; To VA-174, NAS Cecil Field, FL., 20 APR 78 ** Transferred to NATC, NAS Patuxent River, MD., for RDT & E, 22 NOV 78; To NATC, NAS Jacksonville, Fl., 14 AUG 80; To NATC, NAS Patuxent River, MD., 14 AUG 80; To NATC, NAS Jacksonville, Fl., 15 AUG 80; To NATC, NAS Patuxent River, MD., 07 OCT 80 ** Transferred to NATC, FS, NAS Patuxent River, MD., 21 NOV 85 ** Transferred to NATC, NAS Patuxent River, MD., for RDT & E, 04 AUG 86 thru 28 SEP 87 ** End of flight record card ** Transferred to AMARC, Davis Monthan AFB; Tucson, AZ., assigned park code 6A0282, 13 JUL 88 ** 3258.3 flight hours ** TF41A402D engine S/N 141338 ** Aircraft released from storage and prepared for overland and above deck shipment to Greece, 19 AUG 94 ** Transferred to the Helenic Air force (Greece).

E-118 156852 Navy acceptance from NPRO Rep. LTV, Dallas, TX., 10 FEB 70 ** Transferred to VA-113/CVW-3, AC/4XX, NAS LeMoore, CA., 29 APR 70 ** Transferred to VA-192/CVW-11, NH/3XX, NAS LeMoore, CA., 18 MAY 70; To VA-192, USS Kitty Hawk (CVA-63), 19 JUN 70 ** Transferred to FS, NAS LeMoore, CA., 14 SEP 70 ** Transferred to VA-22/ CVW-15, NL/306, NAS LeMoore, CA., 08 MAR 71; To VA-22, USS Coral Sea (CVA-43), 28 JUN 71; To VA-22, NAS LeMoore, CA., 29 JUN 73; To VA-22, USS Coral Sea (CVA-43), 29 NOV 74; To VA-22, NAS LeMoore, CA., 07 JUL 75; To VA-22, NAS Fallon, NV., 01 SEP 75; To VA-22, NAS LeMoore, CA., 28 SEP 75; To VA-22, NAS Jacksonville, FL., 28 MAR 76; To VA-22, NAS Fallon, NV., 31 MAR 76; To VA-22, NAS Jacksonville, FL., 07 MAY 76 ** Transferred to VA-174/FRS, AD/4XX, NAS Cecil Field, FL., 21 MAY 76 ** Transferred to VA-105/CVW-3, AC/4XX, USS Saratoga (CV-60), 27 JUN 77; To VA-105, NAS Cecil Field, FL., 16 JUL 77; To VA-105, USS Saratoga (CV-60), 21 MAY 78; To VA-105, NAS Cecil Field, FL., 17 OCT 78; To VA-105, MCAS Yuma, AZ., 17 OCT 78; To VA-105, NAS Cecil Field, FL., 17 OCT 78; To VA-105, USS Saratoga (CV-60), 17 OCT 78; To VA-105, NAS Cecil Field, FL., 17 OCT 78; To VA-105,

USS Saratoga (CV-60), 20 MAR 80; To VA-105, NAS Cecil Field, FL., 31 DEC 80; To VA-105, NAS Jacksonville, FL., 01 APR 81 ** Transferred to VA-27/CVW-14, NK/4XX, NAS LeMoore, CA., 20 APR 81; To VA-27, USS Coral Sea (CV-43), 21 APR 81; To VA-27, NAS LeMoore, CA., 11 JUN 81; To VA-27, USS Coral Sea (CV-43), 20 AUG 81; To VA-27, NAF Atsugi, JP., 07 JAN 82; To VA-27, USS Coral Sea (CV-43), 19 JAN 82; To VA-27, NAS LeMoore, CA., 22 MAR 82 ** Transferred to VA-147/CVW-9, NG/4XX, NAS LeMoore, CA., 10 JAN 83; To VA-147, NAS Jacksonville, FL., 12 JUL 83; To VA-147, NAS LeMoore, CA., 13 SEP 83; To VA-147, USS Kitty Hawk (CV-63), 13 SEP 83; To VA-147, NAS LeMoore, CA., 15 AUG 84; To VA-147, USS Kitty Hawk (CV-63), 16 MAY 85; To VA-147, NAF Atsugi, JP., 17 SEP 85; To VA-147, USS Kitty Hawk (CV-63), 26 SEP 85; To VA-147, NAS LeMoore, CA., 22 SEP 86 ** Transferred to VA-203/CVWR-20, AF/3XX, NAS Jacksonville, FL., 22 SEP 86; To VA-203, NAS Pensacola, FL., 22 SEP 86; To VA-203, NAS Jacksonville, FL., 01 DEC 86; To VA-203, NAS Pensacola, FL., 18 DEC 86 ** Transferred to VA-205/CVWR-20, AF/5XX, NAS Atlanta, GA., 23 SEP 87 ** End of flight record card ** Transferred to AMARC, Davis Monthan AFB; Tucson, AZ., assigned park code 6A0346; 19 APR 90 ** 6343.9 flight hours ** TF41A402D engine S/N AE141383 ** Project changed per FSO letter, 06 APR 04 ** Engine released to DRMO, Davis Monthan AFB; Tucson, AZ., for disposition, 03 FEB 06.

E-119 156853 Navy acceptance from NPRO Rep. LTV, Dallas, TX., 23 JAN 70 ** Transferred to VA-122/FRS, NJ/2XX, NAS LeMoore, CA. 24 JAN 70 ~ S 1SO strike, 14 OCT 71 ** No data on strike.

E-120 156854 Navy acceptance from NPRO Rep. LTV, Dallas, TX., 26 JAN 70 ** Transferred to VA-122/FRS, NJ/2XX, NAS LeMoore, CA., 29 JAN 70 ~ S 1SO strike, 17 MAR 71 ** No data on strike.

E-121 156855 Navy acceptance from NPRO Rep. LTV, Dallas, TX., 17 MAR 70 ** Transferred to VA-12/CVW-7, AG/4XX, USS Independence (CVA-62), 03 OCT 72; To VA-12, NAS Cecil Field, FL., 27 FEB 73; To VA-12, USS Independence (CV-62), 18 FEB 74; To VA-12 NAS Cecil Field, FL., 10 DEC 74; To VA-12, NAS Jacksonville, FL., 23 JAN 75; To VA-12, NAS Cecil Field, FL., 12 FEB 75; To VA-12, NAS Fallon, NV., 24 FEB 75; To VA-12, NAS Cecil Field, FL., 01 JUL 75; To VA-12, USS Independence (CV-62), 01 OCT 75; To VA-12 NAS Cecil Field, FL., 07 MAY 76; To VA-12, NAS Fallon, NV., 01 AUG 76; To VA-12, USS Independence (CV-62), 01 NOV 76; To VA-12, NAS Cecil Field, FL., 01 NOV 76; To VA-12, USS Independence (CV-62), 01 NOV 76; To VA-12, NAS Cecil Field, FL., 01 FEB 77; To VA-12, NAS Cecil Field, FL., 01 MAY 77; To VA-12, USS Independence (CV-62), 09 AUG 77; To VA-12, NAS Cecil Field, FL., 09 AUG 77; To VA-12, USS Dwight D. Eisenhower (CVN-69), 09 AUG 77; To VA-12, NAS Cecil Field, FL., 15 MAY 78; To VA-12, USS Dwight D. Eisenhower (CVN-69), 29 JUN 78; To VA-12, NAS Cecil Field, FL., 11 SEP 78; To VA-12, USS Dwight D. Eisenhower (CVN-69), 11 SEP 78; To VA-12, NAS Cecil Field, FL., 11 SEP 78; To VA-12, USS Dwight D. Eisenhower (CVN-69), 11 SEP 78; To VA-12, NAS Cecil Field, FL., 12 DEC 79; To VA-12, USS Dwight D. Eisenhower (CVN-69), 12 DEC 79; To VA-12, NAS Cecil Field, FL., 29 AUG 80; To VA-12, NAS Jacksonville, FL., 10 MAR 81; To VA-12, NAS Cecil Field, FL., 12 MAY 81; To VA-12, USS Dwight D. Eisenhower (CVN-69), 12 MAY 81; To VA-12, NAS Cecil Field, FL., 12 MAY 81; To VA-12, USS Dwight D. Eisenhower (CVN-69), 12 MAY 81 ~ S 1SO strike, 04 MAR 82 ** No data on strike.

E-122 156856 Navy acceptance from NPRO Rep. LTV, Dallas, TX., 31 JAN 70 ** Transferred to VA-25/CVW-2, NE/4XX, NAS LeMoore, CA., 01 FEB 70 ** Transferred to VA-97/CVW-14, NK/3XX, USS Enterprise (CVAN-65), 01 JUL 70; To VA-97, NAS LeMoore, CA., 26 JUN 71; To VA-97, USS Enterprise (CVAN-65), 01 MAY 75; To VA-97, NAS LeMoore, CA., 20 MAY 75; To VA-95, NAS Jacksonville, FL., 14 SEP 75; To VA-97, NAS LeMoore, CA., 02 NOV 75; To VA-97, NAS Fallon, NV., 30 NOV 75; To VA-97, NAS LeMoore, CA., 20 FEB 76; To VA-97, USS Enterprise (CVN-65), 20 FEB 76; To VA-97, NAS LeMoore, CA., 29 APR 76; To VA-97, USS Enterprise (CVN-65), 28 JUL 76; To VA-97, NAS LeMoore, CA., 19 JUN 77; To VA-97, USS Enterprise (CVN-65), 23 AUG 77; To VA-97, NAS LeMoore, CA., 01 SEP 77; To VA-97, USS Enterprise (CVN-65), 10 MAR 78; To VA-97, NAF Atsugi, JP., 26 JUN 78; To VA-97, USS Enterprise (CVN-65), 05 JUL 78; To VA-97, NAS LeMoore, CA., 30 OCT 78; To VA-97, NAS Jacksonville, FL., 27 NOV 78; To VA-97, NAS LeMoore, CA., 24 FEB 79; To VA-97, USS Coral Sea (CV-43), 16 OCT 79 ** Transferred to VA-192/CVW-11, NH/3XX, NAS LeMoore, CA., 27 FEB 80 ** To VA-122/FRS, NJ/2XX, NAS LeMoore, CA., 26 SEP 80; To VA-122, NAS Jacksonville, FL., 29 APR 81; To VA-122, NAS LeMoore, CA., 06 JUN 81 ** Transferred to VA-25/CVW-2, NE/4XX, NAS LeMoore, CA., 18 JUN 81; To VA-25, NAS Fallon, NV., 14 SEP 81; To VA-25, USS Ranger (CV-61), 16 OCT 81; To VA-25, NAS LeMoore, CA., 25 OCT 81; To VA-25, USS Ranger (CV-61), 14 JAN 82; To VA-25, NAS LeMoore, CA., 14 JAN 82; To VA-25, USS Ranger (CV-61), 14 JAN 82; To VA-25, NAS Cubi Point, PI., 14 JAN 82 ** Transferred to VA-56/CVW-5, NF/4XX, NAF Atsugi, JP., 21 AUG 82 ** Transferred to VA-22/CVW-11, NH/3XX, USS Enterprise (CVN-65), 21 NOV 84; To VA-22, NAS LeMoore, CA., 21 NOV 84; To VA-22, NAS Fallon, NV., 01 MAR 85; To VA-22, NAS LeMoore, CA., 03 APR 85; To VA-22, NAS Jacksonville, FL., 23 OCT 85 ** Transferred to VA-205/CVWR-20, AF/5XX, NAS Atlanta, GA., 26 NOV 85; To VA-205, NAS Jacksonville, FL., 10 MAR 86; To VA-205, NAS Atlanta, GA., 14 MAR 86 Thru 15 MAY 87 ** End of flight record card ** Transferred to AMARC, Davis Monthan AFB; Tucson, AZ., assigned park code 6A0248; 04 FEB 88 ** 7061.5 flight hours ** TF41A402D engine S/N 141599 ** Engine records released to DRMO for disposition, 05 SEP 05 ** Aircraft deleted from inventory and sent to DRMO for disposition, 09 SEP 05.

E-123 156857 Navy acceptance from NPRO Rep. LTV, Dallas, TX., 23 FEB 70 ** Transferred to VA-192/CVW-11, NH/3XX, NAS LeMoore, CA., 26 FEB 70; To VA-192, USS Kitty Hawk (CVA-63), 24 JUN 70 ** Transferred to FS, NAS LeMoore, CA., 14 SEP 70 ** Transferred to VA-22/CVW-15, NL/3XX, NAS LeMoore, CA., 08 MAR 71; To VA-22, USS Coral Sea (CVA-43), 28 JUN 71 ** Transferred to VA-146/CVW-9, NG/3XX, USS Constellation (CVA-64), 10 NOV 72; To VA-146, NAS LeMoore, CA., 22 DEC 74; To VA-146, NAS Fallon, NV., 25 APR 75; To VA-146, NAS LeMoore, CA., 25 APR 75; To VA-146, NAS Fallon, NV., 10 MAY 75; To VA-146, NAS LeMoore, CA., 10 MAY 75; To VA-146, USS Constellation (CV-64), 20 AUG 76; To VA-146, NAS LeMoore, CA., 15 DEC 76; To VA-146, USS Constellation (CV-64), 15 DEC 76; NAS LeMoore, CA., 05 FEB 77 ** Transferred to VA-27/CVW-14, NK/4XX, NAS LeMoore, CA., 07 APR 77; To VA-27, NAS Jacksonville, FL., 30 APR 77; To VA-27, NAS LeMoore, CA., 29 JUN 77; To VA-27, USS Enterprise (CVN-65), 12 JAN 78; To VA-27, NAS LeMoore, CA., 03 MAR 78; To VA-27, USS Enterprise (CVN-65), 26 JUN 78; To VA-27, NAS Cubi Point, PI., 27 SEP 78; To VA-27, NAF Atsugi, JP., 04 OCT 78; To VA-27, NAS Cecil Field, FL., 10 OCT 78; To VA-27, NPTR El Centro, CA., 08 JAN 79; To VA-27, NAS Jacksonville, FL., 09 JUL 79; To VA-27, NPTR El Centro, CA., 22 AUG 79; To VA-27, NAS LeMoore, CA., 20 SEP 79 ** Transferred to VA-195/CVW-11, NH/4XX, NAS LeMoore, CA., 23 OCT 79 ** Transferred to VA-25/CVW-2, NE/4XX, NAS LeMoore, CA., 10 MAR 80; To VA-25, USS Ranger (CV-61), 29 MAY 80; To VA-25, NAS LeMoore, CA., 02 JUL 80; To VA-25, USS Ranger (CV-61), 18 JUL 80; To VA-25, NAS LeMoore, CA., 07 AUG 80; To VA-25, USS Ranger (CV-61), 10 SEP 80; To VA-25, NAS LeMoore, CA., 18 MAY 81; To VA-25, NAS Jacksonville, FL., 26 AUG 81; To VA-25, NAS LeMoore, CA., 28 NOV 81; To VA-25, USS Ranger (CV-61), 14 JAN 82; To VA-25, NAS LeMoore, CA., 14 JAN 82; To VA-25, USS Ranger (CV-61), 14 JAN 82; To VA-25, NAS Cubi Point, PI., 14 JAN 82; To VA-25, NAF Atsugi, JP., 28 MAY 82; To VA-25, NAS Cubi Point, PI., 11 JUN 82 ** Transferred to VA-56/CVW-5, NF/4XX, NAF Atsugi, JP., 23 AUG 82 ** Transferred to VA-22/CVW-11, NH/3XX, USS Enterprise (CVN-65), 17 NOV 84; To VA-22, NAS LeMoore, CA., 17 NOV 84 ** Transferred to VA-122/FRS, NJ/2XX, NAS LeMoore, CA., 26 FEB 85 ** Transferred to VA-204/CVWR-20, AF/4XX, NAS New Orleans, LA., 06 MAR 86; To VA-204, NAS Jacksonville, FL., 02

JUL 86 ** Transferred to VA-205/CVWR-20, AF/5XX, NAS Atlanta, 03 JUL 86 ** To VA-205, NAS Jacksonville, FL., 25 SEP 86; To VA-205, NAS Atlanta, GA., 01 OCT 86 thru 29 MAY 87 ** End of flight record card ** Transferred to AMARC, Davis Monthan AFB; Tucson, AZ., assigned park code 6A0366, 26 JUN 90 ** 7175.0 flight hours ** TF41A402D engine S/N 141381 ** Project changed per FSO letter, 06 APR 04 ** Engine records released to DRMO for disposition, 29 JUN 05 ** Aircraft deleted from inventory and sent to DRMO for disposition, 01 AUG 05.

E-124 156858 Navy acceptance from NPRO Rep. LTV, Dallas, TX., 26 JAN 70 ** Transferred to VA-122/FRS, NJ/2XX, NAS LeMoore, CA., 12 FEB 70; To VA-122, CRAA, NAS LeMoore, CA., 14 OCT 71; To VA-122, NAS LeMoore, CA., 21 NOV 71; To VA-122, CRAA, NAS LeMoore, CA., 02 DEC 71 ** Transferred to VA-195/CVW-11, NH/4XX, USS Kitty Hawk (CVA-63), 08 FEB 72; To VA-195, NAS LeMoore, CA., 15 JUN 72; To VA-195, USS Kitty Hawk (CV-63), 29 JUN 73 ** Transferred to VA-122/FRS, NJ/2XX, NAS LeMoore, CA., 15 NOV 73 ** Transferred to NATC, NAS Patuxent River, MD. for RDT & E, 21 FEB 75; To NATC, NAS Jacksonville, FL., 11 MAR 75; To NATC, NAS Patuxent River, MD., 01 APR 75; To NATC, NAS Jacksonville, FL., 09 MAY 75; To NATC, NAS Patuxent River, MD., 12 MAY 75; To NATC, NAS Jacksonville, FL., 17 FEB 76 ** Transferred to VA-27/CVW-14, NK/4XX, NAS LeMoore, CA., 12 MAR 76; To VA-27, USS Enterprise (CVN-65), 29 APR 76; To VA-27, NAS LeMoore, CA., 17 MAY 76; To VA-27, USS Enterprise (CVN-65), 30 JUN 76; To VA-27, NAS LeMoore, CA., 30 JUN 76; To VA-27, USS Enterprise (CVN-65), 30 JUN 76 ** Transferred to VA-192/CVW-11, NH/3XX, NAS LeMoore, CA., 09 JUL 76; To VA-192, MCAS Yuma, AZ., 30 NOV 76; To VA-192, NAS LeMoore, CA., 22 JUN 77; To VA-192, USS Kitty Hawk (CV-63), 25 JUL 77; To VA-192, NAS LeMoore, CA., 11 AUG 77; To VA-192, USS Kitty Hawk (CV-63), 31 AUG 77; To VA-192, NAS LeMoore, CA., 30 SEP 77; To VA-192, USS Kitty Hawk (CV-63), 25 OCT 77; To VA-192, NAS LeMoore, CA., 14 MAY 78; To VA-192, USS America (CV-66), 14 DEC 78 ** Transferred to VA-27/CVW-14, NK/4XX, NAS LeMoore, CA., 02 JAN 79; To VA-27, NAS El Centro, CA., 17 MAR 79; To VA-27, NAS LeMoore, CA., 12 NOV 79; To VA-27, USS Coral Sea (CV-43), 23 DEC 79; To VA-27, NAF Atsugi, JP., 31 MAR 80; To VA-27, USS Coral Sea (CV-43), 04 APR 80 ** Transferred to VA-56/CVW-5, NF/4XX, NAF Atsugi, JP., 10 MAY 80; To VA-56, USS Midway (CV-41), 12 MAY 80; To VA-56, NAF Atsugi, JP., 07 JUL 80; To VA-56, USS Midway (CV-41), 24 FEB 81; To VA-56, NAF Atsugi, JP., 27 JUN 81; To VA-56, USS Midway (CV-41), 03 SEP 81; To VA-56, NAF Atsugi, JP., 13 SEP 81 ** Transferred to VA-25/CVW-2, NE/4XX, NAS Cubi Point, PI., 21 AUG 82; To VA-25, NAF Atsugi, JP., 26 AUG 82; To VA-25, USS Ranger (CV-61), 04 OCT 82; To VA-25, NAS LeMoore, CA., 01 OCT 82; To VA-25, NAS Jacksonville, FL., 19 MAY 83 ** Transferred to VFA-25, NAS Jacksonville, FL., 20 MAY 83 9, NE/3XX, NAS LeMoore, CA., 20 JUL 83; To VA-147, USS Kitty Hawk (CV-63), 14 SEP 83; To VA-147, NAS LeMoore, CA., 20 AUG 84; To VA-147, USS Kitty Hawk (CV-63), 15 JUL 85 ** Transferred to VA-27/CVW-15, NL/4XX, NAS LeMoore, CA., 22 JUL 85 ** Transferred to VA-203/CVWR-20, AF/3XX, NAS Jacksonville, FL., 12 DEC 85 thru 01 DEC 86 ** End of flight record card ** Transferred to AMARC, Davis Monthan AFB; Tucson, AZ., assigned park code 6A0257; 28 MAR 88 ** 6177.6 flight hours ** TF41A402D engine S/N 141885 ** Project changed per FSO letter, 06 APR 04 ** Engine records released to DRMO for disposition, 05 OCT 05 ** Aircraft deleted from inventory and sent to DRMO for disposition, 05 AUG 05.

E-125 156859 Navy acceptance from NPRO Rep. LTV, Dallas, TX., 26 JAN 70 ** Transferred to VA-25/CVW-2, NE/4XX, NAS LeMoore, CA., 31 JAN 70 ** Transferred to VA-97/CVW-14, NK/3XX, USS Enterprise (CVAN-65), 13 JUL 70; To VA-97, NAS LeMoore, CA., 20 JUN 71 ** Transferred to VA-192/CVW-11, NH/300, NAS LeMoore, CA., 11 SEP 74; To VA-192, USS Kitty Hawk (CV-63), 13 JAN 75; To VA-192, NAS LeMoore, CA., 28 MAR 75; To VA-192, USS Kitty Hawk (CV-63), 19 MAY 75; To

VA-192, NAS Cubi Point, PI., 27 SEP 75; To VA-192, USS Kitty Hawk (CV-63), 05 NOV 75; To VA-192, NAS LeMoore, CA., 17 FEB 76; To VA-192, NAS Jacksonville, FL., 09 JUL 76; To VA-192, NAS LeMoore, CA., 08 SEP 76; To VA-192, MCAS Yuma, AZ., 30 NOV 76; To VA-192, NAS LeMoore, CA., 16 DEC 76; To VA-192, USS Kitty Hawk (CV-63), 21 JUL 77; To VA-192, NAS LeMoore, CA., 10 AUG 77; To VA-192, USS Kitty Hawk (CV-63), 14 SEP 77; To VA-192, NAS LeMoore, CA., 30 SEP 77; To VA-192, USS Kitty Hawk (CV-63), 17 OCT 77 ~ S 1SO strike, 16 JAN 78 ** No data on strike.

E-126 156860 Navy acceptance from NPRO Rep. LTV, Dallas, TX., 04 FEB 70 ** Transferred to VA-122/FRS, NJ/2XX, NAS LeMoore, CA., ** Transferred to VA-195/CVW-11, NH/4XX, NAS LeMoore, CA., 20 MAY 70; To VA-195, USS Kitty Hawk (CVA-63), 08 JUN 70 ** Transferred to FS, NAS LeMoore, CA., 29 SEP 70 ** Transferred to VA-94/CVW-15, NL/4XX, NAS LeMoore, CA., 08 MAR 71; To VA-94, USS Coral Sea (CVA-43), 02 JUN 71 ~ S 1SO strike, 16 APR 72 ** CDR D.L. Moss, (Squadron C.O.), was rescued after being shot down by a SAM over North Vietnam.

E-127 156861 Navy acceptance from NPRO Rep. LTV, Dallas, TX., 17 MAR 70 ** Transferred to VA-195/CVW-11, NH/4XX, NAS LeMoore, Ca., 02 APR 70; To VA-195, USS Kitty Hawk (CVA-63) 26 JUN 70 ** Transferred to FS, NAS LeMoore, CA., 11 DEC 70 ** Transferred to VA-94/CVW-15, NL/411, NAS LeMoore, CA., 22 MAR 71; To VA-94, USS Coral Sea (CVA-43), 28 JUN 71; To VA-94, NAS LeMoore, CA., 25 JUN 73; To VA-94, USS Coral Sea (CVA-43), 01 FEB 75; To VA-94, NAS Fallon, NV., 01 SEP 75; To VA-94, NAS LeMoore, CA., 02 NOV 75; To VA-94, NAS Fallon, NV., 05 MAR 76; To VA-94, NAS LeMoore, CA., 05 MAY 76; To VA-94, NAS Alameda, CA., 13 MAY 76; To VA-94, NAS LeMoore, CA. 03 JUN 76; To VA-94, NAS Jacksonville, FL., 23 SEP 76; To VA-94, USS Coral Sea (CV-43), 03 DEC 76; To VA-94, NAS LeMoore, CA., 08 JAN 77; To VA-94, USS Coral Sea (CV-43), 07 APR 77; To VA-94, NAF Atsugi, JP., 22 JUN 77; To VA-94, USS Coral Sea, (CV-43), 05 AUG 77; To VA-94, NAF Atsugi, JP., 22 AUG 77; To VA-94, USS Coral Sea, (CV-43), 06 SEP 77; To VA-94, NAS LeMoore, CA., 18 OCT 77; To VA-94, NAS Alameda, CA., 16 AUG 78; To VA-94, NAS LeMoore, CA., 06 OCT 78 ** Transferred to VA-192/CVW-11, NH/3XX, NAS LeMoore, CA., 19 OCT 78; To VA-192, NAS Alameda, CA., 21 DEC 78; To VA-192, NAS LeMoore, CA., 22 DEC 78; To VA-192, USS America (CV-66), 14 FEB 79; To VA-192, NAS LeMoore, CA., 08 MAR 79; To VA-192, NAS Jacksonville, FL., 09 OCT 79; To VA-192, NAS LeMoore, CA., 13 NOV 79; To VA-192, NAS Fallon, NV., 20 OCT 80; To VA-192, NAS LeMoore, CA., 07 NOV 80; To VA-192, USS America (CV-66), 30 NOV 80 ** Transferred to VA-122/FRS, NJ/2XX, NAS LeMoore, CA., 15 JAN 81; To VA-122, NAS Jacksonville, FL., 12 SEP 81 ** Transferred to VA-25/CVW-2, NE/4XX, NAS LeMoore, CA., 20 NOV 81; To VA-25, USS Ranger (CV-61), 20 NOV 81; To VA-25, NAS LeMoore, CA., 18 FEB 82; To VA-25, USS Ranger (CV-61), 18 FEB 82; To VA-25, NAS Cubi Point, PI., 18 FEB 82; To VA-25, USS Ranger (CV-61), 18 FEB 82 ** Transferred to VA-56/CVW-5, NF/4XX, NAF Atsugi, JP., 01 SEP 82 ** Transferred to VA-22/CVW-11, NH/3XX, USS Enterprise (CVN-65), 03 NOV 84; To VA-22, NAF Atsugi, JP., 05 NOV 84; To VA-22, USS Enterprise (CVN-65), 15 NOV 84; To VA-22, NAS LeMoore, CA., 09 DEC 84; To VA-22, NAS Jacksonville, FL., 08 JAN 85 ** Transferred to VA-192/CVW-9, NG/3XX, NAS LeMoore, CA., 16 MAR 85; To VA-192, NAS Cubi Point, PI., 09 SEP 85; To VA-192, NAS LeMoore, CA., 30 DEC 85; To VA-192, NAS Jacksonville, FL., 02 FEB 86 ** Transferred to VA-205/CVWR-20, AF/5XX, NAS Jacksonville, FL., 05 FEB 86 ** Transferred to VA-204/CVWR-20, AF/401, NAS New Orleans, LA., 23 JUL 86 thru 11 SEP 87 ** End of flight record card ** Transferred to AMARC, Davis Monthan AFB; Tucson, AZ., assigned park code 6A0266, 02 MAY 88 ** 6093.6 flight hours ** TF41A402D engine S/N 141933 ** Project changed per FSO letter, 06 APR 04 ** Engine records released to DRMO for disposition, 05 OCT 05 ** Aircraft deleted from inventory and sent to DRMO for disposition, 05 AUG 05.

E-128 156862 Navy acceptance from NPRO Rep. LTV, Dallas, TX., 09 FEB 70 ** Transferred to VA-122/FRS, NJ/2XX, NAS LeMoore, CA., 10 FEB 70 ** Transferred to VA-195/CVW-11, NH/3XX, USS Kitty Hawk (CVA-63), 02 JUL 70 ** Transferred to VA-97/CVW-14, NK/3XX, USS Enterprise (CVAN-65), 21 AUG 70; To VA-97, NAS LeMoore, CA., 19 JUN 71; To VA-97, USS Enterprise (CVAN-65), 01 MAY 75; To VA-97, NAS LeMoore, CA., 20 MAY 75; To VA-97, NAS Fallon, NV., 30 NOV 75; To VA-97, USS Enterprise (CVN-65), 05 DEC 75; To VA-97, NAS LeMoore, CA., 05 DEC 75; To VA-97, USS Enterprise (CVN-65), 28 JUL 76; To VA-97, NAS LeMoore, CA., 19 JUN 77; To VA-97, USS Enterprise (CVN-65), 10 MAR 78; To VA-97, NAF Atsugi, JP., 28 JUN 78; To VA-97, USS Enterprise (CVN-65), 05 JUL 78; To VA-97, NAS LeMoore, CA., 30 OCT 78; To VA-97, NAS Jacksonville, FL., 02 DEC 79 ** Transferred to VA-15/CVW-6, AE/3XX, NAS Cecil Field, FL., 27 MAR 79; To VA-15, USS Independence (CV-62), 27 MAR 79; To VA-15, NAS Cecil Field, FL., 10 MAR 80; To VA-15, USS Independence (CV-62), 10 MAR 80 ** Transferred to VA-105/CVW-3, AC/4XX, USS Saratoga (CV-60) 10 NOV 80; To VA-105, NAS Cecil Field, FL., 10 NOV 80; To VA-105, NAS Fallon, NV., 10 NOV 80; To VA-105, NAS Cecil Field, FL., 10 NOV 80; To VA-105, USS John F. Kennedy (CV-67), 10 NOV 80; To VA-105, NAS Jacksonville, FL., 17 SEP 81 ** Transferred to VA-81/CVW-17, AA/4XX, NAS Cecil Field, FL., 24 NOV 81; To VA-81, NAS Fallon, NV., 24 NOV 81; To VA-81, USS Forrestal (CV-59), 25 NOV 81; To VA-81, NAS Cecil Field, FL., 25 NOV 81 ** To VA-87/CVW-6, AE/4XX, NAS Cecil Field, FL., 25 MAY 82; To VA-87, USS Independence (CV-62), 25 MAY 82; To VA-87, NAS Cecil Field, FL., 25 MAY 82; To VA-87, NAS Jacksonville, FL., 08 JUN 83; To VA-87, NAS Cecil Field, FL., 08 JUN 83; To VA-87, USS Independence (CV-62), 08 JUN 83; To VA-87, NAS Cecil Field, FL., 10 JUN 83; To VA-87, NAS Jacksonville, FL., 30 SEP 83; To VA-87, USS Independence (CV-62), 03 OCT 83; To VA-87, NAS Cecil Field, FL., 03 OCT 83; To VA-87, USS USS Independence (CV-62), 24 JUL 84; To VA-87, NAS Cecil Field, FL., 24 JUL 84; To VA-87, USS USS Independence (CV-62), 24 JUL 84; To VA-87, NAS Cecil Field, FL., 24 JUL 84 ** Transferred to VA-82/CVW-8, AJ/3XX, NAS Jacksonville, FL., 12 NOV 85 ** Transferred to VA-87/CVW-6, AE/4XX, NAS Cecil Field, FL., 23 NOV 85; To VA-87, NAS Jacksonville, FL., 30 JAN 86 ** Transferred to VA-86/CVW-8, AJ/4XX, NAS Cecil Field, FL., 30 JAN 86 ** Transferred to VA-83/CVW-17, AA/303, NAS Cecil Field, FL., 15 MAY 86; To VA-83, USS Saratoga (CV-60), 15 MAY 86 ** Transferred to AMARC, Davis Monthan AFB; Tucson, AZ., assigned park code 6A0196; 03 SEP 86 ** End of flight record card ** 6318.3 flight hours ** TF41A2B engine S/N 141463 ** Project changed per FSO letter, 06 APR 04 ** Engine records released to DRMO for disposition, 22 MAR 05 ** Aircraft deleted from inventory and released to DRMO for disposition, 11 APR 05.

E-129 156863 Navy acceptance from NPRO Rep. LTV, Dallas, TX., 26 JAN 70 ** Transferred to VA-122/FRS, NJ/2XX, NAS LeMoore, CA., 01 FEB 70 ** Transferred to VA-146/CVW-9, NG/3XX, USS Constellation (CVA-64), 05 SEP 72; To VA-146, NAS LeMoore, CA., 22 DEC 74; To VA-146, NAS Jacksonville, FL., 02 MAY 75; To VA-146, NAS LeMoore, CA., 08 JUL 75; To VA-146, USS Constellation (CV-64), 20 SEP 76; To VA-146, NAS LeMoore, CA., 15 DEC 78; To VA-146, USS Constellation (CV-64), 25 DEC 76; To VA-146, NAS LeMoore, CA., 15 DEC 76; To VA-146, NAS Cubi Point, PI., 14 MAY 77; To VA-146, USS Constellation (CV-64), 05 SEP 77; To VA-146, NAS LeMoore, CA., 19 NOV 77; To VA-146, NAS Jacksonville, FL., 26 JAN 78; To VA-146, NAS LeMoore, CA., 10 MAR 78; To VA-146, NAS Fallon, NV., 12 MAY 78; To VA-146, NAS LeMoore, CA., 20 JUN 78; To VA-146, USS Constellation (CV-64), 16 JUL 78; To VA-146, NAS LeMoore, CA., 24 AUG 78; To VA-146, USS Constellation (CV-64), 21 SEP 78; To VA-146, NAS Cubi Point, PI., 21 DEC 78; To VA-146, NAF Atsugi, JP., 26 JAN 79; To VA-146, NAS Cubi Point, PI., 12 FEB 79; To VA-146, NAF Atsugi, JP., 21 FEB 79; To VA-146, NAS Cubi Point, PI., 22 FEB 79; To VA-146, NAS LeMoore, CA. 19 JUN 79 ** Transferred to VA-174/FRS, AD/4XX, NAS Cecil Field, FL., 30 NOV 79 ** Transferred to VA-12/CVW-7, AG/4XX, USS Dwight D. Eisenhower (CVN-69), 12 APR 80; To VA-12, NAS Cecil Field, FL., 12 APR 80; To VA-12, USS Dwight D. Eisenhower (CVN-69), 12 APR 80 ** Transferred to VA-174/FRS, AD/4XX, NAS Cecil Field, FL., 22 OCT 81; To VA-174, NAS Jacksonville, FL., 11 FEB 82; To VA-174, NAS Cecil Field, FL., 29 MAR 82 ** Transferred to VA-12/CVW-7, AG/4XX, NAS Cecil Field, FL., 25 AUG 82; To VA-12, USS Dwight D. Eisenhower (CVN-69), 25 AUG 82; To VA-12, NAS Cecil Field, FL., 25 AUG 82; To VA-12, NAS Jacksonville, FL., 12 JAN 84; To VA-12, NAS Cecil Field, FL., 12 JAN 84; To VA-12, NAS Jacksonville, FL., 17 JAN 84; To VA-12, NAS Cecil Field, FL., 03 APR 84; To VA-12, USS Dwight D. Eisenhower (CVN-69), 03 APR 84; To VA-12, NAS Cecil Field, FL., 03 APR 84; To VA-12, USS Dwight D. Eisenhower (CVN-69), 03 APR 84; To VA-12, NAS Cecil Field, FL., 03 APR 84; To VA-12, USS Dwight D. Eisenhower (CVN-69), 03 APR 84; To VA-12, NAS Cecil Field, FL., 09 OCT 85, Paint is white on light gray, black modex ** Transferred to AMARC, Davis Monthan AFB; Tucson, AZ., assigned park code 6A0199, 09 SEP 86 ** End of flight record card ** 6006.7 flight hours ** TF41A2C engine S/N 142624 ** Aircraft deleted from inventory and released to DRMO for disposition, 20 DEC 95.

E-130 156864 Navy acceptance from NPRO Rep. LTV Dallas, TX., 16 FEB 70 ** Transferred to VA-25/CVW-2, NE/4XX, NAS LeMoore, CA., 17 FEB 70 ~ S 1SO strike, 13 AUG 70 ** No data on strike.

E-131 156865 Navy acceptance from NPRO Rep. LTV Dallas, TX., 09 MAR 70 ** Transferred to VA-195/CVW-11, NH/4XX, NAS LeMoore, CA., 24 APR 70 ~ S 1SO strike, 18 JUN 70 ** No data on strike.

E-132 156866 Navy acceptance from NPRO Rep. LTV, Dallas, TX., 19 FEB 70 ** Transferred to NATC, Service Test, NAS Patuxent River, MD., 20 FEB 70 ** Transferred to VA-192/CVW-11, NH/306, NAS LeMoore, CA., 31 MAR 70 ** Transferred to NATC, Service Test, NAS Patuxent River, MD., 14 AUG 70 ** Transferred to VA-97/CVW-14, NK/3XX, USS Enterprise (CVAN-65), 27 DEC 70; To VA-97, NAS LeMoore, CA., 17 JUN 71 ~ S 1SO strike, 12 OCT 71 ** Due to Landing Gear Failure.

E-133 156867 Navy acceptance from NPRO Rep. LTV, Dallas, TX., 18 MAR 70 ** Transferred to VA-174/FRS, AD/4XX, NAS Cecil Field, FL., 18 MAR 70 ** Transferred to VA-25/CVW-2, NE/4XX, NAS LeMoore, CA., 11 MAY 72 ** Transferred to HMM-262, MCAS Kaneohe Bay, HI., 01 SEP 72 ** Transferred to VA-25/CVW-2, NE/4XX, NAS LeMoore, CA., 22 SEP 72 ~ S 1SO strike, 28 MAY 73 ** No data on strike.

E-134 156868 Navy acceptance from NPRO Rep. LTV, Dallas, TX., 30 JAN 70 ** First A-7E to receive the TF41-A-2 Engine ** Transferred to VA-122/FRS, NJ/2XX, NAS LeMoore, CA., 06 APR 70 ** Transferred to VA-146/CVW-9, NG/305, USS Constellation (CVA-64), 17 JUL 72; To VA-146, NAS Jacksonville, FL., 19 FEB 75; To VA-146, NAS Lemoore, CA., 19 FEB 75; To VA-146, NAS Jacksonville, FL., 24 FEB 75; To VA-146, NAS Lemoore, CA., 20 APR 75; To VA-146, NAS Fallon, NV., 27 MAY 75; To VA-146, NAS LeMoore, CA., 23 JUN 75; To VA-146, NAS Alameda, CA., 11 FEB 76; To VA-146, NAS LeMoore, CA., 12 FEB 76; To VA-146, NAS Alameda, CA., 18 FEB 76; To VA-146, NAS LeMoore, CA., 22 MAR 76; To VA-146, USS Constellation (CV-64), 20 SEP 76; To VA-146, NAS LeMoore, CA., 15 DEC 76; To VA-146, USS Constellation (CV-64), 15 DEC 76; To VA-146, NAS LeMoore, CA., 05 FEB 77; To VA-146, NAS Cubi Point, PI., 14 MAY 77; To VA-146, NAF Atsugi, JP., 24 JUN 77; To VA-146, NAS Cubi Point, PI., 25 JUN 77; To VA-146, USS Constellation (CV-64), 31 AUG 77; To VA-146, NAS Lemoore, CA., 19 NOV 77; To VA-146, NAS Jacksonville, FL., 16 MAR 78; To VA-146, NAS Fallon, NV., 24 MAR 78; To VA-146, NAS LeMoore, CA., 20 MAY 78; To VA-146, USS Constellation (CV-64), 16 JUL 78; To VA-146, NAS LeMoore, CA., 24 AUG 78; To VA-146, USS Constellation (CV-64), 21 SEP 78; To VA-146, NAS Cubi Point, PI., 21 DEC 78; To VA-147/CVW-9, NG/4XX, USS Constellation (CV-64), 11 JUN 79; To VA-147, NAS LeMoore, CA., 11 JUN 79; To VA-147, USS Constellation (CV-64), 11 DEC 79; To VA-147, NAS LeMoore, CA., 10 JAN 80; To VA-147, USS Constellation (CV-64), 29 FEB 80 ** Transferred to VA-174/FRS, AD/4XX, NAS Cecil Field, FL., 05 MAR 80 ** Transferred to VA-12/ CVW-7, AG/4XX, USS Dwight D. Eisenhower (CVN-69), 13 APR 81 ~ S 1SO strike, 01 OCT 81 ** No data on strike.

E-135 156869 Navy acceptance from NPRO Rep. LTV, Dallas, TX., 31 MAR 70 ** Transferred to VA-192/CVW-11, NH/3XX, NAS LeMoore, CA., 06 APR 70; To VA-192, USS Kitty Hawk (CVA-63), 27 APR 70 ** Transferred to FS, NAS LeMoore, CA., 30 SEP 70 ** Transferred to VA-22/CVW-15, NL/3XX, NAS LeMoore, CA., 16 MAR 71; To VA-22, USS Coral Sea (CVA-43) , 17 JUN 71 ** Transferred to VA-122/FRS, NJ/2XX, NAS LeMoore, CA., 22 AUG 72 ** Transferred to VA-94/CVW-15, NL/4XX, NAS LeMoore, CA., 27 NOV 74; To VA-94, USS Coral Sea (CV-43), 10 APR 75; To VA-94, NAS LeMoore, CA., 02 JUL 75; To VA-94, NAS Fallon, NV., 14 AUG 75; To VA-94, NAS LeMoore, CA., 27 SEP 75; To VA-94, NAS Jacksonville, FL., 26 JAN 76; To VA-94, NAS Fallon, NV., 11 MAR 76 ** Transferred to VA-174/FRS, AD/4XX, NAS Cecil Field, FL., 02 APR 76, AJ/3XX, NAS Cecil Field, FL., 08 JUN 76; To VA-82, USS Nimitz (CVN-68), 16 FEB 77; To VA-82, NAS Cecil Field, FL., 24 FEB 77; To VA-82, USS Nimitz (CVN-68), 20 JUL 77; To VA-82, NAS Cecil Field, FL., 20 JUL 77; To VA-82, NAS Jacksonville, FL., 19 SEP 78; To VA-82, NAS Cecil Field, FL., 19 OCT 78 ** Transferred to VA-66/CVW-7, AG/3XX, USS Dwight D. Eisenhower (CVN-69), 23 JUL 79; To VA-66, NAS Cecil Field, FL., 29 OCT 79; To VA-66, USS Dwight D. Eisenhower (CVN-69), 06 DEC 79; To VA-66, NAS Cecil Field, FL., 06 DEC 79; To USS Dwight D. Eisenhower (CVN-69), 27 MAR 80 ** Transferred to VA-174/FRS, AD/4XX, NAS Cecil Field, FL., 11 APR 80 ** Transferred to VA-12/CVW-7, AG/4XX, NAS Cecil Field, FL., 18 FEB 81; To VA-12, USS Dwight D. Eisenhower (CVN-65), 28 MAY 81; To VA-12, NAS Cecil Field, FL., 01 JUN 81; To VA-12, USS Dwight D. Eisenhower (CVN-65), 01 JUN 81; To VA-12, NAS Cecil Field, FL., 01 JUN 81; To VA-12, USS Dwight D. Eisenhower (CVN-65), 16 DEC 82 ** Transferred to VA-174/FRS, AD/4XX, NAS Cecil Field, FL., 18 APR 83; To VA-174, NAS Jacksonville, FL., 11 JAN 81; To VA-174, NAS Cecil Field, FL., 08 MAR 84 ** Transferred to AMARC, Davis Monthan AFB; Tucson, AZ., assigned park code 6A166, 30 MAY 86 ** 3900.4 flight hours ** TF41A402B engine S/N 141243 ** Ejection seat S/N 0268 removed from aircraft, 09 MAR 89 ** Aircraft deleted from inventory and released to DRMO for disposition, 31 OCT 95 ** Sold as surplus to Fritz Enterprises; Taylor, MI., delivered to HVF West's yard; Tucson, AZ., 10 SEP 96.

E-136 156870 Navy acceptance from NPRO Rep. LTV, Dallas, TX., 26 MAR 70 ** Transferred to VA-192/CVW-11, NH/3XX, NAS LeMoore, CA., 09 MAR 70; To VA-192, USS Kitty Hawk (CVA-63), 13 MAY 70 ** Transferred to VA-122/ FRS, NJ/2XX, NAS LeMoore, CA., 31 JUL 70 ** Transferred to VA-192/CVW-11, NH/3XX, USS Kitty Hawk (CVA-63), 01 AUG 70 ** Transferred to FS, NAS LeMoore, CA., 30 SEP 70 ** Transferred to VA-22/CVW-15, NL/3XX, NAS LeMoore, CA., 16 MAR 71; To VA-22, USS Coral Sea (CVA-43), 12 MAY 71 ~ S 1SO strike, 04 FEB 72 ** Pilot killed due to controlled flight into the water.

E-137 156871 Navy acceptance from NPRO Rep. LTV Dallas, TX., 12 FEB 70 ** Transferred to VA-122/FRS, NJ/2XX, NAS LeMoore, CA., 13 FEB 70 ** Transferred to VA-192/CVW-11, NH/3XX, USS Kitty Hawk (CVA-63), 14 SEP 70 ** Transferred to FS, NAS Lemoore, CA., 14 SEP 70 ** Transferred to VA-22/CVW-15, NL/3XX, NAS LeMoore, CA., 16 MAR 71 ** To VA-22, USS Coral Sea (CVA-43), 21 JUN 71 ~ S 1SO strike, 17 NOV 71 ** No data on strike.

E-138 156872 Navy acceptance from NPRO Rep. LTV, Dallas, TX., 28 FEB 70 ** Transferred to VA-25/CVW-2, NE/4XX, NAS LeMoore, CA., 28 FEB 70 ** Transferred to VA-97/CVW-14, NK/300, USS Enterprise (CVAN-65), 20 JUL 70; To VA-97, NAS LeMoore, CA., 26 JUN 71; To VA-97, USS Enterprise (CVAN-65), 06 DEC 74; To VA-97, NAS LeMoore, CA., 20 MAY 75; To VA-97, NAS Fallon, NV., 21 NOV 75; To VA-97, NAS LeMoore, CA., 19 DEC 75; To VA-97, NAS Jacksonville, FL., 22 DEC 75; To VA-97, NAS LeMoore, CA., 16 FEB 76; To VA-97, USS Enterprise (CVN-65), 25 FEB 76; To VA-97, NAS LeMoore, CA., 27 APR 76; To VA-97, USS Enterprise (CVN-65), 28 JUL 76; To VA-97, NAF Atsugi, JP., 02 NOV 76; To VA-97, USS Enterprise (CVN-65), 17 NOV 76; To VA-97, NAS LeMoore, CA., 19 JUN 77; To VA-97, USS Enterprise (CVN-65), 10 MAR 78; To VA-97, NAF Atsugi, JP., 29 JUN 78; To VA-97, USS Enterprise (CVN-65), 01 JUL 78; To VA-97, NAS LeMoore, CA., 30 OCT 78; To VA-97, NAS Jacksonville, FL., 09 FEB 79; To VA-97, NAS LeMoore, CA., 17 JUN 79; To VA-97, USS Coral Sea (CV-43), 17 FEB 80; To VA-97, NAS LeMoore, CA., 23 MAR 80; To VA-97, USS Coral Sea (CV-43), 30 OCT 80; To VA-97, NAS LeMoore, CA., 16 JAN 81; To VA-97, USS Coral Sea (CV-43), 22 APR 81; To VA-97, NAS LeMoore, CA., 11 JUN 81; To VA-97, NAS Jacksonville, FL., 25 JUN 81 ** Transferred to VX-5, XE/XXX, NWC China Lake, CA., 10 SEP 81; To VX-5, NAS Jacksonville, FL., 20 AUG 83 ** Transferred to VA-203/CVWR-20, AF/3XX, NAS Jacksonville, FL., 24 AUG 83 ** Transferred to VA-205/CVWR-20, AF/5XX, NAS Atlanta, GA., 31 JUL 84 thru 04 JUN 87 ** End of flight record card ** Transferred to AMARC, Davis Monthan AFB; Tucson, AZ., assigned park code 6A0277; 23 JUN 88 ** 6733.5 flight hours ** TF41A402D engine S/N 142546 ** Project changed per FSO letter, 06 APR 04 ** Engine records released to DRMO for disposition, 05 OCT 05 ** Aircraft deleted from inventory and released to DRMO for disposition, 05 OCT 05.

E-139 156873 Navy acceptance from NPRO Rep. LTV, Dallas, TX., 26 FEB 70 ** Transferred to VA-195/CVW-11, NH/427, NAS LeMoore, Ca., 12 JUN 70; To VA-195, USS Kitty Hawk (CVA-63), 12 JUN 70 ** Transferred to FS, NAS LeMoore, CA., 28 FEB 71 ** Transferred to VA-94/CVW-15, NL/4XX, NAS LeMoore, CA., 28 FEB 71 ~ S 1SO strike, 18 APR 71 ** No data on strike.

E-140 156874 Navy acceptance from NPRO Rep. LTV, Dallas, TX., 08 APR 70 ** Transferred to VA-192/CVW-11, NH/3XX, NAS LeMoore, CA., 09 APR 70; To VA-192, USS Kitty Hawk (CVA-63), 23 JUN 70 ** Transferred to FS, NAS LeMoore, CA., 24 SEP 70 ** Transferred to VA-22/CVW-15, NL/3XX, NAS LeMoore,CA., 23 FEB 71; To VA-22, USS Coral Sea (CVA-43), 18 JUN 71 ** Transferred to VA-122/FRS, NJ/2XX, NAS LeMoore, CA., 28 JUL 72 ** Transferred to NWC China Lake, CA., NWC/XXX, for RDT & E, 08 AUG 74; To NWC, NAS Jacksonville, FL., 17 FEB 77; To NWC, China Lake, CA., 22 FEB 77 ** Transferred to NAF Warminster, PA., NADC on tail, No modex, RDT & E, 07 NOV 78 ** Transferred to NATC, SD/405, NAS Patuxent River, MD. for, RDT & E, 01 MAY 82; To NATC, NAS Jacksonville, FL., 01 DEC 86; To NATC, NAS Patuxent River, MD., 03 DEC 86 thru 03 APR 87 ** End of flight record card ** Transferred to AMARC, Davis Monthan AFB; Tucson, AZ., assigned park code 6A0408; 03 FEB 92 ** 3769.9 flight hours ** TF41A402D engine S/N 141948 ** Project changed per FSO letter, 06 APR 04 ** At AMARC; Davis Monthan AFB; Tucson, AZ., 11 JAN 06.

E-141 156875 Navy acceptance from NPRO Rep. LTV, Dallas, TX., 10 MAR 70 ** Transferred to VA-192/CVW-11, NH/3XX, NAS LeMoore, CA., 01 MAY 70; To VA-192, USS Kitty Hawk (CVA-63), 16 JUN 70 ** Transferred to FS, NAS LeMoore, CA., 22 SEP 70 ** Transferred to VA-22/CVW-15, NL/312, NAS LeMoore, CA., 22 MAR 71; To VA-22, USS Coral Sea (CVA-43), 29 JUN 71 ** Transferred to VA-122/FRS, NJ/2XX, NAS LeMoore, CA., 18 JAN 73 ** Transferred to VA-22/CVW-15, NL/312, USS Coral Sea (CVA-43), 26 NOV 74 ~ S 1SO strike, 13 APR 75 ** No data on strike.

E-142 156876 Navy acceptance from NPRO Rep. LTV, Dallas, TX., 09 MAR 70 ** Transferred to VA-174/FRS, AD/4XX, NAS Cecil Field, FL., 10 MAR 70 ** Transferred to VA-122/FRS, NJ/2XX, CRAA, NAS LeMoore, CA., 17 MAY 72; To VA-122, NAS LeMoore, CA., 15 JUN 72; To VA-122, NAS Jacksonville, FL., 04 MAR 78; To VA-122, NAS LeMoore, CA., 07 MAY 78; To VA-122, NAS Jacksonville, FL., 18 OCT 79; To VA-122, NAS LeMoore, CA., 21 DEC 79 ** Transferred to VA-97/CVW-14, NK/3XX, NAS LeMoore, CA., 30 MAR 81; To VA-97, USS Coral Sea (CV-43), 22 APR 81; To VA-97, NAS LeMoore, CA., 11 JUN 81; To VA-97, USS Coral Sea (CV-43), 24 JUL 81 ** Transferred to VA-122/ FRS, NJ/2XX, NAS LeMoore, CA., 17 AUG 71 ** Transferred to VA-25/CVW-2, NE/4XX, NAS Fallon, NV., 10 SEP 81; To VA-25, USS Ranger (CV-61), 26 SEP 81; To VA-25, LeMoore, CA., 05 OCT 81; To VA-25, USS Ranger (CV-61), 12 JAN 82; To VA-

25, NAS Jacksonville, FL., 13 JAN 82; To VA-25, NAS LeMoore, CA., 14 FEB 82; To VA-25, USS Ranger (CV-61), 14 FEB 82; To VA-25, NAS Cubi Point, PI., 14 FEB 82 ** Transferred to VA-56/CVW-5, NF/4XX, NAS Atsugi, JP., 21 AUG 82; To VA-56, USS Enterprise (CVN-65), 13 NOV 84 ** Transferred to VA-22/CVW-11, NH/3XX, NAS LeMoore, 13 NOV 84 ** Transferred to VA-122/FRS, NJ/2XX, NAS LeMoore, 20 FEB 85; To VA-122, NAS Jacksonville, FL., 17 APR 86 ** Transferred to VA-204/CVWR-20, AF/4XX, NAS Jacksonville, FL., 17 APR 86; To VA-204, NAS New Orleans, LA., 23 OCT 87 thru 23 DEC 86 ** End of flight record card ** Transferred to AMARC, Davis Monthan AFB; Tucson, AZ., assigned park code 6A0273; 13 JUN 88 ** 5189.3 flight hours ** TF41A402D engine S/N 142516 ** Project changed per FSO letter, 06 APR 04 ** Engine records released to DRMO for disposition, 27 JUL 05 ** Aircraft deleted from inventory and released to DRMO for disposition, 01 AUG 05.

E-143 156877 Navy acceptance from NPRO Rep. LTV, Dallas, TX., 31 MAR 70 ** Transferred to VA-195/CVW-11, NH/4XX, NAS LeMoore, CA., 08 APR 70; To VA-195, USS Kitty Hawk (CVA-63), 01 JUN 70 ** Transferred to FS, NAS LeMoore, CA., 30 SEP 70 ** Transferred to VA-94/CVW-15, NL/410, NAS LeMoore, CA., 31 MAR 71; To VA-94, USS Coral Sea (CVA-43), 23 JUN 71 ~ S 1SO strike, 24 MAY 72 ** LCDR H.A. Eikel ejected and was rescued after being shot down by a SAM 25 Miles east of Haiphong, North Vietnam.

E-144 156878 Navy acceptance from NPRO Rep. LTV, Dallas, TX., 26 FEB 70 ** Transferred to VA-25/CVW-2, NE/4XX, NAS LeMoore, CA., 28 FEB 70 ** Transferred to VA-97/CVW-14, NK/3XX, USS Enterprise (CVAN-65), 19 AUG 70; To VA-97, NAS LeMoore, CA., 23 MAR 71; To VA-97, USS Enterprise (CVAN-65), 01 FEB 75; To VA-97, NAS LeMoore, CA., 20 MAY 75; To VA-97, NAS Jacksonville, FL., 15 AUG 75; To VA-97, NAS LeMoore, CA., 18 OCT 75; To VA-97, NAS Fallon, NV., 18 OCT 75; To VA-97, NAS LeMoore, CA., 18 OCT 75; To VA-97, USS Enterprise (CVN-65), 20 FEB 76; To VA-97, NAS Alameda, CA., 07 APR 76; To VA-97, NAS LeMoore, CA., 10 MAY 76; To VA-97, USS Enterprise (CVN-65), 28 JUL 76; To VA-97, NAS LeMoore, CA., 19 JUN 77; To VA-97, USS Enterprise (CVN-65), 10 MAR 78; To VA-97, NAF Atsugi, JP., 17 JUN 78; To VA-97, USS Enterprise (CVN-65), 25 JUN 78; To VA-97, NAF Atsugi, JP., 29 JUN 78; To VA-97, USS Enterprise (CVN-65), 05 JUL 78; To VA-97, NAS LeMoore, CA., 30 OCT 78; To VA-97, NAS Jacksonville, FL., 03 NOV 78 ** Transferred to VA-174/FRS, AD/421, NAS Cecil Field, FL., 26 JAN 79; To VA-174, NAS Jacksonville, FL., 18 AUG 81; To VA-174, NAS Cecil Field, FL., 28 OCT 81; To VA-174, NAS Jacksonville, FL., 06 DEC 83; To VA-174, Bloomfield, 12 MAR 84; To VA-174, NAS Cecil Field, FL., 12 MAR 84; To VA-174, NAS Jacksonville, FL., 15 JUL 86; To VA-174, NAS Cecil Field, FL., 31 JUL 86 ** Transferred to VA-304/CVWR-30, ND/4XX, NAS Alameda, CA., 31 JUL 86; To VA-304, NAS Jacksonville, FL., 17 DEC 86; To VA-304, NAS Alameda, CA., 14 JAN 87 thru 14 SEP 87 ** End of flight record card.

E-145 156879 Navy acceptance from NPRO Rep. LTV, Dallas, TX., 31 MAR 70 ** Transferred to VA-192/CVW-11, NH/3XX, NAS LeMoore, CA., 02 APR 70; To VA-192, USS Kitty Hawk (CVA-63), 10 APR 70 ** Transferred to FS, NAS LeMoore, CA., 22 SEP 70 ** Transferred to VA-22/CVW-15, NL/313, NAS LeMoore, CA., 22 MAR 71; To VA-22, USS Coral Sea (CVA-43), 23 JUN 71 ~ S 1SO strike, 06 MAY 72 ** LT Marvin B. Wiles ejected when shot down by a SAM near Dong Hoi, NVN ** Killed by NVN.

E-146 156880 Navy acceptance from NPRO Rep. LTV, Dallas, TX., 20 FEB 70 ** Transferred to VA-195/CVW-11, NH/4XX, NAS LeMoore, CA., 21 FEB 70; To VA-195, USS Kitty Hawk (CVA-63), 18 MAY 70 ** Transferred to FS, NAS LeMoore,CA., 28 SEP 80; Transferred to VA-94/CVW-15, NL/4XX, NAS LeMoore, CA., 16 FEB 71; To VA-94, USS Coral Sea (CVA-43), 16 JUN 71 ~ S 1SO strike, 18 JAN 72 ** Pilot ejected and was rescued after the Starboard MLG collaped on launch in the Gulf of Tonkin off the coast of NVN.

E-147 156881 Navy acceptance from NPRO Rep. LTV, Dallas, TX., 09 MAR 70 ** Transferred to VA-195/CVW-11, NH/4XX, NAS LeMoore, CA., 10 MAR 70; To VA-195, USS Kitty Hawk (CVA-63), 09 JUN 70 ** Transferred to FS, NAS LeMoore, CA., 14 SEP 70 ** Transferred to VA-94/CVW-15, NL/4XX, NAS LeMoore, CA., 31 MAR 71; To VA-94, USS Coral Sea (CVA-43), 17 JUN 7 ** Transferred to VA-122/FRS, NJ/2XX, NAS LeMoore, CA., 04 AUG 72 ~ S 1SO strike, 12 FEB 75 ** No data on strike.

E-148 156882 Navy acceptance from NPRO Rep. LTV, Dallas, TX., 12 MAR 70 ** Transferred to VA-174/FRS, AD/4XX, NAS Cecil Field, FL., 13 MAR 70 ** Transferred to VA-122/FRS, NJ/2XX, NAS LeMoore, CA., 21 APR 71; To VA-122, CRAA, NAS LeMoore, CA., 09 JUN 72; To VA-122, NAS LeMoore, CA., 26 JUL 72; To VA-122, CRAA, NAS LeMoore, CA., 21 DEC 72 ** Transferred to VA-113/CVW-2, NE/3XX, NAS LeMoore, CA., 27 JAN 73 ** Transferred to VA-22/CVW-15, NL/3XX, USS Coral Sea (CVA-43), 03 JUN 73; To VA-22, NAS LeMoore, CA., 18 MAY 74; To VA-22 USS Coral Sea (CV-43), 29 NOV 74; To VA-22, NAS LeMoore, CA., 30 JUL 75; To VA-22, NAS Fallon, NV., 01 AUG 75; To VA-22, NAS LeMoore, CA., 01 NOV 75; To VA-22, NAS Jacksonville, FL., 11 MAR 76 ** Transferred to VA-174/FRS, AD/4XX, NAS Cecil Field, FL., 24 MAR 76 ** Transferred to VA-105/CVW-3, AC/415, NAS Cecil Field, FL., 28 OCT 76; To VA-105, USS Saratoga (CV-60), 28 OCT 76; To VA-105, NAS Cecil Field, FL., 18 JUL 77; To VA-105, NAS Jacksonville, FL., 13 JUN 78; To VA-105, USS Saratoga (CV-60, 08 JUL 78; To VA-105, NAS Cecil Field, FL., 08 JUL 78; To VA-105, USS Saratoga (CV-60, 08 JUL 78; To VA-105, NAS Cecil Field, FL., 18 JUL 79; To VA-105, MCAS Yuma, AZ., 18 JUL 79; To VA-105, NAS Cecil Field, FL., 24 OCT 79; To VA-105, USS Saratoga (CV-60), 24 OCT 79; To VA-105, NAS Cecil Field, FL., 24 OCT 79 ** Transferred to AMARC, Davis Monthan AFB; Tucson, AZ., assigned park code 6A0119, 05 FEB 80 ** Transferred to NWEF Kirtland AFB, NM., 13 SEP 82 ** Transferred to VA-205/CVWR-20, AF/5XX, NAS Atlanta, GA., 06 AUG 84; To VA-205, NAS Jacksonville, FL., 31 AUG 84 ** Transferred to VA-203/CVWR-20, AF/3XX, NAS Jacksonville, FL., 01 OCT 84 thru 31 MAR 87 ** End of flight record card ** Transferred to AMARC, Davis Monthan AFB; Tucson, AZ., assigned park code 6A0246, 28 JAN 88 ** 5673.9 flight hours ** TF41A402D engine S/N 14142 ** Project changed per FSO letter 06 APR 04 ** Engine records released to DRMO for disposition, 09 SEP 05 ** Aircraft deleted from inventory and released to DRMO for disposition, 09 SEP 05.

E-149 156883 Navy acceptance from NPRO Rep. LTV, Dallas, TX., 09 MAR 70 ** Transferred to VA-195/CVW-11, NH/4XX, NAS LeMoore, CA., 31 MAR 70; To VA-195, USS Kitty Hawk (CVA-63), 09 JUN 70 ** Transferred to FS, NAS LeMoore, CA., 30 SEP 70 ** Transferred to VA-94/CVW-15, NL/4XX, NAS LeMoore, CA., 31 MAR 71; To VA-94, USS Coral Sea (CVA-43), 08 JUN 71 ** Transferred to VA-122/FRS, NJ/2XX, NAS LeMoore, CA., 25 JUL 72 ** Transferred to NPRO Rep. LTV Dallas, TX., for RDT & E, 21 OCT 74 ** Transferred to NAF China Lake, CA. XX/XXX, for RDT & E, 15 MAR 76 ** Transferred to VX-5, XE/XXX, NAF China Lake, CA., 08 SEP 76 ** Transferred to NAF China Lake, CA., for RDT & E, 08 OCT 76; To NAF China Lake at NAS Jacksonville, FL., 30 NOV 77; To NAF, China Lake, CA., 06 JAN 78 ** Transferred to VX-5, XE/XXX, NAF China Lake, CA., 17 JUL 78; To NAF China Lake, CA., 22 AUG 78; To NAF China Lake at NAS Jacksonville, FL., 21 JAN 82; To NAF China Lake, CA., 08 MAR 82; To NAF China Lake at NAS Jacksonville, FL., 16 JUN 86; To NAF China Lake, CA., 25 SEP 86 thru 09 SEP 87 ** End of flight record card ** Loaned to Hughes Aircraft for tests on the AGM-65 Maverick Missile, date unknown.

E-150 156884 Navy acceptance from NPRO Rep. LTV, Dallas, TX., 17 MAR 70 ** Transferred to VA-174/FRS, AD/4XX, NAS Cecil Field, FL. 18 MAR 70 ** Transferred to NATC, Service Test, NAS Patuxent River, MD., for RDT & E, 12 MAY 72 ** Transferred to NATC, NAS Patuxent River, MD., for RDT & E, 01 SEP 72 ** Transferred to VA-192/ CVW-11, NH/4XX, NAS LeMoore, CA., 01 MAY 73; To VA-192, USS Kitty Hawk (CV-

63), 29 JUN 73; To VA-192, NAS LeMoore, CA., 05 AUG 74; To VA-192, NAS Jacksonville, FL., 30 NOV 74; TO VA-192, NAS LeMoore, CA., 07 FEB 75; To VA-192, USS Kitty Hawk (CV-63), 11 APR 75; To VA-192, NAS Cubi Point, PI., 16 SEP 75; To VA-192, USS Kitty Hawk (CV-63), 19 NOV 75; To VA-192, NAS LeMoore, CA., 07 JAN 76; To VA-192, MCAS Yuma, AZ., 30 NOV 76; To VA-192, NAS LeMoore, CA., 25 APR 77; To VA-192, USS Kitty Hawk (CV-63), 21 JUL 77; To VA-192, NAS LeMoore, CA., 11 AUG 77; To VA-192, USS Kitty Hawk (CV-63), 25 OCT 77; To VA-192, NAS LeMoore, CA., 14 MAY 78; To VA-192, NAS Jacksonville, FL., 25 JUN 78 ** Transferred to VA-87/CVW-6, AE/4XX, NAS Cecil Field, FL., 02 NOV 78; To VA-87, USS Independence (CV-62), 02 NOV 78; To VA-87, NAS Cecil Field, FL., 02 NOV 78, To VA-87, USS Nimitz (CVN-68), 10 JUL 80 ** Transferred to VA-82/CVW-8, AJ/3XX, USS Nimitz (CVN-68), 10 JUL 80; To VA-82, NAS Jacksonville, FL., 08 OCT 80; To VA-82, NAS Cecil Field, FL., 27 JAN 81; To VA-82, USS Nimitz (CVN-68), 29 JAN 81; To VA-82, NAS Cecil Field, FL., 29 JAN 81 ** Transferred to VA-12/CVW-7, AG/4XX, USS Dwight D. Eisenhower (CVN-69), 01 APR 82; To VA-12, NAS Cecil Field, FL., 01 APR 82; Transferred to VA-174/FRS, AD/4XX, NAS Cecil Field, FL., 01 SEP 82; To VA-174, NAS Jacksonville, FL., 07 DEC 83; To VA-174, NAS Cecil Field, FL., 07 DEC 83; To VA-174, NAS Jacksonville, FL., 14 JAN 86; To VA-174, NAS Cecil Field, FL., 23 JAN 86; To VA-174, NAS Jacksonville, FL., 18 MAR 86; To VA-174, NAS Cecil Field, FL., 22 MAR 86; To VA-174, NAS Pensacola, FL., 05 SEP 86; To VA-174, NAS Cecil Field, FL., 06 SEP 86 ** Transferred to VA-204/CVWR-20, AF/400, NAS New Orleans, LA., 09 SEP 86; To VA-204, NAS Pensacola, FL., 09 APR 87; To VA-204, NAS New Orleans, LA., 03 JUN 87 thru 20 SEP 87 ** End of flight record card ** Transferred to AMARC, Davis Monthan AFB; Tucson, AZ., assigned park code 6A0284, 29 JUL 88 ** 5698.7 flight hours ** TF41A402D engine S/N 141950 ** Project changed per FSO letter, 06 APR 04 ** Engine records released to DRMO for disposition, 05 OCT 05 ** Aircraft deleted from inventory and released to DRMO for disposition, 05 OCT 05.

E-151 156885 Navy acceptance from NPRO Rep. LTV, Dallas, TX., 31 MAR 70 ** Transferred to VA-195/CVW-11, NH/4XX, NAS LeMoore, CA., 03 APR 70; To VA-195, USS Kitty Hawk (CVA-63), 28 APR 70 ** Transferred to FS, NAS LeMoore, CA., 30 SEP 70 ** Transferred to VA-94/CVW-15, NL/4XX, NAS LeMoore, CA., 24 MAR 71; To VA-94, USS Coral Sea (CVA-43), 03 JUN 71 ** Transferred to VA-122/FRS, NJ/2XX, NAS LeMoore, CA., 10 AUG 72; To VA-122, NAS Jacksonville, FL., 15 DEC 75; To VA-122, NAS LeMoore, CA., 07 APR 76; To VA-122, NAS Jacksonville, FL., 13 JAN 78; To VA-122, NAS LeMoore, CA., 17 FEB 78; To VA-122, NAS Jacksonville, FL., 14 FEB 80; To VA-122, NAS LeMoore, CA., 18 APR 80; To VA-122, NAS Alameda, CA., 09 FEB 81; To VA-122, NAS LeMoore, CA., 17 FEB 81; To VA-122, NAS Alameda, CA., 10 JUL 81; To VA-122, NAS LeMoore, CA., 14 AUG 81; To VA-122, NAS Alameda, CA., 24 AUG 81; To VA-122, NAS LeMoore, CA., 13 SEP 81; To VA-122, NAS Alameda, CA., 17 SEP 81; To VA-122, NAS LeMoore, CA., 8 SEP 81 ** Transferred to VA-147/CVW-9, NE/3XX, NAS LeMoore, CA., 27 MAY 83; To VA-147, NAS Jacksonville, FL., 23 JUN 83; To VA-147, NAS LeMoore, CA., 22 AUG 83; To VA-147, NAS Alameda, CA., 14 OCT 83; To VA-147, NAS LeMoore, CA., 20 DEC 83; To VA-147, USS Kitty Hawk (CV-63), 20 DEC 83 ** Transferred to VA-122/FRS, NJ/2XX, NAS LeMoore, CA., 03 JAN 84 ** Transferred to VA-147/CVW-9, NE/3XX, USS Kitty Hawk (CV-63), 29 AUG 84; To VA-147, NAS LeMoore, CA., 25 SEP 84; To VA-147, NAS Jacksonville, FL., 08 FEB 85; To VA-147, NAS LeMoore, CA., 19 FEB 85; To VA-147, NAS Jacksonville, FL., 25 MAR 85 ** Transferred to NSWC, Strike/26, NAS Fallon, NV., 26 JUL 85 ** Transferred to AMARC, Davis Monthan AFB; Tucson, AZ., assigned park code 6A0207, 26 SEP 86 ** End of flight record card ** 4919.7 flight hours ** TF41A2C engine S/N 141443 ** Project changed per FSO letter, 06 APR 04 ** Aircraft deleted from inventory and released to DRMO for disposition, 26 MAY 05.

E-152 156886 Navy acceptance from NPRO Rep. LTV, Dallas, TX., 12 MAR 70 ** Transferred to VA-174/FRS, AD/4XX, NAS Cecil Field, FL. 13 MAR 70 ** Transferred to VA-113/CVW-2, NE/302, NAS LeMoore, CA. 07 MAY 72; To VA-113, USS Ranger (CV-61), 21 JUN 73; To VA-113, NAS Jacksonville, FL., 09 NOV 74; To VA-113, NAS LeMoore, CA., 20 JAN 75; To VA-113, USS Ranger (CV-61), 07 JUL 75; To VA-113, NAS LeMoore, CA., 18 APR 77; To VA-113, NAS Jacksonville, FL., 06 JAN 78; To VA-113, NAS LeMoore, CA., 11 JAN 78; To VA-113, USS Ranger, (CV-61), 27 SEP 78; To VA-113, NAS LeMoore, CA., 16 OCT78; To VA-113, USS Ranger, (CV-61), 09 NOV 78; To VA-113, NAS LeMoore, CA., 15 DEC 78 ** Transferred to VA-97/CVW-14, NK/3XX, NAS LeMoore, CA., 23 JAN 79; To VA-97, NAS Jacksonville, FL., 23 JAN 79; To VA-97, NAS LeMoore, CA., 13 AUG 79; To VA-97, USS Coral Sea (CV-43), 13 OCT 79; To VA-97, NAS LeMoore, CA., 13 OCT 79 ** Transferred to VA-66/CVW-7, AG/304, USS Dwight D. Eisenhower (CVN-69), 14 OCT 79; To VA-66, NAS Cecil Field, FL., 14 OCT 79; To VA-66, USS Dwight D. Eisenhower (CVN-69), 20 APR 81; To VA-66, NAS Cecil Field, FL., 20 APR 81; To VA-66, USS Dwight D. Eisenhower (CVN-69), 20 APR 81 ** Transferred to VA-174/FRS, AD/4XX, NAS Cecil Field, FL., 31 JUL 81; To VA-174, NAS Jacksonville, FL., 22 OCT 81; To VA-174, NAS Cecil Field, FL., 28 DEC 81 ** Transferred to VA-37CVW-15, NL/3XX, NAS Cecil Field, FL., 17 SEP 82; To VA-37, USS Carl Vinson (CVN-70), 29 DEC 82; To VA-37, NAS Cecil Field, FL., 30 JAN 83; To VA-37, USS Carl Vinson (CVN-70), 16 MAR 83; Transferred to VA-81/CVW-17, AA/401, NAS Cecil Field, FL., 20 APR 83; To VA-81, NAS Fallon, NV., 12 AUG 83; To VA-81, NAS Cecil Field, FL., 16 AUG 83; To VA-81, USS Saratoga (CV-60), 16 AUG 83; To VA-81, NAS Cecil Field, FL., 24 JAN 84; To VA-81, USS Saratoga (CV-60), 28 MAR 84; To VA-81, NAS Cecil Field, FL., 28 MAR 84; To VA-81, NAS Jacksonville, FL., 23 MAY 85; To VA-81, NAS Cecil Field, FL., 24 MAY 85; To VA-81, USS Saratoga (CV-60), 24 MAY 85; To VA-81, NAS Cecil Field, FL., 01 MAY 86; To VA-81, USS Saratoga (CV-60), 29 MAY 86; To VA-81, NAS Cecil Field, FL., 21 OCT 86 ** Transferred to AMARC, Davis Monthan AFB; Tucson, AZ., assigned park code 6A0215; 15 JAN 87 ** End of flight record card ** 5903.6 flight hours ** TF41A2B engine S/N 141902 ** Project changed per FSO letter, 06 APR 04 ** Aircraft deleted from inventory and released to DRMO for disposition, 11 APR 05.

E-153 156887 Navy acceptance from NPRO Rep. LTV, Dallas, TX., 09 MAR 70 ** Transferred to VA-174/FRS, AD/4XX, NAS Cecil Field, FL., 10 MAR 70 ** Transferred to VA-122/FRS, NJ/2XX, NAS LeMoore, CA., 11 MAY 71; To VA-122, CRAA, NAS LeMoore, CA., 20 JUN 72; To VA-122, NAS LeMOORE, CA., 26 JUL 72; To VA-122, NAS Jacksonville, FL., 31 JUL 77; To VA-122, NAS LeMOORE, CA., 31 JUL 77; To VA-122, NAS Jacksonville, FL., 17 JUL 79; To VA-122, NAS LeMoore, CA., 24 AUG 79 ** Transferred to VA-97/CVW-14, NK/3XX, NAS LeMoore, CA., 06 FEB 81; To VA-97, USS Coral Sea (CV-43), 23 FEB 81; To VA-97, NAS LeMoore, CA., 11 JUN 81; To VA-97, USS Coral Sea (CV-43), 21 JUL 81 ** Transferred to VA-122/FRS, NJ/2XX, NAS LeMoore, CA., 17 AUG 81; To VA-122, NAS Jacksonville, FL., 29 APR 82 ** Transferred to NARF, NAS Jacksonville, FL., 12 AUG 82 ** Transferred to VA-27/CVW-14, NK/4XX, NAS LeMoore, CA., 27 AUG 82; To VA-27, NAS Alameda, CA., 20 OCT 82; To VA-27, NAS LeMoore, CA., 02 NOV 82; To VA-27, USS Coral Sea (CV-43), 23 FEB 83; To VA-27, NAS LeMoore, CA., 23 FEB 83 ** Transferred to VA-174/FRS, AD/410, NAS Cecil Field, FL., 09 SEP 83; To VA-174, NAS Jacksonville, FL., 11 JAN 85; To VA-174, NAS Cecil field, FL., 16 JAN 85 ** Transferred to AMARC, Davis Monthan AFB; Tucson, AZ., assigned park code 6A0210; 24 DEC 86 ** 5788.7 flight hours ** TF41A2B engine S/N 141630 ** End of flight record card ** Ejection seat S/N 0261 removed, 29 MAR 89 ** Project changed per FSO letter, 06 APR 04 ** At AMARC; Davis Monthan AFB; Tucson, AZ., 10 JAN 05.

E-154 156888 Navy acceptance from NPRO Rep. LTV, Dallas, TX., 31 MAR 70 ** Transferred to VA-195/CVW-11, NH/4XX, NAS LeMoore, CA., 06 APR 70; To VA-195, USS Kitty Hawk (CVA-63), 26 JUN 70 ** Transferred to FS, NAS LeMoore, CA., 30 SEP 70 ** Transferred to VA-94/CVW-15, NL/4XX, NAS LeMoore, CA., 19 JAN 71; To VA-94, USS Coral Sea (CVA-43), 14 JUN 71 ~ S 1SO strike, 01 MAY 72 ** LT M.G. Surdyk ejected and was rescued from the Tonkin Gulf after having an electrical system failure due to being hit by a SAM near Deng Hoi, NVN.

E-155 156889 Navy acceptance from NPRO Rep. LTV, Dallas, TX., 07 APR 70 ** Transferred to VA-195/CVW-11, NH/4XX, NAS LeMoore, CA., 08 APR 70; To VA-195, USS Kitty Hawk (CVA-63), 20 MAY 70 ** Transferred to FS, NAS LeMoore, CA., 28 SEP 70 ** Transferred to VA-94/CVW-15, NL/4XX, NAS LeMoore, CA., 02 FEB 71; To VA-94, USSCoral Sea (CVA-43), 10 JUN 71 ** Transferred to VA-122/FRS, NJ/2XX, NAS LeMoore, CA., 17 AUG 72; To VA-122, NAS Jacksonville, FL., 06 JUL 77; To VA-122, NAS LeMoore, CA., 15 SEP 77; To VA-122, NAS Alameda, CA., 19 JUN 79; To VA-122, NAS LeMoore, CA., 06 JUL 79; To VA-122, NAS Alameda, CA., 02 AUG 79; To VA-122, NAS LeMoore, CA., 03 AUG 79; To VA-122, NAS Jacksonville, FL., 23 JAN 80; To VA-122, NAS LeMoore, CA., 25 FEB 80; To VA-122, NAS Jacksonville, FL., 09 MAR 82; To VA-122, NAS LeMoore, CA., 08 MAY 82 ** Transferred to VA-94/CVW-11, NH/4XX, NAS LeMoore, CA., 01 JUL 82; To VA-94, USS Enterprise (CVN-65), 02 AUG 82; To VA-94, NAS Cubi Point, PI., 09 FEB 83; To VA-94, NAS LeMoore, CA., 09 FEB 83 ** Transferred to VA-27/CVW-14, NK/4XX, USS Coral Sea (CV-43), 21 APR 83; To VA-27, NAS LeMoore, CA., 28 SEP 83; To VA-27/CVW-15, NL/4XX, USS Carl Vinson (CVN-70), 29 FEB 84; To VA-27, NAS LeMoore, CA., 19 APR 84; To VA-27, USS Carl Vinson (CVN-70), 19 APR 84 ** Transferred to VA-195/CVW-9, NG/400, NAS LeMoore, CA., 10 MAY 84; To VA-195, NAS Jacksonville, FL., 18 DEC 84; To VA-195, NAS LeMoore, CA., 25 FEB 85 ** Transferred to VA-94/CVW-11, NH/4XX, NAS LeMoore, CA., 08 MAY 85 ** Transferred to VA-174/FRS, AD/311, NAS Cecil Field, FL., 15 AUG 85 ** Transferred to AMARC,Davis Monthan AFB; Tucson, AZ., assigned park code 6A0170, 12 JUN 86 ** End of flight record card ** Ejection seat S/N 0136 removed from aircraft, 17 JUN 86 ** 6193.3 flight hours ** Aircraft deleted from inventory and released to DRMO for disposition, 18 JAN 96 ** Sold as surplus to Fritz Enterprises; Taylor, MI., delivered to HVF West's yard; Tucson, AZ., 10 SEP 96.

E-156 156890 Navy acceptance from NPRO Rep. LTV, Dallas, TX., 18 APR 70 ** Transferred to VA-174/FRS, AD/4XX, NAS Cecil Field, FL., 05 MAY 70; To VA-174, NAS Jacksonville, FL., 10 FEB 78;To VA-174, NAS Cecil Field, FL., 29 MAR 78; To VA-174, NAS Jacksonville, FL., 24 APR 80; To VA-174, NAS Cecil Field, FL., 23 JUN 80 ** Transferred to VA-81/CVW-17, AA/4XX, NAS Cecil Field, FL., 13 AUG 80; To VA-81, USS Forrestal (CV-59), 02 SEP 80; To VA-81, NAS Cecil Field, FL., 02 SEP 80; To VA-81, USS Forrestal (CV-59), 17 FEB 81; To VA-81, NAS Cecil Field, FL., 17 FEB 81; To VA-81, NAS Fallon, NV., 18 FEB 81; To VA-81, USS Forrestal (CV-59), 18 FEB 81; To VA-81, NAS Cecil Field, FL., 17 MAY 82 ** Transferred to VA-174/FRS, AD/4XX, NAS Cecil Field, FL., 28 MAY 82; To VA-174, NAS Jacksonville, FL., 06 DEC 82 ** Transferred toVA-81/CVW-17, AA/4XX, NAS Cecil Field, FL., 17 JAN 83; To VA-81, NAS Fallon, NV., 07 JUL 83; To VA-81, NAS Cecil Field, FL., 07 JUL 83; To VA-81, USS Saratoga (CV-60), 17 NOV 83; To VA-81, NAS Cecil Field, FL., 21 JAN 84; To VA-81, USS Saratoga (CV-60), 21 JAN 84; To VA-81, NAS Cecil Field, FL., 21 JAN 84; To VA-81, USS Saratoga (CV-60), 30 APR 85; To VA-81, NAS Jacksonville, FL., 11 JUN 85; To VA-81, USS Saratoga (CV-60), 11 JUN 85; To VA-81, NAS Jacksonville, FL., 21 OCT 85 ** Transferred to VA-37/CVW-6, AE/3XX, NAS Cecil Field, FL., 23 OCT 85; To VA-37, USS Forrestal (CV-59), 16 JAN 86; To VA-37, NAS Cecil Field, FL., 16 JAN 86; To VA-37, USS Forrestal (CV-59), 28 MAY 86; To VA-37, NAS Cecil Field, FL., date unknown ** Transferred to AMARC, Davis Monthan AFB; Tucson, AZ., assigned park code 6A0222; 17 MAR 87 ** End of flight record card ** 4677.1 flight hours ** TF41A2B engine S/N 142630 ** Project changed per FSO letter 06 APR 04 ** Engine records released to DRMO for disposition, 01 DEC 05 ** Aircraft deleted from inventory and released to DRMO for disposition, 19 JAN 06.

157435/157481 LTV A-7E-6-CV Corsair II (Block VI) Multi-YR 69, Contract N00019-68-C-0075, (160) A-7E; E-158/E-317

E-204 157435 Navy acceptance from NPRO Rep. LTV, Dallas, TX., 23 MAY 70 ** Transferred to VA-122/FRS, NJ/2XX, NAS LeMoore, CA., 27 MAY 70 ** Transferred to VA-27/CVW-14, NK/4XX, USS Enterprise (CVAN-65), 20 MAY 71; To VA-27, NAS LeMoore, CA., 07 JUN 71; To VA-27, USS Enterprise (CVAN-65), 01 APR 75; To VA-27, NAS LeMoore, CA., 20 MAY 75; To VA-27, NAS Fallon, NV., 24 OCT 75; To VA-27, NAS Jacksonville, FL., 03 NOV 75; To VA-27, NAS LeMoore, CA., 07 JAN 76; To VA-27, USS Enterprise (CVN-65), 12 MAR 76; To VA-27, NAS LeMoore, CA., 26 APR 76; To VA-27, USS Enterprise (CVN-65), 30 JUN 76; To VA-27, NAS LeMoore, CA., 30 JUN 76; To VA-27, USS Enterprise (CVN-65), 28 JUL 76; To VA-27, NAS LeMoore, CA., 28 MAR 77; To VA-27, USS Enterprise (CVN-65), 12 JAN 78; To VA-27, NAS LeMoore, CA., 03 MAR 78; To VA-27, USS Enterprise (CVN-65), 26 JUN 78; To VA-27, NAS Cubi Point, PI, 28 SEP 78; To VA-27, NAF Atsugi, JP., 29 SEP 78; To VA-27, NAS Cubi Point, PI., 04 OCT 78; To VA-27, NAS LeMoore, CA., 10 OCT 78; To VA-27, NAS Jacksonville, FL., 08 DEC 78; To VA-27, NAS LeMoore, CA., 22 FEB 79; To VA-27, NPTR El Centro, CA., 22 FEB 79 ** Transferred to VA-22/CVW-15, NL/3XX, NAS LeMoore, CA., 11 APR 79; To VA-22, USS Kitty Hawk (CV-63), 26 APR 79; To VA-22, NAF Atsugi, JP., 12 DEC 79; To VA-22, USS Kitty Hawk (CV-63), 26 DEC 79; To VA-22, NAS LeMoore, CA., 26 DEC 79; To VA-22, USS Kitty Hawk (CV-63), 11 SEP 80; To VA-22, NAS LeMoore, CA., 28 SEP 80 ** Transferred to VA-146/CVW-9, NG/3XX, NAS LeMoore, CA., 03 DEC 80; To VA-146, NAS Jacksonville, FL., 01 FEB 81; To VA-146, NAS LeMoore, CA., 31 MAR 81 ** To VA-147/CVW-9, NG/4XX, NAF El Centro, CA., 23 APR 81; To VA-147, USS Constellation (CV-64), 30 APR 81; To VA-147, NAS LeMoore, CA., 12 JUN 81; To VA-147, USS Constellation (CV-64), 07 JUL 81; To VA-147, NAS LeMoore, CA., 06 AUG 81; To VA-147, USS Constellation (CV-64), 19 OCT 81; To VA-147, NAS Cubi Point, PI., 19 OCT 81; To VA-147, USS Constellation (CV-64), 19 OCT 81; To VA-147, NAS LeMoore, CA., 19 OCT 81; To VA-147, NAS Jacksonville, FL., 15 APR 83; To VA-147, NAS LeMoore, CA., 12 JUL 83; To VA-147, USS Kitty Hawk (CV-63), 22 DEC 83; To VA-147, NAS LeMoore, CA., 29 AUG 84; To VA-147, USS Kitty Hawk (CV-63), 11 APR 85; To VA-147, NAS LeMoore, CA., 03 FEB 86; To VA-147, NAS Jacksonville, FL., 12 JUN 86 ** Transferred to VA-304/CVWR-30, ND/403, NAS Alameda, CA., 18 NOV 86; To VA-304, NAS Jacksonville, FL., 09 DEC 86; To VA-304, NAS Alameda, CA., 31 AUG 87 ** End of flight record card ** Transferred to AMARC, Davis Monthan AFB; Tucson, AZ., as 6A0268; 19 MAY 88 ** 6495.5 flight hours ** TF41A402D engine S/N 142621 ** Aircraft deleted from inventory and released to DRMO for disposition, 02 JUN 99 ** On conditional loan from the National Naval Museum; Pensacola, FL., to the Mayor of Watertown, SD., for display, 15 JUN 99.

E-158 157436 Navy acceptance from NPRO Rep. LTV, Dallas, TX., 11 APR 70 ** Transferred to VA-113/CVW-2, NE/3XX, NAS LeMoore, CA., 14 APR 70 ** Transferred to VA-27/CVW-14, NK/4XX, USS Enterprise (CVAN-65), 03 AUG 70 ~ S 1SO strike, 06 MAY 71 ** No data on strike.

E-159 157437 Navy acceptance from NPRO Rep. LTV, Dallas, TX., 31 MAR 70 ** Transferred to VA-113/CVW-2, NE/3XX, NAS LeMoore, CA., 02 APR 70 ** Transferred to VA-27/CVW-14, NK/4XX, USS Enterprise (CVAN-65), 30 JUN 70; To VA-27, NAS LeMoore, CA., 14 JUN 71 ** Transferred to VA-97/CVW-14, NK/3XX, NAS LeMoore, CA., 26 OCT 71 ** Transferred to VA-22/CVW-15, NL/3XX, USS Coral Sea (CVA-43), 27 JAN 72 ~ S 1SO strike, 25 JUN 72 ** LT Geofrey R. Shumway KIA when shot down over North Vietnam.

E-160 157438 Navy acceptance from NPRO Rep. LTV, Dallas, TX., 18 APR 70 ** Transferred to VA-113/CVW-2, NE/3XX, NAS LeMoore, CA., 19 APR 70 ** Transferred to VA-27/CVW-14, NK/4XX, USS Enterprise (CVAN-65), 07 JUL 70; To VA-27, NAS LeMoore, CA., 27 MAR 71 ** Transferred to VA-146/CVW-

9, NG/310, NAS LeMoore, CA., 28 JAN 72; To VA-146, USS Constellation (CVA-64), 30 JUN 72; To VA-146, NAS LeMoore, CA., 22 DEC 74; To VA-146, NAS Jacksonville, FL., 12 APR 75; To VA-146, NAS Cecil field, FL., 28 MAY 75; To VA-146, NAS Fallon, NV., 02 JUN 75; To VA-146, NAS Jacksonville, FL., 02 JUN 75; To VA-146, NAS LeMoore, CA., 23 JUN 75 ** Transferred to VA-22/CVW-15, NL/3XX, NAS LeMoore, CA., 17 NOV 75; To VA-22, NAS Fallon, NV., 30 APR 76; To VA-22, NAS LeMoore, CA., 30 APR 76; To VA-22, NAF Atsugi, JP., 08 JUN 77; To VA-22, USS Coral Sea (CV-43), 12 JUL 77; To VA-22, NAF Atsugi, JP., 28 JUL 77; To VA-22, USS Coral Sea (CV-43), 18 AUG 77; To VA-22, NAF Atsugi, JP., 08 SEP 77; To VA-22, USS Coral Sea (CV-43), 11 SEP 77; To VA-22, NAS LeMoore, CA., 18 OCT 77; To VA-22, NAS Jacksonville, FL., 12 FEB 78; To VA-22, NAS LeMoore, CA., 05 APR 78; To VA-22, NAS Kingsville, TX., 23 AUG 78; To VA-22, NAS LeMoore, CA., 23 AUG 78; To VA-22, USS Kitty Hawk (CV-63), 21 MAR 79; To VA-22, NAS Cubi Point, PI., 30 MAY 79; To VA-22, NAS LeMoore, CA., 30 JAN 80 ** To VA-97/CVW-14, NK/3XX, USS Coral Sea (CV-43), 22 MAR 80 ** To VA-93/CVW-5, NF/3XX, NAF Atsugi, JP., 20 APR 80; To VA-93, USS Midway (CV-41), 27 MAY 80; To VA-93, NAF Atsugi, JP., 13 NOV 80 ** Transferred to VA-56/CVW-5, NF/4XX, USS Midway (CV-41), 24 FEB 81; To VA-56, NAF Atsugi, JP., 06 JUL 81 ~ S 1SO strike, 29 AUG 81 ** No data on strike.

E-161 157439 Navy acceptance from NPRO Rep. LTV, Dallas, TX., 05 MAY 70 ** Transferred to VA-174/FRS, AD/4XX, NAS Cecil Field, FL., 05 MAY 70 ** Transferred to VA-83/CVW-17, AA/3XX, NAS Cecil Field, FL., 29 JUN 70; To VA-83, USS Forrestal (CVA-59), 29 JUN 70; To VA-83, NAS Cecil Field, FL., 26 JUN 71; To VA-83, USS Forrestal (CVA-59), 22 APR 72; To VA-83, NAS Cecil Field, FL., 13 MAY 74; To VA-83, NAS Jacksonville, FL., 22 NOV 74; To VA-83, USS Forrestal (CVA-59), 05 FEB 75; To VA-83, NAS Cecil Field, FL., 01 SEP 75; To VA-83, USS Forrestal (CV-59), 25 SEP 75; To VA-83, NAS Cecil Field, FL., 25 SEP 75; To VA-83, USS Forrestal (CV-59), 25 SEP 75; To VA-83, NAS Cecil Field, FL., 25 SEP 75; To VA-83, NAS Roosevelt Roads, PR., 25 SEP 75; To VA-83, NAS Cecil Field, FL., 25 SEP 75; To VA-83, USS Forrestal (CV-59), 20 JUL 77; To VA-83, NAS Cecil Field, FL., 20 JUL 77; To VA-83, USS Forrestal (CV-59), 20 JUL 77; To VA-83, NAS Jacksonville, FL., 01 FEB 78; To VA-83, USS Forrestal (CVA-59), 13 MAR 78; To VA-83, NAS Cecil Field, FL., 26 APR 78; To VA-83, USS Forrestal (CV-59), 06 MAR 79 ** Transferred to VA-37/CVW-3, AC/3XX, NAS Cecil Field, FL., 09 JUL 79; To VA-37, MCAS Yuma, AZ., 09 JUL 79; To VA-37, NAS Cecil Field, FL., 09 JUL 79; To VA-37, USS Saratoga (CV-60), 09 JUL 79; To VA-37, NAS Cecil Field, FL., 09 JUL 79; To VA-37, USS Saratoga (CV-60), 09 JUL 79; To VA-37, NAS Cecil Field, FL., 09 JUL 79 ** Transferred to VA-12/CVW-7, AG/4XX, NAS Cecil Field, FL., 20 FEB 81; To VA-12, USS Dwight D. Eisenhower (CVN-69), 20 APR 81 ** Transferred to VA-174/FRS, AD/4XX, 01 AUG 81; To VA-174, NAS Jacksonville, FL., 09 SEP 81; To VA-174, NAS Cecil Field, FL., 02 NOV 81 ** Transferred to VA-12/CVW-7, AG/4XX, NAS Cecil Field, FL., 07 NOV 81; To VA-12, USS Dwight D. Eisenhower (CVN-69), 22 JAN 82; To VA-12, NAS Cecil Field, FL., 18 FEB 82 ** Transferred to VA-174/FRS, AD/4XX, NAS Cecil Field, FL., 14 JAN 83 ~ S 1SO strike, 14 JUN 83 ** Crashed on the USS Lexington (AVT-16) in the Gulf of Mexico, Pilot ejected and landed on the Flight Deck.

E-162 157440 Navy acceptance from NPRO Rep. LTV, Dallas, TX., 01 APR 70 ** Transferred to VA-113/CVW-2, NE/3XX, NAS LeMoore, CA., 07 APR 70 ** Transferred to VA-27/CVW-14, NK/402, USS Enterprise (CVAN-65), 21 AUG 70; To VA-27, NAS LeMoore, CA., 07 JUN 71; To VA-27, USS Enterprise (CVAN-65), 20 OCT 74; To VA-27, NAS LeMoore, CA., 25 MAY 75; To VA-27, NAS Jacksonville, FL., 28 AUG 75; To VA-27, NAS LeMoore, CA., 16 SEP 75; To VA-27, NAS Fallon, NV., 24 OCT 75; To VA-27, NAS LeMoore, CA., 19 FEB 76; To VA-27, USS Enterprise (CVN-65), 12 MAR 76; To VA-27, NAS LeMoore, CA., 24 MAR 76; To VA-27, USS Enterprise (CVN-65), 29 APR 76; To VA-27, NAF Atsugi, JP., 28 DEC 76; To VA-27, USS Enterprise (CVN-65), 29 DEC 76; To VA-27, NAS LeMoore, CA., 17 MAR 77; To VA-27, USS Enterprise (CVN-65), 02 FEB 78; Painted three tone gray with no tail letters

in 78; To VA-27, NAS LeMoore, CA., 03 MAR 78; To VA-27, USS Enterprise (CVN-65), 25 AUG 78; To VA-27, NAF Atsugi, JP., 31 AUG 78; To VA-27, USS Enterprise (CVN-65), 01 SEP 78; To VA-27, NAF Atsugi, JP., 04 SEP 78; To VA-27, NAS Cubi Point, PI., 24 SEP 78; To VA-27, NAS LeMoore, CA., 10 OCT 78; To VA-27, NAS Jacksonville, FL., 25 JAN 79; To VA-27, NAS LeMoore, CA., 15 MAR 79; To VA-27, NPTR El Centro, CA., 15 MAR 79 ** Transferred to VA-22/CVW-15, NL/4XX, NAS LeMoore, CA., 11 APR 79; To VA-22, USS Kitty Hawk (CV-63), 26 APR 79; To VA-22, NAS LeMoore, CA., 30 MAY 79; To VA-27, NAS Alameda, CA., 24 MAR 80; To VA-27, NAS LeMoore, CA., 08 AUG 80; To VA-22, USS Kitty Hawk (CV-63), 11 SEP 80; To VA-27, NAS LeMoore, CA., 13 JAN 81; To VA-22, USS Kitty Hawk (CV-63), 22 JAN 81 ** Transferred to VA-122/FRS, NJ/257, NAS LeMoore, CA., 11 FEB 81; To VA-122, NAS Jacksonville, FL., 25 AUG 81; To VA-122, NAS LeMoore, CA., 23 SEP 81; To VA-122, NAS Jacksonville, FL., 23 OCT 81 ** Transferred to VA-25/CVW-2, NE/4XX, NAS LeMoore, CA., 18 FEB 82; To VA-25, USS Ranger (CV-61), 18 FEB 82; To VA-25, NAS Cubi Point, PI., 18 FEB 82; To VA-25, USS Ranger (CV-61), 18 FEB 82; To VA-25, NAF Atsugi, JP., 29 AUG 82 ** Transferred to VA-94/CVW-11, NH/4XX, USS Enterprise (CVN-65), 10 FEB 83; To VA-94, NAS Cubi Point, PI.,10 FEB 83; To VA-94, NAS LeMoore, CA., 16 APR 83 ** Transferred to VA-37/ CVW-15, NL/3XX, USS Carl Vinson (CVN-70), 12 MAY 83 ** To VA-27/CVW-15, NL/4XX, NAS LeMoore, CA., 31 OCT 83; To VA-27, USS Carl Vinson (CVN-70), 01 APR 84; To VA-27, NAS Jacksonville, FL., 06 APR 84; To VA-27, USS Carl Vinson (CVN-70), 09 APR 84; To VA-27, NAS Jacksonville, FL., 16 JUL 84; To VA-27, NAS LeMoore, CA., 21 JUL 84; To VA-27, USS Carl Vinson (CVN-70), 21 JUL 84; To VA-27, NAS LeMoore, CA., 31 OCT 83 ** Transferred to VA-174/FRS, AD/4XX, NAS Jacksonville, FL., 05 JUN 86; To VA-174, NAS Cecil Field, FL., 20 JUN 86 ** Transferred to VA-204/CVWR-20, AF/411, NAS New Orleans, LA., 21 JUL 86 thru 06 AUG 87 ** End of flight record card ** Transferred to AMARC, Davis Monthan AFB; Tucson, AZ., assigned park code 6A0304; 12 OCT 89 ** 5967.3 flight hours ** TF41A402D engine S/N AE1419?? ** Project changed per FSO letter, 06 APR 04 ** At AMARC; Davis Monthan AFB; Tucson, AZ., 11 JAN 06.

E-163 157441 Navy acceptance from NPRO Rep. LTV, Dallas, TX., 31 MAR 70 ** Transferred to VA-113/CVW-2, NE/3XX, NAS LeMoore, CA., 05 APR 70 ** Transferred to VA-27/CVW-14, NK/4XX, USS Enterprise (CVAN-65), 30 JUN 70; To VA-27, NAS LeMoore, CA., 07 JUN 71; To VA-27, NAS Jacksonville, FL., 17 SEP 75; To VA-27, NAS Fallon, NV., 19 NOV 75; To VA-27, NAS LeMoore, CA., 19 FEB 76; To VA-27, USS Enterprise (CVN-65), 07 MAR 76; To VA-27, NAS Alameda, CA., 15 MAR 76; To VA-27, NAS LeMoore, CA., 31 MAR 76; To VA-27, USS Enterprise (CVN-65), 29 APR 76; To VA-27, NAS LeMoore, CA., 17 MAY 76; To VA-27, USS Enterprise (CVN-65), 30 JUN 76; To VA-27, NAF Atsugi, JP., 20 OCT 76; To VA-27, USS Enterprise (CVN-65), 07 NOV 76; To VA-27, NAS LeMoore, CA., 17 MAR 77; To VA-27, USS Enterprise (CVN-65), 12 JAN 78; To VA-27, NAS LeMoore, CA., 03 MAR 78; To VA-27, USS Enterprise (CVN-65), 10 JUN 78; To VA-27, NAF Atsugi, JP., 22 JUN 78; To VA-27, USS Enterprise (CVN-65), 29 JUN 78; To VA-27, NAF Atsugi, JP., 07 JUL 78; To VA-27, USS Enterprise (CVN-65), 21 JUL 78; To VA-27, NAS Cubi Point, PI., 30 AUG 78; To VA-27, NAS LeMoore, CA., 10 OCT 78; To VA-27, NAS Jacksonville, FL., 15 FEB 79; To VA-27, NPTR El Centro, CA., 30 APR 79; To VA-27, NAS LeMoore, CA., 20 SEP 79; To VA-27, USS Coral Sea (CV-43), 20 SEP 79 ** Transferred to VA-25/CVW-2, NE/4XX, NAS LeMoore, CA., 07 NOV 79; To VA-25, NAS Fallon, NV., 07 NOV 79; To VA-25, NAS LeMoore, CA., 12 JAN 80; To VA-25, USS Ranger (CV-61), 29 MAY 80; To VA-25, NAS LeMoore, CA., 25 JUN 80; To VA-25, USS Ranger (CV-61), 30 JUN 80; To VA-25, NAS LeMoore, CA., 07 AUG 80; To VA-25, USS Ranger (CV-61), 10 SEP 80; To VA-25, NAS LeMoore, CA., 10 SEP 80; To VA-25, NAS Jacksonville, FL., 04 JUN 81; To VA-25, NAS LeMoore, CA., 22 JUL 81; To VA-25, NAS Fallon, NV., 14 SEP 81; To VA-25, USS Ranger (CV-61), 20 OCT 81; To VA-25, NAS LeMoore, CA., 10 NOV 81; To VA-25, NAS Jacksonville, FL., 11 NOV 81; To VA-25, NAS LeMoore, CA., 27 NOV 81; To VA-25,

USS Ranger (CV-61), 14 JAN 82; To VA-25, NAS LeMoore, CA., 14 JAN 82; To VA-25, USS Ranger (CV-61), 11 MAR 82; To VA-25, NAS Cubi Point, PI., 11 MAR 82; To VA-25, USS Ranger (CV-61), 26 JUN 82 ** Transferred to VA-56/CVW-5, NF/4XX, NAF Atsugi, JP., 27 AUG 82 ** Transferred to VA-22/CVW-11, NH/3XX, USS Enterprise (CVN-65), 17 NOV 84; To VA-22, NAS LeMoore, CA., 17 NOV 84 ** Transferred to VA-122/FRS, NJ/2XX, NAS LeMoore, CA., 01 MAR 85 ** Transferred to VA-304/CVWR-30, ND/4XX, NAS Alameda, CA., 28 MAY 86; To VA-304, NAS Pensacola, FL., 04 JUN 86; To VA-304, NAS Alameda, CA., 23 FEB 87; To VA-304, NAS Pensacola, FL., 04 MAR 87; To VA-304, NAS Alameda, CA., 18 MAR 87 thru 25 APR 87 ** End of flight record card ** Transferred to AMARC, Davis Monthan AFB; Tucson, AZ., assigned park code 6A0286; 29 JUL 88 ** 6144.4 flight hours ** TF41A402D engine S/N 141258 ** Engine released to DRMO for disposition, 05 OCT 05 ** Aircraft deleted from inventory and released to DRMO for disposition, 05 OCT 05.

E-164 157442 Navy acceptance from NPRO Rep. LTV, Dallas, TX., 17 APR 70 ** Transferred to VA-113/CVW-2, NE/3XX, NAS LeMoore, CA., 17 APR 70 ** Transferred to VA-27/CVW-14, NK/414, USS Enterprise (CVAN-65), 10 SEP 70; To VA-27, NAS LeMoore, CA., 05 APR 71; To VA-27, USS Enterprise (CVAN-65), 25 AUG 74 ** Transferred to VA-195/CVW-11, NH/4XX, NAS LeMoore, CA., 08 OCT 75; To VA-195, NAS Alameda, CA., 04 DEC 74; To VA-195, NAS LeMoore, CA., 05 DEC 74; To VA-195, USS Kitty Hawk (CV-63), 01 MAR 75; To VA-195, NAS Cubi Point, PI., 21 JUN 75; To VA-195, NAS LeMoore, CA., 19 JAN 76; To VA-195, NAS Jacksonville, FL., 17 MAR 77; To VA-195, NAS LeMoore, CA., 18 MAY 77; To VA-195, USS Kitty Hawk (CV-63), 25 JUL 77; To VA-195, NAS LeMoore, CA., 12 AUG 77; To VA-195, USS Kitty Hawk (CV-63), 16 SEP 77 ** Transferred to VA-25/CVW-2, NE/4XX, USS Ranger (CV-61), 11 MAR 82; To VA-25, NAS Cubi Point, PI., 11 MAR 82; To VA-25, USS Ranger (CV-61), 26 JUN 82 ** To VA-56/CVW-5, NF/4XX, NAF Atsugi, JP., 27 AUG 82 ** Transferred to VA-195/CVW-11, NH/4XX, USS Kitty Hawk (CV-63), 16 SEP 77; To VA-195, NAS LeMoore, CA., 09 MAR 78; To VA-195, USS America (CV-66), 30 APR 79 ~ S 1SO strike, 15 JUN 79 ** No data on strike.

E-165 157443 Navy acceptance from NPRO Rep. LTV, Dallas, TX., 18 APR 70 ** Transferred to VA-174/FRS, AD/4XX, NAS Cecil Field, FL., 21 APR 70 ** Transferred to VA-81/CVW-17, AA/4XX, NAS Cecil Field, FL., 25 MAY 70; To VA-81, USS Forrestal (CVA-59), 25 MAY 70; To VA-81, NAS Cecil Field, FL., 10 JUN 71 ** Transferred to VA-66/CVW-7, AG/300, NAS Cecil Field, FL., 15 SEP 71; To VA-66, USS Independence (CVA-62), 27 JUN 72; To VA-66, NAS Cecil Field, FL., 23 MAR 73; To VA-66, USS Independence (CVA-62), 26 FEB 74; To VA-66, NAS Jacksonville, FL., 03 FEB 75; To VA-66, NAS Cecil Field, FL., 20 FEB 75; To VA-66, USS Independence (CVA-62), 03 SEP 75; To VA-66, NAS Cecil Field, FL., 10 MAY 76; To VA-66, NAS Fallon, NV., 08 SEP 76; To VA-66, USS Independence (CVA-62), 08 SEP 76; To VA-66, NAS Cecil Field, FL., 01 JAN 77; To VA-66, USS Independence (CVA-62), 01 JAN 77; To VA-66, NAS Cecil Field, FL., 01 APR 77; To VA-66, USS Independence (CVA-62), 01 JUL 77; To VA-66, NAS Cecil Field, FL., 20 OCT 77; To VA-66, NAS Jacksonville, FL., 21 OCT 77; To VA-66, Dwight D. Eisenhower (CVN-69), 21 OCT 77; To VA-66, NAS Jacksonville, FL., 24 JAN 78; To VA-66, NAS Cecil Field, FL., 30 JAN 78; To VA-66, Dwight D. Eisenhower (CVN-69), 09 MAY 78; To VA-66, NAS Cecil Field, FL., 09 MAY 78; To VA-66, Dwight D. Eisenhower (CVN-69), 09 MAY 78; To VA-66, NAS Cecil Field, FL., 09 MAY 78; To VA-66, Dwight D. Eisenhower (CVN-69), 09 MAY 78; To VA-66, NAS Cecil Field, FL., 04 JAN 80; To VA-66, Dwight D. Eisenhower (CVN-69), 22 MAR 80; To VA-66, NAS Cecil Field, FL., 01 APR 80; To VA-66, Dwight D. Eisenhower (CVN-69), 01 APR 80; To VA-66, NAS Cecil Field, FL., 01 APR 80; To VA-66, Dwight D. Eisenhower (CVN-69), 01 APR 80 ** Transferred to VA-174/FRS, AD/4XX, NAS Cecil Field, FL., 17 AUG 81 ** Transferred to VA-37/CVW-15, NL/3XX, NAS Cecil Field, FL., 07 OCT 82; To VA-37, USS Carl Vinson (CVN-70), 10 DEC 82; To VA-37, NAS Cecil Field, FL., 10 DEC 82; To VA-37, USS Carl Vinson (CVN-70), 10 DEC 82 ~ S 1SO strike, 26 JUL 83 ** Crashed due to a night ramp strike, pilot ejected safely.

E-166 157444 Navy acceptance from NPRO Rep. LTV, Dallas, TX., 13 APR 70 ** Transferred to VA-113/CVW-2, NE/3XX, NAS LeMoore, CA., 24 APR 70 ** Transferred to VA-27/CVW-14, NK/4XX, USS Enterprise (CVAN-65), 06 JUL 70; To VA-27, NAS LeMoore, CA., 28 JUN 71 ** Transferred to VA-94/CVW-15, NL/403, USS Coral Sea (CVA-43), 28 JAN 72; To VA-94, NAS LeMoore, CA., 21 JUN 73; To VA-94, USS Coral Sea (CVA-43), 24 MAY 75; To VA-94, NAS LeMoore, CA., 09 JUL 75; To VA-94, NAS Fallon, NV., 01 SEP 75; To VA-94, NAS LeMoore, CA., 01 NOV 75; To VA-94, NAS Fallon, NV., 11 MAR 76; To VA-94, NAS LeMoore, CA., 29 APR 76 ** Transferred to VA-12/CVW-7, AG/4XX, NAS Cecil Field, FL., 10 MAY 76; To VA-12, NAS Fallon, NV., 10 MAY 76; To VA-12, USS Independence (CV-62), 10 MAY 76; To VA-12, NAS Cecil Field, FL., 10 MAY 76; To VA-12, USS Independence (CV-62), 10 MAY 76; To VA-12, USS America (CV-66), 03 JAN 77 ** Transferred to VA-174/FRS, AD/4XX, NAS Cecil Field, FL., 26 MAY 77 ** Transferred to VA-83/CVW-17, AA/3XX, USS Forrestal (CV-59), 14 MAR 78; To VA-83, NAS Cecil Field, FL., 27 APR 78; To VA-83, USS Forrestal (CV-59), 16 AUG 78; To VA-83, NAS Cecil Field, FL., 17 AUG 78; To VA-83, NAS Jacksonville, FL., 03 OCT 78; To VA-83, NAS Cecil Field, FL., 13 OCT 78; To VA-83, USS Forrestal (CV-59), 09 NOV 78; To VA-83, NAS Cecil Field, FL., 24 OCT 79; To VA-83, USS Forrestal (CV-59), 24 OCT 79; To VA-83, NAS Cecil Field, FL., 20 MAR 80; To VA-83, NAS Jacksonville, FL., 21 JUL 80; To VA-83, NAS Cecil Field, FL., 22 SEP 80; To VA-83, USS Forrestal (CV-59), 25 SEP 80; To VA-83, NAS Cecil Field, FL., 25 SEP 80; To VA-83, USS Forrestal (CV-59), 25 SEP 80; To VA-83, NAS Cecil Field, FL., 25 SEP 80; To VA-83, NAS Fallon, NV., 09 DEC 81 ** Transferred to VA-81/CVW-17, AA/4XX, USS Forrestal (CV-59), 22 FEB 82; To VA-81, NAS Cecil Field, FL., 25 MAR 82; To VA-81, USS Forrestal (CV-59), 25 MAR 82; To VA-81, NAS Cecil Field, FL., 25 MAR 82; To VA-81, NAS Jacksonville, FL., 14 DEC 82; To VA-81, NAS Cecil Field, FL., 04 FEB 83; To VA-81, NAS Fallon, NV., 05 AUG 83; To VA-81, NAS Cecil Field, FL., 05 AUG 83; To VA-81, USS Saratoga (CV-60), 25 OCT 83; To VA-81, NAS Cecil Field, FL., 27 DEC 83; To VA-81, USS Saratoga (CV-60), 27 DEC 83; To VA-81, NAS Cecil Field, FL., 27 DEC 83; To VA-81, USS Saratoga (CV-60), 30 APR 85; To VA-81, NAS Cecil Field, FL., 01 JUN 85; To VA-81, NAS Jacksonville, FL., 02 AUG 85; To VA-81, USS Saratoga (CV-60), 08 JAN 86; To VA-81, NAS Jacksonville, FL., 27 MAR 86 ** Transferred to VA-174/FRS, AD/413, NAS Cecil Field, FL., 02 APR 86 ** Transferred to AMARC, Davis Monthan AFB; Tucson, AZ., assigned park code 6A0239; 15 AUG 86 thru 15 SEP 87 ** End of flight record card ** 6145.9 flight hours ** TF41A2C engine S/N AE141919 ** Engine released to DRMO for disposition, 05 OCT 05 ** Aircraft deleted from inventory and released to DRMO for disposition, 05 OCT 05.

E-167 157445 Navy acceptance from NPRO Rep. LTV, Dallas, TX., 09 APR 70 ** Transferred to VA-113/CVW-2, NE/3XX, NAS LeMoore, CA., 11 APR 70 ** Transferred to VA-27/CVW-14, NK/4XX, USS Enterprise (CVAN-65), 20 AUG 70; To VA-27, NAS LeMoore, CA., 17 JUN 71; To VA-27, USS Enterprise (CVAN-65), 01 FEB 75; To VA-27, NAS LeMoore, CA., 20 MAY 75; To VA-27, NAS Jacksonville, FL., 13 AUG 75; To VA-27, NAS Fallon, NV., 16 OCT 75; To VA-27, NAS LeMoore, CA., 04 FEB 76; To VA-27, USS Enterprise (CVN-65), 12 MAR 76; To VA-27, NAS LeMoore, CA., 16 APR 76; To VA-27, USS Enterprise (CVN-65), 22 APR 76; To VA-27, NAS LeMoore, CA., 17 MAY 76; To VA-27, USS Enterprise (CVN-65), 30 JUN 76; To VA-27, NAF Atsugi, JP., 11 JAN 77; To VA-27, USS Enterprise (CVN-65), 15 JAN 77; To VA-27, NAS LeMoore, CA., 28 MAR 77; To VA-27, USS Enterprise (CVN-65), 12 JAN 78; To VA-27, NAS LeMoore, CA., 02 FEB 78; To VA-27, USS Enterprise (CVN-65), 25 AUG 78; To VA-27, NAF Atsugi, JP., 15 SEP 78; To VA-27, NAS Cubi Point, PI., 22 SEP 78; To VA-27, NAF Atsugi, JP., 25 SEP 78; To VA-27, NAS Cubi Point, PI., 02 OCT 78; To VA-27, NAS LeMoore, CA., 10 OCT 78; To VA-27, NAS Jacksonville, FL., 10 DEC 78; To VA-27, NAS LeMoore, CA., 11 DEC 78; To VA-27, NAS Jacksonville, FL., 13 MAR 79; To VA-27, NAS LeMoore, CA., 19 MAR 79; To VA-27, NAS Jacksonville, FL., 24 MAR 79; To VA-27, NAS LeMoore, CA., 26 MAR 79; To VA-27, NAS El Centro, CA., 26 MAR 79 ** Transferred to VA-22/

CVW15, NL/3XX, NAS LeMoore, CA., 05 APR 79; To VA-22, USS Kitty Hawk (CV-63), 19 APR 79; To VA-22, NAF Atsugi, JP., 26 OCT 79; To VA-22, NAS LeMoore, 26 OCT 79; To VA-22, USS Kitty Hawk (CV-63), 11 SEP 80; To VA-22, NAS LeMoore, CA., 20 OCT 80 ** Transferred to VA-27/CVW-14, NK/4XX, NAS Jacksonville, FL., 08 APR 81; To VA-27, NAS LeMoore, CA., 04 JUN 81; To VA-27, USS Coral Sea (CV-43), 20 AUG 81; To VA-27, NAS LeMoore, CA., 22 MAR 82 ** Transferred to VA-94/CVW-11, NH/4XX, USS Enterprise (CVN-65), 25 AUG 82; To VA-94, NAS Cubi Point, PI., 06 DEC 82; To VA-94, NAS LeMoore, CA., 16 APR 83; To VA-94, NAF Atsugi, JP., 19 APR 83 ** Transferred to VA-37/ CVW-15, NL/3XX, USS Carl Vinson (CVN-70), 12 MAY 83; To VA-37, NAF Atsugi, JP., 24 JUN 83; To VA-37, USS Carl Vinson (CVN-70), 30 JUN 83 ** Transferred to VA-122/FRS, NJ/2XX, NAS LeMoore, CA., 28 OCT 83; To VA-122, NAS Jacksonville, FL., 03 MAR 84; To VA-122, NAS LeMoore, CA., 18 MAY 84 ** Transferred to AMARC, Davis Monthan AFB; Tucson, AZ., assigned park code 6A0190; 15 AUG 86 ** End of flight record card ** 6025.8 flight hours ** TF41A2B engine S/N 141507 ** Project changed per FSO letter, 06 APR 04 ** Engine released to DRMO for disposition, 05 OCT 05 ** Aircraft deleted from inventory and released to DRMO for disposition, 05 OCT 05.

E-168 157446 Navy acceptance from NPRO Rep. LTV, Dallas, TX., 18 APR 70 ** Transferred to VA-174/FRS, AD/4XX, NAS Cecil Field, FL., 21 APR 70 ** Transferred to VA-81/CVW-17, AA/400, NAS Cecil Field, FL., 25 MAY 70; To VA-81, USS Forrestal (CVA-59), 02 JUN 70; To VA-81, NAS Cecil Field, FL., 17 JUN 71; To VA-81, USS Forrestal (CVA-59), 21 MAY 72; To VA-81, NAS Jacksonville, FL., 11 SEP 74; To VA-81,USS Forrestal (CVA-59), 12 SEP 74; To VA-81, NAS Jacksonville, FL., 17 SEP 74; To VA-81, NAS Cecil Field, FL., 07 NOV 74; To VA-81, USS Forrestal (CVA-59), 07 NOV 74; To VA-81, NAS Cecil Field, FL., 01 SEP 75; To VA-81, USS Forrestal (CVA-59), 20 SEP 75; To VA-81, NAS Cecil Field, Fl., 20 SEP 75; To VA-81, NAS Roosevelt Roads, PR., 05 JAN 77; To VA-81, NAS Cecil Field, Fl., 15 FEB 77; To VA-81, NAS Roosevelt Roads, PR., 07 APR 77; To VA-81, NAS Cecil Field, Fl., 07 APR 77; To VA-81, USS Forrestal (CV-59), 20 JUL 77; To VA-81, NAS Cecil Field, Fl., 20 JUL 77;To VA-81, USS Forrestal (CV-59), 15 JAN 78 ** Transferred to NARF, NAS Jacksonville, FL., 20 MAR 78 ** Transferred to VA-87/CVW-6, AE/4XX, NAS Cecil Field, FL., 03 FEB 82; To VA-87, USS Independence (CV-62), 08 APR 82; To VA-87, NAS Cecil Field, FL., 08 APR 82; To VA-87, USS Independence (CV-62), 09 APR 82; To VA-87, NAS Cecil Field, FL., 09 APR 82 ~ S 1SO strike, 05 APR 83 ** Pilot ejected safely after an engine failure.

E-169 157447 Navy acceptance from NPRO Rep. LTV, Dallas, TX., 07 MAY 70 ** Transferred to VA-174/FRS, AD/4XX, NAS Cecil Field, FL., 10 MAY 70 thru 01 DEC 71 ~ S 1SO strike, 01 DEC 71 ** No data on strike.

E-170 157448 Navy acceptance from NPRO Rep. LTV, Dallas, TX., 18 APR 70 ** Transferred to VA-174/FRS, AD/4XX, NAS Cecil Field, FL., 23 APR 70 ** Transferred to VA-81/CVW-17, AA/403, NAS Cecil Field, FL., 19 MAY 70; To VA-81, USS Forrestal (CV-59), 25 MAY 70; To VA-81, NAS Cecil Field, FL., 27 MAY 71 ~ S 1SO strike, 05 DEC 71 ** No data on strike.

E-171 157449 Navy acceptance from NPRO Rep. LTV, Dallas, TX., 30 APR 70 ** Transferred to VA-174/FRS, AD/4XX, NAS Cecil Field, FL., 01 MAY 70 ** Transferred to VA-66/CVW-7, AG/302, NAS Cecil Field, FL., 23 AUG 71; To VA-66, USS Independence (CVA-62), 30 JUN 72; To VA-66, NAS Cecil Field, FL., 17 APR 73; To VA-66, USS Independence (CVA-62), 15 MAR 74; To VA-66, NAS Jacksonville, FL., 14 JAN 75; To VA-66, NAS Cecil Field, FL., 20 FEB 75; To VA-66, USS Independence (CVA-62), 24 JUL 75; To VA-66, NAS Cecil Field, FL., 12 MAY 76; To VA-66, NAS Fallon, NV., 08 JUL 76; To VA-66, USS Independence (CVA-62), 01 NOV 76; To VA-66, NAS Cecil Field, FL., 01 NOV 76; To VA-66, USS Independence (CVA-62), 01 NOV 76; To VA-66, NAS Cecil Field, FL., 01 FEB 77; To VA-66, USS Independence (CVA-62), 01 FEB

77; To VA-66, NAS Cecil Field, FL., 09 AUG 77; To VA-66, USS Dwight D. Eisenhower (CVN-69), 09 AUG 77; To VA-66, NAS Cecil Field, FL., 09 AUG 77; To VA-66, NAS Jacksonville, FL., 27 MAY 78; To VA-66, USS Dwight D. Eisenhower (CVN-69), 26 JUL 78; To VA-66, NAS Cecil Field, FL., 12 SEP 78; To VA-66, USS Dwight D. Eisenhower (CVN-69), 12 SEP 78; To VA-66, NAS Cecil Field, FL., 12 SEP 78; To VA-66, USS Dwight D. Eisenhower (CVN-69), 12 SEP 78; To VA-66, NAS Cecil Field, FL., 25 OCT 79; To VA-66, USS Dwight D. Eisenhower (CVN-69), 04 DEC 79; To VA-66, NAS Cecil Field, FL., 04 DEC 79; To VA-66, USS Dwight D. Eisenhower (CVN-69), 04 DEC 79 ** Transferred to VA-146/CVW-9, NG/3XX, USS Constellation (CV-64), 27 JUL 80; To VA-146, NAS LeMoore, CA., 27 JUL 80 ** Transferred to VA-174/FRS, AD/4XX, NAS Cecil Field, FL., 31 OCT 80 ** Transferred to VA-66/CVW-7, AG/3XX, NAS Cecil Field, FL., 11 FEB 81; To VA-66, USS Dwight D. Eisenhower (CVN-69), 22 JUN 81; To VA-66, NAS Jacksonville, FL., 26 JUN 81; To VA-66, NAS Cecil Field, FL., 06 JUL 81; To VA-66, USS Dwight D. Eisenhower (CVN-69), 06 JUL 81; To VA-66, NAS Cecil Field, FL., 14 OCT 81; To VA-66, USS Dwight D. Eisenhower (CVN-69), 14 OCT 81; To VA-66, NAS Cecil Field, FL., 14 DEC 81 ** Transferred to VA-174/FRS, AD/4XX, NAS Cecil Field, FL., 20 AUG 82; To VA-174, NAS Jacksonville, FL., 20 SEP 83; To VA-174, NAS Cecil Field, FL., 21 SEP 83 ~ S 1SO strike, 08 NOV 83 ** No data on strike.

E-172 157450 Navy acceptance from NPRO Rep. LTV, Dallas, TX., 20 APR 70 ** Transferred to VA-174/FRS, AD/4XX, NAS Cecil Field, FL., 23 APR 70 ** Transferred to VA-81/CVW-17, AA/404, NAS Cecil Field, FL., 21 JUN 70; To VA-81, USS Forrestal (CV-59), 22 JUN 70; To VA-81, NAS Cecil Field, FL., 17 APR 71; To VA-81, USS Forrestal (CV-59), 02 JUN 72; To VA-81, NAS Cecil Field, FL., 21 OCT 74; To VA-81, USS Forrestal (CV-59), 14 JAN 75 ** Transferred to VA-174/FRS, AD/354, NAS Cecil Field, FL., 31 JAN 75; To VA-174, NAS Jacksonville, FL., 06 FEB 75; To VA-174, NAS Cecil Field, FL., 26 MAR 75 ** Transferred to VA-82/ CVW-8, AJ/3XX, NAS Cecil Field, FL., 15 MAR 77; To VA-82, USS Nimitz (CVN-68), 20 JUL 77; To VA-82, NAS Cecil Field, 16 MAY 78; To VA-82, NAS Jacksonville, FL., 28 AUG 78; To VA-82, NAS Cecil Field, FL., 28 SEP 78; To VA-82, USS Nimitz (CVN-68), 25 JUL 80; To VA-82, NAS Jacksonville, FL., 29 JUL 80; To VA-82, USS Nimitz (CVN-68), 30 SEP 80; To VA-82, NAS Cecil Field, FL., 30 SEP 80; To VA-82, USS Nimitz (CVN-68), 30 SEP 80; To VA-82, NAS Cecil Field, FL., 26 NOV 81 ** Transferred to VA-174/ FRS, AD/4XX, NAS Cecil Field, FL., 23 APR 82; To VA-174, NAS Jacksonville, FL., 10 MAR 83; To VA-174, NAS Cecil Field, FL., 28 MAR 83 ** Transferred to VA-87/CVW-6, AE/4XX, NAS Cecil Field, FL., 05 MAY 83; To VA-87, USS Independence (CV-62), 06 JUN 83; To VA-87, NAS Cecil Field, FL., 17 JUN 83; To VA-87, USS Independence (CV-62), 25 JUL 83; To VA-87, NAS Cecil Field, FL., 09 AUG 83; To VA-87, USS Independence (CV-62), 09 AUG 83; To VA-87, NAS Cecil Field, FL., 02 MAY 84; To VA-87, USS Independence (CV-62), 17 JUL 84; To VA-87, NAS Cecil Field, FL., 20 JUL 84; To VA-87, USS Independence (CV-62), 20 JUL 84 ** Transferred to VA-174/FRS, AD/4XX, NAS Cecil Field, FL., 15 OCT 84; To VA-174, NAS Jacksonville, FL., 28 OCT 85 ** Transferred to VA-12/CVW-7, AG/4XX, NAS Cecil Field, FL., 29 OCT 85 ** Transferred to VA-174/FRS, AD/426, NAS Cecil Field, FL., 27 AUG 86 ** Transferred to AMARC, Davis Monthan AFB; Tucson, AZ., assigned park code 6A0243; 29 SEP 87 ** End of flight record card ** 5961.3 flight hours ** TF41A2C engine S/N 141514 ** Engine released to DRMO for disposition, 05 OCT 05 ** Aircraft deleted from inventory and released to DRMO for disposition, 05 OCT 05.

E-173 157451 Navy acceptance from NPRO Rep. LTV, Dallas, TX., 27 MAY 70 ** Transferred to VA-122/FRS, NJ/2XX, NAS LeMoore, CA., 28 MAY 70 ** Transferred to VA-25/CVW-2, NE/400, NAS LeMoore,CA., 15 JAN 71 ** Transferred to VA-94/CVW-15, NL/4XX, USS Coral Sea (CVA-43), 17 MAY 72 ** Transferred to VA-122/FRS, NJ/2XX, NAS LeMoore, CA., 20 NOV 72 ** Transferred to VA-195/CVW-11, NH/4XX, NAS LeMoore, CA., 27 DEC 73; To VA-195, USS Kitty Hawk (CV-63), 29 JUN

73; To VA-195, NAS LeMoore, CA., 28 AUG 74; To VA-195, USS Kitty Hawk (CV-63), 28 MAR 75; To VA-195, NAS LeMoore, CA., 28 MAR 75; To VA-195, USS Kitty Hawk (CV-63), 19 MAY 75; To VA-195, NAS Cubi Point, PI., 21 JUN 75; To VA-195, NAS LeMoore, CA.,14 DEC 75; To VA-195, NAS Jacksonville, FL., 21 JUN 76; To VA-195, NAS LeMoore, CA., 02 JUL 76; To VA-195, USS Kitty Hawk (CV-63), 25 JUL 77; To VA-195, NAS LeMoore, CA., 12 AUG 77; To VA-195, USS Kitty Hawk (CV-63), 29 SEP 77; To VA-195, NAS LeMoore, CA., 09 MAR 78; To VA-195, NAS Jacksonville, FL., 27 SEP 78; To VA-195, NAS LeMoore, CA., 28 SEP 78; To VA-195, NAS Jacksonville, FL., 26 OCT 78; To VA-195, NAS LeMoore, CA., 01 NOV 78 ~ S 1SO strike, 11 APR 79 ** No data on strike.

E-174 157452 Navy acceptance from NPRO Rep. LTV, Dallas, TX., 19 APR 70 ** Transferred to VA-174/FRS, AD/4XX, NAS Cecil Field, FL., 21 APR 70 ** Transferred to VA-81/CVW-17, AA/4XX, NAS Cecil Field, FL., 31 MAY 70; To VA-81, USS Forrestal (CVA-59), 22 JUN 70; To VA-81, NAS Cecil Field, FL., 25 MAR 71 ** Transferred to VA-174/FRS, AD/4XX, NAS Cecil Field, FL., 19 JUL 72 ** Transferred to VA-81/CVW-17, AA/4XX, USS Forrestal (CVA-59), 10 AUG 72; To VA-81, NAS Cecil Field, FL., 09 OCT 74; To VA-81, USS Forrestal (CVA-59), 17 OCT 74 ** Transferred to VA-174/FRS, AD/4XX, NAS Cecil Field, FL., 21 FEB 75; To VA-174, NAS Jacksonville, FL., 24 FEB 75; To VA-174, NAS Cecil Field, FL., 24 FEB 75; To VA-174, NAS Jacksonville, FL., 25 FEB 75; To VA-174, NAS Cecil Field, FL., 16 APR 75; To VA-174, NAS Jacksonville, FL., 19 JUN 78; To VA-174, NAS Cecil Field, FL., 17 OCT 78; To VA-174, NAS Jacksonville, FL., 21 FEB 81; To VA-174, NAS Cecil Field, FL., 27 JUN 81; To VA-174, NAS Jacksonville, FL., 13 DEC 83; To VA-174, NAS Cecil Field, FL., 01 JAN 84; To VA-174, NAS Jacksonville, FL., 08 MAR 84 ** Transferred to VA-12/CVW-7, AG/4XX, NAS Cecil Field, FL., 09 MAR 84; To VA-12, USS Dwight D. Eisenhower (CVN-69), 12 MAY 84; To VA-12, NAS Cecil Field, FL., 14 MAY 84; To VA-12, USS Dwight D. Eisenhower (CVN-69), 14 MAY 84; To VA-12, NAS Cecil Field, FL., 16 MAY 85; To VA-12, USS Dwight D. Eisenhower (CVN-69), 30 MAY 85; To VA-12, NAS Cecil Field, FL., 23 SEP 85; To VA-12, NAS Jacksonville, FL., 07 MAR 86; To VA-12, NAS Cecil Field, FL., 12 MAR 86; To VA-12, NAS Jacksonville, FL., 07 JUL 86; To VA-12, NAS Cecil Field, FL., 31 JUL 86 ** Transferred to VA-304/CVWR-30, ND/4XX, NAS Alameda, CA., 31 OCT 86 thru 17 MAY 87 ** End of flight record card ** On conditional loan from the National Museum of Naval Aviation; Pensacola, Florida to NAS Atlanta, GA, date unknown.

E-175 157453 Navy acceptance from NPRO Rep. LTV, Dallas, TX., 19 APR 70 ** Transferred to VA-174/FRS, AD/4XX, NAS Cecil Field, FL., 20 APR 70 ** Transferred to VA-81/CVW-17, AA/4XX, NAS Cecil Field, FL., 31 MAY 70; To VA-81, USS Forrestal (CVA-59), 22 JUN 70; To VA-81, NAS Cecil Field, FL., 27 MAY 71; To VA-81, USS Forrestal (CVA-59), 21 MAY 72; To VA-81, NAS Cecil Field, FL., 04 NOV 74; To VA-81, NAS Jacksonville, FL., 03 JAN 75; To VA-81, NAS Cecil Field, FL., 03 JAN 75; To VA-81, USS Forrestal (CVA-59), 04 JAN 75; To VA-81, NAS Cecil Field, FL., 01 SEP 75; To VA-81, USS Forrestal (CVA-59), 03 NOV 75; To VA-81, NAS Cecil Field, FL., 03 NOV 75; To VA-81, NAS Roosevelt Roads, PR., 26 OCT 76; To VA-81, NAS Cecil Field, FL., 26 OCT 76; To VA-81, NAS Roosevelt Roads, PR., 26 OCT 76; To VA-81, NAS Cecil Field, FL., 26 OCT 76; To VA-81, NAS Jacksonville, FL., 01 DEC 77; To VA-81, NAS Cecil Field, FL., 02 JAN 78; To VA-81, USS Forrestal (CV-59), 07 FEB 78; To VA-81, NAS Cecil Field, FL., 01 MAR 78 ** Transferred to VA-174/FRS, AD/4XX, NAS Cecil Field, FL., 16 JAN 79; To VA-174, NAS Jacksonville, FL., 25 FEB 81; Transferred to VA-174, NAS Cecil Field, FL., 22 MAR 81; To VA-174, NAS Jacksonville, FL., 14 JUN 82; Transferred to VA-174, NAS Cecil Field, FL., 23 JUL 82 ** Transferred to VA-37/CVW-15, NL/3XX, NAS Cecil Field, FL., 23 NOV 82; To VA-37, USS Carl Vinson (CVN-70), 10 JAN 83; Transferred to VA-37, NAS Cecil Field, FL., 26 JAN 83; To VA-37, USS Carl Vinson (CVN-70), 26 JAN 83; To VA-37, NAS Roosevelt Roads, PR., 26 JAN 83; To VA-37, NAS Cecil Field, FL., 09 MAR

84; To VA-37, NAS Jacksonville, FL., 09 MAR 84; To VA-37, NAS Cecil Field, FL., 12 MAR 84; To VA-37, NAS Jacksonville, FL., 11 MAY 84; To VA-37, NAS Cecil Field, FL., 14 MAY 84; To VA-37, MCAS Twenty Nine Palms, CA. 24 JUL 84; To VA-37, NAS Cecil Field, FL., 05 SEP 84; To VA-37, MCAS Iwakuni, JP., 11 SEP 84; To VA-37, Korea, 03 MAR 85; To VA-37, MCAS Iwacuni, JP., 05 MAR 85; To VA-37, NAS Cecil Field, Fl., 02 JUL 85; To VA-37, USS Forrestal (CV-59), 03 FEB 86; To VA-37, NAS Cecil Field, Fl., 03 FEB 86; To VA-37, USS Forrestal (CV-59), 09 MAY 86; To VA-37, NAS Cecil Field, FL., 09 DEC 86 ** Transferred to AMARC, Davis Monthan AFB; Tucson, AZ., assigned park code 6A0212; 09 JAN 87 ** End of flight record card ** 6160.7 flight hours ** TF41A2B engine S/N 141235 ** Aircraft deleted from inventory and released to DRMO for dispsition, 18 JAN 96.

E-176 157454 Navy acceptance from NPRO Rep. LTV, Dallas, TX, 17 APR 70 ** Transferred to VA-113/CVW-2, NE/3XX, NAS LeMoore, CA., 19 APR 70 ** Transferred to VA-27/CVW-14, NK/405 & NK/411, USS Enterprise (CVAN-65), 20 JUN 70; To VA-27, NAS LeMoore, CA., 24 MAR 71; To VA-27 USS Enterprise (CVAN-65), 08 NOV 74 ~ S 1SO strike, 29 APR 75 ** No data on strike.

E-177 157455 Navy acceptance from NPRO Rep. LTV, Dallas, TX., 30 APR 70 ** Transferred to VA-174/FRS, AD/4XX, NAS Cecil Field, FL., 02 MAY 70 ** Transferred to VA-83/CVW-17, AA/310, USS Forrestal (CVA-59), 14 JUL 70; To VA-83, NAS Cecil Field, FL., 15 MAY 71; To VA-83, USS Forrestal (CVA-59), 22 APR 72; To VA-83 NAS Field, FL., 16 AUG 74; To VA-83, NAS Jacksonville, FL., 12 DEC 74; To VA-83, USS Forrestal (CVA-59), 20 FEB 75; To VA-83, NAS Cecil Field, FL., 01 SEP 75; To VA-83, USS Forrestal (CV-59), 01 MAR 76; To VA-83, NAS Cecil Field, FL., 17 MAR 76; To VA-83, USS Forrestal (CV-59), 21 MAY 76; To VA-83, NAS Cecil Field, FL., 21 MAY 76; To VA-83, NAS Roosevelt Roads, PR., 16 DEC 76; To VA-83, NAS Cecil Field, FL., 16 DEC 76; To VA-83, USS Forrestal (CV-59), 20 JUL 77; To VA-83, NAS Cecil Field, FL., 20 JUL 77; To VA-83, NAS Jacksonville, FL., 05 JAN 78; To VA-83, USS Forrestal (CV-59), 03 FEB 78; To VA-83, NAS Cecil Field, FL., 14 FEB 78 ** Transferred to VA-174/FRS, AD/4XX, NAS Cecil Field, FL., 17 JAN 79; To VA-174, NAS Jacksonville, FL., 02 NOV 79; To VA-174, NAS Cecil Field, FL., 23 JAN 80 ** Transferred to VA-46/CVW-1, AB/311, NAS Cecil Field, FL., 31 JAN 80; To VA-46, USS John F. Kennedy (CV-67), 20 MAR 80; To VA-46, NAS Cecil Field, FL., 15 APR 81; To VA-46, NAS Jacksonville, FL., 30 MAR 82; To VA-46, NAS Cecil Field, FL., 11 APR 82 ** Transferred to VA-12/CVW-7, AG/406, NAS Cecil Field, FL., 31 AUG 82; To VA-12, USS Dwight D. Eisenhower (CVN-69), 04 MAY 83; To VA-12, NAS Cecil Field, FL., 20 JUN 83; To VA-12, USS Dwight D. Eisenhower (CVN-69), 23 MAY 84; To VA-12, NAS Jacksonville, FL., 07 JUN 84 ** Transferred to VA-174/FRS, AD/4XX, NAS Cecil Field, FL., 12 SEP 84 ** Transferred to VA-37/CVW-6, AE/3XX, NAS Cecil Field, FL., 17 NOV 84; To VA-37, MCAS Iwakuni, JP., 17 NOV 84; To VA-37, Korea, 17 NOV 84; MCAS Iwakuni, JP., 17 NOV 84; To VA-37, NAS Cecil Field, FL., 17 NOV 84; To VA-37, USS Forrestal (CV-59), 21 JAN 86; To VA-37, NAS Cecil Field, FL., 21 JAN 86; To VA-37, USS Forrestal (CV-59), 28 MAY 86 ** Transferred to US Army, 16 JUL 87 thru 17 JUL 87 ** End of flight record card ** On display at the War Eagles Air Museum; Santa Teresa, NM., MAY 01.

E-178 157456 Navy acceptance from NPRO Rep. LTV, Dallas, TX., 28 APR 70 ** Transferred to VA-174/ FRS, AD/4XX, NAS Cecil Field, FL., 01 MAY 70 ** Transferred to VA-37/CVW-3, AC/3XX, NAS Cecil Field, FL., 29 JUN 73 ** Transferred to NATC, NAS Patuxent River, MD., for RDT & E, 17 JUN 74 ** Transferred to VA-174/FRS, AD/4XX, NAS Cecil Field, FL., 06 SEP 74; To VA-174, NAS Jacksonville, FL., 24 APR 75; To VA-174, NAS Cecil Field, FL., 12 JUN 75 ** Transferred to VA-82/CVW-8, AJ/305, USS Nimitz (CVN-68), 15 NOV 77; To VA-82, NAS Jacksonville, FL., 15 AUG 78; To VA-82, NAS Cecil Field, FL., 13 SEP 78; To VA-82, USS Nimitz (CVN-68), 30 APR 80; To VA-82, NAS Jacksonville, FL., 30 MAY 80; To VA-82, USS Nimitz (CVN-68), 30 MAY 80; To VA-82, NAS Cecil Field, FL., 06 AUG 80 ~ S-1SO strike, 02 MAR 81** Pilot ejected after a night ramp strike followed by an explosion.

E-179 157457 Navy acceptance from NPRO Rep. LTV, Dallas, TX., 30 APR 70 ** Transferred to VA-174/FRS, AD/4XX, NAS Cecil Field, FL., 01 MAY 70 ** Transferred to VA-83/CVW-17, AA/305, NAS Cecil Field, FL., 29 JUN 70; To VA-83, USS Forrestal (CVA-59), 29 JUN 70; To VA-83, NAS Cecil Field, FL., 26 APR 71; To VA-83, USS Forrestal (CVA-59), 28 APR 72; To VA-83, NAS Cecil Field, FL., 26 SEP 74; To VA-83, NAS Jacksonville, FL., 04 NOV 74; To VA-83, NAS Cecil Field, FL., 05 NOV 74; To VA-83, NAS Jacksonville, FL., 19 DEC 74; To VA-83, NAS Cecil Field, FL., 31 DEC 74; To VA-83, USS Forrestal (CVA-59), 31 DEC 74; To VA-83, NAS Cecil Field, FL., 31 DEC 74; To VA-83, USS Forrestal (CVA-59), 31 DEC 74; To VA-83, NAS Cecil Field, FL., 17 AUG 75 ~ S 1SO strike, 17 AUG 75 ** No data on strike.

E-180 157458 Navy acceptance from NPRO Rep. LTV, Dallas, TX., 09 MAY 70 ** Transferred to VA-174/FRS, AD/4XX, NAS Cecil Field, FL., 11 MAY 70; Transferred to VA-83/CVW-17, AA/3XX, USS Forrestal (CVA-59), 29 JUL 70; To VA-83, NAS Cecil Field, FL., 27 APR 71; To VA-83, USS Forrestal (CVA-59), 01 APR 72; To VA-83, NAS Cecil Field, FL., 19 FEB 74; To VA-83, NAS Jacksonville, FL., 08 NOV 74; To VA-83, NAS Cecil Field, FL., 08 NOV 74; To VA-83, NAS Jacksonville, FL., 11 NOV 74; To VA-83, NAS Cecil Field, FL., 28 DEC 74; To VA-83, USS Forrestal (CVA-59), 28 DEC 74; To VA-83, NAS Cecil Field, FL., 28 DEC 74; To VA-83, USS Forrestal (CVA-59), 28 DEC 74; To VA-83, NAS Cecil Field, FL., 01 SEP 75; To VA-83, USS Forrestal (CV-59), 23 SEP 75; To VA-83, NAS Cecil Field, FL., 25 SEP 75; To VA-83, USS Forrestal (CV-59), 25 SEP 75; To VA-83, NAS Cecil Field, FL., 25 SEP 75; To VA-83, NAS Roosevelt Roads, PR., 25 SEP 75; To VA-83, NAS Cecil Field, FL., 25 SEP 75; To VA-83, USS Forrestal (CV-59), 20 JUL 77; To VA-83, NAS Cecil Field, FL., 20 JUL 77; To VA-83, NAS Jacksonville, FL., 16 JAN 78; To VA-83, USS Forrestal (CV-59), 07 FEB 78; To VA-83, NAS Cecil Field, FL., 09 OCT 78; To VA-83, NAS Jacksonville, FL., 13 NOV 78; To VA-83, NAS Cecil Field, FL., 15 DEC 78 ** Transferred to VA-174/FRS, AD/4XX, NAS Cecil Field, FL., 22 MAR 79 ** Transferred to VA-72/CVW-1, AB/4XX, NAS Cecil Field, FL., 24 MAR 80; To VA-72, USS John F. Kennedy (CV-67), 22 APR 80; To VA-72, NAS Cecil Field, FL., 22 APR 80 ** Transferred to VA-81/CVW-17, AA/4XX, NAS Cecil Field, FL., 30 APR 82 ** Transferred to VA-87/CVW-6, AE/414, NAS Cecil Field, FL., 26 MAY 82; To VA-87, USS Independence (CV-62), 27 MAY 82; To VA-87, NAS Cecil Field, FL., 27 MAY 82; To VA-87, USS Independence (CV-62), 28 APR 83; To VA-87, NAS Cecil Field, FL., 28 APR 83; To VA-87, USS Independence (CV-62), 25 JUL 85; To VA-87, NAS Cecil Field, FL., 29 SEP 83; To VA-87, USS Independence (CV-62), 05 OCT 83 ~ S 1SO strike, 13 FEB 84 ** Lost due to engine failure, pilot ejected safely.

E-181 157459 Navy acceptance from NPRO Rep. LTV, Dallas, TX., 25 APR 70 ** Transferred to VA-174/FRS, AD/4XX, NAS Cecil Field, FL., 27 APR 70 ** Transferred to VA-83/CVW-17, AA/300, USS Forrestal (CV-59), 07 JUL 70; To VA-83, NAS Cecil Field, FL., 16 JUN 71 ** Transferred to VA-174/FRS, AD/4XX, NAS Cecil Field, FL., 24 MAY 72 ** Transferred to VA-12/CVW-7, AG/414, USS Independence (CVA-62), 18 OCT 72; To VA-12, NAS Cecil Field, FL., 08 FEB 73; To VA-12, USS Independence (CVA-62), 01 JUL 74; To VA-12, NAS Jacksonville, FL., 23 JAN 75; To VA-12, NAS Cecil Field, FL., 24 FEB 75; To VA-12, NAS Fallon, NV., 01 APR 75; To VA-12, NAS Cecil Field, FL., 01 JUL 75; To VA-12, USS Independence (CV-62), 03 SEP 75; To VA-12, NAS Cecil Field, FL., 07 MAY 76; To VA-12, NAS Fallon, NV., 15 JUL 76; To VA-12, USS Independence (CV-62), 01 SEP 76; To VA-12, NAS Cecil Field, FL., 01 DEC 76; To VA-12, USS Independence (CV-62), 01 DEC 76; To VA-12, NAS Cecil Field, FL., 09 AUG 77; To VA-12, NAS Jacksonville, FL., 08 OCT 77; To VA-12, NAS Cecil Field, FL., 28 FEB 78 ** Transferred to VA-174/FRS, AD/404, NAS Cecil Field, FL., 27 APR 78; To VA-174, NAS Jacksonville, FL., 31 DEC 81; To VA-174, NAS Cecil Field, FL., 31 DEC 81; To VA-174, NAS Jacksonville, FL., 05 JAN 82; NAS Cecil Field, FL., 03 MAR 82; To VA-174, NAS Dallas, TX., 09 MAR 82 ** Transferred to VA-86/CVW-8, AJ/401, NAS Cecil Field, FL., 07

JUN 82; To VA-86, USS Nimitz (CVN-68), 07 JUN 82; To VA-86, NAS Cecil Field, FL., 07 JUN 82; To VA-86, USS Nimitz (CVN-68), 07 JUN 82; NAS Cecil Field, FL., 07 JUN 82; To VA-86, USS Nimitz (CVN-68), 07 JUN 82; NAS Cecil Field, FL., 07 JUN 82; To VA-86, NAS Roosevelt Roads, PR., 31 AUG 83 ~ S 1SO, strike, 31 AUG 83 ** No data on crash.

E-182 157460 Navy acceptance from NPRO Rep. LTV, Dallas, TX., 13 MAY 70 ** Transferred to VA-113/CVW-2, NE/3XX, NAS LeMoore, CA., 15 MAY 70 ** Transferred to VA-27/CVW-14, NK/4XX, USS Enterprise (CVAN-65), 28 JUL 70 ** Transferred to VA-113/CVW-2, NE/305, NAS LeMoore, CA., 28 JUL 70 ** Transferred to VA-27/CVW-14, NK/4XX, USS Enterprise (CVAN-65), 28 JUL 70; To VA-27, NAS LeMoore, CA., 17 MAR 71; To VA-27, NAS Fallon, NV., 01 DEC 75; To VA-27, NAS LeMoore, CA., 01 DEC 75; To VA-27, NAS Jacksonville, FL., 28 FEB 76; To VA-27, USS Enterprise (CVN-65), 17 APR 76; To VA-27, NAS LeMoore, CA., 17 MAY 76; To VA-27, USS Enterprise (CVN-65), 30 JUN 76; To VA-27, NAS LeMoore, CA., 30 JUN 76; To VA-27, USS Enterprise (CVN-65), 28 JUL 76; To VA-27, NAS LeMoore, CA., 28 MAR 77; To VA-27, USS Enterprise (CVN-65), 12 JAN 78; To VA-27, NAS LeMoore, CA., 03 MAR 78; To VA-27, USS Enterprise (CVN-65), 26 JUN 78; To VA-27, NAF Atsugi, JP., 28 JUN 78; To VA-27, USS Enterprise (CVN-65), 04 JUL 78; To VA-27, NAS Cubie Point, PI., 22 SEP 78; NAF Atsugi, JP., 29 SEP 78; To VA-27, NAS Cubie Point, PI., 04 OCT 78; To VA-27, NAS LeMoore, CA., 10 OCT 78; To VA-27, NAS Jacksonville, FL., 06 JAN 79; To VA-27, NAS LeMoore, CA., 16 FEB 79; To VA-27, NPTR El Centro, CA., 21 MAR 79; To VA-27, USS Coral Sea (CV-43), 25 JUL 79; To VA-27, NAS LeMoore, CA., 25 JUL 79; To VA-27, USS Coral Sea (CV-43), 12 OCT 79 ** Transferred to VA-192/CVW-11, NH/3XX, NAS LeMoore, CA., 07 JUL 81; To VA-192, NAS Jacksonville, FL., 27 FEB 83; To VA-192, NAS Dallas, TX., 24 MAY 83; To VA-192, USS Ranger (CV-61), 25 MAY 83; To VA-192, NAS Dallas, TX., 27 AUG 83 ** Transferred to VA-146/CVW-9, NG/3XX, 27 AUG 83; To VA-146, NAS Kitty Hawk (CV-63), 08 OCT 83; To VA-146, NAS LeMoore, CA., 27 AUG 84; To VA-146, NAS Jacksonville, FL., 28 MAR 85; To VA-146, NAS LeMoore, CA., 28 MAR 85; To VA-146, NAS Jacksonville, FL., 01 APR 85 ** Transferred to NARF, NAS Jacksonville, FL., 21 JUL 85 ** Transferred to VA-22/CVW-11, NH/3XX, NAS LeMoore, CA., 11 AUG 85 ** Transferred to VA-82/CVW-8, AJ/3XX, NAS Cecil Field, FL., 31 OCT 85; To VA-82, USS Nimitz (CVN-68), 19 FEB 86; To VA-82, NAS Cecil Field, FL., 10 OCT 86; To VA-82, USS Nimitz (CVN-68), 10 OCT 86; To VA-82, NAS Cecil Field, FL., 10 OCT 86 ** Transferred to VA-174/FRS, AD/427, NAS Cecil Field, FL., 15 SEP 87 ** End of flight record card ** Transferred to AMARC, Davis Monthan AFB; Tucson, AZ., assigned park code 6A0256; 23 MAR 88 ** 5987.8 flight hours ** TF41A402D engine S/N 141386 ** Project changed per FSO letter, 06 APR 04 ** At AMARC; Davis Monthan AFB; Tucson, AZ., 11 JAN 06.

E-183 157461 Navy acceptance from NPRO Rep. LTV, Dallas, TX., 20 APR 70 ** Transferred to VA-174/FRS, AD/4XX, NAS Cecil Field, FL., 23 APR 70 ** Transferred to VA-81/CVW-17, AA/4XX, NAS Cecil Field, FL., 18 MAY 70; To VA-81, USS Forrestal (CVA-59), 22 JUN 70; To VA-81, NAS Cecil Field, FL., 07 MAR 71 ** Transferred to VA-82/CVW-6, AE/3XX, USS America (CVA-66), 06 MAR 72 ** Transferred to VA-174/FRS, AD/4XX, NAS Cecil Field, FL., 31 MAR 72 ** Transferred to VA-12/CVW-7, AG/4XX, USS Independence (CVA-62), 16 OCT 72; To VA-12, NAS Cecil Field, FL., 23 MAR 73; To VA-12, USS Independence (CVA-62), 24 MAY 75 ** Transferred to VA-174/FRS, AD/4XX, NAS Cecil Field, FL., 10 JUL 74; To VA-174, NAS Jacksonville, FL., 26 FEB 75; To VA-174, NAS Cecil Field, FL., 23 APR 75 ** Transferred to VA-81/CVW-17, AA/4XX, USS Forrestall (CV-59), 14 MAR 78; To VA-81, NAS Cecil Field, FL., 14 MAR 78; To VA-81, USS Forrestal (CV-59), 22 NOV 78; To VA-81, NAS Cecil Field, FL., 22 NOV 78 ** Transferred to VA-105/CVW-3, AC/4XX, NAS Cecil Field, FL., 07 AUG 79; To VA-105, USS Saratoga (CV-60), 07 AUG 79; To VA-105, NAS Cecil Field, FL., 07 AUG 79; To VA-105, USS Saratoga (CV-60), 07 AUG 79; To VA-105, NAS Cecil Field, FL., 26 FEB

81; To VA-105 NAS Jacksonville, FL., 26 FEB 81; To VA-105, NAS Cecil Field, FL., 26 MAY 81 ** Transferred to VA-86/CVW-8, AJ/4XX, USS Nimitz (CVN-68), 30 MAY 81; To VA-86, NAS Cecil Field, FL., 30 MAY 81; To VA-86, USS Nimitz (CVN-68), 17 JUL 81; To VA-86, NAS Cecil Field, FL., 17 JUL 81 ** Transferred to VA-82/CVW-8, AJ/3XX, USS Carl Vinson (CVN-70), 08 MAY 82; To VA-82, NAS Cecil Field, FL., 27 MAY 82; To VA-82, USS Nimitz (CVN-68), 01 JUL 82; To VA-82, NAS Cecil Field, FL., 01 JUL 82; To VA-82, USS Nimitz (CVN-68), 01 JUL 82; To VA-82, NAS Cecil Field, FL., 16 MAY 83 ~ S 1SO strike, 31 AUG 83 ** No data on strike.

E-184 157462 Navy acceptance from NPRO Rep. LTV, Dallas, TX., 28 MAY 70 ** Transferred to VA-174/FRS, AD/4XX, NAS Cecil Field, FL., 02 JUN 70 ~ S 1SO strike, 28 AUG 73 ** No data on strike.

E-185 157463 Navy acceptance from NPRO Rep. LTV, Dallas, TX., 30 APR 70 ** Transferred to VA-174/FRS, AD/4XX, NAS Cecil Field, FL., 01 MAY 70 ** Transferred to VA-83/CVW-17, AA/3XX, USS Forrestal (CVA-59), 27 JUL 70; To VA-83, NAS Cecil Field, FL., 24 MAY 71 ** Transferred to VA-174/FRS, AD/4XX, NAS Cecil Field, FL., 16 MAY 72 ** Transferred to VA-66/CVW-7, AG/314, USS Forrestal (CVA-59), 25 OCT 72; To VA-66; NAS Cecil Field, FL., 12 DEC 73; To VA-66, USS Independence (CV-62), 23 APR 75; To VA-66; NAS Cecil Field, FL., 27 JAN 75; To VA-66, USS Independence (CV-62), 01 SEP 75; To VA-66; NAS Cecil Field, FL., 10 MAY 76; To VA-66, NAS Fallon, NV., 26 JUL 76; To VA-66, USS Independence (CV-62), 26 JUL 76; To VA-66; NAS Cecil Field, FL., 01 JAN 77; To VA-66, USS Independence (CV-62), 01 JAN 77; To VA-66, NAS Cecil Field, FL., 09 AUG 77; To VA-66, USS Dwight D. Eisenhower (CVN-69), 09 AUG 77; To VA-66, NAS Cecil Field, FL., 09 AUG 77; To VA-66, NAS Jacksonville, FL., 19 APR 78; To VA-66, NAS Cecil Field, FL., 03 AUG 78; To VA-66, USS Dwight D. Eisenhower (CVN-69), 03 AUG 78; To VA-66, NAS Cecil Field, FL., 03 AUG 78; To VA-66, USS Dwight D. Eisenhower (CVN-69), 03 AUG 78; To VA-66, NAS Cecil Field, FL., 03 AUG 78; To VA-66, USS Dwight D. Eisenhower (CVN-69), 03 AUG 78 ** Transferred to VA-82/CVW-8, AJ/3XX, NAS Cecil Field, FL., 08 JAN 79 ** Transferred to VA-174/FRS, AD/4XX, NAS Cecil Field, FL., 24 JAN 80; To VA-174, NAS Jacksonville, FL., 18 AUG 80 ** Transferred to VA-105/CVW-3, AC/4XX, USS Saratoga (CV-60), 28 OCT 80; To VA-105, NAS Cecil Field, FL., 28 OCT 80; To VA-105, NAS Fallon, NV., 17 MAY 81; To VA-105, NAS Cecil Field, FL., 25 JUN 81; To VA-105, USS John F. Kennedy (CV-67), 16 JUL 81; To VA-105, NAS Cecil Field, FL., 17 JUL 81 ** Transferred to VA-37/CVW-3, AC/3XX, NAS Cecil Field, FL., 26 AUG 82; To VA-37/CVW-15, NL/3XX, USS Carl Vinson (CVN-70), 19 JAN 83; To VA-37, NAS Cecil Field, FL., 20 JAN 83 ** Transferred to VA-87/CVW-6, AE/4XX, NAS Cecil field, FL., 22 FEB 83; To VA-87, USS Independence (CV-62), 19 MAY 83 ** Transferred to VA-82/CVW-8, AJ/3XX, NAS Cecil Field, FL., 03 JUN 83; To VA-82, NAS Jacksonville, FL., 30 SEP 83; To VA-82, NAS Cecil Field, FL., 28 JAN 84 ** Transferred to VA-12/CVW-7, AG/413, NAS Cecil Field, FL., 03 APR 84; To VA-12, USS Dwight D. Eisenhower (CVN-69), 03 APR 84; To VA-12, NAS Cecil Field, FL., 03 APR 84; To VA-12, USS Dwight D. Eisenhower (CVN-69), 03 APR 84; To VA-12, NAS Cecil Field, FL., 03 APR 84; To VA-12, USS Dwight D. Eisenhower (CVN-69), 03 APR 84; To VA-12, NAS Cecil Field, FL., 10 SEP 85; To VA-12, NAS Jacksonville, FL., 27 MAR 86; To VA-12, NAS Cecil Field, FL., 14 APR 86; To VA-12, NAS Jacksonville, FL., 16 JUN 86; To VA-12, NAS Cecil Field, FL., 17 JUN 86 ** Transferred to AMARC, Davis Monthan AFB; Tucson, AZ., assigned park code 6A0194; 28 AUG 86 ** End of flight record card ** 4787.9 flight hours ** TF41A402D engine S/N 142379 ** Project changed per FSO letter, 06 APR 04 ** Aircraft deleted from inventory and released to DRMO for disposition, 05 OCT 05.

E-186 157464 Navy acceptance from NPRO Rep. LTV, Dallas, TX., 11 MAY 70 ** Transferred to VA-81/CVW-17, AA/4XX, NAS Cecil Field, FL., 13 MAY 70 ~ S 1SO strike, 04 JUN 70 ** No data on strike.

E-187 157465 Navy acceptance from NPRO Rep. LTV, Dallas, TX., 11 MAY 70 ** Transferred to VA-81/CVW-17, AA/4XX, NAS Cecil Field, FL., 13 MAY 70; To VA-81, USS Forrestal (CVA-59), 22 JUN 70; To VA-81, NAS Cecil Field, FL., 15 JUN 71 ** Transferred to VA-82/CVW-8, AJ/3XX, USS America (CVA-66), 24 MAR 72 ** Transferred to VA-81/ CVW-17, AA/4XX, NAS Cecil Field, FL., 05 MAY 72; To VA-81, USS Forrestal (CVA-,59), 05 MAY 72; To VA-81, NAS Cecil Field, FL., 20 FEB 74; To VA-81, NAS Jacksonville, FL., 10 DEC 74; To VA-81, USS Forrestal (CVA-59), 11 FEB 75; To VA-81, NAS Cecil Field, FL., 01 SEP 75; To VA-81, USS Forrestal (CVA-59), 23 SEP 75; To VA-81, NAS Cecil Field, FL., 23 SEP 75; To VA-81, NAS Roosevelt Roads, PR., 25 AUG 76; To VA-81, NAS Cecil Field, FL., 25 AUG 76; To VA-81, NAS Roosevelt Roads, PR., 06 APR 76; To VA-81, NAS Cecil Field, FL., 06 APR 77; To VA-81, USS Forrestal (CV-59), 20 JUL 77, To VA-81, NAS Cecil Field, FL., 20 JUL 77; To VA-81, NAS Jacksonville, FL., 10 JAN 78; To VA-81, USS Forrestal (CV-59), 14 FEB 78, To VA-81, NAS Cecil Field, FL., 14 MAY 78 ** Transferred to VA-174/FRS, AD/4XX, NAS Cecil Field, FL., 19 JAN 79 ** Transferred to VA-37/CVW-3, AC/3XX, NAS Cecil Field, FL., 28 JUN 79; To VA-37, MCAS Yuma, AZ., 28 JUN 79; To VA-37, NAS Cecil Field, FL., 28 JUN 79; To VA-37, USS Saratoga (CV-60), 15 DEC 79; To VA-37, NAS Cecil Field, FL., 15 DEC 79; To VA-37, USS Saratoga (CV-60), 15 DEC 79; To VA-37, NAS Cecil Field, FL., 15 DEC 79; To VA-37, NAS Fallon, NV., 12 DEC 80; To VA-37, NAS Cecil Field, FL., 12 DEC 80; To VA-37, USS John F. Kennedy (CV-67), 12 DEC 80; To VA-37, NAS Cecil Field, FL., 12 DEC 80 ** Transferred to VA-87/CVW-6, AE/4XX, NAS Cecil Field, FL., 08 OCT 81; To VA-87, NAS Jacksonville, FL., 06 NOV 81; To VA-87, USS Independence (CV-62), 28 DEC 81; To VA-87, NAS Jacksonville, FL., 31 JAN 82; To VA-87, NAS Cecil Field, FL., 02 FEB 82; To VA-87, USS Independence (CV-62), 02 FEB 82; To VA-87, NAS Cecil Field, FL., 02 FEB 82; To VA-87, USS Independence (CV-62), 02 FEB 82; To VA-87, NAS Cecil Field, FL., 02 FEB 82 ~ S 1SO strike, 14 APR 83 ** Crashed due to engine failure, pilot ejected safely.

E-188 157466 Navy acceptance from NPRO Rep. LTV, Dallas, TX., 14 MAY 70 ** Transferred to VA-113/CVW-2, NE/3XX, NAS LeMoore, CA., 15 MAY 70 ** Transferred to VA-27/CVW-14, NK/4XX, USS Enterprise (CVAN-65), 30 JUL 70; To VA-27, NAS LeMoore, CA., 14 JUN 71 ** Transferred to VA-122/FRS, NJ/2XX, NAS LeMoore, CA., 22 JUN 72 ** Transferred to VA-22/CVW-15, NL/300, USS Coral Sea (CV-43), 10 SEP 72; To VA-22, NAS LeMoore, CA., 18 JUN 73; To VA-22, USS Coral Sea (CVA-43), 29 NOV 74; To VA-22, NAS LeMoore, CA., 30 JUL 75; To VA-22, NAS Fallon, NV., 01 SEP 75; To VA-22, NAS LeMoore, CA., 01 NOV 75; To VA-22, NAS Jacksonville, FL., 30 NOV 75; To VA-22, NAS LeMoore, CA., 01 DEC 75; To VA-22, NAS Jacksonville, FL., 27 FEB 76; To VA-22, NAS LeMoore, CA., 05 MAR 76; To VA-22, NAS Fallon, NV., 30 APR 76; To VA-22, NAS LeMoore, CA., 30 APR 76; To VA-22, USS Coral Sea (CV-43), 21 JUN 77; To VA-22, NAF Atsugi, JP., 27 JUN 77; To VA-22, USS Coral Sea (CV-43), 30 JUN 77; To VA-22, NAS LeMoore, CA., 17 OCT 77; To VA-22, NAS Alameda, CA., 30 JAN 78; To VA-22, NAS LeMoore, CA., 23 FEB 78; To VA-22, NAS Jacksonville, FL., 19 AUG 78; To VA-22, NAS Kingsville, TX., 30 SEP 78; To VA-22, NAS LeMoore, CA., 05 MAR 79; To VA-22, USS Kitty Hawk (CV-63), 26 APR 79; To VA-22, NAF Atsugi, JP., 02 OCT 79; To VA-22, USS Kitty Hawk (CV-63), 24 OCT 79; To VA-22, NAS LeMoore, CA., 24 OCT 79; To VA-22, NAS Jacksonville, FL., 23 JUL 80; To VA-22, NAS LeMoore, CA., 23 JUL 80; To VA-22, NAS Jacksonville, FL., 24 JUL 80; To VA-22, USS Kitty Hawk (CV-63), 04 OCT 80; To VA-22, NAS LeMoore, CA., 13 JAN 81; To VA-22, USS Kitty Hawk (CV-63), 22 JAN 81 ** Transferred to VA-94/CVW-15, NL/4XX, NAS LeMoore, CA.,09 MAR 81; To VA-94, NAS Cubi Point, PI., 13 MAY 81; To VA-94, NAF Atsugi, JP., 25 JUN 81; To VA-94, NAS Cubi Point, PI., 27 JUL 81; To VA-94, USS Kitty Hawk (CV-63), 27 JUL 81 ** Transferred to VA-56/CVW-5, NF/4XX, USS Midway (CVA-41), 23 OCT 81; To VA-56, NAF Atsugi, JP., 30 OCT 81 ** Transferred to VA-25/ CVW-2, NE/4XX, NAS Cubi Point, PI.,

23 AUG 82; To VA-25, NAF Atsugi, JP., 13 SEP 82; To VA-25, USS Ranger (CV-61), 04 OCT 82; To VA-25, NAS LeMoore, CA., 04 OCT 82; To VA-25, NAS Jacksonville, FL., 07 FEB 83 ** Transferred to VA-147/CVW-9, NE/3XX, NAS LeMoore, CA., 17 JUN 83; To VA-147, USS Kitty Hawk (CV-63), 06 JUL 83; To VA-147, NAF Atsugi, JP., 08 MAR 84; To VA-147, USS Kitty Hawk (CV-63), 31 MAR 84; To VA-147, NAF Atsugi, JP., 22 JUN 84; To VA-147, USS Kitty Hawk (CV-63), 30 JUN 84; To VA-147, NAS LeMoore, CA., 05 OCT 84; To VA-147, USS Kitty Hawk (CV-63), 12 JUL 85; To VA-147, NAS Jacksonville, FL., 14 JUL 85; To VA-147, NAS LeMoore, CA., 08 JAN 86 ** Transferred to VA-122/FRS, NJ/220, NAS LeMoore, CA., 24 MAR 86 thru 13 SEP 87 ** End of flight record card ** Transferred to AMARC, Davis Monthan AFB; Tucson, AZ., assigned park code 6A0258; 05 APR 88 ** 6330.9 flight hours ** TF41A402D engine S/N 141278 ** Engine released to DRMO for disposition, 21 DEC 04** Aircraft deleted from inventory and released to DRMO for disposition, 19 JAN 05 ** Transferred to NAS Fallon, NV., to be used as a range target, 26 JAN 05.

E-189 157467 Navy acceptance from NPRO Rep. LTV, Dallas, TX., 28 MAY 70 ** Transferred to VA-81/CVW-17, AA/4XX, NAS Cecil Field, FL., 29 MAY 70; To VA-81, USS Forrestal (CVA-59), 15 JUN 70; To VA-81, NAS Cecil Field, FL., 31 MAY 71; To VA-81, USS Forrestal (CVA-59), 21 MAY 72 ~ S 1SO strike, 12 SEP 72 ** No data on strike.

E-190 157468 Navy acceptance from NPRO Rep. LTV, Dallas, TX., 28 MAY 70 ** Transferred to VA-81/CVW-17, AA/4XX, NAS Cecil Field, FL., 29 MAY 70; To VA-81, USS Forrestal (CVA-59), 23 JUN 70; To VA-81, NAS Cecil Field, FL., 27 APR 71 ** Transferred to VA-174/FRS, AD/4XX, NAS Cecil Field, FL., 01 JUN 72 ** Transferred to VA-12/CVW-7, AG/410, USS Independence (CVA-62), 17 NOV 72; To VA-12, NAS Cecil Field, FL., 15 FEB 73; To VA-12, USS Independence (CV-62), 01 JUL 73; To VA-12, NAS Cecil Field, FL., 01 JUL 73; To VA-12, NAS Fallon, NV., 02 APR 73; To VA-12, NAS Cecil Field, FL., 01 JUL 75; To VA-12, USS Independence (CV-62), 03 SEP 75; To VA-12, NAS Cecil Field, FL., 07 MAY 76; To VA-12, NAS Fallon, NV., 31 AUG 76; To VA-12, USS Independence (CV-62), 01 NOV 76; To VA-12, NAS Cecil Field, FL., 01 NOV 76 ** Transferred to VA-15/CVW-6, AE/3XX, USS America (CV-66), 28 DEC 76; To VA-15, MCAS Yuma, AZ., 28 DEC 76; To VA-15, NAS Cecil Field, FL., 01 FEB 77; To VA-15, USS America (CV-66), 01 FEB 77 ** Transferred to VA-174/FRS, AD/4XX, NAS Cecil Field, FL., 13 JUL 77; To VA-174, NAS Jacksonville, FL., 28 SEP 78; Transferred to VA-174, NAS Cecil Field, FL., 30 NOV 78; To VA-174, NAS Jacksonville, FL., 15 MAY 81; Transferred to VA-174, NAS Cecil Field, FL., 20 MAY 81; To VA-174, NAS Jacksonville, FL., 24 JUL 81; To VA-174, NAS Dallas, TX., 18 AUG 81 ** Transferred to VA-15/CVW-6, AE/305, NAS Cecil Field, FL., 28 OCT 81; To VA-15, USS Independence (CV-62), 28 OCT 81; To VA-15, NAS Cecil Field, FL., 28 OCT 81; To VA-15, USS Independence (CV-62), 29 OCT 81; VA-15, NAS Cecil Field, FL., 09 MAR 82; To VA-15, USS Independence (CV-62), 11 MAR 82; To VA-15, NAS Cecil Field, FL., 14 MAR 82; To VA-15, NAS Jacksonville, FL., 21 MAR 83; To VA-15, USS Independence (CV-62), 26 APR 83; To VA-15, NAS Cecil Field, FL., 26 APR 83; To VA-15, NAS Jacksonville, FL., 01 AUG 83; To VA-15, USS Independence (CV-62), 01 AUG 83; To VA-15, NAS Cecil Field, FL., 16 SEP 83; To VA-15, USS Independence (CV-62), 21 SEP 83 ~ S 1SO strike, 04 DEC 83 ** CDR Edward K. "Honiak" Andrews was hit by a Syrian SAM-7 off the coast of Beirut, LE., near Casino du Liban, LE., Pilot was picked up by a Christian Lebanese fisherman and his son near Zouk Mkayel, LE.

E-191 157469 Navy acceptance from NPRO Rep. LTV, Dallas, TX., 07 MAY 70 ** Transferred to VA-174/FRS, AD/4XX, NAS Cecil Field, FL., 09 MAY 70 ** Transferred to VA-83/CVW-17, AA/3XX, USS Forrestal (CVA-59), 17 JUL 70; To VA-83, NAS Cecil Field, FL., 02 JUN 71 ** Transferred to VA-174/FRS, AD/4XX, NAS Cecil Field, FL., 28 JUN 72 ** Transferred to VA-66/CVW-7, AG/3XX, NAS Cecil Field, FL.,

USS Independence (CVA-62), 31 OCT 72; To VA-66, NAS Cecil Field, FL., 15 FEB 73; To VA-66, USS Independence (CV-62), 01 JUL 73; To VA-66, NAS Cecil Field, FL., 01 FEB 75; To VA-66, NAS Jacksonville, FL., 07 MAR 75; To VA-66, NAS Cecil Field, FL., 08 MAR 75; To VA-66, NAS Jacksonville, FL., 10 MAR 75; To VA-66, NAS Cecil Field, FL., 08 APR 75 ** Transferred to VA-174/FRS, AD/4XX, NAS Cecil Field, FL., 12 JUN 75 ** Transferred to VA-66/CVW-7, AG/3XX, NAS Cecil Field, FL. 15 JUN 76; To VA-66, NAS Fallon, NV., 13 JUL 76; To VA-66, USS Independence (CV-62), 13 JUL 76; To VA-66, NAS Cecil Field, FL., 07 JAN 77 ** Transferred to VA-87/CVW-6, AE/4XX, USS America (CV-66), 07 JAN 77; To VA-87, NAS Cecil Field, FL., 01 APR 77, To VA-87, USS America (CV-66), 09 AUG 77 ** Transferred to VA-174/FRS, AD/4XX, NAS Cecil Field, FL., 23 SEP 77; To VA-174, NAS Jacksonville, FL., 27 SEP 78; Transferred to VA-174, NAS Cecil Field, FL., 19 AUG 80; To VA-174, NAS Jacksonville, FL. 08 JUN 81; Transferred to VA-174/FRS, AD/4XX, NAS Cecil Field, FL., 16 JUL 81 ~ S 1SO strike, 11 DEC 83 ** Pilot ejected after he experienced an electrical failure.

E-192 157470 Navy acceptance from NPRO Rep. LTV, Dallas, TX., 27 MAY 70 ** Transferred to VA-81/CVW-17, AA/4XX, NAS Cecil Field, FL., 29 MAY 70; To VA-81, USS Forrestal (CVA-59), 25 JUN 70; To VA-81, NAS Cecil Field, FL., 14 JUN 71 ** Transferred to VA-174/FRS, AD/4XX, NAS Cecil Field, FL., 30 MAY 72 ~ S 1SO strike, 05 JUL 74 ** No data on strike.

E-193 157471 Navy acceptance from NPRO Rep. LTV, Dallas, TX., 19 MAY 70 ** Transferred to VA-113/CVW-2, NE/3XX, NAS LeMoore, CA., 20 MAY 70 ** Transferred to VA-27/CVW-14, NK/4XX, USS Enterprise (CVAN-65), 20 AUG 70; To VA-22, NAS LeMoore, CA., 24 MAR 71 ** Transferred to VA-122/FRS, NJ/2XX, NAS LeMoore, CA., 22 JUN 72 ** Transferred to VA-94/CVW-15, NL/4XX, USS Coral Sea (CVA-43), 13 SEP 72; To VA-94, NAS LeMoore, CA., 25 JUN 73; To VA-94, NAS Alameda, CA., 18 NOV 74; To VA-94, NAS LeMoore, CA., 19 NOV 74; To VA-94, NAS Alameda, CA., 20 NOV 74 ** Transferred to VA-122/FRS, NJ/2XX, NAS LeMoore, CA., 27 NOV 74; To VA-122, NAS Alameda, CA., 21 FEB 75; To VA-122, NAS LeMoore, CA., 23 FEB 75; To VA-122, NAS Jacksonville, FL., 16 MAY 75; To VA-122, NAS LeMoore, CA., 30 JUN 75 ** Transferred to VA-27/CVW-14, NK/4XX, NAS LeMoore, CA., 07 AUG 75; To VA-27, NAS Fallon, NV., 24 OCT 75; To VA-27, NAS LeMoore, CA., 19 FEB 76; To VA-27, USS Enterprise (CVN-65), 12 MAR 76; To VA-27, NAS LeMoore, CA., 16 MAR 76; To VA-27, USS Enterprise (CVN-65), 31 MAR 76; To VA-27, NAS LeMoore, CA., 31 MAR 76; To VA-27, USS Enterprise (CVN-65), 31 MAR 76; To VA-27, NAS LeMoore, CA., 31 MAY 76; To VA-27, NAF Atsugi, JP., 13 SEP 76; To VA-27, USS Enterprise (CVN-65), 20 SEP 76; To VA-27, NAF Atsugi, JP., 31 JAN 77; To VA-27, USS Enterprise (CVN-65), 23 FEB 77; To VA-27, NAS LeMoore, CA., 17 MAR 77; To VA-27, USS Enterprise (CVN-65), 12 JAN 78; To VA-27, NAS LeMoore, CA., 03 MAR 78; To VA-27, USS Enterprise (CVN-65), 12 JUN 78; To VA-27, NAF Atsugi, JP., 28 JUN 78; To VA-27, USS Enterprise (CVN-65), 04 JUL 78; To VA-27, NAF Atsugi, JP., 19 SEP 78; To VA-27, NAS Cubi Point, PI., 29 SEP 78; To VA-27, NAS LeMoore, CA., 10 OCT 78; To VA-27, NPTR El Centro, CA., 13 FEB 79; To VA-27, NAS LeMoore, CA., 29 OCT 79; To VA-27, USS Coral Sea (CV-43), 29 OCT 79; To VA-27, NAS Cubi Point, PI., 12 NOV 79; To VA-27, USS Coral Sea (CV-43), 23 DEC 79; To VA-27, NAS LeMoore, CA., 08 JAN 80; To VA-27, NAS Jacksonville, FL., 09 MAR 81; To VA-27, NAS LeMoore, CA., 07 JUL 81; To VA-27, USS Coral Sea (CV-43), 20 AUG 81; To VA-27, NAS LeMoore, CA., 22 MAR 82; To VA-27, USS Coral Sea (CV-43), 10 MAR 83 ** Transferred to VA-203/CVWR-20, AF/308, NAS Jacksonville, FL., 11 AUG 83 thru 01 DEC 86 ** End of flight record card ** Transferred to AMARC, Davis Monthan AFB; Tucson, AZ., assigned park code 6A0247; 29 JAN 88 ** 7179.4 flight hours ** TF41A402D engine S/N 141887 ** Aircraft demilitarized, 13 JAN 05 ** Engine released to DRMO for disposition, 09 SEP 05 ** Aircraft deleted from inventory and released to DRMO for disposition, 09 SEP 05.

E-194 157472 Navy acceptance from NPRO Rep. LTV, Dallas, TX., 28 MAY 70 ** Transferred to VA-174/FRS, AD/413, NAS Cecil Field, FL., 29 MAY 70 ** Transferred to VA-81/CVW-17, AA/4XX, NAS Cecil Field, FL., 05 JUN 70; To VA-81, USS Forrestal (CVA-59), 22 JUN 70; TO VA-81, NAS Cecil Field, FL., 15 MAY 71 ** Transferred to VA-174/FRS, AD/4XX, NAS Cecil Field, FL., 16 MAY 72 ** Transferred to VF-31, NAS Oceana, VA., 04 OCT 72 ** Transferred to VA-12/CVW-7, AG/400, USS Independence (CV-62), 24 OCT 72; To VA-12, NAS Cecil Field, FL., 14 FEB 73; To VA-12, USS Independence (CV-62), 12 MAR 74; To VA-12, NAS Cecil Field, FL., 30 JAN 75; To VA-12, NAS Jacksonville, FL., 31 JAN 75; To VA-12, NAS Cecil Field, FL., 25 FEB 75; To VA-12, NAS Jacksonville, FL., 21 APR 75; To VA-12, NAS Fallon, NV., 01 MAY 75; To VA-12, NAS Cecil Field, FL., 01 JUN 75; To VA-12, USS Independence (CV-62), 01 SEP 75; To VA-12, NAS Cecil Field, FL., 07 MAY 76; To VA-12, NAS Fallon, NV., 30 AUG 76; To VA-12, USS Independence (CV-62), 01 NOV 76; To VA-12, NAS Cecil Field, FL., 01 NOV 76; To VA-12, USS Independence (CV-62), 01 NOV 76; To VA-12, NAS Cecil Field, FL., 01 FEB 77; To VA-12, USS Independence (CV-62), 01 FEB 77; To VA-12, NAS Cecil Field, FL., 09 AUG 77; To VA-12, USS Dwight D. Eisenhower (CVN-69), 04 JAN 78; To VA-12, NAS Cecil Field, FL., 29 AUG 78; To VA-12, NAS Jacksonville, FL., 30 AUG 78; To VA-12, USS Dwight D. Eisenhower (CVN-69), 30 AUG 78; To VA-12, NAS Cecil Field, FL., 30 AUG 78; To VA-12, USS Dwight D. Eisenhower (CVN-69), 30 AUG 78; To VA-12, NAS Jacksonville, FL., 08 DEC 78 ** Transferred to VA-15/CVW-6, AE/3XX, NAS Cecil Field, FL., 17 DEC 78; To VA-15, USS Independence (CV-62), 18 DEC 78; To VA-15, NAS Cecil Field, FL., 18 DEC 78; To VA-15, USS Independence (CV-62), 18 DEC 78; To VA-15, NAS Cecil Field, FL., 18 DEC 78 ** Transferred to VA-87/CVW-6, AE/4XX, NAS Cecil Field, FL., 29 FEB 80 **Transferred to VA-174/FRS, AD/413, NAS Cecil Field, FL., 17 JUL 80; To VA-174, NAS Jacksonville, FL., 05 JUN 81; To VA-174, NAS Cecil Field, FL., 11 SEP 81 ** Transferred to VA-66/CVW-7, AG/3XX, USS Dwight D. Eisenhower (CVN-69), 20 OCT 81; To VA-66, NAS Cecil Field, FL., 20 OCT 81; To VA-66, Dwight D. Eisenhower (CVN-69), 20 OCT 81; To VA-66, NAS Cecil Field, FL., 20 OCT 81 ** Transferred to VA-174/FRS, AD/413, NAS Cecil Field, FL., 20 AUG 82; To VA-174, NAS Jacksonville, FL., 28 APR 83; To VA-174, NAS Cecil Field, FL., 28 APR 83; To VA-174, NAS Jacksonville, FL., 02 MAY 83; To VA-174, NAS Dallas, TX., 08 AUG 83 ** Transferred to VA-86/CVW-8, AJ/4XX, NAS Cecil Field, FL., 08 NOV 83 ** Transferred to VA-82/CVW-8, AJ/3XX, NAS Cecil Field, FL., 20 JUN 84; To VA-82, USS Nimitz (CVN-68), 20 JUN 84; To VA-82, NAS Cecil Field, FL., 20 JUN 84; To VA-82, USS Nimitz (CVN-68), 20 JUN 84; To VA-82, NAS Cecil Field, FL., 20 JUN 84; To VA-82, NAS Jacksonville, FL., 06 NOV 85; To VA-82, NAS Cecil Field, FL., 04 DEC 85; To VA-82, NAS Jacksonville, FL., 24 JAN 86 ** Transferred to VA-105/CVW-6, AE/408, NAS Cecil Field, FL., 28 JAN 86; To VA-105, USS Forrestal (CV-59), 06 FEB 86; To VA-105, NAS Cecil Field, FL., 06 FEB 86; To VA-105, USS Forrestal (CV-59), 06 JUL 86; To VA-105, NAS Cecil Field, FL., 01 SEP 86; To VA-105, USS Forrestal (CV-59), 17 JUL 87 thru 27 JUL 87 ** End of flight record card ** Transferred to AMARC, Davis Monthan AFB; Tucson, AZ., assigned park code 6A0255; 16 MAR 88 ** 6861.9 flight hours ** TF41A402D engine S/N 142543 ** Project changed per FSO letter, 06 APR 04 ** Engine released to DRMO for disposition, 05 OCT 05 ** Aircraft deleted from inventory and released to DRMO for disposition, 05 OCT 05.

E-195 157473 Navy acceptance from NPRO Rep. LTV Dallas, TX., 05 JUN 70 ** Transferred to VA-174/FRS, AD/4XX, NAS Cecil Field, FL., 06 JUN 70 ** Transferred to VA-83/CVW-17, AA/3XX, USS Forrestal (CVA-59), 14 JUL 70; To VA-83, NAS Cecil field, FL., 31 MAR 71 ~ S 1SO strike, 02 DEC 71 ** No data on strike.

E-196 157474 Navy acceptance from NPRO Rep. LTV, Dallas, TX., 26 MAY 70 ** Transferred to VA-122/FRS, NJ/2XX, NAS LeMoore, CA., 27 MAY 70; To VA-122, COSA, NAS LeMoore, CA., 23 JUN 70; To VA-122, NAS LeMoore, CA., 04 NOV 70 ** Transferred to VA-25/CVW-2, NE/4XX, NAS LeMoore, CA., 15 JAN 71 ** Transferred to VA-113CVW-2, NE/303, NAS LeMoore, CA., 24 APR 71; To VA-

113, USS Ranger (CV-61), 21 JUN 73 ** Transferred to VA-122/FRS, NJ/2XX, NAS LeMoore, 02 APR 74 ** Transferred to VA-146/CVW-9, NG/3XX, USS Constellation (CVA-64), 14 JUN 74 ** Transferred to VA-113/CVW-2, NE/303, USS Ranger (CV-61), 12 JUL 74; To VA-113, NAS LeMoore, CA., 12 JUL 74; To VA-113, NAS Jacksonville, FL., 07 JUN 75; To VA-113, NAS LeMoore, CA., 08 JUN 75; To VA-113, USS Ranger (CV-61), 16 AUG 75; To VA-113, NAS LeMoore, CA., 18 APR 77; To VA-113, NAS Jacksonville, FL., 23 NOV 77; To VA-113, NAS LeMoore, CA., 11 DEC 77; To VA-113, NAS Jacksonville, FL., 09 JAN 78; To VA-113, NAS LeMoore, CA., 10 JAN 78; To VA-113, USS Ranger (CV-61), 27 SEP 78; To VA-113, NAS LeMoore, CA., 18 OCT 78; To VA-113, USS Ranger (CV-61), 09 NOV 78; To VA-113, NAS LeMoore, CA., 09 NOV 78; To VA-113, USS Ranger (CV-61), 22 MAR 79; To VA-113, NAS Cubi Point, PI, 02 JUL 79; To VA-113, NAS Jacksonville, FL., 03 OCT 79; To VA-113, NAS LeMoore, CA., 30 NOV 79; To VA-113, NAS Jacksonville, FL., 17 DEC 79; To VA-113, NAS LeMoore, CA., 20 DEC 79; To VA-113, NAS Fallon, NV., 20 DEC 79; To VA-113, NAS LeMoore, CA., 26 JAN 80; To VA-113, USS Ranger (CV-61), 05 MAY 80; To VA-113, NAS LeMoore, CA., 30 JUN 80; To VA-113, USS Ranger (CV-61), 18 JUL 80; To VA-113, NAS Cubi Point, PI., 24 OCT 80; To VA-113, NAS LeMoore, CA., 04 APR 81 ** Transferred to VA-97/CVW-14, NK/3XX, USS Coral Sea (CV-43), 20 MAY 81; To VA-97, NAS LeMoore, 11 JUN 81; To VA-97, USS Coral Sea (CV-43), 20 AUG 81; To VA-97, NAS LeMoore, 22 MAR 82; To VA-97, USS Coral Sea (CV-43), 17 FEB 83; To VA-97, NAS LeMoore, 28 SEP 83; To VA-97, NAS Jacksonville, FL., 16 FEB 84; To VA-97/CVW-15, NL/3XX, USS Carl Vinson (CVN-70), 16 FEB 84; To VA-97, NAS LeMoore, CA., 16 FEB 84; To VA-97, USS Carl Vinson (CVN-70), 16 FEB 84; To VA-97, NAS Jacksonville, FL., 30 JUN 84; To VA-97, NAS LeMoore, CA., 09 JUL 84; To VA-97, USS Carl Vinson (CVN-70), 30 AUG 84 ** Transferred to VA-146/CVW-9, NE/3XX, NAS LeMoore, CA., 10 OCT 84; To VA-146, USS Kitty Hawk (CV-63), 08 MAY 85; To VA-146, NAS LeMoore, CA., 12 NOV 85 ** Transferred to VX-5, NWC China Lake, CA., 08 JUL 86 ~ S 1SO strike, 05 NOV 86 ** No data on crash ** Transferred to NWC China Lake, CA., to be used as a taget on the survivability range, 04 NOV 04.

E-197 157475 Navy acceptance from NPRO Rep. LTV, Dallas, TX., 20 MAY 70 ** Transferred to VA-122/FRS, NJ/2XX, NAS LeMoore, CA., 21 JUN 70; To VA-122, COSA, NAS LeMoore, CA., 23 JUN 70; To VA-122, NAS LeMoore, CA., 30 MAR 71 ** Transferred to VA-146/CVW-9, NG/3XX, NAS Fallon, NV., 09 JUN 71; To VA-146, NAS LeMoore, CA., 22 JUN 71; To VA-146, USS Constellation (CVA-64), 30 JUN 72 ** Transferred to VA-122/FRS, NJ/2XX, NAS LeMoore, CA., 22 NOV 72; To VA-122, NAS Alameda, CA., 10 NOV 76; To VA-122, NAS LeMoore, CA., 11 NOV 76; To VA-122, NAS Jacksonville, FL., 17 MAR 77; To VA-122, NAS LeMoore, CA., 05 MAY 77 ** To VA-122, NAS Jacksonville, FL., 07 MAY 79; To VA-122, NAS LeMoore, CA., 20 JUN 79; To VA-122, NAS Jacksonville, FL., 30 MAR 81; To VA-122, NAS LeMoore, CA., 09 JUN 81 ** Transferred to VA-27/CVW-14, NK/4XX, NAS LeMoore, CA., 22 JUN 81; To VA-27, USS Coral Sea (CV-43), 20 AUG 81; To VA-27, NAS LeMoore, CA., 22 MAR 82 ** Transferred to VA-25/CVW-2, NE/4XX, NAS LeMoore, CA., 10 JAN 83; To VA-25, NAS Alameda, CA., 16 MAR 83 ** Transferred to VA-94/CVW-11, NH/4XX, NAS LeMoore, CA., 19 MAY 83 ** Transferred to VA-195/CVW-9, NG/4XX, USS Ranger (CV-61), 19 SEP 83; To VA-195, NAF Atsugi, JP., 13 JAN 84; To VA-195, USS Ranger (CV-61), 20 JAN 84; To VA-195, NAS LeMoore, CA., 20 JAN 84; To VA-195, NAS Jacksonville, FL., 07 MAY 84; To VA-195, NAS LeMoore, CA., 27 JUN 84 ** Transferred to VA-122/FRS, NJ/231, NAS LeMoore, CA., 29 MAY 85 ** Transferred to AMARC, Davis Monthan AFB; Tucson, AZ., assigned park code 6A0185; 24 JUL 86 ** End of flight record card ** 5743.6 flight hours ** TF41A2B engine S/N 142596 ** Aircraft demilitarized, 11 JAN 05 ** Aircraft deleted from inventory and released to DRMO for disposition, 09 SEP 05.

E-198 157476 Navy acceptance from NPRO Rep. LTV, Dallas, TX., 17 JUN 70 ** Transferred to VA-83/CVW-17, AA/3XX, NAS Cecil Field, FL., 19 JUN 70; To VA-83, USS Forrestall (CVA-59),

19 JUN 70; To VA-83, NAS Cecil Field, FL., 31 MAR 71; To VA-83, USS Forrestall (CVA-59), 26 APR 72 ** Transferred to VA-174/FRS, AD/4XX, NAS Cecil Field, FL., 24 JAN 74; To VA-174, NAS Jacksonville, FL., 29 JUN 74 ** Transferred to VA-82/CVW-8, AJ/3XX, NAS Cecil Field, FL., 12 NOV 74; To VA-82, USS Nimitz (CVN-68), 03 FEB 76; To VA-82, NAS Cecil Field, Fl., 27 JUL 75; To VA-82, NAS Roosevelt Roads, PR., 28 OCT 75; To VA-82, NAS Cecil Field, FL., 28 OCT 75; To VA-82, USS Nimitz (CVN-68), 03 FEB 76; To VA-82, NAS Cecil Field, Fl., 19 FEB 76; To VA-82, USS Nimitz (CVN-68), 19 APR 76; To VA-82, NAS Cecil Field, Fl., 04 MAY 76 ** Transferred to VA-174/FRS, AD/411, NAS Cecil Field, FL., 27 SEP 77; To VA-174, NAS Jacksonville, FL., 14 NOV 77; To VA-174, NAS Cecil Field, FL., 13 DEC 77 ** Transferred to VA-66/CVW-7, AG/3XX, NAS Cecil Field, FL., 15 JUN 78; To VA-66, USS Dwight D. Eisenhower (CVN-69), 15 JUN 78; To VA-66, NAS Cecil Field, FL., 15 JUN 78; To VA-66, USS Dwight D. Eisenhower (CVN-69), 15 JUN 78; To VA-66, NAS Cecil Field, FL., 15 JUN 78; To VA-66, USS Dwight D. Eisenhower (CVN-69), 15 JUN 78; Transferred to VA-87/CVW-6, AE/4XX, NAS Cecil Field, FL., 06 JAN 79; To VA-87, USS Independence (CV-62), 25 MAY 79; To VA-87, NAS Cecil Field, FL., 21 FEB 80; To VA-87, USS Independence (CV-62), 29 JUL 80 ** Transferred to VA-174/FRS, AD/4XX, NAS Cecil Field, FL., 13 NOV 80 ** Transferred to VA-82/CVW-8, AJ/3XX, NAS Cecil Field, FL., 05 MAY 81; To VA-82, USS Nimitz (CVN-68), 27 MAY 81; To VA-82, NAS Norfolk, VA., 28 MAY 81; To VA-82, USS Nimitz (CVN-68), 03 JUN 81; To VA-82, NAS Norfolk, VA. 09 OCT 81 ** Transferred to NARF, NAS Jacksonville, FL., 18 DEC 81, Transferred to VA-174/FRS, AD/4XX, NAS Cecil Field, FL., 20 JUL 82; To VA-174, NAS Dallas, TX., 29 SEP 82 ** Transferred to VA-66/CVW-7, AG/3XX, NAS Cecil Field, FL., 02 OCT 82; To VA-66, USS Dwight D. Eisenhower (CVN-69), 02 OCT 82; To VA-66, NAS Cecil Field, FL., 02 OCT 82 ** Transferred to VA-86/CVW-8, AJ/4XX, NAS Roosevelt Roads, PR., 14 FEB 84; To VA-86, NAS Cecil Field, FL., 14 FEB 84; To VA-86, NAS Jacksonville, FL., 20 NOV 84; To VA-86, NAS Cecil Field, FL., 19 DEC 84; To VA-86, NAS Jacksonville, FL., 15 JAN 85; To VA-86, USS Nimitz (CVN-68), 09 FEB 85; To VA-86, NAS Cecil Field, FL., 09 FEB 85; To VA-86, USS Nimitz (CVN-68), 22 APR 86; To VA-86, NAS Cecil Field, FL., 22 APR 86 ** Transferred to VA-81/CVW-1, AB/4XX, NAS Cecil Field, FL., 31 JUL 86; To VA-81, USS Saratoga (CV-60), 07 AUG 86; To VA-81, NAS Cecil Field, FL., 07 AUG 86; To VA-81, USS Saratoga (CV-60), 07 AUG 86 ** Transferred to VA-37/CVW-6, AE/3XX, NAS Cecil Field, FL., 19 FEB 87; To VA-37, NAS Jacksonville, FL., 15 MAY 87; To VA-37, USS Forrestal (CV-59), 15 MAY 87; To VA-37, NAS Jacksonville, FL., 18 SEP 87 ** End of flight record card ** Transferred to VA-204?CVWR-20, AF/410, NAS New Orleans LA., date unknown ** Transferred to AMARC, Davis Monthan AFB; Tucson, AZ., assigned park code 6A0364; 18 JUN 90 ** 7070.2 flight hours ** TF41A402D engine S/N 141940 ** Aircraft demilitarized, 13 JAN 05 ** Aircraft deleted from inventory and released to DRMO for disposition, 09 SEP 05.

E-199 157477 Navy acceptance from NPRO Rep. LTV, Dallas, TX., 10 JUN 70 ** Transferred to VA-174/FRS, AD/4XX, NAS Cecil Field, FL., 11 JUN 70 ** Transferred to VA-105/CVW-3, AC/414, NAS Cecil Field, FL., 04 SEP 73; To VA-105, USS Saratoga (CV-60), 29 JUL 74; To VA-105, NAS Cecil Field, FL., 29 JUL 74; To VA-105, USS Saratoga (CV-60), 29 JUL 74; To VA-105, NAS Cecil Field, FL., 29 JUL 74; To VA-105, USS Saratoga (CV-60), 20 SEP 74; To VA-105, NAS Cecil Field, FL., 20 SEP 74; To VA-105, USS Saratoga (CV-60), 20 SEP 74; To VA-105, NAS Cecil Field, FL., 20 SEP 74; To VA-105, MCAS Yuma, AZ., 24 JUL 75, To VA-105, NAS Jacksonville, FL., 15 SEP 75; To VA-105, USS Saratoga (CV-60), 06 OCT 75; To VA-105, NAS Cecil Field, FL., 06 OCT 75; To VA-105, USS Saratoga (CV-60), 01 NOV 76; To VA-105, NAS Cecil Field, FL., 03 MAR 77; To VA-105, USS Saratoga (CV-60), 03 MAR 77; To VA-105, NAS Cecil Field, FL., 16 JUL 77; To VA-105, USS Saratoga (CV-60), 31 MAY 78; To VA-105, NAS Jacksonville, FL., 07 JUN 78; To VA-105, USS Saratoga (CV-60), 29 JUN 78; To VA-105, NAS Cecil Field, FL., 29 JUN 78; To VA-105, USS Saratoga (CV-60), 29 JUN 78; To VA-105, NAS Cecil Field, FL., 29 JUN 78; To VA-105, MCAS Yuma, AZ., 29 JUN 78; To VA-105, NAS Cecil Field, FL., 29 JUN 78; To VA-105,

USS Saratoga (CV-60), 29 JUN 78; To VA-105, NAS Cecil Field, FL., 29 JUN 78 ** Transferred to VA-174/FRS, AD/4XX, NAS Cecil Field, FL., 28 FEB 80; To VA-174, NAS Jacksonville, FL., 03 JUN 80; To VA-174, NAS Cecil Field, FL., 23 JUL 80 ** Transferred to VA-83/CVW-17, AA/3XX, NAS Cecil Field, FL., 04 MAR 81; To VA-83, NAS Fallon, NV., 07 JAN 82 ** Transferred to VA-81/CVW-17, AA/4XX, NAS Cecil Field, FL., 07 JAN 82; To VA-81, NAS Fallon, NV., 07 JAN 82; To VA-81, USS Forrestal (CV-59), 07 JAN 82; To VA-81, NAS Cecil Field, FL., 23 APR 82 ** Transferred to VA-174/FRS, AD/4XX, NAS Cecil Field, FL., 04 MAY 82; To VA-174, NAS Jacksonville, FL., 25 AUG 83; To VA-174, NAS Cecil Field, FL., 19 SEP 83; To VA-174, NAS Jacksonville, FL., 21 FEB 84; To VA-174, NAS Cecil Field, FL., 23 FEB 84; To VA-174, NAS Jacksonville, FL., 28 APR 86 ** Transferred to VA-81/CVW-17, AA/4XX, NAS Cecil Field, FL., 01 MAY 86; To VA-81, USS Saratoga (CV-60), 23 JUL 86; To VA-81, NAS Cecil Field, FL., 21 OCT 86; To VA-81, USS Saratoga (CV-60), 02 MAR 87; To VA-81, NAS Cecil Field, FL., 16 MAR 87; To VA-81, USS Saratoga (CV-60), 15 APR 87; To VA-81, NAS Cecil Field, FL., 12 MAY 87 ** Transferred to VA-87/CVW-6, AE/4XX, USS Saratoga (CV-60), 14 MAY 87 thru 01 JUN 87 ** End of flight record card ** Transferred to VA-203/CVWR-20, AF/3XX, NAS Cecil Field, FL., date unknown ** Transferred to AMAR, Davis Monthan AFB; Tucson, AZ., assigned park code 6A0296; 15 AUG 89 ** 6742.7 flight hours ** TF41A402D engine S/N 141937 ** Engine released to DRMO for disposition, 25 NOV 03 ** Aircraft demilitarized, 11 JAN 05 ** Aircraft deleted from inventory and released to DRMO for disposition, 09 SEP 05.

E-200 157478 Navy acceptance from NPRO Rep. LTV, Dallas, TX., 28 MAY 70 ** Transferred to VA-174/FRS, AD/4XX, NAS Cecil Field, FL., 01 JUN 70 ** Transferred to VA-105/CVW-3, AC/4XX, NAS Cecil Field, FL., 07 MAY 73; To VA-105, USS Saratoga (CV-60), 25 JAN 74; To VA-105, NAS Cecil Field, FL., 25 JAN 74; To VA-105, USS Saratoga (CV-60), 25 JAN 74; To VA-105, NAS Cecil Field, FL., 25 JAN 74; To VA-105, USS Saratoga (CV-60), 25 JAN 74; To VA-105, NAS Cecil Field, FL., 25 JAN 74; To VA-105, MCAS Yuma, AZ., 24 JUL 75; To VA-105, USS Saratoga (CV-60), 23 OCT 75; To VA-105, NAS Cecil Field, FL., 10 NOV 75 ** Transferred to VA-174/FRS, AD/4XX, NAS Cecil Field, FL., 06 DEC 76; To VA-174, NAS Jacksonville, FL., 25 JUN 77; To VA-174, NAS Cecil Field, FL., 22 AUG 77 ** Transferred to VA-37/CVW-3, AC/3XX, NAS Cecil Field, FL., 10 AUG 78; To VA-37, USS Saratoga (CV-60), 10 AUG 78; To VA-37, NAS Cecil Field, FL., 10 AUG 78; To VA-37, MCAS Yuma, AZ., 10 AUG 78 ** Transferred to VA-12/CVW-7, AG/404, USS Dwight D. Eisenhower (CVN-69), 06 SEP 79; To VA-12, NAS Cecil Field, FL., 04 DEC 80 To VA-12, USS Dwight D. Eisenhower (CVN-69), 27 MAR 81; To VA-12, NAS Cecil Field, FL., 27 MAR 81 ** Transferred to VA-174/FRS, AD/2XX, NAS Cecil Field, FL., 23 DEC 81; To VA-174, NAS Jacksonville, FL., 08 FEB 82; To VA-174, NAS Cecil Field, FL., 08 FEB 82; To VA-174, NAS Jacksonville, FL., 10 FEB 82; To VA-174, NAS Cecil Field, FL., 19 APR 82; To VA-174, NAS Dallas, TX., 06 JUL 82 ** Transferred to VA-86/CVW-8, AJ/410, NAS Cecil Field, FL., 06 JUL 82, Paint was light gray on medium gray; To VA-86, USS Nimitz (CVN-68), 06 JUL 82; To VA-86, NAS Cecil Field, FL., 06 JUL 82; To VA-86, USS Nimitz (CVN-68), 06 JUL 82; To VA-86, NAS Cecil Field, FL., 13 MAY 83; To VA-86, NAS Roosevelt Roads, PR., 08 JUL 83; To VA-86, NAS Cecil Field, FL., 08 JUL 83 ** Transferred to VA-72/CVW-1, AB/4XX, NAS Cecil Field, FL., 11 OCT 83; To VA-72, USS America (CV-66), 11 OCT 83; To VA-72 NAS Cecil Field, FL., 11 OCT 83; To VA-72, USS America (CV-66), 11 OCT 83; To VA-72 NAS Cecil Field, FL., 11 OCT 83; To VA-72, NAS Jacksonville, FL., 05 FEB 85; To VA-72 NAS Cecil Field, FL., 08 FEB 85; To VA-72, NAS Jacksonville, FL., 01 APR 85; To VA-72 NAS Cecil Field, FL., 02 APR 85; To VA-72, USS America (CV-66), 26 APR 85; To VA-72, NAS Cecil Field, FL, 16 OCT 85; To VA-72, USS America (CV-66), 01 FEB 86; To VA-72, NAS Cecil Field, FL, 01 FEB 86; To VA-72, NAS Jacksonville, FL., 12 FEB 87; To VA-72, NAS Cecil Field, FL., 12 FEB 87; To VA-72, NAS Jacksonville, FL., 14 APR 87; To VA-72, USS Dwight D. Eisenhower (CVN-69), 14 APR 87; To VA-72, NAS Cecil Field, FL., 14 APR 87; To VA-72, NAS Jacksonville, FL., 15 SEP 87 thru 22 SEP 87 ** End of flight record card.

E-201 157479 Navy acceptance from NPRO Rep. LTV, Dallas, TX., 16 JUN 70 ** Transferred to VA-83/CVW-17, AA/3XX, NAS Cecil Field, FL., 23 MAY 70; To VA-83, USS Forrestal (CVA-59), 23 JUN 70; To VA-83, NAS Cecil Field, FL., 30 MAY 71 ** Transferred to VA-122/FRS, NJ/2XX, CRAA, NAS LeMoore, CA., 13 MAY 72 ** Transferred to VA-147/ CVW-9, NG/4XX, NAS LeMoore, CA., 01 JUN 72; To VA-147, USS Constellation (CVA-64), 03 JUN 72; To VA-147, NAS LeMoore, CA., 21 JAN 75; To VA-147, NAS Jacksonville, FL., 25 FEB 75; To VA-147, NAS LeMoore, CA., 11 MAR 75; To VA-147, NAS Fallon, NV., 15 MAY 75; To VA-147, NAS LeMoore, CA., 05 JUN 75; To VA-147, MCAS Yuma, AZ., 27 OCT 75; To VA-147, NAS LeMoore, CA., 27 OCT 75; To VA-147, USS Constellation (CV-64), 28 SEP 76; To VA-147, NAS LeMoore, CA., 22 OCT 76; To VA-147, NAS LeMoore, CA., 22 OCT 76; To VA-147, NAS Cubi Point, PI., 07 JUL 77; To VA-147, NAF Atsugi, JP., 18 JUL 77; To VA-147, NAS Cubi Point, PI., 23 JUL 77; To VA-147, USS Constellation (CV-64), 31 AUG 77; To VA-147, LeMoore, CA., 19 NOV 77; To VA-147, NAS Jacksonville, FL., 19 JAN 78; To VA-147, NAS LeMoore, CA., 17 FEB 78; To VA-147, USS Constellation (CV-64), 25 SEP 78; To VA-147, NAS Cubi Point, PI., 06 NOV 78; To VA-147, NAF Atsugi, JP., 13 DEC 78, To VA-147, USS Constellation (CV-64), 20 NOV 78; To VA-147, LeMoore, CA., 19 JUN 79; To VA-147, NAS Jacksonville, FL., 02 NOV 79; To VA-147, NAS LeMoore, CA., 03 NOV 79; To VA-147, USS Constellation (CV-64), 13 DEC 79; To VA-147, NAS LeMoore, CA., 23 JAN 80; To VA-147, USS Constellation (CV-64), 26 FEB 80; To VA-147, NAS Cubi Point, PI., 18 APR 80; To VA-147, USS Constellation (CV-64), 18 SEP 80; To VA-147, NAS LeMoore, CA., 18 SEP 80; To VA-147, NAS Alameda, CA., 04 DEC 80; To NAs LeMoore, CA., 12 MAR 81; To VA-147, NAF El Centro, CA., 02 APR 81; To VA-147, USS Constellation (CV-64), 24 MAY 81; To VA-147, NAS LeMoore, CA., 12 JUN 81; To VA-147, USS Constellation (CV-64), 07 JUL 81; To VA-147, NAS LeMoore, CA., 06 AUG 81; To VA-147, USS Constellation (CV-64), 20 SEP 81 ** Transferred to VA-122/FRS, NJ/2XX, NAS LeMoore, CA., 07 OCT 81; To VA-122, NAS Jacksonville, FL., 26 JAN 82 ** Transferred to VA-174/FRS, AD/4XX, NAS Cecil Field, FL., 29 APR 82; To VA-174, NAS Jacksonville, FL., 19 FEB 84; To VA-174, Cecil Field, FL., 19 FEB 84; To VA-174, NAS Jacksonville, FL., 22 FEB 84 ** Transferred to VA-37/CVW-3, AC/3XX, NAS Cecil Field, FL., 02 MAY 84; To VA-37, MCAS Twenty Nine Palms, CA., 03 JUL 84; To VA-37, NAS Cecil Field, FL., 29 AUG 84 ** Transferred to VA-174/ FRS, AD/4XX, NAS Cecil Field, FL., 17 NOV 84; To VA-174, NAS Jacksonville, FL., 22 SEP 86; To VA-174, Cecil Field, FL., 01 OCT 86 ** Transferred to VA-304/CVWR-30, ND/4XX, NAS Alameda, CA., 02 OCT 86 ** Transferred to VA-174, NAS Cecil Field, FL., 31 OCT 86 ** Transferred to VA-304, NAS Alameda, CA., 18 FEB 87 Thru 31 AUG 87 ** End of flight record card.

E-202 157480 Navy acceptance from NPRO Rep. LTV, Dallas, TX., 30 JUN 70 ** Transferred to VA-83/CVW-17, AA/3XX, USS Forrestal (CVA-59), 02 JUL 70; To VA-83, NAS Cecil Field, FL., 26 APR 71; To VA-83, USS Forrestal (CVA-59), 12 MAY 72; To VA-83, NAS Cecil Field, FL., 17 OCT 74; To VA-83, USS Forrestal (CVA-59), 28 JAN 75; Transferred to VA-174/FRS, AD/4XX, NAS Cecil Field, FL., 27 FEB 75; To VA-174, NAS Jacksonville, FL., 07 AUG 75; To VA-174, NAS Cecil Field, FL., 21 OCT 75; To VA-174, NAS Jacksonville, FL., 09 MAR 76; To VA-174, NAS Cecil Field, FL., 02 AUG 78; To VA-174, NAS Jacksonville, FL., 27 MAY 80; To VA-174, NAS Cecil Field, FL., 27 JUN 80 ** Transferred to VA-82/CVW-8, AJ/3XX, USS Nimitz (CVN-68), 18 JUL 80; To VA-82, NAS Cecil Field, FL., 18 JUL 80; To VA-82, USS Nimitz (CNV-68), 18 JUL 80; To VA-82, NAS Cecil field, FL., 18 JUL 80 ** Transferred to VA-174/FRS, AD/4XX, NAS Cecil Field, FL., 09 MAR 82; To VA-174, NAS Jacksonville, FL., 13 AUG 82; To VA-174, NAS Cecil Field, FL., 23 AUG 82 ** Transferred to VA-37/CVW-6, NL/3XX, NAS Cecil Field, FL., 15 DEC 82; To VA-37, USS Carl Vinson (CVN-70), 15 DEC 82; To VA-37, NAS Cecil Field, FL., 15 DEC 82; To VA-37, USS Carl Vinson (CVN-70), 15 DEC 82; To VA-37, NAS Roosevelt Roads, PR., 31 DEC 83; To VA-37, NAS Cecil Field, FL., 11 JAN 84; To VA-37, NWC China Lake, CA., 11 JAN 84 ** Transferred to VA-12/CVW-7, AG/4XX, USS Dwight D. Eisenhower (CVN-69), 16 MAR 84; To VA-12, NAS Cecil Field, FL., 16 MAR 84; To VA-12,

USS Dwight D. Eisenhower (CVN-69), 16 MAR 84; To VA-12, NAS Cecil Field, FL., 16 MAR 84; USS Dwight D. Eisenhower (CVN-69), 16 MAR 84; To VA-12, NAS Jacksonville, FL., 23 SEP 85; To VA-12, NAS Cecil Field, FL., 22 OCT 85; To VA-12, NAS Jacksonville, FL., 10 DEC 85 ** Transferred to VA-82/CVW-8, AJ/3XX, NAS Cecil Field, FL., 11 DEC 85; To VA-82, USS Nimitz (CVN-68), 20 FEB 86 ** Transferred to VA-174/FRS, AD/4XX, NAS Cecil Field, FL., date unknown ** Transferred to AMARC, Davis Monthan AFB, Tucson, AZ., assigned park code 6A0191; 15 AUG 86 ** End of flight record card ** 4954.7 flight hours ** TF41A2B engine S/N 141962 ** Aircraft released from storage and prepared for overland and above deck shipment to the government of Greece, 19 JUL 94 ** Transferred to the Helenic Air force (Greece).

E-203 157481 Navy acceptance from NPRO Rep. LTV, Dallas, TX., 29 JUN 70 ** Transferred to VA-83/CVW-17, AA/3XX, USS Forrestal (CVA-59), 30 JUN 70; To VA-83, NAS Cecil Field, FL., 29 JUN 71; To VA-83, USS Forrestal (CVA-59), 25 MAY 72 ** Transferred to VA-174/FRS, AD/4XX, NAS Cecil Field, FL., 20 JUL 72; To VA-174, NAS Jacksonville, FL., 16 JUN 78; To VA-174, NAS Cecil Field, FL., 25 AUG 78 ** Transferred to VA-72/CVW-1, AB/4XX, NAS Cecil Field, FL., 10 MAY 80; To VA-72, USS John F. Kennedy (CVA-67), 21 JUN 80; To VA-72, NAS Cecil Field, FL., 21 JUN 80; To VA-72, NAS Jacksonville, FL., 09 JUL 81; To VA-72, NAS Cecil Field, FL., 24 SEP 81 ** Transferred to VA-46/CVW-1, AB/304, NAS Cecil Field, FL., 06 OCT 81; To VA-46, USS America (CV-66), 06 OCT 81; To VA-46, NAS Cecil Field, FL., 06 OCT 81; To VA-46, USS America (CV-66), 19 NOV 82 ** Transferred to VA-174/FRS, AD/4XX, NAS Cecil Field, FL., 02 DEC 82; To VA-174, NAS Jacksonville, FL., 30 SEP 83; To VA-174, NAS Cecil Field, FL., 03 OCT 83; To VA-174, NAS Jacksonville, FL., 03 APR 86; To VA-174, NAS Cecil Field, FL., 03 APR 86; To VA-174, NAS Jacksonville, FL., 13 JUN 86; To VA-174, NAS Cecil Field, FL., 23 JUN 86; To VA-174, NAS Jacksonville, FL., 25 JUN 86; To VA-174, NAS Cecil Field, FL., 26 JUN 86; To VA-174, NAS Pensacola, FL,, 23 SEP 86; To VA-174, NAS Cecil Field, FL., 24 SEP 86 ** Transferred to VA-203/CVWR-20, AF/3XX, NAS Jacksonville, FL., 25 SEP 86 ** Transferred to VA-304/CVWR-30, ND/4XX, NAS Alameda, CA., 27 JAN 87; To VA-304, NAS Pensacola, FL., 09 APR 87; To VA-304, NAS Alameda, CA., 06 JUL 87 thru 18 AUG 87 ** End of flight record card ** Transferred to AMARC, Davis Monthan AFB; Tucson, AZ., assigned park code 6A0269, 19 MAY 88 ** 4831.8 flight hours ** TF41A402D engine S/N 141296 ** Aircraft released from storage and prepared for overland shipment, destination unknown, 21 JUN 94.

157482/157537 LTV A-7E-7-CV Corsair II (Block VII)

E-260 157482 Navy acceptance from NPRO Rep. LTV, Dallas, TX. 01 SEP 70 ** Transferred to VA-82/CVW-8, AJ/3XX, NAS Cecil Field, FL., 02 SEP 70; To VA-82 USS America (CVA-66), 29 MAR 71 ** Transferred to VA-174/FRS, AD/4XX, NAS Cecil Field, FL., 31 MAR 72 ** Transferred to VA-83/CVW-17, AA/3XX, USS Forrestal (CVA-59), 20 JAN 74; To VA-83, NAS Cecil Field, FL., 13 AUG 74; To VA-83, USS Forrestal (CVA-59), 13 AUG 74; To VA-83, NAS Cecil Field, FL., 13 AUG 74; USS Forrestal (CVA-59), 13 AUG 74; To VA-83, NAS Cecil Field, FL., 13 AUG 74 ** Transferred to VA-174/ FRS, AD/4XX, NAS Cecil Field, 27 FEB 75 ** Transferred to VA-15/CVW-6, AE/3XX, USS America (CV-66), 14 FEB 76; To VA-15, MCAS Yuma, AZ., 14 DEC 76; To VA-15, USS America (CV-66), 20 JAN 77; To VA-15, NAS Cecil Field, FL., 19 JUL 77; To VA-15, USS America (CV-66), 19 JUL 77; To VA-15, NAS Cecil Field, FL., 23 MAY 78; To VA-15, NAS Jacksonville, FL., 11 SEP 78; To VA-15, NAS Roosevelt Roads, PR., 13 OCT 78; To VA-15, USS America (CV-66), 08 NOV 78; To VA-15, NAS Cecil Field, FL., 08 NOV 78; To VA-15, USS Independence (CV-62), 08 NOV 78; To VA-15, NAS Cecil Field, FL., 08 NOV 78; To VA-15, USS Independence (CV-62), 08 NOV 78; To VA-15, NAS Cecil Field, FL., 08 NOV 78; To VA-15, USS Independence (CV-62), 22 JUL 80 ** Transferred to VA-86/CVW-8, AJ/4XX, USS Nimitz (CVN-68), 30 OCT 80; To VA-86, NAS Jacksonville, FL., 31 DEC 80; To VA-86, USS Nimitz (CVN-68), 31 DEC 80; To VA-86, NAS Cecil Field, FL., 27 JUN 81~ S 1SO strike, 27 JUN 81 ** No data on strike.

E-205 157483 Navy acceptance from NPRO Rep. LTV, Dallas, TX., 18 JUN 70 ** Transferred to VA-25/CVW-2, NE/4XX, NAS LeMoore, CA., 26 JUN 70 ~ S 1SO strike, 03 DEC 70 ** No data on strike.

E-206 157484 Navy acceptance from NPRO Rep. LTV, Dallas, TX., 04 JUN 70 ** Transferred to VA-174/FRS, AD/4XX, NAS Cecil Field, FL., 13 JUN 70 ** Transferred to VA-66/CVW-7, AG/3XX, NAS Cecil Field, FL., 03 SEP 71; To VA-66, USS Independence (CV-62), 15 JUN 72 ** Transferred to VA-12/CVW-7, AG/4XX, USS Independence (CV-62)), 15 JUN 72; To VA-12, NAS Cecil Field, FL., 16 MAR 73; To VA-12, USS Independence (CV-62)), 27 FEB 74; To VA-12, NAS Cecil Field, FL., 04 SEP 74; To VA-12, NAS Jacksonville, FL., 13 MAR 75; To VA-12, NAS Cecil Field, FL., 10 APR 75; To VA-12, NAS Fallon, NV., 10 APR 75; To VA-12, NAS Cecil Field, FL., 01 JUN 75; To VA-12, USS Independence (CV-62), 01 SEP 75; To VA-12, NAS Cecil Field, FL., 01 DEC 75; To VA-12, USS Independence (CV-62), 01 MAR 76; To VA-12, NAS Cecil Field, FL., 07 MAY 76; To VA-12, NAS Fallon, NV., 31 AUG 76; To VA-12, USS Independence (CV-62), 01 NOV 76; To VA-12, NAS Cecil Field, FL., 01 NOV 76; To VA-12, USS Independence (CV-62)), 01 NOV 76; To VA-12, NAS Cecil Field, FL., 01 NOV 76; To VA-12, USS Independence (CV-62)), 01 FEB 77; To VA-12, NAS Cecil Field, FL., 01 MAY 77; To VA-12, USS Independence (CV-62)), 09 AUG 77; To VA-12, NAS Cecil Field, FL., 09 AUG 77; To VA-12, USS Dwight D. Eisenhower (CVN-69), 09 AUG 77; To VA-12, NAS Cecil Field, FL., 22 JUN 78; To VA-12, NAS Jacksonville, FL., 23 JUN 78; To VA-12, USS Dwight D. Eisenhower (CVN-69), 19 SEP 78; To VA-12, NAS Cecil Field, 19 SEP 78; To VA-12, USS Dwight D. Eisenhower (CVN-69), 19 SEP 78; To VA-12, NAS Cecil Field, FL., 19 SEP 78; To VA-12, USS Dwight D. Eisenhower (CVN-69), 19 SEP 78; To VA-12, NAS Cecil Field, FL., 13 DEC 80; To VA-12, USS Dwight D. Eisenhower (CVN-69), 09 JAN 81; To VA-12, NAS Jacksonville, FL., 10 AUG 81; To VA-12, USS Dwight D. Eisenhower (CVN-69), 20 OCT 81; To VA-12, NAS Cecil Fiel, FL., 20 OCT 81; To VA-12, USS Dwight D. Eisenhower (CVN-69),20 OCT 81; To VA-12, NAS Cecil Field, FL., 20 OCT 81 ** Transferred to VA-174/ FRS, AD/4XX, NAS Cecil Field, FL., 09 SEP 82; To VA-174, NAS Jacksonville, FL., 27 OCT 83; To VA-174, NAS Cecil Field, FL., 15 FEB 84 thru 06 SEP 87 ** End of flight record card.

E-207 157485 Navy acceptance from NPRO Rep. LTV, Dallas, TX., 17 JUN 70 ** Transferred to VA-113/CVW-2, NE/3XX, NAS LeMoore, CA., 19 JUN 70 ** Transferred to VA-22/CVW-15, NL/3XX, USS Coral Sea (CVA-43), 14 MAY 72; To VA-22, NAS LeMoore, CA., 22 MAY 73; To VA-22, USS Coral Sea (CVA-43), 28 OCT 74; To VA-22, NAS LeMoore, CA., 28 OCT 74 ** Transferred to VA-122/FRS, NJ/2XX, NAS LeMoore, CA., 14 NOV 74; To VA-122, NAS Alameda, CA., 16 NOV 74; To VA-122, NAS LeMoore, CA., 28 FEB 75; To VA-122, NAS Jacksonville, FL., 04 MAR 76; To VA-122, NAS LeMoore, CA., 20 APR 76; To VA-122, NAS Jacksonville, FL., 07 JUN 78; To VA-122, NAS LeMoore, CA., 07 JUN 78; To VA-122, NAS Jacksonville, FL., 07 JUN 78; To VA-122, NAS LeMoore, CA., 19 JUL 78; To VA-122, NAS Jacksonville, FL., 13 SEP 80; To VA-122, NAS LeMoore, CA., 07 NOV 80 ** Transferred to VA-27/ CVW-14, NK/4XX, NAS LeMoore, CA., 02 FEB 81; To VA-27, USS Coral Sea (CVA-43), 19 MAR 81; To VA-27, NAS LeMoore, CA., 11 JUN 81; To VA-27, USS Coral Sea (CVA-43), 20 AUG 81; To VA-27, NAF Atsugi, JP., 12 JAN 82; To VA-27, USS Coral Sea (CVA-43), 18 JAN 82; To VA-27, NAS LeMoore, CA., 22 MAR 82; To VA-27, NAS Jacksonville, FL., 17 JAN 83; To VA-27, USS Coral Sea (CVA-43), 09 MAR 83; To VA-27, NAS LeMoore, CA., 12 AUG 83 ** Transferred to VA-87/CVW-6, AE/4XX, NAS Cecil Field, FL., 10 SEP 83; To VA-87, USS Independence (CV-62), 10 OCT 83; To VA-87, NAS Cecil Field, FL., 14 FEB 84; To VA-87, USS Independence (CV-62), 18 JUL 84; To VA-87, NAS Cecil Field, FL., 25 JUL 84; To VA-87, USS Independence (CV-62), 07 OCT 84; To VA-87, NAS Cecil Field, FL., 10 OCT 84; To VA-87, NAS Jacksonville, FL., 29 APR 85 ** Transferred to VA-37/CVW-3, AC/312, NAS Cecil Field, FL., Paint was light gray on dark gray with black modex, 23 AUG 85; To VA-37, USS Forrestal (CV-59), 07 FEB 85; To VA-37, NAS Cecil Field, FL., 07 FEB 86 ** Transferred to VA-174/FRS, AD/437, NAS Cecil

Field, FL., 15 SEP 86 ** Transferred to AMARC, Davis Monthan AFB; Tiucson, AZ., assigned park code 6A0233; 18 AUG 87 ** End of flight record card ** 6651.4 flight hours ** TF41A2C engine S/N 141960 ** Engine released to DRMO for disposition, 23 MAY 05 ** Aircraft deleted from inventory and released to DRMO for disposition, 09 SEP 05.

E-208 157486 Navy acceptance from NPRO Rep. LTV, Dallas, TX., 23 JUN 70 ** Transferred to VA-25/CVW-2, NE/4XX, NAS LeMoore, CA., 26 JUN 70 ** Transferred to VA-94/CVW-15, NL/4XX, USS Coral Sea (CVA-43), 14 MAY 72 ** Transferred to VA-122/FRS, NJ/2XX, NAS LeMoore, CA., 06 DEC 72 ** Transferred to VA-146/CVW-9, NG/3XX, NAS LeMoore, CA., 16 JUN 76; To VA-146, USS Constellation (CV-62), 16 SEP 76; To VA-146, NAS LeMoore, CA., 15 DEC 76; To VA-146, USS Constellation (CV-62), 13 JAN 77; To VA-146, NAS LeMoore, CA., 26 JAN 77; To VA-146, NAS Cubi Point, PI., 14 MAY 77; To VA-146, NAF Atsugi, JP., 26 JUL 77; To VA-146, NAS Cubi Point, PI., 28 JUL 77; To VA-146, USS Constellation (CV-62), 25 OCT 77; To VA-146, NAS LeMoore, CA., 19 NOV 77; To VA-146, NAS Jacksonville, FL., 23 JAN 78; To VA-146, NAS LeMoore, CA., 24 FEB 78; To VA-146, NAS Fallon, NV., 10 MAY 78; To VA-146, NAS LeMoore, CA., 30 JUN 78; To VA-146, USS Constellation (CV-62), 16 JUL 78; To VA-146, NAS LeMoore, CA., 24 AUG 78; To VA-146, USS Constellation (CV-62), 21 SEP 78; To VA-146, NAS Cubi Point, PI., 21 DEC 78 ** Transferred to VA-147/ CVW-9, NG/4XX, USS Constellation (CV-62), 21 JUN 79; To VA-147, NAS LeMoore, CA., 21 JUN 79; To VA-147, NAS Jacksonville, FL., 11 NOV 79; To VA-147, NAS LeMoore, CA., 11 NOV 79; To VA-147, NAS Jacksonville, FL., 15 NOV 79; To VA-147, USS Constellation (CV-62), 15 NOV 79; To VA-147, NAS LeMoore, CA., 26 JAN 80; To VA-147, USS Constellation (CV-62), 26 FEB 80; To VA-147, NAS Cubi Point, PI., 18 APR 80; To VA-147, USS Constellation (CV-62), 18 SEP 80; To VA-147, NAS LeMoore, CA., 18 SEP 80; To VA-147, NAF El Centro, CA., 02 APR 81; To VA-147, USS Constellation (CV-62), 30 APR 81; To VA-147, NAS LeMoore, CA., 12 JUN 81; To VA-147, USS Constellation (CV-62), 07 JUL 81; To VA-147, NAS LeMoore, CA., 06 AUG 81; To VA-147, USS Constellation (CV-62), 19 OCT 81; To VA-147, NAS Cubi Point, PI., 19 OCT 81; To VA-147, USS Constellation (CV-62), 19 OCT 81; To VA-147, NAS LeMoore, Ca., 19 OCT 81; To VA-147, NAS Jacksonville, FL., 07 JUN 82; To VA-147, NAS LeMoore, CA., 16 JUL 82 ** Transferred to VA-27/CVW-14, NK/4XX, NAS LeMoore, CA., 30 DEC 82; To VA-27, USS Coral Sea (CV-43), 09 MAR 83; To VA-27, NAS LeMoore, CA., 12 MAR 83; To VA-27/CVW-15, NL/4XX, USS Carl Vinson (CVN-70), 10 MAY 84; To VA-27, NAS Jacksonville, FL., 01 JUN 84 ** Transferred to VA-146/CVW-9, NE/3XX, NAS LeMoore, CA., 30 OCT 84; To VA-146, USS Kitty Hawk (CV-63), 24 JAN 85; To VA-146, NAS LeMoore, CA., 14 OCT 85 ** Transferred to VA-97/CVW-15, NL/3XX, NAS LeMoore, CA., 10 APR 86; To VA-97, USS Carl Vinson (CVN-70), 25 MAY 86; To VA-97, NAS LeMoore, CA., 07 JUN 86; To VA-97, USS Carl Vinson (CVN-70), 07 JUN 86; To VA-97, NAS Alameda, CA., 19 JAN 87 thru 09 SEP 87 ** End of flight record card ** Transferred to AMARC, Davis Monthan AFB; Tucson, AZ., assigned park code 6A0328; 28 MAR 90, with FLIR ** 6367.2 flight hours ** TF41A402D engine S/N 142509 ** Storage location 111219 ** At AMARG, Davis Monthan AFB; Tucson, AZ., 15 JUN 07.

E-209 157487 Navy acceptance from NPRO Rep. LTV, Dallas, TX., 12 JUN 70 ** Transferred to VA-174/FRS, AD/4XX, NAS Cecil Field, FL., 13 JUN 70 ** Transferred to NARF Jacksonville, FL., 14 DEC 70 ** Transferred to VA-122/FRS, NJ/ 2XX, NAS LeMoore, CA., 14 DEC 72; To VA-122, CRAA, NAS LeMoore, CA., 21 DEC 72; To VA-122, NAS LeMoore, CA., 18 JUL 73; To VA-122, NAS Jacksonville, FL., 13 APR 77 ** Transferred to VA-195/CVW-11, NH/4XX, NAS LeMoore, CA., 06 JUN 77; To VA-195, USS Kitty Hawk (CV-63), 28 FEB 77; To VA-195, NAS LeMoore, CA., 12 AUG 77; To VA-195, USS Kitty Hawk (CV-63), 29 SEP 77; To VA-195, NAS LeMoore, CA., 09 MAR 78; To VA-195, USS America (CV-66), 05 JUL 79; To VA-195, NAS LeMoore, CA., 05 JUL 79; To VA-195, NAS Jacksonville, FL., 29 OCT 79, To VA-195, NAS LeMoore,

CA., 14 DEC 79; To VA-195, NAS Fallon, NV., 19 OCT 80; To VA-195, NAS LeMoore, CA., 07 NOV 80; To VA-195, USS America (CV-66), 25 JAN 81; To VA-195, NAS LeMoore, CA., 25 JAN 81 ** Transferred to VA-25/CVW-2, NE/411, NAS LeMoore, CA., 26 JUN 81; To VA-25, NAS Jacksonville, FL., 13 JUL 81; To VA-25, USS Ranger (CV-61), 11 OCT 81; To VA-25, NAS LeMoore, CA., 13 NOV 81; To VA-25, USS Ranger (CV-61), 14 JAN 82; To VA-25, NAS LeMoore, CA., 14 JAN 82; To VA-25, USS Ranger (CV-61), 14 JAN 82; To VA-25, NAS Cubi Point, PI., 14 JAN 82; To VA-25, NAF Atsugi, JP., 30 JUL 82; To VA-25, USS Ranger (CV-61), 16 AUG 82 ** Transferred to VA-56/CVW-5, NF/4XX, NAF Atsugi, JP., 28 AUG 82 ** Transferred to VA-22/CVW-11, NH/3XX, USS Enterprise (CVN-65), 15 NOV 84; To VA-22, NAS LeMoore, CA., 15 NOV 84; To VA-22, NAS Jacksonville, FL., 22 JAN 85 ** Transferred to VA-192/CVW-11, NH/3XX, NAS LeMoore, CA., 23 MAR 85; To VA-192, NAS Cubi Point, PI., 13 SEP 85; To VA-192, NAS LeMoore, CA., 30 DEC 85; To VA-192, NAS Jacksonville, FL., 04 FEB 86 ** Transferred to VA-204/CVWR-20, AF/4XX, NAS New Orleans, LA., 07 FEB 86 thru 01 APR 87 ** W/O, 09 NOV 89.

E-210 157488 Navy acceptance from NPRO Rep. LTV, Dallas, TX., 11 JUN 70 ** Transferred to VA-174/FRS, AD/4XX, NAS Cecil Field, FL., 16 JUN 70 ** Transferred to VA-86/CVW-8, AJ/4XX, NAS Cecil Field, FL., 23 JUN 71; To VA-86, USS America (CVA-66), 23 JUN 71 ** Transferred to VA-66/CVW-7, AG/3XX, NAS Cecil Field, FL., 08 APR 72; To VA-66, USS Independence (CVA-62), 08 APR 72; To VA-66, NAS Cecil Field, FL., 12 MAR 73 ** Transferred to VA-174/FRS, AD/4XX, NAS Cecil Field, FL., 21 JUN 74 ** Transferred to VA-86/CVW-8, AJ/4XX, USS Nimitz (CVN-68), 09 SEP 77; To VA-86, NAS Cecil Field, FL., 09 SEP 77; To VA-86, USS Nimitz (CVN-68), 09 SEP 77; To VA-86, NAS Cecil Field, FL., 23 JAN 78; To VA-86, NAS Roosevelt Roads, PR., 26 SEP 78; To VA-86, NAS Jacksonville, FL., 05 DEC 78; To VA-86, NAS Cecil Field, FL., 11 JAN 79; To VA-86, USS Nimitz (CVN-68), 11 JAN 79; To VA-86, NAS Cecil Field, FL., 11 JAN 79; To VA-86, USS Nimitz (CVN-78), 19 MAR 80 ~ S 1SO strike, 18 AUG 80 ** No data on strike.

E-211 157489 Navy acceptance from NPRO Rep. LTV, Dallas, TX., 27 MAY 70 ** Transferred to VA-174/FRS, AD/4XX, NAS Cecil Field, FL., 29 MAY 70 ** Transferred to VA-82/CVW-8, AJ/3XX, NAS Cecil Field, FL., 24 NOV 70; To VA-82, USS America(CVA-66), 22 APR 71 ** Transferred to VA-174/FRS, AD/4XX, NAS Cecil Field, FL., 04 APR 72 ** Transferred to VA-66/CVW-7, AG/3XX, USS Independence (CVA-62), 27 DEC 72; To VA-66, NAS Cecil Field, FL., 19 FEB 73; To VA-66, USS Independence (CV-62), 11 APR 74; To VA-66, NAS Cecil Field, FL., 22 AUG 74 ** Transferred to VA-174/FRS, AD/4XX, NAS Cecil Field, FL., 11 AUG 75 ** Transferred to VA-66/CVW-7, AG/3XX, NAS Fallon, NV., 30 AUG 76; To VA-66, USS Independence (CV-62), 01 SEP 76; To VA-66, NAS Cecil Field, FL., 01 DEC 76; To VA-66, USS Independence (CV-62), 01 DEC 76 ** Transferred to VA-87/CVW-6, AE/4XX, MCAS Yuma, AZ., 16 JAN 77; To VA-87, USS America (CV-66), 16 JAN 77; To VA-87, NAS Cecil Field, FL., 01 MAR 77 ** Transferred to VA-174/FRS, AD/4XX, NAS Cecil Field, FL., 13 SEP 77 ** Transferred to VA-81/CVW-17, AA/4XX, USS Forrestal (CV-59), 21 MAR 78; To VA-81, NAS Cecil Field, FL., 31 AUG 78; To VA-81, NAS Jacksonville, FL., 01 SEP 78 ** Transferred to VA-174/FRS, AD/401, NAS Cecil Field, FL., 30 JAN 79; To VA-174, NAS Jacksonville, FL., 24 JUL 81; To VA-174, NAS Cecil Field, FL., 01 SEP 81** Transferredc to VA-12/CVW-7, AG/4XX, USS Dwight D. Eisenhower (CVN-69), 20 OCT 81 ** Transferred to VA-174/FRS, AD/4XX, NAS Cecil Field, FL., 24 OCT 81; To VA-174, NAS Jacksonville, FL., 08 SEP 83; To VA-174, NAS Cecil Field, FL., 08 SEP 83; To VA-174, NAS Jacksonville, FL., 13 SEP 83; To VA-174, NAS Cecil Field, FL., 14 SEP 83; To VA-174, NAS Jacksonville, FL., 26 JAN 84 ** Transferred to VA-105/CVW-6, AE/4XX, NAS Cecil Field, FL., 09 APR 84; To VA-105, NAF Kadena, JP., 09 APR 84; To VA-105, NAS Cubi Point, PI., 09 APR 84; To VA-105, MCAS Iwakuni, JP, 09 APR 84; To VA-105, NAS Cecil Field, FL., 09 APR 84 ** Transferred to VA-15/CVW-6, AE/3XX, NAS Cecil Field, FL., 12 MAR 85; To VA-15, MCAS Iwakuni, JP., 22 NOV 85; To VA-15, Korea, 22 NOV 85; To VA-15, NAS Cubi Point, PI., 22 NOV 85; To VA-15, NAS Cecil Field, FL., 22 NOV

85; To VA-15, NAS Jacksonville, FL., 10 JUL 86; To VA-15, NAS Cecil Field, FL., 31 JUL 86; To VA-15, NAS Jacksonville, FL., 26 SEP 86; To VA-15, NAS Cecil Field, FL., 29 SEP 86 ** Transferred to VA-81/CVW-17, AA/4XX, 29 SEP 86; To VA-81, USS Saratoga (CV-60), 26 NOV 86; To VA-81, NAS Cecil Field, FL., 26 NOV 86; To VA-81, USS Saratoga (CV-60), 13 APR 87; To VA-81, NAS Cecil Field, FL., 15 APR 87; To VA-81, USS Saratoga (CV-60), 15 APR 87 ** End of flight record card ** Transferred to VA-204/CVWR-20, AF/4XX, NAS New Orleans, LA., date unknown ** Transferred to AMARC, Davis Monthan AFB; Tucson, AZ., assigned park code 6A0316; 22 FEB 90 ** 6381.4 flight hours ** TF41A402D engine S/N 141453 ** Engine records released to DRMO for disposition, 25 NOV 03 ** Aircraft demilitarized, 11 JAN 05 ** Aircraft deleted from inventory and released to DRMO for disposition, 09 SEP 05.

E-212 157490 Navy acceptance from NPRO Rep. LTV, Dallas, TX., 22 JUL 70 ** Transferred to VA-113/CVW-2, NE/3XX, NAS LeMoore, CA., 23 JUL 70; To VA-113, USS Ranger (CV-61), 21 JUN 73; To VA-113, NAS LeMoore, CA., 07 MAY 74; To VA-113, USS Ranger (CV-61), 07 MAY 74; To VA-113, NAS LeMoore, CA., 26 FEB 75; To VA-113, NAS Jacksonville, FL., 08 APR 75; To VA-113, NAS LeMoore, CA., 14 MAY 75; To VA-113, USS Ranger (CV-61), 03 JUL 76; To VA-113, NAS LeMoore, CA., 18 NOV 7674; To VA-113, USS Ranger (CV-61), 24 AUG 78; To VA-113, NAS LeMoore, CA., 24 AUG 78; To VA-113, USS Ranger (CV-61), 02 DEC 78; To VA-113, NAS LeMoore, CA., 16 DEC 78; To VA-113, USS Ranger (CV-61), 22 MAR 79; To VA-113, NAS Cubi Point, PI., 02 JUL 79; To VA-113, NAS LeMoore, CA., 15 NOV 79; To VA-113, NAS Fallon, NV., 20 DEC 79; To VA-113, NAS LeMoore, CA., 20 DEC 79; To VA-113, NAS Jacksonville, FL., 24 APR 80; To VA-113, USS Ranger (CV-61), 13 MAY 80; To VA-113, NAS LeMoore, CA., 09 JUL 80; To VA-113, USS Ranger (CV-61), 18 JUL 80; To VA-113, NAS Cubi Point, PI., 24 OCT 80 ** Transferred to VA-56/CVW-5, NF/4XX, NAF Atsugi, JP., 06 MAR 81; To VA-56, USS Midway (CV-41), 03 SEP 81; To VA-56, NAF Atsugi, JP., 04 NOV 81 ** Transferred to VA-25/CVW-2, NE/4XX, USS Ranger (CV-61), 27 AUG 82; To VA-25, NAS LeMoore, CA., 15 NOV 82 ** Transferred to VA-147/CVW-9, NG/4XX, 09FEB 83 ** Transferred to VA-27/CVW-14, NK/4XX, USS Coral Sea (CV-43), 08 MAR 83; To VA-27, NAS LeMoore, CA., 01 SEP 83 ** Transferred to VA-82/CVW-8, AJ/3XX, NAS Cecil Field, FL., 11 SEP 83 ** Transferred to VA-37/CVW-15, NL/312, Carl Vinson (CVN-70), 21 NOV 83; To VA-37, NAS Roosevelt Roads, PR., 30 NOV 83; To VA-37, NAS Cecil Field, FL., 30 NOV 83; To VA-37, Carl Vinson (CVN-70), 21 NOV 83; To VA-37, NAS Roosevelt Roads, PR., 30 NOV 83; To VA-37, NAS Cecil Field, FL. 30 NOV 83; To VA-37, NWC China Lake, CA., 05 DEC 83; To VA-37, NAS Cecil Field, FL., 19 MAR 84; To VA-37, MCAS Twenty Nine Palms, CA., 18 JUL 84; To VA-37, NAS Cecil Field, FL., 07 SEP 84; To VA-37, MCAS Iwakuni, JP., 12 SEP 84, To VA-37, Korea, 12 SEP 84; To VA-37, MCAS Iwakuni, JP., 12 SEP 84; To VA-37, NAS Cecil Field, FL., 21 JUN 85; To VA-37, NAS Jacksonville, FL., 15 NOV 85; To VA-37, NAS Cecil Field, FL., 18 NOV 85; To VA-37, USS Forrestal (CV-59), 28 JAN 86; To VA-37, NAS Cecil field, FL., 28 JAN 86; To VA-37, USS Forrestal (CV-59), 28 JAN 86; To VA-37, NAS Cecil Field, FL., 22 DEC 86 ** Transferred to AMARC, Davis Monthan AFB; Tucson, AZ., assigned park code 6A0224; 15 MAY 87 ** End of flight record card ** Aircraft deleted from inventory and released to DRMO for disposition, 18 AUG 05.

E-213 157491 Navy acceptance from NPRO Rep. LTV, Dallas, TX., 19 JUN 70 ** Transferred to VA-113/CVW-2, NE/3XX, NAS LeMoore, CA., 23 JUN 70 ** Transferred to VA-147/CVW-9, NG/4XX, USS Constellation (CVA-64), 14 NOV 72; To VA-147, NAS LeMoore, CA., 01 APR 75; To VA-147, NAS Jacksonville, FL., 18 APR 75; To VA-147, NAS LeMoore, CA., 07 JUN 75; To VA-147, MCAS Yuma, AZ., 29 OCT 75; To VA-147, NAS LeMoore CA., 29 OCT 75; To VA-147, USS Constellation (CV-64), 29 SEP 76; To VA-147, NAS LeMoore, CA., 22 OCT 76; To VA-147, NAS Cubi Point, PI., 07 JUL 77; To VA-147, USS Constellation (CV-64), 12 JUL 77; To VA-147, NAS LeMoore, CA., 19 NOV 77; To VA-147, NAS Jacksonville, FL., 04 MAR 78; To VA-147, NAS LeMoore,

CA., 01 MAY 78; To VA-147, USS Constellation (CV-64), 25 SEP 78; To VA-147, NAS Cubi Point, PI., 06 NOV 78; To VA-147, USS Constellation (CV-64), 31 DEC 78; To VA-147, NAS LeMoore, CA., 11 JUN 79; To VA-147, NAS Jacksonville, FL., 02 NOV 79; To VA-147, NAS LeMoore, CA., 02 NOV 79; To VA-147, NAS Jacksonville, FL., 06 NOV 79; To VA-147, USS Constellation (CV-64), 06 NOV 79; To VA-147, NAS LeMoore, CA., 20 JAN 80; To VA-147, USS Constellation (CV-64), 30 MAR 80; To VA-147, NAF Atsugi, JP., 07 APR 80; To VA-147, NAS Cubi Point, PI., 25 APR 80; To VA-147, NAF Atsugi, JP., 16 JUN 80; To VA-147, NAS Cubi Point, PI., 25 JUN 80; To VA-147, NAF Atsugi, JP., 20 AUG 80; To VA-147, NAS Cubi Point, PI., 21 AUG 80; To VA-147, USS Constellation (CV-64), 08 SEP 80; To VA-147, NAS LeMoore, CA., 11 SEP 80; To VA-147, NAF El Centro, CA., 02 APR 81; To VA-147, USS Constellation (CV-64), 30 APR 81; To VA-147, NAS LeMoore, CA., 12 JUN 81; To VA-147, USS Constellation (CV-64),07 JUL 81; To VA-147, NAS LeMoore, CA., 06 AUG 81; To VA-147, USS Constellation (CV-64), 19 OCT 81; To VA-147, NAS Cubi Point, PI., 19 OCT 81; To VA-147, USS Constellation (CV-64), 19 OCT 81; To VA-147, NAS LeMoore, CA., 19 OCT 81; To VA-147, NAS Jacksonville, FL., 17 JUN 82; To VA-147, NAS LeMoore, CA., 16 AUG 82 ** Transferred to VA-27/CVW-14, NK/4XX, NAS LeMoore, CA., 30 DEC 82; To VA-27, USS Coral Sea (CV-43), 04 MAR 83; To VA-27, NAS LeMoore, CA., 10 SEP 83 ** Transferred to VA-203/CVWR-20, AF/3XX, NAS Jacksonville, FL., 03 OCT 83 ** Transferred to VA-205/CVWR-20, AF/500, NAS Atlanta, GA., 20 JUN 84 thru 15 MAY 87, Paint was light gray on medium gray with black modex ** End of flight record card ** Transferred to AMARC, Davis Monthan AFB; Tucson, AZ., assigned park code 6A0244; 15 JAN 88 ** Transferred to NSWC; Fallon, NV., to be used as a range target on pasture 4755.

E-214 157492 Navy acceptance from NPRO Rep. LTV, Dallas, TX., 09 JUL 70 ** Transferred to VA-195/CVW-11, NH/ 4XX, USS Kitty Hawk (CVA-63), 13 JUL 70 ** Transferred to VA-27/CVW-14, NK/4XX, NAS LeMoore, CA., 12 FEB 72 ** Transferred to VA-195/ CVW-11, NH/4XX, USS Kitty Hawk (CVA-63), 28 FEB 72; To VA-195, NAS LeMoore, CA., 26 JUN 72; To VA-195, USS Kitty Hawk (CV-63), 29 JUN 73; To VA-195, NAS LeMoore, CA., 07 AUG 74; To VA-195, NAS North Island, CA., 31 JAN 75; To VA-195,USS Kitty Hawk (CV-63), 31 JAN 75; To VA-195, NAS North Island, CA., 21 FEB 75; To VA-195, NAS LeMoore, CA., 21 FEB 75 ** Transferred to NARF, NAS Jacksonville, FL., 21 APR 75 ** Transferred to VA-192/CVW-11, NH/3XX, NAS LeMoore, CA., 11 AUG 77; To VA-192, USS Kitty Hawk (CV-63), 25 JUL 77; To VA-192, NAS LeMoore, CA., 11 AUG 77; To VA-192, USS Kitty Hawk (CV-63), 14 OCT 77; To VA-192, NAS LeMoore, CA., 14 MAY 78; To VA-192, USS America (CV-66), 05 JAN 79; To VA-192, NAS LeMoore, CA., 05 JAN 79; To VA-192, NAS Jacksonville, FL., 02 NOV 79; To VA-192, NAS LeMoore, CA., 05 NOV 79 ** Transferred to VA-122/FRS, NJ/2XX, NAS LeMoore, CA., 23 JUL 80 ** Transferred to VA-25/ CVW-2, NE/4XX, NAS LeMoore, CA., 13 JUL 81; To VA-25, NAS Fallon, NV., 27 JUL 81; To VA-25, NAS Jacksonville, FL., 18 SEP 81; To VA-25, NAS LeMoore, CA., 19 NOV 81; To VA-25, USS Ranger (CV-61), 14 JAN 82; To VA-25, NAS LeMoore, CA., 22 FEB 82; To VA-25, USS Ranger (CV-61), 22 FEB 82; To VA-25, NAS Cubi Point, PI., 22 FEB 82 ** Transferred to VA-56/CVW-5, NF,4XX, NAF Atsugi, JP., 22 AUG 82 ** Transferred to VA-22/CVW-11, NH/3XX, USS Enterprise (CVN-65), 13 NOV 84; To VA-22, NAS LeMoore, CA., 15 NOV 84; To VA-22, NAS Jacksonville, FL., 01 FEB 85; To VA-22, NAS Fallon, NV., 01 FEB 85 ** Transferred to VA-147/CVW-9, NE/3XX, NAS LeMoore, CA., 05 APR 85; To VA-147, USS Kitty Hawk (CV-63), 23 APR 85; To VA-147, NAS LeMoore, CA., 15 SEP 86; To VA-147. NAS Jacksonville, FL., 16 SEP 86 ** Transferred to VA-204/CVWR-20, AF/4XX, NAS New Orleans, LA., 17 SEP 86 thru 06 JUN 87 ** End of flight record card ** Transferred to VA-205/CVWR-20, AF/5XX, NAS Atlanta, GA., date unknown ** Transferred to AMARC, Davis Monthan AFB; Tucson, AZ., assigned park code 6A0367; 26 JUN 90 ** 6588.8 flight hours ** TF41A402D engine S/N 141903 ** Project changed per FSO letter, 06 APR 04 ** Engine records released to DRMO for disposition, 05 OCT 05. ** Aircraft deleted from inventory and released to DRMO for disposition, 05 OCT 05.

E-215 157493 Navy acceptance from NPRO Rep. LTV, Dallas, TX., 22 JUN 70 ** Transferred to VA-113/CVW-2, NE/304, NAS LeMoore, CA., 25 JUN 70 ** Transferred to VA-195/CVW-11, NH/4XX, USS Kitty Hawk (CVA-63), 14 MAY 72; To VA-195, NAS LeMoore, CA., 16 JUN 72; To VA-195, USS Kitty Hawk (CV-63), 29 JUN 73; To VA-195, NAS LeMoore, CA., 07 AUG 74; To VA-195, USS Kitty Hawk (CV-63), 28 MAR 85; To VA-195, NAS LeMoore, CA., 09 APR 75; To VA-195, USS Kitty Hawk (CV-63), 19 MAY 75; To VA-195, NAS Cubi Point, PI., 21 JUN 75; To VA-195, NAS LeMoore, CA., 14 DEC 75; To VA-195, NAS Jacksonville, FL., 04 JUL 76; To VA-195, NAS LeMoore, CA., 09 SEP 76; To VA-195, NAS Jacksonville, FL., 14 SEP 76 ** Transferred to VA-37/CVW-3, AC/3XX, NAS Cecil Field, FL., 28 SEP 76; To VA-37, USS Saratoga (CV-60), 18 OCT 76; To VA-37, NAS Cecil Field, FL., 18 OCT 76; To VA-37, USS Saratoga (CV-60), 18 OCT 76; To VA-37, NAS Cecil Field, FL., 16 JUL 77 ** Transferred to VA- 82/CVW-8, AJ/3XX, USS Nimitz (CVN-68), 19 MAR 80; To VA-82, NAS Jacksonville, FL., 24 OCT 80; To VA-82, USS Nimitz (CVN-68), 17 DEC 80; To VA-82, NAS Cecil Field, FL., 18 DEC 80; To VA-82, USS Nimitz (CVN-68), 24 APR 81; To VA-82, NAS Cecil Field, FL., 24 APR 81; To VA-82, USS Carl Vinson(CVN-70), 24 APR 81; To VA-82, NAS Cecil Field, FL., 24 APR 81; To VA-82, USS Nimitz (CVN-68), 24 APR 81; To VA-82, NAS Cecil Field, FL., 24 APR 81; To VA-82, USS Nimitz (CVN-68), 24 APR 81; To VA-82, NAS Cecil Field, FL., 24 APR 81; To VA-82, NAS Jacksonville, FL., 27 JUN 83; To VA-82, NAS Cecil Field, FL., 25 JUL 83; To VA-82, NAS Jacksonville, FL., 19 AUG 83; To VA-82, NAS Cecil Field, FL., 22 AUG 83 ** Transferred to VA-81/CVW-17, AA/4XX, NAS Cecil Field, FL., 25 OCT 83; To VA-81, USS Saratoga (CV-60), 27 OCT 83; To VA-81, NAS Cecil Field, FL., 19 NOV 83; To VA-81, USS Saratoga (CV-60), 19 NOV 83; To VA-81, NAS Cecil Field, FL., 19 NOV 83; To VA-81, USS Saratoga (CV-60), 28 JAN 85 ** Transferred to VA-174/FRS, AD/4XX, NAS Cecil Field, FL., 25 JUN 85; To VA-174, NAS Jacksonville, FL., 22 JAN 86; To VA-174, NAS Cecil Field, FL., 28 JAN 86 ** Transferred to VA-203/ CVWR-20, AF/3XX, NAS Jacksonville, FL., 19 NOV 86 thru 18 SEP 87 ** End of flight record card ** Transferred to VA-205/CVWR-20, AF/507, NAS Atlanta, GA., date unknown ** Transferred to AMARC, Davis Monthan AFB; Tucson, AZ., assigned park code 6A0365; 26 JUN 90 ** 7446.9 flight hours ** TF41A402D engine S/N 142589 ** Aircraft demilitarized, 13 JAN 03 ** Engine records released to DRMO for disposition, 25 NOV 03. ** Aircraft deleted from inventory and released to DRMO for disposition, 09 SEP 05.

E-216 157494 Navy acceptance from NPRO Rep. LTV, Dallas, TX., 24 JUN 70 ** Transferred to VA-25/CVW-2, NE/4XX, NAS LeMoore, CA., 26 JUN 70; To VA-25, USS Ranger (CV-61), 21 JUN 73; To VA-25, NAS LeMoore, CA., 15 NOV 74, To VA-25, NAS Jacksonville, FL., 06 APR 75; To VA-25, NAS LeMoore, CA., 22 MAY 75; To VA-25, NAS Fallon, NV., 13 JUL 75; To VA-25, USS Ranger (CV-61), 14 AUG 74; To VA-25, NAS LeMoore, CA., 23 SEP 75; To VA-25, USS Ranger (CV-61), 25 SEP 75; To VA-25, NAS LeMoore, CA., 23 SEP 76; To VA-25, NAS Fallon, NV., 27 JUL 77; To VA-25, NAS LeMoore, CA., 12 AUG 77; To VA-25, MCAS Yuma, AZ., 31 AUG 77; To VA-25, NAS LeMoore, CA.,31 AUG 77; To VA-25, NAS Jacksonville, FL., 27 FEB 78; To VA-25, NAS LeMoore, CA., 07 APR 78; To VA-25, USS Ranger (CV-61), 01 NOV 78; To VA-25, NAS LeMoore, CA., 07 DEC 78; To VA-25, USS Ranger (CV-61), 24 JAN 79 ** Transferred to NARF, NAS North Island, CA., 15 FEB 79 ** Transferred to VA-192/CVW-11, NH/306, NAS LeMoore, CA., 28 JUL 82; To VA-192, USS Ranger (CV-61), 28 JUL 82; To VA-192, NAS LeMoore, CA., 18 JAN 84; To VA-192, NAS Jacksonville, FL., 02 OCT 84; To VA-192, NAS LeMoore, CA., 20 DEC 84; To VA-192, NAS Cubi Point, PI., 06 SEP 85 ** Transferred to VA-93/CVW-5, NF/304, NAF Atsugi, JP., 08 NOV 85; To VA-93, NAS LeMoore, CA., 04 APR 86 ** Transferred to VA-122/FRS, NJ/226, NAS LeMoore, CA., 13 MAY 86 thru 12 MAY 87 ** End of flight record card ** Transferred to AMARC, Davis Monthan AFB; Tucson, AZ., assigned park code 6A0312; 15 FEB 90 ** 5070.0 flight hours ** TF41A402D engine S/N 14 ** Storage location 211960 ** Engine released to DRMO, Davis Monthan AFB; Tucson, AZ., for disposition, 25 NOV 03 ** Aircraft at AMARG, Davis Monthan AFB; Tucson, AZ., 15 JUN 07.

E-217 157495 Navy acceptance from NPRO Rep. LTV, Dallas, TX., 23 JUL 70 ** Transferred to VA-195/CVW-11, NH/4XX, USS Kitty Hawk (CVA-63), 27 JUL 70; To VA-195, NAS LeMoore, CA., 20 MAY 72 ** Transferred to VA-97/ CVW-14, NK/303, NAS LeMoore, CA., 22 NOV 72; To VA-97, NAS Fallon, NV., 30 NOV 75; To VA-97, USS Enterprise (CVN-65), 20 FEB 76; To VA-97, NAS LeMoore, CA., 30 APR 76 ** Transferred to VA-195/CVW-11, NH/4XX, NAS LeMoore, CA., 13 JUL 76; To VA-195, NAS Jacksonville, FL., 07 APR 77; To VA-195, NAS LeMoore, CA., 31 MAY 77; To VA-195, USS Kitty Hawk (CV-63), 19 JUL 77; To VA-195, NAS LeMoore, CA., 12 AUG 77; To VA-195, USS Kitty Hawk (CV-63), 20 SEP 77; To VA-195, NAS LeMoore, CA., 22 MAR 78; To VA-195, NAS Alameda, CA., 23 DEC 78; To VA-195, USS America (CV-66), 08 JAN 79; To VA-195, NAS Alameda, CA., 27 FEB 79; To VA-195, NAS LeMoore, CA., 28 FEB 79; To VA-195, USS America (CV-66), 28 FEB 79; To VA-195, NAS LeMoore, CA., 28 FEB 79; To VA-195, NAS Jacksonville, FL., 02 NOV 79; To VA-195, NAS LeMoore, CA., 12 DEC 79 ** Transferred to VA-113/CVW-2, NE/3XX, USS Ranger (CV-61), 30 MAY 80; To VA-113, NAS LeMoore, CA., 28 JUN 80; To VA-113, USS Ranger (CV-61), 18 JUL 80, VA-113, NAS Cubi Point, PI., 24 OCT 80; To VA-113, NAS LeMoore, CA., 04 APR 81; To VA-113, NAS Fallon, NV., 28 AUG 81; To VA-113, NAS Jacksonville, FL., 04 SEP 81; To VA-113, USS Ranger (CV-61), 20 NOV 81; To VA-113, NAS Jacksonville, FL., 20 NOV 81 ** Transferred to VA-25/CVW-2, NE/4XX, NAS LeMoore, CA., 25 NOV 81; To VA-25, USS Ranger (CV-61), 25 NOV 81; To VA-25, NAS LeMoore, CA., 25 NOV 81; To VA-25, USS Ranger (CV-61), 25 NOV 81; To VA-25, NAS Cubi Point, PI., 25 NOV 81; To VA-25, NAF Atsugi, JP., 15 JUL 82; To VA-25, NAS Cubi Point, PI., 22 JUL 82; To VA-25, USS Ranger (CV-61), 22 JUL 82 ** Transferre to VA-56/CVW-5, NF/4XX, NAF Atsugi, JP., 01 SEP 82 ~ S 1SO strike, 21 AUG 84 ** No data on strike.

E-218 157496 Navy acceptance from NPRO Rep. LTV, Dallas, TX., 24 JUN 70 ** Transferred to VA-113/CVW-2, NE/310, NAS LeMoore, CA., 26 JUN 70; To VA-113, USS Ranger (CV-61), 21 JUN 73; To VA-113, NAS LeMoore, CA., 07 MAY 74; To VA-113, USS Ranger (CV-61), 07 MAY 74; To VA-113, NAS LeMoore, CA., 15 NOV 74; To VA-113, NAS Jacksonville, FL., 22 JUL 75; To VA-113, NAS LeMoore, CA., 26 JUL 75; To VA-113, NAS Jacksonville, FL., 14 JUN 78; To VA-113, NAS LeMoore, CA., 09 SEP 75; To VA-113, NAS LeMoore, CA., 24 JAN 77; To VA-113, NAS Jacksonville, FL., 02 MAY 78; To VA-113, NAS LeMoore, CA., 01 JUN 78; To VA-113, NAS Jacksonville, FL., 14 JUN 78; To VA-113, NAS LeMoore, CA., 13 AUG 78; To VA-113, USS Ranger (CVA-61), 27 SEP 78; To VA-113, NAS LeMoore, CA., 16 OCT 78; To VA-113, USS Ranger (CV-61), 09 NOV 78; To VA-113, NAS LeMoore, CA., 15 DEC 78; To VA-113, USS Ranger (CV-61), 22 MAR 79; To VA-113, NAS Cubi Point, PI., 02 JUL 79; To VA-113, NAS Fallon, NV., 22 SEP 79; To VA-113, NAS LeMoore, CA., 26 JAN 80; To VA-113, USS Ranger (CV-61), 22 APR 80; To VA-113, NAS Jacksonville, FL., 22 MAY 80; To VA-113, USS Ranger (CV-61), 22 MAY 80; To VA-113, NAS Jacksonville, FL., 23 MAY 80; To VA-113, NAS LeMoore, CA., 23 MAY 80; To VA-113, NAS Jacksonville, FL., 18 JUL 80; To VA-113, USS Ranger (CV-61), 23 JUL 80; To VA-113, NAS Cubi Point, PI., 24 OCT 80 ** Transferred to VA-56/CVW-5, NF/4XX, NAF Atsugi, JP., 03 MAR 81; To VA-56, USS Midway (CV-41), 28 MAY 81; To VA-56, NAF Atsugi, JP., 27 JUN 81; To VA-56, USS Midway (CV-41), 03 SEP 81; To VA-56, NAF Atsugi, JP., 20 OCT 81 ** Transferred to VA-27/CVW-15, NL/4XX, NAS LeMoore, CA., 21 OCT 82; To VA-27, USS Carl Vinson (CVN-70), 24 JAN 84; To VA-27, NAS LeMoore, CA., 24 JAN 84; To VA-27, USS Carl Vinson (CVN-70), 23 MAY 84; To VA-27, NAS LeMoore, CA., 23 MAY 84 ** Transferred to VA-146/CVW-9, NG/3XX, NAS LeMoore, CA., 13 SEP 84; To VA-146, USS Kitty Hawk (CV-63), 18 JUL 85 ** Transferred to VA-97/CVW-15, NL/3XX, NAS LeMoore, CA., 19 JUL 85; To VA-97, USS Carl Vinson (CVN-70), 01 OCT 85 ** To NWEF, Kirtland AFB; Albuquerque, NM., 01 MAY 86 ** Transferred to AMARC, Davis Monthan AFB; Tucson, AZ., assigned park code 6A0217, 06 FEB 87 ** End of flight record card 5145.2 flight hours ** TF41A2B engine S/N 142575 ** Aircraft released from storage and prepared for overland and above deck shipment to the government of Greece, 02 SEP 94 ** Transferred to the Helenic Air force (Greece).

E-219 157497 Navy acceptance from NPRO Rep. LTV, Dallas, TX., 28 JUL 70 ** Transferred to VA-192/CVW-11, NH/311, USS Kitty Hawk (CVA-63), 29 JUL 70; To VA-192, NAS LeMoore, CA., 15 MAY 72; To VA-192, USS Kitty Hawk (CV-63), 29 JUN 73; To VA-192, NAS LeMoore, CA., 24 AUG 74; To VA-192,USS Kitty Hawk (CV-63), 12 DEC 74; To VA-192, NAS LeMoore, CA., 28 MAR 75; To VA-192,USS Kitty Hawk (CV-63), 28 MAR 75; To VA-192, NAS Cubi Point, PI., 01 NOV 75; To VA-192,USS Kitty Hawk (CV-63), 19 NOV 75; To VA-192, NAS LeMoore, CA., 01 FEB 76; To VA-192, NAS Jacksonville, FL., 07 JUL 76; To VA-192, MCAS Yuma, AZ., 30 NOV 76; To VA-192, NAS LeMoore, CA., 23 JUN 77; To VA-192, USS Kitty Hawk (CV-63), 27 JUL 77; To VA-192, NAS LeMoore, CA., 31 AUG 77; To VA-192, USS Kitty Hawk (CV-63), 25 OCT 77; To VA-192, NAS LeMoore, CA., 14 MAY 78 ** Transferred to VA-97/CVW-14, NK/3XX, NAS LeMoore, CA., 21 DEC 78; To VA-97, NAS Jacksonville, FL., 10 APR 79; To VA-97, NAS LeMoore, CA., 14 APR 79; To VA-97, NAS Jacksonville, FL., 23 OCT 79; To VA-97, USS Coral Sea (CV-43), 24 OCT 79 ** Transferred to VA-56/CVW-5, NF/4XX, NAF Atsugi, JP., 15 JUL 80; To VA-56, USS Midway (CV-41), 15 JUL 80; To VA-56, NAF Atsugi, JP., 04 SEP 80; To VA-56, USS Midway (CV-41), 02 FEB 81; To VA-56, NAF Atsugi, JP., 27 APR 81; To VA-56, USS Midway (CV-41), 15 JUL 81; To VA-56, NAF Atsugi, JP., 04 OCT 81 ** Transferred to VA-25/CVW-2, NE/4XX, NAS Cubi Point, PI., 01 SEP 82 ** Transferred to VA-27/CVW-14, NK/4XX, NAS LeMoore, CA., 21 OCT 82 ~ S 1SO strike, 16 FEB 83 ** Crashed during bomb run, pilot ejected safely.

E-220 157498 Navy acceptance from NPRO Rep. LTV, Dallas, TX., 25 JUN 70 ** Transferred to VA-82/CVW-8, AJ/3XX, NAS Cecil Field, FL., 29 SEP 70 ~ S 1SO strike, 15 JUN 71 ** No data on strike.

E-221 157499 Navy acceptance from NPRO Rep. LTV, Dallas, TX., 23 JUN 70 ** Transferred to VA-25/CVW-2, NE/402, NAS LeMoore, CA., 26 JUN 70; To VA-25, USS Ranger (CV-61), 27 JUN 73; To VA-25, NAS LeMoore, CA., 11 DEC 74; To VA-25, NAS Jacksonville, FL., 06 MAR 75; To VA-25, NAS LeMoore, CA., 01 MAY 75; To VA-25, NAS Fallon, NV., 13 JUL 75; To VA-25, USS Ranger (CV-61), 14 AUG 75; To VA-25, NAS LeMoore, CA., 16 SEP 75; To VA-25, USS Ranger (CV-61), 01 NOV 75; To VA-25, NAS LeMoore, CA., 16 SEP 75; To VA-25, USS Ranger (CV-61), 11 NOV 75; To VA-25, NAF Atsugi, JP., 05 APR 76; To VA-25, USS Ranger (CV-61), 12 MAY 76; To VA-25, NAS LeMoore, CA., 13 DEC 76; To VA-25, NAS Fallon, NV., 16 JUL 77; To VA-25, NAS LeMoore, CA., 15 AUG 77; To VA-25, NAS Alameda, CA., 26 AUG 77; To VA-25, NAS LeMoore, CA., 31 AUG 77 ** Transferred to VA-146/CVW-9, NG/3XX, NAS LeMoore, CA., 28 JUN 78; To VA-146, NAS Jacksonville, FL., 09 JUL 78; To VA-146, NAS LeMoore, CA., 20 AUG 78; To VA-146, USS Constellation (CV-64), 21 SEP 78; To VA-146, NAS Cubi Point, PI., 21 DEC 78; To VA-146, NAS LeMoore, CA., 18 JUN 79; To VA-146, USS Constellation (CV-64), 18 JUN 79; To VA-146, NAS LeMoore, CA., 18 JUN 79 ** Transferred to VA-195/ CVW-11, NH/4XX, NAS Jacksonville, FL., 19 JUN 80; To VA-195, NAS LeMoore, CA., 21 AUG 80; To VA-195, NAS Fallon, NV., 19 OCT 80; To VA-195, NAS LeMoore, CA., 07 NOV 80; To VA-195, USS America (CV-66), 25 JAN 81; To VA-195, NAS LeMoore, CA., 09 APR 81; To VA-195, NAF Atsugi, JP., 01 JUN 81; To VA-195, USS America (CV-66), 07 JUN 81; To VA-195, NAS LeMoore, CA., 11 NOV 81 ~ S 1SO strike, 14 DEC 81 ** No data on strike.

E-222 157500 Navy acceptance from NPRO Rep. LTV, Dallas, TX., 28 JUL 70 ** Transferred to VA-113/CVW-2, NE/3XX, NAS LeMoore, CA., 29 JUL 70; To VA-113, USS Ranger (CV-61), 21 JUN 73; To VA-113, NAS LeMoore, CA., 07 MAY 74; To VA-113, USS Ranger (CV-61), 05 AUG 74; To VA-113, NAS LeMoore, CA., 15 NOV 74; To VA-113, USS Ranger (CVA-61), 16 AUG 75 ** Transferred to VA-94/CVW-15, NL/4XX, NAS LeMoore, CA., 02 FEB 76; To VA-94, NAS Fallon, NV., 30 APR 76; To VA-94, NAS LeMoore, CA., 30 APR 76; To VA-94, USS Coral Sea (CV-43), 09 DEC 76; To VA-94, NAS LeMoore, CA., 14 DEC 76; To VA-94, USS Coral Sea (CV-43), 20 JUL 77; To VA-94, NAF Atsugi, JP., 04 AUG 77; To VA-94, USS Coral Sea (CV-43), 18 AUG 77; To VA-94, NAS LeMoore, CA., 29 SEP 77; To VA-94, NAS Jacksonville, FL., 01

DEC 77; To VA-94, NAS LeMoore, CA., 04 APR 78; To VA-94, NAS Cubi Point, PI., 29 MAY 79; To VA-94, USS Kitty Hawk (CV-63), 06 JUN 79; To VA-94, NAS LeMoore, CA., 21 SEP 79; To VA-94, NAS Jacksonville, FL., 05 JUN 80; To VA-94, USS Kitty Hawk (CV-63), 05 JUN 80; To VA-94, NAS Jacksonville, FL., 15 AUG 80; To VA-94, NAS LeMoore, CA., 18 AUG 80; To VA-94, USS Kitty Hawk (CV-63), 11 SEP 80; To VA-94, NAS LeMoore, CA., 06 NOV 80; To VA-94, USS Kitty Hawk (CV-63), 27 FEB 81; To VA-94, NAS Cubi Point, PI., 13 MAY 81; To VA-94, NAF Atsugi, JP., 09 JUN 81; To VA-94, NAS Cubi Point, PI., 18 JUN 81; To VA-94, USS Kitty Hawk (CV-63), 18 JUN 81; To VA-94, NAS LeMoore, CA., 04 OCT 81; To VA-94, NAS Jacksonville, FL., 11 JUN 82; To VA-94, Naples, IT., 13 OCT 82; To VA-94, NAS Jacksonville, FL., 18 OCT 82 ** Transferred to VA-27/CVW-14, NK/401, NAS LeMoore, CA., 02 NOV 82; To VA-27, USS Coral Sea (CV-43), 21 MAR 83; To VA-27, NAS LeMoore, CA., 17 SEP 83; To VA-27, USS Carl Vinson (CVN-70), 14 MAR 84; To VA-27, NAS LeMoore, CA., 14 MAR 84; To VA-27, USS Carl Vinson (CVN-70), 14 MAR 84; To VA-27, NAS LeMoore, CA., 14 MAR 84 ~ S 1SO strike, 11 JUL 84 ** Pilot killed enroute to NWC China Lake, CA.

E-223 157501 Navy acceptance from NPRO Rep. LTV, Dallas, TX., 30 JUN 70 ** Transferred to VA-113/CVW-2, NE/3XX, NAS LeMoore, CA., 01 JUL 70; To VA-113, USS Ranger (CV-61), 21 JUN 73; To VA-113, NAS LeMoore, CA., 07 MAY 74; To VA-113, USS Ranger (CV-61), 08 JUL 74; To VA-113, NAS LeMoore, CA., 14 FEB 75; To VA-113, NAS Jacksonville, FL., 23 MAY 75; To VA-113, NAS LeMoore, CA., 28 JUL 75; To VA-113, USS Ranger (CV-61), 16 AUG 75; To VA-113, NAF Atsugi, JP., 09 JUL 76; To VA-113, USS Ranger ICV-61), 12 AUG 76; To VA-113, NAS LeMoore, CA., 22 MAR 77; To VA-113, NAS Jacksonville, FL., 23 APR 78; To VA-113, NAS LeMoore, CA., 13 AUG 78; To VA-113, USS Ranger (CV-61), 27 SEP 78; To VA-113, NAS LeMoore, CA., 06 OCT 78; To VA-113, USS Ranger (CV-61), 09 NOV 78; To VA-113, NAS LeMoore, CA., 15 DEC 78; To VA-113, USS Ranger (CV-61), 22 MAR 79; To VA-113, NAS Cubi Point, PI., 02 JUL 79; To VA-113, NAS Jacksonville, FL., 14 DEC 79; To VA-113, NAS LeMoore, CA., 16 DEC 79; To VA-113, NAS Jacksonville, FL., 18 DEC 79; To VA-113, NAS Fallon, NV., 18 DEC 79; To VA-113, NAS LeMoore, CA., 18 DEC 79; To VA-113, USS Ranger (CV-61), 05 MAY 80; To VA-113, NAS LeMoore, CA., 09 JUL 80; To VA-113, USS Ranger (CV-61), 18 JUL 80; To VA-113, NAS Cubi Point, PI., 18 JUN 81; To VA-113, NAS LeMoore, CA., 04 APR 81; To VA-113, NAS Fallon, NV., 14 SEP 81; To VA-113, USS Ranger (CV-61), 28 SEP 81; To VA-113, NAS LeMoore, CA., 28 SEP 81; To VA-113, USS Ranger (CV-61), 28 SEP 81; To VA-113, NAS LeMoore, CA., 28 SEP 81; To VA-113, NAS Jacksonville, FL., 16 MAR 82 ** Transferred to VA-94/CVW-15, NL/414, USS Enterprise (CVN-65), Painted light gray on dark gray, 28 JUN 82; To VA-94, NAF Atsugi, JP., 28 MAR 83 ** Transferred to VA-195/ CVW-11, NH/4XX, NAS LeMoore, CA., 02 JUN 83; To VA-195, USS Ranger (CV-61), 02 JUN 83; To VA-195, NAS LeMoore, CA., 16 DEC 83 ** Transferred to VA-94/CVW-11, NH/4XX, NAS LeMoore, CA., 16 MAY 85; To VA-94, USS Enterprise (CVN-65), 09 DEC 85; To VA-94, NAS Jacksonville, FL., 02 APR 86 ** Transferred to NSWC, NAS Fallon, NV., 09 APR 86 thru 08 JUN 87 ** End of flight record card ** Transferred to AMARC, Davis Monthan AFB; Tucson, AZ., assigned park code 6A0267; 16 MAY 88 ** 5511.4 flight hours ** TF41A402D engine S/N 141265 ** Project changed per FSO letter, 06 APR 04 ** Engine records released to DRMO for disposition, 05 OCT 05. ** Aircraft deleted from inventory and released to DRMO for disposition, 05 OCT 05.

E-224 157502 Navy acceptance from NPRO Rep. LTV, Dallas, TX., 26 JUN 70 ** Transferred to VA-25/CVW-2, NE/4XX, NAS LeMoore, CA., 29 JUN 70 ** Transferred to NARF, NAS Alameda, CA., 15 DEC 70 ** Transferred to VA-25/CVW-2, NE/4XX, NAS LeMoore, CA., 15 MAY 72 ** Transferred to VA-146/CVW-9, NG/3XX, USS Constellation (CVA-64), 09 NOV 72 ** Transferred to VA-195/CVW-11, NH, 4XX, NAS LeMoore, CA., 21 DEC 72; To VA-195, USS Kitty Hawk (CV-63), 29 JUN 73; To VA-195, NAS LeMoore, CA., 06 AUG 74; To VA-195, NAS Jacksonville, FL., 12 FEB 75; To VA-195, USS Kitty Hawk (CV-63), 04 APR 75; To VA-

195, NAS LeMoore, CA., 09 APR 75; To VA-195, USS Kitty Hawk (CV-63), 27 APR 75 ** Transferred to VA-122/FRS, NJ/2XX, NAS LeMoore, CA., 15 MAY 75 ** Transferred to VA-27/ CVW-14, NK/4XX, NAS LeMoore, CA., 18 JUN 75; To VA-27, NAS Fallon, NV., 04 SEP 75; To VA-27, NAS LeMoore, CA., 19 FEB 76; To VA-27, USS Enterprise (CVN-65), 12 MAR 76; To VA-27, NAS LeMoore, CA., 31 MAR 76; To VA-27, USS Enterprise (CVN-65), 29 APR 76; To VA-27, NAS LeMoore, CA., 17 MAY 76; To VA-27, USS Enterprise (CVN-65), 30 JUN 76; To VA-27, NAS LeMoore, CA., 30 JUN 76; To VA-27, USS Enterprise (CVN-65), 28 JUL 76; To VA-27, NAS LeMoore, CA., 28 MAR 77; To VA-27, USS Enterprise (CVN-65), 12 JAN 78; To VA-27, NAS LeMoore, CA., 03 MAR 78; To VA-27, NAF Atsugi, JP., 22 MAY 78; To VA-27, USS Enterprise (CVN-65), 12 JUN 78; To VA-27, NAF Atsugi, JP., 31 AUG 78; To VA-27, USS Enterprise (CVN-65), 01 SEP 78; To VA-27, NAS LeMoore, CA., 10 OCT 78; To VA-27, NAS Jacksonville, FL., 23 DEC 78; To VA-27, NAS LeMoore, CA.,29 JAN 79; To VA-27, NPTR El Centro, CA., 29 JAN 79; To VA-27, USS Coral Sea (CV-43), 12 OCT 79; To VA-27, NAS Cubi Point, PI., 12 NOV 79; To VA-27, USS Coral Sea (CV-43), 23 DEC 79; To VA-27, NAS LeMoore, CA., 26 MAR 80; To VA-27, NAS Jacksonville, FL., 07 MAR 81; To VA-27, NAS LeMoore, CA., 29 APR 81; To VA-27, USS Coral Sea (CV-43), 29 APR 81; To VA-27, NAS Cecil Field, FL., 11 JUN 81; To USS Coral Sea (CV-43), 20 AUG 81; To VA-27, NAF Atsugi, JP., 16 SEP 81; To USS Coral Sea (CV-43), 30 SEP 81; To VA-27, NAS LeMoore, CA., 22 MAR 82 ** Transferred to VA-94/CVW-11, NH/4XX, USS Enterprise (CVN-65),05 JUL 82; To VA-94, NAS Cubi Point, PI., 05 JUL 82; To VA-94, NAS LeMoore, CA., 05 JUL 82; To VA-94, NAS Jacksonville, FL., 25 OCT 83; To VA-94, USS Enterprise (CVN-65), 25 OCT 83; To VA-94, NAS LeMoore, CA., 25 OCT 83; To VA-94, USS Enterprise (CVN-65), 25 OCT 83; To VA-94, NAS Jacksonville, FL., 17 APR 84 ** Transferred to VA-22/CVW-11, NH/3XX, NAS LeMoore, CA., 19 APR 84; To VA-22, USS Enterprise (CVN-65), 19 APR 84 ** Transferred to VA-56/CVW-5, NF/4XX, NAF Atsugi, JP., 12 NOV 84; To VA-56, NAS LeMoore, CA., 19 DEC 85; To VA-56, NAS Jacksonville, FL., 10 JUN 86 ** Transferred to VA-146/ CVW-9, NE/3XX, NAS LeMoore, CA., 30 AUG 86 ** Transferred to VX-5, XE/XXX, NWC China Lake, CA., 17 DEC 86 thru 14 MAY 87 ** End of flight record card ** Transferred to AMARC, Davis Monthan AFB; Tucson, AZ., assigned park code 6A0345, 19 APR 90 ** 5517.8 flight hours ** TF41A402D engine S/N 191307 ** Aircraft released from storage and prepared for overland and above deck shipment to the government of Greece, 14 JUL 94 ** Transferred to the Helenic Air force (Greece).

E-225 157503 Navy acceptance from NPRO Rep. LTV, Dallas, TX., 18 JUL 70 ** Transferred to VA-113/CVW-2, NE/3XX, NAS LeMoore, CA. 21 JUL 70 ~ S 1SO strike, 24 DEC 72 ** No data on strike.

E-226 157504 Navy acceptance from NPRO Rep. LTV, Dallas, TX., 30 JUN 70 ** Transferred to VA-113/CVW-2, NE/313, NAS LeMoore, CA. 03 JUL 70; To VA-113, USS Ranger (CV-61), 21 JUN 73; To VA-113, NAS LeMoore, CA., 07 MAY 74; To VA-113, USS Ranger (CV-61), 07 MAY 74; To VA-113, NAS LeMoore, CA., 14 JAN 75; To VA-113, USS Ranger (CV-61), 16 AUG 75 ** Transferred to VA-94/CVW-15, NL/4XX, NAS LeMoore, CA., 13 NOV 75; To VA-94, NAS Fallon, NV., 30 APR 76; To VA-94, NAS LeMoore, CA., 30 APR 76; To VA-94, USS Coral Sea (CV-43), 30 AUG 76 ** Transferred to VA-122/FRS, NJ/2XX, NAS LeMoore, CA., 08 NOV 76; To VA-122, NAS Jacksonville, FL., 19 OCT 77; To VA-122, NAS LeMoore, CA., 05 JAN 78 ** Transferred to VA-195/CVW-11, NH/4XX, NAS LeMoore, CA., 30 APR 79; To VA-195, USS America (CV-66), 30 APR 79; To VA-195, NAS LeMoore, CA., 25 MAY 79; To VA-195, NAS Jacksonville, FL., 29 APR 80 ** Transferred to VA-94/CV-15, NL/4XX, NAS LeMoore, CA., 08 JUN 80; To VA-94, USS Kitty Hawk (CV-63), 27 JUN 80; To VA-94, NAS LeMoore, CA., 27 JUN 80; To VA-94, USS Kitty Hawk (CV-63), 04 SEP 80; To VA-94, NAS LeMoore, CA., 06 NOV 80; To VA-94, USS Kitty Hawk (CV-63), 27 FEB 81; To VA-94, NAS Cubi Point, PI., 13 MAY 81; To VA-94, NAF Atsugi, JP., 09 SEP 81; To VA-94, NAS Cubi Point, PI., 24 SEP 81; To VA-94, USS Kitty Hawk (CV-63), 24 SEP 81; To VA-94, NAS

LeMoore, CA., 04 OCT 81; To VA-94, NAS Alameda, CA., 06 OCT 82; To VA-94, NAS LeMoore, CA., 11 MAR 82; To VA-94, NAS Jacksonville, FL., 20 MAY 82; To VA-94, NAS LeMoore, CA., 28 MAY 82; To VA-94, NAS Jacksonville, FL., 08 JUN 82; To VA-94, USS Enterprise (CVN-65), 24 SEP 82; To VA-94, NAS Jacksonville, FL., 06 OCT 82 ** Transferred to VA-97/CVW-14, NK/3XX, NAS LeMoore, CA., 30 NOV 82; To VA-97, USS Coral Sea (CV-43), 14 FEB 83; To VA-97, NAS LeMoore, CA., 02 AUG 83 ** Transferred to VA-174/FRS, AD/4XX, NAS Cecil Field, FL., 09 SEP 83; To VA-174, NAS Jacksonville, FL., 06 SEP 85; To VA-174, NAS Cecil Field, FL., 16 OCT 85; To VA-174, NAS Jacksonville, FL., 27 NOV 85; To VA-174, NAS Cecil Field, FL., 15 DEC 85 ** Transferred to VA-66/CVW-7, AG/3XX, NAS Cecil Field, FL., 31 JAN 86; To VA-66, USS John F. Kennedy (CV-67), 25 AUG 86; To VA-66, NAS Jacksonville, FL., 09 SEP 86; To VA-66, USS John F. Kennedy (CV-67), 09 SEP 86; To VA-66, NAS Jacksonville, FL., 19 SEP 86 ** Transferred to VA-205/CVWR-20, AF/512, NAS Atlanta, GA., 20 SEP 86 thru 13 SEP 87 ** End of flight record card ** Transferred to AMARC, Davis Monthan AFB; Tucson, AZ., assigned park code 6A0298; 24 AUG 89 ** 6349.8 flight hours ** TF41A402D engine S/N 141560 ** Storage location 210805 ** Under GSA jurisdiction ** Aircrat deleted from inventory and released to DRMO for disposition, 04 MAY 06.

E-227 157505 Navy acceptance from NPRO Rep. LTV, Dallas, TX., 20 JUL 70 ** Transferred to VA-25/CVW-2, NE/4XX, NAS LeMoore, CA., 30 JUL 70; To VA-25, USS Ranger (CV-61), 21 JUN 73; To VA-25, NAS LeMoore, CA., 15 JAN 75; To VA-25, NAS Jacksonville, FL., 23 MAY 75; To VA-25, NAS Fallon, NV., 22 JUL 75; To VA-25, USS Ranger (CV-61), 04 SEP 75; To VA-25, NAS LeMoore, CA., 23 SEP 75; To VA-25, USS Ranger (CV-61), 27 JAN 76; To VA-25, NAS LeMoore, CA., 14 MAR 77; To VA-25, NAS Fallon, NV., 29 JUL 77; To VA-25, NAS LeMoore, CA., 17 AUG 77; To VA-25, USS Ranger (CV-61), 05 NOV 78; To VA-25, NAS LeMoore, CA., 05 NOV 78; To VA-25, NAF Atsugi, JP., 20 MAR 79; To VA-25, USS Ranger (CV-61), 28 MAR 79; To VA-25, NAS Cubi Point, PI., 28 MAR 79; To VA-25, NAS Fallon, NV., 21 SEP 79; To VA-25, NAS LeMoore, CA., 21 SEP 79; To VA-25, NAS Jacksonville, FL., 02 MAY 80; To VA-25, NAS LeMoore, CA., 02 MAY 80; To VA-25, NAS Jacksonville, FL., 05 MAY 80; To VA-25, NAS LeMoore, CA., 06 JUL 80; To VA-25, USS Ranger (CV-61), 18 JUL 80; To VA-25, NAS LeMoore, CA., 06 AUG 80; To VA-25, USS Ranger (CV-61), 10 SEP 80 ** Transferred to VA-87/CVW-6, AE/4XX, NAS Cecil Field, FL., 25 FEB 81; To VA-87, USS Independence (CV-62), 21 JAN 82; To VA-87, NAS Cecil Field, FL., 21 JAN 82; To VA-87, USS Independence (CV-62), 08 APR 82; To VA-87, NAS Cecil Field, FL., 21 APR 82; To VA-87, USS Independence (CV-62), 21 APR 82; To VA-87, NAS Cecil Field, FL., 21 APR 82; To VA-87, NAS Jacksonville, FL., 08 FEB 83; To VA-87, NAS Cecil Field, FL., 26 MAR 83; To VA-87, NAS Jacksonville, FL., 29 APR 83; To VA-87, NAS Cecil Field, FL., 30 APR 83; To VA-87, USS Independence (CV-62), 23 JUN 83; To VA-87, NAS Cecil Field, FL., 23 JUN 83; To VA-87, USS Independence (CV-62), 23 JUL 83; To VA-87, NAS Dallas, TX., 17 AUG 83; ** Transferred to VA-46/CVW-15, NL/3XX, NAS Cecil Field, FL., 17 AUG 83; To VA-46, USS America (CV-66), 14 NOV 83; To VA-46, NAS Cecil Field, FL., 14 DEC 83; To VA-46, USS America (CV-66), 20 JAN 84; To VA-46, NAS Cecil Field, FL., 20 JAN 84; To VA-46, USS America (CV-66), 20 JAN 84; To VA-46, NAS Cecil Field, FL., 20 JAN 84; To VA-46, NAS Jacksonville, FL., 20 MAY 85; To VA-46, USS America (CV-66), 20 MAY 85; To VA-46, NAS Cecil Field, FL., 21 MAY 85; To VA-46, USS America (CV-66), 21 MAY 85; To VA-46, NAS Jacksonville, FL., 30 SEP 85 ** Transferred to VA-105/CVW-6, AE/4XX, NAS Cecil Field, FL., 01 OCT 85; To VA-105, USS Forrestal (CV-59), 11 OCT 85; To VA-105, NAS Cecil Field, FL., 11 OCT 85; To VA-105, USS Forrestal (CV-59), 13 OCT 86; To VA-105, NAS Cecil Field, FL., 13 OCT 86; To VA-105, USS Forrestal (CV-59), 15 MAY 87 thru 02 SEP 87 ** End of flight record card;

E-228 157506 Navy acceptance from NPRO Rep. LTV, Dallas, TX., 27 JUL 70 ** Transferred to VA-25/CVW-2, NE/410, NAS LeMoore, CA., 26 JUL 70; To VA-25, USS Ranger (CV-61), 21 JUN 73; To VA-25, NAS LeMoore, CA., 15 JAN 75; To VA-25, NAS Jacksonville

FL., 03 JUN 75; To VA-25, NAS Fallon, NV., 29 JUL 75; To VA-25, USS Ranger (CV-61), 14 AUG 75; To VA-25, NAS LeMoore, CA., 23 SEP 75; To VA-25, USS Ranger (CV-61), 23 SEP 75; To VA-25, NAS LeMoore, CA., 24 JAN 77; To VA-25, NAS Fallon, NV., 31 JUL 77; To VA-25, NAS LeMoore, CA., 12 AUG 77; To VA-25, MCAS Yuma, AZ., 18 OCT 77; To VA-27, NAS LeMoore, CA., 18 OCT 77; To VA-25, NAS Jacksonville, FL., 31 MAR 78; To VA-25, NAS LeMoore, CA., 16 MAY 78; To VA-25, USS Ranger (CV-61), 13 NOV 78; To VA-25, NAS LeMoore, CA., 15 DEC 78; To VA-25, USS Ranger (CV-61), 31 JAN 79; To VA-25, NAS Cubi Point, PI., 20 FEB 79; To VA-25, NAS LeMoore, CA., 16 NOV 79; To VA-25, NAS Fallon, NV., 16 NOV 79; To VA-25, NAS LeMoore, CA., 26 JAN 80; To VA-25, NAS Jacksonville, FL., 28 MAY 80; To VA-25, NAS LeMoore, CA., 28 MAY 80; To VA-25, NAS Jacksonville, FL., 16 JUL 80; To VA-25, USS Ranger (CV-61), 17 JUL 80; To VA-25, NAS LeMoore, CA., 07 AUG 80; To VA-25, USS Ranger (CV-61), 10 SEP 80; To VA-25, NAS LeMoore, CA., 15 MAY 81 ** Transferred to VA-27/CVW-14, NK/4XX, USS Coral Sea (CV-43), 20 AUG 81; To VA-27, NAF Atsugi, JP., 09 JAN 82; To VA-27, USS Coral Sea (CV-43), 20 JAN 82; To VA-27, NAS LeMoore, CA., 22 MAR 82; To VA-27, NAS Jacksonville, FL., 22 SEP 82; To VA-27, NAS LeMoore, CA., 12 NOV 82; To VA-27, USS Coral Sea (CV-43), 12 NOV 82; To VA-27, NAS LeMoore, CA., 19 JUN 83 ** Transferred to VA-174/FRS, AD/4XX, NAS Cecil Field, FL., 09 SEP 83; To VA-174, NAS Jacksonville, FL., 18 OCT 84; To VA-174, NAS Cecil Field, FL., 18 OCT 84; To VA-174, NAS Jacksonville, FL., 22 OCT 84 ** Transferred to VA-81/CVW-17, AA/4XX, NAS Cecil Field, FL., 07 FEB 85; To VA-81, USS Saratoga (CV-60), 26 MAR 85; To VA-81, NAS Cecil Field, FL., 26 MAR 85; To VA-81, USS Saratoga (CV-60), 26 MAR 85; To VA-81, NAS Cecil Field, FL., 29 APR 86 ** Transferred to VA-174/FRS, AD/4XX, NAS Cecil Field, 25 AUG 86 ** Transferred to NAD Norfolk, VA., 12 JUN 87 ~ S-3SO strike, 18 AUG 87 ** No data 0n strike ** On display at Hampton Air Power Park and museum; Hampton, VA., since at least 98, carries the incorrect Bureau Number of 157500.

E-229 157507 Navy acceptance from NPRO Rep. LTV, Dallas, TX., 17 JUL 70 ** Transferred to VA-25/CVW-2, NE/4XX, NAS LeMoore, CA., 18 JUL 70; To VA-25, USS Ranger (CV-61), 21 JUN 73; To VA-25, NAS LeMoore, CA., 09 MAR 75 ~ S 1SO strike, 28 APR 75 ** No data on strike.

E-230 157508 Navy acceptance from NPRO Rep. LTV, Dallas, TX., 13 JUL 70 ** Transferred to VA-192/CVW-11, NH/301, USS Kitty Hawk (CVA-63) CDR Bud Owens painted on side of cockpit, 16 JUL 70; To VA-192, NAS LeMoore, 16 MAY 72; To VA-192, USS Kitty Hawk (CV-63), 29 JUN 73; To VA-192, NAS LeMoore, 12 AUG 74; To VA-192, USS Kitty Hawk (CV-63), 12 DEC 74 70; To VA-192, NAS LeMoore, 01 MAR 75; To VA-192, USS Kitty Hawk (CV-63), 19 MAY 75; To VA-192, NAS Cubi Point, PI., 27 SEP 75; To VA-192, USS Kitty Hawk (CV-63), 19 NOV 75; To VA-192, NAS LeMoore, 16 MAR 76; To VA-192, MCAS Yuma, AZ., 30 NOV 76; To VA-192, NAS LeMoore, CA., 01 JAN 77; To VA-192, NAS Jacksonville, FL., 29 MAR 77; To VA-192, NAS LeMoore, CA., 01 JAN 77; To VA-192, NAS Jacksonville, FL., 28 JAN 77; To VA-192, NAS LeMoore, CA., 03 FEB 77; To VA-192, NAS Jacksonville, FL., 29 MAR 77; To VA-192, NAS LeMoore, 12 APR 77; To VA-192, USS Kitty Hawk (CV-63), 5 JUL 77; To VA-192, NAS LeMoore, 11 AUG 77; To VA-192, USS Kitty Hawk (CV-63), 25 OCT 77; To VA-192, NAS LeMoore, 14 MAY 78; To VA-192, USS America (CV-66), 14 FEB 79; To VA-192, NAS LeMoore, CA., 08 MAR 79; To VA-192, NAS Jacksonville, FL., 29 OCT 79; To VA-192, NAS LeMoore, CA., 13 APR 80; To VA-192, NAS Alameda., 16 OCT 80; To VA-192, NAS LeMoore, 25 NOV 80; To VA-192, USS America (CV-66), 25 NOV 80 ** Transferred to VA-147/CVW-9, NG/4XX, NAS LeMoore, CA., 07 JAN 81; To VA-147, NAF El Centro, CA., 02 APR 81; To VA-147, USS Constellation (CV-64), 30 APR 81; To VA-147, NAS LeMoore, CA., 12 JUN 81; To VA-147, USS Constellation (CV-64), 07 JUL 81; To VA-147, NAS LeMoore, CA., 06 AUG 81; To VA-147, NAS Jacksonville, FL., 12 AUG 81; To VA-147, NAS LeMoore, CA., 12 AUG 81; To VA-147, NAS Jacksonville, FL., 18 SEP 81; To VA-147, USS Constellation (CV-64), 10 OCT 81; To VA-147, NAS Cubi Point, PI., 19 OCT

81; To VA-147, USS Constellation (CV-64), 19 OCT 81; To VA-147, NAS LeMoore, CA., 19 OCT 81; To VA-147, NAS Jacksonville, FL., 22 NOV 83 ** Transferred to VA-97/CVW-15 NL/3XX, NAS LeMoore, CA., 23 NOV 83; To VA-97, USS Carl Vinson (CVN-70), 07 MAR 84; To VA-97, NAS LeMoore, CA., 07 MAR 84; To VA-97, USS Carl Vinson (CVN-70), 07 MAR 84; NAS LeMoore, CA., 27 JUN 84; To VA-97, USS Carl Vinson (CVN-70), 27 JUN 84; NAS LeMoore, CA., 27 JUN 84 ** Transferred to VA-146/CVW-9, NE/3XX, NAS LeMoore, CA., 07 SEP 84 ** Transferred to VA-22/CVW-11, NH/3XX, NAS LeMoore, CA., 23 JAN 85; To VA-22, NAS Fallon, NV., 25 APR 85, To VA-22, NAS LeMoore, CA., 16 MAY 85; To VA-22, NAS Jacksonville, FL., 17 MAY 85 ** Transferred to VA-97/CVW-15 NL/3XX, NAS LeMoore, CA., 15 AUG 85; To VA-97, USS Carl Vinson (CVN-70), 15 AUG 85 ** Transferred to VA-146/CVW-9, NE/3XX, NAS LeMoore, CA., 02 MAY 86 ** Transferred to NSWC, Strike/XX, NAS Fallon, NV. Strike /22, 19 JUN 86 ** Transferred to AMARC, Davis Monthan AFB; Tucson, AZ., assigned park code 6A0242; 23 SEP 87 ** 6241.9 flight hours ** TF41A2B engine S/N 142653 ** End of flight record card ** Aircraft deleted from inventory and released to DRMO, Davis Monthan AFB; Tucson, AZ., for disposition, 10 AUG 05.

E-231 157509 Navy acceptance from NPRO Rep. LTV, Dallas, TX., 14 JUL 70 ** Transferred to VA-25/CVW-2, NE-4XX, NAS LeMoore, CA., 15 JUL 70 ~ S 1SO strike, 28 DEC 70 ** No data on strike.

E-232 157510 Navy acceptance from NPRO Rep. LTV, Dallas, TX., 13 MAY 70 ** Transferred to NPRO Rep. LTV, Dallas, TX., for RDT & E, 16 MAY 70 ** Transferred to VA-86/CVW-8, AJ/407, NAS Cecil Field, FL., 27 OCT 70; To VA-86, USS America (CVA-66), 14 JUN 71 ** Transferred to VA-66/CVW-7, AG/3XX, NAS Cecil Field, FL., 01 APR 72; To VA-66, USS Independence (CVA-62), 01 APR 72 ** Transferred to VA-174/FRS, AD/4XX,NAS Cecil Field, FL., 19 DEC 72 ** Transferred to VA-86/CVW-8, AJ/407, NAS Cecil Field, FL., 05 DEC 74; To VA-86, USS Nimitz (CVAN-70), 23 JAN 75; To VA-86, NAS Cecil Field, FL., 24 JUL 75; To VA-86, NAS Roosevelt Roads, PR., 24 JUL 75; To VA-86, NAS Cecil Field, FL., 24 JUL 75; To VA-86, USS Nimitz (CVN-70), 24 JUL 75; To VA-86, NAS Cecil Field, FL., 24 JUL 75; To VA-86, USS Nimitz (CVN-70), 24 JUL 75; To VA-86, NAS Cecil Field, FL., 24 JUL 75; To VA-86, NAS Roosevelt Roads, PR., 24 JUL 75; To VA-86, USS Nimitz (CVN-70), 19 JUL 77; To VA-86, NAS Cecil Field, FL., 19 JUL 77; To VA-86, USS Nimitz (CVN-70), 19 JUL 77; To VA-86, NAS Cecil Field, FL., 09 NOV 77; To VA-86, NAS Jacksonville, FL., 22 SEP 78; To VA-86, NAS Roosevelt Roads, PR., 17 NOV 78; To VA-86, NAS Cecil Field, FL., 17 NOV 78; To VA-86, USS Nimitz (CVN-70), 17 NOV 78; To VA-86, NAS Cecil Field, FL., 17 NOV 78; To VA-86, USS Nimitz (CVN-70), 09 JUN 80; To VA-86, NAS Cecil Field, FL., 01 DEC 80; To VA-86, NAS Jacksonville, FL., 07 MAY 81; To VA-86, NAS Cecil Field, FL., 15 MAY 81; To VA-86, USS Nimitz (CVN-70), 01 JUL 81; To VA-86, NAS Cecil Field, FL., 01 JUL 81 ** Transferred to VA-174/FRS, AD/4XX,NAS Cecil Field, FL., 01 MAR 82 ** Transferred to VA-81/CVW-17, AA/403, USS Forrestal (CV-59), 02 MAY 82; To VA-81, NAS Cecil Field, FL., 02 MAY 82; To VA-81, NAS Fallon, NV., 28 JUL 83; To VA-81, NAS Jacksonville, FL., 02 AUG 83; To VA-81, NAS Cecil Field, FL., 02 AUG 83; To VA-81, NAS Jacksonville, FL., 31 OCT 83; To VA-81, USS Saratoga (CV-60), 13 NOV 83; To VA-81, NAS Cecil Field, FL., 22 NOV 83; To VA-81, USS Saratoga (CV-60), 22 NOV 83; To VA-81, NAS Cecil Field, FL., 22 NOV 83 ~ S 1SO strike, 20 FEB 85 ** Pilot ejected safely when engine failed over the Ocala National Forest and crashed near Pinecastle, McCoy AFB; Orlando, FL.

E-233 157511 Navy acceptance from NPRO Rep. LTV, Dallas, TX., 29 JUL 70 ** Transferred to VA-113/CVW-2, NE/3XX, NAS LeMoore, CA. ~ S 1SO strike, 17 APR 71 ** No data on strike.

E-234 157512 Navy acceptance from NPRO Rep. LTV, Dallas, TX., 30 JUL 70 ** Transferred to VA-113/CVW-2, NE/302 & NE/305, NAS LeMoore, CA., 31 JUL 70; To VA-113, USS Ranger (CV-61), 21 JUN 73; To VA-113, NAS LeMoore, CA., 07 MAY 74; To VA-113,

USS Ranger (CV-61), 07 MAY 74; To VA-113, NAS LeMoore, CA., 03 DEC 74; To VA-113, NAS Jacksonville, FL., 29 MAY 75; To VA-113, NAS LeMoore,CA., 29 MAY 75; To VA-113, NAS Jacksonville, FL., 03 JUN 75; To VA-113, NAS LeMoore, CA., 25 JUL 75; To VA-113, USS Ranger (CV-61), 16 AUG 75; To VA-113, NAS LeMoore, CA., 18 APR 77; To VA-113, USS Ranger (CV-61), 27 SEP 78; To VA-113, NAS LeMoore, CA., 19 OCT 78; To VA-113, USS Ranger (CV-61), 09 NOV 78; To VA-113, NAS LeMoore, CA., 15 DEC 78; To VA-113, USS Ranger (CV-61), 22 MAR 79; To VA-113, NAS Cubi Point, PI., 02 JUL 79; To VA-113, NAS Jacksonville, FL., 21 NOV 79; To VA-113, NAS Fallon, NV., 27 NOV 79; To VA-113, NAS LeMoore, CA., 25 JAN 80; To VA-113, USS Ranger (CV-61), 24 APR 80; To VA-113, NAS LeMoore, CA., 09 JUL 80; To VA-113, USS Ranger (CV-61), 18 JUL 80; To VA-113, NAS Cubi Point, PI., 24 OCT 80; To VA-113, NAS LeMoore, CA., 04 APR 81 ** Transferred to VA-97/CVW-14, NK/3XX, USS Coral Sea (CV-43), 27 MAY 81; To VA-97, NAS LeMoore, CA., 11 JUN 81; To VA-97, USS Coral Sea (CV-43), 20 AUG 81; To VA-97, NAS LeMoore, CA., 22 MAR 82; To VA-97, NAS Jacksonville, FL., 24 MAR 82; To VA-97, NAS LeMoore, CA., 29 APR 82; To VA-97, USS Coral Sea (CV-43), 22 FEB 83; To VA-97, NAS LeMoore, CA., 12 AUG 83 ** Transferred to VA-82/CVW-8, AJ/3XX, NAS Cecil Field, FL., 09 SEP 83 ** Transferred to VA-37/CVW-15, NL/3XX, USS Carl Vinson (CVN-70), 18 NOV 83; To VA-37, NAS Roosevelt Roads, PR., 23 DEC 83; To VA-37/CVW-6, AE/3XX, NAS Cecil Field, FL., 02 JAN 84; To VA-37, NAS Jacksonville, FL., 23 MAR 84; To VA-37, NWC China Lake, CA., 23 MAR 84; To VA-37, NAS Jacksonville, FL., 26 MAR 84 ** Transferred to VA-87/CVW-6, AE/4XX, NAS Cecil Field, FL., 19 JUN 84; To VA-87, USS Independence (CV-62), 19 JUN 84; To VA-87, NAS Cecil Field, FL., 18 SEP 84; To VA-87, USS Independence (CV-62), 18 SEP 84; To VA-87, NAS Cecil Field, FL., 25SEP 84 ** Transferred to VA-174/FRS, AD/4XX, NAS Cecil Field, FL., 27 FEB 86; To VA-174, NAS Jacksonville, FL., 17 JUN 86; To VA-174, NAS Cecil Field, FL., 20 JUN 86; To VA-174, NAS Jacksonville, FL., 31 OCT 86 ** Transferred to VA-304/CVWR-30, ND/4XX, NAS Alameda, CA., 11 DEC 86 thru 21 APR 87 ** End of flight record card ** Transferred to VA-205/CVWR-20, AF/5XX, NAS Atlanta, GA., date unknown ** Transferred to AMARC, Davis Monthan AFB; Tucson, AZ., assigned park code 6A0338; 13 APR 90 ** 7517.4 flight hours ** TF41A402D engine S/N 141380 ** Aircraft demilitarized, 13 JAN 05 ** Engine records released to DRMO for disposition, 09 SEP 05. ** Aircraft deleted from inventory and released to DRMO for disposition, 09 SEP 05.

E-235 157513 Navy acceptance from NPRO Rep. LTV, Dallas, TX., 29 JUN 70 ** Transferred to VA-192/CVW-11, NH/3XX, USS Kitty Hawk (CVA-63), 31 JUL 70; To VA-192, NAS LeMoore, CA., 12 MAY 72; To VA-192, USS Kitty Hawk (CV-63), 29 JUN 73; To VA-192, NAS LeMoore, CA., 05 AUG 74 ~ S 1SO, strike, 06 NOV 74 ** No data on strike.

E-236 157514 Navy acceptance from NPRO Rep. LTV, Dallas, TX., 06 AUG 70 ** Transferred to VA-25/CVW-2, NE/402, NAS LeMoore, CA., 07 AUG 70; To VA-25, USS Ranger (CV-61), 21 JUN 73; To VA-25, NAS LeMoore, CA., 27 JAN 75; To VA-25, NAS Fallon, NV., 13 JUL 75; To VA-25, USS Ranger (CV-61), 14 AUG 75; To VA-25, NAS LeMoore, CA., 07 SEP 75; To VA-25, USS Ranger (CV-61), 14 JAN 76; To VA-25, NAS Atsugi, JP., 22 APR 76; To VA-25, USS Ranger (CV-61), 01 MAY 76; To VA-25, NAS LeMoore, CA., 08 OCT 76; To VA-25, NAS Alameda, CA., 09 MAR 77; To VA-25, NAS LeMoore, CA., 15 MAR 77; To VA-25, NAS Fallon, NV., 31 JUL 77; To VA-25, NAS LeMoore, CA., 12 AUG 77; To VA-25, NAS Jacksonville, FL., 24 AUG 77; To VA-25, NAS LeMoore, CA., 12 DEC 77; To VA-25, USS Ranger (CV-61), 04 NOV 78; To VA-25, NAS LeMoore, CA., 15 DEC 78; To VA-25, USS Ranger (CV-61), 25 JAN 79; To VA-25, NAS Cubi Point, PI., 20 FEB 79; To VA-25, NAS Fallon, NV., 21 SEP 79; To VA-25, NAS LeMoore, CA., 26 JAN 80; To VA-25, NAS Jacksonville, FL., 31 MAR 80; To VA-25, NAS LeMoore, CA., 04 APR 80; To VA-25, USS Ranger (CV-61), 30 MAY 80; To VA-25, NAS LeMoore, CA., 03 JUL 80; To VA-25, USS Ranger (CV-61), 18 JUL 80; To VA-25, NAS LeMoore, CA., 06 AUG 80; To VA-25, USS Ranger (CV-61), 10

SEP 80; To VA-25, NAS LeMoore, CA., 10 SEP 80; To VA-25, NAS Fallon, NV., 14 SEP 81; To VA-25, USS Ranger (CV-61), 21 OCT 81; To VA-25, NAS LeMoore, CA., 16 NOV 81; To VA-25, USS Ranger (CV-61), 26 NOV 81; To VA-25, NAS LeMoore, CA., 26 NOV 81 ** Transferred to VA-195/CVW-11, NH/4XX, NAS LeMoore, CA., 23 DEC 81; To VA-195, NAS Jacksonville, FL., 20 APR 82; To VA-195, NAS LeMoore, CA., 02 JUL 82; To VA-195, USS Ranger (CV-61), 05 JUL 83; To VA-195, NAS LeMoore, CA., 29 JAN 84; To VA-195, NAS Jacksonville, FL., 08 NOV 84; NAS LeMoore, CA., 24 JAN 85 ** Transferred to VA-192/CVW-11, NH/3XX, NAS Cubi Point, PI., 06 SEP 85; To VA-192, NAS LeMoore, CA., 10 NOV 85; To VA-192, NAS Jacksonville, FL., 27 JAN 86 ** Transferred to VA-205/CVWR-20, AF/5XX, NAS Atlanta, GA., 11 JUN 86 ** Transferred to VA-204/CVWR-20, AF/4XX, NAS New Orleans, LA., 04 DEC 86 thru 02 SEP 87 ** End of flight record card ** Transferred to AMARC, Davis Monthan AFB; Tucson, AZ., assigned park code 6A0250; 18 FEB 88 ** 6761.4 flight hours ** TF41A402D engine S/N 142607 ** Aircraft demilitarized, 13 JAN 05 Aircraft deleted from inventory and released to DRMO for disposition, 09 SEP 05.

E-237 157515 Navy acceptance from NPRO Rep. LTV, Dallas, TX., 29 JUN 70 ** Transferred to VA-25/CVW-2, NE/405, NAS LeMoore, CA., 01 JUL 70; To VA-25, USS Ranger (CVA-61), 21 JUN 73 ~ S 1SO strike, 19 MAR 74 ** No data on strike.

E-238 157516 Navy acceptance from NPRO Rep. LTV, Dallas, TX., 30 JUL 70 ** Transferred to VA-25/CVW-2, NE/4XX, NAS LeMoore, CA., 31 JUL 70; To VA-25, USS Ranger (CV-61), 21 JUN 73; To VA-25, NAS LeMoore, CA., 19 FEB 75; To VA-25, NAS Jacksonville, FL., 03 JUL 75; To VA-25, NAS Fallon, NV., 09 JUL 75; To VA-25, NAS LeMoore, CA., 11 AUG 75; To VA-25, USS Ranger (CV-61), 21 AUG 75; To VA-25, NAS LeMoore, CA., 23 SEP 75; To VA-25, USS Ranger (CV-61), 30 DEC 75; To VA-25, NAS LeMoore, CA., 30 OCT 76; To VA-25, NAS Fallon, NV., 31 JUL 77; To VA-25, NAS LeMoore, CA., 12 AUG 77; To VA-25, NAS Jacksonville, FL., 25 JUN 78; To VA-25, NAS LeMoore, CA., 16 AUG 78; To VA-25, USS Ranger (CV-61), 13 NOV 78; To VA-25, NAS LeMoore, CA., 07 DEC 78; To VA-25, USS Ranger (CV-61), 07 NOV 79 ** Transferred to VA-113/CVW-2, NE/3XX, NAS Cubi Point, PI., 06 APR 79 ** Transferred to VA-25/CVW-2, NE/4XX, USS Ranger (CV-61), 04 MAY 79; To VA-25, NAS Cubi Point, PI., 04 MAY 79; To VA-25, NAS Fallon, NV., 21 SEP 79; To VA-25, NAS LeMoore, CA., 26 JAN 80; To VA-25, USS Ranger (CV-61), 28 APR 80; To VA-25, NAS LeMoore, CA., 28 APR 80; To VA-25, USS Ranger (CV-61), 28 APR 80; To VA-25, NAS LeMoore, CA., 21 AUG 80; To VA-25, NAS Jacksonville, FL., 22 AUG 80; To VA-25, USS Ranger (CV-61), 28 AUG 80; To VA-25, NAS Jacksonville, FL., 28 OCT 80 ** Transferred to VA-192/CVW-11, NH/3XX, NAS Fallon, NV.,29 OCT 80; To VA-192, NAS LeMoore, CA., 04 NOV 80; To VA-192, USS America (CV-66), 29 JAN 81; To VA-192, NAS LeMoore, CA., 08 APR 81 ** Transferred to VA-94/CVW-11, NH/4XX, USS Enterprise (CVN-65), 11 AUG 82; To VA-94, NAF Atsugi, JP., 22 MAR 83; To VA-94, NAS Jacksonville, FL., 04 MAY 83; To VA-94, NAS LeMoore, CA., 23 JUN 83 ** Transferred to VA-147/CVW-9, NE/3XX, NAS LeMoore, CA., 24 JUN 83; To VA-147, USS Kitty Hawk (CV-63), 28 DEC 83; To VA-147, NAS LeMoore, CA., 21 SEP 84; To VA-147, NAS Jacksonville, FL., 05 DEC 84; To VA-147, NAS LeMoore, CA., 05 DEC 84 84; To VA-147, NAS Jacksonville, FL., 06 DEC 84; To VA-147, NAS LeMoore, CA., 20 MAY 85; To VA-147, USS Kitty Hawk (CV-63), 20 MAY 85 ** Transferred to VA-122/FRS, NJ/2XX, NAS LeMoore, CA., 16 MAY 86; To VA-122, NAS Pensacola, FL., 05 AUG 86 ** Transferred to VA-304/CVWR-30, ND/411, NAS Alameda, CA. 05 AUG 86; To VA-304, NAS Pensacola, FL., 11 AUG 86; To VA-304, NAS Alameda, CA., 17 APR 87 thru 12 JUN 87 ** End of flight record card ** Transferred to AMARC, Davis Monthan AFB; Tucson, AZ., assigned park code 6A0283, 22 JUL 88 ** 6190.1 flight hours ** TF41A402D engine S/N 141335 ** Project changed per FSO letter, 06 APR 04 ** Engine records released to DRMO for disposition, 05 JUL 05 ** Aircraft deleted from inventory and released to DRMO for disposition, 01 AUG 05.

E-239 157517 Navy acceptance from NPRO Rep. LTV, Dallas, TX., 30 JUL 70 ** Transferred to VA-113/CVW-2, NE/3XX, NAS LeMoore, CA., 31 JUL 70; To VA-113, USS Ranger (CV-61), 21 JUN 73; To VA-113, NAS LeMoore, CA., 07 MAY 74; To VA-113, USS Ranger (CV-61), 07 MAY 74; To VA-113, NAS LeMoore, CA., 03 FEB 75; To VA-113, USS Ranger (CV-61), 01 JUL 75; To VA-113, NAF Atsugi, JP., 18 MAY 76; To VA-113, USS Ranger (CV-61), 28 MAY 76; To VA-113, NAS LeMoore, CA., 29 NOV 76; To VA-113, NAS Jacksonville, FL., 29 SEP 77; To VA-113, NAS LeMoore, CA., 29 SEP 77; To VA-113, NAS Jacksonville, FL., 30 SEP 77; To VA-113, NAS LeMoore, CA., 14 DEC 77; To VA-113, USS Ranger (CV-61), 27 SEP 78; To VA-113, NAS LeMoore, CA., 16 OCT 78; To VA-113, USS Ranger (CV-61), 09 NOV 78; To VA-113, NAS LeMoore, CA., 15 DEC 78; To VA-113, USS Ranger (CV-61), 22 MAR 79; To VA-113, NAS Cubi Point, PI., 02 JUL 79; To VA-113, NAS LeMoore, CA., 02 JUL 79; To VA-113, NAS Fallon, NV., 12 DEC 79; To VA-113, NAS LeMoore, CA., 26 JAN 80; To VA-113, USS Ranger (CV-61), 22 APR 80; To VA-113, NAS LeMoore, CA., 30 JUN 80; To VA-113, USS Ranger (CV-61), 18 JUL 80; To VA-113, NAS Cubi Point, PI., 24 OCT 80; To VA-113, NAS LeMoore, CA., 04 APR 81; To VA-113, NAS Fallon, NV. 28 AUG 81; To VA-113, USS Ranger (CV-61), 28 SEP 81** Transferred to VFA-125/FRS, NJ/544, NAS LeMoore, CA., 09 OCT 81; To VFA-125, NAS Alameda, CA., 08 FEB 82; To VFA-125, NAS LeMoore, CA., 26 FEB 82; To VFA-125, NAS Jacksonville, FL., 19 MAY 82; To VFA-125, NAS LeMoore, CA., 20 MAY 82; To VFA-125, NAS Jacksonville, FL., 13 JUL 82 ** Transferred to VA-97/CVW-14, NK/3XX, NAS LeMoore, CA., 25 AUG 82; To VA-97, USS Coral Sea (CV-43), 28 FEB 83; To VA-97, NAS LeMoore, CA., 07 SEP 83 ** Transferred to VA-174/FRS, AD/4XX, NAS Cecil Field, FL., 09 SEP 83; To VA-174, NAS Jacksonville, FL., 22 JAN 85; To VA-174, NAS Cecil Field, FL., 06 FEB 85; To VA-174, NAS Jacksonville, FL., 20 MAR 85; To VA-174, NAS Cecil Field, FL., 22 MAR 85; To VA-174, NAS Jacksonville, FL., 23 SEP 86; To VA-174, NAS Cecil Field, FL., 23 SEP 86 ** Transferred to VA-304/CVWR-30, ND/4XX, NAS Alameda, CA., 26 SEP 86; To VA-304, NAS Jacksonville, FL., 11 MAR 87; To VA-304, NAS Alameda, CA., 24 MAR 87 thru 09 JUL 87 ** End of flight record card ** Transferred to VA-205/CVWR-20, AF/511, NAS Atlanta, GA., date unknown ** Transferred to AMARC, Davis Monthan AFB; Tucson, AZ., assigned park code 6A0334, 03 APR 90 ** 6250.7 flight hours ** TF41A402D engine S/N 141469 ** Engine records released to DRMO for disposition, 09 SEP 05 ** Aircraft deleted from inventory and released to DRMO for disposition, 09 SEP 05.

E-240 157518 Navy acceptance from NPRO Rep. LTV, Dallas, TX., 07 AUG 70 ** Transferred to VA-195/CVW-11, NH/4XX, USS Kitty Hawk (CVA-63), 10 AUG 70; To VA-195, NAS LeMoore, CA., 05 JUN 72; To VA-195, USS Kitty Hawk (CV-63), 29 JUN 73; To VA-195, NAS LeMoore, CA., 19 AUG 74; To VA-195, USS Kitty Hawk (CV-63), 19 MAY 75; To VA-195, NAS Cubi Point, PI., 21 JUN 75; To VA-195, NAF Atsugi, JP., 13 NOV 75; To VA-195, NAS Cubi Point, PI., 16 NOV 75; To VA-195, NAS LeMoore, CA., 14 DEC 75; To VA-195, NAS Jacksonville, FL., 08 DEC 76 ** Transferred to VA-146/CVW-9, NG/3XX, NAS LeMoore, CA., 28 DEC 76; To VA-146, USS Constellation (CV-64), 28 DEC 76; To VA-146, NAS LeMoore, CA., 16 FEB 77; To VA-146, NAS Cubi Point, PI., 14 MAY 77; To VA-146, USS Constellation (CV-64), 05 SEP 77; To VA-146, NAS LeMoore, CA., 19 NOV 77; To VA-146, NAS Fallon, NV., 10 MAY 78; To VA-146, NAS LeMoore, CA., 20 JUN 78; To VA-146, USS Constellation (CV-64), 16 JUL 78; To VA-146, NAS LeMoore, CA., 29 AUG 78; To VA-146, USS Constellation (CV-64), 21 SEP 78; To VA-146, NAS Cubi Point, PI, 21 DEC 78; To VA-146, NAS Jacksonville, FL., 08 JUN 79; To VA-146, NAS Cubi Point, PI., 03 AUG 79; To VA-146, USS Constellation (CV-64), 03 AUG 79 ** Transferred to VA-147/CVW-9, NG/4XX, USS Constellation (CV-64), 03 OCT 79; To VA-147, NAS LeMoore, CA., 02 DEC 79; To VA-147, USS Constellation (CV-64), 13 DEC 79; To VA-147, NAS LeMoore, CA., 23 JAN 80; To VA-147, USS Constellation (CV-64), 26 FEB 80; To VA-147, NAS Cubi Point, PI., 18 APR 80; To VA-147, USS Constellation (CV-64), 18 SEP 80; To VA-147, NAS LeMoore, CA., 18 SEP 80; To VA-147, NAF El Centro, CA., 18 SEP 80; To VA-147, NAS Jacksonville, FL., 19 MAY 81; To VA-147, USS Constellation (CV-64), 22 MAY 81; To VA-147, NAS LeMoore, CA., 12 JUN 81; To VA-147, USS Constellation

(CV-64), 07 JUL 81; To VA-147, NAS LeMoore, CA., 06 AUG 81; To VA-147, USS Constellation (CV-64), 19 OCT 81; To VA-147, NAS Cubi Point, PI., 19 OCT 81; To VA-147, NAF Atsugi, JP., 13 FEB 82; To VA-147, USS Constellation (CV-64), 15 FEB 82; To VA-147, NAF Atsugi, JP., 28 APR 82; To VA-147, NAS LeMoore, CA., 28 APR 82; To VA-147, NAF Atsugi, JP., 17 JUN 82 ** Transaferred to VA-93/CVW-5, NF/3XX, USS Midway (CV-41), 12 JUL 82 ** Transferred to VA-25/CVW-2, NE/4XX, NAS Cubi Point, PI., 05 AUG 82; To VA-25, USS Ranger (CV-61), 16 AUG 82 ** Transferred to VA-97/CVW-14, NK/3XX, NAS LeMoore, CA., 25 OCT 82; To VA-97, USS Coral Sea (CV-43), 11 MAR 83; To VA-97, NAS LeMoore, CA., 08 SEP 83 ** Transferred to VA-82/CVW-8, AJ/3XX, NAS Cecil Field, FL., 09 SEP 83; To VA-82, NAS Jacksonville, FL., 21 FEB 84; To VA-82, NAS Cecil Field, FL., 04 MAR 84; To VA-82, NAS Jacksonville, FL., 14 MAR 84; To VA-82, NAS Cecil Field, FL., 03 APR 84; To VA-82, NAS Jacksonville, FL., 27 APR 84 ** Transferred to VA-37/CVW-6, AE/3XX, NAS Cecil Field, FL., 30 APR 84 ** To VA-37, MCAS Twenty Nine Palms, CA., 24 MAY 84; To VA-37, NAS Cecil Field, FL., 31 AUG 84; To VA-37, MCAS Iwakuni, JP., 26 OCT 84; To VA-37, Korea, 26 OCT 84; To VA-37, MCAS Iwakuni, JP., 26 OCT 84; To VA-37, NAS Cecil Field, FL., 26 OCT 84 ** Transferred to VA-12/CVW-7, AG/4XX, 18 OCT 85 ** Transferred to AMARC, Davis Monthan AFB; Tucson, AZ., assigned park code 6A0183, 16 JUL 86 ** End of flight record card ** 6493.6 flight hours ** TF41A2D engine S/N 142505 ** Aircraft deleted from inventory and released to DRMO for disposition, 18 JAN 96 ** Sold as surplus to Fritz Enterprises; Taylor, MI., delivered to HVF West's yard; Tucson, AZ., 08 AUG 96.

E-241 157519 Navy acceptance from NPRO Rep. LTV, Dallas, TX., 25 AUG 70 ** Transferred to VA-192/CVW-11, NH/3XX, USS Kitty Hawk (CVA-63), 26 AUG 70; To VA-192, NAS LeMoore, CA., 31 MAY 72; To VA-192, USS Kitty Hawk (CV-63), 29 JUN 73; To VA-192, NAS LeMoore, CA., 04 MAY 74; To VA-192, NAS Jacksonville, FL., 03 SEP 74; To VA-192, NAS LeMoore, CA., 04 SEP 74; To VA-192, NAS Jacksonville, FL., 08 NOV 74; To VA-192, NAS LeMoore, CA., 09 NOV 74; To VA-192, USS Kitty Hawk (CV-63), 09 JAN 75; To VA-192, NAS LeMoore, CA., 28 MAR 75; To VA-192, USS Kitty Hawk (CV-63), 11 APR 75; To VA-192, NAS Cubi Point, PI., 16 SEP 75; To VA-192, USS Kitty Hawk (CV-63), 19 NOV 75; To VA-192, NAS LeMoore, CA., 19 JAN 76; To VA-192, MCAS Yuma, AZ., 20 NOV 76; To VA-192, NAS LeMoore, CA., 01 DEC 76; To VA-192, USS Kitty Hawk (CV-63), 25 JUL 77; To VA-192, NAS LeMoore, CA., 11 AUG 77; To VA-192, USS Kitty Hawk (CV-63), 22 SEP 77; To VA-192, NAS LeMoore, CA., 30 SEP 77; To VA-192, USS Kitty Hawk (CV-63), 13 OCT 77; To VA-192, NAS LeMoore, CA., 14 MAY 78; To VA-192, NAS Jacksonville, FL., 11 AUG 78; To VA-192, NAS LeMoore, CA., 11 AUG 78; To VA-192, NAS Jacksonville, FL., 16 AUG 78; To VA-192, NAS LeMoore, CA., 19 DEC 78; To VA-192, USS America (CV-66), 05 JAN 79; To VA-192, NAS LeMoore, CA., 19 DEC 78; To VA-192, NAS Fallon, NV., 20 OCT 80; To VA-192, NAS LeMoore, CA., 07 NOV 80 ** Transferred to VA-27/CVW-14, NK/4XX, NAS LeMoore, CA., 14 NOV 80; To VA-27, NAS Jacksonville, FL., 29 JAN 81; To VA-27, NAS LeMoore, CA., 21 MAR 81; To VA-27, USS Coral Sea (CV-43), 16 APR 81; To VA-27, NAS LeMoore, CA., 11 JUN 81; To VA-27, USS Coral Sea (CV-43), 20 JUL 81 ** Transferred to VA-122/FRS, NJ/2XX, NAS LeMoore, CA., 14 AUG 81; To VA-122, NAS Jacksonville, FL., 12 JUN 83 ** Transferred to VA-203/CVWR-20, AF/3XX, NAS Jacksonville, FL., 15 JUN 83; To VA-203, NAS Pensacola, FL., 22 SEP 86; To VA-203, NAS Jacksonville, FL., 22 NOV 86 thru 01 DEC 86 ** End of flight record card ** Transferred to AMARC, Davis Monthan AFB; Tucson, AZ., assigned park code 6A0249, 17 FEB 88 ** 6702.9 flight hours ** TF41A402D engine S/N 142556 ** Aircraft deleted from inventory and released to DRMO for disposition, 18 OCT 05.

E-242 157520 Navy acceptance from NPRO Rep. LTV, Dallas, TX., 31 AUG 70 ** Transferred to VA-192/CVW-11, NH/307, USS Kitty Hawk (CVA-63), 01 SEP 70 ~ S 1SO strike, 23 MAR 72 ** LT D.S. Pike KIA when shot down Near Phuoc My, SVN next to border with Laos. Pilot ejected but was killed when parachute did not deploy.

E-243 157521 Navy acceptance from NPRO Rep. LTV Dallas, TX., 10 AUG 70 ** Transferred to VA-192/CVW-11, NH/3XX, USS Kitty Hawk (CVA-63), 11 AUG 70 ~ S 1SO strike, 18 SEP 70 ** No data on strike.

E-244 157522 Navy acceptance from NPRO Rep. LTV, Dallas, TX., 04 AUG 70 ** Transferred to VA-195/CVW-11, NH/4XX, USS Kitty Hawk (CVA-63), 05 AUG 70; To VA-195, NAS LeMoore, CA., 10 JUN 72; To VA-195, USS Kitty Hawk (CV-63), 11 JUN 73; To VA-195, NAS Jacksonville, FL., 26 JUL 74; To VA-195, NAS LeMoore, CA., 30 JUL 74; To VA-195, NAS Jacksonville, FL., 30 SEP 74; To VA-195, NAS LeMoore, CA., 16 OCT 74; To VA-195, USS Kitty Hawk (CV-63), 05 NOV 74; To VA-195, NAS LeMoore, CA., 21 FEB 75; To VA-195, USS Kitty Hawk (CV-63), 19 MAY 75; To VA-195, NAS Cubi Point, PI., 20 MAY 75; To VA-195, NAS LeMoore, CA., 14 DEC 75 ** Transferred to VA-122/FRS, NJ/2XX, NAS LeMoore, CA., 24 MAY 77; To VA-122, NAS Jacksonville, FL., 22 APR 78; To VA-122, NAS LeMoore, CA., 22 APR 78; To VA-122, NAS Jacksonville, FL., 24 APR 78; To VA-122, NAS LeMoore, CA., 10 AUG 78 ** Transferred to VA-147/CVW-9, NG/4XX, NAS LeMoore, CA., 10 AUG 78; To VA-147, USS Constellation (CV-64), 25 SEP 78; To VA-147, NAS NAS Cubi Point, PI., 06 NOV 78; To VA-147, USS Constellation (CV-64), 31 DEC 78; To VA-147, NAS LeMoore, CA., 16 MAY 79; To VA-147, USS Constellation (CV-64), 06 DEC 79; To VA-147, NAS LeMoore, CA., 23 JAN 80; To VA-147, USS Constellation (CV-64), 26 FEB 80; To VA-147, NAS NAS Cubi Point, PI., 18 APR 80; To VA-147, USS Constellation (CV-64), 11 SEP 80; To VA-147, NAS LeMoore, CA., 11 SEP 80; To VA-147, NAF El Centro, CA., 19 FEB 81; To VA-147, NAS Alameda, CA., 29 MAY 81; To VA-147, NAS LeMoore, CA., 26 JUN 81; To VA-147, USS Constellation (CV-64), 07 JUL 81; To VA-147, NAS LeMoore, CA., 06 AUG 81; To VA-147, USS Constellation (CV-64), 19 OCT 81; To VA-147, NAS Cubi Point, PI., 19 OCT 81; To VA-147, USS Constellation (CV-64), 19 OCT 81; To VA-147, NAS LeMoore, CA., 19 OCT 81 ** Transferred to VA-203/CVWR-20, AF/3XX, NAS Jacksonville, FL., 01 JUL 83 thru 01 DEC 86 ** End of flight record card ** Transferred to AMARC, Davis Monthan AFB; Tucson, AZ., assigned park code A0253, 14 MAR 88 ** 7776.2 flight hours ** TF41A2C engine S/N 141894 ** Project changed per FSO letter, 06 APR 04 Aircraft deleted from inventory and released to DRMO for disposition, 18 OCT 05.

E-245 157523 Navy acceptance from NPRO Rep. LTV, Dallas, TX., 11 AUG 70 ** Transferred to VA-195/CVW-11, NH/4XX, USS Kitty Hawk (CVA-63), 13 AUG 70; To VA-195, NAS LeMoore, CA., 22 JUN 72 ** Transferred to VA-27/ CVW-14, NK/412, NAS LeMoore, CA., 19 NOV 72; To VA-27, NAS Fallon, NV., 24 OCT 75; To VA-27, NAS LeMoore, CA., 12 JAN 76; To VA-27, USS Enterprise (CVN-65), 12 MAR 76; To VA-27, NAS LeMoore, CA., 23 APR 76; To VA-27, USS Enterprise (CVN-65), 05 MAY 76; To VA-27, NAS LeMoore, CA., 05 MAY 76; To VA-27, USS Enterprise (CVN-65), 05 MAY 76 ** Transferred to VA-192/CVW-11, NH/3XX, NAS LeMoore, CA., 11 JUL 76; To VA-192, MCAS Yuma, AZ., 24 OCT 76; To VA-192, NAS LeMoore, CA., 24 OCT 76 ** Transferred to VA-122/FRS, NJ/2XX, NAS LeMoore, CA., 20 JUN 77; To VA-122, NAS Jacksonville, FL., 16 NOV 77; To VA-122, NAS LeMoore, CA., 02 MAR 78 ** Transferred To VA-94/CVW-15, NL/4XX, NAS LeMoore, CA., 09 APR 79; To VA-94, NAS Cubi Point, PI., 29 MAY 79; To VA-94, USS Kitty Hawk (CV-63), 06 JUN 79; To VA-94, NAS LeMoore, CA., 21 SEP 79; To VA-94, NAS Jacksonville, FL., 22 APR 80 ** Transferred to VA-195/CVW-11, NH/4XX, NAS LeMoore, CA., 10 JUN 80; To VA-195, NAS Fallon, NV., 19 OCT 80; To VA-195, NAS LeMoore, CA., 07 NOV 80; To VA-195, USS America (CV-66), 25 JAN 81; To VA-195, NAS LeMoore, CA., 09 APR 81; To VA-195 NAS Jacksonville, FL., 02 MAY 82; To VA-195, NAS LeMoore, CA., 24 AUG 82; To VA-195/CVW-9, NG/4XX, USS Ranger (CV-61), 17 JAN 83; To VA-195, NAS LeMoore, CA., 28 JAN 84; To VA-195 NAS Jacksonville, FL., 09 OCT 84; To VA-195, NAS LeMoore, CA., 11 DEC 84 ** Transferred to VA-122/FRS, NJ/241, NAS LeMoore, CA., 01 MAY 85 ** Transferred to AMARC, Davis Monthan AFB; Tucson, AZ., assigned park code 6A0202, 15 SEP 86 ** 6277.5 flight hours ** TF41A2C engine S/N 141361 ** Aircraft deleted and released to DRMO for disposition, 18 OCT 05.

E-246 157524 Navy acceptance from NPRO Rep. LTV, Dallas, TX., 17 AUG 70 ** Transferred to VA-192/CVW-11, NH/303, USS Kitty Hawk (CVA-63), 19 AUG 70; To VA-192, NAS LeMoore, CA., 12 MAY 72; To VA-192, USS Kitty Hawk (CV-63), 09 JUN 73; To VA-192, NAS LeMoore, CA., 26 JUL 74; To VA-192, NAS Fallon, NV., 26 OCT 74; To VA-192, NAS LeMoore, CA., 26 OCT 74; To VA-192, USS Kitty Hawk (CV-63), 26 OCT 74; To VA-192, NAS LeMoore, CA., 01 MAR 75; To VA-192, USS Kitty Hawk (CV-63), 02 APR 75; To VA-192, NAS Cubi Point, PI., 27 SEP 75; To VA-192, NAF Atsugi, JP., 10 NOV 75; To VA-192, USS Kitty Hawk (CV-63), 19 NOV 75; To VA-192, NAS LeMoore, CA., 01 MAR 76; To VA-192, NAS Jacksonville, FL., 22 NOV 76; To VA-192, NAS LeMoore, CA., 23 NOV 76; To VA-192, NAS Jacksonville, FL., 24 JAN 77; To VA-192, NAS LeMoore, CA., 04 FEB 77; To VA-192, USS Kitty Hawk (CV-63), 25 JUL 77; To VA-192, NAS LeMoore, CA., 11 AUG 77; To VA-192, USS Kitty Hawk (CV-63), 25 OCT 77; To VA-192, NAS LeMoore, CA., 14 MAY 78 ** Transferred to VA-97/CVW-14, NK/3XX, NAS LeMoore, Ca., 20 DEC 78; To VA-97, NAS Jacksonville, FL., 24 MAR 79; To VA-97, NAS LeMoore, CA., 01 MAY 79 ** Transferred to VA-94/CVW-15, NL/4XX, USS Kitty Hawk (CV-63), 06 JUN 79; To VA-94, NAS LeMoore, CA., 23 NOV 79; To VA-94, USS Kitty Hawk (CV-63), 27 JUN 80; To VA-94, NAS LeMoore, CA., 27 JUN 80; To VA-94, USS Kitty Hawk (CV-63), 11 SEP 80; To VA-94, NAS LeMoore, CA., 06 NOV 80 ** Transferred to VA-146/CVW-9, NG/3XX, USS Constellation (CV-64), 14 JUL 81; To VA-146, NAS Jacksonville, FL., 15 JUL 81; To VA-146, NAS LeMoore, CA., 17 JUL 81; To VA-146, NAS Jacksonville, FL., 11 SEP 81; To VA-146, USS Constellation (CV-64), 08 OCT 81 ** Transferred to VA-147/CVW-9, NG/4XX, NAS LeMoore, CA., 09 OCT 81; To VA-147, USS Constellation (CV-64), 19 OCT 81; To VA-147, NAS Cubi Point, PI., 19 OCT 81; To VA-147, USS Constellation (CV-64), 19 OCT 81; To VA-147, NAS LeMoore, CA., 19 OCT 81 ** Transferred to VA-27/CVW-14, NK/4XX, NAS LeMoore, CA., 09 SEP 82; To VA-27, USS Coral Sea (CV-43), 14 MAR 83 ** Transferred to VA-122/FRS, NJ/2XX, NAS LeMoore, CA., 15 MAR 83; To VA-122, NAS Jacksonville, FL., 29 SEP 84; To VA-122, NAS LeMoore, CA., 10 NOV 84 ~ S 1SO strike, 06 MAY 86 ** No data on strike.

E-247 157525 Navy acceptance from NPRO Rep. LTV, Dallas, TX., 29 SEP 70 ** Transferred to VA-82/CVW-8, AJ/3XX, NAS Cecil Field, 30 SEP 70, To VA-82, USS America (CVA-66), 16 MAY 71 ** Transferred to VA-174/FRS, AD/4XX, NAS Cecil Field, FL., 31 MAR 72 ** Transferred to VA-81/CVW-17, AA/4XX, USS Forrestal (CVA-59), 17 SEP 72; To VA-81, NAS Cecil Field, FL., 15 OCT 74; To VA-81, USS Forrestal CVA-59), 23 OCT 74; To VA-81, NAS Cecil Field, FL., 24 JUL 75; To VA-81, USS Forrestal (CVA-59), 23 DEC 75; To VA-81, NAS Cecil Field, FL., 23 DEC 75; To VA-81, NAS Jacksonville, FL., 02 JUL 76; To VA-81, NAS Cecil Field, FL., 31 AUG 76; To VA-81, NAS Roosevelt Roads, PR., 31 AUG 76; To VA-81, NAS Cecil Field, FL., 31 AUG 76; To VA-81, NAS Roosevelt Roads, PR., 31 AUG 76; To VA-81, NAS Cecil Field, FL., 31 AUG 76; To VA-81, USS Forrestal (CV-59), 20 JUL 77; To VA-81, NAS Cecil Field, FL., 20 JUL 77; To VA-81, USS Forrestal CV-59), 20 JUL 77; To VA-81, NAS Cecil Field, FL., 10 MAR 78 ** Transferred to VA-83/CVW-17, AA/3XX, NAS Cecil Field, FL., 16 JAN 79; To VA-83, USS Forrestal (CV-59), 23 MAR 79; To VA-83, NAS Cecil Field, FL., 11 SEP 79; To VA-83, USS Forrestal (CV-59), 11 SEP 79; To VA-83, NAS Cecil Field, FL., 20 MAR 80; To VA-83, USS Forrestal (CV-59), 29 OCT 80; To VA-83, NAS Jacksonville, FL., 30 OCT 80; To VA-83, NAS Cecil Field, FL., 30 OCT 80 ** Transferred to VA-82/CVW-8, AJ/3XX, NAS Cecil Field, FL., 24 DEC 80; USS Nimitz (CVN-68), 24 DEC 80; To VA-82, NAS Cecil field, FL., 10 FEB 82; To VA-82, USS Carl Vinson (CVN-70), 01 APR 82; To VA-82, NAS Cecil Field, FL., 01 APR 82; To VA-82, USS Nimitz (CVN-68), 01 APR 82; To VA-82, NAS Cecil Field, FL., 03 SEP 82; To VA-82, USS Nimitz (CVN-68), 03 SEP 82; To VA-82, NAS Cecil Field, FL., 16 MAY 83; To VA-82, NAS Jacksonville, FL., 28 JUN 83; To VA-82, NAS Cecil Field, FL., 10 JUL 83; To VA-82, NAS Jacksonville, FL., 09 AUG 83; To VA-82, NAS Cecil Field, FL., 08 SEP 83; To VA-82, NAS Jacksonville, FL., 16 DEC 83; To VA-82, NAS Cecil Field, FL., 27 DEC 83 ** Transferred to VA-86/CVW-8, AJ/4XX, NAS Cecil Field, FL., 14 JUN 84; To VA-86, NAS Roosevelt Roads, PR., 01 AUG 84; To VA-86, NAS Cecil Field, FL., 01 AUG 84; To VA-86, USS Nimitz (CVN-68), 15 NOV 84; To VA-86, NAS Cecil Field, FL., 15 NOV 84; To VA-86,

USS Nimitz (CVN-68), 15 NOV 84; To VA-86, NAS Cecil Field, FL., 23 OCT 85; To VA-86, USS Nimitz (CVN-68), 28 APR 86; To VA-86, NAS Cecil Field, FL., 02 JUN 86; To VA-86, USS Nimitz (CVN-68), 02 JUN 86; To VA-86, NAS Jacksonville, FL., 26 SEP 86 ** Transferred to NARF. NAS Jacksonville, FL., 26 SEP 86 ** Transferred to VA-81/CVW-17, AA/4XX, NAS Cecil Field, FL., 07 OCT 86; To VA-81, USS Saratoga (CV-60), 01 DEC 86; To VA-81, NAS Cecil Field, FL., 01 DEC 86; To VA-81, USS Saratoga (CV-60), 15 APR 87; To VA-81, NAS Cecil Field, FL., 24 APR 87; To VA-81, USS Saratoga (CV-60), 24 APR 87 ** End of flight record card ** Transferred to VA-203/CVWR-30, AF/3XX, date unknown ** Transferred to AMARC, Davis Monthan AFB; Tucson, AZ., assigned park code 6A0301, 15 SEP 89 ** 7490.8 flight hours ** TF41A402D engine S/N 142604 ** Engine released to DRMO, Davis Monthan AFB; Tucson, AZ., for disposition, 17 NOV 05 ** Project changed per FSO letter, 06 APR 04 ** Aircraft at AMARC; Davis Monthan AFB; Tucson, AZ., 16 JAN 06.

E-248 157526 Navy acceptance from NPRO Rep. LTV, Dallas, TX., 31 JUL 70 ** Transferred to VA-195/CVW-11, NH/406, USS Kitty Hawk (CVA-63), 03 AUG 70; To VA-195, NAS LeMoore, CA., 26 JUN 72; To VA-195, USS Kitty Hawk (CV-63), 29 JUN 73; To VA-195, NAS LeMoore, CA., 01 AUG 74; To VA-195, NAS Jacksonville, FL., 12 SEP 74; To VA-195, NAS LeMoore, CA., 29 NOV 74; To VA-195, USS Kitty Hawk (CV-63), 29 NOV 74; To VA-195, NAS LeMoore, CA., 09 APR 75; To VA-195, USS Kitty Hawk (CV-63), 19 MAY 75; To VA-195, NAS Cubi Point, PI., 21 JUN 75; To VA-195, NAS LeMoore, CA., 14 DEC 75; To VA-195, USS Kitty Hawk (CV-63), 25 MAY 77; To VA-195, NAS LeMoore, CA., 09 AUG 77; To VA-195, USS Kitty Hawk (CV-63), 29 SEP 77; To VA-195, NAF Atsugi, JP., 28 FEB 78; To VA-195, USS Kitty Hawk (CV- 63) , 05 MAR 78; To VA-195, NAS LeMoore, CA., 09 MAR 78; To VA-195, NAS Jacksonville, FL., 14 SEP 78; To VA-195, NAS LeMoore, CA., 06 DEC 78; To VA-195, NAS Jacksonville, FL., 09 DEC 78; To VA-195, NAS LeMoore, CA., 10 DEC 78 ~ S 1SO strike, 11 APR 79 ** No data on strike.

E-249 157527 Navy acceptance from NPRO Rep. LTV, Dallas, TX., 18 SEP 70 ** Transferred to VA-82/CVW-8, AJ/3XX, NAS Cecil Field, FL., 19 SEP 70; To VA-82, USS America (CVA-66), 23 JUN 71 ** Transferred to VA-174/FRS, AD/4XX, NAS Cecil Field, FL., 31 MAR 72 ** Transferred to VA-37/CVW-3, AC/3XX, NAS Cecil Field, FL., 24 SEP 75; To VA-37, USS Saratoga (CV-60), 22 APR 74; To VA-37, NAS Cecil Field, FL., 22 APR 74; To VA-37, USS Saratoga (CV-60), 22 APR 74; To VA-37, NAS Jacksonville, FL., 06 AUG 75; To VA-37, NAS Cecil Field, FL., 06 AUG 75; To VA-37, USS Saratoga (CV-60), 21 OCT 75; To VA-37, NAS Cecil Field, FL., 21 OCT 75; To VA-37, USS Saratoga (CV-60), 22 OCT 76; To VA-37, NAS Cecil Field, FL., 22 OCT 76; To VA-37, USS Saratoga (CV-60), 22 OCT 76; To VA-37, NAS Cecil Field, FL., 16 JUL 77; To VA-37, NAS Jacksonville, FL., 03 FEB 78; To VA-37, NAS Cecil Field, FL., 03 APR 78; To VA-37, USS Saratoga (CV-60), 23 OCT 78 ~ S 1SO strike, 23 OCT 78 ** No data on strike.

E-250 157528 Navy acceptance from NPRO Rep. LTV, Dallas, TX., 18 AUG 70 ** Transferred to VA-192/CVW-11, NH/3XX, USS Kitty Hawk (CVA-63), 12 AUG 70; To VA-192, NAS LeMoore, CA., 22 JUN 72; To VA-192, USS Kitty Hawk (CV-63), 31 MAY 73 ** Transferred to VA-122/FRS, NJ/2XX, NAS LeMoore, CA., 19 NOV 73; To VA-122, CRAA, NAS LeMoore, CA., 05 DEC 73; To VA-122, NAS LeMoore, CA., 05 DEC 74; To VA-122, NAS Jacksonville, FL., 08 SEP 78; To VA-122, NAS LeMoore, CA., 22 JAN 79 ** Transferred to VA-192/CVW-11, NH/3XX, NAS LeMoore, CA. 21 SEP 79; To VA-192, NAS Fallon, NV., 20 OCT 80; To VA-192, NAs LeMoore, CA., 07 NOV 80 ** Transferred to VA-97/CVW-14, NK/3XX, USS Coral Sea (CV-43), 12 NOV 80; To VA-97, NAS LeMoore, CA., 17 JAN 81; To VA-97, NAS Jacksonville, FL., 28 JAN 81; To VA-97, NAS LeMoore, CA., 08 MAR 81; To VA-97, USS Coral Sea (CV-43), 04 APR 81; To VA-97, NAS LeMoore, CA., 11 JUN 81; To VA-97, USS Coral Sea (CV-43), 20 AUG 81; To VA-97, NAS LeMoore, CA., 20 AUG 81 ** Transferred to VA-147/CVW-9, NE/3XX, USS Constellation (CV-64), 03 MAR 82; To VA-147, NAS LeMoore, CA., 19 MAR 82; To VA-147, NAS Jacksonville, FL., 23 MAR 83; To VA-147, NAS LeMoore, CA., 23 MAR 83; To VA-147, NAS Jacksonville, FL., 25 MAR 83; NAS LeMoore, CA., 03 JUN

83; To VA-147, USS Kitty Hawk (CV-63), 09 SEP 83; To VA-147, NAS LeMoore, CA., 07 SEP 84; To VA-147, USS Kitty Hawk (CV-63), 27 APR 85; To VA-147, NAS LeMoore, CA., 14 JAN 86; To VA-147, NAS Jacksonville, FL., 15 JAN 86 ** Transferred to VA-122/FRS, NJ/2XX, NAS LeMoore, CA., 15 MAR 86 ** Transferred to AMARC, Davis Monthan AFB; Tucson, AZ., assigned park code 6A0240, 21 SEP 87 ** End of flight record card ** 5874.5 flight hours ** TF41A2B engine S/N 141965 ** Aircraft deleted from inventory and released to DRMO for disposition, 17 OCT 05.

E-251 157529 Navy acceptance from NPRO Rep. LTV, Dallas, TX., 01 AUG 70 ** Transferred to VA-192/CVW-11, NH/3XX, USS Kitty Hawk (CVA-63), 03 AUG 70 ~ S 1SO strike, 19 MAR 72 ** Pilot Ejected and rescued due to engine vibration and failure on a climb out of the Gulf of Tonkin and gliding back to the carrier.

E-252 157530 Navy acceptance from NPRO Rep. LTV, Dallas, TX., 19 AUG 70 ** Transferred to VA-192/CVW-11, NH/300, USS Kitty Hawk (CVA-63), 20 AUG 70; To VA-192, NAS LeMoore, CA., 28 JUN 72 ~ S 1SO strike, 02 NOV 72 ** Pilot ejected and was rescued after being hit by AAA near Tap Phuc.

E-253 157531 Navy acceptance from NPRO Rep. LTV, Dallas, TX., 21 AUG 70 ** Transferred to VA-192/CVW-11, NH/3XX, USS Kitty Hawk (CVA-63), 22 AUG 70 ~ S 1SO strike, 17 JUN 72 ** CDR Darrel D. Owens was rescued after being hit by two SAM's over NVN. Pilot flew back to the carrier but ejected on approach when the aircraft started to roll.

E-254 157532 Navy acceptance from NPRO Rep. LTV, Dallas, TX., 13 JUL 70 ** Transferred to NPRO Rep. LTV, Dallas, TX., for RDT & E, 14 JUL 70 ** Transferred to VA-94/CVW-15, NL/4XX, NAS LeMoore, CA., 18 MAY 71; To VA-94, USS Coral Sea (CVA-43), 22 JUN 71; To VA-94, NAS LeMoore, CA., 25 JUN 73; To VA-94, USS Coral Sea (CVA-43), 24 MAR 75; NAS LeMoore, CA., 08 JUL 75; To VA-94, NAS Fallon, NV., 31 MAR 76; To VA-94, NAS LeMoore, CA., 31 MAR 76; To VA-94, USS Coral Sea (CV-43), 30 NOV 76; To VA-94, NAS LeMoore, CA., 30 NOV 76; To VA-94, USS Coral Sea (CV-43), 31 JAN 77; NAS LeMoore, CA., 11 FEB 77 ** Transferred to VA-122/FRS, NJ/2XX, NAS LeMoore, CA., 11 FEB 77; To VA-122, NAS Jacksonville, FL. 21 APR 78; To VA-122, NAS LeMoore, CA., 21 APR 78; To VA-122, NAS Jacksonville, FL., 27 APR 78; To VA-122, NAS LeMoore, CA., 03 AUG 78 ** Transferred to VA-147/CVW-9, NG/4XX, USS Constellation (CV-64), 25 SEP 78; To VA-147, NAS Cubi Point, PI., 06 NOV 78; To VA-147, USS Constellation (CV-64), 31 DEC 78; To VA-147, NAS LeMoore, CA., 02 DEC 79; To VA-147, USS Constellation (CV-64), 13 DEC 79; To VA-147, NAS LeMoore, CA., 23 JAN 80; To VA-147, USS Constellation (CV-64), 26 FEB 80; To VA-147, NAS Cubi Point, PI., 18 APR 80 ~ S 1SO strike, 02 JUN 80 ** No data on strike.

E-255 157533 Navy acceptance from NPRO Rep. LTV, Dallas, TX., 07 AUG 70 ** Transferred to VA-195/CVW-11, NH/4XX, USS Kitty Hawk (CVA-63), 10 AUG 70; To VA-195, NAS LeMoore, CA., 07 JUN 72; To VA-195, USS Kitty Hawk (CV-63), 29 JUN 73; To VA-195, NAS LeMoore, CA., 16 JUN 74; To VA-195, USS Kitty Hawk (CV-63), 19 MAY 75; To VA-195, NAS Cubi Point, PI., 21 JUN 75; To VA-195, NAS LeMoore, CA.,14 DEC 75; To VA-195, USS Kitty Hawk (CV-63), 08 JUN 77 ** Transferred to VA-122/FRS, NJ/2XX, NAS LeMoore, CA., 15 JUL 77; To VA-122, NAS Jacksonville, FL., 10 MAY 78; To VA-122, NAS LeMoore, CA., 19 MAY 78 ~ S 1SO strike, 30 JUN 78 ** No data on strike.

E-256 157534 Navy acceptance from NPRO Rep. LTV, Dallas, TX., 20 AUG 70 ** Transferred to VA-195/CVW- 11, NH/4XX, USS Kitty Hawk (CVA-63), 26 AUG 70 ~ S 1SO strike, 26 JAN 72 ** No data on strike.

E-257 157535 Navy acceptance from NPRO Rep. LTV, Dallas, TX., 23 OCT 70 ** Transferred to VA-86/CVW-8, AJ/4XX, NAS Cecil Field, FL., 27 OCT 70; To VA-86, USS America (CVA-66), 14 JUN 71 ** Transferred to VA-66/CVW-7, AG/3XX, NAS Cecil Field, FL.,

01 APR 72; To VA-66, USS Independence (CVA-62), 30 JUN 72 ** Transferred to VA-174/FRS, AD/4XX, NAS Cecil Field, FL., 26 SEP 72 ** Transferred to VA-105/CVW-3, AC/4XX, NAS Cecil Field, FL., 04 JUN 73; To VA-105, USS Saratoga (CV-60), 30 JUN 72 ~ S 1SO strike, 14 JUL 75 ** No data on strike.

E-258 157536 Navy acceptance from NPRO Rep. LTV, Dallas, TX., 21 AUG 70 ** Transferred to VA-195/CVW-11, NH/4XX, USS Kitty Hawk (CVA-63), 22 AUG 70; To VA-195, NAS LeMoore, CA. 02 JUN 72 ** Transferred to NARF, NAS Alameda, CA., 06 JUL 72 ** Transferred to NARF, NAS Jacksonville, FL.,17 JAN 73 ** Transferred to VA-122/FRS, NJ/2XX, NAS LeMoore, CA., 06 NOV 73 ** Transferred to NWEF, Kirtland AFB; Albuquerque, NM., 31 OCT 74 ** Transferred to VA-122/FRS, NJ/2XX, NAS LeMoore, CA., 24 JUN 75; To VA-122, NAS Jacksonville, FL., 28 MAR 77; To VA-122, NAS LeMoore, CA., 19 MAY 77 ** Transferred to VA-27/ CVW-14, NK/400, NAS LeMoore, CA., 24 MAY 77; To VA-27, USS Enterprise (CVN-65), 12 JAN 78; To VA-27, NAS LeMoore, CA., 03 MAR 78; To VA-27, NAS Cubi Point, PI., 02 MAY 78; To VA-27, NAS LeMoore, CA., 10 OCT 78; To VA-27, NPTR El Centro, CA., 02 APR 79; To VA-27, NAS Jacksonville, FL., 09 JUN 79; To VA-27, NAF El Centro, CA., 28 JUL 79; To VA-27, NAS LeMoore, CA., 23 OCT 79; To VA-27, USS Coral Sea (CV-43), 24 OCT 79; To VA-27, NAS Cubi Point, PI., 12 NOV 79; To VA-27, USS Coral Sea (CV-43), 23 DEC 79; To VA-27, NAS LeMoore, CA., 26 MAR 80; To VA-27, USS Coral Sea (CV-43), 16 APR 81; To VA-27, NAS LeMoore, CA., 11 JUN 81; To VA-27, USS Coral Sea (CV-43), 30 JUL 81; To VA-27, NAS Jacksonville, FL., 03 AUG 81** Transferred to VA-25/CVW-2, NE/4XX, USS Ranger (CV-61), 11 OCT 81; To VA-25, NAS LeMoore, CA., 20 OCT 81; To VA-25, USS Ranger (CV-61), 14 JAN 82; To VA-25, NAS LeMoore, CA., 14 JAN 82; To VA-25, USS Ranger (CV-61), 14 JAN 82; To VA-25, NAS Cubi Point, PI., 14 JAN 82 ** Transferred to VA-56/CVW-5, NF/4XX, NAF Atsugi, JP., 25 AUG 82 ** Transferred to VA-22/CVW-11, NH/3XX, USS Enterprise (CVN-65), 17 NOV 84; To VA-22, NAS LeMoore, CA., 17 NOV 84 ** Transferred to VA-122/FRS, NJ/243, NAS LeMoore, CA., 21 FEB 85 ** Transferred to AMARC, Davis Monthan AFB; Tucson, AZ., assigned park code 6A0189, 15 AUG 86 ** End of flight record card ** Project changed per FSO letter, 06 APR 04 ** Aircraft deleted from inventory and released to DRMO for disposition, 01 AUG 05.

E-259 157537 Navy acceptance from NPRO Rep. LTV, Dallas, TX., 01 SEP 70 ** Transferred to VA-192/CVW-11, NH/310, USS Kitty Hawk (CVA-63), 03 SEP 70 ** To VA-192, NAS LeMoore, CA., 08 MAY 72; To VA-192, USS Kitty Hawk (CV-63), 29 JUN 73; To VA-192, NAS LeMoore, CA., 01 JUL 74; To VA-192, NAS Jacksonville, FL., 04 SEP 74; To VA-192, NAS LeMoore, CA., 13 NOV 74; To VA-192, USS Kitty Hawk (CV-63), 14 JAN 75; To VA-192, NAS LeMoore, CA., 28 MAR 75; To VA-192, USS Kitty Hawk (CV-63), 11 APR 75; To VA-192, NAF Atsugi, JP., 12 AUG 75; To VA-192, USS Kitty Hawk (CV-63), 10 SEP 75; To VA-192, NAS Cubi Point, PI., 17 OCT 75; To VA-192, USS Kitty Hawk (CV-63), 19 NOV 75; To VA-192, NAS LeMoore, CA., 17 FEB 76; To VA-192, MCAS Yuma, AZ., 30 NOV 76; To VA-192, NAS LeMoore, CA., 24 FEB 77; To VA-192, USS Kitty Hawk (CV-63), 25 JUL 77; To VA-192, NAS LeMoore, CA., 11 AUG 77; To VA-192, USS Kitty Hawk (CV-63), 31 AUG 77; To VA-192, NAS LeMoore, CA., 27 SEP 77; To VA-192, USS Kitty Hawk (CV-63), 25 OCT 77; To VA-192, NAS LeMoore, CA., 14 MAY 78; To VA-192, USS America (CV-66), 05 JAN 79; To VA-192, NAS LeMoore, CA., 05 JAN 79; To VA-192, NAS Jacksonville, FL., 16 OCT 80; To VA-192, NAS LeMoore, CA., 09 DEC 80; To VA-192, USS America (CV-66), 29 JAN 81; To VA-192, NAS LeMoore, CA., 08 APR 81; To VA-192, USS America (CV-66), 12 JUN 81; To VA-192, NAS LeMoore, CA., 13 JUN 81; To VA-192, NAS Jacksonville, FL., 21 JUN 83 ** Transferred to VA-203/CVWR-20, AF/3XX, NAS Jacksonville, FL., 22 JUN 82 ** Transferred to VA-205/CVWR-20, AF/502, NAS Atlanta, GA., 18 JUL 84 thru 18 MAY 87 ** End of flight record card ** Transferred to AMARC, Davis Monthan AFB; Tucson, AZ., assigned park code 6A0260, 22 APR 88 ** 6213.5 flight hours ** TF41A402D engine S/N 141589 ** Aircraft deleted from inventory and released to DRMO for dispositiom, 18 OCT 05.

157538/157594 LTV A-7E-8-CV Corsair II (Block VIII)

E-317 157538 Navy acceptance from NPRO Rep. LTV, Dallas, TX., 30 SEP 70 ** Transferred to VA-82/CVW-8, AJ/313, NAS Cecil Field, FL., 01 OCT 70; To VA-82, USS America (CVA-66), LT Eddie Walsh painted on side of nose, 17 MAY 71 ** Transferred to VA-174/FRS, AD/4XX, NAS Cecil Field, FL., 31 MAR 72; To VA-174, NAS Jacksonville, FL., 09 JUN 78; To VA-174, NAS Cecil Field, FL., 03 AUG 78; To VA-174, NAS Jacksonville, FL., 29 AUG 80; To VA-174, NAS Cecil Field, FL., 07 OCT 80 ** Transferred to VA-66/CVW-7, AG/306, USS Dwight D. Eisenhower (CVN-69), 03 JUN 81; To VA-66, NAS Cecil Field, FL., 17 JUN 81; To VA-66, USS Dwight D. Eisenhower (CVN-69), 17 JUN 81; To VA-66, NAS Cecil Field, FL., 17 JUN 81; USS Dwight D. Eisenhower (CVN-69), 16 DEC 81; To VA-66, NAS Cecil Field, FL., 28 MAY 82 ** Transferred to VA-12/CVW-7, AG/4XX, USS Dwight D. Eisenhower (CVN-69), 13 APR 83; To VA-12, NAS Jacksonville, FL., 15 APR 83 ** Transferred to NARF, NAS Jacksonville, FL., 15 JUL 86 ** Transferred to VA-81/CVW-17, AA/4XX, NAS Fallon, NV., 18 JUL 83; To VA-81, NAS Cecil Field, FL., 11 AUG 83; To VA-81, USS Saratoga (CV-60), 05 OCT 83; To VA-81, NAS Cecil Field, FL., 11 NOV 83; To VA-81, USS Saratoga (CV-60), 11 NOV 83; To VA-81, NAS Cecil Field, FL., 11 NOV 83; To VA-81, USS Saratoga (CV-60), 11 NOV 83 ** Transferred to VA-87/CVW-6, AE/4XX, NAS Cecil Field, FL., 14 MAY 85; To VA-87, NAS Jacksonville, FL., 16 SEP 85; To VA-87, NAS Cecil Field, FL., 17 SEP 85 ** Transferred to VA-86/CVW-8, AJ/4XX, NAS Cecil Field, FL., 29 OCT 85 ** Transferred to VA-83/CVW-17, AA/3XX, NAS Cecil field, FL., 14 MAY 86; To VA-83, USS Saratoga (CV-60), 14 MAY 86 ** Transferred to NSWC, NAS Fallon, NV., date unknown ** Transferred to VA-83/CVW-CVW-17, AA/302, NAS Cecil Field, FL., date unknown ** Transferred to AMARC, Davis Monthan AFB; Tucson, AZ., assigned park code 6A0205, 19 SEP 86, 5389.5 flight hours ** TF41A2B engine S/N 141275 ** End of flight record card ** Project changed per FSO letter, 06 APR 04 ** At AMARC; Davis Monthan AFB; Tucson, AZ., 11 JAN 05.

E-261 157539 Navy acceptance from NPRO Rep. LTV, Dallas, TX., 29 AUG 70 ** Transferred to VA-195/CVW-11, NH/4XX, USS Kitty Hawk (CVA-63), 30 AUG 70; To VA-195, NAS LeMoore, CA., 05 MAY 72 ~ S 1SO strike, 07 FEB 73 ** No data on strike.

E-262 157540 Navy acceptance from NPRO Rep. LTV, Dallas, TX., 19 SEP 70 ** Transferred to VA-192/CVW-11, NH\3XX, USS Kitty Hawk (CVA-63), 21 SEP 70; To VA-192, NAS LeMoore, CA., 02 MAY 72; To VA-192, USS Kitty Hawk (CV-63), 25 JUN 73; To VA-192, NAS LeMoore, CA., 12 AUG 74; To VA-192, NAS Jacksonville, FL., 19 SEP 74; To VA-192, NAS LeMoore, CA., 19 SEP 74; To VA-192, NAS Jacksonville, FL., 25 SEP 74; To VA-192, NAS LeMoore, CA., 20 NOV 74; To VA-192, USS Kitty Hawk (CV-63), 12 DEC 74; To VA-192, NAS LeMoore, CA., 28 MAR 75; To VA-192, USS Kitty Hawk (CV-63), 11 APR 75; To VA-192, NAS Cubi Point, PI., 16 SEP 75; To VA-192, USS Kitty Hawk (CV-63), 19 NOV 75; To VA-192, NAS LeMoore, CA., 25 FEB 76; To VA-192, MCAS Yuma, AZ., 10 NOV 76; To VA-192, NAS LeMoore, CA., 10 NOV 76; To VA-192, USS Kitty Hawk (CV-63), 21 JUL 77; To VA-192, NAS LeMoore, CA., 11 AUG 77; To VA-192, USS Kitty Hawk (CV-63), 25 OCT 77; To VA-192, NAS LeMoore, CA., 14 MAY 78; To VA-192, NAS Jacksonville, FL., 27 MAY 78; To VA-192, NAS LeMoore, CA., 27 MAY 78; To VA-192, NAF Andrews, WA, DC., 31 MAY 78; To VA-192, NAS Jacksonville, FL., 17 JUL 78; To VA-192, NAS LeMoore, CA., 03 OCT 78; To VA-192, USS America (CV-66), 05 JAN 79; To VA-192, NAS LeMoore, CA., 05 JAN 79; To VA-192, NAS Fallon, NV., 08 JUL 80; To VA-192, NAS LeMoore, CA., 05 OCT 80 ~ S 1SO strike, 29 JAN 81 ** No data on strike.

E-263 157541 Navy acceptance from NPRO Rep. LTV, Dallas, TX., 20 AUG 70 ** Transferred to VA-195/CVW-11, NH/401, USS Kitty Hawk (CVA-63), 21 AUG 70; To VA-195, NAS LeMoore, CA., 20 JUN 72; To VA-195, USS Kitty Hawk (CV-63), 29 JUN 73; To VA-195, NAS LeMoore, CA., 23 APR 74; To VA-195, NAS Alameda, CA., 23 OCT 74; To VA-195, USS Kitty Hawk (CV-63), 08 NOV 74; To VA-195, NAS LeMoore, CA., 09 APR 75; To VA-195, USS Kitty Hawk (CV-63), 19 MAY 75; To VA-195, NAS Cubi Point, PI., 21 JUN 75; To VA-195, NAS LeMoore, CA., 01 JAN 76; To VA-195, NAS Jacksonville, FL., 04 JUN 76; To VA-195, NAS LeMoore, CA., 03 AUG 76; To VA-195, NAS Jacksonville, FL., 13 AUG 76 ** Transferred to VA-81/CVW-17, AA/4XX, NAS Cecil Field, FL., 17 AUG 76; To VA-81, NAS Roosevelt Roads, PR., 21 DEC 76; To VA-81, NAS Cecil Field, FL., 21 DEC 76; To VA-81, NAS Roosevelt Roads, PR., 21 DEC 76; To VA-81, NAS Cecil Field, FL., 21 DEC 76; To VA-81, USS Forrestal (CV-59), 20 JUL 77; To VA-81, NAS Cecil Field, FL., 20 JUL 77; To VA-81, USS Forrestal (CV-59), 20 JUL 77; To VA-81, NAS Jacksonville, FL., 27 OCT 78 ** Transferred to VA-83/CVW-17, AA/3XX, NAS Cecil Field, FL., 27 DEC 78; To VA-83, USS Forrestal (CV-59), 27 DEC 78; To VA-83, NAS Cecil Field, FL., 23 APR 79; To VA-83, USS Forrestal (CV-59), 23 APR 79; To VA-83, NAS Cecil Field, FL., 24 OCT 79; To VA-83, USS Forrestal (CV-59), 30 OCT 79; To VA-83, NAS Cecil Field, FL., 07 NOV 79 ** Transferred to VA-86/CVW-8, AJ/4XX, USS Nimitz (CVN-68), 23 JUL 80; To VA-86, NAS Jacksonville, FL., 01 DEC 80; To VA-86, USS Nimitz (CVN-68), 01 DEC 80; To VA-86, NAS Jacksonville, FL., 03 DEC 80; To VA-86, NAS Cecil Field, FL., 18 FEB 81; To VA-86, USS Nimitz (CVN-68), 18 FEB 81; To VA-86, NAS Cecil Field, FL., 18 FEB 81; To VA-86, USS Nimitz (CVN-68), 18 FEB 81; To VA-86, NAS Cecil Field, FL., 18 FEB 81 ** Transferred to VA-82/CVW-8, AJ/3XX, NAS Cecil Field, FL., 09 MAR 82; To VA-82, USS Carl Vinson (CVN-70), 26 MAR 82; To VA-82, NAS Cecil Field, FL., 26 MAR 82; To VA-82, USS Nimitz (CVN-68), 26 MAR 82; To VA-82, NAS Cecil Field, FL., 26 MAR 82; To VA-82, USS Nimitz (CVN-68), 26 MAR 82; To VA-82, NAS Cecil Field, FL., 26 MAR 82; To VA-82, NAS Jacksonville, FL., 02 JUN 83; To VA-82, NAS Cecil Field, FL., 16 JUN 83; To VA-82, NAS Jacksonville, FL., 22 AUG 83; To VA-82, NAS Cecil Field, FL., 24 AUG 83; To VA-82, NAS Dallas, TX., 01 DEC 83 ** Transferred to VA-66/CVW-7, AG/3XX, NAS Cecil Field, FL. 01 DEC 83 To VA-66, USS Dwight D. Eisenhower (CVN-69), 01 DEC 83; To VA-66, NAS Cecil Field, FL., 01 DEC 83; To VA-66, USS Dwight D. Eisenhower (CVN-69), 01 DEC 83; To VA-66, NAS Cecil Field, FL., 01 DEC 83; To VA-66, USS Dwight D. Eisenhower (CVN-69), 01 DEC 83; To VA-66, NAS Cecil Field, FL., 22 APR 85; To VA-66, USS Dwight D. Eisenhower (CVN-69), 22 JUL 85; To VA-66, NAS Cecil Field, FL., 03 OCT 85; To VA-66, NAS Jacksonville, FL., 07 JUL 86 ** Transferred to VA-82/CVW-8, AJ/3XX, NAS Cecil Field, FL., 28 FEB 86; To VA-82, USS Nimitz (CVN-68), 28 JUN 86; To VA-82, NAS Cecil Field, FL., 10 OCT 86; To VA-82, USS Nimitz (CVN-68), 10 OCT 86; To VA-82, NAS Cecil Field, FL., 10 OCT 86 thru 21 SEP 87 ** End of flight record card ** Transferred to AMARC, Davis Monthan AFB; Tucson, AZ., assigned park code 6A0299, 25 AUG 89 ** 6598 flight hours ** Storage location 210445 ** Seat removed ** At AMARG, Davis Monthan AFB; Tucson, AZ., 15 JUN 07.

E-264 157542 Navy acceptance from NPRO Rep. LTV, Dallas, TX., 30 OCT 70 ** Transferred to VA-86/CVW-8, AJ/4XX, NAS Cecil Field, FL., 31 OCT 70; To VA-86, USS America (CVA-66), 20 APR 71 ** Transferred to VA-12/CVW-7, AG/4XX, USS Independence (CVA-62), 31 MAR 72 ** Transferred to VA-174/FRS, AD/4XX, NAS Cecil Field, FL., 17 NOV 72 ~ S 1SO strike, 18 JAN 73 ** No data on strike.

E-265 157543 Navy acceptance from NPRO Rep. LTV Dallas, TX., 16 SEP 70 ** Transferred to VA-82/CVW-8, AJ/3XX, NAS Cecil Field, FL., 18 SEP 70 ~ S 1SO strike, 16 NOV 70 ** No data on strike.

E-266 157544 Navy acceptance from NPRO Rep. LTV, Dallas, TX., 01 NOV 70 ** Transferred to VA-66/CVW-7, AG/300, Independence (CVA-62), 12 NOV 70; To VA-66, NAS Cecil Field, FL. 13 JUN 71 ~ S 1SO strike, 07 SEP 71 ** No data on strike ** On display at the War Eagles Air Museum in St. Teresa, NM., JAN 98.

E-267 157545 Navy acceptance from NPRO Rep. LTV, Dallas, TX., 01 SEP 70 ** Transferred to VA-195/CVW-11, NH/400, USS Kitty Hawk (CVA-63), 06 SEP 70 ~ S 1SO strike, 04 NOV 71 ** No data on strike.

E-268 157546 Navy acceptance from NPRO Rep. LTV, Dallas, TX., 24 SEP 70 ** Transferred to VA-25/CVW-2, NE/4XX, NAS LeMoore, CA., 25 SEP 70; To VA-25, USS Ranger (CV-61), 23 JUN 73; To VA-25, NAS LeMoore, CA., 10 FEB 75, To VA-25, NAS Fallon, NV., 13 JUL 75; To VA-25, USS Ranger (CV-61), 29 JUL 75 ** Transferred to VA-27/CVW-14 NK/4XX, NAS LeMoore, CA., 06 AUG 75; To VA-27, NAS Fallon, NV., 07 OCT 75; To VA-27, NAS LeMoore, CA., 19 FEB 76; To VA-27, USS Enterprise (CVN-65), 12 MAR 76; To VA-27, NAS LeMoore, CA., 17 MAY 76; To VA-27, USS Enterprise (CVN-65), 30 JUN 76; To VA-27, NAS LeMoore, CA., 30 JUN 76; To VA-27, USS Enterprise (CVN-65), 30 JUN 76 ** Transferred to VA-192/CVW-11, NH/3XX, NAS LeMoore, CA., 09 JUL 76; To VA-192, MCAS Yuma, AZ., 25 OCT 76; To VA-192, NAS LeMoore, CA., 14 DEC 76 ** Transferred to VA-122/FRS, NJ/2XX, NAS LeMoore, CA., 14 JUN 77; To VA-122, NAS Jacksonville, FL., 18 MAR 78; To VA-122, NAS LeMoore, CA., 15 JUL 78 ** Transferred to VA-192/CVW-11, NH/3XX, NAS LeMoore, CA., 02 SEP 78; To VA-192, NAS Jacksonville, FL., 29 AUG 80; To VA-192, NAS Fallon, NV., 20 OCT 80; To VA-192, NAS LeMoore, CA., 07 NOV 80; To VA-192, USS America (CV-66), 29 JAN 81; To VA-192, NAS LeMoore, CA., 08 APR 81 ** Transferred to VA-195/CVW-9, NG/4XX, NAS LeMoore, CA., 08 DEC 82; To VA-195, USS Ranger (CV-61), 10 JUL 83; To VA-195, NAS Jacksonville, FL., 18 JUL 83 ** Transferred to NARF, NAS Jacksonville, FL., 02 DEC 83 ** Transferred to VA-203/CVWR-20, AF/3XX, NAS Jacksonville, FL., 19 JUL 83 thru 03 DEC 86 ** End of flight record card ** Transferred to AMARC, Davis Monthan AFB; Tucson, AZ., assigned park code 6A0262; 26 APR 88 ** 6376.5 flight hours ** TF41A402D engine S/N 141898 ** Storage location 210520 ** At AMARG, Davis Monthan AFB; Tucson, AZ., 15 JUN 07.

E-269 157547 Navy acceptance from NPRO Rep. LTV, Dallas, TX., 26 SEP 70 ** Transferred to VA-82/CVW-8, AJ/3XX, NAS Cecil Field, FL., 29 SEP 70; To VA-82, USS America (CVA-66), 13 JUN 71 ** Transferred to NATC, Service Test, NAS Patuxent River, MD., 27 MAR 72 ** Transferred to VA-122/FRS, NJ/2XX, NAS LeMoore, CA., 19 JUN 72 ~ S 1SO strike, 08 JUN 73 ** No data on strike.

E-270 157548 Navy acceptance from NPRO Rep. LTV, Dallas, TX., 24 SEP 70 ** Transferred to VA-195/CVW-11, NH/414, USS Kitty Hawk (CVA-63), 26 SEP 70 ~ S 1SO strike, 27 FEB 71 ** No data on strike.

E-271 157549 Navy acceptance from NPRO Rep. LTV, Dallas, TX., 30 SEP 70 ** Transferred to VA-82/CVW-8, AJ/3XX, NAS Cecil Field, FL., 01 OCT 70; To VA-82, USS America (CVA-66), 23 JUN 71 ** Transferred to VA-174/FRS, AD/4XX, NAS Cecil Field, FL., 31 MAR 72 ** Transferred to VA-37/CVW-3, AC/3XX, NAS Cecil Field, FL., 03 JUL 73; To VA-37, USS Saratoga (CV-60), 23 MAY 74; To VA-37, NAS Cecil Field, FL., 23 MAY 74; To VA-37, NAS Jacksonville, FL., 10 OCT 75; To VA-37, NAS Cecil Field, FL., 10 OCT 75; To VA-37, USS Saratoga (CV-60), 09 NOV 76; To VA-37, NAS Cecil Field, FL., 09 NOV 76; To VA-37, USS Saratoga (CV-60), 09 NOV 76; To VA-37, NAS Cecil Field, FL., 16 JUL 77; To VA-37, NAS Jacksonville, FL., 11 MAY 78; NAS Cecil Field, FL., 07 JUN 78; To VA-37, USS Saratoga (CV-60), 07 JUN 78; To VA-37, NAS Cecil Field, FL., 07 JUN 78 ** Transferred to VA-174/FRS, AD/4XX, NAS Cecil Field, FL., 19 JUL 78; To VA-174, NAS Jacksonville, FL., 23 MAY 80; To VA-174, NAS Cecil Field, FL., 23 MAY 80 ** Transferred to VA-12/CVW-7, AG/4XX, NAS Cecil Field, FL., 09 FEB 81; To VA-12, USS Dwight D. Eisenhower (CVN-69), 09 FEB 81 ** To VA-37, NAS Cecil Field, FL., 09 FEB 81; To VA-12, USS Dwight D. Eisenhower (CVN-69), 23 DEC 81 ** Transferred to VA-86/CVW-8, AJ/4XX, USS Nimitz (CVN-68), 25 JAN 82; To VA-86, NAS Cecil Field, FL., 15 FEB 82 ** Transferred to VA-42, NAS Oceana, VA.,15 JUN 82 ** Transferred to VA-174/FRS, AD/4XX, NAS Cecil Field, FL., 16 JUN 82; To VA-174, NAS Jacksonville, FL., 29 SEP 82 ** Transferred to VA-37/CVW-15, NL/3XX, NAS Cecil Field, 30 SEP 82; To VA-37, USS Carl Vinson (CVN-70); 30 SEP 82; To VA-37, NAS Cecil Field, 30 SEP 82; To VA-37, USS Carl Vinson (CVN-70), 30 SEP 82; To VA-37, NAS Roosevelt Roads, PR., 09 NOV 83; To VA-37, NAS Cecil Field, FL., 09 NOV 83; To VA-37,

NWC China Lake, CA., 09 NOV 83; To VA-37, NAS Cecil Field, FL., 09 NOV 83; To VA-37, MCAS Twenty Nine Palms, CA., 30 JUL 84 ** Transferred to VA-174/FRS, AD/4XX, NAS Cecil Field, FL., 03 AUG 84; To VA-174, NAS Jacksonville, FL., 09 AUG 85; To VA-174, NAS Cecil Field, FL., 13 AUG 85 ** Transferred to VA-12/CVW-7, AG/402, NAS Cecil Field, FL., 16 DEC 85 ** End of flight record card ** Transferred to AMARC, Davis Monthan AFB; Tucson, AZ., assigned park code 6A0193, 21 AUG 86 ** 5404.0 flight hours ** TF41A2B engine S/N 141572 ** Aircraft storage location 210540 ** Aircraft deleted from inventory and released to AMARC for disposition, 03 MAY 06 ** At AMARG, Davis Monthan AFB; Tucson, AZ., 15 JUN 07.

E-272 157550 Navy acceptance from NPRO Rep. LTV, Dallas, TX., 10 SEP 70 ** Transferred to VA-82/CVW-8, AJ/3XX, NAS Cecil Field, FL., 11 SEP 70; To VA-82, USS America (CVA-66), 04 JUN 71 ** Transferred to VA-174/FRS, AD/4XX, NAS Cecil Field, FL., 26 AUG 71 ** Transferred to VA-83/CVW-17, AA/3XX, NAS Cecil Field, FL., 30 OCT 74; To VA-83, USS Forrestal (CVA-59), 09 DEC 74; To VA-83, NAS Cecil Field, FL., 09 DEC 74; To VA-83, USS Forrestal (CVA-59), 09 DEC 74; To VA-83, NAS Cecil Field, FL., 01 SEP 75; To VA-83, USS Forrestal (CV-59), 01 SEP 75; To VA-83, NAS Cecil Field, FL., 09 OCT 75; To VA-83, NAS Roosevelt Roads, PR., 09 OCT 75; To VA-83, NAS Cecil Field, FL., 09 OCT 75; To VA-83, NAS Jacksonville, FL., 23 SEP 77; To VA-83, USS Forrestal (CV-59), 23 SEP 77; To VA-83, NAS Cecil Field, FL., 13 DEC 77; To VA-83, USS Forrestal (CV-59), 13 DEC 77; To VA-83, NAS Jacksonville, FL., 08 FEB 78 ** Transferred to NARF, NAS Norfolk, VA., 09 FEB 78 ** Transferred to VA-105/CVW-3, AC/4XX, NAS Cecil Field, FL., 10 JUL 79; To VA-105, MCAS Yuma, AZ., 10 JUL 79; To VA-105, NAS Cecil Field, FL., 10 JUL 79; To VA-105, USS Saratoga (CV-60), 10 JUL 79; To VA-105, NAS Cecil Field, FL., 10 JUL 79; To VA-105, USS Saratoga (CV-60), 10 JUL 79; To VA-105, NAS Cecil Field, FL., 02 DEC 80; To VA-105, NAS Fallon, NV., 22 MAY 81; To VA-105, NAS Cecil Field, FL., 22 MAY 81; To VA-105, USS John F. Kennedy (CV-67), 09 JUL 81 ** Transferred to VA-72/CVW-1, AB/4XX, NAS Cecil Field, FL., 12 AUG 81; To VA-72, NAS Jacksonville, FL., 07 JAN 82; To VA-72, NAS Cecil Field, FL., 12 FEB 82; To VA-72, NAS Dallas, TX., 25 MAR 82; To VA-72, NAS Cecil Field, FL., 13 APR 82; To VA-72, NAS Dallas, TX., 26 MAY 82 ** Transferred to VA-15/CVW-6, AE/3XX, NAS Cecil Field, FL., 27 MAY 82; To VA-15, USS Independence (CV-62), 27 MAY 82; To VA-15, NAS Cecil Field, FL., 27 MAY 82 ~ S 1SO strike, 03 DEC 82 ** No data on strike.

E-273 157551 Navy acceptance from NPRO Rep. LTV, Dallas, TX., 30 SEP 70 ** Transferred to VA-82/CVW-8, AJ/3XX, NAS Cecil Field, FL., 01 OCT 70; To VA-82, USS America (CVA-66), 03 APR 71 ** Transferred to NATC, Service Test, NAS Patuxent River, MD., 03 APR 72 ** Transferred to VA-122/FRS, NJ/2XX, NAS LeMoore, CA., 09 JUN 72; To VA-122, NAS Jacksonville, FL., 22 JUN 78; To VA-122, NAS LeMoore, CA., 25 JAN 79 ** Transferred to VA-94/CVW-15, NL/4XX, NAS LeMoore, CA., 28 FEB 79; To VA-94, NAS Cubi Point, PI., 29 MAY 79; To VA-94, USS Kitty Hawk (CV-63), 05 JAN 80; To VA-94, NAS LeMoore, CA., 27 JAN 80; To VA-94, USS Kitty Hawk, (CV-63), 15 JUL 80; To VA-94, NAS LeMoore, CA., 27 JUL 80; To VA-94, USS Kitty Hawk, (CV-63), 11 SEP 80; To VA-94, NAS LeMoore, CA., 06 NOV 80 ** Transferred to VA-146/CVW-9, NG/3XX, NAS LeMoore, CA., 09 FEB 81; To VA-146, NAS Jacksonville, FL., 05 MAY 81; To VA-146, NAS LeMoore, CA., 06 MAY 81; To VA-146, NAS Jacksonville, FL., 02 JUN 81; To VA-146, NAS LeMoore, CA., 26 JUN 81; To VA-146, USS Constellation (CV-64), 26 JUN 81 ** Transferred to VA-147/CVW-9, NG/4XX, USS Constellation (CV-64), 02 JUL 81; To VA-147, NAS LeMoore, CA., 06 AUG 81; To VA-147, USS Constellation (CV-64), 19 OCT 81; To VA-147, NAS Cubi Point, PI., 19 OCT 81; To VA-147, NAF Atsugi, JP., 01 DEC 81; To VA-147, NAS Cubi Point, PI., 02 DECT 81; To VA-147, NAF Atsugi, JP., 07 DEC 81; To VA-147, NAS Cubi Point, PI., 11 DEC 81; To VA-147, USS Constellation (CV-64), 11 DEC 81; To VA-147, NAS LeMoore, CA., 11 DEC 81; To VA-147, NAS Jacksonville, FL., 27 MAY 83; To VA-147, NAS LeMoore, CA.,

03 JUN 83; To VA-147, NAS Jacksonville, FL., 31 AUG 83; To VA-147, NAS LeMoore, CA., 06 SEP 83; To VA-147, NAS Dallas, TX., 07 SEP 83 ** Transferred to VA-22/CVW-11, NH/3XX, NAS LeMoore, CA., 22 DEC 83; To VA-22, USS Enterprise (CVN-65), 22 DEC 83; To VA-22, NAS LeMoore, CA., 11 JAN 84; To VA-22, USS Enterprise (CVN-65), 25 JUN 84; To VA-22, NAF Atsugi, JP., 26 JUL 84; To VA-22, USS Enterprise (CVN-65), 02 AUG 84; To VA-22, NAF Atsugi, JP., 07 AUG 84; To VA-22, USS Enterprise (CVN-65), 08 AUG 84; To VA-22, NAF Atsugi, JP., 13 AUG 84; To VA-22, USS Enterprise (CVN-65), 16 AUG 84 ** Transferred to VA-22/CVW-11, NH/3XX, NAF Atsugi, JP., 18 OCT 84; To VA-22, USS Enterprise (CVN-65), 03 NOV 84 ** To VA-56, USS Midway (CV-41), 05 NOV 84; Transferred to VA-56/CVW-5, NF/4XX, NAF Atsugi, JP., 05 NOV 84; To VA-56, NAS LeMoore, CA., 31 JAN 86 ** Transferred to VA-146/CVW-9, NE/3XX, NAS LeMoore, CA., 12 MAY 86; To VA-146, NAS Jacksonville, FL., 22 SEP 86 ** Transferred to VA-22/CVW-11, NH/3XX, NAS LeMoore, CA., 23 DEC 86 thru 05 JUN 87 ** End of flight record card ** Transferred to VA-122/FRS, NJ/2XX, NAS LeMoore, CA., date unknown ** Transferred to AMARC, Davis Monthan AFB, Tucson, AZ., assigned park code 6A0303, 21 SEP 89 ** 7322.2 flight hours ** TF41A402D engine S/N 141267 ** seat removed, S/N and date unknown ** Storage location 210446 ** At AMARG, Davis Monthan AFB; Tucson, AZ., 15 JUN 07.

E-274 157552 Navy acceptance from NPRO Rep. LTV, Dallas, TX., 26 OCT 70 ** Transferred to VA-86/CVW-8, AJ/4XX, NAS Cecil Field, FL., 27 OCT 70; To VA-86, USS America (CVA-66), 03 APR 71 ** Transferred to VA-66/CVW-7, AG/3XX, NAS Cecil Field, FL., 31 MAR 72 ** Transferred to VA-174/FRS, AD/4XX, NAS Cecil Field, FL., 25 OCT 72 ** Transferred to VA-37/CVW-3, AC/304, NAS Cecil Field, FL., 07 MAY 73; To VA-37, USS Saratoga (CV-60), 29 APR 74; To VA-37, NAS Cecil Field, FL., 29 APR 74; To VA-37, USS Saratoga (CV-60), 29 APR 74; To VA-37, NAS Cecil Field, FL., 29 APR 74; To VA-37, NAS Jacksonville, FL., 24 OCT 75; To VA-37, USS Saratoga (CV-60), 24 OCT 75; To VA-37, NAS Jacksonville, FL., 04 OCT 75; To VA-37, NAS Cecil Field, FL., 18 DEC 75; To VA-37, USS Saratoga (CV-60), 24 SEP 76; To VA-37, NAS Cecil Field, FL., 24 SEP 76; To VA-37, USS Saratoga (CV-60), 24 SEP 76; To VA-37, NAS Cecil Field, FL., 16 JUL 77; To VA-37, NAS Jacksonville, FL., 07 MAR 78; To VA-37, NAS Cecil Field, FL., 18 APR 78; To VA-37, USS Saratoga (CV-60), 21 JUL 78; To VA-37, NAS Cecil Field, FL., 13 JUN 79; To VA-37, MCAS Yuma, AZ., 21 JUN 79; To VA-37, NAS Cecil Field, FL., 21 JUN 79; To VA-37, USS Saratoga (CV-60), 21 JUN 79; To VA-37, NAS Cecil Field, FL., 21 JUN 79 ** Transferred to VA-174/FRS, AD/4XX, NAS Cecil Field, FL., 19 FEB 80 ** Transferred to VA-81/CVW-17, AA/4XX, NAS Cecil Field, FL., 11 AUG 80; To VA-81, USS Forrestal (CV-59), 11 AUG 80; To VA-81, NAS Cecil Field, FL., 16 OCT 80; To VA-81, USS Forrestal (CV-59), 11 FEB 81; To VA-81, NAS Cecil Field, FL., 11 FEB 81; To VA-81, NAS Fallon, NV., 11 FEB 81; To VA-81, USS Forrestal (CV-59), 11 FEB 81; To VA-81, NAS Cecil Field, FL., 29 APR 82; To VA-81, USS Forrestal (CV-59), 29 APR 82; To VA-81, NAS Cecil Field, FL., 24 NOV 82 ** Transferred to VA-82/CVW-8, AJ/3XX, USS Nimitz (CVN-68), 05 MAR 83; To VA-82, NAS Cecil Field, FL., 15 MAY 83; To VA-82, NAS Jacksonville, FL., 27 JUL 84; To VA-82, NAS Cecil Field, FL., 27 JUL 84; To VA-82, NAS Jacksonville, FL., 30 JUL 84 ** Transferred to VA-81/CVW-17, AA/4XX, NAS Cecil Field, FL., 27 NOV 84; To VA-81, USS Saratoga (CV-59), 22 JAN 85; To VA-81, NAS Cecil Field, FL., 18 JUN 85; To VA-81, USS Saratoga (CV-59), 26 JUN 85; To VA-81, NAS Cecil Field, FL., 26 JUN 85; To VA-81, USS Saratoga (CV-59), 26 JUN 85; To VA-81, NAS Cecil Field, FL., 21 OCT 86 ** Transferred to VA-174/FRS, AD/4XX, NAS Cecil Field, FL., 17 JAN 87 ** End of flight record card ** Transferred to AMARC, Davis Monthan AFB; Tucson, AZ., assigned park code 6A0227, 15 JUL 87 ** 6125.0 flight hours ** TF41A2B engine S/N 142592 ** Storage location 210528 ** Engine records released to DRMO for disposition, 22 FEB 06 ** Aircraft deleted from inventory and released to DRMO for disposition, 04 MAY 06 ** At AMARG, Davis Monthan AFB; Tucson, AZ., 15 JUN 07.

E-275 157553 Navy acceptance from NPRO Rep. LTV, Dallas, TX., 29 SEP 70 ** Transferred to VA-82/CVW-8, AJ/3XX, NAS Cecil Field, FL., 30 SEP 70; To VA-82, USS America (CVA-66), 23 MAR 71 ** Transferred to VA-81/CVW-17, AA/403, NAS Cecil Field, FL., 22 MAR 72; To VA-81, USS Forrestal (CV-59), 25 MAY 72 ** Transferred to VA-174/FRS, AD/4XX, NAS Cecil Field, FL., 16 AUG 72 ** Transferred to VA-86/CVW-8, AJ/4XX, NAS Cecil Field, FL., 11 FEB 75; To VA-86, USS Nimitz (CVN-68), 11 FEB 75 ** To VA-86, NAS Cecil Field, FL., 24 JUL 75; To VA-86, NAS Roosevelt Roads, PR., 24 JUL 75; To VA-86, NAS Cecil Field, FL., 24 JUL 75; To VA-86, USS Nimitz (CVN-68), 24 JUL 75 ** Transferred to VA-174/FRS, AD/4XX, NAS Cecil Field, FL., 18 FEB 76; To VA-174, NAS Jacksonville, FL., 11 MAY 76; To VA-174, NAS Cecil Field, FL., 29 JUN 76 ** Transferred to VA-105/CVW-3, AC/412, USS Saratoga (CV-59), 28 JUN 77; To VA-105, NAS Cecil Field, FL., 16 JUL 77; To VA-105, USS Saratoga (CV-59), 23 MAY 78; To VA-105, NAS Cecil Field, FL., 17 OCT 78; To VA-105, MCAS Yuma, AZ., 17 OCT 78; To VA-105, NAS Cecil Field, FL., 24 OCT 79; To VA-105, USS Saratoga (CV-59), 20 DEC 79; To VA-105, NAS Cecil Field, FL., 20 DEC 79; To VA-105, USS Saratoga (CV-59), 20 MAR 80; To VA-105, NAS Jacksonville, FL., 10 SEP 80; To VA-105, USS Saratoga (CV-59), 31 OCT 80; To VA-105, NAS Cecil Field, FL., 25 NOV 80; To VA-105, NAS Fallon, NV., 25 NOV 80; To VA-105, NAS Cecil Field, FL., 07 JUL 81; To VA-105, USS John F. Kennedy (CV-67), 09 JUL 81 ** Transferred to VA-81/CVW-17, AA/4XX, NAS Cecil Field, FL., 22 OCT 81; To VA-81, NAS Fallon, NV., 22 OCT 81; To VA-81, USS Forrestal (CV-59), 2 OCT 81; To VA-81, NAS Cecil Fielf, FL., 25 APR 82 ** Transferred to VA-174/FRS, AD/4XX, NAS Cecil Field, FL., 07 MAY 82; To VA-174, NAS Jacksonville, FL., 07 NOV 83; To VA-174, NAS Cecil Field, FL., 18 NOV 83; To VA-174, NAS Jacksonville, FL., 13 JAN 84; To VA-174, NAS Cecil Field, FL., 18 JAN 84 ** Transferred to VA-203/CVWR-20, AF/3XX, NAS Jacksonville, FL., 24 JUL 86 ** Transferred to VA-204/CVWR-20, AF/4XX, NAS Jacksonville, FL., 02 DEC 86; To VA-204, NAS New Orleans, LA., 04 DEC 86; To VA-204, NAS Jacksonville, FL., 23 DEC 86; To VA-204, NAS New Orleans, LA., 23 DEC 86 ** End of flight record card ** Transferred to AMARC, Davis Montan AFB; Tucson, AZ., assigned park code 6A0265, 02 MAY 88 ** 6044.5 flight hours ** TF41A402D engine S/N 142568 ** Storage location 210344 ** At AMARC, Davis Montan AFB; Tucson, AZ., Seat has been removed, 15 NOV 07.

E-276 157554 Navy acceptance from NPRO Rep. LTV, Dallas, TX., 29 OCT 70 ** Transferred to VA-86/CVW-8, AJ/4XX, NAS Cecil Field, FL. 30 OCT 70 ~ S 1SO strike, 08 MAR 71 ** No data on strike.

E-277 157555 Navy acceptance from NPRO Rep. LTV, Dallas, TX., 30 SEP 70 ** Transferred to VA-82/CVW-8, AJ/300, NAS Cecil Field FL., 01 OCT 70; To VA-82, USS America (CVA-66), 17 APR 71 ** Transferred to VA-81/CVW-17, AA/4XX, NAS Cecil Field, FL., 15 FEB 72; To VA-81, USS Forrestal (CVA-59), 05 APR 72; To VA-81, NAS Cecil Field, FL., 17 SEP 74; To VA-81, USS Forrestal (CVA-59), 06 NOV 74; To VA-81, NAS Cecil Field, FL., 24 JUL 75; To VA-81, NAS Jacksonville, FL., 19 FEB 76; To VA-81, NAS Cecil Field, FL., 19 FEB 76; To VA-81, NAS Jacksonville, FL., 20 FEB 76; To VA-81, USS Forrestal (CV-59), 31 MAR 76; To VA-81, NAS Cecil Field, FL., 31 MAR 76 ~ S 1SO strike, 15 DEC 76 ** Aircraft lost when it went over the side. Pilot ejected and was rescued with injuries.

E-278 157556 Navy acceptance from NPRO Rep. LTV, Dallas, TX., 30 SEP 70 ** Transferred to VA-86/CVW-8, AJ/4XX, NAS Cecil Field, FL., 02 OCT 70; To VA-86, USS America (CVA-66), 05 JUN 71 ** Transferred to VA-66/CVW-7, AG/3XX, NAS Cecil Field, FL., 31 MAR 72; To VA-66, USS Independence (CVA-62), 31 MAY 72 ** Transferred to VA-174/FRS, AD/4XX, NAS Cecil Field, FL., 31 OCT 72 ** Transferred to VA-105/CVW-3, AC/4XX, NAS Cecil Field, FL., 31 MAY 73; To VA-105, USS Saratoga (CV-60), 12 AUG 74; To VA-105, NAS Cecil Field, FL., 23 OCT 74; To VA-105, USS Saratoga (CV-60), 23 OCT 74; To VA-105, NAS Cecil Field, FL., 23 OCT 74; To VA-105, USS Saratoga (CV-60),

06 OCT 75; To VA-105, NAS Cecil Field, FL., 21 OCT 75; To VA-105, USS Saratoga (CV-60), 01 NOV 76; To VA-105, NAS Cecil Field, FL., 01 FEB 77 ** Transferred to VA-174/FRS, AD/4XX, NAS Cecil Field, FL., 31 MAY 77; To VA-174, NAS Jacksonville, FL., 30 JUN 78; To VA-174, NAS Cecil Field, FL., 30 AUG 78; To VA-174, NAS Jacksonville, FL., 19 MAR 81 ** Transferred to VA-97/CVW-14, NK/3XX, NAS LeMoore, CA., 29 APR 81; To VA-97, USS Coral Sea (CV-43), 29 APR 81; To VA-97, NAS LeMoore, CA., 03 JUN 81 ** Transferred to VA-174/FRS, AD/4XX, NAS Cecil Field, FL., 26 JUN 81; To VA-174, NAS Jacksonville, FL., 08 NOV 82; To VA-174, NAS Cecil Field, FL., 08 NOV 82; To VA-174, NAS Jacksonville, FL., 09 NOV 82 ** Transferred to VA-81/CVW-17, AA/4XX, NAS Cecil Field, FL., 31 JAN 83; To VA-81, NAS Fallon, NV., 13 JUL 83; To VA-81, NAS Cecil Field, FL., 22 SEP 83; To VA-81, USS Saratoga (CV-60), 01 NOV 83; To VA-81, NAS Cecil Field, FL., 20 MAR 84; To VA-81, NAS Jacksonville, FL., 13 MAY 85; To VA-81, USS Saratoga (CV-60), 15 MAY 85; To VA-81, NAS Cecil Field, FL., 15 MAY 85; To VA-81, USS Saratoga (CV-60), 09 AUG 85; To VA-81, NAS Cecil Field, FL., 12 MAR 86; To VA-81, USS Saratoga (CV-60), 22 SEP 86; To VA-81, NAS Cecil Field, FL., 26 SEP 86 ** Transferred to VA-174/FRS, AD/433, NAS Cecil Field, FL., 07 OCT 86 ** End of flight record card ** Transferred to AMARC, Davis Monthan AFB; Tucson, AZ., assigned park code 6A0238, 08 SEP 87 ** 5555.6 flight hours ** TF41A2C engine S/N AD141925 ** Storage location 210442 ** Under GSA control ** AT AMARG, Davis Monthan AFB; Tucson, AZ., 15 JUN 07.

E-279 157557 Navy acceptance from NPRO Rep. LTV, Dallas, TX., 23 OCT 70 ** Transferred to VA-86/CVW-8, AJ/4XX, NAS Cecil Field, FL., 24 OCT 70; To VA-86, USS America (CVA-66), 20 APR 71 ** Transferred to VA-66/CVW-7, AG/3XX, NAS Cecil Field, FL., 31 MAR 72; To VA-66, USS Independence (CVA-62), 31 MAR 72 ** Transferred to VA-174/FRS, AD/4XX, NAS Cecil Field, FL., 05 OCT 72 ** Transferred to VA-105/ CVW-3, AC/4XX, NAS Cecil Field, FL., 25 JUN 73 ~ S 1SO strike, 31 MAY 74 ** No data on strike.

E-280 157558 Navy acceptance from NPRO Rep. LTV, Dallas, TX., 26 OCT 70 ** Transferred to VA-86/CVW-8, AJ/4XX, NAS Cecil Field, FL., 27 OCT 70; To VA-86, USS America (CVA-66), 05 APR 71 ** Transferred to VA-83/CVW-17, AA/3XX, NAS Cecil Field, FL., 05 APR 72; To VA-83, USS Forrestal (CVA-59), 27 APR 72; To VA-83, NAS Cecil Field, FL., 05 NOV 74; To VA-83, USS Forrestal (CVA-59), 18 NOV 74; To VA-83, NAS Cecil Field, FL., 18 NOV 74; To VA-83, USS Forrestal (CVA-59), 18 NOV 74; To VA-83, NAS Cecil Field, FL., 01 SEP 75; To VA-83, NAS Jacksonville, FL., 13 DEC 75; To VA-83, NAS Cecil Field, FL., 16 DEC 75 ~ S 1SO, strike, 03 FEB 76 ** No data on strike.

E-281 157559 Navy acceptance from NPRO Rep. LTV, Dallas, TX., 27 OCT 70 ** Transferred to VA-66/CVW-7, AG/3XX, NAS Cecil Field, FL., 29 OCT 70; To VA-66, USS Independence (CVA-62), 15 FEB 72 ** Transferred to VA-174/FRS, AD/4XX, NAS Cecil Field, FL., 03 OCT 72 ** Transferred to VA-37/CVW-3, AC/300, NAS Cecil Field, FL.; 18 AUG 73; To VA-37, USS Saratoga (CV-60), 02 APR 74; To VA-37, NAS Cecil Field, FL.; 02 APR 74; To VA-37, USS Saratoga (CV-60), 29 SEP 75; To VA-37, NAS Cecil Field, FL.; 29 SEP 75; To VA-37, USS Saratoga (CV-60), 06 MAY 76; To VA-37, NAS Cecil Field, FL., 01 JUL 76; To VA-37, NAS Jacksonville, FL., 30 SEP 76; To VA-37, NAS Cecil Field, FL.; 28 DEC 76; To VA-37, USS Saratoga (CV-60), 28 DEC 76; To VA-37, NAS Cecil Field, FL.; 28 DEC 76; To VA-37, USS Saratoga (CV-60), 28 DEC 76; To VA-37, NAS Cecil Field, FL., 16 JUL 77; To VA-37, NAS Jacksonville, FL., 18 OCT 78; To VA-37, NAS Cecil Field, FL., 18 OCT 78; To VA-37, NAS Jacksonville, FL., 18 OCT 78; To VA-37, NAS Cecil Field, FL., 13 NOV 78; To VA-37, MCAS Yuma, AZ., 13 NOV 78; To VA-37, USS Saratoga (CV-60), 18 DEC 79; To VA-37, NAS Cecil Field, FL., 22 DEC 79; To VA-37, USS Saratoga (CV-60), 20 FEB 80; To VA-37, NAS Cecil Field, FL., 16 MAR 80; To VA-37, NAS Jacksonville, FL., 05 MAR 81; To VA-37, NAS Cecil Field, FL.,

28 APR 81; To VA-37, NAS Fallon, NV., 28 APR 81; To VA-37, NAS NAS Cecil Field, FL., 28 APR 81; To VA-37; USS John F. Kenndey (CV-67), 28 APR 81; To VA-37, NAS Cecil Field, FL., 28 APR 81; To VA37/CVW-15, NL/3XX, USS Carl Vinson (CVN-70), 10 DEC 82; To VA-37, NAS Cecil Field, FL., 10 DEC 82; To VA-37, USS Carl Vinson (CVN-70), 12 APR 83; To VA-37, NAS Jacksonville, FL., 28 NOV 83; To VA-37, NAS Roosevelt Roads, PR., 28 NOV 83; To VA-37, NAS Cecil Field, FL., 28 NOV 83; To VA-37, NWC China Lake, CA., 28 NOV 83; To VA-37, NAS Jacksonville, FL., 27 APR 84 ** Transferred to VA-82/CVW-8, AJ/3XX, NAS Cecil Field, FL., 01 MAY 84; To VA-82, USS Nimitz (CVN-68), 14 JUN 84; To VA-82, NAS Cecil Field, FL., 14 JUN 84; To VA-82, USS Nimitz (CVN-68), 14 JUN 84; To VA-82, NAS Cecil Field, FL., 28 OCT 85; To VA-82, NAS Jacksonville, FL., 02 JUN 86; To VA-82, NAS Cecil Field, FL., 03 JUN 86; To VA-82, USS Nimitz (CVN-68), 19 JUN 86; To VA-82, NAS Cecil Field, FL., 10 OCT 86; To VA-82, USS Nimitz (CVN-68), 10 NOV 86; To VA-82, NAS Cecil Field, FL., 10 NOV 86 ** Transferred to VA-105/CVW-6, AE/4XX, USS Forrestal (CV-59), 17 JUL 87 thru 31 AUG 87 ** End of flight record card ** Transferred to PMTC, PMTC/83, NAS Point Mugu, CA., date unknown ** Transferred to AMARC, Davis Monthan AFB; Tucson, AZ., assigned park code 6A0309, 12 JAN 90 ** 7032.8 flight hours ** TF41A402D engine S/N 141955 ** Storage location 210523 ** At AMARG, Davis Monthan AFB; Tucson, AZ., 15 JUN 07.

E-282 157560 Navy acceptance from NPRO Rep. LTV, Dallas, TX., 24 OCT 70 ** Transferred to VA-86/CVW-8, AJ/4XX, NAS Cecil Field, FL., 27 OCT 70; To VA-86, USS America (CVA-66), 30 MAR 71 ** Transferred to VA-12/CVW-7, AG/4XX, NAS Cecil Field, FL., 31 MAR 72; To VA-12, USS Independence (CVA-62), 31 MAR 72 ** Transferred to VA-174/FRS, AD/4XX, NAS Cecil Field, FL., 13 NOV 72 ** Transferred to VA-37/CVW-3, AC/3XX, NAS Cecil Field, FL., 01 MAY 73; To VA-37, USS Saratoga (CV-60), 05 APR 74; To VA-37, NAS Cecil Field, FL., 05 APR 74; To VA-37, USS Saratoga (CV-60), 05 APR 74; To VA-37, NAS Cecil Field, FL., 05 APR 74; To VA-37, USS Saratoga (CV-60), 05 APR 74; To VA-37, NAS Cecil Field, FL., 05 APR 74; To VA-37, USS Saratoga (CV-60), 28 OCT 75; To VA-37, NAS Cecil Field, FL., 28 OCT 75; To VA-37, USS Saratoga (CV-60), 01 JAN 77; To VA-37, NAS Cecil Field, FL., 01 JAN 77; To VA-37, USS Saratoga (CV-60), 01 APR 77 ** Transferred to VA-174/FRS, AD/4XX, NAS Cecil Field, FL., 21 JUN 77; To VA-174, NAS Jacksonville, FL., 14 JUL 78; To VA-174, NAS Cecil Field, FL., 30 AUG 78 ** Transferred to NARF, NAS Jacksonville, FL., 12 DEC 80 ~ S 1SO strike, 15 DEC 80 ** No data on strike.

E-283 157561 Navy acceptance from NPRO Rep. LTV, Dallas, TX., 26 OCT 70 ** Transferred to VA-86/CVW-8, AJ/4XX, NAS Cecil Field, FL., 28 OCT 70; To VA-86, USS America (CVA-66), 17 MAY 71 ** Transferred to VA-83/CVW-17, AA/3XX, NAS Cecil Field, FL., 06 APR 72; To VA-83, USS Forrestal (CVA-59), 04 MAY 72; To VA-83, NAS Cecil Field, FL., 24 OCT 74; To VA-83, USS Forrestal (CVA-59), 07 NOV 74; To VA-83, NAS Cecil Field, FL., 07 NOV 74; To VA-83, USS Forrestal (CVA-59), 07 NOV 74; To VA-83, NAS Cecil Field, FL., 01 SEP 75; To VA-83, NAS Jacksonville, FL., 17 NOV 75; To VA-83, NAS Cecil Field, FL., 17 JAN 76; To VA-83, USS Forrestal (CV-59), 17 JAN 76; To VA-83, NAS Cecil Field, FL., 17 JAN 76; To VA-83, USS Forrestal (CV-59), 17 JAN 76; To VA-83, NAS Cecil Field, FL., 17 JAN 76; To VA-83, NAS Roosevelt Roads, PR., 17 JAN 76; To VA-83, NAS Cecil Field, FL., 17 JAN 76; To VA-83, USS Forrestal (CV-59), 20 JUL 77; To VA-83, NAS Cecil Field, FL., 20 JUL 77; To VA-83, NAS Jacksonville, FL., 20 JAN 78; To VA-83, USS Forrestal (CV-59), 16 FEB 78; To VA-83, NAS Cecil Field, FL., 22 FEB 78; To VA-83, USS Forrestal (CV-59), 06 MAR 78 ~ S 1SO strike, 24 JUN 78 ** No data on strike.

E-284 157562 Navy acceptance from NPRO Rep. LTV, Dallas, TX., 27 OCT 70 ** Transferred to VA-66/CVW-7, AG/3XX, USS Independence (CVA-62), 28 OCT 70; To VA-66, NAS Cecil Field, FL., 09 JUN 71 ~ S 1SO strike, 28 JUL 71 ** No data on strike.

E-285 157563 Navy acceptance from NPRO Rep. LTV, Dallas, TX., 18 NOV 70 ** Transferred to VA-12/CVW-7, AG/4XX, USS Independence (CVA-62), 19 NOV 70; To VA-12, NAS Cecil Field, FL., 18 JUN 71; To VA-12, USS Independence (CVA-62), 22 MAY 72 ** Transferred to VA-174/FRS, AD/4XX, NAS Cecil Field, FL., 04 OCT 72 ** Transferred to VA-37/CVW-3, AC/3XX, NAS Cecil Field, FL., 14 JAN 74; To VA-37, USS Saratoga (CV-60), 04 FEB 74; To VA-37, NAS Cecil Field, FL.,04 FEB 74 ~ S 1SO strike, 22 OCT 74 ** No data on strike.

E-286 157564 Navy acceptance from NPRO Rep. LTV, Dallas, TX., 30 OCT 70 ** Transferred to VA-66/CVW-7, NG/3XX, USS Independence (CVA-62), 20 JAN 71; To VA-66, NAS Cecil Field, FL., 19 JUN 71 ** Transferred to VA-83/CVW-17, AA/3XX, NAS Cecil Field, FL., 27 MAR 72; To VA-83, USS Forrestal (CVA-59), 25 MAY 72 ** Transferred to VA-12/CVW-7, AG/4XX, USS Independence (CV-62), 30 AUG 74; To VA-12, NAS Cecil Field, FL., 30 AUG 74; To VA-12, NAS Fallon, NV., 30 AUG 74; To VA-12, NAS Cecil Field, FL., 30 AUG 74; To VA-12, USS Independence (CV-62), 01 JUL 75 ** Transferred to VA-174/FRS, AD/4XX, NAS Cecil Field, FL., 02 JUL 75 ** Transferred to VA-12/CVW-7, AG/410, NAS Cecil Field, FL., 16 JUN 76; To VA-12, NAS Jacksonville, FL., 06 JUL 76; To VA-12, NAS Cecil Field, FL., 27 AUG 76; To VA-12, NAS Fallon, NV., 08 JUL 76; To VA-12, USS Independence (CV-62), 27 AUG 76; To VA-12, NAS Cecil Field, FL. 01 JAN 77; To VA-12, USS Independence (CV-62), 01 JAN 77; To VA-12, NAS Cecil Field, FL., 01 APR 77; To VA-12, USS Independence (CV-62), 01 JUL 77; To VA-12, NAS Cecil Field, FL., 09 AUG 77; To VA-12, Dwight D.Eisenhower (CVN-69), 09 AUG 77; To VA-12, NAS Jacksonville, FL., 30 MAR 78; To VA-12, NAS Cecil Field, FL.,19 MAY 78; To VA-12, Dwight D. Eisenhower (CVN-69), 24 JUN 78; To VA-12, NAS Cecil Field, FL., 24 JUN 78; To VA-12, Dwight D. Eisenhower (CVN-69), 24 JUN 78; To VA-12, NAS Cecil Field, FL., 24 JUN 78; To VA-12, Dwight D. Eisenhower (CVN-69), 24 JUN 78; To VA-12, NAS Cecil Field, FL., 05 NOV 79; To VA-12, Dwight D. Eisenhower (CVN-69), 17 NOV 79 ** Transferred to VA-146/CVW-9, NG/3XX, USS Constellation (CV-64), 27 JUL 80 ** Transferred to VA-147/CVW-9, NG/4XX, NAS Cubi Point, PI., 28 AUG 80; To VA-147, NAF Atsugi, JP., 02 SEP 80; To VA-147, NAS Cubi Point, PI., 03 SEP 80; To VA-147, USS Constellation (CV-64), 04 SEP 80; To VA-147, NAS LeMoore, CA., 23 SEP 80 ** Transferred to VA174/FRS, AD/4XX, NAS Cecil Field, FL., 31 OCT 80; To VA-174, NAS Jacksonville, FL., 06 FEB 81; To VA-174, NAS Cecil Field, FL., 06 FEB 81 ** Transferred to VA-82/CVW-8, AJ/3XX, USS Nimitz (CVN-68), 23 JUL 81; To VA-82, NAS Cecil Field, FL., 23 JUL 81; To VA-82, USS Carl Vinson (CVN-70), 23 JUL 81; To VA-82, NAS Cecil Field, FL., 23 JUL 81; To VA-82, USS Nimitz (CVN-68), 10 AUG 82; To VA-82, NAS Cecil Field, FL., 19 AUG 82; To VA-82, USS Nimitz (CVN-68), 19 AUG 82 ~ S 1SO strike, 11 FEB 83 ** No data on strike.

E-287 157565 Navy acceptance from NPRO Rep. LTV, Dallas, TX., 28 OCT 70 ** Transferred to VA-86/CVW-8, AJ/4XX, NAS Cecil Field, FL., 03 NOV 70 ** Transferred to VA-174/FRS, AD/4XX, NAS Cecil Field, FL., 25 JUN 71 ** Transferred to VA-37/CVW-3, AC/3XX, NAS Cecil Field, FL., 04 JUN 73 ~ S 1SO strike, 14 DEC 73 ** No data on strike.

E-288 157566 Navy acceptance from NPRO Rep. LTV, Dallas, TX., 11 NOV 70 ** Transferred to VA-66/CVW-7, AG/3XX, USS Independence (CVA-62), 14 NOV 70; To VA-66, NAS Cecil Field, FL., 11 JUN 71 ** Transferred to VA-174/FRS, AD/4XX, NAS Cecil Field, FL., 25 AUG 71 ** Transferred to VA-66/CVW-7, AG/3XX, NAS Cecil Field, FL., 25 AUG 71 ** Transferred to VA-174/FRS, AD/4XX, NAS Cecil Field, FL., 25 AUG 71 ** Transferred to VA-66/CVW-7, AG/3XX, USS Independence (CVA-62), 05 OCT 72; To VA-66, NAS CecilField, FL., 13 APR 73; To VA-66, USS Independence (CV-62), 16 MAY 74; To VA-66, NAS Cecil Field, FL., 04 FEB 75; To VA-66, USS Independence (CV-62), 04 SEP 75; To VA-66, NAS Cecil Field, FL., 16 FEB 76; To VA-66, NAS Fallon, NV., 08 JUL 76; To VA-66, USS Independence (CV-62), 08 JUL 76; To VA-66, NAS Cecil Field, FL., 08 JUL 76; To VA-66, USS Independence (CV-62), 08 JUL 76; To VA-66, NAS Cecil Field, FL., 08 JUL 76; To VA-66,

USS Independence (CV-62), 08 JUL 76; To VA-66, NAS Cecil Field, FL., 24 MAY 77; To VA-66, USS Independence (CV-62), 01 JUL 77; To VA-66, NAS Cecil Field, FL., 09 AUG 77; To VA-66, USS Dwight D. Eisenhower (CVN-69), 09 AUG 77; To VA-66, NAS Cecil Field, FL., 09 AUG 77; To VA-66, NAS Jacksonville, FL., 27 JUN 78; To VA-66, USS Dwight D. Eisenhower (CVN-69), 16 AUG 78; To VA-66, NAS Cecil Field, FL., 20 OCT 78; To VA-66, USS Dwight D. Eisenhower (CVN-69), 20 OCT 78; To VA-66, NAS Cecil Field, FL., 20 OCT 78; To VA-66, USS Dwight D. Eisenhower (CVN-69), 20 OCT 78; To VA-66, NAS Cecil Field, FL., 20 OCT 78; To VA-66, USS Dwight D. Eisenhower (CVN-69), 18 MAR 80; To VA-66, NAS Cecil Field, FL., 13 FEB 81; To VA-66, NAS Jacksonville, FL., 17 FEB 81; To VA-66, NAS Cecil Field, FL., 01 APR 81; To VA-66, USS Dwight D. Eisenhower (CVN-69), 28 MAY 81; To VA-66, NAS Cecil Field, FL., 28 MAY 81; To VA-66, USS Dwight D. Eisenhower (CVN-69), 28 MAY 81; To VA-66, NAS Cecil Field, FL., 28 MAY 81; To VA-66, USS Dwight D. Eisenhower (CVN-69), 09 DEC 81; To VA-66, NAS Cecil Field, FL., 02 AUG 82; To VA-66, NAS Jacksonville, FL., 29 DEC 82; To VA-66, NAS Cecil Field, FL., 29 DEC 82; To VA-66, NAS Jacksonville, FL., 04 JAN 83 ** Transferred to VA-87/CVW-6, AE/4XX, NAS Cecil Field, FL., 15 APR 83; To VA-87, USS Independence (CV-62), 15 APR 83; To VA-87, NAS Cecil Field, FL., 15 APR 83; To VA-87, USS Independence (CV-62), 15 APR 83; To VA-87, NAS Cecil Field, FL., 16 APR 83; To VA-87, USS Independence (CV-62), 29 SEP 83; To VA-87, NAS Cecil Field, FL., 02 MAY 84; To VA-87, USS Independence (CV-62), 18 JUL 84; To VA-87, NAS Jacksonville, FL., 30 JUL 84; To VA-87, USS Independence (CV-62), 06 AUG 84; To VA-87, NAS Jacksonville, FL., 14 AUG 84; To VA-87, USS Independence (CV-62), 20 AUG 84; To VA-87, NAS Cecil Field, FL., 09 SEP 84; To VA-87, USS Independence (CV-62), 07 OCT 84 ** Transferred to VA-37/CVW-6, AE/3XX, NAS Cecil Field, FL., 15 OCT 84 ** Transferred to VA-81/CVW-17, AA/4XX, NAS Cecil Field, FL., 13 NOV 84; To VA-81, USS Saratoga (CV-60), 12 MAR 85; To VA-81, NAS Cecil Field, FL., 12 MAR 85; To VA-81, USS Saratoga (CV-60), 12 MAR 85; To VA-81, NAS Jacksonville, FL., 28 MAR 86; To VA-81, NAS Cecil Field, FL., 27 MAY 86; To VA-81, NAS Jacksonville, FL., 11 JUL 86 ** Transferred to VA-174/FRS, AD/400, NAS Cecil Field, FL., 17 JUL 86 ** End of flight record card ** Transferred to AMARC, Davis Monthan AFB; Tucson, AZ., assigned park code 6A0236; 26 AUG 87 ** 5922.3 flight hours ** TF41A2B engine S/N 141355 ** Storage location 210527 ** Aircraft deleted fom inventory and released to DRMO for disposition, 04 MAY 06 ** At AMARG, Davis Monthan AFB;Tucson, AZ., 15 JUN 07.

E-289 157567 Navy acceptance from NPRO Rep. LTV, Dallas, TX., 28 OCT 70 ** Transferred to VA-86/CVW-8, AJ/4XX, NAS Cecil Field, FL., 30 OCT 70; To VA-86, USS America (CVA-66), 12 MAY 71 ** Transferred to VA-12/CVW-7, AG/4XX, NAS Cecil Field, FL., 08 JUN 71; To VA-12, USS Independence (CVA-62), 25 MAY 72 ** Transferred to VA-174/FRS, AD/4XX, NAS Cecil Field, FL., 18 OCT 72 ** Transferred to VA-105/CVW-3, AC/406, NAS Cecil Field, FL., 07 AUG 73; To VA-105, USS Saratoga (CV-60), 06 MAY 74; To VA-105, NAS Cecil Field, FL., 06 MAY 74; To VA-105, USS Saratoga (CV-60), 27 SEP 74; To VA-105, NAS Cecil Field, FL., 27 SEP 74; To VA-105, USS Saratoga (CV-60), 27 SEP 74; To VA-105, NAS Cecil Field, FL., 27 SEP 74; To VA-105, MCAS Yuma, AZ., 30 AUG 75; To VA-105, NAS Jacksonville, FL., 08 SEP 75; To VA-105, MCAS Yuma, AZ., 08 SEP 75; To VA-105, NAS Jacksonville, FL., 09 SEP 75; To VA-105, USS Saratoga (CV-60), 10 NOV 75; To VA-105, NAS Cecil Field, FL., 10 NOV 75; To VA-105, USS Saratoga (CV-60), 07 OCT 76; To VA-105, NAS Cecil Field, FL., 07 OCT 76; To VA-105, USS Saratoga (CV-60), 07 OCT 76; To VA-105, NAS Cecil Field, FL., 16 JUL 77; To VA-105, NAS Jacksonville, FL.,26 APR 78; To VA-105, USS Saratoga (CV-60), 21 JUN 78; To VA-105, NAS Cecil Field, FL., 22 JUN 78; To VA-105, USS Saratoga (CV-60), 20 SEP 78; To VA-105, NAS Cecil Field, FL., 26 SEP 78; To VA-105, MCAS Yuma, AZ., 26 SEP 78; To VA-105, NAS Cecil Field, FL., 26 SEP 78 ** Transferred to VA-174/FRS, AD/4XX, NAS Cecil Field, FL., 28 AUG 79 ** Transferred to VA-81/CVW-17, AA/4XX, NAS Cecil Field, FL., 14 AUG 80; To VA-81, USS Forrestal (CV-59), 14 AUG 80; To VA-81, NAS Cecil Field, FL., 14 AUG 80; To

VA-81, USS Forrestal (CV-59), 12 FEB 81; To VA-81, NAS Cecil Field, FL., 12 FEB 81; To VA-81, NAS Fallon, NV., 09 NOV 81; To VA-81, USS Forrestal (CV-59), 09 NOV 81; To VA-81, NAS Cecil Field, FL., 24 APR 82; To VA-81, USS Forrestal (CV-59), 24 APR 82; To VA-81, NAS Jacksonville, FL., 29 NOV 82; To VA-81, NAS Cecil Field, FL., 31 JAN 83; To VA-81, NAS Fallon, NV., 20 JUN 83; To VA-81, NAS Cecil Field, FL., 20 JUN 83; To VA-81, USS Saratoga (CV-60), 20 JUN 83; To VA-81, NAS Cecil Field, FL., 12 NOV 83; To VA-81, USS Saratoga (CV-60), 23 MAR 84; To VA-81, NAS Cecil Field, FL., 23 MAR 84; To VA-81, Jacksonville, FL., 29 OCT 84; To VA-81, NAS Cecil Field, FL., 29 OCT 84; To VA-81, Jacksonville, FL., 05 NOV 84; To VA-81, NAS Cecil Field, FL., 27 FEB 85; To VA-81, USS Saratoga (CV-60), 01 MAY 85; To VA-81, NAS Cecil Field, FL.,10 MAY 85; To VA-81, USS Saratoga (CV-60), 10 MAY 85 ** Transferred to VA-15/CVW-6, AE/3XX, NAS Cecil Field, FL., 14 AUG 85 ** Transferred to VA-12/CVW-6, AE/3XX, NAS Cecil Field, FL., 12 OCT 85 ** Transferred to VA-174/ FRS, AD/4XX, NAS Cecil Field, FL., 15 SEP 86 ** Transferred to US Army, 13 AUG 87 thru 14 AUG 87 ** End of flight record card ** Transferred to VA-174/FRS, AD/4XX, NAS Cecil Field, FL., date unknown ** Transferred to AMARC, Davis Monthan AFB; Tucson, AZ., assigned park code 6A0414, 22 JUL 92 ** 6648.2 flight hours ** Storage location 210832 ** At AMARG, Davis Monthan AFB; Tucson, AZ., Seat Removed, 15 JUN 07.

E-290 157568 Navy acceptance from NPRO Rep. LTV, Dallas, TX., 28 OCT 70 ** Transferred to VA-66/CVW-7, AG/3XX, USS Independence (CVA-62), 29 OCT 70; To VA-66, NAS Cecil Field, FL., 08 JUN 71; To VA-66, USS Independence (CVA-62), 14 OCT 71 ** Transferred to VA-174/FRS, AD/4XX, NAS Cecil Field, FL., 18 OCT 72 ** Transferred to VA-105/CVW-3, AC/4XX, NAS Cecil Field, FL., 18 JUN 73; To VA-105, USS Saratoga (CV-60), 05 AUG 74; To VA-105, NAS Cecil Field, FL., 05 AUG 74; To VA-105, USS Saratoga (CV-60), 05 AUG 74; To VA-105, NAS Cecil Field, FL., 05 AUG 74; To VA-105, MCAS Yuma, AZ., 24 JUL 75; To VA-105, NAS Jacksonville, FL., 26 AUG 75; To VA-105, USS Saratoga (CV-60), 22 OCT 75; To VA-105, NAS Cecil Field, FL., 10 NOV 75; To VA-105, USS Saratoga (CV-60), 22 OCT 75; To VA-105, NAS Cecil Field, FL., 17 NOV 76; To VA-105, USS Saratoga (CV-60), 17 NOV 76; To VA-105, NAS Cecil Field, FL., 16 JUL 77; To VA-105, NAS Jacksonville, FL., 15 MAY 78; To VA-105, USS Saratoga (CV-60), 16 MAY 78; To VA-105, NAS Cecil Field, FL., 07 JUN 78; To VA-105, USS Saratoga (CV-60), 12 AUG 78; To VA-105, NAS Cecil Field, FL., 06 JAN 79 ** Transferred to VA-174/FRS, AD/4XX, NAS Cecil Field, FL., 06 AUG 79; To VA-174, NAS Jacksonville, FL., 16 MAY 80; To VA-174, NAS Cecil Field, FL., 16 MAY 80; To VA-174, NAS Jacksonville, FL., 20 MAY 80; To VA-174, NAS Cecil Field, FL., 17 JUL 80 ** Transferred to VA-12/CVW-7, AG/403, USS Dwight D. Eisenhower (CVN-69), 15 JAN 81, Paint white on dark and medium gray, modex black; To VA-12, NAS Cecil Field, FL., 15 NOV 81; To VA-12, USS Dwight D. Eisenhower (CVN-69), 15 NOV 82; To VA-12, NAS Cecil Field, FL., 02 AUG 82; To VA-12, NAS Jacksonville, FL., 16 SEP 82; To VA-12, NAS Cecil Field, FL., 17 OCT 82; To VA-12, NAS Jacksonville, FL., 30 OCT 82; To VA-12, NAS Cecil Field, FL., 03 NOV 82; To VA-12, USS Dwight D. Eisenhower (CVN-69), 03 FEB 83; To VA-12, NAS Cecil Field, FL., 20 SEP 73; To VA-12, USS Dwight D. Eisenhower (CVN-69), 27 SEP 83; To VA-12, NAS Cecil Field, FL., 29 JUN 84; To VA-12, NAS Jacksonville, FL., 01 AUG 84; To VA-12, NAS Cecil Field, FL., 27 AUG 84; To VA-12, USS Dwight D. Eisenhower (CVN-69), 27 AUG 84; To VA-12, NAS Jacksonville, FL., 03 JAN 85 ** Transferred to VA-81/CVW-17, AA/4XX, NAS Cecil Field, FL., 03 JAN 85; To VA-81, USS Saratoga (CV-60), 04 MAR 85; To VA-81, NAS Cecil Field, FL., 04 MAR 85; To VA-81, USS Saratoga (CV-69), 04 MAR 85; To VA-81, NAS Cecil Field, FL., 03 APR 86 ** Transferred to NARF, NAS Jacksonville, FL., 17 APR 86 ** End of flight record card.

E-291 157569 Navy acceptance from NPRO Rep. LTV, Dallas, TX., 27 OCT 70 ** Transferred to VA-66/CVW-7, AG/3XX, USS Independence (CVA-62), 29 OCT 70; To VA-66, NAS Cecil Field, FL. 28 MAY 71; To VA-66, USS Independence (CVA-62), 06 MAR 72 ** Transferred to VA-12/CVW-7, AG/4XX, USS Independence (CVA-62), 11 OCT 72 ** Transferred to VA-174/FRS, AD/4XX, NAS Cecil

Field, FL., 02 MAY 73 ** Transferred to VA-82/CVW-8, AJ/3XX, NAS Cecil Field, FL., 20 JAN 75; To VA-82, USS Nimitz (CVN-68), 20 JAN 75; To VA-82, NAS Cecil Field, FL., 27 JUL 75; To VA-82, NAS Roosevelt Roads, PR., 27 JUL 75; To VA-82, NAS Cecil Field, FL., 27 JUL 75; To VA-82, USS Nimitz (CVN-68), 27 JUL 75; To VA-82, NAS Cecil Field, FL., 27 JUL 75; To VA-82, USS Nimitz (CVN-68), 27 JUL 75 ** Transferred to VA-174/FRS, AD/4XX, NAS Cecil Field, FL., 10 JUN 76; To VA-174, NAS Jacksonville, FL., 19 JUL 76; To VA-174, NAS Cecil Field, FL., 28 JUL 76 ** Transferred to VA-105/ CVW-3, AC/4XX, NAS Cecil Field, FL., 06 DEC 76; To VA-105, USS Saratoga (CV-60), 06 DEC 76; To VA-105, NAS Cecil Field, FL., 06 DEC 76; To VA-105, USS Saratoga (CV-60), 06 DEC 76; To VA-105, NAS Cecil Field, FL., 16 JUL 77; To VA-105, USS Saratoga (CV-60),05 MAY 78; To VA-105, NAS Jacksonville, FL., 11 AUG 78; To VA-105, NAS Cecil Field, FL., 08 SEP 78; To VA-105, USS Saratoga (CV-60), 19 SEP 78; To VA-105, NAS Cecil Field, FL., 19 SEP 78; To VA-105, MCAS Yuma, AZ., 19 SEP 78; To VA-105, NAS Cecil Field, FL., 22 OCT 79; To VA-105, USS Saratoga (CV-60), 22 OCT 79; To VA-105, NAS Cecil Field, FL., 22 OCT 79; To VA-105, USS Saratoga (CV-60), 20 MAR 80; To VA-105, NAS Cecil Field, FL., 02 DEC 80; To VA-105, NAS Fallon, NV., 02 DEC 80; To VA-105, NAS Cecil Field, FL., 23 JUL 81; To VA-105, USS John F. Kennedy (CV-67), 10 AUG 81; To VA-105, NAS Cecil Field, FL., 30 SEP 81; To VA-105, USS John F. Kennedy (CV-67), 06 OCT 81; To VA-105, NAS Cecil Field, FL., 23 OCT 81 ** Transferred to VA-37/CVW-15, NL/3XX, NAS Cecil Field, FL., 18 AUG 82; To VA-37, USS Carl Vinson (CVN-70), 18 AUG 82; To VA-37, NAS Cecil Field, FL., 18 AUG 82 ** Transferred to VA-81/CVW-17, AA/4XX, NAS Jacksonville, FL., 24 MAR 83; To VA-81, NAS Cecil Field, FL., 31 MAY 83; To VA-81, NAS Dallas, TX., 01 JUN 83; To VA-81, NAS Fallon, NV., 03 JUN 83; To VA-81, NAS Dallas, TX., 02 SEP 83; To VA-81, USS Saratoga (CV-60), 02 SEP 83 ** Transferred to VA-86/CVW-8, AJ/4XX, NAS Cecil Field, FL., 04 NOV 83; To VA-86, NAS Roosevelt Roads, PR., 11 AUG 84; To VA-86, NAS Cecil Field, FL., 10 SEP 84; To VA-86, USS Nimitz (CVN-68), 29 OCT 84; To VA-86, NAS Cecil field, FL., 05 JAN 85 ** Transferred to VA-82/CVW-8, AJ/3XX, USS Nimitz (CVN-68), 05 FEB 85 ** Transferred to VA-105/CVW-6, AE/4XX, NAS Cecil Field, FL., 28 MAR 85; To VA-105, USS Forrestal (CV-59), 11 JUL 85; To VA-105, NAS Cecil Field, FL., 10 AUG 85; To VA-105, USS Forrestal (CV-59), 24 JAN 86; NAS Cecil Field, FL., 24 JAN 86; To VA-105, NAS Jacksonville, FL., 05 JAN 87; To VA-105, NAS Cecil Field, FL., 29 JUN 87; To NNARF, NAS Jacksonville, FL., 30 JUN 87 ** To VA-105, USS Forrestal (CV-59), 27 JUL 87 thru 24 AUG 87 ** End of flight record card ** Transferred to VA-72/CVW-7, AA/4XX , USS Dwight D. Eisenhower (CVN-69), Date unknown; To VA-72, NAS Cecil Field, FL., date unknown ** Transferred to AMARC, Davis Monthan AFB;Tucson, AZ., assigned park code 6A0354, with FLIR, 17 MAY 90 ** 6222.2 flight hours TF41A402D engine S/N 142624 ** Storage location 111206 ** At AMARG, Davis Monthan AFB; Tucson, AZ., 15 JUN 07.

E-292 157570 Navy acceptance from NPRO Rep. LTV, Dallas, TX., 03 DEC 70 ** Transferred to VA-12/CVW-7, AG/4XX, USS Independence (CVA-62), 04 DEC 70; To VA-12, NAS Cecil Field, FL., 21 JUN 71; To VA-12, USS Independence (CVA-62), 16 MAR 72 ** Transferred to VA-66/CVW-7, AG/300, AG/307, & AG/310, USS Independence (CVA-62), 02 OCT 72; To VA-66, NAS Cecil Field, FL. 18 JUN 73; To VA-66, USS Independence (CV-62), 12 APR 74; To VA-66, NAS Cecil Field, FL., 12 APR 74; To VA-66, USS Independence (CV-62),04 SEP 75; To VA-66, NAS Cecil Field, FL., 13 SEP 75; To VA-66, NAS Jacksonville, FL., 27 JUL 76; To VA-66, NAS Cecil Field, FL., 17 AUG 76; To VA-66, NAS Fallon, NV., 17 AUG 76; To VA-66, USS Independence (CV-62), 17 AUG 76; To VA-66, NAS Cecil Field, FL., 17 AUG 76; To VA-66, USS Independence (CV-62), 17 AUG 76; To VA-66, NAS Cecil Field, FL., 17 AUG 76; To VA-66, USS Independence (CV-62), 17 AUG 76; To VA-66, NAS Cecil Field, FL., 09 AUG 77; To VA-66, Dwight D. Eisenhower (CVN-69), 09 AUG 77; To VA-66, NAS Cecil Field, FL., 09 AUG 77; To VA-66, NAS Jacksonville, FL., 17 JUL 78; To VA-66, Dwight D. Eisenhower (CVN-69), 17 JUL 78; To VA-66, NAS Cecil Field, FL., 13 SEP 78; To VA-66, Dwight D. Eisenhower (CVN-69), 13 SEP 78; To VA-66, Dwight D. Eisenhower

(CVN-69), 13 SEP 78; To VA-66, NAS Cecil Field, FL., 08 DEC 79; To VA-66, Dwight D. Eisenhower (CVN-69), 21 DEC 79; To VA-66, NAS Cecil Field, FL., 21 DEC 79; To VA-66, Dwight D. Eisenhower (CVN-69), 21 MAR 80; To VA-66, NAS Cecil Field, FL., 07 APR 80; To VA-66, NAS Jacksonville, FL., 23 APR 81; To VA-66, Dwight D. Eisenhower (CVN-69), 27 APR 81; To VA-66, NAS Cecil Field, FL., 27 APR 81; To VA-66, Dwight D. Eisenhower (CVN-69), 27 APR 81; To VA-66, NAS Cecil Field, FL., 19 JUN 81; To VA-66, Dwight D. Eisenhower (CVN-69), 19 JUN 81; To VA-66, NAS Cecil Field, FL., 19 JUN 81; To VA-66, NAS Jacksonville, FL., 13 DEC 82; To VA-66, NAS Cecil Field, FL., 13 DEC 82; To VA-66, NAS Jacksonville, FL., 14 DEC 82 ** Transferred to VA-87/CVW-6, AE/4XX, NAS Cecil Field, FL., 22 MAR 83; To VA-87, USS Independence (CV-62), 22 MAR 83; To VA-87, NAS Cecil Field, FL., 22 MAR 83; To VA-87, USS Independence (CV-62), 22 MAR 83; To VA-87, NAS Cecil Field, FL., 23 SEP 83; To VA-87, USS Independence (CV-62), 03 OCT 83; To VA-87, NAS Cecil Field, FL., 04 JAN 84; To VA-87, USS Independence (CV-62), 19 JUL 84; To VA-87, NAS Cecil Field, FL., 19 JUL 84; To VA-87, USS Independence (CV-62), 19 JUL 84 ** Transferred to VA-66/CVW-7, AG/3XX, NAS Cecil Field, FL., 01 OCT 84; To VA-66, USS Dwiight D. Eisenhower (CVN-69), 27 JUN 85; To VA-66, NAS Cecil Field, FL., 04 OCT 85; To VA-66, NAS Jacksonville, FL., 22 JAN 86; To VA-66, NAS Cecil Field, FL., 04 FEB 86; To VA-66, NAS Jacksonville, FL., 05 FEB 86; To VA-66, NAS Cecil Field, FL., 08 FEB 86; To VA-66/CVW-3, AC/301, USS John F. Kennedy (CV-67), 10 MAR 86 ** End of flight record card ** Transferred to AMARC, Davis Monthan AFB;Tucson, AZ., assigned park code 6A0188, 15 AUG 86 ** 5929.6 flight hours ** TF41A2B engine S/N 0142609 ** Storage location 210813 ** At AMARG, Davis Monthan AFB; Tucson, AZ., 15 JUN 07.

E-293 157571 Navy acceptance from NPRO Rep. LTV, Dallas, TX., 16 NOV 70 ** Transferred to VA-66/CVW-7, AG/314, USS Independence (CVA-62), 17 NOV 70; To VA-66, NAS Cecil Field, FL., 28 JUN 71; To VA-66, USS Independence (CVA-62), 04 JAN 72 ** Transferred to VA-12/CVW-7, AG/4XX, USS Independence (CVA-62), 03 OCT 72 ** Transferred to VA-174/FRS, AD/4XX, NAS Cecil Field, FL., 30 APR 73 ** Transferred to VA-82/CVW-8, AJ/3XX, NAS Cecil Field, FL., 11 DEC 74; To VA-82, USS Nimitz (CVN-68), 08 JAN 75; To VA-82, NAS Cecil Field, FL., 27 JUL 75; To VA-82, NAS Roosevelt Roads, PR., 27 JUL 75; To VA-82, NAS Cecil Field, FL., 27 JUL 75; To VA-82, Jacksonville, FL., 02 FEB 76; To VA-82, NAS Cecil Field, FL., 19 MAR 76; To VA-82, USS Nimitz (CVN-68), 19 MAR 76; To VA-82, NAS Cecil Field, FL., 19 MAR 76; To VA-82, USS Nimitz (CVN-68), 15 FEB 77; To VA-82, NAS Cecil Field, FL., 22 FEB 77; To VA-82, USS Nimitz (CVN-68), 20 JUL 77; To VA-82, NAS Cecil Field, FL., 20 JUL 77 ** Transferred to VA-81/CVW-17, AA/4XX, USS Forrestal (CV-59), 09 JUL 78; To VA-81, NAS Jacksonville, FL., 01 NOV 78; To VA-81, NAS Cecil Field, FL., 19 DEC 78 ** Transferred to VA-83/CVW-17, AA/3XX, USS Forrestal (CV-59), 22 FEB 79; To VA-83, NAS Cecil Field, FL., 15 SEP 79; To VA-83, USS Forrestal (CV-59), 15 SEP 79 ** Transferred to VA-174/FRS, AD/4XX, NAS Cecil Field, FL., 16 NOV 79 ** Transferred to VA-37/CVW-3, AC/3XX, NAS Cecil Field, FL., 27 FEB 80; To VA-37, USS Saratoga (CV-60), 27 FEB 80; To VA-37, NAS Cecil Field, FL., 28 AUG 80; To VA-37, NAS Jacksonville, FL., 10 NOV 80; To VA-37, NAS Cecil Field, FL., 27 JAN 81; To VA-37, NAS Fallon, NV., 27 JAN 81; To VA-37, NAS Cecil Field, FL., 27 JAN 81; To VA-37, USS John F. Kennedy (CV-67), 27 JAN 81; To VA-37, NAS Cecil Field, FL., 27 JAN 81; To VA-37, USS John F. Kennedy (CV-67), 27 JAN 81; To VA-37, NAS Cecil Field, FL., 27 JAN 81; To VA-37/CVW-15, NL/3XX, USS Carl Vinson (CVN-70), 14 DEC 82; To VA-37, NARF, NAS Jacksonville, FL., 12 AUG 82 ** To VA-37, NAS Cecil Field, FL., 14 DEC 82; To VA-37, NAS Jacksonville, FL., 04 APR 83; To VA-37/CVW-15, NL/3XX, USS Carl Vinson (CVN-70), 15 JUN 83; To VA-37, NAS Dallas, TX., 27 SEP 83 ** Transferred to VA-86/CVW-8, AJ/4XX, NAS Cecil Field, FL., 27 SEP 87 ** Transferred to VA-66/CVW-7, AG/3XX, USS Dwight D. Eisenhower (CVN-69), 12 MAR 84; To VA-66, NAS Cecil Field, FL., 12 MAR 84; To VA-66, USS Dwight D. Eisenhower (CVN-69), 12 MAR 84; To VA-66, NAS Cecil Field, FL., 24 SEP 84; To VA-66, USS Dwight D. Eisenhower (CVN-69), 24 SEP 84; To VA-66, NAS Cecil Field, FL., 25 SEP 84; To VA-66, NAS Jacksonville, FL., 24 JUN 85; To VA-66, NAS Cecil Field, FL., 24 JUN 85; To VA-66, NAS Jacksonville, FL., 11 JUL 85; To VA-66, NAS Cecil Field, FL., 11 JUL 85; To VA-66, NARF, NAS Jacksonville, FL., 22 NOV 85 ** To VA-66, NAS Jacksonville, FL., 25 NOV 85 ** Transferred to VA-105/CVW-6, AE/4XX, NAS Cecil Field, FL.,25 NOV 85; To VA-105, USS Forrestal (CV-59), 26 MAR 86; To VA-105, NAS Cecil Field, FL., 26 MAR 86 ** Transferred to VA-82/CVW-8, AJ/3XX, NAS Cecil Field, FL., 15 MAY 86; To VA-82, USS Nimitz (CV-68), 01 AUG 86; To VA-82, NAS Cecil Field, FL., 10 OCT 86; To VA-82, NAS Jacksonville, FL., 23 OCT 86; To VA-82, NAS Cecil Field, FL., 24 OCT 86; To VA-82, USS Nimitz (CV-68), 17 NOV 86; To VA-82, NAS Cecil Field, FL., 17 NOV 86 ** Transferred to VA-72/CVW-7, AG/4XX, NAS Cecil Field, FL., 15 SEP 87 ** End of flight record card ** Transferred to AMARC, Davis Monthan AFB; Tucson, AZ., assigned park code 6A0342, with FLIR. 17 APR 90 ** 6760.8 flight hours ** TF41A402D engine S/N 141225 ** Storage location 111511 ** At AMARG, Davis Monthan AFB; Tucson, AZ., 15 JUN 07.

E-294 157572 Navy acceptance from NPRO Rep. LTV, Dallas, TX., 20 NOV 70 ** Transferred to VA-66/CVW-7, AG/3XX, USS Independence (CVA-62), 21 NOV 70; To VA-66, NAS Cecil Field, FL., 27 JUN 71 ** Transferred to VA-83/CVW-17, AA/3XX, NAS Cecil Field, FL., 27 MAR 72; To VA-83, USS Forrestal (CV-59), 21 APR 72; To VA-83, NAS Cecil Field, FL, 30 OCT 74; To VA-83, USS Forrestal (CVA-59), 09 DEC 74; To VA-83, NAS Cecil Field, FL, 09 DEC 74; To VA-83, USS Forrestal (CV-59), 09 DEC 74; To VA-83, NAS Cecil Field, FL, 01 SEP 75; To VA-83, NAS Jacksonville, FL., 31 DEC 75; To VA-83, NAS Cecil Field, FL, 13 DEC 76; To VA-83, USS Forrestal (CV-59), 13 FEB 76; To VA-83, NAS Cecil Field, FL, 13 FEB 76; To VA-83, USS Forrestal (CV-59), 13 FEB 76; To VA-83, NAS Cecil Field, FL, 13 FEB 76; To VA-83, NAS Roosevelt Roads, PR., 13 FEB 76; USS Forrestal (CV-59), To VA-83, NAS Cecil Field, FL, 13 FEB 76 ~ S 1SO strike, 02 JUN 77 ** No data on strike.

E-295 157573 Navy acceptance from NPRO Rep. LTV, Dallas, TX., 16 SEP 70 ** Transferred to VA-12/CVW-7, AG/4XX, USS Independence (CVA-62), 17 DEC 70; To VA-12, NAS Cecil Field, FL., 18 JUN 71; To VA-12, USS Independence (CVA-62), 05 APR 72 ** Transferred to VA-66/CVW-7, AG/3XX, USS Independence (CVA-62), 10 OCT 72 ** Transferred to VA-174/FRS, AD/4XX, NAS Cecil Field, FL., 10 APR 74 ** Transferred to VA-86/CVW-8, AJ/406, NAS Cecil Field, FL., 31 JAN 75; To VA-86, USS Nimitz (CVN-68), 31 JAN 75; To VA-86, NAS Cecil Field, FL., 31 JAN 75; To VA-86, NAS Roosevelt Roads, PR., 31 JAN 75; To VA-86, NAS Cecil Field, FL., 31 JAN 75; To VA-86, USS Nimitz (CVN-68), 31 JAN 75; To VA-86, NAS Cecil Field, FL., 31 JAN 75; To VA-86, USS Nimitz (CVN-68), 31 JAN 75; To VA-86, NAS Cecil Field, FL., 30 JUN 75; To VA-86, NAS Roosevelt Roads, PR., 30 JUN 75; To VA-86, USS Nimitz (CVN-68), 19 JUL 77; To VA-86, NAS Cecil Field, FL., 19 JUL 77; To VA-86, USS Nimitz (CVN-68), 19 JUL 77; To VA-86, NAS Cecil Field, FL., 18 JAN 78; To VA-86, NAS Jacksonville, FL., 07 FEB 78; To VA-86, NAS Cecil Field, FL., 22 MAR 78; To VA-86, NAS Roosevelt Roads, PR., 22 MAR 78; To VA-86, NAS Cecil Field, FL., 22 MAR 78; To VA-86, NAS Jacksonville, FL., 10 JAN 79; To VA-86, USS Nimitz (CVN-68), 09 MAR 79; To VA-86, NAS Cecil Field, FL., 09 MAR 79; To VA-86, USS Nimitz (CVN-68), 10 JUN 80; To VA-86, NAS Cecil Field, FL., 17 JUN 80; To VA-86, USS Nimitz (CVN-68), 17 JUN 80; To VA-86, NAS Cecil Field, FL., 17 JUN 80; To VA-86, USS Nimitz (CVN-68), 17 JUN 80 ** Transferred to VA-174/FRS, AD/416, NAS Cecil Field, FL., 10 JUL 81; To VA-174, NAS Jacksonville, FL., 21 SEP 81; To VA-174, NAS Cecil Field, FL, 11 NOV 81; To VA-174, NAS Jacksonville, FL., 30 NOV 83; To VA-174, NAS Cecil Field, FL, 26 MAR 84; To VA-174, NAS Jacksonville, FL., 07 APR 86; To VA-174, NAS Cecil Field, FL, 11 APR 86; To VA-174, NAS Jacksonville, FL., 13 JUN 86; To VA-174, NAS Cecil Field, FL, 24 JUN 86 ** End of flight record card ** Transferred to AMARC, Davis Monthan AFB; Tucson, AZ., assigned park code 6A0211, 24 DEC 86 ** 5425.7 flight hours ** TF41A2B engine S/N 142596 ** Storage location 210826 ** Under GSA control ** At AMARG, Davis Monthan AFB; Tucson, AZ., 15 JUN 07.

E-296 157574 Navy acceptance from NPRO Rep. LTV, Dallas, TX., 30 NOV 70 ** Transferred to VA-12/CVW-7, AG/4XX, USS Independence (CVA-62), 01 DEC 70; To VA-12, NAS Cecil Field, FL., 10 JUN 71; To VA-12, USS Independence (CVA-62), 27 JUN 72; To VA-12, NAS Cecil Field, FL., 15 FEB 73; To VA-12, USS Independence (CV-62), 13 MAR 74; To VA-12, NAS Cecil Field, FL., 13 MAR 74; To VA-12, NAS Fallon, NV., 13 MAR 74; To VA-12, NAS Jacksonville, FL., 02 JUN 75; To VA-12, NAS Cecil Field, FL., 19 JUN 75; To VA-12, USS Independence (CV-62), 24 JUL 75; To VA-12, NAS Cecil Field, FL., 14 SEP 75; To VA-12, NAS Fallon, NV., 30 JUN 76; To VA-12, USS Independence (CV-62), 01 NOV 76; To VA-12, NAS Cecil Field, FL., 01 NOV 76; To VA-12, USS Independence (CV-62), 01 NOV 76; To VA-12, NAS Cecil Field, FL., 01 NOV 76; To VA-12, USS Independence (CVA-62), 01 FEB 77; To VA-12, NAS Cecil Field, FL., 09 AUG 77; To VA-12, USS Dwight D. Eisenhower (CVN-69), 09 AUG 77; To VA-12, NAS Cecil Field, FL., 15 MAR 78; To VA-12, NAS Jacksonville, FL., 16 MAR 78; To VA-12, NAS Cecil Field, FL., 03 JUN 78; To VA-12, USS Dwight D. Eisenhower (CVN-69), 03 JUN 78; To VA-12, NAS Cecil Field, FL., 03 JUN 78; To VA-12, USS Dwight D. Eisenhower (CVN-69), 03 JUN 78; To VA-12, NAS Cecil Field, FL., 03 JUN 78; To VA-12, USS Dwight D. Eisenhower (CVN-69), 03 JUN 78 ** Transferred to VA-174/FRS, AD/4XX, NAS Cecil Field, FL., 11 APR 80; To VA-174, NAS Jacksonville, FL., 08 JUL 80; To VA-174, NAS Cecil Field, FL., 15 AUG 80 ~ S 1SO strike, 10 DEC 80 ** Pilot ejected after experiencing a hook failure and aircraft went over the side of USS Lexington (AVT-16) into the Gulf of Mexico.

E-297 157575 Navy acceptance from NPRO Rep. LTV, Dallas, TX., 18 NOV 70 ** Transferred to VA-66/CVW-7, AG/3XX, USS Independence (CVA-62), 21 NOV 70; To VA-66, NAS Cecil Field, FL., 19 JUN 71; To VA-66, USS Independence (CVA-62), 22 MAY 72; ** Transferred to VA-174/FRS, AD/4XX, NAS Cecil Field, FL., 18 APR 73 ** Transferred to VA-66/CVW-7, AG/3XX, NAS Cecil Field, FL., 26 JUN 75; To VA-66, USS Independence (CV-62), 04 SEP 75; To VA-66, NAS Cecil Field, FL., 13 SEP 75; To VA-66, NAS Jacksonville, FL., 04 JUN 76; To VA-66, NAS Cecil Field, FL., 02 AUG 76; To VA-66, NAS Fallon, NV., 31 AUG 76; To VA-66, USS Independence (CV-62), 31 AUG 76; To VA-66, NAS Cecil Field, FL., 31 AUG 76; To VA-66, USS Independence (CV-62), 31 AUG 76; To VA-66, NAS Cecil Field, FL., 31 AUG 76; To VA-66, USS Independence (CV-62), 31 AUG 76 ~ S 1SO strike, 26 JUL 77 ** No data on strike.

E-298 157576 Navy acceptance from NPRO Rep. LTV, Dallas, TX., 17 NOV 70 ** Transferred to VA-66/CVW-7, AG/3XX, USS Independence (CVA-62), 21 NOV 70; To VA-66, NAS Cecil Field, FL., 27 JUN 71 ~ SS 1SO strike, 31 JAN 72 ** No data on strike.

E-299 157577 Navy acceptance from NPRO Rep. LTV, Dallas, TX., 16 DEC 70 ** Transferred to VA-122/FRS, NJ/2XX, NAS LeMoore, CA., 18 DEC 70 ** Transferred to VA-25/CVW-2, NE/4XX, NAS LeMoore, CA., 12 JAN 71; To VA-25, USS Ranger (CV-61), 21 JUN 73; To VA-25, NAS LeMoore, CA., 27 JAN 75; To VA-25, NAS Fallon, NV., 13 JUL 75; To VA-25, USS Ranger (CV-61), 26 JUL 75; To VA-25, NAS LeMoore, CA., 19 SEP 75; To VA-25, NAS Fallon, NV., 30 APR 76 ** Transferred to VA-22/CVW-15, NL/300, NAS LeMoore, CA., 30 APR 76; To VA-22, USS Coral Sea (CV-43), 01 AUG 77; To VA-22, NAS LeMoore, CA., 01 AUG 77; To VA-22, NAS Jacksonville, FL., 14 NOV 77; To VA-22, NAS LeMoore, CA., 02 MAR 78; To VA-22, NAS Kingsville, TX., 28 JUL 78; To VA-22, NAS LeMoore, CA., 28 JUL 78; To VA-22, USS Kitty Hawk (CV-63), 19 APR 79; To VA-22, NAF Atsugi, JP., 16 OCT 79; To VA-22, USS Kitty Hawk (CV-63), 21 NOV 79; To VA-22, NAF Atsugi, JP., 02 JAN 80; To VA-22, USS Kitty Hawk (CV-63), 11 JAN 80; To VA-22, NAS LeMoore, CA., 01 NOV 80; To VA-22, NAS Jacksonville, FL., 22 JUL 80; To VA-22, NAS LeMoore, CA., 29 AUG 80; To VA-22, USS Kitty Hawk (CV-63), 11 SEP 80; To VA-22, NAS LeMoore, CA., 13 JAN 81; To VA-22, USS Kitty Hawk (CV-63), 20 MAR 81 ** Transferred to VA-94/CVW-11, NH/4XX, NAF Atsugi, JP., 05 MAY 81; To VA-94, NAS Cubi Point, PI., 29 MAY 81; To VA-94, NAF Atsugi, JP., 17 JUL 81; To VA-94, NAS Cubi Point, PI., 06 AUG 81; To VA-94, USS Kitty Hawk (CV-63), 24 OCT 81; To VA-22, NAS LeMoore, CA., 24 OCT 81 ** Transferred to VA-97/CVW-14, NK/3XX, 18 JUL 82 ** Transferred to VA-25/CVW-2, NE/4XX, NAS LeMoore, CA., 05 JAN 83 ** Transferred to NARF, NAS Jacksonville, FL., 03 MAY 83 ** Transferred to VA-203/CVWR-20, AF/3XX, NAS Jacksonville, FL., 12 MAY 83 thru 24 JUL 87 ** End of flight record card ** Transferred to AMARC, Davis Monthan AFB, Tucson, AZ., assigned park code 6A0261, 25 APR 88 ** 7145.1 flight hours ** TF41A402D engine S/N 141521 ** storage location 210347 ** Under GSA jurisdiction, 06 APR 04 ** At AMARG, Davis Monthan AFB; Tucson, AZ., ejection seat removed, 15 JUN 07.

E-300 157578 Navy acceptance from NPRO Rep. LTV, Dallas, TX., 24 NOV 70 ** Transferred to VA-12/CVW-7, AG/4XX, USS Independence (CVA-62), 25 NOV 70; To VA-12, NAS Cecil Field, FL., 18 JUN 71; To VA-12, USS Independence (CVA-62), 06 JUN 72; To VA-12, NAS Cecil Field, FL., FL., 05 FEB 73; To VA-12, USS Independence (CV-62), 05 APR 74; To VA-12, NAS Cecil Field, FL., 05 FEB 75; To VA-12, NAS Fallon, NV., 05 FEB 75; To VA-12, NAS Cecil Field, FL., 01 JUL 75; To VA-12, USS Independence (CV-62), 03 SEP 75; To VA-12, NAS Cecil Field, FL., 14 SEP 75; To VA-12, NAS Jacksonville, FL., 26 APR 76; To VA-12, NAS Cecil Field, FL., 13 JUL 76; To VA-12, NAS Fallon, NV., 13 JUL 76; To VA-12, USS Independence (CV-62), 13 JUL 76; To VA-12, NAS Cecil Field, FL., 13 JUL 76; To VA-12, USS Independence (CV-62), 13 JUL 76; To VA-12, NAS Cecil Field, FL., 13 JUL 76; To VA-12, USS Independence (CV-62), 13 JUL 76; To VA-12, NAS Cecil Field, FL., 09 AUG 77; To VA-12, USS Dwight D. Eisenhower (CVN-69), 14 DEC 77; To VA-12, NAS Cecil Field, FL., 06 APR 78; To VA-12, NAS Jacksonville, FL., 07 APR 78; To VA-12, NAS Cecil Field, FL., 19 MAY 78; To VA-12, NAS Jacksonville, FL., 15 JUL 78; To VA-12, NAS Cecil Field, FL., 17 JUL 78; To VA-12, USS Dwight D. Eisenhower (CVN-69), 17 JUL 78; To VA-12, NAS Cecil Field, FL., 17 JUL 78; To VA-12, USS Dwight D. Eisenhower (CVN-69), 07 OCT 78; To VA-12, NAS Cecil Field, FL., 09 NOV 78; To VA-12, USS Dwight D. Eisenhower (CVN-69), 09 NOV 78 ~ S 1SO strike, 27 FEB 79 ** No data on strike.

E-301 157579 Navy acceptance from NPRO Rep. LTV, Dallas, TX., 21 NOV 70 ** Transferred to VA-12/CVW-7, AG/4XX, USS Independence (CVA-62), 22 NOV 70; To VA-12, NAS Cecil Field, FL., 11 JUN 71; To VA-12, USS Independence (CVA-62), 26 MAY 72 ** Transferred to VA-174/FRS, AD/4XX, NAS Cecil Field, FL., 16 OCT 72 ** Transferred to VA-37/ CVW-3, AC/3XX, NAS Cecil Field, FL., 24 MAY 73; To VA-37, USS Saratoga (CV-60), 26 JAN 74; To VA-37, NAS Cecil Field, FL., 26 JAN 74; To VA-37, USS Saratoga (CV-60), 26 JAN 74; To VA-37, NAS Cecil Field, FL., 26 JAN 74; To VA-37, USS Saratoga (CV-60), 26 JAN 74; To VA-37, NAS Cecil Field, FL., 26 JAN 74; To VA-37, USS Saratoga (CV-60), 12 NOV 75; To VA-37, NAS Cecil Field, FL., 12 NOV 75; To VA-37, NAS Jacksonville, FL., 10 FEB 77; To VA-37, USS Saratoga (CV-60), 21 APR 77 ** Transferred to VA-174/FRS, AD/4XX, NAS Cecil Field, FL., 03 MAY 77 ** Transferred to VA-105/CVW-3, AC/4XX, NAS Cecil Field, FL., 11 JUL 79; To VA-105, MCAS Yuma, AZ., 11 JUL 79; To VA-105, NAS Cecil Field, FL., 25 OCT 79; To VA-105, USS Saratoga (CV-60), 25 OCT 79; To VA-105, NAS Cecil Field, FL., 25 OCT 79; To VA-105, USS Saratoga (CV-60), 20 MAR 80; To VA-105, NAS Cecil Field, FL., 13 FEB 81; To VA-105, NAS Jacksonville, FL., 10 MAR 81; To VA-105, NAS Cecil Field, FL., 10 MAR 81; To VA-105, NAS Jacksonville, FL., 13 MAR 81; To VA-105, NAS Dallas, TX., 27 MAY 81; To VA-105, NAS Cecil Field, FL., 27 MAY 81; To VA-105, USS John F. Kennedy (CV-67), 27 MAY 81 **Transferred to VA-15/CVW-6, AE/3XX, NAS Cecil Field, CA., 28 JUL 81 ** To VA-15, USS Independence (CV-62), 28 JUL 81; To VA-015, NAS Cecil Field, FL., 28 JUL 81; To VA-15, USS Independence (CV-62), 28 JUL 81; To VA-15, NAS Cecil Field, FL., 28 JUL 81; To VA-15, USS Independence (CV-62), 28 JUL 81; To VA-15, NAS Cecil Field, FL., 28 JUL 81 ** Transferred to VA-66/CVW-7, AG/3XX, USS Dwight D. Eisenhower (CVN-69), 15 APR 83; To VA-66, NAS Cecil Field, FL., 30 JUL 83; To VA-66, NAS Jacksonville, FL., 22 FEB 84 ** Transferred to VA-105/

CVW-6, AE/4XX, NAS Cecil Field, FL., 28 FEB 84; To VA-105, NAF Kadena, JP., 30 APR 84; To VA-105, NAS Cubi, Point, PI., 21 AUG 84; To VA-105, NAF Atsugi, JP., 28 AUG 84; To VA-105, NAS Cubi, Point, PI., 07 SEP 84; To VA-105, MCAS Iwakuni, JP, 07 SEP 84; To VA-105, NAS Cecil Field, FL., 07 SEP 84; To VA-105, USS Forrestal (CV-59), 12 APR 85; To VA-105, NAS Cecil Field, FL., 12 APR 85 ** Transferred to VA-66/CVW-7, AG/3XX, NAS Cecil Field, FL., 24 OCT 85; To VA-66, USS John F.Kennedy (CV-67), 22 MAY 86; To VA-66, NAS Jacksonville, FL., 30 SEP 86 ** Transferred to VA-81/CVW-17, AA/4XX, NAS Cecil Field, FL., 07 OCT 86; To VA-81, USS Saratoga (CV-60), 03 NOV 86; To VA-81, NAS Cecil Field, FL., 03 NOV 86; To VA-81, USS Saratoga (CV-60), 09 APR 87; To VA-81, NAS Cecil Field, FL., 13 APR 87; To VA-81, USS Saratoga (CV-60), 13 APR 87 ** End of flight record card.

E-302 157580 Navy acceptance from NPRO Rep. LTV, Dallas, TX., 19 NOV 70 ** Transferred to VA-66/CVW-7, AG/313, USS Independence (CVA-62), 20 NOV 70; To VA-66, NAS Cecil Field, FL., 09 JUN 71; To VA-66, USS Independence (CVA-62), 21 MAR 72 ** Transferred to VA-174/FRS, AD/4XX, NAS Cecil Field, FL, 18 APR 73 ** Transferred to VA-12/CVW-7, AG/4XX, USS Independence (CV-62), 26 MAY 73; To VA-12, NAS Cecil Field, FL., 26 MAY 73 ** Transferred to VA-174/FRS, AD/4XX, NAS Cecil Field, FL, 22 APR 74 ** Transferred to VA-82/CVW-8, AJ/3XX, NAS Cecil Field, FL., 13 FEB 75; To VA-82, USS Nimitz (CVN-68), 13 FEB 75; To VA-82, NAS Cecil Field, FL., 01 JUL 75; To VA-82, NAS Roosevelt Roads, PR., 01 JUL 75; To VA-82, NAS Cecil Field, FL., 01 JUL 75; To VA-82, USS Nimitz (CVN-68), 01 JUL 75; To VA-82, NAS Cecil Field, FL., 01 JUL 75; To VA-82, USS Nimitz (CVN-68), 23 OCT 77; To VA-82, NAS Cecil Field, FL., 15 NOV 77; To VA-82, NAS Jacksonville, FL., 16 SEP 78; To VA-82, NAS Cecil Field, FL., 20 NOV 78; To VA-82, USS Nimitz (CVN-68), 02 MAR 81; To VA-82, NAS Cecil Field, FL., 14 APR 81 ** Transferred to VA-174/FRS, AD/422, NAS Cecil Field, FL, 12 MAR 82; Transferred to VA-174, NAS Jacksonville, FL., 29 NOV 83; To VA-174, NAS Cecil Field, FL, 30 NOV 83; To VA-174, NAS Jacksonville, FL., 23 JAN 86; To VA-174, NAS Cecil Field, FL, 20 FEB 86; To VA-174, NAS Jacksonville, FL., 28 MAR 86; To VA-174, NAS Cecil Field, FL, 02 APR 86 ** Transferred to AMARC, Davis Monthan AFB; Tucson, AZ., assigned park code 6A0216, 21 JAN 87 ** End of flight record card ** 5979.7 flight hours ** TF41A2B engine S/N 141891 ** Project changed per FSO letter, 06 APR 04 ** Engine records released to DRMO for disposition, 06 JUN 05 ** Aircraft deleted from inventory and released to DRMO for disposition, 01 AUG 05.

E-303 157581 Navy acceptance from NPRO Rep. LTV, Dallas, TX., 30 NOV 70 ** Transferred to VA-12/CVW-7 AG/4XX, USS Independence (CVA-62), 01 DEC 70; To VA-12, NAS Cecil Field, FL., 18 JUN 71; To VA-12, USS Independence (CVA-62), 17 MAR 72; To VA-12, NAS Cecil Field, FL., 21 MAR 73; To VA-12, USS Independence (CV-62), 25 APR 74; To VA-12, NAS Cecil Field, FL., 25 APR 74; To VA-12, NAS Fallon, NV., 01 MAY 74; To VA-12, NAS Cecil Field, FL., 01 MAY 74; To VA-12, NAS Fallon, NV., 01 MAY 74; To VA-12, NAS Cecil Field, FL., 01 JUL 75; To VA-12, USS Independence (CV-62), 03 SEP 75; To VA-12, NAS Cecil Field, FL., 14 SEP 75; To VA-12, NAS Jacksonville, FL., 14 JUN 76; To VA-12, NAS Cecil Field, FL., 30 JUL 76; To VA-12, NAS Fallon, NV., 30 JUL 76; To VA-12, USS Independence (CV-62), 30 JUL 76; To VA-12, NAS Cecil Field, FL., 30 JUL 76; To VA-12, USS Independence (CV-62), 30 JUL 76; To VA-12, NAS Cecil Field, FL., 30 JUL 76; To VA-12, USS Independence (CV-62), 30 JUL 76; To VA-12, NAS Cecil Field, FL., 09 AUG 77; To VA-12, USS Dwight D. Eisenhower (CVN-69), 09 AUG 77; VA-12, NAS Cecil Field, FL., 20 JUN 78; To VA-12, NAS Jacksonville, FL., 21 JUN 78; To VA-12, USS Dwight D. Eisenhower (CVN-69), 09 AUG 78; VA-12, NAS Cecil Field, FL., 09 AUG 78; To VA-12, USS Dwight D. Eisenhower (CVN-69), 09 AUG 78; VA-12, NAS Cecil Field, FL., 09 AUG 78; To VA-12, USS Dwight D. Eisenhower (CVN-69), 09 AUG 78; VA-12, NAS Cecil Field, FL., 31 OCT 79; To VA-12, USS Dwight D. Eisenhower (CVN-69), 15 NOV 79 ** Transferred to VA-174/FRS, AD/437, NAS Cecil Field, FL., 12 APR 80; To VA-174, NAS Jacksonville, FL., 17 JUN 81;

Transferred to VA-174, NAS Cecil Field, FL., 08 SEP 81; Transferred to VA-66/CVW-7, AG/3XX, USS Dwight D. Eisenhower (CVN-69), 20 OCT 81; To VA-66, NAS Cecil Field, FL., 20 OCT 81; To VA-66, USS Dwight D. Eisenhower (CVN-69), 20 OCT 81; To VA-66, NAS Cecil Field, FL., 20 OCT 81; To VA-66, USS Dwight D. Eisenhower (CVN-69), 30 MAY 85; To VA-66, NAS Cecil Field, FL., 30 SEP 85; To VA-66, NAS Jacksonville, FL., 18 DEC 85; To VA-66, NAS Cecil Field, FL., 13 JAN 86; To VA-66, NAS Jacksonville, FL., 28 FEB 86 ** Transferred to VA-105/CVW-6, AE/404, USS Forrestal (CV-59), 05 MAR 86; To VA-105, NAS Cecil Field, FL., 05 MAR 86; To VA-105, USS Forrestal (CV-59), 09 JUL 87 thru 10 JUL 87 ** End of flight record card ** Transferred to AMARC, Davis Monthan AFB; Tucson, AZ., assigned park code 6A0254, 16 MAR 88 ** 6100.8 flight hours ** TF41A402D engine S/N 141523 ** Storage location 210430 ** Aircraft deleted from inventory and released to DRMO for disposition, 03 MAY 06 ** Located at AMARG, Davis Monthan AFB; Tucson, AZ., 15 JUN 07.

E-304 157582 Navy acceptance from NPRO Rep. LTV, Dallas, TX., 30 NOV 70 ** Transferred to VA-12/CVW-7, AG/4XX, USS Independence (CVA-62), 01 DEC 70; To VA-12, NAS Cecil Field, FL., 08 JUN 71; To VA-12, USS Independence (CVA-62), 05 APR 72; To VA-12, NAS Cecil Field, FL., 31 MAR 73; To VA-12, USS Independence (CV-62), 16 APR 74; To VA-12, NAS Jacksonville, FL., 25 OCT 74; To VA-12, NAS Cecil Field, FL., 25 OCT 74; To VA-12, NAS Jacksonville, FL., 05 FEB 75; To VA-12, NAS Fallon, NV., 07 MAY 75; To VA-12, NAS Cecil Field, FL., 07 MAY 75; To VA-12, NAS Fallon, NV., 07 MAY 75 ** Transferred to VA-174/FRS, AD/4XX, NAS Cecil Field, FL., 13 JUN 75 ** Transferred to VA-66/CVW-7, AG/3XX, NAS Cecil Field, FL., 31 JUL 78; To VA-66, USS Dwight D. Eisenhower (CVN-69), 31 JUL 78; To VA-66, NAS Cecil Field, FL., 31 JUL 78; To VA-66, USS Dwight D. Eisenhower (CVN-69), 31 JUL 78; To VA-66, NAS Cecil Field, FL., 18 SEP 79; To VA-66, USS Dwight D. Eisenhower (CVN-69), 18 SEP 79; To VA-66, NAS Cecil Field, FL., 02 FEB 81; To VA-66, USS Dwight D. Eisenhower (CVN-69), 10 APR 81; To VA-66, NAS Cecil Field, FL., 10 APR 81; To VA-66, USS Dwight D. Eisenhower (CVN-69), 10 APR 81; To VA-66, NAS Jacksonville, FL., 08 OCT 81 ** Transferred to VA-87/CVW-6, AE/4XX, NAS Cecil Field, FL., 01 DEC 81;To VA-87, USS Independence (CV-62), 14 DEC 81; To VA-87, NAS Cecil Field, FL., 14 DEC 81; To VA-87, USS Independence (CV-62), 14 DEC 81; To VA-87, NAS Cecil Field, FL., 17 MAY 82; To VA-87, USS Independence (CV-62), 19 MAY 82; To VA-87, NAS Cecil Field, FL., 19 MAY 82; To VA-87, USS Independence (CV-62),05 MAY 83; To VA-87, NAS Cecil Field, FL., 05 MAY 83; To VA-87, USS Independence (CV-62), 05 MAY 83; To VA-87, NAS Cecil Field, FL., 05 MAY 83; To VA-87, USS Independence (CV-62), 05 MAY 83; To VA-87, NAS Jacksonville, FL., 11 OCT 83; To VA-87, USS Independence (CV-62), 14 NOV 83; To VA-87, NAS Jacksonville, FL., 13 APR 84 ** Transferred to VA-66/CVW-7, AG/3XX, NAS Cecil Field, FL., 16 APR 84; To VA-66, USS Dwight D. Eisenhower (CVN-69), 16 APR 84; To VA-66, NAS Cecil Field, FL., 16 APR 84; To VA-66, USS Dwight D. Eisenhower (CVN-69), 16 APR 84; To VA-66, NAS Cecil Field, FL., 16 APR 84; To VA-66, USS Dwight D. Eisenhower (CVN-69), 16 APR 84; To VA-66, NAS Cecil Field, FL., 16 APR 84; To VA-66, USS Dwight D. Eisenhower (CVN-69), 16 APR 84; To VA-66, NAS Cecil Field, FL., 16 APR 84; To VA-66, NAS Jacksonville, FL., 26 MAR 86; To VA-66, NAS Cecil Field, FL., 10 APR 86; To VA-66, NAS Jacksonville, FL., 30 JUN 86; To VA-66, NAS Cecil Field, FL., 034 JUL 86; To VA-66/CVW-3, AC/3XX, USS John F. Kennedy (CV-67), 03 JUL 86; To VA-66, NAS Cecil Field, FL., 02 JAN 87 ** Transferred to VA-105/CVW-6, AE/4XX, NAS Cecil Field, FL., 12 MAR 87; To VA-105, NAS Jacksonville, FL., 18 MAY 87; To VA-105, NAS Cecil Field, FL., 28 MAY 87; To VA-105, USS Forrestal (CV-59), 28 MAY 87 thru 11 SEP 87 ** End of flight record card.

E-305 157583 Navy acceptance from NPRO Rep. LTV, Dallas, TX., 30 NOV 70 ** Transferred to VA-12/CVW-7, AG/4XX, USS Independence (CVA-62), 01 DEC 70; To VA-12, NAS Cecil Field, FL., 09 JUN 71; To VA-12, USS Independence (CVA-62), 26 MAY 72 ** Transferred to VA-174/FRS, AD/4XX, NAS Cecil Field, FL., 27 SEP 72 ~ S 1SO strike, 27 NOV 72 ** No data on strike.

E-306 157584 Navy acceptance from NPRO Rep. LTV, Dallas, TX., 30 NOV 70 ** Transferred to VA-12/CVW-7, AG/4XX, USS Independence (CVA-62), 03 DEC 70; To VA-12. NAS Cecil Field, FL., 30 MAY 71; To VA-12, USS Independence (CVA-62), 08 JUN 72 ** Transferred to VA-174/FRS, AD/4XX, NAS Cecil Field, FL., 13 JUN 73 ** Transferred to VA-86/ CVW-8, AJ/411, NAS Cecil Field, FL., 14 FEB 75; To VA-86, USS Nimitz (CVN-68), 14 FEB 75; To VA-86, NAS Cecil Field, FL., 14 FEB 75; To VA-86, NAS Roosevelt Roads, PR., 14 FEB 75; To VA-86, NAS Cecil Field, FL., 14 FEB 75; To VA-86, USS Nimitz (CVN-68), 12 MAR 76, To VA-86, NAS Cecil Field, FL., 31 MAR 76; To VA-86, USS Nimitz (CVN-68), 31 MAR 76, To VA-86, NAS Cecil Field, FL., 31 MAR 76; To VA-86, NAS Roosevelt Roads, PR., 31 MAR 76, Painted in bicentennial colors, 04 JUL 76; To VA-86, USS Nimitz (CVN-68), 19 JUL 77, To VA-86, NAS Cecil Field, FL., 14 SEP 77; To VA-86, USS Nimitz (CVN-68), 14 SEP 77 ~ S 1SO strike, 17 JAN 78 ** LCDR Kent Ewing killed in crash.

E-307 157585 Navy acceptance from NPRO Rep. LTV, Dallas, TX., 14 DEC 70 ** Transferred to VA-192/CVW-11, NH/ 3XX, USS Kitty Hawk (CVA-63), 30 MAY 70 ** Transferred to VA-122/FRS, NJ/2XX, NAS LeMoore, CA., 15 DEC 70 ** Transferred to VA-192/CVW-11, NH/3XX, USS Kitty Hawk (CVA-63), 12 JAN 71; To VA-192, NAS LeMoore, CA., 09 JUN 72; To VA-192, USS Kitty Hawk (CV-63), 29 JUN 73; To VA-192, NAS LeMoore, CA., 13 MAY 74; To VA-192, USS Kitty Hawk (CV-63), 28 JAN 75; To VA-192, NAS LeMoore, CA., 01 MAR 75; To VA-192, USS Kitty Hawk (CV-63), 19 MAY 75; To VA-192, NAF Atsugi, JP., 01 NOV 75; To VA-192, NAS Cubi Point, PI., 03 NOV 75; To VA-192, USS Kitty Hawk (CV-63), 19 NOV 75; To VA-192, NAS LeMoore, CA., 01 MAR 76; To VA-192, MCAS Yuma, AZ., 30 NOV 76; To VA-192, NAS Jacksonville, FL., 01 DEC 76; To VA-192, NAS Roosevelt Roads, PR., 02 FEB 77 ** Transferred to VA-83/ CVW-17, AA/3XX, NAS Cecil Field, FL., 20 JUL 77; To VA-83, USS Forrestal (CV-59), 20 JUL 77; To VA-83, NAS Cecil Field, FL., 20 JUL 77; To VA-83, USS Forrestal (CV-59), 20 JUL 77; To VA-83, NAS Cecil Field, FL., 09 FEB 78; To VA-83, USS Forrestal (CV-59), 11 APR 79; To VA-83, NAS Cecil Field, FL., 12 APR 79; To VA-83, USS Forrestal (CV-59), 29 MAY 79; To VA-83, NAS Cecil Field, FL., 29 MAY 79; To VA-83, USS Forrestal (CV-59), 29 MAY 79; To VA-83, NAS Cecil Field, FL., 15 APR 80; To VA-83, USS Forrestal (CV-59), 22 SEP 80 ** Transferred to VA-86/CVW-8, AJ/4XX, USS Nimitz (CVN-68), 29 OCT 80 ** Transferred to VA-174/FRS, AD/4XX, NAS Cecil Field, FL., 01 MAY 81; To VA-174, NAS Jacksonville, FL., 10 JUN 81; To VA-174, NAS Cecil Field, FL., 10 JUN 81; To VA-174, NAS Jacksonville, FL., 11 JUN 81; To VA-174, NAS Cecil Field, FL., 21 AUG 81 ** Transferred to VA-82/CVW-8, AJ/3XX, USS Nimitz (CVN-68), 19 DEC 81; To VA-82, NAS Cecil Field, FL., 19 DEC 81; To VA-82, USS Carl Vinson (CVN-70), 19 DEC 81; To VA-82, NAS Cecil Field, FL., 19 DEC 81; To VA-82, Nimitz (CVN-68), 19 DEC 81; To VA-82, NAS Cecil Field, FL., 19 DEC 81; To VA-82, Nimitz (CVN-68), 19 DEC 81; To VA-82, NAS Cecil Field, FL., 19 DEC 81; To VA-82, NAS Jacksonville, FL., 08 DEC 84; To VA-82, NAS Cecil Field, FL., 21 FEB 84; To VA-82, NAS Jacksonville, FL., 27 FEB 84; To VA-82, NAS Cecil Field, FL., 22 MAR 84; To VA-82, NAS Jacksonville, FL., 04 APR 84 ** Transferred to VA-37/CVW-6, AE/3XX, NAS Cecil Field, FL., 30 APR 84; To VA-37, MCAS Twenty Nine Palms, CA., 30 APR 84; To VA-37, NAS Cecil Field, FL., 04 SEP 84; To VA-37, MCAS Iwakuni, JP., 25 OCT 84 ** Transferred to VA-174/FRS, AD/4XX, NAS Cecil Field, FL., 07 DEC 84 ** Transferred to AMARC, Davis Monthan AFB; Tucson, AZ., assigned park code 6A0176; 17 JUN 86 ** Transferred to VA-174/FRS, AD/4XX, NAS Cecil Field, FL., 19 JUN 86 ** End of flight record card ** Transferred to AMARC, Davis Monthan AFB; Tucson, AZ., assigned park code 6A0176, 19 JUN 86 ** 5610.6 flight hours ** TF41A2C engine S/N 142540 ** Storage location 210812 ** At AMARG, Davis Monthan AFB; Tucson, AZ., seat removed, 15 JUN 07.

E-308 157586 Navy acceptance from NPRO Rep. LTV, Dallas, TX., 18 DEC 70 ** Transferredc to VA-12/CVW-7, AG/4XX, USS Independence (CVA-62), 19 DEC 70; To VA-12, NAS Cecil Field, FL., 11 JUN 71; To VA-12, USS Independence (CVA-62), 10 APR 72 ** Transferred to VA-105/CVW-3, AC/411, NAS Cecil Field, FL., 09 MAY 73; To VA-105, USS Saratoga (CV-60), 17 APR 74; To VA-105, NAS Cecil Field, FL., 17 APR 74; To VA-105, USS Saratoga (CV-60), 17 APR 74; To VA-105, NAS Cecil Field, FL., 17 APR 74; To VA-105, USS Saratoga (CV-60), 27 SEP 74; To VA-105, NAS Cecil Field, FL., 27 SEP 74; To VA-105, USS Saratoga (CV-60), 27 SEP 74; To VA-105, NAS Cecil Field, FL., 27 SEP 74; To VA-105, MCAS Yuma, AZ., 24 JUL 75; To VA-105, USS Saratoga (CV-60), 21 SEP 75 ** Transferred to NARF, NAS Jacksonville, FL., 19 DEC 75 ** Transferred to VA-87/ CVW-6, AE/410, NAS Cecil Field, FL., 10 APR 79; To VA-87, USS Independence (CV-62), 25 MAY 79; To VA-87, NAS Cecil Field, FL., 25 MAY 79; To VA-87, USS Independence (CV-62), 04 MAR 80; To VA-87, NAS Cecil Field, FL., 28 OCT 80; To VA-87, NAS Jacksonville, FL., 25 SEP 81; To VA-87, NAS Cecil Field, FL., 30 NOV 81; To VA-87, USS Independence (CV-62), 30 NOV 81; To VA-87, NAS Cecil Field, FL., 30 NOV 81; To VA-87, USS Independence (CV-62), 30 NOV 81; To VA-87, NAS Cecil Field, FL., 30 NOV 81; To VA-87, USS Independence (CV-62), 03 JUN 82; To VA-87, NAS Cecil Field, FL., 03 JUN 82; To VA-87, USS Independence (CV-62), 08 FEB 83; To VA-87, NAS Jacksonville, FL., 11 JUL 83; To VA-87, USS Independence (CV-62), 18 JUL 83; To VA-87, NAS Cecil Field, FL., 18 JUL 83; To VA-87, USS Independence (CV-62), 18 JUL 83; To VA-87, NAS Jacksonville, FL., 22 FEB 84 ** Transferred to VA-86/ CVW-8, AJ/4XX, NAS Cecil Field, FL., 28 FEB 84; To VA-86, NAS Roosevelt Roads, PR., 28 FEB 84; To VA-86, NAS Cecil Field, FL., 28 FEB 84; To VA-86, USS Nimitz (CVN-68), 26 OCT 84; To VA-86, NAS Cecil Field, FL., 25 DEC 84; To VA-86, USS Nimitz (CVN-68), 02 JAN 85 ** Transferred to VA-15/CVW-6, AE/3XX, NAS Cecil Field, FL., 28 FEB 85, Painted White on dark gray; To VA-15, MCAS Iwacini, JP., 19 AUG 85; To VA-15, Korea, 19 AUG 85; To VA-15, NAS Cubi Point, PI., 28 APR 86; To VA-15, NAS Cecil Field, FL., 01 MAY 86; To VA-15, NAS Cecil Field, FL., 06 AUG 86; To VA-15, NAS Cecil Field, FL., 28 AUG 86; To VFA-15, NAS Jacksonville, FL., 17 JAN 86 ** Transferred to VA-72/CVW-7, AG/4XX, NAS Cecil Field, FL., 18 OCT 86; To VA-72, USS Dwight D. Eisenhower (CVN-069), 18 JUN 87; To VA-72, NAS Cecil Field, FL., 07 JUL 87 ** End of flight record card.

E-309 157587 Navy acceptance from NPRO Rep. LTV, Dallas, TX., 18 DEC 70 ** Transferred to VA-174/FRS, AD/4XX, NAS Cecil Field, FL., 19 DEC 70 ** Transferred to VA-66/CVG-7, AG/3XX, USS Independence (CVA-62), 03 OCT 72; To VA-66, NAS Cecil Field, FL., 13 MAR 73; To VA-66, USS Independence (CV-62), 13 MAR 73; To VA-66, NAS Cecil Field, FL., 10 FEB 75; To VA-66, USS Independence (CV-62), 03 SEP 75; To VA-66, NAS Cecil Field, FL., 13 SEP 75; To VA-66, NAS Jacksonville, FL., 18 MAY 76; To VA-66, NAS Cecil Field, FL., 30 JUN 76; To VA-66, NAS Fallon, NV., 30 JUN 76; To VA-66, USS Independence (CV-62), 30 JUN 76; To VA-66, NAS Cecil Field, FL., 30 JUN 76; To VA-66, USS Independence (CV-62), 30 JUN 76; To VA-66, NAS Cecil Field, FL., 30 JUN 76; To VA-66, USS Independence (CV-62), 30 JUN 76; To VA-66, NAS Cecil Field, FL., 09 AUG 77; To VA-66, USS Dwight D. Eisenhower (CVN-69), 09 AUG 77; To VA-66, NAS Cecil Field, FL., 09 AUG 77; To VA-66, NAS Jacksonville, FL., 05 APR 78; To VA-66, NAS Cecil Field, FL., 22 JUN 78; To VA-66, USS Dwight D. Eisenhower (CVN-69), 22 JUN 78; To VA-66, NAS Cecil Field, FL., 22 JUN 78; To VA-66, USS Dwight D. Eisenhower (CVN-69), 22 JUN 78; To VA-66, NAS Cecil Field, FL., 22 JUN 78; To VA-66, USS Dwight D. Eisenhower (CVN-69), 22 JUN 78; To VA-66, NAS Cecil Field, FL., 25 OCT 79; To VA-66, USS Dwight D. Eisenhower (CVN-69), 12 DEC 79; To VA-66, NAS Cecil Field, FL., 12 DEC 79; To VA-66, USS Dwight D. Eisenhower (CVN-69), 12 DEC 79 ** Transferred to VA-174/FRS, AD/4XX, NAS Cecil Field, FL., 11 APR 80; To VA-174, NAS Jacksonville, FL., 15 JUL 80; To VA-174, NAS Cecil Field, FL., 28 AUG 80 ** Transferred to VA-66/CVG-7, AG/3XX, NAS Cecil Field, FL., 26 MAR 81; To VA-66, USS Dwight D. Eisenhower (CVN-69), 04 JUN 81; To VA-66, NAS Cecil Field, FL., 16 JUN 81; To VA-66, USS Dwight D. Eisenhower (CVN-69), 16 JUN 81; To VA-66, NAS Cecil Field, FL., 16 JUN 81; To VA-66, USS Dwight D. Eisenhower (CVN-69), 16 JUN 81; To VA-66, NAS Cecil Field, FL., 16 JUN 81; To VA-66, NAS Jacksonville, FL., 16 AUG 82; To VA-66, NAS Cecil Field, FL., 03 NOV 82 ** Transferred to VA-12/ CVW-7, AG/405, USS Dwight D. Eisenhower (CVN-69), 19 APR 83; To VA-12, NAS Cecil Field, FL., 19 APR 83; To VA-12, USS Dwight

D. Eisenhower (CVN-69), 02 MAR 84; To VA-12, NAS Cecil Field, FL., 02 MAR 84; To VA-12, USS Dwight D. Eisenhower (CVN-69), 02 MAR 84; To VA-12, NAS Cecil Field, FL., 02 MAR 84; To VA-12, USS Dwight D. Eisenhower (CVN-69), 02 MAR 84; To VA-12, NAS Cecil Field, FL., 25 SEP 85; To VA-12, NAS Jacksonville, FL., 11 DEC 85; To VA-12, NAS Cecil Field, FL., 13 DEC 85 ** Transferred to AMARC, as 6A0195; 28 AUG 86 ** 5591 flight hours ** Storage location 210538 ** End of flight record card ** 5519.4 flight hours ** TF41A2B engine S/N 141484 ** Engine records released to DRMO for disposition, 22 FEB 06** Aircraft deleted from inventory and released to DRMO for disposition, 04 MAY 06. At AMARG, Davis Monthan AFB; Tucson, AZ., 15 JUN 07.

E-310 157588 Navy acceptance from NPRO Rep. LTV, Dallas, TX., 03 DEC 70 ** Transferred to VA-12/CVW-7, AG/4XX, USS Independence (CVA-62), 10 DEC 70 ~ S 1SO strike, 24 JUN 71 ** LTJG J.M. Gibson lost at sea shortly after a night launch, Pilot never found.

E-311 157589 Navy acceptance from NPRO Rep. LTV, Dallas, TX., 10 DEC 70 ** Transferred to VA-122/FRS, NJ/2XX, NAS LeMoore, CA., 11 DEC 70 ** Transferred to VA-113/CVW-2, NE/315, NAS LeMoore, CA., 12 JAN 71 ~ S 1SO strike, 13 MAR 71 ** No data on strike.

E-312 157590 Navy acceptance from NPRO Rep. LTV, Dallas, TX., 09 DEC 70 ** Transferred to NATC, Service Test, NAS Patuxent River, MD., 17 DEC 70 ** Transferred to VA-122/FRS, NJ/2XX, COSA, NAS LeMoore, CA., 21 JUN 71; To VA-122, NAS LeMoore, CA., 20 SEP 71 ** Transferred to VA-22/CVW-15, NL/3XX, USS Coral Sea (CVA-43), 18 OCT 71 ~ S 1SO strike, 06 APR 72 ** CDR Thomas E. Dunlop KIA when shot down by a SAM over North Vietnam ** Pilots remains found and identified, returned to U.S. 18 MAR 05.

E-313 157591 Navy acceptance from NPRO Rep. LTV, Dallas, TX., 21 JAN 71 ** Transferred to VA-174/FRS, AD/4XX, NAS Cecil Field, FL., 24 JAN 71 ** Transferred to VA-86/CVW-8, AJ/4XX, NAS Cecil Field, FL., 24 JAN 71; To VA-86, USS America (CVA-66), 16 APR 71 ** Transferred to VA-174/FRS, AD/4XX, NAS Cecil Field, FL., 31 MAR 72 ** Transferred to VA-122/FRS, NJ/2XX, CRAA, NAS LeMoore, CA., 14 MAY 72 ** Transferred to VA-146/CVW-9, NG/3XX, NAS LeMoore, CA., 01 JUN 72 ** Transferred to VA-94/CVW-15, NL/4XX, USS Coral Sea (CVA-43), 15 JUN 72; To VA-94, NAS LeMoore, CA., 25 JUN 73 ~ S 1SO strike, 25 JUN 73 ** No data on strike.

E-314 157592 Navy acceptance from NPRO Rep. LTV, Dallas, TX., 15 JAN 71 ** Transferred to VA-27/CVW-14, NK/3XX, USS Enterprise (CVAN-65), 25 JAN 71; To VA-27 NAS LeMoore, CA., 04 JUN 71 ~ S 1SO strike, 23 NOV 72 ** Pilot Ejected and was rescued after a hard landing and bolter followed by an engine failure on the carrier.

E-315 157593 Navy acceptance from NPRO Rep. LTV, Dallas, TX., 29 JAN 71 ** Transferred to VA-174/FRS, AD/4XX, NAS Cecil Field, FL., 29 JAN 71 ** Transferred to NPRO Rep. LTV, Dallas, TX., 29 JAN 71 ** Transferred to VA-174/FRS, AD/4XX, NAS Cecil Field, FL., 30 JAN 71 ** Transferred to VA-81/CVW-17, AA/401, USS Forrestal (CVA-59), 21 APR 71; To VA-81, NAS Cecil Field, FL., 06 MAY 71; To VA-81, USS Forrestal (CVA-59), 15 MAY 72; To VA-81, NAS Cecil Field, FL., 05 JAN 74; To VA-81, USS Forrestal (CVA-59), 12 NOV 74; To VA-81, NAS Cecil Field, FL., 24 JUL 75; To VA-81, NAS Jacksonville, FL., 11 NOV 75; To VA-81, NAS Cecil Field, FL., 31 DEC 75; To VA-81, USS Forrestal (CV-59), 31 DEC 75; To VA-81, NAS Jacksonville, FL., 25 MAY 76; To VA-81, NAS Cecil Field, FL., 27 MAY 76, painted in Bicentennial paint scheme, 04 JUL 76; To VA-81, NAS Norfolk, VA., 18 AUG 76; To VA-81, NAS Cecil Field, FL., 08 SEP 76; To VA-81, NAS Roosevelt Roads, PR., 08 SEP 76; To VA-81, NAS Cecil Field, FL., 15 FEB 77; To VA-81, NAS Roosevelt Roads, PR., 22 APR 77; To VA-81, NAS Cecil Field, FL., 22 APR 77; To VA-81, USS Forrestal (CV-59), 20 JUL 77; To VA-81, NAS Cecil Field, FL., 16 NOV 77; To VA-81, USS Forrestal (CV-59), 16 NOV 77; To VA-81, NAS Cecil Field, FL., 25 FEB 78; To VA-81, NAS Jacksonville, FL., 15 NOV 78; To VA-81, NAS Cecil

Field, FL., 20 DEC 78; To VA-81, USS Forrestal (CV-59), 11 JAN 79; To VA-81, NAS Cecil Field, FL., 11 JAN 79; To VA-81, USS Forrestal (CV-59), 11 JAN 79; To VA-81, NAS Cecil Field, FL., 04 DEC 79 ** Transferred to VA-174/FRS, AD/4XX, NAS Cecil Field, FL., 09 SEP 80 ** Transferred to VA-105/CVW-3, AC/4XX, USS Saratoga (CV-60), 07 OCT 80; To VA-105, NAS Cecil Field, FL., 07 OCT 80; To VA-105, NAS Fallon, NV., 07 OCT 80; To VA-105, NAS Cecil Field, FL., 07 OCT 80; To VA-105, USS John F. Kennedy (CV-67), 07 OCT 80; To VA-105, NAS Cecil Field, FL., 07 OCT 80 ** Transferred to VA-37/CVW-15, NL/3XX, NAS Cecil Field, FL., 16 SEP 82; To VA-37, NAS Jacksonville, FL., 01 NOV 82; To VA-37, NAS Cecil Field, FL., 30 NOV 82; To VA-37, NAS Jacksonville, FL., 16 DEC 82; To VA-37, NAS Cecil Field, FL., 18 DEC 82; To VA-37, USS Carl Vinson (CVN-70), 04 JAN 83; To VA-37, NAS Cecil Field, FL., 28 JAN 83; To VA-37, USS Carl Vinson (CVN-70), 28 JAN 83; To VA-37, NAS Roosevelt Roads, PR., 29 NOV 83; To VA-37, NAS Cecil Field, FL., 29 NOV 83; To VA-37, NWC China Lake, CA., 13 DEC 83; To VA-37, NAS Cecil Field, FL., 01 MAY 84; To VA-37, MCAS Twenty Nine Palms, CA., 27 JUL 84; To VA-37, NAS Cecil Field, FL., 04 SEP 84; To VA-37, MCAS Iwakuni, JP., 09 OCT 84; To VA-37, Korea, 09 OCT 84; To VA-37, NAS Jacksonville, FL., 18 JUN 85; To VA-37, NAS Cecil Field, FL., 18 JUN 85; To VA-37, NAS Jacksonville, FL., 20 JUN 85; To VA-37, NAS Cecil Field, FL., 14 NOV 85; To VA-37, USS Forrestal (CV-59), 16 JAN 86; VA-81, NAS Cecil Field, FL., 16 JAN 86; To VA-81, USS Forrestal (CV-59), 08 MAY 86; To VA-81, NAS Cecil Field, FL., 23 MAR 87 ** End of flight record card ** Transferred to VA-37/CVW-6, AE/314, NAS Cecil Field, FL., date unknown ** Transferred to AMARC, Davis Monthan AFB; Tucson, AZ., assigned park code 6A0225, 21 MAY 87 ** 5894.7 flight hours ** TF41A2B engine S/N 141902 ** Storage location 210444 ** Aircraft deleted from inventory and released to DRMO for disposition, 03 MAY 06 ** At AMARG, Davis Monthan AFB; Tucson, AZ., 15 JUN 07.

E-316 157594 Navy acceptance from NPRO Rep. LTV, Dallas, TX., 04 JAN 71 ** Transferred to VA-122/FRS, NJ/2XX, NAS Cecil Field, FL., 06 JAN 71 ** Transferred to VA-147/CVW-9, NE/4XX, NAS Fallon, NV., 26 MAR 71; To VA-147, NAS LeMoore, CA., 17 JUN 71 ** Transferred to VA-192/CVW-11, NH/3XX, USS Kitty Hawk (CVA-63), 25 MAR 72; To VA-192, NAS LeMoore, CA., 19 JUN 72; To VA-192, USS Kitty Hawk (CV-63), 29 JUN 73 ** Transferred to VA-122/FRS, NJ/2XX, NAS LeMoore, CA., 31 AUG 73 ~ S 1SO strike, 03 MAR 76 ** No data on strike.

157595/157648 Contract cancelled LTV A-7E Corsair II

E---- 157595 Cancelled	E---- 157596 Cancelled
E---- 157597 Cancelled	E---- 157598 Cancelled
E---- 157599 Cancelled	E---- 157600 Cancelled
E---- 157601 Cancelled	E---- 157602 Cancelled
E---- 157603 Cancelled	E---- 157604 Cancelled
E---- 157605 Cancelled	E---- 157606 Cancelled
E---- 157607 Cancelled	E---- 157608 Cancelled
E---- 157609 Cancelled	E---- 157610 Cancelled
E---- 157611 Cancelled	E---- 157612 Cancelled
E---- 157613 Cancelled	E---- 157614 Cancelled
E---- 157615 Cancelled	E---- 157616 Cancelled
E---- 157617 Cancelled	E---- 157618 Cancelled
E---- 157619 Cancelled	E---- 157620 Cancelled
E---- 157621 Cancelled	E---- 157622 Cancelled
E---- 157623 Cancelled	E---- 157624 Cancelled
E---- 157625 Cancelled	E---- 157626 Cancelled
E---- 157627 Cancelled	E---- 157628 Cancelled
E---- 157629 Cancelled	E---- 157630 Cancelled
E---- 157631 Cancelled	E---- 157632 Cancelled
E---- 157633 Cancelled	E---- 157634 Cancelled
E---- 157635 Cancelled	E---- 157636 Cancelled
E---- 157637 Cancelled	E---- 157638 Cancelled
E---- 157639 Cancelled	E---- 157640 Cancelled
E---- 157641 Cancelled	E---- 157642 Cancelled
E---- 157643 Cancelled	E---- 157644 Cancelled
E---- 157645 Cancelled	E---- 157646 Cancelled
E---- 157647 Cancelled	E---- 157648 Cancelled

158002/158028 LTV A-7E-9-CV Corsair II (Block IX)
FY 70 Contract N00019-70-C-0497, (27) A-7E; E-318/E-344

E-344 158002 Navy acceptance from NPRO Rep. LTV, Dallas, TX., 11 JUN 71 ** Transferred to VA-94/CVW-15, NL/400, & NL/404 NAS LeMoore, CA., 12 JUN 71; To VA-94, USS Coral Sea (CVA-43), 23 MAY 72; To VA-94, NAS LeMoore, CA., 25 JUN 73; To VA-94, USS Coral Sea (CV-43), 01 JUL 75; To VA-94, NAS LeMoore, CA., 02 JUL 75; To VA-94, NAS Fallon, NV., 14 AUG 75; To VA-94, NAS LeMoore, CA., 13 OCT 75; To VA-94, NAS Fallon, NV., 30 APR 76; To VA-94, NAS LeMoore, CA., 30 APR 76; To VA-94, USS Coral Sea (CV-43), 09 DEC 76; To VA-94, NAS LeMoore, CA., 14 DEC 76; To VA-94, NAF Atsugi, JP., 30 MAR 77; To VA-94, USS Coral Sea (CV-43), 01 JUN 77; To VA-94, NAF Atsugi, JP., 22 JUN 77; To VA-94, USS Coral Sea (CV-43), 28 JUN 77; To VA-94, NAS LeMoore, CA., 14 OCT 77; To VA-94, MCAS El Toro, CA., 09 DEC 77; To VA-94, NAS LeMoore, CA., 04 JAN 78; To VA-94, NAS Jacksonville, FL., 30 APR 78; To VA-94, NAS LeMoore, CA., 30 APR 78; To VA-94, NAS Jacksonville, FL., 12 JUN 78; To VA-94, NAS LeMoore, CA., 21 AUG 78; To VA-94, USS Kitty Hawk (CV-63), 30 APR 79 ** Transferred to VA-122/FRS, NJ/2XX, NAS LeMoore, CA., 17 MAY 79; To VA-122, NAS Jacksonville, FL., 10 DEC 80; To VA-122, NAS LeMoore, CA., 25 FEB 81 ** Transferred to VA-27/CVW-14, NK/4XX, NAS LeMoore, CA., 10 MAR 81; To VA-27, USS Coral Sea (CV-43), 16 APR 81; To VA-27, NAS LeMoore, CA., 11 JUN 81; To VA-27, USS Coral Sea (CV-43), 20 AUG 81; To VA-27, NAF Atsugi, JP., 19 JAN 82; To VA-27, USS Coral Sea (CV-43), 02 JAN 82; To VA-27, NAS LeMoore, CA., 22 MAR 82; To VA-27, USS Coral Sea (CV-43), 03 MAR 83 ** Transferred to VA-25/CVW-2, NE/4XX, NAS LeMoore, CA., 10 MAR 83; To VA-25, NAS Jacksonville, FL., 28 APR 83; To VFA-25, NAS Lemoore, CA., 30 APR 83; To VFA-25, NAS Jacksonville, FL., 28 OCT 83 ** Transferred to VA-22/CVW-11, NH/3XX, NAS LeMoore, CA., 29 OCT 83; To VA-22, USS Enterprise (CVN-65), 14 DEC 83; To VA-22, NAS LeMoore, CA., 22 FEB 84; To VA-22, USS Enterprise (CVN-65), 27 FEB 84 ** Transferred to VA-56/CVW-5, NF/4XX, NAF Atsugi, JP., 20 NOV 84; To VA-56, NAS LeMoore, CA., 29 APR 86; To VA-56, NAS Jacksonville, FL., 21 JUL 86; To VA-56, NAS LeMoore, CA., 23 JUL 86 ** Transferred to VA-122/FRS, NJ/246, NAS LeMoore, CA., 24 JUL 86 ** Transferred to VA-94/CVW-11, NH/4XX, NAS LeMoore, CA., 14 APR 87 thru 08 MAY 87 ** End of flight record card ** Transferred to VA-122/FRS, NJ/2XX, NAS LeMoore, CA., date unknown ** Transferred to AMARC, Davis Monthan AFB; Tucson, AZ., assigned park code 6A0287; 24 FEB 89 ** 5714.2 flight hours ** TF41A402D engine S/N 141505 ** Project changed per FSO letter, 06 APR 04 ** Engine records released to DRMO for disposition, 23 MAY 05 ** Aircraft deleted from inventory and released to DRMO for disposition, 01 AUG 05.

E-318 158003 Navy acceptance from NPRO Rep. LTV, Dallas, TX., 22 JAN 71 ** Transferred to VA-122/FRS, NJ/2XX, NAS LeMoore, CA., 08 FEB 71 ** Transferred to VA-147/CVW-9, NG/4XX, NAS Fallon, NV., 22 APR 71; To VA-147, NAS LeMoore, CA., 07 JUN 71; To VA-147, USS Constellation (CVA-64), 30 JUN 72; To VA-147, NAS LeMoore, CA., 27 MAR 75; To VA-147, NAS Fallon, NV., 19 MAY 75; To VA-147, NAS LeMoore, CA., 27 MAY 75; To VA-147, MCAS Yuma, AZ., 28 OCT 75; To VA-147, NAS LeMoore, CA., 28 OCT 75; To VA-147, USS Constellation (CVA-64), 30 SEP 76 ** Transferred to VA-97/CVW-14, NK/3XX, USS Enterprise (CVN-65), 18 APR 77; To VA-97, NAS LeMoore, CA., 06 JUN 77; To VA-97, USS Enterprise (CVN-65), 08 AUG 77; To VA-97, NAS LeMoore, CA., 01 SEP 77; To VA-97, NAS Jacksonville, FL., 03 NOV 77; To VA-97, NAS LeMoore, CA., 07 JAN 78; To VA-97, USS Enterprise (CVN-65), 10 MAR 78; To VA-97, NAF Atsugi, JP., 26 JUN 78; To VA-97, USS Enterprise (CVN-65), 05 JUL 78; To VA-97, NAS LeMoore, CA., 30 OCT 78; To VA-97, USS Coral Sea (CV-43), 29 OCT 79; To VA-97, NAF Atsugi, JP., 06 MAR 80; To VA-97, USS Coral Sea (CV-43), 26 MAR 80 ** Transferred to VA-56/CVW-5, NF/4XX, NAF Atsugi, JP., 15 MAY 80; To VA-56, USS Midway (CV-41), 16 JUL 80; To VA-56, NAF Atsugi, JP., 17 NOV 80; To VA-56, USS Midway (CV-41), 25 NOV 80; To VA-56, NAF Atsugi, JP., 25 NOV 80; To VA-56, USS Midway (CV-41), 24 FEB 81; To VA-56;

NAF Atsugi, JP., 24 FEB 81; To VA-56, USS Midway (CV-41), 16 SEP 81; To VA-56; NAF Atsugi, JP., 04 OCT 81 ** Transferred to VA-25/CVW-2, NE/4XX, USS Ranger (CV-61), 14 SEP 82 ** Transferred to VA-27/CVW-14, NK/4XX, NAS LeMoore, CA., 21 OCT 82 ** Transferred to VA-195/ CVW-9, NG/4XX, NAS LeMoore, CA., 18 FEB 83; To VA-195, USS Ranger (CV-61), 09 APR 83; To VA-195, NAS LeMoore, CA., 14 FEB 84; To VA-195, NAS Jacksonville, FL., 03 JUN 85 ** Transferred to VA-97/CVW-15, NL/4XX, NAS LeMoore, CA., 12 JUN 85; To VA-97, USS Carl Vinson (CVN-70), 09 APR 86 ** Transferred to VA-304/CVWR-30, ND/4XX, NAS Alameda, CA., 24 APR 86; To VA-304, NAS Pensacola, FL., 01 MAY 86 ** Transferred to VA-203/CVWR-20, AF/3XX; NAS Jacksonville, FL., 17 JUN 86; To VA-203, NAS Pensacola, FL., 08 JAN 87; To VA-203, NAS Jacksonville, FL., 09 JAN 87 thru 01 JUL 87 ** End of flight record card ** On display at the Lake City, AP, FL., APR 91.

E-319 158004 Navy acceptance from NPRO Rep. LTV, Dallas, TX., 30 JAN 71 ** Transferred to VA-174/FRS, AD/4XX, NAS Cecil Field, FL., 02 FEB 71 ** Transferred to VA-82/CVW-8, AJ/302 NAS Cecil Field, FL., 03 JUN 71; To VA-82, USS America (CVA-66), 29 JUN 71 ** Transferred to VA-174/FRS, AD/4XX, NAS Cecil Field, FL., 31 MAR 72 ** Transferred to VA-66/CVW-7, AG/3XX, USS Independence (CVA-62), 08 NOV 72; To VA-66, NAS Cecil Field, FL., 26 JAN 73; To VA-66, USS Independence (CV-62), 04 APR 74; To VA-66, NAS Cecil Field, FL., 08 FEB 75; To VA-66, USS Independence (CV-62), 04 SEP 75; To VA-66, NAS Cecil Field, FL., 19 SEP 75; To VA-66, NAS Jacksonville, FL., 04 AUG 76; To VA-66, NAS Cecil Field, FL., 17 AUG 76; To VA-66, NAS Fallon, NV., 17 AUG 76; To VA-66, USS Independence (CV-62), 17 AUG 76; To VA-66, NAS Cecil Field, FL., 17 AUG 76; To VA-66, USS Independence (CV-62), 17 AUG 76; To VA-66, NAS Cecil Field, FL., 17 AUG 76; To VA-66, USS Independence (CV-62), 17 AUG 76; To VA-66, NAS Cecil Field, FL., 09 AUG 77; To VA-66, USS Dwight D. Eisenhower (CVN-69), 09 AUG 77; To VA-66, NAS Cecil Field, FL., 09 AUG 77; To VA-66, NAS Jacksonville, FL., 29 APR 78; To VA-66, NAS Cecil Field, FL., 05 AUG 78; To VA-66, USS Dwight D. Eisenhower (CVN-69), 05 AUG 78; To VA-66, NAS Cecil Field, FL., 05 AUG 78; To VA-66, USS Dwight D. Eisenhower (CVN-69), 05 AUG 78; To VA-66, NAS Cecil Field, FL., 05 AUG 78; To VA-66, USS Dwight D. Eisenhower (CVN-69), 05 AUG 78; To VA-66, NAS Cecil Field, FL., 21 NOV 79; To VA-66, USS Dwight D. Eisenhower (CVN-69), 01 DEC 79; To VA-66, NAS Cecil Field, FL., 01 DEC 79; To VA-66, USS Dwight D. Eisenhower (CVN-69), 27 MAR 80; To VA-66, NAS Cecil Field, FL., 27 JAN 81; To VA-66, NAS Jacksonville, FL., 04 MAR 81; To VA-66, NAS Cecil Field, FL., 20 APR 81; To VA-66, USS Dwight D. Eisenhower (CVN-69), 20 APR 81; To VA-66, NAS Cecil Field, FL., 20 APR 81; To VA-66, USS Dwight D. Eisenhower (CVN-69), 20 APR 81; To VA-66, NAS Cecil Field, FL., 20 APR 81; To VA-66, USS Dwight D. Eisenhower (CVN-69), 20 APR 81; To VA-66, NAS Cecil Field, FL., 20 APR 81; To VA-66, NAS Jacksonville, FL., 15 OCT 82; To VA-66, NAS Cecil Field, FL., 15 OCT 82; To VA-66, NAS Jacksonville, FL., 19 OCT 82; To VA-66, NAS Cecil Field, FL., 10 JAN 83; To VA-66, NAS Dallas, TX., 14 APR 83 ** Transferred to VA-83/CVW-17, AA/3XX, NAS Cecil Field, 14 APR 83 ** Transferred to VA-46/CVW-1, AB/3XX, NAS Cecil Field, FL., 20 JUN 83; To VA-46, USS America (CV-66), 04 AUG 83; To VA-46, NAS Cecil Field, FL., 04 AUG 83; To VA-46, USS America (CV-66), 04 AUG 83; To VA-46, NAS Cecil Field, FL., 04 AUG 83; To VA-46, USS America (CV-66), 04 AUG 83; To VA-46, NAS Cecil Field, FL., 02 AUG 84; To VA-46, USS America (CV-66), 24 MAY 85; To VA-46, NAS Cecil Field, FL., 25 MAY 85; To VA-46, NAS Jacksonville, FL., 09 AUG 85; To VA-46, USS America (CV-66), 10 AUG 85; To VA-46, NAS Cecil Field, FL., 10 AUG 85; To VA-46, USS America (CV-66), 10 AUG 85; To VA-46, NAS Cecil Field, FL., 10 AUG 85 ** Transferred to VA-82/CVW-8, AJ/3XX, USS Nimitz (CVN-68), 06 MAR 87; To VA-82, NAS Cecil Field, FL., 19 APR 87; To VA-82, NAS Jacksonville, FL., 03 AUG 87 thru 04 AUG 87 ** End of flight record card ** Transferred to VA-204/CVWR-20, AF/4XX, NAS New Orleans, LA., date unknown ** Transferred to AMARC, Davis Monthan AFB, Tucson, AZ., assigned park code 6A0350, 27 APR 90 ** 7358.5 flight hours ** TF41A402D engine S/N 142616 ** Storage location 210517 ** At AMARG, Davis Monthan AFB, Tucson, AZ., 15 JUN 07.

E-320 158005 Navy acceptance from NPRO Rep. LTV, Dallas, TX., 25 JAN 71 ** Transferred to VA-122/FRS, NJ/2XX, NAS LeMoore, CA., 10 FEB 71 ** Transferred to VA-146/CVW-9, NG/3XX, NAS Fallon, NV., 27 APR 71; To VA-146, NAS LeMoore, CA., 12 JUN 71 ** Transferred to VA-22/CVW-15, NL/3XX, USS Coral Sea (CVA-43), 16 JUN 72; To VA-22, NAS LeMoore, CA., 21 MAY 73; To VA-22, USS Coral Sea (CVA-43), 29 NOV 74; To VA-22, NAS LeMoore, CA., 30 JUL 75; To VA-22, NAS Fallon, NV., 08 SEP 75; To VA-22, NAS LeMoore, CA., 01 NOV 75; To VA-22, NAS Fallon, NV., 11 DEC 75; To VA-22, NAS LeMoore, CA., 11 DEC 75 ** Transferred to VA-25/CVW-2, NE/4XX, NAS Fallon, NV., 31 JUL 77; To VA-25, NAS LeMoore, CA., 12 AUG 77; To VA-25, NAS Jacksonville, FL., 30 SEP 77; To VA-25, NAS LeMoore, CA., 02 DEC 77; To VA-25, USS Ranger (CV-61), 13 NOV 78; To VA-25, NAS LeMoore, CA., 15 DEC 78; To VA-25, USS Ranger (CV-61), 17 JAN 79; To VA-25, NAS Cubi Point, PI., 20 FEB 79; To VA-25, NAS Fallon, NV., 21 SEP 79; To VA-25, NAS LeMoore, CA., 14 JAN 80; To VA-25, USS Ranger (CV-61), 20 MAY 80; To VA-25, NAS LeMoore, CA., 09 JUL 80; To VA-25, USS Ranger (CV-61), 18 JUL 80; To VA-25, NAS LeMoore, CA., 06 AUG 80; To VA-25, USS Ranger (CV-61), 10 SEP 80; To VA-25, NAS LeMoore, CA., 20 MAY 81 ** Transferred to VA-97/CVW-14, NK/3XX, USS Coral Sea (CV-43), 13 AUG 81; To VA-97, NAF Atsugi, JP., 04 JAN 82; To VA-97, NAS LeMoore, CA., 05 JAN 82; To VA-97, NAS Jacksonville, FL., 24 APR 82; To VA-97, NAS LeMoore, CA., 03 OCT 82; To VA-97, USS Coral Sea (CV-43), 28 FEB 83; To VA-97, NAS LeMoore, CA., 09 JUL 83; To VA-97/CVW-15, NL/3XX, USS Carl Vinson (CVN-79), 29 DEC 83; To VA-97, NAS LeMoore, CA., 29 DEC 83; To VA-97, USS Carl Vinson (CVN-79), 14 MAY 87; To VA-97, NAS LeMoore, CA., 06 JUN 84; To VA-97, USS Carl Vinson (CVN-79), 23 JUL 84; To VA-97, NAS LeMoore, CA., 23 JUL 84 ** Transferred to VA-146/CVW-9, NE/3XX, NAS LeMoore, CA., 10 SEP 84; To VA-146, NAS Jacksonville, FL., 31 JUL 85 ** Transferred to VA-97/CVW-15, NL/3XX, NAS LeMoore, CA., 06 AUG 85; To VA-97, USS Carl Vinson (CVN-70), 12 APR 86 ** Transferred to VA-304/CVWR-30, ND/4XX, NAS Alameda, CA., 08 MAY 86; To VA-304, NAS Pensacola, FL., 30 JUN 86 ** Transferred to VA-204/CVWR-20, AF/4XX, NAS New Orleans, LA., 30 JUN 86 ** Transferred to VA-205/CVWR-20, AF/513, NAS Atlanta, GA., 19 NOV 86 thru 04 JUN 87 ** End of flight record card ** Transferred to AMARC, Davis Monthan AFB; Tucson, AZ. assigned park code 6A0275, 17 JUN 88 ** 5609.6 flight hours ** TF41A402D engine S/N 142612 ** Storage location 210521 ** Aircraft deleted from inventory and released to DRMO for disposition, 04 MAY 06. At AMARG, Davis Monthan AFB; Tucson, AZ. 15 JUN 07.

E-321 158006 Navy acceptance from NPRO Rep. LTV, Dallas, TX., 11 FEB 71 ** Transferred to VA-122/FRS, NJ/2XX, NAS LeMoore, CA., 16 FEB 71 ** Transferred to VA-146/CVW-9, NE/3XX, NAS Fallon, NV., 27 APR 71; To VA-146, NAS LeMoore, CA., 26 JUN 71 ** Transferred to VA-195/CVW-11, NH/4XX, USS Kitty Hawk (CVA-63), 25 MAR 72 ~ S 1SO strike, 06 APR 72 ** CDR M.C. Gilfry, (Squadron C.O.), rescued after being shot down by a SAM over North Vietnam.

E-322 158007 Navy acceptance from NPRO Rep. LTV, Dallas, TX., 25 FEB 71 ** Transferred to VA-174/FRS, AD/4XX, NAS Cecil Field, FL., 26 FEB 71 ** Transferred to NPRO Rep. LTV, Dallas, TX., for RTD & E, 23 MAR 71; Transferred to NATC, Weapons Systems Test , NAS Patuxent River, MD., 30 JUN 72 ** Transferred to VA-12/CVW-7, AG/4XX, NAS Cecil Field, FL., 18 AUG 71; To VA-12, USS Independence (CVA-62), 23 MAY 72 ~ S 1SO strike, 23 JUN 72 ** No Data on strike.

E-323 158008 Navy acceptance from NPRO Rep. LTV, Dallas, TX., 30 JAN 71 ** Transferred to VA-174/FRS, AD/4XX, NAS Cecil Field, FL., 02 FEB 71 ** Transferred to VA-82/CVW-8, AJ/3XX, NAS Cecil Field, FL., 24 JUN 71; To VA-82, USS America (CVA-66), 24 JUN 71** Transferred to VA-81/CVW-17, AA/4XX, NAS Cecil Field, FL., 03 APR 72, To VA-81, USS Forrestal (CVA-59), 21 MAY 72; To VA-81, NAS Cecil Field, FL., 20 OCT 74; To VA-81, NAS Jacksonville, FL., 21 OCT 74; To VA-81, NAS Cecil Field,

FL., 21 OCT 74; To VA-81, NAS Jacksonville, FL., 22 OCT 74; To VA-81, NAS Cecil Field, FL., 09 DEC 74; To VA-81, USS Forrestal (CVA-59), 09 DEC 74; To VA-81, NAS Cecil Field, FL., 01 SEP 75; To VA-81, USS Forrestal (CV-59), 30 SEP 75; To VA-81, NAS Cecil Field, FL., 30 SEP 75; To VA-81, NAS Roosevelt Roads, PR., 06 JAN 77; To VA-81, NAS Cecil Field, FL., 06 JAN 77; To VA-81, NAS Roosevelt Roads, PR., 06 JAN 77; To VA-81, NAS Cecil Field, FL., 06 JAN 77; To VA-81, USS Forrestal (CV-59), 20 JUL 77; To VA-81, NAS Cecil Field, FL., 20 JUL 77; To VA-81, USS Forrestal (CV-59), 05 JAN 78; To VA-81, NAS Jacksonville, FL., 25 JAN 78; To VA-81, USS Forrestal (CV-59), 22 FEB 78; To VA-81, NAS Cecil Field, FL., 22 FEB 78; To VA-81, USS Forrestal (CV-59), 28 FEB 79; To VA-81, NAS Cecil Field, FL., 24 APR 79 ** Transferred to VA-83/CVW-17, AA/304, NAS Cecil Field, FL., 20 JUL 79; To VA-83, USS Forrestal (CV-59), 23 OCT 79; To VA-83, NAS Cecil Field, FL., 23 OCT 79; To VA-83, USS Forrestal (CV-59), 17 SEP 80; To VA-83, NAS Cecil Field, FL., 17 SEP 80; To VA-83, USS Forrestal (CV-59), 17 SEP 80; To VA-83, NAS Cecil Field, FL., 14 AUG 81; To VA-83, NAS Jacksonville, FL., 16 DEC 81; To VA-83, NAS Fallon, NV., 12 JAN 82; To VA-83, NAS Jacksonville, FL., 21 JAN 82; To VA-83, NAS Cecil Field, FL., 21 JAN 82; To VA-83, USS Forrestal (CV-59), 22 JAN 82 ** Transferred to VA-81/CVW-17, AA/4XX, NAS Cecil Field, FL., 25 MAR 82; To VA-81, USS Forrestal (CV-59), 21 MAY 82; To VA-81, NAS Cecil Field, FL., 21 MAY 82; To VA-81, NAS Fallon, NV., 11 JUL 83; To VA-81, NAS Cecil Field, FL., 20 JUL 83; To VA-81, USS Saratoga (CV-60), 20 JUL 83; To VA-81, NAS Cecil Field, FL., 20 JUL 83 ** Transferred to VA-37/ CVW-15, NL/3XX, USS Carl Vinson (CVN-70), 12 JAN 84; To VA-37, NAS Jacksonville, FL., 31 JAN 84; To VA-37, NAS Roosevelt Roads, PR., 31 JAN 84; To VA-37, NAS Cecil Field, FL., 31 JAN 84; To VA-37, NWC China Lake, CA., 06 FEB 84; To VA-37 NAS Jacksonville, FL., 30 APR 84 ** Transferred to VA-87/CVW-6, AE/4XX, NAS Cecil Field, FL., 01 MAY 84; To VA-87, USS Independence (CV-62), 01 MAY 84; To VA-87, NAS Cecil Field, FL., 22 SEP 84; To VA-87, USS Independence (CV-62), 22 SEP 84; NAS Cecil Field, FL., 25 SEP 84 ** Transferred to VA-174/FRS, AD/4XX, NAS Cecil Field, FL., 20 FEB 86; To VA-174, NAS Jacksonville, FL., 25 JUN 86; To VA-174, NAS Cecil Field, FL., 05 JUL 86; To VA-174, NAS Jacksonville, FL., 29 AUG 86 ** End of flight record card ** Transferred to AMARC, Davis Monthan AFB; Tucson, AZ., assigned park code 6A0198, 05 SEP 86 ** 5693.6 flight hours ** TF41A2B engine S/N AE142520 ** Storage location 210428 ** Aircraft deleted from inventory and released to DRMO for disposition, 04 MAY 06 ** At AMARG, Davis Monthan AFB; Tucson, AZ., 15 JUN 07.

E-324 158009 Navy acceptance from NPRO Rep. LTV, Dallas, TX., 18 FEB 71 ** Transferred to VA-147/CVW-9, NG/4XX, NAS Fallon, NV., 20 FEB 71; To VA-147, NAS LeMoore, CA., 13 JUN 71; To VA-147, USS Constellation (CVA-64), 30 JUN 72; To VA-147, NAS Jacksonville, FL., 08 JAN 75; To VA-147, NAS LeMoore, CA., 02 MAR 75; To NAS Fallon, NV., 26 MAY 75; To VA-147, NAS LeMoore, CA., 05 JUN 75; To VA-147, MCAS Yuma, AZ., 17 SEP 75; To VA-147, NAS LeMoore, CA., 17 SEP 75; To VA-147, USS Constellation (CV-64), 02 JUL 76; To VA-147, NAS LeMoore, CA., 02 JUL 76; To VA-147, USS Constellation (CV-64), 23 JUL 77; To VA-147, NAF Atsugi, JP., 26 SEP 77; To VA-147, USS Constellation (CV-64), 29 SEP 77; To VA-147, NAS LeMoore, CA., 19 NOV 77; To VA-147, NAS Jacksonville, FL., 25 APR 78; To VA-147, NAS LeMoore, CA., 04 JUN 78; To VA-147, USS Constellation (CV-64), 25 SEP 78; To VA-147, NAS Cubi Point, PI., 06 NOV 78; To VA-147, USS Constellation (CV-64), 31 DEC 78; To VA-147, NAF Atsugi, JP., 26 FEB 79; To VA-147, USS Constellation (CV-64), 08 MAR 79; To VA-147, NAS LeMoore, CA., 02 DEC 79; To VA-147, USS Constellation (CV-64), 07 DEC 79; To VA-147, NAS LeMoore, CA., 07 DEC 79 ** Transferred to VA-22/CVW-15, NL/3XX, NAS Cubi Point, PI., 15 FEB 80; To VA-22, NAS Jacksonville, FL., 27 APR 80; To VA-22, NAS LeMoore, CA., 21 JUL 80; To VA-22, USS Kitty Hawk (CV-63), 11 SEP 80; To VA-22, NAS LeMoore, CA., 09 JAN 81; To VA-22, USS Kitty Hawk (CV-63), 22 JAN 81 ** Transferred to VFA-125/FRS, NJ/5XX, NAS LeMoore, CA.,12 MAR 81 ** Transferred to VA-97/CVW-14, NK/3XX, NAS LeMoore, CA., 15 APR 82; To VA-97, NAS Jacksonville, FL., 29 SEP 82; To VA-97,

NAS LeMoore, CA., 30 NOV 82; To VA-97, USS Coral Sea (CV-43), 03 MAR 83; To VA-97, NAS LeMoore, CA., 17 AUG 83; To VA-97/CVW-15, NL/3XX, USS Carl Vinson (CVN-70), 14 MAR 84; To VA-97, NAS LeMoore, CA., 22 APR 84; To VA-97, USS Carl Vinson (CVN-70), 25 APR 84; To VA-97, NAS LeMoore, CA., 25 APR 84 ** Transferred to VA-122/FRS, NJ/2XX, NAS LeMoore, CA., 10 JUL 84; To VA-122, NAS Jacksonville, FL., 14 JUN 85; To VA-122, NAS LeMoore, CA., 14 JUN 85; To VA-122, NAS Jacksonville, FL., 17 JUN 85; To VA-122, NAS LeMoore, CA., 01 OCT 85 ** Transferred to AMARC, Davis Monthan AFB; Tucson, AZ., assigned park code 6A0234; 19 AUG 87 ** End of flight record card ** 5023.5 flight hours ** TF41A2B engine S/N 141438 ** Project changed per FSO letter, 06 APR 04 ** ** Engine records released to DRMO for disposition, 27 JUL 05 ** Aircraft deleted from inventory and released to DRMO for disposition, 01 AUG 05.

E-325 158010 Navy acceptance from NPRO Rep. LTV, Dallas, TX., 11 MAR 71 ** Transferred to VA-22/CVW-15, NL/3XX, NAS LeMoore, CA., 17 MAR 71; To VA-22, USS Coral Sea (CVA-43), 28 JUN 71 ** Transferred to NARF, NAS Alameda, CA., 06 JUL 72 ** Transferred to VA-122/FRS, NJ/2XX, NAS LeMoore, CA., 25 MAY 73; To VA-122, NAS Jacksonville, FL., 07 MAY 77; To VA-122, NAS LeMoore, CA., 11 MAY 77; To VA-122, NAS Jacksonville, FL., 13 JUL 77; To VA-122, NAS LeMoore, CA., 13 JUL 77; To VA-122, NAS Alameda, CA., 20 SEP 78; To VA-122, NAS LeMoore, CA., 28 OCT 78 ** Transferred to VA-192/CVW-11, NH/3XX, USS America (CV-66), 07 JUN 79; To VA-192, NAS LeMoore, CA., 07 JUN 79; To VA-192, NAS Jacksonville, FL., 04 JAN 80; To VA-192, NAS LeMoore, CA., 13 FEB 80 ** Transferred to VA-25/CVW-2, NE/401, NAS LeMoore, CA., 30 APR 80; To VA-25, USS Ranger (CV-61), 29 MAY 80; To VA-25, NAS LeMoore, CA., 09 JUL 80; To VA-25, USS Ranger (CV-61), 17 JUL 80; To VA-25, NAS LeMoore, CA., 09 AUG 80; To VA-25, USS Ranger (CV-61), 10 SEP 80; To VA-25, NAS LeMoore, CA., 09 FEB 81; To VA-25, NAS Fallon, NV., 14 SEP 81; To VA-25, USS Ranger (CV-61), 20 OCT 81; To VA-25, NAS LeMoore, CA., 20 OCT 81; To VA-25, USS Ranger (CV-61), 20 OCT 81; To VA-25, NAS LeMoore, CA., 06 JAN 82; To VA-25, NAS Jacksonville, FL., 16 MAR 82 ** Transferred to VA-195/CVW-11, NH/4XX, NAS LeMoore, CA., 23 MAR 82 ~ S 1SO strike, 03 JUN 82 ** No data on strike.

E-326 158011 Navy acceptance from NPRO Rep. LTV, Dallas, TX., 23 MAR 71 ** Transferred to VA-94/CVW-15, NL/400. NAS LeMoore, CA., 31 MAR 71; To VA-94, USS Coral Sea (CVA-43), 16 JUN 71; To VA-94, NAS LeMoore, CA., 30 JUN 73; To VA-94, USS Coral Sea (CV-43), 01 JUL 75; To VA-94, NAS LeMoore, CA., 09 JUL 75; To VA-94, NAS Fallon, NV., 05 AUG 75; To VA-94, NAS LeMoore, CA., 24 OCT 75; To VA-94, NAS Fallon, NV., 10 DEC 75; To VA-94, NAS LeMoore, CA., 10 DEC 75; To VA-94, USS Coral Sea (CV-43), 13 OCT 76; To VA-94, NAS LeMoore, CA., 14 DEC 76; To VA-94, USS Coral Sea (CV-43), 20 APR 77; To VA-94, NAF Atsugi, JP., 28 MAY 77; To VA-94, USS Coral Sea (CV-43), 11 JUN 77; To VA-94, NAS LeMoore, CA., 19 OCT 77; To VA-94, NAS Jacksonville, FL., 20 OCT 77; To VA-94, NAS LeMoore, CA., 10 JAN 78; To VA-94, NAS Cubi Point, PI., 29 MAY 79; To VA-94, USS Kitty Hawk (CV-63), 06 JUN 79; To VA-94, NAS LeMoore, CA., 15 NOV 79; To VA-94, NAS Jacksonville, FL., 08 APR 80 ** Transferred to VA-195/CVW-11, NH/4XX, NAS LeMoore, CA., 25 JUL 80; To VA-195, NAS Jacksonville, FL., 31 AUG 80; To VA-195, NAS LeMoore, CA., 18 SEP 80; To VA-195, NAS Fallon, NV., 22 OCT 80; To VA-195, NAS LeMoore, CA., 30 OCT 80; To VA-195, USS America (CV-66), 30 OCT 80; To VA-195, NAS LeMoore, CA., 30 OCT 80 ** Transferred to VA-122/FRS, NJ/2XX, NAS LeMoore, CA., 03 APR 81; To VA-122, NAS Jacksonville, FL., 14 JUL 82; To VA-122, NAS LeMoore, CA., 04 OCT 82; To VA-122, NAS Dallas, TX., 06 OCT 82 ** Transferred to VA-192/CVW-9, NG/3XX, NAS LeMoore, CA., 10 DEC 82; To VA-192/CVW-9, NG/3XX, USS Ranger (CV-61), 22 FEB 83; To VA-192, NAS LeMoore, CA., 18 NOV 83; To VA-192, NAS Jacksonville, FL., 16 FEB 85; To VA-192, NAS LeMoore, CA., 24 APR 85; To VA-192, NAS Cubi Point, PI., 22 AUG 85; To VA-192, NAS LeMoore, CA., 02 JAN 86 ** Transferred to VA-174/FRS, AD/4XX, NAS Cecil Field, FL., 24 JAN 86 ** Transferred to VA-66/

CVW-3, AC/3XX, NAS Cecil Field, FL., 27 JAN 86; To VA-66, USS John F. Kennedy (CV-67), 05 AUG 86 ** Transferred to VA-174/FRS, AD/4XX, NAS Cecil Field, FL., 02 SEP 86 thru 18 JUL 87 ** End of flight record card ** Transferred to NAD, NAS Jacksonville, FL., 01 APR 88 ** Transferred to VFA-105/CVW-6, AE/415, NAS Cecil Field, FL., date unknown ** Transferred to AMARC, Davis Monthan AFB; Tucson, AZ., assigned park code 6A0393, 27 FEB 91 ** 6207.1 flight hours ** TF41A402D engine S/N 141402 ** Storage location 111211 ** At AMARG, Davis Monthan AFB; Tucson, AZ., 15 JUN 07.

E-327 158012 Navy acceptance from NPRO Rep. LTV, Dallas, TX., 15 APR 71 ** Transferred to VA-146/CVW-9, NG/301 & NG/315, NAS Fallon, NV., 19 APR 71; To VA-146, NAS LeMoore, CA., 18 JUN 71; To VA-146, USS Constellation (CVA-64), 30 JUN 72; To VA-146, NAS LeMoore, CA., 22 DEC 74; To VA-146, NAS Fallon, NV., 27 MAY 75; To VA-146, NAS LeMoore, CA., 01 JUL 75; To VA-146, USS Constellation (CV-64), 22 SEP 76; To VA-146, NAS LeMoore, CA., 15 DEC 76; To VA-146, USS Constellation (CV-64), 15 DEC 76; To VA-146, NAS LeMoore, CA., 05 FEB 77 ** Transferred to VA-97/CVW-14, NK/3XX, USS Enterprise (CVN-65), 06 APR 77; To VA-97, NAS LeMoore, CA., 06 JUN 77; To VA-97, NAS Jacksonville, FL., 06 AUG 77; To VA-97, NAS LeMoore, CA., 30 SEP 77 ** Transferred to VA-192/CVW-11, NH/3XX, NAS LeMoore, CA., 14 MAY 78; To VA-192, NAS LeMoore, CA., 05 OCT 77; To VA-192, USS Kitty Hawk (CV-63), 25 OCT 77; To VA-192, NAS LeMoore, CA., 14 MAY 78; To VA-192, USS America (CV-66), 14 FEB 79; To VA-192, NAS LeMoore, CA., 08 MAR 79; To VA-192, NAS Jacksonville, FL., 09 NOV 79; To VA-192, NAS LeMoore, CA., 06 JAN 80; To VA-192, NAS Fallon, NV., 20 OCT 80; To VA-192, NAS LeMoore, CA., 07 NOV 80; To VA-192, USS America (CV-66), 29 JAN 81; To VA-192, NAS LeMoore, CA., 08 APR 81; To VA-192, NAS Jacksonville, FL., 20 NOV 81; To VA-192, NAS LeMoore, CA., 22 FEB 82 ** Transferred to VA-147/CVW-9, NE/3XX, NAS LeMoore, CA., 22 SEP 82; To VA-147, USS Kitty Hawk (CV-63), 26 JAN 84; To VA-147, NAS Jacksonville, FL., 27 AUG 84; To VA-147, NAS LeMoore, CA., 29 AUG 84; To VA-147, NAS Jacksonville, FL., 09 OCT 84; To VA-147, NAS LeMoore, CA., 10 OCT 84; To VA-147, USS Kitty Hawk (CV-63), 05 APR 85; To VA-147, NAS LeMoore, CA., 04 MAR 86; To VA-147, NAS Jacksonville, FL., 02 SEP 86 ** Transferred to VA-304/CVWR-30, ND/4XX, NAS Alameda, CA., 09 SEP 86 ** Transferred to VA-203/CVWR-20. AF/3XX, NAS Jacksonville, FL., 23 JAN 87 thru 17 SEP 87 ** End of flight record card.

E-328 158013 Navy acceptance from NPRO Rep. LTV, Dallas, TX., 20 APR 71 ** Transferred to VA-147/CVW-9, NG/412 & NG/413, NAS Fallon, NV., 19 APR 71; To VA-147, NAS LeMoore, CA., 09 JUN 71, City of Tulare painted on starboard nose; To VA-147, USS Constellation (CVA-64), 30 JUN 72; To VA-147, NAS LeMoore, CA., 14 APR 75; To V A-147, NAS Fallon, NV., 12 MAY 75; To VA-147, NAS LeMoore, CA., 05 JUN 75 ** Transferred to VA-94/CVW-15, NL/4XX, NAS Fallon, NV., 30 SEP 75; To VA-94, NAS LeMoore, CA., 30 SEP 75; To VA-94, NAS Fallon, NV., 30 APR 76; To VA-94, NAS LeMoore, CA., 30 APR 76; To VA-94, Coral Sea (CV-43), 22 OCT 76 ** Transferred to VA-122/FRS, NJ/2XX, NAS LeMoore, CA., 04 NOV 76; To VA-122, NAS Jacksonville, FL., 03 MAR 78; To VA-122, NAS LeMoore, CA., 15 JUN 78 ** Transferred to VA-195/CVW-11, NH/4XX, NAS LeMoore, CA., 21 JUN 78; To VA-195, USS America (CV-66), 27 APR 79; To VA-195, NAS LeMoore, CA., 07 MAY 79; To VA-195, NAS Jacksonville, FL., 25 JUN 80; To VA-195, NAS LeMoore, CA., 31 JUL 80; To VA-195, NAS Fallon, NV., 19 OCT 80; To VA-195, NAS LeMoore, CA., 07 NOV 80; To VA-195, USS America (CV-66), 23 JAN 81; To VA-195, NAS LeMoore, CA., 09 APR 81; To VA-195, NAS Jacksonville, FL., 25 OCT 82; To VA-195, NAS LeMoore, CA., 12 JAN 85; To VA-195, NAS Dallas, TX., 30 MAR 83 ** Transferred to VA-146/CVW-9, NE/3XX, NAS LeMoore, CA., 03 APR 83; To VA-146, USS Kitty Hawk (CV-63), 03 APR 83; To VA-146, NAS LeMoore, CA., 23 APR 84 ** Transferred to VA-22/CVW-11, NH/3XX, NAS LeMoore, CA., 14 MAR 85; To VA-22, NAS Fallon, NV., 14 MAR 85; To VA-22, NAS LeMoore, CA., 19 MAY 85; To VA-22, NAS Jacksonville, FL.,

19 JUL 85; To VA-22, NAS LeMoore, CA., 22 JUL 85; To VA-22, USS Enterprise (CVN-65), 30 DEC 85; To VA-22, NAS LeMoore, CA., 15 APR 86; Transferred to VA-97/CVW-15, NL/303, NAS Alameda, CA., 20 MAY 87 thru 25 AUG 87 ** End of flight record card ** Transferred to AMARC, Davis Monthan AFB; Tucson, AZ., assigned park code 6A0306, 28 NOV 89 ** 7180.2 flight hours ** TF41A402D engine S/N 141436 ** Storage location 210831 ** At AMARG, Davis Monthan AFB; Tucson, AZ., 15 JUN 07.

E-329 158014 Navy acceptance from NPRO Rep. LTV, Dallas, TX., 03 MAY 71 ** Transferred to VA-146/CVW-9, NG/3XX, NAS Fallon, NV., 06 MAY 71; To VA-146, NAS LeMoore, CA., 08 JUN 71; To VA-146, USS Constellation (CV-64), 30 JUN 72 ** Transferred to NARF, NAS Jacksonville, FL., 24 JAN 73 ** Transferred to VA-87/CVW-6, AE/4XX, 11 JAN 82; To VA-87, NAS Cecil Field, FL., 11 JAN 82; To VA-87, NARF, NAS Jacksonville, FL., 01 FEB 82 ** To VA-87, USS Independence (CV-62), 24 MAY 83; To VA-87, NAS Cecil Field, FL., 24 MAY 83; To VA-87, USS Independence (CV-62), 24 MAY 83; To VA-87, NAS Cecil Field, FL., 24 MAY 83; To VA-87, USS Independence (CV-62), 24 MAY 83 ** Transferred to VA-37/CVW-6, AE/3XX, NAS Cecil Field, FL., 18 FEB 84; To VA-37, NAS Jacksonville, FL., 16 MAR 84; To VA-37, NAS Cecil Field, FL., 20 MAR 84; To VA-37, NAS Jacksonville, FL., 18 MAY 84 ** Transferre to VA-87/CVW-6, AE/4XX, NAS Cecil Field, FL., 22 MAY 84; To VA-87, USS Independence (CV-62), 22 MAY 84; To VA-87, NAS Cecil Field, FL., 23 MAY 84; To VA-87, USS Independence (CV-62), 20 SEP 84; To VA-87, NAS Cecil Field, FL., 22 JAN 85 ** Transferred to VA-174/FRS, AD/4XX, NAS Cecil Field, FL., 11 MAR 86 ** Transferred to AMARC, Davis Monthan AFB; Tucson, AZ., assigned park code 6A0219; 11 FEB 87 ** 3122.3 flight hours ** TF41A2B engine S/N 142570 ** Storage location 210811** End of flight record card ** Transferred to FMS 06 APR 04 ** At AMARG, Davis Monthan AFB; Tucson, AZ., 15 JUN 07.

E-330 158015 Navy acceptance from NPRO Rep. LTV, Dallas, TX., 07 MAY 71 ** Transferred to VA-147/CVW-9, NG/404, NAS Fallon, NV., 08 MAY 71; To VA-147, NAS LeMoore, CA., 15 JUN 71 ~ S 1SO strike, 17 MAY 72 ** No data on strike.

E-331 158016 Navy acceptance from NPRO Rep. LTV, Dallas, TX., 23 JUL 71 ** Transferred to VA-147/CVW-9, NG/401, NAS LeMoore CA., 24 JUL 71 ** Transferred to VA-22/CVW-15, NL/3XX, USS Coral Sea (CVA-43), 28 JUN 72; To VA-22, NAS LeMoore, CA., 18 JUN 73; To VA-22, USS Coral Sea (CVA-43), 29 NOV 74; To VA-22, NAS LeMoore, CA., 30 JUL 75; To VA-22, NAS Fallon, NV., 24 AUG 75; To VA-22, NAS LeMoore, CA., 20 OCT 75; To VA-22, NAS Fallon, NV., 23 APR 76; To VA-22, NAS LeMoore, CA., 23 APR 76; To VA-22, USS Coral Sea (CV-43), 30 AUG 77; To VA-22, NAS LeMoore, CA., 17 OCT 77; To VA-22, NAS Jacksonville, FL., 13 JUN 78; To VA-22, NAS Kingsville, TX., 28 JUL 78; To VA-22, NAS LeMoore, CA., 28 JUL 78 To VA-22, NAS Jacksonville, FL., 11 DEC 78; To VA-22, NAS LeMoore, CA., 18 DEC 78; To VA-22, USS Kitty Hawk (CV-63), 26 APR 79; To VA-22, NAF Atsugi, JP., 18 SEP 79; To VA-22, USS Kitty Hawk (CV-63), 27 SEP 79; To VA-22, NAS Cubi Point, PI., 27 SEP 79; To VA-22, NAS LeMoore, CA., 27 SEP 79 ** Transferred to VA-97/CVW-14, NK/3XX, USS Coral Sea (CV-43), 06 FEB 80 ** Transferred to VA-93/CVW-5, NF/3XX, NAF Atsugi, JP., 20 APR 80; To VA-93, USS Midway (CV-41), 12 JUN 80; To VA-93, NAF Atsugi, JP., 25 NOV 80; To VA-93, USS Midway (CV-41), 29 APR 81 ** Transferred to VA-94/CVW-15, NL/4XX, NAS Cubi Point, PI., 16 MAY 81; To VA-94, USS Kitty Hawk (CV-63), 24 OCT 81; To VA-94, NAS LeMoore, CA., 24 OCT 81; To VA-94, USS Enterprise (CVN-65), 22 JUN 82; To VA-94, NAS Cubi Point, PI., 18 MAR 83; To VA-94, NAS LeMoore, CA., 26 APR 83; To VA-94, NAS Jacksonville, FL., 27 APR 83; To VA-94, NAS LeMoore, CA., 01 AUG 83 ** Transferred to VA-146/CVW-9, NE/3XX, NAS LeMoore, CA., 29 OCT 83; To VA-146, USS Kitty Hawk (CV-43), 29 OCT 83; To VA-146, NAS LeMoore, CA., 29 OCT 83 ** Transferred to VA-97/CVW-15, NL/3XX, NAS LeMoore, CA., 10 SEP 84; To VA-97, USS Carl Vinson (CVN-70), 10 SEP 84; To VA-97, NAS LeMoore, CA., 09 DEC 84; To VA-97, NAS Jacksonville, FL., 30 SEP 85; To VA-97, NAS LeMoore, CA., 14 DEC 85; To VA-97, USS

Carl Vinson (CVN-70), 06 FEB 86; To VA-97, NAS LeMoore, CA., 06 FEB 86; To VA-97, USS Carl Vinson (CVN-70), 06 FEB 86; To VA-97, NAS Alameda, CA., 30 JAN 87 ** Transferred to NAD, NAS Jacksonville, FL., 14 SEP 87 ** End of flight record card ** On display at NAS Jacksonville, FL.

E-332 158017 Navy acceptance from NPRO Rep. LTV, Dallas, TX., 03 AUG 71 ** Transferred to VA-146/CVW-9, NG/3XX, NAS LeMoore, CA., 04 AUG 71 ** Transferred to VA-22/CVW-15, NL/3XX, USS Coral Sea (CVA-43), 25 MAR 72; To VA-22, NAS LeMoore, CA., 11 JUN 73; To VA-22, USS Coral Sea (CVA-43), 29 NOV 74; To VA-22, NAS LeMoore, CA., 30 JUL 75; To VA-22, NAS Fallon, NV., 01 SEP 75; To VA-22, NAS LeMoore, CA., 21 OCT 75; To VA-22, NAS Fallon, NV., 30 APR 76; To VA-22 , NAS LeMoore, CA., 30 APR 76; To VA-22, USS Coral Sea (CV-43), 12 MAY 77; To VA-22 , NAS LeMoore, CA., 26 OCT 77; To VA-22, NAS Jacksonville, FL., 04 NOV 77; To VA-22, NAS North Island, CA., 22 DEC 77; To VA-22, NAS Jacksonville, FL., 27 FEB 78; To VA-22, NAS LeMoore, CA., 02 MAR 78; To VA-22, NAS Kingsville, TX., 28 JUL 78; To VA-22 , NAS LeMoore, CA., 28 JUL 78 ** Transferred to VA-195/CVW-11, NH/4XX, NAS LeMoore, CA., 22 SEP 78; To VA-195, USS America (CV-66), 05 JUL 79; To VA-195, NAS LeMoore, CA., 05 JUL 79; To VA-195, NAS Jacksonville, FL., 16 APR 80 ** Transferred to VA-94/CVW-15, NL/4XX, NAS LeMoore, CA., 15 JUN 80; To VA-94, USS Kitty Hawk (CV-63), 27 JUL 80; To VA-94, NAS LeMoore, CA., 27 JUL 80; To VA-94, USS Kitty Hawk (CV-63), 05 AUG 80; To VA-94, NAS LeMoore, CA., 06 NOV 80; To VA-94, USS Kitty Hawk (CV-63), 27 FEB 81; To VA-94, NAS Cubi Point, PI., 13 MAY 81; To VA-94, USS Kitty Hawk (CV-63), 13 MAY 81; To VA-94, NAS LeMoore, CA., 04 OCT 81; To VA-94, NAS Jacksonville, FL., 27 JAN 82; To VA-94, NAS LeMoore, CA., 05 APR 82; To VA-94, NAS Dallas, TX., 09 JUN 82 ** Transferred to VA-192/CVW-2, NG/4XX, NAS LeMoore, CA., 14 JUN 82; To VA-192, USS Ranger (CV-61), 20 MAR 83; To VA-192, NAS LeMoore, CA., 09 DEC 83; To VA-192, NAS Jacksonville, FL., 08 AUG 84; To VA-192, NAS LeMoore, CA., 22 SEP 84 ** Transferred to VA-22/CVW- 11, NH/302, X.O., NAS LeMoore, CA., 02 APR 85; To VA-22, NAS Fallon, NV., 24 APR 85; To VA-22, NAS LeMoore, CA., 29 APR 85; To VA-22, USS Enterprise (CVN-65), 23 DEC 85; To VA-22, NAS LeMoore, CA., 17 JUL 86; To VA-22, NAS Jacksonville, FL., 15 JAN 87; To VA-22, NAS LeMoore, CA., 15 JAN 87; To VA-22, NAS Jacksonville, FL., 21 JAN 87; To VA-22, NAS LeMoore, CA., 21 MAY 87 thru 05 SEP 87 ** End of flight record card ** Transferred to AMARC, Davis Monthan AFB; Tucson, AZ., assigned park code 6A0333, 02 APR 90 ** 6762.2 flight hours ** TF41A402D engine S/N 142513 ** Storage location 111416 ** Under GSA control ** At AMARG, Davis Monthan AFB; Tucson, AZ., 15 JUN 07.

E-333 158018 Navy acceptance from NPRO Rep. LTV, Dallas, TX., 24 JUN 71 ** Transferred to VA-22/CVW-15, NL/3XX, USS Coral Sea (CVA-43), 26 JUN 71 ** Transferred to NARF, NAS Alameda, CA., 27 OCT 71 ** Transferred to VA-22/CVW-15, NL/3XX, NAS LeMoore, CA., 03 AUG 73; To VA-22, USS Coral Sea (CVA-43), 14 NOV 74; To VA-22, NAS LeMoore, CA., 30 JUL 75; To VA-22, NAS Fallon, NV., 01 SEP 75; To VA-22, NAS LeMoore, CA., 25 NOV 75; To VA-22, NAS Fallon, NV., 30 APR 76; To VA-22, NAS LeMoore, CA., 30 APR 76 ** Transferred to VA-192/CVW-11, NH/3XX, MCAS Yuma, AZ., 30 NOV 76; To VA-192, NAS LeMoore, CA., 01 JAN 77; To VA-192, NAS Jacksonville, FL., 21 FEB 77; To VA-192, NAS LeMoore, CA., 26 APR 77; To VA-192, USS Hitty Hawk (CV-63), 25 JUL 77; To VA-192, NAS LeMoore, CA., 11 AUG 77; To VA-192, USS Kitty Hawk (CV-63), 15 SEP 77; To VA-192, NAS LeMoore, CA., 30 SEP 77; To VA-192, USS Kitty Hawk (CV-63), 25 OCT 77; To VA-192, NAS LeMoore, CA., 14 MAY 78 ** Transferred to VA-27/CVW-14, NK/4XX, NAS LeMoore, CA., 20 DEC 78; To VA-27, NPTR El Centro, CA., 20 DEC 78; To VA-27, NAS Coral Sea (CV-43), 12 OCT 79; To VA-27, NAS Cubi Point, PI., 12 NOV 79; To VA-27, USS Coral Sea (CV-43), 23 DEC 79 ** Transferred to VA-56/CVW-5, NF/4XX, NAF Atsugi, JP., 15 MAY 80; To VA-56, USS Midway (CV-41), 14 JUL 80 ~ S 1SO strike, 04 NOV 80 ** No data on strike.

E-334 158019 Navy acceptance from NPRO Rep. LTV, Dallas, TX., 29 JUL 71 ** Transferred to VA-146/CVW-9, NG/3XX, NAS LeMoore, CA., 30 JUL 71; To VA-146, USS Constellation (CVA-64), 30 JUN 72 ** Transferred to VA-122/FRS, NJ/236, NAS LeMoore, CA., 06 JAN 73; To VA-122, NAS Jacksonville, FL., 27 FEB 78; To VA-122, NAS LeMoore, CA., 06 APR 78; To VA-122, NAS Jacksonville, FL., 23 AUG 79; To VA-122, NAS LeMoore, CA., 22 OCT 79 ** Transferred to VA-195/CVW-11, NH/4XX, NAS LeMoore, CA., 11 DEC 80; To VA-195, USS America (CV-66), 25 JAN 81; To VA-195, NAS LeMoore, CA., 09 APR 81; To VA-195, NAS Jacksonville, FL., 24 NOV 81; To VA-195, NAS LeMoore, CA., 07 JAN 82 ** Transferred to VA-94/CVW-11, NH/4XX, NAS LeMoore, CA., 23 APR 82; To VA-94, USS Enterprise (CVN-65), 17 AUG 82; To VA-94, NAF Atsugi, JP., 29 MAR 83; To VA-94, NAS LeMoore, CA., 24 OCT 83; To VA-94, USS Enterprise (CVN-65), 12 FEB 84; To VA-94, NAS Jacksonville, FL., 12 FEB 84; To VA-94, NAS LeMoore, CA., 12 FEB 84; To VA-94, NAS Jacksonville, FL., 28 FEB 84; To VA-94, USS Enterprise (CVN-65), 28 FEB 84; To VA-94, NAS LeMoore, CA., 28 FEB 84; To VA-94, USS Enterprise (CVN-65), 28 FEB 84; To VA-94, NAS Jacksonville, FL., 07 SEP 84 ** Transferred to VA-97/CVW-15, NL/3XX, NAS LeMoore, CA., 11 SEP 84; To VA-97, USS Carl Vinson (CVN-70), 12 SEP 84; To VA-97, NAS LeMoore, CA., 23 DEC 84 ** Transferred to VA-22/CVW-11, NH/3XX, NAS LeMoore, CA., 27 SEP 85; To VA-22, USS Enterprise (CVN-65), 20 DEC 85; To VA-22, NAS LeMoore, CA., 20 JUN 86 ** Transferred to VA-27/CVW-15, NL/4XX, NAS LeMoore, CA., 29 JUL 87 ** End of flight record card ** Transferred to VA-22/CVW-11, NH/310, NAS LeMoore, CA., date unknown ** Transferred to AMARC, Davis Monthan AFB; Tucson, AZ., assigned park code 6A0318; 12 MAR 90 ** 6572.5 flight hours ** TF41A402D engine S/N 142597 ** Storage location 210829 ** At AMARG, Davis Monthan AFB; Tucson, AZ., 15 JUN 07.

E-335 158020 Navy acceptance from NPRO Rep. LTV, Dallas, TX., 19 AUG 71** Transferred to VA-147/CVW-9, NG/4XX, NAS LeMoore, CA., 20 AUG 71 ** Transferred to VA-192/CVW-11, NH/3XX, USS Kitty Hawk (CVA-63), 25 MAR 72; To VA-192, NAS LeMoore, CA., 19 APR 72; To VA-192, USS Kitty Hawk (CV-63), 30 JUN 73 ** Transferred to VA-122/FRS, NJ/2XX, CRAA, NAS Lemoore, CA., 05 DEC 73; To VA-122, NAS LeMoore, CA., 25 MAR 74 ** Transferred to VA-192/ CVW-11, NH/306, USS Kitty Hawk (CV-63), 11 APR 75; To VA-192, NAS Cubi Point, PI., 16 SEP 75; To VA-192, USS Kitty Hawk (CV-63), 19 NOV 75; To VA-192, NAS LeMoore, CA. 27 JAN 76; To VA-192, MCAS Yuma, AZ., 30 NOV 76; To VA-192, NAS LeMoore, CA., 22 APR 77 ~ S 1SO strike, 22 APR 77 ** No data on strike.

E-336 158021 Navy acceptance from NPRO Rep. LTV, Dallas, TX., 28 SEP 71 ** Transferred to VA-195/CVW-11, NH/414 & NH/406, USS Kitty Hawk (CVA-63), painted white on dark gray, 30 SEP 71; To VA-195, NAS LeMoore, CA., 18 JUN 72; To VA-195, USS Kitty Hawk (CV-63), 29 JUN 73; To VA-195, NAS LeMoore, CA., 01 AUG 74; To VA-195, NAS Jacksonville, FL., 27 AUG 74; To VA-195, NAS LeMoore, CA., 27 OCT 74; To VA-195, USS Kitty Hawk (CV-63), 28 OCT 74; To VA-195, NAS LeMoore, CA., 09 APR 75 To VA-195, USS Kitty Hawk (CV-63), 19 MAY 75; To VA-195, NAS Cubi Point, PI., 21 JUN 75; To VA-195, NAS LeMoore, CA., 14 DEC 75; To VA-195, USS Kitty Hawk (CV-63), 26 JAN 77; To VA-195, NAS LeMoore, CA., 31 AUG 77; To VA-195, USS Kitty Hawk (CV-63), 29 SEP77; To VA-195, NAS LeMoore, CA.,22 MAY 78; To VA-195, NAS Jacksonville, FL., 23 MAY 78; To VA-195, NAS LeMoore, CA., 17 OCT 78; To VA-195, USS America (CV-66), 14 FEB 79; To VA-195, NAS LeMoore, CA., 14 FEB 79; To VA-195, NAS Fallon, NV., 19 OCT 80; To VA-195, NAS Jacksonville, FL., 03 NOV 80; To VA-195, NAS LeMoore, CA., 06 JAN 81; To VA-195, USS America (CV-66), 25 JAN 81; To VA-195, NAS LeMoore, CA., 25 JAN 81; To VA-195, NAS Jacksonville, FL., 21 NOV 82; To VA-195, NAS LeMoore, CA., 21 NOV 82; To VA-195, NAS Jacksonville, FL., 23 NOV 82; To VA-195, NAS Dallas, TX., 11 FEB 83 ** Transferred to VA-146/CVW-9, NE/3XX, NAS LeMoore, CA.,06 MAY 83; To VA-146, USS Kitty Hawk (CV-63), 28 DEC 83; To VA-146, NAS LeMoore, CA., 14 APR 84 ** Transferred to VA-97/CVW-15, NL/307, USS Carl

Vinson (CVN-70), 10 OCT 84; To VA-97, NAS LeMoore, CA., 10 NOV 84; To VA-97, NAS Jacksonville, FL., 31 MAY 85; To VA-97, NAS LeMoore, CA., 07 AUG 85; To VA-97, USS Carl Vinson (CVN-70), 25 MAY 86; To VA-97, NAS LeMoore, CA., 28 MAY 86; To VA-97, USS Carl Vinson (CVN-70), 28 MAY 86; To VA-97, NAS Alameda, CA., 16 JAN 87 Thru 24 APR 87 ** End of flight record card ** Transferred to AMARC Davis Monthan AFB; Tucson, AZ., assigned park code 6A0307, 27 NOV 89 ** 6922.5 flight hours ** TF41A402D engine S/N 141237 ** Aircraft released from storage and prepared for overland and above deck shipment to government of Greece, date unknown ** Transferred to the Helenic Air force (Greece).

E-337 158022 Navy acceptance from NPRO Rep. LTV, Dallas, TX., 15 SEP 71 ** Transferred to VA-147/CVW-9, NG/413, NAS LeMoore, CA., 16 SEP 71; To VA-147, USS Constellation (CVA-64), 30 JUN 72 ~ S 1SO strike, 16 SEP 73 ** No data on strike.

E-338 158023 Navy acceptance from NPRO Rep. LTV, Dallas, TX., 15 OCT 71** Transferred to NATC, Service Test, NAS Patuxent River, MD., 16 OCT 71 ** Transferred to NAF China Lake, CA., XX/XXX, for RDT & E, 19 JAN 72 ~ S 1SO strike, 25 JUN 74 ** LT John P. Esposio was killed in crash while validating a new computer delivery system.

E-339 158024 Navy acceptance from NPRO Rep. LTV, Dallas, TX., 15 SEP 71 ** Transferred to VA-81/CVW-17, AA/4XX, NAS Cecil Field, FL., 20 OCT 71; To VA-81, USS Forrestal (CVA-59), 02 JUN 72; To VA-81, NAS Cecil Field, FL., 29 OCT 74, To VA-81, NAS Jacksonville, FL., 29 OCT 74; To VA-81, NAS Cecil Field, FL., 19 DEC 74; To VA-81, USS Forrestal (CVA-59), 19 DEC 74; To VA-81, NAS Cecil Field, FL., 10 AUG 75 ~ S 1SO strike, 10 AUG 75 ** No data on strike.

E-340 158025 Navy acceptance from NPRO Rep. LTV, Dallas, TX., 08 DEC 71 ** Transferred to VA-83/CVW-17, AA/303, NAS Cecil Field, FL., 09 DEC 71; To VA-83, USS Forrestal (CVA-59), 08 APR 72; To VA-83, NAS Cecil Field, FL., 17 SEP 74; To VA-83, USS Forrestal (CVA-59), 12 NOV 74; To VA-83, NAS Cecil Field, FL., 12 NOV 74; To VA-83, USS Forrestal (CVA-59), 12 NOV 74; To VA-83, NAS Cecil Field, FL., 01 SEP 75; To VA-83, USS Forrestal (CV-59), 24 MAR 76; To VA-83, NAS Cecil Field, FL., 28 APR 76; To VA-83, USS Forrestal (CV-59), 28 APR 76; To VA-83, NAS Cecil Field, FL., 28 APR 76; To VA-83, Roosevelt Roads, PR., 28 APR 76; To VA-83, NAS Cecil Field, FL.,28 APR 76; To VA-83, USS Forrestal (CV-59), 20 JUL 77; To VA-83, NAS Jacksonville, FL., 06 DEC 77; To VA-83, NAS Cecil Field, FL., 06 JAN 78; To VA-83, USS Forrestal (CV-59), 06 JAN 78; To VA-83, NAS Cecil Field, FL.,08 MAR 78; To VA-83, NAS Jacksonville, FL., 04 DEC 78; To VA-83, NAS Cecil Field, FL., 12 MAR 79; To VA-83, USS Forrestal (CV-59), 12 MAR 79; To VA-83, NAS Cecil Field, FL., 12 MAR 79; To VA-83, USS Forrestal (CV-59), 12 MAR 79; To VA-83, NAS Cecil Field, FL., 14 NOV 79 ** Transferred to VA-82/CVW-8, AJ/3XX, USS Nimitz (CVN-68), 04 JUL 80; To VA-82, NAS Cecil Field, FL., 04 JUL 80; To VA-82, USS Nimitz (CVN-68), 04 JUL 80; To VA-82, NAS Jacksonville, FL., 15 JUN 81; To VA-82, NAS Dallas, TX., 04 AUG 81 ** Transferred to VA-15/CVW-6, AE/3XX, NAS Cecil Field, CA., 11 NOV 81; To VA-15, USS Independence (CV-62), 11 NOV 81; To VA-15, NAS Cecil Field, FL., 11 NOV 81; To VA-15, USS Independence (CV-62), 11 NOV 81; To VA-15, NAS Cecil Field, FL., 23 APR 82 ** Transferred to VA-86/CVW-8, AJ/4XX, NAS Cecil Field, FL., 23 APR 82; To VA-86, USS Nimitz (CVN-68), 28 JUN 82; To VA-86, NAS Cecil Field, FL., 28 JUN 82; To VA-86, USS Nimitz (CVN-68), 28 JUN 82; To VA-86, NAS Cecil Field, FL., 13 MAY 83; To VA-86, NAS Roosevelt Roads, PR., 18 MAY 83; To VA-15, NAS Cecil Field, FL., 18 MAY 83; To VA-86, NAS Jacksonville, FL., 18 OCT 83; To VA-86, NAS Cecil Field, FL., 24 JAN 84; To VA-86, NAS Roosevelt Roads, PR., 24 JAN 84; To VA-86, NAS Cecil Field, FL., 24 JAN 84; To VA-86, USS Nimitz (CVN-68) 24 JAN 84; To VA-86, NAS Cecil Field, FL., 24 JAN 84; To VA-86, USS Nimitz (CVN-68); 24 JAN 84; To VA-86, NAS Cecil Field, FL., 24 JAN 84; To VA-86, NAS Jacksonville, FL., 06 JAN 86; To VA-86, NAS Cecil Field, FL., 05 FEB 86; To VA-86,

NAS Jacksonville, FL., 21 MAR 86; To VA-86, Cecil Field, FL., 27 MAR 86; To VA-86, USS Nimitz (CVN-68), 19 APR 86; To VA-86, Cecil Field, FL., 19 APR 86; To VA-86, USS Nimitz (CVN-68), 06 AUG 86; To VA-86, Cecil Field, FL., 07 AUG 86; To VA-86, USS Nimitz (CVN-68), 07 AUG 86; To VA-86, Cecil Field, FL., 01 MAY 87 ** Transferred to VA-174/FRS, AD/4XX, NAS Cecil Field, FL., 19 AUG 87 ** End of flight record card ** Transferred to VA-122/FRS, NJ/232, NAS LeMoore, CA., date unknown ** Transferred to AMARC, Davis Monthan AFB; Tucson, AZ., assigned park code 6A0274, 14 JUN 88 ** 7044.1 flight hours ** TF41A402D engine S/N 141578 ** Storage location 210526 ** Aircraft deleted from inventory and released to DRMO for disposition, 04 MAY 06 ** At AMARG, Davis Monthan AFB; Tucson, AZ., 15 JUN 07.

E-341 158026 Navy acceptance from NPRO Rep. LTV, Dallas, TX., 29 NOV 71 ** Transferred to VA-83/CVW-17, AA/3XX, NAS Cecil Field, FL., 30 NOV 71; To VA-83, USS Forrestal (CVA-59), 12 APR 72; To VA-83, NAS Jacksonville, FL., 22 OCT 74; To VA-83, NAS Cecil Field, FL., 22 OCT 74; To VA-83, NAS Jacksonville, FL., 23 OCT 74; To VA-83, NAS Cecil Field, 18 DEC 74; To VA-83, USS Forrestal (CVA-59), 18 DEC 74; To VA-83, NAS Cecil Field, 18 DEC 74; To VA-83, USS Forrestal (CVA-59), 18 DEC 74; To VA-83, NAS Cecil Field, 01 SEP 75; To VA-83, USS Forrestal (CV-59), 01 SEP 75; To VA-83, NAS Cecil Field, 01 SEP 75; To VA-83, USS Forrestal (CV-59), 01 SEP 75;To VA-83, NAS Cecil Field, 09 OCT 75; To VA-83, NAS Roosevelt Roads, PR., 09 OCT 75; To VA-83, NAS Cecil Field, 09 OCT 75; To VA-83, USS Forrestal (CV-59), 20 JUL 77; To VA-83, NAS Cecil Field, 20 JUL 77; To VA-83, USS Forrestal (CV-59), 23 DEC 77; To VA-83, NAS Cecil Field, 03 MAR 78; To VA-83, USS Forrestal (CV-59) ,04 APR 79; To VA-83, NAS Cecil Field, 04 APR 79; To VA-83, USS Forrestal (CV-59), 30 MAY 79; To VA-83, NAS Cecil Field, 02 JUN 79; To VA-83, USS Forrestal (CV-59), 02 JUN 79; To VA-83, NAS Cecil Field, 02 JUN 79; To VA-83, USS Forrestal (CV-59), 29 SEP 80; To VA-83, NAS Cecil Field, 24 SEP 80; To VA-83, USS Forrestal (CV-59), 02 FEB 81 ** Transferred to VA-174/FRS, AD/4XX, NAS Cecil Field, FL., 04 MAR 81; To VA-174, NAS Jacksonville, FL., 23 JUN 81; To VA-174, NAS Dallas, TX., 04 SEP 81; To VA-174, NAS Cecil Field, FL., 30 NOV 81 ** Transferred to VA-83/CVW-17, AA/3XX, NAS Cecil Field, FL., 03 DEC 81; To VA-83, NAS Fallon, NV., 03 DEC 81; To VA-83, NAS Cecil Field, 03 DEC 81; To VA-83, USS Forrestal (CV-59), 04 DEC 81; To VA-83, NAS Cecil Field, 04 DEC 81; To VA-83, USS Forrestal (CV-59), 04 DEC 81; To VA-83, NAS Cecil Field, 04 DEC 81 ** Transferred to VA-105/CVW-15, NL/ 4XX, USS Carl Vinson (CVN-70), 30 MAR 83; To VA-105, NAS Cecil Field, FL., 30 MAR 83; To VA-105, NAS Jacksonville, FL., 24 JAN 84; To VA-105, NAS Roosevelt roads, PR., 24 JAN 84; To VA-105, NAS Jacksonville, FL., 25 JAN 84; To VA-105, NAS Cecil Field, FL., 25 JAN 84; To VA-105, NAS Jacksonville, FL., 30 APR 84; To VA-105, NAS Cecil Field, FL., 01 MAY 84; To VA-105, NAF Kadena, JP., 08 MAY 84; To VA-105, NAS Cubi Point, PI., 08 MAY 84; To VA-105, MCAS Iwakuni, Japan, 08 MAY 84; To VA-105, NAS Cecil Field, FL., 28 NOV 84 ** Transferred to VA-15/CVW-6, AE/3XX, NAS Cecil Field, FL., 14 MAY 85; To VA-15, MCAS Iwakuni, JP., 04 NOV 85; To VA-15, Korea, 04 NOV 85; To VA-15, NAS Cubi Point, PI., 04 NOV 85; To VA-15, NAS Cecil Field, FL., 28 MAY 86; To VA-15, NAS Jacksonville, FL., 10 SEP 86; To VFA-15, NAS Cecil Field, FL., 09 OCT 86; To VFA-15, NAS Jacksonville, FL., 05 DEC 86; To VFA-15, NAS Cecil Field, FL., 06 DEC 86 ** Transferred to VA-72/CVW-7, AG/4XX, NAS Cecil Field, FL., 09 DEC 86; To VA-72, USS Dwight D. Eisenhower (CVN-69), 24 APR 87; To VA-72, NAS Cecil Field, FL., 24 APR 87 thru 08 SEP 87 ** End of flight record card ** On conditional loan from the National Museum of Naval Aviation; Pensacola, FL., to the Heritage in Flight Museum.

E-342 158027 Navy acceptance from NPRO Rep. LTV, Dallas, TX., 16 DEC 71 ** Transferred to VA-82/CVW-8, AJ/3XX, USS America (CVA-66), 21 DEC 71 ** Transferred to VA-81/CVW-17, AA/4XX, NAS Cecil Field, FL., 03 APR 72; To VA-81, USS Forrestal (CVA-59), 10 APR 72; To VA-81, NAS Cecil Field, FL., 01 OCT 74; To VA-81, NAS Jacksonville, FL., 14 NOV 74; To VA-81, NAS Cecil Field, FL., 03 JAN 75; To VA-81, USS Forrestal (CVA-59), 03 JAN 75; To

VA-81, NAS Cecil Field, FL., 01 SEP 75; To VA-81, USS Forrestal (CV-59), 30 SEP 75; To VA-81, NAS Cecil Field, FL., 30 SEP 75; To VA-81, NAS Roosevelt Roads, PR., 04 NOV 76; To VA-81, NAS Cecil Field, FL., 04 NOV 76; To VA-81, NAS Roosevelt Roads, PR., 07 APR 77; To VA-81, NAS Cecil Field, FL., 07 APR 77; To VA-81, USS Forrestal (CV-59), 20 JUL 77; To VA-81, NAS Jacksonville, FL., 11 DEC 77; To VA-81, NAS Cecil Field, FL., 11 JAN 78 ~ S 1SO strike, 15 JAN 78 ** Crashed on flight deck full of aircraft on USS Forrestal (CV-59). Pilot ejected, two killed, ten injured.

E-343 158028 Navy acceptance from NPRO Rep. LTV, Dallas, TX., 23 NOV 71 ** Transferred to VA-81/CVW-17, AA/4XX, NAS Cecil Field, FL., 24 NOV 71; To VA-81, USS Forrestal (CVA-59), 15 MAY 72; To VA-81, NAS Cecil Field, FL., 01 OCT 74; To VA-81, NAS Jacksonville, FL., 07 OCT 74; To VA-81, NAS Cecil Field, FL., 23 DEC 74; To VA-81, USS Forrestal (CVA-59), 23 DEC 74; To VA-81, NAS Cecil Field, FL., 01 SEP 75; To VA-81, USS Forrestal (CV-59), 06 OCT 75; To VA-81, NAS Cecil Field, FL., 06 OCT 75; To VA-81, NAS Roosevelt Roads, PR., 03 JAN 77; To VA-81, NAS Cecil Field, FL., 25 JAN 77; To VA-81, NAS Roosevelt Roads, PR., 25 JAN 77; To VA-81, NAS Cecil Field, FL., 25 JAN 77; To VA-81, USS Forrestal (CV-59), 09 NOV 77; To VA-81, NAS Jacksonville, FL., 20 DEC 77; To VA-81, USS Forrestal (CV-59), 26 JAN 78 ~ S 1SO strike, 25 JUN 78 ** No data on strike.

158652/158666 LTV A-7E-10-CV Corsair II; (Block X)
FY 72, Contract N00019-71-C-0470, (30) A-7E; E-345/E-374

E-359 158652 Navy acceptance from NPRO Rep. LTV, Dallas, TX., 12 JUL 72 ** Transferred to VA-174/FRS, AD/4XX, NAS Cecil Field, FL., 13 JUL 72; Transferred to VA-12/CVW-7, AG/4XX, USS Independence (CVA-62), 27 SEP 72; To VA-12, NAS Cecil Field, FL., 19 APR 73; To VA-12, USS Independence (CV-62), 01 JUL 73; To VA-12, NAS Cecil Field, FL., 01 JUL 73; To VA-12, NAS Jacksonville, FL., 20 MAR 75; To VA-12, NAS Cecil Field, FL., 19 APR 75; To VA-12, NAS Fallon, NV., 19 APR 75; To VA-12, NAS Cecil Field, FL., 01 JUL 75; To VA-12, USS Independence (CV-62), 03 SEP 75; To VA-12, NAS Cecil Field, FL., 07 MAY 76; To VA-12, NAS Fallon, NV., 31 AUG 76; To VA-12, USS Independence (CV-62), 01 NOV 76; To VA-12, NAS Cecil Field, FL., 01 NOV 76; To VA-12, USS Independence (CV-62), 01 NOV 76; To VA-12, NAS Cecil Field, FL., 01 NOV 76; To VA-12, USS Independence (CV-62), 01 FEB 77; To VA-12, NAS Cecil Field, FL., 09 AUG 77; To VA-12, USS Dwight D. Eisenhower (CVN-69), 09 AUG 77; To VA-12, NAS Cecil field, FL., 01 JUN 78; To VA-12, NAS Jacksonville, FL., 02 JUN 78; To VA-12, NAS Cecil Field, FL., 29 JUL 78; To VA-12, USS Dwight D. Eisenhower (CVN-69), 29 JUL 78; To VA-12, NAS Cecil Field, FL., 29 JUL 78; To VA-12, USS Dwight D. Eisenhower (CVN-69), 29 JUL 78; To VA-12, NAS Cecil Field, FL., 29 JUL 78; To VA-12, USS Dwight D. Eisenhower (CVN-69), 29 JUL 78; To VA-12, NAS Jacksonville, FL., 06 JAN 81; To VA-12, NAS Cecil Field, FL., 07 MAR 81; To VA-12, USS Dwight D. Eisenhower (CVN-69), 07 MAR 81; To VA-12, NAS Cecil Field, FL., 25 NOV 81; To VA-12, USS Dwight D. Eisenhower (CVN-69), 12 NOV 81; To VA-12, NAS Cecil Field, FL., 28 JUL 82; To VA-12, NAS Jacksonville, FL., 30 JUL 82; To VA-12, NAS Cecil Field, FL., 30 SEP 82; To VA-12, NAS Dallas, TX., 15 OCT 82 ** Transferred to VA-105/CVW-15, NL/4XX, NAS Cecil Field, FL., 22 DEC 82; To VA-105, USS Carl Vinson (CVN-70), 22 DEC 82; To VA-105, NAS Cecil Field, FL., 22 DEC 82; To VA-105, USS Carl Vinson (CVN-70), 22 DEC 82; To VA-105, NAS Cecil Field, FL.,22 DEC 82; To VA-105, NAS Roosevelt Roads, PR., 06 JAN 84; To VA-105, NAS Cecil Field, FL., 18 JAN 84; To VA-105, NAF Kadena, JP., 19 JUL 84; To VA-105, Cubi Point, PI., 07 AUG 84; To VA-105. MCAS Iwakuni, JP., 07 AUG 84; To VA-105, NAS Cecil Field, FL., 07 AUG 84; To VA-105, NAS Jacksonville, FL., 26 MAR 85 ** Transferred to VA-15/CVW-6, AE/3XX, NAS Cecil Field, FL., 29 MAR 85; To VA-15, MCAS Iwacuni, JP., 19 NOV 85; To VA-15, Korea, 19 NOV 85; To VA-15, NAS Cubi Point, PI., 07 APR 86; To VA-15, NAF Atsugi, JP., 14 APR 86; To VA-15, NAS Cubi Point, PI., 06 MAY 86; To VA-15, NAS Cecil Field, FL., 06 MAY 86 ** Transferred to VA-81/CVW-17, AA/4XX, NAS Cecil Field, FL., 09 JUL 86; To VA-81, USS Saratoga (CV-60), 29 SEP 86; To VA-81, NAS Cecil Field, FL., 03 OCT 86; To VA-81,

USS Saratoga (CV-60), 19 JAN 87; To VA-81, NAS Cecil Field, FL., 17 FEB 87; To VA-81, USS Saratoga (CV-60), 17 FEB 87; To VA-81, NAS Jacksonville, FL., 21 MAY 87; To VA-81, NAS Cecil Field, FL., 21 MAY 87; To VA-81, NAS Jacksonville, FL., 26 MAY 87; To VA-81, USS Saratoga (CV-60), 26 MAY 87; To VA-81, NAS Jacksonville, FL., 20 AUG 87 ** Transferred to VA-174/FRS, AD/4XX, NAS Cecil Field, FL., 25 AUG 87 ** End of flight record card ** Transferred to VA-204/CVWR-20, AF/4XX, NAS New Orleans, LA., date unknown ** Transferred to AMARC, Davis Monthan AFB; Tucson, AZ., assigned park code 6A0360, 04 JUN 90 ** 6737.7 flight hours ** TF41A402D engine S/N 142614 ** Storage location 210524 ** At AMARG, Davis Monthan AFB; Tucson, AZ., 15 JUN 07.

E-345 158653 Navy acceptance from NPRO Rep. LTV, Dallas, TX., 11 FEB 72 ** Transferred to VA-174/FRS, AD/4XX, NAS Cecil Field, FL., 16 FEB 72 ** Transferred to VA-122/FRS, NJ/2XX, CRAA, NAS LeMoore, CA., 14 MAY 72 ** Transferred to VA-146/CVW-9, NG/3XX, NAS LeMoore, CA., 01 JUN 72 ** Transferred to VA-192/CVW-11 NH/3XX, USS Kitty Hawk (CVA-63), 15 JUN 72; To VA-192, NAS LeMoore, CA., 18 JUN 72 ~ S 1SO strike, 19 SEP 72 ** No data on strike.

E-346 158654 Navy acceptance from NPRO Rep. LTV Dallas, TX., 28 JAN 72 ** Transferred to VA-86/ CVW-8, AJ/4XX, USS America (CVA-66), 29 JAN 72 ** Transferred to VA-83/CVW-17, AA/3XX, NAS Cecil Field, FL., 03 APR 72 ~ S 1SO strike, 22 APR 72 ** No data on strike.

E-347 158655 Navy acceptance from NPRO Rep. LTV Dallas, TX., 28 JAN 72 ** Transferred to VA-195/CVW-11, NH/4XX, USS Kitty Hawk (CVA-63), 29 JAN 72 ~ S 1SO strike, 06 MAR 72 ** CDR Donald L. Hall killed.

E-348 158656 Navy acceptance from NPRO Rep. LTV Dallas, TX., ** 11 MAR 72 ** Transferred to VA-97/CVW-14, NK/3XX, NAS LeMoore, CA., 12 FEB 72 ~ S 1SO strike, 16 MAY 72 ** No data on strike.

E-349 158657 Navy acceptance from NPRO Rep. LTV, Dallas, TX., 24 MAR 72 ** Transferred to VA-27/CVW-14, NK/4XX, NAS LeMoore, CA., 28 MAR 72; To VA-27, USS Enterprise (CVAN-65), 01 FEB 75; To VA-27, NAS LeMoore, CA., 20 MAY 75; To VA-27, NAS Jacksonville, FL., 05 AUG 75; To VA-27, NAS LeMoore, CA., 12 SEP 75; To VA-27, NAS Fallon, NV., 24 OCT 75; To VA-27, NAS LeMoore, CA., 19 FEB 76; To VA-27, USS Enterprise (CVAN-65), 12 MAR 76; To VA-27, NAS LeMoore, CA., 17 MAY 76; To VA-27, USS Enterprise (CVAN-65), 29 JUN 76; To VA-27, NAF Atsugi, JP., 07 SEP 76; To VA-27, USS Enterprise (CVAN-65), 27 SEP 76; To VA-27, NAF Atsugi, JP., 08 OCT 76; To VA-27, USS Enterprise (CVAN-65), 20 OCT 76; To VA-27, NAS LeMoore, CA., 28 MAR 77; To VA-27, USS Enterprise (CVN-65), 12 JAN 78; To VA-27, NAS LeMoore, CA., 03 MAR 78; To VA-27, NAF Atsugi, JP., 26 JUN 78; To VA-27, USS Enterprise (CVN-65), 27 JUN 78;To VA-27, NAS Cubi Point, PI., 30 JUN 78; To VA-27, NAS LeMoore, CA., 10 OCT 78; To VA-27, NAS Jacksonville, FL., 26 JAN 79; To VA-27, NPTR El Centro, CA., 29 MAR 79; To VA-27, NAS LeMoore, CA., 12 NOV 79 To VA-27, NAS Cubi Point, PI., 12 NOV 79; To VA-27, USS Coral Sea (CV-43), 23 DEC 79; To VA-27, NAF Atsugi, JP., 29 APR 80 ** Transferred to VA-56/CVW-5, NF/4XX, USS Midway (CV-41), 14 JUL 80; To VA-56, NAF Atsugi, JP., 25 NOV 80; To VA-56, USS Midway (CV-41), 24 FEB 81; To VA-56, NAF Atsugi, JP., 27 MAY 81; To VA-56, USS Midway (CV-41), 28 MAY 81; To VA-56, NAF Atsugi, JP., 09 JUN 81; To VA-56, USS Midway (CV-41), 03 SEP 81; To VA-56, NAF Atsugi, JP., 04 OCT 81 ** Transferred to VA-25/CVW-2, NE/4XX, USS Ranger (CV-61), 29 AUG 82; To VA-25, NAS LeMoore, CA., 29 AUG 82; To VA-25, Bloomfield, 08 JUN 83; To VA-25, NAS LeMoore, CA., 09 JUN 83; To VFA-25, NAS Jacksonville, FL., 07 SEP 83; To VFA-25, NAS LeMoore, CA., 12 SEP 83; To VFA-25, NAS Dallas, TX., 22 FEB 84 **Transferred to VA-22/CVW-11, NH/305, NAS LeMoore, CA., 22 FEB 84, To VA-22, USS Enterprise (CVN-65), 22 FEB 84 ** Transferred to VA-56/CVW-5, NF/4XX, NAF Atsugi, JP., 18 NOV 84; To VA-56, NAS LeMoore, CA., 21 APR 86; To VA-56, NAS Jacksonville, FL.,

11 JUL 86 ** Transferred to VA-146/CVW-9, NE/3XX, USS Kitty Hawk (CV-63), 12 JUL 86; To VA-146, NAS LeMoore, CA., 20 APR 87 thru 14 SEP 87 ** End of flight record card ** Painted in tan and brown in APR 88, no tail code.

E-350 158658 Navy acceptance from NPRO Rep. LTV, Dallas, TX., 24 APR 72 ** Transferred to VA-27/CVW-14, NK/402, NAS LeMoore, CA., 25 APR 72; To VA-27, USS Enterprise (CVAN-65), 11 DEC 74; To VA-27, NAS LeMoore, CA., 20 MAY 75; To VA-27, NAS Alameda, CA., 22 MAY 75; To VA-27, NAS LeMoore, CA., 28 MAY 75; To VA-27, NAS Fallon, NV., 28 MAY 75; To VA-27, NAS LeMoore, CA., 28 JUL 75; To VA-27, USS Enterprise (CVN-65), 28 JUL 75; To VA-27, NAS Alameda, CA., 30 MAR 76; To VA-27, NAS LeMoore, CA., 30 MAR 76; To VA-27, NAS Alameda, CA., 15 APR 76; To VA-27, NAS LeMoore, CA., 04 MAY 76 ** Transferred to VA-122/FRS, NJ/2XX, NAS LeMoore, CA., 12 MAY 76; To VA-122, NAS Alameda, CA., 18 APR 78; To VA-122, NAS LeMoore, CA., 02 JUN 78; To VA-122, NAS Jacksonville, FL., 29 AUG 78; To VA-122, NAS LeMoore, CA., 23 OCT 78; To VA-122, NAS Jacksonville, FL., 21 NOV 80; To VA-122, NAS LeMoore, CA., 21 NOV 80; To VA-122, NAS Jacksonville, FL., 24 NOV 80; To VA-122, NAS LeMoore, CA., 21 FEB 81** Transferred to VA-27/CVW-14, NK-4XX, NAS LeMoore, CA., 02 MAR 81; To VA-27, USS Coral Sea (CV-43), 16 APR 81; To VA-27, NAS LeMoore, CA., 08 JUN 81; To VA-27, USS Coral Sea (CV-43), 20 AUG 81; To VA-27, NAS LeMoore, CA., 22 MAR 82; To VA-27, NAS Alameda, CA., 27 SEP 82; To VA-27, NAS LeMoore, CA., 13 DEC 82; ** Transferred to VA-147/CVW-9, NG/4XX, NAS LeMoore, CA., 30 DEC 82; To VA-147, NAS Jacksonville, FL., 18 APR 83; To VA-147, NAS LeMoore, 06 JUL 83; To VA-147, NAS Dallas, TX., 07 JUL 83 ** Transferred to VA-146/CVW-9, NE/3XX, NAS LeMoore, CA., 06 OCT 83; To VA-146, USS Kitty Hawk (CV-63), 09 OCT 83; To VA-146, NAF Atsugi, JP., 21 JUN 84; To VA-146, USS Kitty Hawk (CV-63), 24 JUN 84 ** Transferred to VA-93/CVW-5, NF/3XX, NAF Atsugi, JP., 07 JUL 84 ** Transferred to VA-56/CVW-5, NF/4XX, NAS LeMoore, CA., 23 APR 86; To VA-56, NAS Jacksonville, FL., 29 APR 86; To VA-56, NAS LeMoore, CA., 19 AUG 86; To VA-56, NAS Jacksonville, FL., 28 AUG 86 ** Transferred to VA-122/FRS, NJ/2XX, NAS LeMoore, CA., 28 AUG 86 ** Transferred to VA-94/CVW-11, NH/4XX, NAS LeMoore, CA., 13 APR 87 thru 19 MAY 87 ** End of flight record card ** Transferred to VA-27/CVW-15, NL/402, NAS LeMoore, CA., date unknown ** Transferred to AMARC, Davis Monthan AFB; Tucson, AZ., assigned park code 6A0386, 14 NOV 90 ** 6808.6 flight hours ** TF41A402D engine S/N 142553 ** Aircraft released from storage and prepared for overland shipment to FMS, NAS Jacksonville, FL., with final shipment to Thailand government, 31 JAN 95 ** Transferred to the Royal Thai Navy, S/N 1408, JUL 95.

E-351 158659 Navy acceptance from NPRO Rep. LTV, Dallas, TX., 16 MAR 72 ** Transferred to VA-174/FRS, AD/4XX, NAS Cecil Field, FL., 18 MAR 72 ** Transferred to VA-122/FRS, NJ/2XX, CRAA, NAS LeMoore, CA., 14 MAY 72 ** Transferred to VA-195/CVW-11, NH/4XX, USS Kitty Hawk (CVA-63), 28 MAY 72 ** Transferred to VA-122/FRS, NJ/2XX, NAS LeMoore, CA., 20 SEP 73 ** Transferred to VA-192/CVW-11, NH/3XX, NAS LeMoore, CA. Painted light gray on dark gray, 01 JUN 76; To VA-192, MCAS Yuma, AZ., 30 NOV 76 ** Transferred to VA-122/FRS, NJ/2XX, NAS LeMoore, CA., 15 JUN 77; To VA-122, NAS Jacksonville, FL., 18 FEB 78; To VA-122, NAS LeMoore, CA., 21 FEB 78; To VA-122, NAS Jacksonville, FL., 02 FEB 80; To VA-122, NAS LeMoore, CA., 28 MAR 80 ** Transferred to VA-192/CVW-11, NH/3XX, NAS Fallon, NV., 20 OCT 80; To VA-192, NAS LeMoore, CA., 07 NOV 80; To VA-192, USS America (CV-66), 24 DEC 80; To VA-192, NAS LeMoore, CA., 08 APR 81; To VA-192, NAS Jacksonville, FL., 02 FEB 82; To VA-192, NAS LeMoore, CA., 12 APR 82; To VA-192, NAS Dallas, TX., 21 APR 82; To VA-192, NAS LeMoore, CA., 07 JUL 82; To VA-192/CVW-9, NG/3XX, USS Ranger (CV-61), 15 JUL 83 ~ S 1SO strike, 30 OCT 83. No data on strike.

E-352 158660 Navy acceptance from NPRO Rep. LTV, Dallas, TX., 18 APR 72 ** Transferred to NPRO Rep. LTV, Dallas, TX., for RDT & E, 19 APR 72 ** Transferred to VA-174/FRS, AD/444, NAS Cecil Field, FL. 13 APR 73 ~ S 1SO strike, 16 AUG 75 ** No data on strike ** Transferred to AMARC, Davis Monthan AFB; Tucson, AZ., assigned park code 6A0292.

E-353 158661 Navy acceptance from NPRO Rep. LTV, Dallas, TX., 15 MAY 72 ** Transferred to VA-113/CVW-2, NE/3XX, NAS LeMoore, CA., 16 MAY 72; To VA-113, USS Ranger (CV-61), 21 JUN 73; To VA-113, NAS Jacksonville, FL., 01 NOV 74; To VA-113, NAS LeMoore, CA., 04 JAN 75; To VA-113, USS Ranger (CV-61), 16 AUG 75; To VA-113, NAS LeMoore, CA., 30 SEP 76; To VA-113, NAS Jacksonville, FL., 06 JAN 78; To VA-113, NAS LeMoore, CA., 14 JAN 78; To VA-113, NAS Jacksonville, FL., 31 JAN 78; To VA-113, NAS LeMoore, CA., 24 MAR 78; To VA-113, USS Ranger (CV-61), 27 SEP 78; To VA-113, NAS LeMoore, CA., 13 OCT 78; To VA-113, USS Ranger (CV-61), 09 NOV 78; To VA-113, NAS LeMoore, CA., 13 DEC 78; To VA-113, USS Ranger (CV-61), 22 MAR 79; To VA-113, NAS Cubi Point, PI., 02 JUL 79; To VA-113, NAS LeMoore, CA., 02 JUL 79; To VA-113, NAS Fallon, NV., 22 SEP 79; To VA-113, NAS LeMoore, CA., 26 JAN 80; To VA-113, USS Ranger (CV-61), 05 MAY 80; To VA-113, NAS LeMoore, CA., 09 JUL 80; To VA-113, USS Ranger (CV-61), 18 JUL 80; To VA-113, NAS Cubi Point, PI., 24 OCT 80; To VA-113, NAS LeMoore, CA., 04 APR 81; To VA-113, NAS Fallon, NV., 14 SEP 81; To VA-113, USS Ranger (CV-61), 14 OCT 81; To VA-113, NAS LeMoore, CA., 13 NOV 81; To VA-113, USS Ranger (CV-61), 13 DEC 81 ** Transferred to VA-195/CVW-11, NH/4XX, NAS LeMoore, CA., 26 JAN 82; To VA-195, NAS Alameda, CA., 25 FEB 82; To VA-195, NAS LeMoore, CA., 06 APR 82; To VA-195, NAS Jacksonville, FL., 29 JUL 82; To VA-195, NAS LeMoore, CA., 18 OCT 82 ** Transferred to VA-192/CVW-9, NG/4XX, USS Ranger (CV-61), 24 JAN 83; To VA-192, NAS LeMoore, CA., 19 DEC 83 ** Transferred to VA-94/CVW-11, NH/4XX, NAS LeMoore, CA., 08 MAR 85; To VA-94, NAS Fallon, NV., 18 APR 85; To VA-94, NAS LeMoore, CA., 19 APR 85; To VA-94, NAS Jacksonville, FL., 27 JUN 85; To VA-94, NAS LeMoore, CA., 27 JUN 85; To VA-94, NAS Jacksonville, FL., 08 JUL 85; To VA-94, NAS LeMoore, CA., 07 OCT 85; To VA-94, USS Enterprise (CVN-65), 07 OCT 85; To VA-94, NAS LeMoore, CA., 28 FEB 86 thru 02 SEP 87 ** End of flight record card.

E-354 158662 Navy acceptance from NPRO Rep. LTV, Dallas, TX., 11 MAY 72 ** Transferred to VA-174/FRS, AD/4XX, NAS Cecil Field, FL., 12 MAY 72 ** Transferred to VA-86/CVW-8, AJ/4XX, NAS Cecil Field, FL., 15 JAN 75; To VA-86, USS Nimitz (CVN-68), 15 JAN 75; To VA-86, NAS Cecil Field, FL., 15 JAN 75; To VA-86, NAS Roosevelt Roads, PR., 15 JAN 75; To VA-86, NAS Cecil Field, FL., 15 JAN 75; To VA-86, USS Nimitz CVN-68), 15 JAN 75; To VA-86, NAS Cecil Field, FL., 15 JAN 75; To VA-86, USS Nimitz (CVN-68), 08 MAY 76; To VA-86, NAS Cecil Field, FL., 01 NOV 76; To VA-86, NAS Roosevelt Roads, PR., 01 MAY 77; To VA-86, USS Nimitz (CVN-68), 03 AUG 77; To VA-86, NAS Cecil Field, FL., 23 AUG 77; To VA-86, USS Nimitz(CVN-68), 23 AUG 77; To VA-86, NAS Cecil Field, FL., 18 JUL 78; To VA-86, NAS Jacksonville, FL., 19 JUL 78; To VA-86, NAS Cecil Field, FL., 05 OCT 78; To VA-86, NAS Roosevelt Roads, PR., 05 OCT 78; To VA-86, USS Nimitz (CVN-68), 05 OCT 78; To VA-86, NAS Cecil Field, FL., 05 OCT 78; To VA-86, USS Nimitz (CVN-68), 10 JUN 80; To VA-86, NAS Cecil Field, FL., 24 JUN 80; To VA-86, USS Nimitz (CVN-68), 13 MAR 81; To VA-86, NAS Cecil Field, FL., 13 MAR 81; To VA-86, USS Nimitz (CVN-68), 13 MAR 81; To VA-86, NAS Cecil Field, FL., 12 FEB 82 ** Transferred to VA-174/FRS, AD/4XX, NAS Cecil Field, FL., 15 JUN 82; To VA-174, NAS Jacksonville, FL., 03 DEC 82; To VA-174, NAS Cecil Field, FL., 03 DEC 82; To VA-174, NAS Jacksonville, FL., 03 DEC 82; To VA-174, NAS Dallas, TX., 07 MAR 83 ** Transferred to VA-46/CVW-1, AB/3XX, NAS Cecil Field, FL., 02 JUN 83; To VA-46, USS America (CV-66), 19 JUL 83; To VA-46, NAS Cecil Field, FL., 19 JUL 83; To VA-46, USS America (CV-66), 19 JUL 83; To VA-46, NAS Cecil Field, FL., 02 APR 84; To VA-46, USS America (CV-66), 17 APR 84; To VA-46, NAS Cecil Field, FL., 17 APR 84; To VA-46, USS America (CV-66), 06 MAY 85; To VA-46, NAS Cecil Field, FL., 21 MAY 85; To VA-46, USS America (CV-66), 29 JUL 85; To VA-46, NAS Jacksonville, FL., 23 AUG 85; To VA-46, USS America (CV-66), 16 OCT 85; To VA-46, NAS Cecil Field, FL., 16 OCT 85; To VA-46, USS America (CV-66), 16 OCT 85; To VA-46, NAS Cecil Field, FL., 19 SEP 86 ** Transferred to VA-83/CVW-17, AA/3XX, NAS Cecil Field, FL., 14 OCT 86; To VA-83, USS Saratoga (CV-60), 11 MAR 87; To VA-83, NAS Cecil Field, FL., 17 MAR 87; To VA-83, USS Saratoga (CV-60), 28 APR 87; To VA-83, NAS Cecil Field, FL., 28 APR 87; To VA-83, USS Saratoga (CV-60), 04 MAY 87 ** End of flight record card ** On conditional loan from the National Museum of Naval Aviation; Pensacola, FL. to NAS Oceana, VA.

E-355 158663 Navy acceptance from NPRO Rep. LTV, Dallas, TX., 24 MAY 72 ** Transferred to VA-174/FRS, AD/4XX, NAS Cecil Field, FL., 07 JUN 72 ** Transferred to VA-37/CVW-3, AC/3XX, NAS Cecil Field, FL., 23 APR 73; To VA-37, USS Saratoga (CV-60), 19 MAR 74; To VA-37, NAS Cecil Field, FL., 19 MAR 74; To VA-37 USS Saratoga (CV-60), 19 MAR 74; To VA-37, NAS Cecil Field, FL., 19 MAR 74; To VA-37 USS Saratoga (CV-60), 19 MAR 74; To VA-37, NAS Cecil Field, FL., 01 MAR 75; To VA-37, NAS Jacksonville, FL., 30 APR 75; To VA-37, NAS Cecil Field, FL., 07 MAY 75; To VA- 37, USS Saratoga (CV-60), 03 SEP 75; To VA-37, NAS Cecil Field, FL., 03 SEP 75; To VA- 37, USS Saratoga (CV-60), 29 SEP 76; To VA-37, NAS Cecil Field, FL., 29 SEP 76; To VA- 37, USS Saratoga (CV-60), 29 SEP 76; To VA-37, NAS Cecil Field, FL., 16 JUL 77; To VA- 37, NAS Jacksonville, FL., 20 APR 78; To VA-37, NAS Cecil Field, FL., 15 MAY 78; To VA-37 USS Saratoga (CV-60), 21 AUG 78; To VA-37, NAS Cecil Field, FL., 17 MAY 79; To VA-37, USS Saratoga (CV-60), 01 AUG 79; To VA-37, NAS Cecil Field, FL., 01 AUG 79; To VA-37, USS Saratoga (CV-60), 01 AUG 79; To VA-37, NAS Cecil Field, FL., 28 AUG 80; To VA-37, NAS Fallon, NV., 11 SEP 80; To VA-37, NAS Cecil Field, FL., 11 SEP 80; To VA-37, USS John F. Kennedy (CV-67), 11 SEP 80 ** Transferred to VA-174/FRS, AD/4XX, NAS Cecil Field, FL., 01 AUG 81; To VA-174, NAS Jacksonville, FL., 04 SEP 81; To VA-174, NAS Cecil Field, FL., 20 OCT 81 ** Transferred to VA-12/CVW-7, AG/4XX, USS Dwight D. Eisenhower (CVN-69), 26 OCT 81; To VA-12, NAS Cecil Field, FL., 26 OCT 81; To VA-12, NAS Cecil Field, FL., 26 JUL 82 ** Transferred to VA-174/FRS, AD/4XX, NAS Cecil Field, FL., 21 DEC 82; To VA-174, NAS Jacksonville, FL., 28 MAR 84 ** Transferred to VA-66/CVW-7, AG/3XX, NAS Cecil Field, FL., 28 MAR 84; To VA-66, USS Dwight D. Eisenhower (CVN-69), 28 MAR 84; To VA-66, NAS Cecil Field, FL., 28 MAR 84; To VA-66, USS Dwight D. Eisenhower (CVN-69), 28 MAR 84; To VA-66, NAS Cecil Field, FL., 28 MAR 84; To VA-66, USS Dwight D. Eisenhower (CVN-69), 28 MAR 84; To VA-66, NAS Cecil Field, FL., 13 MAY 85; To VA-66, USS Dwight D. Eisenhower (CVN-69), 22 MAY 85; To VA-66, NAS Cecil Field, FL., 26 SEP 85; To VA-66, NAS Jacksonville, FL., 06 FEB 86; To VA-66, NAS Cecil Field, FL., 12 MAR 86 ** Transferred to VA-86/CVW-8, AJ/4XX, NAS Jacksonville, FL., 23 APR 86 ** Transferred to VA-66/CVW-3, AC/3XX, NAS Cecil Field, FL., 24 APR 86; To VA-66, USS John F. Kennedy (CV-67), 24 APR 86; To VA-66, NAS Cecil Field, FL., 24 APR 86 ** Transferred to VA-37/CVW-6, AE/3XX, NAS Cecil Field, FL., 17 MAR 87; To VA-37, USS Forrestal (CV-59), 14 MAY 87 ** End of flight record card ** Transferred to VA-22/CVW-11, NH/306, NAS LeMoore, CA., date unknown ** Transferred to AMARC, Davis Monthan AFB; Tucson, AZ., assigned park code 6A0294; 10 AUG 89 ** 7033.7 flight hours ** TF41A402D engine S/N 141934 ** Storage location 210515 ** At AMARG, Davis Monthan AFB; Tucson, AZ., 15 JUN 07.

E-356 158664 Navy acceptance from NPRO Rep. LTV, Dallas, TX., 30 JUN 72 ** Transferred to VA-113/CVW-2, NE/3XX, NAS LeMoore, CA., 26 JUL 72; To VA-113, USS Ranger (CV-61), 21 JUN 73; To VA-113, NAS LeMoore, CA., 07 MAY 74; To VA-113, USS Ranger (CV-61), 07 MAY 74; To VA-113, NAS LeMoore, CA., 04 DEC 74; To VA-113, NAS Jacksonville, FL., 05 DEC 74; To VA-113, NAS LeMoore, CA., 09 FEB 75; To VA-113, USS Ranger (CV-61), 16 AUG 75, painted in bicentennial colors, 04 JUL 76; To VA-113, NAS LeMoore, CA., 30 SEP 76; To VA-113, NAS Jacksonville, FL., 21 AUG 78; To VA-113, NAS LeMoore, CA., 24 AUG 78; To VA-113, USS Ranger (CV-61), 04 OCT 78; To VA-113, NAS Jacksonville, FL., 15 DEC 78; To VA-113, NAS LeMoore, CA., 15 DEC 78; To VA-113, USS Ranger (CV-61), 22 MAR 79; To VA-113, NAS Cubi Point, PI.,02 JUL 79; To VA-113, NAS Fallon, NV., 22 SEP 79; To VA-113, NAS LeMoore, CA., 26 JAN 80; To VA-113, USS Ranger (CV-61), 05 MAY 80; To VA-113, NAS LeMoore, CA., 28 JUN 80; To VA-113, USS Ranger (CV-61), 18 JUL 80; To VA-113, NAS Cubi Point, PI., 24 OCT 80; To VA-113, NAF Atsugi, JP., 14 NOV 80; To VA-113, NAS Cubi Point, PI., 25 NOV 80; To VA-113, USS Ranger (CV-61), 04 MAY 81; To VA-113, NAS LeMoore, CA., 02 JUN 81; To VA-113, NAS Jacksonville, FL., 03 JUN 81; To VA-113, NAS LeMoore, CA., 18 JUN 81; To VA-113, NAS Jacksonville, FL., 20 JUL 81 ** Transferred to VA-97/CVW-15, NL/3XX, USS Coral Sea (CV-43), 20 AUG 81; To VA-97, NAS LeMoore, CA., 22 MAR 82 ** Transferred to VA-147/CVW-9, NG/4XX, NAS LeMoore, CA., 09 JUL 82; To VA-147, NAS Jacksonville, FL., 15 SEP 83 ** Transferred to VA-22/CVW-11, NH/3XX, NAS LeMoore, CA., 08 MAR 84; To VA-22, USS Enterprise CVN-65), 19 JUN 84; To VA-22, NAF Atsugi, JP., 18 SEP 84; To VA-22, USS Enterprise (CVN-65), 03 OCT 84; To VA-22, NAF Atsugi, JP., 31 OCT 84 ** Transferred to VA-56/CVW-5, NF/4XX, NAF Atsugi, JP., 20 AUG 85; To VA-56, NAS LeMoore, CA., 24 DEC 85 ** Transferred to VA-146/CVW-9, NE/3XX, NAS LeMoore, CA., 09 MAY 86; To VA-146, NAS Jacksonville, FL., 28 AUG 86 ** Transferred to VA-22/CVW-11, NH/3XX, NAS LeMoore, CA. 12 DEC 86 thru 14 APR 87 ** End of flight record card.

E-357 158665 Navy acceptance from NPRO Rep. LTV, Dallas, TX., 13 JUN 72 ** Transferred to VA-97/CVW-14, NK/301, NAS LeMoore, CA., 14 JUN 72; To VA-97, USS Enterprise (CVAN-65), 01 APR 75; To VA-97, NAS LeMoore, CA., 20 MAY 75; To VA-97, NAS Jacksonville, FL., 24 SEP 75; To VA-97, NAS LeMoore, CA.,05 JAN 76; To VA-97, USS Enterprise (CVN-65), 20 FEB 76; To VA-97, NAS LeMoore, CA., 27 APR 76; To VA-97, USS Enterprise (CVN-65), 28 JUL 76 ** Transferred to VA-93/CVW-5, NF/3XX, USS Midway (CV-41), 13 MAR 77; To VA-93, NAF Atsugi, JP., 31 JAN 78; To VA-93, USS Midway (CV-41), 28 MAR 78; To VA-93, NAF Atsugi, JP., 21 MAY 78; To VA-93, USS Midway (CV-41), 29 NOV 79; To VA-93, NAF Atsugi, JP., 29 NOV 79; To VA-93, USS Midway (CV-41), 15 APR 80; To VA-93, NAF Atsugi, JP., 16 SEP 80; To VA-93, USS Midway (CV-41), 17 SEP 80; To VA-93, NAF Atsugi, JP., 05 NOV 80 ** Transferred to VA-56/CVW-5, NF/4XX, USS Midway (CV-41), 12 DEC 80; To VA-56, NAF Atsugi, JP., 06 FEB 81; To VA-56, USS Midway (CV-41), 23 FEB 81; To VA-56, NAF Atsugi, JP., 26 MAY 81; To VA-56, USS Midway (CV-41), 29 MAY 81; To VA-56, NAF Atsugi, JP.,27 JUN 81; To VA-56, USS Midway (CV-41), 06 SEP 81; To VA-56, NAF Atsugi, JP., 17 OCT 81 ** Transferred to VA-25/CVW-2, NE/412, NAS Cubi Point, PI., 30 AUG 82; To VA-25, USS Ranger (CV-61), 30 AUG 82; To VA-25, NAS LeMoore, CA. 30 AUG 82; To VA-25, NAS Jacksonville, FL., 23 FEB 83 ** Transferred to VA-147/CVW-9, NE/3XX, NAS LeMoore, CA., 04 APR 83; To VA-147, USS Kitty Hawk (CV-63), 03 FEB 84; To VA-147, NAS LeMoore, CA., 28 SEP 84; To VA-147, NAS Jacksonville, FL., 08 MAR 85; To VA-147, NAS LeMoore, CA., 08 MAR 85; To VA-147, NAS Jacksonville, FL., 11 MAR 85; To VA-147, NAS LeMoore, CA., 31 MAY 85; To VA-147, USS Kitty Hawk (CV-63), 11 JUL 85; To VA-147, NAS LeMoore, CA., 09 JUL 86; To VA-147, NAS Pensacola, FL., 17 JUL 86 ** Transferred to VA-304/CVWR-30, ND/410, NAS Alameda, CA. 18 JUL 86 ** Transferred to VA-147/CVW-9, NE/3XX, NAS LeMoore, CA., 29 JUL 86 ** Transferred to VA-304/CVWR-30, ND/410, NAS Alameda, CA. 20 NOV 86 thru 10 SEP 87 ** End of flight record card ** Transferred to AMARC, Davis Monthan AFB; Tucson,AZ., assigned park code 6A0285; 29 JUL 88 ** 5175.1 flight hours ** TF41A402D engine S/N 142559 ** Project changed per FSO letter, 06 DEC 04 ** ** Engine records released to DRMO for disposition, 21 DEC 04 ** Aircraft deleted from inventory and released to DRMO for disposition, 19 JAN 05.

E-358 158666 Navy acceptance from NPRO Rep. LTV, Dallas, TX., 13 JUN 72 ** Transferred to VA-25/CVW-2, NE/400, NAS LeMoore, CA.,15 JUN 72; To VA-25, USS Ranger (CV-61), 21 JUN 73; To VA-25, NAS Jacksonville, FL., 06 NOV 74; To VA-25, NAS LeMoore, CA., 14 FEB 75; To VA-25, NAS Fallon, NV., 13 JUL 75; To VA-25, USS Ranger (CV-61), 14 AUG 75; To VA-25, NAS LeMoore, CA., 31 OCT 75; To VA-25, USS Ranger (CV-61), 19 DEC 75; To VA-25, NAF Atsugi, JP., 17 MAY 76; To VA-25, USS Ranger (CV-61), 19 MAY 76; To VA-25, NAS LeMoore, CA., 26 OCT 76; To VA-25, NAS Fallon, NV., 31 JUL 77; To VA-25, NAS LeMoore, CA., 12 AUG 77; To VA-25, NAS Jacksonville, FL., 10 JAN 78; To VA-25, NAS LeMoore, CA., 13 FEB 78; To VA-25, USS Ranger (CV-61), 30 NOV 78; To VA-25, NAS LeMoore, CA., 15 DEC 78; To VA-25, USS Ranger (CV-61), 17 JAN 79; To VA-25, NAS Cubi Point, PI., 20 FEB 79; To VA-25, NAS LeMoore, CA., 07 DEC 79; To VA-25, NAS Jacksonville, FL., 10 DEC 79; To VA-25, NAS Fallon, NV., 11 DEC 79; To VA-25, NAS LeMoore, CA., 30 JAN 80; To VA-25, USS Ranger (CV-61), 29 MAY 80; To VA-25, NAS LeMoore, CA., 26 JUN 80; To VA-25, USS Ranger (CV-61), 18 JUL 80; To VA-25, NAS LeMoore, CA., 07 AUG 80; To VA-25, USS Ranger (CV-61), 10 SEP 80; To VA-25, NAS LeMoore, CA., 17 FEB 81; To VA-25, NAS Fallon, NV., 14 SEP 81; USS Ranger (CV-61), 20 OCT 81; To VA-25, NAS LeMoore, CA., 20 OCT 81; To VA-25, USS Ranger (CV-61), 14 JAN 82; To VA-25, NAS LeMoore, CA., 14 JAN 82; To VA-25, NAS Jacksonville, FL., 27 MAR 82; To VA-25, USS Ranger (CV-61), 30 MAR 82; To VA-25, NAS Jacksonville, FL., 21 MAY 82; To VA-25, NAS Cubi Point, PI., 24 MAY 82; To VA-25, NAS Dallas, TX., 28 JUL 82 ** Transferred to VA-22/CVW-11, NH/3XX, NAS LeMoore, CA., 02 AUG 82; To VA-22, USS Enterprise (CVN-65), 03 AUG 82; To VA-22, NAS LeMoore, CA., 20 APR 83 ** Transferred to VA-97/CVW-15, NL/3XX, NAS LeMoore, CA., 19 DEC 83; To VA-97, USS Carl Vinson (CVN-70), 17 JAN 84; To VA-97, NAS LeMoore, CA., 17 JAN 84; To VA-97, USS Carl Vinson (CVN-70), 17 JAN 84; To VA-97, NAS LeMoore, CA., 18 JAN 84; To VA-97, USS Carl Vinson (CVN-70), 12 JUL 84; To VA-97, NAS LeMoore, CA., 12 JUL 84 ** Transferred to VA-192/CVW-9, NG/3XX, NAS LeMoore, CA., 27 AUG 84 ** Transferred to VA-94/CVW-11, NH/4XX, NAS LeMoore, CA., 27 FEB 85; To VA-94, NAS Fallon, NV., 27 FEB 85; To VA-94, NAS LeMoore, CA., 27 FEB 85; To VA-94, NAS Jacksonville, FL., 20 JUN 85; To VA-94, NAS LeMoore, CA., 24 JUN 85; To VA-94, NAS Jacksonville, FL., 24 SEP 85; To VA-94, NAS LeMoore, CA., 28 SEP 85 thru 03 AUG 87 ** End of flight record card ** Transferred to AMARC, Davis Monthan AFB; Tucson, AZ., assigned park code 6A0291; MAY 90 ** 6172.8 flight hours ** TF41A402D engine S/N 141236 ** Aircraft released from storage and prepared for overland shipment to FMS and NAD, NAS Jacksonville, FL., with final shipment to Thailand government, 29 NOV 95 ** Transferred to the Royal Thai Navy, S/N 158666.

158667/158681 LTV A-7E-11-CV Corsair II; (Block XI)

E-374 158667 Navy acceptance from NPRO Rep. LTV, Dallas, TX., 11 JUL 72 ** Transferred to VX-5, XE/XXX, NAF China Lake, CA., 13 JUL 72; To VX-5, NAS LeMoore, CA., 31 JUL 75; To VX-5, NAF China Lake, CA., 01 SEP 75; To VX-5, NAS Jacksonville, FL., 06 DEC 75; To VX-5, NAF China Lake, CA., 06 DEC 75; To VX-5, NAS Jacksonville, FL., 17 DEC 75; To VX-5, NAF China Lake, CA., 27 FEB 76 ** Transferred to VA-86/CVW-8, AJ/4XX, NAS Cecil Field, FL., 27 FEB 76; To VA-86, USS Nimitz (CVN-68), 27 FEB 76; To VA-86, NAS Cecil Field, FL., 27 FEB 76; To VA-86, NAS Roosevelt Roads, PR., 27 FEB 76; To VA-86, USS Nimitz (CVN-68), 19 JUL 77; To VA-86, NAS Cecil Field, FL., 19 JUL 77; To VA-86, USS Nimitz (CVN-68), 19 JUL 77; To VA-86, NAS Cecil Field, FL.,

19 JUL 77; To VA-86, NAS Jacksonville, FL., 26 SEP 78; To VA-86, NAS Cecil Field, FL., 24 OCT 78; To VA-86, NAS Roosevelt Roads, PR., 24 OCT 78; To VA-86, NAS Cecil Field, FL., 24 OCT 78; To VA-86, USS Nimitz (CVN-68), 24 OCT 78; To VA-86, NAS Cecil Field, FL., 09 MAY 79 ** Transferred to VA-83/CVW-17, AA/314, USS Forrestal (CV-59), 20 MAR 80; To VA-83, NAS Cecil Field, FL., 20 MAR 80; To VA-83, NAS Jacksonville, FL., 27 JUN 80; To VA-83, NAS Cecil Field, FL., 21 AUG 80; To VA-83, USS Forrestal CV-59), 02 OCT 80; To VA-83, NAS Cecil Field, FL., 02 OCT 80; To VA-83, USS Forrestal CV-59), 27 FEB 81; To VA-83, NAS Cecil Field, FL., 27 FEB 81; To VA-83, NAS Fallon, NV., 09 NOV 81; To VA-83, NAS Cecil Field, FL., 09 NOV 81 ** Transferred to VA-81/CVW-17, AA/4XX, NAS Fallom, NV., 18 FEB 82; To VA-81, USS Forrestal (CV-59), 18 FEB 82; To VA-81, NAS Cecil Field, FL., 11 MAY 82; To VA-81, USS Forrestal (CV-59), 22 MAY 82; To VA-81, NAS Cecil Field, FL., 22 MAY 82; To VA-81, NAS Jacksonville, FL., 10 FEB 83; To VA-81, NAS Dallas, TX., 27 JUL 83 ** Transferred to VA-46/CVW-1, AB/3XX, NAS Cecil Field, FL., 27 JUL 83; To VA-46, USS America (CV-66), 31 JUL 83; To VA-46, NAS Cecil Field, FL., 05 JAN 84; To VA-46, USS America (CV-66), 17 JAN 84; To VA-46, NAS Cecil Field, FL., 17 JAN 84; To VA-46, USS America (CV-66), 12 APR 84; To VA-46, NAS Cecil Field, FL., 19 APR 84; To VA-46, NAS Jacksonville, FL., 01 MAR 85; To VA-46, NAS Cecil Field, FL., 01 MAR 85; To VA-46, NAS Jacksonville, FL., 04 MAR 85; To VA-46, USS America (CV-66), 04 MAR 85; To VA-46, NAS Jacksonville, FL., 05 JUN 85; To VA-46, NAS Cecil Field, FL., 07 JUN 85; To VA-46, USS America (CV-66), 07 JUN 85; To VA-46, NAS Cecil Field, FL., 07 JUN 85; To VA-46, USS America (CV-66), 07 JUN 85 ** Transferred to VA-105/CVW-6, AE/4XX, USS Forrestal (CV-59), 19 JUL 86; To VA-105, NAS Cecil Field, FL., 13 OCT 86 ** Transferred to VA-82/CVW-8 AJ/3XX, NAS Cecil Field, FL., 24 NOV 86; To VA-82, USS Nimitz (CVN-68), 27 NOV 86 ~ S 1SO strike, 24 FEB 87 ** Pilot was rescued after crashing into the Mediterranean Sea, shortly after takeoff.

E-360 158668 Navy acceptance from NPRO Rep. LTV, Dallas, TX., 29 JUN 72 ** Transferred to NAF China Lake, CA., for RDT & E, 30 JUN 72 ** Transferred to VA-174/FRS, AD/4XX, NAS Cecil Field, FL., 18 FEB 73 ~ S 1SO strike, 05 JUL 74 ** No data on strike.

E-361 158669 Navy acceptance from NPRO Rep. LTV, Dallas, TX., 25 JUL 72 ** Transferred to VA-174/FRS, AD/4XX, NAS Cecil Field, FL., 27 JUL 72 ** Transferred to VA-66/CVW-7, AG/303, USS USS Independence (CVA-62), 26 SEP 72; To VA-66, NAS Cecil Field, FL., 31 MAR 73; To VA-66, USS USS Independence (CV-62), 17 MAR 74; To VA-66, NAS Jacksonville, FL., 14 JAN 75; To VA-66, NAS Cecil Field, FL., 24 FEB 75; To VA-66, USS USS Independence (CV-62), 13 SEP 75; To VA-66, NAS Cecil Field, FL., 01 NOV 75; To VA-66, USS USS Independence (CV-62), 01 FEB 76; To VA-66, NAS Cecil Field, FL., 01 MAY 76; To VA-66, NAS Fallon, NV., 07 JUL 76; To VA-66, USS USS Independence (CV-62), 01 SEP 76; To VA-66, NAS Cecil Field, FL., 01 DEC 76; To VA-66, USS USS Independence (CV-62), 01 DEC 76; To VA-66, NAS Cecil Field, FL., 01 JUN 77; To VA-66, USS USS Independence (CV-62), 16 JUN 77; To VA-66, NAS Cecil Field, FL., 16 AUG 77; To VA-66, USS Dwight D. Eisenhower (CVN-69), 16 AUG 77; To VA-66, NAS Cecil Field, FL., 16 AUG 77; To VA-66, NAS Jacksonville, FL., 26 AUG 78; To VA-66, NAS Cecil Field, FL., 28 AUG 78; To VA-66, USS Dwight D. Eisenhower (CVN-69), 28 AUG 78; To VA-66, NAS Cecil Field, FL., 28 AUG 78; To VA-66, USS Dwight D. Eisenhower (CVN-69), 28 AUG 78; To VA-66, NAS Cecil Field, FL., 28 AUG 78; To VA-66, USS Dwight D. Eisenhower (CVN-69), 28 AUG 78; To VA-66, NAS Cecil Field, FL., 28 AUG 78; To VA-66, USS Dwight D. Eisenhower (CVN-69), 28 MAR 80; To VA-66, NAS Norfolk, VA., 23 DEC 80; To VA-66, USS Dwight D. Eisenhower (CVN-69), 24 DEC 80; To VA-66, NAS Cecil Field, FL., 29 DEC 80; To VA-66, NAS Jacksonville, FL., 09 MAR 81; To VA-66, USS Dwight D. Eisenhower (CVN-69), 06 APR 81; To VA-66, NAS Cecil Field, FL., 06 APR 81; To VA-66, USS Dwight D. Eisenhower (CVN-69), 06 APR 81; To VA-66, NAS Jacksonville, FL., 14 SEP 81 ** Transferred to VA-174/FRS, AD/4XX, NAS Cecil Field, FL., 15 SEP 81 **Transferred to VA-66/CVW-7, AG/3XX, USS Dwight D. Eisenhower (CVN-69), 15 OCT 81; To VA-66, NAS Cecil Field, FL., 15 OCT 81; To VA-66, USS Dwight D. Eisenhower (CVN-69), 15 OCT 81; To VA-66, NAS Cecil Field, FL., 22 JUL 82; To VA-66, NAS Cecil Field, FL., 26 JUL 82 ** Transferred to VA-12/CVW-7, AG/4XX, NAS Cecil Field, FL., 01 SEP 82; To VA-12, USS Dwight D. Eisenhower (CVN-69), 08 APR 83; To VA-12, NAS Cecil Field, FL., 18 APR 83; To VA-12, USS Dwight D.Eisenhower (CVN-69), 18 APR 83 ** Transferred to VA-174/,FRS, AD/4XX, NAS Cecil Field, FL., 25 MAY 84; To VA-174, NAS Jacksonville, FL., 28 JUN 84; To VA-174, NAS Cecil Field, FL., 19 SEP 84; To VA-174, NAS Jacksonville, FL., 20 MAY 85; To VA-174, NAS Cecil Field, FL., 23 MAY 85; To VA-174, NAS Jacksonville, FL., 23 AUG 85; To VA-174, NAS Cecil Field, FL., 27 AUG 85 ** Transferred to VA-204/CVWR-20, AF/415, NAS New Orleans, LA., 23 SEP 86; To VA-204, NAS Jacksonville, FL., 23 SEP 86; To VA-204, NAS New Orleans, LA., 04 DEC 86; To VA-204, NAS Jacksonville, FL., 29 JAN 87; To VA-204, NAS New Orleans, LA., 11 FEB 87 thru 13 AUG 87 ** End of flight record card ** Transferred to AMARC, Davis Monthan AFB; Tucson, AZ., assigned park code 6A0351, 27 APR 90 ** 5962.2 flight hours ** TF41A402D engine S/N 141904 ** Storage location 210536 ** At AMARG, Davis Monthan AFB; Tucson, AZ., 15 JUN 07.

E-362 158670 Navy acceptance from NPRO Rep. LTV, Dallas, TX., 07 AUG 72 ** Transferred to VA-22/CVW-15, NL/3XX, USS Coral Sea (CVA-43), 08 AUG 72; To VA-22, NAS LeMoore, CA., 31 MAY 73; To VA-22, USS Coral Sea (CVA-43), 29 NOV 74; VA-22, NAS LeMoore, CA., 10 JUL 75; To VA-22, NAS Fallon, NV., 01 SEP 75; VA-22, NAS LeMoore, CA., 01 NOV 75; To VA-22, NAS Jacksonville, FL., 26 NOV 75; VA-22, NAS LeMoore, CA., 26 JAN 76 ** Transferred to VA-81/ CVW-17, AA/4XX, NAS Cecil Field, FL., 26 JAN 76; To VA-81, USS Forrestal (CV-59), 26 JAN 76; To VA-81, NAS Cecil Field, FL., 26 JAN 76 ~ S 1SO strike, 19 JUN 76 ** No data on strike.

E-363 158671 Navy acceptance from NPRO Rep. LTV, Dallas, TX., 13 SEP 72 ** Transferred to VA-146/CVW-9, NG/3XX, USS Constellation (CVA-64), 19 SEP 72 ** Transferred to VA-94/CVW-15, NL/4XX, USS Coral Sea (CVA-43), 20 NOV 72; To VA-94, NAS LeMoore, CA., 24 JUN 73; To VA-94, NAS Alameda, CA., 06 SEP 74; To VA-94, NAS LeMoore, CA., 18 NOV 74; To VA-94, USS Coral Sea (CV-43), 01 JUL 75; To VA-94, NAS Fallon, NV., 01 JUL 75; To VA-94, NAS LeMoore, CA., 29 OCT 75; To VA-94, NAS Jacksonville, FL., 10 NOV 75; To VA-94, NAS LeMoore, CA., 24 JAN 76 ** Transferred to VA-83/CVW-17, AA/3XX, NAS Cecil Field, FL., 24 JAN 76; To VA-83, USS Forrestal (CV-59), 24 JAN 76; To VA-83, NAS Cecil Field, FL., 24 JAN 76; To VA-83, NAS Roosevelt Roads, PR, 17 JUL 76; To VA-83, NAS Cecil Field, FL., 15 JUL 76 ~ S 1SO strike, 02 JUN 77 ** No data on strike.

E-364 158672 Navy acceptance from NPRO Rep. LTV, Dallas, TX., 29 AUG 72 ** Transferred to VA-174/FRS, AD/4XX, NAS Cecil Field, FL., 01 SEP 72 ** Transferred to VA-37/CVW-3, AC/310, NAS Cecil Field, FL., 23 APR 73; To VA-37, USS Saratoga (CV-60), 10 APR 74; To VA-37, NAS Cecil Field, FL., 10 APR 74; To VA-37, USS Saratoga (CV-60), 10 APR 74; To VA-37, NAS Cecil Field, FL., 10 APR 74; To VA-37, NAS Jacksonville, FL., 26 JUN 75; To VA-37, NAS Cecil Field, FL., 13 AUG 75; To VA-37, USS Saratoga (CV-60), 13 AUG 75; To VA-37, NAS Cecil Field, FL., 13 AUG 75; To VA-37, USS Saratoga (CV-60), 15 NOV 76; To VA-37, NAS Cecil Field, FL., 15 NOV 76; To VA-37, USS Saratoga (CV-60), 15 NOV 76; To VA-37, NAS Cecil Field, FL., 16 JUL 77; To VA-37, NAS Jacksonville, FL., 02 MAY 78; To VA-37, NAS Cecil Field, FL., 26 MAY 78; To VA-37, USS Saratoga (CV-60), 24 JUL 78; To VA-37, NAS Cecil Field, FL., 23 MAY 79; To VA-37, USS Saratoga (CV-60), 23 OCT 79; To VA-37, NAS Cecil Field, FL., 23 OCT 79; To VA-37, USS Saratoga (CV-60), 23 OCT 79; To VA-37, NAS Cecil Field, FL., 23 OCT 79 ** Transferred to VA-87/CVW-6, AE/4XX, NAS Cecil Field, FL., 23 OCT 79; To VA-87, USS Independence (CV-62), 13 SEP 80 ** Transferred to VA-174/FRS, AD/415, NAS Cecil Field, FL., 13 NOV 80; To VA-174, NAS Jacksonville, FL., 30 NOV 81; To VA-

174, NAS Cecil Field, FL., 01 DEC 81 ** Transferred to VA-87/ CVW-6, AE/4XX, NAS Cecil Field, FL., 18 DEC 81; To VA-87, USS Independence (CV-62), 18 DEC 81; To VA-87, NAS Cecil Field, FL., 05 JAN 82; To VA-87, USS Independence (CV-62), 09 JAN 82; To VA-87, NAS Cecil Field, FL., 07 MAY 82; To VA-87, USS Independence (CV-62), 19 MAY 82; To VA-87, NAS Cecil Field, FL., 30 SEP 82; To VA-87, USS Independence (CV-62), 14 MAY 83; To VA-87, NAS Cecil Field, FL., 14 MAY 83; To VA-87, USS Independence (CV-62), 14 MAY 83; To VA-87, NAS Cecil Field, FL., 13 JUN 83; To VA-87, USS Independence (CV-62), 13 JUN 83 ** Transferred to VA-86/CVW-8, AJ/4XX, NAS Cecil Field, FL., 29 OCT 83; To VA-86, NAS Jacksonville, FL., 29 OCT 83; To VA-86, NAS Cecil Field, FL., 03 MAY 84 ** Transferred to VA-82/CVW-8, AJ/3XX, NAS Cecil Field, FL., 04 MAY 84; To VA-82, USS Nimitz (CVN-68), 13 JUL 84; To VA-82, NAS Cecil Field, FL, 13 JUL 84; To VA-82, USS Nimitz (CVN-68), 13 JUL 84; To VA-82, NAS Cecil Field, FL, 13 JUL 84; To VA-82, NAS Jacksonville, FL., 29 MAY 86; To VA-82, NAS Cecil Field, FL, 04 JUN 86; To VA-82, USS Nimitz (CVN-68), 04 AUG 86; To VA-82, NAS Jacksonville, FL., 08 AUG 86; To VA-82, USS Nimitz (CVN-68), 09 AUG 86; To VA-82, NAS Cecil Field, FL, 09 AUG 86; To VA-82, USS Nimitz (CVN-68), 25 NOV 86; To VA-82, NAS Cecil Field, FL, 25 NOV 86 ** Transferred to VA-174/FRS, AD/4XX, NAS Cecil Field, FL., 08 SEP 87 ** End of flight record card ** Transferred to VA-205/CVWR-20, AF/5XX, NAS Atlanta, GA., dae unknown ** Transferred to AMARC, Davis Monthan AFB; Tucson, AZ., assigned park code 6A0335, 03 APR 90 ** 6710.2 flight hours ** TF41A402D engine S/N AE142562 ** Storage location 210343 ** Under GSA jurisdiction, 06 APR 04 ** At AMARG, Davis Monthan AFB; Tucson, AZ., 15 JUN 07.

E-365 158673 Navy acceptance from NPRO Rep. LTV, Dallas, TX., 12 SEP 72 ** Transferred to VA-174/FRS, AD/4XX, NAS Cecil Field, FL., 14 SEP 72 ** Transferred to VA-105/CVW-3, AC/4XX, NAS Cecil Field, FL., 14 MAY 73; To VA-105, USS Saratoga (CV-60), 30 MAR 74; To VA-105, NAS Cecil Field, FL., 30 MAR 74; To VA-105, USS Saratoga (CV-60), 30 MAR 74; To VA-105, NAS Cecil Field, FL., 30 MAR 74; To VA-105, USS Saratoga (CV-60), 30 MAR 74; To VA-105, NAS Jacksonville, FL., 19 JUN 75; To VA-105, NAS Cecil Field, FL., 19 JUN 75; To VA-105, NAS Jacksonville, FL., 20 JUN 75; To VA-105, NAS Cecil Field, FL., 08 AUG 75; To VA-105, MCAS Yuma, AZ., 10 SEP 75; To VA-105, NAS Jacksonville, FL., 12 SEP 75; To VA-105, MCAS Yuma, AZ., 30 SEP 75; To VA-105, NAS Cecil Field, FL., 02 OCT 75; To VA-105, USS Saratoga (CV-60), 11 NOV 76; To VA-105, NAS Cecil Field, FL., 11 NOV 76; To VA-105, USS Saratoga (CV-60), 11 NOV 76; To VA-105, NAS Cecil Field, FL., 16 JUL 77; To VA-105, NAS Jacksonville, FL., 30 JUN 78; To VA-105, NAS Cecil Field, FL., 29 JUL 78; To VA-105, USS Saratoga (CV-60), 08 AUG 78; To VA-105, NAS Cecil Field, FL., 08 AUG 78; To VA-105, MCAS Yuma, AZ., 08 AUG 78; To VA-105, NAS Cecil Field, FL., 10 OCT 79; To VA-105, USS Saratoga (CV-60), 03 DEC 79; To VA-105, NAS Cecil Field, FL., 03 DEC 79; To VA-105, USS Saratoga (CV-60), 03 DEC 79; To VA-105, NAS Cecil Field, FL., 09 FEB 81; To VA-105, NAS Fallon, NV., 04 MAR 81 ** Transferred to VA-72/CVW-1, AB/4XX, NAS Cecil Field, FL., 05 JUN 81; To VA-72, NAS Jacksonville, FL., 17 JAN 82 ** Transferred to VA-82/CVW-8, AJ/3XX, NAS Cecil Field, FL., 01 MAR 82 ~ S ISO strike, 22 MAR 82 ** No data on strike.

E-366 158674 Navy acceptance from NPRO Rep. LTV, Dallas, TX., 31 AUG 72 ** Transferred to VA-94/CVW-15, NL/4XX, 05 MAY 72; To VA-94, NAS LeMoore, CA., 03 JUN 73; To VA-94, NAS Alameda, CA., 26 SEP 74; To VA-94, NAS LeMoore, CA., 01 NOV 74; To VA-94, USS Coral Sea (CVA-43), 10 APR 75; To VA-94, NAS Fallon, NV., 01 SEP 75; To VA-94, NAS LeMoore, CA., 02 NOV 75; To VA-94, NAS Jacksonville, FL., 13 APR 76; To VA-94, NAS LeMoore, CA., 03 JUN 76; To VA-94, USS Coral Sea (CV-43), 09 DEC 76; To VA-94, NAS LeMoore, CA., 08 JAN 77; To VA-94, USS Coral Sea (CV-43), 31 AUG 77; To VA-94, NAS LeMoore, CA., 26 OCT 77; To VA-94, NAS Jacksonville, FL., 14 AUG 78; To VA-94, NAS LeMoore, CA., 21 SEP 78; To VA-94, NAS Cubi Point,

PI., 29 MAY 79; To VA-94, USS Kitty Hawk (CV-63), 06 JUN 79; To VA-94, NAS LeMoore, CA., 15 NOV 79; To VA-94, USS Kitty Hawk (CV-63), 27 JUN 80; To VA-94, NAS LeMoore, CA., 07 AUG 80; To VA-94, NAS Jacksonville, FL., 08 AUG 80; To VA-94, USS Kitty Hawk (CV-63), 11 AUG 80; To VA-94, NAS Jacksonville, FL., 17 OCT 80; To VA-94, NAS LeMoore, CA., 07 DEC 80; To VA-94, USS Kitty Hawk (CV-63), 27 FEB 81; To VA-94, NAS Cubi Point, PI., 13 MAY 81; To VA-94, USS Kitty Hawk (CV-63), 24 OCT 81; To VA-94, NAS LeMoore, CA., 24 OCT 81 ** Transferred to VA-195/CVW-11, NH/ 4XX, NAS LeMoore, CA., 27 MAY 82; To VA-195, NAS Dallas, TX., 15 MAR 83 ** Transferred to VA-146/ CVW-9, NE/3XX, NAS LeMoore, CA., 13 JUN 83; To VA-146, USS Kitty Hawk (CV-63), 14 JUN 83; To VA-146, NAS LeMoore, CA., 20 JUL 84 ** Transferred to VA-22/CVW-11, NH/307, NAS LeMoore, CA., 23 JAN 85; To VA-22, NAS Fallon, NV., 10 APR 85; To VA-22, NAS LeMoore, CA., 27 APR 85; To VA-22; NAS Jacksonville, FL., 31 MAY 85; To VA-22, NAS LeMoore, CA., 14 SEP 85; To VA-22, USS Enterprise (CVN-65), 08 JAN 86; To VA-22, NAS LeMoore, CA., 09 OCT 86 thru 05 SEP 87 ** End of flight record card ** Transferred to AMARC, Davis Monthan AFB; Tucson, AZ., assigned park code 6A0295, 14 AUG 89 ** End of flight record card ** 6916.4 flight hours ** TF41A402D engine S/N 141373 ** Project changed per FSO letter, 06 APR 04 ** Engine records released to DRMO for disposition, 29 JUN 05 ** Aircraft deleted from inventory and released to DRMO for disposition, 01 AUG 05.

E-367 158675 Navy acceptance from NPRO Rep. LTV, Dallas, TX., 26 OCT 72 ** Transferred to VA-94/CVW-15, NL/4XX, USS Coral Sea (CVA-43), 01 NOV 72; To VA-94, NAS LeMoore, CA., 25 JUN 73; To VA-94, USS Coral Sea (CV-43), 01 JUL 75; To VA-94, NAS Fallon, NV., 14 AUG 75; To VA-94, NAS Jacksonville, FL., 21 OCT 75; To VA-94, NAS LeMoore, CA., 24 OCT 75; To VA-94, NAS Fallon, NV., 30 APR 76; To VA-94, NAS LeMoore, CA., 30 APR 76; To VA-94, USS Coral Sea (CV-43), 09 DEC 76; To VA-94, NAS LeMoore, CA., 20 DEC 76; To VA-94, USS Coral Sea (CV-43), 31 AUG 77; To VA-94, NAS Jacksonville, FL14 AUG 78; To VA-94, NAS LeMoore, CA., 21 SEP 78; To VA-94, NAS Cubi Point, PI., 29 MAY 79; To VA-94, NAS LeMoore, CA., 21 SEP 79; To VA-94, NAS Jacksonville, FL., 16 MAY 80; To VA-94, NAS LeMoore, CA., 19 MAY 80; To VA-94, USS Kitty Hawk (CV-63), 27 JUL 80; To VA-94, NAS LeMoore, CA., 27 JUL 80; To VA-94, USS Kitty Hawk (CV-63), 11 SEP 80; To VA-94, NAS LeMoore, CA., 06 NOV 80; To VA-94, USS Kitty Hawk (CV-63), 14 JAN 81; To VA-94, NAF Atsugi, JP., 29 APR 81; To NAS Cubi Point, PI., 06 MAY 81; To VA-94, NAF Atsugi, JP., 31 AUG 81; To NAS Cubi Point, PI., 30 SEP 81; To VA-94, NAF Atsugi, JP., 14 OCT 81; To VA-94, USS Kitty Hawk (CV-63), 24 OCT 81; To VA-94, NAS LeMoore, CA., 24 OCT 81 ** Transferred to VA-146/CVW-9, NE/3XX, NAS LeMoore, CA., 23 AUG 82; To VA-146, NAS Jacksonville, FL., 12 OCT 82; To VA-146, NAS Dallas, TX., 07 DEC 82; To VA-146, NAS LeMoore, CA., 08 DEC 82; To VA-146, USS Kitty Hawk (CV-63), 30 DEC 83 ** Transferred to VA-22/ CVW-11, NH/3XX, NAS LeMoore, CA., 06 JAN 84 ** Transferred to VA-122/FRS, NJ/2XX, NAS LeMoore, CA., 25 MAY 84 ** Transferred to VA-22/CVW-11, NH/ 303, NAS LeMoore, CA., 26 FEB 85; To VA-22, NAS Fallon, NV., 26 FEB 85; To VA-22, NAS LeMoore, CA., 17 MAY 85; To VA-22, NAS Jacksonville, FL., 19 NOV 85; To VA-22, NAS LeMoore, CA., 22 NOV 85; To VA-22, USS Enterprise (CVN-65), 23 DEC 85; To VA-22, NAS LeMoore, CA., 02 JUL 86 thru 26 MAY 87 ** End of flight record card ** Transferred to AMARC, Davis Monthan AFB; Tucson, AZ., assigned park code; 6A0288, 27 APR 89 ** 6589.7 flight hours ** TF41A402D engine S/N 141501 ** Project changed per FSO letter, 06 APR 04 ** Engine records released to DRMO for disposition, 20 MAR 05 ** At AMARC; Davis Monthan AFB; Tucson, AZ., 09 MAY 05.

E-368 158676 Navy acceptance from NPRO Rep. LTV, Dallas, TX., 27 SEP 72 ** Transferred to VA-94/CVW-15, NL/4XX, USS Coral Sea (CVA-43), 28 SEP 72; To VA-94, NAS LeMoore, CA., 25 JUN 73; To VA-94, USS Coral Sea (CV-43), 01 JUL 75; To VA-94,

NAS LeMoore, CA., 01 AUG 75; To VA-94, NAS Fallon, NV., 01 SEP 75, To VA-94, NAS Jacksonville, FL., 13 NOV 75; To VA-94, NAS LeMoore, CA., 31 DEC 75; To VA-94, NAS Jacksonville, FL., 07 JAN 76; To VA-94, NAS LeMoore, CA., 31 DEC 75; To VA-94, NAS Fallon, NV., 30 APR 76; To VA-94, NAS LeMoore, CA., 30 APR 76; To VA-94, USS Coral Sea (CV-43), 09 DEC 76; To VA-94, NAS LeMoore, CA., 08 JAN 77; To VA-94, USS Coral Sea (CV-43), 17 JUL 77 ~ S 1SO strike, 17 JUL 77 ** No data on strike.

E-369 158677 Navy acceptance from NPRO Rep. LTV, Dallas, TX., 18 OCT 72 ** Transferred to VA-22/CVW-15, NL/3XX, USS Coral Sea (CVA-43), 20 OCT 72; To VA-22, NAS LeMoore, CA., 02 JUN 73; To VA-22, USS Coral Sea (CVA-43), 29 NOV 74; To VA-22, NAS LeMoore, CA., 30 JUL 75; To VA-22, NAS Fallon, NV., 01 AUG 75, To VA-22, NAS LeMoore, CA., 24 OCT 75; To VA-22, NAS Jacksonville, FL., 21 MAR 76; To VA-22, NAS LeMoore, CA., 04 MAY 76; To VA-22, USS Coral Sea (CV-43), 07 APR 77; To VA-22, NAS LeMoore, CA., 18 OCT 77; To VA-22, NAS Kingsville, TX., 31 AUG 78; To VA-22, NAS LeMoore, CA., 31 AUG 78; To VA-22, USS Kitty Hawk (CV-63), 26 APR 79; To VA-22, NAF Atsugi, JP., 03 NOV 79; To VA-22, USS Kitty Hawk (CV-63), 04 NOV 79; To VA-22, NAS LeMoore, CA., 04 NOV 80; To VA-22, USS Kitty Hawk (CV-63), 20 AUG 80; To VA-22, NAS Jacksonville, FL., 28 OCT 80; To VA-22, NAS LeMoore, CA., 09 JAN 81; To VA-22, USS Kitty Hawk (CV-63), 19 JAN 81 ** Transferred to VA-94/CVW-15, NL/4XX,, NAS Cubi Point, PI., 13 MAY 81; To VA-94, USS Kitty Hawk (CV-63), 13 MAY 81; To VA-94, NAS LeMoore, CA., 04 OCT 81; Transferred to VA-195/CVW-11, NH/4XX, NAS LeMoore, CA., 16 MAR 82; To VA-195, NAS Jacksonville, FL., 20 OCT 82; To VA-195, NAS LeMoore, CA., 05 JAN 83; To VA-195, NAS Dallas, TX., 24 MAR 83; To VA-195/CVW-9, NG/4XX, USS Ranger (CV-61), 27 MAR 83 ** Transferred to VA-146/CVW-9, NE/3XX, NAS LeMoore, CA., 28 MAR 83; To VA-146, USS Kitty Hawk (CV-63), 11 AUG 83; To VA-146, NAS LeMoore, CA., 27 AUG 84 ** Transferred to VA-22/CVW-11, NH/3XX, NAS LeMoore, CA., 23 JAN 85; To VA-22, NAS Fallon, NV., 30 APR 85; To VA-22, NAS Jacksonville, FL., 30 APR 85; To VA-22, NAS LeMoore, CA., 02 AUG 85; To VA-22, USS Enterprise (CVN-65), 18 SEP 85; To VA-22, NAF Atsugi, JP., 05 APR 86; To VA-22, USS Enterprise (CVN-65), 10 APR 86; To VA-22, NAS LeMoore, CA., 17 APR 86 thru 26 JUN 87 ** End of flight record card.

E-370 158678 Navy acceptance from NPRO Rep. LTV, Dallas, TX., 01 NOV 72 ** Transferred to VA-174/FRS, AD/4XX, NAS Cecil Field, FL., 02 NOV 72; To VA-174, NAS Jacksonville, FL., 29 APR 76; To VA-174, NAS Cecil Field, FL., 24 JUN 76 ** Transferred to VA-82/CVW-8, AJ/3XX, NAS Jacksonville, FL., 10 JUL 78; To VA-82, NAS Cecil Field, FL., 01 AUG 78; To VA-82, USS Nimitz (CVN-68), 19 MAR 80; To VA-82, NAS Jacksonville, FL., 08 JUL 80; To VA-82, USS Nimitz (CVN-68), 08 JUL 80; To VA-82, NAS Jacksonville, FL., 10 JUL 80; To VA-82, USS Nimitz (CVN-68), 12 SEP 80; To VA-82, NAS Cecil Field, FL., 12 SEP 80; To VA-82, USS Nimitz (CVN-68), 12 SEP 80 ~ S 1SO strike, 22 NOV 81 ** No data on strike.

E-371 158679 Navy acceptance from NPRO Rep. LTV, Dallas, TX., 03 NOV 72 ** Transferred to VA-122/FRS, NJ/2XX, NAS LeMoore, CA., 07 OCT 72; To VA-122, NAS Jacksonville, FL., 07 JUN 77; To VA-122, NAS LeMoore, CA., 28 AUG 77 ~ S 1SO strike, 18 DEC 77 ** No data on strike.

E-372 158680 Navy acceptance from NPRO Rep. LTV, Dallas, TX., 25 OCT 72 ** Transferred to VA-22/CVW-15, NL/3XX, USS Coral Sea (CVA-43), 27 OCT 72 ~ S 1SO strike, 03 APR 73 ** No data on strike.

E-373 158681 Navy acceptance from NPRO Rep. LTV, Dallas, TX., 30 NOV 72 ** Transferred to VA-174/FRS, AD/4XX, NAS Cecil Field, FL., 12 DEC 72 ~ S 1SO strike, 09 MAY 73 ** No data on strike.

158819/158830 LTV A-7E-12-CV Corsair II; (Block XII)
FY 72 Contract N00019-72-C-0098, (24) A-7E; E-375/E-398

E-386 158819 Navy acceptance from NPRO Rep. LTV, Dallas, TX., 19 APR 73 ** Transferred to VA-174/FRS, AD/4XX, NAS Cecil Field, FL., 20 APR 73 ** Transferred to VA-86/CVW-8, AJ/404, NAS Cecil Field, FL., 10 DEC 74; To VA-86, USS Nimitz (CVN-68), 22 JAN 75; To VA-86, NAS Cecil Field, FL., 22 DEC 75; To VA-86, NAS Roosevelt Roads, PR., 22 JAN 75; To VA-86, NAS Cecil Field, FL., 22 JAN 75; To VA-86, USS Nimitz (CVN-68), 22 JAN 75; To VA-86, NAS Cecil Field, FL., 22 JAN 75; To VA-86, USS Nimitz (CVN-68), 08 MAY 76; in bi-centennial paint, 04 JUL 76; To VA-86, NAS Cecil Field, FL., 01 JAN 77; VA-86, USS Nimitz (CVN-68), 10 AUG 77 ** Transferred to VA-174/FRS, AD/4XX, NAS Cecil Field, FL., 28 SEP 77; To VA-174, NAS Jacksonville, FL., 29 NOV 77; To VA-174, NAS Cecil Field, FL., 08 DEC 77; To VA-174, NAS Jacksonville, FL., 11 DEC 81; To VA-174, NAS Cecil Field, FL., 11 DEC 81; To VA-174, NAS Jacksonville, FL., 15 DEC 81; To VA-174, NAS Cecil Field, FL., 27 FEB 82; To VA-174, NAS Dallas, TX., 05 MAR 82; To VA-174, NAS Cecil Field, FL., 21 MAY 82 ** Transferred to VA-15/CVW-6, AE/3XX, NAS Cecil Field, FL., 24 MAY 82; To VA-15, USS Independence (CV-62), 24 MAY 82; To VA-15, NAS Cecil Field, FL., 24 MAY 82; To VA-15, USS Independence (CV-62), 24 MAY 83; To VA-15, NAS Cecil Field, FL., 24 MAY 83; To VA-15, USS Independence (CV-62), 24 MAY 83; To VA-15, NAS Cecil Field, FL., 24 MAY 83; To VA-15, USS Independence (CV-62), 24 MAY 83; To VA-15, NAS Cecil Field, FL., 03 MAY 84; To VA-15, NAS Jacksonville, FL., 23 MAY 84; To VA-15, USS Independence (CV-62), 18 JUL 84; To VA-15, NAS Cecil Field, FL., 17 SEP 84; To VA-15, USS Independence (CV-62), 24 SEP 84 ** Transferred to VA-82/CVW-8, AJ/3XX, NAS Cecil Field, FL., 10 OCT 84; To VA-82, USS Nimitz (CVN-68), 10 OCT 84; To VA-82, NAS Cecil Field, FL., 10 OCT 84; To VA-82, USS Nimitz (CVN-68), 10 OCT 84 ** Transferred to VA-15/CVW-6, AE/3XX, NAS Cecil Field, FL., 29 MAR 85; To VA-15, MCAS Iwakuni, JP., 18 SEP 85; To VA-15, NAF Atsugi, JP., 03 FEB 86; To VA-15, MCAS Iwakuni, JP., 21 FEB 86; To VA-15, Korea, 21 FEB 86; To VA-15, NAS Cubi Point, PI., 21 FEB 86; To VA-15, NAS Cecil Field, FL., 29 MAY 86; To VA-15, NAS Jacksonville, FL., 06 AUG 86; To VA-15, NAS Cecil Field, FL., 06 AUG 86; To VA-15, NAS Jacksonville, FL., 11 AUG 86; To VFA-15, NAS Jacksonville, FL., 02 DEC 86 ** Transferred to VA-72/CVW-1, AB/4XX, NAS Cecil Field, FL., 09 DEC 86; To VA-72, USS Dwight D. Eisenhower (CVN-69), 29 JUN 87; To VA-72, NAS Cecil Field, FL., 18 JUL 87 thru 13 SEP 87 ** End of Flight record card ** On conditional loan from the National Museum of Naval Aviation; Pensacola, FL., to the Port of Tillamook Bay, OR.

E-375 158820 Navy acceptance from NPRO Rep. LTV, Dallas, TX., 31 JAN 73 ** Transferred to VA-174/FRS, AD/4XX, NAS Cecil Field, FL., 02 FEB 73 ** Transferred to VA-82/CVW-8, AJ/3XX, NAS Cecil Field, FL., 04 FEB 75; To VA-82, USS Nimitz (CV-68), 04 FEB 75; To VA-82, NAS Cecil Field, FL., 04 FEB 75; To VA-82, NAS Roosevelt Roads, PR., 04 FEB 75; To VA-82, NAS Cecil Field, FL., 04 FEB 75; To VA-82, USS Nimitz (CV-68), 04 FEB 75; To VA-82, NAS Cecil Field, FL., 14 MAY 76; To VA-82, USS Nimitz (CV-68), 01 DEC 76 To VA-82, NAS Cecil Field, FL., 28 FEB 77; To VA-82, USS Nimitz (CV-68), 10 AUG 77 ** Transferred to VA-174/FRS, AD/4XX, NAS Cecil Field, FL., 10 NOV 77; To VA-174, NAS Jacksonville, FL., 13 NOV 77; To VA-174, NAS Cecil Field, FL., 04 FEB 78 ** Transferred to VA-37/CVW-3, AC/3XX, USS Saratoga (CV-60), 08 NOV 78; To VA-37, NAS Cecil Field, FL., 08 NOV 78 ** Transferred to VA-174/FRS, AD/4XX, NAS Cecil Field, FL., 12 JUL 79; To VA-174, NAS Jacksonville, FL., 14 MAY 80 ** Transferred to VA-86/CVW-8, AJ/4XX, USS Nimitz (CVN-68), 16 JUL 80; To VA-86, NAS Cecil Field, FL., 16 JUL 80; To VA-86, USS Nimitz (CVN-68), 27 MAY 81; To VA-86, NAS Norfolk, VA., 28 MAY 81; To VA-86, NAS Cecil Field, FL., 21 JUL 81; To VA-86, USS Nimitz (CVN-68), 21 JUL 81; To VA-86, NAS Cecil Field, FL., 21 JUL 81; To VA-86, NAS Jacksonville, FL., 14 APR 82 Transferred to VA-82/CVW8, AJ/3XX, NAS Cecil Field, FL., 30 JUL 82; To VA-82, USS Nimitz (CV-68), 30 JUL 82; To VA-82, NAS Cecil Field, FL., 30 JUL 82; To VA-82, USS Nimitz (CVN-68), 30 JUL 82 ~ S 1SO strike, 23 MAR 83 ** No data on strike.

E-376 158821 Navy acceptance from NPRO Rep. LTV, Dallas, TX., 30 JAN 73 ** Transferred to VA-122/FRS, NJ/2XX, NAS LeMoore, CA., 31 JAN 73; To VA-122, NAS Jacksonville, FL., 20 MAY 77; To VA-122, NAS LeMoore, CA., 16 JUL 77; To VA-122, NAS Jacksonville, FL., 20 JUL 79; To VA-122, NAS LeMoore, CA., 27 AUG 79; To VA-122, NAS Jacksonville, FL., 21 SEP 82 ** Transferred to VA-146/CVW-9, NE/3XX, NAS LeMoore, CA., 26 MAR 83; To VA-146, NWC China Lake, CA., 22 MAY 83; To VA-146, NAS LeMoore, CA., 07 SEP 83; To VA-146, USS Kitty Hawk (CV-63), 28 DEC 83 ** Transferred to VA-22/CVW-11, NH/3XX, NAS LeMoore, CA., 06 JAN 84 ** Transferred to VA-122/FRS, NJ/2XX, NAS LeMoore, CA., 23 FEB 84 ** Transferred to VA-22/CVW-11, NH/3XX, NAS LeMoore, CA., 14 FEB 85; To VA-22, NAS Fallon, NV., 14 FEB 85; To VA-22, NAS LeMoore, CA., 17 MAY 85; To VA-22, NAS Jacksonville, FL., 21 JUL 85; To VA-22, NAS LeMoore, CA., 22 OCT 85; To VA-22, USS Enterprise (CVN-65), 25 OCT 85; To VA-22, NAS LeMoore, CA., 30 JUN 86 thru 03 DEC 86 ** End of flight record card ** Transferred to VA-147/CVW-9, NG/401, NAS LeMoore, CA., date unknown ** Transferred to AMARC, Davis Monthan AFB; Tucson, AZ., assigned park code 6A0293 28 JUL 89 ** 6095.8 flight hours ** TF41A402D engine S/N 142626 ** Storage location 210833 ** At AMARG, Davis Monthan AFB; Tucson, AZ., 15 JUN 07.

E-377 158822 Navy acceptance from NPRO Rep. LTV, Dallas, TX., 02 MAR 73 ** Transferred to VA-195/CVW-11, NH/4XX, NAS LeMoore, CA., 08 MAR 73; To VA-195, USS Kitty Hawk (CVA-63), 08 MAR 73; To VA-195, NAS LeMoore, CA., 26 AUG 74; To VA-195, USS Kitty Hawk (CV-63), 28 MAR 75; To VA-195, NAS LeMoore, CA., 09 APR 75; To VA-195, USS Kitty Hawk (CV-63), 19 MAY 75; To VA-195, NAS Cubi Point, PI., 21 JUN 75; To VA-195, NAS LeMoore, CA., 14 DEC 75; To VA-195, NAS Jacksonville, FL., 24 SEP 76; To VA-195, NAS LeMoore, CA., 26 OCT 76; To VA-195, USS Kitty Hawk (CV-63), 25 JUL 77; To VA-195, NAS LeMoore, CA., 12 AUG 77; To VA-195, USS Kitty Hawk (CV-63), 06 SEP 77; To VA-195, NAS LeMoore, CA., 09 MAR 78; To VA-195, NAS Jacksonville, FL., 11 FEB 79 ** Transferred to VA-22/CVW15, NL/3XX, NAS LeMoore, CA., 19 APR 79; To VA-22, USS Kitty Hawk (CV-63), 26 APR 79; To VA-22, NAS LeMoore, CA., 30 MAY 79; To VA-22, USS Kitty Hawk (CV-63), 27 JUN 80; To VA-22, NAS LeMoore, CA., 15 DEC 80; To VA-22, NAS Jacksonville, FL., 16 DEC 80; To VA-22, USS Kitty Hawk (CV-63), 12 MAR 81; To VA-22, NAS Dallas, TX., 04 MAY 81 ** Transferred to VA-146/CVW-9, NG/3XX, NAS LeMoore, CA., 15 MAY 81; To VA-146, USS Constellation (CV-64), 15 MAY 81; To VA-146, NAS LeMoore, CA., 15 MAY 81; To VA-146, USS Constellation (CV-64), 11 SEP 81; To VA-146, NAS LeMoore, CA., 20 OCT 81; To VA-146, NAS Jacksonville, FL., 02 JUN 83; To VA-146, NAS LeMoore, CA., 30 JUL 83 ** Transferred to VA-94/CVW-11, NH/4XX, NAS LeMoore, CA., 24 AUG 83; To VA-94, USS Enterprise (CVN-65), 05 DEC 83; To VA-94, NAS LeMoore, CA., 15 JAN 84; To VA-94, USS Enterprise (CVN-65), 15 JAN 84; To VA-94, NAS LeMoore, CA., 15 JAN 84 ** Transferred to VA-122/FRS, NJ/2XX,NAS LeMoore, CA.,25 MAY 84 ** Transferred to VA-174/FRS, AD/4XX,NAS Cecil Field, FL., 27 SEP 85; To VA-174, NAS Pensacola, FL., 07 AUG 86 ** Transferred to VA-37/CVW-6, AE/302, NAS Cecil Field, FL., 13 APR 87; To VA-37, USS Forrestal (CV-59), 12 MAY 87 ** End of flight Record card ** Transferred to AMARC, Davis Monthan AFB; Tucson, AZ., assigned park code 6A0379; 20 SEP 90 ** 6458.4 flight hours ** TF41A402D engine S/N 141620 ** Project changed per FSO letter, 06 APR 04 ** Aircraft deleted from inventory and released to DRMO for disposition, 26 MAY 05.

E-378 158823 Navy acceptance from NPRO Rep. LTV, Dallas, TX., 12 FEB 73 ** Transferred to VA-122/FRS, NJ/2XX, NAS LeMoore, CA., 13 FEB 73 ** Transferred to VA-192/CVW-11, NH/3XX, NAS LeMoore, CA., 26 FEB 73; To VA-192, USS Kitty Hawk (CV-63), 11 JUN 73; To VA-192, NAS LeMoore, CA., 04 APR 74; To VA-192, USS Kitty Hawk (CV-63), 12 DEC 74; To VA-192, NAS LeMoore, CA., 20 MAR 75; To VA-192, USS Kitty Hawk (CV-63), 20 MAR 75; To VA-192, NAS LeMoore, CA., 09 MAY 75; To VA-192, USS Kitty Hawk (CV-63), 15 MAY 75; To VA-192, NAS Cubi Point, PI.,

15 MAY 75; To VA-192, USS Kitty Hawk (CV-63), 12 NOV 75; To VA-192, NAS Alameda, CA., 13 NOV 75; To VA-192, USS Kitty Hawk (CV-63), 14 NOV 75 ** Transferred to VA-122/FRS, NJ/2XX, NAS LeMoore, CA., 24 NOV 75; To VA-122, NAS Jacksonville, FL., 29 JUN 77; To VA-122, NAS LeMoore, CA., 03 JUL 77 ** Transferred to VA-195/CVW-11, NH/4XX, NAS LeMoore, CA., 30 APR 79; To VA-195, USS America (CV-66), 05 JUL 79; To VA-195, NAS LeMoore, CA., 05 JUL 79; To VA-195, NAS Jacksonville, FL., 13 NOV 79; To VA-195, NAS LeMoore, CA., 05 MAR 80; To VA-195, NAS Fallon, NV., 19 OCT 80; To VA-195, NAS LeMoore, CA., 07 NOV 80; To VA-195, USS America (CV-66), 04 DEC 80 ** Transferred to VA-122/FRS, NJ/2XX, NAS LeMoore, CA., 07 JAN 81; To VA-122, NAS Jacksonville, FL., 26 OCT 81 ** Transferred to VA-195/CVW-11, NH/4XX, NAS LeMoore, CA., 22 JAN 82; To VA-195/CVW-9, NG/4XX, USS Ranger (CV-61), 06 JUL 83; To VA-195, NAS LeMoore, CA., 07 JUL 83; To VA-195, NAS Jacksonville, FL., 08 MAR 84 ** VA-97/CVW-15, NL/3XX, NAS LeMoore, CA., 31 AUG 84; To VA-97, USS Carl Vinson (CVN-70), 31 AUG 84; To VA-97, NAS LeMoore, CA., 10 NOV 84 ** Transferred to VA-146/CVW-9, NE/3XX, NAS LeMoore, CA., 28 APR 86; To VA-146, NAS Jacksonville, FL., 20 OCT 86; To VA-146, NAS LeMoore, CA., 20 OCT 86; To VA-146, NAS Jacksonville, FL., 18 NOV 86; To VA-146, USS Kitty Hawk (CV-63), 18 NOV 86; To VA-146, NAS Jacksonville, FL., 23 MAR 87 ** Transferred to VA-22/CVW-11, NH/ 3XX, NAS LeMoore, CA., 25 MAR 87 thru 29 JUL 87 ** End of flight record card.

E-379 158824 Navy acceptance from NPRO Rep. LTV, Dallas, TX., 27 MAR 73 ** Transferred to VA-174/FRS, AD/4XX, NAS Cecil Field, FL., 28 MAR 73 ** Transferred to VA-82/CVW-8, AJ/306, NAS Cecil Field, FL., 10 DEC 74; To VA-82, USS Nimitz (CVN-68), 22 JAN 75; To VA-82, NAS Cecil Field, FL., 22 JAN 75; To VA-82, NAS Roosevelt Roads, PR., 22 JAN 75; To VA-82, NAS Cecil Field, FL., 22 JAN 75; To VA-82, USS Nimitz (CVN-68), 22 JAN 75; To VA-82, NAS Cecil Field, FL., 22 JAN 75; To VA-82, USS Nimitz (CVN-68), 22 JAN 75; To VA-82, NAS Cecil Field, FL., 14 MAY 76; To VA-82, USS Nimitz (CVN-68), 08 SEP 77; To VA-82, NAS Cecil Field, FL., 12 APR 78; To VA-82, NAS Jacksonville, FL., 18 OCT 78; To VA-82, NAS Cecil Field, FL., 06 DEC 78 ** Transferred to NARF, NAS Jacksonville, FL., 15 OCT 79 ** Transferred to MASDC, Davis Monthan AFB; Tucson, AZ., assigned park code 6A0120, 25 APR 80 ** Transferred to NWC China Lake, NWC/ XXX, NAS Jacksonville, FL., 13 SEP 82; To NWC, China Lake, CA., 14 SEP 82; To NWC, NAS Jacksonville, FL., 19 NOV 82; To NWC, China Lake, CA., 08 DEC 82; To NWC, NAS Jacksonville, FL., 20 DEC 82; To NWC, China Lake, CA., 03 JAN 83; To NWC, NAS Jacksonville, FL., 19 JAN 83; To NWC, China Lake, CA., 28 FEB 83; To NWC, NAS Jacksonville, FL., 28 MAR 83 ** Transferred to NARF, NAS Jacksonville, FL., 30 MAR 83 ** Transferred to VA-174/ FRS, AD/4XX, NAS Cecil Field, FL., 18 JUL 83; To VA-174, NAS Jacksonville, FL., 22 AUG 85; To VA-174, NAS Cecil Field, FL., 17 OCT 85; To VA-174, NAS Jacksonville, FL., 23 OCT 85 ** Transferred to VA-86/CVW-8, AJ/4XX, NAS Cecil Field, FL., 24 OCT 85; To VA-86, USS Nimitz (CVN-68), 04 MAR 86; To VA-86, NAS Cecil Field, FL., 04 MAR 86; To VA-86, USS Nimitz (CVN-68), 04 MAR 86 ** Transferred to VA-174/FRS, AD/4XX, NAS Cecil Field, FL., 06 AUG 86 ** Transferred to AMARC, Davis Monthan AFB; Tucson, AZ., assigned park code 6A0229, 03 AUG 87 ** End of flight record card ** 3880.0 flight hours ** TF41A2C engine S/N 142581 ** Aircraft released from storage and prepaired for overland and above deck shipping to government of Greece, 25 JUL 94 ** Transferred to the Helenic Air force (Greece).

E-380 158825 Navy acceptance from NPRO Rep. LTV, Dallas, TX., 27 FEB 73 ** Transferred to VA-174/FRS, AD/4XX, NAS Cecil Field, FL., 04 MAR 73 ** Transferred to VA-86/CVW-8, AJ/4XX, NAS Cecil Field, FL., 14 NOV 74; To VA-86, USS Nimitz (CVN-68),16 DEC 74; To VA-86, NAS Cecil Field, FL., 16 DEC 74; To VA-86, NAS Roosevelt Roads, PR., 16 DEC 74; To VA-86, NAS Cecil Field, FL., 16 DEC 74; To VA-86, USS Nimitz (CVN-68), 16 DEC 74; To VA-86, NAS Cecil Field, FL., 16 DEC 74; To VA-86, USS Nimitz (CVN-68), 30 JUN 75; To VA-86, NAS Cecil Field, FL., 30 JUN 75; To VA-

86, NAS Roosevelt Roads, PR., 01 MAY 77; To VA-86, USS Nimitz (CVN-68), 10 AUG 77; To VA-86, NAS Cecil Field, FL., 10 AUG 77; To VA-86, USS Nimitz (CVN-68), 10 AUG 77; To VA-86, NAS Cecil Field, FL., 18 JUL 78; To VA-86, NAS Jacksonville, FL.,19 JUL 78; To VA-86, NAS Cecil Field, FL., 14 SEP 78; To VA-86, NAS Roosevelt Roads, PR., 14 SEP 78; To VA-86, NAS Cecil Field, FL., 14 SEP 78; To VA-86, USS Nimitz (CVN-68), 28 FEB 79; To VA-86, NAS Cecil Field, FL., 06 MAR 79; To VA-86, NAS Jacksonville, FL., 27 FEB 81; To VA-86, USS Nimitz (CVN-68), 27 MAY 81; To VA-86, NAS Norfolk, VA., 28 MAY 81; To VA-86, USS Nimitz (CVN-68), 28 MAY 81 ** Transferred to NARF, NAS Jacksonville, FL., 29 APR 82 ** Transferred to VA-86/CVW-8, AJ/4XX, NAS Cecil Field, FL., 18 NOV 83 ** Transferred to VA-82/CVW-8, AJ/3XX, 22 MAR 84 ** Transferred to VA-15/CVW-6, AE/3XX, USS Independence (CV-62), 09 OCT 84; To VA-15, NAS Cecil Field, FL., 09 OCT 84 ** Transferred to VA-105/CVW-6, AE/4XX, NAS Cecil Field, FL., 01 MAY 85; To VA-105, USS Forrestal (CV-59), 21 JUN 85; To VA-105, NAS Cecil Field, FL., 21 JUN 85; To VA-105, NAS Jacksonville, FL., 03 DEC 85; To VA-105, NAS Cecil Field, FL., 03 JAN 86; To VA-105, NAS Jacksonville, FL., 07 FEB 86; To VA-105, NAS Cecil Field, FL., 11 FEB 86; To VA-105, USS Forrestal (CV-59), 04 MAR 86; To VA-105, NAS Cecil Field, FL., 04 MAR 86; To VA-105, USS Forrestal (CV-59), 04 MAR 86 ** Transferred to VA-174/FRS, AD/4XX, NAS Cecil Field, FL., 23 JUL 87 thru 11 SEP 87 ** End of flight record card ** Transferred to VA-105/CVW-6, AE/412, NAS Cecil Field, FL., date unknown ** Transferred to AMARC, Davis Monthan AFB; Tucson, AZ., assigned park code 6A0382, 24 OCT 90 ** 5967.4 flight hours ** TF41A402D engine S/N 141524 ** Aircraft released from storage and prepaired for overland and above deck shipping to government of Greece, 08 JUL 94 ** Transferred to the Helenic Air force (Greece).

E-381 158826 Navy acceptance from NPRO Rep. LTV, Dallas, TX., 30 APR 73 ** Transferred to VA-174/FRS, AD/4XX, NAS Cecil Field, FL., 02 MAY 73 ** Transferred to VA-37/CVW-3, AC/300, NAS Cecil Field, FL., 07 MAY 73; To VA-37, USS Saratoga (CV-60), 29 JUL 74; To VA-37, NAS Cecil Field, FL., 07 AUG 74; To VA-37, USS Saratoga (CV-60), 24 JUL 75; To VA-37, NAS Cecil Field, FL., 24 JUL 75; To VA-37, USS Saratoga(CV-60), 05 OCT 76; To VA-37, NAS Cecil Field, FL., 01 MAR 77; To VA-37, USS Saratoga (CV-60), 01 MAR 77; To VA-37, NAS Cecil Field, FL., 09 AUG 77; To VA-37, NAS Jacksonville, FL., 04 MAY 78; To VA-37, NAS Cecil Field, FL., 12 JUN 78; To VA-37, NAS Jacksonville, FL., 13 JUN 78; To VA-37, NAS Cecil Field, FL., 21 AUG 78; To VA-37, USS Saratoga (CV-60), 21 AUG 78; To VA-37, NAS Cecil Field, FL., 21 AUG 78; To VA-37, MCAS Yuma, AZ., 16 APR 79; To VA-37, USS Saratoga (CV-60), 24 OCT 79; To VA-37, NAS Cecil Field, FL., 24 OCT 79; To VA-37, USS Saratoga (CV-60), 24 OCT 79; To VA-37, NAS Cecil Field, FL., 24 OCT 79; To VA-37, USS Saratoga (CV-60), 24 OCT 79; To VA-37, NAS Cecil Field, FL., 22 JUL 80; To VA-37, NAS Jacksonville, FL., 01 MAY 81; To VA-37, NAS Fallon, NV., 01 MAY 81; To VA-37, NAS Cecil Field, FL., 10 JUN 81; To VA-37, USS John F. Kennedy (CV-67), 10 JUN 81; To VA-37, NAS Cecil Field, FL., 10 JUN 81 ** Transferred to VA-81/CVW-17, AA/4XX, NAS Cecil Field, FL., 22 OCT 81; To VA-81, NAS Fallon, NV., 22 OCT 81; To VA-81, USS Forrestal (CV-59), 22 OCT 81; To VA-81, NAS Cecil Field, FL., 18 MAY 82; To VA-81, USS Forrestal (CV-59), 18 MAY 82; To VA-81, NAS Jacksonville, FL., 30 NOV 82; To VA-81, NAS Cecil Field, FL., 23 MAR 83; To VA-81, NAS Fallon, NV., 04 AUG 83; To VA-81, NAS Cecil Field, FL., 20 SEP 83; To VA-81, USS Saratoga (CV-60), 28 OCT 83 ~ S 1SO strike, 18 DEC 83 ** No data on strike.

E-382 158827 Navy acceptance from NPRO Rep. LTV, Dallas, TX., 04 APR 73 ** Transferred to VA-192/CVW-11, NH/3XX, NAS LeMoore, CA., 05 APR 73; To VA-192, USS Kitty Hawk (CV-63), 09 JUN 73; To VA-192, NAS LeMoore, CA., 21 FEB 74; To VA-192, USS Kitty Hawk (CV-63), 11 APR 75; To VA-192, NAS Cubi Point, PI., 27 SEP 75; To VA-192, USS Kitty Hawk (CV-63), 19 NOV 75; To VA-192, NAS LeMoore, CA., 05 FEB 76; To VA-192, NAS Jacksonville, FL., 31 OCT 76 ** Transferred to VA-81/CVW-17, AA/4XX, NAS Cecil Field, FL., 07 JAN 77; To VA-81,

NAS Roosevelt Roads, 07 JAN 77; To VA-81, NAS Cecil Field, FL., 07 JAN 77; To VA-81, USS Forrestal](CV-59), 20 JUL 77; To VA-81, NAS Cecil Field, FL., 20 JUL 77; To VA-81, USS Forrestal (CV-59), 20 JUL 77; To VA-81, NAS Cecil Field, FL., 22 FEB 78; To VA-81, NAS Jacksonville, FL., 01 DEC 78; To VA-81, NAS Cecil Field, FL., 20 JAN 79; To VA-81, USS Forrestal (CV-59), 22 FEB 79; To VA-81, NAS Cecil Field, FL., 22 FEB 79; To VA-81, USS Forrestal (CV-59), 22 FEB 79 ** Transferred to VA-83/CVW-17, AA/3XX, USS Forrestal (CV-59), 14 SEP 79; To VA-83, NAS Cecil Field, FL., 15 SEP 79; To VA-83, USS Forrestal (CV-59), 22 FEB 80; To VA-83, NAS Cecil Field, FL., 20 MAR 80; To VA-83, USS Forrestal (CV-59), 16 OCT 80 ** Transferred to VA-82/CVW-8, AJ/3XX, USS Nimitz (CVN-68}, Hawk with CVW-8 painted on side of nose 26 OCT 80; To VA-82, NAS Cecil Field, FL., 26 OCT 80; To VA-82, NAS Jacksonville, FL., 28 APR 81; To VA-82, USS Nimitz (CVN-68}, 28 APR 81; To VA-82, NAS Cecil Field, FL., 25 JUN 81; To VA-82, USS Carl Vinson (CVN-70), 25 JUN 81; To VA-82, NAS Cecil Field, FL., 25 JUN 81; To VA-82, USS Nimitz (CVN-68}, 25 JUN 81; To VA-82, NAS Cecil Field, FL., 25 JUN 81; To VA-82, USS Nimitz (CVN-68}, 25 JUN 81; To VA-82, NAS Cecil Field, FL., 25 JUN 81; To VA-82, NAS Jacksonville, FL., 09 DEC 83; To VA-82, NAS Cecil Field, FL., 07 JAN 84; To VA-82, NAS Jacksonville, FL., 30 MAY 84 ** Transferred to VA-66/CVW-7, AG/3XX, USS Dwight D. Eisenhower (CVN-69), 30 MAY 84; To VA-66, NAS Cecil Field, FL., 30 MAY 84; To VA-66, USS Dwight D. Eisenhower (CVN-69), 30 MAY 84; To VA-66, NAS Cecil Field, FL., 11 SEP 84; To VA-66, USS Dwight D. Eisenhower (CVN-69), 17 SEP 84; To VA-66, NAS Cecil Field, FL., 17 SEP 84; To VA-66, USS Dwight D. Eisenhower (CVN-69), 17 SEP 84; To VA-66, NAS Cecil Field, FL., 24 SEP 85; To VA-66, NAS Jacksonville, FL., 11 JUN 86; To VA-66, NAS Cecil Field, FL., 13 JUN 86; To VA-66, USS John F. Kennedy (CV-67), 13 JUN 86; To VA-66, NAS Cecil Field, FL., 20 OCT 86 ** Transferred to VA-105/CVW-6, AE/4XX, NAS Cecil Field, FL., 13 MAR 87; To VA-105, USS Forrestal (CV-59), 08 MAY 87 ** End of flight record card.

E-383 158828 Navy acceptance from NPRO Rep. LTV, Dallas, TX., 22 MAY 73 ** Transferred to VA-195/CVW-11, NH/400, NAS LeMoore, CA., 23 MAY 73; To VA-195, USS Kitty Hawk (CV-63), 29 JUN 73; To VA-195, NAS LeMoore, CA., 23 APR 74; To VA-195, USS Kitty Hawk (CV-63), 28 MAR 75; To VA-195, NAS LeMoore, CA., 09 APR 75; To VA-195, USS Kitty Hawk (CV-63), 19 MAY 75; To VA-195, NAS Cubi Point, PI., 21 JUN 75; To VA-195, NAS LeMoore, CA., 14 DEC 75; To VA-195, NAS Jacksonville, FL., 03 JAN 77; To VA-195, NAS LeMoore, CA., 03 MAR 77; To VA-195, USS Kitty Hawk (CV-63), 19 JUL 77; To VA-195, NAS LeMoore, CA., 09 AUG 77; To VA-195, USS Kitty Hawk (CV-63), 29 SEP 77; To VA-195, NAF Atsugi, JP., 30 JAN 78; To VA-195, USS Kitty Hawk (CV-63), 11 FEB 78 ** Transferred to VA-56/CVW-5, NF/4XX, USS Midway (CV-41), 22 APR 78; To VA-56, NAF Atsugi, JP., 13 JUN 78; To VA-56, USS Midway (CV-41), 14 JUL 80; To VA-56, NAF Atsugi, JP., 17 DEC 80 ~ S 1SO strike, 17 DEC 80 ** Lost power on take off, pilot ejected safely after pulling full back on stick and pulling lower ejection handle on second attempt.

E-384 158829 Navy acceptance from NPRO Rep. LTV, Dallas, TX., 16 MAY 73 ** Transferred to VA-105/CVW-3, AC/401, NAS Cecil Field, FL., 17 MAY 73; To VA-105, USS Saratoga (CV-60), 18 OCT 74; To VA-105, NAS Cecil Field, FL., \21 OCT 74; To VA-105, USS Saratoga (CV-60), 21 OCT 74; To VA-105, NAS Cecil Field, FL., 21 OCT 74; To VA-105, MCAS Yuma, AZ., 30 AUG 75; To VA-105, USS Saratoga (CV-60), 16 SEP 75; To VA-105, NAS Cecil Field, FL., 01 SEP 76 ** Transferred to VA-174/FRS, AD/4XX, NAS Cecil Field, FL., 18 AUG 77 ** Transferred to VA-105/CVW-3, AC/4XX, USS Saratoga (CV-60), 11 AUG 78; To VA-105, NAS Cecil Field, FL., 19 JUL 79; To VA-105, USS Saratoga (CV-60), 21 AUG 79; To VA-105, NAS Cecil Field, FL., 28 JAN 80; To VA-105, USS Saratoga (CV-60), 20 MAR 80; To VA-105, NAS Cecil Field, FL., 17 NOV 80; To VA-105, NAS Fallon, NV., 11 JUN 81; To VA-105, NAS Jacksonville, FL., 21 JUL 81; To VA-105, USS John F. Kennedy (CV-67), 21 JUL 81; To VA-105, NAS Jacksonville, FL., 15 SEP 81; To VA-105, USS John F. Kennedy (CV-67), 15 SEP 81; To VA-105, NAS Cecil Field,

FL., 10 MAY 82 ** Transferred to VA-37/CVW-15, NL/3XX, NAS Cecil Field, FL., 02 SEP 82; To VA-37, USS Carl Vinson (CVN-70), 01 DEC 82; To VA-37, NAS Cecil Field, FL., 01 DEC 82; To VA-37, USS Carl Vinson (CVN-70), 01 DEC 82; To VA-37, NAS Roosevelt Roads, PI., 07 FEB 84; To VA-37, NAS Cecil Field, FL., 08 MAR 84; To VA-37, NWC China Lake, CA., 07 APR 84; To VA-37, NAS Cecil Field, FL., 24 APR 84; To VA-37, NAS Jacksonville, FL., 24 MAY 84; To VA-37, NAS Cecil Field, FL., 07 AUG 84; To VA-37, MCAS Twenty Nine Palms, CA., 13 AUG 84; To VA-37, NAS Cecil Field, FL., 05 SEP 84; To VA-37, MCAS Iwakuni, JP., 13 SEP 84 ** Transferred to VA-174/FRS, AD/4XX, NAS Cecil Field, FL., 10 DEC 84 ** Transferred to AMARC, Davis Monthan AFB; Tucson, AZ., assigned park code 6A0177; 19 JUN 86; Transferred to VA-174/ RS, AD/4XX, NAS Cecil Field, FL., 19 JUN 86; Transferred to AMARC, Davis Monthan AFB; Tucson, AZ., assigned park code 6A0177, 19 JUN 86 ** End of flight record card ** Ejection seat S/N 0288 removed, 09 FEB 89 ** 5770.7 flight hours ** TF41A2B engine S/N 141294 ** Aircraft released from storage and prepaired for overland and above deck shipping to government of Greece, 19 JUL 94 ** Transferred to the Helenic Air force (Greece).

E-385 158830 Navy acceptance from NPRO Rep. LTV, Dallas, TX., 27 JUN 73 ** Transferred to VA-37/CVW-3, AC/301 & AC/300, NAS Cecil Field, FL., 28 JUN 73; To VA-37, USS Saratoga (CV-60), 03 MAY 74; To VA-37, NAS Cecil Field, FL., 03 MAY 74; To VA-37, USS Saratoga (CV-60), 03 MAY 74; To VA-37, NAS Cecil Field, FL., 03 MAY 74; To VA-37, USS Saratoga (CV-60), 05 AUG 75; To VA-37, NAS Cecil Field, FL., 05 AUG 75; To VA-37, USS Saratoga (CV-60), 01 APR 76; To VA-37, NAS Cecil Field, FL., 22 JUL 76; To VA-37, NAS Jacksonville, FL., 23 JUL 76; To VA-37, NAS Cecil Field, FL., 16 SEP 76; To VA-37, USS Saratoga (CV-60), 03 NOV 76; To VA-37, NAS Cecil Field, FL., 03 NOV 76; To VA-37, USS Saratoga (CV-60), 03 NOV 76; To VA-37, NAS Cecil Field, FL., 16 JUL 77; To VA-37, NAS Jacksonville, FL., 28 JUL 78; To VA-37, NAS Cecil Field, FL., 22 AUG 78; To VA-37, USS Saratoga (CV-60), 22 AUG 78; To VA-37, NAS Cecil Field, FL., 22 AUG 78; To VA-37, MCAS Yuma, AZ., 22 AUG 78; To VA-37, USS Saratoga (CV-60), 25 OCT 79; To VA-37, NAS Cecil Field, FL., 25 OCT 79; To VA-37, USS Saratoga (CV-60), 25 OCT 79; To VA-37, NAS Cecil Field, FL., 25 OCT 79; To VA-37, USS Saratoga (CV-60), 25 OCT 79; To VA-37, NAS Cecil Field, FL., 25 OCT 79; To VA-37, NAS Jacksonville, FL., 17 OCT 80; To VA-37, NAS Cecil Field, FL., 16 DEC 80; To VA-37, NAS Fallon, NV., 16 DEC 80; To VA-37, NAS Cecil Field, FL., 16 DEC 80; To VA-37, USS John F. Kennedy (CV-67), 16 DEC 80; To VA-37, NAS Cecil Field, FL., 16 DEC 80; To VA-37, USS John F. Kennedy (CV-67), 16 DEC 80; To VA-37, NAS Cecil Field, FL., 16 DEC 80; To VA-37/CVW-15, NL/3XX, USS Carl Vinson (CVN-70), 27 DEC 82; To VA-37, NAS Cecil Field, FL., 27 DEC 82 ** Transferred to VA-12/ CVW-7, AG/4XX, NAS Cecil Field, FL., 17 FEB 83; To VA-12, NAS Jacksonville, FL., 20 APR 83; To VA-12, Dwight D. Eisenhower (CVN-69), 23 APR 83; To VA-12, NAS Jacksonville, FL., 01 JUL 83; To VA-12, Dwight D. Eisenhower (CVN-69), 13 JUL 83; To VA-12, NAS Cecil Field, FL., 20 OCT 83 ** Transferred to VA-86/CVW-8, AJ/4XX, NAS Cecil Field, FL., 31 OCT 83 ** Transferred to VA-66/CVW-7, AG/3XX, NAS Cecil Field, FL.,01 MAR 84; To VA-66, USS Dwight D. Eisenhower (CVN-69), 03 APR 84; To VA-66, NAS Cecil Field, FL., 03 APR 84; To VA-66, USS Dwight D. Eisenhower (CVN-69), 03 APR 84; To VA-66, NAS Cecil Field, FL., 03 APR 84; To VA-66, USS Dwight D. Eisenhower (CVN-69), 03 APR 84; To VA-66, NAS Cecil Field, FL., 20 MAY 85; To VA-66, USS Dwight D. Eisenhower (CVN-69), 21 MAY 85; To VA-66, NAS Cecil Field, FL., 23 SEP 85; To VA-66, NAS Jacksonville, FL., 17 JAN 86 ** Transferred to VA-82/CVW-8, AJ/3XX, NAS Cecil Field, FL., 17 JAN 86; To VA-82, USS Nimitz (CVN-68), 10 MAR 86; To VA-82, NAS Cecil Field, FL., 08 OCT 86; To VA-82, USS Nimitz (CVN-68), 12 DEC 86; To VA-82, NAS Cecil Field, FL., 01 DEC 86 ** Transferred to VA-37/ CVW-6, AE/3XX, USS Forrestal (CV-59), 04 AUG 87 thru 20 AUG 87 ** End of flight record card ~ Strike, 91 ** Damaged during Operation Desert Storm and left at Sigonella, IT. ** On display at the Museo dell' Aviazione at Cerbiaola, IT.

158831/158842 LTV A-7E-13-CV Corsair II; (Block XIII)

E-398 158831 Navy acceptance from NPRO Rep. LTV, Dallas, TX., 24 JUL 73 ** Transferred to VA-105/CVW-3, AC/400, NAS Cecil Field, FL., 15 JUL 73; To VA-105, USS Saratoga (CV-60), 28 JUN 74; To VA-105, NAS Cecil Field, FL., 28 JUN 74; To VA-105, USS Saratoga (CV-60), 28 JUN 74; To VA-105, NAS Cecil Field, FL., 28 JUN 74; To VA-105, USS Saratoga (CV-60), 28 JUN 74; To VA-105, NAS Cecil Field, FL., 28 JUN 74; To VA-105, USS Saratoga (CV-60), 28 JUL 75; To VA-105, NAS Cecil Field, FL., 28 JUL 75; Pained in bi-centennial paint scheme, 04 JUL 76; To VA-105, USS Saratoga (CV-60), 01 DEC 76; To VA-105, NAS Cecil Field, FL., 01 MAR 77; To VA-105, USS Saratoga (CV-60), 01 MAR 77 ** Transferred to VA-174/FRS, AD/426, NAS Cecil Field, FL., 27 JUN 77; To VA-174, NAS Jacksonville, FL., 30 SEP 77; To VA-174, NAS Cecil Field, FL., 04 JAN 78 ** Transferred to VA-86/ CVW-8, AJ/4XX, USS Nimitz (CVN-68), 27 MAY 81; To VA-86, NAS Norfolk, VA., 28 MAY 81; To VA-86, USS Nimitz (CVN-68), 28 MAY 81; To VA-86, NAS Cecil Field, FL., 28 MAY 81 ** Transferred to NARF, NAS Jacksonville, FL., 22 JUN 82 ** Transferred to VA-82/ CVW-8, AJ/3XX, NAS Cecil Field, FL., 01 OCT 84 ** Transferred to VA-15/CVW-6, AE/3XX, USS Independence (CV-62), 06 OCT 84; To VA-15, NAS Cecil Field, FL., 06 OCT 84 ** Transferred to VA-46/CVW-1, AB/3XX, USS America (CV-66), 06 MAY 85; To VA-46, NAS Cecil Field, FL., 21 MAY 85; To VA-46, USS America (CV-66), 21 MAY 85; To VA-46, NAS Cecil Field, FL., 21 MAY 85; To VA-46, USS America (CV-66), 21 MAY 85; To VA-46, NAS Cecil Field, FL., 21 MAY 85; To VA-46, USS Dwight D. Eisenhower (CVN-69), 26 MAR 87; To VA-46, NAS Cecil Field, FL., 26 MAR 87; To VA-46, NAS Jacksonville, FL., 24 AUG 87; To VA-46, NAS Cecil Field, FL., 2AUG 87; To VA-46, NAS Jacksonville, FL., 27 AUG 87 ** End of flight record card ** Transferred to PMTC, PMTC/XXX, NAS Point Mugu, CA., date unknown ** Transferred to AMARC, Davis Monthan AFB; Tucson, AZ., assigned park code 6A0310; 12 JAN 90 ** 5006.5 flight hours ** TF41A402D engine S/N 141575 ** Storage location 211963 ** Aircraft deleted from inventory and released to DRMO for disposition, 19 JAN 06 ** At AMARG, Davis Monthan AFB; Tucson, AZ., 15 JUN 07.

E-387 158832 Navy acceptance from NPRO Rep. LTV, Dallas, TX., 11 JUL 73 ** Transferred to VA-27/CVW-14, NK/4XX, NAS LeMoore, CA., 07 SEP 73; To VA-27, NAS Fallon, NV., 08 OCT 75; To VA-27, NAS LeMoore, CA., 08 OCT 75; To VA-27 USS Enterprise (CVN-65), 31 JAN 76; To VA-27, NAS LeMoore, CA., 31 JAN 76; To VA-27, NAS Jacksonville, FL., 17 APR 76; To VA-27 USS Enterprise (CVN-65), 17 APR 76; To VA-27, NAS Jacksonville, FL., 20 APR 76; To VA-27, NAS LeMoore, CA., 20 APR 76; To VA-27, NAS Jacksonville, FL., 08 JUN 76; To VA-27 USS Enterprise (CVN-65), 01 JUL 76; To VA-27, NAF Atsugi, JP., 08 DEC 76; To VA-27, USS Enterprise (CVN-65), 12 DEC 76; To VA-27, NAS LeMoore, CA., 12 DEC 76 ** Transferred to VA-56/ CVW-5, NF/4XX, USS Midway (CV-41), 11 MAR 77; To VA-56, NAF Atsugi, JP., 04 APR 77; To VA-56, USS Midway (CV-41), 08 APR 77; To VA-56, NAF Atsugi, JP., 20 JAN 78; To VA-56, USS Midway (CV-41), 26 JAN 78; To VA-56, NAF Atsugi, JP., 15 JUN 78; To VA-56, USS Midway (CV-41), NAF Atsugi, JP., 07 MAY 80; To VA-56, USS Midway (CV-41), 14 JUL 80; To VA-56, NAF Atsugi, JP., 24 NOV 80; To VA-56, USS Midway (CV-41), 18 FEB 81; To VA-56, NAF Atsugi, JP., 08 JUN 81; To VA-56, USS Midway (CV-41), 02 SEP 81; To VA-56, NAF Atsugi, JP., 05 OCT 81 ~ S 1SO strike, 04 NOV 81 ** No data on strike.

E-388 158833 Navy acceptance from NPRO Rep. LTV, Dallas, TX., 22 AUG 73 ** Transferred to VA-113/CVW-2, NE/3XX, USS Ranger (CV-61), 24 AUG 73; To VA-113, NAS LeMoore, CA., 07 MAY 74; To VA-113, USS Ranger (CV-61), 07 MAY 74; To VA-113, NAS LeMoore, CA., 23 OCT 74; To VA-113, USS Ranger (CV-61), 16 JUL 75 ** Transferred to VA-97/CVW-14, NK/3XX, NAS LeMoore, CA., 18 AUG 75; To VA-97, NAS Fallon, NV., 30 NOV 75; To VA-97, USS Enterprise (CVN-65), 05 DEC 75; To VA-97, NAS LeMoore, CA., 05 DEC 75 ** Transferred to

VA-195/CVW-11, NH/4XX, NAS LeMoore, CA., 21 APR 76; To VA-195, NAS Jacksonville, FL., 16 DEC 76; To VA-195, NAS LeMoore, CA., 02 MAR 77; To VA-195, USS Kitty Hawk (CV-63), 19 JUL 77; To VA-195, NAS LeMoore, CA., 12 AUG 77; To VA-195, USS Kitty Hawk (CV-63), 29 SEP 77; To VA-195, NAS LeMoore, CA., 09 MAR 78 ** Transferred to VA-97/CVW-14, NK/3XX, NAS LeMoore, CA., 07 DEC 78; To VA-97, NAS Jacksonville, FL., 04 MAY 79; To VA-97, NAS LeMoore, CA., 09 MAY 79; To VA-97, USS Coral Sea (CV-43), 10 OCT 79 ** Transferred to VA-56/CVW-5, NF/412, NAF Atsugi, JP., 07 MAY 80; To VA-56, USS Midway (CV-41), 14 JUL 80; To VA-56, NAF Atsugi, JP., 27 JUN 81; To VA-56, USS Midway (CV-41), 03 SEP 81; NAF Atsugi, JP., 24 SEP 81; To VA-56, USS Midway (CV-41), 26 SEP 81; To VA-56, NAF Atsugi, JP., 30 SEP 81 ** Transferred to VA-25/CVW-2, NE/4XX, NAS Cubi Point, PI., 22 AUG 82; To VA-25, USS Ranger (CV-61), 22 AUG 82; To VA-25, NAS LeMoore, CA., 22 AUG 82 ** Transferred to VA-97/CVW-14, NK/3XX, NAS LeMoore, CA., 04 JAN 83; To VA-97, USS Coral Sea (CV-43), 04 JAN 83 ** Transferred to VA-195/CVW-11, NH/4XX, NAS LeMoore, CA., 15 FEB 83; To VA-195, USS Ranger (CV-61), 22 JUN 83; To VA-195, NAS LeMoore, CA-, 29 JAN 84; To VA-195, NAS Jacksonville, FL., 15 MAY 84 ** Transferred to VA-97/CVW-15, NL/3XX, NAS LeMoore, CA., 22 SEP 84; To VA-97, USS Carl Vinson (CVN-70), 22 SEP 84; To VA-97, NAS LeMoore, CA., 10 NOV 84 ** Transferred to VA-22/CVW-11, NH/3XX, NAS LeMoore, CA., 13 JUN 85; To VA-22, USS Enterprise (CVN-65), 28 DEC 85; To VA-22, NAS LeMoore, CA., 17 APR 86; To VA-22, NAS Jacksonville, FL., 12 MAR 87; To VA-22, NAS LeMoore, CA., 12 MAR 87; To VA-22, NAS Jacksonville, FL., 17 MAR 87; To VA-22, NAS LeMoore, CA., 28 JUL 87 ** End of flight record card.** Transferred to AMARC, Davis Monthan AFB; Tucson, AZ., assigned park code 6A0340, 16 APR 90 ** 7012.9 flight hours ** TF41A402D engine S/N AE141582 ** Aircraft released from storage and prepared for overland shipment to FMS and NAD, NAS Jacksonville, FL., with final shipment to government of Thailand, 11 OCT 95 ** Transferred to the Royal Thai Navy, S/N 158833.

E-389 158834 Navy acceptance from NPRO Rep. LTV, Dallas, TX., 21 AUG 73 ** Transferred to VA-25/CVW-2, NE/412, USS Ranger (CV-61), 22 AUG 73; To VA-25, NAS LeMoore, CA., 14 NOV 74; To VA-25, NAS Fallon, NV.,13 JUL 75; To VA-25, USS Ranger (CV-61), 14 AUG 75; To VA-25, NAS LeMoore, CA., 23 SEP 75; To VA-25, USS Ranger (CV-61), 23 SEP 75; To VA-25, NAF Atsugi, JP., 29 MAR 76; To VA-25, USS Ranger (CV-61), 01 APR 76; To VA-25, NAS LeMoore, CA., 01 DEC 76; To VA-25, NAS Jacksonville, FL., 30 APR 77; To VA-25, NAS LeMoore, CA., 10 MAY 77; To VA-25, NAS Fallon, NV., 29 JUL 77; To VA-25, NAS LeMoore, CA., 12 AUG 77; To VA-25, USS Ranger (CV-61), 10 OCT 78; To VA-25, NAS LeMoore, CA., 10 OCT 78; To VA-25, USS Ranger (CV-61), 10 OCT 78 ** Transferred to VA-27/CVW-14, NK/4XX, NAS LeMoore, CA., 12 FEB 79; To VA-27, NPTR El Centro, CA., 02 APR 79; To VA-27, NAS Jacksonville, FL., 02 MAY 79; To VA-27, NNPTR El Centro, CA., 07 JUN 79; To VA-27, USS Coral Sea (CV-43), 12 OCT 79; To VA-27, NAS Cubi Point, PI., 12 NOV 79; To VA-27, USS Coral Sea (CV-43), 23 DEC 79 ** Transferred to VA-56/CVW-5, NF/4XX, NAF Atsugi, JP., 13 MAY 80; To VA-56, USS Midway (CV-41), 19 JUL 80 ~ S 1SO strike, 14 NOV 80 ** No data on strike.

E-390 158835 Navy acceptance from NPRO Rep. LTV, Dallas, TX., 15 AUG 73 ** Transferred to VA-105/CVW-3, AC/403, NAS Cecil Field, FL., 20 AUG 73; To VA-105, USS Saratoga (CV-60), 07 AUG 74; To VA-105, NAS Cecil Field, FL., 30 SEP 74; To VA-105, USS Saratoga (CV-60), 30 SEP 74; To VA-105, NAS Cecil Field, 30 SEP 74; To VA-105, USS Saratoga (CV-60), 30 SEP 74; To VA-105, NAS Cecil Field, 30 SEP 74; To VA-105, USS Saratoga (CV-60), 01 JAN 77; To VA-105, NAS Cecil Field, 01 JAN 77 ** Transferred to VA-25/CVW-2, NE/4XX, USS Saratoga (CV-60), 01 APR 77 ** Transferred to VA-174/FRS, AD/4XX, NAS Cecil Field, FL., 22 JUN 77; To VA-174, NAS Jacksonville, FL., 28 FEB 78; To VA-174, NAS Cecil Field, 01 MAR 78; To VA-174,

NAS Jacksonville, FL., 12 APR 78; To VA-174, NAS Cecil Field, FL., 10 MAY 78 ** Transferred to VA-12/CVW-7, AG/414, NAS Cecil Field, FL., 28 JUN 78, USS Dwight D.Eisenhower (CVN-69), 28 JUN 78; To VA-12, NAS Cecil Field, FL., 28 JUN 78; To VA-12, USS Dwight D. Eisenhower (CVN-69), 28 JUN 78; To VA-12, NAS Cecil Field, FL., 28 JUN 78; To VA-12, USS Dwight D. Eisenhower (CVN-69), 28 JUN 78; To VA-12, NAS Cecil Field, FL., 11 DEC 79; To VA-12, USS Dwight D. Eisenhower (CVN-69), 11 DEC 79; To VA-12, NAS Jacksonville, FL., 02 FEB 81; To VA-12, USS Dwight D. Eisenhower (CVN-69), 13 MAR 81; To VA-12, NAS Cecil Field, FL., 16 MAR 81; To VA-12, USS Dwight D. Eisenhower (CVN-69), 16 MAR 81; To VA-12, NAS Cecil Field, FL., 21 JUL 82; To VA-12, NAS Jacksonville, FL., 19 AUG 82; To VA-12, NAS Cecil Field, FL., 08 NOV 82; VA-12, NARF, NAS Jacksoville, FL., 08 NOV 82 ** To VA-12, USS Dwight D. Eisenhower (CVN-69), 08 NOV 82; To VA-12, NAS Cecil Field, FL., 02 NOV 82; To VA-12, USS Dwight D. Eisenhower (CVN-69), 31 JAN 84; To VA-12, NAS Cecil Field, FL., 31 JAN 84; To VA-12, USS Dwight D. Eisenhower (CVN-69), 12 SEP 84; To VA-12, NAS Cecil Field, FL., 08 APR 85; Paint was white on light gray with black modex, 85; To VA-12, USS Dwight D. Eisenhower (CVN- 69), 08 APR 85; To VA-12, NAS Jacksonville, FL., 17 SEP 85; To VA-12, NAS Cecil Field, FL.,25 SEP 85; To VA-12, NAS Jacksonville, FL., 04 DEC 85; To VA-12, NAS Cecil Field, FL., 06 DEC 85 ** Transferred to AMARC, Davis Monthan AFB; Tucson, AZ., assigned park code 6A0197, 05 SEP 86 ** 559.5 flight hours ** TF41A402D engine S/N 141569 ** Storage location 210806 ** End of flight record card ** Engine Records released to DRMO for disposition, 25 FEB 06 ** Aircraft at AMARG, Davis Monthan AFB; Tucson, AZ., 15 JUN 07.

E-391 158836 Navy acceptance from NPRO Rep. LTV, Dallas, TX., 27 SEP73 ** Transferred to VA-174/FRS, AD/4XX, NAS Cecil Field, FL., 28 SEP 73 ** Transferred to VA-82/CVW-8, AJ/3XX, NAS Cecil Field, FL., 18 DEC 74; To VA-82, USS Nimitz (CVN-68), 16 JAN 75; To VA-82, NAS Cecil Field, FL., 01 JUL 75; To VA-82, NAS Roosevelt Roads, PR., 01 JUL 75; To VA-82, NAS Cecil Field, FL., 01 JUL 75; To VA-82, USS Nimitz (CVN-68), 01 JUL 75; To VA-82, NAS Cecil Field, FL., 01 JUL 75; To VA-82, USS Nimitz (CVN-68), 01 JUL 75; To VA-82, NAS Cecil Field, FL., 01 JUL 75; To VA-82, USS Nimitz (CVN-68), 10 AUG 77 ** Transferred to VA-174/FRS, AD/4XX, NAS Cecil Field, FL., 03 NOV 77; To VA-174, NAS Jacksonville, FL., 13 DEC 77; To VA-174, NAS Cecil Field, FL., 06 APR 78 ** Transferred to VA-82/CVW-8, AJ/3XX, NAS Cecil Field, FL., 25 SEP 79; To VA-82, USS Nimitz (CVN-68), 25 OCT 79; To VA-82, NAS Jacksonville, FL., 30 MAY 80; To VA-82, USS Nimitz (CVN-68), 11 JUN 80; To VA-82, NAS Jacksonville, FL., 10 JUL 80; To VA-82, USS Nimitz (CVN-68), 05 AUG 80; To VA-82, NAS Cecil Field, FL., 05 AUG 80; To VA-82, USS Nimitz (CVN-68), 05 AUG 80; To VA-82, NAS Cecil Field, FL., 05 AUG 80; To VA-82, USS Carl Vinson (CVN-70), 15 APR 82 ** Transferred to VA-174/FRS, AD/4XX, NAS Cecil Field, FL., 01 MAY 82; To VA-174, NAS Jacksonville, FL., 23 JUN 82; To VA-174, NAS Cecil Field, FL., 23 JUN 82; To VA-174, NAS Jacksonville, FL., 25 JUN 82; To VA-174, NAS Cecil Field, FL., 30 AUG 82 ** Transferred to VA-37/CVW-15, NL/3XX, NAS Cecil Field, FL., 09 OCT 82; To VA-37, USS Carl Vinson (CVN-70), 27 DEC 82; To VA-37, NAS Cecil Field, FL., 27 DEC 82; To VA-37, USS Carl Vinson (CVN-70), 23 MAR 83 ** Transferred to VA-81/CVW-17, AA/4XX, NAS Cecil Field, FL., 15 APR 83; To VA-81, NAS Fallon, NV., 28 JUL 83; To VA-81, NAS Cecil Field, FL., 06 SEP 83; To VA-81, USS Saratoga (CV-60), 28 NOV 83; To VA-81, NAS Cecil Field, FL., 27 DEC 83; To VA-81, USS Saratoga (CV-60), 27 DEC 83; To VA-81, NAS Cecil Field, FL., 27 DEC 83; To VA-81, USS Saratoga (CV-60), 22 APR 85 ** Transferred to VA-174/FRS, AD/446, NAS Cecil Field, FL., 23 MAY 85 ** Transferred to AMARC, Davis Monthan AFB; Tucson, AZ., assigned park code 6A0228; 28 JUL 87 ** End of flight record card ** 5338.2 flight hours ** TF41A2C engine S/N 142540 ** Storage location 210346 ** Under GSA control ** At AMARG, Davis Monthan AFB; Tucson, AZ., 15 JUN 07.

E-392 158837 Navy acceptance from NPRO Rep. LTV, Dallas, TX., 01 NOV 73 ** Transferred to VA-147/CVW-9, NG/4XX, USS Constellation (CVA-64), 02 NOV 73; To VA-147, NAS LeMoore, CA., 11 MAR 75; To VA-147, NAS Fallon, NV., 26 MAY 75; To VA-147, NAS LeMoore, CA., 05 JUN 75 ** Transferred to VA-22/CVW-15, NL/3XX, NAS Fallon, NV., 20 AUG 75; To VA-22, NAS LeMoore, CA., 17 OCT 75; To VA-22, NAS Fallon, NV., 30 APR 76; To VA-22, NAS LeMoore, CA., 30 APR 76 ** Transferred to VA-195/CVW-11, NH/4XX, NAS LeMoore, CA., 05 NOV 76; To VA-195, NAS Jacksonville, FL., 17 JAN 77; ** To VA-195, NAS LeMoore, CA., 12 MAR 77; To VA-195, USS Kitty Hawk (CV-63), 19 JUL 77; To VA-195, NAS LeMoore, CA., 12 AUG 77; To VA-195, USS Kitty Hawk (CV-63), 17 SEP 77; To VA-195, NAS LeMoore, CA., 09 MAR 78 ** Transferred to VA-97/CVW-14, NK/3XX, NAS LeMoore, CA., 21 DEC 78; To VA-97, NAS Jacksonville, FL., 03 MAY 79; To VA-97, NAS LeMoore, CA., 17 JUN 79; To VA-97, USS Coral Sea (CV-43), 11 OCT 79 ** Transferred to VA-56/CVW-5, NF/4XX, NAF Atsugi, JP., 14 MAY 80; To VA-56, USS Midway (CV-41), 14 JUL 80; To VA-56, NAF Atsugi, JP., 15 NOV 80; To VA-56, USS Midway (CV-41), 19 NOV 80; To VA-56, NAF Atsugi, JP., 25 NOV 80; To VA-56, USS Midway (CV-41), 23 FEB 81; To VA-56, NAF Atsugi, JP., 01 JUN 81; To VA-56, USS Midway (CV-41), 01 AUG 81; To VA-56, NAF Atsugi, JP., 01 AUG 81 ** Transferred to VA-25/CVW-2, NE/4XX, USS Ranger (CV-61), 26 AUG 82 ** Transferred to VA-27/CVW-14, NK/4XX, NAS LeMoore, CA., 21 OCT 82; To VA-27, USS Coral Sea (CV-43), 03 MAR 83; To VA-27, NAS LeMoore, 26 SEP 83; To VA-27, NAS Jacksonville, FL., 16 DEC 83; To VA-27/CVW-15, NL/4XX, USS Carl Vinson (CVN-70), 19 DEC 83; To VA-27, NAS LeMoore, CA., 19 DEC 83; To VA-27, USS Carl Vinson (CVN-70), 19 DEC 83 ** Transferred to VA-97/CVW-15, NL/3XX, USS Carl Vinson (CVN-70), 17 MAY 84; To VA-97, NAS LeMoore, CA., 18 MAY 84; To VA-97, USS Carl Vinson (CVN-70), 24 JUL 84; To VA-97, NAS LeMoore, CA., 20 AUG 84; To VA-97, NAS Jacksonville, FL., 21 SEP 84; To VA-97, USS Carl Vinson (CVN-70), 21 SEP 84; To VA-97, NAS Jacksonville, FL., 04 FEB 85; To VA-97, NAS LeMoore, CA., 04 FEB 85; To VA-97, NAS Jacksonville, FL., 11 JUN 85 ** Transferred to VA-146/CVW-9, NE/3XX, NAS LeMoore, CA., 14 JUN 85; To VA-146, USS Kitty Hawk (CV-63), 14 JUN 85; To VA-146, NAS LeMoore, CA., 02 JAN 86 ** Transferred to VA-97/CVW-15, NL/3XX, USS Carl Vinson (CVN-70, 16 JUL 86; To VA-97, NAS Alameda, CA., 12 JAN 87; To VA-97, NAS Jacksonville, FL., 18 JUL 87 thru 20 JUL 87 ** End of flight record card ** Transferred to NAD, NAS Jacksonville, FL., 17 DEC 87 ** Transferred to VA-122/FRS, NJ/223, NAS LeMoore, CA., date unknown ** Transferred to AMARC, Davis Monthan AFB; Tucson, AZ., assigned park code 6A0362, 05 JUN 90 ** 6417.4 flight hours ** TF41A402D engine S/N 142598 ** Storage location 111517 ** At AMARG, Davis Monthan AFB; Tucson, AZ., 15 JUN 07.

E-393 158838 Navy acceptance from NPRO Rep. LTV, Dallas, TX., 17 OCT 73 ** Transferred to VA-122/FRS, NJ/246, NAS LeMoore, CA., 18 OCT 73; To VA-122, NAS Jacksonville, FL., 16 MAY 77; To VA-122, NAS LeMoore, CA., 13 JUL 77; To VA-122, NAS Jacksonville, FL., 13 SEP 79; To VA-122, NAS LeMoore, CA., 26 OCT 79; To VA-122, NAS Jacksonville, FL., 29 DEC 82; To VA-122, NAS LeMoore, CA., 04 APR 83; To VA-122, NAS Dallas, TX., 21 JUN 83 ** Transferred to VA-146/CVW-9, NE/3XX, NAS LeMoore, CA., 21 JUN 83; To VA-146, USS Kitty Hawk (CV-63), 28 DEC 83; To VA-146, NAS LeMoore, CA., 16 JUN 84 ** Transferred to VA-97/CVW-15, NL/3XX, NAS LeMoore, CA., 18 SEP 84; To VA-97, USS Carl Vinson (CVN-70), 18 SEP 84; To VA-97, NAS LeMoore, CA., 12 MAY 85; To VA-97, NAS Jacksonville, FL., 20 FEB 86; To VA-97, USS Carl Vinson (CVN-70), 11 MAR 86; To VA-97, NAS Jacksonville, FL., 24 JUN 86; To VA-97, NAS LeMoore, CA., 24 JUN 86 ** Transferred to VA-146/CVW-9, NE/3XX, NAS LeMoore, CA., 03 JUL 86; To VA-146, USS Kitty Hawk (CV-63), 03 JUL 86; To VA-146, NAS LeMoore, CA., 24 MAR 87 ** End of flight record card ** Transferred to VA-94/CVW-11, NH/417, NAS LeMoore, CA., date unknown ** Transferred to AMARC, Davis Monthan AFB; Tucson, AZ., assigned park code 6A0297, 18 AUG 89 ** 5244.6 flight hours ** TF41A402D engine S/N 141411 ** Aircraft released from storage and prepared for overland shipment to FMS, NAS Jacksonville, FL., with final shipment to government of Thailand, 06 DEC 94 ** Transferred to the Royal Thai Navy, S/N 1404.

E-394 158839 Navy acceptance from NPRO Rep. LTV, Dallas, TX., 18 OCT 73 ** Transferred to VA-174/FRS, AD/4XX, NAS Cecil Field, FL., 19 OCT 73 ** Transferred to VA-86/CVW-8, AJ/4XX, NAS Cecil Field, FL., 16 JAN 75; To VA-86, USS Nimitz (CVN-68), 16 JAN 75; To VA-86, NAS Cecil Field, FL., 16 JAN 75; To VA-86, NAS Roosevelt Roads, PR., 16 JAN 75; To VA-86, NAS Cecil Field, FL., 16 JAN 75; To VA-86, USS Nimitz (CVN-68), 16 JAN 75; To VA-86, NAS Cecil Field, FL., 16 JAN 75; To VA-86, USS Nimitz (CVN-68), 16 JAN 75; To VA-86, NAS Cecil Field, FL., 30 JUN 75; To VA-86, NAS Roosevelt Roads, PR., 30 JUN 75; To VA-86, NAS Cecil Field, FL., 10 AUG 77; To VA-86, USS Nimitz (CVN-68), 10 AUG 77; To VA-86, NAS Cecil Field, FL., 10 AUG 77 ** Transferred to VA-174/FRS, AD/4XX, NAS Cecil Field, FL., 20 OCT 77; To VA-174, NAS Jacksonville, FL., 05 DEC 77; To VA-174, NAS Cecil Field, FL., 16 JAN 78 ** Transferred to VA-86/CVW-8, AJ/4XX, USS Nimitz (CVN-68), 30 JAN 78; To VA-86, NAS Cecil Field, FL., 30 JAN 78 ** Transferred to VA-83/CVW-17, AA/3XX, USS Forrestal (CV-59), 09 JUL 78; To VA-83, NAS Cecil Field, FL., 09 JUL 78; To VA-83, USS Forrestal (CV-59), 09 JUL 78; To VA-83, NAS Cecil Field, FL., 14 SEP 79; To VA-83, USS Forrestal (CV-59), 14 SEP 79; To VA-83, NAS Cecil Field, FL., 14 SEP 79; To VA-83, NAS Jacksonville, FL., 19 MAY 80; To VA-83, NAS Cecil Field, FL., 07 JUL 80; To VA-83, USS Forrestal (CV-59), 08 AUG 80; To VA-83, NAS Cecil Field, FL., 08 AUG 80; To VA-83, NAS Jacksonville, FL., 14 JAN 82; To VA-83, NAS Fallon, NV., 14 JAN 82; To VA-83, NAS Jacksonville, FL., 18 JAN 82; To VA-83, NAS Cecil Field, FL., 18 JAN 82; To VA-83, NAS Dallas, TX., 05 APR 82; To VA-83, NAS Cecil Field, FL., 05 APR 82; To VA-83, NAS Dallas, TX., 28 MAY 82; To VA-83, USS Forrestal (CV-59), 28 MAY 82 ** Transferred to VA-86/CVW-8, AJ/4XX, NAS Cecil Field, FL., 02 JUN 82; To VA-86, USS Nimitz (CVN-68), 02 JUN 82; To VA-86, NAS Cecil Field, FL., 02 JUN 82; To VA-86, USS Nimitz (CVN-68), 02 JUN 82; To VA-86, NAS Cecil Field, FL., 02 JUN 82; To VA-86, USS Nimitz (CVN-68), 02 JUN 82; To VA-86, NAS Cecil Field, FL., 13 MAY 83; To VA-86, NAS Roosevelt Roads, PR., 18 MAY 83; To VA-86, NAS Cecil Field, FL., 18 MAY 83 ** Transferred to VA-72/CVW-1, AB/4XX, NAS Cecil Field, FL., 07 OCT 83; To VA-72, USS America(CV-66), 07 OCT 83; To VA-72, NAS Cecil Field, FL., 07 OCT 83 ** Transferred to VA-105/CVW-15, NL/4XX, NAS Roosevelt Roads, PR., 02 FEB 84; To VA-105, NAS Cecil Field, FL., 27 APR 84 ** Transferred to VA-86/CVW-8, AJ/4XX, NAS Cecil Field, FL., 07 JUN 84; To VA-86, NAS Roosevelt Roads, PR., 07 JUN 84; To VA-86, NAS Cecil Field, FL., 19 SEP 84; To VA-86, NAS Jacksonville, FL., 20 SEP 84; To VA-86, USS Nimitz (CVN-68), 20 SEP 84; To VA-86, NAS Cecil Field, FL., 01 NOV 84; To VA-86, USS Nimitz (CVN-68), 01 NOV 84 ** Transferred to VA-15/CVW-6, AE/3XX, NAS Cecil Fielf, FL., 27 MAR 85; To VA-15, MCAS Iwakuni, JP., 26 NOV 85; To VA-15, Korea, 26 NOV 85; To VA-15, NAS Cubi Point, PI., 26 NOV 85; To VA-15, NAS Cecil Field, FL., 05 JUN 86 ** Transferred to VA-174/FRS, AD/4XX, NAS Cecil Field, FL., 01 OCT 86; To VA-174, NAS Jacksonville, FL., 19 MAR 87; To VA-174, NAS Cecil Field, FL., 19 MAR 87; To VA-174, NAS Jacksonville, FL., 23 MAR 87 ** Transferred to VA-37/CVW-6, AE/3XX, USS Forrestal (CV-59), 07 AUG 87 ** End of flight record card ** LT Dano Wise painted on side of cockpit along with 23 combat missions under the name. Shapes of ordnance dropped with numbers under them are 50 Geneneral Purpose bombs, 72 Rockeyes, 17 Harm missiles, & 1 Walleye, 43 Camels are painted under the ordnance, 91.

E-395 158840 Navy acceptance from NPRO Rep. LTV, Dallas, TX., 11 DEC 73 ** Transferred to VA-122/FRS, NJ/2XX, NAS LeMoore, CA., 12 DEC 73; To VA-122, NAS Jacksonville, FL., 27 APR 77; To VA-122, NAS LeMoore, CA., 01 JUL 77; To VA-122, NAS Jacksonville, FL., 04 AUG 79; To VA-122, NAS LeMoore, CA., 02 OCT 79; To VA-122, NAS Jacksonville, FL., 24 JAN 82 ** Transferred to VA-94/CVW-11, NH/4XX, NAS LeMoore, CA., 08 APR 82; To VA-94, USS Enterprise (CVN-65), 14 JUN 82; To VA-94, NAS Jacksonville, FL., 22 NOV 82; To VA-94, NAS Cubi Point, PI., 22 NOV 82; To VA-94, NAS LeMoore, CA., 22 NOV 82 ** Transferred to NARF, NAS Jacksonville, FL., 09 MAY 83 ** Transferred to NAD, NAS Jacksonville, FL., 15 SEP 87 ** End of flight record card.

E-396 158841 Navy acceptance from NPRO Rep. LTV, Dallas, TX., 29 NOV 73 ** Transferred to VA-174/FRS, AD/4XX, NAS Cecil Field, FL., 30 NOV 73 ** Transferred to VA-82/CVW-8, NAS Cecil Field, FL., 23 JAN 75; To VA-82, USS Nimitz (CVN-68), 23 JAN 75; To VA-82, NAS Cecil Field, FL., 01 JUL 75; To VA-82, NAS Roosevelt Roads, PR., 01 JUL 75; To VA-82, NAS Cecil Field, FL., 01 JUL 75; To VA-82, USS Nimitz (CVN-68), 01 JUL 75; To VA-82, NAS Cecil Field, FL., 01 JUL 75; To VA-82, USS Nimitz (CVN-68), 01 JUL 75; To VA-82, NAS Cecil Field, FL., 01 JUL 75; To VA-82, USS Nimitz (CVN-68), 08 JAN 77 ~ S 1SO strike, 08 JAN 77 ** Pilot killed when he flew into the ocean during a practice bombing run on a marker flare.

E-397 158842 Navy acceptance from NPRO Rep. LTV, Dallas, TX., 05 DEC 73 ** Transferred to VA-174/FRS, AD/4XX, NAS Cecil Field, FL., 09 DEC 73; To VA-174, NAS Jacksonville, FL., 08 APR 78; To VA-174, NAS Cecil Field, FL., 26 JUL 78; To VA-174, NAS Jacksonville, FL., 21 OCT 80; To VA-174, NAS Cecil Field, FL., 23 OCT 80; To VA-174, NAS Dallas, TX., 10 JAN 81; To VA-174, NAS Cecil Field, FL., 10 APR 81 ** Transferred to VA-72/CVW-1, AB/4XX, NAS Cecil Field, FL., 01 SEP 81 ** Transferred to VA-83/CVW-17, AA/ 3XX, NAS Cecil Field, FL., 11 JAN 82; To VA-83, USS Forrestal (CV-59), 11 JAN 82; To VA-83, NAS Cecil Field, FL., 11 JAN 82; To VA-83, USS Forrestal (CV-59), 11 JAN 82; To VA-83, NAS Cecil Field, FL., 26 OCT 82; To VA-83, NAS Jacksonville, FL., 28 MAR 83; To VA-83, NAS Cecil Field, FL., 01 JUN 83; To VA-83, NAS Fallon, NV., 01 JUN 83; To VA-83, NAS Cecil Field, FL., 01 JUN 83; To VA-83, USS Saratoga (CV-60), 01 JUN 83; To VA-83, NAS Cecil Field, FL., 28 FEB 84 ** Transferred to VA-46/CVW-1, AB/3XX, NAS Cecil Field, FL., 30 MAR 84; To VA-46, USS America (CV-66), 09 APR 84; To VA-46, NAS Cecil Field, FL., 18 APR 84; To VA-46, USS America (CV-66), 07 FEB 85; To VA-46, NAS Cecil Field, FL., 07 FEB 85; To VA-46, NAS Jacksonville, FL., 16 AUG 85; To VA-46, USS America (CV-66), 08 SEP 85; To VA-46, NAS Jacksonville, FL., 28 OCT 85 ** Transferred to VA-174/FRS, AD/4XX, NAS Cecil Field, FL., 04 NOV 85 thru 21 MAY 87 ** End of flifgt record card ** On conditional loan from the National Museum of Naval Aviation; Pensacola, Fl. to the Air Classics Inc. Museum of Aviation, Aurora MAP; Sugar Grove, IL.

159261/159272 LTV A-7E-14-CV Corsair II; (Block XIV)
FY 73 Contract N00019-73-C-0302, (48) A-7E; E-399/E-446

E-409 159261 Navy acceptance from NPRO Rep. LTV, Dallas, TX., 29 JAN 74 ** Transferred to VA-174/FRS, AD/4XX, NAS Cecil Field, FL., 30 JAN 74 ** Transferred to VA-82/CVW-8, AJ/313, NAS Cecil Field, FL., 06 SEP 77; To VA-82, USS Nimitz (CVN-68), 06 SEP 77; To VA-82, NAS Cecil Field, FL., 01 AUG 78; To VA-82, NAS Jacksonville, FL., 03 SEP 78; To VA-82, NAS Cecil Field, FL., 26 OCT 78; To VA-82, NAS Jacksonville, FL., 12 JAN 81; To VA-82, NAS Cecil Field, FL., 24 FEB 81; To VA-82, NAS Jacksonville, FL., 25 FEB 81; To VA-82, NAS Dallas, TX., 25 MAR 81; To VA-82, USS Nimitz (CVN-68), 25 MAR 81 ** Transferred to VA-37/CVW-3, AC/3XX, NAS Cecil Field, FL., 03 JUN 81; To VA-37, USS John F. Kennedy (CV-67),04 JUN 81; To VA-37, NAS Cecil Field, FL., 04 JUN 81 ** Transferred to VA-105/CVW-3, AC/4XX, NAS Cecil Field, FL., 26 AUG 82; To VA-105, NAS Jacksonville, FL., 05 JAN 83; To VA-105/CVW-15, NL/4XX, USS Carl Vinson (CVN-70), 05 JAN 83; To VA-105, NAS Jacksonville, FL., 06 JAN 83; To VA-105, NAS Cecil Field, FL., 10 FEB 83; To VA-105 USS Carl Vinson (CVN-70), 10 FEB 83; To VA-105, NAS Cecil Field, FL., 10 FEB 83 ** Transferred to VA-83/CVW-17, AA/3XX, NAS Cecil Field, FL., 04 NOV 83; To VA-83, USS Saratoga (CV-60), 04 NOV 83; To VA-83, NAS Cecil Field, FL., 04 NOV 83; To VA-83, USS Saratoga (CV-60), 04 NOV 83; To VA-83, NAS Cecil Field, FL., 04 NOV 83; To VA-83, NAS Fallon, NV., 02 JAN 85; To VA-83, NAS Cecil Field, FL., 30 JAN 85; To VA-83, NAS Jacksonville, FL., 08 MAR 85; To VA-83, NAS Cecil Field, FL., 14 MAR 85; To VA-83, USS Saratoga (CV-60), 13 APR 85; To VA-83, NAS Jacksonville, FL., 08 MAY 85; To VA-83, USS Saratoga (CV-60), 09 MAY 85; To VA-83, NAS Cecil Field, FL., 09 MAY 85; To VA-83, USS Saratoga (CV-60), 09 MAY 85; To VA-83, NAS Cecil Field, FL., 29 APR 86 ** Transferred to VA-66/CVW-3, AC/3XX, John F. Kennedy (CV-67), 25 AUG 86 ** Transferred to VA-46/CVW-1, AB/3XX, NAS Cecil Field, FL., 15 SEP 86; To VA-46/CVW-7, AG/3XX, USS Dwight D. Eisenhower (CVN-69), 05 MAR 87; To VA-46, NAS Jacksonville, FL., 08 JUL 87; To VA-46, NAS Cecil Field, FL., 08 JUL 87; To VA-46, NAS Jacksonville, FL., Paint was light gray on darkgray with black modex ** End of flight record card.

E-399 159262 Navy acceptance from NPRO Rep. LTV, Dallas, TX., 18 JAN 74 ** Transferred to VA-122/FRS, NJ/2XX, NAS LeMoore, CA., 25 JAN 74; To VA-122, NAS Jacksonville, FL., 25 JUL 77; To VA-122, NAS LeMoore, CA., 25 JUL 77; To VA-122, NAS Jacksonville, FL., 27 JUL 77; To VA-122, NAS LeMoore, 24 SEP 77 ** Transferred to VA-195/CVW-11, NH/4XX, NAS LeMoore, CA. 01 MAR 79; To VA-195, USS America (CV-66), 01 MAR 79; To VA-195, NAS LeMoore, CA., 01 MAR 79; To VA-195, NAS Jacksonville, FL., 03 DEC 79; To VA-195, NAS LeMoore, CA., 21 JAN 80 ~ S 1SO strike, 11 SEP 80 ** No data on strike.

E-400 159263 Navy acceptance from NPRO Rep. LTV, Dallas, TX., 24 JAN 74 ** Transferred to VA-174/FRS, AD/4XX, NAS Cecil Field, FL., 25 JAN 74 ** Transferred to VA-86/CVW-8, AJ/4XX, USS Nimitz (CVN-68), 07 SEP 77; To VA-86, NAS Cecil Field, FL., 07 SEP 77; To VA-86, USS Nimitz (CVN-68), 07 SEP 77; To VA-86, NAS Cecil Field, FL., 01 AUG 78; To VA-86, NAS Jacksonville, FL., 23 AUG 78; To VA-86, NAS Cecil Field, FL., 17 OCT 78; To VA-86, NAS Roosevelt Roads, PR., 17 OCT 78; To VA-86, NAS Cecil Field, FL., 17 OCT 78; To VA-86, USS Nimitz (CVN-68), 17 OCT 78; To VA-86, NAS Cecil Field, FL., 17 OCT 78; To VA-86, NAS Jacksonville, FL., 14 JAN 81; To VA-86, NAS Dallas, TX., 24 MAR 81; To VA-86, USS Nimitz (CVN-68), 24 MAR 81 ** Transffered to VA-37/CVW-3, AC/3XX, NAS Cecil Field, FL., 23 MAY 81; To VA-37, NAS Fallon, NV., 23 MAY 81; To VA-37, NAS Cecil Field, FL., 23 MAY 81; To VA-37, USS John F. Kennedy (CV-67), 23 MAY 81; To VA-37, NAS Cecil Field, FL., 24 MAY 81 ** Transferred to VA-83/CVW-17, AA/3XX, NAS Cecil Field, FL., 02 NOV 81; To VA-83, NAS Fallon, NV., 02 NOV 81; To VA-83, NAS Cecil Field, FL., 02 NOV 81; To VA-83, USS Forrestal (CV-67), 08 MAR 82; To VA-83, NAS Cecil Field, FL., 11 MAR 82; To VA-83, USS Forrestal (CV-67), 11 MAR 82; To VA-83, NAS Cecil Field, FL., 11 MAR 82; To VA-83, NAS Jacksonville, FL., 14 DEC 82; To VA-83, NAS Cecil Field, FL., 14 DEC 82; To VA-83, NAS Jacksonville, FL., 17 DEC 82; To VA-83, NAS Cecil Field, FL.,14 MAR 83; To VA-83, NAS Fallon, NV., 14 MAR 83; To VA-83, NAS Cecil Field, FL., 14 MAR 83; To VA-83, USS Saratoga (CV-60), 25 JAN 84; To VA-83, NAS Cecil Field, FL., 25 JAN 84; To VA-83, USS Saratoga (CV-60), 25 JAN 84 ** Transferred to VA-174/FRS, AD/4XX, NAS Cecil Field, FL., 10 SEP 84; To VA-174, NAS Jacksonville, FL., 13 AUG 85; To VA-174, NAS Cecil Field, FL., 11 SEP 85 ** Transferred to VA-15/CVW-6, AE/3XX, NAS Cecil Field, FL., 11 OCT 85; To VA-15, MCAS Iwakuni, JP., 08 NOV 85; To VA-15, Korea, 11 FEB 86; To VA-15, NAS Cubi Point, PI., 11 FEB 86; To VA-15, NAS Cecil Field, FL., 11 FEB 86 ** Transferred to VA-81/CVW-17, AA/4XX, USS Saratoga (CV-60), 11 AUG 86; To VA-81, NAS Cecil Field, FL., 22 OCT 86; To VA-81, USS Saratoga (CV-60), 28 OCT 86 ** Transffered to VA-37/CVW-6, AE/3XX, NAS Cecil Field, FL., 13 FEB 87; To VA-37, NAS Jacksobnville, FL., 30 JUN 87; Top VA-37, NAS Cecil Field, FL., 30 JUN 87; To VA-37, USS Forrestal (CV-59), 30 JUN 87 thru 06 JUL 87 ** End of flight recard card ** Transferred to the Helenic Air force (Greece).

E-401 159264 Navy acceptance from NPRO Rep. LTV, Dallas, TX., 15 FEB 74 ** Transferred to VA-174/FRS, AD/4XX, NAS Cecil Field, FL., 19 FEB 74 ** Transferred to VA-37/CVW-3, AC/302, NAS Cecil Field, FL., 12 MAY 75; To VA-37, USS Saratoga (CV-60), 10 SEP 75; To VA-37, NAS Cecil Field, FL., 10 SEP 75; To VA-37, USS Saratoga (CV-60), 21 SEP 76; To VA-37, NAS Cecil Field, FL., 27 OCT 77; To VA-37, NAS Jacksonville,

FL., 18 DEC 77; To VA-37, NAS Cecil Field, FL., 18 APR 78; To VA-37, USS Saratoga (CV-60), 18 APR 78; To VA-37, NAS Cecil Field, FL., 18 APR 78; To VA-37, MCAS Yuma, AZ., 10 MAY 79; To VA-37, NAS Cecil Field, FL., 10 MAY 79; To VA-37, USS Saratoga (CV-60), 21 NOV 79; To VA-37, NAS Cecil Field, FL., 21 NOV 79; To VA-37, USS Saratoga (CV-60), 21 NOV 79; To VA-37, NAS Cecil Field, FL., 21 NOV 79; To VA-37, NAS Jacksonville, FL., 06 NOV 80; To VA-37, NAS Cecil Field, FL., 07 NOV 80; To VA-37, NAS Jacksonville, FL., 16 DEC 80; To VA-37, NAS Cecil Field, FL., 17 DEC 80; To VA-37, NAS Fallon, NV., 17 DEC 80; To VA-37, NAS Cecil Field, FL., 17 DEC 80 ** Transferred to VA-86/CVW-8, AJ/4XX, USS Nimitz (CVN-68), 16 JUL 81; To VA-86, NAS Cecil Field, FL., 16 JUL 81; To VA-86, NAS Jacksonville, FL., 23 JUN 82; To VA-86, USS Nimitz (CVN-68), 23 JUN 82; To VA-86, NAS Cecil Field, FL., 23 JUN 82; To VA-86, USS Nimitz (CVN-68), 13 AUG 82; To VA-86, NAS Jacksonville, FL., 18 SEP 82; To VA-86, NAS Cecil Field, FL., 24 SEP 82 ** Transferred to VA-37/CVW-15, NL/3XX, NAS Cecil Field, FL., 08 OCT 82; To VA-37, USS Carl Vinson (CVN-70), 19 NOV 83; To VA-37, NAS Cecil Field, FL., 19 JAN 83; To VA-37, USS Carl Vinson (CV-70), 19 JAN 83; To VA-37, NAS Roosevelt Roads, PR., 02 SEP 83; To VA-37, NAS Cecil Field, FL., 02 SEP 83; To VA-37, NWC China Lake, CA., 02 SEP 83; To VA-37, NAS Cecil Field, FL., 02 SEP 83 ** Transferred to VA-12/CVW-7, AG/4XX, NAS Cecil Field, FL., 01 MAY 84; To VA-12, USS Dwight D. Eisenhower (CVN-69), 01 MAY 84; To VA-12, NAS Cecil Field, FL., 09 MAY 85; To VA-12, NAS Jacksonville, FL., 10 MAY 85; To VA-12, NAS Cecil Field, FL., 21 JUN 85; To VA-12, USS Dwight D. Eisenhower (CVN-69), 21 JUN 85; To VA-12, NAS Cecil Field, FL., 21 JUN 85 ** Transferredc to VA-174/FRS, AD/408, NAS Cecil Field, FL., 19 AUG 86 ** End of flight record card ** Transferred to AMARC, Davis Monthan AFB; Tucson, AZ., assigned park code 6A0235, 26 AUG 87 ** 5546.4 flight hours ** TF41A2B engine S/N 141962 ** Storage location 210342 ** Under GSA control ** At AMARG, Davis Monthan AFB; Tucson, AZ., 15 JUN 07.

E-402 159265 Navy acceptance from NPRO Rep. LTV, Dallas, TX., 06 FEB 74 ** Transferred to VA-122/FRS, NJ/2XX, NAS LeMoore, CA., 08 FEB 74; To VA-122, NAS Jacksonville, FL., 17 JUL 77; To VA-122, NAS LeMoore, CA., 21 JUL 77; To VA-122, NAS Jacksonville, FL., 30 AUG 77; To VA-122, NAS LeMoore, 14 OCT 77 ** Transferred to VA-192/CVW-11, NH/3XX, NAS LeMoore, CA., 29 NOV 78; To VA-192, USS America (CV-66), 26 APR 79 ~ S 1SO strike, 26 APR 79 ** No data on strike.

E-403 159266 Navy acceptance from NPRO Rep. LTV, Dallas, TX., 17 JAN 74 ** Transferred to VA-22/CVW-15, NL/3XX, NAS LeMoore, CA., 18 JAN 74 ** Transferred to VA-25/CVW-2, NE/407, NAS LeMoore, CA., 06 NOV 74; To VA-25, NAS Fallon, NV., 13 JUL 75; To VA-25, USS Ranger (CV-61), 14 AUG 75; To VA-25, NAS LeMoore, CA., 23 SEP 75; To VA-25, USS Ranger (CV-61), 27 JAN 76; To VA-25, NAS LeMoore, CA., 01 JAN 77; To VA-25, NAS Jacksonville, FL., 26 MAY 77; To VA-25, NAS Fallon, NV., 01 JUN 77; To VA-25, NAS LeMoore, CA., 12 AUG 77; To VA-25, USS Ranger (CV-61), 27 OCT 78; To VA-25, NAS LeMoore, CA., 15 DEC 78; To VA-25, USS Ranger (CV-61), 24 JAN 79; To VA-25, NAS Cubi Point, PI., 20 FEB 79; To VA-25, NAS LeMoore, CA., 07 DEC 79; To VA-25, NAS Fallon, NV., 07 DEC 79; To VA-25, NAS LeMoore, CA., 26 JAN 80; To VA-25, USS Ranger (CV-61), 29 MAY 80; To VA-25, NAS LeMoore, CA., 26 JUN 80; To VA-25, USS Ranger (CV-61), 13 JUL 80; To VA-25, NAS LeMoore, CA., 24 JUL 80; To VA-25, USS Ranger (CV-61), 10 SEP 80; To VA-25, NAS LeMoore, CA., 18 JAN 81; To VA-25, NAS Fallon, NV., 14 SEP 81; To VA-25, USS Ranger (CV-61), 20 OCT 81; To VA-25, NAS LeMoore, CA., 12 NOV 81; To VA-25, NAS Jacksonville, FL., 13 NOV 81; To VA-25, NAS LeMoore, CA., 14 NOV 81; To VA-25, NAS Jacksonville, FL., 19 JAN 82; To VA-25, NAS Dallas, TX., 20 JAN 82; To VA-25, USS Ranger (CV-61), 21 JAN 82; To VA-25, NAS LeMoore, CA., 26 JAN 82; To VA-25, NAS Dallas, TX., 30 MAR 82; To VA-25, USS Ranger (CV-61), 30 MAR 82 ** Transferred to VA-22/CVW-

11, NH/3XX, NAS LeMoore, CA., 05 APR 82; To VA-22, USS Enterprise (CVN-65), 05 APR 82; To VA-22, NAS LeMOORE, CA., 05 APR 82; To VA-22, USS Enterprise (CVN-65), 05 APR 82; To VA-22, NAS LeMoore, CA., 05 APR 82 ** Transferred to VA-97/CVW-15, NL/3XX, NAS LeMoore, CA., 19 APR 84; To VA-97, USS Carl Vinson (CVN-70), 25 MAY 84; To VA-97, NAS Jacksoinville, FL., 29 MAY 84; To VA-97, NAS LeMoore, CA., 14 JUL 84; To VA-97, USS Carl Vinson (CVN-70), 14 JUL 84; To VA-97, NAS LeMoore, CA., 14 JUL 84 ** Transferred to VA-146/CVW-9, NE/3XX, NAS LeMoore, CA., 10 SEP 84 ~ S 1SO strike, 26 MAR 85 ** Engine failure, pilot ejected safely.

E-404 159267 Navy acceptance from NPRO Rep. LTV, Dallas, TX., 14 FEB 74 ** Transferred to VA-122/FRS, NJ/2XX, NAS LeMoore, CA., 15 FEB 74 ** Transferred to VA-195/CVW-11, NH/4XX, NAS LeMoore, CA., 09 JUN 76; To VA-195, USS Kitty Hawk (CV-63), 23 JUL 77; To VA-195, NAS LeMoore, CA., 12 AUG 77; To VA-195, USS Kitty Hawk (CV-63), 29 SEP 77; NAS LeMoore, CA., 30 MAY 78; To VA-195, NAS Jacksonville, FL., 05 JUN 78; To VA-195, NAS LeMoore, CA., 05 JUN 78; To VA-195, NAS Jacksonville, FL., 08 JUN 78; To VA-195, NAS LeMoore, CA., 05 DEC 78; To VA-195, USS America (CV-66), 05 JAN 79; To VA-195, NAS LeMoore, CA., 05 JAN 79; To VA-195, NAS Fallon, NV., 19 OCT 80; To VA-195, NAS LeMoore, CA., 07 NOV 80; To VA-195, NAS Jacksonville, FL., 08 JAN 81; To VA-195, USS America (CV-66), 24 FEB 81; To VA-195, NAS LeMoore, CA., 09 APR 81; To VA-195, NAS Jacksonville, FL., 09 OCT 82; To VA-195, NAS Dallas, TX., 20 DEC 82; ** Transferred to VA-146/CVW-9, NE/3XX, NAS LeMoore, CA., 23 MAR 83; To VA-146, USS Kitty Hawk (CV-63), 23 MAR 83; To VA-146, NAS LeMoore, CA., 23 MAR 83; To VA-146, NAS Jacksonville, FL., 07 MAR 85; To VA-146, NAS LeMoore, CA., 08 MAR 85; To VA-146, NAS Jacksonville, FL., 25 APR 85; To VA-146, NAS LeMoore, CA., 07 MAY 85; To VA-146, USS Kitty Hawk (CV-63), 17 JUL 85 ~ S 1SO strike, 17 JUL 85 ** Crashed into the Pacific after an engine failure, pilot ejected safely.

E-405 159268 Navy acceptance from NPRO Rep. LTV, Dallas, TX., 21 MAR 74 ** Transferred to VA-66/CVW-7, AG/3XX, NAS Cecil Field, FL., 22 MAR 74; To VA-66, USS Independence (CV-62), 22 MAR 74; To VA-66, NAS Cecil Field, FL., 22 MAR 74; To VA-66, USS Independence (CV-62), 03 SEP 75; To VA-66, NAS Cecil Field, FL., 10 MAY 76; To VA-66, NAS Fallon, NV., 19 JUL 76; To VA-66, USS Independence (CV-62), 19 JUL 76; To VA-66, NAS Cecil Field, FL., 19 JUL 76; To VA-66, USS Independence (CV-62), 19 JUL 76; To VA-66, NAS Cecil Field, FL., 19 JUL 76; To VA-66, USS Independence (CV-62), 19 JUL 76; To VA-66, NAS Cecil Field, FL., 09 AUG 77; To VA-66, USS Dwight D. Eisenhower (CVN-69), 09 AUG 77; To VA-66, NAS Cecil Field, FL., 01 FEB 78; To VA-66, NAS Jacksonville, FL., 24 MAR 78; To VA-66, NAS Cecil Field, FL., 06 JUN 78; To VA-66, USS Dwight D. Eisenhower (CVN-69), 06 JUN 78; To VA-66, NAS Cecil Field, FL., 06 JUN 78; To VA-66, USS Dwight D. Eisenhower (CVN-69), 06 JUN 78; To VA-66, NAS Cecil Field, FL., 06 JUN 78; To VA-66, USS Dwight D. Eisenhower (CVN-69), 06 JUN 78; To VA-66, NAS Cecil Field, FL., 10 NOV 79; To VA-66, USS Dwight D. Eisenhower (CVN-69), 21 DEC 79; To VA-66, NAS Cecil Field, FL., 15 JAN 80; To VA-66, USS Dwight D. Eisenhower (CVN-69), 15 JAN 80; To VA-66, NAS Cecil Field, FL., 01 APR 80 ** Transferred to NARF, NAS Jacksonville, FL., 01 APR 80 ** Transferred to VA-174/FRS, AD/4XX, NAS Cecil Field, FL., 10 AUG 82 ** Transferred to VA-66/CVW-7, AG/3XX, NAS Cecil Field, FL., 08 NOV 82; To VA-66, USS Dwight D. Eisenhower (CVN-69), 28 DEC 82; To VA-66, NAS Cecil Field, FL., 01 AUG 83 ** Transferred to VA-105/CVW-15, NL/4XX, NAS Cecil Field, FL., 02 APR 84 ** Transferred to VA-15/CVW-6, AE/3XX, NAS Cecil Field, FL., 05 JUN 84; To VA-15, USS Independence (CV-62), 05 JUN 84; To VA-15, NAS Cecil Field, FL., 20 SEP 84; To VA-15, USS Independence (CV-62), 20 SEP 84 ** Transferred to VA-82/CVW-8, AJ/3XX, NAS Cecil Field, FL., 11 OCT 84; To VA-82, USS Nimitz (CVN-68), 20 OCT 84; To VA-82, NAS Jacksonville, FL., 17 DEC 84; To VA-82,

NAS Cecil Field, FL., 23 DEC 84; To VA-82, NAS Jacksonville, FL., 11 FEB 85 ** Transferred to VA-46/VW-1, AB/3XX, NAS Cecil Field, FL., 12 FEB 85; To VA-46, USS America (CV-66), Paint was light gray on dark gray with black modex, 17 APR 85; To VA-46, NAS Cecil Field, FL., 17 APR 85; To VA-46, USS America (CV-66), 17 APR 85; To VA-46, NAS Cecil Field, FL., 17 APR 85; To VA-46, USS America (CV-66), 17 APR 85; To VA-46, NAS Cecil Field, FL., 17 APR 85; To VA-46, NAS Jacksonville, FL., 23 APR 87; To VA-46, NAS Cecil Field, FL., 23 APR 87; To VA-46, NAS Jacksonville, FL., 28 APR 87; To VA-46/CVW-7, AG/3XX,, USS Dwight D, Eisenhower (CVN- 69), 28 APR 87; To VA-46, NAS Cecil Field, FL., 28 APR 87; To VA-46, NAS Jacksonville, FL., 01 SEP 87; To VA-46, NAS Cecil Field, FL., 02 SEP 87 ** End of flight record card ** On display at the Intrepid Sea-Air-Space Museum; New York City, NY. ** Moved to the Maps Air Museum; Canto, OH, 04.

E-406 159269 Navy acceptance from NPRO Rep. LTV, Dallas, TX., 19 FEB 74 ** Transferred to VA-174/FRS. AD/4XX, NAS Ceciul Field, FL., 20 FEB 74 ** Transferred to VA-105/CVW-3, AC/4XX, USS Saratoga (CV-60), 06 OCT 75; To VA-105, NAS Cecil Field, FL., 27 MAR 76; To VA-105, USS Saratoga (CV-60), 21 OCT 76; To VA-105, NAS Cecil Field, FL., 28 MAR 77; To VA-105, USS Saratoga (CV-60), 12 MAY 77; To VA-105, NAS Cecil Field, FL., 09 AUG 77; To VA-105, NAS Jacksonville, FL., 19 MAY 78; To VA-105, NAS Cecil Field, FL., 29 AUG 78; To VA-105, USS Saratoga (CV-60), 29 AUG 78; To VA-105, NAS Cecil Field, FL., 29 AUG 78; To VA-105, MCAS Yuma, AZ.,29 AUG 78; To VA-105, NAS Cecil Field, FL., 29 AUG 78; To VA-105, USS Saratoga (CV-60), 29 AUG 78; To VA-105, NAS Cecil Field, FL., 29 AUG 78; To VA-105, USS Saratoga (CV-60), 26 FEB 80; To VA-105, NAS Jacksonville, FL., 06 NOV 80; To VA-105, NAS Dallas, TX., 27 JAN 81; To VA-105, NAS Fallon, NV., 26 MAY 81; To VA-105, NAS Cecil Field, FL., 23 JUN 81; To VA-105, USS John F. Kennedy (CV-67), 02 JUL 81 ** Transferred to VA-83/CVW-17, AA/3XX, NAS Cecil Field, FL.02 NOV 81; To VA-83, NAS Fallon, NV., 02 NOV 81; To VA-83, NAS Cecil Field, FL., 02 NOV 81; To VA-83, USS Forrestal (CV-59), 08 MAR 82; To VA-83, NAS Cecil Field, FL., 11 MAR 82; To VA-83, USS Forrestal (CV-59), 11 MAR 82; To VA-83, NAS Cecil Field, FL., 22 NOV 82; To VA-83, NAS Fallon, NV., 01 JUL 83; To VA-83, NAS Jacksonville, FL., 06 SEP 83; To VA-83, NAS Cecil Field, FL., 06 SEP 83; To VA-83, NAS Jacksonville, FL., 07 SEP 83; To VA-83, NAS Cecil Field, FL., 23 NOV 83; To VA-83, USS Saratoga (CV-60), 23 NOV 83; To VA-83, NAS Cecil Field, FL., 23 NOV 83; To VA-83, USS Saratoga (CV-60), 23 NOV 83; To VA-83, NAS Cecil Field, FL. 31 AUG 84; To VA-83, NAS Fallon, NV., 26 DEC 84; To VA-83, NAS Cecil Field, FL., 26 DEC 84; To VA-83, USS Saratoga (CV-60), 08 MAY 85 ~ S 1SO strike, 03 JUN 85 ** No data on strike.

E-407 159270 Navy acceptance from NPRO Rep. LTV, Dallas, TX., 17 APR 74 ** Transferred to VA-27/CVW-14, NK/4XX, NAS LeMoore, CA., 19 APR 74 ** Transferred to VA-192/CVW-11, NH/3XX, NAS LeMoore, CA., 29 AUG 74; To VA-192, USS Kitty Hawk (CV-63), 12 DEC 74; To VA-192, NAS LeMoore, CA., 28 MAR 75; To VA-192, USS Kitty Hawk (CV-63), 11 APR 75 ** Transferred to VA-122/FRS, NJ/2XX, NAS LeMoore, CA., 15 MAY 75 ** Transferred to VA-22/CVW-15, NL/3XX, NAS LeMoore, CA., 20 MAY 76; To VA-22, USS Coral Sea (CV-43), 10 JUL 77 ** Transferred to VA-93/CVW-5, NF/313, USS Midway (CV-41), 29 AUG 77; To VA-93, NAF Atsugi, JP., 19 NOV 77; To VA-93, USS Midway (CV-41), 29 NOV 77; To VA-93, NAF Atsugi, JP., 12 MAY 78; To VA-93, USS Midway (CV-41), 23 JUN 80; To VA-93, NAF Atsugi, JP., 10 JAN 81; To VA-93, NAS Cubi Point, PI., 21 JAN 81 ** Transferred to VA-113/CVW-2, NE/3XX, NAS Cubi Point, PI., 18 FEB 81; To VA-113, NAF Atsugi, JP., 03 MAR 81; To VA-113, NAS Cubi Point, PI., 16 MAR 81; To VA-113, USS Ranger (CV-61), 04 MAY 81; To VA-113, NAS LeMoore, CA., 26 MAY 81; To VA-113, NAS Jacksonville, FL., 27 MAY 81; To VA-113, NAS LeMoore, CA., 18 JUN 81; To VA-113, NAS Jacksonville, FL., 10 JUL 81; To VA-113, NAS LeMoore, CA., 18

JUL 81; To VA-113, NAS Jacksonville, FL., 27 JUL 81; To VA-113, NAS LeMoore, CA., 30 JUL 81** Transferred to VA-122/FRS, NJ/2XX, NAS LeMoore, CA., 03 AUG 81 ** Transferred to VA-94/CVW-11, NH/4XX, NAS LeMoore, CA., 05 FEB 82; To VA-94, USS Enterprise (CVN-65), 19 AUG 82; To VA-94, NAS Cubi Point, PI., 03 FEB 83; To VA-94, NAS LeMoore, CA., 05 MAR 83; To VA-94, NAS Jacksonville, FL., 22 JUL 83; To VA-94, NAS LeMoore, CA., 14 FEB 84; To VA-94, USS Enterprise (CVN-65), 14 FEB 84; To VA-94, NAS LeMoore, CA., 14 FEB 84; To VA-94, USS Enterprise (CVN-65), 14 FEB 84; To VA-94, NAF Atsugi, JP., 24 JUL 84; To VA-94, USS Enterprise (CVN-65), 03 AUG 84 ** Transferred to VA-93, NAF Atsugi, JP., 26 OCT 84; To VA-93, NAS LeMoore, CA., 10 JAN 86; To VA-93, NAS Jacksonville, FL., 04 JUN 86 ** Transferred to VA-147/CVW-9, NE/3XX, NAS LeMoore, CA., 03 SEP 86 ** Transferred to VA-94/CVW-11, NH/4XX, NAS LeMoore, CA., 17 DEC 86 ** Transferred to VA-122/FRS, NJ/2XX, NAS LeMoore, CA., 13 APR 87 ** End of flight record card ** Transferred to PMTC, NAS Point Mugu, CA., date unknown ** Transferred to AMARC, Davis Monthan AFB; Tucson, AZ., assigned park code 6A0407, 27 SEP 91 ** 6132.9 flight hours ** TF41A402D engine S/N AE142597 ** Storage location 210824 ** Located at AMARG, Davis Monthan AFB; Tucson, AZ., 15 JUN 07.

E-408 159271 Navy acceptance from NPRO Rep. LTV, Dallas, TX., 07 MAR 74 ** Transferred to VA-122/FRS, NJ/2XX, NAS LeMoore, CA. 08 MAR 74; To VA-122, NAS Alameda, CA., 01 NOV 76; To VA-122, NAS LeMoore, CA., 28 NOV 76; To VA-122, NAS Alameda, CA., 29 DEC 76; To VA-122, NAS LeMoore, CA., 27 JAN 77 ** Transferred to VX-5, XE/XXX, NAF China Lake, CA., 16 MAR 77; To VX-5, NAS Jacksonville, FL., 04 APR 78 ** To VX-5, NAF China Lake, CA., 04 APR 78; To VX-5, NAS Jacksonville, FL., 05 APR 78 ** To VX-5, NAF China Lake, CA., 26 JUL 78; To VX-5, NAS LeMoore, CA., 07 JUL 80; To VX-5, NWC China Lake, CA., 11 JUL 80 ~ S 1SO strike, 05 NOV 80 ** No data on strike.

E-409 159272 Navy acceptance from NPRO Rep. LTV, Dallas, TX., 13 MAR 74 ** Transferred to VA-122/FRS, NJ/2XX, NAS LeMoore, CA., 15 MAR 74 ** Transferred to VA-94/CVW-15, NL/4XX, NAS LeMoore, CA., 08 JUN 76; To VA-94, USS Coral Sea (CV-43), 09 DEC 76; To VA-94, NAS LeMoore, CA., 15 DEC 76; To VA-94, USS Coral Sea (CV-43), 31 MAY 77; To VA-94, NAF Atsugi, JP., 11 JUN 77 ** Transferred to VA-56/CVW-5, NF/4XX, USS Midway (CV-41), 29 AUG 77; To VA-66, NAF Atsugi, JP., 10 NOV 77; To VA-56, USS Midway (CV-41), 11 NOV 78; To VA-56, NAF Atsugi, JP., 26 APR 78 ** Transferred to VA-27/CVW-14, NK/4XX, USS Coral Sea (CV-43), 15 MAY 80; To VA-27, NAS LeMoore, CA., 21 MAY 80; To VA-27, NAS Jacksonville, FL., 24 MAR 81; To VA-27, USS Coral Sea (CV-43), 03 JUN 81; To VA-27, NAS Dallas, TX., 08 JUN 81 ** Transferred to VA-113/CVW-9, NG/3XX, NAS LeMoore, CA., 14 AUG 81; To VA-113, NAS Fallon, NV., 14 AUG 81; To VA-113 USS Ranger (CV-61), 14 AUG 81; To VA-113, NAS LeMoore, CA., 14 AUG 81; To VA-113 USS Ranger (CV-61), 14 JAN 82; To VA-113, NAS LeMoore, CA., 14 JAN 82; To VA-113 USS Ranger (CV-61), 26 FEB 82; To VA-113, NAS Cubi Point, PI., 26 FEB 82; To VA-113, NAF Atsugi, JP., 26 FEB 82 ** Transferred to VA-93/ CVW-5, NF/3XX, NAS Cubi Point, PI., 27 SEP 82; To VA-93, NAF Atsugi, JP., 28 SEP 82; To VA-93, NAS Cubi Point, PI., 05 NOV 82; To VA-93, USS Midway (CV-41), 14 NOV 82; To VA-93, NAF Atsugi, JP., 16 OCT 83; To VA-93, NAS LeMoore, CA., 27 JAN 86 ** Transferred to VA-147/CVW-9, NE/3XX, NAS LeMoore, CA., 14 MAY 86; To VA-147, NAS Jacksonville, FL., 09 OCT 86 ** Transferred to VA-94/CVW-11, NH/405, NAS LeMoore, CA., 13 JAN 87 thru 07 AUG 87 ** End of flight record card ** Transferred to AMARC, Davis Monthan AFB; Tucson, AZ., assigned park code 6A0300, 25 AUG 89 ** 5028.3 flight hours ** TF41A402D engine S/N 141011 ** Aircraft released from storage and prepared for overland shipment to FMS and NAD, NAS Jacksonville, FL., with final shipment to government of Thailand, 17 JUN 05 ** Transferred to the Royal Thai Navy, S/N 159272.

159273/159284 LTV A-7E-15-CV Corsair II; (Block XV)

E-422 159273 Navy acceptance from NPRO Rep. LTV, Dallas, TX., 16 APR 74 ** Transferred to VA-66/CVW-7, AG/301, NAS Cecil Field, FL., 19 APR 74; To VA-66, USS Independence (CV-62), 19 APR 74; To VA-66, NAS Cecil Field, FL., 19 APR 74; To VA-66, USS Independence (CV-62), 03 SEP 75; To VA-66, NAS Cecil Field, FL., 13 SEP 75; To VA-66, NAS Fallon, NV., 08 JUL 76; To VA-66, USS Independence (CV-62), 08 JUL 76; To VA-66, NAS Cecil Field, FL., 08 JUL 76; To VA-66, USS Independence (CV-62), 08 JUL 76; To VA-66, NAS Cecil Field, FL., 08 JUL 76; To VA-66, USS Independence (CV-62), 08 JUL 76; To VA-66, NAS Cecil Field, FL., 27 OCT 77; To VA-66, NAS Jacksonville, FL., 28 OCT 77; To VA-66, Dwight D. Eisenhower (CVN-69), 28 OCT 77; To VA-66, NAS Jacksonville, FL., 31 JAN 78 ** Transferred to VA-22/CVW-15, NL/3XX, NAS LeMoore, CA., 27 FEB 78; To VA-22, NAS Kingsville, TX., 05 MAY 78; To VA-22, NAS LeMoore, CA., 05 MAY 78; To VA-22, USS Kitty Hawk (CV-63), 24 APR 79; To VA-22, NAS LeMoore, CA., 30 MAY 79; To VA-22, NAS Jacksonville, FL., 24 APR 80; To VA-22, NAS LeMoore, CA., 26 APR 80; To VA-22, USS Kitty Hawk (CV-63), 11 SEP 80 ** Transferred to VA-192/CVW-11, NH/3XX, NAS Fallon,NV., 16 OCT 80; To VA-192, LeMoore, CA., 27 OCT 80; To VA-192, USS America (CV-66), 29 JAN 80; To VA-192, LeMoore, CA., 21 FEB 81; To VA-192, USS America (CV-66), 11 JUL 81; To VA-192, NAS Jacksonville, FL., 18 SEP 81; To VA-192, LeMoore, CA., 18 SEP 81; To VA-192, NAS Jacksonville, FL., 14 JAN 82; To VA-192, LeMoore, CA., 19 JAN 82; To VA-192, NAS Jacksonville, FL., 01 FEB 83; To VA-192, LeMoore, CA., 01 FEB 83; To VA-192, NAS Jacksonville, FL., 04 FEB 83; To VA-192, NAS Dallas, TX., 22 APR 83; To VA-192/CVW-9, NG/3XX, USS Ranger (CV-61), 26 APR 83 ** Transferred to VA-146/CVW-9, NE/3XX, NAS LeMoore, CA., 15 JUL 83; To VA-146, USS Kitty Hawk (CV-63), 30 DEC 83; To VA-146, NAS LeMoore, CA., 14 AUG 84 ** Transferred to VA-97/CVW-15, NL/4XX, NAS LeMoore, CA., 10 SEP 84; To VA-97, USS Carl Vinson (CVN-70), 10 SEP 84; To VA-97, NAS LeMoore, CA.,05 JAN 85; To VA-97, NAS Jacksonville, FL., 19 AUG 85; To VA-97, NAS LeMoore, CA., 25 NOV 85; To VA-97, USS Carl Vinson (CVN-70), 06 FEB 86; To VA-97, NAS LeMoore, CA., 06 FEB 86; To VA-97, USS Carl Vinson (CVN-70), 06 FEB 86; To VA-97, NAS Alameda, CA., 31 DEC 86 ** End of flight record card.

E-411 159274 Navy acceptance from NPRO Rep. LTV, Dallas, TX., 16 APR 74 ** Transferred to VA-12/CVW-7, AG/405, NAS Cecil Field, FL., 19 APR 74; To VA-12, USS Independence (CV-62), 19 APR 74; To VA-12, NAS Cecil Field, Fl., 30 JAN 75; To VA-12, NAS Fallon, NV., 10 FEB 75; To VA-12, NAS Cecil Field, Fl., 10 FEB 75; To VA-12, NAS Fallon, NV., 10 FEB 75; To VA-12, NAS Cecil Field, Fl., 01 JUL 75; To VA-12, USS Independence (CV-62), 01 JUL 75; To VA-12, NAS Cecil Field, Fl., 01 JUL 75; To VA-12, NAS Fallon, NV., 24 AUG 76; To VA-12, USS Independence (CV-62), 24 AUG 76; To VA-12, NAS Cecil Field, Fl., 24 AUG 76; To VA-12, USS Independence (CV-62), 24 AUG 76; To VA-12, NAS Cecil Field, Fl., 24 AUG 76; To VA-12, USS Independence (CV-62), 24 AUG 76; To VA-12, NAS Cecil Field, Fl., 09 AUG 77; To VA-12, USS Dwight D. Eisenhower (CVN-69), 09 AUG 77; To VA-12, NAS Cecil Field, Fl., 27 MAR 78; To VA-12, NAS Jacksonville, FL., 28 MAR 78; To VA-12, NAS Cecil Field, Fl., 06 JUN 78; To VA-12, USS Dwight D. Eisenhower (CVN-69), 06 JUN 78; To VA-12, NAS Cecil Field, Fl., 06 JUN 78; To VA-12, USS Dwight D. Eisenhower (CVN-69), 06 JUN 78; To VA-12, NAS Cecil Field, Fl., 27 DEC 78; To VA-12, USS Dwight D. Eisenhower (CVN-69), 04 OCT 79; To VA-12, NAS Cecil Field, Fl., 16 NOV 79; To VA-12, USS Dwight D. Eisenhower (CVN-69), 28 NOV 79; To VA-12, NAS Cecil Field, Fl., 28 JAN 81; To VA-12, NAS Jacksonville, FL., 29 JAN 81; To VA-12, NAS Cecil Field, Fl., 07 MAR 81; To VA-12, USS Dwight D. Eisenhower (CVN-69), 07 MAR 81; To VA-12, NAS Cecil Field, Fl., 07 MAR 81; To VA-12, USS Dwight D. Eisenhower (CVN-69), 07 MAR 81; To VA-12, NAS Cecil Field, Fl., 07 MAR 81; To VA-12, NAS Jacksonville, FL., 24 AUG 82; To VA-12, NAS Cecil Field, Fl., 05 NOV 82; To VA-12, USS Dwight D. Eisenhower (CVN-69), 03 MAR 83; To VA-12, NAS Cecil Field, Fl., 03 MAR 83; To VA-12, USS Dwight D. Eisenhower (CVN-69), 30 MAR 84; To VA-12, NAS Cecil Field, Fl., 22 JUN 84;

To VA-12, USS Dwight D. Eisenhower (CVN-69), 18 SEP 84; To VA-12, NAS Jacksonville, FL., 09 MAY 85; To VA-12, NAS Cecil Field, Fl., 22 JUN 85; To VA-12, USS Dwight D. Eisenhower (CVN-69), 22 JUN 85; To VA-12, NAS Cecil Field, Fl., 22 JUN 85 ** Transferred to VA-174/FRS, NJ/2XX, NAS Cecil Field, FL., 25 AUG 86; To VA-174, NAS Pensacola, FL., 06 MAR 87; To VA-174, NAS Cecil Field, FL., 06 MAR 87; To VA-174, NAS Pensacola, FL., 10 MAR 87 thru 10 APR 87 ** End of flight record card.

E-412 159275 Navy acceptance from NPRO Rep. LTV, Dallas, TX., 22 MAR 74 ** Transferred to VA-12/CVW-7, AG/401, NAS Cecil Field, FL., 22 MAR 74; To VA-12, USS Independence (CV-62), 22 MAR 74; To VA-12, NAS Cecil Field, FL., 24 JAN 75; To VA-12, NAS Fallon, NV., 06 FEB 75; To VA-12, NAS Cecil Field, FL., 06 FEB 75; To VA-12, USS Independence (CV-62), 03 SEP 75 ~ S 1SO strike, 11 DEC 75 ** No data on strike.

E-413 159276 Navy acceptance from NPRO Rep. LTV, Dallas, TX., 04 APR 74 ** Transferred to VA-122/FRS, NJ/2XX, NAS LeMoore, CA., 08 APR 74; To VA-122, NAS Alameda, CA., 16 JUL 75; To VA-122, NAS LeMoore, CA., 12 NOV 75 ~ S 1SO strike, 02 APR 76 ** No data on strike.

E-414 159277 Navy acceptance from NPRO Rep. LTV, Dallas, TX., 09 MAY 74 ** Transferred to VA-37/CVW-3, AC/3XX, NAS Cecil Field, FL., 15 MAY 74; To VA-37, USS Saratoga (CV-60), 15 MAY 74; To VA-37, NAS Cecil Field, FL., 15 MAY 74; To VA-37, USS Saratoga (CV-60), 15 MAY 74; To VA-37, NAS Cecil Field, FL., 15 MAY 74; To VA-37, USS Saratoga (CV-60), 15 MAY 74; To VA-37, NAS Cecil Field, FL., 15 MAY 74; To VA-37, USS Saratoga (CV-60), 03 SEP 75; To VA-37, NAS Cecil Field, FL., 03 SEP 75; To VA-37, USS Saratoga (CV-60), 12 OCT 76; To VA-37, NAS Cecil Field, FL., 12 OCT 76; To VA-37, USS Saratoga (CV-60), 12 OCT 76; To VA-37, NAS Cecil Field, FL., 09 AUG 77; To VA-37, NAS Jacksonville, FL., 25 APR 78; To VA-37, NAS Cecil Field, FL., 12 AUG 78; To VA-37, USS Saratoga (CV-60), 12 AUG 78; To VA-37, NAS Cecil Field, FL., 12 AUG 78; To VA-37, USS Saratoga (CV-60), 18 DEC 79; To VA-37, NAS Cecil Field, FL., 21 DEC 79; To VA-37, USS Saratoga (CV-60), 16 FEB 80; To VA-37, NAS Cecil Field, FL., 16 FEB 80; To VA-37, NAS Jacksonville, FL., 02 DEC 80; To VA-37, NAS Cecil Field, FL., 21 JAN 81; To VA-37, NAS Jacksonville, FL., 22 JAN 81; To VA-37, NAS Dallas, TX., 19 FEB 81; To VA-37, NAS Cecil Field, FL., 27 APR 81; To VA-37, NAS Fallon, NV., 10 JUN 81; To VA-37, NAS Cecil Field, FL., 10 JUN 81; To VA-37, USS John F. Kennedy (CV-67), 10 JUN 81; To VA-37, NAS Cecil Field, FL., 10 JUN 81; To VA-37, USS John F. Kennedy (CV-67), 02 OCT 81; To VA-37, NAS Cecil Field, FL., 02 OCT 81 ** Transferred to VA-105/CVW-3, AC/4XX, NAS Cecil Field, FL., 18 AUG 82; To VA-105, NAS Jacksonville, FL., 05 JAN 83; To VA-105/CVW-15, NL/4XX., USS Carl Vinson (CVN-70), 05 JAN 83; To VA-105, NAS Jacksonville, FL., 06 JAN 83; To VA-105, NAS Cecil Field, FL., 09 FEB 83; To VA-105, USS Carl Vinson (CVN-70), 09 FEB 83; To VA-105, NAS Cecil Field, FL., 09 FEB 83 ~ S 1SO strike, 06 DEC 83 ** No data on strike ** On display at the Southern Museum of Flight; Birmingham, AL.

E-415 159278 Navy acceptance from NPRO Rep. LTV, Dallas, TX., 01 MAY 74 ** Transferred to VA-97/CVW-14, NK/3XX, NAS LeMoore, CA., 03 MAY 74 ** Transferred to VA-195/CVW-11, NH/4XX, NAS LeMoore, CA., 30 AUG 74; To VA-195, USS Kitty Hawk (CV-63), 28 MAR 75; To VA-195, NAS LeMoore, CA., 09 APR 75; To VA-195, USS Kitty Hawk (CV-63), 19 MAY 75; To VA-195, NAS Cubi Point, PI., 21 JUN 75; To VA-195, NAS LeMoore, CA., 14 DEC 75 ** Transferred to VA-122/FRS, NJ/2XX, NAS LeMoore, CA., 16 JUN 77; To VA-122, NAS Jacksonville, FL., 05 JAN 78; To VA-122, NAS LeMoore, CA., 06 APR 78 ** Transferred to VA-146/CVW-9, NG/3XX, NAS LeMoore, CA., 10 APR 78; To VA-146, NAS Fallon, NV., 10 MAY 78; To VA-146, NAS LeMoore, CA., 20 JUN 78; To VA-146, USS Constellation (CV-64), 21 SEP 78; To VA-146, NAS Cubi Point, PI., 21 DEC 78 ** Transferred to VA-94/CVW-15, NL/4XX, NAS LeMoore, CA., 17 MAY 79; To VA-94, NAS Cubi Point, PI., 29 MAY 79; To VA-94, USS Kitty Hawk (CV-63), 06 JUN 79; To VA-94, NAS

LeMoore, CA., 21 SEP 79; To VA-94, NAS Jacksonville, FL., 09 APR 80; To VA-94, NAS LeMoore, CA., 16 APR 80; To VA-94, USS Kitty Hawk (CV-63), 17 JUN 80; To VA-94, NAS LeMoore, CA., 18 AUG 80; To VA-94, USS Kitty Hawk (CV-63), 11 SEP 80; To VA-94, NAS LeMoore, CA., 29 SEP 80; Transferred to VA-195/CVW-11, NH/4XX, NAS LeMoore, CA., 12 NOV 80; To VA-195, USS America (CV-66), 25 JAN 81; To VA-195, NAS LeMoore, CA., 09 APR 81; To VA-195, NAS Jacksonville, FL., 01 SEP 82; To VA-195, NAS LeMoore, CA., 11 NOV 82; To VA-195, NAS Dallas, TX., 04 FEB 85 ** Transferred to NWC China Lake, CA., 04 FEB 83 ** Transferred to VX-5, XE/XXX, NWC China Lake, CA., 16 MAY 83 ** Transferred to VA-146/CVW-9, NG/3XX, NAS LeMoore, CA., 07 SEP 83, NE/3XX, NASLeMoore, CA., 07 SEP 83; To VA-146, USS Kitty Hawk (CV-63), 18 OCT 83; To VA-146, NAS LeMoore, CA., 23 MAR 84; To VA-146, USS Kitty Hawk (CV-63), 16 MAY 85; To VA-146, NAS LeMoore, CA., 14 SEP 85 ** Transferred to VA-97/ CVW-15, NL/3XX, NAS LeMoore, CA., 02 APR 86; To VA-97, USS Carl Vinson (CVN-70), 02 APR 86; To VA-97, NAS LeMoore, CA., 02 APR 86; To VA-97, USS Carl Vinson (CVN-70), 05 AUG 86; To VA-97, NAS Alameda, CA., 15 JAN 87; To VA-97, NAS Jacksonville, FL., 27 JUL 87 thru 28 JUL 87 ** End of flight record card ** On conditional loan from the National Museum of Naval Aviation; Pensacola, FL. to the Southern Museum of Flight; Birmingham, AL.

E-416 159279 Navy acceptance from NPRO Rep. LTV, Dallas, TX., 10 MAY 74 ** Transferred to VA-174/FRS, AD/4XX, NAS Cecil Field, FL., 20 MAY 74 ** Transferred to VA-87/CVW-6, AE/4XX, NAS Cecil Field, FL., 08 AUG 77; To VA-87, USS America (CV-66), 08 AUG 77; To VA-87, NAS Jacksonville, FL., 03 AUG 78, To VA-87, NAS Cecil Field, FL., 30 AUG 78; To VA-87, NAS Roosevelt Roads, PR., 13 SEP 78; To VA-87, NAS Cecil Field, FL., 13 SEP 78; To VA-87, USS Independence (CV-62), 13 SEP 78; To VA-87, NAS Cecil Field, FL., 29 FEB 80; To VA-87, USS Independence (CV-62), 23 AUG 80; To VA-87, NAS Cecil Field, FL., 16 JAN 81; To VA-87, USS Independence (CV-62) 03 AUG 81; To VA-87, NAS Cecil Field, FL., 03 AUG 81; To VA-87, USS Independence (CV-62), 03 AUG 81 ** Transferred to VA-174/FRS, AD/4XX, NAS Cecil Field, FL., 08 MAR 82; To VA-174, NAS Jacksonville, FL., 30 JUN 82; To VA-174, NAS Cecil Field, FL., 07 SEP 82; To VA-174, NAS Dallas, TX., 16 NOV 82 ** Transferred to VA-105/CVW-6, AE/4XX, NAS Cecil Field, FL., 16 NOV 82; To VA-105, USS Carl Vinson (CVN-70), 17 NOV 82; To VA-105, NAS Cecil Field, FL., 17 NOV 82; To VA-105, USS Carl Vinson (CVN-70), 17 NOV 82; To VA-105, NAS Cecil Field, FL., 18 NOV 82; To VA-105, NAS Roosevelt Roads, PR., 18 NOV 82; To VA-105, NAS Cecil Field, FL., 18 NOV 82; To VA-105, NAF Kadena, JP., 09 MAY 84; To VA-105, NAS Cubi Point, PI., 09 MAY 84; To VA-105, MCAS Iwakuni, JP., 09 MAY 84; To VA-105, NAS Cecil Field, FL., 09 MAY 84; To VA-105, NAS Jacksonville, FL., 21 JUN 85; To VA-105, NAS Cecil Field, FL., 22 JUN 85; To VA-105, USS Forrestal (CV-59), 22 JUN 85; To VA-105, NAS Cecil Field, FL., 22 JUN 85; To VA-105, USS Forrestal (CV-59), 16 JAN 86; To VA-105, NAS Cecil Field, FL., 16 JAN 86; To VA-105, USS Forrestal (CV-59), 13 OCT 86; To VA-105, NAS Cecil Field, FL., 13 OCT 86 ** Transferred to VA-66/CVW-3, AC/3XX, USS John F. Kennedy (CV-67), 29 OCT 86; To VA-66, NAS Cecil Field, FL., 29 OCT 86 ** Transferred to VA-37/CVW-6, AE/3XX, NAS Cecil Field, FL., 17 MAR 87; To VA-37, USS Forrestal (CV-59), 07 JUL 87 thru 13 JUL 87 ** End of flight record card.

E-417 159280 Navy acceptance from NPRO Rep. LTV, Dallas, TX., 02 MAY 74 ** Transferred to VA-27/CVW-14, NK/4XX, NAS LeMoore, CA., 06 MAY 74 ** Transferred to VA-192/CVW-11, NH/3XX, NAS LeMoore, CA., 29 AUG 74; To VA-192, USS Kitty Hawk (CV-63), 12 DEC 74; To VA-192, NAS LeMoore, CA., 28 MAR 75; To VA-192, USS Kitty Hawk (CV-63), 11 APR 75 ** Transferred to VA-122/FRS, NJ/2XX, NAS LeMoore, CA., 15 MAY 75; To VA-122, NAS Alameda, CA., 22 JUL 76; To VA-122, NAS LeMoore, CA., 10 AUG 76; To VA-122, NAS Jacksonville, FL., 18 OCT 77; To VA-122, NAS LeMoore, CA., 24 OCT 77 ** Transferred to VA-97/ CVW-14, NK/3XX, NAS LeMoore, CA., 26 OCT 77; To VA-97, USS Enterprise (CVN-65), 10 MAR 78; To VA-97, NAF Atsugi, JP., 29 JUN 78; To VA-97, USS Enterprise (CVN-65), 05 JUL 78; To VA-97, NAS Jacksonville, FL., 30 OCT 78; To VA-97, NAS Jacksonville,

FL., 17 AUG 79; To VA-97, NAS LeMoore, CA., 18 AUG 79; To VA-97, NAS Jacksonville, FL., 20 SEP 79; To VA-97, NAS LeMoore, CA., 22 SEP 79; To VA-97, USS Coral Sea (CV-43), 15 OCT 79; To VA-97, NAS LeMoore, CA., 12 NOV 79; To VA-97, USS Coral Sea (CV-43), 17 OCT 80; To VA-97, NAS LeMoore, CA., 19 JAN 81; To VA-97, USS Coral Sea (CV-43), 04 APR 81; To VA-97, NAS LeMoore, CA., 12 JUN 81 ** Transferred to VA-122/FRS, NJ/2XX, NAS LeMoore, CA., 26 JUN 81; To VA-122, NAS Jacksonville, FL., 10 DEC 81; To VA-122, NAS Dallas, TX., 10 FEB 82; To VA-122, NAS LeMoore, CA., 11 FEB 82; To VA-122, NAS Dallas, TX., 12 APR 82 ** Transferred to VA-22/CVW-11, NH/3XX, NAS LeMoore, CA., 19 APR 82; To VA-22, USS Enterprise (CVN-65), 19 APR 82; To VA-22, NAS LeMoore, CA., 27 APR 83; To VA-22, USS Enterprise (CVN-65), 27 APR 83; To VA-22, NAS LeMoore, CA., 21 FEB 84 ** Transferred to VA-27/CVW-15, NL/4XX, NAS LeMoore, CA., 24 APR 84; To VA-27, USS Carl Vinson (CVN-70), 24 APR 84; To VA-27, NAS LeMoore, CA., 27 JUN 84; To VA-27, NAS Jacksonville, FL., 28 JUN 84; To VA-27, NAS LeMoore, CA., 24 AUG 84; To VA-27, USS Carl Vinson (CVN-70), 24 AUG 84; To VA-27, NAS LeMoore, CA., 10 APR 85; To VA-27, USS Carl Vinson (CVN-70), 23 APR 86 ** Transferred to VA-122/FRS, NJ/224, NAS LeMoore, CA., 01 MAY 86; To VA-122, NAS Jacksonville, FL., 27 AUG 86; To VA-122, NAS LeMoore, CA., 27 AUG 86; To VA-122, NAS Jacksonville, FL., 28 AUG 86; To VA-122, NARF, NAS Jacksonville, FL., 25 NOV 86 ** To VA-122, NAS LeMoore, CA., 02 DEC 86 ** End of flight record card ** Transferred to AMARC, Davis Monthan AFB; Tucson, AZ., assigned park code 6A0313, 16 FEB 90 ** 6899.0 flight hours ** TF41A402D engine S/N 141987 ** Storage location 111211 ** placed on FMS list with FLIR ** At AMARG, Davis Monthan AFB; Tucson, AZ., 15 JUN 07.

E-418 159281 Navy acceptance from NPRO Rep. LTV, Dallas, TX., 18 JUN 74 ** Transferred to VA-174/FRS, AD/4XX, NAS Cecil Field, FL., 20 JUN 74 ** Transferred to VA-12/CVW-7, AG/4XX, USS Independence (CV-62), 12 NOV 74; To VA-12, NAS Cecil Field, FL., 12 NOV 74; To VA-12, NAS Fallon, NV., 12 NOV 74; To VA-12, NAS Cecil Field, FL., 12 NOV 74 ** Transferred to VA-66/CVW-7, NG/3XX, NAS Fallon, NV.,12 NOV 74 ** Transferred to VA-12/CVW-7, AG/4XX, NAS Fallon, NV., 12 NOV 74; To VA-12, NAS Cecil Field, FL., 01 JUL 75; To VA-12, USS Independence (CV-62), 03 SEP 75; To VA-12, NAS Cecil Field, FL., 14 SEP 75; To VA-12, NAS Fallon, NV., 16 JUL 76; To VA-12, USS Independence (CV-62), 16 JUL 76; To VA-12, NAS Cecil Field, FL., 16 JUL 76; To VA-12, USS Independence (CV-62), 16 JUL 76; To VA-12, NAS Cecil Field, FL., 16 JUL 76; To VA-12, USS Independence (CV-62), 16 JUL 76; To VA-12, NAS Cecil Field, FL., 09 AUG 77; To VA-12, NAS Jacksonville, FL., 03 NOV 77 ** Transferred to VA-147/CVW-9, NG/4XX, NAS LeMoore, CA., 25 JAN 78; To VA-147, USS Constellation (CV-64), 25 SEP 78; To VA-147, NAS Cubi Point, PI., 06 NOV 78; To VA-147, USS Constellation (CV-64), 31 DEC 78; To VA-147, NAS LeMoore, CA., 30 JUL 79; To VA-113, NAS LeMoore, CA.,19 DEC 79, To VA-113, NAS Fallon, NV., 19 DEC 79 ** Transferred to VA-113/CVW-2, NE/3XX, NAS LeMoore, CA., 30 JAN 80; To VA-113, USS Ranger (CV-61), 05 MAY 80; To VA-113, NAS LeMoore, CA., 09 JUL 80; To VA-113, USS Ranger (CV-61), 18 JUL 80; To VA-113, NAS Cubi Point, PI., 24 OCT 80; To VA-113, NAS LeMoore, CA., 04 APR 81 ** Transferred to VA-97/CVW-14, NK/3XX, NAS LeMoore, CA., 09 JUN 81; To VA-97, USS Coral Sea (CV-43), 20 AUG 81; To VA-97, NAS LeMoore, CA., 22 MAR 82; To VA-97, NAS Jacksonville, FL., 09 APR 82; To VA-97, NAS LeMoore, CA., 11 JUN 82; To VA-97, NAS Dallas, TX., 16 JUN 82 ** Transferred to VA-192/CVW-9, NG/3XX, NAS leMoore, CA., 14 SEP 82; To VA-192, USS Ranger (CV-61), 17 FEB 83; To VA-192, NASLeMoore, CA., 03 SEP 83; To VA-192, NAS Jacksonville, FL., 05 NOV 84; To VA-192, NAS LeMoore, CA., 02 APR 85; To VA-192, NAS Cubi Point, PI., 05 SEP 85; To VA-192, NAS LeMoore, CA., 02 JAN 86 ** Transferred to VA-27/CVW-15, NL/4XX, NAS LeMoore, CA., 24 JAN 86; To VA-27, USS Carl Vinson (CVN-70), 29 APR 86; To VA-27, NAS LeMoore, CA., 15 JUL 86; To VA-27, USS Carl Vinson (CVN-70), 05 AUG 86; To VA-27, NAS LeMoore, CA., 17 NOV 86; To VA-27, NAS Jacksonville, FL., 07 AUG 87; To VA-27, NAS LeMoore, CA., 07 AUG 87; To VA-27, NAS Jacksonville, FL., 11 AUG 87 ** End of flight record card.

E-419 159282 Navy acceptance from NPRO Rep. LTV, Dallas, TX., 05 JUN 74 ** Transferred to VA-97/CVW-14 NK/3XX, NAS LeMoore, CA., 06 JUN 74 ** Transferred to VA-195/CVW-11, NH/4XX, NAS LeMoore, CA., 29 AUG 74; To VA-195, USS Kitty Hawk (CV-63), 18 MAR 75 ** Transferred to VA-122/FRS, NJ/2XX, NAS LeMoore, CA., 14 MAY 75; To VA-122, NAS Jacksonville, FL., 28 SEP 77; To VA-122, NAS LeMoore, CA., 30 NOV 77 ** Transferred to VA-192/CVW-11, NH/3XX, NAS LeMoore, CA., 28 NOV 78; To VA-192, USS America (CV-66), 05 JAN 79; To VA-192, NAS LeMoore, CA., 05 JAN 79; To VA-192, NAS Jacksonville, FL., 13 DEC 79; To VA-192, NAS LeMoore, CA., 28 JAN 80; To VA-192, NAS Alameda, CA., 20 AUG 80; To VA-192, NAS LeMoore, CA., 15 SEP 80; To VA-192, NAS Fallon, NV., 20 OCT 80; To VA-192, NAS LeMoore, CA., 31 OCT 80; To VA-192, USS America (CV-66), 29 JAN 81; To VA-192, NAS LeMoore, CA., 08 APR 81; To VA-192, NAS Jacksonville, FL., 11 NOV 81; To VA-192, NAS LeMoore, CA., 11 NOV 81; To VA-192, NAS Jacksonville, FL., 13 JAN 82; To VA-192, NAS Dallas, TX., 15 JAN 82 ** Transferred to VA-22/CVW-11, NH/3XX, NAS LeMoore, CA., 01 JUN 82; To VA-22, USS Enterprise (CVN-65), 01 JUN 82; To VA-22, NAS LeMoore, CA., 02 MAR 83; To VA-22, USS Enterprise (CVN-65), 22 DEC 83; To VA-22, NAS LeMoore, CA., 30 JAN 84; To VA-22, USS Enterprise (CVN-65), 19 MAY 84 ** Transferred to VA-56/CVW-5, NF/4XX, NAF Atsugi, JP., 17 NOV 84; To VA-56, NAS LeMoore, CA., 16 JUL 85 ** Transferred to VA-97/CVW-15, NL/3XX, USS Carl Vinson (CVN-70), 24 APR 86; To VA-97, NAS LeMoore, CA., 02 JUL 86; To VA-97, USS Carl Vinson (CVN-70), 25 JUL 86; To VA-97, NAS Alameda, CA., 25 JUL 86; To VA-97, NAS Jacksonville, FL., 05 APR 87; To VA-97, NAS Alameda, CA., 03 JUL 87 ** End of flight record card.

E-420 159283 Navy acceptance from NPRO Rep. LTV, Dallas, TX., 14 JUN 74 ** Transferred to VA-105/CVW-3, AC/4XX, NAS Cecil Field, FL., 15 JUN 74; To VA-105, USS Saratoga (CV-60), 15 JUN 74; To VA-105, NAS Cecil Field, FL., 15 JUN 74; To VA-105, USS Saratoga (CV-60), 15 JUN 74; To VA-105, NAS Cecil Field, FL., 15 JUN 74; To VA-105, USS Saratoga (CV-60), 15 JUN 74; To VA-105, NAS Cecil Field, FL., 15 JUN 74; To VA-105, USS Saratoga (CV-60), 15 JUN 74; To VA-105, NAS Cecil Field, FL., 15 JUN 74; To VA-105, MCAS Yuma, AZ., 30 AUG 75; To VA-105, USS Saratoga (CV-60), 16 SEP 75; To VA-105, NAS Cecil Field, FL., 16 SEP 75; To VA-105, USS Saratoga (CV-60), 21 OCT 76; To VA-105, NAS Cecil Field, FL., 21 OCT 76; To VA-105, USS Saratoga (CV-60), 21 OCT 76; To VA-105, NAS Cecil Field, FL., 09 AUG 77; To VA-105, NAS Jacksonville, FL., 05 JAN 78; To VA-105, NAS Cecil Field, FL., 13 MAY 78; To VA-105, USS Saratoga (CV-60), 13 MAY 78; To VA-105, NAS Cecil Field, FL., 13 MAY 78; To VA-105, USS Saratoga (CV-60), 13 MAY 78; To VA-105, NAS Cecil Field, FL., 25 JUL 79; To VA-105, MCAS Yuma, AZ., 30 JUL 79; To VA-105, NAS Cecil Field, FL., 22 OCT 79; To VA-105, USS Saratoga (CV-60), 31 OCT 79; To VA-105, NAS Cecil Field, FL., 31 OCT 79; To VA-105, USS Saratoga (CV-60), 26 FEB 80; To VA-105, NAS Jacksonville, FL., 12 DEC 80; To VA-105, NAS Dallas, TX., 24 FEB 81 ** Transferred to VA-15/CVW-6, AE/3XX, USS independence (CV-62), 23 MAY 81; To VA-15, NAS Cecil Field, FL., 23 MAY 81; To VA-15, USS Independence (CV-62), 29 SEP 81; To VA-15, NAS Cecil Field, FL., 29 SEP 81; To VA-15, USS Independence (CV-62), 29 SEP 81; To VA-15, NAS Cecil Field, FL., 29 SEP 81; To VA-15, USS Independence (CV-62), 29 SEP 81; To VA-15, NAS Cecil Field, FL., 29 SEP 81; To VA-15, NAS Jacksonville, FL., 17 JAN 83; To VA-15, NARF, NAS Jacksonville, FK., 26 MAR 83; To VA-15, NAS Cecil Field, FL., 27 MAR 83; To VA-15, USS Independence (CV-62), 03 MAY 83; To VA-15, NAS Cecil Field, FL., 03 MAY 83; To VA-15, USS Independence (CV-62), 03 MAY 83; To VA-15, NAS Cecil Field, FL., 03 MAY 83; To VA-15, USS Independence (CV-62), 29 SEP 81; 03 MAY 83; To VA-15, NAS Cecil Field, FL., 03 MAY 83; To VA-15, USS Independence (CV-62), 29 SEP 81; 03 MAY 83; To VA-15, NAS Cecil Field, FL., 17 SEP 84; To VA-15, USS Independence (CV-62), 20 SEP 84 ** Transferred to VA-83/CVW-17, AA/3XX, NAS Cecil Field, FL., 12 OCT 84; To VA-83, NAS Fallon, NV., 14 DEC 84; To VA-83, NAS Cecil Field, FL., 15 JAN 85; To VA-83, USS Saratoga (CV-60), 17 JAN 85; To VA-83, NAS Cecil Field, FL., 17 JAN 85 ** Transferred To VA-174/ FRS, AD/432, NAS Cecil Field, FL., 03 JUL 85; To VA-174, NAS Jacksonville, FL., 16 OCT 85; To VA-174, NAS Cecil Field, FL., 01 NOV 85; To VA-174, NAS Jacksonville, FL., 17 JAN 86; To VA-174, NAS Cecil Field, FL., 22 JAN 86 thru 03 SEP 87 ** End of flight record card ** Transferred to AMARC, Davis Monthan AFB; Tucson, AZ., assigned park code 6A0271; 27 MAY 88 ** 4934.3 flight hours ** TF41A402D engine S/N 142569 ** Engine records released to DRMO, Davis Monthan AFB; Tucson, AZ., 22 FEB 06 ** Aircraft storage location 210522 ** Aircraft at AMARG, Davis Monthan AFB; Tucson, AZ., 15 JUN 07.

E-421 159284 Navy acceptance from NPRO Rep. LTV, Dallas, TX., 07 JUN 74 ** Transferred to VA-22/CVW-15 NL/ 3XX,10 JUN 74 ** Transferred to VA-25/CVW-2, NE/4XX, NAS LeMoore, CA., 23 JUN 75; To VA-25, NAS Fallon, NV., 13 JUL 75; To VA-25, USS Ranger (CV-61), 14 AUG 75; To VA-25, NAS LeMoore, CA., 24 OCT 75; To VA-25, USS Ranger (CV-61), 29 OCT 75; To VA-25, NAF Atsugi, JP., 14 APR 76; To VA-25, USS Ranger (CV-61), 15 APR 76; To VA-25, NAF Atsugi, JP., 11 JUL 76; To VA-25, USS Ranger (CV-61), 12 JUL 76; To VA-25, NAS LeMoore, CA., 14 MAR 77; To VA-25, NAS Fallon, NV., 31 JUL 77; To VA-25, NAS LeMoore, CA., 12 AUG 77; To VA-25, NAS Jacksonville, FL., 07 MAR 78; To VA-25, NAS LeMoore, CA., 12 JUN 78; To VA-25, USS Ranger (CV-61), 13 NOV 78; To VA-25, NAS LeMoore, CA., 15 DEC 78; To VA-25, USS Ranger (CV-61), 17 NOV 79; To VA-25, NAS Cubi Point, PI., 20 FEB 79; To VA-25, NAS LeMoore, CA., 25 DEC 79; To VA-25, NAS Fallon, NV., 25 DEC 79; To VA-25, NAS LeMoore, CA., 26 JAN 80; To VA-25, USS Ranger (CV-61), 29 MAY 80; To VA-25, NAS LeMoore, CA., 09 JUL 80; To VA-25, USS Ranger (CV-61), 13 JUL 80; To VA-25, NAS LeMoore, CA., 20 AUG 80; To VA-25, NAS Alameda. CA., 25 AUG 80 ** Transferred to VA-122/FRS, NJ/240, NAS LeMoore, CA., 16 OCT 80; To VA-122, NAS Jacksonville, FL., 02 APR 81; To VA-122, NAS Dallas, TX., 13 JUL 81; To VA-122, NAS LeMoore, CA., 04 AUG 81; To VA-122, NAS Dallas, TX., 16 SEP 81; To VA-122, NAS LeMoore, CA., 03 OCT 81; To VA-122, NAS Jacksonville, FL., 11 JUN 84; To VA-122, NAS LeMoore, CA., 28 AUG 84 thru 16 JUL 87 ** End of flight record card ** Transferred to VA-122, NARF NAS LeMoore, CA., 12 DEC 88; To VA-122, NAS LeMoore, CA., date unknown ** Transferred to AMARC, Davis Monthan AFB; Tucson, AZ., assigned park code 6A0314, 22 FEB 90 ** 5772.6 flight hours ** TF41A402D engine S/N 141406 ** Storage location 111215 ** At AMARG, Davis Monthan AFB; Tucson, AZ., 15 JUN 07.

159285/159308 LTV A-7E-16-CV Corsair II; (Block XVI)

E-446 159285 Navy acceptance from NPRO Rep. LTV, Dallas, TX., 17 JUL 74 ** Transferred to VA-174/ FRS, AD/4XX, NAS Cecil Field, FL., 20 AUG 74 ** Transferred to VA-66/CVW-7, AG/3XX, NAS Cecil Field, FL., 01 MAR 75; To VA-66, USS Independence (CV-62), 03 SEP 75; To VA-66, NAS Cecil Field, FL., 14 SEP 75; To VA-66, NAS Fallon, NV., 08 JUL 76; To VA-66, USS Independence (CV-62), 08 JUL 76; To VA-66, NAS Cecil Field, FL., 08 JUL 76; To VA-66, USS Independence (CV-62), 08 JUL 76; To VA-66, NAS Cecil Field, FL.,08 JUL 76; To VA-66, USS Independence (CV-62), 08 JUL 76; To VA-66, NAS Cecil Field, FL., 09 AUG 77; To VA-66, USS Dwight D. Eisenhower (CVN-69), 09 AUG 77; To VA-66, NAS Cecil Field, FL., 09 AUG 77; To VA-66, NAS Jacksonville, FL., 08 MAR 78; To VA-66, NAS Cecil Field, FL., 23 MAY 78; To VA-66, USS Dwight D. Eisenhower (CVN-69), 23 MAY 78; To VA-66, NAS Cecil Field, FL., 23 MAY 78; To VA-66, USS Dwight D. Eisenhower (CVN-69), 23 MAY 78; To VA-66, NAS Cecil Field, FL., 23 MAY 78; To VA-66, USS Dwight D. Eisenhower (CVN-69), 23 MAY 78; To VA-66, NAS Cecil Field, FL., 28 JAN 80; To VA-66, USS Dwight D. Eisenhower (CVN-69), 08 FEB 80; To VA-66, NAS Cecil Field, FL., 26 FEB 81; To VA-66, NAS Jacksonville, FL., 22 MAY 81; To VA-66, USS Dwight D. Eisenhower (CVN-69), 22 MAY 81; To VA-66, NAS Cecil Field, FL., 22 MAY 81; To VA-66, NAS Dallas, TX., 11 AUG 81 ** Transferred to VA-15/CVW-6, AE/3XX, USSIndependence (CV-62), 04 JUN 83; To VA-15, NAS Cecil Field, FL., 04 JUN 83; To VA-15, USS Independence (CV-62), 04 JUN 83; To VA-15, NAS Cecil Field, FL.,04 JUN 83; To VA-15, USS Independence (CV-62),

04 JUN 83; To VA-15, NAS Cecil Field, FL., 04 JUN 83; To VA-15, NAS Jacksonville, FL., 19 JUN 84; To VA-15, NAS Cecil Field, FL., 20 JUN 84; To VA-15, USS Independence (CV-62), 20 JUN 84; To VA-15, NAS Cecil Field, FL., 20 SEP 84; To VA-15, USS Independence (CV-62), Paint was white on light gray with black modex, 25 SEP 84; To VA-15, NAS Cecil Field, FL., 25 SEP 84; To VA-15, MCAS Iwakuni, JP., 18 NOV 85 ** Transferred to VA-174/FRS, AD/4XX, NAS Cecil Field, FL., 09 DEC 85; To VA-174, NAS Jacksonville, FL., 26 SEP 86 ** Transferred to VA-46/CVW-7, AG/306, NAS Cecil Field, FL., 29 SEP 86; To VA-46, USS Dwight D. Eisenhower (CVN-69), 20 APR 87; To VA-46, NAS Cecil Field, FL., 20 APR 87 ** End of flight record card ** Transferred to the Helenic Air force (Greece).

E-423 159286 Navy acceptance from NPRO Rep. LTV, Dallas, TX., 05 AUG 74 ** Transferred to VA-94/CVW-15, NL/4XX, NAS LeMoore, CA., 09 AUG 74 ** Transferred to VA-113/CVW-2, NE/3XX, NAS LeMoore, CA., 25 NOV 74; To VA-113, USS Ranger (CV-61), 16 AUG 75; To VA-113, NAF Atsugi, JP., 02 JUL 76; To VA-113, USS Ranger (CV-61), 11 AUG 76; To VA-113, NAS LeMoore, CA., 29 SEP 76; To VA-113, NAS Jacksonville, FL., 16 MAY 78; To VA-113, USS Ranger (CV-61), 15 SEP 78; To VA-113, NAS LeMoore, CA., 16 OCT 78; To VA-113, USS Ranger (CV-61), 09 NOV 78; To VA-113, NAS Cubi Point, PI., 28 MAR 79; To VA-113, NAS Fallon, NV., 22 SEP 79; To VA-113, NAS LeMoore, CA., 26 JAN 80; To VA-113, USS Ranger (CV-61), 20 APR 80; To VA-113, NAS LeMoore, CA., 07 JUL 80; To VA-113, USS Ranger (CV-61), 16 JUL 80 ** Transferred to VA-122/FRS, NJ/2XX, NAS LeMoore, CA., 18 SEP 80; To VA-122, NAS Jacksonville, FL., 20 MAR 81; To VA-122, NAS LeMoore, CA., 21 MAR 81; To VA-122, NAS Jacksonville, FL., 23 MAR 81; To VA-122, NAS LeMoore, CA., 26 MAY 81; To VA-122, NAS Dallas, TX., 03 AUG 81; To VA-122, NAS LeMoore, CA., 04 AUG 81; To VA-122, NAS Dallas, TX., 11 AUG 81 ** Transferred to VA-113/CVW-2, NE/3XX, USS Ranger (CV-61), 18 OCT 81; To VA-113, NAS LeMoore, CA., 12 NOV 81; To VA-113, USS Ranger (CV-61), 14 JAN 82; To VA-113, NAS LeMoore, CA., 14 JAN 82; To VA-113, USS Ranger (CV-61), 26 FEB 82; To VA-113, NAS Cubi Point, PI., 26 FEB 82; To VA-113, NAF Atsugi, JP., 26 FEB 82 ** Transferred to VA-93/CVW-5, NF/3XX, NAS Cubi Point, PI., 27 SEP 82; To VA-93, NAF Atsugi, JP., 01 NOV 82; To VA-93, NAS Cubi Point, PI., 08 NOV 82; To VA-93, NAF Atsugi, JP., 24 NOV 82; To VA-93, NAS Cubi Point, PI., 05 DEC 82; To VA-93, NAF Atsugi, JP., 09 MAY 83; To VA-93, USS Midway (CV-41), 09 MAY 83; To VA-93, NAF Atsugi, JP., 09 MAY 83; To VA-93, NAS LeMoore, CA., 01 MAY 86 ** Transferred to VA-122/FRS, NJ/227, NAS LeMoore, CA., 13 MAY 86 thru 24 SEP 87 ** End of flight record card ** Transferred to AMARC, Davis Monthan AFB; Tucson, AZ., assigned park code 6A0363, 05 JUN 90 ** 5604.4 flight hours ** TF41A402D engine S/N 141528 ** Project changed per FSO letter, 06 APR 04 ** Engine released to DRMO for disposition, 27 JUL 05 ** Aircraft deleted from inventory and released to DRMO for disposition, 01 AUG 05.

E-424 159287 Navy acceptance from NPRO Rep. LTV, Dallas, TX., 08 JUL 74 ** Transferred to VA-22/CVW-15, NL/3XX, NAS LeMoore, CA., 06 AUG 74; To VA-22, USS Coral Sea (CVA-43), 11 NOV 74 ** Transferred to VA-25/CVW-2, NE/4XX, NAS LeMoore, CA., 12 NOV 74; To VA-25, NAS Fallon, NV., 13 JUL 75; To VA-25, USS Ranger (CV-61), 14 AUG 75; To VA-25, NAS LeMoore, CA., 23 SEP 75; To VA-25, USS Ranger (CV-61), 27 JAN 76; To VA-25, NAF Atsugi, JP., 03 APR 76; To VA-25, USS Ranger (CV-61), 06 APR 76 ~ S 1SO strike, 23 JUN 76 ** No data on strike.

E-425 159288 Navy acceptance from NPRO Rep. LTV, Dallas, TX., 08 JUL 74 ** Transferred to VA-94/CVW-15, NL/4XX, NAS LeMoore, CA., 06 AUG 74 ** Transferred to VA-113/CVW-2, NE/3XX, NAS LeMoore, CA., 19 NOV 74; To VA-113, USS Ranger (CV-61), 16 AUG 75; To VA-113, NAS LeMoore, CA., 21 MAR 77; To VA-113, NAS Jacksonville, FL., 23 SEP 77; To VA-113, NAS LeMoore, CA., 16 NOV 77; To VA-113, USS Ranger (CV-61), 27 SEP 78; To VA-113, NAS LeMoore, CA., 16 OCT 78; To VA-113, USS Ranger (CV-61), 09 NOV 78; To VA-113, NAS LeMoore, CA., 15 DEC 78; To VA-113, USS Ranger (CV-61), 22 MAR 79; To VA-

113, NAS Cubi Point, PI., 02 JUL 79; To VA-113, NAS LeMoore, CA., 21 DEC 79; To VA-113, NAS Jacksonville, FL., 31 DEC 79; To VA-113, NAS Fallon, NV., 31 DEC 79; To VA-113, NAS LeMoore, CA., 31 JAN 80; To VA-113, USS Ranger (CV-61), 22 APR 80; To VA-113, NAS LeMoore, CA., 30 JUN 80; To VA-113, USS Ranger (CV-61), 21 JUL 80; To VA-113, NAS Cubi Point, PI., 24 OCT 80; To VA-113, NAS LeMoore, CA., 08 APR 81 ** Transferred to VA-97/CVW-14, NK/3XX, NAS LeMoore, CA., 22 MAR 82, 10 AUG 81; To VA-97, NAS LeMoore, CA., 22 MAR 82; To VA-97, NAS Jacksonville, FL., 17 JUL 82; To VA-97, NAS Dallas, TX., 22 SEP 82 ** Transferred to VA-192/CVW-9, NG/3XX, NAS LeMoore, CA., 09 DEC 82; To VA-192, USS Ranger (CV-61), 06 JUL 83; To VA-192, NAS LeMoore, CA., 17 NOV 83; To VA-192, NAS Jacksonville, FL., 08 FEB 85; To VA-192, NAS LeMoore, CA., 03 APR 85; To VA-192, NAS Cubi Point, PI., 06 SEP 85; To VA-192, NAS LeMoore, CA., 30 DEC 85 ** Transferred to VA-147/CVW-9, NE/3XX, NAS LeMoore, CA., 14 FEB 86 ** Transferred to VA-27/CVW-15, NL/401, USS Carl Vinson (CVN-70), 14 AUG 86; To VA-27, NAS LeMoore, CA., 05 MAR 87; To VA-27, NAS Jacksonville, FL., 24 JUN 87; To VA-27, NAS LeMoore, CA., 24 JUN 87 87; To VA-27, NAS Jacksonville, FL., 26 JUN 87 ** End of flight record card ** Transferred to AMARC, Davis Monthan AFB; Tucson, AZ., assigned park code 6A0384, 30 OCT 90 ** 7181.5 flight hours ** TF41A402D engine S/N 141488 ** Aircraft released from storage and prepared for overland shipment to FMS and NAD, NAS Jacksonville, FL., with final shipment to government of Thailand, 31 JAN 95 ** Transferred to the Royal Thai Navy, S/N 1407.

E-426 159289 Navy acceptance from NPRO Rep. LTV, Dallas, TX., 21 AUG 74 ** Transferred to VA-174/FRS, AD/4XX, NAS Cecil Field, FL., 26 AUG 74 ** Transferred to VA-82/CVW-8, AJ/300, NAS Cecil Field, FL., 07 NOV 74; To VA-82, USS Nimitz (CVN-68), 06 DEC 74; To VA-82, NAS Cecil Field, FL., 01 JUL 75; To VA-82, NAS Roosevelt Roads, PR., 01 JUL 75; To VA-82, NAS Cecil Field, FL., 01 JUL 75; To VA-82, USS Nimitz (CVN-68), 01 JUL 75; To VA-82, NAS Cecil Field, FL.,01 JUL 75; To VA-82, USS Nimitz (CVN-68), 01 JUL 75; To VA-82, NAS Cecil Field, FL., 01 JUL 75; To VA-82, USS Nimitz (CVN-68), 10 AUG 77; To VA-82, NAS Cecil Field, FL., 20 JUL 78; To VA-82, NAS Jacksonville, FL., 21 JUL 78; To VA-82, NAS Cecil Field, FL., 24 OCT 78 ** Transferred to VA-174/FRS, AD/4XX, NAS Cecil Field, FL., 24 JAN 80; To VA-174, NAS Dallas, TX., 12 JUN 81 ** Transferred to VA-15/CVW-6, AE/3XX, NAS Cecil Field, FL., 17 AUG 81; To VA-15, USS Independence (CV-62), 17 DEC 81 ** Transferred to VA-83/CVW-17, AA/3XX, NAS Fallon, NV., 19 JAN 82; To VA-83, NAS Cecil Field, FL., 19 JAN 82; To VA-83, USS Forrestal (CV-59), 19 JAN 82 ** Transferred to VA-86/CVW-8, AJ/4XX, NAS Cecil Field, FL., 29 APR 82; To VA-86, USS Nimitz (CVN-68), 24 JUN 82; To VA-86, NAS Cecil Field, FL., 24 JUN 82; To VA-86, USS Nimitz (CVN-68), 24 JUN 82; To VA-86, NAS Cecil Field, FL., 24 JUN 82; To VA-86, USS Nimitz (CVN-68), 24 JUN 82; To VA-86, NAS Cecil Field, FL., 24 JUN 82; To VA-86, NAS Jacksonville, FL., 22 JUL 83; To VA-86, NAS Roosevelt Roads, PR., 22 JUL 83; To VA-86, NAS Cecil Field, FL., 22 JUL 83; To VA-86, NAS Roosevelt Roads, PR., 03 FEB 84; To VA-86, NAS Cecil Field, FL., 03 FEB 84; To VA-86, USS Nimitz (CVN-68), 03 FEB 84; To VA-86, NAS Cecil Field, FL., 03 FEB 84; To VA-86, USS Nimitz (CVN-68), 08 FEB 85; To VA-86, NAS Cecil Field, FL., 08 FEB 85; To VA-86, NAS Jacksonville, FL., 03 DEC 85; To VA-86, NAS Cecil Field, FL., 29 DEC 85; To VA-86, NAS Jacksonville, FL., 07 FEB 86; To VA-86, NAS Cecil Field, FL., 12 FEB 86; To VA-86, USS Nimitz (CVN-68), 19 FEB 86; To VA-86, NAS Cecil Field, FL., 19 FEB 86; To VA-86, USS Nimitz (CVN-68), 06 AUG 86; To VA-86, NAS Cecil Field, FL., 07 AUG 86; To VA-86, USS Nimitz (CVN-68), 07 AUG 86; To VA-86, NAS Cecil Field, FL., 07 AUG 86 ** Transferred to VA-174/FRS, AD/4XX, NAS Cecil Field, FL., 20 JUL 87 ** End of flight record card ** Transferred to NAD, NAS Jacksonville, FL., 25 MAR 88 ** Transferred to VA-46/CVW-7, AG312, USS Dwight D. Eisenhower (CVN-69), date unknown; To VA-46, NAS Cecil Field, FL, date unknown ** Transferred to AMARC, Davis Monthan AFB; Tucson, AZ., assigned park code 6A0375, 02 AUG 90 ** 6376.1 flight hours ** TF41A402D engine S/N 141911 ** Storage location 210817 ** At AMARG, Davis Monthan AFB; Tucson, AZ., 15 JUN 07.

E-427 159290 Navy acceptance from NPRO Rep. LTV, Dallas, TX., 02 AUG 74 ** Transferred to VA-122/FRS, NJ/2XX, NAS LeMoore, CA., 08 AUG 74; To VA-122, NAS Jacksonville, FL., 12 SEP 77; To VA-122, NAS LeMoore, CA., 14 SEP 77; To VA-122, NAS Jacksonville, FL., 21 MAR 80; To VA-122, NAS LeMoore, CA., 21 APR 80; To VA-122, NAS Jacksonville, FL., 24 MAR 82; To VA-122, NAS LeMoore, CA., 07 JUN 82; To VA-122, NAS Dallas, TX., 10 SEP 82 ** Transferred to VA-192/CVW-11, NH/3XX, NAS LeMoore, CA., 15 SEP 82; To VA-192, NAS Alameda, CA., 13 JAN 83; To VA-192, NAS LeMoore, CA., 28 JAN 83; To VA-192/CVW-9, NG/4XX, USS Ranger (CV-61), 01 JUN 83; To VA-192, NAS LeMoore, CA., 01 JUN 83; To VA-192, NAS Cubi Point, PI., 06 SEP 85; To VA-192, NAS LeMoore, CA., 20 NOV 85 ** Transferred to VA-27/CVW-15, NL/404, NAS LeMoore, CA., 03 JAN 86; To VA-27, USS Carl Vinson (CVN-70), 15 MAY 86; To VA-27, NAS LeMoore, CA., 08 JUN 86; To VA-27, USS Carl Vinson (CVN-70), 06 JUN 86; To VA-27, NAS LeMoore, CA., 02 JAN 87; To VA-27, NAS Jacksonville, FL., 13 AUG 87; To VA-27, NAS LeMoore, CA., 13 AUG 87; To VA-27, NAS Jacksonville, FL., 17 AUG 87 ** End of flight record card ** Transferred to AMARC, Davis Monthan AFB; Tucson, AZ., assigned park code 6A0308; 29 NOV 89 ** 6468.2 flight hours ** TF41A402D engine S/N 141631 ** Project changed per FSO letter, 06 APR 04 ** Project changed per FSO letter, 06 APR 04 ** Engine released to DRMO for disposition, 27 JUL 05 ** Aircraft deleted from inventory and released to DRMO for disposition, 01 AUG 05.

E-428 159291 Navy acceptance from NPRO Rep. LTV, Dallas, TX., 18 JUL 74 ** Transferred to VA-105/CVW-3, AC/4XX, USS Saratoga (CV-60), 19 JUL 74; To VA-105, NAS Cecil Field, FL., 19 JUL 74; To VA-105, USS Saratoga, (CV-60), 19 JUL 74; To VA-105, NAS Cecil Field, FL., 19 JUL 74; To VA-105, USS Saratoga (CV-60), 19 JUL 74; To VA-105, NAS Cecil Field, FL., 19 JUL 74; To VA-105, MCAS Yuma, AZ., 30 AUG 75; To VA-105, USS Saratoga, (CV-60), 18 SEP 75; To VA-105, NAS Cecil Field, FL., 15 MAY 76; To VA-105, USS Saratoga, (CV-60), 19 OCT 76; To VA-105, NAS Cecil Field, FL., 19 OCT 76; To VA-105, USS Saratoga, (CV-60), 19 OCT 76; To VA-105, NAS Cecil Field, FL., 09 AUG 77; To VA-105, NAS Jacksonville, FL., 21 APR 78; To VA-105, USS Saratoga, (CV-60), 12 AUG 78; To VA-105, NAS Cecil Field, FL., 18 SEP 78; To VA-105, MCAS Yuma, AZ., 18 SEP 78; To VA-105, NAS Cecil Field, FL., 18 SEP 78; To VA-105, USS Saratoga, (CV-60), 18 SEP 78; To VA-105, NAS Cecil Field, FL., 18 SEP 78; To VA-105, USS Saratoga, (CV-60), 20 FEB 80; To VA-105, NAS Cecil Field, FL., 24 FEB 81; To VA-105, NAS Dallas, TX., 03 MAR 81; To VA-105, NAS Fallon, NV., 24 JUN 81; To VA-105, NAS Cecil Field, FL., 24 JUL 81; To VA-105, USS John F. Kennedy (CV-67), 24 JUL 81; To VA-105, NAS Cecil Field, FL., 20 APR 82; To VA-105/CVW-15, NL/4XX, USS Carl Vinson (CVN-70), 06 DEC 82; To VA-105, NAS Jacksonville, FL., 06 DEC 82; To VA-105, USS Carl Vinson (CVN-70), 07 JAN 83; To VA-105, NAS Jacksonville, FL., 10 JAN 83; To VA-105, NAS Cecil Field, FL., 16 FEB 83; To VA-105, USS Carl Vinson (CVN-70), 16 FEB 83; To VA-105, NAS Cecil Field, FL., 16 FEB 83; To VA-105, NAS Roosevelt Roads, PR., 16 FEB 83; To VA-105, NAS Cecil Field, FL., 16 FEB 83; To VA-105, NAF Kadena, JP., 03 MAY 84; To VA-105 Cubi Point, PI., 03 MAY 84; To VA-105, MCAS Iwakuni, JP., 03 MAY 84; To VA-105, NAS Cecil Field, FL., 03 MAY 84; To VA-105, NAS Jacksonville, FL., 13 JUN 85; To VA-105, NAS Cecil Field, FL., 27 JUN 85; To VA-105/CVW-6, AE/4XX, USS Forrestal (CV-59), 02 AUG 85; To VA-105, NAS Jacksonville, FL., 07 AUG 85 ** Transferred to VA-37/CVW-6, AE/3XX, NAS Cecil Field, FL., 13 AUG 85 ** Transferred to VA-15/CVW-6, AE/3XX, NAS Cecil Field, FL., 16 SEP 85; To VA-15, MCAS Iwakuni, JP., 16 SEP 85; To VA-15, Korea, 16 MAR 86; To VA-15, NAS Cubi Point, PI., 31 MAR 86; To VA-15, NAS Cecil Field, FL., 09 MAY 86 ** Transferred to VA-81/CVW-17, AA/4XX, NAS Cecil Field, FL., 14 JUL 86; To VA-81, USS Saratoga (CV-60), 16 SEP 86; To VA-81, NAS Cecil Field, FL., 25 OCT 86; To VA-81, USS Saratoga (CV-60), 05 DEC 86; To VA-81, NAS Cecil Field, FL., 06 FEB 87; To VA-81, USS Saratoga (CV-60), 09 APR 87; To VA-81, NAS Cecil Field, FL., 13 MAY 87; To VA-81, USS Saratoga (CV-60), 19 MAY 87 ** End of flight record card ** On conditional loan from the National Museum of Naval Aviation; Pensacola, FL., to the Patriots Point Naval Maritime Museum; Mt. Pleasant, SC., as Bureau Number 153176.

E-429 159292 Navy acceptance from NPRO Rep. LTV, Dallas, TX., 23 AUG 74 ** Transferred to VA-174/FRS, AD/4XX, NAS Cecil Field, FL., 27 AUG 74 ** Transferred to VA-86/CVW-8, AJ/400, NAS Cecil Field, FL., 21 NOV 74; To VA-86, USS Nimitz (CVN-68), 18 DEC 74; To VA-86, NAS Cecil Field, FL., 18 DEC 74; To VA-86, NAS Roosevelt Roads, PR., 18 DEC 74; To VA-86, NAS Cecil Field, FL., 18 DEC 74; To VA-86, USS Nimitz (CVN-68), 18 DEC 74; To VA-86, NAS Cecil Field, FL., 18 DEC 74; To VA-86, USS Nimitz (CVN-68), 18 DEC 74; To VA-86, NAS Cecil Field, FL., 30 JUN 75; To VA-86, NAS Roosevelt Roads, PR., 30 JUN 75; To VA-86, NAS Cecil Field, FL., 10 AUG 77; To VA-86, USS Nimitz (CVN-68), 10 AUG 77; To VA-86, NAS Cecil Field, FL., 10 AUG 77; To VA-86, USS Nimitz (CVN-68), 10 AUG 77; To VA-86, NAS Cecil Field, FL., 03 AUG 78; To VA-86, NAS Jacksonville, FL., 04 AUG 78; To VA-86, NAS Cecil Field, FL., 25 SEP 78; To VA-86, NAS Roosevelt Roads, PR., 25 SEP 78; To VA-86, NAS Cecil Field, FL., 25 SEP 78; To VA-86, USS Nimitz (CVN-68), 22 MAR 79; To VA-86, NAS Cecil Field, FL., 26 MAR 79; To VA-86, USS Nimitz (CVN-68), 24 JUN 80; To VA-86, NAS Cecil Field, FL., 17 FEB 81; To VA-86, NAS Jacksonville, FL., 19 FEB 81; To VA-86, NAS Dallas, TX., 22 APR 81; To VA-86, USS Nimitz (CVN-68), 22 APR 81; To VA-86, NAS Dallas, TX., 16 JUN 81; To VA-86, NAS Cecil Field, FL., 24 JUN 81 ** Transferred to VA-105/CVW-3, AC/4XX, NAS Fallon, NV., 26 JUN 81; To VA-105, NAS Cecil Field, FL., 26 JUN 81; To VA-105, USS John F. Kennedy (CV-67), 26 JUN 81; To VA-105, NAS Cecil Field, FL., 27 JUN 81; To VA-105, USS John F. Kennedy (CV-67), 27 JUN 81; To VA-105, NAS Cecil Field, FL., 12 APR 82; To VA-105/CVW-15, NL/4XX, USS Carl Vinson (CVN-70), 05 JAN 83; To VA-105, NAS Jacksonville, FL., 07 JAN 83; To VA-105, NAS Cecil Field, FL., 15 FEB 83; To VA-105/USS Carl Vinson (CVN-70), 15 FEB 83; To VA-105, NAS Cecil Field, FL., 15 FEB 83; To VA-105, NAS Roosevelt Roads, PR., 01 DEC 83; To VA-105, NAS Cecil Field, FL., 30 JAN 84; To VA-105, NAF Kadena, JP., 08 JUN 84; To VA-105, NAS Cubi Point, PI., 08 JUN 84; To VA-105, MCAS Iwakuni, JP., 08 JUN 84; To VA-105, NAS Cecil Field, FL., 08 JUN 84; To VA-105/CVW-6, AE,4XX, USS Forrestal (CV-59), 12 FEB 85; To VA-105, NAS Jacksonville, FL., 22 AUG 85; To VA-105, NAS Cecil Field, FL., 07 OCT 85; To VA-105, NAS Jacksonville, FL., 25 OCT 85 ** Transferred to VA-66/CVW-7, AG/3XX, NAS Cecil Field, FL., 25 OCT 85; To VA-66, USS John F. Kennedy (CV-67), 25 AUG 86 ** Transferred to VA-83/CVW-17, AA/3XX, USS Saratoga (CV-60), 25 SEP 86; To VA-83, NAS Cecil field, FL., 14 OCT 86; To VA-83, USS Saratoga (CV-60), 16 MAR 87; To VA-83, NAS Cecil Field, FL., 21 MAR 87; To VA-83, USS Saratoga (CV-60), 21 MAR 87; To VA-83, NAS Cecil Field, FL., 21 MAR 87; To VA-83, USS Saratoga (CV-60), 21 MAR 87 ** End of flight record card ** Transferred to the Helinic Air Force (Greece) ** Transferred to 335 MV ~ Strike, 10 OCT 01 ** No data on strike.

E-430 159293 Navy acceptance from NPRO Rep. LTV, Dallas, TX., 10 SEP 74 ** Transferred to VX-5, XE/XXX, NAF China Lake, CA., 16 SEP 74; To VX-5, NAS Alameda, CA., 23 NOV 76; To VX-5, NAF China Lake, CA., 05 JAN 77; To VX-5, NAS Jacksonville, FL., 17 JAN 79; To VX-5, NWC China Lake, CA., 01 APR 79; To VX-5, NAS Jacksonville, FL., 13 JUL 81; To VX-5, NWC China Lake, CA., 22 JUL 81; To VX-5, NAS Jacksonville, FL., 04 SEP 81; To VX-5, NAS Dallas, TX., 09 SEP 81; To VX-5, NWC China Lake, CA., 20 SEP 81; To VX-5, NAS Dallas, TX., 06 OCT 81; To VX-5, NWC China Lake, CA., 20 OCT 81; To VX-5, NAS Dallas, TX., 22 DEC 81 ** Transferred to VA-192/CVW-11, NH/3XX, NAS LeMoore, CA., 28 DEC 81 ** Transferred to VA-22/CVW-15 NL/3XX, NAS LeMoore, CA., 25 FEB 82 ** Transferred to VA-122/FRS, NJ/2XX, NAS LeMoore, CA., 25 MAY 82 ** Transferred to VA-97/CVW-15, NL/3XX, NAS LeMoore, CA., 14 OCT 83; To VA-97, USS Carl Vinson (CVN-70), 05 APR 84; To VA-97, NAS Jacksonville, FL., 11 APR 84; To VA-97, USS Carl Vinson (CVN-70), 29 JUN 84; To VA-97, NAS LeMoore, CA., 29 JUN 84 ** Transferred to VA-122/FRS, NJ/2XX, NAS LeMoore, CA., 11 SEP 84 ** Transferred to VA-192/CVW-9, NG/3XX, NAS Cubi Point, PI., 06 SEP 85; To VA-192, NAF Atsugi, JP., 28 OCT 85; To VA-192, NAS Cubi Point, PI., 31 OCT 85; To VA-192, NAS LeMoore, CA., 31 OCT 85 ** Transferred to VA-27/CVW-15, NL/4XX, NAS LeMoore, CA., 27 DEC 85 **

Transferred to VA-122/FRS, NJ/201, NAS LeMoore, CA., 30 APR 86 thru 16 SEP 87 ** End of flight record card ** Transferred to AMARC, Davis Monthan AFB; Tucson, AZ., assigned park code 6A0358; 29 MAY 90 ** 5539.4 flight hours ** TF41A402D engine S/N 142582 ** Storage location 210345 ** Project changed per FSO letter, 06 APR 04 ** Aircraft deleted from inventory and released to DRMO for disposition, 01 AUG 05 ** At AMARG, Davis Monthan AFB; Tucson, AZ., 15 JUN 07.

E-431 159294 Navy acceptance from NPRO Rep. LTV, Dallas, TX., 27 SEP 74 ** Transferred to VA-83/CVW-17, AA/3XX, NAS Cecil Field, FL., 27 SEP 74; To VA-83, USS Forrestal (CV-59), 05 DEC 74; To VA-83, NAS Cecil Field, FL., 05 DEC 74; To VA-83, USS Forrestal (CV-59), 05 DEC 74; To VA-83, NAS Cecil Field, FL., 01 SEP 75; To VA-83, USS Forrestal (CV-59), 22 MAR 76; To VA-83, NAS Cecil Field, FL., 24 MAR 76; To VA-83, USS Forrestal (CV-59), 22 JUL 76; To VA-83, NAS Cecil Field, FL., 29 JUL 76; To VA-83, NAS Roosevelt Roads, PR., 29 JUL 76; To VA-83, NAS Cecil Field, FL., 09 JUL 76; To VA-83, NAS Jacksonville, FL., 05 OCT 77; To VA-83, USS Forrestal (CV-59), 29 NOV 77; To VA-83, NAS Cecil Field, FL., 29 NOV 77; To VA-83, USS Forrestal (CV-59), 29 NOV 77; To VA-83, NAS Cecil Field, FL., 29 NOV 77; To VA-83, USS Forrestal (CV-59), 29 NOV 77; To VA-83, NAS Cecil Field, FL., 29 NOV 77; To VA-83, USS Forrestal (CV-59), 29 NOV 77; To VA-83, NAS Cecil Field, FL., 23 OCT 79; To VA-83, USS Forrestal (CV-59), 24 OCT 79 ** Transferred to VA-37/CVW-3, AC/3XX, NAS Cecil Field, Fl., 30 NOV 79; To VA-37, USS Saratoga (CV-60), 14 FEB 80; To VA-37, NAS Cecil Field, FL., 14 FEB 80; To VA-37, NAS Fallon, NV., 11 MAR 81; To VA-37, NAS Cecil Field, FL., 11 MAR 81; To VA-37, USS John F. Kennedy (CV-67), 11 MAR 81 ** Transferred to VA-174/FRS, AD/4XX, NAS Cecil Field, FL., 06 AUG 81; To VA-174, NAS Jacksonville, FL., 02 FEB 82 ** Transferred to VA-15/CVW-6, AE/3XX, NAS Cecil Field, FL., 17 MAY 82; To VA-15, USS Independence (CV-62), 17 MAY 82; To VA-15, NAS Cecil Field, FL., 17 MAY 82; To VA-15, USS Independence (CV-62),09 MAY 83; To VA-15, NAS Cecil Field, FL., 09 MAY 83; To VA-15, USS Independence (CV-62), 09 MAY 83; To VA-15, NAS Cecil Field, FL., 09 MAY 83; To VA-15, USS Independence (CV-62), 09 MAY 83; To VA-15, NAS Cecil Field, FL., 05 MAR 84; To VA-15, NAS Jacksonville, FL., 13 JUN 84; To VA-15, USS Independence (CV-62), 13 JUN 84; To VA-15, NAS Jacksonville, FL., 09 AUG 84 ** Transferred to VA-86/CVW-8, AJ/4XX, NAS Roosevelt Roads, PR., 10 AUG 84; To VA-86, NAS Cecil Field, FL., 23 AUG 84; To VA-86, USS Nimitz (CVN-69), 23 AUG 84; To VA-86, NAS Cecil Field, FL., 26 SEP 84; To VA-86, USS Nimitz (CVN-69), 26 SEP 84; To VA-86, NAS Cecil Field, FL., 10 OCT 85 ** Transferred to VA-15/CVW-6, AE/3XX, NAS Cecil Field, FL., 08 NOV 85; To VA-15, MCAS Iwakuni, JP., 27 NOV 85; To VA-15, Korea, 27 NOV 85; To VA-15, NAF Atsugi, JP., 24 APR 86; To VA-15, NAS Cubi Point, PI., 29 APR 86; To VA-15, NAS Cecil Field, FL., 29 APR 86 ** Transferred to VA-174/FRS, AD/4XX, NAS Cecil Field, FL., 11 SEP 86; To VA-174, NAS Jacksonville, FL., 22 JAN 87; To VA-174, NAS Cecil Field, FL., 22 JAN 87; To VA-174, NAS Jacksonville, FL., 27 JAN 87 ** Transferred to VA-37/CVW-6, AE/3XX, NAS Cecil Field, Fl., 08 JUN 87; To VA-37, USS Forrestal (CV-59), 16 JUN 87 ** End of flight record card ** Transferred to VA-105/CVW-6, AE/405, NAS Cecil Field, FL., date unknown ** Transferred to AMARC, Davis Monthan AFB; Tucson, AZ., assigned park code 6A0390; 07 JAN 91 ** 7301.5 flight hours ** TF41A402D engine S/N 141551 ** Storage location 111319 ** At AMARG, Davis Monthan AFB; Tucson, AZ., 15 JUN 07.

E-432 159295 Navy acceptance from NPRO Rep. LTV, Dallas, TX., 12 SEP 74 ** Transferred to VA-174/FRS, AD/4XX, NAS Cecil Field, FL., 13 SEP 74 ** Transferred to VA-12/CVW-7, AG/4XX, NAS Cecil Field, FL., 07 JUN 76; To VA-12, NAS Fallon, NV., 05 AUG 76; To VA-12, USS Independence (CV-62), 05 AUG 76; To VA-12, NAS Cecil Field, FL., 05 AUG 76; To VA-12, USS Independence (CV-62), 05 AUG 76; To VA-12, NAS Cecil Field, FL., 05 JAN 77; To VA-12, USS Independence (CV-62), 05 JAN 77; To VA-12, NAS Cecil Field, FL., 09 AUG 77; To VA-12, USS Dwight D. Eisenhower

(CVN-69), 09 AUG 77; To VA-12, NAS Cecil Field, FL., 24 FEB 78; To VA-12, NAS Jacksonville, FL., 25 APR 78; To VA-12, NAS Cecil Field, FL., 17 MAY 78; To VA-12, USS , USS Dwight D. Eisenhower (CVN-69), 17 MAY 78; To VA-12, NAS Cecil Field, FL., 17 MAY 78; To VA-12, USS Dwight D. Eisenhower (CVN-69), 17 MAY 78; To VA-12, NAS Cecil Field, FL., 31 OCT 79; To VA-12, USS Dwight D. Eisenhower (CVN-69), 07 NOV 79 ~ S 1SO strike, 26 OCT 80 ** No data on strike.

E-433 159296 Navy acceptance from NPRO Rep. LTV, Dallas, TX., 05 SEP 74 ** Transferred to NATC, NAS Patuxent River, MD., for RDT & E, NATC/296, 12 SEP 74, Transferred NATC, Weapons Systems Test, NAS Patuxent River, MD., Paint was white with orange tail and wing tips, 01 MAR 79; Transferred to NATC, NAS Patuxent River, MD., for RDT & E, 07 MAY 79; To NATC, Jacksonville, FL., for RDT & E, 11 MAY 83; Transferred to NATC, NAS Patuxent River, MD., for RDT & E, 01SEP 83; To NATC, Jacksonville, FL., for RDT & E, 08 JUL 86; Transferred to NATC, NAS Patuxent River, MD., for RDT & E, 19 SEP 86 thru 02 FEB 87 ** End of flight record card ** Transferred to NAD, NAS Jacksonville, FL., 29 DEC 88** Transferred to NAWC, SD/401, NAS Patuxent River, MD., date unknown ** Transferred to AMARC, Davis Monthan AFB; Tucson, AZ., assigned park code 6A0409; 03 FEB 92 ** 4427.6 flight hours ** TF41A402D engine S/N 142635 ** Storage location 111313 ** Placed on FMS list with D-704 Buddy store, 06 APR 04 ** At AMARG, Davis Monthan AFB; Tucson, AZ., 15 JUN 07.

E-434 159297 Navy acceptance from NPRO Rep. LTV, Dallas, TX., 17 OCT 74 ** Transferred to VA-81/CVW-17, AA/4XX, NAS Cecil Field, FL., 18 OCT 74; To VA-81, USS Forrestal (CVA-59), 21 NOV 74; To VA-81, NAS Cecil Field, FL., 01 SEP 75; To VA-81, USS Forrestal (CVA-59), 23 SEP 75; To VA-81, NAS Cecil Field, FL., 23 SEP 75; To VA-81 NAS Roosevelt Roads, PR, 23 SEP 75; To VA-81, NAS Cecil Field, FL., 23 SEP 75; To VA-81 NAS Roosevelt Roads, PR, 23 SEP 75; To VA-81, NAS Cecil Field, FL., 23 SEP 75; To VA-81 NAS Roosevelt Roads, PR, 22 AUG 77; To VA-81,USS Forrestal (CV-59), 22 AUG 77; To VA-81, NAS Cecil Field, FL., 22 AUG 77; To VA-81,USS Forrestal (CV-59), 22 AUG 77; To VA-81, NAS Jacksonville, FL., 27 JAN 78; To VA-81, USS Forrestal (CV-59), 10 MAR 78; To VA-81, NAS Cecil Field, FL., 10 MAR 78; To VA-81,USS Forrestal (CV-59), 11 APR 79; To VA-81, NAS Cecil Field, FL., 27 JUL 79 ** Transferred to VA-97/CVW-14, NK/3XX, NAS LeMoore, CA., 01 AUG 79; To VA-97, USS Coral Sea (CV-43), 10 OCT 79 ~ S 1SO strike, 08 JAN 80 ** Aircraft stalled on final and struck ramp, pilot ejected.

E-435 159298 Navy acceptance from NPRO Rep. LTV, Dallas, TX., 23 OCT 74 ** Transferred to VA-83/CVW-17, AA/300, NAS Cecil Field, Fl., 30 OCT 74; To VA-83, USS Forrestal (CVA-59), 25 NOV 74; To VA-83, NAS Cecil Field, FL., 25 NOV 74; To VA-83, USS Forrestal (CVA-59), 25 NOV 74; To VA-83, NAS Cecil Field, FL., 01 SEP 75; To VA-83, USS Forrestal (CV-59), 06 OCT 75; To VA-83, NAS Cecil Field, FL., 04 MAY 76; To VA-83, USS Forrestal (CV-59), 08 JUN 76; To VA-83, NAS Cecil Field, FL., 08 JUN 76; To VA-83, NAS Roosevelt Roads, PR., 08 JUN 76; To VA-83, NAS Cecil Field, FL., 08 JUN 76; To VA-83, USS Forrestal (CV-59), 20 JUL 77; To VA-83, NAS Jacksonville, FL., 16 DEC 77; To VA-83, USS Forrestal (CV-59), 19 DEC 77; To VA-83, NAS Jacksonville, FL., 27 FEB 78; To VA-83, USS Forrestal (CV-59), 17 MAR 78; To VA-83, NAS Cecil Field, FL., 17 MAR 78; To VA-83, USS Forrestal (CV-59), 29 MAY 79 ~ S 1SO strike, 14 DEC 79 ** No data on strike.

E-436 159299 Navy acceptance from NPRO Rep. LTV, Dallas, TX., 18 OCT 74 ** Transferred to NPRO LTV, Dallas, TX., for RDT & E, 19 OCT 74 ** Transferred to NAF China Lake, CA., China Lake/ XXX, 15 MAR 76 ** Transferred to VX-5, XE/20, NAF China Lake, CA., 07 JUL 76 ~ S 1SO strike, 30 AUG 76 ** Mid air collision with A-6E 152953 on night approach, pilot ejected, crashed inside the fence on Inyokern RD.

CVWA-20 (top to bottom): VAQ-208 A-3, VF-201 F-4, VF-202 F-4, VFP-206 RF-8, VA-203 A-7, and VA-205 A-4L over NAS Fallon, NV.

...7s (front to back): NL/01 USS Coral Sea, NE/03 USS Ranger, NL/00, NE/05, NG/11, ...G/60, AH/11, NH/11, NG/XX, and XXXX

VA-215 A-7 154460 and VA-146 A-7 NG/311

A-7Bs from USS Roosevelt (clockwise from top): VA-15 154512 AE/310, VA-215 154538 AE/401, and VA-15's 154415 AE/301 and 154412 AE/303

...WR-20 (from top clockwise): (2) VA-204 A-7s, VAK-208 A-3, VA-203 A-7, VAQ-209 ...-6, and (2) VA-205 A-7s

VA-215 A-7B 154536 AE/401, VA-15 A-7B 154415 AE/301, and VFP-63 RF-8A 146858 AE/601, all USS Roosevelt

VA-94 A-7E NL/404 USS Coral Sea and VA-27 A-7E NK/410 USS Enterprise

VA-305 A-7A ND/504 and VA-304 A-7A ND/402 on the cat of USS Ranger

CVWR-30 A-7As on USS Ranger, 1976: VA-304 ND/412, VA-303 ND/306, VA-304 154356 ND/402, VA-304 ND/400, and VA-305 ND/505

Background: VA-305 A-7A ND/505 launching. Foreground: VA-303 A-7As ND/305, 314

CVWR-80 (l-r): VF-301 F-8 149204 ND/101, VF-302 F-8 ND/213, VA-303 A-7A 154354 ND/303, VA-304 A-7A 154852 ND/401, VA-305 A-7A 153138 ND/504, VFP-306 RF-149616 ND/601, and VAQ-308 138914 ND/634

A-7 port main landing gear

A-7 VA-93 #2 and #3 ordnance stations

A-7 port wing #1 ordnance station with bomb rack

Sarboard wing fold with lock in place

A-7 engine exhaust turbine

A-7 RAT (Ram Air Turbine)

A-7 port fuselage nose launch bar and access doors/panels

A-7 TF-41 engine

A-7 ejection seat

A-7 cockpit

A-7 nose landing gear and launch bar with tow bar attached

TA-7C display

TA-7C display

A-7E Gatling gun port nose

A-7 on cat

A-7 taking the wire

A-7 gun site on another A-7

A-7 on approach to the carrier

A-7

A-7 firing rocket

A-7s lining up for an inflight refuel

A-7 formation

A-7s lining up for an inflight refuel

A-7 being chased by another A-7

A-7 launch

A-7s: USAF A-7D 71-293 and USN A-7E 157551

A-7 taxiing

A-7 on approach to carrier

A-7 in turn

A-7 launch

A-7 with ordnance

F-8, F-16, and VA-94 A-7 404

A-7A 152661 USS Eisenhower/U.S. Naval Sea Cadets display

A-7E on flight deck

A-7 on flight deck

A-7 on cat

A-7s on flight deck

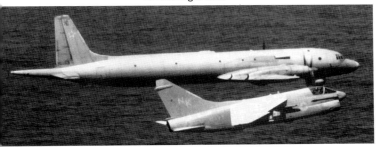

A-7 escorting a Russian aircraft

A-7s on a sand blower

A-7B 154423 AH/300

A-7 HUD (Heads Up Display)

A-7s in formation with 2 Blue Angels, A-4s #3 and #4

Two A-7s in formation with Blue Angels #3 and #4

A-7 display

A-7 hits the round down, E-2 in the foreground

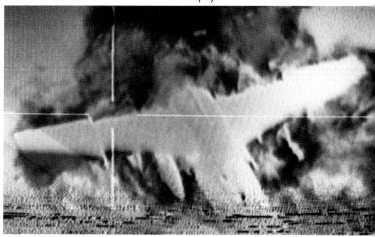

A-7 hits the round down and into flight deck

A-7 explodes on flight deck after hitting the round down, E-2 in foreground

HAF A-7H Tiger

HAF A-7H Tiger

HAF A-7H Tiger

HAF A-7H Tiger

HAF A-7H Tiger

HAF A-7H Tiger

HAF A-7H Tiger

HAF A-7H Tiger

HAF A-7H in boneyard

HAF A-7H refueling from USN S-3

HAF TA-7H

Three HAF A-7Hs

HAF A-7H weapons display

Two HAF A-7Hs

Two HAF A-7Hs in hangar

HAF TA-7H in hangar, mothballed and with wing removed

HAF A-7H

HAF A-7H

HAF A-7H

HAF TA-7H

HAF A-7H

HAF A-7E 160552

HAF TA-7H 154477

HAF TA-7H 154477

HAF TA-7H 154489

HAF TA-7C 155774

HAF TA-7C 156747

HAF TA-7C 156747

HAF TA-7C 156767

HAF TA-7C 156768

HAF TA-7H 155774

HAF TA-7Hs 159658, 156787

HAF TA-7H 156787

HAF A-7E 158824

HAF A-7E 158021

HAF A-7H 158824

HAF A-7H 159274

HAF A-7E 159640

HAF A-7E 159658

HAF A-7E 159658

HAF A-7H 159938 in boneyard

HAF A-7H 159926

HAF A-7H 159664

HAF A-7Hs 159927, 159916, and 159926 in boneyard

HAF A-7H 159914

HAF A-7H 159959 and 159931 in boneyard

HAF A-7H 159916 in boneyard

HAF A-7H 159932 in boneyard

HAF A-7H 159918 in boneyard

HAF A-7H 159939

HAF A-7H in boneyard

HAF A-7H 159959 in boneyard

HAF A-7Hs 159962 and 159965

HAF A-7H 159980

HAF A-7H 159939

HAF A-7E 160541

HAF A-7H 159949

HAF A-7E 160552

HAF A-7H 159975

HAF A-7E 160557

HAF A-7E 160560

HAF A-7E 160566

HAF A-7H 160648

HAF A-7H 160728

HAF A-7E 160736

HAF A-7H 160736

HAF A-7H 160736

HAF A-7E 170537

HAF A-7E 160857

HAF A-7E 160865

HAF A-7H 160866

HAF A-7E 160867

HAF A-7E 160867

HAF A-7H 160873

HAF A-7H 160873

HAF TA-7H

161218

HAF TA-7H 161219

HAF TA-7H 161220

HAF TA-7C 161220

HAF TA-7H 161221

HAF TA-7H 161222

PAF A-7P PAF 5521 from 153134

PAF A-7P PAF 5521 from 153134

PAF A-7Ps PAF 5521 from 153170

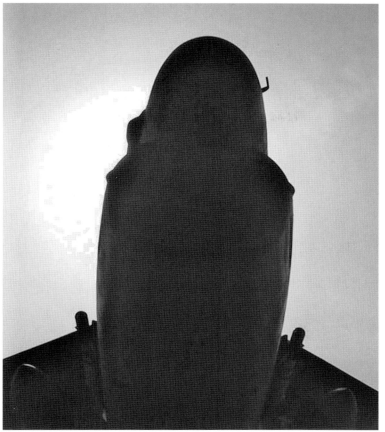

PAF A-7P

PAF TA-7P PAF 5521 from 153134

PAF A-7P PAF 5523 from 153159

PAF A-7P PAF 5503 from 153272

PAF A-7Ps PAF 5536 from 153208

PAF A-7P PAF 5529 from 153191

PAF TA-7P PAF 15547 from 153224

PAF TA-7P PAF 5547 from 153224

PAF TA-7P PAF 5549 from 153268

PAF A-7P PAF 15503 from 153272

PAF A-7P avionics bay, door open with air start recepticle panel off

PAF A-7P avionics bay, door open with sidewinder

PAF A-7P PAF 5534 from 153229

PAF A-7P PAF 5544 from 153245

PAF A-7P

PAF A-7Ps PAF 5522 from 153155

PAF A-7P PAF 5501 from 154352

PAF A-7P PAF 15545 from 153201

PAF A-7Ps PAF 5502 from 153200

PAF A-7Ps PAF 5518 from 153248

PAF A-7P formation

PAF A-7P PAF 5547 from 153224

PAF A-7P PAF 15512 from 153170

PAF TA-7P PAF 5549 from 153268

PAF A-7P PAF 5537 from 153254

PAF A-7P PAF 5508 from 153219

PAF A-7P PAF 5537 from 153254

PAF A-7P PAF 5509 from 153244

PAF TA-7P PAF 15549 from 153268

RTN TA-7C 156794 RTN 1418

RTN TA-7C unknown

RTN TA-7C 156788 RTN 1417

RTN A-7E 160542 RTN 1401

292

AMARG A-7s, F-4s in right foreground

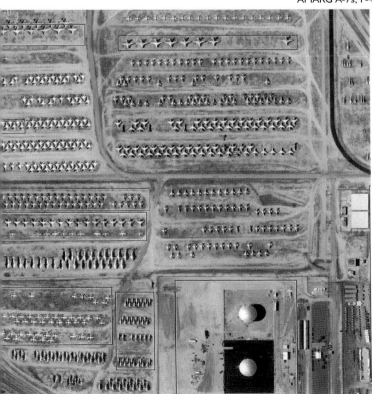

AMARG satellite photo

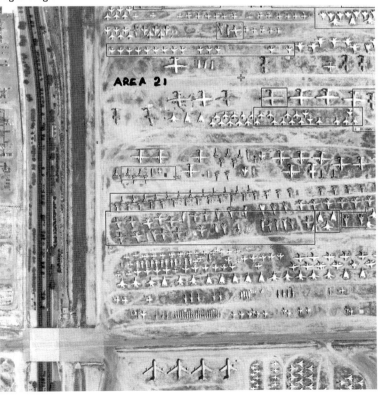

AMARG satellite photo

AMARG A-7s

AMARG A-7s

AMARG A-7s

AMARG A-7s

AMARG A-7s

AMARG A-7s

AMARG A-7s

AMARG A-7s

AMARG A-7B 154491 AF/411 Park code 6A0158

AMARG 157585 Park Code 6A176

AMARG A-7B 154491 VA-204 AF/411 Park code 6A0158

AMARG A-7E 158835 VA-12 AG/414 Park Code 6A197

AMARG A-7B 154491 VA-204 AF/411 Park code 6A0158

AMARG A-7E 151573 Va-174 AD/415

AMARG A-7E 158014 VA-174 AL/303 Park Code 6A219

AMARG A-7B 154484 VA-205 AF/511 Park Code 6A140

AMARG A-7E 157566 VA-174 AD/400 Park Code 6A236

AMARG A-7E 158821 VA-147 NG/401 Park Code 6A293

AMARG A-7 VA-72 Park Code 6A370

AMARG A-7E 157504 VA-205 AF/512 Park Code 6A298

AMARG A-7E 157494 VA-122 NJ/226 Park Code 6A312

AMARG A-7E 159997 VA-66 AG/311 Park Code 6A302

AMARG A-7E 158019 VA-97 Park Code 6A318

AMARG A-7E 158013 VA-97 NL/305 Park Code 6A306

AMARG A-7E 156822 VA-205 AF/500 Park Code 6A324

AMARG A-7E 159308 VA-72 AC/401 Park Code 6A541

AMARG A-7E 159656 NSWC 24 Park Code 6A403

AMARG TA-7C 156784 VAQ-33 GD/116 Park Code 6A3768

AMARG EA-7L 158761 NAWC 84 Park Code 6A0418

AMARG A-7E 159985 NSWC 21 Park Code 6A406

AMARG TA-7C PMTC 86 Park Code 6A0471

AMARG A-7E 159270 PMTC-82 Park Code 6A407

AMARG A-7K 79466 AZ ANG AAAE0021

AMARG A-7K ED 80 290 Park Code AAAE290

AMARG A-7D ED Park Code AE429

AMARG A-7K AF 80 286 IA ANG Park Code AAAE0286

AMARG A-7K OK ANG Park Code AV6A0444

AMARG A-7K OH ANG Park Code AV6A0445

AMARG A-7B 154516 VA-204 AF/412 Park Code 6A160

AMARG A-7B 154505 VA-304 ND/402 Park Code 6A201

AMARG TA-7C N164TB Thunderbird Aviation

AMARG A-7D OH ANG Park Code AE133

AMRAG A-7A 152656 PMTC 63 Park Code 6A079

AMARG A-7E 156806 VA-205 Park Code 6A252

AMARG A-7E 157585 (foreground) VA-174 Park Code 6A176

AMARG A-7D PT 742

AMARG A-7D OH 992

AMARG A-7B 154439 VA-305 ND/507

AMARG A-7A 152665

AMARG A-7E 157581 VA-105 Park Code 6A254

AMARG A-7E 158669 VA-72 Park Code 6A251

AMARG A-7D DM 355

AMARG A-7A 153171 Park Code 6A026

AMARG A-7s

AMARG A-7B 154360 NJ/521 Park Code 6A050

AMARG A-7B VA-204 AF/41

AMARG A-7B 152660 Park

AMARG A-7A 153177 VA-305 ND/515

AMARG TA-7C NAWC 84

AMARG TA-7C PMTC Park Code 6A400

AMARG A-7E PMTC Park Code 6A407

AMARG A-7A 152676 VA-304 ND/406

AMARG A-7 153215 being placed in a guppy

AMARG A-7 153215 being shipped in a guppy

AMARG A-7

AMARG A-7E

AMARG A-7E 159289 VA-46 AC/312 Park Code 6A375

AMARG A-7E

AMARG A-7E

AMARG TA-7C

AMARG TA-7C being shipped by rail

Haveco A/C salvage. Upper part of satellite photo shows A-7Ds.

Haveco A/C Salvage A-7Ds

Haveco A/C Salvage A-7Ds

Haveco A/C Salvage A-7Ds

Haveco A/C Salvage A-7Ds

Haveco A/C Salvage A-7Ds

Haveco A/C Salvage A-7D tail sections

Yanks Air Museum A-7B 154538

Haveco A/C Salvage A-7D

Haveco A/C Salvage A-7D cockpit

Thunderbird Aviation TA-7C N165TB

A-7 fuselage at unknown location

Haveco A/C Salvage A-7D

Yanks Air Museum A-7B 154538

E-437 159300 Navy acceptance from NPRO Rep. LTV, Dallas, TX., 11 OCT 74 ** Transferred to VX-5, XE/XXX, NAF China Lake, CA., 11 OCT 74; To VX-5, NAS Alameda, CA., 15 OCT 76; To VX-5, NAF China Lake, 22 OCT 76; To VX-5, NAS Jacksonville, FL., 16 MAR 79; To VX-5, NAS LeMoore, CA., 24 JUN 80; To VX-5, NAF China Lake, 27 JUN 80; To VX-5, NAS Jacksonville, FL., 30 JUN 83; To VX-5, NAF China Lake, 30 JUN 83; To VX-5, NAS Jacksonville, FL., 05 JUL 83 ** Transferred to VA-27/CVW-15, NL/4XX, NAS LeMoore, CA., 10 JAN 84; To VA-27, USS Carl Vinson, CVN-70, 10 JAN 84; To VA-27, NAS LeMoore, CA., 10 JAN 84; To VA-27, USS Carl Vinson, (CVN-70), 04 MAY 84; To VA-27, NAS LeMoore, CA., 08 MAY 84; To VA-27, USS Carl Vinson, (CVN-70), 08 MAY 84; To VA-27, NAS LeMoore, CA., 22 MAR 85; To VA-27, NAS Jacksonville, FL., 19 FEB 86; To VA-27, NAS LeMoore, CA., 26 APR 86; To VA-27, USS Carl Vinson, (CVN-70), 26 APR 86; To VA-27, NAS LeMoore, CA., 26 APR 86; To VA-27, USS Carl Vinson, (CVN-70), 26 APR 86; To VA-27, NAS LeMoore, CA., 26 APR 86 thru 23 AUG 87 ** End of flight record card ** Transferred to VA-22/CVW-11, NH/313, NAS LeMoore, CA., date unknown ** Transferred to AMARC, Davis Monthan AFB; Tucson, AZ., assigned park code 6A0290, 28 JUN 89 ** 4958.8 flight hours ** TF41A402D engine S/N 141328 ** Aircraft released from storage and prepared for overland shipment to FMS, NAS Jacksonville, FL., with final shipment to government of Thailand, 06 JUN 94 ** Transferred to Royal Thai Navy as spare parts for the A-7 program ** Located at the dump in Thailand, 04 JAN 06.

E-438 159301 Navy acceptance from NPRO Rep. LTV, Dallas, TX., 19 NOV 74 ** Transferred to VA-82/CVW-8, AJ/301, NAS Cecil Field, FL., 22 NOV 74; To VA-82, NAS Jacksonville, FL., 01 MAR 75; To VA-82, USS Nimitz (CVN-68), 01 MAR75; To VA-82, NAS Cecil Field, FL., 01 MAR 75; To VA-82, NAS Jacksonville, FL., 13 NOV 75; To VA-82, NAS Roosevelt Roads, PR., 17 NOV 75; To VA-82, NAS Cecil Field, FL.,17 NOV 75; To VA-82, USS Nimitz (CVN-68), 17 NOV 75; To VA-82, NAS Cecil Field, FL., 17 NOV 75; To VA-82, USS Nimitz (CVN-68), 17 NOV 75; To VA-82, NAS Cecil Field, FL., 17 NOV 75; To VA-82, USS Nimitz (CVN-68), 04 OCT 76; To VA-82, NAS Cecil Field, FL., 01 DEC 76; To VA-82, USS Nimitz (CVN-68), 20 JUL 77; To VA-82, NAS Jacksonville, FL., 28 JUL 78; To VA-82, NAS Cecil Field, FL., 25 AUG 78; To VA-82, USS Nimitz (CVN-68), 19 MAR 80; To VA-82, NAS Jacksonville, FL., 03 JUN 80; To VA-82, USS Nimitz (CVN-68), 03 JUN 80; To VA-82, NAS Cecil Field, FL., 31 JUL 80; To VA-82, USS Nimitz (CVN-68), 31 JUL 80; To VA-82, NAS Cecil Field, FL., 31 JUL 80; To VA-82, USS Carl Vinson (CVN-70), 31 JUL 80; To VA-82, NAS Cecil Field, FL., 31 JUL 80; To VA-82, USS Nimitz (CVN-68), 31 JUL 80 ** Transferred to VA-174/FRS, AD/4XX, NAS Cecil Field, FL., 15 SEP 82; To VA-174, NAS Jacksonville, FL., 16 JAN 83; To VA-174, NAS Cecil Field, FL., 15 FEB 83; To VA-174, NAS Jacksonville, FL., 24 MAR 83; To VA-174, NAS Cecil Field, FL., 25 MAR 83 ** Transferred to VA-46/CVW-1, AB/3XX, NAS Cecil Field, FL., 13 JUN 83; To VA-46, USS America (CV-66), 13 JUN 83; To VA-46, NAS Cecil Field, FL., 20 DEC 83; To VA-46, USS America (CV-66), 22 DEC 83; To VA-46, NAS Cecil Field, FL., 22 DEC 83; To VA-46, USS America (CV-66), 22 DEC 83; To VA-46, NAS Cecil Field, FL., 22 DEC 83; To VA-46, NAS Jacksonville, FL., 17 DEC 84; To VA-46, NAS Cecil Field, FL.,17 DEC 84; To VA-46, NAS Jacksonville, FL., 21 DEC 84; To VA-46, NAS Cecil Field, FL., 19 MAR 85; To VA-46, USS America (CV-66), 19 MAR 85; To VA-46, NAS Cecil Field, FL., 19 MAR 85; To VA-46, USS America (CV-66), 19 MAR 85; To VA-46, NAS Cecil Field, FL., 01 NOV 85; To VA-46, USS America (CV-66), 06 JAN 86; To VA-46, NAS Cecil Field, FL., 06 JAN 86 ** Transferred to VA-83/CVW-17, AA/3XX, NAS Cecil Field, FL., 20 DEC 86; To VA-83, USS Saratoga (CV-60), 10 MAR 87; To VA-83, NAS Cecil Field, FL., 20 MAR 87; To VA-83, USS Saratoga (CV-60), 20 MAR 87; To VA-83, NAS Cecil Field, FL., 20 MAR 87; To VA-83, USS Saratoga (CV-60), 20 MAR 87 ** End of flight record card ** On conditional loan from the National Museum of Naval Aviation; Pensacola, FL., to the Western Aerospace Museum, San Francisco-Oakland IAP, CA.

E-439 159302 Navy acceptance from NPRO Rep. LTV, Dallas, TX., 13 NOV 74 ** Transferred to VA-81/CVW-17, AA/4XX, NAS Cecil Field, FL., 14 NOV 74; To VA-81, USS Forrestal (CVA-59), 29 NOV 74; To VA-81, NAS Cecil Field, FL., 01 SEP 75; To VA-81, USS Forrestal (CV-59), 23 SEP 75; To VA-81, NAS Cecil Field, FL., 23 SEP 75; To VA-81, NAS Rooevelt Roads, PR., 23 SEP 75; To VA-81, NAS Cecil Field, FL., 23 SEP 75; To VA-81, NAS Rooevelt Roads, PR., 23 SEP 75; To VA-81, NAS Cecil Field, FL., 23 SEP 75; To VA-81, USS Forrestal (CV-59), 20 JUL 77; To VA-81, NAS Cecil Field, FL., 20 JUL 77; To VA-81, USS Forrestal (CV-59), 19 JAN 78; To VA-81, NAS Cecil Field, FL., 03 MAR 78; To VA-81, NAS Jacksonville, FL., 07 FEB 79; To VA-81, NAS Cecil Field, FL., 23 MAR 79; To VA-81, USS Forrestal (CV-59), 23 MAR 79 ** Transferred to VA-97/CVW-14, NK/3XX, NAS LeMoore, CA., 05 APR 79; To VA-97, USS Coral Sea (CV-43), 23 AUG 79; To VA-97, NAS LeMoore, CA., 12 NOV 79; To VA-97, NAS Alameda, CA., 24 OCT 80; To VA-97, USS Coral Sea (CV-43), 26 NOV 80; To VA-97, NAS LeMoore, CA., 05 JAN 81; To VA-97, USS Coral Sea (CV-43), 17 APR 81; To VA-97, NAS LeMoore, CA., 11 JUN 81; To VA-97, USS Coral Sea (CV-43), 21 JUL 81 ** Transferred to VA-122/FRS, NJ/2XX, NAS LeMoore, CA., 04 AUG 81; To VA-122, NAS Jacksonville, FL., 08 JAN 82; To VA-122, NAS LeMoore, CA., 09 MAR 82; To VA-122, NAS Dallas, TX., 18 MAY 82 ** Transferred to VA-22/CVW-11, NH/3XX, NAS LeMoore, CA., 20 MAY 82; To VA-22, USS Enterprise (CVN-65), 20 AUG 82; To VA-22, NAS LeMoore, CA., 20 AUG 82; To VA-22, USS Enterprise (CVN-65), 26 JAN 84; To VA-22, NAS Jacksonville, FL., 27 JAN 84 ** Transferred to VA-94/CVW-11, NH/4XX, NAS LeMoore, CA., 20 APR 84; To VA-94, USS Enterprise (CVN-65), 27 JUN 84; To VA-94, NAS LeMoore, CA., 03 JAN 85; To VA-94, NAS Fallon, NV., 26 APR 85; To VA-94, NAS LeMoore, CA., 03 MAY 85 ** Transferred to VA-122/FRS, NJ/2XX, NAS LeMoore, CA., 26 DEC 85 ** Transferred to VA-27/CVW-15, NL/403, NAS LeMoore, CA., 28 APR 86; To VA-27, USS Carl Vinson (CVN-70), 28 APR 86; To VA-27, NAS LeMoore, CA., 28 APR 86; To VA-27, USS Carl Vinson (CVN-70), 28 APR 86; To VA-27, NAS LeMoore, CA., 30 JAN 87; To VA-27, NAS Jacksonville, FL., 27 AUG 87; To VA-27, NAS LeMoore, CA., 27 AUG 87; To VA-27, NAS Jacksonville, FL., 02 SEP 87 ** End of flight record card ** Transferred to AMARC, Davis Monthan AFB; Tucson, AZ., assigned park code 6A0311; 29 JAN 90 ** 5680.0 flight hours ** TF41A402D engine S/N 141927 ** Storage location 210825 ** At AMARG, Davis Monthan AFB; Tucson, AZ., 15 JUN 07.

E-440 159303 Navy acceptance from NPRO Rep. LTV, Dallas, TX., 26 NOV 74 ** Transferred to VA-82/CVW-8, AJ/303, NAS Cecil Field, FL., 04 DEC 74; To VA-82, USS Nimitz (CVN-68), 19 DEC 74; To VA-82, NAS Cecil Field, FL., 01 JUL 75; To VA-82, NAS Roosevelt Roads, PR., 01 JUL 75; To VA-82, NAS Cecil Field, FL., 01 JUL 75; To VA-82, USS Nimitz (CVN-68), 01 JUL 75; To VA-82, NAS Cecil Field, FL., 01 JUL 75; To VA-82, USS Nimitz (CVN-68), 01 JUL 75; To VA-82, NAS Cecil Field, FL., 01 JUL 75; To VA-82, USS Nimitz (CVN-68), 20 JUL 77; To VA-82, NAS Cecil Field, FL., 28 JUL 78; To VA-82, NAS Jacksonville, FL., 29 JUL 78; To VA-82, NAS Cecil Field, FL., 19 SEP 78; To VA-82, USS Nimitz (CVN-68), 18 NOV 80; To VA-82, NAS Jacksonville, FL., 08 JAN 81; To VA-82, NAS Dallas, TX., 19 MAR 81** Transferred to VA-37/ CVW-3, AC/3XX, NAS Cecil Field, FL., 19 JUN 81; To VA-37, USS John F. Kennedy (CV-67), 19 JUN 81; To VA-37, NAS Cecil Field, FL., 20 JUN 81; To VA-37, USS John F. Kennedy (CV-67), 20 JUN 81; To VA-37, NAS Cecil Field, FL., 20 JUN 81 ** Transferred to VA-105/CVW-15, NL/4XX, NAS Cecil Field, FL., 16 SEP 82; To VA-105, USS Carl Vinson (CVN-70), 16 SEP 82; To VA-105, NAS Cecil Field, FL., 16 SEP 82 ** Transferred to VA-83/CVW-17, AA/3XX, NAS Cecil Field, FL., 23 FEB 83; To VA-83, NAS Fallon, NV., 05 AUG 83; To VA-83, NAS Cecil Field, FL., 06 AUG 83; To VA-83, NAS Jacksonville, FL., 30 SEP 83; To VA-83, USS Saratoga (CV-60), 27 JAN 84; To VA-83, NAS Cecil Field, FL., 27 JAN 84; To VA-83, NAS Fallon, NV., 07 DEC 84; To VA-83, NAS Cecil Field, FL., 07 DEC 84; To VA-83, USS Saratoga (CV-60), 19 APR 85; To

VA-83, NAS Cecil Field, FL.,19 APR 85; To VA-83, USS Saratoga (CV-60), 19 APR 85; To VA-83, NAS Jacksonville, FL., 05 MAY 86; To VA-83, NAS Cecil Field, FL., 29 MAY 86; To VA-83, NAS Jacksonville, FL., 10 JUN 86; To VA-83, NAS Cecil Field, FL., 12 JUL 86; To VA-83, USS Saratoga (CV-60), 12 JUL 86; To VA-83, NAS Cecil Field, FL., 03 OCT 86; To VA-83, USS Saratoga (CV-60), 09 OCT 86; To VA-83, NAS Cecil Field, FL., 09 OCT 86; To VA-83, USS Saratoga (CV-60), 09 OCT 86; To VA-83, NAS Cecil Field, FL., 06 MAY 87; To VA-83, USS Saratoga (CV-60), 20 MAY 87 ** End of flight record card ** On display at Edwardsville Township, IL.

E-441 159304 Navy acceptance from NPRO Rep. LTV, Dallas, TX., 06 DEC 74 ** Transferred to VA-113/CVW-2, NE/3XX, NAS LeMoore, CA., 10 DEC 74; To VA-113, USS Ranger (CV-61), 16 AUG 75; To VA-113, NAS LeMoore, CA., 23 JUN 77; To VA-113, NAS Jacksonville, FL., 18 JUN 78; To VA-113, USS Ranger (CV-61), 03 AUG 78; To VA-113, NAS LeMoore, CA., 03 AUG 78; To VA-113, NAS Jacksonville, FL.,30 NOV 78; To VA-113, NAS LeMoore, CA., 30 NOV 78; To VA-113, USS Ranger (CV-61), 22 MAR 79; To VA-113, NAS Cubi Point, PI., 02 JUL 79; To VA-113, NAS LeMoore, CA., 11 DEC 79; To VA-113, NAS Fallon, NV., 28 DEC 79; To VA-113, NAS LeMoore, CA., 26 JAN 80; To VA-113, USS Ranger (CV-61), 05 MAY 80; To VA-113, NAS LeMoore, CA., 09 JUL 80; To VA-113, USS Ranger (CV-61), 18 JUL 80; To VA-113, NAS Cubi Point, PI., 24 OCT 80; To VA-113, USS Ranger (CV-61), 04 MAY 81; To VA-113, NAS LeMoore, CA., 22 MAY 81; To VA-113, NAS Jacksonville, FL., 13 JUL 81; To VA-113, NAS Dallas, TX., 15 JUL 81; To VA-113, NAS LeMoore, CA., 28 JUL 81; To VA-113, NAS Dallas, TX., 29 JUL 81; To VA-113, Fallon, NV., 29 JUL 81; To VA-113, USS Ranger (CV-61), 29 JUL 81; To VA-113, NAS LeMoore, CA., 05 OCT 81; To VA-113, USS Ranger (CV-61), 14 JAN 82; To VA-113, NAS LeMoore, CA., 14 JAN 82; To VA-113, USS Ranger (CV-61), 26 FEB 82; To VA-113, NAS Cubi Point, PI., 26 FEB 82; To VA-113, NAF Atsugi, JP., 26 AUG 82 ** Transferred to VA-93/CVW-5, NF/3XX, NAS Cubi Point, PI., 27 SEP 82; To VA-93, NAF Atsugi, JP., 13 OCT 82; To VA-93, NAS Cubi Point, PI., 25 OCT 82; To VA-93, NAF Atsugi, JP., 15 NOV 82; To VA-93, USS Midway (CV-41), 12 DEC 82; To VA-93, NAF Atsugi, JP., 27 AUG 83 ** Transferred to VA-147/CVW-9, NE/3XX, 23 APR 86; To VA-147, NAS Jacksonville, FL., 18 AUG 86; To VA-147, NAS LeMoore, CA., 30 OCT 86; To VA-147, USS Kitty, Hawk (CV-63), 30 OCT 86; To VA-147, NAS LeMoore, CA., 16 APR 87 thru 16 SEP 87 ** End of flight record card ** Transferred to VA-94/CVW-11, NH/4XX, NAS LeMoore, CA., date unknown ** Transferred to AMARC, Davis Monthan AFB; Tucson, AZ., assigned park code 6A0289; 19 MAY 89 ** 5835.7 flight hours ** TF41A402D engine S/N 142541 ** Storage location 210427 ** Aircraft deleted from inventory and released to DRMO for disposition, 03 MAY 06 ** At AMARG, Davis Monthan AFB; Tucson, AZ., 15 JUN 07.

E-442 159305 Navy acceptance from NPRO Rep. LTV, Dallas, TX., 19 NOV 74 ** Transferred to VA-86/CVW-8, AJ/402, NAS Cecil Field, FL., 25 NOV 74; To VA-86, USS Nimitz (CVN-68), 23 DEC 74; To VA-86, NAS Cecil Field, FL., 23 DEC 74; To VA-86, NAS Roosevelt Roads, PR., 23 DEC 74; To VA-86, NAS Cecil Field, FL., 23 DEC 74; To VA-86, USS Nimitz (CVN-68), 23 DEC 74; To VA-86, NAS Cecil Field, FL., 23 DEC 74; To VA-86, USS Nimitz (CVN-68), 23 DEC 74; To VA-86, NAS Cecil Field, FL., 30 JUN 75; To VA-86, NAS Roosevelt Roads, PR., 19 JUL 77; To VA-86, USS Nimitz (CVN-68), 19 JUL 77; To VA-86, NAS Cecil Field, FL., 19 JUL 77; To VA-86, USS Nimitz (CVN-68), 19 JUL 77; To VA-86, NAS Jacksonville, FL., 18 JUL 78; To VA-86, NAS Cecil Field, FL., 16 AUG 78; To VA-86, NAS Roosevelt Roads, PR., 16 AUG 78; To VA-86, NAS Cecil Field, FL., 16 AUG 78; To VA-86, USS Nimitz (CVN-68), 16 AUG 78; To VA-86, NAS Cecil Field, FL., 16 AUG 78; To VA-86, USS Nimitz (CVN-68), 22 APR 80 ~ S 1SO, strike, 22 APR 80 ** Crashed in Indian Ocean on takeoff, pilot ejected.

E-443 159306 Navy acceptance from NPRO Rep. LTV, Dallas, TX., 12 DEC 74 ** Transferred to VA-86/CVW-8, AJ-402, NAS Cecil Field, FL., 17 DEC 74; To VA-86, USS Nimitz (CVN-68), 29 JAN 75; To VA-86, NAS Cecil Field, FL., 29 JAN 75; To VA-86, NAS Roosevelt Roads, PR., 29 JAN 75; To VA-86, NAS Cecil Field, FL., 29 JAN 75; To VA-86, USS Nimitz (CVN-68), 29 JAN 75; To VA-86, NAS Cecil Field, FL., 29 JAN 75; To VA-86, USS Nimitz (CVN-68), 29 JAN 75; To VA-86, NAS Cecil Field, FL., 30 JUN 75; To VA-86, NAS Roosevelt Roads, PR., 30 JUN 75; To VA-86, USS Nimitz (CVN-68), 19 JUL 77; To VA-86, NAS Cecil Field, FL., 19 JUL 77; To VA-86, USS Nimitz (CVN-68), 19 JUL 77; To VA-86, NAS Cecil Field, FL., 18 APR 78; To VA-86, NAS Jacksonville, FL., 09 SEP 78; To VA-86, NAS Roosevelt Roads, PR., 16 NOV 78; To VA-86, NAS Cecil Field, FL., 16 NOV 78; To VA-86, USS Nimitz (CVN-68), 16 NOV 78; To VA-86, NAS Cecil Field, FL., 16 NOV 78; To VA-86, USS Nimitz (CVN-68), 18 JUN 80; To VA-86, NAS Cecil Field, FL., 01 JUL 80; To VA-86, NAS Jacksonville, FL., 20 APR 81; To VA-86, USS Nimitz (CVN-68), 21 APR 81; To VA-86, NAS Cecil Field, FL., 21 APR 81; To VA-86, NAS Dallas, TX., 07 JUL 81 ** Transferred to VA-15/CVW-6, AE/3XX, NAS Cecil Field, FL., 09 SEP 81; To VA-15, USS Independence (CV-62), 10 SEP 81; To VA-15, NAS Cecil Field, Fl. 10 SEP 81; To VA-15, USS Independence (CV-62), 10 SEP 81 ** Transferred to VA-86/CVW-8, AJ-402, NAS Cecil Field, FL., 09 MAR 82; To VA-86, USS Nimitz (CVN-68), 10 MAY 82; To VA-86, NAS Cecil Field, FL., 31 AUG 82; To VA-86, USS Nimitz (CVN-68), 31 AUG 82; To VA-86, NAS Cecil Field, FL., 25 OCT 82; To VA-86, USS Nimitz (CVN-68), 30 OCT 82; To VA-86, NAS Cecil Field, FL., 27 MAY 83; To VA-86, NAS Jacksonville, FL., 28 OCT 83; To VA-86, NAS Cecil Field, FL., 07 FEB 84 ** Transferred to VA-105/CVW-15, NL/ 4XX, NAS Cecil Field, FL., 27 MAR 84; To VA-105, NAF Kadena, JP., 27 MAR 84; To VA-105, NAS Cubi Point, PI., 27 MAR 84; To VA-105, MCAS Iwakuni, JP., 27 MAR 84; To VA-105, NAS Cecil Field, FL., 27 MAR 84 ** Transferred to VA-174/FRS, AD/4XX, NAS Cecil Field, FL., 30 JAN 85; To VA-174, NAS Jacksonville, FL., 19 FEB 86; To VA-174, NAS Cecil Field, FL., 07 MAR 86; To VA-174, NAS Jacksonville, FL., 21 APR 86 ** Transferred to VA-81/CVW-17, AA/4XX, NAS Cecil Field, FL., 22 APR 86; To VA-81, USS Saratoga (CV-60), 25 SEP 86; To VA-81, NAS Cecil Field, FL., 05 OCT 86; To VA-81, USS Saratoga (CV-60), 09 OCT 86; To VA-81, NAS Cecil Field, FL., 07 APR 87; To VA-81, USS Saratoga (CV-60), 09 APR 87; To VA-81, NAS Cecil Field, FL., 09 APR 87; To VA-81, USS Saratoga (CV-60), 09 APR 87 ** End of flight record card ** Transferred to NAD Jacksonville, FL., 23 JUN 88 ** Transferred to VA-46/CVW-7, AG/311, USS Dwight D. Eisenhower (CVN-69), date unknown; To VA-46, NAS Cecil Field, FL., date unknown ** Transferred to AMARC, Davis Monthan AFB; Tucson, AZ., assigned park code 6A0374, 02 AUG 90 ** 6280.4 flight hours ** TF41A402D engine S/N 141243 ** Storage location 111519 ** At AMARG, Davis Monthan AFB; Tucson, AZ., 15 JUN 07.

E-444 159307 Navy acceptance from NPRO Rep. LTV, Dallas, TX., 17 DEC 74 ** Transferred to VA-82/CVW-8, AJ/3XX, NAS Cecil Field, FL., 18 DEC 74; To VA-82, USS Nimitz (CVN-68), 27 JAN 75; To VA-82, NAS Cecil Field, FL., 01 JUL 75; To VA-82, NAS Roosevelt Roads, PR., 05 NOV 75; To VA-82, NAS Cecil Field, FL., 06 NOV 75; To VA-82, USS Nimitz (CVN-68), 06 NOV 75; To VA-82, NAS Cecil Field, FL., 06 NOV 75; To VA-82, USS Nimitz (CVN-68), 06 NOV 75; To VA-82, NAS Cecil Field, FL., 07 JUN 76; To VA-82, USS Nimitz (CVN-68), 22 JUN 76; To VA-82, NAS Cecil Field, FL., 22 JUN 76; To VA-82, USS Nimitz (CVN-68), 20 JUL 77; To VA-82, NAS Cecil Field, FL., 03 AUG 78; To VA-82, NAS Jacksonville, FL., 04 AUG 78; To VA-82, NAS Cecil Field, FL., 28 SEP 78; To VA-82, USS Nimitz (CVN-68), 09 OCT 79; To VA-82, NAS Cecil Field, FL., 26 AUG 80; To VA-82, USS Nimitz (CVN-68), 26 MAR 81 ** Transferred to VA-174/ FRS, AD/4XX, NAS Cecil Field, FL., 06 MAY 81; To VA-174, NAS Jacksonville, FL., 19 OCT 81; To VA-174, NAS Dallas, TX., 08 JAN 82 ** Transferred to VA-86/CVW-8, AJ/4XX, NAS Cecil Field, FL., 22 MAR 82; To VA-86, USS Nimitz (CVN-68), 22 MAR 82; To

VA-86, NAS Cecil Field, FL., 22 MAR 82; To VA-86, USS Nimitz (CVN-68), 22 MAR 82; To VA-86, NAS Cecil Field, FL., 05 JUL 83; To VA-86, NAS Roosevelt Roads, PR., 30 AUG 83; To VA-86, NAS Cecil Field, FL., 30 AUG 83; To VA-86, NAS Cecil Field, FL., 11 JAN 84; To VA-86, NAS Roodevelt Roads, PR., 10 AUG 84; To VA-86, NAS Cecil Field, FL., 09 SEP 84 ** Transferred to NARF, NAS Jacksonville, FL., 03 OCT 84 ** Transferred to VA-86/CVW-8, AJ/4XX, NAS Cecil Field, FL., 10 FEB 86; To VA-86, USS Nimitz (CVN-68), 12 MAR 86; To VA-86, NAS Cecil Field, FL., 2 MAR 86; To VA-86, USS Nimitz (CVN-68), 12 MAR 86; To VA-86, NAS Cecil Field, FL., 10 OCT 86; To VA-86, USS Nimitz (CVN-68), 10 OCT 86; To VA-86, NAS Cecil Field, FL., 10 OCT 86 ** Transferred to VA-174/FRS, AD/4XX, NAS Cecil Field, FL., 17 AUG 87 ~ S 1SO strike, 02 SEP 87 ** Crashed on Takeoff, pilot ejected safely.

E-445 159308 Navy acceptance from NPRO Rep. LTV, Dallas, TX., 16 DEC 74 ** Transferred to VA-86/CVW-8, AJ/4XX, Cecil Field, FL., 18 DEC 74; To VA-86, USS Nimitz (CVAN-68), 18 DEC 74; To VA-86, NAS Cecil Field, FL., 18 DEC 74; To VA-86, NAS Roosevelt Roads, PR., 18 DEC 74; To VA-86, NAS Cecil Field, FL., 18 DEC 74; To VA-86, USS Nimitz (CVAN-68), 18 DEC 74; To VA-86, NAS Cecil Field, FL., 18 DEC 74; To VA-86, USS Nimitz (CVAN-68), 18 DEC 74; To VA-86, NAS Cecil Field, FL., 30 JUN 75; To VA-86, NAS Roosevelt Roads, PR., 30 JUN 75; To VA-86, USS Nimitz (CVN-68), 19 JUL 77; To VA-86, NAS Cecil Field, FL., 19 JUL 77; To VA-86, USS Nimitz (CVN-68), 19 JUL 77; To VA-86, Cecil Field, FL., 10 AUG 78; To VA-86, NAS Jacksonville, FL., 11 AUG 78; To VA-86, Cecil Field, FL., 26 SEP 78; To VA-86. USS Nimitz (CVN-68), 26 SEP 76; To VA-86, NAS Cecil Field, FL., 26 SEP 78; To VA-86, NAS Roosevelt Roads, PR., 26 SEP 78; To VA-86, NAS Cecil Field, FL., 26 SEP 78; To VA-86, USS Nimitz (CVN-68), 26 SEP 78; To VA-86, NAS Cecil Field, FL., 26 SEP 78; To VA-86, USS Nimitz (CVN-68), 17 DEC 80; To VA-86, NAS Cecil Field, FL., 23 DEC 80; To VA-86, NAS Jacksonville, FL., 10 MAR 81; To VA-86, NAS Cecil Field, FL., 23 APR 81; To VA-86, USS Nimitz CVN-68), 14 MAY 81; To VA-86, NAS Cecil Field, FL., 14 MAY 81; To VA-86, USS Nimitz (CVN-68), 14 MAY 81; To VA-86, NAS Cecil Field, FL., 14 MAY 81 ** Transferred to VA-12/CVW-7, AG/4XX, USS Dwight D. Eisenhower (CVN-69), 25 JAN 82; To VA-12, NAS Cecil Field, FL., 25 JAN 82; To VA-12, NAS Jacksonville, FL., 14 SEP 82; To VA-12, NAS Cecil Field, FL., 22 NOV 82; To VA-12, USS Dwight D. Eisenhower (CVN-69), 30 NOV 82 ** Transferred to VA-83/CVW-17, AA/3XX, NAS Cecil Field, FL., 02 MAR 83 ** Transferred to VA-46/CVW-1, AB/3XX, NAS Cecil Field, FL., 16 SEP 83; To VA-46, USS America (CV-66), 16 SEP 83; To VA-46, NAS Cecil Field, FL., 16 SEP 83; To VA-46, USS America (CV-66), 16 SEP 83; To VA-46, NAS Cecil Field, FL., 16 SEP 83; To VA-46, USS America (CV-66), 16 SEP 83; To VA-46, NAS Cecil Field, FL., 16 SEP 83 ** Transferred to VA-83/CVW-17, AA/3XX, NAS Fallon, NV., 04 DEC 84; To VA-83, NAS Cecil Field, FL., 04 DEC 84; To VA-83, NAS JacksonVille, FL., 16 APR 85; To VA-83, USS Saratoga (CV-60), 29 APR 85; To VA-83, NAS Cecil Field, FL., 29 MAY 85; To VA-83, NAS JacksonVille, FL., 29 JUN 85; To VA-83, NAS Cecil Field, FL., 02 JUL 85; To VA-83, USS Saratoga (CV-60), 05 AUG 85; To VA-83, NAS Cecil Field, FL., 12 AUG 85 ** Transferred to VA-66/CVW-7, AG/3XX, NAS Cecil Field, FL., 12 JUN 86; To VA-66, USS John F. Kennedy (CV-67), 29 JUL 86 ** Transferred to VA-105/ CVW-6, AE/4XX, USS Forrestal (CV-59), 29 OCT 86; To VA-105, NAS Cecil Field, FL., 10 NOV 86; To VA-105, USS Forrestal (CV-59), 01 JUN 87; Transferred to VA-174/ FRS, AD/4XX, NAS Cecil Field, FL., 13 AUG 87 thru 27 AUG 87 ** End of flight record card ** Transferred to NAD, NAS Jacksonville, FL., 20 APR 88 ** Transferred to VA-72/CVW-7, AG/401, USS Dwight D. Eisenhower (CVN-69), date unknown; To VA-72, NAS Cecil Field, FL., date unknown ** Transferred to AMARC, Davis Monthan AFB; Tucson, AZ., assigned park code 6A0341, 17 APR 90 ** 6735.1 flight hours ** TF41A402D engine S/N AE141475 ** Storage location 211844 ** At AMARC, Davis Monthan AFB; Tucson, AZ., 15 JUN 07.

159638/159661 LTV A-7E Corsair II; (Block XVII)
FY 74 Contract N00019-74-C-0126, (24) A-7E; E-447/E-470

E-470 159638 Navy acceptance from NPRO Rep. LTV, Dallas, TX., 09 JAN 75 ** Transferred to VA-82/CVW-8, AJ/3XX, NAS Cecil Field, FL., 11 JAN 75; To VA-82, USS Nimitz (CVAN-68), 11 JAN 75; To VA-82, NAS Cecil Field, FL., 01 JUL 75; To VA-82, NAS Roosevelt Roads, PR., 01 JUL 75 ** Transferred to VA-15/CVW-6, AE/3XX, NAS Cecil Field, FL., 11 NOV 75; To VA-15, USS America (CV-66), 11 NOV 75; To VA-15, MCAS Yuma, AZ., 07 JAN 77; To VA-15, USS America (CV-66), 07 JAN 77; To VA-15, NAS Jacksonville, FL., 30 AUG 77; To VA-15, USS America (CV-66), 21 SEP 77; To VA-15, NAS Jacksonville, FL., 08 MAY 78; To VA-15, NAS Cecil Field, FL., 10 MAY 78; To VA-15, NAS Jacksonville, FL., 02 JUN 78; To VA-15, NAS Cecil Field, FL., 05 JUN 78; To VA-15, NAS Roosevelt Roads, PR., 14 AUG 78; To VA-15, USS America (CV-66), 14 AUG 78; To VA-15, NAS Cecil Field, FL., 14 AUG 78; To VA-15, USS Independence (CV-62), 14 AUG 78; To VA-15, NAS Cecil Field, FL., 14 AUG 78 ** Transferred to VA-37/CVW-3, AC/3XX, USS Saratoga (CV-60), 22 OCT 79; To VA-37, NAS Cecil Field, FL., 22 OCT 79 ** Transferred to VA-83/CVW-17, AA/315, NAS Cecil Field, FL., 08 NOV 79; To VA-83, USS Forrestal (CV-59), 07 SEP 80; To VA-83, NAS Cecil Field, FL. 07 SEP 80; To VA-83, USS Forrestal (CV-59), 07 SEP 80; To VA-83, NAS Cecil Field, FL., 14 AUG 81 ** Transferred to VA-174/FRS, AD/4XX, NAS Cecil Field, FL., 04 NOV 81; To VA-174, NAS Jacksonville, FL., 21 MAY 82; Transferred to VA-82/CVW-8, AJ/3XX, NAS Cecil Field, FL., 07 JUL 82; To VA-82, USS Nimitz (CVN-68), 07 JUL 82; To VA-82, NAS Cecil Field, FL., 07 JUL 82; To VA-82, USS Nimitz (CVN-68), 07 JUL 82; To VA-82, NAS Cecil Field, FL., 07 JUL 82; To VA-82, NAS Jacksonville, FL., 28 MAR 84; To VA-82, NAS Cecil Field, FL., 28 MAR 84; To VA-82, NAS Jacksonville, FL., 29 MAR 84 ** Transferred to VA-37/CVW-6, AE/300, NAS Cecil Field, FL., 08 JUN 84; To VA-37, MCAS Twenty Nine Palms, CA., 19 AUG 84; To VA-37, NAS Cecil Field, FL., 06 SEP 84; To VA-37, MCAS Iwakuni, JP., 06 SEP 84; To VA-37, Korea, 06 SEP 84; To VA-37, MCAS Iwakuni, JP., 06 SEP 84; To VA-37, NAS Cecil Field, FL., 06 SEP 84; To VA-37, USS Forrestal (CV-59), 17 DEC 85; To VA-37, NAS Cecil Field, FL., 17 DEC 85; To VA-37, USS Forrestal (CV-59), 17 DEC 85; To VA-37, NAS Cecil Field, FL., 25 NOV 86; To VA-37, USS Forrestal (CV-59), 16 DEC 86; To VA-37, NAS Ceil Field, FL., date unknown ** End of flight record card ** Transferred to AMARG, Davis Monthan AFB; Tucson, AZ., assigned park code 6A0231; 14 AUG 87 ** 5731.1 flight hours ** TF41A2C engine S/N 142573 ** Storage location 210532 ** At AMARG, Davis Monthan AFB; Tucson, AZ., 15 JUN 07.

E-447 159639 Navy acceptance from NPRO Rep. LTV, Dallas, TX., 16 JAN 75 ** Transferred to VA-147/CVW-9, NG/4XX, USS Constellation (CV-64), 22 JAN 75; To VA-147, NAS LeMoore, CA., 17 MAR 75; To VA-147, NAS Fallon, NV., 26 MAY 75; To VA-147, NAS LeMoore, CA., 05 JUN 75; To VA-147, MCAS Yuma, AZ., 21 OCT 75; To VA-147, NAS LeMoore, CA., 28 OCT 75; To VA-147, USS Constellation (CV-64), 24 AUG 76; To VA-147, NAS LeMoore, CA., 24 AUG 76; To VA-147, USS Constellation (CV-64), 23 JUL 77; To VA-147, NAS LeMoore, CA., 26 OCT 77 ** Transferred to VA-93/ CVW-5, NF/3XX, USS Midway (CV-41), 03 NOV 77; To VA-93, NAF Atsugi, JP., 16 JAN 78; To VA-93, USS Midway (CV-41), 18 JAN 78; To VA-93, NAF Atsugi, JP., 05 JUN 78; To VA-93, USS Midway (CV-41), 30 SEP 79; To VA-93, NAF Atsugi, JP., 30 SEP 79 ** Transferred to VA-147/CVW- 9, NG/4XX, NAS Cubi Point, PI., 21 APR 80; To VA-147, USS Constellation (CV-64), 18 SEP 80; To VA-147, NAS LeMoore, CA., 18 SEP 80; To VA-147, NAS Jacksonville, FL., 13 NOV 80; To VA-147, NAS Dallas, TX., 21 JAN 80; To VA-147, USS Constellation (CV-64), 30 APR 81; To VA-147, NAS LeMoore, CA., 24 MAY 81 ** Transferred to VA-122/ FRS, NJ/2XX, NAS LeMoore, CA.., 05 JUN 81; To VA-122, NAS Jacksonville, FL., 09 DEC 82; To VA-122, NAS LeMoore, CA., 18 MAR 83; To VA-122, NAS Jacksonville, FL., 09 NOV 84; To VA-122, NAS LeMoore, CA., 03 APR 85; To VA-122, NAS Jacksonville, FL., 07 DEC 85; To VA-122, NAS LeMoore, CA., 16 DEC 85; To VA-122, NAS Jacksonville, FL., 24 JAN 86; To VA-122, NAS LeMoore, CA., 28 JAN 86; To VA-122, NAS Jacksonville, FL., 12 MAR 86; To

VA-122, NAS LeMoore, CA., 15 MAR 86 thru 20 JAN 87 ** End of flight record card ** Transferred to AMARC, Davis Monthan AFB; Tucson, AZ., assigned park code 6A0373, 01 AUG 90 ** 5745.3 flight hours ** TF41A402D engine S/N 141483 ** Aircraft released from storage and prepared for overland above deck shipment to the government of Greece, 11 AUG 94 ** Transferred to the Helenic Air force (Greece).

E-448 159640 Navy acceptance from NPRO Rep. LTV, Dallas, TX., 14 FEB 75 ** Transferred to VA-174/FRS, AD/4XX, NAS Cecil Field, FL., 22 FEB 75 ** Transferred to VA-87/CVW-6, AE/4XX, NAS Cecil Field, FL., 17 NOV 75; To VA-87, USS Saratoga (CV-60), 17 NOV 75; To VA 87, USS America (CV-66), 24 JAN 76; To VA-87, NAS Cecil Field, FL., 24 MAR 76; To VA-87, MCAS Yuma, AZ., 20 APR 76; To VA-87, NAS Jacksonville, FL., 24 JAN 77; To VA 87, USS America (CV-66), 25 FEB 77; To VA-87, NAS Cecil Field, FL., 25 FEB 77; To VA 87, USS America (CV-66), 19 JUL 77; To VA-87, NAS Cecil Field, FL., 01 AUG 78; To VA-87, NAS Jacksonville, FL., 20 SEP 78; To VA-87, NAS Roosevelt Roads, PR., 23 OCT 78; To VA-87, NAS Cecil Field, FL., 23 OCT 78; To VA-87, USS Independence (CV-62), 23 OCT 78; To VA-87, NAS Cecil Field, FL., 23 OCT 78; To VA-87, USS Independence (CV-62), 04 AUG 80; To VA-87, NAS Cecil Field, FL., 04 AUG 80; To VA-87, USS Independence (CV-62), 11 JUL 81; To VA-87, NAS Cecil Field, FL., 11 JUL 81; To VA-87, NAS Jacksonville, FL., 01 APR 82; To VA-87, NAS Dallas, TX., 02 JUN 82; To VA-87, USS Independence (CV-62), 09 JUN 82 ** Transferred to VA-66/CVW-7, AG/3XX, NAS Cecil Field, 01 SEP 82; To VA-66, USS Dwight D. Eisenhower (CVN-69), 02 SEP 82; To VA-66, NAS Cecil Field, FL., 03 JUL 83 ** Transferred to VA-15/CVW-6, AE/3XX, USS Independence CV-62), 11 DEC 83 ** Transferred to VA-105/CVW-15, NL/4XX, NAS Cecil Field, FL., 01 MAR 84 ** Transferred to VA-15/CVW-6, AE/3XX, NAS Cecil Field, FL., 09 MAY 84; To VA-15, USS Independence (CV-62), 20 JUL 84; To VA-15, NAS Jacksonville, FL., 11 SEP 84; To VA-15, USS Independence (CV-62), 11 SEP 84; To VA-15, NAS Jacksonville, FL., 29 NOV 84 ** Transferred to VA-72/CVW-1, AB/4XX, NAS Cecil Field, FL., 29 NOV 84; To VA-72, USS America (CV-66), 05 FEB 85; To VA-72, NAS Cecil Field, FL., 03 FEB 85; To VA-72, USS America (CV-66), 05 FEB 85; To VA-72, NAS Cecil Field, FL., 05 FEB 85 ** Transferred to VA-86/CVW-8, AJ/4XX, USS Nimitz (CVN-68), 02 DEC 86; To VA-86, NAS Cecil Field, FL., 02 DEC 86 ** Transferred to VA-174/FRS, AD/4XX, NAS Cecil Field, FL., 04 AUG 87; To VA-174, NAS Jacksonville, FL., 09 SEP 87 ** End of flight record card ** Transferred to the Helinic Air Force (Greece).

E-449 159641 Navy acceptance from NPRO Rep. LTV, Dallas, TX., 17 JAN 75 ** Transferred to VA-174/FRS, AD/4XX, NAS Cecil Field, FL., 22 JAN 75 ** Transferred to VA-87/CVW-6, AE/406, USS Saratoga (CV-60), 06 DEC 75; To VA-87, NAS Cecil Field, FL., 06 DEC 75; To VA-87, USS America (CV-66), 06 DEC 75; To VA-87, NAS Cecil Field, FL., 06 DEC 87; To VA-87, MCAS Yuma, AZ., 06 DEC 75; To VA-87, USS America (CV-66), 06 DEC 75 ~ S 1SO strike, 18 MAY 77 ** No data on strike.

E-450 159642 Navy acceptance from NPRO Rep. LTV, Dallas, TX., 04 FEB 75 ** Transferred to VA-174/FRS, AD/4XX, NAS Cecil Field, FL., 06 FEB 75 ** Transferred to VA-15/CVW-6, AE/307, NAS Cecil Field, FL., 11 DEC 75; To VA-15, USS America (CV-66), 11 DEC 75; To VA-15, MCAS Yuma, AZ., 19 NOV 76; To VA-15, NAS Cecil Field, FL., 31 JAN 77; To VA-15, USS America (CV-66), 28 FEB 77; To VA-15, NAS Cecil Field, FL., 19 JUL 77; To VA-15, USS America (CV-66), 19 JUL 77; To VA-15, NAS Cecil Field, FL., 02 FEB 78; To VA-15, NAS Jacksonville, FL., 20 MAR 78; To VA-15, USS America (CV-66), 21 MAR 78; To VA-15, NAS Cecil Field, FL., 20 APR 78; To VA-15, NAS Roosevelt Roads, PR., 09 AUG 78; To VA-15, USS America (CV-66), 09 AUG 78; To VA-15, NAS Cecil Field, FL., 09 AUG 78; To VA-15, USS Independence (CV-62), 09 AUG 78; To VA-15, NAS Cecil Field, FL., 09 AUG 78; To VA-15, USS Independence (CV-62), 09 AUG 78; To VA-15, NAS Cecil Field, FL., 10 MAR 80; To VA-15, USS Independence (CV-62), 11 MAR 80 ** Transferred to VA-22/CVW-15, NL/3XX, USS Kitty Hawk (CV-63), 24 OCT 80;

To VA-22, NAS LeMoore, CA., 13 JAN 81; To VA-22, USS Kitty Hawk (CV-63), 30 JAN 81; To VA-22, NAS LeMoore, CA., 25 MAR 81 ** Transferred to VA-122/FRS, NJ/2XX, NAS LeMoore, CA., 07 JUN 82; To VA-122, NAS Jacksonville, FL., 17 DEC 82; To VA-122, NAS LeMoore, CA., 18 DEC 82; To VA-122, NAS Jacksonville, FL., 27 DEC 82; To VA-122, NAS LeMoore, CA., 01 MAR 83; To VA-122, NAS Jacksonville, FL., 27 MAR 85 ** Transferred to VA-192/CVW-11, NH/3XX, NAS LeMoore, CA., 09 APR 85; To VA-192, NAS Cubi Point, PI., 09 SEP 85; To VA-192, NAS LeMoore, CA., 09 SEP 85 ** Transferred to VA-27/CVW-15, NL/4XX, NAS LeMoore, CA., 19 DEC 85; To VA-27, USS Carl Vinson (CVN-70), 23 APR 86; To VA-27, NAS LeMoore, CA., 23 APR 86; To VA-27, USS Carl Vinson (CVN-70), 12 AUG 86 ~ S 1SO strike, 12 AUG 86 ** No data on strike.

E-451 159643 Navy acceptance from NPRO Rep. LTV, Dallas, TX., 14 MAR 75 ** Transferred to VA-174/FRS, AD/4XX, NAS Cecil Field, FL., 15 MAR 75 ** Transferred to VA-87/CVW-6, AE/4XX, USS Saratoga (CV-60), 11 NOV 75; To VA-87, USS America (CV-66), 19 FEB 76; To VA-87, NAS Cecil Field, FL., 12 MAR 76; To VA-87, USS America (CV-66), 12 MAR 76; To VA-87, NAS Cecil Field, FL., 12 MAR 76; To VA-87, MCAS Yuma, AZ., 12 MAR 76; To VA-87, NAS Cecil Field, FL., 19 FEB 77; To VA-87, USS America (CV-66), 22 FEB 77; To VA-87, NAS Cecil Field, FL., 23 MAR 77; To VA-87, USS America (CV-66), 19 JUL 77; To VA-87, NAS Jacksonville, FL., 19 APR 78; To VA-87, NAS Cecil Field, FL., 12 MAY 78; To VA-87, NAS Roosevelt Roads, PR., 13 SEP 78; To VA-87, NAS Cecil Field, FL., 13 SEP 78 ~ S 1SO strike, 06 FEB 79 ** No data on strike.

E-452 159644 Navy acceptance from NPRO Rep. LTV, Dallas, TX., 16 APR 75 ** Transferred to VA-147/CVW-9, NG/ 4XX, NAS LeMoore, CA., 19 APR 75; To VA-147, NAS Fallon, NV., 26 MAY 75; To VA-147, NAS LeMoore, CA., 05 JUN 75; To VA-147, MCAS Yuma, AZ., 31 OCT 75; To VA-147, NAS LeMoore, CA., 31 OCT 75; To VA-147, USS Constellation (CV-64), 30 SEP 76; To VA-147, NAS LeMoore, CA., 22 OCT 76; To VA-147, USS Constellation (CV-64), 23 JUL 77; To VA-147, NAS LeMoore, CA., 19 NOV 77; To VA-147, NAS Jacksonville, FL., 20 JAN 78; To VA-147, NAS LeMoore, CA., 16 FEB 78; To VA-147, USS Constellation (CV-64), 28 AUG 78 ** Transferred to VA-192/CVW-11, NH/3XX, NAS LeMoore, CA., 05 SEP 78 ** Transferred to VA-27/CVW-14, NK/4XX, NAS LeMoore, CA., 23 NOV 78; To VA-27, NPTR El Centro, CA., 09 MAR 79; To VA-27, NAS LeMoore, CA., 24 OCT 79; To VA-27, USS Coral Sea (CVA- 43), 3 DEC 79; To VA-27, NAS LeMoore, CA., 27 MAR 80; To VA-27, USS Coral Sea (CVA- 43), 16 APR 81; To VA-27, NAS LeMoore, CA., 11 JUN 81; To VA-27, NAS Jacksonville, FL., 07 JUL 81 ** Transferred to VFA-125/FRS, NJ/5XX, NAS LeMoore, CA., 25 AUG 81 ** Transferred to VA-122/FRS, NJ/2XX, NAS LeMoore, CA., 29 APR 82; To VA-122, NAS Jacksonville, FL., 01 OCT 83 ** Transferred to VA-22/CVW-11, NH/3XX, NAS LeMoore, CA., 05 MAR 84; To VA-22, USS Enterprise (CVN-65), 21 MAY 84 ** Transferred to VA-56/CVW-5, NF/4XX, NAF Atsugi, JP., 18 NOV 84; To VA-56, NAS LeMoore, CA., 27 MAR 86 ** Transferred to FS FAWPRA, NAF Atsugi, JP., 28 APR 86 ** Transferred to VA-22/CVW-11, NH/3XX, USS Enterprise (CVN-65), 19 JUL 86; To VA-22, NAS LeMoore, CA., 27 AUG 86 thru 04 MAY 87 ** End of flight record card.

E-453 159645 Navy acceptance from NPRO Rep. LTV, Dallas, TX., 26 FEB 75 ** Transferred to VA-146/CVW-9, NG/3XX, NAS LeMoore, CA., 28 FEB 75; To VA-146, NAS Fallon, NV., 27 MAY 75; To VA-146, NAS LeMoore, CA., 23 JUN 75; To VA-146, USS Constellation (CV-64), 14 MAY 76; To VA-146, NAS LeMoore, CA., 15 DEC 76; To VA-146, USS Constellation (CV-64), 13 JAN 77; To VA-146, NAS LeMoore, CA., 21 JAN 77; To VA-146, NAS Cubi Point, PI., 14 MAY 77; To VA-146, USS Constellation (CV-64), 31 AUG 77; To VA-146, NAS LeMoore, CA., 19 NOV 77; To VA-146, NAS Jacksonville, FL., 10 APR 78; To VA-146, NAS Fallon, NV., 13 APR 78; To VA-146, NAS Jacksonville, FL., 31 MAY 78; To VA-146, NAS LeMoore, CA., 18 JUN 78; To VA-146, USS Constellation (CV-64), 16 JUL 78; To VA-146, NAS LeMoore, CA., 29 AUG 78; To VA-146, USS Constellation (CV-64), 21 SEP 78; To VA-146, NAS Cubi

Point, PI., 21 DEC 78 ** Transferred to VA-97/CVW-14, NK/3XX, NAS LeMoore, CA., 10 JUL 79; To VA-97, USS Coral Sea (CV-43), 11 OCT 79; To VA-97, NAS LeMoore, CA., 21 MAY 80; To VA-97, USS Coral Sea (CV-43), 18 NOV 80; To VA-97, NAS Jacksonville, FL., 19 NOV 80; To VA-97, NAS Dallas, TX., 25 JAN 81; To VA-97, USS Coral Sea (CV-43), 01 APR 81; To VA-97, NAS LeMoore, CA., 11 JUN 81** Transferred to VA-122/FRS, NJ/2XX, NAS LeMoore, CA., 29 JUN 81; To VA-122, NAS Alameda, CA., 13 JUL 82; To VA-122, NAS LeMoore, CA., 14 JUL 82; To VA-122, NAS Jacksonville, FL., 22 APR 83; To VA-122, NAS LeMoore, CA., 29 JUL 83 ** Transferred to VA-27/CVW-15, NL/4XX, NAS LeMoore, CA., 20 DEC 83; To VA-27, USS Carl Vinson (CVN-70), 12 MAR 84; To VA-27, NAS LeMoore, CA., 14 MAR 84; To VA-27, USS Carl Vinson (CVN-70), 14 MAR 84; To VA-27, NAS LeMoore, CA., 17 JUL 84; To VA-27, USS Carl Vinson (CVN-70), 09 OCT 84; To VA-27, NAS LeMoore, CA., 06 OCT 85; To VA-27, NAS Jacksonville, FL., 29 AUG 85; To VA-27, NAS LeMoore, CA., 26 NOV 85; To VA-27, USS Carl Vinson (CVN-70), 13 FEB 86; To VA-27, NAS LeMoore, CA., 13 FEB 86; To VA-27, USS Carl Vinson (CVN-70), 13 FEB 86; To VA-27, NAS LeMoore, CA., 17 FEB 87 thru 09 SEP 87 ** End of flight record card ** Transferred to the Helenic Air force (Greece).

E-454 159646 Navy acceptance from NPRO Rep. LTV, Dallas, TX., 05 MAR 75 ** Transferred to VA-174/FRS, AD/4XX, NAS Cecil Field, FL., 14 MAR 75 ** Transferred to VA-15/CVW-6, AE//3XX, NAS Cecil Field, FL., 08 OCT 75; To VA-15, USS America (CV-66), 08 OCT 75; To VA-15, MCAS Yuma, AZ., 29 DEC 76; To VA-15, NAS Jacksonville, FL., 16 FEB 77; To VA-15, USS America (CV-66), 16 FEB 77; To VA-15, NAS Cecil Field, FL., 19 JUL 77; To VA-15, USS America (CV-66), 19 JUL 77; To VA-15, NAS Cecil Field, FL., 09 MAY 78; To VA-15, NAS Jacksonville, FL., 11 SEP 78; To VA-15, NAS Cecil Field, FL., 13 SEP 78; To VA-15, NAS Roosevelt Roads, PR., 13 SEP 78; To VA-15, USS America (CV-66), 13 SEP 78; To VA-15, NAS Cecil Field, FL., 13 SEP 78; To VA-15, USS Independence (CV-62), 13 SEP 78; To VA-15, NAS Cecil Field, FL., 13 SEP 78 ** Transferred to VA-87/CVW-6, AE/4XX, USS Independence (CV-62), 13 FEB 80; To VA-87, NAS Cecil Field, FL., 22 OCT 80 ** Transferred to VA-81/CVW-17, AA/4XX, USS Forrestal (CV-59), 05 DEC 80; To VA-81, NAS Cecil Field, FL., 04 AUG 81; To VA-81, NAS Fallon, NV., 28 OCT 81; To VA-81, USS Forrestal (CV-59), 28 OCT 81; To VA-81, NAS Cecil Field, FL., 11 MAY 82; To VA-81, USS Forrestal (CV-59), 25 MAY 82; To VA-81, NAS Cecil Field, FL., 25 MAY 82; To VA-81, NAS Jacksonville, FL., 27 JAN 83; To VA-81, NAS Cecil Field, FL., 15 APR 83 ** Transferred to VA-46/CVW-1, AB/3XX, NAS Cecil Field, FL., 13 JUL 83; To VA-46, USS America (CV-66), 30 OCT 83; To VA-46, NAS Cecil Field, FL., 30 OCT 83; To VA-46, USS America (CV-66), 30 OCT 83; To VA-46, NAS Cecil Field, FL., 30 OCT 83; To VA-46, USS America (CV-66), 30 OCT 83; To VA-46, NAS Cecil Field, FL., 01 MAY 85; To VA-46, USS America (CV-66), 29 APR 85 ** Transferred to VA-105/CVW-6, AE/4XX, NAS Cecil Field, FL., 01 MAY 85; To VA-105, USS Forrestal (CV-59), 12 JUN 85; To VA-105, NAS Cecil Field, FL., 12 JUN 85; To VA-105, NAS Jacksonville, FL., 20 DEC 85; To VA-105, NAS Cecil Field, FL., 03 JAN 86; To VA-105, NAS Jacksonville, FL., 20 FEB 86 ** Transferred to VA-82/CVW-8, AJ/3XX, NAS Cecil Field, FL., 21 FEB 86; To VA-82, USS Nimitz (CVN-68), 14 MAY 86 ~ S 1SO strike, 04 SEP 86 ** Crashed in bad weather near Floroe, Norway, Pilot and aircraft not found.

E-455 159647 Navy acceptance from NPRO Rep. LTV, Dallas, TX., 02 APR 75 ** Transferred to VA-174/FRS, AD/4XX, NAS Cecil Field, FL., 04 APR 75 ** Transferred to VA-15/CVW- 6, AE/3XX, NAS Cecil Field, FL., 18 NOV 75; To VA-15, USS America (CV-66), 18 NOV 75; To VA-15, MCAS Yuma, AZ., 17 NOV 76; To VA-15, USS America (CV-66), 24 NOV 76; To VA-15, NAS Cecil Field, FL., 19 JUL 77; To VA-15, USS America (CV-66), 19 JUL 77; To VA-15, NAS Cecil Field, FL., 05 JUL 78; To VA-15, NAS Jacksonville, FL., 13 JUL 78; To VA-15, NAS Cecil Field, FL., 09 AUG 78; To VA-15, NAS Roosevelt Roads, PR., 09 AUG 78; To VA-15, USS America (CV-66), 09 AUG 78; To VA-15, NAS Cecil Field, FL., 09 AUG 78; To VA-15, USS Independence (CV-62), 09 AUG 78; To VA-15, NAS Cecil Field, FL., 09 AUG 78; To VA-15, USS Independence (CV-

62), 09 AUG 78; To VA-15, NAS Cecil Field, FL., 09 AUG 78 ** Transferred to VA-25/CVW-2, NE/4XX, NAS LeMoore, CA., 03 MAY 80; To VA-25, USS Ranger (CV-61), 02 JUN 80; To VA-25, NAS LeMoore, CA., 02 JUL 80; To VA-25, USS Ranger (CV-61), 18 JUL 80; To VA-25, NAS LeMoore, CA., 19 MAY 81; To VA-25, NAS Fallon, NV., 14 SEP 81; To VA-25, USS Ranger (CV-61), 20 OCT 81; To VA-25, NAS LeMoore, CA., 29 OCT 81 ** Transferred to VA-22/CVW-11, NH/3XX, NAS LeMoore, CA., 22 DEC 81; To VA-22, NAS Jacksonville, FL., 26 MAY 82; To VA-22, NAS LeMoore, CA., 09 AUG 82; To VA-22, USS Enterprise (CVN-65)., 10 AUG 82; To VA-22, NAS Dallas, TX., 15 OCT 82 ** Transferred to VA-192/CVW-9, NG/3XX, NAS LeMoore, CA., 19 OCT 82; To VA-192, USS Ranger (CV-61), 26 APR 83; To VA-192, NAS LeMoore, CA., 19 FEB 84 ** Transferred to VA-122/FRS, NJ/2XX, NAS LeMoore, CA., 01 APR 85; To VA-122, NAS Jacksonville, FL., 20 NOV 85 ** Transferred to VA-22/CVW-11, NH/3XX, NAS LeMoore, CA., 21 DEC 85; To VA-22, USS Enterprise (CVN-65), 21 DEC 85; To VA-22, NAS LeMoore, CA., 12 MAY 86 ** Transferred to VA-122/FRS, NJ/2XX, NAS LeMoore, CA., 07 OCT 86 thru 12 FEB 87 ** End of flight record card ** On display at NAS Fallon, NV.

E-456 159648 Navy acceptance from NPRO Rep. LTV, Dallas, TX., 03 APR 75 ** Transferred to VA-146/CVW-9, NG/3XX, NAS LeMoore, CA., 05 APR 75; To VA-146, NAS Fallon, NV., 27 MAY 75; To VA-146, NAS LeMoore, CA., 23 JUN 75; To VA-146, USS Constellation (CV-64), 14 MAY 76; To VA-146, NAS LeMoore, CA., 15 DEC 76; To VA-146, USS Constellation (CV-64), 15 DEC 76; To VA-146, NAS LeMoore, CA., 09 FEB 77; To VA-146, NAS Cubi Point, PI., 04 MAY 77; To VA-146, NAF Atsugi, JP., 23 AUG 77; To VA-146, NAS Cubi Point, PI., 31 AUG 77; To VA-146, USS Constellation (CV-64), 31 AUG 77; To VA-146, NAS LeMoore, CA., 19 NOV 77; To VA-146, NAS Jacksonville, FL., 29 APR 78; To VA-146, NAS Fallon, NV., 29 APR 78; To VA-146, NAS Jacksonville, FL., 23 JUN 78; To VA-146, NAS LeMoore, CA., 27 JUN 78; To VA-146, USS Constellation (CV-64), 16 JUL 78; To VA-146, NAS LeMoore, CA., 29 AUG 78; To VA-146, USS Constellation (CV-64), 29 SEP 78; To VA-146, NAS Cubi Point, PI., 21 DEC 78 ** Transferred to VA-27/CVW-14, NK/4XX, NAF El Centro, CA., 03 AUG 79; To VA-27, USS Coral Sea (CV-43), 12 OCT 79; To VA-27, NAS Cubi Point, PI., 12 NOV 79; To VA-27, USS Coral Sea (CV-43), 23 DEC 79; To VA-27, NAS LeMoore, CA., 24 JUN 80; To VA-27, NAS Jacksonville, FL., 17 OCT 80; To VA-27, NAS LeMoore, CA., 19 DEC 80; To VA-27, NAS Dallas, TX., 11 MAR 81 ** Transferred to VA-94/CVW-15, NL/4XX, NAS LeMoore, CA., 19 MAR 81; To VA-94, NAS Cubi Point, PI., 13 MAY 81 ** Transferred to VA-93/CVW-5, NF/3XX, USS Midway (CV-41), 16 MAY 81; To VA-93, NAF Atsugi, JP., 27 JUN 81; To VA-93, Korea, 15 JUL 81; To VA-93, USS Midway (CV-43), 03 SEP 81; To VA-93, NAF Atsugi, JP., 04 OCT 81; To VA-93, USS Midway (CV-43), 30 OCT 81; To VA-93, NAF Atsugi, JP., 04 JAN 82; To VA-93, USS Midway (CV-43), 07 JAN 82; To VA-93, NAF Atsugi, JP., 20 APR 82 ** Transferred to VA-146/CVW-9, NG/3XX, USS Constellation (CV-62), 23 APR 82; To VA-146, NAS LeMoore, CA., 23 APR 82 ** Transferred to VA-122/FRS, NJ/2XX, NAS LeMoore, CA., 06 JUL 82; To VA-122, NAS Jacksonville, FL., 06 MAR 83; To VA-122, NAS LeMoore, CA., 29 MAY 83 ** Transferred to VA-27/CVW-15, NL/4XX, NAS LeMoore, CA., 25 JUL 84; To VA-27, USS Carl Vinson (CVN-70), 30 SEP 84; To VA-27, NAS LeMoore, CA., 28 APR 85; To VA-27, NAS Jacksonville, FL., 14 MAR 86; To VA-27, NAS LeMoore, CA., 30 APR 86; To VA-27, USS Carl Vinson (CVN-70), 30 APR 86; To VA-27, NAS LeMoore, CA., 30 APR 86; To VA-27, USS Carl Vinson (CVN-70), 30 APR 86; To VA-27, NAS LeMoore, CA., 30 JAN 87 thru 18 SEP 87 ** End of flight record card ** Transferred to the Helenic Air force (Greece).

E-457 159649 Navy acceptance from NPRO Rep. LTV, Dallas, TX., 26 MAR 75 ** Transferred to VA-147/CVW-9, NG/415, NAS LeMoore, CA., 31 MAR 75; To VA-147, NAS Fallon, NV., 26 MAY 75; To VA-147, NAS LeMoore, CA., 05 JUN 75; To VA-147, MCAS Yuma, AZ., 28 OCT 75; To VA-147, NAS LeMoore, CA., 28 OCT 75; To VA-147, USS Constellation (CV-62), 30 SEP 76; To VA-147, NAS LeMoore, CA., 22 OCT 76; To VA-147, USS Constellation

(CV-62), 23 JUL 77; To VA-147, NAS LeMoore, CA., 19 NOV 77; To VA-147, NAS Jacksonville, FL., 05 JUN 78; To VA-147, NAS LeMoore, CA., 29 JUL 78; To VA-147, USS Constellation (CV-62), 25 SEP 78; To VA-147, NAS Cubi Point, PI., 06 NOV 78; To VA-147, USS Constellation (CV-62), 31 DEC 78; To VA-147, NAS LeMoore, CA., 02 DEC 79; To VA-147, USS Constellation (CV-62), 13 DEC 79; To VA-147, NAS LeMoore, CA., 23 JAN 80 ** Transferred to VA-94/CVW-15, NL/4XX, USS Kitty Hawk (CV-63), 15 FEB 80; To VA-94, NAS LeMoore, CA., 08 APR 80; To VA-94, USS Kitty Hawk (CV-63), 27 JUL 80; To VA-94, NAS LeMoore, CA., 27 JUL 80; To VA-94, USS Kitty Hawk (CV-63), 05 SEP 80; To VA-94, NAS Jacksonville, FL., 07 SEP 80; To VA-94, NAS LeMoore, CA., 05 NOV 80; To VA-94, NAS Dallas, TX., 19 FEB 81; To VA-94, USS Kitty Hawk (CV-63), 24 FEB 81 ** Transferred to VA-22/CVW-15, NL/3XX, USS Kitty Hawk (CV-63), 01 MAR 81; To VA-22, NAS LeMoore, CA., 25 MAR 81 ** Transferred to VA-192/CVW-11, NH/3XX, NAS LeMoore, CA., 11 FEB 82 ** Transferred to VA-122/FRS, NJ/2XX, NAS Jacksonville, FL.,, 06 MAR 83 ** Transferred to VA-94/CVW-11, NH/4XX, NAS LeMoore, CA., 20 JUN 83; To VA-94, USS Enterprise (CVN-65), 28 SEP 83 ** Transferred to NARF, NAS Jacksonville, FL., 10 JAN 84 ** End of flight record card ** On display at Charleston, SC., AUG 94.

E-458 159650 Navy acceptance from NPRO Rep. LTV, Dallas, TX., 05 MAY 75 ** Transferred to VA-174/FRS, AD/4XX, NAS Cecil Field, FL., 13 MAY 75 ** Transferred to VA-87/CVW-6, AE/4XX, USS Saratoga (CV-60), 07 OCT 75; To VA-87, NAS Cecil Field, FL., 07 OCT 75; To VA-87, USS America (CV-66), 07 OCT 75; To VA-87, NAS Cecil Field, FL., 07 OCT 75; To VA-87, MCAS Yuma, AZ., 07 OCT 75; To VA-87, USS America (CV-66), 07 OCT 75; To VA-87, NAS Cecil Field, FL., 07 OCT 75; To VA-87, USS America (CV-66), 19 JUL 77; To VA-87, NAS Cecil Field, FL., 22 MAY 78; To VA-87, NAS Jacksonville, FL., 23 MAY 78 ** Transferred to VA-147/CVW-9, NE/3XX, NAS LeMoore, CA., 25 JUL 78; To VA-147, USS Constellation (CV-64), 25 SEP 78; To VA-147, NAS Cubi Point, PI., 06 NOV 78; To VA-147, USS Constellation (CV-64), 31 DEC 78; To VA-147, NAS LeMoore, CA., 09 JUN 79; To VA-147, USS Constellation (CV-64), 13 DEC 79 ** Transferred to VA-113/CVW-2, NE/3XX, NAS LeMoore, CA., 08 JAN 80; To VA-113, USS Ranger (CV-61), 05 MAY 80; To VA-113, NAS LeMoore, CA., 05 MAY 80 ** Transferred to VA-195/CVW-11, NH/4XX, NAS LeMoore, CA., 01 JUN 80; To VA-195, NAS Jacksonville, FL., 20 AUG 80; To VA-195, NAS LeMoore, CA., 24 OCT 80; To VA-195, NAS Dallas, TX., 29 JAN 81 ** Transferred to VA-22/CVW-15, NL/3XX, NAS LeMoore, CA., 06 FEB 81; To VA-22, USS Kitty Hawk (CV-63), 25 MAR 81; To VA-22, NAF Atsugi, JP., 07 OCT 81; To VA-22, NAS LeMoore, CA., 31 OCT 81; To VA-22, NAF Atsugi, JP., 02 NOV 81; To VA-22, NAS LeMoore, CA., 24 NOV 81 ** Transferred to VA-122/FRS, NJ/2XX, NAS LeMoore, CA., 23 APR 82 ** Transferred to VA-27/CVW-15, NL/4XX, NAS LeMoore, CA., 24 OCT 83; To VA-27, NAS Jacksonville, FL., 22 DEC 83; To VA-27, USS Carl Vinson (CVN-70), 31 MAR 84; To VA-27, NAS LeMoore, CA., 03 MAY 84; To VA-27, USS Carl Vinson (CVN-70), 03 MAR 84; To VA-27, NAS LeMoore, CA., 10 JAN 85; To VA-27, USS Carl Vinson (CVN-70), 30 MAY 86; To VA-27, NAS LeMoore, CA., 31 MAY 86; To VA-27, USS Carl Vinson (CVN-70), 31 MAY 86; To VA-27, NAS LeMoore, CA., 05 MAR 87; To VA-27, NAS Jacksonville, FL., 18 SEP 87; To VA-27, NAS LeMoore, CA., 18 SEP 87; To VA-27, NAS Jacksonville, FL., 22 SEP 87 ** End of flight record card ** Transferred to VAQ-34/FEWSG, GD/XXX, NAS Point Mugu, CA., date unknown ** Transferred to AMARC, Davis Monthan AFB; Tucson, AZ., assigned park code 6A0402; 12 SEP 91 ** 6038.6 flight hours ** TF41A402D engine S/N 141323 ** Engine released to DRMO for disposition, 29 JUN 05 ** Aircraft deleted from inventory and released to DRMO for disposition 01 AUG 05 ** Transferred to NSWC, NAS Fallon, NV., area 4755, pasture road, 25 AUG 05.

E-459 159651 Navy acceptance from NPRO Rep. LTV, Dallas, TX., 30 MAY 75 ** Transferred to VA-27/CVW-14, NK/401, NAS LeMoore, CA., CDR Jim Newkey painted on side of cockpit, 18 JUN 75; To VA-27, NAS Fallon, NV., 24 OCT 75; To VA-27, NAS LeMoore, CA., 19 FEB 76; To VA-27, USS Enterprise (CVN-65),

12 MAR 76; To VA-27, NAS LeMoore, CA., 06 APR 76; To VA-27, USS Enterprise (CVN-65), 29 APR 76; To VA-27, NAS LeMoore, CA., 17 MAY 76; To VA-27, USS Enterprise (CVN-65), 30 JUN 76; To VA-27, NAS LeMoore, CA., 28 JUL 76 ** Transferred to VA-56/CVW-5, NF/4XX, USS Midway (CV-41), 12 MAR 77; To VA-56, NAF Atsugi, JP., 11 APR 77; To VA-56, USS Midway (CV-41), 13 APR 77; To VA-56, NAF Atsugi, JP., 14 FEB 78; To VA-56, USS Midway (CV-41), 10 APR 78; To VA-56, NAF Atsugi, JP., 15 JUN 78; To VA-56, USS Midway (CV-41), 30 MAR 79; To VA-56, NAF Atsugi, JP., 30 SEP 79; To VA-56, USS Midway (CV-41), 27 JUL 80; To VA-56, NAF Atsugi, JP., 27 NOV 80; To VA-56, USS Midway (CV-41), 24 FEB 81; To VA-56, NAF Atsugi, JP., 27 JUN 81; To VA-56, USS Midway (CV-41), 25 JUL 81; To VA-56, NAF Atsugi, JP., 30 OCT 81 ** Transferred to VA-25/CVW-2, NE/4XX, NAS Cubi Point, PI., 24 AUG 82; To VA-25, USS Ranger (CV-61), 24 AUG 82; To VA-25, NAS LeMoore, CA., 24 AUG 82 ** Transferred to VA-122/FRS, NJ/2XX, NAS LeMoore, CA., 15 JUN 83; To VA-122, NAS Jacksonville, FL., 16 JAN 84 ** Transferred to VA-97/CVW-15, NL/3XX, NAS LeMoore, CA., 27 JUN 84; To VA-97, USS Carl Vinson (CVN-70), 27 JUN 84; To VA-97, NAS LeMoore, CA., 27 JUN 84; To VA-97, USS Carl Vinson (CVN-70), 27 JUN 84; To VA-97, NAS LeMoore, CA., 05 JAN 85 ** Transferred to VA-22/CVW-11, NH/3XX, NAS LeMoore, CA., 29 SEP 85; To VA-22, USS Enterprise (CVN-65), 16 JAN 86; To VA-22, NAS LeMoore, CA., 27 AUG 86 ** Transferred to VX-5, XE/XXX, NWC China Lake, CA., 12 MAY 87; To VX-5, NAS Jacksonville, FL., 16 SEP 87; To VX-5, NWC China Lake, CA., 16 SEP 87; To VX-5, NAS Jacksonville, FL., 17 SEP 87 ** End of flight record card ** Transferred to VA-122/FRS, NJ/222, NAS LeMoore, CA., date unknown ** Transferred to AMARC, Davis Monthan AFB; Tucson, AZ., assigned park code 6A0359, 29 MAY 90 ** 6456.3 flight hours ** TF41A402D engine S/N 141883 ** Storage location 210518 ** Aircraft deleted from inventory and released to DRMO for disposition, 04 MAY 06 ** At AMARG, Davis Monthan AFB; Tucson, AZ., 15 JUN 07.

E-460 159652 Navy acceptance from NPRO Rep. LTV, Dallas, TX., 06 JUN 75 ** Transferred to VA-174/FRS, AD/4XX, NAS Cecil Field, FL., 12 JUN 75 ** Transferred to VA-87/CVW-6, AE/4XX, NAS Cecil Field, FL., 18 NOV 75; To VA-87, USS Saratoga (CV-60), 18 NOV 75; To VA-87, NAS Cecil Field, FL., 18 NOV 75; To VA-87, USS America (CV-66), 18 NOV 75; To VA-87, NAS Cecil Field, FL., 18 NOV 75; To VA-87, MCAS Yuma, AZ., 18 NOV 75; To VA-87, NAS Cecil Field, FL., 03 FEB 77; To VA-87, NAS Jacksonville, FL., 08 FEB 77; To VA-87, USS America (CV-66), 02 MAR 77; To VA-87, NAS Cecil Field, FL., 04 MAR 77; To VA-87, USS America (CV-66), 19 JUL 77; To VA-87, NAS Jacksonville, FL., 12 JUL 78; To VA-87, NAS Cecil Field, FL., 13 JUL 78; To VA-87, NAS Jacksonville, FL., 23 AUG 78; To VA-87, NAS Roosevelt Roads, PR., 18 SEP 78; To VA-87, NAS Cecil Field, FL., 18 SEP 78; To VA-87, USS Indepedence (CV-62), 20 SEP 78; To VA-87, NAS Cecil Field, FL., 13 FEB 80; To VA-87, USS Indepedence (CV-62), 20 AUG 80; To VA-87, NAS Cecil Field, FL., 20 AUG 80; To VA-87, USS Indepedence (CV-62), 09 NOV 81; To VA-87, NAS Cecil Field, FL., 09 NOV 81; To VA-87, USS Indepedence (CV-62), 09 NOV 81 ** Transferred to VA-174/FRS, AD/4XX, NAS Cecil Field, FL., 07 MAR 82; To VA-174, NAS Jacksonville, FL., 18 MAY 82; To VA-174, NAS Dallas, TX., 28 JUL 82; To VA-174, NAS Cecil Field, FL., 30 JUL 82; To VA-174, NAS Dallas, TX., 05 OCT 82 ** Transferred to VA-66/CVW-7, AG/3XX, NAS Cecil Field, FL., 11 OCT 82; To VA-66, USS Dwight D. Eisenhower (CVN-69), 12 OCT 82; To VA-66, NAS Cecil Field, FL., 12 OCT 82 ** Transferred to VA-15/CVW-6, AE/3XX, USS Independence (CV-62), 14 DEC 83; To VA-15, NAS Cecil Field, FL., 26 APR 84; To VA-15, USS Independence (CV-62), 20 JUN 84; To VA-15, NAS Jacksonville, FL., 13 SEP 84 ** Transferred to VA-86/CVW-8, AJ/4XX, NAS Cecil Field, FL., 14 SEP 84; To VA-86, USS Nimitz (CVN-68), 14 SEP 84; To VA-86, NAS Cecil Field, FL., 14 SEP 84; To VA-86, USS Nimitz (CVN-68), 04 FEB 85; To VA-86, NAS Cecil Field, FL., 16 OCT 85 ** Transferred to VA-72/CVW-1, AB/4XX, USS America (CV-66), 23 DEC 85; To VA-72, NAS Cecil Field, FL., 28 APR 86; To VA-72/CVW7, AG/4XX, USS Dwight D. Eisenhower (CVN-69), 23 JUN 87; To VA-72, NAS Cecil Field, FL., 07 JUL 87 ** End of flight record card.

E-461 159653 Navy acceptance from NPRO Rep. LTV, Dallas, TX., 24 JUN 75 ** Transferred to VA-174/FRS, AD/4XX, NAS Cecil Field, FL., 27 JUN 75 ** Transferred to VA-87/CVW-6, AE/4XX, NAS Cecil Field, FL., 11 NOV 75; To VA-87, USS Saratoga (CV-69), 11 NOV 75; To VA-87, NAS Cecil Field, FL., 11 NOV 75; To VA-87, USS America (CV-66), 11 NOV 75; To VA-87, NAS Cecil Field, FL., 11 NOV 75; To VA-87, MCAS, AZ., 11 NOV 75; To VA-87, USS America (CV-66), 11 NOV 75; To VA-87, NAS Cecil Field, FL., 27 MAY 77; To VA-87, NAS Jacksonville, FL., 28 MAY 77; To VA-87, USS America (CV-66), 19 JUL 77; To VA-87, NAS Jacksonville, FL., 22 MAY 78; To VA-87, NAS Cecil Field, FL., 27 JUN 78; To VA-87, NAS Roosevelt Roads, PR., 06 JUL 78; To VA-87, NAS Cecil Field, FL., 06 JUL 78; To VA-87, NAS Jacksonville, FL., 06 DEC 78; To VA-87, NAS Cecil Field, FL., 13 DEC 78; To VA-87, USS Independence (CV-62), 19 DEC 78; To VA-87, NAS Cecil Field, FL., 30 APR 80; To VA-87, USS Independence (CV-62), 27 AUG 80; Transferred to VA-174/FRS, AD/4XX, NAS Cecil Field, FL., 13 NOV 80 ** Transferred to VA-86/CVW-8, AJ/406; USS Nimitz (CVN-68), Paint was light gray on medium gray, 30 MAY 81; To VA-86, NAS Cecil Field, FL., 30 MAY 81; To VA-86, USS Nimitz (CVN-68), 19 JUL 81; To VA-86, NAS Cecil Field, FL., 19 JUL 81; To VA-86, NAS Jacksonville, FL., 27 MAY 82 ** Transferred to VA-82/CVW-8, AJ/3XX, NAS Cecil Field, FL., 28 JUL 82; To VA-82, USS Nimitz (CVN-68), 28 JUL 82; To VA-82, NAS Cecil Field, FL., 18 OCT 82; To VA-82, USS Nimitz (CVN-68), 26 OCT 82; To VA-82, NAS Cecil Field, FL., 09 MAY 83 ** Transferred to VA-87/CVW-6, AE/4XX, USS Independence (CV-62), 05 JAN 84; To VA-87, NAS Jacksonville, FL., 30 APR 84; To VA-87, NAS Cecil Field, FL., 30 APR 84; To VA-87, NAS Jacksonville, FL., 02 MAY 84; To VA-87 USS Independence (CV-62), 25 JUL 84; To VA-87, NAS Cecil Field, FL., 25 JUL 84; To VA-87, USS Independence (CV-62), 25 JUL 84; To VA-87, NAS Cecil Field, FL., 18 FEB 85 ** Transferred to VA-174/FRS, AD/430, NAS Cecil Field, FL., 12 MAR 86; To VA-174, NAS Jacksonville, FL., 30 JUL 86; To VA-174, NAS Cecil Field, FL., 10 AUG 86; To VA-174, NAS Jacksonville, FL., 30 SEP 86; To VA-174, NAS Cecil Field, FL., 07 OCT 86 ** Transferred to AMARC, Davis Monthan AFB; Tucson, AZ., assigned park code 6A0230; 11 AUG 87 ** End of flight record card ** 4864.8 flight hours ** TF41A2C engine S/N 141613 ** Storage location 210530 ** Aircraft deleted from inventory and released to DRMO for disposition, 04 MAY 06 ** At AMARG, Davis Monthan AFB; Tucson, AZ., 15 JUN 07.

E-462 159654 Navy acceptance from NPRO Rep. LTV, Dallas, TX., 18 JUN 75 ** Transferred to VA-174/FRS, AD/4XX, NAS Cecil Field, FL., 21 JUN 75 ** Transferred to VA-15/CVW-6, AE/3XX, NAS Cecil Field, FL., 11 NOV 75; To VA-15, USS America (CV-66), 17 JUL 75; To VA-15, MCAS Yuma, AZ., 07 DEC 76; To VA-15, NAS Jacksonville, FL., 13 JAN 77; To VA-15, MCAS Yuma, AZ., 17 JAN 77; To VA-15, NAS Cecil Field, FL., 18 JAN 77; To VA-15, NAS Jacksonville, FL., 09 FEB 77; To VA-15, NAS Cecil Field, FL., 11 FEB 77; To VA-15, USS America (CV-66), 11 FEB 77; To VA-15, NAS Cecil Field, FL., 19 JUL 77; To VA-15, USS America (CV-66), 19 JUL 77; To VA-15, NAS Cecil Field, FL., 17 MAY 78; To VA-15, NAS Jacksonville, FL., 07 JUN 78; To VA-15, NAS Cecil Field, FL., 12 JUN 78; To VA-15, NAS Roosevelt Roads, PR., 25 JUL 78; VA-15, USS America (CV-66), 25 JUL 78; To VA-15, NAS Cecil Field, FL., 25 JUL 78; To VA-15, USS Independence (CV-62), 25 JUL 78; To VA-15, NAS Cecil Field, FL., 09 FEB 79; To VA-15, USS Independence (CV-62), 09 FEB 79; To VA-15, NAS Cecil Field, FL., 01 MAR 80; To VA-15, USS Independence (CV-62), 07 MAY 80 ** Transferred to VA-86/CVW-8, AJ/4XX, USS Nimitz (CVN-68), 13 NOV 80; To VA-86, NAS Cecil Field, FL., 13 NOV 80; To VA-86, USS Nimitz (CVN-68), 17 APR 81; To VA-86, NAS Cecil Field, FL., 17 APR 81; To VA-86, USS Nimitz (CVN-68), 17 APR 81; To VA-86, NAS Cecil Field, FL., 17 APR 81 ** Transferred to VA-174/FRS, AD/4XX, NAS Cecil Field, FL., 31 MAR 82 ~ S 1SO strike, 18 AUG 82 ** No Data on strike.

E-463 159655 Navy acceptance from NPRO Rep. LTV, Dallas, TX., 17 JUL 75 ** Transferred to VA-15/CVW-6, AE/300, NAS Cecil Field, FL., 17 JUL 75; To VA-15, USS America (CV-66), 17 JUL 75; Painted in bicentennial colors, 04 JUL 76; To VA-15, MCAS Yuma,

AZ. 09 DEC 76; To VA-15, USS America (CV-66), 16 DEC 76; To VA-15, NAS Cecil Field, Fl., 19 JUL 77; To VA-15, USS America (CV-66), 19 JUL 77; To VA-15, NAS Cecil Field, Fl. 26 JUN 78; To VA-15, NAS Jacksonville, FL., 21 AUG 78; To VA-15, NAS Cecil Field, Fl., 14 SEP 78; To VA-15, NAS Roosevelt Roads, PR., 14 SEP 78; To VA-15, USS America (CV-66), 14 SEP 78; To VA-15, NAS Cecil Field, Fl., 14 SEP 78; To VA-15, USS Independence (CV-62), 14 SEP 78; To VA-15, NAS Cecil Field, Fl., 14 SEP 78; To VA-15, USS Independence (CV-62), 14 SEP 78; To VA-15, NAS Cecil Field, Fl., 18 MAR 80 ** Transferred to VA-22/CVW-15, NL/3XX, NAS Cubi Point, PI., 19 MAR 80; To VA-22, NAS LeMoore, CA., 24 APR 80; To VA-22, USS Kitty, HAWK (CV-63), 11 SEP 80 ** Transferred to VA-192/CVW-11, NH/315, NAS Fallon, NV., 20 OCT 80; To VA-192, LeMoore, CA., 07 NOV 80; To VA-192, USS America (CV-66), 29 JAN 81; To VA-192, LeMoore, CA., 08 APR 81; To VA-192, Jacksonville, FL., 28 APR 82 ** Transferred to VA-27/CVW-14, NK/4XX, NAS LeMoore, CA., 08 JUL 82; To VA-27, USS Coral Sea (CV-43), 08 MAR 83; To VA-27, NAS LeMoore, CA., 03 MAY 83; To VA-27, USS Carl Vinson (CVN-70), 03 MAY 83; To VA-27, NAS LeMoore, CA., 03 MAY 83; To VA-27, USS Carl Vinson (CVN-70), 03 MAY 83; To VA-27, NAS Jacksonville, FL., 12 JUL 84; To VA-27, NAS LeMoore, CA., 12 JUL 84; To VA-27, NAS Jacksonville, FL., 16 JUL 84; To VA-27, USS Carl Vinson (CVN-70), 16 JUL 84; To VA-27, NAS Jacksonville, FL., 10 JAN 85 ** Transferred to VA-146/CVW-9, NE/3XX, NAS LeMoore, CA., 10 JAN 85; To VA-146, USS Kitty Hawk (CV-63), 24 JAN 85; To VA-146, NAS LeMoore, CA., 01 OCT 85; To VA-146, USS Kitty Hawk (CV-63), 27 OCT 86; To VA-146, NAS LeMoore, CA., 27 OCT 86 thru 26 SEP 87 ** End of flight record card.

E-464 159656 Navy acceptance from NPRO Rep. LTV, Dallas, TX., 30 JUN 75 ** Transferred to VA-97/CVW-14, NK/3XX, NAS LeMoore, CA., 03 JUL 75; To VA-97, NAS Fallon, NV., 30 NOV 75; To VA-97, USS Enterprise (CVN-65), 20 FEB 76; To VA-97, NAS LeMoore, CA., 16 APR 76; To VA-97, USS Enterprise (CVN-65), 28 JUL 76 ** Transferred to VA-93/CVW-5, NF/3XX, USS Midway (CV-41), 13 MAR 77; To VA-93, NAF Atsugi, JP., 22 MAR 78; To VA-93, USS Midway (CV-41), 27 MAR 78; To VA-93, NAF Atsugi, JP., 08 MAY 78; To VA-93, USS Midway (CV-41), 23 JUN 80; To VA-93, NAF Atsugi, JP., 25 NOV 80; To VA-93, NAS Cubi Point, PI., 25 NOV 80 ** Transferred to VA-56/CVW-5, NF/4XX, NAF Atsugi, JP., 16 FEB 81; To VA-56, USS Midway (CV-41), 24 FEB 81 ** Transferred to VA-25/CVW-2, NE/4XX, USS Ranger (CV-61), 28 MAR 81; To VA-25, NAS LeMoore, CA., 15 MAY 81; To VA-25, NAS Fallon, NV., 14 SEP 81; To VA-25, USS Ranger (CV-61), 26 SEP 81; To VA-25, NAS LeMoore, CA., 26 SEP 81; To VA-25, USS Ranger (CV-61), 26 SEP 81; To VA-25, NAS LeMoore, CA., 26 SEP 81 ** Transferred to VA-192/CVW-11, NH/3XX, NAS LeMoore, CA., 29 MAR 82; To VA-192, NAS Norfolk, VA., 09 JUN 82; To VA-192, NAS Jacksonville, FL., 10 JUN 82; To VA-192, NAS Dallas, TX., 27 AUG 82; To VA-197, NAS LeMoore, CA., 11 NOV 82; To VA-192, USS Ranger (CV-61), 29 JUN 83; To VA-192, NAF Atsugi, JP., 24 OCT 83; To VA-192, USS Ranger (CV-61), 01 NOV 83; To VA-197, NAS LeMoore, CA., 01 NOV 83 ** Transferred to VA-122/FRS, NJ/2XX, NAS LeMoore, CA., 01 MAR 84 ** Transferred to VA-97/CVW-15, NL/3XX, USS Carl Vinson (CVN-70), 09 MAY 84; To VA-97, NAS LeMoore, CA., 28 SEP 84; To VA-97, USS Carl Vinson (CVN-70), 28 SEP 84; To VA-97, NAS Jacksonville, FL., 09 OCT 85 ** Transferred to VA-146/CVW-9, NG/3XX, NAS LeMoore, CA., 09 JAN 85; To VA-146, USS Kitty Hawk (CV-63), 28 FEB 85; To VA-146, NAS LeMoore, CA., 28 FEB 85; To VA-146, USS Kitty Hawk (CV-63), 01 OCT 86; To VA-146, NAS LeMoore, CA., 01 OCT 86 ** End of flight record card ** Transferred to NAD, NAS Jacksonville, FL., 07 MAR 89 ** Transferred to NSWC, Strike/24, NAS Fallon, NV, date unknown ** Transferred to AMARC, Davis Monthan AFB; Tucson, AZ., assigned park code 6A0403, 19 SEP 91 ** 5684.1 flight hours ** TF41A402D engine S/N AE141259 ** Engine records released to DRMO, Davis Monthan AFB; Tucson, AZ., for disposition, 22 FEB 06 ** Aircraft storage location 210525 ** Aircraft at AMARG, Davis Monthan AFB; Tucson, AZ., 15 JUN 07.

E-465 159657 Navy acceptance from NPRO Rep. LTV, Dallas, TX., 28 AUG 75 ** Transferred to VA-87/CVW-6, AE/4XX, NAS Cecil Field, FL., 03 OCT 75; To VA-87, USS Saratoga (CV-60), 03 OCT 75; To VA-87, NAS Cecil Field, FL., 03 OCT 75; To VA-87, USS America (CV-66), 01 MAY 76; To VA-87, NAS Cecil Field, FL., 14 JUN 76; To VA-87, MCAS Yuma, AZ., 14 JUN 76; To VA-87, USS America (CV-66), 14 JUN 76; To VA-87, NAS Cecil Field, FL., 14 JUN 76; To VA-87, NAS Jacksonville, FL., 26 JUL 77; To VA-87, NAS Cecil Field, FL., 28 JUL 77; To VA-87, USS America (CV-66), 28 JUL 77; To VA-87, NAS Jacksonville, FL., 10 MAY 78; To VA-87, NAS Cecil Field, FL., 08 JUN 78; To VA-87, NAS Roosevelt Roads, PR., 12 AUG 78; To VA-87, NAS Cecil Field, FL., 12 AUG 78; To VA-87, USS Independence (CV-62), 12 AUG 78 ** Transferred to VA-27/CVW-14, NK/4XX, NAF El Centro, CA., 06 SEP 79; To VA-27, NAS LeMoore, CA., 06 SEP 79 ** Transferred to VA-122/FRS, NJ/240, NAS LeMoore, CA., 11 OCT 79 ~ S 1SO strike, 27 APR 81 ** Mid air during in flight refueling, pilot ejected.

E-466 159658 Navy acceptance from NPRO Rep. LTV, Dallas, TX., 30 SEP 75 ** Transferred to VA-15/CVW-6, AE/3XX, NAS Cecil Field FL., 03 OCT 75; To VA-15, USS America (CV-66), 03 OCT 75; To VA-15, MCAS Yuma, AZ., 15 DEC 76; To VA-15, USS America (CV-66), 22 DEC 76; To VA-15, NAS Cecil Field, FL., 19 JUL 77; To VA-15, USS America (CV-66), 19 JUL 77; To VA-15, NAS Jacksonville, FL., 08 MAY 78; To VA-15, NAS Cecil Field, FL., 02 JUN 78; To VA-15, NAS Roosevelr Roads, PR., 22 AUG 78; To VA-15, USS America (CV-66), 22 AUG 78; To VA-15, NAS Cecil Field, FL., 22 AUG 78; To VA-15, USS Independence CV-62), 22 AUG 78; To VA-15, NAS Cecil Field, FL., 08 MAY 79; To VA-15, USS Independence (CV-62), 09 MAY 79; Transferred to VA-27/CVW-14, NK/4XX, NAF El Centro, CA., 29 AUG 79; To VA-27, USS Coral Sea (CV-43), 12 OCT 79; To VA-27, NAS Cubi Point, PI., 12 NOV 79; To VA-27, USS Coral Sea (CV-43), 23 DEC 79; To VA-27, NAS LeMoore, CA., 08 JAN 80; To VA-27, USS Coral Sea (CV-43), 19 MAR 81; To VA-27, NAS LeMoore, CA., 11 JUN 81 ** Transferred VA-122/FRS, NJ/2XX, NAS LeMoore, CA., 20 JUL 81; To VA-122, NAS Jacksonville, FL., 18 SEP 81; To VA-122, NAS LeMoore, CA., 17 OCT 81; To VA-122, NAS Jacksonville, FL., 30 OCT 81; To VA-122, NAS LeMoore, CA., 10 NOV 81 ** Transferred to VA-94/CVW-11, NH/410, NAS LeMoore, CA. 08 JUN 82; To VA-94, USS Enterprise (CVN-65), 07 SEP 82; To VA-94, NAS Cubi Point, PI., 07 SEP 82; To VA-94, NAS LeMoore, CA., 07 SEP 82; To VA-94, NAS Jacksonville, FL., 03 NOV 83; To VA-94, USS Enterprise (CVN-65), 03 NOV 83; To VA-94, NAS LeMoore, CA., 03 NOV 83; To VA-94, NAS Jacksonville, FL., 28 MAR 84; To VA-94, NAS LeMoore, CA., 30 MAR 84 ** Transferred to VA-22/CVW-11, NH/3XX, NAS LeMoore, CA., 31 MAR 84; To VA-22, USS Enterprise (CVN-65), 18 APR 84 ** Transferred to VA-56/CVW-5, NF/4XX, NAF Atsugi, JP., 17 NOV 84; To VA-56, NAS LeMoore, CA., 07 JUL 85; To VA-56, NAS Jacksonville, FL., 28 MAY 86 ** Transferred to VA-146/CVW-9, NG/3XX, NAS LeMoore, CA., 28 AUG 86; To VA-146, USS Kitty Hawk (CV-63), 28 AUG 86; To VA-146, NAS LeMoore, CA., 24 MAY 87 ** End of flight record card ** Transferred to the Helenic Air force (Greece).

E-467 159659 Navy acceptance from NPRO Rep. LTV, Dallas, TX., 24 OCT 75 ** Transferred to VA-87/CVW-6, AE/403, USS America (CV-66), 31 OCT 75; To VA-87, NAS Cecil Field, FL., 31 OCT 75; To VA-87, USS America (CV-66), 31 OCT 75; To VA-87, NAS Cecil Field, FL., 31 OCT 75; To VA-87, MCAS Yuma, AZ.,31 OCT 75; To VA-87, USS America (CV-66), 31 OCT 75; To VA-87, NAS Cecil Field, FL., 31 OCT 75; To VA-87, USS America (CV-66), 19 JUL 77; To VA-87, NAS Cecil Field, FL., 22 JUN 78; To VA-87, NAS Jacksonville, FL., 13 JUL 78; To VA-87, NAS Cecil Field, FL., 09 AUG 78; To VA-87, NAS Roosevelt Roads, PR., 09 AUG 78; To VA-87, NAS Cecil Field, FL., 09 AUG 78; To VA-87, USS Independence (CV-62), 09 AUG 78; To VA-87, NAS Cecil Field, FL., 27 FEB 80; To VA-87, USS Independence (CV-62), 21 JUL 81; To VA-87, NAS Cecil Field, FL., 21 JUL 81; To VA-87, NAS Jacksonville, FL., 04 MAR 82; To VA-87, NAS Cecil Field,

FL., 08 MAR 82; To VA-87, NAS Dallas, TX., 01 JUN 82; To VA-87, USS Independence (CV-62), 01 JUN 82 ** Transferred to VA-66/CVW-7, AG/3XX, NAS Cecil Field, FL., 13 AUG 82; To VA-66, USS Dwight D. Eisenhower (CVN-69), 14 AUG 82; To VA-66, NAS Cecil Field, FL., 14 AUG 82 ** Transferred to VA-86/CVW-8, AJ/4XX, NAS Cecil Field, FL., 29 MAR 84; To VA-86, NAS Roosevelt Roads, PR., 28 AUG 84 ~ S 1SO strike, 28 AUG 84 ** Crashed on takeoff, pilot ejected safely.

E-468 159660 Navy acceptance from NPRO Rep. LTV, Dallas, TX., 13 NOV 75 ** Transferred to VA-15/CVW-6, AE/3XX, NAS Cecil Field, FL., 14 NOV 75; To VA-15, USS America (CV-66), 14 NOV 75; To VA-15, MCAS Yuma, AZ., 17 DEC 76; To VA-15, USS America (CV-66), 24 DEC 76; To VA-15, NAS Cecil Field, FL., 19 JUL 77; To VA-15, USS America (CV-66), 19 JUL 77; To VA-15, NAS Jacksonville, FL., 01 JUN 78; To VA-15, NAS Cecil Field, Fl., 23 JUN 78; To VA-15, NAS Roosevelt, Roads, PR., 17 JUL 78; To VA-15, USS America (CV-66), 17 JUL 78; To VA-15, NAS Cecil Field, FL., 17 JUL 78; To VA-15, USS Independence (CV-62), 17 JUL 78; To VA-15, NAS Cecil Field, FL., 17 JUL 78; To VA-15, USS Independence (CV-62), 17 JUL 78; To VA-15, NAS Cecil Field, FL., 17 JUL 78 ** Transferred to VA-81/CVW-17, AA/4XX, NAS Cecil Field, FL., 19 JUN 80; To VA-81, USS Forrestal (CV-59), 24 JUL 80; To VA-81, NAS Cecil Field, FL., 24 JUL 80; To VA-81, USS Forrestal (CV-59), 24 JUL 80; To VA-81, NAS Cecil Field, FL., 24 JUL 80; To VA-81, NAS Fallon, NV., 24 JUL 80; To VA-81, USS Forrestal (CV-59), 24 JUL 80 ** Transferred to VA-174/FRS, AD/4XX, NAS Cecil Field, FL., 16 APR 82; To VA-174, NAS Jacksonville, FL., 13 JUL 82; To VA-174, NAS Cecil Field, FL., 15 SEP 82; To VA-174, NAS Dallas, TX., 16 NOV 82 ** Transferred to VA-105/CVW-3, NL/4XX, NAS Cecil field, FL., 19 NOV 82; To VA-105, USS Carl Vinson, (CVN-70), 19 NOV 82; To VA-105, NAS Cecil Field, FL., 19 NOV 82; To VA-105, USS Carl Vinson, (CVN-70), 19 NOV 82; To VA-105, NAF Atsugi, JP., 15 SEP 83; To VA-105, USS Carl Vinson, (CVN-70), 17 SEP 83; To VA-105, NAS Cecil Field, FL., 17 SEP 83; To VA-105, NAS Roosevelt Roads, PR., 17 SEP 83; NAS Cecil Field, FL., 17 SEP 83 ** Transferred to VA-82/CVW-8, AJ/3XX, NAS Cecil Field, FL., 14 MAR 84; To VA-82, USS Nimitz (CVN-70), 23 SEP 84; To VA-82, NAS Jacksonville, FL., 06 DEC 84 ** Transferred to VA-46/CVW-1, AB/3XX, NAS Cecil Field, FL., 26 MAR 85; To VA-46, USS America (CV-66), 26 MAR 85; To VA-46, NAS Cecil Field, FL., 26 MAR 85; To VA-46, USS America (CV-66), 26 MAR 85; To VA-46, NAS Cecil Field, FL., 26 MAR 85; To VA-46, USS America (CV-66), 26 MAR 85; To VA-46, NAS Cecil Field, FL., 26 MAR 85 ** Transferred to VA-83/CVW-17, AA/3XX, NAS Cecil Field, FL.,05 FEB 87; To VA-83, USS Saratoga (CV-60), 04 MAR 87; To VA-83, NAS Cecil Field, FL., 17 MAR 87; To VA-83, USS Saratoga (CV-60), 17 MAR 87; To VA-83, NAS Cecil Field, FL., 17 MAR 87; To VA-83, USS Saratoga (CV-60), 17 MAR 87 ** End of flight record card ** Transferred to VA-146/CVW-9, NG/3XX, NAS LeMoore, CA., date unknown ** Transferred to AMARC, Davis Monthan AFB; Tucson, AZ., assigned park code 6A0202; 25 JUL 89 ** Changed park code to 6A0292 ** 6048.7 flight hours ** TF41A402D engine S/N 141597 ** Project changed per FSO letter, 06 APR 04 ** Engine records released to DRMO for disposition, 26 MAY 05 ** Aircraft deleted from inventory and released to DRMO for disposition, 01 AUG 05.

E-469 159661 Navy acceptance from NPRO Rep. LTV, Dallas, TX., 17 DEC 75 ** Transferred to VA-15/CVW-6, AE/302, NAS Cecil Field, FL., 19 DEC 75; To VA-15, USS America (CV-66), 19 DEC 75; To VA-15, MCAS Yuma, AZ., 28 DEC 76; To VA-15, USS America (CV-66), 07 JAN 77; To VA-15, NAS Cecil Field, FL., 19 JUL 77; To VA-15, USS America (CV-66), 19 JUL 77; To VA-15, NAS Jacksonville, FL., 09 JUN 78; To VA-15, NAS Cecil Field, FL., 06 JUL 78; To VA-15, NAS Roosevelt Roads, PR., 13 JUL 78; To VA-15, USS America (CV-66), 13 JUL 78; To VA-15, NAS Cecil Field, FL., 13 JUL 78; To VA-15, USS Independence (CV-62), 13 JUL 78; To VA-15, NAS Cecil Field, FL., 13 JUL 78; To VA-15, USS Independence (CV-62), 13 JUL 78; To VA-15, NAS Cecil Field,

FL., 13 JUL 78 ** Transferred to VA-174/FRS, AD/4XX, NAS Cecil Field, FL., 23 JAN 80 ** Transferred to VA-81/CVW-17, AA/4XX, NAS Cecil Field, FL., 07 JUL 80; To VA-81, USS Forrestal (CV-59), 22 JUL 80; To VA-81, NAS Cecil Field, FL., 22 JUL 80; To VA-81, USS Forrestal (CV-59), 22 JUL 80; To VA-81, NAS Cecil Field, FL., 22 JUL 80 ** Transferred to VA-12/CVW-7, AG/4XX, USS Dwight D. Eisenhower (CVN-69), 26 OCT 81; To VA-12, NAS Cecil Field, FL., 02 NOV 81; To VA-12, USS Dwight D. Eisenhower (CVN-69), 23 NOV 81; To VA-12, NAS Jacksonville, FL., 19 JUL 82; To VA-12, NAS Cecil Field, FL., 28 AUG 82; To VA-12, USS Dwight D. Eisenhower (CVN-69), 31 MAR 83; To VA-12, NAS Cecil Field, FL., 13 JUL 83; To VA-12, USS Dwight D. Eisenhower (CVN-69), 13 JUL 83 ** Transferred to VA-174/FRS, AD/4XX, NAS Cecil Field, FL., 16 MAY 84 ** Transferred to NARF, NAS Jacksonville, FL., 27 SEP 84 ** Transferred to VA-37/CVW-6, AE/305, NAS Cecil Field, FL., 08 NOV 84; To VA-37, MCAS Iwakuni, JP., 08 NOV 84; To VA-37, Korea, 05 MAR 85; To VA-37, MCAS Iwakuni, JP., 08 MAR 85; To VA-37, NAF Atsugi, JP., 31 MAY 85; To VA-37, NAS Cecil Field, FL., 01 JUN 85; To VA-37, USS Forrestal (CV-59), 06 DEC 85; To VA-37, NAS Cecil Field, FL., 06 DEC 85; To VA-37, USS Forrestal (CV-59), 06 DEC 85 ** End of flight record card ** To VA-37, NAS Cecil Field, FL., date unknown ** Transferred to AMARC, Davis Monthan AFB; Tucson, AZ., assigned park code 6A0226; 08 JUL 87 ** 5112.7 flight hours ** TF41A402D engine S/N 142633 ** Engine records released to DRMO, Davis Monthan AFB; Tucson, AZ., for disposition, 22 FEB 06 ** Aircraft storage location 210807 ** End of flight record card ** Aircraft at AMARG, Davis Monthan AFB; Tucson, AZ., 15 JUN 07.

159967/159984 LTV A-7E Corsair II; (Block XIX)
FY 75 Contract N00019-75-C-0056, (18) A-7E; from E-471/E-488
FY 75 Contract N00019-75-C-0164, (18) A-7E; from E-489/E-506

E-492 159967 Navy acceptance from NPRO Rep. LTV, Dallas, TX., 28 JAN 76 ** Transferred to VA-15/CVW-6, AE/3XX, USS America (CV-66), 29 JAN 76; To VA-15, NAS Cecil Field, FL., 29 JAN 76; To VA-15, USS America (CV-66), 29 JAN 76; To VA-15, MCAS Yuma, AZ., 30 NOV 76; To VA-15, NAS Jacksonville, FL., 28 FEB 77; To VA-15, USS America (CV-66), 28 MAR 77; To VA-15, NAS Cecil Field, FL., 19 JUL 77; To VA-15, USS America (CV-66), 19 JUL 77; To VA-15, NAS Cecil Field, FL., 14 JUN 78; To VA-15, NAS Jacksonville, FL., 10 JUL 78; To VA-15, NAS Cecil Field, FL., 17 JUL 78; To VA-15, NAS Roosevelt Roads, PR., 18 JUL 78; To VA-15, USS America (CV-66), 18 JUL 78; To VA-15, NAS Cecil Field, FL., 18 JUL 78; VA-15, USS Independence (CV-62), 18 JUL 78; To VA-15, NAS Cecil Field, FL., 18 JUL 78; VA-15, USS Independence (CV-62), 20 JUL 78; To VA-15, NAS Cecil Field, FL., 21 FEB 80 ** VA-174/FRS, AD/4XX, NAS Jacksonville, FL., 23 SEP 80; To VA-174, NAS Cecil Field, FL., 23 SEP 80; To VA-174, NAS Dallas, TX., 12 DEC 80 ** Transferred to VA-105/CVW-3, AC/4XX, NAS Cecil Field, FL., 12 MAR 81; To VA-105, NAS Fallon, NV., 19 MAY 81; To VA-105, NAS Cecil Field, FL., 19 MAY 81; To VA-105, USS John F. Kennedy (CV-67), 19 MAY 81; To VA-105, NAS Cecil Field, FL., 14 MAR 82; To VA-105/CVW-15, NL/4XX, USS Carl Vinson (CVN-70), 14 MAR 82; To VA-105, NAS Cecil Field, FL., 14 MAR 82; To VA-105, USS Carl Vinson (CVN-70), 14 MAR 82; To VA-105, NAS Cecil Field, FL., 14 MAR 82; To VA-105, USS Carl Vinson (CVN-70), 14 MAR 82 ** Transferred to VA-83/CVW-17, AA/3XX, NAS Cecil Field, FL., 15 MAR 83; To VA-83, NAS Fallon, NV., 15 MAR 83; NAS Cecil Field, FL., 30 SEP 83; To VA-83, USS Saratoga (CV-60), 01 NOV 83; To VA-83, NAS Cecil Field, FL., 01 NOV 83; To VA-83, USS Saratoga (CV-60), 13 MAR 84; To VA-83, NAS Cecil Field, FL., 16 MAR 84; To VA-83, NAS Fallon, NV., 12 DEC 84; To VA-83, NAS Cecil Field, FL., 12 DEC 84; To VA-83, USS Saratoga (CV-60), 12 DEC 84; To VA-83, NAS Cecil Field, FL., 01 JUN 85; To VA-83, NAS Jacksonville, FL., 06 AUG 85 ** Transferred to VA-174/FRS, AD/4XX, NAS Cecil Field, FL., 26 NOV 85 ** Transferred to VA-37/CVW-6, AE/3XX, 12 JAN 87; To VA-37, USS Forrestal (CV-59), 16 JUL 87 thru 19 SEP 87 ** End of flight record card ** Transferred to the Helinic Air Force (Greece).

E-471 159968 Navy acceptance from NPRO Rep. LTV, Dallas, TX., 19 JAN 76 ** Transferred to VA-87/CVW-6, AE/4XX, USS America (CV-66), 21 JAN 76; To VA-87, NAS Cecil Field, FL., 21 JAN 76; To VA-87, USS America (CV-67), 21 JAN 76; To VA-87, MCAS Yuma, AZ., 21 JAN 76; To VA-87, USS America (CV-66), 21 JAN 76; To VA-87, NAS Cecil Field, FL., 21 JAN 76; To VA-87, USS America (CV-67), 19 JUL 76; To VA-87, NAS Jacksonville, FL., 01 JUN 78; To VA-87, NAS Cecil Field, FL., 27 JUN 78; To VA-87, NAS Roosevelt Roads, PR., 06 SEP 78; To VA-87, NAS Cecil Field, FL., 06 SEP 78; To VA-87, USS Independence (CV-62), 06 SEP 78; To VA-87, NAS Cecil Field, FL., 27 FEB 80; To VA-87, USS Independence (CV-62), 08 AUG 80; To VA-87, NAS Cecil Field, FL., 12 JAN 81 ** Transferred to VA-174/FRS, AD/4XX, NAS Cecil Field, FL., 28 DEC 81; To VA-174, NAS Jacksonville, FL., 29 OCT 82 ** Transferred to VA-83/CVW-17, AA/3XX, NAS Cecil Field, FL., 11 FEB 83 ** Transferred to VA-46/CVW-1, AB/3XX, NAS Cecil Field, FL., 22 SEP 83; To VA-46, USS America (CV-66), 22 SEP 83; To VA-46, NAS Cecil Field, FL., 16 JAN 84; To VA-46, USS America (CV-66), 20 JAN 84; To VA-46, NAS Cecil Field, FL., 20 JAN 84; To VA-46, USS America (CV-66), 01 MAY 84; To VA-46, NAS Cecil Field, FL., 19 NOV 84; To VA-46, USS America (CV-66), 17 MAY 85; To VA-46, NAS Cecil Field, FL., 20 MAY 85; To VA-46, NAS Jacksonville, FL., 19 AUG 85 ** Transferred to VA-105/CVW-6, AE/4XX, NAS Cecil Field, FL., 22 AUG 85; To VA-105, USS Forrestal (CV-59), 17 OCT 85; To VA-105, NAS Cecil Field, FL., 17 OCT 85; To VA-105, USS Forrestal (CV-59), 13 OCT 86; To VA-105, NAS Cecil Field, FL., 13 OCT 86 ** Transferred to VA-46/CVW-1, AB/3XX, NAS Cecil Field, FL., 09 JAN 87; To VA-46, USS Dwight D. Eisenhower (CVN-69), 14 APR 87; To VA-46, NAS Cecil Field, FL., 14 APR 87 ** End of flight record card Transferred to NAD, NAS Jacksonville, FL., 28 JUL 89 ** Transferred to VX-5, NWC China Lake, CA., date unknown ** Transferred to AMARC, Davis Monthan AFB; Tucson, AZ., assigned park code 6A0397; 16 JUL 91 ** 6466.7 flight hours ** TF41A402D engine S/N 141269 ** Aircraft deleted from inventory and released to DRMO for disposition ** Storage location 210529 ** At AMARG, Davis Monthan AFB; Tucson, AZ., 15 JUN 07.

E-472 159969 Navy acceptance from NPRO Rep. LTV, Dallas, TX., 10 FEB 76 ** Transferred to VA-87/CVW-6, AE/4XX, USS America (CV-66), 12 FEB 76; To VA-87, NAS Cecil Field, FL., 12 FEB 76; To VA-87, USS America (CV-66), 12 FEB 76; To VA-87, NAS Cecil Field, FL., 12 FEB 76; To VA-87, MCAS Yuma, AZ., 12 FEB 76; To VA-87, USS America (CV-66), 12 FEB 76; To VA-87, NAS Cecil Field, FL., 12 FEB 76; To VA-87, USS America (CV-66), 19 JUL 76; To VA-87, NAS Jacksonville, FL., 12 JUN 78 ** To VA-87, NAS Cecil Field, FL., 11 JUL 78; To VA-87, NAS Roosevelt Roads, PR., 20 JUL 78; To VA-87, NAS Cecil Field, FL., 20 JUL 78; To VA-87, USS Independence (CV-62), 20 JUL 78; To VA-87, NAS Cecil Field, FL., 19 MAR 80; To VA-87, USS Independence (CV-62), 28 AUG 80; To VA-87, NAS Cecil Field, FL., 28 AUG 80; To VA-87, USS Independence (CV-62), 24 AUG 81; To VA-87, NAS Cecil Field, FL., 24 AUG 81; To VA-87, USS Independence (CV-62), 24 AUG 81; To VA-87, NAS Cecil Field, FL., 24 AUG 81; To VA-87, USS Independence (CV-62), 24 AUG 81; To VA-87, NAS Jacksonville, FL., 22 DEC 82; To VA-87, NAS Dallas, TX., 23 FEB 83; To VA-87, NAS Cecil Field, FL., 24 MAR 83; To VA-87, NAS Dallas, TX., 19 MAY 83; To VA-87, NAS Cecil Field, FL., 22 MAY 83 ** Transferred to VA-46/CVW-1, AB/3XX, USS America (CV-66), 24 MAY 83; To VA-46, NAS NAS Cecil Field, FL., 15 JUN 83; To VA-46, USS America (CV-66), 22 SEP 83; To VA-46, NAS Cecil Field, FL., 22 SEP 83; To VA-46, USS America (CV-66), 22 SEP 83; To VA-46, NAS Cecil Field, FL., 22 SEP 83; To VA-46, USS America (CV-66), 22 SEP 83; To VA-46, NAS Cecil Field, FL., 19 NOV 84; To VA-46, NAS Jacksonville, FL., 04 JAN 85; To VA-46, NAS Cecil Field, FL., 25 MAR 85; To VA-46, USS America (CV-66), 25 MAR 85; To VA-46, NAS Cecil Field, FL., 25 MAR 85; To VA-46, USS America (CV-66), 25 MAR 85; To VA-46, NAS Cecil Field, FL., 25 AUG 85; To VA-46, USS America (CV-66), 25 AUG 85; To VA-46, NAS Cecil Field,

FL., 25 AUG 85 ** Transferred to VA-83/CVW-17, AA/3XX, USS Saratoga (CV-60), 18 SEP 86; To VA-83, NAS Cecil Field, FL., 15 OCT 83; To VA-83, USS Saratoga (CV-60), 15 OCT 86; To VA-83, NAS Cecil Field, FL., 17 MAR 87; To VA-83, USS Saratoga (CV-60), 12 APR 87; To VA-83, NAS Cecil Field, FL., 17 MAY 87; To VA-83, USS Saratoga (CV-60), 17 MAY 87 ** Transferred to VA-37/CVW-6, AE/3XX, NAS Cecil Field, FL., 04 JUN 87; To VA-37, USS Forrestal (CV-59), 21 JUL 87 thru 27 JUL 87 ** End of flight record card ** Transferred to NAD, NAS Jacksonville, FL., 08 DEC 88 ** Transferred to VA-205/CVWR-30, AF/5XX, NAS Atlanta, GA., date unknown ** Transferred to AMARC, Davis Monthan AFB; Tucson, AZ., assigned park code 6A0326, 23 MAR 90 ** 6047.1 flight hours ** TF51A402D engine S/N 141181 ** Storage location 111506 ** At AMARG, Davis Monthan AFB; Tucson, AZ., 15 JUN 07.

E-473 159970 Navy acceptance from NPRO Rep. LTV, Dallas, TX., 30 JAN 76 ** Transferred to VA-94/CVW- 15, NL/4XX, NAS LeMoore, CA., 02 FEB 76; To VA-94, NAS Fallon, NV., 30 APR 76; To VA-94, NAS LeMoore, CA., 30 APR 76; To VA-94, USS Coral Sea (CV-43), 09 DEC 76; To VA-94, NAS LeMoore, CA., 15 DEC 76; To VA-94, USS Coral Sea (CV-43), 31 UG 77; To VA-94, NAS LeMoore, CA., 17 OCT 77; To VA-94, NAS Jacksonville, FL., 19 FEB 78; To VA-94, NAS LeMoore, CA., 04 APR 78; To VA-94, USS Kitty Hawk (CV-63), 27 APR 79 ** Transferred to VA-97/CVW-14, NK/3XX, NAS LeMoore, CA., 14 MAY 79; To VA-97, USS Coral Sea (CV-43), 17 OCT 79; To VA-97, NAS LeMoore, CA., 20 DEC 79; To VA-97, NAS Jacksonville, FL., 23 SEP 80; To VA-97, NAS Dallas, TX., 05 JAN 81; To VA-97, USS Coral Sea (CV-43), 31 MAR 81; To VA-97, NAS LeMoore, CA., 31 MAR 81 ** Transferred to VA-105/CVW-3, AC/400, NAS Fallon, NV., 14 APR 81; To VA-105, NAS Cecil Field, FL., 24 JUL 81; To VA-105, USS John F. Kennedy (CV-67), 20 AUG 81; To VA-105, NAS Cecil Field, FL., 11 DEC 81 81; To VA-105, USS John F. Kennedy (CV-67), 16 DEC 81; To VA-105, NAS Cecil Field, FL., 18 MAR 82; To VA-105/CVW-15, NL/4XX, USS Carl Vinson (CVN-70), 18 MAR 82; To VA-105, NAS Cecil Field, FL., 18 MAR 82; To VA-105, USS Carl Vinson (CVN-70), 18 MAR 82; To VA-105, NAS Cecil Field, FL., 28 OCT 83; To VA-105, NAS Jacksonville, FL., 17 NOV 83; To VA-105, NAS Cecil Field, FL., 05 DEC 83 83; To VA-105, NAS Jacksonville, FL., 24 JAN 84; To VA-105, NAS Roosevelt Roads, PR., 25 JAN 84; To VA-105, NAS Cecil Field, FL., 25 JAN 84; To VA-105, NAF Kadena, JP., 10 MAY 84; To VA-105, Cubi Point, PI., 10 MAY 84; To VA-105, MCAS Iwakuni, JP., 10 MAY 84; To VA-105, NAS Cecil Field, FL., 10 MAY 84; To VA-105, USS Forrestal (CV-59), 12 JUN 85; To VA-105, NAS Cecil Field, FL., 12 JUN 85; To VA-105, USS Forrestal (CV-59), 26 MAR 86; To VA-105, NAS Cecil Field, FL., 31 MAR 86; To VA-105, NAS Jacksonville, FL., 19 JUN 86 ** Transferred to NARF, NAS Jacksonville, FL., 30 JUN 90 ** Transferred to VA-86/CVW-8, AJ/4XX, USS Nimitz (CVN-68), 01 JUL 86; To VA-86, NAS Cecil Field, FL., 10 OCT 86; To VA-86, USS Nimitz (CVN-68), 10 OCT 86; To VA-86, NAS Cecil Field, FL., 10 OCT 86 ** Transferred to NSWC, Strike/XX, NAS Fallon, NV., 23 SEP 87 ** End of flight record card ** Transferred to AMARC, Davis Monthan AFB; Tucson, AZ., assigned park code 6A0319; 15 MAR 90 ** 6200.9 flight hours ** TF41A402D engine S/N 141952 ** Project changed per FSO letter, 06 DEC 04 ** Aircraft deleted from inventory and released to DRMO for disposition, 17 SEP 04, ** Located at AMARG; Davis Monthan AFB; Tucson, AZ., 15 AUG 05.

E-474 159971 Navy acceptance from NPRO Rep. LTV, Dallas, TX., 09 MAR 76 ** Transferred to NATC, NAS Paxtuxent River, MD, for RDT & E, 09 MAR 76 ** Transferred to VA-174/FRS, AD/4XX, NAS Cecil Field, FL., 02 AUG 76 ** Transferred to VA-72/CVW-1, AB/4XX, NAS Cecil Field, FL., 13 SEP 77; To VA-72, NAS Jacksonville, FL., 12 APR 78; To VA-72, NAS Cecil Field, FL., 10 MAY 78; To VA-72, USS John F. Kennedy (CV-67), 10 MAY 78; To VA-72, NAS Cecil Field, FL., 10 MAY 78; Transferred to VA-174/FRS, AD/4XX, NAS Cecil Field, FL., 09 JUL 80; To VA-174, NAS Jacksonville, FL., 16 SEP 80; To VA-

174, NAS Cecil Field, FL., 16 SEP 80; To VA-174, NAS Dallas, TX., 08 DEC 80 ** Transferred to VA-37/CVW-3, AC/3XX, NAS Cecil Field, FL., 02 MAR 81; To VA-37, NAS Fallon, NV., 02 MAR 81; To VA-37, USS John F. Kennedy (CV-67), 02 MAR 81; To VA-37, NAS Cecil Field, FL., 02 MAR 81; To VA-37, USS John F. Kennedy (CV-67), 02 MAR 81; To VA-37, NAS Cecil Field, FL., 02 MAR 81 ** Transferred to VA-105/CVW-15, NL/4XX, NAS Cecil Field, FL., 02 SEP 82; To VA-105, USS Carl Vinson (CVN-70), 11 OCT 82; To VA-105, NAS Cecil Field, FL., 11 OCT 82 ** Transferred to VA-15/CVW-6, AE/3XX, NAS Cecil Field, FL., 24 FEB 83; To VA-15, NAS Jacksonville, FL., 16 MAY 83; To VA-15, USS Independence (CV-62), 26 MAY 83; To VA-15, NAS Cecil Field, FL., 13 JUN 83; To VA-15, NAS Jacksonville, FL., 08 AUG 83; To VA-15, USS Independence (CV-62), 09 AUG 83; To VA-15, NAS Cecil Field, FL., 09 AUG 83; To VA-15, USS Independence (CV-62), 09 AUG 83; To VA-15, NAS Cecil Field, FL., 09 AUG 83; To VA-15, USS Independence (CV-62), 13 JUN 84; To VA-15, NAS Cecil Field, FL., 13 SEP 84; To VA-15, USS Independence (CV-62), 19 SEP 84; To VA-15, NAS Cecil Field, FL., 19 SEP 84 ** Transferred to VA-66/CVW-7, AG/3XX, NAS Cecil Field, FL., 02 JUL 85; To VA-66, NAS Jacksonville, FL., 16 JAN 86 ** Transferred to VA-72/CVW-1, AB/4XX, NAS Cecil Field, FL., 17 JAN 86; To VA-72, USS America (CV-66), 27 JAN 86; To VA-72, NAS Cecil Field, FL., 18 JUN 86; To VA-72/CVW-7, AG/4XX, USS Dwight D. Eisenhower (CVN-69), 09 FEB 87; To VA-72, NAS Cecil Field, FL., 09 FEB 87 thru 17 SEP 87 ** End of flight record card ** On loan from National Museum of Naval Aviation, Pensacola, FL., to the Carolinas Historic Aviation Commission Museum; Charlotte, NC.

E-475 159972 Navy acceptance from NPRO Rep. LTV, Dallas, TX., 22 JAN 76 ** Transferred to VA-87/CVW-6, AE/4XX, USS America (CV-66), 23 JAN 76; To VA-87; NAS Cecil Field, FL., 23 JAN 76; To VA-87, USS America (CV-66), 14 APR 76; To VA-87, NAS Cecil Field, FL., 14 APR 76; To VA-87, MCAS Yuma, AZ., 14 APR 76; To VA-87, USS America (CV-66), 14 APR 76; To VA-87, NAS Cecil Field, FL., 14 APR 76; To VA-87, USS America (CV-66), 19 JUL 77; To VA-87, NAS Jacksonville, FL., 19 JUN 78; To VA-87, NAS Cecil Field, FL., 17 JUL 78; To VA-87, NAS Roosevelt Roads, PR., 18 JUL 98; To VA-87, NAS Cecil Field, FL., 18 JUL 78; To VA-87, USS Independence (CV-62), 24 MAY 79; To VA-87, NAS Cecil Field, FL., 24 MAY 79; To VA-87, USS Independence (CV-62), 30 MAY 80 ~ S 1SO strike, 13 FEB 81** No data on strike.

E-476 159973 Navy acceptance from NPRO Rep. LTV, Dallas, TX., 23 MAR 76 ** Transferred to NAVPRO Rep. LTV Dallas, TX., for RDT & E, 24 MAR 76 ** Transferred to NATC, NAS Patuxent River, MD., for RDT & E, 22 JUL 77 ** Transferred to VA-94/CVW-15, NL/403, NAS LeMoore, CA., 18 OCT 77; To VA-94, NAS Cubi Point, PI., 29 MAY 79; To VA-94, USS Kitty Hawk (CV-63), 06 JUN 79; To VA-94, NAS LeMoore, CA., 21 SEP 79; To VA-94, NAS Jacksonville, FL., 03 APR 80; To VA-94, NAS LeMoore, CA., 10 APR 80; To VA-94, USS Kitty Hawk (CV-63), 28 APR 80; To VA-94, NAS LeMoore, CA., 28 APR 80; To VA-94, USS Kitty Hawk (CV-63), 28 APR 80; To VA-94, NAS LeMoore, CA., 28 APR 80; To VA-94, USS Kitty Hawk (CV-63), 28 APR 80 ** Transferred to NWEF Kirtland AFB; Albuquerque, NM., 20 MAY 80 ** Transferred to VA-122/FRS, NJ/2XX, NAS LeMoore, CA., 01 APR 81 ** Transferred to NWC China Lake, CA., 01 JUN 82; To NWC, NAS Jacksonville, FL., 19 APR 83; To NWC, China Lake, CA., 28 JUL 83 ** Transferred to VA-122/FRS, NJ/2XX, NAS LeMoore, CA., 29 JUL 83 ** Transferred to VA-93/CVW-5, NF/3XX, USS Midway (CV-41), 06 SEP 83; To VA-93, NAF Atsugi, JP., 06 SEP 83 ** Transferred to VA-94/CVW-11, NH/4XX, USS Enterprise (CVN-65), 29 OCT 84; To VA-94, NAS LeMoore, CA., 23 NOV 84; To VA-94, NAS Fallon, NV., 11 APR 85; To VA-94, NAS LeMoore, CA., 17 APR 85; To VA-94, NAS Jacksonville, FL., 25 SEP 85; To VA-94, NAS LeMoore, CA., 04 OCT 85; To VA-94, USS Enterprise (CVN-65), 22 JAN 86 ~ S 1SO strike, 08 MAR 86 ** No data on strike.

E-477 159974 Navy acceptance from NPRO Rep. LTV, Dallas, TX., 26 JAN 76 ** Transferred to VA-15/CVW-6, AE/3XX, USS America (CV-66), 30 JAN 76; To VA-15, NAS Cecil Field, FL., 30 JAN 76; To VA-15, USS America (CV-66), 30 JAN 76; To VA-15, MCAS Yuma, AZ., 14 JAN 77; To VA-15, USS America (CV-66), 14 JAN 77; To VA-15, NAS Cecil Field, Fl., 19 JUL 77; To VA-15, USS America (CV-66), 19 JUL 77; To VA-15, NAS Cecil Field, Fl., 19 JUN 78; To VA-15, NAS Jacksonville, FL., 23 JUN 78; To VA-15, NAS Roosevelt Roads, PR., 26 JUN 78; To VA-15, USS America (CV-66), 26 JUN 78; To VA-15, NAS Cecil Field, Fl., 26 JUN 78; To VA-15, USS Independence (CV-62), 26 JUN 78; To VA-15, NAS Cecil Field, Fl., 26 JUN 78; To VA-15, USS Independence (CV-62), 26 JUN 78; To VA-15, NAS Cecil Field, Fl., 26 JUN 78; To VA-15, USS Independence (CV-62), 19 JUN 80 ** Transferred to VA-86/CVW-8, AJ/4XX, USS Nimitz (CVN-68), 12 NOV 80; To VA-86, NAS Cecil Field, FL., 12 NOV 80; To VA-86, USS Nimitz (CVN-68), 19 MAR 81; To VA-86, NAS Cecil Field, FL., 19 MAR 81; To VA-86, USS Nimitz (CVN-68), 19 MAR 81; To VA-86, NAS Cecil Field, FL., 19 MAR 81 ** Transferred to VA-81/CVW-17, AA/4XX, USS Forrestal (CV-59), 25 FEB 82; To VA-81, NAS Cecil Field, FL., 25 FEB 82; To VA-81, USS Forrestal (CV-59), 25 FEB 82; To VA-81, NAS Jacksonville, FL., 18 NOV 82; To VA-81, NAS Cecil Field, FL., 02 FEB 83; To VA-81, NAS Dallas, TX., 19 APR 83 ** Transferred to VA-15/CVW-6, AE/3XX, NAS Cecil Field, FL., 20 APR 83; To VA-15, USS Independence (CV-62), 02 JUN 83; To VA-15, NAS Cecil Field, FL., 02 JUN 83 ** Transferred to VA-46/CVW-1, AB/300, NAS Cecil Field, FL., 14 JUL 83; To VA-46, USS America (CV-66), 08 SEP 83; To VA-46, NAS Cecil Field, FL., 08 SEP 83; To VA-46, USS America (CV-66), 08 SEP 83; To VA-46, NAS Cecil Field, FL., 08 SEP 83; To VA-46, USS America (CV-66), 08 SEP 83; To VA-46, NAS Cecil Field, FL., 27 NOV 84; To VA-46, NAS Jacksonville, FL., 30 APR 85; To VA-46, USS America (CV-66), 03 MAY 85; To VA-46, NAS Cecil Field, FL., 03 MAY 85; To VA-46, USS America (CV-66), 03 MAY 85; To VA-46, NAS Cecil Field, FL., 03 MAY 85; To VA-46, USS America (CV-66), 14 JAN 86; To VA-46, NAS Cecil Field, FL., 15 JAN 86 ** Transferred to VA-83/CVW-17, AA/3XX, USS Saratoga (CV-60), 18 SEP 86; To VA-83, NAS Cecil Field, FL., 15 OCT 86; To VA-83, USS Saratoga (CV-60), 12 JAN 87; To VA-83, NAS Cecil Field, FL., 06 FEB 87; USS Saratoga (CV-60), 06 FEB 87; To VA-83, NAS Cecil Field, FL., 06 FEB 87; USS Saratoga (CV-60), 18 SEP 86 ** End of flight record card ** On conditional loan from the National Museum of Naval Aviation; Pensacola, FL., to NAS, JRB, New Orleans, LA.

E-478 159975 Navy acceptance from NPRO Rep. LTV, Dallas, TX., 23 FEB 76 ** Transferred to VA-22/CVW-15, NL/3XX, NAS LeMoore, CA., 24 FEB 76; To VA-22, NAS Fallon, NV., 30 APR 76; To VA-22, NAS LeMoore, CA., 30 APR 76; Painted In bicentennial colors, 04 JUL 76; To VA-22, USS Coral Sea (CV-43), 13 AUG 77; To VA-22, NAS LeMoore, CA., 02 SEP 77; To VA-22, NAS Jacksonville, FL., 26 MAY 78; To VA-22, NAS LeMoore, CA., 01 JUL 78; To VA-22, NAS Kingsville, TX., 23 AUG 78; To VA-22, NAS LeMoore, CA, 23 AUG 78; To VA-22, USS Kitty Hawk (CV-63), 20 APR 79 ** Transferred to VA-97/CVW-14, NK/302, NAS LeMoore, CA., 19 JUN 79; To VA-97, USS Coral Sea (CV-43), 11 OCT 79; To VA-97, NAS LeMoore, CA., 12 NOV 79; To VA-97, USS Coral Sea (CV-43), 18 NOV 80; To VA-97, NAS LeMoore, CA., 18 NOV 80; To VA-97, NAS Jacksonville, FL., 18 FEB 81; To VA-97, NAS LeMoore, CA., 27 APR 81; To VA-97, USS Coral Sea (CV-43), 27 APR 81; To VA-97, NAS Dallas, TX., 16 JUN 81; To VA-97, NAS LeMoore, CA., 28 JUN 81** Transferred to VA-113/ CVW-2, NE/3XX, NAS LeMoore, CA., 01 JUL 81; To VA-113, NAS Fallon, NV., 14 SEP 81; To VA-113, USS Ranger (CV-61), 18 OCT 81; To VA-113, NAS LeMoore, CA., 12 NOV 81; To VA-113, USS Ranger (CV-61), 12 NOV 81; To VA-113, NAS LeMoore, CA., 12 NOV 81; To VA-113, USS Ranger (CV-61), 26 FEB 82; To VA-113, NAS Cubi Point, PI., 26 FEB 82; To VA-113, NAF Atsugi, JP., 26 FEB 82 ** Transferred to VA-93/CVW-5, NF/3XX, NAS Cubi Point, PI., 27 SEP 82; To VA-93, NAF Atsugi, JP., 01 OCT 82; To VA-93, NAS Cubi Point, PI., 05 OCT 82; To VA-93, USS Midway (CV-41), 10 DEC 82; To VA-93, NAF Atsugi, JP., 16 SEP 83; To VA-93, USS Midway (CV-41), 17 SEP 83; To VA-93, NAF Atsugi, JP., 25 OCT 83 ** Transferred to VA-146/CVW-9, NE/3XX, NAS LeMoore, CA., 07 JUL 84; To VA-146, USS Kitty Hawk (CV-63), 29 OCT 84; To VA-146, NAS LeMoore, CA., 02 JAN 86; To VA-146, NAS Jacksonville, FL., 17 JAN 86; To VA-146, NAS LeMoore, CA., 17 APR 86 ** Transferred to VA-97/CVW-15, NL/3XX, NAS LeMoore, CA., 28 APR 86; To VA-97, USS Carl Vinson (CVN-70), 28 APR 86; To VA-97, NAS LeMoore, CA., 28 APR 86; To VA-97, USS Carl Vinson (CVN-70), 28 APR 86; To VA-97, NAS Alameda, CA., 18 FEB 87 thru 02 MAR 87 ** End of flight record card ** Transferred to the Helenic Air force (Greece).

E-479 159976 Navy acceptance from NPRO Rep. LTV, Dallas, TX., 27 APR 76 ** Transferred to VA-94/CVW-15, NL/4XX, NAS LeMoore, CA., 07 MAY 76; Painted in bicentennial colors, 04 JUL 76; To VA-94, USS Coral Sea (CV-43), 09 DEC 76; To VA-94, NAS LeMoore, CA., 22 DEC 76; To VA-94, USS Coral Sea (CV-43), 31 AUG 77; To VA-94, NAS LeMoore, CA., 26 OCT 77; To VA-94, NAS Jacksonville, FL., 10 MAY 78; To VA-94, NAS LeMoore, CA., 22 MAY 78 ** Transferred to VA-122/FRS, NJ/2XX, NAS LeMoore, CA., 10 APR 79 ** Transferred to VA-27/CVW-14, NK/4XX, NAF, El Centro, CA., 11 OCT 79; To VA-27, USS Coral Sea (CV-43), 11 OCT 79; To VA-27, NAS Cubi Point, PI., 12 NOV 79; To VA-27, USS Coral Sea (CV-43), 23 DEC 79; To VA-27, NAS LeMoore, CA., 08 JAN 80; To VA-27, NAS Jacksonville, FL., 31 DEC 80; To VA-27, NAS Dallas, TX., 02 MAR 81; To VA-27, USS Coral Sea (CV-43), 09 MAR 81 ** Transferred to VA-146/CVW-9, NG/3XX, NAS LeMoore, CA., 13 MAY 81; To VA-146, USS Constellation (CV-64), 08 JUL 81; To VA-146, NAS LeMoore, CA., 06 AUG 81; To VA-146, USS Constellation (CV-64), 06 AUG 81; To VA-146, NAS LeMoore, CA., 15 MAY 82; To VA-146, NAS Jacksonville, FL., 30 AUG 83; Transferred to VA-27/CVW-15, NL/4XX, NAS LeMoore, CA., 28 NOV 83 ** Transferred to VA-146/CVW-9, NG/3XX, USS Kitty Hawk (CV-63), 29 NOV 83 ** Transferred to VA-27/CVW-15, NL/4XX, USS Carl Vinson (CVN-70), 30 NOV 83; To VA-27, NAS LeMoore, CA., 01 DEC 83; To VA-27, USS Carl Vinson (CVN-70), 01 DEC 83; To VA-27, NAS LeMoore, CA., 01 DEC 83; To VA-27, NAS Jacksonville, FL., 11 FEB 86; To VA-27, NAS LeMoore, CA., 11 FEB 86; To VA-27, NAS Jacksonville, FL., 18 FEB 86 ** Transferred to NARF, NAS Jacksonville, FL., 28 APR 86 ** Transferred to VA-27/CVW-15, NL/410, NAS LeMoore, CA., 30 APR 86; To VA-27, USS Carl Vinson (CVN-70), 30 APR 86; To VA-27, NAS LeMoore, CA., 30 APR 86; To VA-27, USS Carl Vinson (CVN-70), 30 APR 86; To VA-27, NAS LeMoore, CA., 01 OCT 86 thru 19 MAR 87 ** End of flight record card ** Transferred to AMARC, Davis Monthan AFB; Tucson, AZ., assigned park code 6A0305, 27 NOV 89 ** 6188.0 flight hours ** TF41A402 engine S/N 141273 ** Aircraft released from storage and prepared for overland shipment to FMS and NAD, NAS Jacksonville, FL., with final shipment to government of Thailand, 17 JUN 05 ** Transferred to the Royal Thai Navy.

E-480 159977 Navy acceptance from NPRO Rep. LTV, Dallas, TX., 18 FEB 76 ** Transferred to VA-87/CVW-6, AE/413, USS America (CV-66), 20 FEB 76; To VA-87, NAS Cecil Field, FL., 20 FEB 76; To VA-87, USS America (CV-66), 20 FEB 76; To VA-87, NAS Cecil Field, FL., 20 FEB 76; To VA-87, MCAS Yuma, AZ., 20 FEB 76 ** To VA-87, USS America (CV-66), 20 FEB 76; To VA-87, NAS Cecil Field, FL., 20 FEB 76; To VA-87, USS America (CV-66), 19 JUL 77; To VA-87, NAS Jacksonville, FL., 23 MAY 78; To VA-87, NAS Cecil Field, FL., 25 MAY 78; To VA-87, NAS Jacksonville, FL., 26 JUN 78; To VA-87, NAS Cecil Field, FL., 24 JUL 78; To VA-87, NAS Roosevelt Roads, PR., 28 JUL 79; To VA-87, NAS Cecil Field, FL., 28 JUL 78; To VA-87, NAS Jacksonville, FL., 07 DEC 78; To VA-87, NAS Cecil Field, FL., 15 DEC 78; To VA-87, USS Independence (CV-62), 15 DEC 78; To VA-87, NAS Cecil Field, FL., 19 MAR 80; To VA-87, NAS Jacksonville, FL., 02 JUN 80; To VA-87, NAS Cecil Field, FL., 11 JUN 80; To VA-87, USS Independence (CV-62), 05 AUG 80 ~ S ISO strike, 12 NOV 80 ** No data on strike.

E-481 159978 Navy acceptance from NPRO Rep. LTV, Dallas, TX., 30 MAR 76 ** Transferred to VA-174/FRS, AD/4XX, NAS Cecil Field, FL., 02 APR 76 ** Transferred to VF-101, NAS Oceana, VA., 13 SEP 77 ** Transferred to VA-46/CVW-1, AB/3XX, NAS Cecil Field, FL., 14 SEP 77; To VA-46, NAS Jacksonville, FL., 08 MAY 78; To VA-46, USS John F. Kennedy (CV-67), 08 MAY 78; To VA-46, NAS Cecil Field, FL., 09 MAY 78; To VA-46, USS John F. Kennedy (CV-67), 14 FEB 80; To VA-46, NAS Cecil Field, FL., 14 FEB 80; To VA-46, NAS Jacksonville, FL., 23 FEB 82; To VA-46, NAS Cecil Field, FL., 25 MAR 82; To VA-46, USS America (CV-66), 01 APR 82; To VA-46, NAS Cecil Field, FL., 01 APR 82; To VA-46, USS America (CV-66), 01 APR 82; To VA-46, NAS Cecil Field, FL., 18 APR 83; Transferred to VA-82/CVW-8, AJ/3XX, NAS Cecil Field, FL., 18 APR 83; To VA-82, NAS Jacksonville, FL., 28 MAR 84; To VA-82, NAS Cecil Field, FL., 28 MAR 84; To VA-82, NAS Jacksonville, FL., 30 MAR 84 ** Transferred to VA-37/CVW-15, NL/3XX, NAS Cecil Field, Fl., 06 JUN 84; To VA-37, MCAS Twenty Nine Palms, CA., 15 AUG 84 ~ S 1SO strike, 15 AUG 84 ** No data on strike.

E-482 159979 Navy acceptance from NPRO Rep. LTV, Dallas, TX., 23 FEB 76 ** Transferred to VA-15/CVW-6, AE/3XX, USS America (CV-66), 26 FEB 76; To VA-15, NAS Cecil Field, FL., 26 FEB 76; To VA-15, USS America (CV-66), 26 FEB 76 ~ S 1SO strike, 07 JUN 76 ** No data on strike.

E-483 159980 Navy acceptance from NPRO Rep. LTV, Dallas, TX., 31 MAR 76 ** Transferred to VA-22/CVW-15, NL/ 3XX, NAS LeMoore, CA., 06 APR 76; To VA-22, NAS Fallon, NV., 30 APR 76; To VA-22, NAS LeMoore, CA., 30 APR 76; To VA-22, USS Coral Sea (CV-43), 30 AUG 77 77; To VA-22, NAS LeMoore, CA., 18 OCT 77; To VA-22, NAS Jacksonville, FL., 22 MAY 78; To VA-22, NAS LeMoore, CA., 21 JUN 78; To VA-22, NAS Kingsville, TX., 23 AUG 78; To VA-22, NAS LeMoore, CA., 23 AUG 78 ** Transferred to VA-27/CVW-14, NK/4XX, NPTR El Centro, CA., 09 APR 79; To VA-27, NAS Alameda, CA., 11 JUL 79; To VA-27, USS Coral Sea (CV-43), 11 JUL 79; To VA-27, NAS LeMoore, CA., 22 OCT 79; To VA-27, USS Coral Sea (CV-43), 22 OCT 79; To VA-27, NAS Cubi Point, PI., 12 NOV 79; To VA-27, USS Coral Sea (CV-43), 23 DEC 79; To VA-27, NAF Atsugi, JP., 02 MAY 80; To VA-27, USS Coral Sea (CV-43), 05 MAY 80; To VA-27, NAS LeMoore, CA., 21 MAY 80; To VA-27, NAS Jacksonville, FL., 29 JAN 81; To VA-27, NAS LeMoore, CA., 13 APR 81; To VA-27, USS Coral Sea (CV-43), 16 APR 81; To VA-27, NAS Dallas, TX., 16 JUN 8 ** Transferred to VA-113/ CVW-2, NE/ 3XX, NAS LeMoore, CA., 01 JUL 81; To VA-113, NAS Fallon, NV., 11 SEP 81; To VA-113, USS Ranger (CV-61), 18 OCT 81; To VA-113, NAS LeMoore, CA., 12 NOV 81; To VA-113, USS Ranger (CV-61),12 NOV 81; To VA-113, NAS LeMoore, CA., 12 NOV 81; To VA-113, USS Ranger (CV-61), 23 MAR 82; To VA-113, NAS Cubi Point, PI., 23 MAR 82; To VA-113, NAF Atsugi, JP., 23 MAR 82 ** Transferred to VA-93/ CVW-5, NF/3XX, NAS Cubi Point, PI., 27 SEP 82; To VA-93, USS Midway (CV-41), 27 SEP 82; To VA-93, NAF Atsugi, JP., 28 OCT 83 ** Transferred to VA-192/ CVW-11, NH/3XX, NAS Cubi Point, PI., 20 NOV 85; To VA-192, NAS LeMoore, CA., 30 DEC 85; To VA-192, NAS Jacksonville, FL., 24 APR 86 ** Transferred to VA-27/CVW-15, NL/4XX, NAS LeMoore, CA., 24 APR 86; To VA-27, USS Carl Vinson (CVN-70), 24 APR 86; To VA-27, NAS LeMoore, CA., 24 APR 86; To VA-27, USS Carl Vinson (CVN-70), 24 APR 86; To VA-27, NAS LeMoore, CA., 04 MAR 87 thru 22 MAY 87 ** End of flight record card ** Transferred to the Helenic Air force (Greee).

E-484 159981 Navy acceptance from NPRO Rep. LTV, Dallas, TX., 22 MAR 76 ** Transferred to VA-94/CVW-15, NL/4XX, NAS LeMoore, CA., 26 MAR 76; To VA-94, NAS Fallon, NV., 30 APR 76; To VA-94, NAS LeMoore, CA., 30 APR 76; To VA-94, USS Coral Sea (CV-43), 09 DEC 76; To VA-94, NAS LeMoore, CA., 08 JAN 77; To VA-94, USS Coral Sea (CV-43), 07 APR 77; To VA-94, NAS LeMoore, CA., 31 AUG 77; To VA-94, NAS Jacksonville, FL., 16 MAR 78; To VA-94, NAS LeMoore, CA., 22 APR 78; Transferred to VA-97/CVW14, NK/3XX, NAS LeMoore, CA., 26 SEP 79; To VA-97, USS Coral Sea (CV-43), 16 OCT 79; To VA-97, NAS LeMoore, CA., 14 DEC 79; To VA-97, NAS Jacksonville, FL., 01 OCT 81; To VA-97, NAS Dallas, TX., 01 DEC 80; To VA-97, NAS LeMoore, CA., 23 FEB 81; To VA-97, NAS Dallas, TX., 04 MAR 81 ** To VA-22/CVW-15, NL/3XX, USS Kitty Hawk (CV-63), 05 MAR 81 ** Transferred to VA-93/CVW-5, NF/3XX, NAF Atsugi, JP., 09 OCT 81; To VA-93, USS Midway (CV-41), 10 NOV 81; To VA-93, NAS Cubi Point, PI., 10 NOV 81 ** Transferred to VA-113/CVW-2, NE/3XX, NAF Atsugi, JP., 22 SEP 82; To VA-113, NAS LeMoore, CA., 22 SEP 82 ** Transferred to VA-146/CVW-9, NG/3XX, NAS LeMoore, CA., 28 MAR 83 ** Transferred to VA-94/CVW-11, NH/4XX, NAS LeMoore, CA., 03 JUN 83; To VA-94, USS Enterprise (CVN-65), 13 JUL 83; To VA-94, NAS LeMoore, CA., 13 FEB 84; To VA-94, NAS Jacksonville, FL., 14 FEB 84; To VA-94, USS Enterprise (CVN-65), 31 MAR 84; To VA-94, NAS LeMoore, CA., 18 APR 84; To VA-94, USS Enterprise (CVN-65), 10 MAY 84; To VA-94, NAS LeMoore, CA., 10 MAY 84 ** Transaferred to VA-192/ CVW-11, NH/3XX, NAS LeMoore, CA., 07 MAR 85; To VA-192, NAS Cubi Point, PI., 12 SEP 85; To VA-192, NAS LeMoore, CA., 30 DEC 85; To VA-192, NAS Jacksonville, FL., 14 FEB 86; To VA-192, NAS LeMoore, CA., 14 FEB 86; To VA-192, NAS Jacksonville, FL., 18 MAR 86 ** Transferred to NARF, NAS Jacksonville, FL., 30 JUN 86 ** Transferred to VA-147/CVW-9, NE/3XX, NAS LeMoore, CA., 09 JUL 86; To VA-147, USS Kitty Hawk (CV-63), 01 OCT 86; To VA-147, NAS LeMoore, CA., 01 OCT 86 ** End of flight record card ** Transferred to NSWC, NAS Fallon, NV., date unknown ** Transferred to AMARC, Davis Monthan AFB; Tucson, AZ., assigned park code 6A0325, 22 MAR 90 ** 1409.6 flight hours ** TF41A402D engine S/N 141926 ** Project changed per FSO letter, 06 DEC 04 ** Engine records released to DRMO for disposition, 21 DEC 04 ** Aircraft deleted from inventory and released to DRMO dor disposition, 19 JAN 05.

E-485 159982 Navy acceptance from NPRO Rep. LTV, Dallas, TX., 28 APR 76 ** Transferred to VA-22/CVW-15, NL/3XX, NAS LeMoore, CA., 04 MAY 76 ** Transferred to VA-122/FRS, NJ/2XX, NAS LeMoore, CA., 07 JAN 77 ** Transferred to VA-56/CVW-5, NF/4XX, USS Midway (CV-41), 25 APR 77 ~ S 1SO strike, 15 MAR 78 ** No data on strike.

E-486 159983 Navy acceptance from NPRO Rep. LTV, Dallas, TX., 15 APR 76 ** Transferred To VA-94/CVW-15, NL/3XX, NAs Fallon, NV., 21 APR 76; To VA-94, NAS LeMoore, CA., 30 APR 76; To VA-94, USS Coral Sea (CV-43), 09 DEC 76; To VA-94, NAS LeMoore, CA., 08 JAN 77 ** Transferred to VA-122/FRS, NJ/2XX, NAS LeMoore, CA., 26 JAN 77 ** Transferred to VA-93/CVW-5, NF/3XX, USS Midway (CV-41), 24 APR 77 ~ S 1SO strike, 01 JUL 77 ** No data on strike.

E-487 159984 Navy acceptance from NPRO Rep. LTV, Dallas, TX., 27 APR 76 ** Transferred to VA-174/FRS, AD/4XX, NAS Cecil Field, FL., 01 MAY 76; To VA-174, NAS Jacksonville, FL., 24 MAY 78; To VA-174, NAS Cecil Field, FL., 26 JUN 78 ** Transferred to VA-46/CVW-1, AB/3XX, NAS Cecil Field, FL., 19 MAR 80 ** Transferred to VA-174/FRS, AD/4XX, NAS Cecil Field, FL., 27 JUN 80; To VA-174, NAS Jacksonville, FL., 21 AUG 80; To VA-174, NAS Dallas, TX., 31 OCT 80 ** Transferred to VA-22/CVW-15, NL/3XX, USS Kitty Hawk (CV-63), 18 MAR 81; To VA-22, NAS LeMoore, CA., 23 AUG 81 ** Transferred to VA-122/FRS, NJ/2XX, NAS Jacksonville, FL., 01 JUL 83 ** Transferred to VA-27/CVW-15, NL/4XX, NAS LeMoore, 04 OCT 83; To VA-27, USS Carl Vinson (CVN-70), 03 FEB 84; To VA-27, NAS LeMoore, CA., 03 FEB 84; To VA-27, USS Carl Vinson (CVN-70), 03 FEB 84; To VA-27, NAS LeMoore, CA., 03 FEB 84; To VA-27, USS Carl Vinson (CVN-70), 03 FEB 84; To VA-27, NAS LeMoore, CA., 24 NOV 84; To VA-27, NAS Jacksonville, FL., 30 OCT 85; To VA-27, NAS LeMoore, CA., 30 OCT 85; To VA-27, NAS Jacksonville, FL., 01 NOV 85; To VA-27, NAS North Island, CA., 15 FEB 86; To VA-27, NAS LeMoore, CA., 15 FEB 86; To VA-27, USS Carl Vinson (CVN-70), 14 MAY 86; To VA-27, NAS LeMoore, CA., 24 JUL 86; To VA-27, USS Carl Vinson (CVN-70), 25 JUL 86; To VA-27, NAS LeMoore, CA., 05 MAR 87 thru 13 AUG 87 ** End of flight record card.

159985/159988 LTV A-7E Corsair (Block XX)
FY 75 Contract N00019-75-C-0164, (18) A-7E;
from E-481/491

E-488 159985 Navy acceptance from NPRO Rep. LTV, Dallas, TX., 22 MAY 76 ** Transferred to VA-146/CVW-9, NG/3XX, NAS LeMoore, CA., 23 MAY 76; To VA-146, USS Constellation (CV-64), 17 JUN 76; To VA-146, NAS LeMoore, CA., 27 DEC 76; To VA-146, USS Constellation (CV-64), 28 DEC 76; To VA-146, NAS LeMoore, CA., 05 FEB 77; To VA-146, USS Constellation (CV-64),14 MAR 77; To VA-146, NAS LeMoore, CA., 22 MAR 77 ** Transferred to VA-93/CVW-5, NF/3XX, USS Midway (CV-41), 24 APR 77; To VA-93, NAF Atsugi, JP., 22 MAY 78 ** Transferred to VA-147/ CVW-9, NG/4XX, NAS Cubi Point, PI., 21 APR 80; To VA-147, USS Constellation (CV-64), 20 SEP 80; To VA-147, NAS LeMoore, CA., 20 SEP 80; To VA-147, NAS Jacksonville, FL., 26 JAN 81; To VA-147, NAS Dallas, TX., 09 APR 81; To VA-147, NAS LeMoore, CA., 13 APR 81 ** Transferred to VA-146/CVW-9, NG/3XX, USS Constellation (CV-64), 08 JUL 81; To VA-146, NAS LeMoore, CA., 06 AUG 81; To VA-146, USS Constellation (CV-64), 11 SEP 81; To VA-146, NAS LeMoore, CA., 20 OCT 81; To VA-146, NAS Jacksonville, FL., 11 AUG 83 ** Transferred to VA-94/CVW-11, NH/4XX, NAS LeMoore, CA., 11 OCT 83; To VA-94, USS Enterprise (CVN-65), 12 OCT 83; To VA-94, NAS LeMoore, CA., 12 OCT 83; To VA-94, USS Enterprise (CVN-65), 12 OCT 83; To VA-94, NAS LeMoore, CA., 04 MAY 84; To VA-94, USS Enterprise (CVN-65), 16 MAY 84; To VA-94, NAS LeMoore, CA., 16 MAY 84; To VA-94, NAS Fallon, NV., 17 NOV 85; To VA-94, NAS LeMoore, CA., 17 JAN 85; To VA-94, NAS Jacksonville, FL., 03 OCT 85; To VA-94, NAS LeMoore, CA., 03 OCT 85; To VA-94, NAS Jacksonville, FL., 10 OCT 85; To VA-94, NAS LeMoore, CA., 17 DEC 85; To VA-94, USS Enterprise (CVN-65), 17 DEC 85; To VA-94, NAF Atsugi, JP., 26 FEB 86; To VA-94, USS Enterprise (CVN-65), 04 MAR 86; To VA-94, NAF Atsugi, JP., 02 JUL 86; To VA-94, USS Enterprise (CVN-65), 03 JUL 86; To VA-94, NAS LeMoore, CA., 17 JUL 86 thru 04 SEP 87 ** End of flight record card ** Transferred to NAD, NAS Jacksonville, FL., 06 JAN 90 ** Transferred to NSWC, Strike/XX, NAS Fallon, NV., date unknown ** Transferred to AMARC, Davis Monthan AFB; Tucson, AZ., assigned park code 6A0406, 27 SEP 91 ** 5542.2 flight hours ** TF41A402D engine S/N AD141312 ** Storage location 210808 ** Located at AMARG, Davis Monthan AFB; Tucson, AZ., 15 JUN 07.

E-489 159986 Navy acceptance from NPRO Rep. LTV, Dallas, TX., 14 MAY 76 ** Transferred to VA-174/FRS, AD/4XX, NAS Cecil Field, FL., 15 MAY 76 ** Transferred to VA-72/CVW-1, AB/4XX, NAS Cecil Field, FL., 12 OCT 77; To VA-72, USS Dwight D. Eisenhower (CVN-69), 12 OCT 77; To VA-72, NAS Cecil Field, FL., 12 OCT 77; To VA-72, USS John F. Kennedy (CV-67), 12 OCT 77; To VA-72, NAS Cecil Field, FL., 12 OCT 77; To VA-72, NAS Jacksonville, FL., 30 MAR 78; To VA-72, NAS Cecil Field, FL., 01 MAY 78; To VA-72, USS John F. Kennedy (CV-67), 02 MAY 78; To VA-72, NAS Cecil Field, FL., 02 MAY 78; To VA-72, USS John F. Kennedy (CV-67), 01 FEB 80; To VA-72, NAS Cecil Field, FL., 01 FEB 80 ** Transferred to VA-46/CVW-1, AB/3XX, NAS Cecil Field, FL., 31 AUG 81; To VA-46, NAS Jacksonville, FL., 01 FEB 82; To VA-46, NAS Cecil Field, FL., 09 MAR 82; To VA-46, USS America (CV-66), 09 MAR 82; To VA-46, NAS Cecil Field, FL., 09 MAR 82; To VA-46, USS America (CV-66), 09 MAR 82; To VA-46, NAS Cecil Field, FL., 16 APR 83 ** Transferred to VA-82/CVW-8, AJ/301, NAS Cecil Field, FL., 20 JUN 83; To VA-82, USS Nimitz (CVN-68), 31 MAR 84; To VA-82, NAS Cecil Field, FL., 31 MAR 84; To VA-82, USS Nimitz (CVN-68), 31 JAN 85; To VA-82, NAS Jacksonville, FL., 19 APR 85 ** Transferred to NARF, NAS Jacksonville, FL., 19 APR 85 ** Transferred to VA-81/CVW-17, AA/4XX, USS Saratoga (CV-60), 01 MAY 85; To VA-81, NAS Cecil Field, FL., 12 JUN 85; To VA-81, USS Saratoga (CV-60), 12 JUN 85; To VA-81, NAS Cecil Field, FL., 21 APR 86; To VA-81, USS Saratoga (CV-60), 27 MAY 86; To VA-81, NAS Cecil Field, FL., 21 OCT 86; Transferred to VA-174/FRS, AD/411, NAS Cecil Field, FL., 29 OCT 86 ** Transferred to AMARC, Davis Monthan AFB; Tucson, AZ., assigned park code 6A0241, 22 SEP 87 ** End of flight record card ** 4465.3 flight hours ** TF41A2C engine S/N unknown ** Aircraft placed on FMS list with D-704 Buddy Store

** Storage location 111202 ** Engine records released to DRMO for disposition, 29 JUL 05 ** Aircraft deleted from inventory and released to DRMO for disposition, 01 AUG 05 ** At AMARG, Davis Monthan AFB; Tucson, AZ., 15 JUN 07.

E-490 159987 Navy acceptance from NPRO Rep. LTV, Dallas, TX., 14 MAY 76 ** Transferred to VA-174/FRS, AD/4XX, NAS Cecil Field, FL., 15 MAY 76 ** Transferred to VA-72/CVW-1, AB/4XX, NAS Cecil Field, FL., 12 APR 78; To VA-72, USS John F. Kennedy (CV-67), 12 APR 78; To VA-72, NAS Jacksonville, FL., 22 FEB 79; To VA-72, NAS Cecil Field, FL., 31 MAR 79; To VA-72, USS John F. Kennedy (CV-67), 19 MAR 80 ** Transferred to VA-87/CVW-6, AE/4XX, NAS Cecil Field, FL., 22 DEC 80 ** Transferred to VA-72/CVW-1, AB/4XX, NAS Jacksonville, FL., 18 JUN 81; To VA-72, NAS Cecil Field, FL., 24 AUG 81; To VA-72, NAS Dallas, TX., 11 SEP 81; To VA-72, NAS Cecil Field, FL., 17 NOV 81; To VA-72, USS America (CV-66), 18 NOV 81 ~ S 1SO strikie, 28 DEC 82 ** No data on strike.

E-491 159988 Navy acceptance from NPRO Rep. LTV, Dallas, TX., 14 JUN 76 ** Transferred to VA-174/FRS, AD/4XX, NAS Cecil Field, FL., 15 JUN 76 ** Transferred to VA-46/CVW-1, AB/312, NAS Cecil Field, FL., 20 SEP 77; To VA-46, USS John F. Kennedy (CV-67), 20 SEP 77; To VA-46, NAS Cecil Field, FL., 20 SEP 77; To VA-46, USS John F. Kennedy (CV-67), 20 SEP 77; To VA-46, NAS Cecil Field, FL., 20 SEP 77; To VA-46, NAS Jacksonville, FL., 13 APR 78; To VA-46, NAS Cecil Field, FL., 18 MAY 78; To VA-46, USS John F. Kennedy (CV-67), 18 MAY 78; To VA-46, NAS Cecil Field, FL., 18 MAY 78; To VA-46, USS John F. Kennedy (CV-67), 01 MAR 80; To VA-46, NAS Cecil Field, FL., 15 APR 81; To VA-46, NAS Jacksonville, FL., 12 APR 82; To VA-46, NAS Cecil Field, FL., 19 APR 82; To VA-46, USS America (CV-66), 12 MAY 82; To VA-46, NAS Cecil Field, FL., 12 MAY 82; To VA-46, USS America (CV-66), 12 MAY 82; To VA-46, NAS Cecil Field, FL., 14 APR 83; Transferred to VA-87/CVW-6, AE/4XX, USS Independence (CV-62), 17 JUN 83; To VA-87, NAS Cecil Field, FL., 07 JUL 83; To VA-87, USS Independence (CV-62), 29 JUL 83; To VA-87, NAS Cecil Field, FL., 29 JUL 83; To VA-87, USS Independence (CV-62), 29 JUL 83; To VA-87, NAS Cecil Field, FL., 02 MAY 84; To VA-87, USS Independence (CV-62), 21 MAY 84; To VA-87, NAS Cecil Field, FL., 21 MAY 84; To VA-87, USS Independence (CV-62), 21 MAY 84 ** Transferred to NARF, NAS Jacksonville, FL., 30 MAY 85 ** Transferred to VA-174/FRS, AD/420, NAS Cecil Field, FL., 01 OCT 84; To VA-174, NAS Jacksonville, FL., 30 MAY 85; To VA-174, NAS Cecil Field, FL., 31 MAY 85 ** Transferred to AMARC, Davis Monthan AFB; Tucson, AZ., assigned park code 6A0232; 17 AUG 87 ** 4696.8 flight hours ** TF41A2C engine S/N 142634 ** Storage location 111516 ** End of flight record card ** At AMARG, Davis Monthan AFB; Tucson, AZ., 15 JUN 07.

159989/159996 LTV A-7E Corsair (Block XXI)
FY 75 Contract N00019-75-C-0164, (18) A-7E;
from E-506/E-499

E-506 159989 Navy acceptance from NPRO Rep. LTV, Dallas, TX., 22 JUN 76 ** Transferred to VA-195/CVW-11, NH/4XX, NAS LeMoore, CA., 22 JUN 76 ** Transferred to VA-56/CVW-5, NF/4XX, USS Midway (CV-41), 25 APR 77; To VA-56, NAF Atsugi, JP., 09 JAN 78; To VA-56, USS Midway (CV-41), 11 JAN 78; To VA-56, NAF Atsugi, JP., 21 APR 76 ** Transferred to VA-27/CVW-14, NK/4XX, USS Coral Sea (CV-43), 15 MAY 80; To VA-27, NAS LeMoore, CA., 21 MAY 80; To VA-27, NAS Jacksonville, FL., 25 JAN 81; To VA-27, USS Coral Sea (CV-43), 29 MAY 81; To VA-27, NAS Dallas, TX., 08 JUN 81; To VA-27, NAS LeMoore, CA., 11 JUN 81 ** Transferred to VA-146/CVW-9, NG/3XX, USS Constellation (CV-64), 01 JUL 81; To VA-146, NAS LeMoore, CA., 06 AUG 81; To VA-146, USS Constellation (CV-64), 11 SEP 81; To VA-146, NAS LeMoore, CA., 20 OCT 81 ** Transferred to VA-94/CVW-11, NH/4XX, NAS LeMoore, CA., 26 MAY 83; To VA-94, NAS Jacksonville, FL., 19 AUG 83; To VA-94, NAS LeMoore, CA., 26 OCT 83; To VA-94, USS Enterprise (CVN-65), 26 OCT 83; To VA-94, NAS LeMoore,

CA., 09 MAR 84; To VA-94, USS Enterprise (CVN-65), 12 MAR 84; To VA-94, NAS LeMoore, CA., 12 MAR 84; To VA-94, USS Enterprise (CVN-65), 12 MAR 84; To VA-94, NAS LeMoore, CA., 12 MAR 84; To VA-94, NAS Fallon, NV., 10 JAN 85; To VA-94, NAS LeMoore, CA., 10 JAN 85 ** Transferred to NARF, NAS Jacksonville, FL., 12 MAR 85 ** Transferred to VA-94/CVW-11, NH/400, NAS Jacksonville, FL., 04 SEP 85; To VA-94, NAS LeMoore, CA., 04 SEP 85; To VA-94, NAS Jacksonville, FL., 09 SEP 85; To VA-94, NAS LeMoore, CA., 08 DEC 85; To VA-94, USS Enterprise (CVN-65), 08 DEC 85; To VA-94, NAS LeMoore, CA., 20 AUG 86 thru 17 JUN 87 ** End of flight record card ** Transferred to AMARC, Davis Monthan AFB; Tucson, AZ., assigned park code 6A0317; 12 MAR 90 ** 6019.1 flight hours ** TF41A402D engine S/N 141250 ** Engine records deleted from inventory and released to DRMO for disposition, 19 JAN 05 ** Transferred to NAS Fallon, NV., to be used as a range target, 26 JAN 05.

E-493 159990 Navy acceptance from NPRO Rep. LTV, Dallas, TX., 28 JUN 76 ** Transferred to VA-147/CVW-9, NG/4XX, NAS LeMoore, CA., 06 JUL 76; To VA-147, USS Constellation (CV-64), 28 SEP 76; To VA-147, NAS LeMoore, CA., 22 OCT 76 ** Transferred to VA-93/CVW-5, NF/3XX, USS Midway (CV-41), 24 APR 77; To VA-93, NAF Atsugi, JP., 17 JAN 78; To VA-93, USS Midway (CV-41), 28 JAN 78; To VA-93, NAF Atsugi, JP., 07 JUL 78 ** Transferred to VA-97/ CVW-14, NK/ 3XX, USS Coral Sea (CV-43), 21 APR 80; To VA-97, NAS LeMoore, CA., 21 MAY 80; To VA-97, USS Coral Sea (CV-43), 18 NOV 80; To VA-97, NAS LeMoore, CA., 16 JAN 81; To VA-97, NAS Dallas, TX., 30 APR 81; To VA-97, USS Coral Sea (CV-43), 30 APR 81; To VA-97, NAS Dallas, TX., 16 JUN 81; Transferred to VA-113/CVW-2, NE/3XX, NAS Fallon, NV., 31 AUG 81; To VA-113, USS Ranger (CV-61), 21 OCT 81; To VA-113, NAS LeMoore, CA., 12 NOV 81; To VA-113, USS Ranger (CV-61), 14 JAN 82; To VA-113, NAS LeMoore, CA., 14 JAN 82 ** Transferred to VA-82/CVW-8, AJ/3XX, NAS LeMoore, CA., 24 MAR 82 ** Transferred to VA-22/CVW-11, NH/3XX, USS Enterprise (CVN-65), 24 MAR 82; To VA-22, NAS LeMoore, CA., 17 APR 83; To VA-22, NAS Jacksonville, FL., 22 SEP 83; To VA-22, NAS LeMoore, CA., 06 NOV 83; To VA-22, USS Enterprise (CVN-65), 07 NOV 83; To VA-22, NAS LeMoore, CA., 30 JAN 84; To VA-22, USS Enterprise (CVN-65), 25 JUN 84 ** Transferred to VA-56/CVW-5, NF/4XX, NAF Atsugi, JP., 16 NOV 84 ~ S 1SO strike, 13 JUL 85 ** Crashed into the sea due to engine failure, Pilot ejected safely.

E-494 159991 Navy acceptance from NPRO Rep. LTV, Dallas, TX., 30 JUL 76 ** Transferred to VA-122/FRS, NJ/2XX, NAS LeMoore, CA., 31 JUL 76 ** Transferred to VA-56/CVW-5, NF/4XX, USS Midway (CV-41), 25 APR 77; To VA-56, NAF Atsugi, JP., 23 DEC 77; To VA-56, USS Midway (CV-41), 19 JAN 78 ** Transferred to VA-192/CVW-11, NH/3XX, USS Kitty Hawk (CV-63), 08 FEB 78 ** Transferred to VA-56/CVW-5, NF/4XX, USS Midway (CV-41), 21 APR 78; To VA-56, NAF Atsugi, JP., 12 MAY 78 ** Transferred to VA-97/CVW-14, NK/3XX, USS Coral Sea (CV-43), 12 MAY 80; To VA-97, NAS LeMoore, CA., 21 MAY 80; To VA-97, USS Coral Sea (CV-43), 17 OCT 80; To VA-97, NAS LeMoore, CA., 16 JAN 81; To VA-97, NAS Jacksonville, FL., 24 APR 81; To VA-97, USS Coral Sea (CV-43), 24 APR 81; To VA-97, NAS LeMoore, CA., 01 MAY 81; To VA-97, NAS Dallas, TX., 14 JUL 81 ** Transferred to VA-113/CVW-2, NE/3XX, NAS LeMoore, CA., 16 JUL 81; To VA-113, NAS Fallon, NV., 14 SEP 81; To VA-113, USS Ranger (CV-61), 21 OCT 81; To VA-113, NAS LeMoore, CA., 12 NOV 81; To VA-113, USS Ranger (CV-61), 14 JAN 82; To VA-113, NAS LeMoore, CA., 14 JAN 82; To VA-113, USS Ranger (CV-61), 14 JAN 82; To VA-113, NAS Cubi Point, PI., 14 JAN 82; To VA-113, NAF Atsugi, JP., 24 AUG 82 ** Transferred to VA-93/CVW-5, NF/3XX, NAS Cubi Point, PI., 27 SEP 82; To VA-93, NAF Atsugi, JP., 12 OCT 82; To VA-93, NAS Cubi Point, PI., 21 OCT 82; To VA-93, USS Midway (CV-41), 25 NOV 82; To VA-93, NAF Atsugi, JP., 22 JUN 83; To VA-93, USS Midway

(CV-41), 25 JUN 83; To VA-93, NAF Atsugi, JP., 03 SEP 83; To VA-93, NAS LeMoore, CA., 09 NOV 85 ** Transferred to VA-122/FRS, NJ/2XX, NAS LeMoore, 13 MAY 86; To VA-122, NAS Pensacola, FL., 09 DEC 86; To VA-122, NAS LeMoore, CA., 24 SEP 87 ** End of flight record card.

E-495 159992 Navy acceptance from NPRO Rep. LTV, Dallas, TX., 02 DEC 76 ** Transferred to VA-174/FRS, AD/2XX, NAS Cecil Field, FL., 03 DEC 76 ** Transferred to VA-72/CVW-1, AB/402, NAS Cecil Field, FL., 27 SEP 77; To VA-72, USS Dwight D. Eisenhower (CVN-69), 25 OCT 77; To VA-72, NAS Cecil Field, FL., 10 NOV 77; To VA-72, USS John F. Kennedy (CV-67), 10 NOV 77; To VA-72, NAS Cecil Field, FL., 10 NOV 77; To VA-72, USS John F. Kennedy (CV-67), 10 NOV 77; To VA-72, NAS Jacksonville, FL., 12 FEB 79; To VA-72, NAS Cecil Field, FL., 20 MAR 79; To VA-72, USS John F. Kennedy (CV-67), 19 MAR 80; To VA-72, NAS Cecil Field, FL., 03 FEB 81; To VA-72, NAS Jacksonville, FL., 24 JUN 81; To VA-72, NAS Cecil Field, FL., 28 AUG 81; To VA-72, NAS Dallas, TX., 17 SEP 81; To VA-72, NAS Cecil Field, FL., 23 NOV 81; To VA-72, USS America (CV-66), 04 DEC 81 ** Transferred to VA-83/CVW-17, AA/3XX, NAS Cecil Field, FL., 02 DEC 82 ** Transferred to VA-86/CVW-8, AJ/4XX, USS Nimitz (CVN-68), 05 MAR 83; To VA-86, NAS Cecil Field, FL., 05 MAR 83; To VA-86, NAS Roosevelt Roads, PR., 05 MAR 83; To VA-86, NAS Cecil Field, FL., 05 MAR 83; To VA-86, NAS Jacksonville, FL., 03 JUL 84; To VA-86, NAS Cecil Field, FL., 31 AUG 84; To VA-86, USS Nimitz (CVN-68), 31 AUG 84; To VA-86, NAS Cecil Field, FL., 31 AUG 84; To VA-86, USS Nimitz (CVN-68), 20 FEB 85; To VA-86, NAS Cecil Field, FL., 20 FEB 85; To VA-86, USS Nimitz (CVN-68), 15 APR 86 ** Transferred to NARF, NAS Jacksonville, FL., 15 JUL 86 ** Transferred to VA-86/CVN-8, AJ/4XX, NAS Cecil Field, FL., 22 JUL 86; To VA-86, USS Nimitz (CVN-68), 22 JUL 86; To VA-86, NAS Cecil Field, FL., 10 OCT 86 To VA-86, USS Nimitz (CVN-68), 10 OCT 86; To VA-86, NAS Cecil Field, FL., 10 OCT 86 ** Transferred to VA-22/CVW-11, NH/3XX, 23 SEP 87 ** End of flight record card ** Transferred to VA-122/FRS, NJ/220, NAS LeMoore, CA., date unknown ** Transferred to AMARC, Davis Monthan AFB; Tucson, AZ., assigned park code 6A0355; 22 MAY 90 ** Project changed per FSO letter, 06 APR 04 ** Aircraft deleted from inventory and released to DRMO for disposition, 01 AUG 05.

E-496 159993 Navy acceptance from NPRO Rep. LTV, Dallas, TX., 27 JUL 76 ** Transferred to VA-174/FRS, AD/4XX, NAS Cecil Field, FL., 30 JUL 76 ** Transferred to VA-46/CVW-1, AB/3XX, NAS Cecil Field, FL., 15 SEP 77; To VA-46, USS Dwight D. Eisenhower (CVN-69), 15 SEP 77; To VA-46, NAS Cecil Field, FL., 15 SEP 77; To VA-46, USS John F. Kennedy (CV-67), 15 SEP 77; To VA-46, NAS Jacksonville, FL., 13 FEB 78; To VA-46, NAS Cecil Field, FL., 29 MAR 78; To VA-46, USS John F. Kennedy (CV-67), 22 JUN 78 ~ S 1SO strike, 22 JUN 78 ** No data on strike.

E-497 159994 Navy acceptance from NPRO Rep. LTV, Dallas, TX., 29 OCT 76 ** Transferred to VA-174/FRS, AD/4XX, NAS Cecil Field, FL., 30 OCT 76 ** Transferred to VA-72/CVW-1, AB/4XX, NAS Cecil Field, FL., 27 OCT 77; To VA-72, USS John F. Kennedy (CV-67), 27 OCT 77; To VA-72, NAS Cecil Field, FL.,27 OCT 77; To VA-72, NAS Jacksonville, FL., 13 APR 78; To VA-72, NAS Cecil Field, FL., 08 MAY 78; To VA-72, USS John F. Kennedy (CV-67), 31 MAY 78; To VA-72, NAS Cecil Field, FL., 31 MAY 78 ** Transferred to VA-174/FRS, AD/4XX, NAS Cecil Field, FL., 27 JUN 80; To VA-174, NAS Jacksonville, FL., 13 NOV 80; To VA-174, NAS Dallas, TX., 16 JAN 81; To VA-174, NAS Cecil Field, FL., 02 APR 81 ** Transferred to VA-72/CVW-1, AB/4XX, NAS Cecil Field, FL., 22 SEP 81; To VA-72, USS America (CV-66), 22 SEP 81; To VA-72, NAS Cecil Field, FL., 24 JUN 83; To VA-72, NAS Jacksonville, FL., 13 JUL 83; To VA-72, NAS Cecil Field, FL., 20 SEP 83; To VA-72, USS America (CV-66), 20 SEP 83; To VA-72, NAS Cecil Field, FL., 20 SEP 83; To VA-72, USS America (CV-66), 20 SEP 83; To VA-72, NAS

Cecil Field, FL., 05 JUN 84; To VA-72, USS America (CV-66), 19 JUN 85 ** Transferred to VA-105/CVW-6, AE/4XX, NAS Cecil Field, FL., 03 JUL 85; To VA-105, NAS Jacksonville, FL., 12 DEC 85 ** Transferred to VA-72/CVW-1, AB/4XX, NAS Cecil Field, FL., 16 DEC 85; To VA-72, USS America (CV-66), 16 DEC 85; To VA-72, NAS Cecil Field, FL., 16 DEC 85; To VA-72/CVW-7, AG/4XX, USS Dwight D. Eisenhower (CVN-69), 04 MAR 87; To VA-72, NAS Cecil Field, FL., 04 MAR 87 thru 21 SEP 87 ** End of flight card ** Transferred to NAD, NAS Jacksonville, FL., date unknown ** Transferred to VA-105/CVW-6, AE/402, NAS Cecil Field, FL., date unknown ** Transferred to AMARC, Davis Monthan AFB; Tucson, AZ., assigned park code 6A0383; 24 OCT 90 ** 6462.8 flight hours ** TF41A402D engine S/N 141366 ** Storage location 111314 ** At AMARG, Davis Monthan AFB; Tucson, AZ., 15 JUN 07.

E-498 159995 Navy acceptance from NPRO Rep. LTV, Dallas, TX., 23 JUL 76 ** Transferred to VA-174/FRS, AD/4XX, NAS Cecil Field, FL., 24 JUL 76 ** Transferred to VA-46/CVW-1, AB/3XX, NAS Cecil Field, FL., 27 SEP 77; To VA-46, USS Dwight D. Eisenhower (CVN-69), 27 SEP 77; To VA-46, NAS Cecil Field, FL., 27 SEP 77; To VA-46, USS John F. Kennedy (CV-67), 27 SEP 77; To VA-46, NAS Cecil Field, FL., 27 SEP 77; To VA-46, NAS Jacksonville, FL., 06 APR 78; To VA-46, NAS Cecil Field, FL., 01 MAY 78; To VA-46, USS John F. Kennedy (CV-67), 01 MAY 78; To VA-46, NAS Cecil Field, FL., 01 MAY 78 ** Transferred to VA-174/FRS, AD/4XX, NAS Cecil Field, FL., 31 JUL 80; To VA-174, NAS Jacksonville, FL., 27 AUG 80; To VA-174, NAS Dallas, FL., 04 NOV 80 ** Transferred to VA-37/CVW-3, AC/3XX, 04 FEB 81 ** Transferred to VA-46/CVW-1, AB/3XX, NAS Cecil Field, FL., 01 MAY 81 ** Transferred to VA-72/CVW-1, AB/4XX, NAS Cecil Field, FL., 29 OCT 81; To VA-72, USS America (CV-66), 29 OCT 81; To VA-72, NAS Cecil Field, FL., 24 JUN 83; To VA-72, NAS Jacksonville, FL., 13 JUL 83; To VA-72, NAS Cecil Field, FL., 23 SEP 83; To VA-72, USS America (CV-66), 23 SEP 83; To VA-72, NAS Cecil Field, FL., 23 SEP 83; USS America (CV-66), 28 APR 84; To VA-72, NAS Cecil Field, FL., 28 APR 84 ~ S 1SO strike, 11 DEC 84 ** No data on strike.

E-499 159996 Navy acceptance from NPRO Rep. LTV, Dallas, TX., 15 JUL 76 ** Transferred to VA-174/FRS, AD/2XX, NAS Cecil Field, FL., 16 DEC 76 ** Transferred to VA-72/CVW-1, AB/404, NAS Cecil Field, FL., 13 SEP 77; To VA-72, USS John F. Kennedy (CV-67), 13 SEP 77; To VA-72, NAS Cecil Field, FL., 13 SEP 77; To VA-72, USS John F. Kennedy (CV-67), 13 SEP 77; VA-72, NAS Jacksonville, FL., 01 MAR 79; To VA-72, NAS Cecil Field, FL., 12 APR 79; To VA-72, USS John F. Kennedy (CV-67), 19 MAR 80; To VA-72, NAS Cecil Field, FL., 03 FEB 81; To VA-72, NAS Jacksonville, FL., 08 JUL 81; To VA-72, NAS Cecil Field, FL., 08 SEP 81; To VA-72, NAS Dallas, TX., 30 SEP 81; To VA-72, NAS Cecil Field, FL., 01 OCT 81; To VA-72, USS America (CV-66), 16 DEC 81; To VA-72, NAS Cecil Field, FL., 16 DEC 81; To VA-72, USS America (CV-66), 26 SEP 83; To VA-72, NAS Cecil Field, FL., 26 SEP 83; To VA-72, USS America (CV-66), 26 SEP 83; To VA-72, NAS Jacksonville, FL., 20 NOV 84; To VA-72, NAS Cecil Field, FL., 20 NOV 84; To VA-72, NAS Jacksonville, FL., 26 NOV 84; To VA-72, NAS Cecil Field, FL., 31 JAN 85; To VA-72, USS America (CV-66), 04 JUN 85; To VA-72, NAS Cecil Field, FL., 04 JUN 85; To VA-72, USS America (CV-66), 18 JAN 86; To VA-72, NAS Cecil Field, FL., 18 JAN 86; To VA-72, USS Dwight D. Eisenhower (CVN-69), 20 APR 87; To VA-72, NAS Cecil Field, FL., 16 JUL 87 ** Transferred to VA-174/FRS, AD/2XX, NAS Cecil Field, FL., 11 AUG 87 ** End of flight record card ** Transferred to NADEP , NAS Jacksonville, FL., date unknown ** Transferred to VA-37/CVW-6, AE/305, NAS Cecil Field, FL., date unknown ** Transferred to AMARC, Davis Monthan AFB; Tucson, AZ., assigned park code 6A0378, 04 SEP 90 ** 6135.2 flight hours ** TF41A402D engine S/N 142579 ** Storage location 111412 ** Placed on FMS list with FLIR and D-704 Buddy Store, 31 DEC 97 ** At AMARG, Davis Monthan AFB; Tucson, AZ., 15 JUN 07.

159997/160002 LTV A-7E Corsair (Block XXII)
FY 75 Contract N00019-75-C-0164, (18) A-7E;
***   from E-505/E-505***

E-500 159997 Navy acceptance from NPRO Rep. LTV, Dallas, TX., 24 AUG 76 ** Transferred to VA-174/FRS, AD/2XX, NAS Cecil Field, FL., 25 AUG 76 ** Transferred to VA-46/CVW-1, AB/307, NAS Cecil Field, FL., 26 SEP 77; To VA-46, USS Dwight D. Eisenhower (CVN-69), 26 SEP 77; To VA-46, NAS Cecil Field, FL., 16 DEC 77; To VA-46, USS John F. Kennedy (CV-67), 16 DEC 77; To VA-46, NAS Cecil Field, FL., 16 DEC 77; To VA-46, NAS Jacksonville, FL., 29 MAR 78; To VA-46, NAS Cecil Field, FL., 24 APR 78; To VA-46, USS John F. Kennedy (CV-67), 24 APR 78; To VA-46, NAS Cecil Field, FL., 24 APR 78; To VA-46, USS John F. Kennedy (CV-67), 19 MAR 80; To VA-46, NAS Cecil Field, FL., 01 NOV 80; To VA-46, NAS Dallas, TX., 23 JUL 81 ** Transferred to VA-72/CVW-1, AB/4XX, NAS Cecil Field, FL., 30 SEP 81; To VA-72, USS America (CV-66), 30 SEP 81; To VA-72, NAS Cecil Field, FL., 15 APR 83; To VA-72, USS America (CV-66), 05 NOV 83; To VA-72, NAS Cecil Field, FL., 04 JAN 84; To VA-72, NAS Jacksonville, FL., 23 JAN 84; To VA-72, NAS Cecil Field, FL., 24 JAN 84; To VA-72, USS America (CV-66), 24 JAN 84; To VA-72, NAS Cecil Field, FL., 24 JAN 84; To VA-72, USS America (CV-66), 30 APR 85; To VA-72, NAS Cecil Field, FL., 21 OCT 85; To VA-72, USS America (CV-66), 27 JAN 86; To VA-72, NAS Jacksonville, FL., 15 APR 86 ** Transferred to NARF, NAS Jacksonville, FL., 15 APR 86 ** Transferred to VA-66/CVW-7, AG/3XX, NAS Cecil Field, FL.,19 APR 86; To VA-66, USS John F. Kennedy (CV-67), 19 APR 86 ** Transferred to VA-81/CVW#-17, AA/4XX, USS Saratoga (CV-60), 04 SEP 86; To VA-81, NAS Cecil Field, FL., 21 OCT 86; To VA-81, USS Saratoga (CVA-60), 26 FEB 87; To VA-81, NAS Cecil Field, FL., 20 MAR 87; To VA-81, USS Saratoga (CVA-60), 20 APR 87; To VA-81, NAS Cecil Field, FL., 26 APR 87; To VA-81, USS Saratoga (CVA-60), 26 APR 87 ** End of flight record card ** Transferred to VA-203/CVWR-30, AF/3XX, NAS Cecil Field, FL., date unknown ** Transferred to AMARC, Davis Monthan AFB; Tucson, AZ., assigned park code 6A0302; 15 SEP 89 ** 5474.1 flight hours ** TF41A402D engine S/N 141605 ** Placed on FMS list, 31 DEC 97 ** Storage location 210804 ** Transferred to the Helenic Air force (Greece).

E-501 159998 Navy acceptance from NPRO Rep. LTV, Dallas, TX., 16 SEP 76 ** Transferred to VA-192/CVW-11, NH/3XX, NAS LeMoore, CA., 17 SEP 76; To VA-192, MCAS Yuma, AZ., 30 NOV 76; To VA-192, NAS Lemoore, CA., 14 DEC 76 ** Transferred to VA-56/CVW-5, NF/4XX, USS Midway (CV-41), 25 APR 77; To VA-56, NAF Atsugi, JP., 28 SEP 77; To VA-56, USS Midway (CV-41), 02 NOV 77; To VA-56, NAF Atsugi, JP., 22 MAY 78 ** Transferred to VA-97/ CVW-14, NK/3XX, USS Coral Sea (CV-43), 08 MAY 80; To VA-97, NAS LeMoore, CA., 21 MAY 80; To VA-97, USS Coral Sea (CV-43), 17 OCT 80; To VA-97, NAS LeMoore, CA., 15 DEC 80; To VA-97, NAS Jacksonville, FL., 18 FEB 81; To VA-97, NAS LeMoore, CA., 30 APR 81; To VA-97, NAS Dallas, TX., 12 MAY 81; To VA-97, Nas LeMoore, CA., 12 MAY 81; To VA-97, NAS Dallas, TX., 15 JUL 81 ** Transferred to VA-113/CVW-2, NE/3XX, NAS LeMoore, CA., 20 JUL 81; To VA-113, NAS Fallon, NV., 14 SEP 81; To VA-113, USS Ranger (CV-61), 28 SEP 81; To VA-113, NAS LeMoore, CA., 28 SEP 81; To VA-113, USS Ranger (CV-61), 14 JAN 82; To VA-113, NAS LeMoore, CA., 14 JAN 82 ** Transferred to VA-22/CVW-15, NL/3XX, NAS LeMoore, CA., 17 MAR 82 ~ S 1SO strike, 15 JUL 82 ** No data on strike.

E-502 159999 Navy acceptance from NPRO Rep. LTV, Dallas, TX., 16 SEP 76 ** Transferred to VA-122/FRS, NJ/2XX, NAS LeMoore, CA., 17 SEP 76 ** Transferred to VA-93/CVW-5, NF/3XX, USS Midway (CV-41), 27 APR 77; To VA-93, NAF Atsugi, JP., 12 MAY 78 ** Transferred to VA-97/CVW-14, NK/3XX, USS Coral Sea (CV-43), 21 APR 80; To VA-97, NAS LeMoore, CA., 21 MAY 80; To VA-97, USS Coral Sea (CV-43), 17 OCT 80; To VA-97, NAS LeMoore, CA., 16 JAN 81; To VA-97, NAS Jacksonville, FL., 27 FEB 81; To VA-97, NAS LeMoore, CA., 04 MAY 81; To VA-97, NAS Dallas, TX., 18 MAY 81; To VA-97, NAS LeMoore, CA., 18 MAY 81; To VA-97, NAS Dallas, TX., 15 JUL 81** Transferred to VA-113/CVW-2, NE/3XX,

NAS LeMoore, CA., 23 JUL 81; To VA-113, NAS Fallon, NV., 23 JUL 81; To VA-113, USS Ranger (CV-61), 21 OCT 81; To VA-113, NAS LeMoore, CA., 12 NOV 81; To VA-113, USS Ranger (CV-61), 14 JAN 82; To VA-113, NAS LeMoore, CA., 14 JAN 82; To VA-113, USS Ranger (CV-61), 26 FEB 82; To VA-113, NAS Cubi Point, PI., 26 FEB 82; To VA-113, NAF Atsugi, JP., 04 JUL 82 ** Transferred to VA-93/CVW-5, NF/3XX, NAS Cubi Point, PI., 27 SEP 82; To VA-93, NAF Atsugi, JP., 22 NOV 82; To VA-93, NAS Cubi Point, PI., 25 NOV 82; To VA-93, USS Midway (CV-41), 25 NOV 82; To VA-93, NAF Atsugi, JP., 12 SEP 83; To VA-93, USS Midway (CV-41), 26 SEP 83; To VA-93, NAF Atsugi, JP., 25 OCT 83; To VA-93, NAS LeMoore, CA., 09 NOV 85 ** Transferred to VA-147/CVW-9, NE/3XX, NAS LeMoore, CA., 24 APR 86; To VA-147, NAS Jacksonville, FL., 06 JAN 87 ** Transferred to VA-94/CVW-11, NH/4XX, NAS LeMoore, CA., 12 JAN 87 thru 24 JUN 87 ** End of flight record card ** Transferred to the Helenic Air force (Greee).

E-503 160000 Navy acceptance from NPRO Rep. LTV, Dallas, TX., 25 OCT 76 ** Transferred to VA-25/CVW-2, NE/4XX, NAS LeMoore, CA., 28 OCT 76 ** Transferred to VA-56/CVW-5, NF/406, USS Midway (CV-41), 25 APR 77; To VA-56, NAF Atsugi, JP., 17 JUN 68; To VA-56, USS Midway (CV-41), 13 SEP 79; To VA-56, NAF Atsugi, JP., 09 NOV 79 ** Transferred to VA-27CVW-14, NK/4XX, USS Coral Sea (CV-43), 06 MAY 80; To VA-27, NAS LeMoore, CA., 30 JUN 80; To VA-27, NAS Jacksonville, FL., 02 APR 81; To VA-27, USS Coral Sea (CV-43), 03 APR 81; To VA-27, NAS Jacksonville, FL., 05 JUN 81; To VA-27, NAS LeMoore, CA., 18 JUN 81; To VA-27, NAS Dallas, TX., 21 AUG 81 ** Transferred to VA-113/ CVW-2, NE/3XX, NAS LeMoore, CA., 27 AUG 81; To VA-113, NAS Fallon, NV., 14 SEP 81; To VA-113, USS Ranger (CV-61), 21 OCT 81; To VA-113, NAS LeMoore, CA., 12 NOV 81; To VA-113, USS Ranger (CV-61), 21 JAN 82; To VA-113, NAS LeMoore, CA., 04 FEB 82; To VA-113, USS Ranger (CV-61), 21 MAR 82; To VA-113, NAS Cubi Point, PI., 21 MAR 82; To VA-113, NAF Atsugi, JP., 16 SEP 82 ** Transferred to VA-93/CVW-5, NF/3XX, NAS Cubi Point, PI., 27 SEP 82; To VA-93, USS Midway (CV-41), 27 SEP 82; To VA-93, NAF Atsugi, JP., 28 MAY 83; To VA-93, USS Midway (CV-41), 18 JUN 83; To VA-93, NAF Atsugi, JP., 11 JUL 83; To VA-93, NAS LeMoore, CA., 18 SEP 85 ** Transferred to VA-147/ CVW-9, NE/3XX, NAS LeMoore, CA., 14 MAY 86; To VA-147, USS Kitty Hawk (CV-63), 16 DEC 86; To VA-147, NAS LeMoore, CA., 16 DEC 86 ** End of flight record card.

E-504 160001 Navy acceptance from NPRO Rep. LTV, Dallas, TX., 02 DEC 76 ** Transferred to VA-113/CVW-2, NE/3XX, NAS LeMoore, CA., 03 DEC 76 ** Transferred to VA-93/CVW-5, NF/305, USS Midway (CV-41), 24 APR 77; To VA-93, NAF Atsugi, JP., 22 MAY 78; To VA-93, USS Midway (CV-41), 27 JUL 80; Transferred to VA-146/CVW-9, NG/3XX, USS Constellation (CV-64), 22 SEP 80; To VA-146, NAS LeMoore, CA., 22 SEP 80; To VA-146, NAS Jacksonville, FL., 13 APR 81; To VA-146, NAS LeMoore, CA., 30 JUN 81; To VA-146, USS Constellation (CV-64), 22 SEP 80; To VA-146, NAS LeMoore, CA., 22 SEP 80; To VA-146, NAS Jacksonville, FL., 13 APR 81; To VA-146, NAS LeMoore, CA., 30 JUN 81; To VA-146, USS Constellation (CV-64), 30 JUN 81; To VA-146, NAS LeMoore, CA., 30 JUN 81; To VA-146, NAS Dallas, TX., 24 AUG 81; To VA-146, USS Constellation (CV-64), 08 SEP 81 ** Transferred to VA-122/FRS, NJ/2XX, NAS LeMoore, CA., 24 SEP 81 ** Transferred to VA-97/CVW-15, NL/3XX, USS Carl Vinson (CVN-70), 30 MAY 84; To VA-97, NAS LeMoore, CA., 09 JUL 84; To VA-97, USS Carl Vinson (CVN-70), 11 JUL 84; To VA-97, NAS LeMoore, CA., 31 AUG 84 ** Transferred to VA-122/FRS, NJ/2XX, NAS LeMoore, CA., 01 SEP 84 ** Transferred to VA-94/CVW-11, NH/4XX, NAS LeMoore, CA., 27 DEC 85; To VA-94, USS Enterprise (CVN-65), 27 DEC 85; To VA-94, NAS LeMoore, CA., 27 DEC 85; To VA-94, NAS Jacksonville, FL., 15 APR 87; To VA-94, NAS LeMoore, CA., 15 APR 87; To VA-94, NAS Jacksonville, FL., 21 APR 87; To VA-94, NAD, NAS Jacksonville, FL., 30 JUL 87; To VA-94, NAS LeMoore, CA., 04 AUG 87 ** End of flight record card ** Transferred to AMARC, Davis Monthan AFB; Tucson, AZ., assigned park code 6A0329; 28 MAR 90 ** 5221.6 flight hours ** TF41A402D engine S/N 141632 ** Storage location 111218 ** At AMARG, Davis Monthan AFB; Tucson, AZ., 15 JUN 07.

E-505 160002 Navy acceptance from NPRO Rep. LTV, Dallas, TX., 12 DEC 76 ** Transferred to VA-25/CVW-2, NE/4XX, NAS LeMoore, CA., 13 DEC 76 ** Transferred to VA-56/CVW-5, NF/4XX, USS Midway (CV-41), 25 APR 77; To VA-56, NAF Atsugi, JP., 07 SEP 77; To VA-56, USS Midway (CV-41), 13 SEP 77; To VA-56, NAF Atsugi, JP., 22 MAY 78 ** Transferred to VA-27/CVW-14, NK/4XX, NAS LeMoore, CA., 21 MAY 80; To VA-27, USS Coral Sea (CV-43)., 25 MAR 81; To VA-27, NAS Jacksonville, FL., 05 JUN 81; To VA-27, NAS LeMoore, CA., 24 JUN 81; To VA-27, NAS Dallas, TX., 26 AUG 81 ** Transferred to VA-113/CVW-2, NE/3XX, NAS Fallon, NV., 30 AUG 81; To VA-113, USS Ranger (CV-61), 18 OCT 81; To VA-113, NAS LeMoore, CA., 12 NOV 81; To VA-113, USS Ranger (CV-61), 14 JAN 82; To VA-113, NAS LeMoore, CA., 14 JAN 82; To VA-113, USS Ranger (CV-61), 26 FEB 82; To VA-113, NAS Cubi Point, PI., 26 FEB 82; To VA-113, NAF Atsugi, JP., 26 FEB 82 ** Transferred To VA-93/CVW-5, NF/3XX, NAS Cubi Point, PI., 27 SEP 82; To VA-93, NAF Atsugi, JP., 09 NOV 82; To VA-93, NAS Cubi Point, PI., 21 NOV 82; To VA-93, USS Midway (CV-41), 21 NOV 82; To VA-93, NAF Atsugi, JP., 01 JUL 83; To VA-93, USS Midway (CV-41), 16 AUG 83; To VA-93, NAF Atsugi, JP., 12 SEP 83 ** Transferred to VA-192/CVW- 11, NH/3XX, NAS LeMoore, CA., 30 DEC 85 ** Transferred to VA-147/CVW-9, NE/3XX, NAS LeMoore, CA., 11 FEB 86; To VA-147, NARF, NAS Jacksonville, FL., 30 OCT 86; To VA-147, NAS LeMoore, CA., 31 OCT 86; To VA-147, USS Kitty Hawk (CV-63), 31 OCT 86; To VA-147, NAS LeMoore, CA., 31 OCT 86 ** End of flight record card ** Transferred to NAD, NAS Jacksonville, FL., date unknown ** Transferred to AMARC, Davis Monthan AFB; Tucson, AZ., assigned park code 6A0380, 21 SEP 90 ** 52171.1 flight hours ** TF41A402D engine 142549 ** Aircraft released from storage and prepared for overland and above deck shipmeny to the government of Greece, 12 JUL 94 ** Transferred to the Helenic Air Force (Greece).

160537/160554 LTV A-7E Corsair II; (Block XXIII)
   FY 76-7T Contract N00019-76-C-0152,
   (30) FLIR-2 A-7E E-507/E-536

E-524 160537 Navy acceptance from NPRO Rep. LTV, Dallas, TX., 31 JAN 77 ** Transferred to VA-113/CVW-2, NE/3XX, NAS LeMoore, CA., 01 FEB 77 ** Transferred to VA-93/CVW-5, NF/3XX, USS Midway (CV-41), 24 APR 77; To VA-93, NAF Atsugi, JP., 21 MAY 78; To VA-93, USS Midway (CV-41), 16 JUL 80 ** Transferred to VA-146/CVW-9, NG/3XX, USS Constellation (CV-64), 22 SEP 80; To VA-146, NAS LeMoore, CA., 22 SEP 80; To VA-146, NAS Jacksonville, FL., 21 NOV 80; To VA-146, NAS LeMoore, CA., 22 JAN 81; To VA-146, NAS Dallas, TX., 17 MAR 81; To VA-146, NAS LeMoore, CA., 18 MAR 81 ** Transferred to VA-93/CVW-5, NF/3XX, USS Midway (CV-41), 28 MAY 81; To VA-93, NAF Atsugi, JP., 27 JUN 81; To VA-93, Korea, 15 JUL 81; To VA-93, USS Midway (CV-41), 03 SEP 81; To VA-93, NAF Atsugi, JP., 04 OCT 81; To VA-93, USS Midway (CV-41), 30 OCT 81; To VA-93, NAF Atsugi, JP., 11 JAN 82; To VA-93, USS Midway (CV-41), 15 JAN 82; To VA-93, NAS Cubi Point, PI., 28 AUG 82 ** Transferred to VA-113/CVW-2, NE/3XX, NAF Atsugi, JP., 23 SEP 82; To VA-113, NAS Jacksonville, FL., 04 NOV 82; To VA-113, NAS LeMoore, CA., 21 DEC 82 ** Transferred to VA-122/FRS, NJ/2XX, NAS LeMoore, CA., 24 FEB 83 ** Transferred to VA-22/CVW-11, NH/3XX, NAS LeMoore, CA., 31 JAN 85; To VA-22, NAS Fallon, NV., 11 APR 85; To VA-22, NAS LeMoore, CA., 11 APR 85; To VA-22, NAS Jacksonville, FL., 24 JUL 85; To VA-22, NAS LeMoore, CA., 25 JUL 85; To VA-22, USS Enterprise (CVN-65), 25 JUL 85; To VA-22, NAS LeMoore, CA., 11 JUN 86 thru 08 MAY 87 ** End of flight record card ** Transferred to the Helenic Air force (Greee).

E-507 160538 Navy acceptance from NPRO Rep. LTV, Dallas, TX., 15 FEB 77 ** Transferred to VA-113/CVW-2, NE/3XX, NAS LeMoore, CA., 17 FEB 77 ** Transferred to VA-93/CVW-5, NF/3XX, USS Midway (CV-41), 24 APR 77; To VA-93, NAF Atsugi, JP., 21 MAY 78; To VA-93, USS Midway (CV-41), 16 JUL 80 ** Transferred to VA-146/CVW-9, NG/3XX, USS Constellation (CV-64), 22 SEP 80; To VA-146, NAS LeMoore, CA., 22 SEP 80; To VA-146, NAS Jacksonville, FL., 24 APR 81; To VA-146, NAS LeMoore,

CA., 24 APR 81; To VA-146, NAS Jacksonville, FL., 11 JUN 81; To VA-146, NARF, NAS Jacksonville, FL., 14 AUG 81; To VA-146, NAS Dallas, TX., 17 AUG 81; To VA-146, NAS LeMoore, CA., 18 AUG 81; To VA-146, USS Constellation (CV-64), 08 SEP 81; To VA-146, NAS Dallas, TX., 12 NOV 81 ** Transferred to VA-192/ CVW-11, NH/3XX, NAS LeMoore, CA., 13 NOV 81 ** Transferred to VA-22/CVW-11, NH/303, NAS Lemoore, CA., 18 FEB 82; To VA-22, USS Enterprise (CVN-65), 18 FEB 82; To VA-22, NAS LeMoore, CA., 18 JAN 83; To VA-22, NAS Jacksonville, FL., 19 DEC 83; To VA-22, NAS LeMoore, CA., 23 DEC 83; To VA-22, USS Enterprise (CVN-65), 23 DEC 83; To VA-22, NAS LeMoore, CA., 17 FEB 84; To VA-22, USS Enterprise (CVN-65), 06 MAY 84 ** Transferred to VA-56/CVW-5, NF/4XX, NAF Atsugi, JP., 14 NOV 84; To VA-56, NAS Jacksonville, FL., 24 APR 86; To VA-56, NAS LeMoore, CA., 24 APR 86; To VA-56, NAS Jacksonville, FL., 08 MAY 86 ** Transferred to VA-146/CVW-9, NE/3XX, NAS LeMoore, CA., 05 SEP 86; To VA-146, USS Kitty Hawk (CV-63), 01 OCT 86; To VA-146, NAS LeMoore, CA., 01 OCT 86 ** Transferred to VA-97/CVW-15, NL/3XX, NAS Alameda, CA., 15 JUL 87 thru 21 SEP 87 ** End of flight record card ** Transferred to VA-122/FRS, NJ/231, NAS LeMoore, CA., date unknown ** Transferred to AMARC, Davis Monthan AFB; Tucson, AZ., assigned park code 6A0356, 22 MAY 90 ** 5624.5 flight hours ** TF41A402D engine S/N 141518 ** Storage location 111208 ** At AMARC, Davis Monthan AFB; Tucson, AZ.,15 JUN 07.

E-508 160539 Navy acceptance from NPRO Rep. LTV, Dallas, TX., 02 MAR 77 ** Transferred to VA-122/FRS, NJ/2XX, NAS LeMoore, CA., 17 MAR 77 ** Transferred to VA-56/ CVW-5, NF/4XX, USS Midway (CV-41), 25 APR 77; To VA-56, NAF Atsugi, JP., 22 MAY 78 ** Transferred to VA-97/CVW-14, NK/3XX, USS Coral Sea (CV-43), 15 MAY 80; To VA-97, NAS LeMoore, CA., 21 MAY 80; To VA-97, USS Coral Sea (CV-43), 08 OCT 80; To VA-97, NAS LeMoore, CA., 16 JAN 81; To VA-97, NAS Jacksonville, FL., 22 APR 81; To VA-97, USS Coral Sea (CV-43), 23 APR 81; To VA-97, NAS Jacksonville, FL., 30 JUN 81; To VA-97, NAS LeMoore, CA., 17 JUL 81; To VA-97, USS Coral Sea (CV-43), 17 JUL 81; To VA-97, NAS Dallas, TX., 21 SEP 81 ** Transferred to VA-113/CVW-2, NE/3XX, NAS Fallon, NV., 28 SEP 81 CA., To VA-113, USS Ranger (CV-61), 26 OCT 81; To VA-113, NAS LeMoore, CA., 12 NOV 81; To VA-113, USS Ranger (CV-61), 14 JAN 82; To VA-113, NAS LeMoore, CA., 14 JAN 82; To VA-113, USS Ranger (CV-61), 26 FEB 82; To VA-113, NAS Cubi Point, PI., 26 FEB 82; To VA-113, NAF Atsugi, JP., 26 FEB 82 ** Transferred to VA-93/CVW-5, NF/3XX, NAS Cubi Point, PI., 27 SEP 82; To VA-93, NAF Atsugi, JP., 28 SEP 82; To VA-93, NAS Cubi Point, PI., 06 OCT 82; To VA-93, USS Midway (CV-41), 06 OCT 82; To VA-93, NAF Atsugi, JP., 30 JUL 83; To VA-93, NAS LeMoore, CA., 08 OCT 85 ** Transferred to VA-122/FRS, NJ/2XX, NAS LeMoore, CA., 13 MAY 86; To VA-122, NAS Jacksonville, FL., 16 SEP 86; To VA-122, NAS LeMoore, CA., 16 SEP 86; To VA-122, NARF, NAS Jacksonville, FL., 20 SEP 86; To VA-122, NAS LeMoore, CA., 23 JAN 87 thru 26 JUN 87 ** End of flight record card ** Transferred to AMARC, Davis Monthan AFB; Tucson, AZ., assigned park code 6A0349, 24 APR 90 ** 5004.2 flight hours ** TF41A402D engine S/N 142511 ** Aircraft released from storage and prepared for shipment to FL., 19 MAY 94.

E-509 160540 Navy acceptance from NPRO Rep. LTV, Dallas, TX., 03 MAR 77 ** Transferred to VA-122/FRS, NJ/2XX, NAS LeMoore, CA., 05 MAR 77 ** Transferred to VA-56/CVW-5, NF/4XX, USS Midway (CV-41), 25 APR 77; To VA-56, NAF Atsugi, JP., 22 MAY 78; To VA-56, USS Midway (CV-41), 14 JUL 80 ** Transferred to VA-146/CVW-9, NG/3XX, USS Constellation (CV-64), 22 SEP 80; To VA-146, NAS LeMoore, CA., 22 SEP 80; To VA-146, NAS Jacksonville, FL., 21 APR 81; To VA-146, NAS Dallas, TX., 06 JUL 81; To VA-146, NAS LeMoore, CA., 14 JUL 81; To VA-146, NAS Dallas, TX., 17 SEP 81 ** Transferred to VA-122/FRS, NJ/XXX, NAS LeMoore, CA., 24 SEP 81 ** Transferred to VA-146/CVW-9, NG/3XX, NAS LeMoore, CA., 14 JUL 82 ** Transferred to VA-105/CVW-15, NL/4XX, USS Carl Vinson

(CVN-70), 03 MAY 83; To VA-105, NAS Cecil Field, FL., 03 MAY 85 ** Transferred to VA-97/CVW-15, NL/3XX, NAS LeMoore, CA., 28 OCT 83; To VA-97, NAS Jacksonville, FL., 09 FEB 84; To VA-97, NAS LeMoore, CA., 15 FEB 84; To VA-97, USS Carl Vinson (CVN-70), 16 FEB 84; To VA-97, NAS LeMoore, CA., 26 APR 84; To VA-97, USS Carl Vinson (CVN-70), 27 MAY 84; To VA-97, NAS LeMoore, CA., 06 JUN 84; To VA-97, USS Carl Vinson (CVN-70), 20 JUL 84; To VA-97, NAS LeMoore, CA., 20 JUL 84; To VA-97, USS Carl Vinson (CVN-70), 20 JUL 84; To VA-97, NAS LeMoore, CA., 29 MAR 85 ~ S 1SO strike, 27 JUN 85 ** Pilot ejected safely when engine failed on approach to NAS LeMoore, CA.

E-510 160541 Navy acceptance from NPRO Rep. LTV, Dallas, TX., 01 MAR 77 ** Transferred to VA-122/FRS, NJ/2XX, NAS LeMoore, CA., 17 MAR 77 ** Transferred to VA-93/ CVW-5, NF/3XX, USS Midway (CV-41), 24 APR 77; To VA-93, NAF Atsugi, JP., 22 MAY 78 ** Transferred to VA-93, USS Midway (CV-41), 23 JUN 80 ** Transferred to VA-146/CVW-9, NG/3XX, USS Constellation (CV-64), 22 SEP 80; To VA-146, NAS LeMoore, CA., 22 SEP 80; To VA-146, NAS Jacksonville, FL., 15 JUL 81; To VA-146, NAS LeMoore, CA., 22 JUL 81; To VA-146, USS Constellation (CV-64), 22 JUL 81; To VA-146, NAS Jacksonville, FL., 28 SEP 81; To VA-146, Bloomfield, 30 SEP 81; To VA-146, NAS Dallas, TX., 12 OCT 81 ** Transferred to VA-192/CVW-11, NH/3XX, NAS LeMoore, CA., 29 DEC 81 ** Transferred to VA-22/CVW-11, NH/3XX, NAS LeMoore, CA., 09 FEB 82; To VA-22, USS Enterprise (CVN-65), 09 FEB 82; To VA-22, NAS LeMoore, CA., 13 JUN 83; To VA-22, USS Enterprise (CVN-65), 13 JUN 83; To VA-22, NAS LeMoore, CA., 06 MAR 84; To VA-22, NAS Jacksonville, FL., 07 MAR 84 ** Transferred to VA-27/CVW-15, NL/4XX, NAS LeMoore, CA., 30 APR 84; To VA-27, USS Carl Vinson (CVN-70), 01 MAY 84; To VA-27, NAS LeMoore, CA., 01 MAY 84; To VA-27, USS Carl Vinson (CVN-70), 01 MAY 84; To VA-27, NAS LeMoore, CA., 01 MAY 84; To VA-27, NAS Jacksonville, FL., 05 MAR 86 ** Transferred to VA-122/ FRS, NJ/2XX, NAS LeMoore, CA., 30 MAY 86 ** Transferred to VA-147/CVW-9, NE/3XX, NAS LeMoore, CA., 25 AUG 86; To VA-147, USS Kitty Hawk (CV-63), 01 OCT 86; To VA-147, NAS LeMoore, CA., 01 OCT 86 thru 15 SEP 87 ** End of flight record card ** Transferred to the Helenic Air force (Greee).

E-511 160542 Navy acceptance from NPRO Rep. LTV, Dallas, TX., 01 APR 77 ** Transferred to VA-122/FRS, NJ/2XX, NAS LeMoore, CA., 04 APR 77; To VA-122, NAS North Island, CA., 31 MAY 77 ** Transferred to VA-56/CVW-5, NF/4XX, USS Midway (CV-41), 25 JUN 77; To VA-56, NAF Atsugi, JP., 20 SEP 77; To VA-56, USS Midway (CV-41), 23 SEP 77; To VA-56, NAF Atsugi, JP., 22 MAY 78; To VA-56, USS Midway (CV-41), 14 JUL 80 ** Transferred to VA-146/CVW-9, NG/3XX, USS Constellation (CV-64), 22 SEP 80; To VA-146, NAS LeMoore, CA., 22 SEP 80; To VA-146, NAS Jacksonville, FL., 06 JUN 81; To VA-146, NAS LeMoore, CA., 13 AUG 81; To VA-146, NAS Dallas, TX., 31 AUG 81 ** Transferred to VA-122/FRS, NJ/260, NAS LeMoore, CA., 01 NOV 81; To VA-122, NAS Jacksonville, FL., 10 DEC 84; To VA-122, NAS LeMoore, CA., 09 FEB 85 ** Transferred to VA-192/CVW-9, NG/3XX, NAS LeMoore, CA., 14 FEB 85; To VA-192, NAS Cubi Point, PI., 06 SEP 85 ** Transferred to VA-93/CVW-5, NF/3XX, NAF Atsugi, JP., 08 NOV 85; To VA-93, NAS LeMoore, CA., 21 DEC 85 ** Transferred to VA-122/FRS, NJ/2XX, NAS LeMoore, CA., 15 MAY 86 ** Transferred to VA-192/CVW-9, NG/3XX, NAS Cubi Point, PI., 09 SEP 85 ** Transferred to VA-93/CVW-5, NF/3XX, NAF Atsugi, JP., 08 NOV 85; To VA-93, NAS LeMoore, CA., 21 NOV 85 ** Transferred to VA-122/FRS, NJ/2XX, NAS LeMoore, CA., 15 MAY 86 thru 23 SEP 87 ** End of flight record card ** Transferred to NAD, NAS Jacksonville, FL., 02 JUN 88 ** Transferred to VA-122/ FRS, NJ/236, NAS LeMoore, CA., date unknown ** Transferred to AMARC, Davis Monthan AFB; Tucson, AZ., assigned park code 6A0391, 24 JAN 91 ** 4682.4 flight hours ** TF41A402D engine S/N 142527 ** Aircraft released from storage and prepared for overland and above deck shipment to the government of Thailand, 20 JUN 94 ** Transferred to the Royal Thai Navy, S/N 1401.

E-512 160543 Navy acceptance from NPRO Rep. LTV, Dallas, TX., 12 APR 77 ** Transferred to VA-122/FRS, NJ/2XX, NAS LeMoore, CA., 14 APR 77; To VA-122, NAS North Island, CA., 18 MAY 77 ** Transferred to VA-56/CVW-5, NF/4XX, NAF Atsugi, JP., USS Midway (CV-41), 25 JUN 77; To VA-56, NAF Atsugi, JP., 09 MAY 78 ** Transferred to VA-97/CVW-14, NK/3XX, USS Coral Sea (CV-43), 16 MAY 80; To VA-97, NAS LeMoore, CA., 21 MAY 80; To VA-97, USS Coral Sea (CV-43), 04 APR 81; To VA-97, NAS LeMoore, CA., 04 JUN 81; To VA-97, NAS Jacksonville, FL., 06 JUL 81; To VA-97, USS Coral Sea (CV-43), 16 OCT 81; To VA-97, NAS Norfolk, VA., 28 JAN 82; To VA-97, NAS Dallas, TX., 04 FEB 82; To VA-97, NAS LeMoore, CA., 04 FEB 82 ** Transferred to VA-22/CVW-11, NH/303, NAS Lemoore, CA., 04 FEB 82; To VA-22, USS Enterprise, (CVN-65), 17 MAR 82; To VA-22, NAS LeMoore, CA., 28 MAR 83 ** Transferred to VA-97/CVW-15, NL/3XX, NAS LeMoore, CA., 14 OCT 83; To VA-97, USS Carl Vinson (CVN-70), 06 FEB 84; To VA-97, NAS LeMoore, CA., 06 FEB 84; To VA-97, USS Carl Vinson (CVN-70), 17 MAY 84 ** Transferred to VA-122/FRS, NJ/2XX, NAS LeMoore, CA., 30 MAY 84; To VA-122, NAS Jacksonville, FL., 28 JUN 84 ** Transferred to VA-97/CVW-15, NL/3XX, USS Carl Vinson (CVN-70), 09 AUG 84; To VA-97, NAS LeMoore, CA., 09 AUG 84; To VA-97, USS Carl Vinson (CVN-70), 09 AUG 84; To VA-97, NAS LeMoore, CA., 10 NOV 84; To VA-97, NAS Jacksonville, FL., 08 APR 86; To VA-97, NAS LeMoore, CA., 08 APR 86; To VA-97, NAS Jacksonville, FL., 10 APR 86; To VA-97, USS Carl Vinson (CVN-70), 10 APR 86; To VA-97, NAS Jacksonville, FL., 01 JUL 86 ** Transferred to VA-146/CVW-9, NE/3XX, NAS LeMoore, CA., 13 JUL 86; To VA-146, USS Kitty Hawk (CV-63), 01 OCT 86; To VA-146, NAS LeMoore, CA., 16 JUN 87 ** Transferred to VA-97/CVW-15, NL/3XX, NAS Alameda, CA., 20 JUL 87 ** End of flight record card ** Transferred to the Helenic Air force (Greee).

E-513 160544 Navy acceptance from NPRO Rep. LTV, Dallas, TX., 04 MAY 77 ** Transferred to VA-122/FRS, NJ/2XX, NAS LeMoore, CA., 06 MAY 77; To VA-122, NAS North Island, CA., 24 MAY 77 ** Transferred to VA-93/CVW-5, NF/301, USS Midway (CV-41), 24 JUN 77; To VA-93, NAF Atsugi, JP., 25 MAY 78; To VA-93, USS Midway (CV-41), 30 SEP 79; To VA-93, NAF Atsugi, JP., 30 SEP 79; To VA-93, USS Midway (CV-41), 23 JUN 80 ** Transferred to VA-66/CVW-7, AG/3XX, USS Dwight D. Eisenhower (CVN-69), 04 NOV 80; To VA-66, NAS Cecil Field, FL., 04 NOV 80 ** Transferred to VA-122/FRS, NJ/2XX, NASLeMoore, CA., 28 JAN 81; To VA-122, NAS Jacksonville, FL., 12 MAY 81; To VA-122, NAS LeMoore, CA., 05 AUG 81; To VA-122, NAS Dallas, TX., 07 OCT 81; To VA-122, NAS LeMoore, CA., 16 OCT 81 ** Transferred to VA-146/CVW-9, NG/3XX, NAS LeMoore, CA., 06 JUL 82 ** Transferred to VA-94/ CVW-11, NH/4XX, NAS LeMoore, CA., 21 OCT 83; To VA-94, NAS Jacksonville, FL., 28 NOV 83; To VA-94, USS Enterprise (CVN-65), 25 JAN 84; To VA-94, NAS LeMoore, CA., 30 JAN 84; To VA-94, USS Enterprise (CVN-65), 20 APR 84; To VA-94, NAF Atsugi, JP., 24 JUL 84; To VA-94, USS Enterprise (CVN-65), 02 AUG 84; To VA-94, NAF Atsugi, JP., 05 OCT 84; To VA-94, USS Enterprise (CVN-65), 11 NOV 84 ** Transferred to VA-93/CVW-5, NF/3XX, NAF Atsugi, JP., 12 NOV 84; To VA-93, NAS LeMoore, CA., 05 FEB 86 ** Transferred to VA-147/CVW-9, NE/3XX, NAS LeMoore, CA., 14 MAY 86; To VA-147, NAS Jacksonville, FL., 29 JUL 86; To VA-147, NAS LeMoore, CA., 29 JUL 86; To VA-147, NAS Jacksonville, FL., 31 JUL 86; To VA-147, NAS LeMoore, CA., 23 OCT 86; To VA-97, USS Kitty Hawk (CV-63), 23 OCT 86 ** Transferred to NARF, NAS Jacksonville, FL., 23 OCT 86 ** Transferred to VA-147/CVW-9. NE/3XX, NAS LeMoore, CA., 19 APR 87 ** End of flight record card ** Transferred to VA-22/CVW-11, NH/3XX, NAS LeMoore, CA., date unknown ** Transferred to AMARC, Davis Monthan AFB; Tucson, AZ., assigned park code 6A0347, 23 APR 90 ** 5336.0 flight hours ** TF41A402D engine S/N 141482 ** Aircraft released from storage and prepared for overland and above deck shipment to the government of Thailand, 17 DEC 94 ** Transferred to the Royal Thai Navy, S/N 1405.

E-514 160545 Navy acceptance from NPRO Rep. LTV, Dallas, TX., 01 APR 77 ** Transferred to VA-122/FRS, NJ/2XX, NAS LeMoore, CA., 03 APR 77; To VA-122, NAS North Island, CA., 31 MAY 77 ** Transferred to VA-93/CVW-5, NF/3XX, USS Midway (CV-41), 24 JUN 77; To VA-93, NAF Atsugi, JP., 25 MAY 78; To VA-93, USS Midway (CV-41), 23 JUN 80 ** Transferred to VA-12/CVW-7, AG/4XX, USS Dwight D. Eisenhower (CVN-69), 04 NOV 80; To VA-12, NAS Cecil Field, FL., 04 NOV 80 ** Transferred to VA-122/FRS, NJ/XXX, NAS LeMoore, CA., 22 JAN 81; To VA-122, NAS Jacksonville, FL., 23 JUL 81; To VA-122, NAS LeMoore, CA., 04 OCT 81; To VA-122, NARF, NAS Jacksonville, FL., 21 OCT 81; To VA-122, NAS Dallas, TX., 28 JAN 82 ** Transferred to VA-22/CVW-11, NH/3XX, NAS LeMoore, CA., 02 FEB 82; To VA-22, USS Enterprise (CVN-65), 02 FEB 82; To VA-22, NAS LeMoore, CA., 02 FEB 82; To VA-22, USS Enterprise (CVN-65), 08 SEP 83; To VA-22, NAS LeMoore, CA., 08 SEP 83 ** Transferred to VA-122/FRS, NJ/2XX, NAS LeMoore, CA., 17 FEB 84; To VA-122, NAS Jacksonville, FL., 10 APR 84 ** Transferred to VA-195/CVW-9, NG/4XX, NAS LeMoore, CA., 30 MAY 84 ** Transferred to VA-94/CVW-11, NH/4XX, NAS Fallon, NV., 19 APR 85; To VA-94, NAS LeMoore, CA., 25 MAY 85; To VA-94, USS Enterprise (CVN-65), 28 JAN 86; To VA-94, NAS LeMoore, CA., 23 MAY 86; To VA-94, NAS Jacksonville, FL., 11 SEP 86; To VA-94, NAS LeMoore, CA., 17 DEC 86 thru 31 AUG 87 ** End of flight record card ** Transferred to AMARC, Davis Monthan AFB; Tucson, AZ., assigned park code 6A0348 ** 5956.4 flight hours ** TF41A402D engine S/N AE141294 ** Aircraft released from storage and prepared for overland and above deck shipment to the government of Thailand, 23 NOV 94 ** Transferred to the Royal Thai Navy, S/N 1406.

E-515 160546 Navy acceptance from NPRO Rep. LTV, Dallas, TX., 12 MAY 77 ** Transferred to VA-174/FRS, AD/4XX, NAS Cecil Field, FL., 13 MAY 77 ** Transferred to VA-72/CVW-7, AG/4XX, NAS Cecil Field, FL., 12 OCT 77; To VA-72, USS Dwight D. Eisenhower (CVN-69), 12 OCT 77; To VA-72, NAS Cecil Field, FL., 03 DEC 77 ~ S 1SO strike, 03 DEC 77 ** No data on strike.

E-516 160547 Navy acceptance from NPRO Rep. LTV, Dallas, TX., 14 JUN 77 ** Transferred to VA-174/FRS, AD/4XX, NAS Cecil Field, FL., 15 JUN 77 ** Transferred to VA-46/CVW-1, AB/3XX, NAS Cecil Field, FL., 27 SEP 77; To VA-46, USS Dwight D. Eisenhower (CVN-69), 27 SEP 77; To VA-46, NAS Cecil Field, FL., 27 SEP 77; To VA-46, USS John F. Kennedy (CV-67), 27 SEP 77; To VA-46, NAS Cecil Field, FL., 27 SEP 77; To VA-46, USS John F. Kennedy (CV-67), 27 SEP 77; To VA-46, NAS Cecil Field, FL., 27 SEP 77; To VA-46, USS John F. Kennedy (CV-67), 19 MAR 80; To VA-46, NAS Cecil Field, FL., 19 MAR 80; To VA-46, NAS Jacksonville, FL., 06 AUG 81; To VA-46, NAS Cecil Field, FL., 02 OCT 81; To VA-46, NAS Dallas, TX., 16 OCT 81 ** Transferred to VA-72/CVW1, AB/4XX, NAS Cecil Field, FL., 27 DEC 81; To VA-72, USS America (CV-66), 27 DEC 81; To VA-72, NAS Cecil Field, FL., 22 JUN 83; To VA-72, USS America (CV-66), 31 OCT 83; To VA-72, NAS Jacksonville, FL., 30 NOV 83; To VA-72, USS America (CV-66), 02 DEC 83; To VA-72, NAS Cecil Field, FL., 14 DEC 83; To VA-72, USS America (CV-66), 23 JAN 84; To VA-72, NAS Cecil Field, FL., 23 JAN 84; To VA-72, USS America (CV-66), 23 MAY 85; To VA-72, NAS Cecil Field, FL., 23 MAY 85; To VA-72, USS America (CV-66), 24 JAN 86; To VA-72, NAS Jacksonville, FL., 01 APR 86 ** Transferred to NARF, NAS Jacksonville, FL., 25 JUN 86 ** Transferred to VA-86/CVW-8, AJ/406, USS Nimitz (CVN-68), 26 JUN 86; To VA-86, NAS Cecil Field, FL., 26 JUN 86; To VA-86, USS Nimitz (CVN-68), 26 JUN 86; To VA-86, NAS Cecil Field, FL., 10 OCT 86; To VA-86, USS Nimitz (CVN-68), 10 OCT 86; To VA-86, NAS Cecil Field, FL., 10 OCT 86 thru 17 AUG 87 ** End of flight record card ** Transferred to VA-174/FRS, AD/4XX, NAS Cecil Field, FL., date unknown ** Transferred to AMARC, Davis Monthan AFB; Tucson, AZ., assigned park code 6A0272, 27 MAY 88 ** Park Code changed to 6A0343 ** 4762.8 flight record ** TF41A402D engine 142637 ** Aircraft released from storage and prepared for overland shipment to FMS and NAD, NAS Jacksonville, FL., with final shipment to government of Thailand, 18 SEP 95 ** Transferred to the Royal Thai Navy, S/N 160547.

E-517 160548 Navy acceptance from NPRO Rep. LTV, Dallas, TX., 24 MAY 77 ** Transferred to VA-174/FRS, AD/4XX, NAS Cecil Field, FL., 27 MAY 77 ** Transferred to VA-72/CVW-1, AB/4XX, NAS Cecil Field, FL., 29 SEP 77; To VA-72/ CVW-7, AG/4XX, USS Dwight D. Eisenhower (CVN-69), 29 SEP 77; To VA-72, NAS Cecil Field, FL., 29 SEP 77; To VA-72, USS John F. Kennedy (CV-67), 29 SEP 77; To VA-72, NAS Cecil Field, FL., 29 SEP 77; To VA-72, USS John F. Kennedy (CV-67), 29 SEP 77 ** Transferred to VA-46/ CVW-1, AB/3XX, NAS Cecil Field, FL., 29 SEP 77 ** Transferred to VA-72/ CVW-1, AB/4XX, NAS Cecil Field, FL., 25 JUL 79; To VA-72, USS John F. Kennedy (CV-67), 02 JUL 80; To VA-72, NAS Cecil Field, FL., 02 JUL 80; To VA-72, NAS Jacksonville, FL., 16 JUL 81; To VA-72, NAS Cecil Field, FL., 02 OCT 81; To VA-72, NAS Dallas, TX., 22 OCT 81; To VA-72, NAS Cecil Field, FL., 15 JAN 82 ~ S 1SO strike, 02 FEB 82 ** No data on strike.

E-518 160549 Navy acceptance from NPRO Rep. LTV, Dallas, TX., 02 JUN 77 ** Transferred to VA-174/FRS, AD/4XX, NAS Cecil Field, FL., 06 JUN 77 ** Transferred to VA-46/CVW-1, AB/305, NAS Cecil Field, FL., 05 OCT 77; To VA-46, USS Dwight D. Eisenhower (CVN-69), 05 OCT 77; To VA-46, NAS Cecil Field, FL., 05 OCT 77; To VA-46, USS John F. Kennedy (CV-67), 05 OCT 77; To VA-46, NAS Cecil Field, FL., 05 OCT 77; To VA-46, USS John F. Kennedy (CV-67), 05 OCT 77; To VA-46, NAS Cecil Field, FL., 05 OCT 77; To VA-46, USS John F. Kennedy (CV-67), 19 MAR 80; To VA-46, NAS Cecil Field, FL., 19 MAR 80; To VA-46, NAS Jacksonville, FL., 13 AUG 81; To VA-46, NAS Dallas, TX., 28 OCT 81 ** Transferred to VA-72/CVW-1, AB/4XX, NAS Cecil Field, FL., 16 FEB 82; To VA-72, USS America (CV-66), 12 MAR 82; To VA-72, NAS Cecil Field, FL., 28 JUN 83; To VA-72, USS America (CV-66), 16 NOV 83; To VA-72, NAS Cecil Field, FL., 16 NOV 83; To VA-72, USS America (CV-66), 16 NOV 83; To VA-72, NAS Jacksonville, FL., 06 DEC 84; To VA-72, NAS Cecil Field, FL., 08 DEC 84; To VA-72, NAS Jacksonville, FL., 24 JAN 85; To VA-72, NAS Cecil Field, FL., 15 FEB 85; To VA-72, USS America (CV-66), 22 APR 85; To VA-72, NAS Cecil Field, FL., 22 APR 85; To VA-72, USS America (CV-66), 06 MAR 86; To VA-72 NAS Cecil Field, FL., 18 MAY 86; To VA-72, NAS Jacksonville, FL., 02 FEB 87; To VA-72, NAS Cecil Field, FL., 02 FEB 87; To VA-72, NAS Jacksonville, FL., 03 FEB 87; To VA-72, NADEP, NAS Jacksonville, FL., 03 FEB 87; To VA-72, USS Dwight D. Eisenhower (CVN-69), 12 JUN 87; To VA-72, NAS Cecil Field, FL., 12 JUN 87 thru 21 SEP 87 ** End of flight record card ** Transferred to AMARC, Davis Monthan AFB; Tucson, AZ., assigned park code 6A0343; 17 APR 90 ** 5318.6 flight hours ** TF41A402D engine S/N 142515 ** storage location 111515 ** At AMARG, Davis Monthan AFB; Tucson, AZ., 15 JUN 07.

E-519 160550 Navy acceptance from NPRO Rep. LTV, Dallas, TX., 23 JUN 77 ** Transferred to VA-174/FRS, AD/4XX, NAS Cecil Field, FL., 25 JUN 77 ** Transferred to VA-72/CVW-1, AB/4XX, USS Dwight D. Eisenhower (CVN-69), 29 SEP 77; To VA-72, NAS Cecil Field, FL., 29 SEP 77; To VA-72, USS John F. Kennedy (CV-67), 29 SEP 77; To VA-72, NAS Cecil Field, FL., 29 SEP 77; To VA-72, USS John F. Kennedy (CV-67), 29 SEP 77; To VA-72, NAS Cecil Field, FL., 16 JAN 79; To VA-72, USS John F. Kennedy (CV-67), 19 MAR 80; To VA-72, NAS Cecil Field, FL., 19 MAR 80; To VA-72, NAS Jacksonville, FL., 28 AUG 81; To VA-72, NAS Cecil Field, FL., 28 AUG 81; To VA-72, NAS Jacksonville, FL., 01 SEP 81; To VA-72, NAS Dallas, TX., 02 NOV 81; To VA-72, NAS Cecil Field, FL., 24 NOV 81; To VA-72, USS America (CV-66), 21 FEB 82; To VA-72, NAS Cecil Field, FL., 21 FEB 82; To VA-72, USS America (CV-66), 29 OCT 83; To VA-72, NAS Cecil Field, FL., 19 JAN 84; To VA-72, USS America (CV-66), 25 JAN 84; To VA-72, NAS Jacksonville, FL., 27 JAN 84; To VA-72, NAS Cecil Field, FL., 29 NOV 84; To VA-72, NAS Jacksonville, FL., 25 JAN 85; To VA-72, NAS Cecil Field, FL., 29 JAN 85; To VA-72, USS America (CV-66), 28 FEB 85; To VA-72, NAS Cecil Field, FL., 28 FEB 85; To VA-72, USS America (CV-66), 14 JAN 86; To VA-72, NAS Cecil Field, FL., 29 SEP 86; To VA-72, NAS Jacksonville, FL., 29 SEP 86; Transferred to VA-37/CVW-6, AE/3XX, NAS Cecil Field, FL., 20 JAN 87; To VA-37, USS Forrestal (CV-59), 09 JUL 87 ** End of flight record card ** Transferred to the Helenic Air force (Greee).

E-520 160551 Navy acceptance from NPRO Rep. LTV, Dallas, TX., 11 JUL 77 ** Transferred to VA-174/FRS, AD/4XX, NAS Cecil Field, FL., 16 JUL 77 ** Transferred to VA-46/CVW-1, AB/3XX, USS Dwight D. Eisenhower (CVN-69), 06 OCT 77; To VA-46, NAS Cecil Field, FL., 06 OCT 77; To VA-46, USS John F. Kennedy (CV-67), 06 OCT 77; To VA-46, NAS Cecil Field, FL., 06 OCT 77; To VA-46, USS John F. Kennedy (CV-67), 06 OCT 77; Transferred to VA-72/CVW-1, AB/4XX, NAS Cecil Field, FL., 06 OCT 77; To VA-72, USS John F. Kennedy (CV-67), 26 FEB 80; Transferred to VA-46/ CVW-1, AB/3XX, NAS Cecil Field, FL., 26 FEB 80; To VA-46, NAS Jacksonville, FL., 20 AUG 81; To VA-46, NAS Cecil Field, FL., 20 AUG 81; To VA-46, NAS Jacksonville, FL., 24 AUG 81; To VA-46, NAS Dallas, TX., 18 NOV 81 ** Transferred to VA-72/CVW-1, AB/4XX, NAS Cecil Field, FL., 25 FEB 82; To VA-72, USS America (CV-66), 25 FEB 82; To VA-72, NAS Cecil Field, FL., 15 APR 83; To VA-72, USS America (CV-66), 22 NOV 83; To VA-72, NAS Cecil Field, FL., 22 DEC 83; To VA-72, USS America (CV-66), 16 APR 84; To VA-72, NAS Cecil Field, FL., 19 NOV 84; To VA-72, NAS Jacksonville, FL., 20 MAY 85; To VA-72, NAS Cecil Field, FL., 21 MAY 85; To VA-72, USS America (CV-66), 21 MAY 85 ** Transferred to VA-174/FRS, AD/4XX, NAS Cecil Field, FL., 22 AUG 85 ** Transferred to VA-15/CVW-6, AE/3XX, NAS Cecil Field, FL., 12 OCT 85; To VA-15, MCAS Iwakuni, JP., 12 OCT 85; To VA-15, Korea, 12 OCT 85; To VA-15, NAS Cubi Point, PI., 12 OCT 85; To VA-15, NAS Cecil Field, FL., 12 OCT 85 ** Transferred to VA-46/CVW-1, AB/315, NAS Cecil Field, FL., 18 SEP 86; To VA-46/CVW-7, AG/3XX, USS Dwight D. Eisenhower (CVN-69), 12 MAY 87; To VA-46, NAS Cecil Field, FL., 03 JUN 87 ** End of flight record card.

E-521 160552 Navy acceptance from NPRO Rep. LTV, Dallas, TX., 18 JUL 77 ** Transferred to VA-174/FRS, AD/4XX, NAS Cecil Field, FL., 20 JUL 77 ** Transferred to VA-72/CVW-1, AB/4XX, NAS Cecil Field, FL., 27 OCT 77; To VA-72, USS Dwight D. Eisenhower (CVN-69), 27 OCT 77; To VA-72, NAS Cecil Field, FL., 27 OCT 77; To VA-72, USS John F. Kennedy (CV-67), 27 OCT 77; To VA-72, NAS Cecil Field, FL., 27 OCT 77; To VA-72, USS John F. Kennedy (CV-67), 27 OCT 77; To VA-72, USS John F. Kennedy (CV-67), 14 JUL 80; To VA-72, NAS Cecil Field, FL., 14 JUL 80; To VA-72, NAS Jacksonville, FL., 14 SEP 81; To VA-72, NAS Cecil Field, FL., 28 NOV 81; To VA-72, NAS Dallas, TX., 15 DEC 81; To VA-72, NAS Cecil Field, FL., 28 FEB 82; To VA-72, USS America (CV-66), 28 FEB 82; To VA-72, NAS Cecil Field, FL., 28 FEB 82; To VA-72, USS America (CV-66), 28 OCT 83; To VA-72, NAS Cecil Field, FL., 30 OCT 83; To VA-72, USS America (CV-66), 30 OCT 83; To VA-72, NAS Cecil Field, FL., 07 DEC 84; To VA-72, NAS Jacksonville, FL., 19 FEB 85; To VA-72, NAS Cecil Field, FL., 19 FEB 85; To VA-72, USS America (CV-66), 05 MAR 85; To VA-72, NAS Cecil Field, FL., 25 MAR 85; To VA-72, USS America (CV-66), 24 MAR 86; To VA-72, NAS Cecil Field, FL., 01 JUL 86; To VA-72, NAS Jacksonville, FL., 30 JAN 87; To VA-72, NAS Cecil Field, FL., 30 JAN 87; To VA-72, NAS Jacksonville, FL., 09 FEB 87; To VA-72/CVW-7, AG/4XX, USS Dwight D. Eisenhower (CVN-69), 09 FEB 87; To VA-72, NAS Cecil Field, FL., 10 JUN 87 thru 15 SEP 87 ** End of flight record card ** Painted in two tone desert camoflouge with CAPT (CAG) White painted on nose, with 31 camels, 91 ** Transferred to the Helenic Air force (Greee).

E-522 160553 Navy acceptance from NPRO Rep. LTV, Dallas, TX., 30 JUN 77 ** Transferred to VA-174/FRS, AD/4XX, NAS Cecil Field, FL., 03 JUL 77 ** Transferred to VA-46/CVW-1, AB/3XX, NAS Cecil Field, FL., 04 OCT 77; To VA-46, USS Dwight D. Eisenhower (CVN-69), 04 OCT 77; To VA-46, NAS Cecil Field, FL., 04 OCT 77; To VA-46, USS John F. Kennedy (CV-67), 04 OCT 77; To VA-46, NAS Cecil Field, FL., 04 OCT 77; To VA-46, USS John F. Kennedy (CV-67), 04 OCT 77; To VA-46, NAS Cecil Field, FL., 04 OCT 77; To VA-46, USS John F. Kennedy (CV-67), 18 MAR 80 ** Transferred to VA-72/CVW-1, AB/4XX, NAS Cecil Field, FL., 18 MAR 80; To VA-72, NAS Jacksonville, FL., 11 AUG 81 ** Transferred to VA-46/CVW-1, AB/3XX, NAS Cecil Field, FL., 09 OCT 81; To VA-46, USS America (CV-66), 09 OCT 81; To VA-46, NAS Cecil Field, FL., 09 OCT 81; To VA-46, USS America (CV-66), 09 OCT 81; To VA-46, NAS Cecil Field, FL., 21 APR 83 ** Transferred to VA-174/FRS, AD/4XX, NAS Cecil Field, FL., 01 JUL 83; To VA-174, NAS Jacksonville, FL., 03

FEB 84; To VA-174, NAS Cecil Field, FL., 04 FEB 84; To VA-174, NAS Jacksonville, FL., 23 FEB 84; To VA-174, NAS Cecil Field, FL., 02 MAR 84 ** Transferred to VA-82/CVW-8, AJ/3XX, NAS Cecil Field, FL., 20 JUN 84 ** Transferred to VA-15/CVW-6, AE/3XX, USS Independence (CV-62), 10 OCT 84; To VA-15, NAS Cecil Field, FL., 10 OCT 84 ** Transferred to VA-66/CVW-7, AG/3XX, USS Dwight D. Eisenhower (CVN-69), 08 JUL 85; To VA-66, NAS Cecil Field, FL., 03 OCT 85; To VA-66, USS John F. Kennedy (CV-67), 24 JUN 86; To VA-66, NAS Jacksonville, FL., 12 SEP 86 ** Transferred to VA-83/CVW-17, AA/3XX, USS Saratoga (CV-60), 12 SEP 86; To VA-83, NAS Cecil Field, FL., 15 OCT 86; To VA-83, USS Saratoga (CV-60), 10 MAR 87; To VA-83, NAS Cecil Field, FL., 10 MAR 87; To VA-83, USS Saratoga (CV-60), 10 MAR 87 ** End of flight record card.

E-523 160554 Navy acceptance from NPRO Rep. LTV, Dallas, TX., 08 JUL 77 ** Transferred to VA-174/FRS, AD/4XX, NAS Cecil Field, FL., 18 JUL 77 ** Transferred to VA-72/CVW-1, AB/4XX, NAS Cecil Field, FL., 22 SEP 77; To VA-72, USS Dwight D. Eisenhower (CVN-69), 22 SEP 77; To VA-72, NAS Cecil Field, FL., 22 SEP 77; To VA-72, USS John F. Kennedy (CV-67), 22 SEP 77; To VA-72, USS John F. Kennedy (CV-67), 07 JUN 78; To VA-72, NAS Cecil Field, FL., 26 JUN 78; To VA-72, USS John F. Kennedy (CV-67), 19 JUL 78; To VA-72, NAS Cecil Field, FL., 02 AUG 78; To VA-72, USS John F. Kennedy (CV-67), 18 APR 80; To VA-72, NAS Cecil Field, FL., 18 APR 80 ** Transferred to VA-46/CVW-1, AB/3XX, NAS Cecil Field, FL., 08 OCT 81; To VA-46, NAS Jacksonville, FL., 01 APR 82; To VA-46, NAS Cecil Field, FL., 01 APR 82; To VA-46, NAS Jacksonville, FL., 06 APR 82; To VA-46, NAS Cecil Field, FL., 27 MAY 82; To VA-46, USS America (CV-66), 27 MAY 82; To VA-46, NAS Cecil Field, FL., 27 MAY 82; To VA-46, USS America (CV-66), 27 MAY 82; To VA-46, NAS Cecil Field, FL., 27 MAY 82 ** Transferred to VA-87/CVW-6, AE/4XX, USS Independence (CV-62), 10 JUN 83; To VA-87, NAS Cecil Field, FL., 10 JUN 83; To VA-87, USS Independence (CV-62), 03 OCT 83; To VA-87, NAS Cecil Field, FL., 26 APR 84; To VA-87, NAS Jacksonville, FL., 12 JUN 84; To VA-87, NAS Cecil Field, FL., 21 JUN 84; To VA-87, USS Independence (CV-62), 21 JUL 84; To VA-87, NAS Jacksonville, FL., 20 AUG 84; To VA-87, USS Independence (CV-62), 21 AUG 84; To VA-87, NAS Cecil Field, FL., 22 AUG 84; To VA-87, USS Independence (CV-62), 13 SEP 84; To VA-87, NAS Cecil Field, FL., 18 FEB 85 ** Transferred to VA-174/FRS, AD/4XX, NAS Cecil Field, FL., 13 MAR 86 thru 30 AUG 87 ** End of flight record card.

160555/160566 LTV A-7E Corsair II (Block XXIV)
FY 75 Contract N00019-76-C-0152, (18) A-7E;
from E-536/E-535 (Block XXIV)

E-536 160555 Navy acceptance from NPRO Rep. LTV, Dallas, TX., 21 JUL 77 ** Transferred to VA-174/FRS, AD/4XX, NAS Cecil Field, FL., 21 JUL 77 ** Transferred to VA-46/CVW-1, AB/3XX, NAS Cecil Field, FL., 04 OCT 77; To VA-46, USS Dwight D. Eisenhower (CVN-69), 04 OCT 77; To VA-46, NAS Cecil Field, FL., 04 OCT 77; To VA-46, USS John F. Kennedy (CV-67), 04 OCT 77; To VA-46, NAS Cecil Field, FL., 04 OCT 77; To VA-46, USS John F. Kennedy (CV-67), 04 OCT 77; To VA-46, USS John F. Kennedy (CV-67), 06 MAR 80; To VA-46, NAS Cecil Field, FL., 06 MAR 80; To VA-46, NAS Jacksonville, FL., 26 AUG 81; To VA-46, NAS Cecil Field, FL., 23 NOV 81; To VA-46, USS America (CV-66), 04 MAR 82; To VA-46, NAS Cecil Field, FL., 04 MAR 82; To VA-46, USS America (CV-66), 04 MAR 82; To VA-46, NAS Cecil Field, FL., 20 JUN 83 ** Transferred to VA-174/FRS, AD/4XX, NAS Cecil Field, FL., 04 AUG 83; To VA-174, NAS Jacksonville, FL., 06 MAR 84; To VA-174, NAS Cecil Field, FL., 07 MAR 84; To VA-174, NAS Jacksonville, FL., 22 MAR 84 ** Transferred to VA-82/CVW-8, AJ/3XX, NAS Cecil Field, FL., 30 JUL 84; To VA-82, USS Nimitz (CVN-68), 30 JUL 84; To VA-82, NAS Cecil Field, FL., 30 JUL 84; To VA-82, USS Nimitz (CVN-68), 30 JUL 84; To VA-82, NAS Cecil Field, FL., 24 OCT 85; To VA-82, NAS Jacksonville, FL., 05 AUG 86; To VA-82, NARF, NAS Jacksonville, FL,m 27 OCT 86; To VA-82, NAS Cecil Field, FL., 28 OCT 86; To VA-82, USS Nimitz (CVN-68), 18 NOV 86; To VA-82, NAS Cecil Field, FL., 18 NOV 86 ** Transferred to VA-46/CVW-7, AG/316, USS Dwight D. Eisenhower (CVN-69), 16 JUN 87; To VA-

46, NAS Cecil Field, FL., 05 AUG 87 thru 14 SEP 87 ** End of flight record card ** Transferred to AMARC, Davis Monthan AFB; Tucson, AZ., assigned park code 6A0353; 04 MAY 90 ** 6044.3 flight hours ** TF41A402D engine S/N 141490 ** Storage location 111318 ** At AMARG, Davis Monthan AFB; Tucson, AZ., 15 JUN 07.

E-525 160556 Navy acceptance from NPRO Rep. LTV, Dallas, TX., 22 JUL 77 ** Transferred to VA-174/FRS, AD/4XX, NAS Cecil Field, FL., 22 JUL 77 ** Transferred to VA-72/CVW-1, AB/4XX, NAS Cecil Field, FL., 14 OCT 77; To VA-72, USS Dwight D. Eisenhower (CVN-69), 14 OCT 77; To VA-72, NAS Cecil Field, FL., 14 OCT 77; To VA-72, USS John F. Kennedy (CV-67), 14 OCT 77; To VA-72, NAS Cecil Field, FL., 14 OCT 77; To VA-72, USS John F. Kennedy (CV-67), 14 OCT 77; To VA-72, NAS Cecil Field, FL., 14 OCT 77; To VA-72, USS John F. Kennedy (CV-67), 07 JUL 80; To VA-72, NAS Cecil Field, FL., 07 JUL 80; To VA-72, NAS Jacksonville, FL., 21 AUG 81; To VA-72, NAS Cecil Field, FL., 23 OCT 81 ** Transferred to VA-46/CVW-1, AB/3XX, USS America (CV-66), 30 APR 82; To VA-46, NAS Cecil Field, FL., 30 APR 82; To VA-46, USS America (CV-66), 30 APR 82; To VA-46, NAS Cecil Field, FL., 20 JUN 83 ** Transferred to VA-174/FRS, AD/4XX, NAS Cecil Field, FL., 28 JUL 83; To VA-174, NAS Jacksonville, FL., 28 FEB 84; To VA-174, NAS Cecil Field, FL., 09 MAR 84; To VA-174, NAS Jacksonville, FL., 19 MAR 84; To VA-174, NAS Cecil Field, FL., 08 APR 84; To VA-174, NAS Jacksonville, FL., 30 JUL 84 ** Transferred to VA-82/CVW-8, AJ/3XX, NAS Cecil Field, FL., 31 JUL 84; To VA-82, USS Nimitz (CVN-68), 15 AUG 84; To VA-82, NAS Cecil Field, FL.,15 AUG 84; To VA-82, USS Nimitz (CVN-68), 15 AUG 84; To VA-82, NAS Cecil Field, FL., 15 AUG 84; To VA-82, USS John F. Kennedy (CV-67), 17 JUL 86 ** Transferred to VA-66/ CVW-3, AC/3XX, USS John F. Kennedy (CV-67), 17 JUL 86; To VA-66, NAS Jacksonville, FL., 10 OCT 86 ** Transferred to NARF, NAS Jacksonville, FL., 10 OCT 86 ** Transferred to VA-82/ CVW-8, AJ/3XX, NAS Cecil Field, FL., 14 OCT 86; To VA-82, USS Nimitz (CVN-68), 07 NOV 86; To VA-82, NAS Cecil Field, FL., 07 NOV 86 thru 09 SEP 87 ** End of flight record card ** Transferred to VA-105/CVW-6, AE/400, NAS Cecil Field, FL., date unknown ** Transferred to AMARC, Davis Monthan AFB; Tucson, AZ., assigned park code 6A0388, 03 DEC 90 ** 5384.6 flight hours ** TF41A402D engine S/N 141302 ** Aircraft released from storage and prepared for overland and above deck shipment to the government of Greece, 28 JUL 94 ** Transferred to the Helenic Air Force (Greece).

E-526 160557 Navy acceptance from NPRO Rep. LTV, Dallas, TX., 20 SEP 77 ** Transferred to VA-174/FRS, AD/4XX, NAS Cecil Field, FL., 03 OCT 77 ** Transferred to VA-12/CVW-7, AG/4XX, NAS Cecil Field, FL., 27 APR 78; To VA-12; USS Dwight D. Eisenhower (CVN-69), 27 APR 78; To VA-12, NAS Cecil Field, FL., 27 APR 78; To VA-12; USS Dwight D. Eisenhower (CVN-69), 27 APR 78; To VA-12, NAS Cecil Field, FL., 27 APR 78; To VA-12; USS Dwight D. Eisenhower (CVN-69), 27 APR 78; To VA-12, NAS Cecil Field, FL., 13 NOV 79; To VA-12; USS Dwight D. Eisenhower (CVN-69), 13 NOV 79; To VA-12, NAS Cecil Field, FL., 25 MAR 80; To VA-12; USS Dwight D. Eisenhower (CVN-69), 25 MAR 80; To VA-12, NAS Jacksonville, FL., 05 AUG 81; To VA-12; USS Dwight D. Eisenhower (CVN-69), 13 OCT 81; To VA-12, NAS Cecil Field, FL., 13 OCT 81; To VA-12; USS Dwight D. Eisenhower (CVN-69), 13 OCT 81; To VA-12, NAS Cecil Field, FL., 13 OCT 81; To VA-12; USS Dwight D. Eisenhower (CVN-69), 15 FEB 83; To VA-12, NAS Cecil Field, FL., 15 FEB 83; To VA-12, NAS Jacksonville, FL., 06 MAR 84; To VA-12; USS Dwight D. Eisenhower (CVN-69), 14 MAY 84; To VA-12, NAS Cecil Field, FL., 13 JUN 84; To VA-12, NAS Jacksonville, FL., 28 JUN 84; To VA-12, NAS Cecil Field, FL., 02 JUL 84 ** Transferred to VA-82/CVW-8, AJ/302, NAS Cecil Field, FL. 02 JUL 84; To VA-82, USS Nimitz (CVN-68), 13 JUL 84; To VA-82, NAS Cecil Field, FL., 13 JUL 84; To VA-82, USS Nimitz (CVN-68), 13 JUL 84; To VA-82, NAS Cecil Field, FL., 9 OCT 85; To VA-82, USS Nimitz (CVN-68), 11 JUN 86; To VA-82, NAS Jacksonville, FL., 12 SEP 86; To VA-82, NAS Cecil Field, FL., 16 SEP 86; To VA-82, USS Nimitz (CVN-68), 03 NOV 86; To VA-82, NAS Cecil Field, FL., 03 NOV 86 ** Transferred to VA-105/CVW-6, AE/4XX, USS Forrestal (CV-59), 14 JUL 87 thru 10 AUG 87 ** End of flight record card ** Transferred to the Helenic Air force (Greee).

E-527 160558 Navy acceptance from NPRO Rep. LTV, Dallas, TX., 22 SEP 77 ** Transferred to VA-46/CVW-1, AB/3XX, NAS Cecil Field, FL., 23 SEP 77; To VA-46, USS Dwight D. Eisenhower (CVN-69), 11 OCT 77; To VA-46, NAS Cecil Field, FL., 11 OCT 77; To VA-46, USS John F. Kennedy (CV-67), 11 OCT 77; To VA-46, NAS Cecil Field, FL., 11 OCT 77; To VA-46, USS John F. Kennedy (CV-67), 11 OCT 77; To VA-46, NAS Cecil Field, FL., 11 OCT 77; To VA-46, USS John F. Kennedy (CV-67), 19 FEB 80; To VA-46, NAS Cecil Field, FL., 19 FEB 80; To VA-46, NAS Jacksonville, FL., 08 OCT 81; To VA-46, NAS Cecil Field, FL., 08 OCT 81; To VA-46, NAS Jacksonville, FL., 13 OCT 81; To VA-46, NAS Cecil Field, FL., 11 DEC 81; To VA-46, USS America (CV-66), 11 DEC 81; To VA-46, NAS Cecil Field, FL., 11 DEC 81; To VA-46, USS America (CV-66), 11 DEC 81; To VA-46, NAS Cecil Field, FL., 18 APR 83 ** Transferred to VA-174/FRS, AD/4XX, NAS Cecil Field, FL., 05 AUG 83; To VA-174, NAS Jacksonville, FL., 17 MAY 84; To VA-174, NAS Cecil Field, FL., 14 JUN 84; To VA-174, NAS Jacksonville, FL., 21 SEP 84 ** Transferred to VA-82/CVW-8, AJ/3XX, NAS Cecil Field, FL., 23 SEP 84 ** Transferred to VA-15/CVW-6, AE/3XX, USS Independence (CV-62), 09 OCT 84; To VA-15, NAS Cecil Field, FL., 09 OCT 84; To VA-105/CVW-6, AE/4XX, NAS Cecil Field, FL., 12 MAR 85 ** Transferred to VA-82/CVW-8, AJ/3XX, USS Nimitz (CVN-68), 30 MAR 85; To VA-82, NAS Cecil Field, FL., 30 MAR 85; To VA-82, USS Nimitz (CVN-68), 14 FEB 86; To VA-82, NAS Cecil Field, FL., 14 FEB 86; To VA-82, USS Nimitz (CVN-68), 04 NOV 86; To VA-82, NAS Jacksonville, FL., 24 FEB 87 ** Transferred to NARF, NAS Jacksonville, FL., 24 FEB 87 ** Transferred to VA-46/CVW-7, AG/315, NAS Cecil Field, FL., 02 MAR 87; To VA-46, USS Dwight D. Eisenhower (CVN-69), 29 MAY 87; To VA-46, NAS Cecil Field, FL., 29 MAY 87 ** End of flight record card ** Transferred to AMARC, Davis Monthan AFB; Tucson, AZ., assigned park code 6A0352, 04 MAY 90 ** 5877.6 flight hours ** TF41A402D engine S/N AE141295 ** Storage location 111204 ** At AMARG, , Davis Monthan AFB; Tucson, AZ., 15 JUN 07.

E-528 160559 Navy acceptance from NPRO Rep. LTV, Dallas, TX., 20 SEP 77 ** Transferred to VA-72/CVW-1, AB/413, NAS Cecil Field, FL., 03 OCT 77; To VA-72, USS Dwight D. Eisenhower (CVN-69), 28 OCT 77; To VA-72, NAS Cecil Field, FL., 28 OCT 77; To VA-72, USS John F. Kennedy (CV-67), 28 OCT 77; To VA-72, NAS Cecil Field, FL., 28 OCT 77; To VA-72, USS John F. Kennedy (CV-67), 28 OCT 77; To VA-72, NAS Cecil Field, FL., 28 OCT 77; To VA-72, USS John F. Kennedy (CV-67), 16 APR 80; To VA-72, NAS Cecil Field, FL., 16 APR 80; To VA-72, NAS Jacksonville, FL., 17 DEC 81 ** Transferred to VA-46/CVW-1, AB/3XX, NAS Cecil Field, FL., 22 FEB 82; To VA-46, USS America (CV-66), 08 SEP 82 ~ S 1SO strike, 08 SEP 82 ** No data on strike.

E-529 160560 Navy acceptance from NPRO Rep. LTV, Dallas, TX., 22 SEP 77 ** Transferred to VA-46/CVW-1, AB/3XX, NAS Cecil Field, FL., 28 SEPT 77; To VA-46, USS Dwight D. Eisenhower (CVN-69), 19 OCT 77; To VA-46, NAS Cecil Field, FL., 19 OCT 77; To VA-46, USS John F. Kennedy (CV-67), 19 OCT 77; To VA-46, NAS Cecil Field, FL., 19 OCT 77; To VA-46, USS John F. Kennedy (CV-67), 19 OCT 77; To VA-46, NAS Cecil Field, FL., 19 OCT 77; To VA-46, USS John F. Kennedy (CV-67), 25 JAN 80; To VA-46, NAS Cecil Field, FL., 25 JAN 80; To VA-46, NAS Jacksonville, FL., 12 NOV 81; To VA-46, NAS Cecil Field, FL., 12 NOV 81; To VA-46, NAS Jacksonville, FL., 13 NOV 81; To VA-46, NAS Cecil Field, FL., 19 JAN 82; To VA-46, USS America (CV-66), 11 FEB 82; To VA-46, NAS Cecil Field, FL., 11 FEB 82; To VA-46, USS America (CV-66), 11 FEB 82; To VA-46, NAS Cecil Field, FL., 11 APR 83 ** Transferred to VA-87/CVW-6, AE/4XX, USS Independence (CV-62), 10 JUN 83; To VA-87, NAS Cecil Field, FL., 01 AUG 83; To VA-87, USS Independence (CV-62), 01 AUG 83; To VA-87, NAS Cecil Field, FL., 23 APR 84; To VA-87, NAS Jacksonville, FL., 28 JUN 84; To VA-87, USS Independence (CV-62), 28 JUN 84; To VA-87, NAS Cecil Field, FL., 03 JUL 84; To VA-87, USS Independence (CV-62), 03 JUL 84; To VA-87, NAS Cecil Field, FL., 03 JUL 84 ** Transferred to VA-81/CVW-17, AA/3XX, USS Saratoga (CV-60), 10 MAY 85; To VA-81, NAS Cecil Field, FL., 10 MAY 85; To VA-81, USS Saratoga (CV-60), 10 MAY 85; To VA-81, NAS Cecil Field, FL., 05 MAY 86; To VA-81, USS Saratoga (CV-60), 09 MAY 86; To VA-81,

NAS Cecil Field, FL., 09 MAY 86; To VA-81, USS Saratoga (CV-60), 09 DEC 86; To VA-81, NAS Cecil Field, FL., 09 DEC 86; To VA-81, NAS Jacksonville, FL., 09 APR 87 ** Transferred to VA-46/CVW-7, AG/3XX, NAS Cecil Field, FL., 13 APR 87; To VA-46, USS Dwight D. Eisenhower (CVN-69), 13 APR 87; To VA-46, NAS Cecil Field, FL., 13 APR 87 ** Transferred to VA-203/CVWR-20, AF/3XX, NAS Jacksonville, FL., 30 JUL 87 thru 10 SEP 87 ** End of flight record card ** Transferred to the Helenic Air force (Greee).

E-530 160561 Navy acceptance from NPRO Rep. LTV, Dallas, TX., 06 OCT 77 ** Transferred to VA-174/FRS, AD/4XX, NAS Cecil Field, FL., 18 NOV 77 ** Transferred to VA-46/CVW-1, AB/3XX, USS John F. Kennedy (CV-67), 28 JUN 78; To VA-46, NAS Cecil Field, FL., 28 JUN 78 ** Transferred to VA-174/FRS, AD/4XX, NAS Cecil Field, FL., 23 MAR 79; To VA-174, NAS Jacksonville, FL., 07 NOV 79 ** Transferred to VA-46/CVW-1, AB/3XX, NAS Cecil Field, FL., 24 APR 80; To VA-46, USS John F. Kennedy (CV-67), 24 APR 80; To VA-46, NAS Cecil Field, FL., 24 APR 80; To VA-46, NAS Jacksonville, FL., 23 SEP 81; To VA-46, NAS Cecil Field, FL., 23 SEP 81; To VA-46, NAS Jacksonville, FL., 24 SEP 81; To VA-46, NAS Cecil Field, FL., 30 NOV 81; To VA-46, USS America (CV-66), 01 DEC 81; To VA-46, NAS Cecil Field, FL., 01 DEC 81; To VA-46, USS America (CV-66), 01 DEC 81; To VA-46, NAS Cecil Field, FL., 23 MAY 83 ** Transferred to VA-174/FRS, AD/4XX, NAS Cecil Field, FL., 07 SEP 83; To VA-174, NAS Jacksonville, FL., 18 JUL 84; To VA-174, NAS Cecil Field, FL., 03 SEP 84; To VA-174, NAS Jacksonville, FL., 24 OCT 84 ** Transferred to VA-82/CVW-8, AJ/3XX, NAS Cecil Field, FL., 24 OCT 84; To VA-82, USS Nimitz (CVN-68), 24 OCT 84; To VA-82, NAS Cecil Field, FL., 24 OCT 84; To VA-82, USS Nimitz (CVN-68), 24 OCT 84; NAS Cecil Field, FL., 09 MAR 85; To VA-82, USS Nimitz (CVN-68), 13 FEB 86; NAS Cecil Field, FL., 27 OCT 86; To VA-82, USS Nimitz (CVN-68), 28 OCT 86; To VA-82, Naples, IT., 02 FEB 87; To VA-82, NAS Jacksonville, FL., 03 FEB 87 ** Transferred to VA-83/CVW-17, AA/3XX, NAS Cecil Field, FL., 03 FEB 87; To VA-83, USS Saratoga (CV-60), 10 MAR 87; To VA-83, NAS Cecil Field, FL., 22 MAR 87; To VA-83, USS Saratoga (CV-60), 22 MAR 87; To VA-83, NAS Cecil Field, FL., 22 MAR 87; To VA-83, USS Saratoga (CV-60), 22 MAR 87 ** End of flight record card.

E-531 160562 Navy acceptance from NPRO Rep. LTV, Dallas, TX., 28 OCT 77 ** Transferred to VA-174/FRS, AD/4XX, NAS Cecil Field, FL., 18 NOV 77 ** Transferred to VA-12/CVW-7, AG/4XX, NAS Cecil Field, FL., 26 APR 78; To VA-12, USS Dwight D. Eisenhower (CVN-69), 26 APR 78; To VA-12, NAS Cecil Field, FL., 26 APR 78; To VA-12, USS Dwight D. Eisenhower (CVN-69), 26 APR 78; To VA-12, NAS Cecil Field, FL., 26 APR 78; To VA-12, USS Dwight D. Eisenhower (CVN-69), 26 APR 78; To VA-12, NAS Cecil Field, FL., 31 OCT 79; To VA-12, USS Dwight D. Eisenhower (CVN-69), 26 NOV 79 ~ S 1SO strike, 12 FEB 80 ** No data on strike.

E-532 160563 Navy acceptance from NPRO Rep. LTV, Dallas, TX., 27 OCT 77 ** Transferred to VA-174/FRS, AD/4XX, NAS Cecil Field, FL., 28 OCT 77 ** Transferred to VA-66/CVW-7, AG/300, NAS Cecil Field, FL., 03 MAY 78; To VA-66, USS Dwight D. Eisenhower (CVN-69), 03 MAY 78; To VA-66, NAS Cecil Field, FL.,03 MAY 78; To VA-66, USS Dwight D. Eisenhower (CVN-69), 03 MAY 78; To VA-66, NAS Cecil Field, FL., 03 MAY 78; To VA-66, USS Dwight D. Eisenhower (CVN-69), 03 MAY 78; To VA-66, NAS Cecil Field, FL., 13 NOV 79; To VA-66, USS Dwight D. Eisenhower (CVN-69), 14 DEC 79; To VA-66, NAS Cecil Field, FL., 14 DEC 79; To VA-66, USS Dwight D. Eisenhower (CVN-69), 27 MAR 80; To VA-66, NAS Cecil Field, FL., 04 FEB 81; To VA-66, USS Dwight D. Eisenhower (CVN-69), 10 MAR 81; To VA-66, NAS Cecil Field, FL., 10 MAR 81; To VA-66, USS Dwight D. Eisenhower (CVN-69), 10 MAR 81; To VA-66, NAS Jacksonville, FL., 16 OCT 81; To VA-66, USS Dwight D. Eisenhower (CVN-69), 16 OCT 81; To VA-66, NAS Jacksonville, FL., 20 OCT 81; To VA-66, NAS Cecil Field, FL., 20 OCT 81; To VA-66, NAS Jacksonville, FL., 31 DEC 81; To VA-66, NAS Cecil Field, FL., 05 JAN 82; To VA-66, NAS Dallas, TX., 07 JAN 82 ** Transferred to VA-86/CVW-8, AJ/4XX, NAS Cecil Field, FL., 13 MAR 82; To VA-86, USS Nimitz (CVN-68), 13 MAR 82; To VA-86, NAS Cecil Field, FL., 13 MAR 82; To VA-86, USS Nimitz (CVN-68), 13 MAR 82; To VA-86, NAS Cecil Field,

FL., 13 MAR 82; To VA-86, USS Nimitz (CVN-68), 13 MAR 82; To VA-86, NAS Cecil Field, FL., 13 MAY 83; To VA-86, NAS Roosevelt Roads, PR., 18 MAY 83; To VA-86, NAS Cecil Field, FL., 18 MAY 83; To VA-86, NAS Jacksonville, FL., 13 AUG 84; To VA-86, NAS Cecil Field, FL., 24 SEP 84; To VA-86, USS Nimitz (CVN-68), 24 SEP 84; To VA-86, NAS Cecil Field, FL., 16 JUL 85; To VA-86, USS Nimitz (CVN-68), 23 APR 86; To VA-86, NAS Jacksonville, FL., 31 JUL 86; To VA-86, USS Nimitz (CVN-68), 05 AUG 86; To VA-86, NAS Cecil Field, FL., 10 OCT 86; To VA-86, USS Nimitz (CVN-68), 25 NOV 86; To VA-86, NAS Cecil Field, FL., 02 DEC 86 ** End of flight record card ** Transferred to VA-122/FRS, NJ/232, NAS LeMoore, CA., date unknown ** Transferred to AMARC, Davis Monthan AFB; Tucson, AZ., assigned park code 6A0372, 01 AUG 90 ** 5904.2 flight hours ** TF41A402D engine S/N 141275 ** Aircraft released from storage and prepared for overland shipment to FMS and NAD, NAS Jacksonville, FL., with final shipment to government of Thailand, 18 SEP 95 ** Transferred to the Royal Thai Navy, S/N 1411.

E-533 160564 Navy acceptance from NPRO Rep. LTV, Dallas, TX., 22 NOV 77 ** Transferred to VA-66/CVW-7, AG/301, NAS Cecil Field, FL., 28 NOV 77; To VA-66, USS Dwight D. Eisenhower (CVN-69), 28 NOV 77; To VA-66, NAS Cecil Field, FL., 28 NOV 77; To VA-66, USS Dwight D. Eisenhower (CVN-69), 24 APR 78; To VA-66, NAS Cecil Field, FL., 24 APR 78; To VA-66, USS Dwight D. Eisenhower (CVN-69), 24 APR 78; To VA-66, NAS Cecil Field, FL., 24 APR 78; To VA-66, USS Dwight D. Eisenhower (CVN-69), 24 APR 78; To VA-66, NAS Cecil Field, FL., 31 JAN 80; To VA-66, USS Dwight D. Eisenhower (CVN-69), 22 MAR 80 ~ S 1SO strike, 20 OCT 80 ** CDR Kent Ewing ejected into the N. Arabian Sea.

E-534 160565 Navy acceptance from NPRO Rep. LTV, Dallas, TX., 21 DEC 77 ** Transferred to NAF, NAF/XXX, China Lake, CA., 26 DEC 77 ** Transferred to NATC, NATC/XXX, NAS Patuxent River, MD., for RDT & E, 13 FEB 78 ** Transferred to NWEF, NWEF/XXX, Kirtland AFB; Albuquerque, NM., 28 OCT 78 ** Transferred to NATC, NATC/XXX, NAS Patuxent River, MD., for RDT & E, 25 APR 79; To NATC, NAS Jacksonville, FL., for RDT & E, 14 MAY 79; To NATC, NAS Patuxent River, MD., for RDT & E, 25 JUL 79 ** Transferred to VX-5, XE/XXX, NWC, China Lake, CA., 15 JUL 81; To VX-5, NAS Jacksonville, FL., 08 MAR 82 ** Transferred to NWC, NWC/XXX, China Lake, CA., 17 MAY 82 ** Transferred to NATC, NATC/XXX, N AS Patuxent River, MD., for RDT & E, 25 AUG 82 ** Transferred to NATC, FS, NAS Patuxent River, MD., 21 JAN 86 ** Transferred to NATC, SD/406, NAWC Patuxent River, MD., for RDT & E, 13 JUN 86 thru 28 APR 87 ** End of flight record card ** To NATC, NAD, NAS Jacksonville, FL., 28 MAR 88; To NATC, SD/406, NAWC Patuxent River, MD., date unknown ** Transferred to AMARC, Davis Monthan AFB; Tucson, AZ., assigned park code 6A0372, date unknown ** Changed park code to 6A0411; 03 FEB 92 ** 3280.3 flight hours TF41A402D engine S/N 142655 ** Storage location 150915 ** Placed on FMS list with D-704 Buddy store, 06 APR 04 ** At AMARG, Davis Monthan AFB; Tucson, AZ.,15 JUN 07.

E-535 160566 Navy acceptance from NPRO Rep. LTV, Dallas, TX., 26 OCT 77 ** Transferred to NPRO Rep. LTV, Dallas, TX., for RDT & E, 27 OCT 77 ** Transferred to NATC, NATC/XXX, NAS Patuxent River, MD., for RDT & E, 13 JUN 78 ** Transferred to NAF, NAF/XXX, China Lake, CA., 07 SEP 78 ** Transferred to VA-122/FRS, NJ/2XX, NAS LeMoore, CA., 28 FEB 80; To VA-122, NAS Jacksonville, FL., 14 JUL 80; To VA-122, NAS LeMoore, CA., 19 AUG 80 ** Transferred to VA-94/CVW-15, NL/4XX, NAS LeMoore, CA., 23 AUG 80; To VA-94, USS Kitty Hawk (CV-63), 11 SEP 80; To VA-94, NAS LeMoore, CA.,06 NOV 80; To VA-94, USS Kitty Hawk (CV-63), 27 FEB 81 ** Transferred to VA-122/FRS, NJ/2XX, NAS LeMoore, CA., 25 MAR 81; To VA-122, NAS Jacksonville, FL., 15 NOV 82; To VA-122, NAS LeMoore, CA., 15 NOV 82; To VA-122, NAS Jacksonville, FL., 19 NOV 82; To VA-122, NAS LeMoore, CA., 04 FEB 83; To VA-122, NAS Jacksonville, FL., 14 JUN 85; To VA-122, NAS LeMoore, CA., 07 AUG 85; To VA-122, NAS Jacksonville, FL., 11 SEP 85; To VA-122, NAS LeMoore, CA., 10 NOV 85 thru 22 SEP 87 ** End of flight record card ** Transferred to the Helinic Air Force (Greece).

160613/160618 LTV A-7E Corsair II (C/N E-482/E-487); (Block XXV)
FY 76-7T Contract N00019-76-C-0152, (6) A-7E; E-537/E-542

E-542 1606613 Navy acceptance from NPRO Rep. LTV, Dallas, TX., 23 JAN 78 ** Transferred to VA-12/CVW-7, AG/401, USS Dwight D. Eisenhower (CVN-69), 27 JAN 78 ** Transferred to VA-174/FRS, AD/4XX, NAS Cecil Field, FL., 27 APR 78 ** Transferred to VA-81/CVW-17, AA/4XX, NAS Cecil Field, FL., 25 JAN 79; To VA-81, USS Forrestal (CV-59), 09 FEB 79; To VA-81, NAS Cecil Field, FL., 08 AUG 79; To VA-81, NAS Jacksonville, FL., 07 MAY 80; To VA-81, NAS Cecil Field, FL., 09 JUN 80 ** Transferred to VA-15/CVW-6, AE/3XX, USS Independence (CV-62), 18 JUN 80; To VA-15, NAS Cecil Field, FL., 04 MAR 81; To VA-15, NAS Jacksonville, FL., 15 JAN 82; To VA-15, USS Independence (CV-62), 15 JAN 82; To VA-15, NAS Jacksonville, FL., 20 JAN 82 ** Transferred to VA-83/CVW-17, AA/3XX, USS Forrestal (CV-59), 16 MAR 82; To VA-83, NAS Cecil Field, FL., 16 MAR 82; To VA-83, USS Forrestal (CV-59), 16 MAR 82; To VA-83, NAS Cecil Field, FL., 16 MAR 82; To VA-83, NAS Fallon, NV., 28 JUL 83; To VA-83, NAS Cecil Field, FL., 28 JUL 83; To VA-83, USS Saratoga (CV-60), 28 DEC 83; To VA-83, NAS Cecil Field, FL., 28 DEC 83 ** Transferred to VA-66/CVW-7, AG/305, NAS Cecil Field, FL., 09 FEB 84; To VA-66, USS Dwight D. Eisenhower (CVN-69), 14 MAY 84; To VA-66, NAS Cecil Field, FL., 14 MAY 84; To VA-66, NAS Jacksonville, FL., 04 AUG 84; To VA-66, USS Dwight D. Eisenhower (CVN-69), 08 AUG 84; To VA-66, NAS Jacksonville, FL., 22 AUG 84; To VA-66, NAS Cecil Field, FL., 07 SEP 84; To VA-66, USS Dwight D. Eisenhower (CVN-69), 07 SEP 84 ** Transferred to VA-83/CVW-17, AA/3XX, USS Saratoga (CV-60), 01 OCT 84 ** Transferred to VA-15/CVW-6, AE/3XX, USS Independence (CV-62), 09 OCT 84; To VA-15, NAS Cecil Field, FL., 09 OCT 84 ** Transferred to VA-46/CVW-1, AB/3XX, NAS Cecil Field, FL., 21 FEB 85; To VA-46, USS America (CV-66), 19 MAR 85; To VA-46, NAS Cecil Field, FL., 19 MAR 85; To VA-46, USS America (CV-66), 19 MAR 85; To VA-46, NAS Cecil Field, FL., 25 OCT 85; To VA-46, USS America (CV-66), 27 JAN 86; To VA-46, NAS Cecil Field, FL., 11 JUN 86; To VA-46, NAS Jacksonville, FL., 15 DEC 86; To VA-46, NAS Cecil Field, FL., 15 DEC 86; To VA-46, NAS Jacksonville, FL., 16 DEC 86; To VA-46, NAS Cecil Field, FL., 20 APR 87; To VA-46/CVW-7, AG/3XX, USS Dwight D. Eisenhower (CVN-69), 20 APR 87; To VA-46, NAS Cecil Field, FL., 20 APR 87 ** End of flight record card ** On conditional loan from the National Museum of Naval Aviation; Pensacola, Fl. to the Empire State Aerosciences Museum, NY., FEB 02.

E-537 160614 Navy acceptance from NPRO Rep. LTV, Dallas, TX., 26 JAN 78 ** Transferred to VA-66/CVW-7, AG/3XX, NAS Cecil Field, FL., 12 FEB 78 ** Transferred to VA-174/FRS, AD/4XX, NAS Cecil Field, FL., 17 MAY 78 ** Transferred to VA-81/CVW-17, AA/4XX, NAS Cecil Field, FL., 09 JAN 79; To VA-81, USS Forrestal (CV-59), 13 MAR 79; To VA-81, NAS Cecil Field, FL., 25 JUL 79; To VA-81, USS Forrestal (CV-59), 25 JUL 79; To VA-81, NAS Cecil Field, FL., 30 JUL 79; To VA-81, NAS Jacksonville, FL., 07 MAY 80; To VA-81, NAS Cecil Field, FL., 12 JUN 80 ** Transferred to VA-83/CVW-17, AA/3XX, USS Forrestal (CV-59), 17 JUL 80; To VA-83, NAS Cecil Field, FL., 17 JUL 80; To VA-83, USS Forrestal (CV-59), 09 FEB 81; To VA-83, NAS Cecil Field, FL., 09 FEB 81; To VA-83, NAS Fallon, NV., 10 JAN 82; To VA-83, NAS Cecil Field, FL., 03 FEB 82; To VA-83, USS Forrestal (CV-59), 25 FEB 82; To VA-83, NAS Jacksonville, FL., 01 MAR 82; To VA-83, USS Forrestal (CV-59), 27 APR 82; To VA-83, NAS Cecil Field, FL., 27 APR 82 ** Transferred to VA-86/CVW-8, AJ/4XX, NAS Cecil Field, FL., 27 MAY 82; To VA-86, USS Nimitz (CVN-68), 27 MAY 82; To VA-86, NAS Cecil Field, FL., 27 MAY 82; To VA-86, USS Nimitz (CVN-68), 27 MAY 82; To VA-86, NAS Cecil Field, FL., 27 MAY 82; To VA-86, USS Nimitz (CVN-68), 27 MAY 82; To VA-86, NAS Cecil Field, FL., 27 MAY 83; To VA-86, NAS Roosevelt Roads, PR., 01 JUN 83; To VA-86, NAS Cecil Field, FL., 01 JUN 83 ** Transferred to VA-72/CVW-1, AB/4XX, NAS Cecil Field, FL, 28 OCT 83; To VA-72, USS America (CV-66), 28 OCT 83; To VA-72, NAS Cecil Field, FL., 28 OCT 83 ** Transferred to VA-105/CVW-15, NL/4XX, NAS Roosevelt Roads, PR., 31 JAN 84; To VA-105, NAS Cecil Field, FL., 31 JAN 84 ** Transferred to VA-86/CVW-8, AJ/4XX, NAS Cecil Field, FL., 12 MAR 84; To VA-86, NAS

Roosevelt Roads, PR., 12 MAR 84; To VA-86, NAS Cecil Field, FL., 20 SEP 84; To VA-86, NAS Jacksonville, FL., 25 SEP 84; To VA-86, USS Nimitz (CVN-68), 13 NOV 84; To VA-86, NAS Jacksonville, FL., 16 NOV 84; To VA-86, NAS Cecil Field, FL., 11 DEC 84; To VA-86, USS Nimitz (CVN-68), 11 DEC 84; To VA-86, NAS Cecil Field, FL., 11 DEC 84; To VA-86, USS Nimitz (CVN-68), 25 FEB 86; To VA-86, NAS Cecil Field, FL., 25 FEB 86; To VA-86, USS Nimitz (CVN-68), 07 AUG 86; To VA-86, NAS Cecil Field, FL., 25 AUG 86; To VA-86, USS Nimitz (CVN-68), 26 NOV 86 ** Transferred to VA-37/CVW-6, AE/3XX, NAS Cecil Field, FL., 04 DEC 86; To VA-37, NAS Jacksonville, FL., 07 JAN 87; To VA-37, NAS Cecil Field, FL., 08 JAN 87; To VA-37, USS Forrestal (CV-59), 13 JUL 87 thru 12 SEP 87 ** End of flight record card ** On conditional loan from the National Museum of Naval Aviation; Pensacola, FL., to the NJROTC Unit at Mountain Home, AR.

E-538 160615 Navy acceptance from NPRO Rep. LTV, Dallas, TX., 23 FEB 78 ** Transferred to VA-174/FRS, AD/4XX, NAS Cecil Field, FL., 24 FEB 78 ** Transferred to VA-46/CVW-1, AB/3XX, NAS Cecil Field, FL., 19 JUN 79 ** Transferred to VA-15/CVW-6, AE/3XX, USS Independence (CV-62), 19 FEB 80; To VA-15, NAS Cecil Field, FL., 25 FEB 80; To VA-15, USS Independence (CV-62), 26 MAR 80; To VA-15, NAS Cecil Field, FL., 26 MAR 80 ** Transferred to VA-72/ CVW-1, AB/4XX, NAS Cecil Field, FL., 05 OCT 81; To VA-72, NAS Jacksonville, FL., 14 FEB 82; To VA-72, NAS Cecil Field, FL., 14 FEB 82; To VA-72, NAS Jacksonville, FL., 17 FEB 82; To VA-72, NAS Cecil Field, FL., 23 APR 82; To VA-72, USS America (CV-66), 19 AUG 82 ** Transferred to VA-83/CVW-17, AA/3XX, NAS Cecil Field, FL., 02 DEC 82 ** Transferred to VA-72/CVW-1, AB/4XX, USS America (CV-66), 22 JAN 83; To VA-72, NAS Cecil Field, FL., 22 JAN 83; To VA-72, USS America (CV-66), 22 JAN 83; To VA-72, NAS Cecil Field, FL., 22 JAN 83; To VA-72, USS America (CV-66), 22 JAN 83; To VA-72, NAS Cecil Field, FL., 22 JAN 83; To VA-72, NAS Jacksonville, FL., 13 DEC 84; To VA-72, NAS Cecil Field, FL., 05 JAN 85; To VA-72, NAS Jacksonville, FL., 25 FEB 85; To VA-72, NAS Cecil Field, FL., 27 FEB 85; To VA-72, USS America (CV-66), 20 MAR 85; To VA-72, NAS Cecil Field, FL., 20 MAR 85 ** Transferred to VA-86/CVW-8, AJ/415, NAS Cecil Field, FL., 15 JAN 86; To VA-86, USS Nimitz (CVN-68), Painted light gray on medium gray with black modex, 08 MAY 86; To VA-86, NAS Cecil Field, FL., 08 MAY 86; To VA-86, USS Nimitz (CVN-68), 07 AUG 86; To VA-86, NAS Cecil Field, FL., 13 AUG 86; To VA-86, NAS Jacksonville, FL., 31 OCT 86 ** Transferred to VA-105/CVW-6, AE/4XX, NAS Cecil Field, FL., 12 NOV 86; To VA-105, USS Forrestal (CV-59), 06 JUL 87 thru 16 JUL 87 ** End of flight record card.

E-539 160616 Navy acceptance from NPRO Rep. LTV, Dallas, TX., 23 FEB 78 ** Transferred to NPRO Rep. at LTV, Dallas, TX. for RDT & E, 23 FEB 78 ** Transferred to NATC, NATC/XXX, NAS Patuxent River, MD, for RDT & E, 13 JUN 78 ** Transferred to VX-5, XE/XXX, NAF China Lake, CA., 25 AUG 78; To VX-5, NAS Jacksonville, FL., 31 OCT 80; To VX-5, NWC China Lake, CA., 09 NOV 80; To VX-5, NAS Jacksonville, FL., 09 FEB 83; To VX-5, NWC China Lake, CA., 22 APR 83; To VX-5, NAS Alameda, CA., 30 OCT 84; To VX-5, NWC China Lake, CA., 04 JAN 85 thru 14 SEP 87 ** End of flight record card ** Transferred to the Helenic Air force (Greee).

E-540 160617 Navy acceptance from NPRO Rep. LTV, Dallas, TX., 31 MAR 78 ** Transferred to NATC, NATC/XXX, NAS Patuxent River, MD. for RDT & E, 02 MAY 78 ** Transferred to VA-81/CVW-17, AA/4XX, NAS Cecil Field, FL., 06 NOV 78; To VA-81, USS Forrestal (CV-59), 24 JAN 79; To VA-81, NAS Cecil Field, FL., 30 AUG 79; To VA-81, USS Forrestal (CV-59), 31 JUL 80; To VA-81, NAS Cecil Field, FL., 31 JUL 80; To VA-81, USS Forrestal (CV-59), 31 JUL 80; To VA-81, NAS Cecil Field, FL., 31 JUL 80 ** Transferred to VA-174/FRS, AD/4XX, NAS Cecil Field, FL., 29 OCT 81 ** Transferred to VA-66/CVW-7, AG/3XX, NAS Cecil Field, FL., 29 SEP 82; To VA-66, NAS Jacksonville, FL., 29 OCT 82; To VA-66, NAS Cecil Field, FL., 29 OCT 82; To VA-66, NAS Jacksonville, FL., 01 NOV 82; To VA-66, NAS Cecil Field, FL., 30 DEC 82; To VA-

66, USS Dwight D. Eisenhower (CVN-69), 30 DEC 82; To VA-66, NAS Cecil Field, FL., 30 AUG 83 ** Transferred to VA-82/CVW-8, AJ/3XX, NAS Cecil Field, FL., 02 FEB 84; To VA-82, USS Nimitz (CVN-68), 02 FEB 84; To VA-82, NAS Cecil Field, FL., 02 FEB 84 ** Transferred to VA-174/FRS, AD/4XX, NAS Cecil Field, FL., 20 FEB 85; To VA-174, NAS Jacksonville, FL., 19 JUN 85; To VA-174, NAS Cecil Field, FL., 28 JUN 85 ** Transferred to VA-15/CVW-6, AE/3XX, NAS Cecil Field, FL., 02 OCT 85; To VA-15, MCAS Iwakuni, JP., 25 NOV 85; To VA-15, Korea, 25 NOV 85; To VA-15, NAS Cubi Point, PI., 25 NOV 85; To VA-15, NAS Cecil Field, FL., 25 NOV 85 ** Transferred to VA-174/FRS, AD/4XX, NAS Cecil Field, FL., 07 OCT 86; To VA-174, NAS Pensacola, FL., 04 MAR 87; To VA-174, NAS Cecil Field, FL., 04 MAR 87; To VA-174, NAS Pensacola, FL., 05 MAR 87 thru 10 SEP 87 ** End of flight record card ** Transferred to the Helenic Air force (Greee).

E-541 160618 Navy acceptance from NPRO Rep. LTV, Dallas, TX., 31 MAR 78 ** Transferred to VA-174/FRS, AD/4XX, NAS Cecil Field, FL., 20 APR 78 ** Transferred to VA-81/CVW-17, AA/4XX, NAS Cecil Field, FL., 22 JAN 79; To VA-81, USS Forrestal (CV-59), 22 JAN 79; To VA-81, NAS Cecil Field, FL., 22 JAN 79; To VA-81, USS Forrestal (CV-59), 22 JAN 79 ~ S 1SO strike, 05 FEB 80 ** No data on strike.

160710/160721 LTV A-7E Corsair II; (Block XXVI)
160722/160739 LTV A-7E Corsair II; (Block XXVII)
FY 77, Contract N00019-77-C-0498, (30) A-7E E-543/E-571

E-554 160710 Navy acceptance from NPRO Rep. LTV, Dallas, TX., 06 APR 78 ** Transferred to NAF, NAF/ XXX, China Lake, CA., 13 APR 78 ** Transferred to NATC, NATC/XXX, NAS Patuxent River, MD., for RDT & E, 17 OCT 80 ** Transferred to NWC, NWC/XXX, China Lake, CA., 23 DEC 80 ** Transferred to PMTC, PMTC/XXX, NAS Point Mugu, CA., 30 APR 81 ** Transferred to VX-5, XE/XXX, NWC China Lake, CA., 12 NOV 81; To VX-5, NAS Jacksonville, FL., 28 NOV 82 ** Transferred to NWC, NWC/XXX, China Lake, CA., 28 NOV 82; To NWC, NAS Jacksonville, FL., 03 FEB 83; To NWC, China Lake, CA., 01 APR 83 thru 04 AUG 87 ** End of flight record card ** Transferred to the Helenic Air force (Greee).

E-543 160711 Navy acceptance from NPRO Rep. LTV, Dallas, TX., 12 APR, 78 ** Transferred to VA-174/FRS, AD/4XX, NAS Cecil Field, FL., 15 APR 78 ~ S 1SO strike, 23 MAY 78 ** No data on strike.

E-544 160712 Navy acceptance from NPRO Rep. LTV, Dallas, TX., 17 MAY 78 ** Transferred to VA-174/FRS, AD/4XX, NAS Cecil Field, FL., 23 MAY 78 ** Transferred to VA-81/CVW-17, AA/4XX, NAS Cecil Field, FL., 21 DEC 78; To VA-81, USS Forrestal (CV-59), 21 DEC 78; To VA-81, NAS Cecil Field, FL., 31 JUL 79; To VA-81, NAS Jacksonville, FL., 08 MAY 80; To VA-81, NAS Cecil Field, FL., 17 JUN 80 ** Transferred to VA-83/CVW-8, AJ/3XX, NAS Cecil Field, FL., 30 SEP 80; To VA-83, USS Forrestal (CV-59), 30 SEP 80; To VA-83, NAS Cecil Field, FL., 30 SEP 80; To VA-83, USS Forrestal (CV-59), 30 SEP 80; To VA-83, NAS Cecil Field, FL., 26 AUG 81 ** Transferred to NARF, NAS Jacksonville, FL., 31 DEC 81 ** Transferred to VA-66/CVW-7, AG/3XX, NAS Cecil Field, FL., 01 SEP 82; To VA-66, USS Dwight D. Eisenhower (CVN-69), 29 SEP 82; To VA-66, NAS Cecil Field, FL., 29 SEP 82 ** Transferred to VA-105/CVW-15, NL/4XX, NAS Cecil Field, FL., 08 MAR 84; To VA-105, NAF Kadena, JP., 15 MAY 84; To VA-105, Cubi Point, PI., 15 MAY 84; To MCAS Iwakuni, JP., 15 MAY 84; To VA-105, NAS Jacksonville, FL., 02 JAN 85; To VA-105/CVW-6, AE/4XX, NAS Cecil Field, FL., 25 JAN 85; To VA-105, NAS Jacksonville, FL., 19 FEB 85; To VA-105, NAS Cecil Field, FL., 20 FEB 85; To VA-105, USS Forrestal (CV-59), 28 FEB 85; To VA-105, NAS Cecil Field, FL., 28 FEB 85 ** Transferred to VA-15/CVW-6, AE/3XX, NAS Cecil Field, FL., 20 SEP 85; To VA-15, MCAS Iwakuni, JP., 20 SEP 85; To VA-15, Korea, 20 SEP 85; To VA-15, NAS Cubi Point, PI., 20 SEP 85; To VA-15, NAS Cecil Field, FL., 20 SEP 85; To VA-15, NAS Jacksonville, FL., 31 JUL 86; To VA-15, NAS Cecil Field, FL., 31 JUL 86; To VA-15, NAS Jacksonville, FL., 13 AUG 86; To VFA-

15, NAS Jacksonville, FL., 14 AUG 86 ** Transferred to VA-72/CVW-1, AB/4XX, NAS Cecil Field, FL., 05 NOV 86 ** Transferred to NARF, NAS Jacksonville, FL., 05 NOV 86 ** Transferred to To VA-72/CVW-7, AG/4XX, USS Dwight D. Eisenhower (CVN-69), 27 MAR 87; To VA-72, NAS Cecil Field, FL., 27 MAR 87 ** End of flight record card ** Transferred to VA-94/ CVW-11, NH/4XX, NAS LeMoore, CA., date unknown ** Transferred to AMARC, Davis Monthan AFB; Tucson, AZ., assigned park code 6A0332; 02 APR 90 ** 5162.1 flight hours ** TF41A402D engine S/N 141610 ** Placed on FMS list at NAS Fallon, NV., at N69190, 25 AUG 05.

E-545 160713 Navy acceptance from NPRO Rep. LTV, Dallas, TX., 05 MAY 78 ** Transferred to VA-174/FRS, AD/4XX, NAS Cecil Field, FL., 06 MAY 78 ** Transferred to VA-81/CVW-17, AA/4XX, NAS Cecil Field, FL., 06 MAY 80 ** Transferred to VA-83/CVW-17, AA/3XX, NAS Cecil Field, FL., 24 SEP 80; To VA-83, USS Forrestal (CV-59), 24 SEP 80; To VA-83, NAS Cecil Field, FL., 29 DEC 80; To VA-83, USS Forrestal (CV-59), 29 DEC 80; To VA-83, NAS Cecil Field, FL., 29 DEC 80; To VA-83, NAS Fallon, NV., 29 DEC 80; To VA-83, NAS Cecil Field, FL., 03 FEB 82; To VA-83, USS Forrestal (CV-59), 16 FEB 82 ** Transferred to VA-86/CVW-8, AJ/4XX, NAS Cecil Field, FL., 31 MAR 82; To VA-86, NAS Jacksonville, FL., 24 MAY 82; To VA-86, NAS Cecil Field, FL., 24 MAY 82; To VA-86, NAS Jacksonville, FL., 26 MAY 82; To VA-86, USS Nimitz (CVN-68), 03 SEP 82; To VA-86, NAS Cecil Field, FL., 03 SEP 82; To VA-86, USS Nimitz (CVN-68), 03 SEP 82; To VA-86, NAS Cecil Field, FL., 03 SEP 82; To VA-86, NAS Roosevelt Roads, PR., 03 SEP 82; To VA-86, NAS Cecil Field, FL., 03 SEP 82 ** Transferred to VA-83/CVW-17, AA/3XX, NAS Cecil Field, 28 SEP 83; To VA-83, USS Saratoga (CV-60), 24 OCT 83; To VA-83, NAS Cecil Field, FL., 28 FEB 84; To VA-83, USS Saratoga (CV-60), 12 MAR 84; To VA-83, NAS Cecil Field, FL., 12 MAR 84; To VA-83, NAS Jacksonville, FL., 15 NOV 84; To VA-83, NAS Cecil Field, FL., 20 NOV 84; To VA-83, NAS Jacksonville, FL., 07 JAN 85; To VA-83, NAS Fallon, NV., 08 JAN 85; To VA-83, NAS Cecil Field, FL., 21 JAN 85; To VA-83, USS Saratoga (CV-60), 26 MAR 85; To VA-83, NAS Cecil Field, FL., 26 MAR 85; To VA-83, USS Saratoga (CV-60), 26 MAR 85; To VA-83, NAS Cecil Field, FL., 27 AUG 85; To VA-83, USS Saratoga (CV-60), 17 SEP 86; To VA-83, NAS Jacksonville, FL., 19 FEB 87; To VA-83, USS Saratoga (CV-60), 23 FEB 87; To VA-83, NAS Cecil Field, FL., 23 FEB 87; To VA-83, USS Saratoga (CV-60), 23 FEB 87; To VA-83, NAS Cecil Field, FL., 23 FEB 87; To VA-83, NAS Jacksonville, FL., 25 JUN 87 ** Transferred to VA-46/CVW-7, AG/307, USS Dwight D. Eisenhower (CVN-69), 25 JUN 87; To VA-46, NAS Cecil Field, FL., 25 JUN 87; To VA-46 thru 22 SEP 87 ** End of flight record card ** Transferred to AMARC, Davis Monthan AFB; Tucson, AZ., assigned park code 6A0395; 10 JUN 91 ** 5587.8 flight hours ** TF41A402D engine S/N 141340 ** On conditional loan from the National Museum of Naval Aviation; Pensacola, FL., to the Pima Air and Space Museum, Tucson, AZ., 16 APR 98.

E-546 160714 Navy acceptance from NPRO Rep. LTV, Dallas, TX., 24 MAY 78 ** Transferred to VA-174/FRS, AD/4XX, NAS Cecil Field, FL., 30 MAY 78 ** Transferred to VA-81/CVW-1, AB/4XX, NAS Cecil Field, FL., 20 JAN 79; To VA-81, USS Forrestal (CV-59), 20 JAN 79; To VA-81, NAS Cecil Field, FL., 20 JAN 79; To VA-81, USS Forrestal (CV-59), 20 JAN 79; To VA-81, NAS Cecil Field, FL., 14 SEP 79; To VA-81, USS Forrestal (CV-59), 06 OCT 80; To VA-81, NAS Jacksonville, FL., 09 OCT 80; To VA-81, USS Forrestal (CV-59), 14 NOV 80; To VA-81, NAS Cecil Field, FL., 17 NOV 80; To VA-81, USS Forrestal (CV-59), 17 NOV 80; To VA-81, NAS Cecil Field, FL., 17 NOV 80; To VA-81, NAS Fallon, NV., 29 FEB 81 ** Transferred to VA-83/CVW-17, AA/3XX, NAS Cecil Field, FL., 23 FEB 82; To VA-83, USS Forrestal (CV-59), 23 FEB 82; To VA-83, NAS Cecil Field, FL., 23 FEB 82; To VA-83, USS Forrestal (CV-59), 23 FEB 82; To VA-83, NAS Cecil Field, FL., 13 AUG 82; To VA-83, NAS Jacksonville, FL., 07 JAN 83; To VA-83, NAS Cecil Field, FL., 07 JAN 83; To VA-83, NAS Jacksonville, FL., 10 JAN 83; To VA-83, NAS Cecil Field, FL., 11 FEB 83; To VA-83, NAS Fallon, NV., 29 MAR 83; To VA-83, NAS Cecil Field, FL., 27 SEP 83; To VA-83, USS Saratoga (CV-60), 05 OCT 83; To VA-83, NAS Cecil Field, FL., 05 OCT 83; To VA-83, USS Saratoga (CV-60), 05 OCT 83; To VA-83,

NAS Cecil Field, FL., 05 OCT 83; To VA-83, NAS Fallon, NV., 06 DEC 84; To VA-83, NAS Cecil Field, FL., 06 DEC 84; To VA-83, USS Saratoga (CV-60), 17 MAY 85; To VA-83, NAS Cecil Field, FL., 24 JUN 85; To VA-83, NAS Jacksonville, FL., 26 JUL 85; To VA-83, USS Saratoga (CV-60), 17 AUG 85; To VA-83, NAS Jacksonville, FL., 23 SEP 85 ** Transferred to VA-66/CVW-7, AG/3XX, NAS Cecil Field, FL., 27 SEP 85 ** Transferred to VA-83/CVW-17, AA/3XX, NAS Cecil Field, FL., 30 JUL 86; To VA-83, USS Saratoga (CV-60), 30 JUL 86; To VA-83, NAS Cecil Field, FL., 30 JUL 86; To VA-83, USS Saratoga (CV-60), 21 JAN 87 ** Transferred to VA-72/CVW-7, AG/4XX, NAS Cecil Field, FL., 23 FEB 87; To VA-72, USS Dwight D. Eisenhower (CVN-69), 28 MAY 87; To VA-72, NAS Cecil Field, FL., 10 JUN 87 thru 02 SEP 87 ** End of flight record card ** On display at National Museum of Naval Aviation, Pensacola, FL.

E-547 160715 Navy acceptance from NPRO Rep. LTV, Dallas, TX., 24 MAY 78 ** Transferred to VA-174/FRS, AD/4XX, NAS Cecil Field, FL., 22 JUN 78 ** Transferred to VA-81/CVW-17, AA/4XX, USS Forrestal (CV-59), 11 APR 79; To VA-81, NAS Cecil Field, FL., 11 AUG 79; To VA-81, USS Forrestal (CV-59), 31 OCT 79; To VA-81, NAS Cecil Field, FL., 18 JUN 80; To VA-81, NAS Jacksonville, FL., 19 JUN 80; To VA-81, NAS Cecil Field, FL., 21 JUL 80; To VA-81, USS Forrestal (CV-59), 22 JUL 80; To VA-81, NAS Cecil Field, FL., 22 JUL 80; To VA-81, USS Forrestal (CV-59), 03 FEB 81; To VA-81, NAS Cecil Field, FL., 03 FEB 81; Transferred to VA-174/FRS, AD/4XX, NAS Cecil Field, FL., 29 OCT 81 ** Transferred to VA-86/CVW-8, AJ/4XX, NAS Cecil Field, FL., 17 MAY 82; To VA-86, USS Nimitz (CVN-68), 17 MAY 82; To VA-86, NAS Cecil Field, FL., 17 MAY 82; To VA-86, USS Nimitz (CVN-68), 17 MAY 82 ** Transferred to VA-66/CVW-7, AG/303, NAS Cecil Field, FL., 17 MAY 82; To VA-66, NAS Jacksonville, FL., 01 OCT 82; To VA-66, NAS Jacksonville, FL., 04 OCT 82; To VA-66, NAS Cecil Field, FL., 13 DEC 82; To VA-66, USS Dwight D.Eisenhower (CVN-69), 13 DEC 82; To VA-66, NAS Cecil Field, FL., 13 DEC 82; To VA-66, USS Dwight D. Eisenhower (CVN-69), 26 MAR 84; To VA-66, NAS Cecil Field, FL., 04 MAY 84; To VA-66, USS Dwight D. Eisenhower (CVN-69), 04 MAY 84; To VA-66, NAS Cecil Field, FL., 10 SEP 84; To VA-66, USS Dwight D. Eisenhower (CVN-69), 14 SEP 84 ** Transferred to VA-83/CVW-17, AA/304, USS Saratoga (CV-60), Painted light gray on medium gray with black modex, 04 OCT 84; To VA-83, NAS Cecil Field, FL., 10 OCT 84; To VA-83, NAS Fallon, NV., 06 NOV 84; To VA-83, NAS Cecil Field, FL.,06 NOV 84; To VA-83, NAS Jacksonville, FL., 22 APR 85; To VA-83, USS Saratoga (CV-60), 06 MAY 85; To VA-83, NAS Cecil Field, FL., 05 JUN 85; To VA-83, NAS Jacksonville, FL., 20 JUN 85; To VA-83, NAS Cecil Field, FL., 22 JUN 85; To VA-83, USS Saratoga (CV-60), 07 AUG 85; To VA-83, NAS Cecil Field, FL., 12 AUG 85; To VA-83, USS Saratoga (CV-60), 12 AUG 85; To VA-83, NAS Cecil Field, FL., 12 AUG 85 ** Transferred to VA-46/CVW-1, AB/3XX, NAS Jacksonville, FL., 29 APR 87; To VA-46/CVW-7, AG/3XX,, NAS Cecil Field, FL., 29 APR 87; To VA-46, NAS Jacksonville, FL., 07 MAY 87; To VA-46, USS Dwight D. Eisenhower (CVN-69), 07 MAY 87; To VA-46, NAS Jacksonville, FL., 31 JUL 87; To VA-46, NAS Cecil Field, FL., 31 JUL 87 thru 17 SEP 87 ** End of flight record card ** On conditional loan from the National Museum of Naval Aviation; Pensacola, FL., to the Jacksonville University, JROTC, FL.

E-548 160716 Navy acceptance from NPRO Rep. LTV, Dallas, TX., 07 JUN 78 ** Transferred to VA-174/FRS, AD/4XX, NAS Cecil Field, FL., 08 JUN 78 ** Transferred to VA-81/CVW-17, AA/4XX, NAS Cecil Field, FL., 27 JUN 80 ** Transferred to VA-83/CVW-17, AA/303, NAS Cecil Field, FL., 11 AUG 80; To VA-83, USS Forrestal (CV-59), CDR Mike Mears painted on nose under the windscreen, 11 SEP 80, To VA-83, NAS Cecil Field, FL., 11 SEP 80; To VA-83, To VA-83, USS Forrestal (CV-59), 11 SEP 80, To VA-83, NAS Cecil Field, FL., 11 SEP 80; To VA-83, NAS Fallon, NV., 09 NOV 81; To VA-83, NAS Cecil Field, FL., 09 NOV 81; To VA-83, USS Forrestal (CV-59), 09 NOV 81 ** Transferred to VA-86/CVW-8, AJ/4XX, NAS Cecil Field, FL., 01 MAR 82; To VA-86, NAS Jacksonville, FL., 13 JUL 82; To VA-86, USS Nimitz (CVN-68), 02 SEP 82; To VA-86, NAS Cecil Field, FL., 02 SEP 82; To VA-86, USS Nimitz (CVN-

68), 02 SEP 82; NAS Cecil Field, FL., 02 SEP 82; To VA-86, NAS Roosevelt Roads, PR., 02 SEP 82 ** Transferred to VA-83/CVW-17, AA/3XX, NAS Fallon, NV., 03 AUG 83; To VA-83, NAS Cecil Field, FL., 03 AUG 83; To VA-83, USS Saratoga (CV-60), 03 AUG 83; To VA-83, NAS Cecil Field, FL., 03 AUG 83; To VA-83, USS Saratoga (CV-60), 03 AUG 83; To VA-83, NAS Fallon, NV., 29 NOV 84; To VA-83, NAS Cecil Field, FL., 26 FEB 85; To VA-83, NAS Jacksonville, FL., 27 FEB 85; To VA-83, NAS Cecil Field, FL., 28 MAR 85; To VA-83, NAS Jacksonville, FL., 10 APR 85; To VA-83, NAS Cecil Field, FL., 12 APR 85; To VA-83, USS Saratoga (CV-60), 02 MAY 85; To VA-83, NAS Cecil Field, FL., 03 JUN 85; To VA-83, USS Saratoga (CV-60), 03 JUN 85; To VA-83, NAS Cecil Field, FL., 03 JUN 85; To VA-83, USS Saratoga (CV-60), 21 AUG 86; To VA-83, NAS Cecil Field, FL., 06 OCT 86; To VA-83, NAS Jacksonville, FL., 20 FEB 87; To VA-83, NAS Cecil Field, FL., 20 FEB 87; To VA-83, USS Saratoga (CV-60), 06 MAR 87; To VA-83, NAS Cecil Field, FL., 06 MAR 87; To VA-83, NAS Jacksonville, FL., 24 JUN 87 ** Transferred to VA-46/CVW-7, AG/3XX, USS Dwight D. Eisenhower (CVN-69), 25 JUN 87; To VA-46, NAS Cecil Field, FL., 25 JUN 87 thru 22 SEP 87 ** End of flight record card** Transferred to VA-105/CVW-6, AE/4XX, NAS Cecil Field, FL., 19 AUG 94 ** Transferred to AMARC, Davis Monthan AFB; Tucson, AZ., assigned park code 6A0389, 05 DEC 90 ** 5342.1 flight hours ** TF41A402D engine S/N 142530 ** Aircraft released from storage to be prepared for overland and above deck shipment to the government og Greece ** Transferred to the Helenic Air force (Greee).

E-549 160717 Navy acceptance from NPRO Rep. LTV, Dallas, TX., 21 JUL 78 ** Transferred to VA-174/FRS, AD/4XX, NAS Cecil Field, FL., 25 JUL 78 ** Transferred to VA-81/CVW-17, AA/4XX, NAS Cecil Field, FL., 08 DEC 78; To VA-81, USS Forreastal (CV-59), 08 DEC 78; To VA-81, NAS Cecil Field, FL., 19 JUL 79; To VA-81, USS Forreastal (CV-59), 26 JUL 79; To VA-81, NAS Cecil Field, FL., 06 JAN 80; To VA-81, NAS Jacksonville, FL., 09 SEP 80; To VA-81, USS Forreastal (CV-59), 09 SEP 80; To VA-81, NAS Cecil Field, FL., 17 OCT 80; To VA-81, USS Forreastal (CV-59), 01 APR 81; To VA-81, NAS Cecil Field, FL., 27 MAY 81 ** Transferred to VA-83/CVW-17, AA/310, NAS Cecil Field, FL., 28 DEC 81; To VA-83, NAS Fallon, NV., 18 JAN 82; To VA-83, NAS Cecil Field, FL., 12 FEB 82; To VA-83, USS Forrestal (CV-59), 12 FEB 82; To VA-83, NAS Cecil Field, FL., 12 FEB 82; To VA-83, USS Forrestal (CV-59), 12 FEB 82; ToVA-83, NAS Cecil Field, FL., 12 FEB 82; To VA-83, NAS Jacksonville, FL., 05 JAN 83; To VA-83, NAS Cecil Field, FL., 07 FEB 83; To VA-83, NAS Fallon, NV., 07 FEB 83; To VA-83, NAS Cecil Field, FL., 07 FEB 83; To VA-83, USS Saratoiga (CV-60), 07 FEB 73; To VA-83, NAS Cecil Field, FL., 07 FEB 83; To VA-83, USS Saratoga (CV-60), 07 FEB 83; To VA-83, NAS Cecil Field, FL., 09 OCT 84; To VA-83, NAS Fallon, NV., 12 DEC 84; To VA-83, NAS Jacksonville, FL., 12 FEB 85; To VA-83, NAS Cecil Field, FL., 14 FEB 85; To VA-83, NAS Jacksonville, FL., 16 APR 85; To VA-83, NAS Cecil Field, FL., 18 APR 85; To VA-83, USS Saratoga (CV-60), 18 APR 85; To VA-83, NAS Cecil Field, FL., 18 APR 85; To VA-83, USS Saratoga (CV-60), 18 APR 85; To VA-83, NAS Cecil Field, FL., 18 APR 85; To VA-83, USS Saratoga (CV-60), 16 AUG 85; To VA-83, NAS Cecil Field, FL., 22 SEP 86; To VA-83, USS Saratoga (CV-60), 22 SEP 86; To VA-83, NAS Cecil Field, FL., 20 FEB 87; To VA-83, USS Saratoga (CV-60), 20 FEB 87; To VA-83, NAS Cecil Field, FL., 20 FEB 87, USS Saratoga (CV-60), 20 FEB 87 ** End of flight record card ** Transferred to the Helenic Air force (Greee).

E-550 160718 Navy acceptance from NPRO Rep. LTV, Dallas, TX., 25 JUL 78 ** Transferred to VA-174/FRS, AD/4XX, NAS Cecil Field, FL., 28 JUL 78 ** Transferred to VA-81/CVW-17, AA/404, NAS Cecil Field, FL., 01 FEB 79; To VA-81, USS Forrestal (CV-59), 01 FEB 79; To VA-81, NAS Cecil Field, FL., 17 JUL 79; To VA-81, USS Forrestal (CV-59), 25 JUL 79; To VA-81, NAS Cecil Field, FL., 25 JUL 79; To VA-81, NAS Jacksonville, FL., 26 SEP 80; To VA-81, USS Forrestal (CV-59), 23 OCT 80; To VA-81, NAS Cecil Field, FL., 05 NOV 80; To VA-81, USS Forrestal (CV-59), 05 NOV 80; To VA-81, NAS Cecil Field, FL., 05 NOV 80; To VA-81, NAS Fallon, NV., 05 JAN 82; To VA-81, USS Forrestal (CV-59), 05

JAN 82 ** Transferred to VA-83/CVW-17, AA/303, USS Forrestal (CV-59), 11 MAR 82; To VA-83, NAS Cecil Field, FL., 11 MAR 82 ** Transferred to VA-86/CVW-8, AJ/4XX, NAS Cecil Field, FL., 27 MAY 82 ** Transferred to VA-66/CVW-7, AG/3XX, NAS Cecil Field, FL., 19 AUG 82; To VA-66, NAS Jacksonville, FL., 04 OCT 82; To VA-66, NAS Cecil Field, FL., 04 OCT 82; To VA-66, NAS Jacksonville, FL., 05 OCT 82; To VA-66, NAS Cecil Field, FL., 16 DEC 82; To VA-66, USS Dwight D. Eisenhower (CVN-69), 16 DEC 82; To VA-66, NAS Cecil Field, FL., 16 DEC 82 ** Transferred to VA-86/CVW-8, AJ/4XX, USS Dwight D. Eisenhower (CV-69), 02 APR 84 ** Transferred to VA-66/CVW-7, AG/3XX, NAS Cecil Field, FL., 02 APR 84; To VA-66, USS Dwight D. Eisenhower (CVN-69), 02 APR 84; To VA-66, NAS Cecil Field, FL., 02 APR 84; To VA-66, USS Dwight D. Eisenhower (CVN-69), 02 APR 84; To VA-66, NAS Cecil Field, FL., 09 MAY 85; To VA-66, NAS Jacksonville, FL., 14 MAY 85; To VA-66, NAS Cecil Field, FL., 15 MAY 85; To VA-66, NAS Jacksonville, FL., 09 JUL 85 ** Transferred to VA-83/CVW-17, AA/3XX, NAS Cecil Field, FL., 09 JUL 85; To VA-83, USS Saratoga (CV-60), 08 AUG 85; To VA-83, NAS Cecil Field, FL., 23 APR 86; To VA-83, USS Saratoga (CV-60), 02 JUN 86; To VA-83, NAS Cecil Field, FL., 02 JUN 86; To VA-83, USS Saratoga (CV-60), 17 JAN 87 ** Transferred to VA-46/CVW-7, AG/3XX, NAS Cecil Field, FL., 11 FEB 87; To VA-46, NAS Jacksonville, FL., 10 JUN 87; To VA-46, NAS Cecil Field, FL., 19 JUN 87; To VA-46, NAS Jacksonville, FL., 17 SEP 87; To VA-46, NAS Cecil Field, FL., 18 SEP 87 ** End of flight record card ** Transferred to the Helenic Air force (Greee).

E-551 160719 Navy acceptance from NPRO Rep. LTV, Dallas, TX., 21 JUL 78 ** Transferred to VA-174/FRS, AD/4XX, NAS Cecil Field, FL., 25 JUL 78 ** Transferred to VA-81/CVW-17, AA/400, USS Forrestal CV-59), Painted light gray on a darker gray with black darter on tail, 23 MAY 79; To VA-81, NAS Cecil Field, FL., 30 AUG 79; To VA-81, NAS Jacksonville, FL., 08 AUG 80; To VA-81, NAS Cecil Field, FL., 12 AUG 80; To VA-81, NAS Jacksonville, FL., 15 SEP 80; To VA-81, NAS Cecil Field, FL., 16 SEP 80; To VA-81, USS Forrestal (CV-59), 18 SEP 80; To VA-81, NAS Cecil Field, FL., 23 SEP 80; To VA-81, USS Forrestal (CV-59), 18 SEP 80; To VA-81, NAS Cecil Field, FL., 23 SEP 80; To VA-81, USS Forrestal (CV-59), 23 SEP 80; To VA-81, NAS Cecil Field, FL., 23 SEP 80; To VA-81, NAS Fallon, NV., 23 SEP 80 ** Transferred to VA-83/ CVW-17, AA/3XX., NAS Cecil Field, FL., 17 FEB 82; To VA-83, USS Forrestal (CV-59), 18 FEB 82; To VA-83, NAS Cecil Field, FL., 18 FEB 82 ** Transferred to VA-86/CVW-8, AJ/4XX, NAS Cecil Field, FL., 27 MAY 82; To VA-86, USS Nimitz (CVN-68), 27 MAY 82; To VA-86, NAS Cecil Field, FL., 27 MAY 82; To VA-86, USS Nimitz (CVN-68), 27 MAY 82 ** Transferred to VA-66/CVW-7, AG/3XX, NAS Cecil Field, FL., 01 SEP 82; To VA-66, NAS Jacksonville, FL., 24 SEP 82; To VA-66, NAS Cecil Field, Fl., 24 SEP 82; To VA-66, NAS Jacksonville, FL., 28 SEP 82; To VA-66, NAS Cecil Field, Fl., 01 DEC 82; To VA-66, USS Dwight D. Eisenhower (CVN-69), 01 DEC 82; To VA-66, NAS Cecil Field, Fl., 01 DEC 82; To VA-66, USS Dwight D. Eisenhower (CVN-69), To VA-66, NAS Cecil Field, Fl., 29 FEB 84; To VA-66, USS Dwight D. Eisenhower (CVN-69), 27 JUL 84; To VA-66, NAS Cecil Field, Fl., 27 JUL 84; To VA-66, USS Dwight D. Eisenhower (CVN-69), 27 JUL 84 ~ S 1SO strike, 14 APR 85 ** No data on strike.

E-552 160720 Navy acceptance from NPRO Rep. LTV, Dallas, TX., 14 AUG 78 ** Transferred to VA-174/FRS, AD/4XX, NAS Cecil Field, FL., 19 AUG 78 ** Transferred to VA-72/CVW-1, AB/4XX, NAS Cecil Field, FL., 14 JUN 79 ** Transferred to VA-81/CVW-17, AA/4XX, USS Forrestal (CV-59), 21 FEB 80; To VA-81, NAS Cecil Field, FL., 21 FEB 80; To VA-81, NAS Jacksonville, FL., 15 SEP 80; To VA-81, USS Forrestal (CV-59), 22 OCT 80; To VA-81, NAS Cecil Field, FL., 17 JAN 81 ~ S 1SO strike, 17 JAN 81 ** No data on strike.

E-553 160721 Navy acceptance from NPRO Rep. LTV, Dallas, TX., 28 SEP 78 ** Transferred to VA-22/CVW-15, NL/3XX, NAS LeMoore, CA., 17 OCT 78; To VA-22, USS Kitty Hawk (CV-63), 26 APR 79 ** Transferred to VA-146/CVW-9, NG/ 3XX, NAS Cubi Point, PI., 03 MAY 79; To VA-146, NAS LeMoore, CA., 03 MAY 79; To VA-146, USS Constellation (CV-64), 25 OCT 79; To VA-146, NAS LeMoore, CA., 10

NOV 79; To VA-146, USS Constellation (CV-64), 06 DEC 79; To VA-146, NAS LeMoore, CA., 23 JAN 80; To VA-146, USS Constellation (CV-64), 28 FEB 80; To VA-146, NAS LeMoore, CA., 28 FEB 80; To VA-146, NAS Jacksonville, FL., 18 NOV 80; To VA-146, NAS LeMoore, CA., 24 JAN 81 ** Transferred to VA-22/CVW-15, NL/3XX, NAS LeMoore, CA., 30 JAN 81; To VA-22, USS Kitty Hawk (CV-63), 02 MAR 81; To VA-22, NAS LeMoore, CA., 25 MAR 81; To VA-22/CVW-11, NH/3XX, USS Enterprise (CVN-65), 13 JUL 82 ** Transferred to VA-122/FRS, NJ/2XX, NAS LeMoore, CA., 02 SEP 82 ** Transferred to NARF, NAS Jacksonville, FL., 18 DEC 84 thru 29 JAN 87 ** End of flight record card ** Transferred to NAD, NAS Jacksonville, FL., 30 DEC 87 ** Transferred to VA-97, NL/3XX, NAS LeMoore, CA., Date unknown ** Transferred to AMARC, Davis Monthan AFB; Tucson, AZ., assigned park code 6A0412; 13 JUL 92 ** 2953.9 flight hours ** TF41A402D engine S/N 141505 ** Engine removed, date unknown ** Project changed per FSO letter, 06 APR 04 ** Aircraft deleted from inventory and released to DRMO for disposition, 17 SEP 04 ** Transferred to U.S. Army at Fort Sill; Lawton, OK., MICOM Modex 029, to be used as a target on the Falcon range, 28 JAN 05.

E-572 160722 Navy acceptance from NPRO Rep. LTV, Dallas, TX., 30 AUG 78 ** Transferred to VX-5, XE/XXX, NAF China Lake, CA., 14 SEP 78; To VX-5, NAS LeMoore, CA., 29 JAN 80; To VX-5, NWC China Lake, CA., 22 FEB 80; To VX-5, NAS Jacksonville, FL., 10 MAY 83; To VX-5, NWC China Lake, CA., 13 AUG 83; To VX-5, NAS Jacksonville, FL., 12 JAN 84; To VX-5, NWC China Lake, CA., 26 JAN 84 thru 23 SEP 87 ** End of flight record card ** On display at the Pacific Coast Division of the United States Aviation Museum; Inyokern, CA. ** The Inyokern museum was closed, the aircraft are no longer there ** Located at VX-31, Preservation Yard, NAWC China Lake, CA., NOV 04.

E-555 160723 Navy acceptance from NPRO Rep. LTV, Dallas, TX., 23 AUG 78 ** Transferred to VA-22/CVW-15, NL3XX, NAS LeMoore, CA., 26 AUG 78; To VA-22, NAS Kingsville, TX., 26 AUG 78; To VA-22, NAS LeMoore, CA., 26 AUG 78; To VA-22, USS Kitty Hawk (CV-63), 26 APR 79 ** Transferred to VA-146/CVW-9, NG/3XX, NAS Cubi Point, PI., 18 MAY 79; To VA-146, USS Constellation (CV-64), 26 OCT 79; To VA-146, NAS LeMoore, CA., 26 OCT 79; To VA-146, USS Constellation (CV-64), 13 DEC 79; To VA-146, NAS LeMoore, CA., 13 DEC 79; To VA-146, USS Constellation (CV-64), 06 APR 80; To VA-146, NAF Atsugi, JP., 07 APR 80; To VA-146, USS Constellation (CV-64), 14 APR 80; To VA-146, NAS LeMoore, CA., 14 APR 80; To VA-146, NAS Jacksonville, FL., 07 NOV 80; To VA-146, NAS LeMoore, CA., 29 DEC 80 ** Transferred to VA-22/CVW-15, NL3XX, USS Kitty Hawk (CV-63), 02 MAR 81; To VA-22, NAS LeMoore, CA., 04 AUG 81 ** Transferred to VA-192/CVW-11, NH/3XX, NAS LeMoore, CA., 16 MAR 82; To VA-192, NAS Jacksonville, FL., 11 NOV 82; To VA-192, NAS LeMoore, CA., 11 NOV 82; To VA-192, NAS Jacksonville, FL., 15 NOV 82; To VA-192, NAS LeMoore, CA., 25 JAN 83; To VA-192/CVW-9, NG/3XX, USS Ranger (CV-61), 24 JUL 83; To VA-192, NAS LeMoore, CA., 30 DEC 83 ** Transferred to VA-146/CVW-9, NG/3XX, NAS LeMoore, CA., 06 FEB 85; To VA-146, USS Kitty Hawk (CV-63), 23 JUN 85; To VA-146, NAS LeMoore, CA., 05 DEC 85; To VA-146, NAS Jacksonville, FL., 11 FEB 86; To VA-146, NAS LeMoore, CA., 25 APR 86 ** Transferred to VA-97/CVW-15, NL/3XX, NAS LeMoore, CA., 28 APR 86; To VA-97, USS Carl Vinson (CVN-70), 28 APR 86; To VA-97, NAS LeMoore, CA., 28 APR 86; To VA-97, USS Carl Vinson (CVN-70), 28 APR 86 ~ S 1SO strike, 27 DEC 86 ** Pilot ejected safely as brakes failed while taxiing the catapult.

E-556 160724 Navy acceptance from NPRO Rep. LTV, Dallas, TX., 14 SEP 78 ** Transferred to VX-5, XE/XXX, NAF China Lake, CA., 15 SEP 78; To VX-5, NAS LeMoore, CA., 07 JAN 80; To VX-5, NWC China Lake, CA., 04 FEB 80; To VX-5, NAS Jacksonville, FL., 02 NOV 82; To VX-5, NWC China Lake, CA., 03 JAN 85; To VX-5, NAS Pensacola, FL., 16 MAR 87; To VX-5, NWC China Lake, CA., 19 MAR 87; To VX-5, NAS Pensacola, FL., 10 APR 87 thru 18 SEP 87 ** End of flight record card ** On conditional loan from the National Museum of Naval Aviation; Pensacola, Fl. to the Louisiana Naval War Memorial; Baton Rouge, LA.

E-557 160725 Navy acceptance from NPRO Rep. LTV, Dallas, TX., 14 SEP 78 ** Transferred to VA-94/CVW-15, NL/4XX, NAS LeMoore, CA., 16 SEP 78; To VA-94, USS Kitty Hawk (CV-63), 25 APR 79 ** Transferred to VA-146/CVW-9, NG/3XX, NAS Cubi Point, PI., 10 MAY 79; To VA-146, NAS LeMoore, CA., 10 MAY 79; To VA-146, USS Constellation (CV-64), 26 OCT 79; To VA-146, NAS LeMoore, CA., 26 OCT 79; To VA-146, USS Constellation (CV-64), 30 DEC 79; To VA-146, NAS LeMoore, CA., 23 JAN 80; To VA-146, USS Constellation (CV-64), 28 FEB 80; To VA-146, NAS LeMoore, CA., 28 FEB 80; To VA-146, NAS Jacksonville, FL., 07 NOV 80; To VA-146, NAS LeMoore, CA., 30 DEC 80 ** Transferred to VA-94/CVW-15, NL/4XX, NAS LeMoore, CA., 08 JAN 81 ~ S 1SO strike, 24 FEB 81 ** No data on strike.

E-558 160726 Navy acceptance from NPRO Rep. LTV, Dallas, TX., 31 OCT 78 ** Transferred to VA-22/CVW-15, NL/3XX, NAS LeMoore, CA., 10 NOV 78; To VA-22, USS Kitty Hawk (CV-63), 29 APR 79 ** Transferred to VA-146/CVW-9, NG/3XX, NAS Cubi Point, PI., 17 MAY 79; To VA-146, NAS LeMoore, CA., 17 MAY 79; To VA-146, USS Constellation (CV-64), 21 DEC 79; To VA-146, NAS LeMoore, 23 JAN 80; To VA-146, USS Constellation (CV-64), 28 FEB 80 ** Transferred to VA-93/CVW-5, NF/3XX, USS Midway (CV-41), 01 SEP 80; To VA-93, NAF Atsugi, JP., 25 NOV 80; To VA-93, NAS Cubi Point, PI., 27 FEB 81; To VA-93, USS Midway (CV-41), 27 FEB 81; To VA-93, NAF Atsugi, JP., 04 JUN 81; To VA-93, Korea, 15 JUL 81; To VA-93, USS Midway (CV-41), 03 SEP 81; To VA-93, NAF Atsugi, JP., 04 OCT 81; To VA-93, USS Midway (CV-41), 30 OCT 81; To VA-93, NAF Atsugi, JP., 02 FEB 82; To VA-93, USS Midway (CV-41), 10 FEB 82 ** Transferred to VA-146/CVW-9, NG/3XX, USS Constellation (CV-64), 20 APR 82; To VA-146, NAS LeMoore, CA., 20 APR 82 ** Transferred to VA-122/FRS, NJ/2XX, NAS LeMoore, CA., 02 JUL 82; To VA-122, NAS Jacksonville, FL., 17 JAN 83; To VA-122, NAS LeMoore, CA., 17 JAN 83; To VA-122, NAS Jacksonville, FL., 20 JAN 83; To VA-122, NAS LeMoore, CA., 01 APR 83 ** Transferred to VA-97/CVW-15, NL/3XX, NAS LeMoore, CA., 01 FEB 84; To VA-97, USS Carl Vinson (CVN-70), 01 FEB 84; To VA-97, NAS LeMoore, CA., 01 FEB 84; To VA-97, USS Carl Vinson (CVN-70), 01 FEB 84; To VA-97, NAS LeMoore, CA., 16 JUN 84 ** Transferred to VA-66/CVW-8, AJ/4XX, USS Carl Vinson (CVN-70), 09 AUG 84 ** Transferred to VA-192/CVW-9, NG/3XX, NAS LeMoore, CA., 10 AUG 84 ** Transferred to VA-22/CVW-11, NH/3XX, NAS LeMoore, CA., 12 FEB 85; To VA-22, NAS Fallon, NV., 25 APR 85; To VA-22, NAS LeMoore, CA., 22 MAY 85; To VA-22, NAS Jacksonville, FL., 25 JUN 85; To VA-22, NAS LeMoore, CA., 30 AUG 85; To VA-22, USS Enterprise (CVN-65), 30 AUG 85; To VA-22, NAS LeMoore, CA., 20 JUL 86 thru 05 SEP 87 ** End of flight record card ** Seen at the DMI Aviation Yard, 28 AUG 00.

E-559 160727 Navy acceptance from NPRO Rep. LTV, Dallas, TX., 03 NOV 78 ** Transferred to VA-94/CVW-15, NL/4XX, NAS LeMoore, CA., 15 NOV 78; To VA-94, USS Kitty Hawk (CV-63), 25 APR 79 ** Transferred to VA-146/CVW-9, NG/ 3XX, NAS Cubi Point, PI., 14 MAY 79; To VA-146, NAS LeMoore, CA., 24 JUL 79; To VA-146, USS Constellation (CV-64), 25 OCT 79; To VA-146, NAS LeMoore, CA., 25 OCT 79; To VA-146, USS Constellation (CV-64), 14 DEC 79; To VA-146, NAS LeMoore, CA., 04 DEC 80; To VA-146, USS Constellation (CV-64), 28 FEB 80 ** Transferred to VA-93/CVW-5, NF/3XX, USS Midway (CV-41), 22 SEP 80; To VA-93, NAF Atsugi, JP., 04 NOV 80; To VA-93, USS Midway (CV-41), 24 NOV 80; To VA-93, NAF Atsugi, JP., 17 DEC 80; To VA-93, NAS Cubi Point, PI., 28 JAN 81; To VA-93, USS Midway (CV-41), 24 FEB 81; To VA-93, NAF Atsugi, JP., 04 JUN 81; To VA-93, Korea, 15 JUL 81; To VA-93, USS Midway (CV-41), 03 SEP 81; To VA-93, NAF Atsugi, JP., 04 OCT 81; To VA-93, USS Midway (CV-41), 30 OCT 81; To VA-93, NAF Atsugi, JP., 21 JAN 82; To VA-93, USS Midway (CV-41), 02 FEB 82; To VA-93, NAS Cubi Point, PI., 02 FEB 82 ** Transferred to VA-113/CVW-2, NE/3XX, NAF Atsugi, JP., 25 SEP 82; To VA-113, NAS LeMoore, CA., 25 SEP 82; To VA-113, NAS Jacksonville, FL., 16 MAR 83; To VFA-113, NAS Jacksonville, FL., 25 MAY 83 ** Transferred to VA-122/FRS, NJ/2XX, NAS LeMoore, CA., 31 MAY 83; To VA-122, NAS Jacksonville, FL., 02 JUL 85; To

VA-122, NAS LeMoore, CA., 20 AUG 85 ** Transferred to VA-27/ CVW-15, NL/4XX, NAS LeMoore, CA., 28 APR 86 ** Transferred to VA-122/FRS, NJ/2XX, NAS LeMoore, CA., 29 APR 86 ~ S 1SO strike, 06 MAY 86 ** No data on strike.

E-560 160728 Navy acceptance from NPRO Rep. LTV, Dallas, TX., 19 OCT 78 ** Transferred to VA-94/CVW-15, NL/4XX, NAS LeMoore, CA., 24 OCT 78; To VA-94, USS Kitty Hawk (CV-63), 25 APR 79 ** Transferred to VA-146/CVW-9, NG/ 3XX, NAS Cubi Point, PI., 22 MAY 79; To VA-146, NAS LeMoore, CA., 22 MAY 79; To VA-146, USS Constellation (CV-64), 25 OCT 79; To VA-146, NAS LeMoore, CA., 25 OCT 79; To VA-146, USS Constellation (CV-64), 28 FEB 80; To VA-146, NAS LeMoore, CA., 28 FEB 80; To VA-146, NAS Jacksonville, FL., 22 NOV 80; To VA-146, NAS LeMoore, CA., 02 JAN 81 ** Transferred to VA-94/CVW-15, NL/4XX, NAS LeMoore, CA., 09 JAN 81; To VA-94, USS Kitty Hawk (CV-63), 27 FEB 81 ** Transferred to VA-22/CVW-15, NL/3XX, USS Kitty Hawk (CV-63), 03 APR 81; To VA-22, NAS LeMoore, CA., 03 APR 81 ** Transferred to VA-192/CVW-11, NH/3XX, NAS LeMoore, CA., 01 MAR 82 ** Transferred to VA-122/FRS, NJ/2XX, NAS LeMoore, CA., 28 FEB 83; To VA-122, NAS Jacksonville, 03 MAR 83; To VA-122, NAS LeMoore, CA., 18 MAY 83 ** Transferred to VA-192/ CVW-11, NH/3XX, NAS LeMoore, CA., 29 JUN 84 ** Transferred to VA-97/CVW-15, NL/3XX, USS Carl Vinson (CVN-70), 09 AUG 84; To VA-97, NAS LeMoore, CA., 01 SEP 84; To VA-97, USS Carl Vinson (CVN-70), 21 SEP 84; To VA-97, NAS LeMoore, CA., 29 APR 85; To VA-97, NAS Jacksonville, FL., 09 SEP 85; To VA-97, NAS LeMoore, CA., 07 DEC 85; To VA-97, USS Carl Vinson (CVN-70), 07 DEC 85; To VA-97, NAS LeMoore, CA., 07 DEC 85; To VA-97, USS Carl Vinson (CVN-70), 07 DEC 85; To VA-97, NAS Alameda, CA., 06 NOV 86 thru 09 SEP 87 ** End of flight record card ** Transferred to the Helinic Air Force (Greece) with S/N 160728.

E-561 160729 Navy acceptance from NPRO Rep. LTV, Dallas, TX., 14 NOV 78 ** Transferred to VA-27/CVW-14, NK/4XX, NAS LeMoore, CA., 18 NOV 78; To VA-27, NPTR El Centro, CA., 18 NOV 78 ** Transferred to VA-146/CVW-9, NG/3XX, NAS Cubi Point, PI., 26 JUN 79; To VA-146, NAS LeMoore, CA., 16 JUN 79; To VA-146, USS Constellation (CV-64), 25 OCT 79; To VA-146, NAS LeMoore, CA., 25 OCT 79; To VA-146, USS Constellation (CV-64), 27 DEC 79; To VA-146, NAS LeMoore, CA., 23 JAN 80; To VA-146, USS Constellation (CV-64), 28 FEB 80** Transferred to VA-93/ CVW-5, NF/3XX, USS Midway (CV-41), 22 SEP 80; To VA-93, NAF Atsugi, JP., 21 NOV 80; To VA-93, NAS Cubi Point, PI., 23 FEB 81; To VA-93, USS Midway (CV-41), 23 FEB 81; To VA-93, NAF Atsugi, JP., 04 JUN 81; To VA-93, Korea, 15 JUL 81; To VA-93, USS Midway (CV-41), 03 SEP 81; To VA-93, NAF Atsugi, JP., 04 OCT 81; To VA-93, USS Midway (CV-41), 04 OCT 81; To VA-93, NAF Atsugi, JP., 04 OCT 81; To VA-93, USS Midway (CV-41), 21 JAN 82; To VA-93, NAF Atsugi, JP., 01 SEP 82; To VA-93, NAS Cubi Point, PI., 13 SEP 82 ** Transferred to VA-113/CVW-2, NE/3XX, NAF Atsugi, JP., 24 SEP 82; To VA-113, NAS LeMoore, CA., 27 SEP 82; To VA-113, NAS Jacksonville, FL., 21 MAR 83; To VFA-113, NAS Jacksonville, FL., 20 MAY 83 ** Transferred to VA-122/FRS, NJ/2XX, NAS LeMoore, CA., 26 MAY 83 ** Transferred to VX-5, XE/XXX, NWC China Lake, CA., 15 JUL 83 thru 21 SEP 87 ** End of flight record card ** Transferred to NADEP, NAS Jacksonville, FL., 11 OCT 88 ** Transferred to VA-122/FRS, NJ/244, NAS LeMoore, CA., date unknown ** Transferred to AMARC, Davis Monthan AFB; Tucson, AZ., assigned park code 6A0315, with FLIR, 22 FEB 90 ** 4202.3 flight hours ** TF41A402D engine S/N unknown ** Storage location 111212 ** At AMARG, Davis Monthan AFB; Tucson, AZ., 15 JUN 07.

E-562 160730 Navy acceptance from NPRO Rep. LTV, Dallas, TX., 08 DEC 78 ** Transferred to VA-97/CVW-14, NK/3XX, NAS LeMoore, CA., 17 DEC 78 ** Transferred to VA-146/CVW-9, NG/3XX, NAS Cubi Point, PI., 10 JUL 79; To VA-146, USS Constellation (CV-64), 25 OCT 79; To VA-146, NAS LeMoore, CA., 25 OCT 79; To VA-146, USS Constellation (CV-64), 13 DEC 79; To VA-146, NAS LeMoore, CA., 23 JAN 80; To VA-146, USS Constellation (CV-64), 28 FEB 80 ** Transferred to VA-56/CVW-5,

NF/4XX, USS Midway (CV-41), 22 SEP 80; To VA-56, NAF Atsugi, JP., 22 DEC 80 ** Transferred to VA-93/ CVW-5, NF/3XX, NAF Atsugi, JP., 16 FEB 81; To VA-93, NAS Cubi Point, PI., 24 FEB 81; To VA-93, USS Midway (CV-41), 24 FEB 81; To VA-93, NAF Atsugi, JP., 04 JUN 81; To VA-93, Korea, 15 JUL 81; To VA-93, USS Midway (CV-41), 03 SEP 81; To VA-93, NAF Atsugi, JP., 04 OCT 81; To VA-93, USS Midway (CV-41), 30 OCT 81; To VA-93, NAF Atsugi, JP., 13 JAN 82; To VA-93, USS Midway (CV-41), 18 JAN 82; To VA-93, NAS Cubi Point, PI., 18 JAN 82 ** Transferred to VA-113/CVW-2, NE/3XX, NAF Atsugi, JP., 22 SEP 82; To VA-113, NAS LeMoore, CA., 22 SEP 82 ** Transferred to VA-25/ CVW-2, NE/4XX, NAS LeMoore, CA., 05 APR 83; To VFA-25, NAS LeMoore, CA., 15 JUL 83 ** Transferred to VA-22/CVW-11, NH/3XX, NAS LeMoore, CA., 20 JUL 83; To VA-22, USS Enterprise (CVN-65), 08 DEC 83; To VA-22, NAS LeMoore, CA., 08 DEC 83 ** Transferred to VA-97/CVW-15, NL/3XX, USS Carl Vinson (CVN-70), 27 MAR 84; To VA-97, NAS LeMoore, CA., 27 MAR 84; To VA-97, USS Carl Vinson (CVN-70), 27 MAR 84; To VA-97, NAS LeMoore, CA., 27 MAR 84; To VA-97, USS Carl Vinson (CVN-70), 27 MAR 84; To VA-97, NAS LeMoore, CA., 27 MAR 84; ** Transferred to VA-147/CVW-9, NE/3XX, NAS LeMoore, CA., 14 SEP 84; To VA-147, USS Kitty Hawk (CV-63), 14 MAY 85; To VA-147, NAS LeMoore, CA., 04 FEB 86; To VA-147, NAS Jacksonville, FL., 03 JUL 86; To VA-147, NAS LeMoore, CA., 12 SEP 86; To VA-147, USS Kitty Hawk (CV-63), 12 SEP 86; To VA-147, NAS LeMoore, CA., 12 SEP 86 ** End of flight record card.

E-563 160731 Navy acceptance from NPRO Rep. LTV, Dallas, TX., 18 JAN 79 ** Transferred to VA-27/CVW-14, NK/4XX, NAS LeMoore, CA., 02 DEC 79; To VA-27, NPTR El Centro, CA., 02 APR 79 ** Transferred to VA-146/CVW-9, NG/3XX, NAS Cubi Point, PI., 27 JUN 79; To VA-146, NAS LeMoore, CA., 27 JUN 79; To VA-146, USS Constelletion (CV-64), 25 OCT 79; To VA-146, NAS LeMoore, CA., 25 OCT 79; To VA-146, USS Constelletion (CV-64), 13 DEC 79; To VA-146, NAS LeMoore, CA., 23 JAN 80; To VA-146, USS Constelletion (CV-64), 28 FEB 80 ** Transferred to VA-56/ CVW-5, NF/4XX, USS Midway (CV-41), 22 SEP 80; To VA-56, NAF Atsugi, JP., 12 NOV 80; To VA-56, USS Midway (CV-41), 18 NOV 80; To VA-56, NAF Atsugi, JP., 16 JAN 81 ** Transferred to VA-93/ CVW-5, NF/3XX, NAS Cubi Point, PI., 28 JAN 81; To VA-93, USS Midway (CV-41), 23 FEB 81; To VA-93, NAF Atsugi, JP., 04 JUN 81; To VA-93, Korea, 15 JUL 81; To VA-93, NAF Atsugi, JP., 31 JUL 81; To VA-93, USS Midway (CV-41), 31 JUL 81; To VA-93, NAS Cubi Point, PI., 30 OCT 81 ** Transferred to VA-113/CVW-2, NE/3XX, NAF Atsugi, JP., 22 SEP 82; To VA-113, NAS LeMoore, CA., 22 SEP 83 ** Transferred to VA-25/CVW-2, NE/4XX, NAS LeMoore, CA., 09 MAR 83; To VA-25, NAS Jacksonville, FL., 30 MAR 83 ** Transferred to VA-94/CVW-11, NH/4XX, NAS LeMoore, CA., 30 JUN 83; To VA-94, USS Enterprise (CVN-65), 30 JUN 83; To VA-94, NAS LeMoore, CA., 30 JUN 83; To VA-94, USS Enterprise (CVN-65), 30 JUN 83; To VA-94, NAS LeMoore, CA., 30 JUN 83; To VA-94, USS Enterprise (CVN-65), 14 JUN 84; To VA-94, NAS LeMoore, CA., 19 JUN 84; To VA-94, NAS Fallon, NV., 13 MAR 85; To VA-94, NAS LeMoore, CA., 13 MAR 85; To VA-94, NAS Jacksonville, FL., 09 JUN 85; To VA-94, NAS LeMoore, CA., 16 JUN 85; To VA-94, USS Enterprise (CVN-65), 25 DEC 85; To VA-94, NAS LeMoore, CA., 06 MAY 86 ** Transferred to VA-122/ FRS, NJ/ 2XX, NAS LeMoore, 27 MAR 87 thru 03 JUN 87 ** End of flight record card ~ S 1SO strike, 29 OCT 87 ** No data on strike.

E-564 160732 Navy acceptance from NPRO Rep. LTV, Dallas, TX., 06 FEB 79 ** Transferred to VA-97/CVW-14, NK/3XX, NAS LeMoore, CA., 08 FEB 79 ** Transferred to VA-146/CVW-9, NG/3XX, NAS Cubi Point, PI., 05 JUL 79; To VA-146, NAS LeMoore, CA., 05 JUL 79; To VA-146, USS Constellation (CV-64), 25 OCT 79; To VA-146, NAS LeMoore, CA., 25 OCT 79; To VA-146, USS Constellation (CV-64), 19 DEC 79; To VA-146, NAS LeMoore, CA., 23 JAN 80; To VA-146, USS Constellation (CV-64), 28 FEB 80 ** Transferred to VA-93/CVW-5, NF/3XX, USS Midway (CV-41), 01 SEP 80; To VA-93, NAF Atsugi, JP., 15 NOV 80; To VA-93, USS Midway (CV-41), 25 NOV 80; To VA-93, NAF

Atsugi, JP., 25 NOV 80; To VA-93, NAS Cubi Point, PI., 24 FEB 81; To VA-93, USS Midway (CV-41), 24 FEB 81; To VA-93, NAF Atsugi, JP., 04 JUN 81; To VA-93, USS Midway (CV-41), 15 SEP 81; To VA-93, NAF Atsugi, JP., 15 SEP 81; To VA-93, USS Midway (CV-41), 15 SEP 81; To VA-93, NAS Cubi Point, PI, 15 SEP 81 ** Transferred to VA-113/CVW-2, NE/3XX, NAF Atsugi, JP., 22 SEP 82; To VA-113, NAS LeMoore, CA., 22 SEP 82 ** Transferred to VA-25/CVW-2, NE/4XX, NAS LeMoore, CA., 10 MAR 83 ** Transferred to VA-122/FRS, NJ/ 2XX, NAS LeMoore, CA., 06 JUL 83; To VA-122, NAS Jacksonville, FL., 02 NOV 83; To VA-122, NAS LeMoore, CA, 29 FEB 84 ** Transferred to VA-146/CVW-9, NE/3XX, NAS LeMoore, CA., 27 MAR 85; To VA-146, USS Kitty Hawk (CV-63), 27 MAR 85; To VA-146, NAS LeMoore, CA., 22 SEP 85; To VA-146, NAS Jacksonville, FL., 12 AUG 86; To VA-146, NAS LeMoore, CA., 22 OCT 86; To VA-146, USS Kitty Hawk (CV-63), 22 OCT 86; To VA-146, NAS LeMoore, CA., 22 OCT 86 Thru 24 AUG 87 ** End of flight record card ** Transferred to NADEP, NAS Jacksonville, FL., 08 JUN 89 ** Transferred to VA-22/CVW-11, NH/312, NAS LeMoore, CA., date unknown ** Transferred to AMARC, Davis Monthan AFB; Tucson, AZ., assigned park code 6A0339, 13 APR 90 ** 4323.8 flight hours ** TF41A402D engine S/N 141317 ** Storage location 111504 ** Placed on the FMS list, 06 APR 04 ** At AMARG, Davis Monthan AFB; Tucson, AZ., 15 NOV 07.

E-565 160733 Navy acceptance from NPRO Rep. LTV, Dallas, TX., 20 APR 79 ** Transferred to VA-122/FRS, NJ/201, NAS LeMoore, CA., 26 APR 79 ** Transferred to VA-147/CVW-9, NG/3XX, NAS LeMoore, CA., 17 DEC 79; To VA-147, USS Constellation (CV-64), 17 DEC 79; To VA-147, NAS LeMoore, CA., 23 JAN 80; To VA-147, USS Constellation (CV-64), 26 FEB 80; To VA-147, NAS Cubi Point, PI., 18 APR 80 ** Transferred to VA-93/CVW-5, NF/3XX, NAF Atsugi, JP., 21 APR 80; To VA-93, USS Midway (CV-41), 23 JUN 80; To VA-93, NAF Atsugi, JP., 20 DEC 80; To VA-93, NAS Cubi Point, PI., 28 JAN 81; To VA-93, USS Midway (CV-41), 24 FEB 81; To VA-93, NAF Atsugi, JP., 27 MAY 81; To VA-93, Korea, 26 JUL 81; To VA-93, USS Midway (CV-41), 03 SEP 81; To VA-93, NAF Atsugi, JP., 04 OCT 81; To VA-93, USS Midway (CV-41), 30 OCT 81; To VA-93, NAF Atsugi, JP., 13 APR 82; To VA-93, USS Midway (CV-41), 17 APR 82; To VA-93, NAS Cubi Point, PI., 27 AUG 82 ** Transferred to VA-113/CVW-2, NE/3XX, NAS Atsugi, JP., 24 SEP 82; To VA-113, NAS LeMoore, CA., 24 SEP 82 ** Transferred to VA-122/FRS, NJ/2XX, NAS LeMoore, CA., 07 MAR 83; To VA-122, NAS Jacksonville, FL., 23 JUN 83 ** Transferred to VA-97/CVW-15, NL/3XX, NAS LeMoore, CA., 11 OCT 83; To VA-97, USS Carl Vinson (CVN-70), 22 NOV 83; To VA-97, NAS LeMoore, CA., 22 NOV 83; To VA-97, USS Carl Vinson (CVN-70), 22 NOV 83; To VA-97, NAS LeMoore, CA., 13 JUL 84; To VA-97, USS Carl Vinson (CVN-70), 31 AUG 84; To VA-97, NAS LeMoore, CA., 31 AUG 84; To VA-97, USS Carl Vinson (CVN-70), 31 AUG 84; To VA-97, NAS LeMoore, CA., 13 APR 85; To VA-97, NAS Jacksonville, FL., 22 NOV 85; To VA-97, NAS LeMoore, CA., 14 FEB 86; To VA-97, USS Carl Vinson (CVN-70), 14 FEB 86; To VA-97, NAS Alameda, CA., 03 JUL 86; To VA-97, To VA-97, USS Carl Vinson (CVN-70), 03 JUL 86; To VA-97, NAS Alameda, CA., 03 JUL 86 ** Transferred to NARF, NAS Jacksonville, FL., 13 JAN 87 ** Transferred to NAD, NAS Jacksonville, FL., 08 JUN 87 ** End of flight record card.

E-566 160734 Navy acceptance from NPRO Rep. LTV, Dallas, TX., 21 MAR 79 ** Transferred to VA-27/CVW-14, NK/4XX, NAS LeMoore, CA., 23 MAR 79; To VA-27, NPTR El Centro, CA., 23 MAR 79 ** Transferred to VA-146/CVW-9, NG/312, NAS Cubi Point, PI., 13 JUN 79; To VA-146, NAS LeMoore, CA., 29 JUN 79; To VA-146, USS Constellation (CV-64), 13 DEC 79; To VA-146, NAS LeMoore, CA., 23 JAN 80; To VA-146, USS Constellation (CV-64), 28 FEB 80 ** Transferred to VA-93/CVW-5, NF/3XX, USS Midway (CV-41), 22 SEP 80; To VA-93, NAF Atsugi, JP., 31 DEC 80; To VA-93, NAS Cubi Point, PI., 28 JAN 81; To VA-93; USS Midway (CV-41), 28 JAN 81; To VA-93, NAF Atsugi, JP., 27 JUN 81; To VA-93, Korea, 15 JUL 81; To VA-93, NAF Atsugi, JP., 20 AUG 81; To VA-93; USS Midway (CV-41), 21 AUG 81; To VA-93, NAF Atsugi, JP., 05 OCT 81; To VA-93; USS Midway (CV-41), 22 OCT 81 ~ S 1SO strike, 18 MAR 82

** No data on strike, **E-567 160735** Navy acceptance from NPRO Rep. LTV, Dallas, TX., 03 MAY 79 ** Transferred to VA-146/CVW-9, NG/3XX, NAS Cubi Point, PI., 08 MAY 79; To VA-146, NAS LeMoore, CA., 01 JUN 79; To VA-146, USS Constellation (CV-64), 13 DEC 79; To VA-146, NAS LeMoore, CA., 23 JAN 80; To VA-146, USS Constellation (CV-64), 28 FEB 80 ** Transferred to VA-93/CVW-5, NF/3XX, USS Midway (CV-41), 22 SEP 80; To VA-93, NAF Atsugi, JP., 30 DEC 80; To VA-93, NAS Cubi Point, PI., 28 JAN 81; To VA-93, USS Midway (CV-41), 24 FEB 81; To VA-93, NAF Atsugi, JP., 04 JUN 81; To VA-93, Korea, 23 JUN 81; To VA-93, NAF Atsugi, JP., 24 AUG 81; To VA-93, USS Midway (CV-41), 03 SEP 81; To VA-93, NAF Atsugi, JP., 04 OCT 81; To VA-93, USS Midway (CV-41), 30 OCT 81; To VA-93, NAS Cubi Point, PI., 30 OCT 81 ** Transferred to VA-113/CVW-2, NE/3XX, NAF Atsugi, JP., 23 SEP 82; To VA-113, NAS LeMoore, CA., 23 SEP 82 ** Transferred to VA-122/FRS, NJ/224, NAS LeMoore, CA., 24 FEB 83; To VA-122, NAS Jacksonville, FL., 21 OCT 83 ** Transferred to VA-97/CVW-15, NL/3XX, NAS LeMoore, CA., 13 JAN 84; To VA-97, USS Carl Vinson (CVN-70), 13 JAN 84; To VA-97, NAS LeMoore, CA., 22 APR 84; To VA-97, USS Carl Vinson (CVN-70), 26 APR 84; To VA-97, NAS LeMoore, CA., 26 APR 84; To VA-97, USS Carl Vinson (CVN-70), 26 APR 84 ** Transferred to VA-147/CVW-9, NE/3XX, NAS LeMoore, CA., 14 SEP 84; To VA-147, USS Kitty Hawk (CV-63), 17 JAN 85; To VA-147, NAS LeMoore, CA., 14 APR 86; To VA-147, NAS Jacksonville, FL., 11 JUN 86; To VA-147, NAS LeMoore, CA., 04 SEP 86; To VA-147, USS Kitty Hawk (CV-63), 04 SEP 86; To VA-147, NAS LeMoore, CA., 04 SEP 86 ** End of flight record card ** Transferred to NAD, NAS Jacksonville, FL., 02 AUG 89 ** Transferred to VX-5, NWC China Lake, CA., date unknown ** Transferred to AMARC, Davis Monthan AFB; Tucson, AZ., assigned park code 6A0398; 16 JUL 91 ** 4707.1 flight hours ** TF41A402D engine S/N AE142504 ** Engine records released to DRMO for disposition ** Placed on FMS list with D704 Buddy Store at NAS Fallon, NV., 10 MAY 05.

E-568 160736 Navy acceptance from NPRO Rep. LTV, Dallas, TX., 01 JUN 79 ** Transferred to VA-174/FRS, AD/4XX, NAS Cecil Field, FL., 03 JUN 79 ** Transferred to VA-15/CVW-6, AE/3XX, NAS Cecil Field, FL., 26 FEB 80; To VA-15, USS Independence (CV-62), 26 FEB 80; To VA-15, NAS Cecil Field, FL., 26 FEB 80; To VA-15, NAS Jacksonville, FL., 25 SEP 81; To VA-15, NAS Cecil Field, FL., 10 NOV 81; To VA-15, USS Independence (CV-62), 10 NOV 81; To VA-15, NAS Cecil Field, FL., 10 NOV 81; To VA-15, USS Independence (CV-62), 10 NOV 81; To VA-15, NAS Cecil Field, FL., 10 NOV 81; To VA-15, USS Independence (CV-62), 10 NOV 81; To VA-15, NAS Cecil Field, FL., 10 NOV 81 ** Transferred to VA-66/CVW-7, AG/3XX, USS Dwight D. Eisenhower (CVN-69), 06 MAR 83; To VA-66, NAS Cecil Field, FL., 08 DEC 83; To VA-66, NAS Jacksonville, FL., 08 DEC 83; To VA-66, NAS Cecil Field, FL., 28 MAR 84; To VA-66, USS Dwight D. Eisenhower (CVN-69), 28 MAR 84; To VA-66, NAS Cecil Field, FL., 28 MAR 84; To VA-66, USS Dwight D. Eisenhower (CVN-69), 28 MAR 84; To VA-66, NAS Cecil Field, FL., 28 MAR 84; To VA-66, USS Dwight D. Eisenhower (CVN-69), 28 MAR 84; To VA-66, NAS Cecil Field, FL., 28 MAR 84; To VA-66, USS Dwight D. Eisenhower (CVN-69), 28 MAR 84; To VA-66, NAS Cecil Field, FL., 28 MAR 84; To VA-66, USS Dwight D. Eisenhower (CVN-69), 28 MAR 84; To VA-66, NAS Jacksonville, FL., 30 JAN 86; To VA-66, NAS Cecil Field, FL., 24 FEB 86; To VA-66, NAS Jacksonville, FL., 07 APR 86; To VA-66, NAS Cecil Field, FL., 09 APR 86; To VA-66, USS John F. Kennedy (CV-67), 09 APR 86; To VA-66, NAS Cecil Field, FL., 20 NOV 86 ** Transferred to VA-37/CVW-3, AC/307, NAS Cecil Field, FL., 19 MAR 87; To VA-37, USS Forrestal (CV-59), 07 JUN 87 ** End of flight record card ** Transferred to the Helenic Air force (Greee).

E-569 160737 Navy acceptance from NPRO Rep. LTV, Dallas, TX., 24 JUL 79 ** Transferred to VA-122/FRS, NJ/2XX, NAS LeMoore, CA., 25 JUL 79 ** Transferred to VA-22/CVW-15, NL/3XX, NAS LeMoore, CA., 23 APR 80; To VA-22, USS Kitty Hawk (CV-63), 11 SEP 80; To VA-22, NAS LeMoore, CA., 13 JAN

81; To VA-22, USS Kitty Hawk (CV-63), 22 JAN 81; To VA-22, NAS LeMoore, CA., 25 MAR 81; To VA-22, NAS Jacksonville, FL., 15 DEC 81; To VA-22, NAS LeMoore, CA., 27 JAN 82; To VA-22, USS Enterprise (CVN-65), 15 MAR 82; To VA-22, NAS LeMoore, CA., 15 MAR 82; To VA-22/CVW-11, NH/3XX, USS Enterprise (CVN-65), 17 DEC 83; To VA-22, NAS LeMoore, CA., 14 FEB 84; To VA-22, NAS Jacksonville, FL., 27 FEB 84; To VA-22, NAS LeMoore, CA., 27 APR 84; To VA-22, USS Enterprise (CVN-65), 27 APR 84 ** Transferred to VA-56/CVW-5, NF/4XX, NAF Atsugi, JP., 11 NOV 84; To VA-56, NAS LeMoore, CA., 27 JUL 85 ** Transferred to VA-146/CVW-9, NE/3XX, NAS LeMoore, CA., 25 APR 86; To VA-146, NAS Jacksonville, FL., 23 JUL 86; To VA-146, NAS LeMoore, CA., 19 SEP 86; To VA-146, USS Kitty Hawk (CV-63), 08 DEC 86; To VA-146, NAS LeMoore, CA., 14 APR 87 ** End of flight record card.

E-570 160738 Navy acceptance from NPRO Rep. LTV, Dallas, TX., 12 SEP 79 ** Transferred to VA-174/FRS, AD/4XX, NAS Cecil Field, FL., 21 SEP 79 ** Transferred to VA-15/CVW-6, AE/300, NAS Cecil Field, FL., 21 MAR 80; To VA-15, USS Independence (CV-62), 14 APR 80; To VA-15, NAS Cecil Field, FL., 14 APR 80; To VA-15, NAS Jacksonville, FL., 08 DEC 81; To VA-15, NAS Cecil Field, FL., 23 DEC 81; To VA-15, USS Independence (CV-62), 19 JAN 82; To VA-15, NAS Cecil Field, FL., 19 JAN 82; To VA-15, USS Independence (CV-62), 19 JAN 82; To VA-15, NAS Cecil Field, FL., 19 JAN 82; To VA-15, USS Independence (CV-62), 19 JAN 82; To VA-15, NAS Cecil Field, FL., 19 JAN 82; To VA-15, USS Independence (CV-62), 25 FEB 83; To VA-15, NAS Cecil Field, FL., 25 FEB 83; To VA-15, USS Independence (CV-62), 25 JUL 83; To VA-15, NAS Cecil Field, FL., 08 AUG 83; To VA-15, USS Independence (CV-62), 01 OCT 83; To VA-15, NAS Cecil Field, FL., 01 MAY 84; To VA-15, NAS Jacksonville, FL., 21 MAY 84; To VA-15, USS Independence (CV-62), 03 AUG 84; To VA-15, NAS Cecil Field, FL., 13 SEP 84; To VA-15, USS Independence (CV-62), 28 SEP 84 ~ S 1SO strike, 24 DEC 84 ** Pilot saved after the aircraft crashed into the Sea.

E-571 160739 Navy acceptance from NPRO Rep. LTV, Dallas, TX., 27 SEP 79 ** Transferred to VA-122/FRS, NJ/2XX, NAS LeMoore, CA., 04 OCT 79 ** Transferred to VA-147/CVW-9, NG/4XX, NAS LeMoore, CA., 17 DEC 79; To VA-147, USS Constellation (CV-64), 17 DEC 79; To VA-147, NAS LeMoore, CA., 23 JAN 80; To VA-147, USS Constellation (CV-64), 26 FEB 80; To VA-147, NAS Cubi Point, PI., 18 APR 80 ** Transferred to VA-93/CVW-5, NF/3XX, NAF Atsugi, JP., 21 APR 80; To VA-93, USS Midway (CV-41), 23 JUN 80; To VA-93, NAF Atsugi, JP., 20 DEC 80; To VA-93, NAS Cubi Point, PI., 28 JAN 81; To VA-93, USS Midway (CV-41), 24 FEB 81; To VA-93, NAF Atsugi, JP., 04 JUN 81; To VA-93, Korea, 15 JUL 81; To VA-93, USS Midway (CV-41), 03 SEP 81; To VA-93, NAF Atsugi, JP., 04 OCT 81; To VA-93, USS Midway (CV-41), 30 OCT 81; To VA-93, NAF Atsugi, JP., 18 JAN 82; To VA-93, USS Midway (CV-41), 18 MAR 82; To VA-93, NAF Atsugi, JP., 27 MAY 82; To VA-93, USS Midway (CV-41), 04 JUN 82; To VA-93, NAS Cubi Point, PI., 04 APR 82 ** Transferred to VA-113/CVW-2, NE/3XX, NAF Atsugi, JP., 23 SEP 82; To VA-113, NAS LeMoore, CA., 23 SEP 82 ** Transferred to VA-122/FRS, NJ/2XX, NAS LeMoore, CA., 25 MAR 83; To VA-122, NAS Jacksonville, FL., 29 MAY 84; To VA-122, NAS LeMoore, CA., 17 AUG 84 ** Transferred to VA-146/CVW-9, NE/3XX, NAS LeMoore, CA., 10 MAY 85; To VA-146, USS Kitty Hawk (CV-63), 10 MAY 85; To VA-146, NAS LeMoore, CA., 28 MAY 85; To VA-146, USS Kitty Hawk (CV-63), 18 JAN 87; To VA-146, NAS LeMoore, CA., 21 FEB 87 thru 25 AUG 87 ** End of flight record card ** Transferred to NAD, NAS Jacksonville, FL., 23 APR 88 ** Transferred to VA-27/CVW-15, NL/412, NAS LeMoore, CA., date unknown ** Transferred to AMARC, Davis Monthan AFB; Tucson, AZ., assigned park code 6A0387, 14 NOV 90 ** 5248.3 flight hours ** TF41A402D engine S/N 142522 ** Aircraft released from storage and prepared for overland shipping to FMS and NAD, NAS Jacksonville, FL., with final shipping to the government of Thailand, 20 JUN 94 ** Transferred to the Royal Thai Navy, S/N 1402.

160857/160868 LTV A-7E Corsair II; (Block XXVIII)
FY 78 Contract N00019-77-C-0437 (12) A-7E; E-573/E-584

E-584 160857 Navy acceptance from NPRO Rep. LTV, Dallas, TX., 27 SEP 79 ** Transferred to NATC, NATC/XXX, NAS Patuxent River, MD, for RDT & E, 19 FEB 80; Transferred to NWC China Lake, CA., NWC/XXX, 20 FEB 80; Transferred to VX-5, XE/XXX, NWC China Lake, CA., 01 FEB 84 ** Transferred to NWC China Lake, CA., NWC/XXX, 15 MAY 84 thru 22 JUL 87 ** End of flight record card ** Transferred to the Helenic Air force (Greee).

E-573 160858 Navy acceptance from NPRO Rep. LTV, Dallas, TX., 16 NOV 79 ** Transferred to VA-122/FRS, NJ/2XX, NAS LeMoore, CA., 18 NOV 79 ** Transferred to VA-94/CVW-15, NL/4XX, USS Kitty Hawk (CV-63), 30 SEP 80; To VA-94, NAS LeMoore, CA., 30 OCT 80; To VA-94, USS Kitty Hawk (CV-63), 27 FEB 81 ** Transferred to VA-22/CVW-15, NL/3XX, USS Kitty Hawk (CV-63), 09 APR 81; To VA-22, NAS LeMoore, CA., 09 APR 81; To VA-22, NAS Jacksonville, FL., 14 DEC 81 ** Transferred to VA-192/CVW-11, NH/3XX, NAS LeMoore, CA., 03 FEB 82 ** Transferred to VA-25/CVW-2, NE/4XX, NAS LeMoore, CA., 07 DEC 82 ** Transferred to VA-97/CVW-15, NL/3XX, NAS LeMoore, CA., 03 OCT 83; To VA-97, NAS Jacksonville, FL., 06 FEB 84; To VA-97, USS Carl Vinson, (CVN-70), 08 FEB 84; To VA-97, NAS Jacksonville, FL., 26 APR 84; To VA-97, USS Carl Vinson, (CVN-70), 26 APR 84 ** Transferred to VA-27/CVW-15, NL/4XX, USS Carl Vinson (CVN-70), 04 MAY 84; To VA-27, NAS LeMoore, CA., 30 MAY 84; To VA-27, USS Carl Vinson (CVN-70), 20 SEP 84; To VA-27, NAS LeMoore, CA., 20 SEP 84; To VA-27, USS Carl Vinson (CVN-70), 30 APR 86 ** Transferred to VA-122/FRS, NJ/2XX, NAS LeMoore, CA., 13 MAY 86 ~ S 1SO strike, 20 MAY 86 ** No data on crash.

E-574 160859 Navy acceptance from NPRO Rep. LTV, Dallas, TX., 19 DEC 79 ** Transferred to VA-15/CVW-6, AE/305, USS Independence (CV-62), 23 DEC 79; To VA-15, NAS Cecil Field, FL., 21 OCT 80; To VA-15, NAS Jacksonville, FL., 28 JAN 82; To VA-15, USS Independence (CV-62), 12 FEB 82; To VA-15, NAS Cecil Field, FL., 10 MAR 82; To VA-15, USS Independence (CV-62), 10 MAR 82; To VA-15, NAS Cecil Field, FL., 10 MAR 82; To VA-15, USS Independence (CV-62), 22 MAR 83; To VA-15, NAS Cecil Field, FL., 22 MAR 83; To VA-15, USS Independence (CV-62), 22 MAR 83; To VA-15, NAS Cecil Field, FL., 22 MAR 83; To VA-15, USS Independence (CV-62), 22 MAR 83; To VA-15, NAS Cecil Field, FL., 20 APR 84; To VA-15, USS Independence (CV-62), 16 MAY 84; To VA-15, NAS Cecil Field, FL., 19 SEP 84; To VA-15, USS Independence (CV-62), 24 SEP 84; To VA-15, NAS Jacksonville, FL., 30 NOV 84 ** Transferred to NAD, NAS Jacksonville, FL., 02 DEC 84 ** Transferred to VA-72/CVW-1, AB/4XX, NAS Cecil Field, FL., 03 DEC 84; To VA-72, USS America (CV-66), 01 MAR 85; To VA-72, NAS Cecil Field, FL., 22 OCT 85; To VA-72, USS America (CV-66), 15 NOV 85; To VA-72, NAS Cecil Field, FL., 11 JUN 86; To VA-72, USS Dwight D. Eisenhower (CVN-69), 15 OCT 86; To VA-72, NAS Cecil Field, FL., 15 OCT 86 thru 15 SEP 87 ** End of flight record card ** Transferred to AMARC, Davis Monthan AFB; Tucson, AZ., assigned park code 6A0251, 25 FEB 88 ** 3941.3 flight hours ** TF41A402D engine S/N 141457 ** Aircraft released from storage and prepared for overland shipping to FMS and NAD, NAS Jacksonville, FL., with final shipping to the government of Thailand, 06 DEC 94 ** Transferred to the Royal Thai Navy, S/N 1403.

E-575 160860 Navy acceptance from NPRO Rep. LTV, Dallas, TX., 15 JAN 80 ** Transferred to VA-15/CVW-6, AE/3XX, USS Independence (CV-62), 19 JAN 80; To VA-15, NAS Cecil Field, FL., 03 JUN 80; To VA-15, USS Independence (CV-62), 02 JUL 80 ~ S 1SO strike, 15 JAN 81 ** No data on strike.

E-576 160861 Navy acceptance from NPRO Rep. LTV, Dallas, TX., 11 FEB 80 ** Transferred to VA-15/CVW-6, AE/3XX, USS Independence (CV-62), 12 FEB 80; To VA-15, NAS Cecil Field, FL., 22 AUG 80; To VA-15, USS Independence (CV-62), 16 SEP 80 ~ S 1SO strike, 20 FEB 81 ** No data on strike.

E-577 160862 Navy acceptance from NPRO Rep. LTV, Dallas, TX., 12 MAR 80 ** Transferred to VA-122/FRS. NJ/2XX, NAS LeMoore, CA., 02 APR 80 ** Transferred to VA-94/CVW-15, NL/4XX, NAS LeMoore, CA., 15 APR 80; To VA-94, USS Kitty Hawk (CV-63), 27 JUL 80; To VA-94, NAS LeMoore, CA., 27 JUL 80; To VA-94, USS Kitty Hawk (CV-63), 11 SEP 80; To VA-94, NAS LeMoore, CA., 27 FEB 81 ** Transferred to VA-22/CVW-15, NL/3XX, USS Kitty Hawk (CV-63), 02 APR 81; To VA-22, NAF Atsugi, JP., 29 APR 81; To VA-22, USS Kitty Hawk (CV-63), 08 MAY 81; To VA-22, NAS LeMoore, CA., 08 MAY 81; To VA-22, NAS Jacksonville, FL., 21 MAR 82; To VA-22, NAS LeMoore, CA., 28 APR 82; To VA-22/CVW-11, NH/3XX, USS Enterprise (CVN-65), 28 APR 82 ** To VA-22, NAS LeMoore, CA., 31 JAN 83 ** Transferred to VA-192/ CVW-9, NG/3XX, NAS LeMoore, CA., 30 JUN 83; To VA-192, USS Ranger (CV-61), 06 JUL 83; To VA-192, NAS LeMoore, CA., 26 AUG 83 ** Transferred to VA-97/CVW-15, NL/3XX, USS Carl Vinson (CVN-70), 14 MAR 84; To VA-97, NAS LeMoore, CA., 22 APR 84; To VA-97, USS Carl Vinson (CVN-70), 27 APR 84; To VA-97, NAS LeMoore, CA., 27 APR 84; To VA-97, USS Carl Vinson (CVN-70), 21 JUL 84 ** Transferred to VA-192/CVW-9, NG/3XX, NAS LeMoore, CA., 13 AUG 84; To VA-192, NAS Jacksonville, FL., 13 JUN 85 ** Transferred to VA-94/CVW-11, NH/4XX, NAS LeMoore, CA., 17 JUN 85 ** Transferred to VA-146/CVW-9, NE/3XX, USS Kitty Hawk (CV-63), 19 JUL 85; To VA-146, NAS LeMoore, CA., 14 SEP 85 ** Transferred to VA-147/CVW-9, NE/3XX, NAS LeMoore, CA., 30 SEP 86; To VA-147, USS Kitty Hawk (CV-63), 16 OCT 86; To VA-147, NAS LeMoore, CA., 16 OCT 86 ** Transferred to VA-27/ CVW-15, NL/4XX, NAS LeMoore, CA., 05 AUG 87 ** End of flight record card ** Transferred to the Helenic Air force (Greee).

E-578 160863 Navy acceptance from NPRO Rep. LTV, Dallas, TX., 29 APR 80 ** Transferred to VA-15/CVW-6, AE/3XX, NAS Cecil Field, FL., 30 APR 80; To VA-15, USS Independence (CV-62), 30 APR 80; To VA-15, NAS Cecil Field, FL., 30 APR 80; To VA-15, USS Independence (CV-62), 24 JAN 82; To VA-15, NAS Cecil Field, FL., 24 JAN 82; To VA-15, USS Independence (CV-62), 24 JAN 82 ** Transferred to VA-86/CVW-8, AJ/4XX, NAS Cecil Field, FL., 01 APR 82; To VA-86, NAS Jacksonville, FL., 24 MAY 82; To VA-86, USS Nimitz (CVN-68), 27 JUL 82; To VA-86, NAS Cecil Field, FL., 27 JUL 82; To VA-86, USS Nimitz (CVN-68), 27 JUL 82; To VA-86, NAS Cecil Field, FL.,27 JUL 82; To VA-86, USS Nimitz (CVN-68), 27 JUL 82 ~ S 1SO strike, 11 FEB 83 ** Pilot ejected safely after a mid air collosion with another VA-86 A-7E which landed at Akrotin in eastern Mediteranian.

E-579 160864 Navy acceptance from NPRO Rep. LTV, Dallas, TX., 24 APR 80 ** Transferred to VA-22/CVW-15, NL/3XX, NAS LeMoore, CA., 28 APR 80; To VA-22, USS Kitty Hawk (CV-63), 11 SEP 80; To VA-22, NAS LeMoore, CA., 13 JAN 81; To VA-22, USS Kitty Hawk (CV-63), 05 MAR 81; To VA-22, NAS LeMoore, CA., 25 MAR 81; To VA-22, NAS Alameda, CA., 25 FEB 82; To VA-22, NAS LeMoore, CA., 26 FEB 82 ** Transferred to NARF, NAS Alameda, CA., 23 APR 82 ** Transferred to VA-192/CVW-11, NH/3XX, NAS LeMoore, CA., 07 JUL 84; To VA-192, NAS Jacksonville, FL. 15 OCT 84; To VA-192, NAS LeMoore, CA., 07 DEC 84 ** Transferred to VA-146/CVW-9, NE/3XX, NAS LeMoore, CA., 11 DEC 84; To VA-146, USS Kitty Hawk (CV-63), 13 FEB 85; To VA-146, NAS LeMoore, CA., 24 AUG 85 ** Transferred to VA-97/CVW-15, NL/3XX, USS Carl Vinson (CVN-70), 24 APR 86; To VA-97, NAS LeMoore, CA., 24 APR 86; To VA-97, USS Carl Vinson (CVN-70), 31 AUG 86; To VA-97, NAS Alameda, CA., 18 JAN 87; To VA-97, NAS Jacksonville, FL., 09 JUN 87; To VA-97, NAS Alameda, CA., 09 JUN 87; To VA-97, NAS Jacksonville, FL., 11 JUN 87; To VA-97, NAS Alameda, CA., 04 SEP 87 ** End of flight record card ** Transferred to the U.S. Army at Holloman AFB; Alamogordo, NM., for the Patriot missile program, date unknown ** Transferred to AMARC, Davis Monthan AFB; Tucson, AZ., assigned park code 6A0385, 30 OCT 90 ** 3873.3 flight hours ** TF41A402D engine S/N 141403 ** Aircraft released from storage and prepared for overland and above deck shipping to the government of Greece, 11 AUG 94 ** Transferred to the Helenic Air force (Greee).

E-580 160865 Navy acceptance from NPRO Rep. LTV, Dallas, TX., 23 MAY 80 ** Transferred to VA-15/CVW-15, NL/ 3XX, NAS Cecil Field, FL., 11 JUL 80; To VA-15, USS Independence (CV-62), 11 JUL 80; To VA-15, NAS Cecil Field, FL.., 11 JUL 80; To VA-15, USS Independence (CV-62), 11 JUL 80; To VA-15, NAS Cecil Field, FL.., 11 JUL 80; To VA-15, USS Independence (CV-62), 11 JUL 80; To VA-15, NAS Cecil Field, FL.., 11 JUL 80; To VA-15, USS Independence (CV-62), 11 JUL 80; To VA-15, NAS Cecil Field, FL.., 11 JUL 80; To VA-15, NAS Jacksonville, FL., 27 JAN 83; To VA-15, NAS Cecil Field, FL.., 11 MAR 83; To VA-15, USS Independence (CV-62), 03 JUN 83; To VA-15, NAS Cecil Field, FL.., 03 JUN 83; To VA-15, USS Independence (CV-62), 03 JUN 83; To VA-15, NAS Cecil Field, FL.., 03 JUN 83; To VA-15, USS Independence (CV-62), 03 JUN 83; To VA-15, NAS Cecil Field, FL.., 03 JUN 83; To VA-15, USS Independence (CV-62), 10 MAY 84; To VA-15, NAS Cecil Field, FL.., 19 SEP 84; To VA-15, USS Independence (CV-62), 24 SEP 84 ** Transferred to VA-82/CVW-8, AJ/3XX, NAS Cecil Field, 09 OCT 84; To VA-82, USS Nimitz (CVN-68), 23 NOV 84 ** Transferred to VA-46/CVW-1, AB/ 3XX, NAS Cecil Field, FL., 26 NOV 84; To VA-46, NAS Jacksonville, FL., 05 APR 85; To VA-46, USS America (CV-66), 08 APR 85; To VA-46, NAS Jacksonville, FL., 26 JUN 85; To VA-46, NAS Cecil Field, FL., 27 JUN 85; To VA-46, USS America (CV-66), 27 JUN 85; To VA-46, NAS LeMoore, CA., 27 JUN 85 ** Transferred to VA-174/FRS, AD/4XX, NAS Cecil Field, FL., 27 JUN 85 ** Transferred to VA-81/CVW-17, AA/4XX, NAS Cecil Field, FL., 14 NOV 86; To VA-81, USS Saratoga (CV-60), 16 DEC 86; To VA-81, NAS Cecil Field, FL., 07 APR 87; To VA-81, USS Saratoga (CV-60), 09 APR 87; To VA-81, NAS Cecil Field, FL., 09 APR 87; To VA-81, USS Saratoga (CV-60), 09 APR 87 ** End of flight record card ** Transferred to the Helinic Air Force (Greece).

E-581 160866 Navy acceptance from NPRO Rep. LTV, Dallas, TX., 24 JUN 80 ** Transferred to VA-22/CVW-15, NL/3XX, USS Kitty Hawk (CV-63), 21 NOV 80; To VA-22, NAS LeMoore, CA., 13 JAN 81; To VA-22, USS Kitty Hawk (CV-63), 06 MAR 81; To VA-22, NAS Dallas, TX., 11 MAR 81 ** Transferred to VA-146/CVW-9, NG/3XX, NAS LeMoore, CA., 06 APR 81 ** To VA-146, USS Constellation (CV-64) 08 JUL 81; To VA-146, NAS LeMoore, CA., 06 AUG 81; To VA-146, USS Constellation (CV-64) 11 SEP 81; To VA-146, NAS LeMoore, CA., 20 OCT 81; To VA-146, NAS Jacksonville, FL., 13 DEC 82; To VA-146, NAS LeMoore, CA., 31 JAN 83 ** Transferred to VA-94/ CVW-11, NH/4XX, NAS LeMoore, CA., 28 JUN 83; To VA-94, USS Enterprise (CVN-65), 02 DEC 83; To VA-94, NAS LeMoore, CA., 02 DEC 83; To VA-94, USS Enterprise (CVN-65), 02 DEC 83; To VA-94, NAS LeMoore, CA., 02 DEC 83; To VA-94, USS Enterprise (CVN-65), 02 DEC 83; To VA-94, NAS LeMoore, CA., 21 DEC 84; To VA-94, NAS Jacksonville, FL., 10 JAN 85; To VA-94, NAS Fallon, NV., 13 APR 85; To VA-94, NAS LeMoore, CA., 13 APR 85; To VA-94, USS Enterprise (CVN-65), 18 SEP 85; To VA-94, NAS LeMoore, CA., 19 FEB 86 thru 11 JUN 87 ** Transferred to PMTC, NAS Point Mugu, CA., Modex 81, date unknown ** End of flight record card ** Transferred to AMARC, Davis Monthan AFB; Tucson, AZ., assigned park code 6A0401, 10 SEP 91 ** 4939.2 flight hours ** TF41A402D engine S/N AE142583 ** Prepare for overland and above deck shipment to Stellar Freight; Galveston, TX., for the government of Greece, no later than, 30 SEP 95 ** Transferred to the Helenic Air Force (Greece) ~ S 1SO strike, 29 OCT 87 ** No data on strike.

E-582 160867 Navy acceptance from NPRO Rep. LTV, Dallas, TX., 24 JUN 80 ** Transferred to VA-83/CVW-17, AA/3XX, USS Forrestal (CV-59), 04 NOV 80; To VA-83, NAS Cecil Field, FL., 04 NOV 80; To VA-83, USS Forrestal (CV-59), 04 NOV 80; To VA-83, NAS Cecil Field,FL., 04 NOV 80; To VA-83, NAS Fallon, NV., 04 NOV 80; To VA-83, NAS Cecil Field,FL., 04 NOV 80; To VA-83, USS Forrestal (CV-59), 04 NOV 80; To VA-83, NAS Cecil Field,FL., 04 NOV 80; To VA-83, USS Forrestal (CV-59), 04 NOV 80; To VA-83, NAS Cecil Field,FL., 04 NOV 80; To VA-83, NAS Jacksonville, FL., 03 JAN 83; To VA-83, NAS Cecil Field,FL., 17 FEB 83; To VA-83, NAS Jacksonville, FL., 16 FEB 83; To VA-83, NAS Cecil Field, FL., 17 FEB 83; To VA-83, NAS Fallon, NV., 26 AUG 83; To VA-83, NAS Cecil Field, FL., 01 SEP 83; To VA-83, USS Saratoga (CV-60),

02 SEP 83; To VA-83, NAS Cecil Field, FL., 02 SEP 83; To VA-83, USS Saratoga (CV-60), 02 SEP 83; To VA-83, NAS Cecil Field,FL., 02 SEP 83; To VA-83, NAS Jacksonville, FL., 31 OCT 84; To VA-83, NAS Fallon, NV., 02 NOV 84; To VA-83, NAS Jacksonville, FL., 29 JAN 85; To VA-83, NAS Cecil Field, FL., 31 JAN 85; To VA-83, USS Saratoga (CV-60), 06 MAY 85; To VA-83, NAS Cecil Field, FL., 08 MAY 85; To VA-83, USS Saratoga (CV-60), 08 MAY 85; To VA-83, NAS Cecil Field, FL., 08 MAY 85 ** Transferred to VA-82/CVW-8, AJ/3XX, NAS Cecil Field, FL., 25 JUL 86; To VA-82, USS Nimitz (CVN-68), 03 AUG 86; To VA-82, NAS Cecil Field, FL., 10 OCT 86; To VA-82, USS Nimitz (CVN-68), 10 OCT 86; To VA-82, NAS Cecil Field, FL., 10 OCT 86 thru 21 SEP 87 ** End of flight record card ** Transferred to the Helenic Air force (Greee).

E-583 160868 Navy acceptance from NPRO Rep. LTV, Dallas, TX., 23 JUL 80 ** Transferred to VA-122/FRS, NJ/2XX, NAS LeMoore, CA., 27 DEC 80 ** Transferred to VA-146/CVW-9, NG/3XX, NAS LeMoore, CA.,, 12 MAY 81; To VA-146, USS Constellation (CV-64), 08 JUL 81; To VA-146, NAS LeMoore, CA., 06 AUG 81; To VA-146, USS Constellation (CV-64), 11 SEP 80 ** Transferred to VA-93/CVW-5, NF/3XX, USS Midway (CV-41), 20 APR 82; To VA-93, NAS Cubi Point, PI., 20 APR 82; To VA-93, NAF Atsugi, JP., 15 NOV 82; To VA-93, NAS Cubi Point, PI., 17 NOV 82; To VA-93, NAF Atsugi, JP., 09 DEC 82; To VA-93, USS Midway (CV-41), 28 JAN 83; To VA-93, NAF Atsugi, JP., 30 SEP 83; To VA-93, NAS LeMoore, CA., 17 APR 86 ** Transferred to VA-122/FRS, NJ/2XX, NAS LeMoore, CA., 15 MAY 86; To VA-122, NAS Pensacola, FL., 18 MAR 87; To VA-122, NAS LeMoore, CA., 22 SEP 87 ** End of flight record card ** Transferred to the Helenic Air force (Greee).

160869/160880 LTV A-7E Corsair II (Block XXIX)
FY 79 Contract N00019-79-C-0034 (12) A-7E; E-585/E-596

E-596 160869 Navy acceptance from NPRO Rep. LTV, Dallas, TX., 20 OCT 80 ** Transferred to VA-15/CVW-6, AE/3XX, USS Independence (CV-62), 21 OCT 80; To VA-15, NAS Cecil Field, FL., 21 OCT 80; To VA-15, USS Independence (CV-62), 21 OCT 80; To VA-15, NAS Cecil Field, FL., 21 OCT 80; To VA-15, USS Independence (CV-62), 21 OCT 80; To VA-15, NAS Cecil Field, FL., 21 OCT 80; To VA-15, USS Independence (CV-62), 21 OCT 80; To VA-15, NAS Cecil Field, FL., 21 OCT 80; To VA-15, NAS Jacksonville, FL., 14 FEB 83; To VA-15, NAS Cecil Field, FL., 08 APR 83; To VA-15, USS Independence (CV-62), 13 JUN 83; To VA-15, NAS Cecil Field, FL., 20 JUN 83; To VA-15, USS Independence (CV-62), 20 JUN 83; To VA-15, NAS Cecil Field, FL., 20 JUN 83; To VA-15, USS Independence (CV-62), 20 JUN 83; To VA-15, NAS Cecil Field, FL., 20 JUN 83; To VA-15, USS Independence (CV-62), 25 MAY 84; To VA-15, NAS Cecil Field, FL., 25 MAY 84; To VA-15, USS Independence (CV-62), 25 MAY 84 ** Transferred to VA-83/CVW-17, AA/3XX, NAS Cecil Field, FL., 08 OCT 84; To VA-83, NAS Fallon, NV., 06 NOV 84; To VA-83, NAS Jacksonville, FL., 22 FEB 85; To VA-83, NAS Cecil Field, FL., 22 FEB 85; To VA-83, NAS Jacksonville, FL., 25 FEB 85; To VA-83, USS Saratoga (CV-60), 02 MAY 85; To VA-83, NAS Cecil Field, FL., 13 MAY 85; To VA-83, USS Saratoga (CV-60), 13 MAY 85 ** Transferred to VA-174/FRS, AD/4XX, NAS Cecil Field, FL., 22 AUG 85 ** Transferred to VA-105/CVW-6, AE/4XX, NAS Cecil Field, FL., 20 OCT 85; To VA-105, USS Forrestal (CV-59), 20 OCT 85; To VA-105, NAS Cecil Field, FL., 20 OCT 85; To VA-105, USS Forrestal (CV-59), 13 OCT 86; To VA-105, NAS Cecil Field, FL., 13 OCT 86; To VA-105, USS Forrestal (CV-59), 13 JUL 87 thru 16 JUL 87 ** End of flight record card ** On conditional loan from the National Museum of Naval Aviation; Pensacola, FL., to the Dyersburg Arm, Air Base Memorial.

E-585 160870 Navy acceptance from NPRO Rep. LTV, Dallas, TX., 09 OCT 80 ** Transferred to VA-122/FRS, NJ/2XX, NAS LeMoore, CA., 10 OCT 80 ** Transferred to VA-146/CVW-9, NG/3XX, NAS LeMoore, CA., 23 APR 81; To VA-146, USS Constellation (CV-64), 08 JUL 81; To VA-146, NAS LeMoore, CA., 06 AUG 81; To VA-146, USS Constellation (CV-64), 11 SEP 81; To VA-146, NAS LeMoore, CA., 20 OCT 81; To VA-146, NAS Jacksonville, FL., 28 MAR 83; To VA-146, NAS LeMoore, CA., 12 MAY 83 ** Transferred to VA-94/CVW-11, NH/4XX, NAS LeMoore, CA., 24 OCT 83; To VA-94, USS Enterprise (CVN-65), 24 OCT 83; To VA-94, NAS LeMoore, CA., 28 FEB 84; To VA-94, USS Enterprise (CVN-65), 28 FEB 84; To VA-94, NAS LeMoore, CA., 04 MAR 84; To VA-94, USS Enterprise (CVN-65), 04 MAR 84; To VA-94, NAS LeMoore, CA., 27 DEC 84; To VA-94, NAS Jacksonville, FL., 10 JAN 85; To VA-94, NAS LeMoore, CA., 10 JAN 85; To VA-94, NAS Jacksonville, FL., 14 JAN 85; To VA-94, NAS LeMoore, CA., 29 MAR 85; To VA-94, NAS Fallon, NV., 29 MAR 85; To VA-94, NAS LeMoore, CA., 29 MAR 85; To VA-94, USS Enterprise (CVN-65), 12 SEP 85; To VA-94, NAS LeMoore, CA., 25 JUN 86 thru 17 JUN 87 ** End of flight record card.

E-586 160871 Navy acceptance from NPRO Rep. LTV, Dallas, TX., 07 NOV 80 ** Transferred to VA-83/CVW-17, AA/3XX, NAS Cecil Field, FL., 10 NOV 80 ** Transferred to VA-174/FRS, AD/4XX, NAS Cecil Field, FL., 30 DEC 80 ** Transferred to VA-105/CVW-3, AC/402, NAS Fallon,NV., 07 APR 81; To VA-105, NAS Cecil Field, FL., 07 APR 81; To VA-105, USS John F. Kennedy (CV-67), 07 APR 81; To VA-105, NAS Cecil Field, FL., 07 APR 81; To VA-105, NAS Jacksonville, FL., 18 OCT 82; To VA-105, NAS Cecil Field, FL., 30 NOV 82; To VA-105/CVW-15, NL/4XX, USS Carl Vinson (CVN-70), 30 NOV 82; To VA-105, NAS Cecil Field, FL., 30 NOV 82; To VA-105, USS Carl Vinson (CVN-70), 30 NOV 82; To VA-105, NAS Cecil Field, FL., 28 OCT 83; To VA-105, NAS Roosevelt Roads, PR., 28 OCT 83; To VA-105, NAS Cecil Field, FL., 28 OCT 83; To VA-105, NAF Kadena, JP., 15 MAY 84; To VA-105, NAS Cubi Point, PI., 15 MAY 84; To VA-105, MCAS Iwakuni, JP., 15 MAY 84; To VA-105/CVW-6, AE/4XX, NAS Cecil Field, FL., 15 MAY 84; To VA-105, NAS Jacksonville, FL., 16 MAY 85; To VA-105, NAS Cecil Field, FL., 20 MAY 85; To VA-105, USS Forrestal (CV-59), 28 MAY 85; To VA-105, NAS Cecil Field, FL., 29 AUG 85 ** Transferred to VA-66/CVW-7, AG/3XX, NAS Cecil Field, FL., 11 DEC 85 ** Transferred to VA-81/CVW-17, AA/3XX, NAS Cecil Field, FL., 06 JUN 86; To VA-81, USS Saratoga (CV-60), 28 JUL 86; To VA-81, NAS Cecil Field, FL., 09 OCT 86; To VA-81, USS Saratoga (CV-60), 17 DEC 86; To VA-81, NAS Cecil Field, FL., 17 DEC 86; To VA-81, USS Saratoga (CV-60), 13 APR 87; To VA-81, NAS Cecil Field, FL., 15 APR 87; To VA-81, USS Saratoga (CV-60), 15 APR 87 thru 05 AUG 87 ** End of flight record card ** Transferred to the Helenic Air Force (Greece) ** Pilot ejected safely, when it crashed on a test flight from Araxos, GR., 26 Mar 02.

E-587 160872 Navy acceptance from NPRO Rep. LTV, Dallas, TX., 20 NOV 80 ** Transferred to VA-94/CVW-15, NL/4XX, NAS LeMoore, CA., 20 NOV 80; To VA-94, USS Kitty Hawk (CV-63), 27 FEB 81 ** Transferred to VA-146/CVW-9, NG/ 3XX, NAS LeMoore, CA., 09 MAR 81; To VA-146, USS Constellation (CV-64), 08 JUL 81; To VA-146, NAS LeMoore, CA., 06 AUG 81; To VA-146, USS Constellation (CV- 64), 11 SEP 81; To VA-146, NAS LeMoore, CA., 20 OCT 81; To VA-146, NAS Jacksonville, FL., 04 MAR 83; To VA-146, NAS LeMoore, CA., 07 APR 83 ** Transferred to VA-94/CVW-11, NH/4XX, NAS LeMoore, CA., 01 SEP 83; To VA-94, USS Enterprise (CVN-65), 11 DEC 83; To VA-94, NAS LeMoore, CA., 11 DEC 83; To VA-94, USS Enterprise (CVN-65), 11 DEC 83; To VA-94, NAS LeMoore, CA., 11 DEC 83; To VA-94, USS Enterprise (CVN-65), 11 DEC 83; To VA-94, NAS LeMoore, CA., 03 JAN 85; To VA-94, NAS Jacksonville, FL., 01 FEB 85; To VA-94, NAS LeMoore, CA., 12 APR 85; To VA-94, USS Enterprise (CVN-65), 24 OCT 85; To VA-94, NAS LeMoore, CA., 02 JUL 86 thru 21 SEP 87 ** End of flight record card ** Transferred to NAD, NAS Jacksonville, FL., 22 FEB 89 ** Transferred to MICOM U.S. Army, Modex 028, Holloman AFB; Alamogordo, NM., date unknown ** Transferred to AMARC, Davis Monthan AFB; Tucson, AZ., assigned park code 6A0413, 14 JUL 92 ** 4516.3 flight hours ** TF41A402D engine S/N 141339 ** Project changed per FSO letter, 06 APR 04 ** Engine records released to DRMO for disposition 17 SEP 04 ** Transferred to Fort Sill; Lawton, OK., to be used as a target on the Falcon range, 25 JAN 05.

E-588 160873 Navy acceptance from NPRO Rep. LTV, Dallas, TX., 02 DEC 80 ** Transferred to VA-37/CVW-3, AC/3XX, NAS Cecil Field, FL., 02 DEC 80; To VA-37, NAS Fallon, NV., 02 DEC 80; To VA-37, NAS Cecil Field, FL., 02 DEC 80; To VA-37, USS John F. Kennedy (CV-67), 02 DEC 80; To VA-37, NAS Cecil Field, FL., 02 DEC 80; To VA-37, USS John F. Kennedy (CV-67), 02 DEC 80; To VA-37, NAS Cecil Field, FL., 02 DEC 80 ** Transferred to VA-105/ CVW-15, NL/4XX, NAS Cecil Field, FL., 30 SEP 82; To VA-105, USS Carl Vinson (CVN-70), 30 SEP 82; To VA-105, NAS Jacksonville, FL., 18 FEB 83 ** Transferred to VA-15/CVW-6, AE/3XX, NAS Cecil Field, FL., 05 APR 83; To VA-15, USS Independence (CV-62), 19 MAY 83; To VA-15, NAS Cecil Field, FL., 19 MAY 83; To VA-15, USS Independence (CV-62), 19 MAY 83; To VA-15, NAS Cecil Field, FL., 29 SEP 83; To VA-15, USS Independence (CV-62), 03 OCT 83; To VA-15, NAS Cecil Field, FL., 03 OCT 83; To VA-15, USS Independence (CV-62), 25 MAY 84; To VA-15, NAS Cecil Field, FL., 17 SEP 84; To VA-15, USS Independence (CV-62), 24 SEP 84 ** Transferred to VA-82/CVW-8, AJ/3XX, NAS Cecil Field, FL., 09 OCT 84; To VA-82, USS Nimitz (CVN-68), 09 OCT 84; To VA-82, NAS Cecil Field, FL., 19 DEC 84; To VA-82, USS Nimitz (CVN-68), 03 MAR 85; To VA-82, NAS Cecil Field, FL., 18 OCT 85; To VA-82, NAS Jacksonville, FL., 22 JAN 86 ** Transferred to VA-105/CVW-6, AE/4XX, NAS Cecil Field, FL., 24 JAN 86; To VA-105, USS Forrestal (CV-59), 04 FEB 86; To VA-105, NAS Cecil Field, FL., 04 FEB 86; To VA-105, USS Forrestal (CV-59), 13 OCT 86; To VA-105, NAS Cecil Field, FL., 13 OCT 86; To VA-105, USS Forrestal (CV-59), 13 JUL 87 ** End of flight record card ** Transferred to the Helenic Air Force (Greee).

E-589 160874 Navy acceptance from NPRO Rep. LTV, Dallas, TX., 14 JAN 81 ** Transferred to VA-122/FRS, NJ/2XX, NAS LeMoore, CA., 15 JAN 81 ** Transferred to VA-146/CVW-9, NG/3XX, NAS LeMoore, CA., 15 MAY 81; To VA-146, USS Constellation (CV-64), 08 JUL 81; To VA-146, NAS LeMoore, CA., 06 AUG 81; To VA-146, USS Constellation (CV-64), 11 SEP 81 ** Transferred to VA-93/CVW-5, NF/3XX, USS Midway (CV-41), 20 APR 82; To VA-93, NAS Cubi Point, PI., 20 APR 82; To VA-93, USS Midway (CV-41), 20 APR 82; To VA-93, NAF Atsugi, JP., 04 FEB 83; To VA-93, USS Midway (CV-41), 29 MAR 83; To VA-93, NAF Atsugi, JP., 15 SEP 83; To VA-93, NAS LeMoore, CA., 25 APR 86 ** Transferred to FAWPRA, NAF Atsugi, JP., 25 APR 86 ** Transferred to VA-147/ CVW-9, NE/3XX, NAS LeMoore, CA., 12 MAY 86; To VA-147, USS Kitty Hawk (CV-63), 27 OCT 86; To VA-147, NAS LeMoore, CA., 27 OCT 86 ** End of flight record, card ** Transferred to VA-72/ CVW-7, AG/4XX, USS Dwight D. Eisenhower (CVN-69), 29 FEB 88; To VA-72, NAS Cecil Field, FL., date unknown ** Transferred to AMARC, Davis Monthan AFB; Tucson, AZ., assigned park code 6A0344, 17 APR 90, with FLIR ** 4334.7 flight hours ** TF41A402D engine S/N 142603 ** Storage location 111201 ** At AMARC, Davis Monthan AFB; Tucson, AZ., 15 JUN 07

E-590 160875 Navy acceptance from NPRO Rep. LTV, Dallas, TX., 18 DEC 80 ** Transferred to VA-83/ CVW-17, AA/305, NAS Cecil Field, FL., 23 DEC 80, Painted light gray on medium gray with black modex; To VA-83, USS Forrestal (CV-59), 30 JAN 81; To VA-83, NAS Cecil Field, FL., 30 JAN 81; To VA-83, NAS Fallon, NV., 30 JAN 81; To VA-83, NAS Cecil Field, FL., 30 JAN 81; To VA-83, USS Forrestal (CV-59), 30 JAN 81; To VA-83, NAS Cecil Field, FL., 30 JAN 81; To VA-83, USS Forrestal (CV-59), 30 JAN 81; To VA-83, NAS Cecil Field, FL., 30 JAN 81; To VA-83, NAS Jacksonville, FL., 04 JAN 83; To VA-83, NAS Cecil Field, FL., 31 JAN 83; To VA-83, NAS Jacksonville, FL., 09 MAR 83; To VA-83, NAS Cecil Field, FL., 10 MAR 83; To VA-83, NAS Fallon, NV., 10 MAR 83; To VA-83, NAS Cecil Field, FL., 10 MAR 83; To VA-83, USS Saratoga (CV-60), 10 MAR 83; To VA-83, NAS Cecil Field, FL., 07 FEB 84; To VA-83, USS Saratoga CV-60), 08 MAR 84; To VA-83, NAS Cecil Field, FL., 08 MAR 84; To VA-83, NAS Fallon, NV., 07 NOV 84; To VA-83, NAS Cecil Field, FL., 07 NOV 84; To VA-83, USS Saratoga (CV-60), 07 NOV 84; To VA-83, NAS Cecil Field, FL., 07 FEB 84; To VA-83, USS Saratoga (CV-60), 22 AUG 85; To VA-83, NAS Jacksonville, FL., 03 SEP 85 ** Transferred to NARF, NAS Jacksonville, FL., 06 DEC 85 ** Transferred to VA-86/CVW-8, AJ/4XX, NAS Cecil Field, FL., 10 DEC 85; To VA-86, USS Nimitz (CVN-68), 10 DEC 85; To

VA-86, NAS Cecil Field, FL., 10 DEC 85; To VA-86, USS Nimitz (CVN-68), 10 DEC 85; To VA-86, NAS Cecil Field, FL., 10 OCT 86; To VA-86, USS Nimitz (CVN-68), 10 OCT 86; To VA-86, NAS Cecil Field, FL., 10 OCT 86 ** Transferred to VA-174/FRS, AD/4XX, NAS Cecil Field, FL., 27 AUG 87 ** End of flight record card ** Transferred to VA-122/FRS, NJ/225, NAS LeMoore, CA., date unknown ** Transferred to AMARC, Davis Monthan AFB, Tucson, AZ., Assigned park code 6A0371, 01 AUG 90 ** 3726.0 flight hours ** TF41A402D engine S/N 141286 ** Storage location 150916 ** At AMARG, Davis Monthan AFB; Tucson, AZ., 15 JUN 07.

E-591 160876 Navy acceptance from NPRO Rep. LTV, Dallas, TX., 23 JAN 81** Transferred to VA-122/FRS, NJ/2XX, NAS LeMoore, CA., 30 JAN 81 ** Transferred to VA-146/CVW-9, NG/3XX, NAS LeMoore, CA., 08 JUN 81; To VA-146, USS Constellation (CV-64), 08 JUL 81; To VA-146, NAS LeMoore, CA., 06 AUG 81; To VA-146, USS Constellation (CV-64), 25 AUG 81; To VA-146, NAS LeMoore, CA., 20 OCT 81; To VA-146, NAS Jacksonville, FL., 28 APR 83 ** Transferred to VA-94/CVW-11, NH/4XX, NAS LeMoore, CA., 09 JUN 83; To VA-94, USS Enterprise (CVN-65), 21 JUL 83; To VA-94, NAS LeMoore, CA., 28 FEB 84; To VA-94, USS Enterprise (CVN-65), 10 MAR 84; To VA-94, NAS LeMoore, CA., 21 MAR 84; To VA-94, USS Enterprise (CVN-65), 21 MAR 84; To VA-94, NAS LeMoore, CA., 27 DEC 84; To VA-94, NAS Jacksonville, FL., 13 FEB 85; To VA-94, NAS LeMoore, CA., 01 MAY 85; To VA-94, USS Enterprise (CVN-65), 14 SEP 85; To VA-94, NAS LeMoore, CA., 10 JUN 86 thru 09 SEP 87 ** End of flight record card.

E-592 160877 Navy acceptance from NPRO Rep. LTV, Dallas, TX., 23 FEB 81 ** Transferred to VA-105/CVW-3, AC/4XX, NAS Cecil Field, FL., 24 FEB 81; To VA-105, NAS Fallon, NV.,08 MAY 81; To VA-105, NAS Cecil Field, FL., 08 MAY 81; To VA-105, USS John F. Kennedy (CV-67), 08 MAY 81; To VA-105, NAS Cecil Field, FL., 21 DEC 81; To VA-105, USS John F. Kennedy (CV-67), 23 DEC 81; To VA-105, NAS Cecil Field, FL., 23 DEC 81 ** Transferred to NATC, NATC/XXX, NAS Patuxent River, MD., for RDT & E, 12 OCT 82 ** Transferred to VA-105/CVW-15, NL/4XX, USS Carl Vinson (CVN-70), 13 JAN 83; To VA-105, NAS Cecil Field, FL., 13 JAN 83; To VA-105, USS Carl Vinson (CVN-70), 08 FEB 83; To VA-105, NAS Cecil Field, FL., 28 OCT 85; To VA-105, NAS Jacksonville, FL., 05 DEC 83; To VA-105, NAS Cecil Field, FL., 26 DEC 83; To VA-105, NAS Roosevelt Roads, PR., 25 JAN 84; To VA-105, NAS Jacksonville, FL., 13 FEB 84; To VA-105, NAS Cecil Field, FL., 14 FEB 84; To VA-105, NAF Kadena, JP., 14 MAY 84; To VA-105, NAS Cubi Point, PI., 14 MAY 84; To VA-105, MCAS Iwakuni, JP., 14 MAY 84; To VA-105/CVW-6, AE/4XX, NAS Cecil Field, FL., 14 MAY 84; To VA-105, USS Forrestal (CV-59), 28 MAY 85; To VA-105, NAS Cecil Field, FL., 28 MAY 85; To VA-105, USS Forrestal (CV-59), 14 JAN 86; To VA-105, NAS Jacksonville, FL., 31 MAR 86 ** Transferred to VA-86/CVW-8, AJ/4XX, NAS Cecil Field, FL., 07 APR 86; To VA-86, USS Nimitz (CVN-68), 07 APR 86; To VA-86, NAS Cecil Field, FL., 07 APR 86; To VA-86, USS Nimitz (CVN-68), 07 APR 86; To VA-86, NAS Cecil Field, FL., 10 OCT 86; To VA-86, USS Nimitz (CVN-68), 19 NOV 86; To VA-86, NAS Cecil Field, FL., 19 NOV 86 ** Transferred to VA-174/FRS, AD/4XX, NAS Cecil Field, FL., 31 AUG 87 ** End of flight record card.

E-593 160878 Navy acceptance from NPRO Rep. LTV, Dallas, TX., 18 FEB 81 ** Transferred to VA-122/FRS, NJ/2XX, NAS LeMoore, CA., 25 FEB 81 ** Transferred to VA-146/CVW-9, NG/3XX, NAS LeMoore, CA., 07 MAY 81; To VA-146, USS Constellation (CV-64), 08 JUL 81; To VA-146, NAS LeMoore, CA., 06 AUG 81; To VA-146, USS Constellation (CV-64), 11 SEP 81 ~ S 1SO strike, 08 MAR 82 ** No data on strike.

E-594 160879 Navy acceptance from NPRO Rep. LTV, Dallas, TX., 13 MAR 81 ** Transferred to VA-37/CVW-3, AC/300, NAS Cecil Field, FL., 14 MAR 81; To VA-37, NAS Fallon, NV., 14 MAR 81; To VA-37, NAS Cecil Field, FL., 14 MAR 81; To VA-37, USS John F. Kennedy (CV-67), 14 MAR 81; To VA-37, NAS Cecil Field, FL.,14 MAR 81; To VA-37, USS John F. Kennedy (CV-67), 14 MAR 81; To VA-37, NAS Cecil Field, FL., 14 MAR 81 ** Transferred to VA-105/

CVW-15, NL/4XX, NAS Cecil Field, FL., 07 OCT 82; To VA-105, USS Carl Vinson (CVN-70), 07 OCT 82; To VA-105, NAS Cecil Field, FL., 07 OCT 82 ** Transferred to VA-15/CVW-6, AE/306, NAS Cecil Field, FL., 18 FEB 83; To VA-15, NAS Jacksonville, FL., 04 MAY 83; To VA-15, USS Independence (CV-62), 17 MAY 83, Painted white on two tone gray with black modex; To VA-15, NAS Cecil Field, FL., 07 JUL 83; To VA-15, USS Independence (CV-62), 07 JUL 83; To VA-15, NAS Cecil Field, FL., 27 SEP 83; To VA-15, USS Independence (CV-62), 05 OCT 83; To VA-15, NAS Cecil Field, FL., 05 OCT 83; To VA-15, USS Independence (CV-62), 05 JUN 84; To VA-15, NAS Cecil Field, FL., 25 SEP 84; To VA-15, USS Independence (CV-62), 28 SEP 84; To VA-15, NAS Cecil Field, FL., 28 SEP 84; To VA-15, NAS Jacksonville, FL., 16 MAY 85; To VA-15, NAS Cecil Field, FL., 07 AUG 85; To VA-15, MCAS Iwacuni, JP., 13 AUG 85 ** Transferred to VA-86/CVW-8, AJ/4XX, NAS Cecil Field, FL., 09 DEC 85; To VA-86, USS Nimitz (CVN-68), 09 DEC 85; To VA-86, NAS Cecil Field, FL., 09 DEC 85; To VA-86, USS Nimitz (CVN-68), 09 DEC 86; To VA-86, NAS Cecil Field, FL., 10 OCT 86; To VA-86, USS Nimitz (CVN-68), 27 OCT 86; To VA-86, NAS Cecil Field, FL., 27 OCT 86 ** Transferred to VA-174/FRS, AD/4XX, NAS Cecil Field, FL., 10 AUG 87 ** End of flight record card ** Transferred to NAD, NAS Jacksonvill, FL., 19 DEC 88 ** Transferred to AMARC, Davis Monthan AFB; Tucson, AZ., assigned park code 6A0396, 20 JUN 91 ** 3796.7 flight hours ** TF41A402D engine S/N 141956 ** Placed on FMS list with D704 Buddy Store at NAS Fallon, NV., 10 MAY 05.

E-595 160880 Navy acceptance from NPRO Rep. LTV, Dallas, TX., 24 MAR 81 ** Transferred to VA-122/FRS, NJ/2XX, NAS LeMoore, CA., 25 MAR 81 ** Transferred to VA-146/CVW-9, NG/3XX, NAS LeMoore, CA., 29 APR 81; To VA-146, USS Constellation (CV-64), 08 JUL 81; To VA-146, NAS LeMoore, CA., 06 AUG 81; To VA-146, USS Constellation (CV-64), 11 SEP 81 ** Transferred to VA-93/CVW-5, NF/3XX, USS Midway (CV-41), 19 APR 82; To VA-93, NAS Cubi Point, PI., 19 APR 82; To VA-93, USS Midway (CV-41), 19 APR 82; To VA-93, NAF Atsugi, JP., 04 APR 83; To VA-93, USS Midway (CV-41), 31 MAY 83; To VA-93, NAF Atsugi, JP., 18 JUN 83 ~ S 1SO strike, 15 MAR 84 ** Pilot Ejected and rescued after a slow launch into the Arabian Sea.

160881/160886 Contract cancelled LTV A-7E Corsair II (Block XXIX)
Cancelled delivery of 160881 THRU 160886

E---- 160881 Cancelled	E---- 160882 Cancelled
E---- 160883 Cancelled	E---- 160884 Cancelled
E---- 160885 Cancelled	E---- 160886 Cancelled

APPENDIX 1

A-7 Odd Aircraft Assignments

Model	Bureau Number	Command	Location	Date
A-7A	152655	VC-2 Det	NAS Quanset Point	21 AUG 67
A-7A	153171	NAS	NAS Cubi Point	05 OCT 68
A-7A	153177	VAW-121 Det 9	USS Essex (CVS-9)	07 JUN 67
A-7A	153180	VAW-121 Det 9	USS Essex (CVS-9)	07 JUN 67
A-7A	153181	VAW-121 Det 9	USS Essex (CVS-9)	08 JUN 67
A-7A	153199	NAS	NAS Cubi Point	13 JUL 68
A-7A	153208	NAS	NAS Cubi Point	13 JUL 68
A-7A	153215	NAS	NAS Cubi Point	05 OCT 68
A-7A	153244	NAS	NAS Cubi Point	02 OCT 68
A-7A	153250	VMO-6	MCAS Futenma	27 JUL 77
A-7B	154370	VA-87	USS Intrepid (CVS-11)	08 APR 69
A-7B	154384	VA-87	USS Intrepid (CVS-11)	26 MAR 69
"	"	"	"	19 JUN 69
A-7B	154401	VA-15	USS Intrepid (CVS-11)	17 APR 69
A-7B	154402	VA-15	USS Intrepid (CVS-11)	14 MAR 69
A-7B	154403	VA-15	USS Intrepid (CVS-11)	14 MAR 69
TA-7C	154404	HC-7	NAS Imperial Beach	30 SEP 85
A-7B	154406	VA-15	USS Intrepid (CVS-11)	09 APR 69
A-7B	154410	VA-15	USS Intrepid (CVS-11)	11 MAR 69
A-7B	154414	VA-15	USS Intrepid (CVS-11)	07 JUN 69
A-7B	154415	VA-15	USS Intrepid (CVS-11)	14 APR 69
A-7B	154416	VA-15	USS Intrepid (CVS-11)	14 APR 69
A-7B	154518	VF-114	USS Kitty Hawk (CVA-63)	10 DEC 68
A-7B	154462	VA-15	USS Intrepid (CVS-11)	11 MAR 69
A-7B	154492	VA-15	USS Intrepid (CVS-11)	17 APR 69
A-7B	154500	NAS	NAS Miramar	17 DEC 68
A-7B	154552	VMFA-251	MCAS Beaufort	24 AUG 77
TA-7C	156741	VAQ-34	NAS Pt. Mugu	26 JAN 83
TA-7C	156743	VAQ-34	NAS Pt. Mugu	12 MAY 83
TA-7C	156745	VAQ-34	NAS Pt. Mugu	03 JUN 83
TA-7C	156757	VAQ-34	NAS Pt. Mugu	19 AUG 83
TA-7C	156761	VAQ-34	NAS Pt. Mugu	18 MAY 84
TA-7C	156786	VAQ-34	NAS Pt. Mugu	12 JUL 83
A-7E	156828	VFA-125	NAS Jacksonville	06 JUN 81
A-7E	156832	VFA-87	NAS Jacksonville	19 JUN 86
A-7E	156838	VFA-125	NAS LeMoore	18 OCT 81
A-7E	156867	HMM-262	MCAS Kaneohe Bay	01 SEP 72
A-7E	157455	U.S. Army	Unknown	06 JUL 87
A-7E	157473	VF-31	NAS Oceana	04 OCT 72
A-7E	157517	VFA-125	NAS Jacksonville	09 OCT 81
A-7E	157549	VA-42	NAS Oceana	15 JUN 82
A-7E	157567	U.S. Army	Unknown	13 AUG 87
A-7E	157586	VFA-15	NAS Jacksonville	17 OCT 86
A-7E	158002	VFA-25	NAS LeMoore	30 APR 83
A-7E	158009	VFA-125	NAS LeMoore	12 MAR 81
A-7E	158026	VFA-15	NAS Cecil Field	09 OCT 86
A-7E	158657	VFA-25	NAS Jacksonville	07 SEP 83
A-7E	158819	VFA-15	NAS Jacksonville	02 DEC 86
A-7E	159644	VFA-125	NAS LeMoore	25 AUG 81
A-7E	159978	VF-101	NAS Oceana	13 SEP 77
A-7E	160712	VFA-15	NAS Jacksonville	14 AUG 86
A-7E	160721	U.S. Army MICOM	Unknown	Unknown
A-7E	160727	VFA-113	NAS Jacksonville	25 MAY 83
A-7E	160729	VFA-113	NAS Jacksonville	15 JUL 83
A-7E	160730	VFA-25	NAS Jacksonville	15 JUL 83
A-7E	160864	U.S. Army MICOM	Holloman AFB	Unknown
A-7E	160872	U.S. Army MICOM	Unknown	Unknown

APPENDIX 2

Unidentified A-7 Corsair IIs

1. Eight Corsair II aircraft, Models unknown, Bureau Numbers unknown, used as artificial reefs on 10 JUL 97, within 9 Miles of the Mayport, FL, Jetties. Preliminary Loran Coordinates are 45174.0 and 61995.5

2. One A-7, destroyed and disposed of at the target range in Warren, NJ. Model and Serial number unknown. Probably an Air Force D or K model.

3. One A-7, Bureau Number unknown, skeleton at the Kenosha Military museum, Kenosha, WI.

4. One A-7, Bureau Number unknown, at the National Atomic museum at Kirtland AFB, NM.

5. One A-7A or B, Bureau Number unknown, both wings cut at the root, for sale on E-Bay, auction ending 29 NOV 05. Price $15,500.00, plus shipping, located in Orlando, FL, by aircraftstock@aol.com.

6. One A-7 airframe Bureau Number unknown being sold as spare parts on E-Bay along with A-7A 153241 for $275,000.00, 25 JUL 06. Aircraft & spare airframe located in Scottsdale, AZ, by Andy Taylor at Controller.com.

7. Three A-7E fuselages located near the Civil Terminal at RTND Base, U-tapao, Thailand.

APPENDIX 3

TA-7C / EA-7L

TA-7C List

154361/154417 Ling - Temco - Vought A-7B-1-CV Corsair II

CSN	Bureau Number	Conversion TA-7C Date	First Command	Location	Date
TB-06	154361	24 JUL 75	VA-122	NAS LeMoore	28 DEC 78
TB-08	154377	04 DEC 75	VA-122	NAS LeMoore	14 OCT 78
TB-26	154379	07 AUG 76	VA-122	NAS LeMoore	23 MAY 78
TB-18	154402	30 JUN 76	VA-122	NAS LeMoore	26 MAY 79
TB-11	154404	06 FEB 76	NPRO	LTV Dallas	02 APR 79
TB-14	154407	30 APR 76	VA-122	NAS LeMoore	01 SEP 78
TB-30	154410	07 OCT 76	VA-122	NAS LeMoore	06 JUN 78
TB-29	154412	03 SEP 76	NATC	NAS Patuxent River	02 MAY 78

154418/154474 Ling - Temco - Vought A-7B-2-CV Corsair II

CSN	Bureau Number	Conversion TA-7C Date	First Command	Location	Date
TB-09	154424	17 JAN 76	VA-174	NAS Cecil Field	26 FEB 79
TB-27	154425	09 AUG 76	NWC	NWC China Lake	19 APR 78
TB-07	154437	03 OCT 76	VA-174	NAS Cecil Field	14 DEC 78
TB-13	154450	05 APR 76	VA-174	NAS Cecil Field	06 AUG 78
TB-04	154455	04 SEP 76	VA-122	NAS LeMoore	15 OCT 78
TB-28	154458	02 SEP 76	VX-5	NWC China Lake	25 APR 78
TB-02	154464	06 JUL 75	NPRO	LTV Dallas	03 MAR 77
TB-12	154467	01 MAR 76	VA-122	NAS LeMoore	05 OCT 78
TB-25	154471	01 AUG 76	VA-174	NAS LeMoore	09 JAN 79

154475/154522 Ling - Temco - Vought A-7B-3-CV Corsair II

CSN	Bureau Number	Conversion TA-7C Date	First Command	Location	Date
TB-01	154477	09 MAR 75	NATC	NAS Patuxent River	29 NOV 82
TB-17	154489	21 JUN 76	VA-174	NAS Cecil Field	17 OCT 78
TB-19	154500	01 JUL 76	VA-174	NAS Cecil Field	01 DEC 78
TB-16	154507	29 MAY 76	VA-174	NAS Cecil Field	23 JUL 78

154523/154556 Ling - Temco - Vought A-7B-4-CV Corsair II

CSN	Bureau Number	Conversion TA-7C Date	First Command	Location	Date
TB-31	154536	08 OCT 76	VA-122	NAS LeMoore	31 JUL 79
TB-05	154537	24 JUL 75	VA-174	NAS Cecil Field	31 OCT 78
TB-03	154544	30 NOV 75	NPRO	LTV Dallas	30 MAR 78

156734/156740 Ling - Temco - Vought A-7C-1-CV Corsair II

CSN	Bureau Number	Conversion TA-7C Date	First Command	Location	Date
TE-20	156737	15 JAN 76	VA-174	NAS Cecil Field	20 APR 79
TE-23	156738	01 APR 76	NWC	NWC China Lake	23 MAR 78
TE-15	156740	15 JAN 75	NPRO	LTV Dallas	03 OCT 78

156741/156761 Ling - Temco - Vought A-7C-2-CV Corsair II

CSN	Bureau Number	Conversion TA-7C Date	First Command	Location	Date
TE-42	156741	30 JUN 77	VA-122	NAS LeMoore	31 JAN 79
TE-33	156743	26 NOV 76	VA-174	NAS Cecil Field	23 JUN 78
TE-37	156744	07 APR 77	VA-174	NAS Cecil Field	08 OCT 78
TE-41	156745	28 JUN 77	VA-122	NAS LeMoore	19 MAY 79
TE-47	156746	17 NOV 77	VA-174	NAS Cecil Field	31 OCT 79
TE-48	156747	17 NOV 77	VA-122	NAS LeMoore	19 SEP 79
TE-10	156748	24 SEP 75	VX-5	NWC China Lake	08 MAY 78
TE-43	156750	26 JUL 77	NWEF	Kirtland AFB	09 APR 79
TE-44	156751	26 JUL 77	VA-174	NAS Cecil Field	27 MAY 79
TE-54	156753	28 FEB 78	VA-122	NAS LeMoore	01 APR 80
TE-22	156757	03 MAY 76	VA-174	NAS Cecil Field	09 JUN 78
TE-24	156761	23 MAY 76	NATC	NAS Patuxent River	28 APR 78

156762/156800 Ling - Temco - Vought A-7C-3-CV Corsair II

CSN	Bureau Number	Conversion TA-7C Date	First Command	Location	Date
TE-52	156765	16 DEC 77	VA-122	NAS LeMoore	27 NOV 79
TE-21	156766	08 FEB 76	VA-122	NAS LeMoore	23 JUN 78
TE-46	156767	26 JUL 77	VA-174	NAS Cecil Field	21 JUN 79
TE-49	156768	15 NOV 77	NWC	NWC China Lake	20 DEC 79
TE-57	156770	25 MAY 78	NTPS	NAS Patuxent River	09 JUN 80
TE-39	156773	01 JUN 77	VA-122	NAS LeMoore	06 DEC 78
TE-59	156774	23 AUG 78	VA-174	NAS Cecil Field	02 AUG 80
TE-51	156777	23 NOV 77	PMTC	NAS Point Mugu	18 DEC 79
TE-55	156779	24 MAR 78	VA-174	NAS Cecil Field	19 APR 80
TE-56	156782	01 MAY 78	VA-122	NAS LeMoore	29 MAR 80
TE-40	156784	01 JUN 77	VA-174	NAS Cecil Field	22 DEC 78
TE-35	156786	06 DEC 76	VA-174	NAS Cecil Field	02 AUG 78
TE-53	156787	08 FEB 78	PMTC	NAS Point Mugu	09 FEB 80
TE-50	156788	18 NOV 77	VA-122	NAS LeMoore	01 NOV 79
TE-45	156789	26 JUL 77	VA-174	NAS Cecil Field	29 APR 79
TE-38	156790	24 MAY 77	VA-122	NAS LeMoore	24 OCT 78
TE-60	156791	05 SEP 78	VA-122	NAS LeMoore	29 AUG 80
TE-58	156793	22 JUN 78	VX-5	NWC China Lake	27 JUN 80
TE-36	156794	22 FEB 77	VA-174	NAS Cecil Field	02 OCT 78
TE-32	156795	11 SEP 76	VA-122	NAS LeMoore	19 JUN 78
TE-34	156800	30 OCT 76	VA-174	NAS Cecil Field	18 AUG 78

EA-7L List

TA-7C CSN	Bureau Number	EA-7L Conversion Date	First Command	Location	Date
TE-42	156741	01 MAY 84	VAQ-34 GD/201	NAS Point Mugu	26 JAN 83
TE-33	156743	01 MAY 84	VAQ-34 GD/202	NAS Point Mugu	26 JAN 83
TE-47	156745	01 MAY 84	VAQ-34 GD/200	NAS Point Mugu	26 JAN 83
TE-22	156757	01 MAY 84	VAQ-34 GD/204	NAS Point Mugu	26 JAN 83
TE-24	156761	01 MAY 84	VAQ-34 GD/205	NAS Point Mugu	26 JAN 83
TE-35	156786	01 MAY 84	VAQ-34 GD/203	NAS Point Mugu	26 JAN 83
TE-60	156791	01 MAY 84	VAQ-34 GD/206	NAS Point Mugu	26 JAN 83

APPENDIX 4

A-7 Deployment History

VA-12 Flying Ubangis then Clinchers; NAS Cecil Field, FL.

Squadron Air Wing	Model	Tail Code/ Modex	Carrier		Date
VA-12/CVW-7	A-7E	AG/4XX	USS Independence	(CVA-62)	16 SEP 71 - 16 MAR 72
VA-12/CVW-7	A-7E	AG/4XX	USS Independence	(CV-62)	21 JUN 73 - 19 JAN 74
VA-12/CVW-7	A-7E	AG/4XX	USS Independence	(CV-62)	19 JUL 74 - 21 JAN 75
VA-12/CVW-7	A-7E	AG/4XX	USS Independence	(CV-62)	17 AUG 75 - 02 OCT 75
VA-12/CVW-7	A-7E	AG/4XX	USS Independence	(CV-62)	15 OCT 75 - 05 MAY 76
VA-12/CVW-7	A-7E	AG/4XX	USS Independence	(CV-62)	31 MAR 77 - 21 OCT 77
VA-12/CVW-7	A-7E	AG/4XX	USS D. D. Eisenhower	(CVN-69)	05 JAN 78 - 01 FEB 78
VA-12/CVW-7	A-7E	AG/4XX	USS D. D. Eisenhower	(CVN-69)	04 AUG 78 - 20 AUG 78
VA-12/CVW-7	A-7E	AG/4XX	USS D. D. Eisenhower	(CVN-69)	18 SEP 78 - 26 OCT 78
VA-12/CVW-7	A-7E	AG/4XX	USS D. D. Eisenhower	(CVN-69)	14 NOV 78 - 04 DEC 78
VA-12/CVW-7	A-7E	AG/4XX	USS D. D. Eisenhower	(CVN-69)	16 JAN 79 - 13 JUL 79
VA-12/CVW-7	A-7E	AG/4XX	USS D. D. Eisenhower	(CVN-69)	04 JAN 80 - 09 FEB 80
VA-12/CVW-7	A-7E	AG/4XX	USS D. D. Eisenhower	(CVN-69)	20 FEB 80 - 21 MAR 80
VA-12/CVW-7	A-7E	AG/4XX	USS D. D. Eisenhower	(CVN-69)	15 APR 80 - 22 DEC 80
VA-12/CVW-7	A-7E	AG/4XX	USS D. D. Eisenhower	(CVN-69)	20 AUG 81 - 07 OCT 81
VA-12/CVW-7	A-7E	AG/4XX	USS D. D. Eisenhower	(CVN-69)	05 JAN 82 - 13 JUL 82
VA-12/CVW-7	A-7E	AG/4XX	USS D. D. Eisenhower	(CVN-69)	28 FEB 83 - 01 APR 83
VA-12/CVW-7	A-7E	AG/4XX	USS D. D. Eisenhower	(CVN-69)	27 APR 83 - 30 NOV 83
VA-12/CVW-7	A-7E	AG/4XX	USS D. D. Eisenhower	(CVN-69)	07 MAY 84 - 20 JUN 84
VA-12/CVW-7	A-7E	AG/4XX	USS D. D. Eisenhower	(CVN-69)	09 JUL 84 - 09 SEP 84
VA-12/CVW-7	A-7E	AG/4XX	USS D. D. Eisenhower	(CVN-69)	11 OCT 84 - 08 MAY 85
VA-12/CVW-7	A-7E	AG/4XX	USS D. D. Eisenhower	(CVN-69)	08 JUL 85 - 07 SEP 85

VA-15 Valions; NAS Cecil Field, FL.

Squadron Air Wing	Model	Tail Code/ Modex	Carrier		Date
VA-15/CVW-6	A-7B	AE/3XX	USS F.D. Roosevelt	(CVA-42)	02 JAN 70 - 27 JUL 70
VA-15/CVW-6	A-7B	AE/3XX	USS F.D. Roosevelt	(CVA-42)	29 JAN 71 - 28 JUL 71
VA-15/CVW-6	A-7B	AE/3XX	USS F.D. Roosevelt	(CVA-42)	15 FEB 72 - 08 DEC 72
VA-15/CVW-6	A-7B	AE/3XX	USS F.D. Roosevelt	(CVA-42)	14 SEP 73 - 17 MAR 74
VA-15/CVW-6	A-7B	AE/3XX	USS F.D. Roosevelt	(CVA-42)	03 JAN 75 - 19 JUL 75
VA-15/CVW-6	A-7E	AE/3XX	USS America	(CV-66)	17 NOV 75 -16 DEC 75
VA-15/CVW-6	A-7E	AE/3XX	USS America	(CV-66)	15 APR 76 - 25 OCT 76
VA-15/CVW-6	A-7E	AE/3XX	USS America	(CV-66)	03 MAY 77 - 24 MAY 77
VA-15/CVW-6	A-7E	AE/3XX	USS America	(CV-66)	10 JUN 77 - 19 JUL 77
VA-15/CVW-6	A-7E	AE/3XX	USS America	(CV-66)	29 SEP 77 - 25 APR 78
VA-15/CVW-6	A-7E	AE/3XX	USS Independence	(CV-62)	28 JUN 79 - 14 DEC 79
VA-15/CVW-6	A-7E	AE/3XX	USS Independence	(CV-62)	19 NOV 80 - 11 JUN 81
VA-15/CVW-6	A-7E	AE/3XX	USS Independence	(CV-62)	07 JAN 82 - 22 DEC 82
VA-15/CVW-6	A-7E	AE/3XX	USS Independence	(CV-62)	06 JUN 83 - 21 JUL 83
VA-15/CVW-6	A-7E	AE/3XX	USS Independence	(CV-62)	15 AUG 83 - 16 SEP 83
VA-15/CVW-6	A-7E	AE/3XX	USS Independence	(CV-62)	18 OCT 83 - 11 APR 84
VA-15/CVW-6	A-7E	AE/3XX	USS Independence	(CV-62)	20 AUG 84 - 09 SEP 84
VA-15/CVW-6	A-7E	AE/3XX	USS Independence	(CV-62)	16 OCT 84 - 19 FEB 85

VA-22 Fighting Redcocks; NAS LeMoore, CA.

Squadron Air Wing	Model	Tail Code/ Modex	Carrier		Date
VA-22/CVW-15	A-7E	NL/3XX	USS Coral Sea	(CVA-43)	12 NOV 71 - 17 JUL 72
VA-22/CVW-15	A-7E	NL/3XX	USS Coral Sea	(CVA-43)	09 MAR 73 - 08 NOV 73
VA-22/CVW-15	A-7E	NL/3XX	USS Coral Sea	(CVA-43)	12 NOV 71 - 17 JUL 72
VA-22/CVW-15	A-7E	NL/3XX	USS Coral Sea	(CVA-43)	09 MAR 73 - 08 NOV 73
VA-22/CVW-15	A-7E	NL/3XX	USS Coral Sea	(CVA-43)	05 DEC 74 - 02 JUL 75
VA-22/CVW-15	A-7E	NL/3XX	USS Coral Sea	(CV-43)	15 FEB 77 - 05 OCT 77
VA-22/CVW-15	A-7E	NL/3XX	USS Kitty Hawk	(CV-63)	30 MAY 79 - 25 FEB 80
VA-22/CVW-15	A-7E	NL/3XX	USS Kitty Hawk	(CV-63)	01 APR 81 - 23 NOV 81
VA-22/CVW-11	A-7E	NH/3XX	USS Enterprise	(CVN-65)	30 MAY 84 - 20 DEC 84
VA-22/CVW-11	A-7E	NH/3XX	USS Enterprise	(CVN-65)	12 JAN 86 - 13 AUG 86
VA-22/CVW-11	A-7E	NH/3XX	USS Enterprise	(CVN-65)	25 OCT 87 - 24 NOV 87
VA-22/CVW-11	A-7E	NH/3XX	USS Enterprise	(CVN-65)	05 JAN 88 - 03 JUL 88

VA-25 Fist of the Fleet; NAS LeMooere, CA.

Squadron Air Wing	Model	Tail Code/ Modex	Carrier		Date
VA-25/CVW-16	A-7B	AH/5XX	USS Ticonderoga	(CVS-14)	01 FEB 69 - 18 SEP 69
VA-25/CVW-2	A-7E	NE/4XX	USS Ranger	(CVA-61)	27 OCT 70 - 17 JUN 71
VA-25/CVW-2	A-7E	NE/4XX	USS Ranger	(CV-61)	16 NOV 72 - 22 JUN 73
VA-25/CVW-2	A-7E	NE/4XX	USS Ranger	(CV-61)	07 MAY 74 - 18 OCT 74
VA-25/CVW-2	A-7E	NE/4XX	USS Ranger	(CV-61)	30 JAN 76 - 07 SEP 76
VA-25/CVW-2	A-7E	NE/4XX	USS Ranger	(CV-61)	09 NOV 76 - 19 NOV 76
VA-25/CVW-2	A-7E	NE/4XX	USS Ranger	(CV-61)	21 FEB 79 - 22 SEP 79
VA-25/CVW-2	A-7E	NE/4XX	USS Ranger	(CV-61)	10 SEP 80 - 05 MAY 81
VA-25/CVW-2	A-7E	NE/4XX	USS Ranger	(CV-61)	07 APR 82 - 18 OCT 82

VA-27 Royal Maces; NAS LeMoore, CA.

Squadron Air Wing	Model	Tail Code/ Modex	Carrier	?????	Date
VA-27/CVW-14	A-7A	NK/6XX	USS Constellation	(CVA-64)	29 MAY 68 - 31 JAN 69
VA-27/CVW-14	A-7A	NK/4XX	USS Constellation	(CVA-64)	11 AUG 69 - 08 MAY 70
VA-27/CVW-14	A-7E	NK/4XX	USS Enterprise	(CVAN-65)	04 FEB 71 - 07 MAR71
VA-27/CVW-14	A-7E	NK/4XX	USS Enterprise	(CVAN-65)	11 JUN 71 - 12 FEB 72
VA-27/CVW-14	A-7E	NK/4XX	USS Enterprise	(CVAN-65)	12 SEP 72 - 12 JUN 73
VA-27/CVW-14	A-7E	NK/4XX	USS Enterprise	(CVAN-65)	17 SEP 74 - 20 MAY 75
VA-27/CVW-14	A-7E	NK/4XX	USS Enterprise	(CVN-65)	30 JUL 76 - 28 MAR 77
VA-27/CVW-14	A-7E	NK/4XX	USS Enterprise	(CVN-65)	04 APR 78 - 30 OCT 78
VA-27/CVW-14	A-7E	NK/4XX	USS Coral Sea	(CV-43)	13 NOV 79 - 11 JUN 80
VA-27/CVW-14	A-7E	NK/4XX	USS Coral Sea	(CV-43)	20 AUG 81 - 23 MAR 82
VA-27/CVW-14	A-7E	NK/4XX	USS Coral Sea	(CV-43)	21MAR 83 - 12 SEP 83
VA-27/CVW-15	A-7E	NL/4XX	USS Carl Vinson	(CVN-70)	13 MAY 84 - 29 JUN 84
VA-27/CVW-15	A-7E	NL/4XX	USS Carl Vinson	(CVN-70)	18 OCT 84 - 24 MAY 85
VA-27/CVW-15	A-7E	NL/4XX	USS Carl Vinson	(CVN-70)	02 MAY 86 - 02 JUL 86
VA-27/CVW-15	A-7E	NL/4XX	USS Carl Vinson	(CVN-70)	12 AUG 86 - 05 FEB 87
VA-27/CVW-15	A-7E	NL/4XX	USS Carl Vinson	(CVN-70)	15 JUN 88 - 14 DEC 88
VA-27/CVW-15	A-7E	NL/4XX	USS Carl Vinson	(CVN-70)	05 SEP 89 - 08 NOV 89
VA-27/CVW-15	A-7E	NL/4XX	USS Carl Vinson	(CVN-70)	01 FEB 90 - 31 JUL 90

VA-37 Bulls; NAS Cecil Field, FL.

Squadron Air Wing	Model	Tail Code/ Modex	Carrier		Date
VA-37/CVW-11	A-7A	NH/3XX	USS Kitty Hawk	(CVA-63)	30 DEC 68 - 04 SEP 69
VA-37/CVW-3	A-7A	AC/3XX	USS Saratoga	(CVA-60)	17 JUN 70 - 11 NOV 70
VA-37/CVW-3	A-7A	AC/3XX	USS Saratoga	(CVA-60)	07 JUN 71 - 19 OCT 71
VA-37/CVW-3	A-7A	AC/3XX	USS Saratoga	(CVA-60)	03 APR 72 - 07 APR 72
VA-37/CVW-3	A-7A	AC/3XX	USS Saratoga	(CV-60)	11 APR 72 - 13 FEB 73
VA-37/CVW-3	A-7E	AC/3XX	USS Saratoga	(CV-60)	27 SEP 74 - 19 MAR 75
VA-37/CVW-3	A-7E	AC/3XX	USS Saratoga	(CV-60)	06 JAN 76 - 28 JUL 76
VA-37/CVW-3	A-7E	AC/3XX	USS Saratoga	(CV-60)	11 JUL 77 - 23 DEC 77
VA-37/CVW-3	A-7E	AC/3XX	USS Saratoga	(CV-60)	03 OCT 78 - 05 APR 79
VA-37/CVW-3	A-7E	AC/3XX	USS Saratoga	(CV-60)	11 MAR 80 - 27 AUG 80

VA-37/CVW-3	A-7E	AC/3XX	USS John F. Kennedy	(CV-67)	04 JAN 82 - 14 JUL 82
VA-37/CVW-15	A-7E	NL/3XX	USS Carl Vinson	(CVN-70)	01 MAR 83 - 29 OCT 83
VA-37/CVW-6	A-7E	AE/3XX	USS Forrestal	(CV-59)	10 JUL 85 - 19 AUG 85
VA-37/CVW-6	A-7E	AE/3XX	USS Forrestal	(CV-59)	02 JUN 86 - 10 NOV 86
VA-37/CVW-6	A-7E	AE/3XX	USS Forrestal	(CV-59)	28 AUG 87 - 09 OCT 87
VA-37/CVW-6	A-7E	AE/3XX	USS Forrestal	(CV-59)	08 APR 88 - 20 APR 88
VA-37/CVW-6	A-7E	AE/3XX	USS Forrestal	(CV-59)	25 APR 88 - 07 OCT 88
VA-37/CVW-6	A-7E	AE/3XX	USS Forrestal	(CV-59)	04 NOV 89 - 12 APR 90

VA-46 Clansmen; NAS Cecil Field, FL.

Squadron Air Wing	Model	Tail Code/ Modex	Carrier		Date
VA-46/CVW-3	A-7B	AC/3XX	USS Saratoga	(CVA-60)	09 JUL 69 - 22 JAN 70
VA-46/CVW-1	A-7B	AB/3XX	USS John F. Kennedy	(CVA-67)	14 SEP 70 - 28 FEB 71
VA-46/CVW-1	A-7B	AB/3XX	USS John F. Kennedy	(CVA-67)	01 DEC 71 - 06 OCT 72
VA-46/CVW-1	A-7B	AB/3XX	USS John F. Kennedy	(CV-67)	16 APR 73 - 01 DEC 73
VA-46/CVW-1	A-7B	AB/3XX	USS John F. Kennedy	(CV-67)	28 JUN 75 - 27 JAN 76
VA-46/CVW-1	A-7B	AB/3XX	USS John F. Kennedy	(CV-67)	02 SEP 76 - 09 NOV 76
VA-46/CVW-1	A-7B	AB/3XX	USS John F. Kennedy	(CV-67)	15 JAN 77 - 01 AUG 77
VA-46/CVW-1	A-7E	AB/3XX	USS D.D. Eisenhower	(CVN-69)	07 NOV 77 - 13 DEC 77
VA-46/CVW-1	A-7E	AB/3XX	USS John F. Kennedy	(CV-67)	20 JAN 78 - 22 MAR 78
VA-46/CVW-1	A-7E	AB/3XX	USS John F. Kennedy	(CV-67)	29 JUN 78 - 08 FEB 79
VA-46/CVW-1	A-7E	AB/3XX	USS John F. Kennedy	(CV-67)	04 AUG 80 - 28 MAR 81
VA-46/CVW-1	A-7E	AB/3XX	USS America	(CV-66	30 MAY 82 - 08 JUL 82
VA-46/CVW-1	A-7E	AB/3XX	USS America	(CV-66)	29 AUG 82 - 04 NOV 82
VA-46/CVW-1	A-7E	AB/3XX	USS America	(CV-66)	08 DEC 82 - 02 JUN 83
VA-46/CVW-1	A-7E	AB/3XX	USS America	(CV-66)	06 FEB 84 - 22 MAR 84
VA-46/CVW-1	A-7E	AB/3XX	USS America	(CV-66)	24 APR 84 - 14 NOV 84
VA-46/CVW-1	A-7E	AB/3XX	USS America	(CV-66)	24 AUG 85 - 09 OCT 85
VA-46/CVW-1	A-7E	AB/3XX	USS America	(CV-66)	08 FEB 86 - 28 FEB 86
VA-46/CVW-1	A-7E	AB/3XX	USS America	(CV-66)	10 MAR 86 - 10 SEP 86
VA-46/CVW-7	A-7E	AG/3XX	USS D.D. Eisenhower	(CVN-69)	16 JUN 87 - 28 JUL 87
VA-46/CVW-7	A-7E	AG/3XX	USS D.D. Eisenhower	(CVN-69)	29 FEB 88 - 29 AUG 88
VA-46/CVW-3	A-7E	AC/3XX	USS John F. Kennedy	(CV-67)	04 JAN 90 - 09 FEB 90
VA-46/CVW-3	A-7E	AC/3XX	USS John F. Kennedy	(CV-6)	15 AUG 90 - 28 MAR 91

VA-56 Champions; NAS LeMoore, CA., NAF Atsugi, JP.

Squadron Air Wing	Model	Tail Code/ Modex	Carrier		Date
VA-56/CVW-2	A-7B	NE/4XX	USS Ranger	(CVA-61)	14 OCT 69 - 01 JUN 70
VA-56/CVW-5	A-7B	NF/4XX	USS Midway	(CVA-41)	16 APR 71 - 01 NOV 71
VA-56/CVW-5	A-7B	NF/4XX	USS Midway	(CVA-41)	10 APR 72 - 03 MAR 73
VA-56/CVW-5	A-7A	NF/4XX	USS Midway	(CVA-41)	11 SEP 73 - 05 OCT 73
VA-56/CVW-5	A-7A	NF/4XX	USS Midway	(CVA-41)	16 NOV 73 - 22 DEC 73
VA-56/CVW-5	A-7A	NF/4XX	USS Midway	(CVA-41)	29 JAN 74 - 05 MAR 74
VA-56/CVW-5	A-7A	NF/4XX	USS Midway	(CVA-41)	26 MAR 74 - 05 MAY 74
VA-56/CVW-5	A-7A	NF/4XX	USS Midway	(CVA-41)	15 JUN 74 - 27 JUN 74
VA-56/CVW-5	A-7A	NF/4XX	USS Midway	(CVA-41)	09 JUL 74 - 22 JUL 74
VA-56/CVW-5	A-7A	NF/4XX	USS Midway	(CVA-41)	02 AUG 74 - 14 AUG 74
VA-56/CVW-5	A-7A	NF/4XX	USS Midway	(CVA-41)	27 SEP 74 - 09 OCT 74
VA-56/CVW-5	A-7A	NF/4XX	USS Midway	(CVA-41)	19 OCT 74 - 19 DEC 74
VA-56/CVW-5	A-7A	NF/4XX	USS Midway	(CVA-41)	13 JAN 75 - 18 FEB 75
VA-56/CVW-5	A-7A	NF/4XX	USS Midway	(CVA-41)	31 MAR 75 - 28 MAY 75
VA-56/CVW-5	A-7A	NF/4XX	USS Midway	(CV-41)	07 JUN 75 - 15 JUL 75
VA-56/CVW-5	A-7A	NF/4XX	USS Midway	(CV-41)	04 AUG 75 - 15 AUG 75
VA-56/CVW-5	A-7A	NF/4XX	USS Midway	(CV-41)	12 SEP 75 - 21 SEP 75
VA-56/CVW-5	A-7A	NF/4XX	USS Midway	(CV-41)	04 OCT 75 - 18 DEC 75
VA-56/CVW-5	A-7A	NF/4XX	USS Midway	(CV-41)	13 JAN 76 - 22 JAN 76
VA-56/CVW-5	A-7A	NF/4XX	USS Midway	(CV-41)	09 FEB 76 - 28 FEB 76
VA-56/CVW-5	A-7A	NF/4XX	USS Midway	(CV-41)	13 MAR 76- 26 APR 76
VA-56/CVW-5	A-7A	NF/4XX	USS Midway	(CV-41)	19 MAY 76 - 21 JUN 76
VA-56/CVW-5	A-7A	NF/4XX	USS Midway	(CV-41)	09 JUL 76 - 04 AUG 76
VA-56/CVW-5	A-7A	NF/4XX	USS Midway	(CV-41)	21 AUG 76 - 16 SEP 76
VA-56/CVW-5	A-7A	NF/4XX	USS Midway	(CV-41)	04 OCT 76 - 18 OCT 76
VA-56/CVW-5	A-7A	NF/4XX	USS Midway	(CV-41)	01 NOV 76 - 17 DEC 76
VA-56/CVW-5	A-7A	NF/4XX	USS Midway	(CV-41)	11 JAN 77 - 01 MAR 77
VA-56/CVW-5	A-7A	NF/4XX	USS Midway	(CV-41)	19 APR 77 - 05 MAY 77
VA-56/CVW-5	A-7E	NF/4XX	USS Midway	(CV-41)	08 AUG 77 - 02 SEP 77

Squadron Air Wing	Model	Tail Code/ Modex	Carrier		Date
VA-56/CVW-5	A-7E	NF/4XX	USS Midway	(CV-41)	27 SEP 77 - 21 DEC 77
VA-56/CVW-5	A-7E	NF/4XX	USS Midway	(CV-41)	11 APR 78 - 23 MAY 78
VA-56/CVW-5	A-7E	NF/4XX	USS Midway	(CV-41)	09 NOV 78 - 23 DEC 78
VA-56/CVW-5	A-7E	NF/4XX	USS Midway	(CV-41)	11 JAN 79 - 20 FEB 79
VA-56/CVW-5	A-7E	NF/4XX	USS Midway	(CV-41)	07 APR 79 - 18 JUN 79
VA-56/CVW-5	A-7E	NF/4XX	USS Midway	(CV-41)	20 AUG 79 - 14 SEP 79
VA-56/CVW-5	A-7E	NF/4XX	USS Midway	(CV-41)	30 SEP 79 - 20 FEB 80
VA-56/CVW-5	A-7E	NF/4XX	USS Midway	(CV-41)	14 JUL 80 - 26 NOV 80
VA-56/CVW-5	A-7E	NF/4XX	USS Midway	(CV-41)	24 FEB 81 – 05 JUN 81
VA-56/CVW-5	A-7E	NF/4XX	USS Midway	(CV-41)	25 JUN 81 - 16 JUL 81
VA-56/CVW-5	A-7E	NF/4XX	USS Midway	(CV-41)	03 SEP 81 - 06 OCT 81
VA-56/CVW-5	A-7E	NF/4XX	USS Midway	(CV-41)	25 OCT 81 - 16 NOV 81
VA-56/CVW-5	A-7E	NF/4XX	USS Midway	(CV-41)	07 MAR 82 - 05 APR 82
VA-56/CVW-5	A-7E	NF/4XX	USS Midway	(CV-41)	26 APR 82 - 18 JUN 82
VA-56/CVW-5	A-7E	NF/4XX	USS Midway	(CV-41)	11 AUG 82 - 20 AUG 82
VA-56/CVW-5	A-7E	NF/4XX	USS Midway	(CV-41)	14 SEP 82 - 10 DEC 82
VA-56/CVW-5	A-7E	NF/4XX	USS Midway	(CV-41)	12 JAN 83 - 27 JAN 83
VA-56/CVW-5	A-7E	NF/4XX	USS Midway	(CV-41)	25 FEB 83 - 22 MAR 83
VA-56/CVW-5	A-7E	NF/4XX	USS Midway	(CV-41)	30 APR 83 - 09 MAY 83
VA-56/CVW-5	A-7E	NF/4XX	USS Midway	(CV-41)	02 JUN 83 - 13 AU 83
VA-56/CVW-5	A-7E	NF/4XX	USS Midway	(CV-41)	25 OCT 83 - 11DEC 83
VA-56/CVW-5	A-7E	NF/4XX	USS Midway	(CV-41)	28 DEC 83 - 23 MAY 84
VA-56/CVW-5	A-7E	NF/4XX	USS Midway	(CV-41)	07 JUN 84 - 13 JUN 84
VA-56/CVW-5	A-7E	NF/4XX	USS Midway	(CV-41)	15 AUG 84 - 09 SEP 84
VA-56/CVW-5	A-7E	NF/4XX	USS Midway	(CV-41)	16 SEP 84 - 30 SEP 84
VA-56/CVW-5	A-7E	NF/4XX	USS Midway	(CV-41)	15 OCT 84 - 13 DEC 84
VA-56/CVW-5	A-7E	NF/4XX	USS Midway	(CV-41)	01 FEB 85 - 28 MAR 85
VA-56/CVW-5	A-7E	NF/4XX	USS Midway	(CV-41)	10 JUN 85 - 14 OCT 85
VA-56/CVW-5	A-7E	NF/4XX	USS Midway	(CV-41)	17 JAN 86 - 30 MAR 86

VA-66 Mod Squad, then Roadrunners; NAS Cecil Field, FL.

Squadron Air Wing	Model	Tail Code/ Modex	Carrier		Date
VA-66/CVW-7	A-7E	AG/3XX	USS Independence	(CVA-62)	16 SEP 71 - 16 MAR 72
VA-66/CVW-7	A-7E	AG/3XX	USS Independence	(CV-62)	21 JUN 73 - 19 JAN 74
VA-66/CVW-7	A-7E	AG/3XX	USS Independence	(CV-62)	19 JUL 74 - 21 JAN 75
VA-66/CVW-7	A-7E	AG/3XX	USS Independence	(CV-62)	17 AUG 75 - 02 OCT 75
VA-66/CVW-7	A-7E	AG/3XX	USS Independence	(CV-62)	15 OCT 75 - 05 MAY 76
VA-66/CVW-7	A-7E	AG/3XX	USS Independence	(CV-62)	31 MAR 77 - 21 OCT 77
VA-66/CVW-7	A-7E	AG/3XX	USS D.D. Eisenhower	(CVN-69)	05 JAN 78 - 01 FEB 78
VA-66/CVW-7	A-7E	AG/3XX	USS D.D. Eisenhower	(CVN-69)	04 AUG 78 - 20 AUG 78
VA-66/CVW-7	A-7E	AG/3XX	USS D.D. Eisenhower	(CVN-69)	18 SEP 78 - 26 OCT 78
VA-66/CVW-7	A-7E	AG/3XX	USS D.D. Eisenhower	(CVN-69)	14 NOV 78 - 04 DEC 78
VA-66/CVW-7	A-7E	AG/3XX	USS D.D. Eisenhower	(CVN-69)	16 JAN 79 - 13 JUL 79
VA-66/CVW-7	A-7E	AG/3XX	USS D.D. Eisenhower	(CVN-69)	20 FEB 80 - 21 MAR 80
VA-66/CVW-7	A-7E	AG/3XX	USS D.D. Eisenhower	(CVN-69)	15 APR 80 - 22 DEC 80
VA-66/CVW-7	A-7E	AG/3XX	USS D.D. Eisenhower	(CVN-69)	20 AUG 81 - 07 OCT 81
VA-66/CVW-7	A-7E	AG/3XX	USS D.D. Eisenhower	(CVN-69)	05 JAN 82 - 13 JUL 82
VA-66/CVW-7	A-7E	AG/3XX	USS D.D. Eisenhower	(CVN-69)	28 FEB 83 - 01 APR 83
VA-66/CVW-7	A-7E	AG/3XX	USS D.D. Eisenhower	(CVN-69)	27 APR 83 - 30 NOV 83
VA-66/CVW-7	A-7E	AG/3XX	USS D.D. Eisenhower	(CVN-69)	07 MAY 84 - 20 JUN 84
VA-66/CVW-7	A-7E	AG/3XX	USS D.D. Eisenhower	(CVN-69)	09 JUL 84 - 09 SEP 84
VA-66/CVW-7	A-7E	AG/3XX	USS D.D. Eisenhower	(CVN-69)	11 OCT 84 - 08 MAY 85
VA-66/CVW-7	A-7E	AG/3XX	USS D.D. Eisenhower	(CVN-69)	08 JUL 85 - 07 SEP 85
VA-66/CVW-3	A-7E	AC/3XX	USS John F. Kennedy	(CV-67)	18 AUG 86 - 03 MAR 87

VA-67 became VA-15; NAS Cecil Field, FL., 02 JUN 69

VA-72 Blue Hawks; NAS Cecil Field, FL.

Squadron Air Wing	Model	Tail Code/ Modex	Carrier		Date
VA-72/CVW-1	A-7B	AB/4XX	USS John F. Kennedy	(CVA-67)	14 SEP 70 - 28 FEB 71
VA-72/CVW-1	A-7B	AB/4XX	USS John F. Kennedy	(CVA-67)	01 DEC 71 - 06 OCT 72
VA-72/CVW-1	A-7B	AB/4XX	USS John F. Kennedy	(CV-67)	16 APR 73 - 01 DEC 73
VA-72/CVW-1	A-7B	AB/4XX	USS John F. Kennedy	(CV-67)	28 JUN 75 - 27 JAN 76
VA-72/CVW-1	A-7B	AB/4XX	USS John F. Kennedy	(CV-67)	02 SEP 76 - 09 NOV 76
VA-72/CVW-1	A-7B	AB/4XX	USS John F. Kennedy	(CV-67)	15 JAN 77 - 01 AUG 77
VA-72/CVW-1	A-7E	AB/4XX	USS D.D. Eisenhower	(CVN-69)	07 NOV 77 - 13 DEC 77

VA-72/CVW-1	A-7E	AB/4XX	USS John F. Kennedy	(CV-67)	20 JAN 78 - 22 MAR 78
VA-72/CVW-1	A-7E	AB/4XX	USS John F. Kennedy	(CV-67)	29 JUN 78 - 08 FEB 79
VA-72/CVW-1	A-7E	AB/4XX	USS John F. Kennedy	(CV-67)	04 AUG 80 - 28 MAR 81
VA-72/CVW-1	A-7E	AB/4XX	USS America	(CV-66)	30 MAY 82 - 08 JUL 82
VA-72/CVW-1	A-7E	AB/4XX	USS America	CV-66)	22 AUG 82 - 04 NOV 82
VA-72/CVW-1	A-7E	AB/4XX	USS America	(CV-66)	08 DEC 82 - 02 JUN 83
VA-72/CVW-1	A-7E	AB/4XX	USS America	(CV-66)	06 FEB 84 - 22 MAR 84
VA-72/CVW-1	A-7E	AB/4XX	USS America	(CV-66)	24 APR 84 - 14 NOV 84
VA-72/CVW-1	A-7E	AB/4XX	USS America	(CV-66)	24 AUG 85 - 09 OCT 85
VA-72/CVW-1	A-7E	AB/4XX	USS America	(CV-66)	08 FEB 86 - 28 FEB 86
VA-72/CVW-1	A-7E	AB/4XX	USS America	(CV-66)	10 MAR 86 - 10 SEP 8
VA-72/CVW-7	A-7E	AG/4XX	USS D.D. Eisenhower	(CVN-69)	16 JUN 87 - 28 JUL 87
VA-72/CVW-7	A-7E	AG/4XX	USS D.D. Eisenhower	(CVN-69)	29 FEB 88 - 29 AUG 88
VA-72/CVW-3	A-7E	AC/4XX	USS John F. Kennedy	(CV-67)	04 JAN 90 - 09 FEB 90
VA-72/CVW-3	A-7E	AC/4XX	USS John F. Kennedy	(CV-67)	15 AUG 90 - 28 MAR 91

VA-81 Sunliners; NAS Cecil Field, FL.

Squadron Air Wing	Model	Tail Code/ Modex	Carrier		Date
VA-81/CVW-17	A-7E	AA/4XX	USS Forrestal	(CVA-59)	05 JAN 71 - 02 JUL 71
VA-81/CVW-17	A-7E	AA/4XX	USS Forrestal	(CVA-59)	22 SEP 72 - 06 JUL 73
VA-81/CVW-17	A-7E	AA/4XX	USS Forrestal	(CVA-59)	11 MAR 74 - 11 SEP 74
VA-81/CVW-17	A-7E	AA/4XX	USS Forrestal	(CV-59)	05 MAR 75 - 22 SEP 75
VA-81/CVW-17	A-7E	AA/4XX	USS Forrestal	(CV-59)	04 APR 78 - 26 OCT 78
VA-81/CVW-17	A-7E	AA/4XX	USS Forrestal	(CV-59)	27 NOV 79 - 07 MAY 80
VA-81/CVW-17	A-7E	AA/4XX	USS Forrestal	(CV-59)	02 MAR 81 - 15 SEP 81
VA-81/CVW-17	A-7E	AA/4XX	USS Forrestal	(CV-59)	28 APR 82 - 17 MAY 82
VA-81/CVW-17	A-7E	AA/4XX	USS Forrestal	(CV-59)	08 JUN 82 - 16 NOV 82
VA-81/CVW-17	A-7E	AA/4XX	USS Saratoga	(CV-60)	09 MAY 83 - 11 JUN 83
VA-81/CVW-17	A-7E	AA/4XX	USS Saratoga	(CV-60)	26 JAN 84 - 21 FEB 84
VA-81/CVW-17	A-7E	AA/4XX	USS Saratoga	(CV-60)	02 APR 84 - 20 OCT 84
VA-81/CVW-17	A-7E	AA/4XX	USS Saratoga	(CV-60)	26 AUG 85 - 16 APR 86
VA-81/CVW-17	A-7E	AA/4XX	USS Saratoga	(CV-60)	05 JUN 87 - 16 NOV 87

VA-82 Marauders; NAS Cecil Field, FL.

Squadron Air Wing	Model	Tail Code/ Modex	Carrier		Date
VA-82/CVW-6	A-7A	AE/3XX	USS America	(CVA-66)	16 JAN 68 - 17 FEB 68
VA-82/CVW-6	A-7A	AE/3XX	USS America	(CVA-66)	07 MAR 68 - 23 MAR 68
VA-82/CVW-6	A-7A	AE/3XX	USS America	(CVA-66)	10 APR 68 - 16 DEC 68
VA-82/CVW-15	A-7A	NL/3XX	USS Coral Sea	(CVA-43)	23 SEP 69 - 01 JUL 70
VA-82/CVW-8	A-7C	AJ/3XX	USS America	(CVA-66)	06 JUL 71 - 16 DEC 71
VA-82/CVW-8	A-7C	AJ/3XX	USS America	(CVA-66)	05 JUN 72 - 24 MAR 73
VA-82/CVW-8	A-7C	AJ/3XX	USS America	(CVA-66)	29 OCT 73 - 21 NOV 73
VA-82/CVW-8	A-7C	AJ/3XX	USS America	(CVA-66)	30 NOV 73 - 13 DEC 73
VA-82/CVW-8	A-7C	AJ/3XX	USS America	(CVA-66)	03 JAN 74 - 03 AUG 74
VA-82/CVW-8	A-7C	AJ/3XX	USS America	(CVA-66)	06 SEP 74 - 12 OCT 74
VA-82/CVW-8	A-7E	AJ/3XX	USS Nimitz	(CVN-68)	15 JUN 75 - 15 SEP 75
VA-82/CVW-8	A-7E	AJ/3XX	USS Nimitz	(CVN-68)	07 JUL 76 - 07 FEB 77
VA-82/CVW-8	A-7E	AJ/3XX	USS Nimitz	(CVN-68)	01 DEC 77 - 20 JUL 78
VA-82/CVW-8	A-7E	AJ/3XX	USS Nimitz	(CVN-68)	10 SEP 79 - 26 MAY 80
VA-82/CVW-8	A-7E	AJ/3XX	USS Nimitz	(CVN-68)	29 AUG 80 - 17 OCT 80
VA-82/CVW-8	A-7E	AJ/3XX	USS Nimitz	(CVN-68)	03 AUG 81 - 13 FEB 82
VA-82/CVW-8	A-7E	AJ/3XX	USS Carl Vinson	(CVN-70)	07 MAY 82 - 11 JUN 82
VA-82/CVW-8	A-7E	AJ/3XX	USS Nimitz	(CVN-68)	10 NOV 82 - 20 MAY 83
VA-82/CVW-8	A-7E	AJ/3XX	USS Nimitz	(CVN-68)	08 MAR 85 - 03 OCT 85
VA-82/CVW-8	A-7E	AJ/3XX	USS Nimitz	(CVN-68)	15 AUG 86 - 16 OCT 86
VA-82/CVW-8	A-7E	AJ/3XX	USS Nimitz	(CVN-68)	30 DEC 86 - 02 JUL 87

VA-83 Rampagers; NAS Cecil Field, FL.

Squadron Air Wing	Model	Tail Code/ Modex	Carrier		Date
VA-83/CVW-17	A-7E	AA/3XX	USS Forrestal	(CVA-59)	05 JAN 71 - 02 JUL 71
VA-83/CVW-17	A-7E	AA/3XX	USS Forrestal	(CVA-59)	22 SEP 72 - 06 JUL 73
VA-83/CVW-17	A-7E	AA/3XX	USS Forrestal	(CVA-59)	11 MAR 74 - 11 SEP 74
VA-83/CVW-17	A-7E	AA/3XX	USS Forrestal	(CV-59)	05 MAR 75 - 22 SEP 75

Squadron Air Wing	Model	Tail Code/ Modex	Carrier		Date
VA-83/CVW-17	A-7E	AA/3XX	USS Forrestal	(CV-59)	04 APR 78 - 26 OCT 78
VA-83/CVW-17	A-7E	AA/3XX	USS Forrestal	(CV-59)	27 NOV 79 - 07 MAY 80
VA-83/CVW-17	A-7E	AA/3XX	USS Forrestal	(CV-59)	02 MAR 81 - 15 SEP 81
VA-83/CVW-17	A-7E	AA/3XX	USS Forrestal	(CV-59)	28 APR 82 - 17 MAY 82
VA-83/CVW-17	A-7E	AA/3XX	USS Forrestal	(CV-59)	08 JUN 82 - 16 NOV 82
VA-83/CVW-17	A-7E	AA/3XX	USS Saratoga	(CV-60)	09 MAY 83 - 11 JUN 83
VA-83/CVW-17	A-7E	AA/3XX	USS Saratoga	(CV-60)	26 JAN 84 - 21 FEB 84
VA-83/CVW-17	A-7E	AA/3XX	USS Saratoga	(CV-60)	02 APR 84 - 20 OCT 84
VA-83/CVW-17	A-7E	AA/3XX	USS Saratoga	(CV-60)	26 AUG 85 - 16 APR 86
VA-83/CVW-17	A-7E	AA/3XX	USS Saratoga	(CV-60)	05 JUN 87 - 16 NOV 87

VA-86 Sidewinders; NAS Cecil Field, FL.

Squadron Air Wing	Model	Tail Code/ Modex	Carrier		Date
VA-86/CVW-6	A-7A	AE/4XX	USS America	(CVA-66)	16 JAN 68 - 17 FEB 68
VA-86/CVW-6	A-7A	AE/4XX	USS America	(CVA-66)	07 MAR 68 - 23 MAR 68
VA-86/CVW-6	A-7A	AE/4XX	USS America	(CVA-66)	10 APR 68 - 16 DEC 68
VA-86/CVW-15	A-7A	NL/4XX	USS Coral Sea	(CVA-43)	23 SEP 69 - 01 JUL 70
VA-86/CVW-8	A-7C	AJ/4XX	USS America	(CVA-66)	06 JUL 71 - 16 DEC 71
VA-86/CVW-8	A-7C	AJ/4XX	USS America	(CVA-66)	05 JUN 72 - 24 MAR 73
VA-86/CVW-8	A-7C	AJ/4XX	USS America	(CVA-66)	29 OCT 73 - 21 NOV 73
VA-86/CVW-8	A-7C	AJ/4XX	USS America	(CVA-66)	05 JUN 72 - 24 MAR 73
VA-86/CVW-8	A-7C	AJ/4XX	USS America	(CVA-66)	30 NOV 73 - 13 DEC 73
VA-86/CVW-8	A-7C	AJ/4XX	USS America	(CVA-66)	03 JAN 74 - 03 AUG 74
VA-86/CVW-8	A-7C	AJ/4XX	USS America	(CVA-66)	06 SEP 74 - 12 OCT 74
VA-86/CVW-8	A-7E	AJ/4XX	USS Nimitz	(CVN-68)	15 JUN 75 - 15 SEP 75
VA-86/CVW-8	A-7E	AJ/4XX	USS Nimitz	(CVN-68)	07 JUL 76 - 07 FEB 77
VA-86/CVW-8	A-7E	AJ/4XX	USS Nimitz	(CVN-68)	01 DEC 77 - 20 JUL 78
VA-86/CVW-8	A-7E	AJ/4XX	USS Nimitz	(CVN-68)	10 SEP 79 - 26 MAY 80
VA-86/CVW-8	A-7E	AJ/4XX	USS Nimitz	(CVN-68)	29 AUG 80 - 17 OCT 80
VA-86/CVW-8	A-7E	AJ/4XX	USS Nimitz	(CVN-68)	03 AUG 81 - 13 FEB 82
VA-86/CVW-8	A-7E	AJ/4XX	USS Carl Vinson	(CVN-70)	07 MAY 82 - 11 JUN 82
VA-86/CVW-8	A-7E	AJ/4XX	USS Nimitz	(CVN-68)	10 NOV 82 - 20 MAY 83
VA-86/CVW-8	A-7E	AJ/4XX	USS Nimitz	(CVN-68)	08 MAR 85 - 03 OCT 85
VA-86/CVW-8	A-7E	AJ/4XX	USS Nimitz	(CVN-68)	15 AUG 86 - 16 OCT 86
VA-86/CVW-8	A-7E	AJ/4XX	USS Nimitz	(CVN-68)	30 DEC 86 - 02 JUL 87

VA-87 Golden Warriors; NAS Cecil Field, FL.

Squadron Air Wing	Model	Tail Code/ Modex	Carrier		Date
VA-87/CVW-16	A-7B	AH/3XX	USS Ticonderoga	(CVS-14)	01 FEB 69 - 18 SEP 69
VA-87/CVW-6	A-7B	AE/4XX	USS F.D. Roosevelt	(CVA-42)	29 JAN 71 - 28 JUL 71
VA-87/CVW-6	A-7B	AE/4XX	USS F.D. Roosevelt	(CVA-42)	15 FEB 72 - 08 DEC 72
VA-87/CVW-6	A-7B	AE/4XX	USS F.D. Roosevelt	(CVA-42)	14 SEP 73 - 17 MAR 74
VA-87/CVW-6	A-7B	AE/4XX	USS F.D. Roosevelt	(CVA-42)	03 JAN 75 - 19 JUL 75
VA-87/CVW-6	A-7E	AE/4XX	USS America	(CV-66)	17 NOV 75 - 16 DEC 75
VA-87/CVW-6	A-7E	AE/4XX	USS America	(CV-66)	15 APR 76 - 25 OCT 76
VA-87/CVW-6	A-7E	AE/4XX	USS America	(CV-66)	03 MAY 77 - 24 MAY 77
VA-87/CVW-6	A-7E	AE/4XX	USS America	(CV-66)	10 JUN 77 - 19 JUL 77
VA-87/CVW-6	A-7E	AE/4XX	USS America	(CV-66)	29 SEP 77 - 25 APR 78
VA-87/CVW-6	A-7E	AE/4XX	USS Independence	(CV-62)	28 JUN 79 - 14 DEC 79
VA-87/CVW-6	A-7E	AE/4XX	USS Independence	(CV-62)	19 NOV 80 - 11 JUN 81
VA-87/CVW-6	A-7E	AE/4XX	USS Independence	(CV-62)	07 JUN 82 - 22 DEC 82
VA-87/CVW-6	A-7E	AE/4XX	USS Independence	(CV-62)	06 JUN 83 - 21 JUL 83
VA-87/CVW-6	A-7E	AE/4XX	USS Independence	(CV-62)	15 AUG 83 - 16 SEP 83
VA-87/CVW-6	A-7E	AE/4XX	USS Independence	(CV-62)	18 OCT 83 - 11 APR 84
VA-87/CVW-6	A-7E	AE/4XX	USS Independence	(CV-62)	20 AUG 84 - 09 SEP 84
VA-87/CVW-6	A-7E	AE/4XX	USS Independence	(CV-62)	16 OCT 84 - 19 FEB 85

VA-93 Blue Blasters; NAS LeMoore, CA., NAF Atsugi, JP.

Squadron Air Wing	Model	Tail Code/ Modex	Carrier		Date
VA-93/CVW-2	A-7B	NE/3XX	USS Ranger	(CVA-61)	14 OCT 69 - 01 JUN 70
VA-93/CVW-5	A-7B	NF/3XX	USS Midway	(CVA-41)	16 APR 71 - 01 NOV 71
VA-93/CVW-5	A-7B	NF/3XX	USS Midway	(CVA-41)	10 APR 72 - 03 MAR 73
VA-93/CVW-5	A-7A	NF/3XX	USS Midway	(CVA-41)	11 SEP 73 - 05 OCT 73

VA-93/CVW-5	A-7A	NF/3XX	USS Midway	(CVA-41)	16 NOV 73 - 22 DEC 73
VA-93/CVW-5	A-7A	NF/3XX	USS Midway	(CVA-41)	29 JAN 74 - 05 MAR 74
VA-93/CVW-5	A-7A	NF/3XX	USS Midway	(CVA-41)	26 MAR 74 - 05 MAY 74
VA-93/CVW-5	A-7A	NF/3XX	USS Midway	(CVA-41)	15 JUN 74 - 27 JUN 74
VA-93/CVW-5	A-7A	NF/3XX	USS Midway	(CVA-41)	09 JUL 74 - 22 JUL 74
VA-93/CVW-5	A-7A	NF/3XX	USS Midway	(CVA-41)	02 AUG 74 - 14 AUG 74
VA-93/CVW-5	A-7A	NF/3XX	USS Midway	(CVA-41)	27 SEP 74 - 09 OCT 74
VA-93/CVW-5	A-7A	NF/3XX	USS Midway	(CVA-41)	19 OCT 74 - 19 DEC 74
VA-93/CVW-5	A-7A	NF/3XX	USS Midway	(CVA-41)	13 JAN 75 - 18 FEB 75
VA-93/CVW-5	A-7A	NF/3XX	USS Midway	(CVA-41)	31 MAR 75 - 28 MAY 75
VA-93/CVW-5	A-7A	NF/3XX	USS Midway	(CV-41)	07 JUN 75 - 15 JUL 75
VA-93/CVW-5	A-7A	NF/3XX	USS Midway	(CV-41)	04 AUG 75 - 15 AUG 75
VA-93/CVW-5	A-7A	NF/3XX	USS Midway	(CV-41)	12 SEP 75 - 21 SEP 75
VA-93/CVW-5	A-7A	NF/3XX	USS Midway	(CV-41)	04 OCT 75 - 18 DEC 75
VA-93/CVW-5	A-7A	NF/3XX	USS Midway	(CV-41)	13 JAN 76 - 22 JAN 76
VA-93/CVW-5	A-7A	NF/3XX	USS Midway	(CV-41)	09 FEB 76 - 28 FEB 76
VA-93/CVW-5	A-7A	NF/3XX	USS Midway	(CV-41)	13 MAR 76- 26 APR 76
VA-93/CVW-5	A-7A	NF/3XX	USS Midway	(CV-41)	19 MAY 76 - 21 JUN 76
VA-93/CVW-5	A-7A	NF/3XX	USS Midway	(CV-41)	09 JUL 76 - 4 AUG 76
VA-93/CVW-5	A-7A	NF/3XX	USS Midway	(CV-41)	21 AUG 76 - 16 SEP 76
VA-93/CVW-5	A-7A	NF/3XX	USS Midway	(CV-41)	04 OCT 76 - 18 OCT 76
VA-93/CVW-5	A-7A	NF/3XX	USS Midway	(CV-41)	01 NOV 76 - 17 DEC 76
VA-93/CVW-5	A-7A	NF/3XX	USS Midway	(CV-41)	11 JAN 77 - 01 MAR 77
VA-93/CVW-5	A-7A	NF/3XX	USS Midway	(CV-41)	19 APR 77 - 05 MAY 77
VA-93/CVW-5	A-7E	NF/3XX	USS Midway	(CV-41)	08 AUG 77 - 02 SEP 77
VA-93/CVW-5	A-7E	NF/3XX	USS Midway	(CV-41)	27 SEP 77 - 21 DEC 77
VA-93/CVW-5	A-7E	NF/3XX	USS Midway	(CV-41)	11 APR 78 - 23 MAY 78
VA-93/CVW-5	A-7E	NF/3XX	USS Midway	(CV-41)	09 NOV 78 - 23 DEC 78
VA-93/CVW-5	A-7E	NF/3XX	USS Midway	(CV-41)	11 JAN 79 - 20 FEB 79
VA-93/CVW-5	A-7E	NF/3XX	USS Midway	(CV-41)	07 APR 79 - 18 JUN 79
VA-93/CVW-5	A-7E	NF/3XX	USS Midway	(CV-41)	20 AUG 79 - 14 SEP 79
VA-93/CVW-5	A-7E	NF/3XX	USS Midway	(CV-41)	30 SEP 79 - 20 FEB 80
VA-93/CVW-5	A-7E	NF/3XX	USS Midway	(CV-41)	14 JUL 80 - 26 NOV 80
VA-93/CVW-5	A-7E	NF/3XX	USS Midway	(CV-41)	24 FEB 81 - 05 JUN 81
VA-93/CVW-5	A-7E	NF/3XX	USS Midway	(CV-41)	25 JUN 81 - 16 JUL 81
VA-93/CVW-5	A-7E	NF/3XX	USS Midway	(CV-41)	03 SEP 81 - 06 OCT 81
VA-93/CVW-5	A-7E	NF/3XX	USS Midway	(CV-41)	25 OCT 81 - 16 NOV 81
VA-93/CVW-5	A-7E	NF/3XX	USS Midway	(CV-41)	07 MAR 82 - 05 APR 82
VA-93/CVW-5	A-7E	NF/3XX	USS Midway	(CV-41)	26 APR 82 - 18 JUN 82
VA-93/CVW-5	A-7E	NF/3XX	USS Midway	(CV-41)	11 AUG 82 - 20 AUG 82
VA-93/CVW-5	A-7E	NF/3XX	USS Midway	(CV-41)	14 SEP 82 - 10 DEC 82
VA-93/CVW-5	A-7E	NF/3XX	USS Midway	(CV-41)	12 JAN 83 - 27 JAN 83
VA-93/CVW-5	A-7E	NF/3XX	USS Midway	(CV-41)	25 FEB 83 - 22 MAR 83
VA-93/CVW-5	A-7E	NF/3XX	USS Midway	(CV-41)	30 APR 83 - 09 MAY 83
VA-93/CVW-5	A-7E	NF/3XX	USS Midway	(CV-41)	02 JUN 83 - 13 AU 83
VA-93/CVW-5	A-7E	NF/3XX	USS Midway	(CV-41)	25 OCT 83 - 11DEC 83
VA-93/CVW-5	A-7E	NF/3XX	USS Midway	(CV-41)	28 DEC 83 - 23 MAY 84
VA-93/CVW-5	A-7E	NF/3XX	USS Midway	(CV-41)	07 JUN 84 - 13 JUN 84
VA-93/CVW-5	A-7E	NF/3XX	USS Midway	(CV-41)	15 AUG 84 - 09 SEP 84
VA-93/CVW-5	A-7E	NF/3XX	USS Midway	(CV-41)	16 SEP 84 - 30 SEP 84
VA-93/CVW-5	A-7E	NF/3XX	USS Midway	(CV-41)	15 OCT 84 - 13 DEC 84
VA-93/CVW-5	A-7E	NF/3XX	USS Midway	(CV-41)	01 FEB 85 - 28 MAR 85
VA-93/CVW-5	A-7E	NF/3XX	USS Midway	(CV-41)	10 JUN 85 - 14 OCT 85
VA-93/CVW-5	A-7E	NF/3XX	USS Midway	(CV-41)	17 JAN 86 - 30 MAR 86

VA-94 Mighty Shrikes; NAS LeMoore, CA.

Squadron Air Wing	Model	Tail Code/ Modex	Carrier		Date
VA-94/CVW-15	A-7E	NL/4XX	USS Coral Sea	(CVA-43)	12 NOV 71 - 17 JUL 72
VA-94/CVW-15	A-7E	NL/4XX	USS Coral Sea	(CVA-43)	09 MAR 73 - 08 NOV 73
VA-94/CVW-15	A-7E	NL/4XX	USS Coral Sea	(CVA-43)	05 DEC 74 - 02 JUL 75
VA-94/CVW-15	A-7E	NL/4XX	USS Coral Sea	(CV-43)	15 FEB 77 - 05 OCT 77
VA-94/CVW-15	A-7E	NL/4XX	USS Kitty Hawk	(CV-63)	30 MAY 79 - 25 FEB 80
VA-94/CVW-15	A-7E	NL/4XX	USS Kitty Hawk	(CV-63)	01 APR 81 - 23 NOV 81
VA-94/CVW-11	A-7E	NH/4XX	USS Enterprise	(CVN-65)	01 SEP 82 - 28 APR 83
VA-94/CVW-11	A-7E	NH/4XX	USS Enterprise	(CVN-65)	30 MAY 84 - 20 DEC 84
VA-94/CVW-11	A-7E	NH/4XX	USS Enterprise	(CVN-65)	12 JAN 86 - 13 AUG 86
VA-94/CVW-11	A-7E	NH/4XX	USS Enterprise	(CVN-65)	25 OCT 87 - 24 NOV 87
VA-94/CVW-11	A-7E	NH/4XX	USS Enterprise	(CVN-65)	05 JAN 88 - 03 JUL 88

VA-97 Warhawks; NAS LeMoore, CA.

Squadron Air Wing	Model	Tail Code/ Modex	Carrier		Date
VA-97/CVW-14	A-7A	NK/5XX	USS Constellation	(CVA-64)	29 MAY 68 - 31 JAN 69
VA-97/CVW-14	A-7A	NK/3XX	USS Constellation	(CVA-64)	11 AUG 69 - 08 MAY 70
VA-97/CVW-14	A-7E	NK/3XX	USS Enterprise	(CVAN-65)	11 JUN 71 - 12 FEB 72
VA-97/CVW-14	A-7E	NK/3XX	USS Enterprise	(CVAN-65)	12 SEP 72 - 12 JUN 73
VA-97/CVW-14	A-7E	NK/3XX	USS Enterprise	(CVAN-65)	17 SEP 74 - 20 MAY 75
VA-97/CVW-14	A-7E	NK/3XX	USS Enterprise	(CVN-65)	30 JUL 76 - 28 MAR 77
VA-97/CVW-14	A-7E	NK/3XX	USS Enterprise	(CVN-65)	04 APR 78 - 30 OCT 78
VA-97/CVW-14	A-7E	NK/3XX	USS Coral Sea	(CV-43)	13 NOV 79 - 11 JUN 80
VA-97/CVW-14	A-7E	NK/3XX	USS Coral Sea	(CV-43)	20 AUG 81 - 23 MAR 82
VA-97/CVW-14	A-7E	NK/3XX	USS Coral Sea	(CV-43)	21 MAR 83 - 12 SEP 83
VA-97/CVW-15	A-7E	NL/3XX	USS Carl Vinson	(CVN-70)	13 MAY 84 - 29 JUN 84
VA-97/CVW-15	A-7E	NL/3XX	USS Carl Vinson	(CVN-70)	31 JUL 84 - 23 AUG 84
VA-97/CVW-15	A-7E	NL/3XX	USS Carl Vinson	(CVN-70)	18 OCT 84 - 24 MAY 85
VA-97/CVW-15	A-7E	NL/3XX	USS Carl Vinson	(CVN-70)	02 MAY 86 - 02 JUL 86
VA-97/CVW-15	A-7E	NL/3XX	USS Carl Vinson	(CVN-70)	12 AUG 86 - 05 FEB 87
VA-97/CVW-15	A-7E	NL/3XX	USS Carl Vinson	(CVN-70)	15 JUN 88 - 14 DEC 88
VA-97/CVW-15	A-7E	NL/3XX	USS Carl Vinson	(CVN-70)	01 FEB 90 - 31 JUL 90

VA-105 Gunslingers; NAS Cecil Field, FL.

Squadron Air Wing	Model	Tail Code/ Modex	Carrier		Date
VA-105/CVW-11	A-7A	NH/4XX	USS Kitty Hawk	(CVA-63)	30 DEC 68 - 04 SEP 69
VA-105/CVW-3	A-7A	AC/4XX	USS Saratoga	(CV-60)	17 JUN 70 - 11 NOV 70
VA-105/CVW-3	A-7A	AC/4XX	USS Saratoga	(CV-60)	07 JUN 71 - 19 OCT 71
VA-105/CVW-3	A-7A	AC/4XX	USS Saratoga	(CV-60)	03 APR 72 - 07 APR 72
VA-105/CVW-3	A-7A	AC/4XX	USS Saratoga	(CV-60)	11 APR 72 - 13 FEB 73
VA-105/CVW-3	A-7E	AC/4XX	USS Saratoga	(CV-60)	27 SEP 74 - 19 MAR 75
VA-105/CVW-3	A-7E	AC/4XX	USS Saratoga	(CV-60)	06 JAN 76 - 28 JUL 76
VA-105/CVW-3	A-7E	AC/4XX	USS Saratoga	(CV-60)	11 JUL 77 - 23 DEC 77
VA-105/CVW-3	A-7E	AC/4XX	USS Saratoga	(CV-60)	03 OCT 78 - 05 APR 79
VA-105/CVW-3	A-7E	AC/4XX	USS Saratoga	(CV-60)	11 MAR 80 - 27 AUG 80
VA-105/CVW-3	A-7E	AC/4XX	USS John F. Kennedy	(CV-67)	04 JAN 82 - 14 JUL 82
VA-105/CVW-15	A-7E	NL/4XX	USS Carl Vinson	(CVN-70)	01 MAR 83 - 29 OCT 83
VA-105/CVW-6	A-7E	AE/4XX	USS Forrestal	(CV-59)	10 JUL 85 - 19 AUG 85
VA-105/CVW-6	A-7E	AE/4XX	USS Forrestal	(CV-59)	02 JUN 86 - 10 NOV 86
VA-105/CVW-6	A-7E	AE/4XX	USS Forrestal	(CV-59)	28 AUG 87 - 09 OCT 87
VA-105/CVW-6	A-7E	AE/4XX	USS Forrestal	(CV-59)	08 APR 88 - 20 APR 88
VA-105/CVW-6	A-7E	AE/4XX	USS Forrestal	(CV-59)	25 APR 88 - 07 OCT 88
VA-105/CVW-6	A-7E	AE/4XX	USS Forrestal	(CV-59)	04 NOV 89 - 12 APR 90

VA-113 Stingers; NAS LeMoore, CA.

Squadron Air Wing	Model	Tail Code/ Modex	Carrier		Date
VA-113/CVW-3	A-7B	AC/4XX	USS Saratoga	(CVA-60)	09 JUL 69 - 22 JAN 70
VA-113/CVW-2	A-7E	NE/3XX	USS Ranger	(CVA-61)	27 OCT 70 - 17 JUN 71
VA-113/CVW-2	A-7E	NE/3XX	USS Ranger	(CV-61)	16 NOV 72 - 22 JUN 73
VA-113/CVW-2	A-7E	NE/3XX	USS Ranger	(CV-61)	07 MAY 74 - 18 OCT 74
VA-113/CVW-2	A-7E	NE/3XX	USS Ranger	(CV-61)	30 JAN 76 - 07 SEP 76
VA-113/CVW-2	A-7E	NE/3XX	USS Ranger	(CV-61)	09 NOV 76 - 19 NOV 76
VA-113/CVW-2	A-7E	NE/3XX	USS Ranger	(CV-61)	21 FEB 79 - 22 SEP 79
VA-113/CVW-2	A-7E	NE/3XX	USS Ranger	(CV-61)	10 SEP 80 - 05 MAY 81
VA-113/CVW-2	A-7E	NE/3XX	USS Ranger	(CV-61)	07 APR 82 - 18 OCT 82

VA-146 Blue Diamonds; NAS LeMoore, CA.

Squadron Air Wing	Model	Tail Code/ Modex	Carrier		Date
VA-146/CVW-9	A-7B	NG/3XX	USS Enterprise	(CVAN-65)	06 JAN 69 - 02 JUL 69
VA-146/CVW-9	A-7E	NG/3XX	USS America	(CVA-66)	05 JAN 70 - 08 MAR 70
VA-146/CVW-9	A-7E	NG/3XX	USS America	(CVA-66)	10 APR 70 - 21 DEC 70
VA-146/CVW-9	A-7E	NG/3XX	USS Constellation	(CVA-64)	01 OCT 71 - 01 JUL 72

Squadron Air Wing	Model	Tail Code/ Modex	Carrier		Date
VA-146/CVW-9	A-7E	NG/3XX	USS Constellation	(CVA-64)	05 JAN 73 - 11 OCT 73
VA-146/CVW-9	A-7E	NG/3XX	USS Constellation	(CVA-64)	21 JUN 74 - 23 DEC 74
VA-146/CVW-9	A-7E	NG/3XX	USS Constellation	(CV-64)	19 JAN 77 - 05 FEB 77
VA-146/CVW-9	A-7E	NG/3XX	USS Constellation	(CV-64)	16 FEB 77 - 13 MAR 77
VA-146/CVW-9	A-7E	NG/3XX	USS Constellation	(CV-64)	12 APR 77 - 21 NOV 77
VA-146/CVW-9	A-7E	NG/3XX	USS Constellation	(CV-64)	26 SEP 78 - 17 MAY 79
VA-146/CVW-9	A-7E	NG/3XX	USS Constellation	(CV-64)	26 FEB 80 - 15 OCT 80
VA-146/CVW-9	A-7E	NG/3XX	USS Constellation	(CV-64)	20 OCT 81 - 23 MAY 82
VA-146/CVW-9	A-7E	NE/3XX	USS Kitty Hawk	(CV-63)	13 JAN 84 - 01 AUG 84
VA-146/CVW-9	A-7E	NE/3XX	USS Kitty Hawk	(CV-63)	24 JUL 85 - 21 DEC 85
VA-146/CVW-9	A-7E	NE/3XX	USS Kitty Hawk	(CV-63)	03 JAN 87 - 30 JUN 87
VA-146/CVW-9	A-7E	NG/3XX	USS Nimitz	(CVN-68)	10 JUN 88 - 01 AUG 88
VA-146/CVW-9	A-7E	NG/3XX	USS Nimitz	(CVN-68)	02 SEP 88 - 02 MAR 89
VA-146/CVW-9	A-7E	NG/3XX	USS Nimitz	(CVN-68)	15 JUN 89 - 09 JUL 89

VA-147 Argonauts; NAS LeMoore, CA.

Squadron Air Wing	Model	Tail Code/ Modex	Carrier		Date
VA-147/CVW-2	A-7A	NE/3XX	USS Ranger	(CVA-61)	04 NOV 67 - 25 MAY 68
VA-147/CVW-2	A-7A	NE/3XX	USS Ranger	(CVA-61)	26 OCT 68 - 17 MAY 69
VA-147/CVW-9	A-7E	NG/4XX	USS America	(CVA-66)	05 JAN 70 - 08 MAR 70
VA-147/CVW-9	A-7E	NG/4XX	USS America	(CVA-66)	10 APR 70 - 21 DEC 70
VA-147/CVW-9	A-7E	NG/4XX	USS Constellation	(CVA-64)	01 OCT 71 - 01 JUL 72
VA-147/CVW-9	A-7E	NG/4XX	USS Constellation	(CVA-64)	05 JAN 73 - 11 OCT 73
VA-147/CVW-9	A-7E	NG/4XX	USS Constellation	(CVA-64)	21 JUN 74 - 23 DEC 74
VA-147/CVW-9	A-7E	NG/4XX	USS Constellation	(CV-64)	19 JAN 77 - 05 FEB 77
VA-147/CVW-9	A-7E	NG/4XX	USS Constellation	(CV-64)	6 FEB 77 - 13 MAR 77
VA-147/CVW-9	A-7E	NG/4XX	USS Constellation	(CV-64)	12 APR 77 - 21 NOV 77
VA-147/CVW-9	A-7E	NG/4XX	USS Constellation	(CV-64)	26 SEP 78 - 17 MAY 79
VA-147/CVW-9	A-7E	NG/4XX	USS Constellation	(CV-64)	26 FEB 80 - 15 OCT 80
VA-147/CVW-9	A-7E	NG/4XX	USS Constellation	(CV-64)	20 OCT 81 - 23 MAY 82
VA-147/CVW-9	A-7E	NE/3XX	USS Kitty Hawk	(CV-63)	13 JAN 84 - 01 AUG 84
VA-147/CVW-9	A-7E	NE/3XX	USS Kitty Hawk	(CV-63)	24 JUL 85 - 21 DEC 85
VA-147/CVW-9	A-7E	NE/3XX	USS Kitty Hawk	(CV-63)	03 JAN 87 - 30 JUN 87
VA-147/CVW-9	A-7E	NG/4XX	USS Nimitz	(CVN-68)	10 JUN 88 - 01 AUG 88
VA-147/CVW-9	A-7E	NG/4XX	USS Nimitz	(CVN-68)	02 SEP 88 - 02 MAR 89

VA-153 Blue Tail Flies; NAS LeMoore, CA.

Squadron Air Wing	Model	Tail Code/ Modex	Carrier		Date
VA-153/CVW-19	A-7A	NM/3XX	USS Oriskany	(CVA-34)	14 MAY 70 - 10 DEC 70
VA-153/CVW-19	A-7A	NM/3XX	USS Oriskany	(CVA-34)	14 MAY 71 - 18 DEC 71
VA-153/CVW-19	A-7A	NM/3XX	USS Oriskany	(CVA-34)	05 JUN 72 - 30 MAR 73
VA-153/CVW-19	A-7B	NM/3XX	USS Oriskany	(CVA-34)	18 OCT 73 - 05 JUN 74
VA-153/CVW-19	A-7B	NM/3XX	USS Oriskany	(CV-34)	03 MAR 75 - 03 MAR 76
VA-153/CVW-19	A-7B	NM/3XX	USS F.D. Roosevelt	(CV-42)	04 OCT 76 - 21 APR 7

VA-155 Silver Foxes; NAS LeMoore, CA.

Squadron Air Wing	Model	Tail Code/ Modex	Carrier		Date
VA-155/CVW-19	A-7B	NM/5XX	USS Oriskany	(CVA-34)	14 MAY 70 - 10 DEC 70
VA-155/CVW-19	A-7B	NM/5XX	USS Oriskany	(CVA-34)	14 MAY 71 - 18 DEC 71
VA-155/CVW-19	A-7B	NM/5XX	USS Oriskany	(CVA-34)	05 JUN 72 - 30 MAR 73
VA-155/CVW-19	A-7B	NM/5XX	USS Oriskany	(CVA-34)	18 OCT 73 - 05 JUN 74
VA-155/CVW-19	A-7B	NM/5XX	USS Oriskany	(CV-34)	03 MAR 75 - 03 MAR 76
VA-155/CVW-19	A-7B	NM/5XX	USS F.D. Roosevelt	(CV-42)	04 OCT 76 - 21 APR 77

VA-192 Golden Dragons; NAS LeMoore, CA.

Squadron Air Wing	Model	Tail Code/ Modex	Carrier		Date
VA-192/CVW-11	A-7E	NH/3XX	USS Kitty Hawk	(CVA-63)	06 NOV 70 - 17 JUL 71
VA-192/CVW-11	A-7E	NH/3XX	USS Kitty Hawk	(CV-63)	17 FEB 72 - 28 NOV 72
VA-192/CVW-11	A-7E	NH/3XX	USS Kitty Hawk	(CV-63)	05 SEP 73 - 30 SEP 73

VA-192/CVW-11	A-7E	NH/3XX	USS Kitty Hawk	(CV-63)	23 NOV 73 - 09 JUL 74
VA-192/CVW-11	A-7E	NH/3XX	USS Kitty Hawk	(CV-63)	25 FEB 75 - 29 MAR 75
VA-192/CVW-11	A-7E	NH/3XX	USS Kitty Hawk	(CV-63)	21 MAY 75 - 15 DEC 7
VA-192/CVW-11	A-7E	NH/3XX	USS Kitty Hawk	(CV-63)	25 OCT 77 - 15 MAY 78
VA-192/CVW-11	A-7E	NH/3XX	USS Enterprise	(CVN-65)	28 NOV 78 - 15 DEC 78
VA-192/CVW-11	A-7E	NH/3XX	USS America	(CV-66)	05 JAN 79 - 12 FEB 79
VA-192/CVW-11	A-7E	NH/3XX	USS America	(CV-66)	13 MAR 79 - 22 SEP 79
VA-192/CVW-11	A-7E	NH/3XX	USS America	(CV-66)	14 APR 81 - 12 NOV 81
VA-192/CVW-9	A-7E	NG/3XX	USS Ranger	(CV-61)	15 JUL 83 - 29 FEB 84

VA-195 Dambusters; NAS LeMoore, CA.

Squadron Air Wing	Model	Tail Code/ Modex	Carrier		Date
VA-195/CVW-11	A-7E	NH/4XX	USS Kitty Hawk	(CVA-63)	06 NOV 70 - 17 JUL 71
VA-195/CVW-11	A-7E	NH/4XX	USS Kitty Hawk	(CV-63)	17 FEB 72 - 28 NOV 72
VA-195/CVW-11	A-7E	NH/4XX	USS Kitty Hawk	(CV-63)	05 SEP 73 - 30 SEP 73
VA-195/CVW-11	A-7E	NH/4XX	USS Kitty Hawk	(CV-63)	23 NOV 73 - 09 JUL 74
VA-195/CVW-11	A-7E	NH/4XX	USS Kitty Hawk	(CV-63)	25 FEB 75 - 29 MAR 75
VA-195/CVW-11	A-7E	NH/4XX	USS Kitty Hawk	(CV-63)	21 MAY 75 - 15 DEC 75
VA-195/CVW-11	A-7E	NH/4XX	USS Kitty Hawk	(CV-63)	25 OCT 77 - 15 MAY 78
VA-195/CVW-11	A-7E	NH/4XX	USS Enterprise	(CVN-65)	28 NOV 78 - 15 DEC 78
VA-195/CVW-11	A-7E	NH/4XX	USS America	(CV-66)	05 JAN 79 - 12 FEB 79
VA-195/CVW-11	A-7E	NH/4XX	USS America	(CV-66)	13 MAR 79 - 22 SEP 79
VA-195/CVW-11	A-7E	NH/4XX	USS America	(CV-66)	14 APR 81 - 12 NOV 81
VA-195/CVW-9	A-7E	NG/4XX	USS Ranger	(CV-61)	15 JUL 83 - 29 FEB 84

VA-203 Blue Dolphin's; NAS Jacksonville, FL., NAS Cecil Field, FL.

Squadron Air Wing	Model	Tail Code/ Modex	Carrier		Date
VA-203/CVWR-20	A-7B	AF/3XX	USS Independence	(CV-62)	27 NOV78 - 01 DEC 78
VA-203/CVWR-20	A-7B	AF/3XX	USS D.D. Eisenhower	(CVN-69)	23 JUN 84 - 02 JUL 84
VA-203/CVWR-20	A-7E	AF/3XX	USS Forrestal	(CV-59)	14 JUN 87 - 26 JUN 87

VA-204 River Rattlers; NAS New Orleans, LA.

Squadron Air Wing	Model	Tail Code/ Modex	Carrier		Date
VA-204/CVWR-20	A-7B	AF/4XX	USS Independence	(CV-62)	27 NOV 78 - 01 DEC 78
VA-204/CVWR-20	A-7E	AF/4XX	USS D,D. Eisenhower	(CVN-69)	23 JUN 84 - 02 JUL 84
VA-204/CVWR-20	A-7E	AF/4XX	USS Forrestal	(CV-59)	14 JUN 87 - 26 JUN 87
VA-204/CVWR-20	A-7E	AF/4XX	USS D.D. Eisenhower	(CVN-69)	24 JUL 89 - 03 AUG 89

VA-205 Falcons; NAS Atlanta, GA.

Squadron Air Wing	Model	Tail Code/ Modex	Carrier		Date
VA-205/CVWR-20	A-7B	AF/5XX	USS Independence	(CV-62)	27 NOV 78 - 01 DEC 78
VA-205/CVWR-20	A-7E	AF/5XX	USS D.D. Eisenhower	(CVN-69)	23 JUN 84 - 02 JUL 84
VA-205/CVWR-20	A-7E	AF/5XX	USS Forrestal	(CV-59)	14 JUN 87 - 26 JUN 87
VA-205/CVWR-20	A-7E	AF/5XX	USS D.D. Eisenhower	(CVN-69)	24 JUL 89 - 03 AUG 89

VA-215 Barn Owls; NAS LeMoore, CA.

Squadron Air Wing	Model	Tail Code/ Modex	Carrier		Date
VA-215/CVW-9	A-7B	NG-4XX	USS Enterprise	(CVAN-65)	06 JAN 69 - 02 JUL 69
VA-215/CVW-6	A-7B	NM/4XX	USS Oriskany	(CVA-34)	14 MAY 71 - 18 DEC 71
VA-215/CVW-19	A-7B	NM/4XX	USS Oriskany	(CVA-34)	05 JUN 72 - 30 MAR 73
VA-215/CVW-19	A-7B	NM/4XX	USS Oriskany	(CVA-34)	18 OCT 73 - 05 JUN 74
VA-215/CVW-19	A-7B	NM/4XX	USS Oriskany	(CV-34)	03 MAR 75 - 03 MAR 76
VA-215/CVW-19	A-7B	NM/4XX	USS F.D. Roosevelt	(CV-42)	04 OCT 76 - 21 APR 77

VA-303 Golden Hawks; NAS Alameda, CA.

Squadron Air Wing	Model	Tail Code/ Modex	Carrier		Date
VA-303/CVWR-30	A-7A	ND/3XX	USS Ranger	(CV-61)	09 NOV 76 - 19 NOV 76
VA-303/CVWR-30	A-7B	ND/3XX	USS Ranger	(CV-61)	1977

VA-304 Firebirds; NAS Alameda, CA.

Squadron Air Wing	Model	Tail Code/ Modex	Carrier		Date
VA-304/CVWR-30	A-7A	ND/4XX	USS Ranger	(CV-61)	09 NOV 76 - 19 NOV 76
VA-304/CVWR-30	A-7B	ND/4XX	USS Ranger	(CV-61)	1977
VA-304/CVWR-30	A-7B	ND/4XX	USS Ranger	(CV-61)	15 JAN 86 - 26 JAN 86
VA-304/CVWR-30	A-7B	ND/4XX	USS Ranger	(CV-61)	1988

VA-305 Hackers, then Lobos; NAS Point Mugu, CA.

Squadron Air Wing	Model	Tail Code/ Modex	Carrier		Date
VA-305/CVWR-30	A-7A	ND/5XX	USS Ranger	(CV-61)	09 NOV 76 - 19 NOV 76
VA-305/CVWR-30	A-7B	ND/5XX	USS Ranger	(CV-61)	1977
VA-305/CVWR-30	A-7B	ND/5XX	USS Ranger	(CV-61)	15 JAN 86 - 26 JAN 86
VA-305/CVWR-30	A-7E	ND/5XX	USS Ranger	(CV-61)	1988

Tailhook Association

APPENDIX 5

PATCH GALLERY

USN

'DESERT STORM'

IRAQ

A-7E

PERSIAN GULF '91

Saudi Arabia

A-7 CORSAIR II

FLEETS FINEST 1966-1991

WESTPAC "1969"

USS KITTY HAWK

BAGHDAD URBAN RE-DEVELOPMENT

A-7E

A-7 CORSAIR

A-7 PILOTS DO IT ON THE FIRST PASS

A-7 PILOTS DO IT BETTER

CORSAIR II

1963   1990

End of an Era

A-7 PILOTS DO IT BETTER

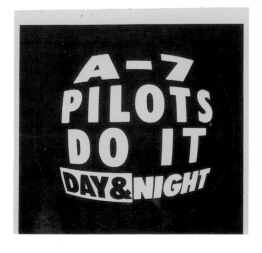

A-7 PILOTS DO IT DAY & NIGHT

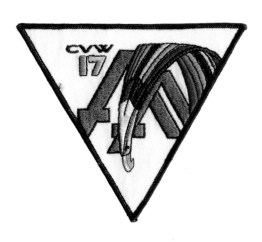

CVW 17

NAVAL AIR DEVELOPMENT CENTER
NADC
WARMINSTER

NAVAL AIR TEST CENTER
STRIKE AIRCRAFT TEST

Naval Air Engineering Center
LAKEHURST, N.J.

US NAVAL AIR TEST FACILITY (SI)
LAKEHURST, N.J.
NARDAC

ATTACK CARRIER AIR WING
RESERVE

NAVAL AIR TEST CENTER
FLIGHT TEST

U.S. NAVAL MISSILE CENTER

AIR WING 30

SERVICE TEST
N.A.T.C.

NSAWC
STRIKE
FROM THE AIR AND SEA

356

NAWC
Weapons Division
NAVAL AIR WARFARE CENTER

PACIFIC MISSILE TEST CENTER

VA-25

U.S.N.T.P.S.

ATTACK SQUADRON TWELVE

ATTACK SQUADRON 27

NWC
NAVAL WEAPONS CENTER-CHINA LAKE, CALIFORNIA

ATTACK SQUADRON 15

CNO · BATTLE · E
SAFETY "S" · GRAMPAW PETTIBONE · AWARD
CHARGERS
'9 ATTACK SQUADRON 27 86

NAVAL WEAPONS EVALUATION FACILITY
NWEF

VA-22

A-7 CORSAIR II 1967-1991
LIGHT ATTACK-END OF AN ERA

357

LAST CORSAIR CRUISE

CV-60

SUNLINERS 1987

GOLDEN WARRIORS

ATKRON-87

ATKRON 82

RAMPAGERS

ATTACK SQUADRON-83

A-7E CORSAIR II

GONE BUT NOT FORGOTTEN

ATKRON 86

ATTACK SQUADRON 93

ATTACK SQUADRON 94

89 WORLD CRUISE 90
CVN-65 CVW-11
END OF AN ERA

MAINT TEAM
WITH PRIDE AND PROFESSIONALISM
400
E
GUNSLINGERS

VA-122

ATKRON-97

ATTACK SQUADRON 125

VA-146

GUNSLINGERS
ATKRON 105

STINGERS

BLUE DIAMONDS
VA-146

ATKRON 147

ARGONAUTS
VA-147
ULTRALIGHT ATTACK

ATKRON 153

END OF AN ERA • A-7 CORSAIR
VA-174 HELLRAZORS

ATTACK SQUADRON 155

PORTUGAL PAF

THAI NAVY

APPENDIX 6

A -7 Aircraft Losses

Note: The U.S. Navy Aircraft History Cards were discontinued as of September 1987 due to budgetary restraints, and when the Navy Regional Data Center (NARDAC) eliminated its secure computer, the Chief of Naval Operations (Air Warfare) office, responsible for maintaining the Aircraft Inventory (OP-515, Aircraft Readiness and Analysis Branch), no longer had a computer system to manage the Naval Aircraft Inventory System. Aircraft History Branch, Naval Historical Center.

This list represents the 445 USN A-7 aircraft losses through September 1987, the 7 unknown USN losses, and the 30 known foreign losses through October 2003. The U.S. Navy losses after September 1987 are not known.

A-7A
199 Built 100 Losses

Model	Bureau Number	Command	Location	Loss Date
YA-7A	152580	China Lake	NAF China Lake	23 MAR 66
YA-7A	152582	NPRO	LTV Dallas, TX	16 FEB 68
A-7A	152652	NATC	NAS Patuxent River	02 AUG 67
A-7A	152653	NATC	NAS Patuxent River	15 NOV 78
A-7A	152654	NWEF	Kirtland AFB	26 JUL 76
A-7A	152662	VA-122	NAS LeMoore	18 MAR 69
A-7A	152663	VA-174	NAS Cecil Field	23 JUN 70
A-7A	152664	VA-122	NAS LeMoore	07 MAY 69
A-7A	152665	VA-56	USS Midway	13 JAN 77
A-7A	152666	VA-122	NAS LeMoore	17 MAY 68
A-7A	152670	VA-122	NAS LeMoore	08 DEC 66
A-7A	152671	VA-122	NAS LeMoore	24 SEP 68
A-7A	152672	VA-174	NAS Cecil Field	26 JAN 67
A-7A	152674	VX-5	NAF China Lake	01 AUG 67
A-7A	152679	VA-86	USS Coral Sea	02 MAY 69
A-7A	152680	VA-82	USS Coral Sea	01 MAY 70
A-7A	152683	VA-122	NAS LeMoore	03 AUG 68
A-7A	152684	VA-174	NAS Cecil Field	28 DEC 67
A-7A	152685	VA-56	USS Midway	24 MAY 75
A-7A	153136	VA-86	USS Coral Sea	04 MAR 70
A-7A	153137	VA-122	NAS LeMoore	08 MAR 68
A-7A	153139	VA-174	NAS Cecil Field	14 JAN 69
A-7A	153141	VA-125	NAS LeMoore	12 FEB 72
A-7A	153143	VA-27	NAS LeMoore	01 MAR 70
A-7A	153146	VA-82	USS Coral Sea	14 JUN 69
A-7A	153147	VA-105	NAS Cecil Field	06 AUG 72
A-7A	153149	VA-174	NAS Cecil Field	15 JUN 70
A-7A	153153	VA-97	USS Constellation	07 APR 70
A-7A	153154	VA-122	NAS LeMoore	14 JUN 68
A-7A	153156	VA-125	NAS LeMoore	15 NOV 69
A-7A	153158	VA-305	USS Ranger	16 NOV 76
A-7A	153160	VA-93	USS Midway	11 JUL 74
A-7A	153161	VA-37	NAS Cecil Field	10 NOV 72
A-7A	153164	VA-37	USS Kitty Hawk	28 APR 69
A-7A	153165	VA-122	NAS LeMoore	21 JAN 69
A-7A	153167	NARF	NAS Jacksonville	27 AUG 73
A-7A	153168	VA-147	NAS LeMoore	28 SEP 67
A-7A	153169	VA-174	NAS Cecil Field	06 APR 73
A-7A	153172	VA-122	NAS LeMoore	17 MAY 68
A-7A	153174	VA-122	NAS LeMoore	11 FEB 68
A-7A	153175	VA-27	USS Constellation	31 OCT 68
A-7A	153176	VA-153	USS Oriskany	29 JUN 70
A-7A	153178	VA-93	USS Midway	06 OCT 75
A-7A	153180	VA-105	USS Kitty Hawk	02 MAY 69

Model	Bureau Number	Command	Location	Loss Date
A-7A	153181	VA-105	USS Kitty Hawk	15 FEB 69
A-7A	153182	VA-37	USS Saratoga	21 MAR 71
A-7A	153183	VA-125	NAS LeMoore	29 JAN 74
A-7A	153185	VA-37	USS Saratoga	02 AUG 69
A-7A	153189	VA-153	USS Oriskany	01 NOV 71
A-7A	153191	VA-93	USS Midway	30 MAR 77
A-7A	153192	VA-105	USS Kitty Hawk	03 OCT 68
A-7A	153193	VA-105	NAS Cecil Field	31 JUL 72
A-7A	153197	VA-105	USS Saratoga	16 JUN 72
A-7A	153198	VA-105	USS Saratoga	10 JUL 70
A-7A	153202	VA-147	NAS LeMoore	26 SEP 67
A-7A	153203	VX-5	NAF China Lake	08 JAN 69
A-7A	153204	VA-56	USS Midway	22 DEC 73
A-7A	153205	VA-153	USS Oriskany	09 JUN 71
A-7A	153206	VA-37	USS Saratoga	14 JUN 72
A-7A	153207	VA-37	NAS Cecil Field	17 AUG 72
A-7A	153209	VA-37	USS Saratoga	03 MAY 71
A-7A	153210	VA-37	NAS Cecil Field	10 JUN 68
A-7A	153211	VA-122	NAS LeMoore	07 JUN 68
A-7A	153213	VA-37	NAS Cecil Field	13 SEP 72
A-7A	153214	VA-97	USS Constellation	18 SEP 68
A-7A	153222	VA-147	NAS LeMoore	12 APR 69
A-7A	153223	VA-153	USS Oriskany	08 SEP 71
A-7A	153225	VA-86	NAS Cecil Field	02 SEP 68
A-7A	153230	VA-105	USS Saratoga	18 JUN 72
A-7A	153231	VA-86	USS Coral Sea	07 JAN 70
A-7A	153232	VA-125	NAS LeMoore	12 NOV 70
A-7A	153233	VA-97	USS Constellation	06 APR 70
A-7A	153234	VA-97	USS Constellation	16 JUL 68
A-7A	153239	VA-147	NAS LeMoore	22 DEC 67
A-7A	153243	VA-147	NAS LeMoore	17 JUN 69
A-7A	153246	VA-82	USS Coral Sea	22 AUG 69
A-7A	153247	VA-174	NAS Cecil Field	04 JUN 71
A-7A	153251	VA-97	USS Constellation	09 MAR 66
A-7A	153252	VA-97	USS Constellation	02 OCT 69
A-7A	153253	VA-82	NAS Cecil Field	24 JUL 68
A-7A	153255	VA-82	USS America	31 MAY 68
A-7A	153256	VA-93	USS Midway	12 NOV 73
A-7A	153257	VA-82	USS America	22 JUN 68
A-7A	153258	VA-82	USS America	31 MAY 68
A-7A	153259	VA-82	USS America	27 APR 68
A-7A	153262	VA-303	NAS Alameda	06 APR 75
A-7A	153264	VA-203	NAS Jacksonville	22 JUL 76
A-7A	153265	VA-86	USS America	11 JUN 68
A-7A	153267	VA-304	NAS Alameda	21 OCT 72
A-7A	153269	VA-86	USS America	21 JUN 68
A-7A	153271	VA-86	USS America	26 JUN 68
A-7A	153273	VA-27	USS Constellation	06 OCT 68
A-7A	154344	VA-27	USS Constellation	25 SEP 68
A-7A	154347	VX-5	NAF China Lake	08 JAN 69
A-7A	154348	VA-97	USS Constellation	09 MAR 68
A-7A	154350	VA-304	NAS Alameda	28 SEP 74
A-7A	154353	VA-56	NAF Atsugi	22 OCT 75
A-7A	154357	VA-125	NAS LeMoore	02 OCT 70
A-7A	154358	VA-97	USS Constellation	03 APR 70
A-7A	154359	VA-27	USS Constellation	25 AUG 68

A -7B
196 Built 102 Losses

Model	Bureau Number	Command	Location	Loss Date
A-7B	154362	VA-304	NAS Alameda	23 APR 86
A-7B	154363	VA-155	USS Oriskany	20 SEP 72
A-7B	154364	VA-125	NAS LeMoore	26 FEB 70
A-7B	154365	VA-125	NAS LeMoore	15 JUN 71
A-7B	154367	VA-122	NAS LeMoore	19 JUN 69
A-7B	154369	VA-122	NAS LeMoore	23 APR 73
A-7B	154374	VA-15	NAS Cecil Field	19 AUG 74
A-7B	154376	VA-122	NAS LeMoore	07 MAR 69
A-7B	154378	VA-122	NAS LeMoore	06 MAY 69
A-7B	154380	VA-153	NAS LeMoore	04 DEC 78
A-7B	154383	VA-215	USS Enterprise	08 JUN 69
A-7B	154384	VA-15	NAS Cecil Field	10 JUL 72
A-7B	154385	VA-122	NAS LeMoore	13 NOV 69
A-7B	154386	VA-72	USS John F. Kennedy	20 MAY 72
A-7B	154387	VA-122	NAS LeMoore	06 MAY 69
A-7B	154391	VA-93	NAS LeMoore	05 FEB 70
A-7B	154392	VA-122	NAS LeMoore	09 JUN 69
A-7B	154393	VA-93	NAS LeMoore	08 SEP 72
A-7B	154394	VA-125	NAS LeMoore	08 MAR 70
A-7B	154395	VA-203	NAS Jacksonville	26 NOV 82
A-7B	154399	VA-56	NAS LeMoore	11 NOV 72
A-7B	154400	VA-153	USS F.D. Roosevelt	10 MAR 77
A-7B	154401	VA-15	USS F.D. Roosevelt	01 MAR 70
A-7B	154403	VA-15	USS F.D. Roosevelt	12 NOV 69
A-7B	154405	VA-93	USS Midway	23 MAY 72
A-7B	154408	VA-15	USS F.D. Roosevelt	04 SEP 69
TA-7C	154410	VA-122	NAS LeMoore	17 JAN 84
A-7B	154414	VA-15	USS F.D. Roosevelt	04 SEP 69
A-7B	154417	VA-174	NAS Cecil Field	25 NOV 68
A-7B	154418	VA-122	NAS LeMoore	03 JUN 69
A-7B	154419	VA-125	NAS LeMoore	30 JAN 72
A-7B	154420	VA-204	NAS New Orleans	12 OCT 83
A-7B	154421	VA-87	NAS Cecil Field	22 OCT 72
A-7B	154422	VA-215	USS Oriskany	07 DEC 70
A-7B	154423	VA-87	NAS Cecil Field	20 JUL 69
A-7B	154426	VA-146	USS Enterprise	14 JAN 69
A-7B	154427	VA-205	NAS Jacksonville	03 JUN 78
A-7B	154428	VA-174	NAS Cecil Field	01 JUN 70
A-7B	154429	VA-146	USS Enterprise	14 JAN 69
A-7B	154430	VA-215	USS Oriskany	22 SEP 71
A-7B	154432	VA-87	USS F. D. Roosevelt	23 JUN 72
A-7B	154434	VA-87	USS F. D. Roosevelt	19 FEB 72
A-7B	154435	VA-87	NAS LeMoore	25 JUL 72
A-7B	154436	VA-155	NAS LeMoore	24 SEP 72
TA-7C	154437	VA-174	NAS Cecil Field	24 AUG 82
A-7B	154441	VA-25	USS Ticonderoga	13 MAY 69
A-7B	154442	VA-153	USS Oriskany	20 JAN 76
A-7B	154444	VA-146	USS Enterprise	14 JAN 69
A-7B	154445	VA-304	NAS Alameda	27 MAR 86
A-7B	154446	VA-215	USS Enterprise	14 JAN 69
A-7B	154447	VA-215	USS Oriskany	18 NOV 70
TA-7C	154450	VA-174	NAS Cecil Field	29 NOV 84
A-7B	154457	VA-215	USS Enterprise	14 JAN 69
A-7B	154459	VA-146	USS Enterprise	07 DEC 68
A-7B	154461	VA-215	USS Enterprise	14 JAN 69
A-7B	154465	VA-204	NAS New Orleans	24 AUG 79
A-7B	154470	VA-174	NAS Cecil Field	01 APR 70
A-7B	154473	VA-25	USS Ticonderoga	09 MAR 69
A-7B	154480	VA-125	NAS LeMoore	27 AUG 70
A-7B	154482	VA-204	NAS New Orleans	06 MAR 81
A-7B	154483	VA-174	NAS Cecil Field	10 APR 69
A-7B	154486	VA-46	NAS Cecil Field	11 APR 69
A-7B	154487	VA-46	USS John F Kennedy	06 JUL 75
A-7B	154492	VA-15	USS F. D. Roosevelt	25 MAY 75
A-7B	154495	VA-46	NAS Cecil Field	25 JAN 71
A-7B	154496	VA-46	NAS Cecil Field	23 MAR 70

Model	Bureau Number	Command	Location	Loss Date
A-7B	154497	VA-204	NAS New Orleans	11 FEB 79
A-7B	154499	VA-113	USS Saratoga	16 APR 69
A-7B	154501	NATC	NAS Patuxent River	03 AUG 74
A-7B	154503	VA-46	NAS Cecil Field	17 APR 71
A-7B	154504	VA-46	NAS Cecil Field	16 MAR 70
A-7B	154506	VA-93	NAS LeMoore	10 NOV 72
A-7B	154508	VA-56	NAS LeMoore	06 AUG 72
A-7B	154510	VA-25	USS Ticonderoga	07 JAN 69
A-7B	154511	VA-113	NAS LeMoore	10 NOV 69
A-7B	154513	VA-15	NAS Cecil Field	08 MAY 74
A-7B	154514	VA-113	USS Saratoga	03 JAN 69
A-7B	154515	VA-174	NAS Cecil Field	25 JAN 69
A-7B	154517	VA-56	NAS LeMoore	26 DEC 69
A-7B	154518	VA-155	NAS LeMoore	12 MAY 74
A-7B	154519	NARF	NAS Alameda	16 NOV 76
A-7B	154521	VA-155	NAS LeMoore	17 JUL 72
A-7B	154522	VA-174	NAS Cecil Field	06 MAY 69
A-7B	154524	VA-113	USS Saratoga	24 JUN 69
A-7B	154525	VA-155	USS Oriskany	25 JUN 70
A-7B	154526	VA-155	USS F.D. Roosevelt	05 DEC 76
A-7B	154528	VA-155	USS Oriskany	14 APR 72
A-7B	154530	VA-155	USS Oriskany	09 APR 70
A-7B	154531	VA-56	NAS LeMoore	23 JUL 72
A-7B	154532	VA-56	NAS LeMoore	23 JUL 72
A-7B	154533	VA-153	NAS LeMoore	19 MAR 74
A-7B	154534	VA-72	USS John F. Kennedy	27 JUN 72
TA-7C	154536	VA-122	NAS LeMoore	02 OCT 79
TA-7C	154537	NARF	NAS Jacksonville	28 JUN 84
A-7B	154539	VA-56	USS Midway	19 OCT 71
A-7B	154540	VA-56	NAS LeMoore	06 NOV 72
A-7B	154541	VA-56	USS Midway	19 MAY 72
A-7B	154542	VA-56	NAS LeMoore	18 DEC 69
A-7B	154543	VA-56	NAS LeMoore	06 JAN 73
A-7B	154546	VA-93	NAS LeMoore	21 OCT 69
A-7B	154549	VA-304	NAS Alameda	12 JAN 84
A-7B	154555	VA-93	NAS LeMoore	09 MAY 70

A-7C
67 Built 31 Losses

Model	Bureau Number	Command	Location	Loss Date
A-7C	156735	NPRO	LTV Dallas	17 JUL 69
A-7C	156736	NATC	NAS Patuxent River	02 JUL 75
TA-7C	156737	VA-174	NAS Cecil Field	10 NOV 83
TA-7C	156740	VA-122	NAS LeMoore	21 SEP 83
A-7C	156742	NATC	NAS Patuxent River	23 SEP 70
EA-7L	156743	VAQ-34	NAS Point Mugu	19 JUL 90
TA-7C	156748	VX-5	NWC China Lake	21 NOV 79
A-7C	156749	VA-122	NAS LeMoore	19 JUN 72
A-7C	156755	VA-82	NAS Cecil Field	02 DEC 74
A-7C	156756	VA-174	NAS Cecil Field	30 JUN 75
A-7C	156758	VA-122	NAS LeMoore	13 AUG 70
A-7C	156759	VX-5	NAF China Lake	25 JUL 74
A-7C	156760	VA-86	NAS Cecil Field	26 JUL 73
A-7C	156762	VA-86	NAS Cecil Field	29 OCT 72
A-7C	156763	NARF	NAS Alameda	06 NOV 75
A-7C	156764	VA-86	NAS Cecil Field	09 NOV 72
TA-7C	156766	VA-122	NAS LeMoore	13 OCT 81
A-7C	156769	VA-122	NAS LeMoore	07 DEC 70
TA-7C	156770	VA-174	NAS Cecil Field	13 JAN 83
A-7C	156771	VA-86	NAS Cecil Field	17 JUL 72
A-7C	156775	VA-86	NAS Cecil Field	28 OCT 72
TA-7C	156777	PMTC	NAS Point Mugu	29 SEP 81
A-7C	156778	VA-122	NAS LeMoore	15 JUN 70
A-7C	156780	VA-122	NAS LeMoore	07 JUN 72
A-7C	156781	NARF	NAS Jacksonville	15 JUN 78
A-7C	156783	VA-82	NAS Cecil Field	20 DEC 72

A-7C	156792	VA-86	NAS Cecil Field	17 JUL 72
TA-7C	156793	VA-122	NAS LeMoore	17 AUG 83
A-7C	156796	VA-174	NAS Cecil Field	24 JUN 70
A-7C	156798	VA-82	NAS Cecil Field	10 SEP 72
A-7C	156799	NARF	NAS Jacksonville	15 JUN 78

A-7D
459 Built 38 Losses

Model	Bureau Number	Command	Location	Loss Date
A-7D	67-14586	3246 TW	Eglin AFB	DEC 75,
A-7D	69-6207	355 TFS	Myrtle Beach AFB	Unknown
A-7D	69-6211	333 TFTS	Davis Monthan AFB	25 NOV 70
A-7D	70-0949	355 TFS	Myrtle Beach AFB	02 DEC 72
A-7D	70-0968	355 TFS	Myrtle Beach AFB	31 JAN 78
A-7D	70-1045	112 TFS	McIntire ANGB	17 MAY 91
A-7D	70-1050	198 TFS	Muniz ANGB	12 JAN 81
A-7D	71-0300	Unknown	Nellis AFB	01 MAY 78
A-7D	71-0305	3 TFS	Korat RTAB	04 MAY 73
A-7D	71-0310	355 TFS	Myrtle Beach AFB	02 DEC 72
A-7D	71-0316	355 TFS	Myrtle Beach AFB	11 JAN 75
A-7D	71-0328	355 TFS	Korat RTAB	23 DEC 75
A-7D	71-0346	Unknown	Singer, West Germany	30 AUG 74
A-7D	71-0348	Unknown	Panama Canal Zone	07 FEB 78
A-7D	71-0351	Unknown	Cloverdale, CA.	20 SEP 76
A-7D	71-0355	333 TFTS	Davis Monthan AFB.	OCT 77
A-7D	72-0172	76 TFS	England AFB	05 AUG 75
A-7D	72-0181	Unknown	Unknown	14 JAN 80
A-7D	72-0184	Unknown	Unknown	22 JUN 88
A-7D	72-0187	Unknown	Unknown	17 JAN 81
A-7D	72-0189	198 TFS	Muniz ANGB	12 JAN 81
A-7D	72-0207	Unknown	Mansfield, LA.	26 OCT 76
A-7D	72-0219	198 TFS	Muniz ANGB	12 JAN 81
A-7D	72-0221	198 TFS	Muniz ANGB	12 JAN 81
A-7D	72-0222	198 TFS	Muniz ANGB	12 JAN 81
A-7D	72-0233	333 TFTS	Davis Monthan AFB	09 FEB 82
A-7D	72-0246	Unknown	Unknown	03 MAR 89
A-7D	72-0257	Unknown	Unknown	05 AUG 88
A-7D	72-0263	Unknown	Nellis AFB	01 MAY 78
A-7D	73-0993	333 TFTS	Davis Monthan AFB	75
A-7D	73-0994	198 TFS	Muniz ANGB	12 JAN 81
A-7D	73-0995	157 TFS	McIntire ANGB	09 DEC 77
A-7D	73-1005	198 TFS	Muniz ANGB	12 JAN 81
A-7D	74-1748	198 TFS	Muniz ANGB	12 JAN 81
A-7D	74-1755	198 TFS	Muniz ANGB	12 JAN 81
A-7D	75-0391	Unknown	Unknown	05 JUL 88
A-7D	75-0396	Unknown	Santa Rosa, NM	11 JAN 92
A-7D	75-0404	Unknown	Sioux City ANGB	APR 77

A-7E
529 Built 212 Lost

Model	Bureau Number	Command	Location	Loss Date
A-7E	156803	VA-147	NAS LeMoore	31 MAY 82
A-7E	156809	VA-22	USS Coral Sea	18 MAY 73
A-7E	156820	VA-81	NAS Cecil Field	07 AUG 85
A-7E	156825	VA-113	USS Ranger	10 MAY 74
A-7E	156826	VA-146	NAS Fallon	29 JUN 71
A-7E	156837	VA-147	USS Constellation	29 JAN 73
A-7E	156838	NSWC	NAS Fallon	20 AUG 85
A-7E	156839	VA-97	USS Enterprise	03 MAR 71
A-7E	156841	VA-122	NAS LeMoore	04 APR 84
A-7E	156842	VA-46	NAS Cecil Field	18 APR 82
A-7E	156843	VA-97	NAS LeMoore	30 SEP 71
A-7E	156844	VA-12	USS D. D. Eisenhower	05 SEP 81
A-7E	156846	VA-22	NAS LeMoore	02 SEP 73
A-7E	156848	VA-22	USS Enterprise	23 NOV 84

Model	Bureau Number	Command	Location	Loss Date
A-7E	156849	VA-146	NAS LeMoore	02 DEC 72
A-7E	156850	VA-122	NAS LeMoore	10 FEB 72
A-7E	156853	VA-122	NAS LeMoore	14 OCT 71
A-7E	156854	VA-122	NAS LeMoore	17 MAR 71
A-7E	156855	VA-12	USS D. D. Eisenhower	04 MAR 82
A-7E	156859	VA-192	USS Kitty Hawk	16 JAN 78
A-7E	156860	VA-94	USS Coral Sea	16 APR 72
A-7E	156864	VA-25	NAS LeMoore	13 AUG 70
A-7E	156865	VA-195	NAS LeMoore	18 JUN 70
A-7E	156866	VA-97	NAS LeMoore	12 OCT 71
A-7E	156867	VA-25	NAS LeMoore	28 MAY 73
A-7E	156868	VA-12	USS D. D. Eisenhower	01 OCT 81
A-7E	156870	VA-22	USS Coral Sea	04 FEB 72
A-7E	156871	VA-22	USS Coral Sea	17 NOV 71
A-7E	156873	VA-94	NAS LeMoore	18 APR 71
A-7E	156875	VA-22	USS Coral Sea	13 APR 75
A-7E	156877	VA-94	USS Coral Sea	24 MAY 72
A-7E	156879	VA-22	USS Coral Sea	06 MAY 72
A-7E	156880	VA-94	USS Coral Sea	18 JAN 72
A-7E	156881	VA-122	NAS LeMoore	12 FEB 75
A-7E	156888	VA-94	USS Coral Sea	01 MAY 72
A-7E	157436	VA-27	USS Enterprise	06 MAY 71
A-7E	157437	VA-22	USS Coral Sea	25 JUN 72
A-7E	157438	VA-56	NAF Atsugi	29 AUG 81
A-7E	157439	VA-174	NAS Cecil Field	14 JUN 83
A-7E	157442	VA-195	USS America	15 JUN 79
A-7E	157443	VA-37	USS Carl Vinson	26 JUL 83
A-4E	157446	VA-87	NAS Cecil Field	05 APR 83
A-7E	157447	VA-174	NAS Cecil Field	01 DEC 71
A-7E	157448	VA-81	NAS Cecil Field	05 DEC 71
A-7E	157449	VA-174	NAS Cecil Field	08 NOV 83
A-7E	157451	VA-195	NAS LeMoore	11 APR 79
A-7E	157454	VA-27	USS Enterprise	29 APR 75
A-7E	157456	VA-82	NAS Cecil Field	02 MAR 81
A-7E	157457	VA-83	NAS Cecil Field	17 AUG 75
A-7E	157458	VA-87	USS Independence	13 FEB 84
A-7E	157459	VA-86	NAS Roosevelt Roads	31 AUG 83
A-7E	157461	VA-82	NAS Cecil Field	31 AUG 83
A-7E	157462	VA-174	NAS Cecil Field	28 AUG 73
A-7E	157464	VA-81	NAS Cecil Field	04 JUN 70
A-7E	157465	VA-87	NAS Cecil Field	14 APR 83
A-7E	157467	VA-81	USS Forrestal	12 SEP 72
A-7E	157468	VA-15	USS Independence	04 DEC 83
A-7E	157469	VA-174	NAS Cecil Field	11 DEC 83
A-7E	157470	VA-174	NAS Cecil Field	05 JUL 74
A-7E	157473	VA-83	NAS Cecil Field	02 DEC 71
A-7E	157474	VX-5	NWC China Lake	05 NOV 86
A-7E	157482	VA-86	NAS Cecil Field	27 JUN 81
A-7E	157483	VA-25	NAS LeMoore	03 DEC 70
A-7E	157488	VA-86	USS Nimitz	18 AUG 80
A-7E	157495	VA-56	NAF Atsugi	21 AUG 84
A-7E	157497	VA-27	NAS LeMoore	16 FEB 83
A-7E	157498	VA-82	NAS Cecil Field	15 JUN 71
A-7E	157499	VA-195	NAS LeMoore	14 DEC 81
A-7E	157500	VA-27	NAS LeMoore	11 JUL 84
A-7E	157503	VA-113	NAS LeMoore	24 DEC 72
A-7E	157507	VA-25	NAS LeMoore	28 APR 75
A-7E	157509	VA-25	NAS LeMoore	28 DEC 70
A-7E	157510	VA-81	NAS Cecil Field	20 FEB 85
A-7E	157511	VA-113	NAS LeMoore	17 APR 71
A-7E	157513	VA-192	NAS LeMoore	06 NOV 74
A-7E	157515	VA-25	USS Ranger	21 JUN 73
A-7E	157520	VA-192	USS Kitty Hawk	23 MAR 72
A-7E	157521	VA-192	USS Kitty Hawk	18 SEP 70
A-7E	157524	VA-122	NAS LeMoore	06 MAY 86
A-7E	157526	VA-195	NAS LeMoore	11 APR 79
A-7E	157527	VA-37	USS Saratoga	23 OCT 78
A-7E	157529	VA-192	USS Kitty Hawk	19 MAR 72
A-7E	157530	VA-192	NAS LeMoore	02 NOV 72
A-7E	157531	VA-192	USS Kitty Hawk	17 JUN 72

Model	Bureau Number	Command	Location	Loss Date
A-7E	157532	VA-147	NAS Cubi Point	02 JUN 80
A-7E	157533	VA-122	NAS LeMoore	30 JUN 78
A-7E	157534	VA-195	USS Kitty Hawk	26 JAN 72
A-7E	157535	VA-105	USS Saratoga	14 JUL 75
A-7E	157539	VA-195	NAS LeMoore	07 FEB 73
A-7E	157540	VA-192	NAS LeMoore	29 JAN 81
A-7E	157542	VA-174	NAS Cecil Field	18 JAN 83
A-7E	157543	VA-82	NAS Cecil Field	16 NOV 70
A-7E	157544	VA-66	NAS Cecil Field	07 SEP 71
A-7E	157545	VA-195	USS Kitty Hawk	04 NOV 71
A-7E	157547	VA-122	NAS LeMoore	08 JUN 73
A-7E	157548	VA-195	USS Kitty Hawk	27 FEB 71
A-7E	157550	VA-15	NAS Cecil Field	03 DEC 82
A-7E	157554	VA-86	NAS Cecil Field	30 OCT 70
A-7E	157555	VA-81	NAS Cecil Field	15 DEC 76
A-7E	157557	VA-105	NAS Cecil Field	31 MAY 74
A-7E	157558	VA-83	NAS Cecil Field	03 FEB 76
A-7E	157560	NARF	NAS Jacksonville	15 DEC 80
A-7E	157561	VA-83	USS Forrestal	24 JUN 78
A-7E	157562	VA-66	USS Independence	28 JUL 71
A-7E	157563	VA-37	NAS Cecil Field	22 OCT 74
A-7E	157564	VA-82	USS Nimitz	11 FEB 83
A-7E	157565	VA-37	NAS Cecil Field	14 DEC 73
A-7E	157572	VA-83	NAS Cecil Field	02 JUN 77
A-7E	157574	VA-174	NAS Cecil Field	10 DEC 80
A-7E	157575	VA-66	USS Independence	26 JUL 77
A-7E	157576	VA-66	NAS Cecil Field	31 JAN 72
A-7E	157578	VA-12	USS D. D. Eisenhower	27 FEB 79
A-7E	157583	VA-174	NAS Cecil Field	27 NOV 72
A-7E	157584	VA-86	USS Nimitz	17 JAN 78
A-7E	157588	VA-12	USS Independence	27 JUN 71
A-7E	157589	VA-113	NAS LeMoore	13 MAR 71
A-7E	157590	VA-22	USS Coral Sea	06 APR 72
A-7E	157591	VA-94	NAS LeMoore	25 JUN 73
A-7E	157592	VA-27	NAS LeMoore	23 NOV 72
A-7E	157594	VA-122	NAS LeMoore	03 MAR 76
A-7E	158006	VA-195	USS Kitty Hawk	06 APR 72
A-7E	158007	VA-12	USS Independence	23 JUN 72
A-7E	158010	VA-195	NAS LeMoore	03 JUN 82
A-7E	158015	VA-147	NAS LeMoore	17 MAY 72
A-7E	158018	VA-56	USS Midway	04 NOV 80
A-7E	158020	VA-192	NAS LeMoore	22 APR 77
A-7E	158022	VA-147	USS Constellation	16 SEP 73
A-7E	158023	China Lake	NAF China Lake	25 JUN 74
A-7E	158024	VA-81	NAS Cecil Field	10 AUG75
A-7E	158027	VA-81	NAS Cecil Field	15 JAN 78
A-7E	158028	VA-81	USS Forrestal	25 JUN 78
A-7E	158653	VA-192	NAS LeMoore	19 SEP 72
A-7E	158654	VA-83	NAS Cecil Field	22 APR 72
A-7E	158655	VA-195	USS Kitty Hawk	06 MAR 72
A-7E	158656	VA-97	NAS LeMoore	16 MAY 72
A-7E	158659	VA-192	USS Ranger	30 OCT 83
A-7E	158660	VA-174	NAS Cecil Field	16 AUG 75
A-7E	158667	VA-82	USS Nimitz	24 FEB 87
A-7E	158668	VA-174	NAS Cecil Field	05 JUL 74
A-7E	158670	VA-81	NAS Cecil Field	19 JUN 76
A-7E	158671	VA-83	NAS Cecil Field	02 JUN 77
A-7E	158673	VA-82	NAS Cecil Field	22 MAR 82
A-7E	158676	VA-94	USS Coral Sea	17 JUL 77
A-7E	158678	VA-82	USS Nimitz	22 NOV 81
A-7E	158679	VA-122	NAS LeMoore	18 DEC 77
A-7E	158680	VA-22	USS Coral Sea	03 APR 73
A-7E	158681	VA-174	NAS Cecil Field	04 MAY 73
A-7E	158820	VA-82	USS Nimitz	23 MAR 83
A-7E	158826	VA-81	USS Saratoga	18 DEC 83
A-7E	158828	VA-56	NAF Atsugi	17 DEC 80
A-7E	158830	Unknown	Operation Desert Storm	-----------91
A-7E	158832	VA-56	NAF Atsugi	04 NOV 81
A-7E	158834	VA-56	USS Midway	14 NOV 80
A-7E	158841	VA-82	USS Nimitz	08 JAN 77

Model	Bureau Number	Command	Location	Loss Date
A-7E	159262	VA-195	NAS LeMoore	11 SEP 80
A-7E	159265	VA-192	USS America	26 APR 79
A-7E	159266	VA-146	NAS LeMoore	26 MAR 85
A-7E	159267	VA-146	USS Kitty Hawk	17 JUL 85
A-7E	159269	VA-85	USS Saratoga	03 JUN 85
A-7E	159271	VX-5	NWC China Lake	05 NOV 80
A-7E	159275	VA-12	USS Independence	11 DEC 75
A-7E	159276	VA-122	NAS LeMoore	02 APR 76
A-7E	159277	VA-105	NAS Cecil Field	06 DEC 83
A-7E	159287	VA-25	USS Ranger	23 JUN 76
A-7E	159295	VA-12	USS D.D. Eisenhower	26 DEC 80
A-7E	159297	VA-97	USS Coral Sea	08 JAN 80
A-7E	159298	VA-83	USS Forrestal	14 DEC 79
A-7E	159299	VX-5	NAF China Lake	30 AUG 76
A-7E	159305	VA-86	USS Nimitz	22 APR 80
A-7E	159307	VA-174	NAS Cecil Field	02 SEP 87
A-7E	159641	VA-87	USS America	18 MAY 77
A-7E	159642	VA-27	USS Carl Vinson	12 AUG 86
A-7E	159643	VA-87	NAS Cecil Field	06 FEB 79
A-7E	159646	VA-82	USS Nimitz	04 SEP 86
A-7E	159654	VA-174	NAS Cecil Field	18 AUG 82
A-7E	159657	VA-122	NAS LeMoore	27 APR 81
A-7E	159659	VA-86	NAS Roosevelt Roads	28 AUG 84
A-7E	159972	VA-87	USS Independence	13 FEB 81
A-7E	159973	VA-94	USS Enterprise	08 MAR 86
A-7E	159977	VA-87	USS Independence	12 NOV 80
A-7E	159978	VA-37	MCAS 29 Palms	15 AUG 84
A-7E	159979	VA-15	USS America	07 JUN 76
A-7E	159982	VA-56	USS Midway	15 MAR 78
A-7E	159983	VA-93	USS Midway	01 JUL 77
A-7E	159987	VA-72	USS America	28 DEC 82
A-7E	159990	VA-56	NAF Atsugi	13 JUL 85
A-7E	159993	VA-46	USS John F. Kennedy	22 JUN 78
A-7E	159995	VA-72	NAS Cecil Field	11 DEC 84
A-7E	159998	VA-22	NAS LeMoore	15 JUL 82
A-7E	160540	VA-97	NAS LeMoore	27 JUN 85
A-7E	160546	VA-72	NAS Cecil Field	03 DEC 77
A-7E	160548	VA-72	NAS Cecil Field	02 FEB 82
A-7E	160559	VA-46	USS America	08 SEP 82
A-7E	160562	VA-12	USS D. D. Eisenhower	12 FEB 80
A-7E	160564	VA-66	USS D. D. Eisenhower	20 OCT 80
A-7E	160618	VA-81	USS Forrestal	05 FEB 80
A-7E	160711	VA-174	NAS Cecil Field	23 MAY 78
A-7E	160719	VA-66	USS D. D. Eisenhower	14 APR 85
A-7E	160720	VA-81	NAS Cecil Field	17 JAN 81
A-7E	160723	VA-97	USS Carl Vinson	29 DEC 86
A-7E	160725	VA-94	NAS LeMoore	24 FEB 81
A-7E	160727	VA-122	NAS LeMoore	06 MAY 86
A-7E	160731	VA-122	NAS LeMoore	29 OCT 87
A-7E	160734	VA-93	USS Midway	18 MAR 82
A-7E	160738	VA-15	USS Independence	24 DEC 84
A-7E	160858	VA-122	NAS LeMoore	20 MAY 86
A-7E	160860	VA-15	USS Independence	15 JAN 81
A-7E	160861	VA-15	USS Independence	20 FEB 81
A-7E	160863	VA-86	USS Nimitz	11 FEB 83
A-7E	160866	AMARC	AMARC	29 OCT 8
A-7E	160878	VA-146	USS Constellation	08 MAR 82
A-7E	160880	VA-93	NAF Atsugi	15 MAR 84

Unidentified USN A-7 Losses

Model	Bureau Number	Command	Location	Loss Date	Remarks
Unknown	Unknown	Unknown	USS Lexington	Unknown	Crashed into the sea upon receiving a cold catapult shot ** Located 17 miles south of Pensacola pass and is sitting upside down at a depth of 108. to 111.5'. Approximate datam: WGS 84, GPS Latitude: 29° Degrees 58.995, GPS Longitude: 87° degrees, 11.784 West.
Unknown	Unknown	VA-204	NAS New Orleans	Unknown	Crashed near Empire, LA. Oyster bed due to improper AIMD maintenance, pilot had a successful ejection, AF/4XX
Unknown	Unknown	VA-204	NAS New Orleans	Unknown	Crashed after pilot made a flaps up landing at El Paso, TX.. The brakes failed, (when they melted), tailhook was dropped, tore up railroad tracks, chain link fence and ended up in the middle of Interstate 10. A photo in the local paper showed the aircraft laying on its side next to a, watch out for low flying aircraft, sign. Due to pilot error, AF/4XX.
Unknown	Unknown	VA-204	NAS New Orleans	Unknown	CDR Phelps successfully ejected while shooting FCLP's at the Gulfport ANG Training Field due to an engine fire. The aircraft crashed a few hundred feet short of the beach, AF/4XX.
Unknown	Unknown	VA-204	NAS New Orleans	Unknown	CDR DeFillipo ejected as he lost power on the catapult shot and went into the water off the USS Lexington (CVT-16), salvage operations were about to start when they lost it due to a hurricane, AF/4XX.
Unknown	Unknown	VA-304	NAS Fallon, NV.	Unknown	LCDR M. "Muddy" Rivers shot himself down, with ricocheting 20MM, on a low level strafing run, at a target range outside of Fallon, NV., pilot ejected safely, ND/4XX.
Unknown	Unknown	VA-305	NAS Point Mugu, CA.	Unknown	LCDR Barry Reiney made a wheels up landing, reason unknown.

Elliniki Palamiki Aeroporia
Helenic Air Force (HAF)
Greece

TA-7C, A-7E, A-7H
64 Built 8 Lost
58 TA-7C/E Received 5 Lost

Model	HAF #	Command	Location	Loss Date
TA-7C	156784	116 Pteriga Makhis	Araxos	09 OCT 03
TA-7C	156800	116 Pteriga Makhis	Araxas	09 DEC 99
A-7E	159292	115 Pteriga Makhis	Unknown	10 OCT 01
A-7H	159918	116 Pteriga Makhis	Unknown	26 NOV 03
A-7H	159940	Unknown	Unknown	04 MAY 00
A-7H	159951	115 Pteriga Makhis	Unknown	13 AUG 98
A-7H	159963	116 Pteriga Makhis	Sperhaida	05 JUL 05
A-7H	159966	Unknown	Unknown	01 NOV 00
A-7E	160871	116 Pteriga Makhis	Araxos.	26 MAR 02
A-7H	Unknown	Unknown	Unknown	05 JUL 05
A-7E	Unknown	Unknown	Unknown	20 SEP 06

Unknown

Model	HAF #	Command	Location	Loss Date	Remarks
Unknown	A-7H	Unknown	Unknown	~ Strike, 05 JUL 05	** Aircraft crashed in the uninhabited area of Sperhiada, northwest of Lamia, central Greece, during a training flight. The 27-year-old Pilot Officer Nikos Danias, ejected safely and was rescued by helicopter and taken to a nearby hospital as a precaution. There were no injuries on the ground. The plane had taken off from 116 Combat Wing, based in Araxos. The cause of the crash was not immediately clear.
Unknown	A-7E	Unknown	Unknown	~ Strike, 20 SEP 06	** Crashed soon after take-off from 116 CW airbase at Araxos. The pilot, Lieutenant Colonel Petros Hatziris ejected safely. There were no injuries on the ground. The cause of the crash was not immediately clear.

Forca Aerea Portuguesa
Portuguese Air Force (PAF)
Portugal

A-7P, TA-7P
50 Built 16 Lost

Mod.	FAP #	Command	Location	Loss Date
A-7P	5501	Esquadra 302	Monte Real	1985
A-7P	5505	Esquadra 302	Monte Real	1985
A-7P	5510	Esquadra 302	Monte Real	1989
A-7P	5516	Esquadra 302	Monte Real	1988
A-7P	5518	Esquadra 302	Monte Real	1985
A-7P	5520	Esquadra 302	Monte Real	1989
A-7P	5523	Esquadra 304	Monte Real	1992
A-7P	5525	Esquadra 304	Monte Real	1992
A-7P	5530	Esquadra 304	Monte Real	1987
A-7P	5535	Esquadra 304	Monte Real	1986
A-7P	5540	Esquadra 304	Dallas, TX.	1985
A-7P	5541	Esquadra 304	Monte Real	1987
TA-7P	5548	Unknown	Monte Real	13 MAY 94
A-7P	15533	Esquadra 304	Monte Real	24 JUL 95
A-7P	15542	Esquadra 304	Monte Real	1994
A-7P	15543	Esquadra 304	Monte Real	1986

Kang Tha Nan Lur Thai
Royal Thailand Navy Division (RTND)
Thailand

TA-7C, A-7E
14 Received 3 Lost

Mod.	FAP #	Command	Location	Loss Date
A-7E	Unknown	Unknown	Unknown	Unknown
A-7E	Unknown	Unknown	Unknown	Unknown
A-7E	Unknown	Unknown	Unknown	Unknown

APPENDIX 7

A-7 Combat Cruise History

Vietnam

Carrier	Air Wing & Tail Code	Date	Squadron & A-7 Model
USS Ranger (CVA-61)	CVW-2 **NE**	04 NOV 67 thru 25 MAY 68	VA-147 A-7A
		26 OCT 68 thru 17 MAY 69	VA-147 A-7A
		14 OCT 69 thru 01 JUN 70	VA-56 A-7B, VA-93, A-7B
		27 OCT 70 thru 17 JUN 71	VA-25 A-7E, VA-113, A-7E
USS Ranger (CV-61)	CVW-2 **NE**	16 NOV 72 thru 23 JUN 73	VA-25 A-7E, VA-113, A-7E
		07 MAY 74 thru 18 OCT 74	VA-25 A-7E, VA-113, A-7E
USS America (CVA-66)	CVW-6 **AE**	10 APR 68 thru 16 DEC 68	VA-82 A-7A, VA-86 A-7A
	CVW-9 **NG**	10 APR 70 thru 21 DEC 70	VA-146 A-7E, VA -147 A-7E
	CVW-8 **AG**	05 JUN 72 thru 24 MAR 73	VA-82 A-7C, VA-86 A-7C
USS Constellation (CVA-64)	CVW-14 **NG**	29 MAY 68 thru 31 JAN 69	VA-27 A-7A, VA-97 A-7A
		11 AUG 69 thru 08 MAY 70	VA-27 A-7A, VA-97 A-7A
	CVW-9 **NG**	01 OCT 71 thru 30 JUN 72	VA-146 A-7E, VA-147 A-7E
		05 JAN 73 thru 11 OTCT 73	VA-146 A-7E, VA-147 A-7E
		21 JUN 74 thru 22 DEC74	VA-146 A-7E, VA-147 A-7E
USS Kitty Hawk (CVA-63)	CVW-1 **NH**	30 DEC 68 thru 04 SEP 69	VA-37 A-7A, VA-105 A-7A
		06 NOV 70 thru 17 JUL 71	VA-192 A-7E, VA-195 A-7E
		17 FEB 72 thru 28 NOV 72	VA-192 A-7E, VA-195 A-7E
USS Kitty Hawk (CV-63)	CVW-11 **NH**	23 NOV 73 thru 09 JUL 74	VA-192 A-7E, VA-195 A-7E
		21 MAY 75 thru 15 DEC 75	VA-192 A-7E, VA-195 A-7E
USS Midway (CVA-41)	CVW-5 **NF**	16 APR 71 thru 06 NOV 71	VA-56 A-7B, VA-93 A-7B
		10 APR 72 thru 03 MAR 73	VA-56 A-7B, VA-93 A-7B
		11 SEP 73 thru 31 DEC 73	VA-56 A-7A, VA-93 A-7A
		01 JAN 74 thru 31 DEC 74	VA-56 A-7A, VA-93 A-7A
USS Midway (CV-41)	CVW-5 **NF**	01 JAN 75 thru 31 DEC 75	VA-56 A-7A, VA-93 A-7A
USS Enterprise (CVAN-65)	CVW-9 **NG**	06JAN 69 thru 02 JUL 69	VA-146 A-7B, VA-215 A-7B
	CVW-14 **NK**	11 JUN 71 thru 12 FEB 72	VA-27 A-7E, VA-97 A-7E
		12 SEP 72 thru 12 JUN 73	VA-27 A-7E, VA-97 A-7E
		17 SEP 74 thru 20 MAY 75	VA-27 A-7E, VA-97 A-7E

Carrier	Air Wing & Tail Code	Date	Squadron & A-7 Model
USS Ticonderoga (CVA-14)	CVW-16 **AH**	01 FEB 69 thru 18 SEP 69	VA-25 A-7B, VA -87 A-7B
USS Saratoga (CV-60)	CVW-3 **AC**	01 APR 72 thru 13 FEB 73	VA-37 A-7A, VA-105 A-7A
USS Coral Sea (CVA-43)	CVW-15 **NL**	23 SEP 69 thru 01 JUL 70	VA-82 A-7A, VA-86 A-7A
		12 NOV 71 thru 17 JUL 72	VA-22 A-7E, VA-94 A-7E
		09 MAR 73 thru 08 NOV 73	VA-22 A-7E, VA-94 A-7E
		05 DEC 74 thru 02 JUL 75	VA22 A-7E, VA-94 A-7E
USS Oriskany (CVA-34)	CVW-19 **NM**	14 MAY 70 thru 10 DEC 70	VA-153 A-7A, VA -155 A-7B
		14 MAY 71 thru 18 DEC 71	VA-153 A-7A, VA-155 A-7B, VA-215 A-7B
		05 JUN 72 thru 30 MAR 73	VA-153 A-7A, VA-155 A-7B, VA-215 A-7B
		18 OCT 73 thru 05 JUN 74	VA-153 A-7B, VA-155 A-7B, VA-215 A-7B
USS Oriskany (CV-34)	CVW-19 **NM**	16 SEP 75 thru 03 MAR 76	VA-153 A-7B, VA-155 A-7B, VA-215 A-7B

Grenada

Carrier	Air Wing & Tail Code	Date	Squadron & A-7 Model
USS Independence (CV-62)	CVW-6 **AE**	24 OCT 83 thru 02 NOV 83	VA-15 A-7E, VA-87 A-7E

Libya

Carrier	Air Wing & Tail Code	Date	Squadron & A-7 Model
USS America (CV-66)	CVW-1 **AB**	24 MAR 86 thru 15 APR 86	VA-46 A-7E, VA-72 A-7E
USS Saratoga (CV-60)	CVW-17 **AA**	26 AUG 85 thru 16 APR 86	VA-81 A-7E, VA-83 A-7E

Lebanon

Carrier	Air Wing & Tail Code	Date	Squadron & A-7 Model
USS Independence (CV-62)	CVW-7 **AG**	17 AUG 75 thru 02 OCT 75	VA-12 A-7E VA-66 A-7E
	CVW-6 **AE**	18 OCT 83 thru 11 APR 84	VA-15 A-7E VA-87 A-7E
USS America (CV-66)	CVW-6 **AE**	15 APR 76 thru 25 OCT 76	VA-15 A-7E VA-87 A-7E
USS John F. Kennedy (CV-67)	CVW-1 **AB**	28 JUN 75 thru 27 JAN 75	VA-46 A-7B, VA-72 A-7B
USS Nimitz (CVN-68)	CVW-8 **AJ**	07 JUL 76 thru 07 FEB 77	VA-82 A-7E VA-86 A-7E
	CVW-8 **AJ**	10 NOV 82 thru 20 MAY 83	VA-82 A-7E VA-86 A-7E

Iraq

Carrier	Air Wing & Tail Code	Date	Squadron & A-7 Model
USS John F. Kennedy (CV-67)	CVW-3 **AC**	16 JAN 91 thru 28 MAR 91	VA-46 A-7E VA-72 A-7E

APPENDIX 8

U.S. NAVY
FOREIGN MILITARY SALES, (FMS)

Elliniki Polemiki Aeroporia
Helenic Air Force (HAF)
Greece

TA-7C, A-7E, A-7H, TA-7H

HAF S/N	MOD	CSN	BUNO	Remarks
154379	TA-7C	TB-23	154379	From B-018
154424	TA-7C	TB-26	154424	From B-063
156747	TA-7C	TE-48	156747	From E-013
156753	TA-7C	TE-54	156753	From E-019
156767	TA-7C	TE-45	156767	From E-033
156768	TA-7C	TE-49	156768	From E-034
156774	TA-7C	TE-59	156774	From E-040
156784	TA-7C	TE-40	156784	From E-050 ** Transferred to 116 Pteriga Makhis ~ Strike, 09 OCT 03 ** Crashed near Araxos AB, Greece, Due to the pilot losing control during a training mission ** Both crew ejected safely.
156800	TA-7C	TE-34	156800	From E-066 ** Transferred to 336 Mira ~ Strike, 09 DEC 99 ** Crashed near Araxos, Greece due to engine failure ** Both crew ejected safely.
156805	A-7E	E-071	156805	
156827	A-7E	E-093	156827	
156833	A-7E	E-099	156833	
156851	A-7E	E-117	156851	
157480	A-7E	E-202	157480	
157486	A-7E	E-208	157486	
157496	A-7E	E-218	157496	
157502	A-7E	E-224	157502	
158021	A-7E	E-336	158021	
158824	A-7E	E-379	158824	
158825	A-7E	E-380	158825	
158829	A-7E	E-384	158829	
159263	A-7E	E-400	159263	
159285	A-7E	E-446	159285	
159292	A-7E	E-429	159292	Transferred to 335 Mv ~ Strike, 10 OCT 01 ** No data on strike.
159639	A-7E	E-447	159639	
159640	A-7E	E-448	159640	
159645	A-7E	E-453	159645	
159648	A-7E	E-456	159648	
159658	A-7E	E-466	159658	

159662/159667 LTV A-7H Corsair II for the Helinic Air Force (Greece)
FY 74 FMS Contract N00019-74-C-0126, (6) A-7H; H-1/H-6. (Block XVIII)

HAF S/N	MOD	CSN	BUNO	Remarks
159662	A-7H	H-01	159662	A-7 First of sixty A-7H for the Helinic Air Force, (Greece), delivered in 77
159663	A-7H	H-02	159663	
159664	A-7H	H-03	159664	
159665	A-7H	H-04	159665	
159666	A-7H	H-05	159666	
159667	A-7H	H-06	159667	

159913/159966 LTV A-7H Corsair II For Greece;
FY 75 FMS Contract N00019-75-C-0056, (42) A-7H; H-07/H-18. (Block I)

HAF S/N	MOD	CSN	BUNO	Remarks
159913	A-7H	H-07	159913	
159914	A-7H	H-08	159914	
159915	A-7H	H-09	159915	
159916	A-7H	H-10	159916	
159917	A-7H	H-11	159917	
159918	A-7H	H-12	159918	Transferred to 116 Pteriga Mahis/336 Mira Vombardismou ~ Strike, 26 NOV 03 ** Crashed at 1100 hrs, near the 117 CW base at Andravida. The pilot, Wing Commander Konstantinos Mitsopoulos C. O. of SOT (Scholio Oplon Taktikis) reported fuel loss, while flying over the sea between Zakynthos Island and the Peloponese. He was instructed to fly to Andravida and land immediately. When the pilot experienced fuel starvation on the final approach and in view of the runway, he tried to avoid residential areas up to the last moment, until the aircraft stalled, he ejected safely and was taken to an HAF hospital for check-up. The A-7H hit the ground 800m short of the runway and skidded 500m coming to a stop by a ditch, very near a warehouse. It appears that the aircraft almost landed itself despite the landing gear not having been lowered, the damage was minimal so may be repaired. In storage at Araxos, SEP 05.
159919	A-7H	H-13	159919	
159920	A-7H	H-14	159920	
159921	A-7H	H-15	159921	
159922	A-7H	H-16	159922	
159923	A-7H	H-17	159923	
159924	A-7H	H-18	159924	

159913/159966 LTV A-7H Corsair II For Greece;
FY 75 FMS Contract N00019-75-C-0056, (42) A-7H; H-19/H-30. (Block II)

HAF S/N	MOD	CSN	BUNO	Remarks
159925	A-7H	H-19	159925	
159926	A-7H	H-20	159926	
159927	A-7H	H-21	159927	
159928	A-7H	H-22	159928	
159929	A-7H	H-23	159929	
159930	A-7H	H-24	159930	
159931	A-7H	H-25	159931	
159932	A-7H	H-26	159932	
159933	A-7H	H-27	159933	
159934	A-7H	H-28	159934	
159935	A-7H	H-29	159935	
159936	A-7H	H-30	159936	

159913/159966 LTV A-7H Corsair II For Greece;
FY 75 FMS Contract N00019-75-C-0056, (42) A-7H; H-31/H-60. (Block III)

HAF S/N	MOD	CSN	BUNO	Remarks
159937	A-7H	H-31	159937	
159938	A-7H	H-32	159938	
159939	A-7H	H-33	159939	
159940	A-7H	H-34	159940	~ Strike, 04 MAY 00 ** W/O ** No data on strike.
159941	A-7H	H-35	159941	
159942	A-7H	H-36	159942	
159943	A-7H	H-37	159943	
159944	A-7H	H-38	159944	
159945	A-7H	H-39	159945	
159946	A-7H	H-40	159946	
159947	A-7H	H-41	159947	
159948	A-7H	H-42	159948	
159949	A-7H	H-43	159949	
159950	A-7H	H-44	159950	
159951	A-7H	H-45	159951	Transferred to 115 Pteriga Makhis ~ Strike, 13 AUG 98 ** Crashed into the Messinian Gulf due to pilot error ** Pilot ejected but drowned.
159952	A-7H	H-46	159952	
159953	A-7H	H-47	159953	
159954	A-7H	H-48	159954	

HAF S/N	MOD	CSN	BUNO	Remarks
159955	A-7H	H-49	159955	
159956	A-7H	H-50	159956	
159957	A-7H	H-51	159957	Based at Larissa, Greece.
159958	A-7H	H-52	159958	
159959	A-7H	H-53	159959	
159960	A-7H	H-54	159960	
159961	A-7H	H-55	159961	
159962	A-7H	H-56	159962	
159963	A-7H	H-57	159963	Transferred to 116 PM, 336Mv ~ Strike, 09 JUL 05 ** 2nd LT Wikolas Danias survived the crash near Sperheiada, Macrocom Region, GR.
159964	A-7H	H-58	159964	
159965	A-7H	H-59	159965	
159966	A-7H	H-60	159966	Took off from the AFB at Suda, Crete on a routine training flight ~ Strike, 01 NOV 00 ** Crashed on the Peleponnessos Peninsula in an area between Tainaros mountain and Cape Tainaros, Pilot escaped unhurt ** Aircraft W/O.

161218/161222 LTV TA-7H Corsair II for the Helinic Air Force (Greece)
FY 78/79 Contract N00019-78-C-0184 (5) TA-7H; H-1/H-5; (Block I)

HAF S/N	MOD	CSN	BUNO	Remarks
161218	TA-7H	TH-5	161218	
161219	TA-7H	TH-1	161219	
161220	TA-7H	TH-2	161220	
161221	TA-7H	TH-3	161221	
161222	TA-7H	TH-4	161222	
159967	A-7E	E-492	159967	
159975	A-7E	E-478	159975	
159980	A-7E	E-483	159980	
159997	A-7E	E-500	159997	
159999	A-7E	E-502	159999	
160537	A-7E	E-524	160537	
160541	A-7E	E-510	160541	
160543	A-7E	E-512	160543	
160550	A-7E	E-519	160550	
160552	A-7E	E-521	160552	
160557	A-7E	E-526	160557	
160560	A-7E	E-529	160560	
160566	A-7E	E-535	160566	
160616	A-7E	E-539	160616	
160617	A-7E	E-540	160617	
160710	A-7E	E-554	160710	
160716	A-7E	E-548	160716	
160717	A-7E	E-549	160717	
160718	A-7E	E-550	160718	
160728	A-7E	E-560	160728	
160736	A-7E	E-568	160736	
160857	A-7E	E-584	160857	
160862	A-7E	E-577	160862	
160864	A-7E	E-579	160864	
160865	A-7E	E-580	160865	
160867	A-7E	E-582	160867	
160868	A-7E	E-583	160868	
160871	A-7E	E-586	160871	~ Strike, 26 MAR 02 ** Crashed, on test flight from Araxos ** Pilot ejected safely.
160873	A-7E	E-588	160873	

HAF S/N	MOD	CSN	BUNO	Remarks
Unknown	A-7H	Unknown	Unknown	~ Strike, 05 JUL 05 ** Aircraft crashed in the uninhabited area of Sperhiada, northwest of Lamia, central Greece, during a training flight. The 27-year-old Pilot Officer Nikos Danias, ejected safely and was rescued by helicopter and taken to a nearby hospital as a precaution. There were no injuries on the ground. The plane had taken off from 116 Combat Wing, based in Araxos. The cause of the crash was not immediately clear.
Unknown	A-7E	Unknown	Unknown	~ Strike, 20 SEP 06 ** Crashed soon after take-off from 116 CW airbase at Araxos. The pilot, Lieutenant Colonel Petros Hatziris ejected safely. There were no injuries on the ground. The cause of the crash was not immediately clear.

APPENDIX 9

U.S. Navy
Foreign Mtilitary Sales, (FMS)

Forca Aerea Portuguesa
Portuguese AF (FAP)
Portugal

A-7P and TA-7P List

OLD SYSTEM

PAF #	MOD	From CSN	BUNO	Remarks
-------	TA-7C	B-043	154404	Transferred to Portuguese Air Force for lease, 1982 ** Transferred back to U.S. Navy, 1985.
5501	A-7P	A-191	154352	Transferred to Esquadra 302 "Falcões", BA-5; Monte Real, PO. 1981 ~ Strike 1985 ** W/O, destroyed in accident in Belgium.
5502	A-7P	A-108	153200	Transferred to Esquadra 302 "Falcões", BA-5; 1981 ** WO, and transferred to BA11; Beja, PO., for storage 1990
5503	A-7P	A-181	153272	Transferred to Esquadra 302 "Falcões", BA-5; Monte Real, PO., 1981.
5504	A-7P	A-092	153184	Transferred to Esquadra 302 "Falcões", BA-5; Monte Real, PO., 1981.
5505	A-7P	A-098	153190	Transferred to Esquadra 302 "Falcões", BA-5; Monte Real, PO., 1981 ~ Strike 1985 ** WO, destroyed in accident in Belgium
5506	A-7P	A-159	153250	Transferred to Esquadra 302 "Falcões", BA-5; Monte Real, PO., 1981.
5507	A-7P	A-102	153194	Transferred to Esquadra 302 "Falcões", BA-5; Monte Real, PO., 1982
5508	A-7P	A-127	153219	Transferred to Esquadra 302 "Falcões", BA-5; Monte Real, PO., 1981 ** Retired 1999 ** On display at Alverca Pole Museum, PO. 1999.
5509	A-7P	A-153	153244	Transferred to Esquadra 302 "Falcões", BA-5; Monte Real, PO., 1981.
5510	A-7P	A-060	153152	Transferred to Esquadra 302 "Falcões", BA-5; Monte Real, PO., 1982 ~ Strike, 1989, Destroyed in accident near Vila Vicosa, PO.
5511	A-7P	A-199	154360	Transferred to Esquadra 302 "Falcões", BA-5; Monte Real, PO., 1981
5512	A-7P	A-078	153170	Transferred to Esquadra 302 "Falcões", BA-5; Monte Real, PO., 1982
5513	A-7P	A-096	153188	Transferred to Esquadra 302 "Falcões", BA-5; Monte Real, PO., 1982 ** Transferred to BA11; Beja, PO., for storage, 1990
5514	A-7P	A-123	153215	Transferred to Esquadra 302 "Falcões", BA-5; Monte Real, PO., 1982.
5515	A-7P	A-129	153221	Transferred to Esquadra 302 "Falcões", BA-5; Monte Real, PO., 1982.
5516	A-7P	A-135	153227	Transferred to Esquadra 302 "Falcões", BA-5; Monte Real, PO., 1982 ~ Strike, 1988, Crashed near Peniche, PO.

PAF #	MOD	From CSN	BUNO	Remarks
5517	A-7P	A-136	153228	Transferred to Esquadra 302 "Falcões", BA-5; Monte Real, PO., 1982 ** WO, transferred to DGMFA Alverca, PO., for storage, 1994
5518	A-7P	A-146	153237	Transferred to Esquadra 302 "Falcões", BA-5; Monte Real, PO., 1982 ~ Strike, 1983 ** WO, crashed near Leiria, PO.
5519	A-7P	A-157	153248	Transferred to Esquadra 302 "Falcões", BA-5; Monte Real, PO., 1982.
5520	A-7P	A-170	153261	Transferred to Esquadra 302 "Falcões", BA-5; Monte Real, PO., 1982 ~ Strike, 1989 ** WO, crashed near Monte Real, PO.
5521	A-7P	A-090	153134	Transferred to Esquadra 304 "Magnificos", BA-5; Monte Real, PO., 1984.
5522	A-7P	A-063	153155	Transferred to Esquadra 304 "Magnificos", BA-5; Monte Real, PO., 1984.
5523	A-7P	A-067	153159	Transferred to Esquadra 304 "Magnificos", BA-5; Monte Real, PO., 1984 ~ Strike, 1992 WO, destroyed in accident near Montijo, PO. ** Located at the dump in Montijo, PO.
5524	A-7P	A-070	153162	Transferred to Esquadra 304 "Magnificos", BA-5; Monte Real, PO., 1984.
5525	A-7P	A-079	153171	Transferred to Esquadra 304 "Magnificos", BA-5; Monte Real, PO., 1984.
5526	A-7P	A-085	153177	Transferred to Esquadra 304 "Magnificos", BA-5; Monte Real, PO., 1984 ** Transferred to DGMFA Alverca, PO., for storage, 1994.
5527	A-7P	A-087	153179	Transferred to Esquadra 304 "Magnificos", BA-5; Monte Real, PO., 1985.
5528	A-7P	A-095	153187	Transferred to Esquadra 304 "Magnificos", BA-5; Monte Real, PO., 1985 ** Transferred to BA11; Beja. PO., for storage, 1989.
5529	A-7P	A-103	153195	Transferred to Esquadra 304 "Magnificos", BA-5; Monte Real, PO., 1985 ** WO and located at DGMFA Alverca, PO., 1994.
5530	A-7P	A-059	153151	Transferred to Esquadra 304 "Magnificos", BA-5; Monte Real, PO., 1985 ~ Strike, 1987 ** WO, crashed near Mira d'Aire, PO.
5531	A-7P	A-120	153212	Transferred to Esquadra 304 "Magnificos", BA-5; Monte Real, PO., 1985.
5532	A-7P	A-124	153216	Transferred to Esquadra 304 "Magnificos", BA-5; Monte Real, PO., 1985.
5533	A-7P	A-081	153173	Transferred to Esquadra 304 "Magnificos", BA-5; Monte Real, PO., 1985.
5534	A-7P	A-137	153229	Transferred to Esquadra 304 "Magnificos", BA-5; Monte Real, PO., 1985.
5535	A-7P	A-149	153240	Transferred to Esquadra 304 "Magnificos", BA-5; Monte Real, PO., 1985 ~ Strike, 1986 ** WO, crashed near Pocarica, PO.
5536	A-7P	A-116	153208	Transferred to Esquadra 304, "Magnificos", BA-5; Monte Real, PO., 1985.
5537	A-7P	A-163	153254	Transferred to Esquadra 304, "Magnificos", BA-5; Monte Real, PO., 1985.
5538	A-7P	A-169	153260	Transferred to Esquadra 304, "Magnificos", BA-5; Monte Real, PO., 1985 ** Transferred to BA11; Beja, PO., for storage, 1990.
5539	A-7P	A-134	153226	Transferred to Esquadra 304, "Magnificos", BA-5; Monte Real, PO., 1985 ** Transferred to BA11; Beja, PO., for storage, 1990.
5540	A-7P	A-185	154346	~ Strike, 1985 ** Crashed during test flight from Vought; Dallas, TX.
5541	A-7P	A-188	154349	Transferred to Esquadra 304 Magnificoes", BA-5; Monte Real, PO., 1985 ~ Strike, 1987 ** WO, crashed near Boticus, PO.
5542	A-7P	A-190	154351	Transferred to Esquadra 304 "Magnificos", BA-5; Monte Real, PO., 1985.
5543	A-7P	A-194	154355	Transferred to Esquadra 304 "Magnificos", BA-5; Monte Real, PO., 1985 ** Strike 1986 ** WO, crashed near Pocarica, PO.
5544	A-7P	A-154	153245	Transferred to Esquadra 304 "Magnificos", BA-5; Monte Real, PO., 1985.

5545	TA-7P	A-109	153201	Transferred to BA5; Monte Real, PO., BA-5; 1985
5546	TA-7P	A-104	153196	Transferred to BA5; Monte Real, PO., BA-5; 1985.
5547	TA-7P	A-132	153224	Transferred to BA5; Monte Real, PO., BA-5; 1985.
5548	TA-7P	A-158	153249	Transferred to BA-5 Monte Real, PO., BA-5; 1985 ~ Strike, 13 MAY 94 ** WO, crashed near Rosas, Spain., Both crew killed.
5549	TA-7P	A-177	153268	Transferred to BA5; Monte Real, PO., BA-5; 1985.
5550	TA-7P	A-198	154354	Transferred to BA5; Monte Real, PO., BA-5; 1985.

NEW SYSTEM

PAF #	MOD	CSN	BUNO	Remarks
15502	A-7P	A-108	153200	Transferred to Esquadra 302 "Falcões", BA-5; Monte Real, PO., 1981 ** WO, transferred to BA-1 Beja, PO., for storage, 1990.
15503	A-7P	A-181	153272	Transferred to Esquadra 302 "Falcões", BA-5; Monte Real, PO. 1981 ** Transferred to Museu do Ar; BA-1; Sintrus, PO., for display, 1996.
15504	A-7P	A-092	153184	Transferred to Esquadra 302 "Falcões", BA-5; Monte Real, PO. 1981 ** Transferred to AM1; Figo Maduro, PO., 1997.
15506	A-7P	A-159	153250	Transferred to Esquadra 302 "Falcões", BA-5; Monte Real, PO., 1981 ** Transferred to CFMTFA; Ota, PO., for storage, 1996.
15507	A-7P	A-102	153194	Transferred to Esquadra 302 "Falcões", BA-5; Monte Real, PO. 1982 ** Transferred to DGMFA; Alverca, PO., for storage, 1997.
15508	A-7P	A-127	153219	Transferred to Esquadra 302 "Falcões", BA-5; Monte Real, PO. 1981 ** WO, transferred to Museu do Ar; Alverca, PO., for display, 1999.
15509	A-7P	A-153	153244	Transferred to Esquadra 302 "Falcões", BA-5; Monte Real, PO., 1981 ** ** WO, located at BA-5; Monte Real, PO., 1999.
15511	A-7P	A-199	154360	Transferred to Esquadra 302 "Falcões", BA-5; Monte Real, PO., 1981 ** WO, located at BA-5; Monte Real, PO., 1998.
15512	A-7P	A-078	153170	Transferred to Esquadra 302 "Falcões", BA-5; Monte Real, PO. 1982 ** Transferred to DGMFA; Alverca, PO., for storage, 1988.
15513	A-7P	A-096	153188	Transferred to Esquadra 302 "Falcões", BA-5; Monte Real, PO., 1982 ** WO, transferred to BA-11; Beja, PO., for storage, 1990.
15514	A-7P	A-123	153215	Transferred to Esquadra 302 "Falcões", BA-5; Monte Real, PO. 1982 ** WO, transferred to DGMFA; Alverca, PO., for storage, 1998.
15515	A-7P	A-129	153221	Transferred to Esquadra 302 "Falcões", BA-5; Monte Real, PO. 1982 ** WO, transferred to DGMFA; Alverca, PO., for storage, 1996.
15517	A-7P	A-136	153228	Transferred to Esquadra 302 "Falcões", BA-5; Monte Real, PO. 1982 ** WO, transferred to DGMFA; Alverca, PO., for storage, 1994.
15519	A-7P	A-157	153248	Transferred to Esquadra 302 "Falcões", BA-5; Monte Real, PO.., 1982 ** WO, transferred to BA-5; Monte Real, PO., for storage, 1998.
15521	A-7P	A-090	153134	Transferred to Esquadra 304 "Magnificos", BA-5; Monte Real, PO., 1984, Special paint scheme on starboard on side of aircraft, "64,000 horas", 2000 ** WO, on display at Monte Real, PO., 2000.
15522	A-7P	A-063	153155	Transferred to Esquadra 304 "Magnificos", BA-5; Monte Real, PO., 1984 ** WO, transferred to DGMFA; Alverca, PO., for storage, 1994.
15524	A-7P	A-070	153162	Transferred to Esquadra 304 "Magnificos", BA-5; Monte Real, PO., 1984 ** Transferred to BA-5; Monte Real, PO., for display, 1999.
15525	A-7P	A-079	153171	Transferred to Esquadra 304 "Magnificos", BA-5; Monte Real, PO., 1984 ~ Strike, 1992, WO, destroyed in accident in Germany.

PAF #	MOD	CSN	BUNO	Remarks
15526	A-7P	A-085	153177	Transferred to Esquadra 304 "Magnificos", BA-5; Monte Real, PO., 1984 ** Transferred to DGMFA; Alverca, PO., for storage, 1994.
15527	A-7P	A-087	153179	Transferred to Esquadra 304 "Magnificos", BA-5; Monte Real, PO., 1985 ** WO, transferred to DGMFA; Alverca, PO., for storage, 1995.
15528	A-7P	A-095	153187	Transferred to Esquadra 304 "Magnificos", BA-5; Monte Real, PO., 1985 ** WO, transferred to BA-11; Beja, PO., for storage, 1989.
15529	A-7P	A-099	153191	Transferred to Esquadra 304 "Magnificos", BA-5; Monte Real, PO., 1985 ** WO, transferred to DGMFA Alverca, PO., for storage, 1994.
15531	A-7P	A-120	153212	Transferred to Esquadra 304 "Magnificos", BA-5; Monte Real, PO., 1985 ** WO, transferred to BA-5; Monte Real, PO., 1999.
15532	A-7P	A-124	153216	Transferred to Esquadra 304 "Magnificos", BA-5; Monte Real, PO., 1985 ** WO, transferred to DGMFA Alverca., PO., for storage, 1995.
15533	A-7P	A-081	153173	Transferred to Esquadra 304 "Magnificos", BA-5; Monte Real, PO., 1985 ~ Strike, 1995 ** WO, destroyed in accident near Baliezao, PO,.
15534	A-7P	A-137	153229	Transferred to Esquadra 304 "Magnificos", BA-5; Monte Real, PO., 1985 ** WO, transferred to DGMFA; Alverca, PO., for storage, 1995.
15536	A-7P	A-116	153208	Transferred to Esquadra 304 "Magnificos", BA-5; Monte Real, PO., 1985 ** WO, transferred to DGMFA; Alverca, PO., for storage 1995.
15537	A-7P	A-163	153254	Transferred to Esquadra 304 "Magnificos", BA-5; Monte Real, PO., 1985 ** WO, transferred to Alcochete Firing Range, PO., for display as a gate guard, 1995.
15538	A-7P	A-169	153260	Transferred to Esquadra 304 "Magnificos", BA-5; Monte Real, PO., 1985 ** WO, transferred to BA-11 Beja, PO., for storage, 1990.
15539	A-7P	A-134	153226	Transferred to Esquadra 304 "Magnificos", BA-5; Monte Real, PO., 1985 ** WO, transferred to BA-11; Beja, PO., for storage, 1990.
15542	A-7P	A-190	154351	Transferred to Esquadra 304 "Magnificos", BA-5; Monte Real, PO., 1985 ~ Strike, 1994 ** WO, destroyed in Crash near Monte Real, PO.
15543	A-7P	A-194	154355	Transferred to Esquadra 304 "Magnificos", BA-5; Monte Real, PO. 1985 ~ Strike, 1986 ** WO, crashed near Pocarica, PO.
15544	A-7P	A-154	153245	Transferred to Esquadra 304 "Magnificos", BA5; Monte Real, PO., 1986 ** WO, transferred to BA-5; Monte Real, PO., for storage, 1996.
15545	TA-7P	A-109	153201	Transferred to BA-5; Monte Real, PO., 1985 ** WO, transferred to DGMFA; Alverca, PO., for storage, 1995.
15546	TA-7P	A-104	153196	Transferred to BA-5; Monte Real, PO., 1985 ** WO, transferred to BA-5; Monte Real, PO., 1999.
15547	TA-7P	A-132	153224	Transferred to BA-5; Monte Real, PO., 1985 ** WO, located in Monte Real, PO., 1995.
15549	TA-7P	A-177	153268	Transferred to BA-5; Monte Real, PO., 1985 ** Retired 1999.
15550	TA-7P	A-198	154354	Transferred to BA-5; Monte Real, PO., 1986 ** WO, transferred to DGMFA; Alverca, PO., for storage, 1997.

Note: These A-7A's were shipped to the Portuguese Air Force to be used as spare parts for the A-7P program.

152651	152655	152656	152657
152667	152669	152675	152676
152678	152682	153138	153140
153144	153199	153217	154356

Note: The Portuguese Air Force has been trying to locate A-7 maintenance manuals to update their Library in an attempt to re-start their A-7 program to a flying status again, as of 2007.

APPENDIX 10

U.S. NAVY
FOREIGN MILITARY SALES, (FMS)

Kang Tha Han Lur Thai
Royal Thailand Navy Division, (RTND)
Thailand

A-7E, TA-7C List
24 Received Unknown Lost

RTND S/N	MOD	CSN	BUNO	Remarks
1401	A-7E	E-511	160542	Transferred to the 1ST Wing, 104TH "White Shark" Squadron at U-Tapao, TH., Summer of 1995 ** Out of service and stored.
1402	A-7E	E-571	160739	Transferred to the 1ST Wing, 104TH "White Shark" Squadron at U-Tapao, TH., Summer of 1995 ** Out of service and stored.
1403	A-7E	E-574	160859	Transferred to the 1ST Wing, 104TH "White Shark" Squadron at U-Tapao, TH., Summer of 1995 ** Out of service and stored.
1404	A-7E	E-393	158838	Transferred to the 1ST Wing, 104TH "White Shark" Squadron at U-Tapao, TH., Summer of 1995 ** Out of service and stored.
1405	A-7E	E-513	160544	Transferred to the 1ST Wing, 104TH "White Shark" Squadron at U-Tapao, TH., Summer of 1995 ** Out of service and stored.
1406	A-7E	E-514	160545	Transferred to the 1ST Wing, 104TH "White Shark" Squadron at U-Tapao, TH., Summer of 1995 ** Out of service and stored.
1407	A-7E	E-425	159288	Transferred to the 1ST Wing, 104TH "White Shark" Squadron at U-Tapao, TH., Summer of 1995 ** Out of service and stored.
1408	A-7E	E-350	158658	Transferred to the 1ST Wing, 104TH "White Shark" Squadron at U-Tapao, TH., Summer of 1995 ** Out of service and stored.
1409	A-7E	E-----	---------	Transferred to the 1ST Wing, 104TH "White Shark" Squadron at U-Tapao, TH., Summer of 1995 ** Out of service and stored.
1410	A-7E	E-----	---------	Transferred to the 1ST Wing, 104TH "White Shark" Squadron at U-Tapao, TH., Summer of 1995 ** Out of service and stored.
1411	A-7E	E-532	160563	Transferred to the 1ST Wing, 104TH "White Shark" Squadron at U-Tapao, TH., Summer of 1995 ** Out of service and stored.
1412	A-7E	E-----	---------	Transferred to the 1ST Wing, 104TH "White Shark" Squadron at U-Tapao, TH., Summer of 1995 ** Out of service and stored.
1413	A-7E	E-----	---------	Transferred to the 1ST Wing, 104TH "White Shark" Squadron at U-Tapao, TH., Summer of 1995 ** Out of service and stored.
1414	A-7E	E-----	---------	Transferred to the 1ST Wing, 104TH "White Shark" Squadron at U-Tapao, TH., Summer of 1995 ** Out of service and stored.

RTND S/N	MOD	CSN	BUNO	Remarks
1415	TA-7C	TE-47	156746	From A-7E, E-012 ** Transferred to the 1ST Wing, 104TH "White Shark" Squadron at U-Tapao, TH., Summer of 1995 ** Out of service and stored.
1416	TA-7C	TE-55	156779	From A-7E, E-045 ** Transferred to the 1ST Wing, 104TH "White Shark" Squadron at U-Tapao, TH., Summer of 1995 ** Out of service and stored.
1417	TA-7C	TE-50	156788	From A-7E, E-054 ** Transferred to the 1ST Wing, 104TH "White Shark" Squadron at U-Tapao, TH., Summer of 1995 ** Out of service and stored.
1418	TA-7C	TE-12	156794	From A-7E, E-060 ** Transferred to the 1ST Wing, 104TH "White Shark" Squadron at U-Tapao, TH., Summer of 1995 ** Out of service and stored.
158666	A-7E	E-358	158666	Transferred to the 1ST Wing, 104TH "White Shark" Squadron at U-Tapao, TH., Summer of 1995 ** Out of service and stored.
158833	A-7E	E-388	158833	Transferred to the 1ST Wing, 104TH "White Shark" Squadron at U-Tapao, TH., Summer of 1995 ** Out of service and stored.
159272	A-7E	E-409	159272	Transferred to the 1ST Wing, 104TH "White Shark" Squadron at U-Tapao, TH., Summer of 1995 ** Out of service and stored.
159300	A-7E	E-437	159300	Transferred to the 1ST Wing, 104TH "White Shark" Squadron at U-Tapao, TH., Summer of 1995, to be used as spare parts for the A-7 program ** Located at the dump, 04 JAN 06.
---------	A-7E	E-479	159976	Transferred to the 1ST Wing, 104TH "White Shark" Squadron at U-Tapao, TH., Summer of 1995 ** Out of service and stored.
160547	A-7E	E-516	160547	Transferred to the 1ST Wing, 104TH "White Shark" Squadron at U-Tapao, TH., Summer of 1995 ** Out of service and stored.

Note: Three A-7E fuselages located near the Civil Terminal at RTND Base at U-Tapao, Thailand. 159300 and two S/N's unknown. To be used as spare parts for the RTND A-7 program.

APPENDIX 11

BUREAU (SERIAL) NUMBER HISTORY

Serial numbers and bureau numbers are synonymous terms for the identifying number assigned to individual naval aircraft. The earliest system was a letter-number combination which segregated the aircraft by manufacturer (or designer) and general type. As this scheme developed, the letter "A" was used with Curtiss hydroaeroplanes, "B" for Wright type hydroaeroplanes, "C" for Curtiss Flying boats, "D" for Burgess, and "E" for the Cutiss Amphibian flying boats. Sequential numbers beginning with 1 were assigned to each set of aircraft. That scheme was replaced by AH numbers which were assigned aircraft in service. A system of construction numbers was then initiated to identify aircraft on order. The two co-existed for some 15 months when the service numbers were abandoned.

Construction numbers began with A-51 and, as Serial numbers or bureau numbers, ran through A-9206, after which the letter "A" was dropped, although sequential numbering continued through 9999; a second series of four digit numbers began with 0001 and ran through 7303 assigned in December 1940. Beginning in 1941 a series of five digit numbers, beginning with 00001 was adopted, and numbers assigned through 99999. A sixth digit was then added beginning with 100001 and is still in use. To summarize, the bureau numbers assigned to naval aircraft are five different series, they are as follows:

A-51 to A-9206

9207 to 9999 (the A prefix was dropped)

0001 to 7303

00001 to 100000 (99991- 100000 were cancelled)

100001 to (numbers still being assigned to this system)

There are several major exceptions to the assignment of numbers in the six digit number system. In the 1960s a block of six digit numbers, beginning with 00, were assigned to the DASH vehicle (Drone Antisubmarine Helicopter). Production models of the DSN were designated QH-50C and QH-50D. All of these helos had six digit bureau numbers that began with 00. The double zeros were part of the bureau number. These numbers obviously do not fit into the regular six digit numbering system that began with 100001. Documentation has not been found that explains why the normal six digit numbering system was not employed for these aircraft.

The other major exception to the normal sequential assignment of bureau numbers in the six digit system involves numbers beginning with 198003 and ranging up to 999794. This group of six digit numbers is not sequentially assigned. Almost all of the aircraft in this group of numbers were acquired by the Navy from the Army, Air Force, or some other organizations, and not directly from the manufacturer. There appears to be no logical sequence or reasoning for the assignment of these six digit numbers. It is believed that some of the numbers may have been derived by modifying the Air Force aircraft numbering system. However, this is only conjecture since there is no documentation to verify this explanation.

Aside from the very sizable overlap stemming from the numbering schemes, most numbers were only used once. However, there are some limited cases where the same number was assigned for two different types of aircraft. During the planning and contracting processes, however, numbers were often assigned to aircraft that were never obtained following the cancellation of the contract. Sometimes some of these cancelled numbers were reassigned to other aircraft.

Naval Historical Center

BIBLIOGRAPHY

U.S. Government Documents:

AMARC Register Sheets   AMARC Form 9   DEC 85 Declassified

AMARC Inactive Navy Aircraft, NavAir 4850-1, 31 DEC. 1997
Declassified

AMARC Inactive Navy Aircraft, NavAir 4850-2, 31 DEC. 1997
Declassified

AMARC Inactive Navy Aircraft, NavAir 4850-3, 31 DEC. 1997
Declassified

AMARC Inactive Navy Aircraft, NavAir 4850-3, 04 NOV. 2004
Declassified

AMARC Inactive Navy Aircraft, NavAir 4850-4, 31 DEC. 1997
Declassified

AMARC Inactive Navy Aircraft, NavAir 4850-5, 31 DEC. 1997
Declassified

AMARC Inactive Navy Aircraft, NavAir 4850-7, 31 DEC. 1997
Declassified

AMARC Inactive Navy Aircraft Report, JUL. 1984 thru JUN. 2001
Declassified

AMARC Inactive Navy Aircraft Report, MAR. 1997 thru APR. 2002
Declassified

Bureau Number Checklist Report Number 5442-65D 19 APR. 1982,
Declassified

Naval Aircraft Listing by Bureau Number, (Inv-12), 31 DEC. 1971,
Declassified

Naval Aircraft Listing by Bureau Number, (Inv-12), 30 JUN. 1972,
Declassified

Naval Aircraft Listing by Bureau Number, (Inv-12), 13 DEC. 1973,
Declassified

Naval Aircraft Listing by Bureau Number, (Inv-12), 31 DEC. 1975,
Declassified

Naval Aircraft Listing by Bureau Number, (Inv-12), 31 JUL. 1976,
Declassified

Naval Aircraft Listing by Bureau Number, (Inv-12), 31 JAN. 1977,
Declassified

Naval Aircraft Listing by Bureau Number, (Inv-12), 31 MAY 1978,
Declassified

Naval Aircraft Listing by Bureau Number, (Inv-12), 31 MAR. 1979,
Declassified

Naval Aircraft Listing by Bureau Number, (Inv-12), 31 AUG. 1981,
Declassified

Naval Aircraft Listing by Bureau Number, (Inv-12), 31 DEC. 1981,
Declassified

Naval Aircraft Listing by Bureau Number, (Inv-12), 31 MAR. 1983,
Declassified

Naval Aircraft Listing by Bureau Number, (Inv-12), 30 NOV. 1984,
Declassified

Naval Aircraft Listing by Model, (Inv-14), 28 FEB. 1981,
Declassified

Unit Inventory Report Number 5442-61D, 19 APR. 1982,
Declassified

Department of Defense, (DOD), Microfilm by the Defense Printing Service:

USN Microfilm M97; Reel 13, Declassified

USN Microfilm M97; Reel 25, Declassified

USN Microfilm M569; Reel 6, Declassified

USN Microfilm M576; Reel 2, Declassified

USN Microfilm M576; Reel 3, Declassified

USN Microfilm M577; Reel 2, Declassified

USN Op-515 Aircraft History Card Microfilm, Reel 115, DEC 62- JUN 65, Declassified

USN Op-515 Aircraft History Card Microfilm, Reel 128, JUN 65, Declassified

USN Op-515 Aircraft History Card Microfilm, Reel 135, JUL 65 - JUN 66, Declassified

USN Op-515 Aircraft History Card Microfilm, Reel 141, JUL 66 - JUN 67, Declassified

USN Op-515 Aircraft History Card Microfilm, Reel 146, JUL 67 - JUN 68, Declassified

USN Op-515 Aircraft History Card Microfilm, Reel 147, JUL 67 - JUN 68, Declassified

USN Op-515 Aircraft History Card Microfilm, Reel 150, JUL 68 - JUN 69, Declassified

USN Op-515 Aircraft History Card Microfilm, Reel 151, JUL 68 - JUN 69, Declassified

USN Op-515 Aircraft History Card Microfilm, Reel 154, JUL 69 - JUN 70, Declassified

USN Op-515 Aircraft History Card Microfilm, Reel 155, JUL 69 - JUN 70, Declassified

USN Op-515 Aircraft History Card Microfilm, Reel 157, JUL 70 - JUN 71, Declassified

USN Op-515 Aircraft History Card Microfilm, Reel 158, JUL 70 - JUN 71, Declassified

USN Op-515 Aircraft History Card Microfilm, Reel 160, JUL 71 - JUN 72, Declassified

USN Op-515 Aircraft History Card Microfilm, Reel 161, JUL 71 - JUN 72, Declassified

USN Op-515 Aircraft History Card Microfilm, Reel 162, JUL 72 - JUN 73, Declassified

USN Op-515 Aircraft History Card Microfilm, Reel 163, JUL 72 - JUN 73, Declassified

USN Op-515 Aircraft History Card Microfilm, Reel 165, JUL 73 - JUN 74, Declassified

USN Op-515 Aircraft History Card Microfilm, Reel 166, JUL 73 - JUN 74, Declassified

USN Op-515 Aircraft History Card Microfilm, Reel 167, JUL 74 - JUN 75, Declassified

USN Op-515 Aircraft History Card Microfilm, Reel 168, JUL 74 - JUN 75, Declassified

USN Op-515 Aircraft History Card Microfilm, Reel 169, JUL 75 - JUN 76, Declassified

USN Op-515 Aircraft History Card Microfilm, Reel 170, JUL 75 - JUN 76, Declassified

USN Op-515 Aircraft History Card Microfilm, Reel 171, JUL 76 - SEP 76, Declassified

USN Op-515 Aircraft History Card Microfilm, Reel 172, OCT 76 - SEP 77, Declassified

USN Op-515 Aircraft History Card Microfilm, Reel 173, OCT 76 - SEP 77, Declassified

USN Op-515 Aircraft History Card Microfilm, Reel 174, OCT 77 - SEP 78, Declassified

USN Op-515 Aircraft History Card Microfilm, Reel 175, OCT 77 - SEP 78, Declassified

USN Op-515 Aircraft History Card Microfilm, Reel 176, OCT 78 - SEP 79, Declassified

USN Op-515 Aircraft History Card Microfilm, Reel 177, OCT 78 - SEP 79, Declassified

USN Op-515 Aircraft History Card Microfilm, Reel 178, OCT 79 - SEP 80, Declassified

USN Op-515 Aircraft History Card Microfilm, Reel 179, OCT 79 - SEP 80, Declassified

USN Op-515 Aircraft History Card Microfilm, Reel 180, OCT 80 - SEP 81, Declassified

USN Op-515 Aircraft History Card Microfilm, Reel 181, OCT 80 - SEP 81, Declassified

USN Op-515 Aircraft History Card Microfilm, Reel 182, OCT 81 - SEP 82, Declassified

USN Op-515 Aircraft History Card Microfilm, Reel 183, OCT 81 - SEP 82, Declassified

USN Op-515 Aircraft History Card Microfilm, Reel 184, OCT 82 - SEP 83, Declassified

USN Op-515 Aircraft History Card Microfilm, Reel 185, OCT 82 - SEP 83, Declassified

USN Op-515 Aircraft History Card Microfilm, Reel 186, OCT 83 - SEP 84, Declassified

USN Op-515 Aircraft History Card Microfilm, Reel 187, OCT 83 - SEP 84, Declassified

USN Op-515 Aircraft History Card Microfilm, Reel 188, OCT 84 - SEP 85, Declassified

USN Op-515 Aircraft History Card Microfilm, Reel 189,
OCT 84 - SEP 85, Declassified

USN Op-515 Aircraft History Card Microfilm, Reel 190,
OCT 85 - SEP 86, Declassified

USN Op-515 Aircraft History Card Microfilm, Reel 191,
OCT 85 - SEP 86, Declassified

USN Op-515 Aircraft History Card Microfilm, Reel 192,
OCT 86 - SEP 87, Declassified

Text:

A-7 Corsair II in Action, Squadron/Signal publications No. 22, 1975

A-7 Corsair II in Detail & Scale, Vol. 22, Bert Kenzey, 1986

A-7 Corsair II, Aero Series, William G. Holder, 1990

A-7 Corsair II in Action Squadron/Signal Publications, 1991

Colors & Markings of the A-7E Corsair II, Vol.9, Bert Kinzey & Ray
Leader, Detail & Scale, 1988

Colors & Markings of the A-7 Corsair II, Part 2, Vol. 15, Bert Kenzey
& Ray Leader, Detail & Scale, 1990

Colors & Markings of the A-7 Corsair II, Part 3, Vol. 19, Bert Kenzey
& Ray Leader, Detail & Scale, 1991

Famous Airplanes of the World No. 131, (Japan), 1982.

Flight Log Book, Captain R. Hodson USN, Ret.

Flight Log Book, Captain E. Jackson USN Ret. 3RD C.O. VA-305

Koku~Fan Oct., (Japan) 1975

Lockdown No. 9, A-7D/K Corsair II Aircraft Photo File, Willy Peeters,
Verlinden Pubs., (Belgium), 1990

LTV A-7 Corsair II, Navy Version, No. 18, (Japan), 1989

LTV A-7 Corsair II, (Japan) Oct. 1972

LTV (Vought) A-7A/E Corsair II, David A. Anderton, (England)
Aircraft Profile Number 239

MASDC II AMARC, Martyn Swann & Barry Fryer, (England), 1998

The A-7 Corsair II in Detail & Scale, Series II, Bert Kenzey, 1979

The Illustrated Encyclopedia of Aircraft, Vol.4, Issue 41, Orbis
Publishing Ltd. (UK), 82

Tonkin Gulf Yahct Club, Naval Institute Press, Rene J. Francillon, 1988

U.S. Navy Combat Aircraft in the 1970's, Lindsay T. Peacock, Warbird
Illustrated NO. 4, (England), 1982

U.S. Navy A-7 Corsair II Units of the Vietnam War, Norman Birzer &
Peter Mersky, Osprey Combat Aircraft, 2004

Vought A-7 Corsair II, Robert F. Dorr, Osprey Air Combat, 1985

Warplane Vol.4, Issue 42, Orbis Publishing Ltd. (UK), 1986

Vought Corporation:

Report number 2-51133 / 8R-8136, A-7 Aircraft correlation list, Revised, 15 JUL 81

Web Sites:

http://aircraftresourcecenter.com/awal/001walk090_a7/walk090.htm

http://en.wikipedia.org/wiki/a-7_corsair_II

http://en.wikipediapedia.org/wiki/aircraft_losses_of_the_Vietnam_war

http://en.wikipedia.org/wiki/list_of_A-7_corsair_II_operators

http://home.att.net/~jbaugher/1972.html

http://home.att.net/~jbaugher/navyserials.html

http://www.aviation-hobby-site.com/oldahs/a7sn.html

http://www.chinalakealumni.org/

http://www.defensetalk.com/pictures/show photo.php?photo=27210

http://www. Globalsecurity.org/military/systems/aircraft/a-7.htm

http://gonavy.jp/cvw19-nm1972.htm

http://www.militaryphotos.net/forums/showthread?t=53823&page=181

http://www..scramble.nl/min/showreport/memphis89.htm

http://www.thai_aviation.net/accidents%203.htm

INDEX

Photographs:

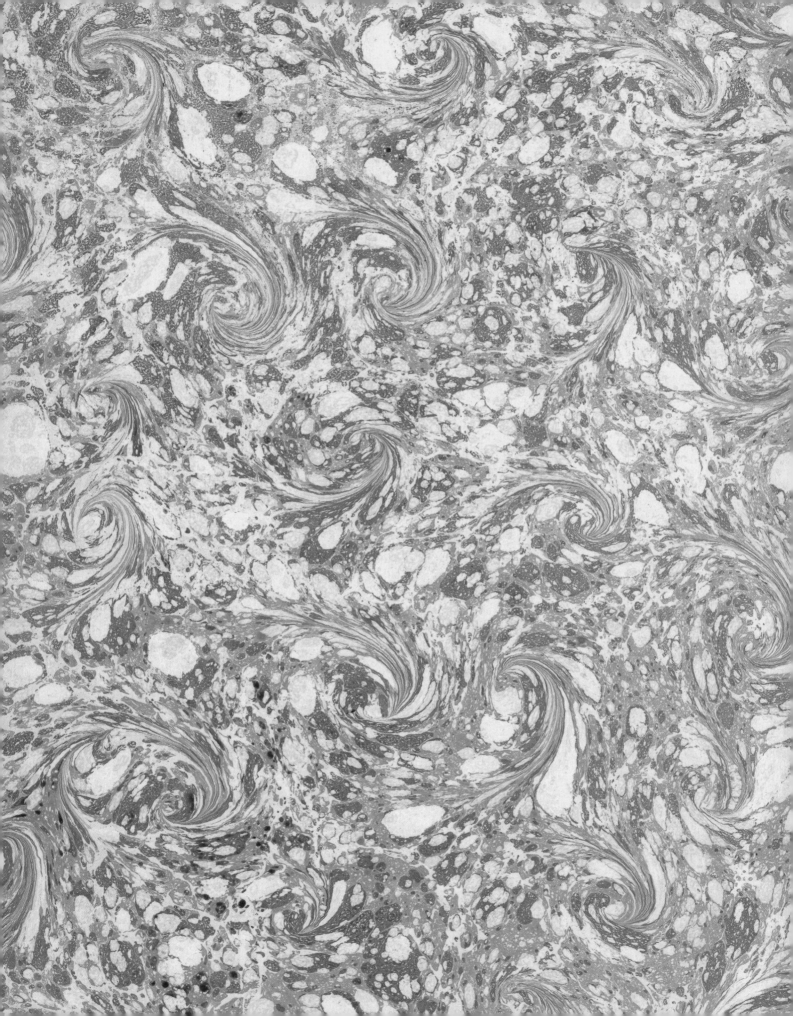